Ninth Edition

Constitutional and Administrative Law

ALEX CARROLL

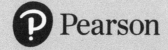 **Pearson**

Harlow, England • London • New York • Boston • San Francisco • Toronto • Sydney • Dubai • Singapore • Hong Kong
Tokyo • Seoul • Taipei • New Delhi • Cape Town • São Paulo • Mexico City • Madrid • Amsterdam • Munich • Paris • Milan

PEARSON EDUCATION LIMITED
Edinburgh Gate
Harlow CM20 2JE
United Kingdom
Tel: +44 (0)1279 623623
Web: **www.pearson.com/uk**

————————————————

First published 1998 (print)
Second edition published 2002 (print)
Third edition published 2003 (print)
Fourth edition published 2007 (print)
Fifth edition published 2009 (print)
Sixth edition published 2011 (print)
Seventh edition published 2013 (print and electronic)
Eighth edition published 2015 (print and electronic)
Ninth edition published 2017 (print and electronic)

ISBN: 978-1-292-17604-8 (print)
       978-1-292-17605-5 (PDF)
       978-1-292-17606-2 (ePub)

British Library Cataloguing-in-Publication Data
A catalogue record for the print edition is available from the British Library

Library of Congress Cataloging-in-Publication Data
Carroll, Alex, 1947– author.
  Constitutional and administrative law / Alex Carroll, Manchester Metropolitan University.
  Ninth edition. | Harlow, England : Pearson Education Limited, 2017. | Includes bibliographical references.
  LCCN 2017011135| ISBN 9781292176048 (Print) | ISBN 9781292176055
    (PDF) | ISBN 9781292176062 (ePub)
  LCSH: Constitutional law—Great Britain. | Administrative law—Great Britain.
  LCC KD3930 .C37 2017 | DDC 342.41—dc23
  LC record available at https://lccn.loc.gov/2017011135

10 9 8 7 6 5 4 3 2
21 20 19 18

Print edition typeset in 9/12pt Stone Serif ITC Pro by SPi Global
Printed by Ashford Colour Press Ltd, Gosport

NOTE THAT ANY PAGE CROSS REFERENCES REFER TO THE PRINT EDITION

This book is dedicated to the memory of
Robert Alan Carroll 1949–2011

Brief contents

Contents

Part 4 The Executive   249

Part 5 Judicial supervision of executive power   337

14 Judicial review: nature and grounds for   339

15 Judicial review: applications for, exclusion of, and exclusivity   386

Acknowledgement

We are grateful to the following for permission to reproduce copyright material:

Text

Extracts on page 6, page 7 from *Town Investments Ltd v Department of the Environment* [1978] AC 359; Extract on page 7 from *D v National Society for Prevention of Cruelty to Children* [1978] AC 171; Extract on page 30 from *AXA General Insurance Ltd v Lord Advocate* [2012] 1 AC 868; Extract on page 65 from *Liversidge v Anderson* [1942] AC 206; Extract on page 90 from 'The Principle of Proportionality in the Case-Law of the German Federal Constitutional Court', Lubbe-Wolff, quoted in *R (Pham) v Secretary of State for the Home Department* [2015] 1 WLR 1591; Extract on page 103 from *Lee v Bude and Torrington Railway Co* (1871) LR 6 CP 577; Extract on page 104 from *Ellen Street Estates v Minister of Health* [1934] 1 KB 590; Extract on page 105 from *Hunt v London Borough of Hackney; Thoburn v Sunderland City Council; Harman v Cornwall County Council; Collins v London Borough of Sutton* [2003] QB 151; Extract on page 106 from *Phillips v Eyre* (1870) LR 6 QB 1; Extracts on page 106, page 281 from *Burmah Oil v Lord Advocate* [1965] AC 75; Extract on page 120 from *Blackburn v Attorney-General* [1971] 1 WLR 1037; Extracts on page 124, page 125, page 126 from *Jackson v Attorney-General* [2006] 1 AC 262; Extract on page 126 from *Axa General Insurance Ltd & Ors v Lord Advocate & Ors (Scotland)* [2012] 1 AC 868; Extract on page 227 from *Adam v Ward* [1917] AC 309; Extract on page 231 from *Wason v Walter* (1868) LR 4 QB 73; Extract on page 231 from *Cook v Alexander* [1974] QB 279; Extract on page 232 from *Pepper v Hart* [1992] 3 WLR 1032; Extracts on page 232 from *Prebble v Television New Zealand Ltd* [1995] 1 AC 321; Extract on page 237 from *Bradlaugh v Gossett* (1884) LR 12 QBD 271; Extract on page 281 from *Chandler v Director of Public Prosecutions* [1964] AC 763; Extract on page 282 from *Kuwait Airways Corporation v Iraqi Airways Corporation (Nos 4 and 5)* [2002] AC 883; Extract on page 284 from *Council of Civil Service Unions v Minister for Civil Service* [1985] AC 374; Extract on page 285 from *BBC v Johns* [1965] Ch 32; Extract on page 287 from *Attorney-General v De Keyser's Royal Hotel* [1920] AC 508; Extract on page 290 from *Laker Airways v Department of Trade* [1977] QB 643; Extracts on page 290, page 362 from *Council of Civil Service Unions v Minister for the Civil Service* [1985] AC 374; Extract on page 292 from *R (on application of Sandiford) v Secretary of State for Foreign and Commonwealth Affairs* [2014] 1 WLR 2697; Extract on page 297 from *Rederiaktiebolaget Amphitrite v R* [1921] 3 KB 500; Extract on page 298 from *Crown Lands Commissioners v Page* [1960] 2 QB 274; Extract on page 299 from *Dunn v R* [1896] QB 116; Extract on page 300 from *Dunn v MacDonald* [1897] 1 QB 401; Extract on page 305 from *Serder Mohammed v Secretary of State for Defence* [2016] 2 WLR 247; Extracts on page 308, page 309 from *Gorringe v Calderdale Metropolitan Borough Council* [2004] 1 WLR 1057; Extracts on page 309, page 312 from *X (minors) v Bedfordshire County Council* [1995] 2 AC 633; Extract on page 310 from *Phelps v Hillingdon London Borough Council* [2001] 2 AC 619; Extract on page 310 from *Stovin v Wise* [1996] AC 923; Extract on page 311 from *Connor v Surrey County Council* [2011] QB 429; Extract on page 313 from *Barrett v Enfield London Borough Council* [1999] 3 WLR 79; Extract on page 319 from *Anufrijeva v Southwark London Borough Council* [2004] QB 1124; Extract on page 327 from *Campbell v Tameside Metropolitan Borough Council* [1982] QB 1065; Extracts on page 328 from *Burmah Oil v Bank of England* [1980] AC 1090; Extract on page 328 from *Air Canada v Secretary of State for Trade* [1963] 3 AC 304; Extract on page 328 from *Alfred Crompton Amusement Machines Ltd v Customs and Excise Commissioners (No. 2)* [1974] AC 405; Extract on page 328 from *D v NSPCC* [1978] AC 171; Extract on page 329 from *R (on application of Binyam Mohamed) v Secretary of State for Foreign and Commonwealth Affairs* [2011] QB 218; Extract on page 333 from *R v H* [2004] 2 AC 134; Extract on page 342 from *R v Central Criminal Court JJ* (1886) 17 QBD 598; Extract on page 342 from *Ashbridge Investments Ltd v Minister of Housing and Local Government* [1965] 1 WLR 1320; Extract on page 342 from *Padfield v Minister of Agriculture* [1968] AC 997;

ACKNOWLEDGEMENT

Extract on page 343 from *Anisminic v Foreign Compensation Commission (No. 2)* [1969] 2 AC 147; Extract on page 344 from *R v Cambridge Health Authority, ex parte B* [1995] 1 WLR 898; Extract on page 347 from *White and Collins v Minister of Health* [1939] 2 KB 838; Extract on page 347 from *R v Secretary of State for the Home Department, ex parte Khawaja* [1984] AC 74; Extract on page 348 from *Runa Begum v Tower Hamlets London Borough Council* [2003] 2 AC 430; Extract on page 349 from *R v Northumberland Compensation Appeal Tribunal, ex parte Shaw* [1952] 1 KB 338; Extracts on page 349, page 390 from *O'Reilly v Mackman* [1983] 2 AC 237; Extract on page 351 from *R v Race Relations Board, ex parte Selvarajaran* [1975] 1 WLR 1686; Extract on page 352 from *R v Skinner* [1968] 2 QB 700; Extract on page 353 from *Lavender v Minister of Housing and Local Government* [1970] 1 WLR 1231; Extract on page 354 from *R v Port of London Authority, ex parte Kynoch Ltd* [1919] 1 KB 176; Extract on page 354 from *British Oxygen Co Ltd v Minister of Technology* [1971] AC 610; Extract on page 356 from *Birkdale District Supply Co v Southport Corporation* [1926] AC 355; Extract on page 357 from *R v Hammersmith and Fulham Borough Council, ex parte Beddowes* [1987] QB 1050; Extract on page 358 from *Southend Corporation v Hodgson (Wickford) Ltd* [1962] 1 QB 416; Extract on page 359 from *R v East Sussex County Council, ex parte Reprotech (Pebsham) Ltd* [2003] 1 WLR 348; Extract on page 361 from *Earl Fitzwilliams Wentworth Estates Co Ltd v Minister of Town and Country Planning* [1951] 2 KB 284; Extract on page 362 from *Associated Provincial Picture Houses v Wednesbury Corporation* [1948] 1 KB 223; Extract on page 365 from *R v Secretary of State for Home Affairs, ex party Bugdaycay* [1987] AC 514; Extract on page 372 from *Kanda v Government of Malaya* [1962] AC 322; Extract on page 373 from *R v Thames Magistrates, ex parte Polemis* [1974] 1 WLR 1371; Extract on page 374 from *R v Army Board of the Defence Council, ex parte Anderson* [1992] 1 QB 169; Extracts on page 374, page 689 from *Bushell v Secretary of State for the Environment* [1981] AC 75; Extract on page 375 from *Save Britain's Heritage v No. 1 Poultry Ltd* [1991] 1 WLR 153; Extract on page 375 from *R v Secretary of State for the Home Department, ex parte Swati* [1986] 1 WLR 477; Extract on page 376 from in *R v Secretary of State for the Home Department, ex parte Doody* [1993] 3 WLR 154; Extract on page 376 from *R v Higher Education Funding Council, ex parte Institute of Dental Surgery* [1994] 1 WLR 242; Extract on page 377 from *R v Sussex Justices, ex parte McCarthy* [1924] 1 KB 256; Extracts on page 377, page 379 from *R v Gough* [1993] AC 646; Extract on page 380 from *Attorney-General for Hong Kong v Ng Yuen Shiu* [1983] 2 AC 629; Extract on page 381 from *R v British Coal Corporation, ex parte Vardy* [1993] ICR 720; Extract on page 388 from *R v Inland Revenue Commissioners, ex parte National Federation of Self-Employed and Small Businesses Ltd* [1982] AC 617; Extract on page 388 from *R v Greater London Council, ex parte Blackburn* [1976] 1 WLR 550; Extract on page 392 from *R v Bristol Corporation, ex parte Hendry* [1974] 1 WLR 498; Extract on page 392 from *Boyce v Paddington Borough Council* [1903] 1 Ch 109; Extract on page 397 from *Smith v East Elloe RDC* [1956] AC 736; Extract on page 398 from *R v Secretary of State for the Environment, ex parte Ostler* [1976] 3 WLR 288; Extract on page 398 from *Attorney-General v Ryan* [1980] AC 718; Extract on page 399 from *R v Medical Appeal Tribunal, ex parte Gilmore* [1975] 1 QB 574; Extract on page 399 from *Robinson v Minister of Town and Country Planning* [1947] KB 702; Extract on page 400 from *Secretary of State for Education and Science v Metropolitan Borough of Tameside* [1977] AC 1014; Extract on page 401 from *Meade v Haringey London Borough Council* [1979] 1 WLR 637; Extract on page 401 from *Secretary of State for the Home Department v Rehman* [2001] 3 WLR 877; Extract on page 402 from *R v Secretary of State for the Environment, ex parte Hammersmith and Fulham* London Borough Councils [1991] 1 AC 521; Extract on page 403 from *R v Halliday* [1917] AC 260; Extract on page 404 from *R v Secretary of State for the Home Department, ex parte Hosenball* [1977] 1 WLR 766; Extract on page 405 from *R (on application Carlile) v Secretary of State for Home Department* [1977] 1 WLR 766; Extract on page 408 from *McClaren v Home Office* [1990] ICR 824; Extract on page 528 from *R (on application of McCann) v Manchester Crown Court* [2003] 1 AC 787; Extract on page 536 from *Campbell v MGM* [2004] 2 WLR 1232; Extract on page 536 from *Venables and Thompson v News Group Newspapers Ltd* [2001] Fam 430; Extract on page 540 from *Ashworth Security Hospital v MGN Ltd* [2001] 1 WLR 515; Extract on page 559 from *R v Self* [1992] 1 WLR 657; Extract on page 603 from *O'Kelly v Harvey* (1883) 14 LR Ir 105; Extract on page 604 from *R (on application of Laporte) v Chief Constable of Gloucestershire* [2007] AC 105; Extract on page 623 from *DPP v Whyte* [1972] AC 849; Extract on page 624 from *Calder (John) Publications Ltd v Powell* [1965] 1 QB 509; Extract on page 625 from *R v Calder and Boyars Ltd* [1969] 1 QB 151; Extract on page 626 from *R v Stanley* [1965] 2 QB 327; Extract on page 629 from *Shaw v DPP* [1962] AC 220; Extract on page 630 from *Knuller v DPP* [1973] AC 435; Extract on page 630 from *R v Gibson* [1990] 2 QB 619; Extract on page 631 from *Re Lonrho plc* [1980] 2 AC 154; Extracts on page 639, page 640 from *Attorney-General v Guardian Newspapers Ltd (No. 2)* [1990] 1 AC 109.

Contains public sector information licensed under the Open Government Licence v3.0.
Contains information licensed under European Union. © European Union, 1995–2017

Preface

This book has been written for students undertaking legal studies at undergraduate level and those pursuing similar courses which include constitutional and administrative law as a core component (e.g. the Postgraduate Diploma in Law). It is intended also to be of use and interest to those who, for whatever purpose, are seeking an easily comprehensible introduction to the legal foundations of the British system of government and to the rights and freedoms to those subject to it. The book's content is based on over thirty years' experience of teaching the subject on A-level, undergraduate and postgraduate courses. Particular attention has been paid to the views of students concerning the strengths and weaknesses of pre-existing and alternative textbooks in this discipline.

As with most law books, many of the legal principles included are explained by reference to particular judicial decisions. The approach taken here has been to discuss those cases which illustrate the principles in issue most clearly or those which exemplify their most recent application.

No attempt has been made to produce an exhaustive reference book covering all those issues which might conceivably fall within the boundaries of the subject. Rather the book concentrates on the subject's key issues and those topics which form the essential core of most constitutional and administrative law syllabi currently taught in further and higher education institutions.

Few legal disciplines have witnessed change and development on the scale, and with the rapidity, that has occurred within constitutional and administrative law within recent years. It follows that much of the subject is concerned with matters of great topicality and modernity. As such, in addition to those learning its elements for mainly academic purposes, it has direct utility for those engaged by the changing fortunes of national and public affairs in general. Change, crisis, and controversy in the process of government, politics, and constitutional development, and any relevant legal intervention or reform which may have followed, all fall within the subject's proper remit.

Some of the more significant recent developments covered, and which have occurred since the last edition of the textbook was published, would include:

- introduction of the new 'English votes for English laws' (EVEL) legislative process;
- implementation of the new system for electoral registration (Individual Electoral Registration);
- re-assessment of the extent of the Crown's legal immunity for acts of state (exercise of prerogative power overseas);
- further judicial consideration of the extent of police liabilityfor negligent performance of their duties;
- review of the content and requirements of the conventional rules regulating the relationship between the House of Commons and the House of Lords (the Strathclyde Review);

- extended use of the power to exclude claimants for legal proceedings involving sensitive aspects of public policy;
- refinement of the meaning of the doctrine of proportionality in the context of English law; EU law, and the law of the European Convention of Human Rights;
- extensions of police powers in relation to communications data;
- the latest anti-terrorist legislation;
- the extent of the executive power to override judicial decisions;
- introduction of new powers enabling a local electorate to 'recall' its MP thereby causing a by-election to be held;
- the latest ministerial code of practice.

All of these matters, and other important developments, particularly in the burgeoning case-law relating to human rights, are explained, where relevant, to a level of depth and detail commensurate with their constitutional significance.

Further details relating to the progress and effects of these modern developments will be provided in the spring and autumn updates to this textbook which may be found on the accompanying website.

Constitutional and administrative law cannot be fully understood without reference to the national's political history and its social and cultural development. This is particularly so in a nation where the constitutional and political systems have been evolving, in a largely uninterrupted fashion, for at least a thousand years. Hence, while every attempt has been made to explain the necessary principles as precisely and succinctly as possible, it has also been the author's intention to do so in a way which places these in their contextual framework. This approach is intended to give insight into the relationship between the subject and those various political historical and cultural factors which have influenced and shaped its nature and content.

The author is greatly indebted to all those who have helped in the book's compilation and production. Particular and belated thanks are due to the late Mr R.H. Buckley, one-time Principal Lecturer in Law at Manchester Metropolitan University, for all his help and advice over the year and for exciting the author's interest in the subject.

Alex Carroll

Table of cases

Table of statutes

Table of statutory instruments

Table of treaties and conventions

Part 1

Fundamental principles

1

Introduction to constitutional and administrative law

Objectives

After reading this chapter you should:

1. Understand what a constitution is.

2. Recognise the difference between 'written' and 'unwritten' constitutions and the historical, cultural and social origins of the British constitution.

3. Understand the institutional terminology of the British constitution and the difference between central and local government.

4. Understand the constitutional development of the 'United Kingdom' and its principal elements.

What is a constitution?

Objective 1

In a purely formal sense a constitution consists of the laws, rules (e.g. conventions) and other practices which identify and explain:

(a) the institutions of government;

(b) the nature, extent and distribution of powers within those institutions;

(c) the forms and procedures through which such powers should be exercised;

(d) the relationship between the institutions of government and the individual citizen, often expressed in terms of a 'Bill of Rights'.

Hence, for example, the first three articles of the Constitution of the United States (1789) – the earliest and perhaps most revered of the modern world's written constitutions – provide for and specify the respective roles and powers of the Congress (Art I); the President (Art II); and the Supreme Court (Art III). The famous American Bill of Rights may be found in the same document in a series of later amendments to the original version written in 1787. Thus, for example, Amendment I provides that 'Congress shall make no law respecting an establishment of religion, or prohibiting the free exercise thereof, or abridging the freedom of speech, or of the press, or the right of people peacefully to assemble, and to petition the Government for a redress of grievances.'

The British constitution

Objective
2

In the majority of nations, as in the United States, such constitutional prescriptions have been set down or 'codified' into a single written document. The constitution may be said, therefore, to exist in a physically tangible form. It is possible to go into a bookshop and buy a copy or to visit the museum or library where the original may be on display albeit closely guarded. This is not the case, however, in the United Kingdom. Here the constitution has simply evolved and been added to by Acts of Parliament, judicial decisions and the growth of constitutional conventions and other political practices. The United Kingdom does not have a constitution, therefore, in the narrow sense of a formal document in which all the fundamental rules relating to the process of government are articulated. For all practical purposes, however, it does possess a body of legal and other rules by which that process is regulated and does, therefore, have a 'constitution' in the functional sense.

For details of constitutional conventions, see Chapter 3.

The cultural dimension

Within the nation-state to which it applies, the constitution will usually be regarded as both the ultimate source of legitimacy and authority for the practice of government and as a framework for the application of that society's political beliefs concerning how the process of government should be conducted and by whom. Thus, except in those circumstances where a particular form of government has been imposed by force, perhaps by some external authority, a society's constitutional arrangements will, to a considerable extent, be a product of its political culture. Thus the constitution of the United Kingdom seeks to give expression and protection to many of the values and beliefs now generally associated with that form of government often referred to as liberal democracy. The values of liberal democracy may be summarised as freedom of thought, expression, association and assembly, and a preference for limited representative and responsible government according to which those in power are answerable:

(a) in regular General Elections: to a fully enfranchised adult population;

(b) on a day-to-day basis to a Parliament or representative assembly freely created by that electorate;

(c) in matters of law and jurisdiction, to an independent system of courts.

It follows that the authority and status of a constitution may usually be understood as having cultural as well as legal foundations. Hence, in addition to the legal duty of allegiance which it may impose, the constitution will be something which also attracts considerable respect and loyalty in a more personal sense. This will be so because the people in a particular society may often regard the constitution, or at least its physical manifestations – e.g. in the United Kingdom, the Monarch and Parliament – as part of their cultural heritage and identity.

Where it exists this sense of cultural affinity with the nation's constitutional arrangements will usually contribute to the general level of political stability and order. Perversely, however, this may make the constitution more difficult to change, at least in any abrupt or substantial way, as people tend to be more 'comfortable' with that with which they are familiar. This may help to explain, to some extent, the tensions experienced in recent times in the United Kingdom concerning the constitutional implications of greater European integration.

Given the usual close relationship between a constitution and the political culture which it mirrors, it is axiomatic that few constitutions are static or immutable. As a society's expectations and beliefs concerning the process of government evolve, so must its constitution respond and develop. Otherwise it atrophies and becomes increasingly irrelevant to prevailing social and political attitudes. This in turn may lead to dissension and conflict over the validity of the very arrangements through which such dissent is supposed to be channelled and resolved.

Distinguishing between constitutional law and administrative law

Constitutional law deals with the legal foundations of the institutional hierarchy through which the state is governed. It concentrates in particular on the rules, both legal and conventional, which explain and regulate the composition, powers, immunities, procedures of, and relationships between, those institutions – hence, for example, the subject's concern with the composition, workings and powers of Parliament, the legal authority and immunities of the executive, and the balance of legal and political power between the two.

Constitutional law also seeks to delineate those individual rights which, according to cultural traditions, are the inalienable attributes of a genuinely free society and upon which the state should not transgress except where an overwhelming public interest so requires (e.g. the defence of the realm). Such rights would include the freedom of the person (i.e. from arbitrary arrest and detention), freedom of association and assembly, and freedom of speech. These matters are now defined and set out in the Human Rights Act 1998.

Administrative law, on the other hand, directs greater attention to the control and regulation of government power by both public and private law and through the workings of the various extra-judicial appeals and complaints procedures created in recent times to supplement the judicial and political mechanisms for dealing with individual grievances against the state. Central to the subject, therefore, is the process of judicial review, whereby alleged government excesses may be brought before the courts and condemned as abuses of power and of no legal effect. The subject also deals, inter alia, with the jurisdiction and workings of statutory tribunals and inquiries which deal largely with appeals against decisions made by central and local government officials, and with the activities of the increasing number of 'ombudspersons' or complaints commissioners dealing with allegations of 'maladministration' in the public services and the execution of public policy.

For the law and procedure of judicial review, see Chapters 14–15.

The terminology of constitutional and administrative law

Objective 3

Not all of those who come to the study of constitutional and administrative law for the first time will be entirely familiar with its language and terminology. Thus, for example, difficulty may be found in giving exact definition to, and distinguishing between, such concepts as the Crown, the Monarch, the government, Parliament, etc. Such conceptual problems are understandable as not all of these are capable of being given entirely distinctive and particular meanings. It is hoped, however, that the text that follows will help to dispel some of these uncertainties and make for greater comprehension of the institutional context in which the subject operates.

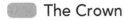 The Monarch

This is the person who occupies the throne and who, by virtue of which, is recognised by law and tradition as Head of State. For many years the right of succession to the throne currently was determined both by traditional hereditary principles (i.e. is reserved to the eldest male heir and, in the absence of which, to the eldest female) and by conditions laid down by Parliament in various enactments – principally the Act of Settlement 1700. This provided that in the absence of any issue by Queen Anne (1701–14), the right of succession should be confined to the Princess Sophia of Hanover 'and the heirs of her body being protestants'. It was by virtue of this enactment that the first of the Hanoverian monarchs, George I (1714–27), succeeded to the throne after Queen Anne's death.

The Succession to the Crown Act 2013 contained provisions seeking to bring to an end the rule giving precedence in the right of succession to the Monarch's male heirs. The effect of the Act is that, henceforth, succession to the throne will depend on age and relationship to the sitting Monarch, without the reference to gender (s 1). Other major provisions of the Act are as follows:

1 A person is not disqualified from succession to the throne as a result of marriage to a Roman Catholic (s 2);

2 The Royal Marriages Act 1772, requiring the Monarch's consent to the marriage of any person in the first six positions of the line of succession, is repealed.

The 2013 Act leaves in place the rule that succession to the throne is limited to confessing members of the Anglican Church (Act of Settlement 1700, s 3).

As Head of State, the executive, legislative and judicial functions of government are all performed in the Monarch's name and by his or her appointees. The Prime Minister and other Members of the government are the King or Queen's Ministers. Law is made by the King or Queen in Parliament, i.e. with the consent of the House of Commons, Lords and Monarch. The same law is administered in the Royal Courts of Justice by the King or Queen's judges.

More will be said about the constitutional role and status of the Monarch in Chapter 2.

In this personal sense, it is still accepted that 'the King can do no wrong'. Hence the Monarch may not be prosecuted for any criminal offence or sued for breach of any civil obligation.

The Crown

As the following quotation explains, the term has been given various meanings.

> The expression 'the Crown' may sometimes be used to designate Her Majesty [HM] in a purely personal capacity. It may sometimes be used to designate Her Majesty in Her capacity as Head of the Commonwealth. It may sometimes be used to designate Her Majesty in Her capacity as the constitutional Monarch of the United Kingdom . . . The expression may sometimes be used in a somewhat broad sense in reference to the functions of government and the administration. It may sometimes be used in reference to the Rule of Law . . . The case for the prosecution is the case for the Crown (*per* Lord Diplock, ***Town Investments Ltd* v *Department of the Environment*** [1978] AC 359).

For all practical purposes, however, and in terms of everyday usage and understanding, it is the fourth of these meanings which should be preferred. Thus when 'the Crown' is spoken of in constitutional law, this is normally for the purpose of referring to all those institutions and, in particular, central government departments and those who work within them (civil or 'Crown' servants), who are responsible for managing public affairs at a national level.

Where . . . we are concerned with the legal nature of the exercise of executive powers of government, I believe that some of the more Athanasian-like features of the debate in your Lordships' House could have been eliminated if instead of speaking of 'the Crown' we were to speak of the 'government' – a term appropriate to embrace both collectively and individually all the Ministers of the Crown and parliamentary secretaries under whose direction the administrative work of government is carried on by the civil servants employed in the various government departments . . . Execution of acts of government that are done by any of them are acts done by 'the Crown' in the fictional sense in which that expression is now used in English public law (*ibid*).

In this institutional rather than personal sense, the Crown is a 'corporation sole'. This means that, unlike the Monarch, it has a definable legal capacity and may sue and be sued in the ordinary courts of law.

The Sovereign

The word 'Sovereign' is employed, generally, in one of two senses. First, it may be used as a synonym for the Monarch – i.e. the person who, in purely legal terms, is at the apex of the constitutional pyramid. In this sense the word denotes little in terms of legislative or actual political power, but much in terms of status and symbolism. Second, it is also frequently used to mean that which in terms of legal or political authority has no superior. Hence, in the United Kingdom, Parliament has long been regarded as the 'sovereign' law-making body – i.e. the law as made by Parliament prevails over all other legal rules whatever their source. In the political sense, however, it is often said that it is 'the people' who are sovereign, i.e. the legislative power of Parliament and the authority of the government is derived from the 'will' of the people as expressed through the ballot box.

The state

English constitutional law contains no exact or fixed definition of the above term. Once again, therefore, a variety of meanings may be attributed to it.

It may be used, for example, to describe the geographical entity over which the institutions of government of a particular society exercise independent political authority. In this sense the state which is referred to as the United Kingdom would be said to consist of England, Wales, Scotland and Northern Ireland.

Alternatively, the word may be used to characterise the entire structure of institutions and organisations through which a particular society is regulated and protected.

The state is the whole organisation of the body politic for civil rule and government – the whole political organisation which is the basis of civil government. As such it certainly extends to local and . . . statutory-bodies in so far as they are exercising autonomous rule (*per* Lord Simon, *D* v *National Society for Prevention of Cruelty to Children* [1978] AC 171).

The realm

The fact that the concept of the state does not have any great political or legal significance in the language of English constitutional law is largely due to historical factors and to the ancient nature of the institutions around which the constitution has developed. Just as these have survived, so has the language of those earlier times in which such institutions were founded. Hence, according to what may be called the language of tradition, the territory over which the King or Queen (now the Crown in the form of the central government) exercised political power by right of succession and/or battle was properly referred to as 'the realm'. In constitutional law, therefore, the term has a similar meaning to that of 'the state' when the latter is used to describe the area over which the government has authority.

The government

This is yet another term capable of various meanings. It may be used, for example, as a collective noun for all those who hold Ministerial office at any particular time. These will all be persons with seats in the House of Commons (HC) or House of Lords (most in the Commons). The number of Ministers of which any government may consist is not fixed, but will usually be in the region of 100 to 130. These will range from the heads of major departments ('Secretaries of State'), to second-rank Ministers, usually referred to as 'Ministers of State', down to the more junior Ministers with titles such as 'Under Secretaries of State' or 'Parliamentary Secretaries'.

The 'government', in this sense, should not be confused with the political party which 'won' the last General Election and holds a majority of the seats in the House of Commons. Hence, after the 2015 General Election, the party 'in power' was the Conservatives with 331 MPs and an overall majority of 12. Those given Ministerial office by Mr Cameron became members of the government. Those not chosen remained merely backbenchers of the parliamentary Conservative party.

The word 'government' is also sometimes given a more extensive meaning which includes all of those institutions and persons at a national level who are concerned with the making and execution of policy. In this sense the term is not dissimilar to the institutional meaning of 'the Crown' and would encompass all those Ministers and civil servants who comprise the central administration.

Government also has a functional meaning in that it may be used to refer to the process through which the nation's affairs are regulated and protected. In this sense government means an activity rather than a particular combination of individuals or institutions.

The Cabinet

This refers to that group of senior Ministers (usually 20 to 24) who meet weekly or twice weekly with the Prime Minister to determine government policy and action. Most of these will be the heads of major government departments (e.g. Foreign Secretary, Chancellor of the Exchequer, Secretary of State for the Home Department). Others will have responsibility for a variety of activities which must be discharged effectively if the government is to survive and prosper. Hence the Cabinet will usually include Ministers with responsibility for managing government business in the House of Commons (Leader of the House of Commons) and in the House of Lords (Leader of the House of Lords). The Deputy Prime Minister and the Chief Secretary to the Treasury would also expect to be given Cabinet positions.

The executive

This is a term used collectively to refer to all those institutions and persons concerned primarily with the implementation of law and policy. Hence all central and local government departments would generally be included as would the police and the armed forces. Precluded from the definition are all those engaged in making law as opposed to enforcing it. Hence it would be improper to regard Parliament or the judiciary as falling within the term's usual meaning.

The legislature

When the term is used in domestic constitutional and administrative law, normally it may be understood as referring to the Parliament. For the purposes of enacting legislation the Parliament of the United Kingdom consists of the House of Commons, the House of Lords and the Monarch.

Not all law in the United Kingdom is made by Parliament. Many important legal rules are made by the judges and become part of the common law. Others are made by government Ministers and local authorities under powers Parliament has delegated to them (delegated or subordinate legislation). In the context of their law-making functions, neither the judges, Ministers nor local authorities should be understood as parts of the legislature.

The judiciary

Traditionally, in the United Kingdom, the term 'judiciary' was accepted as referring to all those employed to preside over a court of law at whatever level within the established legal system. Currently, therefore, and according to this approach, the domestic judiciary would consist of: District Judges (County and Magistrates' Courts), Circuit Judges (Crown Courts), High Court Judges, Lords Justices of Appeal (Court of Appeal), and the Justices of the Supreme Court.

Consequent, however, on the growth and proliferation of the modern system of administrative tribunals, and their increased importance in terms of the official process for the resolution of disputes, many would now probably regard the above definition as unduly restrictive. It is likely, therefore, that many of those taking this approach would regard the judiciary as properly extending to those senior presiding officers and chairpersons operating professionally within the tribunal system. These would include the Senior President of Tribunals and the Presidents of the various Chambers within the Upper and First Tier tribunals. These are appointed from the ranks of existing High Court judges or through open selection by the Judicial Appointments Board.

For the current system of statutory tribunals and inquiries, see Chapter 22.

Local government

Local government in England and Wales is the responsibility of the elected councils which direct the affairs of the various county, district and 'unitary' authorities in their provision of essential public services. Such authorities are created by and receive their powers from Acts of Parliament. The employees of local authorities are paid out of local funds and are not civil or crown servants.

Local authorities are funded by local taxation ('council tax'), government grants and through borrowing. In strict constitutional terms, such authorities are not under the direct control of central government. The latter does, however, exercise considerable influence over local government affairs through various statutory procedures, including the inspection of local government services, the requirements for Ministerial consent prior to the implementation of certain decisions (e.g. the application of a compulsory purchase order or the closure of a school), the issuing of directions to authorities not fulfilling their statutory obligations and the power to assume responsibility for certain local government functions should an authority be found to be 'in default' (see Education Act 1944, s 199). The central government may also seek to exert its will through its control of Treasury grants to local authorities and its ultimate, albeit seldom used, power to withhold moneys where dissatisfied by the standards of service provided by a particular authority.

To a considerable extent the structure of local government in England and Wales remains based on the reforms introduced in 1974 by the Local Government Act 1972. Outside the large conurbations these produced a simplified two-tier system with responsibility for the provision of services being divided between 47 County Councils and 333 District Councils. County Councils were given overall responsibility for such services as education, policing, planning, highways and personal social services. District Councils were to provide certain services in their own right (e.g. housing, public health, parks and cemeteries) with others being provided in partnership with and subject to the overall policy direction of the counties (e.g. local planning). The six major urban areas other than London (Manchester, Merseyside, West Yorkshire, South Yorkshire, West Midlands, Tyne and Wear) were put under the control of new Metropolitan County Councils, working again on a two-tier system with Metropolitan District Councils. This was modelled to a considerable extent on the system of local government for London introduced by the Local Government Act 1963 which created the Greater London Council (the 'GLC') and 32 London Borough Councils. This system of 'big city' government continued until 1986 when the GLC and the Metropolitan County Councils were dissolved and their functions largely devolved to the Metropolitan Districts which remained in existence (Local Government Act 1985). Where this was not feasible for strategic reasons, e.g. as in the case of the police, functions were devolved to joint committees consisting of **councillors** from the related Metropolitan Districts.

The system so prevailed until the passage of the Local Government Act 1992. This established a Local Government Commission for England and Wales to review existing boundaries and structures and gave the Secretary of State power by order made under section 17 of the Act to implement the Commission's recommendations. The functions of the Local Government Commission were passed to the Electoral Commission by the Political Parties, Elections and Referendums Act 2000.

The current procedure for making local government boundary changes is contained in the Local Government and Public Investment in Health Act 2007. This increased the power of the Minister and allows him or her to invite or direct local authorities to submit boundary reform proposals and to order the implementation of these with or without the advice of the Electoral Commission acting through its Boundary Committee.

The principal change to the structure of local government effected under these powers has been the creation, in parts of the country, of single tier or 'unitary' authorities, each providing the full range of local government services. Where this has been done, these have replaced the two-tier system of local administration in which, as explained above, services were shared between county and local district authorities.

As of January 2017, there were 406 local authorities in the United Kingdom. These consisted of 27 county councils and 201 county district councils, 55 English unitary authorities, 36 metropolitan boroughs, and 32 London boroughs. Scotland and Wales had 32 and 22 unitary authorities, respectively. Northern Ireland has 11 district councils. These worked alongside 5 education and library boards.

Local government in London is founded currently on the Greater London Authority Act 1999. The system was approved in a referendum of London elections in May 1998.

The Act established the **Greater London Authority** with a separately elected Mayor and Assembly, each to serve for four years. The Mayor has responsibility for, *inter alia*, transport, planning, the environment, setting the Authority's budget and the approval of economic development and cultural strategies. Election is by simple majority where there are only two candidates or by the additional member system where three or more compete.

The Mayor is accountable to the Assembly, which may override his/her decisions by a majority of two-thirds or more of its total membership.

The Assembly consists of 25 members. Fourteen are elected from the London constituencies and eleven by the electorate of London as a whole. Voters have two votes – a constituency vote and a London vote. The latter may be cast for an individual London candidate or for a party list. Constituency members are returned by the simple majority system. London members are elected by the De Hondt formula (see Greater London Authority Bill, Explanatory Notes, paras 48–53).

Outside the Greater London area a framework for the discharge of local executive functions through elected mayors or other forms of local executives was introduced by the Local Government Act 2000. The Act required local authorities to draw up proposals for the adoption of one of the following options:

(a) a directly elected mayor who appoints two or more councillors, up to a maximum of ten, to the executive (a 'mayor and cabinet executive');

(b) a councillor elected by the authority (the 'executive leader') and two or more councillors (a 'leader and cabinet executive');

(c) an elected mayor and an officer of the authority (a 'mayor and council manager executive').

Option (c) was later removed by the Local Government and Public Investment in Health Act 2007, section 62.

An executive headed by a directly elected mayor may not be established unless this is the will of the local electorate expressed in a referendum. Such a referendum should be held where:

- an authority's proposal included a directly elected mayor;
- five per cent or more of the council's electorate have petitioned for a directly elected mayor;
- the Secretary of State requires an authority to hold a referendum on any of the forms of executives available under the Act.

The purpose of the 2000 Act was to introduce a new system of decision-making into local government. This involves a distinct separation of personnel between those responsible for the formulation and implementation of policy and those engaged in the scrutiny of it.

Prior to the Act and since the inception of elected local government in the nineteenth century, local administration was the responsibility of committees of councillors (e.g. education committees, social services committees), either making decisions or submitting recommendations to the full council. This system is now perceived to be out of date. Under the new system an authority's policy framework and general budget proposals will be drawn up by the local executive and put before the full council for approval. It is claimed that this will lead to greater efficiency, transparency and accountability.

The geography of the constitution

Objective 4

The constitutional principles explained in the text that follows are those applicable to the geographical and political entity known as the United Kingdom. This consists of:

(a) England and Wales;

(b) Scotland;

(c) Northern Ireland.

Wales

For the creation of the modern Welsh Assembly and system of government, see pp. 24–5.

From the time of the military defeat of the Welsh prince Llywelyn in 1282, English monarchs claimed political authority over Wales by right of battle. Initially, however, the Welsh retained their own language, laws and customs. By Act of Parliament in 1536 England and Wales were united into a single kingdom with English as the common and official language. In 1543 the English common law was extended to Wales. Thereafter, England and Wales existed as a single political and administrative unit.

Scotland and the formation of Great Britain

At the time of the English and Welsh union, Scotland was a separate and independent 'state' with its own monarchy, Parliament, administrative and legal systems.

In 1603, Elizabeth I, the last of the Tudors and one of England's most renowned monarchs, died without issue. With her prior agreement the throne of England descended to James VI of Scotland. He became James I of England by right of succession owing to his direct descent from Henry VII, who was his grandfather. However, Scotland retained its existing Parliament and systems of law and government. In strict constitutional terms, therefore, the Kingdom of England and Wales and the Kingdom of Scotland remained as separate political and administrative entities but with a shared monarchy.

For the constitutional status of the Acts of Union, see Chapter 5, pp. 115–19.

Genuine political union between the two kingdoms did not occur until 1707. In that year Acts of Union were passed by both the English and Scottish Parliaments. Thus a single unified Parliament was created with authority over what was to be known thereafter as the Kingdom of Great Britain.

A referendum on the future constitutional and political status of Scotland was conducted on 18 September 2014. The question put to the Scottish electorate was 'should Scotland become an independent country'. In a turnout of 84.59 per cent the votes cast were as follows:

For the creation of the Scottish Parliament and system of government, see pp. 22–4.

Yes, 46.7%

No, 53.3%.

Ireland and the formation of the United Kingdom

The troubled political relationship between England and Ireland dates back to the twelfth century when English intrusion into Irish affairs, and attempts to exert political influence there, began. Initially, however, and despite the claim by Henry II (1154–89) and his successors to be 'Lords of Ireland', effective English government was largely confined to 'the pale', a strip of territory along Ireland's eastern seaboard that was most easily accessible from 'the mainland'.

Genuine military subjugation of Ireland was not effected until the end of the sixteenth century. This followed Henry VIII's decree in 1541 that he and his successors would be recognised, not simply in name but in political fact, as Kings of Ireland. Throughout the century that followed, therefore, each king occupied three separate thrones – those of England and Wales, Scotland, and Ireland. Ireland was allowed to retain its own Parliament and a limited measure of political autonomy. Roman Catholics and Protestant dissenters (i.e. the majority of the population) were, however, entirely excluded from the processes of government.

Political domination of Ireland was finally placed on a formal legal and institutional basis in 1800. In that year, following the precedent set in 1707, Acts of Union were passed by the

Irish Parliament and by the Parliament of Great Britain. Thus the United Kingdom of Great Britain and Ireland was created. The Irish Parliament in Dublin was thereby extinguished. Thereafter, legislative authority in Ireland was to be exercised by the Parliament of the United Kingdom at Westminster to which Ireland would send its elected representatives.

Ireland in its entirety remained within the United Kingdom until the Irish Free State (Agreement) Act 1922. The Act gave effect to the political agreement (the 'Treaty') reached by nationalist leaders and the British government following 'the Troubles' or Irish War of Independence 1919–21. The Free State consisted of twenty-six of the thirty-two counties of Ireland. It was deemed to be a self-governing dominion within the British Empire and given status similar to that of Canada, Australia and New Zealand. The Monarch continued to be recognised as titular head of state with their functions being performed by a Governor-General. In 1948 the new Irish State declared itself a Republic. Thereafter, the position of head of state was filled by an elected President. All formal constitutional links with the United Kingdom were thus severed.

The six northern counties of Ireland excluded from the Free State in 1922 remained within the United Kingdom. Under the terms of the Government of Ireland Act 1920, Northern Ireland was to have its own government and Parliament with authority over domestic affairs but subject at all times to the 'supreme authority of the Parliament of the United Kingdom' (s 75). Excluded from the legislative and executive jurisdiction of the institutions thus created were, *inter alia*, all matters relating to defence, foreign affairs and the armed forces.

The experiment with self-government in Northern Ireland did not prove entirely successful. Due to the religious and political composition of the province's population, the institutions of government were at all times in the control of the Unionist party, supported by its largely protestant electorate. Those of different political persuasions were thus doomed to permanent opposition and exclusion from the process of government. This was one of the reasons for the political discontent, and eventual disorder, which broke out in the late 1960s.

For more detail concerning the creation of the Northern Ireland Assembly and system of government, see pp. 26–30.

As the violence escalated, and increasing numbers of British military personnel were committed to the province, it was decided that the Northern Ireland government and Parliament should be abolished and that, henceforth, all matters concerning Northern Ireland should be determined by the central government in London ('direct rule'). This was effected by the Northern Ireland Constitution Act 1973.

Since that time a number of attempts have been made to restore to the province a measure of self-government. The latest of these was concluded in April 1998 by the Irish and UK governments and by the representatives of the rival political and paramilitary factions. It provided for an Assembly of 108 (reduced to 90 from 2017) members elected by proportional representation. From this is drawn a 'government' headed by a First Minister and Deputy First Minister, with ten other Ministers consisting of representatives from all the main political groups. The membership of the committees through which the Assembly operates is in numerical proportion to the elected representation of the parties on the floor of the Assembly. The Assembly has legislative authority in certain devolved matters. Voting is 'weighted' so that a measure of cross-party support will be needed before any proposal may be enacted.

For more on the Assembly, see Chapter 2.

In consultation and agreement with the government of the Irish Republic, the Assembly will seek to establish areas in which common policies or cooperation may be developed and, where appropriate, administered by bodies representing both the northern and southern governments. Ministers from the Assembly and the Irish government also meet regularly in a North–South Ministerial Council 'to develop . . . cooperation and action within the island of Ireland . . . on matters of mutual interest within the competence of the Administrations North and South'. Matters of common concern are also discussed in a larger British–Irish Council consisting of representatives from the Assembly, the British and Irish governments, and the Parliaments of Scotland, Wales, the Isle of Man and the Channel Islands.

The European dimension

Since its formation in 1801, the United Kingdom had been an entirely independent self-governing entity. This was affected significantly by the UK's accession to the European Community in 1973 and by its signature of the European Convention of Human Rights in 1952. By these actions the UK agreed to allow the government and law-making for parts of its hitherto internal affairs to be undertaken by the two pan-European organisations of which it had agreed to become a member. Thus, the institutions of the European Community became responsible for issues relating to trade, industry, commerce and agriculture with the European Court of Human Rights overseeing the observance by national governments of its human rights obligations. The United Kingdom, in effect, therefore, became subject to three processes of government and law: its ancient indigenous system, and the two new European systems, the EC/EU and the ECHR. For purposes of law and government Brussels and Strasbourg thereby became almost as important as the UK's traditional capital and seat of power.

Matters remained so until the EU referendum of June, 2016. This appeared to presage a possible reversal of these European influences with the UK's constitution and make-up. The question put before the UK electorate was:

'Should the United Kingdom remain a member of the European Union?'

Of those who voted (72.2 per cent of the total electorate), 52 per cent voted to leave the EU (48 per cent of all eligible voters) with 48 per cent voting to remain within it (35 per cent of all eligible voters).

The vote did not apply to and did not affect, therefore, the UK's treaty obligations under the European Convention on Human Rights.

Summary

This chapter:

- introduces the reader to the language and terminology of the British constitution and of constitutional and administrative law;
- provides a basic explanation of the history and development of the United Kingdom as a single entity;
- identifies the principal institutions and procedures through which the process of government is conducted at national and local level, including the effects of the process of devolution.

References

Bradley and Ewing (2014) *Constitutional and Administrative Law* (16th edn), London: Pearson.

Hood, Phillips and Jackson (2001) *Constitutional and Administrative Law* (8th edn), London: Sweet & Maxwell.

Further reading

Turpin (2011) *British Government and the Constitution* (7th edn), London: Cambridge University Press, Ch. 1.

The Characteristics of the Constitution

Objectives

After reading this chapter you should:

1. Appreciate the reasons why the British constitution is unwritten and the benefits and disadvantages of unwritten constitutions.
2. Recognise the difference between 'unitary' and 'federal' constitutions.
3. Understand the extent of the devolution of governmental powers to Northern Ireland, Scotland and Wales.
4. Be aware of the constitutional role of the Monarch.
5. Understand the nature and content of the United Kingdom's principal constitutional doctrines and the requirements of representative government.
6. Recognise the extent to which the British constitution has been influenced by membership of the European Union and the content of the European Convention on Human Rights.

Introduction

It is helpful to begin any examination of the constitutional law of the United Kingdom with a general survey of the various theories, principles and institutions of which the constitution itself is composed. This contributes to an understanding of how the various features relate to each other in a functional sense and how they operate collectively to achieve, however imperfectly, the liberal democratic objectives which underpin the present constitutional arrangement.

The unwritten constitution

Meaning

Objective 1

Although many of the rules of the British constitution may be found in law reports and parliamentary enactments, it remains true to say that no comprehensive attempt has ever been made to collect and codify these into a single defining instrument. As has been the case for centuries, therefore, the constitution's principal contents may still be traced to what may sometimes seem to be myriad judicial decisions, Acts of Parliament and established political practices (conventions). It is in this sense, therefore, that the constitution may be defined as 'unwritten'.

General awareness of the constitution's comparatively disparate nature should not be allowed, however, to obscure the efforts made in recent times to consolidate or 'tidy up' those elements perceived to be particularly lacking in clarity. Hence, for example, by the end of the twentieth century much of the law relating to the relationship between the individual and state in matters pertaining to personal liberty had been cast into statutory form by a series of key enactments including the Obscene Publications Act 1959, the Police and Criminal Evidence Act 1984 (PACE), the Public Order Act 1986, the Official Secrets Act 1989 and the Criminal Justice and Public Order Act 1994. Further codification in this general area has been effected by the Human Rights Act 1998 (HRA), the Regulation of Investigatory Powers Act 2000 (RIPA), the Terrorism Acts 2000, 2006 and 2011, the Serious and Organised Crime and Police Act 2005 and the Investigatory Powers Act 2017.

For more on the Constitutional Reform Act 2005, see pp. 47–8.

Also of significance in this context is the Constitutional Reform Act 2005, which has cast into statutory form a number of important rules relating to the doctrine of the separation of powers and the independence of the judiciary.

Reasons for

Only two other states in the world (Israel and New Zealand) have constitutions which may be described as unwritten. The reasons typically advanced for survival of such in the United Kingdom usually relate to the degree of political continuity evident in the development of the state and consist of a mixture of historical, social and cultural factors – all of which have combined to avoid the sort of cathartic political events (e.g. defeat in war or civil insurrection) which, in many other countries, have led to the abandonment and replacement of a pre-existing constitutional order.

Historical considerations

The 'mainland' of England was last invaded successfully in 1066 (the Norman Conquest). This can be explained, to some extent, by the country's geographical position and separation from Europe by the English Channel – a physical feature which has played no small part in maintaining the nation's political integrity. The last actual 'invasion' took place in 1745 when the Scottish Jacobite army led by the 'Young Pretender', Charles Stuart (grandson of James II), penetrated as far south as Derby. Subsequently, foreign troops entered the United Kingdom for belligerent purposes in 1798 when French troops landed on the West Coast of Ireland to assist the rebellion there, and in 1940 when German forces occupied the Channel Islands.

English history could not, of course, be described as a complete continuum of peace and tranquillity. The seventeenth century, in particular, was a period of great constitutional crisis and witnessed two major rebellions or Civil Wars, both of which led to the demise of individual monarchs. Neither conflict, however, led to the adoption of a permanent written constitution in the modern sense. Indeed, many of the great doctrines and conceptions of the attributes of civil government, including notions of representation, freedom and equality which were to spur the American and French revolutions of the late eighteenth century, and to which their constitutions sought to give expression, had not yet been articulated. The English Civil Wars did, however, directly lead to the creation of the most significant statutory elements of the post-revolutionary constitutional settlement, viz. the Bill of Rights 1689 which sought to regulate the relationship between the Crown and Parliament, and the Act of Settlement 1700 which sought to regulate the relationship between the Crown and Parliament. These remain fundamental elements of the modern constitution and give practical effect to the principles of parliamentary sovereignty and constitutional monarchy.

Towards the end of the eighteenth century relative economic prosperity and the very real threat of invasion by France combined to reduce the potentially destabilising influences of the American and French revolutions. As the nineteenth century dawned and the social and economic deprivations of the Industrial Revolution produced conditions ripe for political disorder, the established order was initially maintained by a policy of oppression. From the 1830s onwards, however, a sufficient blend of self-interest and enlightenment amongst the landed and industrial establishment combined to facilitate the type of moderate political and social reforms necessary to ensure uninterrupted economic development within the established legal and constitutional arrangements. This pragmatic and expedient attitude, sometimes referred to as the philosophy of reform to preserve, helped to avoid duplication of the revolutionary crises encountered by more intransigent regimes elsewhere in Europe. Prominent amongst these nineteenth-century reforms were the Representation of the People Acts 1832, 1867 and 1884, which enfranchised the male rate-paying population, the repeal of the Combination Acts which prohibited trade unions, and the various social and economic measures, including Public Health, Local Government and Factories legislation which attempted to introduce some minimum standards in terms of health, sanitation and working conditions.

During the ensuing years the United Kingdom has survived two World Wars and serious domestic industrial unrest (including the General Strike in 1926, the depression of the 1930s, the Miners' Strikes of 1974 and 1984 and the 'Poll Tax' riots of the early 1990s), but without significant constitutional disruption or rearrangement. Where changes to the relationships and the distribution of power between the institutions of government have occurred, this has been achieved by modifications of the relevant conventional and legal rules (e.g. the removal of the House of Lords' legislative veto by the Parliament Acts 1911 and 1949), thereby allowing the traditional framework to remain in place.

It is, of course, implicit in the above that not all the nations of the world have enjoyed an equally uninterrupted process of political development. Thus, in many countries, older systems of government have been abandoned after wars, revolutions or decolonialisation. These have then been replaced by government according to the political principles of whichever force – external or internal, popular or sectional – has been able to exert its will. In such circumstances it has seldom been possible for the new regime simply to wait for the appropriate rules and institutions of government to evolve. In order to avoid the danger of continued instability and insecurity these have been created, and given the requisite degree of legal authority to ensure peace, order and the continuity of the new system. In the vast majority of cases this has been done through the adoption of a written constitution.

Example

Examples of the institution of written constitutions in recent history in circumstances similar to those described would include that of the Federal Republic of Germany which came into effect in 1949 and recreated the German state after the fall of the Third Reich in 1945, and the constitutions devised for the various elements of the former Yugoslavia and for the states of Eastern Europe following the breaking up of the Soviet Union. It is also interesting and perhaps paradoxical to note that the government and Parliament of the United Kingdom were responsible for the formulation of a number of written constitutions, particularly in the 1960s, given to ex-colonial territories as part of their grants of independence (see, for example, the Independence Acts of Nigeria, Kenya and Malawi, 1960, 1963 and 1964 respectively).

Social and cultural factors

The relatively stable conditions in which the United Kingdom's unwritten constitution has developed are not something which can be explained, however, purely by reference to defining historical events or the lack of them. Social and cultural attributes have also had considerable influence in reducing the likelihood of political tensions. The dominant English society, it has been said, until recent times at least, displayed a marked degree of homogeneity, particularly in the racial and religious senses. Such significant differences as existed tended to be confined to the geographical margins, i.e. to those places (sometimes referred to as the 'Celtic Twilight') to which English influence was extended in order to create the wider political community known as the United Kingdom.

Attention has also been drawn to the contribution of some of the innate cultural preferences which, it has been claimed, for so long typified the attitude of the indigenous majority in political matters. These would include:

(a) a considerable level of agreement concerning the role of government and a reluctance to allow political partisanship to interfere with personal relationships;

(b) a general tendency to favour gradual development and moderate change with a correlative suspicion of ideological or 'quick fix' solutions;

(c) a high level of deference towards those responsible for the nation's affairs, and a related respect for authority and its political symbols, e.g. the monarchy, which in turn has encouraged a greater sense of national identity and loyalty.

The certainty of some of these culture assumptions is, of course, now under question. Racial and religious homogeneity has been affected by post-war immigration from British Commonwealth and former colonial territories. Trust in the political élite and even in the monarchy has been diminished by scandals, sleaze and exposés by an aggressive media. The parliamentary and party system is perceived by some as having 'failed to deliver', and being 'out of touch' particularly in social, economic and environmental terms. Individual 'cause' groups have increased in popularity at the expense of the established political parties. The very structure of the United Kingdom itself has even been challenged by a rise in nationalism.

All of this could, of course, be understood as demonstrating nothing more than the fact that a society's political culture is inevitably in a constant state of change and evolution. This might be to understate, however, the pressures to which the United Kingdom's venerable constitution is currently exposed. Perhaps all that can be said at present is that, although there is no clearly articulated popular campaign for a radical constitutional reform programme beyond that pursued by the post-1997 Labour government, signs of dissatisfaction with the workings of the established political and constitutional order are becoming increasingly apparent. These would include:

● low election 'turnouts' in recent general elections – 2005, 61.4 per cent; 2010, 61.1 per cent; 2015, 66.1 per cent;

● loss of confidence in the traditional 'two party' system – e.g. 12.6 per cent of national vote for United Kingdom Independence Party in 2015 General Election;

- the movement for Scottish independence and the possible break-up of the United Kingdom;
- lack of popular support for continued membership of the European Union.

Flexibility

Meaning

There are three principal ways in which the British constitution may be changed:

(a) by legislation enacted according to normal parliamentary procedure;

(b) by judicial decisions;

(c) by a change in existing conventional practices.

It follows that the constitution has no entrenched provisions, i.e. fundamental or basic laws which cannot be altered except in accordance with a special legislative procedure and/or approval in a referendum.

Entrenchment

Examples of this way of protecting constitutional fundamentals may be found in many of the world's leading liberal democratic constitutions. In the United States the requirement is that any amendment must be approved by majorities of two-thirds in both Houses of Congress and by the legislatures of 'three fourths of the several states' (Art V). Entrenchment is also commonplace in the constitutions of Europe. The French prescription is for amendments to be passed by both Houses of Parliament (National Assembly and Senate) supported by a referendum. Alternatively amendments may be made by Parliament, without a referendum, providing these receive the support of three-fifths of the votes cast (Art 89).

The purpose of such entrenchment is to protect key provisions (e.g. those relating to basic civil liberties) from the passing whims and caprice of those who may hold political office from time to time. The degree of flexibility of written constitutions will therefore depend, to a considerable extent, on the method of entrenchment, if any, which is used. Hence, it is perfectly possible for a written constitution to have no entrenched provisions whatsoever and be subject, therefore, to amendment by ordinary legislative process or, at the other extreme, to contain clauses which are to be regarded as immutable (e.g. the basic human rights requirements of the 1949 German Constitution).

Evolution

In the absence of such restraining procedures it is clear that the British constitution may be changed relatively easily and quickly and may be described, therefore, as having a greater degree of flexibility than many of its written counterparts. This ready susceptibility to change has, however, been both praised and criticised. Hence, those supportive of the existing model have tended to emphasise the way in which the constitution has been able both to adapt to changing times and expectations about the practice of government and, on occasions, to respond to the needs of moment; as in 1975 when the Labour Prime Minister, Harold Wilson, suspended the convention of collective ministerial responsibility to enable Ministers to speak freely on the referendum concerning British membership of the European Community – an approach repeated by the Conservative premier David Cameron prior to the 2016 referendum on the same matter. More sceptical opinions have suggested, however, that unqualified assertions of the benefits of flexibility could be based on the possibly dubious assumption that governments can be trusted not to use their political control of Parliament (through their majority in the House of Commons) to impose constitutional change purely for reasons of political expediency or ephemeral ideology.

Much depends, therefore, on the view that is taken of the effectiveness of the domestic democratic process to deter politicians from unwarranted interference with the constitution's primary rules, i.e. those which underpin contemporary political values and those 'constituent' enactments which brought the state into existence, e.g. the Bill of Rights 1689, the Act of Settlement 1700 and the Acts of Union 1707. At present the assumption appears to be that those tempted to 'meddle' with these crucial provisions do so in the knowledge that this may excite the type of widespread and sustained opposition which is impossible to either ignore or overcome.

The ideal

All constitutions do, of course, need to be changed from time to time. If they are not, they atrophy and become irrelevant to the needs of the times. Radical alterations may then be occasioned by political tensions. The ideal appears to be, therefore, a constitutional arrangement which avoids 'the Scylla of total rigidity and the Charybidis of total flexibility' (Calvert, *An Introduction to British Constitutional Law*, 1985). Some constitutions, as illustrated, seek this through formal restraints. The British preference is for reliance more on informal political and cultural pressures. What really matters, however, is whether the correct balance is struck and that required constitutional change is able to take place within a framework which provides sufficient protection for those fundamentals which retain their functional and ideological validity.

Unitary

Meaning

Objective 2

The principal distinction between unitary and federal systems of government is that in the former ultimate legal authority is not divided between the central and regional authorities.

The relationship between central and local government

In the United Kingdom all sovereign or ultimate legal power is vested in one omnipotent central legislative assembly, viz. the Westminster Parliament. There are, therefore, no regional or state assemblies possessing autonomous authority, i.e. that which cannot be overridden by Parliament.

Local government is conducted by county, district and unitary councils. These do not equate, however, with the regional bodies which might be found in a federal system. Local authorities in the United Kingdom are created by Parliament (the present local government structure deriving from the Local Government Acts 1972 and 1992) and receive their powers from Parliament (in Housing Acts, Education Acts, Highways Acts, etc.). Hence Parliament has the power to abolish all or any type of authority (e.g. Metropolitan County Councils by the Local Government Act 1985) and to make radical alterations – in recent years usually reductions – to the powers allocated to them. In a federal arrangement, by contrast, the existence and partial autonomy of the state's regional components will usually originate and receive protection from the founding constitutional document. In other words, the relevant provisions are entrenched 'so that they cannot be amended at the sole discretion of the federation or of any province or combination of provinces' (Hood Phillips and Jackson, *Constitutional and Administrative Law*, 2001).

Local authorities in the United Kingdom also have the power to make law (by-laws) for the good rule and government of the districts for which they are responsible. Again, however, such power is derived from Parliament and may be revoked or altered at any time. Also, any by-laws which are inconsistent with an Act of Parliament are deemed to be invalid.

Central government and the regions

The United Kingdom does, of course, consist of a number of regions or provinces in the geographical and ethnic sense (particularly Scotland, Wales and Northern Ireland). Prior to the creation of national assemblies in Scotland and Wales in 1998, only Northern Ireland had previously been allowed to have its own Parliament (located at Stormont in East Belfast). It was created by the Government of Ireland Act 1920 but ceased to exist as a result of the Northern Ireland (Temporary Provisions) Act 1972. The existence of the Stormont Parliament was, therefore, at all times, subject to the will of the imperial Parliament at Westminster. Its legislative powers were contained in and delimited by the 1920 Act. Any legislation outside the prescribed limits or inconsistent with Westminster legislation was deemed to be invalid. This sole experiment in regional government in the United Kingdom did not represent, therefore, a significant departure from the essence of the unitary principle.

For the Scottish, Welsh, and Northern Ireland Assemblies, see below, pp. 22–30.

At the time of writing, Scotland, Wales and Northern Ireland each continue to elect and send representatives to the sovereign Westminster Parliament. Each does have its own central government department (the Scottish, Welsh and Northern Ireland Offices). These again, however, are directly accountable to Westminster. The creation of representative assemblies for Scotland, Wales, and Northern Ireland is dealt with below.

Attitudes to federalism

The unitary principle and its expression in the current structure of the United Kingdom has been, of course, a matter of political and national preference. By definition it has been either partly or wholly inimical to the aspirations of nationalist movements. It seems likely, however, that any grants of autonomy precipitated by nationalist pressures, at least in Scotland or Wales, would be effected within the parameters, both geographical and legal, of the unitary state and would, therefore, remain subject to the ultimate authority of Westminster (see below, however, for comments concerning the new Assembly for Northern Ireland).

The relevance of federalism to the United Kingdom was considered by the Royal Commission on the Constitution which reported in 1973 (Cmnd 5460). The essence of its conclusions were contained in the following paragraph of its report:

> Although there are some circumstances in which the benefits to be derived from federalism may outweigh those of any practical alternative, in our view such circumstances do not exist in the United Kingdom. We believe that to most people a federal system would appear strange and artificial. It would not provide continuity with the past or sufficient flexibility for the future. It would be dominated by the overwhelming political importance and wealth of England. The English Parliament would rival the United Kingdom Federal Parliament; and in the Federal Parliament the representation of England could hardly be scaled down in such a way as to enable it to be outvoted by Scotland, Wales and Northern Ireland. A United Kingdom Federation of the four countries, with a Federal Parliament and provincial Parliaments . . . is not, therefore, a realistic proposition (*ibid.*, paras 530–31).

Devolution to Scotland, Wales and Northern Ireland

As explained, the government which took office following the General Election of May 1997 was committed to a programme of constitutional reform. In its agenda were proposals for the creation of elected assemblies in Scotland, Wales and Northern Ireland. Popular approval for these was secured in a series of referenda conducted in 1997 and 1998.

The Scottish Parliament

Background

The government's White Paper, 'Scotland's Parliament', was published on 24 July 1997. In a referendum of Scottish electors on its proposals, 74.3 per cent were in favour with 65.5 per cent also in favour of vesting the Parliament with limited tax-varying powers. The referendum turnout was 60.4 per cent. The first elections for the Scottish Parliament were held on 6 May 1999, with the first meeting of the Parliament taking place on 12 May.

Creation

Statutory authority for the establishing and working of the Scottish Parliament was provided by the Scotland Act 1998, as amended by the Scotland Act 2012. The framework for Scottish self-government as contained therein is as follows.

Composition and election

The Parliament is composed of 129 members. Seventy-three are directly elected from existing parliamentary constituencies by simple majority vote (s 1). A further 56 members are elected by proportional representation from eight regional constituencies. These are the same constituencies used for elections to the European Parliament. Each regional constituency returns seven members (s 1 and Sched 1).

Electors cast two votes each – one for a constituency candidate and one for either an individual regional candidate or for a regional party list (ss 6, 7 and 8).

The age at which people qualify to vote in Scottish Assembly elections is sixteen (Scottish Elections (Reduction of Voting Age) Act 2015). As in the rest of the United Kingdom the qualifying age previously was eighteen.

Persons disqualified from the House of Commons are disqualified from membership of the Scottish Parliament. Peers of the realm, ordained priests and ministers of religion are eligible, however, as are European Union citizens resident in the United Kingdom (ss 15 and 16).

The behaviour and activities of Members of the Scottish Parliament are regulated by a Code of Conduct. This extends to such matters as the declaration and registration of interests, payments from outside sources, lobbying, etc. Complaints alleging breach of the Code may be made to the Scottish Parliamentary Standards Commissioner. After investigating a complaint he/she may issue a report to the Scottish Parliament's Standards, Procedures and Public Appointments Committee or, where the Member's conduct, if proven, appears to amount to a criminal offence, notify the Committee and submit a report to the Procurator Fiscal.

Duration and dissolution

The Parliament sits for fixed terms of five years. In between such 'ordinary' General Elections an 'extraordinary' General Election may occur where:

(a) the Parliament so resolves by a majority of two-thirds of its total membership;

(b) the First Minister resigns and is not replaced within 28 days (i.e. the Parliament is unable to form an alternative administration) (ss 2, 3 and 46).

Legislative authority

Laws enacted by the Scottish Parliament are valid only so far as they relate to matters within its legislative competence ('devolved matters') and are compatible with European Union law and the Human Rights Act 1998 (s 29).

The principal matters devolved to the Scottish Parliament were agriculture, forestry and fisheries, education, environment, health and social services, housing, law and order, local government, sport and the arts, tourism and economic development, and transport. A power to increase or reduce income tax by 3p in the pound was also provided for but was not used. Powers to increase or reduce rates of income tax in all bands was contained in the Scotland Act 2012. The relevant provisions took effect in 2016.

Issues put specifically beyond the competence of the Scottish Parliament are known as 'reserved matters'. These extend to the Crown, Parliament and the constitution, foreign and European affairs, defence and national security, and immigration and nationality. Beyond these limitations, the validity of an enactment is not open to question solely on the ground of procedural error during its parliamentary stages (s 28).

Questions of competence and validity are determined by the Judicial Committee of the Privy Council upon reference thereto either by the Advocate-General for Scotland or the Lord Advocate (s 33).

Power is also given to the Secretary of State for Scotland to prohibit any Scottish Bill from being submitted for the Royal Assent where there are reasonable grounds to believe that it would be incompatible with any international obligations, the interests of defence or national security, or would have an adverse effect on the law relating to any reserved matter (s 35).

Any provision in a Bill before the Scottish Parliament which seeks to modify the law relating to the electoral franchise or system, the number of constituencies or electoral regions or to the number of members to be returned from a particular constituency or electoral region should be approved by a parliamentary majority consisting of not less than two-thirds of all the Parliament's members.

In terms of its internal proceedings the Parliament has power to require the attendance of any person to give evidence relating to any matter within its competence and to require the production of any documentation relating to the same over which the person has control (s 23).

The Scottish Parliament's proceedings and authorised publications relating thereto attract absolute privilege for the purposes of the law of defamation (s 41). Qualified privilege extends to fair and accurate reports of the same (Defamation Act 1996, s 15 and Sched 1).

The legislative relationship between the Scottish Parliament and the sovereign Parliament at Westminster is regulated by an arrangement known as the Sewel Convention. This is to the effect that the Westminster Parliament will not enact certain types of legislation for Scotland without the prior consent of the Scottish Parliament. The types of legislative provision covered by the Convention are those which:

- relate to a devolved matter;
- alter the legislative competence of the Scottish Parliament;
- alter competence of Scottish Ministers.

Scottish approval for any such measure is known as a Legislative Consent Motion (LCM).

The Convention is named after Lord Sewel, the government Minister who announced during the Scotland Act's passage through Parliament that: 'Westminster would not normally legislate with regard to devolved matters in Scotland without the consent of the Scottish Parliament'.

The executive

This consists of:

(a) the First Minister;

(b) such other Ministers as he/she may appoint;

(c) the Lord Advocate and the Solicitor-General for Scotland (s 44).

The First Minister is to be a person who commands a majority among Members of the Parliament. He or she will appoint Ministers from Members of the Parliament with its approval (s 47).

The activities of Scottish Ministers are subject to restrictions similar to those applying to the legislative power. Hence Scottish Ministers are forbidden from making any subordinate legislation or taking any other action incompatible with the law of the European Union or the Human Rights Act 1998 (s 57). In addition, the Secretary of State for Scotland is given authority to prohibit the making or execution of any decision or subordinate legislation reasonably believed to be incompatible with any international obligations and to revoke any subordinate legislation reasonably believed to be incompatible with the interests of defence or national security or which modifies and, which it is reasonably believed, has adverse effect on the law relating to any reserved matter (ss 57 and 58).

The Welsh Assembly

Background

The government's proposals for the above were published on 22 July 1997 in its White Paper, 'A Voice for Wales'. These were approved in a referendum on 18 September 1997. The first elections to the Assembly were held on 6 May 1999. Its first meeting took place on 12 May 1999. Authority for creation of the Assembly was provided by the Government of Wales Act 1998 as amended by the Wales Act 2006.

Composition, election and duration

The Welsh Assembly is composed of 40 constituency members and 20 regional members (Wales Act 2006, s 1). Elections take place every five years (s 3). Each elector casts two votes – one for a constituency member and one for either a regional candidate or a regional party list (s 6). Constituency members are elected by the simple majority system. Regional members are returned by the additional member system of proportional representation.

In order to make the Welsh Assembly government genuinely answerable to the Welsh Assembly, the Wales Act 2006 provided that Welsh Assembly elections should continue to take place every four years, but that 'extraordinary' elections should also be possible within such four-year periods if so resolved by at least two-thirds of all Assembly Members (i.e. at least 40).

The general disqualifications applying to the House of Commons are applicable to membership of the Welsh Assembly (s 16). Disputes as to qualifications are dealt with by the High Court (s 19).

Powers and functions

Under the 1998 Act the Assembly was not possessed of any primary legislative power but had the right to be consulted by the Secretary of State for Wales concerning any proposed legislation of the Westminster government which had implications for Wales (s 33) and to have transferred to it:

(a) any function so far exercisable by a Minister of the Crown in relation to Wales, including powers to make subordinate legislation;

(b) any or all of the functions of a Welsh Health Authority or other public body specified in Sched 4 to the Act.

Significant extensions to the Welsh Assembly's legislative competence were effected by the Wales Act 2006. This gave the Assembly the power to make laws for Wales known as 'Measures of the Welsh Assembly' (s 93). The power to pass such Measures was limited to particular aspects of the twenty general areas or 'Fields' of government responsibility devolved to Wales (Sched 5). Such aspects or 'Matters' were not fully identified in the Act but were to be allotted to the Assembly's legislative competence on a piecemeal basis as and when felt appropriate. This was to be done by Order in Council ('Legislative Competence Orders'), usually at the behest of the Welsh government, or by Act of Parliament.

The 2006 Act further provided for the Assembly to be endowed with full primary legislative authority over the twenty devolved areas of government (s 101 and Sched 7). This was designed to allow the Welsh Assembly to make laws for Wales without the requirement for a specific grant of legislative competence, as in the cases of Measures made under section 93. Any such grant of full legislative authority was, however, made subject to the precondition that it was supported by a majority of the Welsh electorate voting in a referendum (s 103). Accordingly, a referendum to this effect was conducted in Wales on 11 March 2011. The question put to Welsh voters was: 'Do you want the Assembly to make laws on all matters in the twenty subject-areas it has powers for?' In a turnout of 31 per cent, 65.5 per cent voted 'yes'; 36.5 per cent voted 'no'. The Welsh Assembly's new and enhanced legislative competence took effect as from 5 May 2011. Since that date, laws passed by the Assembly qualified for the title of 'Acts of the National Assembly of Wales'. These replaced and brought to an end the process of Welsh legislation by way of Assembly 'Measures'. Questions of whether an Act of the Welsh Assembly falls within its legislative competence may be referred to the Supreme Court by the Welsh Counsel-General or the Attorney-General (s 112).

In addition to being confined to the competencies devolved to it, the Welsh Assembly is also prohibited from passing legislation which is incompatible with the law of the European Convention on Human Rights or with EU law. It should be noted too that, in the final analysis, the sovereign Parliament at Westminster reserves the right to legislate on Welsh affairs in general, including the devolved areas of government (s 107).

The Assembly has no power to make legislation of any type or take any other action incompatible with European Union law or the Human Rights Act 1998.

The Welsh Ombudsman has the power to investigate complaints relating to administrative action taken by the Assembly or other Welsh public authorities.

The Assembly has authority to require any person to attend its proceedings for the purpose of giving evidence and to require the production of documents relating to the same (ss 37–40). Absolute privilege for the purposes of the law of defamation applies to its proceedings and to authorised reports of the same (s 42). Qualified privilege extends to other fair and accurate reports of its proceedings (e.g. newspaper reports) (s 40 and Defamation Act 1996, s 15 and Sched 1).

Complaints about the behaviour of Welsh Assembly Members may be made to the National Assembly for Wales Commissioner for Standards. The findings of his/her investigations are reported to the Assembly's committee on Conduct. Where criminality appears to have been revealed, the Committee is informed and the matter is referred to the police.

Wales Bill 2016–17

The degree of legislative competence entrusted to the Welsh Assembly in 1998 was different to that applicable the Northern Irish and Scottish Assemblies. Hence, while the latter two assemblies may legislate on any issues that may come before them providing that these do not relate to 'reserved matters', the legislative activity of the Welsh Assembly was been limited to those specific subject areas or legislative competencies specifically allocated to it. The intention of the Bill was that the Welsh Assembly should be put into a similar position as those for Northern Ireland and Scotland with the extent of its legislative remit being circumscribed solely by the reserved matters withheld from it.

In addition, the Bill set out to lay down a series of tests for determining when a piece of Welsh legislation should be regarded as having no effect. Thus a legislative provision would be outside the Assembly's legislative authority if:

- it was to apply outside of England and Wales;
- its practical or 'day-to-day' effects would extend beyond Wales;
- it related to any reserved matter;
- it was incompatible with EU law or the European Convention of Human Rights;
- it contravened one of the restrictions in Schedule 2 by allowing the modification by way of subordinate legislation of any reserved matter, private law or criminal law or any amendment of various key pieces of primary Westminster legislation (e.g. EC Act 1972, Human Rights Act 1998, Wales Act 1998, Civil Contingencies Act 2004).

The executive

The Welsh Assembly government consists of the Assembly First Minister and other Ministers assembly appointed by him or her (ss 45–51). The First Minister is elected by the Assembly. In the areas for which they are responsible, the activities of each Welsh Minister are scrutinised by Assembly committees which, in their composition, should, 'so far as it is practicable', reflect the 'balance of parties in the Assembly' (ss 29–30). As with the Assembly, Welsh Ministers may not take any action which is incompatible with EU law or the requirements of the ECHR (ss 80–81).

The Northern Ireland Assembly

Background

Creation of the Assembly was one of the central pillars of the Good Friday Agreement concluded on 10 April 1998. The Agreement was supported by 71.2 per cent of those voting in the referendum of 22 May 1998. The first meeting of the Assembly took place on 1 July 1998, when it elected its First and Deputy First Ministers.

The statutory framework for the Assembly was provided by the Northern Ireland Act 1998. The Act restated Northern Ireland's constitutional guarantee as part of the United Kingdom and provides that this status shall not be altered without the consent of a majority of the people of Northern Ireland voting in a border poll (s 1).

Election, composition and duration

Elections to the Assembly are for fixed periods of five years and are conducted according to the 'Single Transferable Vote' (s 33). Within such periods, however, an 'extraordinary election' may take place if so resolved by at least two-thirds of the Assembly's total constituencies.

These are the same as for elections to the Westminster Parliament. Each of these returns five Members (Members of the Legislative Assembly – MLAs) to an Assembly of ninety members in total. A person holding a seat in the Northern Ireland Assembly may not, at the same time, be a member of Dail Eireann (the parliament of the Republic).

Disqualifications apply according to the provisions of the Northern Ireland Assembly Disqualification Act 1975 (s 36). Disputes as to qualification are to be dealt with by the Northern Ireland High Court (s 38).

The Parliamentary Voting Systems and Constituencies Act 2011 provided for a reduction of the number of Westminster constituencies in Northern Ireland from 18 to 16. The first Northern Ireland elections to be conducted on this basis were those of March, 2017.

Legislative and other powers

Legislation enacted by the Assembly is not valid if it is outside its competence as prescribed by the 1998 Act. That is, if it:

(a) relates to the law of any country or territory outside Northern Ireland;

(b) deals with an excepted or reserved matter (Scheds 2 and 3);

(c) is incompatible with the European Convention on Human Rights;

(d) is incompatible with European Union law;

(e) discriminates between persons on religious or political grounds (s 6).

Excepted matters are areas of legislative jurisdiction which are unlikely to be transferred to the competence of the Assembly. This list includes such matters as the Crown, Parliament and constitution of the United Kingdom; parliamentary elections, including those for the Assembly itself; international relations and those within the European Union; the defence of the realm; the armed forces; nationality and immigration; and national security.

Reserved matters are those which may be transferred by order of the Secretary of State to the Assembly depending on the political circumstances.

The Attorney-General for Northern Ireland may refer questions of validity for determination by the Judicial Committee of the Privy Council (s 11). The Assembly may also seek the opinion of the Northern Ireland Human Rights Commission as to the compatibility of particular Bills with the requirements of human rights obligations (s 13).

Bills passed by the Assembly are submitted for Royal Assent by the Secretary of State for Northern Ireland. A Bill may not be submitted if it appears to be outside the Assembly's competence or if it is the subject of a reference to the Privy Council. The Secretary of State may also refuse to submit any Bill which deals with an excepted or reserved matter (i.e. matters which, unlike excepted matters, may be transferred to the Assembly, see Sched 3) or which contains a provision which would be incompatible with any international obligations, the interests of defence or national security, the protection of safety or public order, or which would have an adverse effect 'on the operation of the single market in goods and services within the United Kingdom' (s 14).

Where thirty or more members of the Assembly so petition on any matter to be voted on (a 'Petition of Concern'), the vote on that matter requires 'cross-community support' (s 42), viz.:

(a) a majority of all those voting and of both the designated Nationalists and Unionists voting ('parallel consent'); or

(b) 60 per cent of all those voting, including 40 per cent of the Nationalists voting and 40 per cent of the Unionists voting ('weighted majority') (s 4).

Other matters designated by the 1998 Act for cross-community support included:

- changes to the categories of reserved and transferred matters;
- decisions relating to the number of Ministers and their responsibilities;
- exclusion of a Minister or member from holding office;
- a vote on the draft budget;
- election of the Speaker and deputies;
- financial votes, resolutions or Acts;
- votes on making or amending standing orders.

Further matters for cross-community support designated by Standing Order of the Assembly extend to:

- motions for the suspension of a Standing Order;
- application of cross-community support to any matter not already identified by the Northern Ireland Act 1998.

The Assembly is empowered to require any person to attend its proceedings to give evidence and to produce any documents relating thereto (s 44). Failure to do so constitutes an offence (s 45).

Absolute privilege in defamation applies to 'the making of a statement in the Assembly' and to 'the publication of a statement under the Assembly's authority' (s 50). Other fair and accurate reports of its proceedings are protected by qualified privilege (Defamation Act 1996, s 15 and Sched 1).

Complaints about injustice in the actions and decisions of Northern Ireland's twelve executive departments and other public bodies may be made to the Northern Ireland Ombudsman. The Ombudsman fulfils the offices and functions of both Northern Ireland's principal statutory complaints systems, viz. the Northern Ireland Assembly Ombudsman (see the Ombudsman (NI) Order 1996) and the Northern Ireland Commission for Complaints (see Commissioner for Complaints (NI) Order 1996). The jurisdiction of the Assembly Ombudsman covers primarily Northern Ireland's 'central' executive departments while the jurisdiction of the Commission for Complaints extends to 'local' and other public authorities not accompanied by the central executive.

Complaints about the conduct and activities of Northern Ireland Assembly Members may be made to the Northern Ireland Assembly Commissioner for Standards. The office was created by the Assembly Members (Independent Financial Review and Standards) Act (NI) 2011. The main function of the Commissioner is to investigate alleged breaches of the Assembly's Code of Conduct. This is a detailed set of prescriptions which identifies 11 different categories of prohibited payments, interests, and benefits. Completed investigations are submitted to the Assembly's Committee on Standards and Privileges.

The executive

This is headed by a First Minister and a Deputy First Minister elected jointly with the support of:

(a) a majority of all Assembly Members;

(b) a majority of Nationalist Assembly Members;

(c) a majority of Unionist Assembly Members.

Should either of the above Ministers resign, the other also ceases to hold office (s 16). The executive also includes ten other Ministers determined jointly by the First and Deputy First Minister and approved by the Assembly with cross-community support (s 18). Party representation in the executive reflects the principal political groupings in the Assembly according to the formula contained in section 18.

Members of the executive have no power to make any subordinate legislation or take any other action incompatible with European Union law or the European Convention on Human Rights (s 24). In addition, the Secretary of State may prohibit the making of any such legislation or any other action which would not be consistent with any international obligations.

Ministers may be excluded from office, and entire political parties from the Assembly, if the Assembly resolves that the Minister or party 'is not committed to non-violence and exclusively peaceful and democratic means'. Such exclusion will be of twelve months' duration (s 30).

The Hillsborough Agreement

The initial transfer of powers to the new Northern Ireland government did not include those relating to policing and justice.

In political terms this was not effected until 2010 under the terms of an agreement between Northern Ireland's political leaders reached at Hillsborough Castle, County Down, on 24 February of that year. The Agreement was approved on 9 March 2010, by 'cross-community' vote in the Northern Ireland Assembly. The Westminster legislation used for the transfer was the Northern Ireland Act 1998, s 4 and the Northern Ireland Act 2008. The practical structure for the implementation of the Agreement was contained in the Department of Justice Act 2009, enacted by the Northern Ireland Assembly. The Hillsborough Agreement was made possible by a number of factors. These included:

- an increased readiness amongst Northern Ireland's political leaders to work together;
- a commitment by Sinn Fein to support the forces of law and order and by the Democratic Unionist Party (DUP) to share power with nationalists and republicans;
- reform of the police and the replacement of the Royal Ulster Constabulary (RUC) by the Police Service of Northern Ireland (PSNI);
- decommissioning of arms by the main paramilitary groupings and the IRA's announcement in 2005 that henceforth its objectives would be pursued by peaceful means.

Implementation of the Agreement was further facilitated by the provision that no persons from either of the main political parties, the DUP and Sinn Fein, should be nominated for the post of Minister of Justice. A single candidate was, therefore, put forward. This was David Ford, the leader of the Alliance Party, which seeks to draw its support from both sides of the sectarian divide.

Human rights and discrimination

The Northern Ireland Act 1998 created two supervisory bodies in the area of human rights and discrimination. These were:

(a) the Northern Ireland Human Rights Commission (s 68);

(b) the Equality Commission of Northern Ireland (s 73).

The principal functions of the Human Rights Commission are to:

(i)   keep under review the adequacy and effectiveness in Northern Ireland of the law and practice relating to the protection of human rights and to advise the Secretary of State and Assembly in related matters;

(ii) to assist those bringing legal proceedings in human rights matters;

(iii) to generally promote awareness and understanding of the importance of human rights (ss 68, 69 and 70).

The Equality Commission took over the functions of the Fair Employment Commission for Northern Ireland, the Equal Opportunities Commission for Northern Ireland, the Commission for Racial Equality for Northern Ireland and the Northern Ireland Disability Council.
The Commission is charged to:

- promote equality of opportunity in Northern Ireland;
- work for the elimination of unlawful discrimination and harassment;
- keep under review and recommend changes to Northern Ireland's fair employment and treatment legislation;
- promote affirmative action in matters relating to the above.

Further protection for human rights and equality issues was provided by section 75, which imposes a duty on all public bodies in Northern Ireland to have due regard to the need to promote equality of opportunity between persons of different religious belief, political opinion, racial group, age, marital status or sexual orientation, between men and women generally, between persons with a disability and persons without, and between persons with dependants and those without. Discrimination by a public body on the grounds of religion or politics is a civil offence remedied by damages and/or injunction (s 76).

The devolved assemblies and judicial review

Legislation of the devolved assemblies is subject to judicial review on the grounds, and to the extent, specified in the legislation by which they were created. As indicated above, this, in general, permits the courts to review and question such legislation if it affects matters not devolved to the Assembly in question, or transgresses the requirements of the law of the European Union or the European Convention on Human Rights. No guidance is offered in the devolution Acts on the further question of whether the legislation of the devolved assemblies may also be questioned on the traditional common law grounds of review. This issue was, however, considered by the Supreme Court in *AXA General Insurance Ltd* v *Lord Advocate* [2012] 1 AC 868. The essential guiding principle enunciated by the court was that the power of review of devolved legislation was limited to those unlikely but conceivable circumstances where such legislation sought to undermine the constitutional fundamentals of the rule of law.

For more on judicial review, see Chapters 14–15.

We now have in Scotland a government which enjoys a large majority in the Scottish Parliament. Its party dominates the only chamber in that Parliament and the committees by which Bills that are in progress are scrutinised. It is not entirely unthinkable that a government which has that power may seek to use it to abolish judicial review or diminish the role of the courts in protecting the interests of the individual. Whether this is likely to happen is not the point. It is enough that it might conceivably do so. The rule of law requires that the judges must retain the power to insist that legislation of that extreme kind is not law which the courts will recognise (Lord Hope).

Beyond this, and due to their representative authority, it was agreed that it should not be open to the courts of law to question the legislation of the devolved assemblies on the well-established grounds of unreasonableness, irrationality or arbitrariness.

> . . . it would be quite wrong for the judges to substitute their views on these issues for the considered judgment of a democratically elected legislature (*ibid*).

The overall judicial approach to the devolution statutes has been that these should be 'interpreted generously and purposively, bearing in mind the values which the constitutional provisions are intended to embody' (Lord Bingham, *Robinson* v *Secretary of State for Northern Ireland* [2002] UKHL 32). Put less diplomatically, this would appear to mean that judges should keep in mind the political background to the present constitutional arrangements for the north of Ireland when interpreting the legislation which gives effect to them and should do so in a way which best facilitates the political objective behind the settlement.

The first example of a Bill from a devolved assembly being found to be outside of its competence occurred in *Recovery of Medical Costs for Asbestos Diseases (Wales)* [2015] UKSC 3. The Bill was intended to make employers and insurers liable for the medical costs incurred by persons who had suffered from certain types of asbestos-related industrial diseases. In this instance, the majority of the court were not prepared to hold that the Welsh Assembly's legislative jurisdiction over the 'organisation and funding of the National Health Service' (Government of Wales Act 1998, s 18) was sufficient to empower it to impose such costs on business and financial concerns operating in the private sector of the economy.

Constitutional monarchy

Definition and general characteristics

Objective
4

Western Europe has eight surviving monarchies, all of which qualify to be regarded as constitutional monarchies. The most essential attribute of a constitutional monarchy is that it exercises its power and authority subject to the demands of the state's law and constitution, whether written or unwritten. In the constitutional dimension of the United Kingdom this means according to the will of Parliament.

Other general attributes of the role and purpose of a constitutional monarch would be:

1 to personify the nation as a whole;

2 to personify the constitutional authority of the state;

3 to act as the ultimate guardian and guarantor of the constitution and constitutional behaviour;

4 to represent the primacy of the constitution over political ideology, and the passing whims of party politics;

5 to reflect the shared history, traditions, values and aspirations of the people over which the state claims authority;

6 to provide a practical 'a-political' means of resolving any constitutional dilemma or deadlock (see below, 'Constitutional crises and royal discretion');

7 to act as the secular head of the state's national religion.

In the British context this means that the monarchy accepts the limitations imposed upon it by statute, convention and the common law. It presupposes, therefore, a monarchy which retains its status and symbolic importance but which is no longer directly involved in the political process.

Evolution

It was not always thus. English monarchs were once very much involved in the practicalities of government. Even after the events of 1689 had demonstrated that the throne was held at the will of Parliament, individual monarchs continued to exercise considerable influence at least until the earlier part of the nineteenth century. Queen Victoria (1837–1901) also attempted to influence policy and appointments and was not averse to expressing partisan political views in matters relating to national affairs. However, as the influence and status of Parliament increased with the extension of the franchise, and it became accepted that the prime political responsibility of Ministers was owed to the representative assembly rather than the Monarch, the latter's political significance began to diminish. The change to genuine constitutional monarchy was therefore almost imperceptible and has never been recognised or expressed in any formal sense.

The Monarch's formal role

The residue of former days is that the Monarch is still recognised as Head of State, Head of the Commonwealth, Monarch of those Commonwealth countries which are not republics, Head of the Church of England and Commander-in-Chief of the armed forces. The terminology of monarchy also has continued to pervade the British system of government. Hence the government is His or Her Majesty's Government, its main parliamentary rival is His or Her Majesty's Loyal Opposition, Ministers are the King or Queen's Ministers, central government employees are Crown servants and justice is dispensed in the Royal Courts of Law. Even the fiction that the government exists merely to advise the Monarch is preserved by the Prime Minister's weekly audiences with the King or Queen.

Constitutional crises and residual royal discretion

Despite the above, however, and the United Kingdom's modern status as a liberal democracy, the Monarch, in strictly legal terms, retains a great deal of power extending, *inter alia*, to appointing the Prime Minister, summoning and dissolving Parliament, assenting to legislation and to making declarations of war.

For more on the royal prerogative, see Chapter 12.

The only significant formal reduction in the powers which attach to the Monarch (the royal prerogative) was effected by the Bill of Rights 1689 (see below). The expectation is, however, that the prerogative will be used in accordance with convention – the principal requirement being that the powers will be exercised on the advice of the Prime Minister speaking on behalf of the government. This, in turn, presumes that such advice will be given in ways which uphold the constitution and other vital national interests. Should this not be the case then it has been suggested that the Monarch might still retain a degree of personal discretion to use the prerogative in ways which best served these concerns. Given, however, that public trust and confidence in the institution depends on the Monarch remaining aloof from ordinary political issues, it is unlikely that such intervention would be contemplated except in the most extreme circumstances. In the second half of the twentieth century and early part of the present century, informed speculation about what these circumstances might be tended to be restricted to the power to grant or refuse a dissolution of Parliament (the prerogative of dissolution). Here, although generally accepted that a decision to dissolve Parliament without or in opposition to Prime Ministerial wishes would be almost inconceivable, tentative support could be found for the view that a dissolution might still be refused if:

(a) an alternative and viable government could be formed from the existing Parliament (or at very least, the grant delayed while deliberations to this end were pursued);

(b) the request was to be made during a period of grave national emergency, e.g. wartime.

Fascinating as these contentious issues may have been, any validity attaching to them would appear to have been reduced to a matter of historical interest only as a result of the passing of the Fixed Term Parliaments Act 2011.

The overall effect of the Act was to replace any political and prerogative discretion relating to the dissolution of Parliament with a rubric of statutory rules ('Parliament cannot otherwise be dissolved', section 3(2)). This, in turn, appears to have put the prerogative in this matter into abeyance. In other words, any pre-existing prerogative power to dissolve Parliament may not be used by the Monarch for so long as the fixed parliaments legislation remains in force. Accordingly, and henceforth, the calling of General Elections will be conducted as per the legislation's prescriptions. These are:

For more on prerogative powers, see Chapter 12, pp. 268–88.

- subsequent General Elections will be held on the first Thursday in May every five years (s 1(3));
- the Prime Minister may defer an election for up to two months where this appears to be in the public interest (s 1(5));
- Parliament is to 'dissolve' automatically twenty-five days before the day 'fixed' for the next election (s 3(1)).

Further provision is made for 'early' elections in two situations. These are:

- where at least two-thirds of all MPs vote in favour (s 2(1));
- where the government is defeated in a vote of confidence which is not overturned within fourteen days (s 2(3)).

Beyond all of this, it remains conceivable that the Monarch could be drawn into the political process should the electorate return a 'hung' Parliament (i.e. one in which no single party had an overall majority). In this scenario the convention requiring the Monarch to appoint as Prime Minister the person commanding a majority in the House of Commons would not be immediately applicable. Royal participation, presumably with the support of advisers and senior representatives from the major parties, might therefore be necessary to broker some sort of coalition prepared to unite behind a person whose appointment as Prime Minister would then follow.

No single party won an overall majority in the General Election of May 2010. The House of Commons seats gained by the three main parties were as follows: Conservatives, 306; Labour, 258; Liberal Democrats, 57. Due, however, to the willingness of the Liberal Democrats to accept the terms for coalition government offered to them by the Conservatives (the largest single party), no significant level of royal intervention or attempts to broker an agreement was required.

The monarchy's modern relevance

Monarchy in the United Kingdom has both advocates and detractors. Those who tend to favour the institution stress what they perceive to be the crucial position of the Monarch, not just in the constitutional hierarchy, but also in the very social and cultural consciousness of the nation. The institution, it is said, has helped to sustain the traditional inclination towards strong central government. It has encouraged a sense of national identity and unity which transcends political divisions. In time of war and national emergency it has provided a focal point of patriotism and loyalty and, on a more continuous basis, has lent a sense of dignity to the process of government which has given added authority and status to those who carry it out. On a wider international basis it has provided a uniquely prestigious and dignified ceremonial figurehead around which Commonwealth nations can unite and which adds an extra dimension to the head of state's ambassadorial role.

In more tangible or practical political terms reference has also been made to the fact that the present Monarch has been served by no fewer than thirteen Prime Ministers in a reign which has extended over seven decades. All of these administrations have, therefore, been able to benefit from her advice and experience. Direct influence is hard to prove but this may represent yet another of the many subtle forces in the constitution's complex and informal structure which underpin and reinforce its central cultural imperatives.

Example

For more on the Belfast peace agreement, see p. 26.

By way of illustration of the extent to which royal 'influence' may still be used for positive political and constitutional purposes, reference could perhaps be made to the role played by the current Monarch in the Irish peace process as effected, in particular, by the Queen's state visit to the Irish Republic in 2011 and her meeting and handshake with the ex-IRA commander Martin McGuinness in Belfast in 2012. Commentators on both sides of the Irish Sea would appear to be agreed that these actions did much to help salve the wounds of the divided community there, thereby shoring up the foundations of the Belfast peace agreement and enhancing its future success.

For the sake of balance, however, some attention should be given to those more critical perspectives of British constitutional monarchy. Hence the Monarch has been accused of personifying and symbolising the class structure and the belief that the right to participate in the process of government may be inherited rather than granted by popular will. Greater concentration on, and media exposure of the personal lives of, members of the Royal Family, accompanied by a feeling in some quarters that not all its members have conducted themselves according to popular expectations, also appears to have damaged the mystique of monarchy and affected respect for it.

For all this, evidence to date suggests that any increased dissatisfaction has not yet crystallised into a significant level of popular support for replacing the monarchy with some other form of head of state (e.g. a presidency). Reform of the monarchy may therefore be on the agenda, but it appears that its abolition, as yet, is not.

In 1992, in response to some of these concerns and to criticisms of the Royal Family's financial status and immunities, it was announced that, in future, Civil List payments would be requested in respect of the Queen and Prince Philip only; further that the Queen would take responsibility for supporting the activities of other members of the Royal Family and that both she and the Prince of Wales would pay tax on their private incomes.

Bicameral sovereign Parliament

Meaning

Objective 5

A Parliament with two chambers or 'houses' may be described as bicameral. In the United States these are the House of Representatives and the Senate; in France, the National Assembly and the Senate; in the Republic of Ireland, the Dáil and the Seanad.

The two chambers of the United Kingdom Parliament are the House of Commons and the House of Lords – the unique feature being that the latter is entirely unelected and until the House of Lords Act 1999 the majority of members succeeded to their seats by right of birth. The elected chamber, the House of Commons, is regarded as having the greater authority. This is given constitutional recognition by the convention that, in the event of a conflict (e.g. concerning amendments to a Bill), the Lords should 'give way' and by the Parliament Acts 1911 and 1949 which allow Bills to be enacted without the consent of the upper chamber.

For the House of Commons, see Chapter 8.

For the House of Lords, see Chapter 9.

The word 'sovereignty' is generally understood as referring to an ultimate source of authority. In most democratic states it is possible to distinguish between what may be called political sovereignty and legal sovereignty. Political sovereignty or ultimate political power, it may be argued, remains with the people (or, at least, the electorate). Indeed, where a written constitution has been approved by referendum, it may be regarded as an expression of that sovereign will (viz. in terms of the way the people wish to be governed). Legal sovereignty, on the other hand, has a somewhat narrower meaning and is generally understood as referring to the location of supreme constitutional authority or legitimation within the state. In the United Kingdom this is Parliament or, in traditional language, the Queen in Parliament (i.e. Commons, Lords and Monarch). In some states, as in the United States, legal sovereignty may vest in the written constitution itself; hence the power of the US Supreme Court to invalidate legislative and executive actions, including those of the Congress and the President, inconsistent with the founding constitutional document. In others, as in France, the distinction between political and legal sovereignty may be more difficult to draw. Thus the French Constitution provides that 'national sovereignty belongs to the people which shall exercise it through its representatives and by way of referendums' (Art 3). This helps to explain the French tendency to refer major constitutional issues to the people in contrast to the British tradition of seeking no greater authority than that of Parliament.

For the domestic doctrine of parliamentary sovereignty, see Chapter 5.

Representative democracy

Meaning

This may be defined as a system of government in which the composition of the legislature and the political complexion of the executive are determined by the popular will expressed in regular and free elections and where, between elections, the government is expected to address popular concerns as expressed by elected representatives. Pure democracy, where all citizens are directly involved in political decision-making, for reasons of scale, is not possible in a modern state. Autocracy or, alternatively, government which represents only a small section of the populace (as in the United Kingdom prior to the extension of the franchise), is now culturally and ideologically unacceptable. Representative democracy may be seen, therefore, as an attempted compromise between these extremes.

The United Kingdom approach is for both the legislature and the executive to be reconstituted by each General Election. These are not elected separately as in many other states. Successful candidates in General Elections become Members of Parliament (MPs). None are directly elected to be head or Members of the government. By convention the government is formed from the party or coalition which has won a majority of seats in the House of Commons (except in the rare cases where a minority government is formed from the largest single party without an overall majority). The leader of this party or coalition then becomes the Prime Minister and chooses the other Members of the government.

The effectiveness and validity of this system is underpinned by certain essential prerequisites.

Universal adult suffrage

The exact details of the franchise, i.e. those who have the right to vote, are set out below. Suffice to say for the moment that, subject to certain disqualifications found in the Representation of the People Acts, the right attends to all British and Commonwealth citizens, and citizens of the Irish Republic resident in the United Kingdom.

For those who have the right to vote, see Chapter 6.

Regular elections and secret ballot

Granting all citizens the right to vote is of little use unless the right can be exercised and in a way which reduces the fear of intimidation or reprisal. In modern history in the British system these needs were addressed by the Parliament Act 1911, which provided for an election to be held at least every five years (previously every seven, Septennial Act 1714), and the Secret Ballot Act 1872. As mentioned above, the Fixed Term Parliaments Act 2011, replaces the requirement for a General Election to be held no less than once every five years with a provision that such elections should be held on the first Thursday in May at fixed five-yearly intervals. The first such 'fixed' election was held on 7 May 2015.

Party political plurality and freedom of speech and assembly

Even the right to vote regularly and secretly is reduced in democratic value unless there is a free and wide choice of parties and representatives to vote for and those engaged in the political process are able to meet, debate and criticise each other's policies and objectives.

The general rule pertaining in the United Kingdom is that political parties and cause groups have the right to exist and participate in national and local affairs providing they do not seek to further their objectives by violent means. Membership of certain paramilitary organisations is, therefore, prohibited by the Terrorism Act 2000.

For the Terrorism Act 2000, see Chapter 21.

It is also possible for political matters to be debated freely unless the words used might, *inter alia*, provoke violence, inflame racial, religious or sexual hatred, incite disaffection amongst the police or members of the armed forces or amount to sedition, defamation, or contempt of court.

The extent of the freedom of assembly in the United Kingdom, i.e. the right to meet for the purposes of such debate, is a matter of greater uncertainty. This will be considered in more detail in the chapter devoted to restrictions on civil liberties. However, the general premise underlying the relevant legal rules is that the right exists unless serious disorder, damage to property or disruption to the life of the community is the likely result.

For civil liberties, see Chapter 18.

The electoral system

An obvious essential of representative democracy is a system of electoral law and practice which seeks to:

(a) control electoral abuses (e.g. bribery, intimidation, etc.);

(b) ensure that parties and candidates for election are given fair access to and treatment by the media;

(c) guarantee that the 'weight' or value of each vote is relatively equal;

(d) ensure that party political preferences expressed in the election are reflected in the composition of Parliament.

Electoral abuses in the United Kingdom are dealt with by the Representation of the People Acts (principally those of 1983 and 2000) which specify a wide range of corrupt and illegal electoral practices. These are criminal offences for which the perpetrator may be fined or imprisoned, and, if committed by the successful candidate, may invalidate their election.

Provisions also exist to minimise bias and unfair discrimination by the broadcast media. These may be found in the Representation of the People Act 1983, the Broadcasting Acts 1990 and 1996, the Communications Act 2003, and the licensing conditions of the BBC. No such restraints, however, apply to the press or other written comment.

The problem of the differential weighting of votes is dealt with by the Boundary Commissions for England, Wales, Scotland and Northern Ireland, operating according to rules in the Parliamentary Constituencies Act 1986 as amended by the Parliamentary Voting and Constituencies Act 2011. Clearly, if there are 120,000 voters in one constituency and only 30,000 in another, votes in the latter have greater weight or value. Only 15,001 would secure an absolute majority; 60,001 would be required in the former. The Boundary Commissions are, therefore, charged to make recommendations for the redrawing of constituency boundaries every five years and, in so doing, attempt to ensure that the numbers of electors in different constituencies vary by no more than 5 per cent number of constituencies) ÷ from the electoral quota (number of electors (*ibid.*, s 6).

The current method of voting in the United Kingdom is usually referred to as the simple majority or 'first past the post' system. It does not result in proportional representation, i.e. close proximity between the proportion of the vote cast for a particular party and the proportion of seats that party acquires in the new Parliament. This is an aspect of the United Kingdom's version of representative democracy which has attracted particular controversy. The 1979, 1983, 1987 and 1992 elections were all 'won' by the Conservative party. On each occasion the party secured more than 57 per cent of the seats in the House of Commons. On no occasion, however, did the Conservatives poll more than 43 per cent of the votes cast or 32 per cent of the total votes of those entitled to vote.

The figures for all subsequent elections are as set out below:

For the current Broadcasting Codes, see Chapter 20, pp.616–8.

General Election 2001

Electorate	44,374,047
Turnout	59.4%
Most votes	Labour
Number of votes	10,724,953
Seats won	412
Percentage of seats	65.5
Percentage of votes cast	40.7
Percentage of total electorate	24.1

General Election 2005

Electorate	44,180,243
Turnout	61.4
Most votes	Labour
Number of votes	9,567,589
Seats won	356
Percentage of seats	54.7
Percentage of votes cast	35.2
Percentage of total electorate	21.6

General Election 2010

Electorate	45,597,461
Turnout	65.1
Most votes	Conservative
Number of votes	10,703,744
Seats won	306
Percentage of seats	47
Percentage of votes cast	36.1
Percentage of total electorate	23.4

General Election 2015

Electorate	46,425,386
Turnout	66.1
Most votes	Conservative
Number of votes	11,334.576
Seats won	331
Percentage of seats	50.9
Percentage of votes cast	36.9
Percentage of total electorate	24.4

After much debate concerning the fairness of the first past the post system, the issue of whether to replace it with the alternative votes system was put to a popular vote in a referendum held on 5 May 2011. This was one of the major conditions insisted upon by the Liberal Democrats in return for agreeing to enter coalition government with the larger Conservative party following the inconclusive General Election of May 2010. The referendum was conducted according to the provisions of the Parliamentary Voting Systems and Constituencies Act 2011. The question put to the electorate was:

At present, the UK uses 'the first past the post' system to elect MPs to the House of Commons. Should the 'alternative vote' system be used instead?

In an electoral turnout of 42 per cent, 67.90 per cent (13,013,123) voted 'no'; 32.10 per cent (6,152,607) voted 'yes'.

The alternative vote system relies on single member constituencies, thus retaining the link between an MP and his/her local electorate. Voters rank candidates on the ballot paper in order of preference, e.g., 1, 2, 3, etc. In order to 'win' the particular seat in which he/she is standing, a candidate must receive an absolute majority of the votes cast, i.e. more than 50 per cent. If, in the first count, none of the candidates has achieved an absolute majority, the vote proceeds to a further count. The candidate who comes last is eliminated and his or her votes are re-allocated according to the second preference expressed on that candidate's ballot papers. If this produces an absolute majority for any of the remaining candidates, he or she is declared to have been elected. If not, then a further round of counting takes place. The candidate now in last place is also eliminated and his/her second preference votes are redistributed in the same way.

The alternative vote is not a system of proportional representation. It is claimed, however, that its adoption would be a first step towards a fairer system and would have the immediate advantages of:

- reducing the numbers of 'wasted' votes, e.g. in a safe seat, those not cast for the sitting MP;
- ensuring that all MPs have some level of support from a majority of their constituents;
- avoiding the need for a wholesale redrawing of constituency boundaries;
- as with the first past the post system, minimising the likelihood of coalition government.

Responsible government

Meaning

Responsible government should not be understood as suggesting that the British government can always be expected to behave in a sensible and reasonable way. It refers instead to the fact that the government in the United Kingdom is answerable to Parliament for its stewardship of the nation's affairs. This concept of responsibility is founded on two constitutional conventions: collective and individual ministerial responsibility.

Collective ministerial responsibility

This encapsulates the following rules.

(a) In Parliament and in public all Ministers must support government policy. Should a Minister feel unable to do so, and wish to speak freely on a particular issue, he/she is expected to resign.

(b) Ministers should not divulge the contents of Cabinet or Ministerial deliberations.

(c) If defeated in a vote of confidence in the House of Commons, the government must resign.

This requirement that the government should resign if so defeated is part of the very essence of the British constitution and the relationship between government and Parliament. In states where the executive and Parliament are elected separately (e.g. the United States and France), the tenure of the government may not be directly affected by adverse votes in the legislature. In the United Kingdom, however, the government must maintain the confidence of the elected assembly which retains the ultimate power of dismissal over any administration whose competence or propriety is deemed beyond redemption.

It is, however, a power which, for party political reasons and the need for government stability, Parliament uses extremely sparingly. Only three governments resigned pursuant to adverse confidence votes in the twentieth century (in 1924 (twice), and 1979). On each of these occasions the government was in a minority. No majority government has been put out of office since 1885. It follows that a government with a secure majority is in little danger of dismissal. The power is, however, by no means obsolete or politically moribund. It remains a potentially potent reminder of the government's obligation to explain and justify its actions to the nation's representatives and to secure parliamentary legitimacy for the implementation of its policies and decisions.

In modern political and constitutional history some of the more prominent examples of ministerial resignations on grounds of inability to support collective Cabinet or government policy would be:

- Michael Heseltine, then Minister of Defence, 1986, opposition to government decision to supply British military forces with helicopters made in the USA (Sikorsky's) in preference to those made in Britain (Westlands);

- Geoffrey Howe, 1990, Deputy Prime Minister and previously Foreign Secretary and Chancellor of the Exchequer, dispute with Prime Minister (Mrs Thatcher) concerning policy towards the European Union;

- Robin Cook, 2003, Leader of the House of Commons and previously Foreign Secretary, opposition to government decision to go to war in Iraq.

The rules relating to ministerial responsibility are of conventional force only. Accordingly, these may, and have been, suspended on those exceptional occasions where it is felt that Ministers should be allowed to vote on a particular matter in compliance with the dictates of their personal convictions. In modern constitutional history this has happened on just five occasions – the most famous instances being the referendum in 1975 on continued membership of the European Community, the referendum of 2011 on the Alternative Voting System, and the 2016 referendum on membership of the European Union.

Individual ministerial responsibility

This contains the rule that each Minister is responsible to Parliament for the conduct of their department or sphere of responsibility and for all actions and decisions relating thereto. The Minister is expected to 'take the blame' for mistakes and errors of judgement and not to 'point the finger' at individual civil servants. In the final analysis, in cases of significant failure, the Minister is expected to resign.

It is increasingly apparent, however, that compliance with this convention is largely a matter of political expediency rather than of honour or constitutional propriety. Hence, if the government and its parliamentary party are prepared to support a Minister who is 'under fire', it is unlikely that the Minister will resign. If, however, for whatever reasons, and these may have little to do with the specific issue of controversy, this support is not forthcoming, the Minister may feel little option but to leave the government.

The separation of powers

Meaning

The doctrine of the separation of powers was developed to guard against abuses of power and the danger of tyrannical government. The essence of the doctrine is that the responsibility for the three main functions of government, viz. the executive, legislative and judicial processes, should be divided between separate but dependent institutions so that no one of these can dominate or function effectively without the others.

Writing in 1748, the French jurist, Montesquieu, argued that 'there can be no liberty' and there would be an end of everything 'if the legislative, executive and judicial powers of government were to be exercised by the same person or authority' (*L'Esprit des Lois*, 1748).

Similar sentiments had been expressed previously by the English political philosopher John Locke. He wrote that it 'may be too great a temptation to human frailty . . . for the same person to have the power of making laws, to have also in their hands the power to execute them, whereby they may exempt themselves from obedience to the laws they make, and suit the law both in its making and execution, to make their own private advantage' (*Second Treatise of Civil Government*, 1690).

The American model

These teachings had a marked effect on the makers of the American Constitution of 1787. They sought to provide a constitutional framework which separated the composition and functions of the three principal organs of state (executive: the presidency; legislature: the Congress; judiciary: the Supreme Court) as far as was compatible with governmental practicability. Hence the President is not elected at the same time as the Congress. He does not have a seat in the Congress and is not directly answerable to it. By the same token, members of Congress are not appointed to the executive. The President's election is for a fixed term (two four-year terms maximum) with the result that the Congress has no power to remove the incumbent from office (unless through impeachment by the Senate for 'treason, bribery, high crimes or . . . misdemeanours': Art 2(4)). The President and his/her cabinet do not control the business of the Congress in the way that the government in the United Kingdom is able to dominate Parliament. They may recommend legislation but cannot ensure that it is enacted. The President may veto legislation but such veto, may, in turn, be overridden by majorities of two-thirds in the House of Representatives and the Senate. Members of the Supreme Court are appointed by the President but their nominations may be overruled by the Senate. Supreme Court judges do not sit in Congress and may not be members of the executive. The Supreme Court, as stated, may invalidate unconstitutional acts of the President or Congress (*Marbury* v *Madison* (1803) 5 US (Cranch) 137).

The existence of rules regulating the relationships between President, Congress and Supreme Court and, in particular, giving the Congress ultimate power to overcome the President, illustrates that, although the US model constitutes a clearer separation of powers than that pertaining domestically, absolute separation does not exist, nor was it ever intended. It can be seen, therefore, that the principal political difference between the American and British systems lies in the relationship between the executive and the legislature. Responsible government, in the British sense, is not replicated in the American system. On the other hand, unlike their British counterparts, an American President will seldom be able to regard the legislature as a compliant ally in the execution of their policies. Hence, if a President is to be anything more than a 'lame-duck', an effective working relationship with Congress is essential. Negotiation and compromise is, therefore, built into the system; it is the only way it can work. The ideal of the separation of powers, viz. a balancing of the authority of state institutions, is thus achieved in a way which is at least as effective as that in the United Kingdom.

The British model: limited separation of powers

The British constitution has long displayed features and characteristics in sharp contradiction of the more exacting expositions of Montesquieu's original prescriptions. Such contradictions could be found both in the composition of the different government bodies, i.e. by persons holding positions in more than one of the three main institutions (government,

Parliament, and the judiciary), and in the lack of any clear functional distinctions between the activities which such institutions performed. The following would be amongst the more blatant transgressions, some of which remain:

(a) Government Ministers are also Members of Parliament having either been elected to the House of Commons or appointed as a life peer and, therefore, eligible to sit in the House of Lords. As Members of the government, such persons are responsible for the key executive functions of formulating and implementing government policy – while, as Members of Parliament, they play a full role in the deliberation and scrutiny of legislative proposals passing through the House of Commons or House of Lords.

For appointment of life peers, see Chapter 9, pp. 199–200.

(b) The government determines Parliament's legislative programme and the content of most primary legislation. Through its parliamentary majority in the House of Commons, the government is able to ensure that its legislative proposals will pass through Parliament and receive the Royal Assent with little amendment or alteration. This has led some to argue that in political reality it is the government, rather than Parliament, which plays the more significant role in the legislative process.

For Public Bills, see Chapter 8, pp. 154–58.

(c) Due to Parliament's inability to pass all the legislation required for the effective regulation of a complex, advanced, modern society, it has been necessary for Parliament to delegate extensive legislative powers to the government – normally to named Ministers. While this ensures that legislative rules can be made as and when they are required, it means also a great many of the laws which regulate the nation's affairs are made in government departments with only minimal parliamentary involvement or supervision.

For delegated legislation, see Chapter 8, pp. 167–76.

(d) Until 2009, and the creation of the Supreme Court, the nation's senior judges, the 'Law Lords', were members of the Appellate Committee of the House of Lords, the UK's final court of appeal, and were eligible to sit in the chamber of the House when it exercised its legislative and deliberative functions.

(e) Until the passing of the Constitutional Reform Act 2005, the Lord Chancellor was traditionally a Cabinet Minister, had a seat in the chamber of the House of Lords and chaired its proceedings. He/she was also a participating member of the Appellate Committee of the House of Lords for the purpose of exercising its judicial functions.

For more details of the 2005 Act, see pp. 47–8.

Checks and balances

Whatever the validity of these alleged defects in the British constitution and of the contention that it was and remains incompatible with Montesquieu's doctrine, the British system has long contained a detailed series of rules designed to provide some reasonable measure of protection against the types of excess and abuse of power with which Montesquieu was concerned.

Restraints on the executive

(a) Attention has already been drawn to the conventions of collective and individual Ministerial responsibility and to Parliament's conventional authority to make a government resign.

(b) The House of Commons Disqualification Act 1975 provides that no more than 95 holders of Ministerial offices may sit and vote in the House of Commons at any one time. This limits the number of Members of Parliament bound by the convention of collective responsibility and, therefore, obliged to vote with the government (the 'pay-roll' vote).

For the rules of natural justice see Chapter 14, pp. 369–71.

(c) The use of statutory and prerogative powers by government Ministers is subject to the supervisory jurisdiction of the courts. The validity of actions and decisions for which there is no legal authority or source (ultra vires), which offend the Human Rights Act or which were taken in flagrant abuse of the requirements of procedural fairness (natural justice) may be challenged through an application for judicial review.

(d) The government must submit itself to the electorate at regular intervals. In theory, at least, this is expected to make Ministers sensitive and responsive to public opinion.

(e) The House of Lords retains the power to veto any Bill purporting to extend the life of Parliament (Parliament Act 1911, s 2(1)). This is to protect against government use of its Commons majority to enact legislation postponing the next election thereby keeping the government in power. The credibility of this 'check' is, however, qualified to some extent by the fact that the upper House is unelected and, therefore, has no representative basis.

(f) Subject to what has already been said about the meaning of constitutional monarchy, in extreme circumstances it remains legally possible for the Monarch to use the royal prerogative to deal with a government which is behaving unconstitutionally.

Restraints on Parliament

(a) Despite its legislative authority, Parliament is not, in a political sense, a unified body. Rather it is a crucible for conflicting political interests. This operates as a force for moderation for, without a considerable degree of 'behind the scenes' cooperation and compromise between political parties, Parliament would be unable to function effectively.

(b) The composition of the House of Commons is, of course, determined ultimately by the electorate.

(c) Following the decision *R v Secretary of State for Transport*, ex parte *Factortame Ltd (No. 2)* [1991] 1 AC 603, and for so long as the UK remains a member of the European Union, English courts will refuse to apply Acts of Parliament which are inconsistent with the law of the EU.

For Declarations of Incompatibility see Chapter 17, pp. 505–6.

(d) In the case of legislation which is incompatible with the requirements of the European Convention on Human Rights, the Human Rights Act 1997 empowers the senior courts, in so far as the language of the statute permits, to 'read down' the offending provision(s) to remove the incompatibility or, where this is not possible, to issue a Declaration of Incompatibility.

(e) All Acts of Parliament are subject to judicial interpretation; the assumption being that this is simply a matter of determining and applying Parliament's will. In this regard, however, the law reports are replete with examples of judicial 'creativity' – particularly in relation to loosely worded or ambiguous legislation. Many examples of this inarticulate legislative tension between Parliament and the courts are considered in the text that follows.

(f) As a general rule, cases pending or being considered in a court of law should not be debated or commented on in either House.

Restraints on the judiciary

(a) Judicial decisions may be modified or rendered ineffective by legislation. Hence, when the House of Lords ruled that the Crown was bound to pay compensation for property destroyed by British Forces in the Second World War in order to deny it to the enemy (*Burmah Oil Co Ltd* v *The Lord Advocate* [1965] AC 75), this was quickly overturned by Act of Parliament (War Damages Act 1965).

(b) The final authority to dismiss a judge resides in Parliament since this can only be done with the consent of both Houses (see judicial independence, below).

(c) Judges may not sit in either House of Parliament or express party-political views.

(d) Judges cannot question the validity of Acts of Parliament nor the conduct of proceedings in either House of Parliament (***Pickin* v *British Railways Board*** [1974] AC 765).

An over-mighty executive?

Despite such checks and balances, there remains a major feature of the British constitution which, in both form and practice, appears irreconcilable with Montesquieu's original doctrine. This was and remains the principle of the government in Parliament and the consequent blurring, to the point almost of extinction, of the particular composition and functions of the executive and the legislature.

The conventions of the British constitution require all Members of the executive government to have a seat in Parliament – in either the House of Commons or the House of Lords. The modern expectation is that the more senior Cabinet Ministers should have seats in the House of Commons.

Traditionally, this was justified on the grounds that such partial fusion of the two institutions was a necessary part of ensuring direct government accountability to the nation's elected representatives. Government Ministers, it was said, could be questioned and criticised in the chamber of the House of Commons. If found wanting or culpable, they could be forced to resign. The government as a whole could be put out of office if defeated by a majority of MPs in a vote of confidence.

The reality, however, has proved to be very different and a variety of factors have combined to render such assertions of parliamentary control of the executive to be less than wholly convincing.

Most MPs on the government side, i.e. the majority in the chamber, will be well aware that their election was due to the popular image of their party and of its leaders, rather than any particular attributes of their own. Perhaps inevitably, therefore, they tend to link the security of their positions in Parliament, and hopes of political advancement, with the fate of the government itself. Any exercise of the power to vote the government out of office could, it is realised, precipitate a General Election, and the end of the parliamentary careers of some of the MPs responsible. The inclination, therefore, of MPs from the party 'in power', is to support 'their' government through 'thick and thin', i.e. regardless of incidents of Ministerial misjudgement or impropriety, or the changing moods of public opinion. As explained above, this means that majority governments in the United Kingdom are unlikely to be defeated in parliamentary votes and can look forward to a secure and uninterrupted period in office for a full parliamentary term (i.e. up to five years).

Such general precepts are supported by the record of recent history. Notwithstanding Parliament's conventional powers, no majority government was defeated in a confidence vote in the House of Commons during the entire twentieth century. It is the case that one government was forced to resign in 1979. This, however, was James Callaghan's minority Labour government which was defeated by a single vote following a motion of no confidence in March of that year.

Such statistics are at the basis of the contention that governments in the United Kingdom are not subject to adequate and meaningful parliamentary controls. The point is also made that this is exacerbated by the fact that, for general constitutional purposes, the British system does not possess a sovereign written constitution against which the validity of executive actions can be tested. Moreover, in the absence of any genuine freedom of information ('sunshine') legislation, real decision making has tended to be conducted in an atmosphere of remoteness and secrecy which inevitably hampers effective scrutiny by both Parliament and the media.

These arguments and concerns about the effectiveness of Parliament have sometimes been linked to the workings of the United Kingdom's 'first past the post' voting system. This, as the figures already quoted illustrate, tends to give the party which has secured the largest share of the popular vote, a significantly increased and disproportionate number of parliamentary seats. Thus, 43.2 per cent of the vote in 1997 gave Mr Blair's New Labour government 63.6 per cent of the seats contested.

For the relevant figures, see p. 37 above.

In practical terms, all of this means, it is said, that the government, with its secure parliamentary majority, can be sure of having its way in all matters which come before the House of Commons and can, if necessary, force its policies onto the statute book regardless of public opinion, questions of popular consent or the counter-arguments of what may be, from time to time, the combined forces of opposition parties, interest groups and the media.

An independent judiciary?

According to the separation of powers and most contemporary concepts of liberal democracy, it is essential that judges are able to make their decisions free of political interference and fear of reprisal. If this was not so, those who might wish to challenge the legality of executive actions would have little hope of their complaints being dealt with objectively.

This explains why the tenure and independence of senior judges is protected by the provisions in the Act of Settlement 1700, now re-enacted in the Senior Courts Act 1981, section 11 (for judges in the High Court and Court of Appeal) and the Constitutional Reform Act 2005, s 33 (for the Supreme Court), that judges hold office during good behaviour and may only be dismissed pursuant to resolutions (in the form of addresses to the Monarch) passed by both Houses of Parliament. Put simply, this means that although the executive appoints the judiciary, it cannot, of its own volition, rid itself of a senior judge whose decisions and opinions may be regarded as an irritation.

Most commentators express Parliament's authority in this regard to be exclusive. It should be noted, however, that there are those (including the authors of Hood Phillips and Jackson, *Constitutional and Administrative Law*) who suggest that the Crown might still be able to dismiss a judge without an address from Parliament for 'official misconduct, neglect of official duties, or (probably) conviction for a serious offence'.

The last and only occasion a judge was removed by parliamentary resolutions was in 1830 (Judge Jonah Barrington). This was for embezzling money which had been paid into court. The last time a motion for removal was put down was in 1973 and involved Sir John Donaldson, then President of the controversial and now defunct National Industrial Relations Court.

Judges may also lose office as a result of retirement (now set at the age of 70 by the Judicial Pensions and Retirement Act 1993), resignation, or incapacity (Senior Court Acts 1981, s 11).

The requirement for resolutions of both Houses of Parliament does not apply to the dismissal of judges below the High Court. Such judges may be dismissed by the Lord Chancellor but this discretion is used very sparingly.

The Act of Settlement reinforced judicial security of tenure by the requirement that judges' salaries should be 'ascertained and established' and not left to executive discretion. This is currently given practical effect by the Senior Courts Act 1981, section 12, which makes the moneys for judicial salaries a standing charge on the Consolidated Fund. In this way the payments are not subject to annual review or legislative renewal and are thus removed from the area of political controversy.

Rules underpinning judicial independence

(a) **Stipendiary magistrates, circuit judges**, and all those in the High Court, Court of Appeal and Supreme Court are disqualified from membership of the House of Commons (House of Commons (Disqualification) Act 1975, s 1 and Sched 1).

(b) By convention Ministers do not criticise judges or their decisions – although in recent times some have found it hard to resist doing so in response to parliamentary questions relating to controversial cases.

(c) The rules of debate in the House of Commons forbid criticism of a judge unless pursuant to a substantive motion for dismissal. Adverse comment on judicial decisions appears to be permissible providing this does not reflect on a judge's character or competence.

(d) Ministers and MPs are expected not to comment on that which is *sub judice* (except where issues of major national importance are involved).

(e) Judges are immune from all civil liability in respect of what is said or done in the exercise of judicial functions (***Scott v Mansfield*** (1868) LR 3 Ex 220).

(f) Any comment which impugns the impartiality of a judge may amount to a criminal contempt of court, as may any conduct or words calculated to interfere with the administration of justice.

Judicial neutrality

The existence of rules to protect judges from political interference does not guarantee that judicial decisions will be free from subliminal political influences. Judges, like the rest of us, are a product of their social environment and it is probably inevitable that their approach to certain issues will be influenced by the attitudes of the group from which their majority is drawn – in this case what has been called the social and educational élite.

This does not mean that they are prejudiced in a party political sense. It has been suggested, however, that they bring to bear on their decisions a political philosophy which prefers the existing distribution of social and economic influence.

> The judges here by their education and training and the pursuit of their profession as barristers, acquire a strikingly homogenous collection of attitudes, beliefs and principles, which to them represent the public interest. They do not always express it as such. But it is the lodestar by which they navigate (Griffith, *The Politics of the Judiciary*, 1991).

This is something which it is hard to prove or disprove. It cannot be denied, however, that judges in the United Kingdom are predominantly white, male and from the social and educational group indicated.

While of course it is impossible to eradicate entirely any effect such influences may have, certain rules do exist to try to preserve the necessary appearance of neutrality.

Rules underpinning judicial neutrality

(a) In addition to their statutory disqualification from the House of Commons, there is a convention that judges do not participate in political activities and refrain from expressing political views.

(b) Justice must be dispensed in public. The conduct of judges is, therefore, open to public scrutiny. Fair and balanced media reports of such proceedings are protected by the defence of qualified privilege.

Constitutional Reform Act 2005

The practical and legal operation of the doctrine of the separation of powers within the British constitution were given greater clarity and effect by the Constitutional Reform Act 2005. The primary purpose of the Act was to achieve a more distinct separation of functions and personnel between the legislature, in the form of the House of Lords, and the judiciary. This was achieved by the creation of the Supreme Court of the United Kingdom, to replace the Appellate Committee of the House of Lords, and by removing the Lord Chancellor from the judicial process.

Functions of the Lord Chancellor

By virtue of Part 2 of the Act, the Lord Chancellor ceased to be a member of the judiciary and relinquished the judicial functions traditionally associated with the office. Holders of the office may continue to sit in the House of Lords when it exercises its legislative functions. The Lord Chancellor's responsibilities as head of the judiciary were transferred to the Lord Chief Justice (LCJ), who also becomes President of the Courts of England and Wales.

The Lord Chief Justice will be responsible for representing the views of the judiciary to Parliament and the government.

Future Lord Chancellors may be drawn from either the House of Lords or the House of Commons. Persons without judicial or legal qualifications will be eligible for the office.

It was intended originally that the 2005 Act would abolish the office of Lord Chancellor altogether, and that, following the Act, any remaining functions would be exercised by the newly created Secretary of State for Constitutional Affairs. During the Bill's passage through Parliament, however, the government had a change of heart and decided that such a drastic alteration to its traditional Ministerial personnel might inhibit its executive effectiveness. Currently, the functions and responsibilities of the Lord Chancellor are performed by the Secretary of State for Justice.

The Act provided also for a 'Speaker of the House of Lords' to preside over the legislative sessions of that House. Holders of the office are to be chosen by the House itself and may or may not be the person who holds the office of Lord Chancellor.

The Supreme Court of the United Kingdom

As of 1 October 2009, the judicial work of the Appellate Committee of the House of Lords was transferred to a Supreme Court consisting of twelve 'Justices of the Supreme Court'. When the court was first established, these were the same twelve judges who had been exercising the judicial functions of the Appellate Committee of the House of Lords (the 'Law Lords'). Judges of the Supreme Court are prohibited from sitting or voting in the House of Lords and from membership of the House of Commons. Appointments to the Supreme Court will be made by the Monarch on the advice of the Prime Minister. Prior to submitting a nomination for royal approval, an elaborate consultative and selection process will be undertaken by an *ad hoc* Selection Commission of five members. The Commission will include the Lord Chief Justice and other senior judicial figures. Commission proposals will then be transmitted to the Lord Chancellor who may, at that stage:

(i) notify the name(s) to the Prime Minister;

(ii) reject the name(s) if considered unsuitable;

(iii) require further consideration by the Commission.

Justices of the Supreme Court will hold office during good behaviour and may not be removed from office save pursuant to resolutions of both Houses of Parliament.

Appointments to other senior courts, including the Court of Appeal and High Court, will continue to be by the Monarch on the advice of the Lord Chancellor. The Lord Chancellor is required to tender such advice in accordance with the recommendations of a Judicial Appointments Commission of fourteen members (see, for composition, Sched 12).

The Act does not abolish the right of appeal to the Judicial Committee of the Privy Council from the courts of those remaining overseas legal systems which still recognise its jurisdiction.

Judicial independence

The rules relating to judicial independence received further underpinning by a number of statutory duties cast by section 3 of the 2005 Act on the Lord Chancellor and other government Ministers. These provisions impose:

- a duty on the Lord Chancellor and all other Ministers to uphold judicial independence;
- a requirement that Ministers should not use their special status to seek to influence judicial decisions;
- a duty on the Lord Chancellor to ensure that the judiciary receive all the support necessary to secure the effective administration of justice.

The rule of law

Meaning

At the outset, and for the sake of clarity, and to avoid confusion, it should be understood that the Rule of Law is not simply a legal rule or principle. Nor is its content limited to the proposition that each individual should at all times obey the law regardless of its requirements. Rather, it is a doctrine of political morality formulated or originating from what have been referred to as 'western liberal democracies' and which seeks to identify the minimum standards and requirements of civilised government in a genuinely free society.

Some have proposed that it is derived from the view held by many of the ancient Greek philosophers that the proper purpose of law was to advance the common good.

> He who bids law to rule seems to bid God and intelligence alone to rule, but he who bids that man rules puts forward a beast as well, for that is the sort of thing desire is, and spiritness twists rulers even when they are the best of men (Aristotle).

Content

This has been variously described. In liberal democracies, however, the assumption is that adherence to the doctrine requires more than simply government according to law. Otherwise, in states where the executive controls the law-making process, it would be possible for the government to secure whatever powers it saw fit and to have these phrased in the vaguest possible terms (see, for example, 'The Law for the Relief of the People and the Reich', 1933, which gave the Hitler regime the powers it needed to stifle free speech and opposition in order to enforce the policies of the Third Reich). Government according to law is, therefore, not necessarily equivalent to government under law and is perfectly compatible with the sort of ordered but unfree systems of government typical of dictatorships and military junta.

Only in a country where the rule of law means more than formal, legal validity will subjects enjoy real protection from official tyranny and abuse (Mathews, *The Rule of Law in an Apartheid Society*).

Accordingly, some interpretations have sought to give the doctrine greater content. One approach has been to propose minimum standards in terms of the way laws are expressed and administered. Here the emphasis has tended to be on the need for rules and procedures which ensure that laws may be used for the protection of rights and freedoms and not just as a means of legitimising the use of powers. Such conceptions may say very little, however, about the substantive nature and extent of the rights in question.

One of the most respected proponents of this approach is legal philosopher Joseph Raz. His procedurally orientated version of the doctrine, explained in 1977, contained eight postulates ('The Rule of Law and Its Virtues' (1977) 93 LQR 195).

1　The law should be general (i.e. not discriminate), prospective, open and clear.

2　The law should be relatively stable (i.e. should not be subject to frequent and unnecessary alteration).

3　Open, stable, clear and general rules should govern executive law-making (i.e. the law should identify the jurisdictional limits to the exercise of delegated legislative powers).

4　The independence of the judiciary should be guaranteed.

5　The application of the law should accord with the rules of natural justice (i.e. the rule against bias and the right to a fair hearing).

6　The courts should have a power of review over law-making and administrative action to ensure compliance with these principles.

7　The courts should be easily accessible (i.e. individual recourse to justice should not be hindered by excessive delays and expense).

8　The discretion of the crime preventing agencies should not be allowed to pervert the law (i.e. such agencies should not be able to choose which laws to enforce and when).

Other interpretations of the doctrine have gone beyond the requirements of form and procedure and have extended the doctrine to the recognition of certain liberal political values. Of these perhaps the most renowned was that propounded by the International Commission of Jurists in 1959 (usually referred to as the Declaration of Delhi). This declared that the purpose of all law should be respect for the 'supreme value of human personality' and that observance of the rule of law should entail:

(a)　the existence of representative government;

For content of the European Convention on Human Rights, see Chapter 16.

(b)　respect for the type of basic human freedoms contained in the United Nations' 1948 Universal Declaration of Human Rights and the 1950 European Convention on Human Rights;

(c)　absence of retrospective penal laws;

(d)　the right to bring proceedings against the state;

(e)　the right to a fair trial including the presumption of innocence, legal representation, bail and the right to appeal;

(f)　an independent judiciary;

(g)　adequate control of delegated legislation.

The 1959 Declaration also broke new ground by contemplating that, if the value of human personality was to be fully realised, it might not be enough to limit the protection of the law to traditional concepts of rights (i.e. freedom of the person, expression, association, etc.). It might also be necessary, it was suggested, for the state to have regard to man's 'economic and social needs in addition to his spiritual and political freedom'. Two years later, at their Lagos Conference in 1961, the International Commission gave more specific expression to these ideas.

> The Rule of Law is a dynamic concept which should be employed to safeguard and advance the will of the people and the political rights of the individual and to establish social, economic, educational and cultural conditions under which the individual may achieve his dignity and realise his legitimate aspirations in all countries, whether dependent or independent.

This clearly prescribes a contentious political role to the law and the law-making agencies and would appear to allow the judiciary the right to interpret legislation and formulate law in ways which might best achieve the objectives stipulated. This in turn, however, raises major questions about traditional conceptions of judicial neutrality and the extent to which judges are accountable for the exercise of their functions.

Professor Dicey's traditional conception

It is normal in studies of English constitutional law for the meaning of the rule of law to be considered by reference to the views of Professor A.V. Dicey published in 1885 (*Introduction to the Study of the Law of the Constitution*). Professor Dicey (1835–1922) was an academic and jurist of some considerable repute. He contended that the essential ingredients of the doctrine were already manifest in the British constitution. These were as follows.

Absence of arbitrary power

Arbitrary power is that which has no identifiable legal origins or limits. It is inherent in such notions as government by decree or the doctrine of state necessity. To Dicey such ideas were alien to the British constitutional tradition and had been roundly condemned as such in *Entick* v *Carrington* (1765) 19 State Tr 1029, where Cambden CJ refused to accept that a government Minister, in the absence of any common law or statutory authority, had any power to grant warrants permitting entry and search of private premises. In more modern times this judicial aversion to arbitrariness was evident in the refusal by the Northern Ireland Court of Appeal to accept that British soldiers dealing with the emergency there should be exempt from the normal legal requirements for the execution of a valid arrest (*Kelly* v *Faulkner* [1973] NI 31).

Absence of wide discretionary power

Dicey felt that the powers of government should be clearly specified and predictable. He did not feel that public officials should be allowed a wide degree of choice in terms of when and how powers should be used. His was a *laissez-faire*, individualist view of the relationship between citizen and the state. To him the state was not simply a public benefactor. Except for its traditional responsibilities, it represented a potential threat to the less-established personal and proprietary rights of the individual. Its activities were, therefore, to be confined as narrowly as possible while the individual was left to pursue their own destiny with the minimum of regulation and interference.

In the period Dicey expressed these views the positive role of the **regulatory state** was clearly not so well developed or understood as it was to become. It is generally accepted, however, that, even in his own time, Dicey understated the functions of both central and local government and the degree to which public officials were already engaged in the exercise of discretionary power – particularly in the spheres of housing and public health.

Dicey also appeared to underestimate the degree of discretionary power available to the government in the royal prerogative and paid little regard to the emergency powers for the government and containment of Ireland contained in a succession of nineteenth-century Coercion Acts.

Dicey's fears were not, however, completely without foundation. Hence, while it is clear that the modern state could not function efficiently without a wide range of discretionary powers, some of which may be phrased in wide **subjective** language, concerns remain over the extent to which such powers are subject to adequate parliamentary and judicial controls. As will become apparent, part of the modern problem relates to the inability of Parliament to scrutinise effectively the work of the vast departments of state and the reluctance of the courts to challenge the legality of executive decisions in certain areas of government activity, e.g. defence and national security.

For parliamentary control of the executive, see Chapter 8, pp. 177–87.

No person to be punished except for a breach of law

This was another aspect of Dicey's rejection of arbitrary power. Penalties should only be imposed on an individual where a breach of an established legal rule had been proved in the ordinary courts of law. The proposition was of considerable contemporary validity but again was affected by its author's rather idealistic view of the British system. By the time Dicey was writing, powers already existed to interfere with both personal and proprietary rights – regardless of the repository's behaviour – where this was in the public interest. These included the **statutory powers** of imprisonment without trial used in Ireland, those authorising the compulsory purchase of property for public works, and the wide prerogative powers relating to the keeping of the peace and the defence of the realm.

For judicial supervision of defence and security issues, see Chapter 15, pp. 403–5.

The notion that law-abiding citizens should be free of executive interference is still deeply embedded in the nation's political psyche. Statutory powers do exist, however, to detain terrorist suspects for up to fourteen days (Prevention of Terrorism Acts). Also the ultimate power of unlimited detention without trial has been used in both World Wars and in Northern Ireland; the last occasion being between 1971 and 1976. Compulsory detention of psychiatric patients is also authorised by the Mental Health Acts 1983 and 2007. Beyond this, the executive retains wide powers of compulsory purchase of property and the extensive prerogatives already mentioned.

The equal subjection of all classes to the ordinary law of the land

Dicey was implacably opposed to government officials having special legal privileges and immunities. He was particularly unimpressed by the French *droit administratif*, a separate system of administrative law and courts for dealing with alleged abuses by government personnel. Such matters, he felt, should be dealt with in the ordinary courts, thus avoiding partiality whether real or apparent.

For more on government permission, see Chapter 13.

It would not be true to say, however, either then or now, that English law treated those in government in exactly the same way as private citizens. Indeed, until the **Crown Proceedings** Act 1947, the Crown could not be sued in contract as of right (the government's permission was required) and was not vicariously liable for the torts of its employees.

For conduct of parliamentary proceedings, see Chapter 10.

Members of Parliament possessed, and still possess, extensive privileges, including complete legal immunity for that said in the conduct of parliamentary proceedings. Also, by virtue of the Diplomatic Privileges Act 1964 foreign diplomats in the United Kingdom are not subject to the full rigour of the law.

The constitution is the result of the ordinary law

Dicey's view was that civil liberties in the United Kingdom did not, as in many other states, derive from a constitutional document. They were, in effect, fundamental social traditions which had been recognised by the judiciary and given protection by the common law:

> ... with us the law of the constitution, the rules which in foreign countries naturally form part of a constitutional code, are not the source but the consequence of the rights of individuals, as defined and enforced by the courts.

He believed that it was this close link between the social origins of rights and their judicial articulation which gave the liberties of the subject in this country their necessary degree of permanence and stability. They were something which could not be interfered with except by a 'thorough revolution in the institutions and manners of the nation'.

As with the other elements of Dicey's understanding of the doctrine, these assertions have not met with universal approval. It has been said, for example, that Dicey underestimated the effectiveness of written constitutions in restraining executive power; also that he put too much faith in the ability and readiness of the judiciary to withstand a sovereign Parliament and to apply a positive libertarian perspective to the task of developing individual freedom. Thus it is not hard to find examples of major and permanent legislative incursions into the rights of individuals (e.g. the loss of the absolute right to silence occasioned by the Criminal Justice and Public Order Act 1994), or cases in which judicial protection of such rights has been criticised as ineffective or unimaginative (see *Malone* v *Commissioner of Police of the Metropolis (No. 2)* [1979] Ch 344; *Council of Civil Service Unions* v *Minister for the Civil Service* [1985] AC 374).

A more modern construction

What might be regarded as a version of the Rule of Law for the twenty-first century was given by Lord Bingham of Cornhill in a lecture delivered to the Centre for Public Law on 16 November 2006. In the years 1992–2008 Lord Bingham served successively as Master of the Rolls, Lord Chief Justice, and senior Law Lord. He was generally regarded as one of the most distinguished judges of the modern era. A hundred and twenty-one years separated his views from those of Professor Dicey. This notwithstanding, it will be noticed that a remarkable level of consistency in some key parts attends the two interpretations of this founding constitutional doctrine.

Lord Bingham's exposition consisted of a basic 'core principle' attached to which were eight more detailed 'sub-rules'.

The core principle

All persons and authorities within the state, whether public or private, should be bound by and entitled to benefit of laws publicly and prospectively promulgated and publicly administered in the courts.

First sub-rule

If everyone is bound by the law they must be able without undue difficulty to find out what it is.

Second sub-rule

Questions of legal right and liability should be reached by application of the law and not the exercise of discretion.

Third sub-rule

The law of the land should apply equally to all, save to the extent that objective differences justify differentiation.

Fourth sub-rule

The law must afford adequate protection of fundamental human rights.

Fifth sub-rule

In the last resort, every person, regardless of financial circumstances, should have access to a court of law, as distinct from arbitration or other more informal means of dispute resolution for the determination of their civil rights or obligations.

Sixth sub-rule

Minsters and public officials at all levels must exercise the powers conferred on them reasonably, in good faith, for the purpose for which the powers were conferred and without exceeding the limits of such powers.

Seventh sub-rule

Adjudicative procedures provided by the state should be fair.

Eighth sub-rule

The state should conduct its affairs in compliance with the obligations of international law.

Practical impact of the rule of law

Despite any imperfections, the importance of the rule of law is that it is a doctrine of considerable intellectual pedigree, dating back in embryonic form to the Greek city states, which provides a rational philosophical basis for the regulation of state power and the promotion of individual liberty. It represents, therefore, an ideological framework for the legislature and those who have to interpret the law. In this country it can be seen in particular operation in the principles of judicial review (see the finding of the House of Lords in *Roberts* v *Hopwood* [1925] AC 578, that there is no such thing in English law as an unfettered discretion) and in the judicial presumptions that, in the absence of a clear contrary intent, statutes should not be given retrospective effect or allowed to restrict established civil liberties.

It is also widely accepted that Dicey's understanding of the doctrine has reinforced suspicions about the ways in which other states deal with government power – particularly through written constitutions and specialised systems of administrative law.

The European dimension

The European Community/European Union

Objective
6

United Kingdom membership of the European Community was effected by:

(a) The Brussels Treaty of Accession 1972 – by which the UK's application for membership was accepted by the existing member states;

(b) The European Economic Communities Act 1972 which ratified the treaty and gave effect to the law and processes of the EC in the domestic state.

Few doubted that this represented the most significant constitutional development affecting the UK certainly since the Glorious Revolution of 1688. Henceforth, the UK's system of law and government was to be conducted according to two distinct sets of principles and rules, i.e. those of its own ancient 'unwritten' constitution and that of the supra-national European organisation.

For immediate practical purposes, this involved an acceptance that the making of executive policy, administrative decisions, and of laws in those areas covered by the various EC treaties – at this stage concerned largely with industry, trade, commerce and agriculture – would henceforth be the responsibility of the EC's executive and law-making institutions. At about the same time a further important step was taken by the Appellate Committee of the House of Lords when it ruled that, in any conflict between an EC law and a provision in an English statute, it was the EU law which should be preferred and applied (*R v Secretary of State for Transport, ex parte Factortame Ltd (No. 1)* [1989] 2 CMLR 3530.

The foundation for further convergence by European states in political, social and economic matters was laid by the Treaty of European Union 1992 (the 'Maastricht Treaty'). By this, member states agreed to make progress towards the formulation of 'common policies' relating to home, judicial, defence, and foreign affairs. Subject to certain qualifying economic criteria, agreement was reached also for the adoption of a single European currency and monetary system.

The decision of the United Kingdom to leave the European Union and its legal, political, and constitutional implications following the referendum of June, 2016, is considered in greater detail below.

The European Convention on Human Rights

The European Convention on Human Rights was formulated in 1949, signed by the UK in 1950, and came into effect in 1953.

Following from the ravages of World War II, the purpose of the Convention was to impose a rubric of human rights laws and standards on European states and to create a legal system through which these could be enforced. To this extent, therefore, the Convention created significant additional constraints on the power of government and gave individuals a right of redress in respect of abuses of power by the governments of European states and their agents.

Although a signatory to it, the UK did not formally ratify and give direct effect to the Convention until the Human Rights Act 1998. This came into full force in October 2000. Accordingly, for the first forty-seven years of its existence the Convention had only 'persuasive effect' on the courts and government of the domestic state, i.e. although these were expected to exercise their powers in accordance with the Convention, contravention of it could not be used as the basis of legal or other proceedings in the UK.

Summary

The chapter identifies and defines the principal distinctive features of the British constitution and laws and explains how these have been moulded and adapted to provide an effective institutional and doctrinal framework for a modern, liberal democracy whilst preserving much of the language and forms of the constitution's ancient beginnings. The chapter also explains and assesses the continuing utility of the constitution's fundamental doctrines and principles, developed since the end of the seventeenth century, for the legal and political control of those holding and exercising the powers of government.

References

Calvert (1985) *An Introduction to British Constitutional Law,* London: Financial Training.

Dicey (1989) *Introduction to the Study of the Law of the Constitution* (10th edn), ed. Wade, E.C.S., London: Macmillan.

Griffith (1997) *The Politics of the Judiciary* (5th edn), London: Fontana.

Hood Phillips and Jackson (2001) *Constitutional and Administrative Law* (8th edn), London: Sweet & Maxwell.

Locke (1956) *Second Treatise of Civil Government,* Oxford: Blackwell.

Mathews (1986) *The Rule of Law in an Apartheid Society,* Cape Town: Jute Press.

Montesquieu (1961) *L'Esprit des Lois,* Paris: Garnier Frères.

Raz (1977) *The Rule of Law and its Virtues* 93 LQR 195.

Report of the House of Lords Select Committee on the Constitution (2005–6) HL 83.

Report of the Royal Commission on the Constitution (1973) Cmnd 5460.

Further reading

Allen and Thompson (2014) *Cases and Materials on Constitutional and Administrative Law* (11th edn), Oxford: Oxford University Press, Ch. 1.

Angelis and Harrison (2003) *History and Importance of the Rule of Law,* World Justice Project.

Bingham (2011) *The Rule of Law,* London: Penguin.

Electoral Reform Society (2015) *The 2015 General Election: A voting system in crisis.*

House of Commons Library, *The Separation of Powers,* Standard Note SN/PC 06053, 15.8.11.

Lord Neuberger (2015) 'What is the Rule of Law', http://worldjusticeproject.org/blog/right-honourable-lord-neubgerger-abbotsbury-speech-aba-london-sessions-800th-anniversary-magna-carta

Loveland (2015) *Constitutional Law, Administrative Law and Human Rights* (7th edn), Oxford: Oxford University Press, Chs 1 and 3.

Turpin and Tompkins (2011) *British Government and the Constitution* (7th edn), London: Cambridge University Press.

World Justice Project (2015) *What is the Rule of Law* http://worldjusticeproject.org/opengovernment-index

3

Sources of constitutional and administrative law

Objectives

After reading this chapter you should:

1. Understand the comparative importance of judicial decisions, Acts of Parliament and constitutional conventions, as the founding rules of the British constitution, and those particular areas of the constitution in which each of these sources is of greatest significance.

2. Be aware of the nature of constitutional conventions, the distinction between constitutional conventions and laws, and the reasons why constitutional conventions are adhered to.

3. Appreciate the extent to which the law of the European Union and of the European Convention on Human Rights now form parts of the British constitution.

Introduction

This chapter will concentrate on the traditional constitutional source material provided by Acts of Parliament, judicial decisions and constitutional conventions. Reference will also be made to European Union law, the European Convention on Human Rights, the law and custom of Parliament and to books of authority.

Acts of Parliament and judicial decisions remain the principal sources of the United Kingdom's system of constitutional and administrative law. Other important constitutional prescriptions may be found in conventions. Conventions are not laws. They are the non-legal rules of the constitution. Strictly speaking, therefore, they should be regarded as a source of the constitution but not of constitutional law. The importance of EU law and the European Convention on Human Rights as sources of domestic constitutional law should not be underestimated. The two European elements of the British constitution have continued to increase in content and significance following the UK's accession to the European Community in 1972 and the more recent full implementation in the domestic jurisdiction of the Convention on Human Rights (Human Rights Act 1998). Given their constitutional impact, individual chapters have been devoted to these developments.

Legislation

Meaning

This consists of rules of law made by Parliament either directly in the form of statute (sometimes referred to as 'primary' legislation) or indirectly by those other authorities on which Parliament has conferred the power to legislate (delegated, subordinate or 'secondary' legislation).

It has been said that legislation is now the most important source of constitutional and administrative law. To the extent that this is so, it would tend to undermine many of the assumptions associated with the notion that the United Kingdom does not have a constitution in the formal written sense.

Classification

The following brief synopsis of some of the more important enactments in this context will serve to illustrate the significance of legislation in all major aspects of the constitution.

Statutes relating to the structure of the United Kingdom and Commonwealth

(a) Acts of Union with Scotland 1707: by which the pre-existing British and Scottish Parliaments both passed Acts of Union and brought into existence the Parliament of Great Britain.

(b) Acts of Union with Ireland 1800: by which the pre-existing English and Irish Parliaments passed Acts of Union bringing into existence the Parliament of the United Kingdom of Great Britain and Ireland.

(c) European Communities Act 1972: which gave effect to the United Kingdom's accession to the European Community.

(d) The Northern Ireland Act 1998, Scotland Act 1998 and Government of Wales Act 1998 and Wales Act 2006, by which devolved powers of self-government were granted to these elements of the United Kingdom.

Statutes relating to the Monarch and the royal prerogative

(a) **Bill of Rights 1689**: which provided, *inter alia*, that the Monarch could not tax, make law, or maintain a standing army in peacetime without parliamentary consent, and could not suspend or dispense with laws made by Parliament.

(b) Act of Settlement 1700: which settled the throne on the Electress Sophia of Hanover (granddaughter of James I) and the heirs of her body being communicants of the Church of England and provided, *inter alia*, that the prerogative to remove judges' commissions should be exercised only on addresses by both Houses of Parliament.

Statutes relating to the election, composition and workings of Parliament

(a) Representation of the People Acts 1983–2000: which enacted the current rules relating to the conduct of parliamentary and local elections, the franchise and the control of electoral abuses.

(b) Parliament Acts 1911 and 1949: which allowed that the Royal Assent could be given to a Bill not approved by the House of Lords.

(c) Life Peerages Act 1958: which allowed for royal creation of 'life peers'.

(d) House of Lords Act 1999: which removed the hereditary element from the upper chamber save for a possible temporary remission for 90 'excepted peers'.

Statutes relating to the judicial system

(a) Supreme Court of Judicature Acts 1873–75 and Appellate Jurisdiction Act 1876: by which the pre-existing system of courts was rationalised into the High Court, Court of Appeal and House of Lords.

(b) Senior Court Act 1981: determined the current structure, personnel and powers of the Supreme Court of Judicature (High Court and Court of Appeal).

For constitutional Reform Act 2005, see pp. 46–8.

(c) Constitutional Reform Act 2005: transferred the functions of the Appellate Committee of the House of Lords to the Supreme Court of the United Kingdom.

Statutes relating to civil liberties and human rights

(a) Habeas Corpus Acts 1640–1862: prohibited imprisonment without just cause.

(b) Obscene Publications Acts 1959 and 1964: limited the freedom of expression by prohibiting the publication or possession for gain of obscene articles.

(c) Official Secrets Acts 1911 and 1989: limited the freedom of movement in relation to 'prohibited places' (viz. those having to do with defence and national security), and the freedom of expression in terms of the communication of information which could be prejudicial to certain key national interests (e.g. defence, national security and the investigation of crime).

(d) Terrorism Acts 2000, 2006 and 2011, and Anti-Terrorism, Crime, and Security Act 2001: introduced a whole new range of offences for terrorist-related activity in or outside the UK.

(e) Police and Criminal Evidence Act 1984, Serious Organised Crime and Police Act 2005 (SOCPA), Regulation of Investigatory Power Act 2000 and Investigatory Powers Act 2016: codified and clarified the law relating to individual freedoms and police powers.

(f) Human Rights Act 1998: extended the rights of the individual against the state by giving legal effect to the European Convention on Human Rights.

Judicial decisions

Meaning

The judicial contribution to the formulation of constitutional and administrative law is performed through interpretation of statutory provisions having to do with the process of government and by the declaration and development of relevant aspects of the common law.

Statutory interpretation

The modern judicial approach to statutory interpretation is to seek to give effect to the literal meaning of the words used by Parliament except where this would produce an absurd result or is not possible due to uncertainty or ambiguity. In these circumstances the usual expectation is that the provision in question will be given a meaning which is compatible both with its linguistic content and the purpose which it appears designed to achieve.

To assist in this sometimes difficult task judges may sometimes have resort to a number of interpretative presumptions (i.e. normative judicial suppositions of parliamentary intention), some of which are of particular significance to constitutional and administrative law. These would include the presumptions that in the absence of express words or necessary implication Parliament does not intend to:

(a) alter the existing rights and privileges of the Crown (*Lord Advocate* v *Dumbarton DC* [1990] 2 AC 580);

(b) reduce or extinguish the pre-existing rights of the citizen (*Secretary of State for Defence* v *Guardian Newspapers Ltd* [1985] AC 339; *HM Treasury* v *Mohammed Jabar Ahmed* [2010] UKSC 2);

(c) *legislate* contrary to the Rule of Law (*R* v *Secretary of State for the Home Department, ex parte Pierson* [1998] AC 539;

(d) impose any taxation (*Attorney-General* v *Wilts United Dairies* (1921) 37 TLR 884);

(e) restrict the citizen's access to the courts (*Chester* v *Bateson* [1920] 1 KB 829), or exclude the power of judicial review (*Anisminic Ltd* v *Foreign Compensation Commission (No. 2)* [1969] 2 AC 147); ·

(f) give retrospective effect to penal enactments (*Waddington* v *Miah* [1974] 1 WLR 683);

(g) extinguish proprietary rights without compensation (*Central Control Board* v *Cannon Brewery Co Ltd* [1919] AC 744);

(h) alter the constitution by a 'sidewind' (i.e. effect major changes indirectly or surreptitiously: *Nairn* v *University of St Andrews*: [1909] AC 147); *Thoburn* v *Sunderland City Council* [2002] EWHC Admin 195.

Common law

This consists of rules of law formulated to deal with those disputes for which there are no statutory prescriptions. This remains a significant source of law in relation to certain elements of the constitution.

The royal prerogative

For nearly 400 years since Coke CJ declared that the 'King hath no prerogative but what the law of the land allows him' (*Case of Proclamations* (1611) 12 Co Rep 74), the courts have claimed the authority to declare the content of the prerogative (i.e. the powers contained within it), the extent of particular prerogatives (*Burmah Oil* v *Lord Advocate* [1965] AC 75), and the relationship between prerogative and statute (*Attorney-General* v *De Keyser's Royal Hotel* [1920] AC 508).

For details of prerogative powers, see Chapter 12.

Judicial supervision of executive action

Persons aggrieved by alleged unlawful uses of government power have long had a right of access to the courts to challenge the actions or decisions in question. The resulting judgments have led to the formulation of the rules which determine when authorities have abused their powers in both the substantive or procedural senses (i.e. acted *ultra vires* or in breach of the rules of natural justice). This body of law includes the basic principles that official decisions may be quashed for unreasonableness (*Associated Provincial Picture Houses Ltd* v *Wednesbury Corporation* [1948] 1 KB 223), or for unfairness if a person whose rights or interests were seriously affected was not given a fair hearing (*Ridge* v *Baldwin (No. 1)* [1964] AC 40).

For details of the scope of judicial review, see Chapter 15.

Civil liberties and human rights

As illustrated, much of the law relating to the rights of the individual has now been cast into statutory form. Complete codification has, however, neither been achieved nor attempted. Some significant elements of constitutional law in this context may still be found, therefore, in the common law. These would include:

(a) the restrictions on the freedom of speech imposed by the tort of defamation and the criminal offences of sedition and conspiracy to corrupt public morals;

(b) the powers of the police to interfere with the freedoms of the person, assembly and movement in order to prevent breaches of the peace.

Reference should, perhaps, also be made to the developing doctrine of confidentiality, which enables the courts to restrict the publication and dissemination of information entrusted in confidence to government employees and agents where this would damage the public interest.

Public interest immunity

For the doctrine of public interest immunity, see Chapter 13, pp. 324–33.

This is a common law doctrine with implications for both the law of evidence and the freedom of information. Essentially it consists of a body of rules which enable any party, and this may often be the government, to withhold relevant evidence from legal proceedings if, once again, its revelation would damage the public interest.

Parliamentary privilege

For the rules of parliamentary privilege, see Chapter 10.

As a result of Parliament being the sovereign body, the courts have no jurisdiction to question its decisions or the way it regulates its composition and proceedings. The common law which determines whether a dispute relates to the affairs of Parliament, and is, therefore, beyond the cognisance of the courts, comprises the rules of parliamentary privilege.

Constitutional conventions

Some definitions

Objective 2

These include some of the constitution's most important rules. In *Reference Re Amendment of the Constitution of Canada* (1982) 125 DLR (3rd) 1, the Canadian Supreme Court's view was that 'while they are not laws some conventions may be more important than laws'.

Dicey defined conventions as 'rules which although they regulate the conduct of the several members of the sovereign power, of the ministers or the other officials, are not in reality laws at all since they are not enforced by the courts'. He also said that conventions could be described as rules of 'constitutional morality'.

Despite its antiquity this definition makes two essential points. First, although conventions are rules, they do not impose legal obligations and no English court will grant a remedy in respect of non-compliance. Second, they should properly be regarded as constituting a value system for the guidance of those engaged in the process of government and politics.

The nature and purpose of conventions

Consistent with Dicey's view of conventions as rules of 'constitutional morality', it has been said that they provide a 'moral framework within which government ministers or the Monarch should exercise the non-justiciable powers' of the constitution (Loveland, *Constitutional Law: A Critical Introduction*, 1996). This value-orientated perspective on conventions may also be found in the Canadian Supreme Court's view that the 'main purpose of conventions is to ensure that the legal framework of the constitution will be operated in accordance with the principal constitutional values or principles of the period' (*Re Amendment of the Constitution of Canada, supra*). Hence, in the domestic context, the rule that a government which loses the confidence of the House of Commons must resign may be seen as an obvious requirement of a representative and responsible parliamentary system.

Conventions are also regarded as giving the constitution a necessary degree of flexibility. In particular, they allow it to change and develop without significant alteration of the existing legal rules – many of which are of ancient origins and, in isolation to conventional practice, of little modern relevance. Thus, for example, the legal rules relating to the summoning of Parliament require that it meets 'frequently' (Bill of Rights 1689) and at least once every three years (Meeting of Parliament Act 1694). Taken and applied literally these bare legal requirements would be wholly inimical to contemporary assumptions about representative democracy and the proper relationship between the executive and Parliament – particularly that the former should conduct its activities subject to constant supervision by the latter acting on behalf of the electorate – hence the convention that Parliament should be summoned annually.

The inevitable corollary of the flexibility of conventions is that some of these tend to be expressed in rather inspecific terms and, accordingly, may not easily be applied to the particulars of individual cases. This was well-illustrated by the events of October, 2015, when the House of Lords voted down a statutory instrument which had passed through the House of Commons. The instrument in question was intended to implement government policy changes in relation to the availability of income tax credits. This was to be achieved by restricting the number of persons eligible to claim the benefit. All of this, in turn, led to the accusation the House had acted in breach of one of the more important conventional rules governing the relationship between the two Houses, i.e. that the Lords should give way to the Commons in financial matters. The issue was forcefully argued but no clear decision was forthcoming. Amongst other things, this was because no consensus could be found as to:

- whether financial privilege applied to instrumental legislation;
- whether the measure in question was financial in nature or primarily an instrument for giving effect to the government's social welfare policies.

Classification

Conventions regulating the exercise of the royal prerogative

As has been made clear, the law of the constitution continues to repose a great deal of legal authority in the person of the Monarch. This is, however, subject to the following conventions.

(a) The Monarch's prerogative to appoint the Prime Minister must be exercised in favour of the person who commands a majority in the House of Commons.

(b) The prerogative to appoint other members of the government must be exercised on the advice of the Prime Minister.

(c) The prerogative to grant or refuse the Royal Assent must be exercised in favour of all Bills approved by the Commons and the Lords.

(d) The prerogative to summon Parliament must be exercised annually.

(e) The prerogative to dissolve Parliament must be exercised on the advice of the Prime Minister subject to the terms of the Fixed Term Parliaments Act 2011.

The conventional regulation of royal power is not just of functional significance. It is this which has enabled the prerogative to remain largely intact and which has, therefore, preserved the Monarch's formal constitutional role (i.e. the Monarch assents to legislation, summons and appoints the Prime Minister, etc.). This, in turn, has done much to sustain the credibility and status of the institution of monarchy itself. It has also helped to synthesise, in a practical sense, two essentially incompatible political concepts, viz. monarchical and **representative parliamentary government**.

Conventions regulating the practice of Cabinet government

The law of the constitution makes only peripheral reference to the offices of Prime Minister and **Cabinet** (see Ministerial and Other Salaries Act 1975). Both exist by virtue of convention. Their powers, relationship and *modus operandi* are also determined by conventional rules, the principal ones being as follows:

For the conduct of Cabinet government, see Chapter 11.

(a) The Prime Minister should be a member of the House of Commons.

(b) The Prime Minister decides national policy in consultation with a Cabinet (i.e. a committee of senior ministers).

(c) The composition of the Cabinet, and the distribution of portfolios within it, is determined by the Prime Minister.

(d) The Cabinet is chosen from MPs and peers who support the party or parties in power.

(e) The Prime Minister, Cabinet and government are collectively responsible to the House of Commons for their conduct of national affairs and must resign if defeated in a vote of censure or no confidence (last occurred in 1979).

(f) Ministers are individually responsible and answerable for the conduct of their particular departments or areas of responsibility and should be prepared to resign if they, their department, or any of their civil servants are guilty of any serious errors of judgement.

(g) The Prime Minister calls Cabinet meetings and determines their agenda.

(h) The Prime Minister determines the number, subject-matter and composition of **Cabinet Committees**.

Conventions regulating the work of Parliament

It is generally agreed that the rules of parliamentary practice and privilege, which are recognised and enforced by **the Speaker**, and which may be embodied in standing orders of either House, should properly be regarded as part of the law and custom of Parliament and, as such, not be classified as conventions. Subject to this, the following rules of parliamentary conduct are founded in conventions:

For the workings of Parliament, see Chapters 8 and 9.

(a) The House of Lords should give way to the House of Commons.

(b) Financial measures should be introduced in the House of Commons and should not be altered by the Lords.

(c) The government arranges the business of the House of Commons in **consultation** with the parties in opposition, particularly **Her Majesty's Official Opposition** ('behind the Speaker's chair').

(d) The government always provides parliamentary time for opposition censure motions.

(e) In the event of a 'tied' vote in the House of Commons, the Speaker's casting vote is cast for the government.

(f) The composition of parliamentary committees should reflect each party's representation in the House of Commons.

Conventions regulating the relationship between the United Kingdom and the Commonwealth

The following rules may be understood as deriving from agreements reached between the United Kingdom and the independent members of the Commonwealth.

(a) Any alteration relating to the Royal Style and Titles or the succession to the throne requires the assent of all the independent Commonwealth states in which the Monarch is the Head of State (e.g. Canada, New Zealand, Australia).

(b) The Governors-General of independent Commonwealth states are appointed by the Monarch on the advice of the Prime Minister of the state in question.

(c) Governors-General represent the Monarch but not the British government.

Rules of recognition

The fact that a particular political practice has been repeated over a period of time or in a given set of circumstances does not, of itself, elevate it to the status of convention. Thus the traditional ritualistic activities of the Chancellor of the Exchequer on budget day are too trivial and lacking in constitutional significance to merit the title of convention. Other 'usual' practices such as the expectation that the Prime Minister will include in the Cabinet persons from the various wings (left, right, centre, etc.) of the party in power, although of greater significance, may be regarded as too imprecise and laden with political discretion to be defined as 'rules'.

Various formulae have been offered, therefore, to assist in determining which political practices qualify to be treated as conventions. The most cited of these is that provided by Sir Ivor Jennings in *The Law of the Constitution* (5th edn), 1959. Jennings proposed three essential tests:

(a) Are there sufficient precedents?

(b) Did those involved believe they were bound by a rule?

(c) Is there a good constitutional reason for the rule?

Few would dispute that the accepted practice of the Prime Minister having a seat in the House of Commons has acquired the status and force of convention. No peer has held the office of Prime Minister since Lord Salisbury resigned in 1902. The precedents usually cited for this convention normally relate to events that occurred in 1923 and 1940. In 1923, when the incumbent premier (Bonar Law) resigned for ill health, the choice was between Lord Curzon and Stanley Baldwin. The latter was chosen. In 1940 the choice appeared to be between Lord Halifax and **Winston Churchill**. Again it was the 'commoner' who was appointed.

The exact grounds for the 1923 decision remain unclear. It cannot be said, therefore, that it represented unequivocal recognition of the existence of a convention based on the diminished significance of the House of Lords following the Parliament Act 1911. It is generally accepted, however, that Lord Halifax's status counted against him in 1940. Halifax himself expressed the view that 'having no access to the House of Commons' he would have 'speedily become a more or less honorary Prime Minister living in a kind of twilight just outside the things that really mattered' (Lord Halifax, *The Fullness of Days*, 1957).

Any remaining doubts about whether the 1923 and 1940 incidents had come to be regarded as binding political precedents appeared to have disappeared by 1963 when both Lords Home and Hailsham announced their intention to renounce their titles in order to compete for the vacant premiership (after the resignation of Harold Macmillan). Lord Home became Sir Alec Douglas-Home and was the successful candidate.

By the middle of the twentieth century the precedents appeared to suggest that a similar and related practice, i.e. that prime ministerial appointments to senior posts in the Cabinet should be limited to persons with seats in the House of Commons, was sufficiently well established to be regarded as a conventional rule. Hence, in 1955, the Prime Minister, Sir Anthony Eden, refrained from appointing his first choice, Lord Salisbury, as Foreign Secretary, as Salisbury was an hereditary peer and did not hold a seat in the democratically elected Lower House. Eden's understanding of the developing status and effect of the above was shown, however, to have been somewhat ahead of its time. Hence, in 1960, another hereditary peer, Lord Home, was appointed Foreign Secretary by the then premier, Harold MacMillan and, in 1979, Lord Carrington was appointed to the same post by Mrs Thatcher.

Suggestions that a further conventional rule was emerging to the effect that no further hereditary peerages would be created also proved precipitous through decisions of Mrs Thatcher to confer such on Harold MacMillan, (Prime Minister, 1967–63), William Whitelaw (Home Secretary, 1979–83) and George Thomas (Speaker, 1974–76).

The reasons for this convention are immediately apparent. The United Kingdom is a representative democracy. The nation's representatives sit in the House of Commons. It is there that the government must account for its conduct of national affairs. As Halifax acknowledged, therefore, it is axiomatic that the leader of the government should be a member of the forum which Professor de Smith has described as the 'grand inquest of the nation'.

It is clear that conventions can also come into existence by agreement. The agreement in 1930 that the royal power to appoint the Governor-General of a dominion would be exercised exclusively on the advice of the government of the dominion concerned, is generally accepted to have created a convention to that effect. Hence it would be regarded as unconstitutional for the Crown to act in this matter without or contrary to such advice.

The relationship between law and convention

In a functional sense law and convention are very closely connected. Most conventions presuppose the existence of particular constitutional laws and have been formulated to regulate the way these legal rules are exercised. Hence Hood Phillips' statement that 'conventions would be meaningless without their legal context' (*op. cit.*).

There are also considerable similarities between the attributes of law and convention. Both are regarded as rules and make use of precedent for the purposes of validity. Those affected accept that both impose a degree of obligation and that adverse consequences may result from disobedience.

For all these jurisprudential musings, however, it remains clear that the courts will not enforce conventions and, where a convention and a legal rule conflict, courts will always apply the latter.

In 1965 Parliament enacted the Southern Rhodesia Act and did so in contravention of the convention that Parliament would not legislate for a dominion unless so requested by the dominion concerned. The Act was the UK's response to Rhodesia's unilateral declaration of independence. It declared that Rhodesia remained a British dominion and invalidated all legislation promulgated by the illegal regime. In *Madzimbamuto* v *Lardner-Burke* [1969] 1 AC 645, the complainant challenged the legality of his detention under Rhodesian emergency regulations. The Privy Council refused to accept the argument that the 1965 Act should not be applied because of the breach of convention or that 'moral, political and other reasons' presented any barrier to the enforcement of a valid legal rule. The 1965 Act was applied and the complainant's detention was found to be illegal.

A further useful example of judicial refusal to give effect to convention was provided by the decision in *Manuel* v *Attorney-General* [1983] Ch 77. On this occasion a group of Canadian Indians took exception to the Canada Act 1982. This conferred authority on the Canadian Federal Parliament to alter certain founding parts of the Canadian constitution contained in nineteenth-century British North America Acts. The Indians believed that this would endanger the protection given by these enactments to rights granted to them in treaties agreed with the original British colonial administration.

The case raised issues similar to those canvassed in *Madzimbamuto*. The Indians argued breach of a convention that the Westminster Parliament would not amend the Canadian constitution except with the consent of all the provinces and peoples of Canada including the Indian nations. The Court of Appeal was firmly of the opinion that it could not inquire into whether a particular convention had been complied with and that purported non-compliance was not something which could impair the effectiveness of that which had been approved by Commons, Lords and Monarch. A further example of the Court of Appeal refusing to enforce a convention may be found in *R (on application of Southall)* v *Secretary of State for Foreign and Commonwealth Affairs* [2003] EWCA Civ 1002, where it felt unable to grant a declaration that, absent a referendum, it would be 'unconstitutional' for the UK government to adopt the proposed new European constitution.

For the new European constitution, see pp. 94–6.

Example

Judicial recognition of the utility of convention in regulating Ministerial powers was evident in the famous wartime decision of **Liversidge** v **Anderson** [1942] AC 206. On this occasion the House of Lords felt that during a national emergency it would be inappropriate for a court to question the reasonableness of the way the Secretary of State for the Home Department had used his power to intern any person believed to be 'of hostile origins or associations' (contained in reg 18B of the Defence (General) Regulations 1939). Viscount Maugham's view was that 'the person who is primarily entrusted with these important duties is one of the principal Secretaries of State, and a member of government answerable to Parliament for a proper discharge of his duties'.

In more recent history during the first Gulf Crisis of 1991 the Court of Appeal refused to question the grounds on which the Secretary of State for the Home Department had exercised his discretion to deport a person whose presence in the United Kingdom was deemed not to be 'conducive to the public good' (Immigration Act 1971, s 3). Lord Donaldson MR commented that the Secretary of State for the Home Department was 'fully accountable to Parliament for his decisions whether or not to deport'; thus demonstrating again the judicial preference for conventional control of Ministerial powers in this politically delicate context (**R** v **Secretary of State for the Home Department, ex parte Cheblak** [1991] 2 All ER 319).

For the freedom of expression, see Chapter 20.

It is interesting to note, however, that the same court did appear to contemplate enforcing a convention in ***Attorney-General* v *Jonathan Cape Ltd*** [1976] QB 752. On this occasion the decision was that a court could grant injunctive relief to prevent an ex-Cabinet Minister from including details of Cabinet meetings in his memoirs. This opinion was founded principally, however, on the equitable doctrine of confidentiality and should not be understood, therefore, as giving legal force to the convention of collective ministerial responsibility.

That conventions are not laws and are not, therefore, legally binding is further illustrated by the events of 1975 and 2016–17 and the referendums concerning the UK's membership of the European Community, latterly the European Union. On each occasion, and because of entrenched opposing views on the issue within the governments of the day, and for this matter alone, the convention of collective ministerial responsibility and unity was suspended for the duration of the referendum campaigns. This was done to allow Ministers to adopt different positions on this crucial question as their consciences directed.

It would be misleading, however, to represent judicial refusal to enforce convention as symptomatic of a reluctance to recognise the existence and significance of non-legal rules in the workings of the constitution. Hence many examples exist of judges citing particular conventions in order to explain the general constitutional coherence of their decisions. Thus the convention of individual Ministerial responsibility has frequently been referred to in a series of cases in which the courts have refused to question Ministerial decisions relating to matters of national security. Here, judicial reservations about interfering with such sensitive policy issues have tended to be accompanied by references to the Minister's conventional responsibility to Parliament – thus implying a preference for alleged abuses of such powers to be dealt with in the chamber of the House of Commons rather than in the courts.

For details of judicial review of emergency and security powers, see Chapter 14.

Reasons for obedience

Various theories have been advanced for the general level of compliance with convention. In any given circumstance obedience is probably secured through a combination of influences.

Moral opprobrium

As already explained, one of the main objectives of convention is to ensure that power is used in accordance with the ideological principles on which the constitution is based. By definition, therefore, the stability of the constitution is prejudiced by unconventional behaviour. It follows that those responsible risk the opprobrium both of colleagues and the media, and may incite the type of public criticism and disapproval which serves to reinforce the effectiveness of any value system and the social and political order which it seeks to sustain.

Breach of the law

Dicey's view was that a breach of convention 'would almost immediately bring the offender into conflict with the courts and the law of the land'. Most commentators would accept that this is a proposition of some validity but one which does not have universal application. Hence, if the Monarch were to renege on the conventional obligation to summon Parliament every year, the annual financial legislation legalising the collection and expenditure of revenue could not be enacted. The same consequence would probably follow if a government refused to resign after losing the confidence and support of the House of Commons. On the other hand, it is difficult to envisage what state of illegality would result if a member of the government were to launch a verbal attack on the competence of a member of the judiciary or were to criticise a decision of the Cabinet.

Political difficulties

Jennings argued that conventions are obeyed 'because of the political difficulties which follow if they are not'. There is little doubt that breach of some of the major conventional rules would have substantial political ramifications. Thus, an immediate constitutional crisis would probably result if the Monarch attempted to use the royal prerogative without or contrary to Ministerial advice. In the longer term, this would be bound to precipitate questions concerning the wisdom of retaining a constitutional monarchy that was not prepared to behave constitutionally. Similarly a government could hardly hope to survive and function effectively if ministers wantonly ignored the conventions of collective and individual responsibility.

Result in legislation

In addition to that proposed by Dicey, a further legal consequence of breach of convention may be that the rule in question will be given legislative force. This is illustrated by the events of 1909–11 when the House of Lords voted against the Finance Bill 1909 – a flagrant breach of the conventional rule requiring the unelected chamber to 'give way' to the House of Commons. The matter was dealt with by the Parliament Act 1911 which gave the rule legal force in respect of all **Public Bills** (except if designed to prolong the life of Parliament).

For the Parliament Act 1911, see Chapter 9, pp. 203–4.

Self-interest

Ambition for high public office is rarely well served by refusal to comply with the ethics of the political and constitutional system. A Minister may be tempted to 'put on record' a sense of dissatisfaction with the Prime Minister or other Cabinet colleagues but will be aware that this could presage the end of a promising political career. An aspirant to high judicial office will know that controversial **extra-curial** comment will do little for the cause of personal advancement. As in any organisation, participants cannot hope to progress within it unless they are prepared to accept the rules by which it is conducted.

Codification of conventions

At first glance it might not seem entirely satisfactory that so many of the constitution's primary rules are not subject to either judicial enforcement or definition. This state of affairs is, however, usually explained by reference to a number of practical justifications.

The most obvious of these is that any comprehensive transformation of conventions into legal rules would inevitably inhibit the constitution's traditional potential to respond to political experience and to changing beliefs about the practice of government. Legislative intervention would then be needed to deal with rules expressive of outdated constitutional values. Legal certainty and authority might be bought, therefore, at the price of flexibility and political relevance. Also, history shows that laws are often not changed until long after they have ceased to fulfil any useful function and even then may be defended for purely symbolic or sentimental reasons. In terms of the ideals of government, therefore, organic constitutional growth and legal specificity may not be entirely compatible notions.

A further consequence of converting convention to law would be that disputes or uncertainty as to the exact content and requirements of the rules in question would become legal rather than political matters. This would have the effect of drawing the judiciary into overtly political controversies – something which would appear to be in direct contradiction of British constitutional tradition. It is also difficult to imagine that those aggrieved or politically disadvantaged by judicial interpretation of contentious constitution rules would be able to desist from allegations, however veiled, of party-political bias.

It might be, of course, that the judges would simply refuse to get involved and would prefer instead to take the view that legal rules relating to high affairs of state and laden with political discretion should be regarded as non-justiciable (i.e. as matters falling outside the proper sphere of judicial competence), an approach which has already been adopted in relation to some of the more important prerogative powers (see the House of Lords in *Council of Civil Service Unions* v *Minister for the Civil Service* [1985] AC 374). This in itself, however, might be another reason for leaving conventions as they are, since, apart from the issue of clarity, there would appear to be little point in giving legal status to that which the judges might not be prepared to enforce.

For discussion of the case, see Chapter 12.

These arguments notwithstanding, it still has to be conceded that some conventions are fraught with uncertainty and it is not possible to state the obligations they impose with any exactitude or confidence. Hence, for example, does the convention that Ministers are responsible for their departments and should resign if serious mistakes are made admit of any exceptions and, if so, what are they? And what are the conventional requirements resting on the Monarch when appointing a Prime Minister from a 'hung' Parliament?

As something of a compromise, therefore, between the present state of uncertainty and the disadvantages of over-formalisation, it has been suggested that conventions could be declared and clarified without alteration of their existing non-legal nature. This has been done, for example, in Australia, where a Constitutional Conference consisting of representatives from the federal and state Parliaments meets at regular intervals for this express purpose.

An alternative approach worthy of mention is that of the Canadian constitution. This gives the Supreme Court there the jurisdiction to pronounce on the existence and content of a convention but not to give it legal force or effect. In Canada, therefore, government action in breach of convention may not be defined as illegal but could be declared to be unconstitutional. The likelihood of breach of convention is thus diminished as no government in a democratic state relishes having its actions condemned by the supreme judicial authority.

Domestically, however, such classification of conventions is unlikely to take place in isolation from some more general programme of constitutional reform – perhaps as part of the replacement of the existing model by a comprehensive written document. At present this is not something which appears to be a matter of immediate political priority, and may yet be 'a bridge too far' in terms of the current state of the prevailing political culture.

European Union law

European law and institutions

Objective 3

Currently, and so long as the United Kingdom remains a member of the EU, the nation's processes of law and government may be said to derive from three principal sources:

(a) the United Kingdom's national courts and Parliament and the established rules of constitutional practice (conventions) within which they operate;

(b) the policy, administrative and law-making institutions of the European Union, and the EU treaties on which these are founded;

(c) the Articles of the European Convention on Human Rights and the jurisprudence of the European Court of Human Rights.

The European Union

For domestic UK purposes, as for all member states, the powers of government, administration and law-making for those activities falling within the EU's spheres of authority – as determined by the various EU treaties, are vested in:

(a) the European Council (all EU prime ministers – general EU policy and development);

(b) the Council of the European Union (Ministers from each member state depending on the subject-matter of particular meetings – policy and law-making for particular EU competencies);

(c) the European Commission (one member from each EU state – enforcement of treaty objections, implementation of legislative proposals);

(d) the Court of Justice of the European Union (one judge from each member state – legal interpretation of EU law).

For the Treaty of Lisbon and the EU Charter of Fundamental Rights, see Chapter 4, pp. 96–99, and Chapter 16, pp. 417–8.

The treaties on which the EU is founded may also be regarded as a source of important constitutional principles, particularly in the sphere of the rights of the individual. These would extend to: freedom of movement within the Union (TFEU Art 21), the right to various benefits following from the right to EU citizenship (TFEU Art 20), and the prohibition of discrimination on grounds of nationality, gender, racial or ethnic origin, religion, age, disability or sexual orientation. All of these were supplemented significantly by the EU's adoption of the Charter of Fundamental Rights as part of the Treaty of Lisbon 2009.

European Convention on Human Rights

For detailed coverage of the Convention, see Chapter 16.

The European Convention of Human Rights and the European Court of Human Rights outdate the European Community, later European Union (per existence from 1953 and 1957, respectively) and, in its origins constitutes an independent and distinct body of legal rights and procedures. These represent a comprehensive framework of broad human rights principles and standards which, as a result of the Human Rights Act 1998, are directly enforceable within the domestic legal system.

The law and custom of Parliament

This consists, in the main, of the rules which regulate the conduct of parliamentary proceedings, the behaviour and the activities of members of both Houses, and which also contain the powers of both Houses to deal with those who are guilty of breaches of parliamentary privilege or whose words or behaviour are contemptuous of either House.

The majority of these rules may be found in parliamentary standing orders, resolutions and rulings from the chair. These are matters which are generally recognised as being beyond the competence of the courts. Compliance is, therefore, a matter for parliamentary rather than judicial enforcement.

Summary

The chapter identifies and provides detailed comment on the three main, traditional sources of English constitutional and administrative law and practice, viz. Acts of Parliament, judicial decisions and constitutional conventions. It also directs readers' attention to the impact on the British constitution of the two 'new' legal and institutional systems to which the United Kingdom is now a party, i.e. the European Union and the European Convention on Human Rights.

References

Halifax (1957) *The Fullness of Days*, London: Collins.

Hood Phillips and Jackson (2001) *Constitutional and Administrative Law* (8th edn), London: Sweet & Maxwell.

Jennings (1959) *The Law of the Constitution* (5th edn), London: University of London Press.

Loveland (1996) *Constitutional Law: A Critical Introduction*, London: Butterworths.

Loveland (2006) *Constitutional Law, Administrative Law and Human Rights* (4th edn), Oxford: Oxford University Press.

Further reading

Allen and Thompson (2014) *Cases and Materials on Constitutional and Administrative Law* (11th edn), Oxford University Press, Ch. 5.

Butler, Bogdanor and Summers (2004) *The Law, Politics and the Constitution: Essays in Honour of Geoffrey Marshall*, Oxford University Press, Chs 5, 6 and 7.

Elliot and Thomas (2014) *Public Law*, Oxford: Oxford University Press.

Loveland (2015) *Constitutional Law, Administrative Law and Human Rights* (7th edn), Oxford: Oxford University Press.

Marshall (1984) *Constitutional Conventions: The Rules and Forms of Political Accountability*, Oxford: Clarendon Press.

Monaghan ((2015) *Blueprints: Constitutional and Administrative Law*, Harlow: Pearson Education

Monro (1999) *Studies in Constitutional Law* (4th edn), London: Butterworths, Ch. 3.

Ryan and Foster (2014 *Unlocking Constitutional Law*, Abingdon, Oxford, Oxford University Press.

Turpin and Tompkins (2011) *British Government and the Constitution* (7th edn), London: Cambridge University Press, Ch. 1.

Part 2

Parliament and the European Union

4

The European Union: institutions of government and sources of law

Objectives

After reading this chapter you should:

1. Understand the evolution and development of the European Union and the principal elements of the treaties on which the EU is founded.

2. Be aware of the process of EU enlargement and related institutional reforms.

3. Appreciate the nature and functions of the main law-making and executive institutions of the EU and the EU's law-making processes.

4. Be aware of the different types of EU law.

5. Understand the reasons for, and the effects of, the Treaty of Lisbon 2007.

Introduction

In the national referendum of 23 June 1916, a majority of those who cast their vote (51.9 per cent) expressed the wish that the United Kingdom should cease to be a member of the European Union. The vote itself, however, did not give immediate legal effect to that intent. This could be achieved only through the process of negotiation required by the Treaty of the European Union, Article 50, followed by final ratification by all other EU member states and by legislation enacted by the Westminster Parliament. During this process, therefore, and until its conclusion and ratification, as described, the United Kingdom remains a full member of the European Union and subject to its treaties with all that this entails including:

1 continued adherence to the founding fundamentals of the EU, viz. the freedom of movement of persons, goods, services, and capital (the 'four freedoms');

2 continued representation and participation in the work of the European Council (save for discussion of the UK's exit from the Union), the Council of Europe (previously the Council of Ministers), the European Commission, the European Parliament, and the Court of Justice of the European Union (CJEU);

3 continued application of the law of the European Union in the domestic courts;

4 continued recognition of the CJEU as the final arbiter of the content, meaning and requirements of EU law and of the authority of the EU's principal policy, executive and law-making institutions as set out above.

Details of the referendum vote and its legal and constitutional implications may be found in the Appendix at pp. 722–3.

Origins and development

The EEC and the European Community

Objective 1

In 1951 – by the Treaty of Paris – Belgium, France, Germany, Italy, Holland and Luxembourg formed the European Coal and Steel Community (ECSC). Six years later, by virtue of the Treaty of Rome, the same six nations created two further communities (i.e. integrated economic and industrial systems). These were the European Economic Community and the European Atomic Energy Community (EAEC or Euratom). The three organisations were referred to collectively as the European Economic Communities (EEC).

Their legal and executive institutions were merged by the Treaty of Merger 1965. Thereafter the European Council of Ministers, the European Commission, the European Court of Justice and the European Assembly acted on behalf of all three organisations.

The United Kingdom joined the EEC by virtue of the Brussels Treaty of Accession 1972. Under the European Communities Act 1972, EEC law was incorporated into the law of the United Kingdom. Both the Treaty and the Act became effective on 1 January 1973. The United Kingdom thus became a member of a supranational organisation with power to make law taking effect within the domestic jurisdiction without reference to Parliament. Thus was effected the most significant change to the British constitution since the Glorious Revolution of 1688.

The European Economic Community was renamed the European Union by the Maastricht Treaty on European Union 1992 (TEU). This gave express recognition to the fact that the legislative and policy-making activities of the organisation had developed and extended beyond purely economic matters. The Maastricht Treaty was given effect in English law by the European Communities (Amendment) Act 1993.

The purposes of the Community were set out in Art 2 of the Treaty. These were:

by establishing a common market and an economic and monetary union . . . to promote throughout the Community a harmonious and well balanced development of economic activities, sustainable and non-inflationary growth . . . a high degree of convergence of economic performance, a high level of employment and of social protection, the raising of the standard of living and the quality of life, and economic and social cohesion and solidarity among members.

Article 3 of the Treaty made it abundantly clear that the activities of the Community extended well beyond purely economic and commercial matters and included:

a policy in the social sphere . . . a policy in the sphere of the environment . . . a contribution to the attainment of a high level of health protection . . . a contribution to education and training of quality and to the flowering of cultures of Member States.

The European Union

Prior to the Maastricht Treaty, the European Community's policy and law-making authority, as founded on the Treaty of Rome, was concerned primarily with European economic integration through the creation and maintenance of a tariff-free European trading zone (the 'Common Market') and the development of common European policies for agriculture and fisheries. The principal effect of Maastricht was to extend the areas of concern of the European organisation to include:

1 foreign affairs and security;
2 justice and home affairs.

The organisation which emerged from the Treaty encompassing all three areas of activity, i.e. the European Community and the Common Market, foreign affairs and security, and justice and home affairs, was given the name the European Union. The three dimensions of the EU were to be referred to as 'Pillars', viz.:

Pillar 1, the European Community and Common Market;

Pillar 2, foreign affairs and security;

Pillar 3, justice and home affairs.

At this stage all of the European policy and law-making institutions, i.e. the Council of Ministers, the Commission, and the ECJ, operated within Pillar 1, the European Community. The European Union had no direct policy- or law-making authority within Pillars 2 and 3. Matters arising in these areas were to be dealt with on an 'intergovernmental basis', i.e. by arrangements between the EU and member states directed towards the development of 'common' or shared positions. The Treaty of Lisbon 2007, provided for the replacement of the 'pillar' structure and terminology by three competences ('exclusive', 'shared', and 'supporting') as from 2014.

For detailed content of the three competences, see p. 100.

The Lisbon Treaty also consolidated the Union's previous and founding treaties into the Treaty on the European Union (TEU), which sets out the general objectives of the Union and its institutional, legislative and policy making framework, and the Treaty on the Functioning of the European Union (TFEU), which, amongst other things, identifies the areas or competences for which the EU's institutions are authorised to make law and policy.

In relation to the European Union, it is important to note that:

(i) As indicated, the Maastricht Treaty did not seek to confer on existing European institutions any law-making authority in the matters covered by the two new pillars.

(ii) The Treaty did not impose any obligation on signatory states to give effect in their domestic law to any developments, agreements or further treaties which might arise from the aforementioned government cooperation in these matters.

(iii) To the extent that the Treaty created any legal obligations, these, and agreements under the two intergovernmental pillars, were binding in international law only between the parties to the Treaty and any such agreements.

(iv) Prior to the Treaty of Lisbon, the European Union did not have any international legal personality and was therefore not capable of making binding international agreements with other states or organisations of states.

It should also be mentioned that the Maastricht Treaty:

(a) created the concept of citizenship of the European Union with the rights specified in Arts 8(a)–(d) of the Treaty;

(b) committed the European Union to economic and monetary union by 1999;

(c) added to the EC Treaty the Protocol on Social Policy (the 'Social Chapter') to be implemented by relevant legislation by the EU's law-making institutions;

(d) made substantial amendments to and altered the name of the founding treaty of the EEC (viz. the Treaty of Rome) to the EC Treaty.

The Maastricht Summit concluded with a commitment to keep the future development of the Union under review to be considered further at the next intergovernmental conference (IGC). This was based on an awareness of the differing perspectives concerning the Union's future political direction, the pace of development and the problems of enlargement. At the Brussels European Council of December 1998 it was agreed that, within this general debate, key matters for consideration should include:

(a) the future role of the European Parliament in decision-making procedures;

(b) the implications of enlargement for the size and composition of the Commission and for voting procedures within the Council of Ministers;

(c) the general issue of how to reconcile the needs of democracy in an enlarged Union with those of institutional efficiency.

An agenda of potential options for reform was prepared by a 'Reflection Group' composed of representatives from the Council of Ministers, the Commission and the Parliament.

The ensuing IGC was held in Amsterdam in 1997 and resulted in the Treaty of Amsterdam 1997. The Treaty took effect on 1 May 1999. Its principal effects were as follows:

(a) a wholesale renumbering of the Articles of the Treaty of Rome as amended by the Treaty on European Union;

(b) the third pillar of the Union entitled Justice and Home Affairs to be renamed Police and Judicial Cooperation in Criminal Matters and its provisions relating to aspects of the freedom of movement including visas, asylum and immigration to be transferred to the jurisdiction of the European Community (Pillar no. 1);

(c) the role of the European Parliament in the legislative process to be enhanced by a significant increase in the number of matters to be decided according to the Co-Decision procedure, i.e. with the consent of both the Council of Ministers and the European Parliament;

(d) the Common Foreign and Security Policy Pillar to be extended to include humanitarian and rescue missions and peacekeeping.

No firm conclusions were reached at Amsterdam concerning the implications of enlargement for institutional reform either in terms of composition generally or the weighting and distribution of votes within the Council of Ministers. These matters were to be taken forward by the next IGC, scheduled to be held in Nice in 2000. For detailed content of the Treaty of Nice, see below.

The process of enlargement

History

Objective 2

As explained above, the original European Community formed in 1957 consisted of just six states (Belgium, France, Germany, Holland, Italy and Luxembourg). These were joined by Ireland, Denmark and the United Kingdom in 1973, Greece in 1981, Portugal and Spain in 1986, and Austria, Finland and Sweden in 1995. The most dramatic enlargement took place in 2004. This saw the accession of a further ten states: Cyprus, Czech Republic, Estonia, Hungary, Malta, Latvia, Lithuania, Poland, Slovakia and Slovenia. A further two states, Bulgaria and Romania, became members from 1 January 2007. This brought the number of EU states to 27. This increased to 28 with the accession of Croatia in 2013.

Institutional changes

The institutional reforms necessitated by the 2004 and 2007 enlargements, particularly for the purposes of presenting the Union's decision-making efficiency, were contained in the Treaty of Nice 2001. The principal changes effected by the Treaty were as follows.

(a) The European Parliament

The distribution of seats following the enlargements of 2004 and 2007, and 2013, is set out on p. 84.

The maximum number of members of the Parliament was increased from 700 to 732 (plus 53 in 2007 with the accession of Bulgaria and Romania). Prior to the Treaty taking effect, national representation in the Parliament was: Germany 99, France 87, Italy 87, United Kingdom 87, Spain 64, Netherlands 31, Belgium 25, Greece 25, Portugal 25, Sweden 22, Austria 21, Denmark 16, Finland 16, Ireland 15, Luxembourg 6.

(b) Council of Ministers

The post-enlargement allocation of votes to member states is set out on p. 82.

Membership of the Council was increased from 15 to 25 (plus 2 in 2007 and 1 in 2013) with one seat for each member state. The previous allocation was France 10, Germany 10, Italy 10, United Kingdom 10, Spain 8, Belgium 5, Greece 5, Holland 5, Portugal 5, Austria 4, Spain 4, Denmark 3, Finland 3, Ireland 3, Luxembourg 2. The threshold for the Council's system of qualified majority voting was changed to 255 from 345 (previously, with 15 states, 169 from 237).

(c) The European Commission

The pre-2004 Commission had 20 members. All 15 states were represented but the larger entities, France, Italy, Germany, Spain and the United Kingdom were allowed two Commissioners each.

After 2004, the Commission had 25 members with just one Commissioner for each member state. Two more were added: one each for Bulgaria and Romania in 2007 and one for Croatia in 2013.

(d) The European Court of Justice

The number of judges was increased from 15 to 25 (2004), 27 in 2007 and 28 in 2013. It was also provided that for important cases the court could function through 'Grand Chambers' of 13 rather than in plenary sessions.

Other significant reforms to increase the court's efficiency were:

- allowing litigants direct access to it;
- the creation of specialised chambers to relieve the court's workload in specialised areas;
- allowing the court to give preliminary rulings in appropriate matters.

(e) The Court of Auditors

The Treaty stipulated that the court should continue to consist of one officer for each member state (i.e. 28) appointed by the Council for six years by qualified majority vote. The court was also given the authority to set up chambers to dispose of different aspects of its work.

These matters are dealt with below, see pp. 93–101.

Further changes to the composition and workings of the EU's institutions were proposed by the ill-fated EU Constitution 2004 and the Treaty of Lisbon 2007.

The future

The process of EU enlargement and the admission of new states are not yet complete. The most recent entrant was Croatia in the summer of 2013. At the time of writing (autumn 2016), there were five fully recognised candidates for EU membership. These, and their dates of application, were: Turkey (1987), Macedonia (2004), Montenegro (2008), Serbia (2009), Albania (2009). Bosnia Herzegovina and Kosovo are classified as 'potential candidates'. A Stabilisation and Accession Agreement was signed by Bosnia-Herzegovina in 2008. Such agreements are preconditional to the making of an EU membership application proper by any of the former states of Yugoslavia.

Due to ongoing political difficulties, the position of Turkey remains uncertain. In 2016 its application for membership was 'suspended' by the European Parliament following the Turkish government's response to an attempted coup. Beyond the geographical fact that only a small part of Turkey's land mass (3 per cent) actually falls within the boundaries of Europe proper, problems complicating progress towards membership have included deficiencies in its human rights record and alleged discrimination in its treatment of minorities. Kosovo's progress to applicant status remains complicated by the failure of a number of EU members to recognise it as a fully independent nation state.

The only major European states not currently in the EU are Switzerland, Norway and Iceland. Switzerland applied for membership in 1992 but the proposition was rejected by the Swiss electorate in referenda in 1992 and 2001. Norway has applied for membership on four occasions. The applications of 1962 and 1967 were vetoed by France. Subsequent applications in 1972 and 1994 were rejected in referenda. Iceland applied for membership in 2009 but subsequently suspended its application.

The Copenhagen Criteria

Entry to the EU is conditional on a prospective member satisfying the 'Copenhagen Criteria'. These are a set of political and economic tests used to measure an applicant state's stage of development and rate of progression towards EU membership requirements. The criteria were formulated by the Copenhagen European Council of 1993. Principal amongst the requirements are the need for:

1 stable institutions of democratic government;

2 respect for rule of law, human rights, and the protection of minorities;

3 a functioning market economy capable of coping with the competitive market forces operating within the Union;

4 the capacity to fulfil the obligations of membership, including compliance with the EU's overall political and economic objectives.

Further progress beyond this has, however, been complicated by what the European Commission has referred to as a failure to achieve the required standards in 'the effectiveness and stability of democratic institutions'.

Institutions of law and government

Objective 3

The treaties provide for six principal institutions through which the executive, legislative and judicial work of the Union is carried out.

These are:

(a) the European Council;

(b) the Council of the European Union (previously the Council of Ministers);

(c) the European Commission;

(d) the European Parliament;

(e) the Court of Justice of the European Union (CJEU);

(f) the Court of Auditors.

The European Council

Composition

The Council is the EU's primary policy-making body. It consists of the heads of government of the various member states sitting with its own President and the President of the European Commission. Meetings of the Council take place in Brussels, generally four times each year. The European Council was not given formal legal recognition as a distinct institution until so provided by the Treaty of Lisbon. This is now embodied in Art 13 of the TEU.

Prior to the Treaty of Lisbon, the European Council was chaired by the head of government of the member state which held the presidency of the Council of Ministers according to the principle of six-monthly rotation. The Treaty of Lisbon provided for a more permanent and dedicated President of the European Council elected by a qualified majority of Council members and serving for one renewable term of two-and-a-half years (i.e. five years maximum). The first President to be elected according to the new procedure was Herman Van Rompuy, formerly Prime Minister of Belgium. Mr Rompuy took office on 1 December 2009, the day the Treaty of Lisbon took effect.

Functions

The principal functions of the European Council include:

1 identifying the EU's strategic interests and objectives;

2 initiation of proposed changes to the EU's founding treaties;

3 formulating the EU's policy priorities and political agenda;

4 determining the EU's overall direction in external affairs and in relation to the exercise of its common foreign and security jurisdiction;

5 providing the impetus and general policy framework for the process of EU enlargement and integration;

6 acting as a forum for debate in times of crisis and assisting in the resolution of disputes between member states.

Powers

Notwithstanding its recognition in the Treaty of Lisbon, the European Council has no formal law-making or executive powers. It is, however, recognised as the EU's supreme political authority and draws its unique authority from its composition of Europe's heads of government. It follows that its decisions and proposals will, almost invariably, be put into effect by the EU's executive and legislative institutions.

The Council of the European Union

Composition and configurations

This is composed of ministerial representatives from all member states (28) and is led by the President of the European Union. The Council's composition at particular meetings is determined by the subject-matter for discussion. If dealing with matters of general substance and Union policy it will be attended by foreign ministers. If a more specific or limited Union competence is under consideration, say agriculture, it will be the states' ministers of agriculture who will be present.

In EU terminology, such subject-specific dimensions of the Council are known as configurations. Ten of these exist at present:

1 General Affairs;

2 Foreign Affairs;

3 Economic and Financial Affairs;

4 Agriculture and Fisheries;

5 Justice and Home Affairs;

6 Employment, Social Policy, Health and Consumer Affairs;

7 Competitiveness;

8 Transport, Telecommunications and Energy;

9 Environment;

10 Education, Youth and Culture.

According to the provisions of the Treaty of Lisbon, Foreign Affairs meetings of the Council of the European Union are chaired by the High Representative of the European Union for Foreign Affairs. Meetings of the Council in its other configurations are chaired by the President. The presidency of the Council 'rotates' and is held for six months by each member state in turn.

The concept of joint presidencies was also introduced by the Treaty of Lisbon. This aims to give greater continuity to the implementation of EU policies. According to this arrangement the functions of the presidency of the council in all its configurations, other than that relating to foreign affairs, are undertaken successively by groups of three member states ('the trio'), each of which uses its six-month tenure of the presidency to pursue a common or shared programme.

Powers

The Council has extensive legislative powers. According to the ordinary legislative procedure, which is used for the vast bulk (90 per cent) of EU legal instruments, the Council's consent, with that of the European Parliament, is required before any such laws may be adopted. These may be in the form of regulations, directives and legally binding decisions.

The Council has six key responsibilities. These are:

1 to make law;

2 to coordinate the broad economic policies of the member states;

3 to conclude international agreements between the EU and nation-states or other inter-national organisations with the European Parliament;

4 with the European Parliament to approve the EU's annual budget;

5 to develop the EU's common foreign and security policy based on the guidelines set by the European Council;

6 to coordinate cooperation between national courts and police forces in criminal matters.

Voting procedures

Prior to 2014 the Council made its decisions by qualified majority votes, simple majority votes or unanimous votes, depending on the subject-matter. Most decisions were taken by qualified majority. When the Council was deciding on a proposal from the Commission, the required qualified majority was to consist of a majority of all member states represent-ing 62 per cent of the population of the entire Union and casting 73.9 per cent of the votes allocated to them (i.e. 260 of 352). After 2007, the votes cast by each state were as follows: France 29, Germany 29, Italy 29, United Kingdom 29, Poland 27, Spain 27, Romania 14, Netherlands 13, Belgium 12, Czech Republic 12, Greece 12, Hungary 12, Portugal 12, Austria 10, Bulgaria 10, Sweden 10, Croatia 7, Denmark 7, Finland 7, Ireland 7, Lithuania 7, Slovakia 7, Cyprus 4, Estonia 4, Latvia 4, Luxembourg 4, Slovenia 4, Malta 3.

When the Council was not dealing with a proposal from the Commission, the require-ment was for the support of at least two-thirds of all member states, rather than, as above, a simple majority.

Significant changes to the Council's decision-making processes were embodied in the Treaty of Lisbon 2007. These took effect on 1 November 2014. The principal change was the replacement of the then existing system of qualified majority voting (as above), based on weighted allocations of votes, by a system of 'double majorities'. According to this, in order to be approved, a measure proposed by the Commission requires the support of 55 per cent of member states (i.e. at least 15 states) representing at least 65 per cent of the EU's popula-tion. An enhanced double majority, i.e. 72 per cent of member states, representing 65 per cent of the EU's population, is required for proposals not emanating from the Commission. The Lisbon Treaty also provided for a blocking minority of at least four member states with a population in excess of 35 per cent of the Union's population.

The Council is aided in its work by a Committee of Permanent Representatives (COREPER). This consists of the member states' permanent representatives or ambassadors to the EU. The Committee is charged with 'preparing the work of the Council and . . . carrying out the tasks assigned to it by the Council' (Art 240 TFEU). More specifically, one of its most important functions is to determine whether agreement can be reached concerning any policy or legislative proposals about to be considered by the Council. Where this is the case, such proposals may be formally adopted by the Council without further debate.

Depending on their subject-matter and significance, issues before the Council may also be decided by simple majorities or by unanimity. A simple majority is reached if fifteen Council members vote in favour of a particular proposal. Such votes tend to be limited to matters such as the Council's own procedural rules and to the organisation and workings of the Council Secretariat. Examples of subjects which must be decided by unanimous votes would include accession of new EU members, common foreign and security policy, EU financial policy, harmonisation of national legislation in the spheres of taxation and social security and protection, and EU citizenship. The Council should also vote unanimously should it wish to decide in opposition to a proposal of the Commission.

The European Commission

Composition

The Commission has 28 members – one for each member state. A new Commission is appointed every five years within six months of elections to the European Parliament. This is done as follows:

(a) member states acting through the European Council and by double majority vote agree a Commission President designate;

(b) their choice must be approved by the European Parliament;

(c) other Commissioners are nominated by the Council acting by double majority vote and in accord with the President designate;

(d) those nominations must be approved 'en bloc' by the European Parliament.

The long-term intent is for the total membership of the Commission to be reduced below the number of member states. The Treaty of Lisbon proposal was that, as of 2014, the number of Commissioners should be fixed at 18 or two-thirds of its present number. This was the response to the process of enlargement and the attendant fears of deadlock and delay in a Commission of then 27 members, rather than 15 as was the case prior to 2004. Progression towards implementing these changes was, however, interrupted by the Irish referendum of 2008. On that occasion, the majority against the Lisbon Treaty was generally believed to have been a result of concerns about the possibility of smaller member states no longer being guaranteed membership of this key European institution. In return, however, for the Irish government committing itself to holding a second referendum on the Lisbon Treaty, the European Council agreed that the number of commissioners in the post-2014 Commission would be increased above the original proposal. No exact figure was, however, set, nor was the overall Treaty commitment to reduce the size of the commission expressly abandoned. The eventual compromise was that the post-2014 Commission should have 27 members, with the state not awarded a seat in a particular Commission (i.e. once every five years) being given the post of High Representative of the Union for Foreign Affairs and Security Policy.

Individual Commissioners serve the Union and not the particular interests of their member states. Their specific portfolios are determined by the Commission President. They must be 'completely independent in the performance of their duties' and 'neither seek nor take instructions from any government or from any other body' (TEU Art 17(3)). Members of the Commission serve for five years and may only be dismissed by a decision of the Court of Justice pursuant to an application by the Council of Ministers or the Commission itself. The grounds for removal are incapacity or misconduct.

Voting Procedure

Decisions of the Commission are taken by majority vote. Proposals must, therefore, be agreed by 15 of the 28 Commissioners before these can be sent for approval to the Council of the EU and to the Parliament. Notwithstanding these requirements, most Commission decisions are made without a formal vote.

The Commission has been described as the 'government' of the European Union. It attends all parliamentary sessions where it must explain and justify its policies and respond to questions by MEPs. In extreme circumstances it may be put out of office by a vote of censure by the Parliament. This must consist of an absolute majority of all MEPs and two-thirds of those voting. The power has not been used to date. In 1999, however, the threat alone was sufficient to precipitate the resignation of the then Commission President, Jacques Santer. Following this, the rest of the Commission resigned of its own accord.

Functions

The Commission's principal functions are:

(a) to act as 'guardian of the treaties' by ensuring that member states act in accordance with their legal obligations under the Treaty and, where this cannot be achieved by less formal means, by commencing legal proceedings before the European Court of Justice to secure compliance with the same;

(b) in matters that cannot be dealt with effectively at national, regional or local level, to initiate proposals for the making of secondary legislation (principally regulations and directives) by the Council of the European Union (the 'right of initiation');

(c) to ensure compliance with policy decisions taken by the Council;

(d) to represent and negotiate on behalf of the Union in its dealings with non-member states and other international organisations;

(e) to prepare draft budget proposals for submission to the Council and the European Parliament;

(f) to execute the EU budget and manage its financial programmes.

The Commission shall promote the general interest of the Union and take appropriate initiatives to that end. It shall ensure the application of the Treaties and of measures adopted by institutions pursuant to them. It shall oversee the application of Union law under the control of the Court of Justice of the European Union. It shall execute the budget and manage programmes. It shall exercise coordinating, executive and management functions, as laid down by the Treaties. With the exception of the common foreign and security policy and other areas provided for in the Treaties, it shall ensure the Union and external representation. It shall initiate the Union's annual and multiannual programming with a view to achieving inter-institutional agreement. (TEU Art 16)

Role of the President

The principal functions of the President of the European Commission are to:

1 lay down the guidelines within which the Commission is to work;

2 decide on the internal organisation of the Commission, ensuring that it acts consistently, efficiently and as a collegiate body;

3 appoint Vice-Presidents, other than the High Representative of the Union for Foreign Affairs and Security Policy, from among the members of the Commission.

The European Parliament

Composition

Pending any further EU enlargement, the Parliament has 751 members (MEPs). There is a minimum threshold of 6 seats for smaller states. At the other end of the spectrum, no state may be allocated more than 96 seats. Elections to the Parliament are held once every five years on the basis of universal adult suffrage. The number of seats allocated to individual states is determined by reference to population and the principle of 'digressive proportionality'. This enables smaller states to be given more seats than would be justified by rigid insistence on exact proportionality between seats and population. In 2004, 732 MEPs were elected in the European elections and a further 53 were added with the accession of Bulgaria and Romania in 2007 (18 and 35 respectively). The 2009 elections returned 736 MEPs – a reduction of 49 in line with the prescriptions of the Treaty of Nice. Seventy-two of these came from the United Kingdom. For the future, and in accordance with the Treaty of Lisbon, the intention is to fix the maximum number of members at 750. The state allocations of seats until 2009, from 2009 to 2014, and from 2014 onwards are set out in Table 4.1.

In 2010, as a temporary measure pending the 2014 elections, and for the purpose of achieving greater parity with the Lisbon proposals, 18 additional seats were distributed between 12 of the current member states. This brought the complement of the 2009 Parliament to 754. One of these was given to the United Kingdom bringing its number of MEPs to 73. The seat was allocated to the West Midlands European parliamentary constituency.

Table 4.1 State allocation of seats

Member state	Population (millions)	Population (as per cent)	Seats (until 2009)	Seats (2009–14)	Seats (after 2014)
Germany	82,438	16.73	99	99	96
France	62,886	12.76	78	72	74
UK	60,422	12.26	78	72	73
Italy	58,752	11.92	78	72	73
Spain	43,758	8.88	54	50	54
Poland	38,157	7.74	54	50	51
Romania	21,610	4.38	35	33	32
Holland	16,334	3.31	27	25	26
Greece	11,125	2.26	24	22	21
Portugal	10,570	2.14	24	22	21
Belgium	10,511	2.13	24	22	21
Czech Rep	10,251	2.08	24	22	21
Hungary	10,077	2.04	24	22	21
Sweden	9,048	1.84	19	18	20
Austria	8,266	1.68	18	17	18
Bulgaria	7,719	1.57	18	17	17
Denmark	5,428	1.10	14	13	13
Slovakia	5,389	1.09	14	13	13
Finland	5,256	1.07	14	13	13
Croatia	4443	0.90	–	12	11
Ireland	4,209	0.85	13	12	11
Lithuania	3,403	0.69	13	12	11
Latvia	2,295	0.47	9	8	8
Slovenia	2,003	0.41	7	7	8
Estonia	1,344	0.27	6	6	6
Cyprus	0.766	0.16	6	6	6
Luxembourg	0.460	0.09	6	6	6
Malta	0.404	0.08	5	5	6
Total	492,881	100.00	785	736	751

Political allegiances

MEPs tend to sit and vote in political rather than national groupings. As of early 2017, the different political groups and alliances were as set out in Table 4.2.

Following the European elections of 2014, the UK's 73 MEPs returned for each electoral region or European parliamentary constituency were as follows: South East 10, London 8, North West 8, East England 7, South West 6, West Midlands 7, East Midlands 5, Yorkshire and Humber 6, North East 3, Scotland 6, Wales 4, Northern Ireland 3. The party politics/allegiances between the 73 members were: United Kingdom Independence Party 24; Labour 20; Conservative 19; Greens 3; Scottish Nationalist 2; Sein Fein 1; Democratic Unionist 1; Plaid Cymru 1; Ulster Unionist 1.

Powers and procedures

The European Parliament does not have the type of exclusive law-making authority generally associated with national legislatures. It does, however, play an important role in the EU's primary law-making process, viz. 'the ordinary legislature procedure'. In most cases, therefore, its consent is needed before new EU legislation may be adopted.

Ordinary legislative procedure

The essential elements of the procedure are as follows:

1 The legislation is formulated and proposed by the European Commission.

2 The proposals are submitted to the European Parliament and to the Council of the European Union for First Reading.

3 Consultations take place between representatives of those member states particularly affected or concerned, interest groups and the public.

4 The proposed legislation is adopted by the Parliament with or without amendments. In relatively rare circumstances, the Parliament voting by an absolute majority may reject a legislative proposal in its entirety.

5 The legislation is considered by the Council. It may accept or reject the amendments made by the Parliament. If these are accepted, the legislation is approved. If the amendments are rejected, the Council's view or 'position' on the amendments is returned to the Parliament for a second reading. The Parliament may approve the Council's position or propose yet more amendments. As mentioned above, should neither of these options appear viable, and should the Parliament wish to reject the Council's position, it may do so only by an absolute majority.

Table 4.2 MEPs' political groupings (as of early 2017)

Political Group	Representatives
European People's Party	217
Progressive Alliance of Socialists and Democrats	189
European Conservatives and Reformists Group	74
Alliance of Liberals and Democrats for Europe	68
European United Left/Nordic Green Left	52
European Free Alliance/Greens	51
Europe of Freedom and Direct Democracy Group	42
Europe of Nations and Freedom	40
Non-aligned	18

6 If no agreement can be reached between Parliament and Council, the legislative proposals will be submitted to a Conciliation Committee composed of equal numbers of MEPs and Members of the Council. The function of such Committee is to determine whether a joint text may be agreed. If this is so, and such text is approved by both the Parliament and the Council, the proposal is adopted and becomes law. If this is not possible, the proposal is abandoned.

7 In those instances where amendments have been proposed by the European Parliament, the European Commission will also be asked to express its position. Should the Council and the Commission be unable to agree on these the amendments may only be adopted by the Council voting unanimously, not by qualified majority.

Special legislative procedures

Procedures other than the ordinary legislative procedure may be used for EU law-making in particularly sensitive or politically contentious areas. There are two such procedures.

1 Consultation procedure

In a limited number of matters the EU Treaty permits the Council, voting unanimously or by qualified majority, depending on the subject-matter, to make law without the EU Parliament's consent. In these instances, the Parliament should be consulted before the proposed legislation is finally adopted. The Council is, however, not bound to accept the EU Parliament's position and, as stated, may proceed to adopt the legislation notwithstanding the Parliament's opposition to it.

It is, however, not open to the Council to proceed with the legislative proposal before receiving the EU Parliament's opinion. Any attempt to do so would result in the legislation being invalidated by the European Court of Justice (*Roquette Frères SA v Council* [1980] ECR 3333).

2 Consent procedure

The legislation is proposed by the Commission. The EU Parliament may give or refuse its consent to it. There is no provision for the proposing or making of amendments. If approved by the Parliament, the legislation may be adopted by the Council.

There is also provision in limited circumstances for the Council and Commission to legislate without parliamentary consent and for the Commission to legislate alone.

The first of these procedures (i.e. proposal by Commission and adoption by Council) applies to measures setting out the common external tariff (TFEU Art 31) and to approval of proposals for trade agreements under the Common Commercial Policy (TFEU Art 207(3)).

The Commission may legislate alone in a number of matters relating to monopolies and the rights of workers to remain in a member state having been employed there (TFEU Art 45(3)).

EU legislation and the role of national parliaments

In the case of EU legislation to be adopted or passed according to the Ordinary or Special legislative procedures, a period of eight weeks must elapse from the time the measure was drafted, normally by the Commission, and its submission to the Council of the EU. This is to allow national parliaments sufficient time to consider both the proposed legislation and the position their particular government intends to adopt towards it. Within this eight-week period any national Parliament may submit a reasoned opinion to the originating institution explaining why, in its view, the proposed legislation does not accord with the principle of subsidiarity. Should such reasoned opinions be submitted by at least a third of all national parliaments, the originating institution, usually the Commission, is required to review the draft legislation with a view to determining whether to amend, retain or withdraw it. Should more than half of all member state parliaments submit such opinions, and in circumstances where the originating EU institution wishes to proceed with it, the matter must be referred to the Council and to the European Parliament either of which may decide that the legislative proposals in question should not be allowed to proceed.

Other powers

The European Parliament also has the power to:

(a) receive and debate annual general reports from the Commission and to question individual Commissioners;

(b) by a majority of all MEPs and two-thirds of the vote cast require the Commission to resign;

(c) initiate legal proceedings in the Court of Justice in respect of any failure of the Council or Commission to fulfil their obligations under the Treaty;

(d) establish Committees of Inquiry to investigate alleged contraventions or mal-administration in the implementation of EU law;

(e) propose (but not insist on) amendments to budget proposals for 'compulsory expenditure' (i.e. that which the Union is obliged to spend to implement its laws and decisions) and, by a majority vote of all MEPs and two-thirds of the vote cast, to insist on amendments to budget proposals for 'non-compulsory expenditure' (i.e. discretionary expenditure);

(f) approve the annual EU budget;

(g) appoint an ombudsman to investigate allegations of maladministration by Union institutions;

(h) receive and consider petitions from natural or legal persons subject to its jurisdiction concerning any aspect of EU law, policy or administration;

(i) debate and express its views on any economic, social or political issue of relevance to the Union.

The Court of Justice of the European Union (CJEU)

The Court has three elements. These are the European Court of Justice, the General Court, and the European Union Civil Service Tribunal.

The Court of Justice

The court consists of 28 judges appointed for renewable terms of six years. Each member state has the power to nominate one judge. Appointment is by common accord amongst all member states. In most instances the court functions through 'chambers' of three to five members. Particularly important cases may, however, be remitted to a full court with a quorum of 15 or to a Grand Chamber of 13 members.

The judges of the court appoint a President who then has overall responsibility for the proper disposal of the court's judicial and administrative functions. Persons appointed to the court must be qualified to hold senior judicial positions in their own countries or be 'jurisconsults' of recognised standing (e.g. eminent academic lawyers). They must also be persons whose 'independence is beyond doubt' (TFEU Art 253). Removal from office may only be effected by a unanimous decision of the other members of the court and the Advocates-General. There are nine such Advocates-General. Their function is, at the conclusion of the parties' submissions, to present the court with a reasoned opinion as to how the case might be decided:

> with complete impartiality and independence, to make . . . reasoned submissions . . . in order to assist the court in the performance of the task assigned to it. (EC Treaty, Art 166)

The court has jurisdiction to entertain proceedings:

(a) brought by the Commission or a member state alleging breach of EU obligations by another member state;

(b) brought by an EU institution or member state challenging the legality of any act or failure to act by the Council, Commissioner or Parliament;

(c) referred by a court of a member state seeking a ruling as to the proper interpretation of EU law relevant to a question before it;

(d) brought by member states and natural or legal persons seeking compensation in respect of the acts or decisions of any EU institution;

(e) appealing against a decision of the Court of First Instance.

The General Court

The court was established in 1988 and was known originally as the Court of First Instance. It was renamed in 2009 by the Treaty on the Functioning of the European Union. The court's primary function was, and remains, to ease the burden of work in the Court of Justice. Like that court, the General Court is composed of at least one judge from each member state, appointed for renewable terms of six years. The General Court has jurisdiction to hear:

1 actions brought by natural or legal persons directly affected by allegedly illegal 'regulatory acts' or acts or omissions of EU institutions, bodies or agencies;

2 actions brought by member states against the Commission;

3 actions for damages alleging unlawful conduct by an EU institution;

4 actions based on contracts made by the EU which expressly give jurisdiction to the General Court;

5 actions relating to EU trade marks;

6 appeals on points of law from decisions of the EU Civil Service Tribunal.

Decisions of the General Court are appealable to the Court of Justice on points of law only. Both courts present their decisions in the form of single judgments. Dissenting judgments are not delivered. The General Court is bound by the decisions of the CJEU. Neither court, however, is bound by its own previous decisions.

The European Union Civil Service Tribunal

The tribunal comprises seven judges appointed by the Council of the European Union. These serve for periods of six years which are renewable. The judges of the tribunal elect a President from among their own number. Each President serves for three years. Again, the term is renewable.

The tribunal sits in chambers of three. Complex cases, or those raising an important point of law, may be referred to a full court.

The tribunal has jurisdiction over disputes between the EU and its employees. These constitute the approximately 35,000 persons who staff its various institutions, bodies and agencies. The types of disputes in question include those relating to pay and conditions of service, disciplinary issues, accidents at work, also sickness, old age and invalidity benefits.

The tribunal has no jurisdiction to hear complaints against member states. Tribunal decisions may be appealed on points of law only to the General Court.

The Court of Auditors

This is not so much a court as an audit commission. Its findings are published in an annual report. The court has 28 members, one for each member state. These are appointed for renewable terms of six years. Appointment is by the Council of the EU acting by qualified majority. The court may set up sub-groups or 'chambers' to dispose of different aspects of its work. Its principal function is to audit the EU's accounts and identify any mismanagement or unlawful use of the Union's financial resources.

The European Ombudsman

The office of European Ombudsman was created by the Maastricht Treaty 1992. He or she serves for renewable periods of five years. Upon taking office the Ombudsman is required to give a solemn undertaking to the CJEU that he/she will perform the duties of the office with complete independence and impartiality. Appointment and dismissal are by the European Parliament. To be effective, motions for dismissal should be approved by the Court of Justice.

The Ombudsman may hear complaints from natural or legal persons resident or registered in the EU. Complaints should relate to the institutions or bodies of the Union and should be made within two years of the complainant becoming aware of the alleged incident of maladministration. The Ombudsman has no jurisdiction in relation to the merits of decisions or the policies on which these were founded. Nor can he/she inquire into the decisions or findings of the Court of Justice of the European Union.

Maladministration is nowhere defined in the Union treaties or the decisions of the Court. The Ombudsman's 1995 report stated that an incident of maladministration occurred where an EU body or institution failed to 'act in accordance with a rule or principle which is binding upon it'. Otherwise, maladministration has been said to be an 'expansive concept' and to include breaches of the principles of good administration such as 'courtesy, efficiency, timeliness, and accuracy' (Cadeddu, 'The Proceedings of the European Ombudsman', *Law and Contemporary Problems* 68(1) (2004)).

Where maladministration is found, and no friendly solution can be reached, the Ombudsman may make recommendations to the body or institution concerned setting out how the problem might be resolved. Should these not be complied with, the Ombudsman may submit a report to the European Parliament.

Subsidiarity and proportionality

Decision-making by EU institutions must be according to the principles of subsidiarity and proportionality.

The principle of subsidiarity was embodied in the Maastricht Treaty. This provided that, in matters relating to the implementation of EU law and policy, where exclusive jurisdiction does not vest in EU institutions, decisions should be taken at the lowest appropriate level of national government which is easily accessible to individual citizens. EC Art 5 of the Maastricht Treaty (now TEU Art 5) stated that 'the Community shall take action in accordance with the principle of subsidiarity only if and so far as the objectives of the proposed action cannot be sufficiently achieved by member states and can, therefore, by reason of the scale or effects of the proposed action, be better achieved by the Community'.

The Treaty of Amsterdam 1997 provided that EU action should be confined to those circumstances where the objective is achievable by the Union, but not by a member state acting alone. In such circumstances the form of the EU action should be as simple or as general as possible, leaving the maximum legitimate scope for flexibility in national implementation.

The taking of any action by the EU within the jurisdictional limits imposed by the principle of subsidiarity is further restricted by the requirements of proportionality.

Proportionality in EU law requires the reviewing court to apply three tests to what was done. First, was the measure in issue appropriate to achieve the objective pursued? Second, was it necessary to achieve that objective or could it have been achieved by a less onerous means? Third, was the interference caused proportionate to the benefits secured? (Lord Reid (*R (on application of Lumsden and Others)* v *Legal Services Board* [2015] UKSC 41).)

Cases of proportionality relating to the legislative or administrative measures of EU institutions themselves are dealt with by the Court of Justice of the European Union. These may not be heard in the courts of member states. Proportionality cases in such national courts are limited to measures of that state's national authorities in the exercise of its obligations to give effect to, and act in accordance with, EU law. The Court of Justice allows European institutions a wide margin of discretion in matters relating to the more politically sensitive or policy-laden areas of decision-making, e.g. those where political, economic or social priorities are involved, and will intervene only where a measure or decision is considered to be 'manifestly inappropriate' (*R* v *Secretary of State for Health, ex parte British American Tobacco Ltd and Imperial Tobacco Ltd* (Case C-491/01)). A measure will be 'manifestly inappropriate' if there is 'a clear and material error, in law or in reasoning, or in the assessment of the facts which goes to the heart of the measure or where the word manifestly appears to describe the degree of obviousness with which the impugned measure fails the proportionality test' (*Lumsden, supra*).

Where a measure is challenged before the CJEU on grounds that it interferes with fundamental rights, e.g. those provided by the European Charter of Fundamental Rights, it should be: (a) 'necessary and genuinely meet objectives recognised by the Union' and (b) 'not constitute a disproportionate and intolerable interference, impairing the very substance of the rights guaranteed' (*British American Tobacco, supra*).

In applying the proportionality test, the Court has insisted that it is exercising a power of judicial review and not of appeal, i.e. that it is 'considering' the legality of the decision only and not whether it agrees with it. Accordingly, it will not seek to substitute opinions or preferences for those of the authority. Nor will it attempt to intervene merely because it feels a better balance could have been struck between the various interests, policy priorities and community needs involved. It will, however, consider in depth the factual foundations and processes of reasoning underlying the authority's decision to determine whether any of these were flawed.

In the final analysis, however, and perhaps it has long been so, the only 'really effective force in controlling the exercise of judicial review is not so much the content and terminology of the test or the context in which it is being used, but the degree of judicial restraint practised in applying it' (*The Principle of Proportionality in the Case-Law of the German Federal Constitutional Court*, Lubbe-Wolff, quoted in **R (Pham) v Secretary of State for the Home Department** [2015] 1 WLR 1591).

Alleged breaches of the restrictions imposed by the rules of subsidiarity and proportionality by any EU institutions may be brought before the European Court of Justice.

Sources of EU law

Primary EU law

Objective 4

This is composed of the Articles of the various treaties on which the EU is founded. Since the ratification of the Treaty of Lisbon in 2009, these are the Treaty on European Union (TEU) and the Treaty on the Functioning of the European Union (TFEU).

Secondary EU law

Regulations

These are directly applicable in the sense that they take effect without further legislative action or implementation by national parliaments or governments. They are also binding in their entirety (Art 285 TFEU). In addition, where sufficiently clear and unconditional, so that they may be applied by national courts without unacceptably wide variations in interpretation, they are also said to be 'directly effective', i.e. they create rights immediately enforceable by individuals. In **Leonesio v Italian Ministry of Agriculture and Forestry** [1973] CMLR 343, the European Court of Justice explained that a regulation 'produces immediate effects and is, as such, apt to attribute to individuals rights which national courts must uphold'. Such rights may be enforced:

(a) 'vertically', i.e. against the state (**van Gend En Loos v Netherlands Fiscal Administration** [1963] CMLR 105);

(b) 'horizontally', i.e. between individuals (**Defrenne v SABENA** [1976] 2 CMLR 98).

Directives

These are not directly applicable but are binding on states as to their objectives or the results to be achieved (Art 288 TFEU). Member states to which they are addressed are obliged to take legislative action (either primary or secondary) to give effect to them by the notified date or, in the case of directives applying to all member states where no particular date for implementation is given, within twenty days of the directive's publication.

A directive which has not been so implemented, or which has been implemented only partially or defectively, may still be capable of having direct effect – i.e. of conferring enforceable rights on individuals.

> A member state which has not adopted the implementing measures required by the directive in the prescribed period may not rely, as against individuals, on its failure to perform the obligation which the directive entails (**Pubblico Ministero v Ratti** [1980] 1 CMLR 96).

The circumstances in which this will pertain are as follows.

(a) The content of the directive is clear and concise and does not permit of any discretion in the manner of its implementation (**Van Duyn v The Home Office** [1974] ECR 1337).

(b) The directive is relied upon by an individual in proceedings against an 'emanation of the state' whether acting in its public or private capacity (***Marshall v Southampton and South-West Hampshire Area Health Authority*** [1986] 1 CMLR 688). In addition to central and local government authorities, the term 'emanation of the state' has been held to extend to any 'body, whatever its legal form, which has been made responsible, pursuant to a measure adopted by the state, for providing a public service under the control of the state and for that purpose has special powers beyond those which result from the normal rules applicable in the relations between individuals' (***Foster v British Gas*** [1990] 2 CMLR 833). This includes health authorities (***Marshall***, *supra*), police authorities (***Johnston v Chief Constable of the Royal Ulster Constabulary*** [1986] 3 CMLR 240), and service-providing public corporations (***Foster***, *supra*). It is also probable that the ***Foster*** definition of emanations of the state is sufficiently wide to encompass 'privatised' public utilities (***Griffin v South West Water Services Ltd*** [1995] IRLR 15). Directives, therefore, are capable of having vertical direct effect only. They are not enforceable by one individual against another – i.e. horizontally (***Johnston***, *supra*) – and are not enforceable by the state against an individual (***Officier van Justitie v Kolpinghuis Nijmegen BV*** [1989] 2 CMLR 18). Note, however, the view of the European Court of Justice in ***Marleasing SA v Comercial Internacional de Alimentación SA*** [1992] 1 CMLR 305, that, even though no public body may be involved in a particular dispute, the relevant domestic legal principles should be interpreted to avoid any conflict with EU law including directives not yet implemented. In this sense, therefore, although the content of a directive not yet given effect by national law may not be used as a cause of action between individuals, it could affect the outcome of a case by influencing the domestic rules applied.

The CJEU has also expressed the view that an individual might be able to rely on a directive which had not yet been implemented in circumstances in which the state was attempting to subject an individual to an inconsistent domestic provision.

> Thus, wherever the provisions of a directive appear, as far as their subject-matter is concerned, to be unconditional and sufficiently precise, these provisions may, in the absence of implementing measures adopted within the prescribed period, be relied upon as against any national provision which is incompatible with the directive . . . (***Becker v Finanzamt Munster-Innenstadt*** [1982] ECR 53).

The fact that a directive which has not been transcribed into national law is not directly enforceable as between individuals does not mean that a person who has suffered financial loss through being unable to enforce the rights contained therein has no remedy. In such circumstances the individual may bring an action against the state in respect of loss incurred as a result of its failure to comply with its obligation under EU law to give effect to directives addressed to it within any prescribed date. Providing the directive in question was intended to confer rights on individuals, and there was a reasonable causal link between the state's failure and the loss suffered, such loss is recoverable (***Francovich v Italy*** [1993] 2 CMLR 66).

National courts do not have the jurisdiction to rule over the validity of EU legislation. This power is reserved to the CJEU. Moreover, where such issue is pending before that Court, a national court may not suspend the operation of national legislation giving effect to the impugned EU measure unless:

The issue of state liability for failure to implement, and breach of, EU law is dealt with in more detail in Chapter 13.

(a) there exists serious doubts as to the validity of the measure in question;

(b) not to suspend the operation would cause 'serious and irreparable damage' to the party seeking interim relief (***R v Secretary of State for Health, ex parte Imperial Tobacco*** [2001] 1 WLR 127).

Decisions

These may be made by the Council or, with the Council's authority, by the Commission. They may be addressed to states, individuals or companies, and are binding in their entirety – i.e. no discretion is permitted in terms of their mode of application. Decisions may relate, for example, to implementation of EC competition policy or to whether member states are complying with EU obligations. Although this has not been settled unequivocally, it would appear that such decisions may be directly enforceable by individuals against those to whom they are addressed (*Grad* v *Finanzamt Traunstein* [1971] CMLR 1).

Decisions of the Court of Justice of the European Union

These also constitute a secondary source of EU law and are the means by which greater definition is given to the requirements of the CJEU Treaties and those regulations and directives made in pursuance of it. Although the ECJ need not follow its own decisions, these are binding on the General Court (Court of First Instance) and on national courts in matters relating to the proper interpretations of European legal principles.

The European Constitution and the Treaty of Lisbon

History and formation

The decision to formulate a European Constitution was taken at the Nice intergovernmental conference (IGC) in 2000. The next step was the agreement of the European Council at its Laeken meeting in 2001 to set up a European Convention to formulate a set of proposals. The Convention had 105 members consisting of 16 representatives of the existing 15 member states, 13 representatives from the applicant states (one per state); 30 representatives from the national parliaments of the member states (two per state), 26 representatives from the parliaments of the applicant states (two per state), 16 representatives from the European Parliament, and representatives from the European Commission, with a chairman and two vice-chairmen – all three former senior European politicians. The Convention convened in February, 2002, under the chairmanship of the former President of France, Valéry Gisgard d'Estaing. Its deliberations were completed and the drafts submitted to the European Council in June 2003. The final text was agreed in 2004.

Founding principles

The opening articles of the Constitution set out the values on which the Union is founded and the objectives which it should seek to pursue.

The Union's values were said to be:

● respect for human dignity, the rule of law, human rights, and the rights of minorities;
● pluralism, non-discrimination, tolerance, justice, solidarity and equality between men and women.

The Union's principal objectives should be:

● to promote peace and the well-being of its peoples;
● to guarantee freedom, security and justice to all within its frontiers;
● a genuinely free internal market ensuring free movement of persons, goods, services and capital and the freedom of establishment;
● sustainable economic growth, price stability, full employment, and lucid progress;
● a high level of protection for, and improvement in, the quality of the environment;

- scientific and technological advance;
- social justice and protection including equality between men and women, solidarity between the generations and protection of the rights of the child;
- respect for cultural and linguistic diversity;
- international peace, security, and the development of the earth, mutual respect amongst peoples, free and fair trading, the eradication of poverty, and the development of, and respect for, international law.

Institutional changes

(a) The European Council

The Constitution sought to draw a clearer distinction between the European Council and the Council of Ministers. Article 1–21 provided that:

- the European Council should consist of the heads of state or government of the member states together with its President (see below) and the President of the European Commission;
- the European Council should meet on a quarterly basis;
- its decisions, in the main, should be based on unanimity and consensus.

The Council's principal functions were defined as providing the Union with the necessary impetus for its development, and defining its general political direction and priorities. The Council should also be concerned with important constitutional issues, including institutional reform and development of the Union's common foreign and security policy. Article 1–22 contained provisions for the creation of a permanent President of the European Council. The President would be elected by the Council acting by qualified majority and would serve a renewable term of two-and-a-half years. This would replace the current system, whereby the presidency of the Union 'rotates' on a six-monthly basis between the political leaders of the different member states.

(b) The Council of Ministers

Article 1–23 of the Constitution required that the Council of Ministers should consist of a representative of each member state at ministerial level who could 'commit the government of the member state . . . and cast its vote'. Decision-making by qualified majority would be the norm with the range of matters to be decided by unanimity being, therefore, significantly reduced. A qualified majority was defined as 'at least 55 per cent of the members of the Council consisting of at least fifteen of them and representing member states comprising of at least 65 per cent of the population of the Union'. The presidency of the Council of Ministers would be held by 'member state representatives in the Council on the basis of equal rotations' in accordance with prescriptions laid down by the European Council acting by qualified majority.

(c) The European Commission

For the most part the Constitution confirmed the composition and power of the Commission as laid down in the Treaty of Nice. Article 1–26 gave a classic exposition of the role of the Commission in the newly enlarged Union:

- To provide the general interests of the Union.
- To ensure the application of the Constitution.

- To oversee the application of Union law.
- To execute and manage the Union's budget programmes.
- To coordinate the Union's various executive agencies.
- To ensure the Union's external representation.

The Constitution confirmed that, for the time being, the Commission should continue to consist of one Commissioner for each member state but that from 2014 it should be reduced in size to a number of members equivalent to two-thirds of the number of member states at that time. The exact arrangement for the post-2014 Commission would be made by the European Council acting unanimously. The objective would be a system of 'equal rotation' by member states 'as regards the determination of the sequence of, and time spent by their nationals as members of the Commission' with regard being had to the need to 'reflect satisfactorily the demographic and geographical range of all the member states' (*ibid.*).

The President of the Commission would continue to be chosen according to the process laid down by the Treaty of Nice.

(d) The European Parliament

In relation to the composition of the European Parliament, Article 1–20 of the Constitution set out the following prescriptions:

- The maximum number of seats should be 750.
- The distribution of seats between member states should be determined by the principle of digressive proportionality.
- No state should have more than 90 seats or fewer than 6.

The Constitution sought to significantly enhance the power of the European Parliament and the extent of its involvement in the European legislative process. This was to be done by the requirement that the majority of law-making proposals emanating from the Commission would be dealt with according to the co-decision procedure. This would be referred to henceforth as the 'ordinary legislative procedure'. The effect of the change would have been that most European legislation would have required the consent of both the Council of Ministers and the Parliament.

(e) The European Court of Justice

Article 1–29 confirmed the changes made to the judicial system by the Treaty of Nice. In addition, it proposed that the term 'Court of Justice of the European Union' should be understood as encompassing both the Court of Justice and the Court of First Instance, with the latter being known as the 'General Court'.

Foreign affairs, security and defence

The Constitution envisaged that the European Council, acting by qualified majority, and in agreement with the Commission President, would appoint a European Minister of Foreign Affairs (Art 1–28). The European Council would identify the Union's strategic interests and determine the objectives of its common foreign and security policy. The policy would then be 'put into effect by the Union's Minister for Foreign Affairs' (Art 1–40).

Member states would be obliged to 'actively and unreservedly support the Union's common foreign and security policy in a spirit of loyalty and mutual solidarity and comply with the Union's actions in this area' (Art 1–16).

European decisions relating to the common foreign and security policy would be made by the European Council acting unanimously (Art 1–40).

Those provisions contemplating the development of a European military competence were, perhaps, some of the most controversial of the entire Constitution. Thus it was provided that the common security and defence policy should give the Union an 'operational capacity drawing on civil and military assets' which could be deployed 'outside the Union for peace-keeping, conflict prevention, and strengthening international security in accordance with the principles of the United Nations Charter' (Art 1–41). It was also envisaged that 'member states should make civilian and military capabilities available to the Union for the implementation of the common security and defence policy' (*ibid*.). The operational requirements of such a European defence force would be identified by a 'European Defence Agency'.

Legal changes

The Constitution proposed a number of important changes to the current rules relating to the Union's legal status and competencies. Paramount amongst these were the following:

- The EU should have a distinct legal personality enabling it to enter into international agreements in its own right (Art 1–7).
- EU law should recognise and adopt the fundamental rights in the European Convention of Human Rights and the Charter of Fundamental Rights proclaimed by the Nice European Council of December 2000. The latter contains a range of social and employment rights not found in the ECHR (Art 1–9).
- EU law should be recognised as superior to the national law of member states (Art 1–6).
- The EU's law-making power should be extended into the areas of justice, asylum, immigration and border control (Art 1–42).

The Treaty of Lisbon

Despite the high hopes and ideals of those who formulated and proposed it, the EU Constitution did not survive the ratification process. In the event, its adoption was deferred after it was rejected by referenda in France (May 2005) and Holland (June 2005). Amongst the main reasons for these 'no-votes', the following concerns appear to have had particular effect:

- in France, particularly, dissatisfaction with the national government's handling of a range of domestic social and economic problems;
- fears that increased economic liberalism and acceptance of the rigours of the 'global market' could have damaging consequences on the European economy and job security;
- fears of dilution of national sovereignty consequent on the enhanced powers of EU institutions and, particularly, the move towards a common European foreign and defence policy with the attendant development of a European military competence.

The rejection of the Constitution posed a dilemma for the leaders of the EU and of its member states. This was so as, notwithstanding any unease about the EU's course of development, it remained the case that the forms and procedures designed for a Union of 15 members could not be expected to function with the necessary efficacy in an enlarged organisation of 27.

A compromise was, therefore, required and, after a period of consultation and intense negotiations, this came in the form of the Treaty of Lisbon.

The Treaty was signed in December 2007. Its full title is the Treaty of Lisbon Amending the Treaty on European Union and the Treaty Establishing the European Community.

The Treaty proposed the removal of some of the more politically sensitive and 'symbolic' elements of the Constitution, i.e. those widely associated with a move towards a European 'super-state'. Beyond this, it sought to preserve many of the constitution's proposed institutional reforms. The retained elements included a permanent EU President, a European Representative for Foreign Affairs, increased powers for the European Parliament and a limit on the number of MEPs, a new system and extension of qualified majority voting in the Council of Ministers, a smaller European Commission, full EU legal and international personality and adoption of the European Charter of Fundamental Rights.

Amongst the proposals in the Constitution not repeated in the Lisbon Treaty were: formal adoption of an EU flag and 'national' anthem, the term 'EU Constitution' itself and the description of the EU's representative in foreign affairs as a 'foreign minister'. Proposals to rename EU regulations and directives as 'EU laws' were also abandoned.

The original intention was for the Treaty to have been ratified by the then 27 member states, and, thereby, ready for implementation by the end of 2008. This became impossible, however, when the Treaty proposals were rejected by the Irish electorate in a national referendum held on 13 June 2008. As explained above, the Irish 'no-vote' appeared to have been precipitated by fears that smaller member states might lose their representation on the European Commission if the proposal to reduce its size were to be put into practice. Following, however, a commitment by the European Council to modify this aspect of the Treaty, the 2008 'no-vote' was reversed in a second Irish referendum in 2009.

With the ratification process thus completed, the Treaty of Lisbon finally came into effect on 1 December 2009. The main provisions of the Treaty and the corresponding articles in the EU treaties in which they are embodied, are set out below.

An elected President

The Treaty of Lisbon largely repeated the proposal in the ill-fated European Constitution for a permanent President of the European Council elected in the Council by qualified majority and serving for one renewable term of two-and-a-half years. The President was allowed no significant executive powers and was to be bound by the Council's decisions and policies.

These provisions may now be found in Art 15(4)–(6) of the amended Treaty on the European Union (TEU). These set out the exact procedure for electing the President (Art 15(5)); the President's term of office (*ibid.*); and the particular functions attaching to the office (Art 15(6)).

Formal recognition of the European Council

In addition to the creation of a permanent presidency, the Treaty provided formal recognition of the European Council as a distinct EU institution, separate from the Council of Ministers, with a more clearly defined role and areas of executive activity.

This was effected by TEU Art 13. The Article identifies and lists the EU's principal decision-making bodies. The European Council appears at second place in the list after the European Parliament. As indicated above, this constituted the first occasion on which any of the EU's founding treaties had included the European Council in provisions relating to the Union's institutional and constitutional structure.

TEU Art 13 also sets out the Council's usual composition and the various voting configurations of the Council for the purpose of making formal decisions.

No attempt was made in the Treaty of Lisbon, or the amended TEU, to identify and categorise the European Council's principal executive powers and other functions. To the extent, therefore, that these have been embodied in the TEU at all, they tend to be found in a range of provisions in various parts of the Treaty, and couched in the widest possible of terms. Thus, TEU Art 22 provides that the 'European Council shall identify the strategic interest and the objectives of the Union', while TEU Art 26 declares that the 'European Council shall . . . determine the objectives and define general guidelines for the common foreign and security policy . . . including matters with defence implications'.

A High Representative of the Union for Foreign Affairs and Security Policy

Although not termed an EU Foreign Minister, the Treaty proposed that the occupant of the above post would fulfil most of the tasks previously envisaged for such an official by the 2004 Constitution. The post would combine the positions and functions of the current High Representative for the Common Foreign and Security Policy, previously held by the Secretary-General of the European Council, with that of the European Commissioner for External Affairs. The High Representative of the Union would be appointed by the European Council and sworn in by the European Parliament. He or she would be a Vice-President of the European Commission and would chair the Foreign Affairs Council of the Council of Ministers and would be supported by a designated diplomatic corps.

The Treaty recognised that the EU's foreign and security policy should not operate to diminish or circumscribe the existing legal capacities and political responsibilities of member states in this important sphere of governmental activity. Also, EU decisions in relation to foreign and security affairs would continue to be taken by unanimity.

Formal recognition and validation of these proposals was given by TEU Arts 18 and 27. The first EU High Representative for Foreign Affairs was Catherine Ashton from the United Kingdom. Ms Ashton took office on 1 December 2009. Prior to this appointment, Ms Ashton had served as a Minister in the post-1997 Labour governments and, from 2008, as the EU Commissioner for Trade.

The High Representative is supported by the newly established European External Action Service. This has been described as the EU's diplomatic and foreign affairs department. The Action Service's legal authority and functions are set out in TEU 27(3).

The EU Parliament: increased powers

In terms similar to the Constitution, the Treaty contained provisions for enhancing the EU Parliament's legislative role and powers. This would be done by extending the range of issues on which law would be made by the ordinary legislative procedure (previously the co-decision process), i.e. the process by which legislative proposals require the consent of both the Parliament and Council of Ministers. Legal rules under a further 40 articles of the Treaty would be dealt with in this way thus taking the number of articles subject to co-decision from 37 to 77.

The numerical composition of the Parliament would be limited to 750, with a minimum of 6 and a maximum of 96 per member state.

These various provisions were incorporated in TFEU Arts 14 and 294.

The Council of Ministers: a new and extended system of qualified majority voting

The Treaty retained the Constitution's core provisions concerning the extended use of qualified majority voting and changes to the system's numerical requirements. Under its provisions, decisions in 20 additional policy areas would be taken by qualified majorities. This would leave only the most important and politically sensitive areas to be dealt with by unanimity (e.g. proposals relating to taxation, foreign affairs and security, social welfare and amendment of the treaties themselves).

From 2014, the basis for calculating qualified majorities in the Council would be changed. The formula contained in the Treaty of Nice requiring a majority of all states representing 62 per cent of the Union's population and polling 255 of the total 345 'weighted' allocations of votes, would be replaced by a simple 'double majority' system. According to this, a measure would be approved if supported by at least 55 per cent of member states (i.e. 15 of 27) representing a minimum of 65 per cent of the Union's population. A 'blocking minority' would require a combination of at least four countries.

In those small number of instances where the Council would not be acting on a proposal from the Commission, the Treaty proposed that the necessary majority of all member states should be increased to 72 per cent (at least 19).

In total, the Treaty of Lisbon proposed the extension of qualified majority voting (QMV) to a further 33 articles of the EU Treaty. Added to the 66 articles to which QMV already applies, this would mean that decisions under 99 articles would have to be made in this way.

Amongst those major competencies affected would be freedom, security and justice. As a result, this would be the decision-making method for matters relating to immigration, asylum and general control of the Union's external borders. Acting in co-decision with the EU Parliament, the Council would thereby be empowered to deal directly with such issues as terrorism, the smuggling of drugs, human trafficking, etc. The United Kingdom did not accede to this particular extension of the jurisdiction.

As a compromise transitional measure, during the period 2014–17, any member state would be able to request that a particular proposal be dealt with by the pre-existing voting formula (i.e. that laid down by the Treaty of Nice). In addition, small minorities of EU states (at least three or more) would be able to call for re-examination of Council decisions about which they had remaining concerns.

The proposals relating to qualified majority voting may be seen as the most significant practical element of the Lisbon Treaty and serve two main purposes. First, they represented a response to fears of small EU states that, with the existing system, Union affairs might be too readily dominated by the voting power of the major states. Second, at the other extreme, they constituted an attempt to ensure that enlargement does not result in the sort of paralysis which could ensue if, on a wide range of issues, the veto of one member could frustrate the legal and policy initiatives of the then 26 EU states.

The provisions giving effect to these new procedures are currently contained in TEU Art 16.

A smaller EU Commission

From 2014, the Treaty proposed departure from the long-established principle that each state should be represented in the composition of the Commission. Following ratification in 2009, a Commission of 27 members (one for each member state) would be sworn for the period 2009–14. As from 2014, the number of Commissioners would be reduced to 18, i.e. two-thirds of the Union's 27 states. Commissioners would be selected on the basis of equal rotation and without bias towards the larger states.

The President of the Commission would be nominated by the European Council acting by qualified majority subject to approval by the European Parliament. For the rest of the Commission, as at present, the Council of the European Union and the Commission President-elect would adopt the list of Commissioners proposed by member states following which the whole Commission would be appointed by the European Council if approved by the European Parliament.

The above proposals, including that relating to the size of the Commission, may now be found in TEU Art 16. Due, however, to the compromise formulated after the Irish 'no-vote' in the referendum of 2008, the proposed reduction in the number of commissioners did not take place in 2014 as originally intended.

For more on the Irish no-vote, see p. 97.

Adoption of the Charter of Fundamental Rights

The Treaty of Lisbon recognised the Charter of Fundamental Rights and stated that it should have 'the same legal value' as the treaties on which the Union is based.

For further comments on the relationship between human rights jurisdictions of the EU and the ECHR, see Chapter 16.

The Charter requires that all EU laws should comply with the requirements of the European Convention on Human Rights and contains a further range of social and economic rights. For the purposes of the United Kingdom, a protocol was attached to the Treaty to prevent the European Court of Justice from using the Charter to invalidate domestic legislation.

The Charter was formally adopted into the EU legal system by TEU Art 6.

Other proposed developments

Pillars and competences

While not seeking to massively extend the authority or policy-making areas open to the EU's institutions, the Lisbon Treaty did seek to clarify the distribution of powers between the Union and member states. In addition, the existing nomenclature and distribution of matters of policy- and law-making jurisdiction into 'pillars', as laid down by the Maastricht Treaty, were replaced by three broad 'competences'. These were:

- 'exclusive' competences including customs union; competition rules; monetary policy for the eurozone; conservation of biological marine resources within the common fisheries policy; common trading policy; relevant international agreements (Art 3 TFEU);

- 'shared' competences including the internal market; social policy; economic, social and territorial cohesion; agriculture and fisheries; the environment; consumer protection; transport, energy, trans-European networks, freedom, security and justice; joint security and safety concerns in public health matters; research, technological development and space; development, cooperation and humanitarian aid (Art 4 TFEU);

- supporting competences including protection and improvement of human health; industry, culture, tourism, education, youth, sport and vocational training; civil protection; administrative protection (Art 6 TFEU).

Mutual assistance and solidarity

Given national sensitivities in these matters, the Treaty's proposals were limited to just two tentative steps towards common European action in matters of security and civil defence. These were phrased in the form of mutual assistance and solidarity clauses. The mutual assistance clause requires member states to offer help to any state which is attacked. The solidarity clause requires the giving of assistance to any fellow member state affected by human or natural catastrophe or terrorist attack.

For the implications of the 2011 Act on the doctrine of parliamentary sovereignty, see p. 113.

In response to concerns relating to the perceived diminution of national sovereignty, the Treaty contained provisions designed to protect the role of national parliaments. Central to these was the proposal for an 'early-warning' mechanism whereby the Commission must look again at any proposal which is causing concern in at least one third of national parliaments or a quarter of such parliaments in matters of justice and internal affairs.

UK recognition of EU treaty amendment

The European Union (Amendment) Act 2008 required any amendment of the treaties of the European Union, particularly the TEU and TFEU, to be approved by an Act of Parliament before final ratification. The European Union Act 2011 further provided for the holding of a referendum in respect of any treaty change seeking to increase or extend the Union's existing powers and competences. The referendum requirement may be activated only in those situations where the UK government wishes to approve the amendment sought. A referendum would not be required, therefore, where the government is opposed to the treaty change in question.

Summary

The chapter gives an appreciation of the extent to which the British constitution and domestic constitutional and administrative law has been affected and changed by membership of the European Union. Matters dealt with include:

- the composition, powers and functions of the EU's institutions of law and government;
- the different types of legal rules made by these institutions and how such rules take effect in the United Kingdom;
- the emergence and development of the EU through its inception and evolution from the European Community to the European Union;
- the process of enlargement and institutional reform including the European Union Constitution and the Treaty of Lisbon.

References

Cadeddu (2004) *The Proceedings of the European Ombudsman, Law and Contemporary Problems* 68(1).

Craig and de Burca (2015) *EU Law: Text Cases and Materials* (6th edn), Oxford: Oxford University Press.

Further reading

Chalmers, Davies and Monti (2014) *European Union Law: Text and Materials* (3rd edn), London: Cambridge University Press.

Steiner and Woods (2014) *EU Law* (12th edn), Oxford: Oxford University Press, Chs 1–5.

Turpin and Tompkins (2011) *British Government and the Constitution* (7th edn), London: Cambridge University Press, Ch. 5.

5

The legislative sovereignty of the Westminster Parliament

Objectives

After reading this chapter you should:

1. Understand the meaning and development of the traditional doctrine of the legislative sovereignty of Parliament.

2. Recognise the legal and political implications of the doctrine for the British constitution.

3. Appreciate the potential political and legal limitations on the doctrine.

4. Be aware of proposed modifications of the doctrine.

Introduction

Definition

Objective
1

The theory of 'continuing' sovereignty, as explained by Professor Dicey, is that there are no limits to the legislative competence of Parliament. Each Parliament is absolutely sovereign in its own time and may legislate as it wishes on any topic and for any place. That which has been enacted by Parliament has supreme force and cannot be invalidated or changed by any other domestic or external authority. As so outlined, the doctrine has been the very foundation of the British constitution since at least the latter days of the nineteenth century. Recent dicta suggest, however, that judicial attitudes may be changing and that support for the doctrine, at least in this wholly unqualified form, may not be as assured or predictable as has for long been assumed. These matters are considered in greater depth towards the end of the chapter.

The United Kingdom has no overriding written constitution against which the validity of Parliament's enactments may be tested. It follows that the function of the courts in relation to Acts of Parliament is limited to interpreting and applying that which has been placed before them bearing on its face the official consents of the Commons, Lords and Monarch.

> All that a Court of Justice can do is to look at the 'parliamentary role'; if from that it should appear that a Bill has passed both Houses and received the Royal Assent, no Court of Justice can inquire into the mode in which was introduced in Parliament, not what was done previous to its introduction, or what passed in Parliament during its stages through both Houses (*per* Lord Campbell, ***Edinburgh and Dalkeith Railway Co*** v ***Wauchope*** (1842) 8 Cl & F 710).

It has also been said that even if 'an Act has been obtained improperly, it is for the legislature to correct it by repealing it: but so long as it exists as law, the courts are bound to obey it' (*per* Willis J, *Lee* v *Bude and Torrington Railway Co* (1871) LR 6 CP 577). The reluctance of the courts to 'go behind' how a statute was enacted is well illustrated by the facts of *Manuel* v *Attorney-General* [1983] Ch 77. The case concerned a challenge made by representatives of the Indian nations of Canada to the Canada Act 1982. Their challenge was based, *inter alia*, on the Statute of Westminster, s 4, which provided that the Westminster Parliament would not legislate for a dominion 'unless it is expressly stated in the Act that the Dominion has requested, and consented to, the enactment . . .' The Canadian Indians argued that as neither they nor all of the Canadian provinces had given their consent to the Canadian government's request for the legislation, the enactment was inconsistent with the 1931 Act and therefore invalid.

The argument did not convince the Court of Appeal. The court pointed out that all the 1931 Act required was that legislation affecting a dominion should simply *state* that it had been requested and consented to by the dominion concerned, and that a formula of words to this effect was contained in the preamble to the 1982 Act. It was not open to the court, therefore, to question the quality, validity, or even factual existence of this consent. If the Act stated that it had been given, that was not something a court could inquire into notwithstanding the substance of allegations to the contrary.

History

The doctrine of the unlimited sovereignty of Parliament really began to evolve in response to the political settlement of 1688. Prior to this, in a less secular society than exists today, examples may be found of judicial dicta suggesting that parliamentary enactments were subordinate to divine law or the law of natural reason.

> Whatsoever is not consonant to the law of God or to right reason which is maintained by scripture, be it Acts of Parliament, customs, or any judicial acts of the Court, it is not the law of England (*per* Keble J, *R* v *Lowe* (1853) 5 St Tr 825).

Other well-known cases in which courts claimed the authority to regard legislation as void if it offended against 'common right or reason' or against 'natural equity' would include *Dr Bonham's Case* (1610) 8 Co Rep 114, and *Day* v *Savadge* (1615) Hob 85.

The 'revolutionaries' of 1688 had, however, no intention of transferring sovereign power from the King to a Parliament genuinely representative of the people. Legal sovereignty was indeed to be vested in Parliament, but in a Parliament which, at the time, was returned by a tiny electorate consisting of the propertied and landed élite. Parliament's sovereign status did not, therefore, derive from its democratic authority in the modern sense.

The 1689 settlement did succeed, however, in establishing a 'balanced constitution' – that is, one dominated by a sovereign Parliament representative of the three principal estates or interests of the realm: Monarch, Lords and Commons. The enactment of valid legislation required the assent of each element. Hence no single estate could entirely dominate the others or legislate purely in its own interests.

Legal and political sovereignty distinguished

According to Dicey and others, while legal sovereignty or the power to issue commands in the form of laws which prevail against all others resides in Parliament, political sovereignty – particularly with the existence of universal adult suffrage – lies with the people. This is either expressed or generally implicit in the various doctrines of the social contract promulgated by Hobbes, Paine, Locke and others (see respectively *The Leviathan* (1615), *The Rights of Man* (1791), *The Treatises of Government* (1690)). The essence of the social contract is that individuals voluntarily submit themselves to the authority of government, and agree to limits on their freedom, in return for peace, order and a system of government which accords with the popular will. Should the government act in ways which abuse the trust and authority deposed in it, then 'the people have a right to act as supreme, and continue the legislative in themselves or place it in a new form, or new hands, as they think good' (Locke, (*op. cit.*)).

Application

Express repeal

Objective 2

Parliament is not bound by its predecessors and may amend or repeal any previous enactments by passing legislation stating its intentions to that end. Hence, were an Act to provide that it was not to be repealed, or to be repealed only according to some special parliamentary procedure, it is generally agreed that this would not bind a subsequent Parliament which could repeal or alter it in the normal way.

Implied repeal

As a general rule, if an Act is partially or wholly inconsistent with a previous Act, then the previous Act is repealed to the extent of the inconsistency. It does not matter that the later Act contains no express words to affect the repeal or alteration. This is known as the doctrine of implied repeal.

Vauxhall Estates v *Liverpool Corporation* [1932] 1 KB 733

> The plaintiffs claimed compensation for property which had been compulsorily purchased from them. According to the defendants, this was to be assessed in compliance with the Housing act 1925. This was refuted by the plaintiffs. They argued that the assessment should be calculated according to the more generous terms contained in the Acquisition of land (Assessment of Compensation) Act 1919 which stipulated expressly that its provisions were to prevail over any others passed or to be passed. The court felt bound to apply the 1925 enactment. It was not within the competence of the Parliament of 1919 to impose fetters on the legislative authority of those which followed it. The fact that the 1925 Act made no express reference to the 1919 Act provisions was irrelevant. These had, by implication, been repealed.

The doctrine was given succinct expression in a much quoted dictum from a case with similar facts two years later:

> The Legislative cannot, according to our constitution, bind itself as to the form of subsequent legislation, and it is impossible for Parliament to enact that in a subsequent statute dealing with the same subject-matter there can be no implied repeal (*per* Maugham LJ, **Ellen Street Estates v Minister of Health** [1934] 1 KB 590).

Clearly, as was evident in the language of Maugham LJ, the doctrine as originally conceived was understood to permit of no significant exceptions. Recent developments suggest, however, that it should now be understood as describing a general rather than an absolute rule and that a major departure from it is in the process of development in relation to what have been called 'constitutional statutes'. The argument here appears to be that those statutes which were of fundamental importance in the shaping of the constitution, and the rights guaranteed to those subject to it, should only be repealed or altered by a clearly expressed intent to that end in subsequent legislation – an idea obviously premised on the view that, as the doctrine of sovereignty in general is judge-made, it remains open to the judges to adapt it to changing political and historical circumstances.

This modified version of the doctrine of implied repeal was articulated most clearly by Laws LJ in **Hunt v London Borough of Hackney; Thoburn v Sunderland City Council; Harman v Cornwall County Council; Collins v London Borough of Sutton** [2003] QB 151 (Admin) 195 (the 'Metric Martyrs' case).

Hunt v London Borough of Hackney; Thoburn v City of Sunderland; Harman v Cornwall County Council; Collins v London Borough of Sutton [2002] EWHC (Admin) 195

The case concerned a number of market traders who had been convicted of selling goods by imperial measurements, i.e. pounds and ounces, contrary to regulations made under the European Communities Act 1972, s 2 (ECA). These regulations gave effect to a European directive requiring the sale of goods in metric measurement only. By way of defence, the traders relied on the Weights and Measures Act 1985, which expressly permitted the use of both the imperial and metric systems. This, it was claimed, repealed impliedly any power in s 2 of the 1972 Act to make any regulations prohibiting the use of imperial measurements and to insist on pain of legal penalty that traders must use the metric system.

In terms of the traditional doctrine of implied repeal, this argument had much to commend it. Laws LJ, however, was of the view that the 1972 Act was a 'constitutional statute' and, as such, not subject to implied repeal. Given their clarity, significance and modernity, his reasons are worth quoting in full:

> In the present state of its maturity the common law has come to recognise that there exist rights which should be properly classified as constitutional or fundamental ... We should recognise a hierarchy of Acts of Parliament: as it were 'ordinary' statutes and 'constitutional' statutes ... In my opinion a constitutional statute is one which (a) conditions the legal relationship between the citizen and the state in some general, overarching manner, or (b) enlarges or diminishes the scope of what we would now regard as fundamental constitutional rights ... The special status of constitutional statutes follows the constitutional status of constitutional rights. Examples are the Magna Carta, the Bill of Rights 1689, the Act of Union, the Reform Acts which distributed and enlarged the franchise, the Human Rights Act 1998, the Scotland Act 1998 and the Government of Wales Act 1998. The ECA clearly belongs in this category. It incorporated the whole corpus of Community rights and obligations, and gave overriding domestic effect to the judicial and administrative machinery of Community Law. It may be that there has never been a statute having such profound effect on so many dimensions of our daily lives. The ECA is, by force of the common law, a constitutional statute ... Ordinary statutes may be impliedly repealed. Constitutional statutes may not. For the repeal of a constitutional Act or the abrogation of a fundamental right to be effected by statute, the court would apply this test: is it shown that the legislature's actual – not imputed, constructed or presumed – intention was to affect the repeal or abrogation? I think the test could only be met by express words in the later statute, or by words so specific that the inference of an actual determination to the effect of the result contended for was irresistible.

Retrospective legislation

Parliament has the power to legislate retrospectively as well as prospectively. This means that Parliament can render illegal and impose penalties on actions which were perfectly lawful when they were committed. Also, actions which were unlawful at the time of commission may be rendered lawful or not subject to any legal sanction or proceedings.

Retrospective legislation which imposes criminal penalties is inconsistent with the European Convention on Human Rights, Article 7, and with most modern conceptions of the rule of law. It contradicts the principle that persons should only be expected to regulate their conduct according to laws which are in existence and should not be punished 'on account of any action or omission which did not constitute a criminal offence . . . when it was committed' (Art 7). The constitutionally dubious nature of this type of legislation was recognised long before any of these more modern prescriptions were formulated. Hence in *Phillips* v *Eyre* (1870) LR 6 QB 1, Willes J stated that retrospective legislation was 'contrary to the general principle that legislation by which the conduct of mankind is to be regulated ought . . . to deal with future acts and ought not to change the character of past transactions carried on upon the faith of their existing law'. He also emphasised the still existing rule that a court 'will not ascribe legislative force to new laws affecting rights unless by express words or necessary implication it appears that such was the intention of the legislative'.

For ECHR Art 7, see Chapter 16, pp. 414–6.

Examples

In *R* v *Londonderry Justices, ex parte Hume* [1972] NI 91, the Court of Appeal in Northern Ireland ruled that the Civil Authorities (Special Powers) Act 1922 (the principal emergency powers statute in force in Northern Ireland when the recent 'Troubles' began), conferred powers of arrest and detention on members of the RUC (the Northern Irish police) but not on British military personnel. This rendered illegal the arrests and detention of all those who had been taken into custody by the army – including those hundreds of suspects who had been 'rounded-up' in the internment operation of August 1971 and who were being held in internment camps. Within 48 hours of the decision the Westminster Parliament had enacted the Northern Ireland Act 1972. This provided that the armed forces were possessed of the necessary powers of arrest at the relevant time. The alternative would have been to release all the detainees.

Another famous example of legislation overruling an 'awkward' judicial decision occurred in 1965. In *Burmah Oil* v *Lord Advocate* [1965] AC 75, the House of Lords held that the Crown was bound to compensate those whose property had been destroyed by British forces during the Second World War – except where this had occurred during the course of a battle. The decision would have resulted in a massive drain on the country's financial resources. Retrospective parliamentary intervention followed in the form of the War Damages Act 1965. The preamble to the Act recited that its purpose was to 'abolish rights at common law to compensation in respect of damage to property affected by the Crown during war'. Rights which existed prior to the Act were thus extinguished.

Acts of Parliament and international law

Parliament is not bound by international law. Should a parliamentary enactment be inconsistent with a rule of international law, the statute prevails. International treaties have only persuasive force in the United Kingdom. The judges assume that Parliament does not intend to legislate inconsistently with them. Hence ambiguities or uncertainties in English law will usually be interpreted in ways which accord with international rules. Where, however, there is a clear and unavoidable inconsistency, the parliamentary provision takes precedence. To the extent that customary international law (international common law) is part of the law of England, it, like any other common law provision, gives way to statute.

Mortensen v Peters (1906) 14 SLT 227

In this case, the captain of a Norwegian trawler was convicted of fishing in the Moray Firth contrary to the Herring Fishery (Scotland) Act 1889. The court felt bound to apply the Act even though it restricted fishing beyond the three-mile territorial limit recognised by international law.

A challenge to the validity of elements of the annual Finance Act was mounted in *Cheney* v *Conn* [1968] 1 All ER 779. The argument was that the Act authorised the collection of revenue some of which would be used for purposes contrary to the Geneva Convention 1957, viz. the construction of nuclear weapons. The court's conclusion was:

> What the statute itself enacts cannot be unlawful, because what the statute says is itself the law, and the highest form of law, that is known in this country. It is the law which prevails over every other form of law, and it is not for the court to say that a parliamentary enactment . . . is illegal (*per* Ungoed-Thomas J).

Parliament's territorial competence

Parliament can and does legislate for places outside the executive competence of the British government. Professor Jennings once said that Parliament could, should it so wish, make it an offence to smoke in the streets of Paris. Jennings was not suggesting that the British government could seek to implement domestic legislation in foreign jurisdictions but that the British courts and law enforcement agencies could enforce such legislation against allegedly guilty persons if, and when, they entered the United Kingdom.

Examples

Famous examples of statutes having extra-territorial effect would include the Continental Shelf Act 1964, which asserted British exploration and mining rights over the continental shelf beyond British waters, and the War Crimes Act 1991 which gave British courts the power to try war crimes committed outside the United Kingdom providing the accused had become a British citizen or was resident in the United Kingdom.

Parliament's extra-territorial competence was manifest as early as the fourteenth century in the Treason Felony Act 1351. This ancient statute, which is still in force, created the offence of adhering to the Crown's enemies in any place inside *or outside* the realm. Until 1998 the offence carried the death penalty. The Act was used in the two most famous treason trials of the twentieth century. In *R* v *Casement* [1917] 1 KB 98, the defendant, an Irish Nationalist and ex-member of the British diplomatic service, was convicted of treason and sentenced to death after he had tried to persuade Irish prisoners of war in Germany to join the German armed forces. The 1351 Act was also used to secure the conviction and execution of William Joyce ('Lord Haw Haw'), who was employed by the Germans to make propaganda broadcasts to the United Kingdom during the Second World War (*Joyce* v *DPP* [1946] AC 347).

In the case of some ex-colonies which were given their constitutions and independent dominion status by Acts of the Westminster Parliament, it was provided that alterations to key elements of those constitutions could be made only by further enactments from Westminster following a request from the dominion parliament concerned – according to the procedure in the Statute of Westminster 1931, s 4. Hence in relatively recent times the Westminster Parliament has, pursuant to the appropriate requests, legislated for both Canada (Canada Act 1982) and Australia (Australia Act 1986). In both cases the purposes of the legislation was to transfer ('repatriate') to the countries concerned the power to legislate in all matters relating to their own constitutions. These two enactments may be regarded, therefore, as examples of Parliament exercising its extra-territorial jurisdiction albeit, in both cases, for the purposes of surrendering that jurisdiction to the appropriate national assemblies.

The extra-territorial competence of the Human Rights Act 1998 is considered in detail in Chapter 17, p. 500.

The succession to the throne

Since the revolutionary settlement of 1688, Parliament has regulated and controlled the succession to the throne. This right was embodied in the Act of Settlement 1700 which, following the death of the childless Queen Anne (1702–14), conferred the succession onto the House of Hanover in the person of George I (1714–27). From subsequent events it would also appear that parliamentary consent is necessary for any alteration in the normal line of succession. Hence when Edward VIII decided that he wished to abdicate in order to marry the divorcee Mrs Wallis Simpson, this, and his replacement by his brother George VI, was authorised by His Majesty's Declaration of Abdication Act 1936.

> Immediately upon the Royal Assent being signified to this Act . . . His Majesty shall cease to be King and there shall be a demise of the Crown and accordingly the member of the Royal Family then next in succession to the throne shall succeed . . .

The most recent development in this context was the Succession to the Crown Act 2013. The main effect of the Act was to remove the common law rule giving primacy to the Monarch's male heirs in the line of succession.

Defining the meaning of Parliament

Parliament is capable of redefining its constituent elements for the purpose of enacting legislation. Thus, for most Bills Parliament will consist of the Commons, Lords and Monarch. By virtue of the Parliament Acts, however, a Bill rejected by the House of Lords in two successive sessions may go for the Royal Assent after one year has elapsed. 'Parliament', for such a Bill, would consist of the House of Commons and the Monarch – two elements rather than three. It has also been argued that, by the provision in the Statute of Westminster making a request from a dominion legislature a precondition to Westminster legislation affecting its territory, Parliament has again effectively redefined itself by adding a fourth element to its composition (viz. Commons, Lords, Monarch and the dominion parliament). Also note the provision in the Northern Ireland Constitution Act 1973, s 1, requiring the consent of the Northern Ireland people by referendum to any change in the province's constitutional status. This could be understood as redefining Parliament to include the Northern Ireland electorate for any relevant legislation.

For more on the Parliament Acts 1911 and 1949, see Chapter 9, pp. 203–4.

Composition and membership

For content of the 1975 Act, see Chapter 7.
Exclusion by resolution is considered in Chapter 10.
The 1958 and 1999 Acts are explained in Chapter 9.

Parliament may decide who is and who is not qualified to sit and participate in its proceedings. This may be done by legislation or by mere resolution of either House. As such resolutions relate to the internal affairs of the sovereign body, they cannot be questioned by the courts. The measure which currently identifies those categories of persons disqualified from membership of the House of Commons is the House of Commons (Disqualification) Act 1975. Statutes relating to the composition of the House of Lords include the Life Peerages Act 1958 and House of Lords Act 1999.

Procedure

Parliament is master of its own procedure and may, therefore, change the procedural process according to which Bills are enacted or any other parliamentary business is conducted. Hence, if, for reasons of expediency, the House of Commons were to dispense with the Committee and Third Reading Stages of a Bill, it is unlikely that this would prevent the measure from becoming a valid Act of Parliament – providing, that is, it was approved by the House of Lords and received the Royal Assent. According to the enrolled Bill rule, a court would be limited to inquiring whether the Bill had been assented to by Parliament as currently defined and recognised by the common law, i.e. Commons, Lords and Monarch. To go beyond this would involve the court inquiring into the validity of the processes through which Parliament had exercised its sovereign legislative power.

Pickin v *British Railways Board* [1974] AC 765

In this case, a challenge was made to the British Railways Act 1968. The Act sought to extinguish certain rights given to the owners of property on either side of a railway line. These rights had been granted by the Acts which had originally authorised acquisition of the land for the railway's construction. They provided that in the event of the line becoming disused, ownership of the land on which it ran should revert to the adjoining landowners. The standing orders of both Houses required that the promoters of Private Bills should give notice of the proposed legislation to any persons whose private interests would be affected thereby. Pickin alleged that this had not been done and that, as a result, the Bill had been put before and dealt with by Parliament, in error, as an unopposed Private Bill (i.e. according to the wrong procedure).

In a purely factual sense, Pickin's case was not without substance. The House of Lords, however, could not be persuaded that it had any constitutional authority to investigate the allegations.

The rule against judicial inquiry into the workings of the sovereign body was again in issue, but on this occasion not applied, in *R (on application of HS2 Action Alliance Ltd)* v *Secretary of State for Transport* [2014] UKSC 3. This was the case dealing with the challenge to the proposed high speed rail link between London, the Midlands, and the North, and the government's stated intention to authorise the scheme by way of a Hybrid Bill (see High Speed Rail Bill 2013–14).

For fuller explanation of Parliament's legislative procedures, see pp. 152–74.

For the opponents of HS2, it was argued that the parliamentary legislative process was not the appropriate mechanism for examining and assessing the project's environmental impact and was not capable of complying with the relevant requirements of EU law, i.e. that the environmental impact assessment for such major public works should be detailed, fully informed and provide for effective public participation (see EIA Directive 2011/92/EU).

This view was based largely on the politically partisan nature of parliamentary proceedings in both the chamber of the House of Commons itself and in its committees. More specific contentions made in this context were:

(a) the environmental impact statement to be considered by the House would have been prepared by the Minister;

(b) it would not be open to the Select Committee on the Bill to consider alternative proposals;

(c) few MPs would be qualified to fully comprehend the voluminous amount of complex information which would be put before the House;

(d) debate would be stifled by the party whips system which required MPs to speak and vote according to the dictates of party policy;

(e) all of those Members holding Ministerial office would be bound to support the government or resign.

The Supreme Court was clearly aware that, by even entertaining the case at all, it would be treading perilously close to the dividing line between the proper constitutional spheres of the judicial and legislative branches of government. It concluded, however, on the facts before it, that it would not be drawn into any unwarranted intrusion upon Parliament's sovereign and exclusive sphere of jurisdiction. This was because:

(i) the proposed Bill had not yet been placed before Parliament;

(ii) the Court was not being asked to express any view or to take any action concerning a decision to lay a Bill before Parliament or relating to parliamentary approval of such a Bill;

(iii) the Court's attention would be directed primarily towards the interpretation and meaning of the relevant elements of the EIA Directive.

On the general question of the capability of the Westminster or other EU legislatures to fulfil the requirements of the Directive, the Supreme Court made the following comments:

(i) the Directive in Art 1(4) permitted ratification of major schemes of public works by legislation provided this satisfied its prescriptions;

(ii) it would be surprising if the Directive had been drafted in ignorance of the party-political way in which most European legislatures operated;

(iii) a decision whether to proceed with a project of this type or scale would inevitably have major political as well as environmental implications;

(iv) the influence of party policy and discipline would not prevent the members of national legislatures from giving careful and responsible consideration to the information relevant to matters to be decided.

Length of existence

Each Parliament may determine the length of its own existence. The Parliament Act 1911 provided that parliaments could continue in existence for a maximum period of five years (previously seven years by virtue of the Septennial Act 1714). Twice in the twentieth century, however, Parliament remained in existence without a dissolution beyond the five-year period. On both occasions this was to avoid the divisive effects of an election during wartime. Thus, the Parliament of 1910 continued until 1918 and the Parliament of 1935 until 1945 (Prolongation of Parliament Acts 1940, 1941, 1942, 1943, 1944).

The position is regulated currently by the Fixed Term Parliaments Act 2011. This provides for the next parliamentary election to take place on 7 May 2015. Subsequent General Elections are scheduled for the first Thursday in May at five-yearly intervals. Within these 'fixed' five-year periods, provision is made for 'early elections' in two circumstances. These are:

(a) where this is the will of Parliament as expressed by a vote of two-thirds of its Members;

For more detail on the 2011 Act, see p. 33.

(b) where the government is defeated in a vote of confidence by the House of Commons which is not overturned within 14 days.

Civil liberties and human rights

Since the United Kingdom has no overriding written constitution, Parliament, by ordinary legislative procedure, may alter or reduce that which might be regarded as the citizen's basic civil liberties or human rights. Thus, in *W (Algeria)* v *Secretary of State for the Home Department* [2010] EWCA Civ 898, it was accepted that, where national security was involved, the Special Immigration Appeals Act 1997 had removed the right to a fair hearing from those challenging deportation orders before the Special Immigration Appeals Commission. This general position has not been altered by the Human Rights Act 1998. Major deprivations of long-established rights were effective in both World Wars when the executive was given powers to intern without trial (Defence of the Realm Act 1914 and Emergency Powers (Defence) Act 1939). Similar powers of unlimited detention were provided by the Northern Ireland (Emergency Provisions) Acts. The power of detention in the Prevention of Terrorism Act 1989 was limited to seven days. A more extensive power was conferred by the Terrorism Act 2006 (28 days later reduced to 14). Other significant and relatively recent enactments restricting individual freedoms would include the Police and Criminal Evidence Act 1984, the Public Order Act 1986, the Criminal Justice and Public Order Act 1994, the Serious Organised Crime and Police Act 2005 and the Investigatory Powers Act 2016.

For discussion of the Human Rights Act see Chapter 17.

For this and anti-terrorist power in general, see Chapter 21, pp. 662–69.

Parliament's sovereign status means that legislative curtailment of the freedoms of the individual is not of itself a ground for judicial intervention (*R* v *Jordan* [1967] Crim LR 483).

Resolutions of the House and subordinate legislation

Mere resolutions of the House of Commons or the House of Lords do not make law and are not binding on the courts. Such resolutions are not made by Parliament as it is defined by the common law.

Stockdale v *Hansard* (1839) 9 Ad & E 1

In this case, the plaintiff sued for libel in respect of the contents of an official parliamentary report. The defendants pleaded a House of Commons resolution of 1839 to the effect that all such publications should be treated as absolutely privileged. The court refused to recognise the resolution as having any legal effect and awarded damages to the plaintiff. Lord Denham CJ explained the court's decision as follows:

> . . . The House of Commons is not Parliament but only a co-ordinate and component part of the Parliament. That sovereign power can make and unmake the laws; but the concurrence of the three legislative estates is necessary; the resolution of any one of them cannot alter the law, or place anyone beyond its control.

This distinction between Acts of Parliament and parliamentary resolutions was also applied in *Bowles* v *Bank of England* [1913] 1 Ch 57. On this occasion it was held that the

Bank was not entitled to deduct income tax from dividends owed to the plaintiff. The only authority for the tax in question was a Budget resolution of the House of Commons. For many years, and until this case, it had been the practice for tax proposals contained in the Budget (usually delivered in March) to be collected immediately or from the beginning of the new financial year and until the enactment of the annual Finance Act (late July/early August) merely on the authority of resolutions of the House. The court had no doubt that this was clearly unlawful and offended against the principle, recognised by the Bill of Rights, that taxation should not be imposed without statutory authority. The immediate result of the decision was the passing of the Provisional Collection of Taxes Act 1913. This gave legal effect to resolutions of the House approving variations of taxation during the period until the annual Finance Act came into force (see now, Provisional Collection of Taxes Act 1968).

The rule that the courts may not question or invalidate legislation applies only to Acts of Parliament or 'primary' legislation. Where, however, Parliament has delegated legislative power to subordinate bodies such as Ministers or local authorities, legislation made by them ('secondary' legislation) is open to judicial review if it exceeds the powers delegated by the 'parent' or 'enabling' legislation (***Attorney-General* v *Wilts United Dairies*** (1921) 37 TLR 881), or was not made according to the correct procedure (***R* v *Secretary of State for Social Services, ex parte Association of Metropolitan Authorities*** [1986] 1 All ER 164).

For further discussion of judicial review of subordinate legislation, see Chapter 8, pp. 174–6.

Where secondary or subordinate legislation has been laid before and approved by Parliament, judicial intervention may appear to come close to questioning a decision of the sovereign body. The rule here appears to be that review of such legislation is restricted to procedural error, bad faith, improper motive or manifest absurdity (***R* v *Secretary of State for the Environment, ex parte Hammersmith and Fulham LBC*** [1991] 1 AC 521).

Possible legal limitations

The doctrine of manner and form

Origins and essence

Objective 3

It has been suggested that if a statute were to prescribe a particular procedure or 'manner and form' for its amendment or repeal, any subsequent legislative provisions seeking to achieve such alteration except by that method would be ineffective. This suggestion is sometimes said to be supported by the decisions in ***Attorney-General for New South Wales* v *Trethowan*** [1932] AC 526, and ***Harris* v *Minister of the Interior*** (1952) 2 SA 428.

Attorney-General for New South Wales v *Trethowan* [1932] AC 526

This case was concerned with the Constitution (Legislative Council Amendment) Act 1929, an Act of the New South Wales Parliament. The Act provided that the Parliament's upper House could not be abolished except by a Bill approved in a referendum after completing its parliamentary stages. In 1930, after an election in New South Wales had changed the political complexion of the state Parliament, a Bill to abolish the upper House was approved by both Houses but was not put to a referendum. An injunction was granted by the High Court of Australia and upheld by the Judicial Committee of the Privy Council to prevent the Bill going for the Royal Assent. It was held that since the Westminster Parliament was sovereign and had decreed in the Colonial Laws Validity Act 1865 that all colonial legislatures should legislate in accordance with 'such manner and form as might from time to time be required by an Act of Parliament or other law for the time being in force in the state', it was incumbent on the New South Wales Parliament to comply with the procedure contained in the 1929 Act.

Harris v *Minister of the Interior* (1952) 2 SA 428

In this case, the South African Supreme Court refused to accept the constitutional validity of one of the pieces of legislation introduced by the post-1948 Nationalist government for the purpose of establishing apartheid. The modern state of South Africa was given its first constitution by the South Africa Act 1909, an Act of the Westminster Parliament. This Act sought to protect the political rights of black citizens in the Cape Province. Section 152 provided that they could not be removed from the electoral register except by a Bill passed by a majority of two-thirds of both Houses of the South African Parliament sitting unicamerally. In 1951 the Nationalist-dominated Parliament sought to remove this guarantee by the Separate Registration of Voters Act. The Act was passed by simple majorities in both Houses with the requirement in s 152 of the 1909 Act being simply ignored.

South Africa's most senior court held that since the South African Parliament had been created and given its powers by the 1909 Act, it was bound to exercise its legislative powers in accordance with the Act's requirements. Legislation seeking to alter the rights protected by s 152 was, therefore, invalid unless the prescribed procedure was adhered to.

Some academic and judicial opinions

It was for long assumed that the only sure principle which could be derived from the *Trethowan* and *Harris* cases was that subordinate parliaments were bound to legislate within the procedural restraints imposed by the 'mother' Parliament at Westminster, but that neither case could be regarded as conclusive authority for the view that the Westminster Parliament could also impose procedural fetters upon itself. There are clear indications, however, that the assumption is no longer reliable as was once the case. That it is now being questioned at the highest level is evidenced by dicta from the House of Lords in *Jackson* v *Attorney-General* [2006] 1 AC 262, and, in particular, Lord Steyn's clearly expressed approval for a relevant academic argument first advanced in 1935:

> The very power of constitutional alteration cannot be exercised except in the form and manner which the law for the time being prescribes. Unless the legislative observes that manner and form, its attempt to alter its constitution is void. It may amend or abrogate for the future the law which prescribes that form or that manner. But in doing so it must comply with its very requirements (Dixson, 'The Law and the Constitution', (1935) 51 LQR 590).

Lord Steyn's comment on this was:

> The law and custom of Parliament regulates what the constituent elements [Monarch, Lords and Commons] must do to legislate: all three must signify their consent to the measure. But apart from the traditional method of law-making, Parliament acting as ordinarily constituted, may functionally redistribute legislative power in different ways. For example, Parliament could for specific purposes provide for a two-thirds majority in the House of Commons and the House of Lords. This would involve a redefinition of Parliament for a specific purpose. Such redefinition could not be disregarded.

For a more detailed analysis of the Jackson case, see, pp. 123–27.

Implications of the European Union Act 2011

The likelihood of such academic and judicial opinions, and of the doctrine of manner and form itself, being put to the test, probably in the higher courts of law, was greatly increased by the passing of the European Union Act 2011.

The principal intent behind the Act was to prevent future UK governments and parliaments from acceding to significant increases in the power or competences of the European Union without the approval of the domestic electorate. The Act provided, therefore, that no such change should be ratified by the United Kingdom unless and until this has been authorised by both an Act of Parliament and by a majority of the electorate voting in a referendum.

In constitutional terms, all this begs the question what would the domestic courts do were a future Parliament to pass legislation giving effect to a major EU Treaty change without reference to the referendum requirement. How would the courts react? Would they recognise and give effect to the legislation in question or would they refuse to apply it until the referendum requirement had been satisfied?

The question has generated considerable, but largely inconclusive, debate. Some have taken the view that, in the absence of any seismic change in the fundamentals of the British constitution, the courts would be bound to accept and apply the doctrine of sovereignty in its traditional sense, i.e. that each individual Parliament is sovereign in its own time and cannot be bound by its predecessors in any matter of form or of substance. Hence it has been argued that it is not for the judges to simply 'tear up the fundamental rule of the system [and] attempt to replace it with a rule of judicial supremacy capable of imposing fundamental constitutional changes on the nation' (Goldsworthy, 'Parliamentary Sovereignty's Premature Obituary', UK Constitutional Law Group, 9 March 2012, http://ukconstitutionallaw.org).

Others, however, have been more prepared to accept the doctrine of manner and form as descriptive of a valid constitutional rule and, on this basis, to argue that, so long as it remains in force, the 2011 Act has created an additional element to the manner and form of the legislative process required to accede to the type of European changes described (see Bogdanor, 'Imprisoned by a doctrine: the modern defence of parliamentary sovereignty' (2011) *Oxford Journal of Legal Studies* 179).

Such debate about the validity of the manner and form doctrine, and its application to the 2011 Act, could, of course, be rendered otiose were a future Parliament simply to repeal the Act in its entirety or to remove from it the referendum prescription. Should this be done, it would appear unlikely that any effective objection could be raised on the basis of existing constitutional law and practice. In practical political terms, however, the matter might not be quite so straightforward. Hence, it has been suggested that having gifted the 'final say' on this controversial issue to the electorate, any attempt to reverse the position and return the power to Westminster might prove to be of great unpopularity and have potentially serious consequences at the ballot box for the government and party responsible.

The self-embracing theory of parliamentary sovereignty

More convincing and perhaps substantial support – albeit purely academic – for the relevance of the manner and form argument in the British context may perhaps be found in the 'self-embracing' theory of parliamentary sovereignty as originally advanced by Sir Ivor Jennings (*The Law of the Constitution* (5th edn), 1959).

According to this approach, and given the importance of statute as a source of English law, the common law requires and has developed a rule or formula for determining what constitutes a valid Act of Parliament. This has been referred to as the common law's 'rule of recognition' and is satisfied by that which has been consented to by the Commons, Lords and Monarch. Judicial statements that the court must simply interpret and apply that which had been so enacted, and may not question the procedure by which these consents were given, represent, therefore, no more than the rule of recognition in practice. It follows, according to Jennings, that if a statute were to prescribe an alternative definition of Parliament for the purpose of amending or repealing a particular enactment – say a requirement for two-thirds majorities in both Houses – this would lay down a new rule of recognition for the purpose of altering the Act in question. Moreover, since this would have been imposed by statute, it would be bound to prevail over the otherwise generally applicable common law rule. Essentially, therefore, the self-embracing theory of sovereignty is founded on the straightforward principle that the common law must give way to statute.

The essence of Jennings' theory is contained in the following statement:

> Legal sovereignty is merely a name indicating that the established legislature has for the time being power to make laws of any kind in the manner prescribed by law. That is, a rule expressed to be made by the Queen, 'with the advice and consent of the Lords spiritual and temporal, and the Commons in this present Parliament assembled . . .' will be recognised by the courts including a rule which alters this law itself. If this be so, the legal sovereign may impose legal limitations upon itself, because its power to change the law includes the power to change the law affecting itself (*ibid*).

Academics differ on the validity of this theory. Professor Wade has pointed out that its validity depends on the assumption that the rule of recognition is indeed nothing more than a common law principle. His view, explained in 1955, was that the supremacy of Parliament in its traditional and accepted form was of greater authority than that normally attributed to a common law rule and was one of the basic political facts which resulted from the 1688 revolution. This was then accepted and applied by the judiciary through the evolution of the doctrine of sovereignty in its traditional or continuing sense. As a result, only something equivalently momentous in the political sense – perhaps a further revolution or major constitutional rearrangement – would be sufficient to break the continuity of the post-1688 government order, and thus entrench and give constitutional authority to a redefined version of the power of Parliament (see Wade; 'The Legal Basis of Sovereignty' (1955) CLJ 172).

The Acts of Union

While most would accept that Parliament has the sovereign power to repeal and alter almost every other type of legislation, regardless of content, it has been suggested that this same legislative authority might not apply to those major statutes which gave effect to the political settlements which brought the United Kingdom and its existing constitutional arrangements into existence. In turn, this has led to considerable speculation about the position of the Acts of Union with Scotland (1707) and with Ireland (1800) which provide the legal basis of the political entity known as the United Kingdom. The issue for debate is whether these statutes may be amended or repealed in the normal way or whether their special constitutional status gives them added authority and, therefore, protection from parliamentary interference.

Although the arguments in this context tend to be couched in legalistic terms, the issue is essentially political. Hence the particular perspective taken on whether such Acts are repealable tends to depend on the advocate's view of the validity of the present structure of the United Kingdom. It is not unusual, therefore, to find unionists – whether Scottish or Irish – taking the view that the Acts of Union are beyond the legislative competence normally attributed to the Westminster Parliament. Nationalists, on the other hand, may be more inclined to believe that Parliament has the legal authority to do that which its Members regard as politically expedient in the circumstances and that the Acts in question, therefore, impose no absolute fetter on Parliament's authority to undo the Union.

Acts of Union with Scotland 1707

These were enacted by the pre-existing Parliaments of England and Scotland and brought into existence 'one Kingdom by the name of Great Britain' (Art 1). The Scottish and English Parliaments thus extinguished themselves and formed the Parliament of Great Britain sitting at Westminster. The Acts provided that the Union was to remain in being 'forever' (Art 1) and attempted to impose certain limits to the legislative competence of the Parliament thus created. In particular it was stipulated that the private law of Scotland was not to be altered except for the 'evident utility' of the Scottish people (Art 18). Other articles were to remain in force 'for all time coming'. These included provisions seeking to guarantee the separate existence of the Scottish courts and legal system (Art 19) and the position of the Presbyterian religion and Church of Scotland (Protestant Religion and Presbyterian Church Act 1707).

These prescriptions, it has been suggested, could be interpreted to mean that the Westminster Parliament was born 'unfree' and that its authority can be no greater than that allocated to it by its founding instruments. The limits on the Westminster Parliament's freedom should thus be understood as being the conditions upon which the two Parliaments, and particularly the Scottish one, agreed to abandon their separate identities. It is this which gives the Acts their special constitutional status and provides the guarantee for the provisions outlined above.

Whatever the weight of this argument, it has not proved entirely effective to give the Acts the type of protection which those responsible for their formulation might have intended. Hence a number of statutes have been passed which would appear to be inconsistent with the guaranteed provisions. The most notable of these was the Scottish Universities Act 1853. This reduced the special position of the Church of Scotland by abolishing the requirement that professors in Scottish universities should be members of the Presbyterian Church. It is not possible to say, however, at least with any certainty, that such post-1707 legislative intrusions have completely undermined the case for regarding the Acts of Union as being constituent or entrenched elements of the constitution. De Smith and Brazier, for example, have argued that, although it may be difficult to discern any strictly legal impediment to their repeal, the Acts may be regarded as the basis of a general conventional principle that Parliament will not enact legislation which substantially undermines their principal provisions, i.e. those relating to the Scottish Church and legal system. Nor is it possible to be absolutely sure about how the Scottish courts would react to such legislation if it were to be approved by the Westminster Parliament as presently constituted. Thus in ***MacCormick* v *Lord Advocate*** 1953 SC 396, Scotland's most senior judge, the Lord President, opined that although the Scottish courts might generally be reluctant to question an Act of Parliament, this did not mean that legislation of the type in issue would automatically be regarded as constitutionally valid:

> The principle of the unlimited sovereignty of Parliament is a distinctively English principle which has no counterpart in Scottish Constitutional Law . . . Considering that the Union legislation extinguished the Parliaments of Scotland and England and replaced them by a new Parliament, I have difficulty in seeing why the new Parliament of Great Britain must inherit all the peculiar characteristics of the English Parliament but none of the Scottish Parliament as if all that happened in 1707 was that Scottish representatives were admitted to the Parliament of England. That is not what was done. Further, the Treaty and the associated legislation, by which the Parliament of Great Britain was brought into existence as the successor of the separate Parliaments . . . contain some clauses which expressly reserve to the Parliament of Great Britain powers of subsequent modification, and other clauses which contain no such

power or emphatically exclude subsequent alteration by declarations that the provision shall be fundamental and unalterable in all time coming . . . I have not found in the Union legislation any provision that the Parliament of Great Britain should be 'absolutely sovereign' in the sense that Parliament should be free to alter the Treaty at will (*per* Lord Cooper).

To date, however, no Scottish court has crossed the Rubicon (point of no return) and openly questioned the validity of any public general Act relating to the issues protected by the Acts of Union. In *Gibson v Lord Advocate* [1975] 1 CMLR 563, the Court of Session was asked whether permitting EEC nationals to fish in Scottish waters pursuant to the European Communities Act 1972 could be for the 'evident utility of the Scottish people'. Lord Keith's opinion was that questions of this type should be resolved by political rather than legal means:

> I am . . . of the opinion that the question whether a particular Act of the United Kingdom Parliament altering a particular aspect of Scots private law is or is not for the evident utility of the subjects within Scotland is not a justiciable issue in this court. The making of decisions upon what must essentially be a political matter is no part of the function of the court.

He was, however, more circumspect about how the Scottish courts would receive an Act seeking to alter substantially or eradicate the Union's essential provisions:

> I prefer to preserve my opinion on what the position would be if the United Kingdom Parliament passed an Act purporting to abolish the Court of Session or the Church of Scotland or to substitute English Law for the whole body of Scots Law.

Scottish independence

The existing Scottish Parliament as created by the Scotland Act 1998, an Act of the UK Parliament, has no authority of its own to create an independent Scottish state outside of the United Kingdom. Accordingly, should the Scottish electorate at some future date vote in favour of independence, the perceived wisdom appears to be that this could be effected only by legislation of both the Parliaments affected, i.e. the devolved Scots Parliament and the 'sovereign' UK Parliament at Westminster – and this only after the latter had delegated to the Scots Parliament the power to legislate on such constitutional matters. This having been done, such concurrent enactments would provide the constitutional and legal basis for both the new state and its institutions of government and for the Scottish independence settlement as agreed between the governments in London and Edinburgh. In strictly legal terms, therefore, this would mean that the consent of the two founding parliaments would be required for any future alterations or amendment of the essentials of the settlement – according to which approach the argument could be made that Scotland would not be a truly sovereign state in the sense of having complete control over its constitutional destiny.

A brief glance at the history of the twentieth century will show that this type of reasoning was also advanced at the time of the Irish Free State (Agreement) Act 1922 when the 26 counties of Southern Ireland were granted dominion status by Westminster but within the auspices of the British Commonwealth. This, however, proved to be no realistic political or legal barrier to Ireland's unilateral adoption of a new constitution in 1949 by which it severed all constitutional links with the United Kingdom, left the British Commonwealth, and declared itself to be a republic. No serious attempt was made then, or at any subsequent time, to postulate that without the UK Parliament's consent, the Irish state was not 'sovereign' to act in this way.

Similarly, therefore, in the Scottish context, a less theoretical position might be that the sovereignty or ultimate authority of the new Scottish state would lie in the will of the Scots people as expressed in a referendum vote and that this, and this only, would be the pre conditional constitutional requirement to any further and future decisions concerning the way in which Scotland wished to be governed.

Acts of Union with Ireland 1800

These Acts created the United Kingdom of Great Britain and Ireland. They declared that the Union was to last forever and sought to guarantee the position of the Anglican Church in Ireland. Despite being adhered to by only a minority of the population, this was to remain the established church in Ireland 'forever', being deemed as an 'essential and fundamental part of the Union' (Art 5). The separate Irish Parliament was thereby extinguished and Ireland given increased representation in the United Kingdom Parliament at Westminster.

History proved, however, that the guarantees contained in the Acts of Union were inadequate to withstand the determination of the majority of Irish people to have a degree of political and religious freedom not envisaged when the Union was created. This may give support to the view that constitutions can do little more than recognise and give expression to political facts and cannot prevent political evolution from taking place. In 1869 the Irish Church Act disestablished the Church of Ireland. In *Ex parte Canon Selwyn* (1872) 36 JP 54, an attempt to question the validity of the Act was found to be non-justiciable. In 1922 the Irish Free State (Agreement) Act gave effect to the political settlement which brought to an end 'The Troubles' or Irish War of Independence 1919–21. The 26 southern counties were given dominion status and the Union, at least as envisaged in 1800, was effectively brought to an end. The Irish Constitution of 1937 asserted that the country was a sovereign independent state. Its status as a republic was recognised by the Ireland Act 1949.

It is significant, however, that the 1949 Act provided that Northern Ireland – the six counties excluded from the Free State in 1922 – should not cease to be part of the United Kingdom without the consent of the Parliament of Northern Ireland. The Northern Ireland Parliament having been abolished in 1972, the Northern Ireland Constitution Act 1973 stipulated that Northern Ireland would remain in the United Kingdom until a majority of its electorate should decide and vote otherwise. This guarantee was repeated in the Anglo-Irish Agreement 1985 and in the Joint Declaration of the British and Irish Governments on the Future of Northern Ireland in 1994.

The intention behind these guarantees appears to be that the unionist majority in Northern Ireland should be able to veto any proposed change to the status of the province which does not have their consent. How a court would, or should, view a statute affecting Northern Ireland's position in the United Kingdom and which was clearly opposed by the majority there remains, however, a matter of debate. The previous history of the Union and the events of 1922 clearly suggest that the traditional doctrine of absolute sovereignty would determine the issue. On the other hand, those with unionist sympathies might be tempted to argue that, for the purpose of altering the union with Northern Ireland, Parliament has changed the rule of recognition by adding the requirement of a referendum amongst the Northern Ireland electorate. It is, therefore, remotely conceivable that some judges might be reluctant to recognise legislation which blatantly ignored the requirement of consent which has been the basis of British policy towards Ireland since 1922. What is perhaps more certain is that the repeated assertions of the need for consent have established, at least for the time being, a convention that Parliament will not seek to legislate contrary to or without this requirement. As has been pointed out, however, conventions are flexible rules of political behaviour. They can and have been abandoned or modified when it was deemed politically expedient so to do. This may explain why there are those in the majority community in Northern Ireland who remain unconvinced as to the practical political reliability of the assurances which they have been given.

Constitutional statutes

The recent development of the concept of constitutional statutes was considered above in the context of the doctrine of implied repeal.

A constitutional statute is one which is of fundamental importance in the creation of the state and/or in determining the relationship between the state and the individuals within it. Examples have been said to include Magna Carta 1215, the Bill of Rights 1689, the Act of Union 1707, the nineteenth-century Reform Acts, the European Communities Act 1972, the Government of Wales Act 1998 and the Scotland Act 1998 (Laws LJ, *Thoburn v Sunderland City Council*, *supra*). This list was not intended to be exhaustive and the concept would probably extend to such enactments as the legislation determining the relationship between Great Britain and Northern Ireland. In particular, given the importance of the political agreement to which it gave effect, it would be difficult to argue that the Northern Ireland Act 1998 does not also fall into this special category.

It is not argued that this special status leaves such enactments immune from repeal or amendment. Rather the contention is that, for this to be effected, express words must be used. In this way such basic constitutional prescriptions are given a degree of entrenchment. They may not be altered unless this is the open and declared intent of the legislation in question as formulated by governments in power at the time the issue arises.

International Transport Roth GmbH and Others v Secretary of State for the Home Department [2002] EWCA Civ 158 was one of the first cases in which the concept of constitutional statutes was considered by the Court of Appeal. On that occasion, with the Human Rights Act 1998 in mind, Law LJ put the emerging rule as follows:

> Here the courts protect the right in question, while acknowledging the legislative sovereignty of Parliament, by means of a rule of construction. The rule is that while the legislature possesses the power to override fundamental rights, general words will not suffice. It can only be done by express or specific provision.

Political restraints

In an everyday sense, the forces which restrain Parliament from extreme uses of its sovereign power are essentially political. They are both subtle and diverse and thus beyond precise definition. Some of the more obvious factors, however, would include the following.

The party system

The House of Commons does not conduct its affairs as a united entity. It is composed of a variety of political parties within which there are further subdivisions on policy generally and on specific issues (e.g. European integration). It is necessary, therefore, for the government to maintain the support of the parliamentary majority and to keep its own party united if it is to get its legislative programme through Parliament. This, to some extent, operates as a restraining influence on the subject-matter and content of legislation. Governments will be reluctant to propose measures so controversial as to precipitate dissension or even defection within their own ranks.

The electorate

There is no constitutional or political rule in the United Kingdom which formally inhibits Parliament from legislating contrary to the apparent wishes of the electorate nor is there any requirement for controversial measures to be put to a referendum. What Parliament is asked to do in the legislative sense is, however, affected by the government's knowledge that, as Dicey put it, ultimate political sovereignty lies with the people. The electorate may change the composition of Parliament when its opinion is sought at least once every five years. Too many unpopular legislative measures may be a factor in determining the opinion expressed by the electorate.

The doctrine of the mandate

The essence of this is that since the majority group in a particular Parliament has been elected to execute a declared political and legislative programme (the party 'manifesto'), it has no authority to introduce important measures not included therein. This is primarily a political argument of limited constitutional significance. Governments must be free to respond to unforeseen and changing circumstances and to any emergencies which may arise by promoting the appropriate legislation. The argument may, however, have some validity in the early days of a new government and in relation to the making of major constitutional changes (e.g. leaving the European Union) without some further reference to the electorate (e.g. referendum).

Territorial competence and grants of independence

Despite what has already been said on this issue, Parliament is unlikely to enact legislation for places where the executive power of the British government does not operate. Hence, although in theory it could repeal the various statutory grants of independence to former colonial territories, it would do so in the sure knowledge that such legislation would be likely to be ignored.

The futility, if not the illegality, of such legislative action, and the fact that such grants of independence are now beyond Parliament's competence, has been recognised in judicial comment. Hence in ***British Coal Corporation v The King*** [1935] AC 500, the attitude of the Privy Council was that, while 'in abstract law' Parliament could revoke the undertaking in the Statute of Westminster 1931, s 4 not to legislate for a dominion without its consent, legal theory was bound to 'march alongside political reality'. This sentiment was repeated by Lord Denning MR, ***Blackburn v Attorney-General*** [1971] 1 WLR 1037.

> Take the Statute of Westminster 1931, which takes away the power of Parliament to legislate for the Dominions. Can anyone imagine that Parliament could or would reverse that statute? Take the Acts which have granted independence to the Dominions and territories overseas. Can anyone imagine that Parliament could or would reverse these laws and take away their independence? Most clearly not. Freedom once given cannot be taken away.

International law

Parliament is unlikely to enact legislation which, by contravening international legal standards, could cause diplomatic and political embarrassment in the United Kingdom's relationships with foreign states. When such legislation has been introduced, generally without intent to offend international rules, it has usually been amended forthwith (see *Golder* v *United Kingdom* (1975) 1 EHRR 524, *X* v *United Kingdom* (1982) 4 EHRR 188, and *Malone* v *United Kingdom* (1985) 7 EHRR 14).

Example

This may be illustrated by the facts of *Dudgeon* v *United Kingdom (No. 2)* (1982) 4 EHRR 149, where the European Court of Human Rights found legislation in Northern Ireland criminalising homosexual relationships between consenting adult males to be contrary to the right to respect for private life in Art 8 of the European Convention on Human Rights. This was followed by the Homosexual Offences (Northern Ireland) Order 1982, which removed the offending restrictions.

The relationship between EU law and Acts of Parliament

The sovereignty of Parliament and the law of the European Union

The United Kingdom acceded to the European Economic Community, as it then was, by virtue of the Brussels Treaty of Accession 1972. As a condition of membership, this obliged the UK, *inter alia*, to abide by and give effect to EU law in its domestic legal systems (i.e. those of England and Wales, Scotland, and of Northern Ireland).

By this time it was already an established principle of EU law that in the event of a conflict or inconsistency between the law of a member state and that of the EEC, the EEC rule in issue should be preferred and applied:

Costa v *ENEL* [1964] ECR 585

By creating a community of unlimited duration having . . . real powers stemming from a limitation of sovereignty or a transfer of powers from the states to the Community, the member states have limited their sovereign rights . . . and have created a body of law which binds both their nationals and themselves.

International Handelgesllschaft mbH v *Einfuhr und Vorratsstelle fur Getreide* [1970] ECR 1125

The law stemming from the treaty cannot by its very nature be overridden by rules of national law, however framed.

Simmenthal SpA v *Italian Minister for Finance* [1976] ECR 1871

Every national court must apply Community law in its entirety and must accordingly set aside national law which may conflict with it, whether prior or subsequent to the Community rule.

The European Economic Communities Act 1972

The United Kingdom incorporated the details of its EEC obligations, and conditions of membership under the Brussels Treaty, into the European Economic Communities Act 1972. This came into force on 1 January, 1973. Accordingly, and from that date, the UK became a full member of the European Community and the law of the EC/EU took effect within its national boundaries. In strictly legal terms, therefore, recognition of the precedence of EU law over English statute was an exercise of Parliament's sovereign power and not an abrogation of it – i.e., if Parliament was absolutely sovereign then it could use that limitless power to gift, share, or reclaim that power or any part of it, as and when it so wished. Accordingly, any sharing of its sovereign power with the EU by the Act of 1972 or any other enactment, could be brought to an end, at any time, by a further Act of Parliament to that effect.

> If the time should come when our Parliament deliberately passes an Act – with the intention of repudiating the Treaty – or intentionally of acting inconsistently with it – and says so in express terms, then I should have thought that it would be the duty of our courts to follow the statute of our Parliament (Lord Denning, *Macarthys Ltd* v *Smith* [1979] 3 All ER 325).

Conflict between EU law and statute: disapplication of an Act of Parliament

In *R* v *Secretary of State for Transport, ex parte Factortame Ltd (No. 1)* [1989] 2 CMLR, the House of Lords made clear that if and when a domestic court was dealing with a case to which both a statutory provision and a rule of EU law applied, but these had different meanings, the duty of the court was to 'disapply' the statutory provision in question. This was, at the time, a novel, and, for some controversial finding as it represented the first occasion in modern legal history on which a senior UK court had claimed the authority not to simply interpret and give effect to Parliament's will as indicated in its legislative enactments.

It is perhaps not surprising, therefore, that, in the years since, the courts have chosen to exercise the 'disapplication' power with considerable caution. A modern and perhaps the most well-known example of its use is provided by the decision in *R (on application of Davis and Others)* v *Secretary of State for the Home Department* [2015] EWHC 2092 (Admin).

This followed directly from the decision of the Court of Justice of the European Union in *Digital Rights Ireland Ltd* v *Minister for Communications, Marine and Natural Resources* [2015] QB 127. Here the Court was asked to consider the validity of the EU Data Retention Directive 2006'24/EC. The Directive required providers of publicly available communications services or networks to retain specified types of communications data for periods of six months to two years. The Directive's purpose was to harmonise data protection rules across EU member states thereby to ensure the better availability of such material for the purpose of investigating serious crime.

The CJEU found the Directive to be incompatible with EU law in that it failed to strike a proportionate balance between the public interest pursued and the individual's right to the privacy and protection of personal data (European Charter of Fundamental Rights, Articles 7 and 8) and the requirement that any interference with such rights should be only so far as was 'strictly necessary' for that end.

The Court's principal concern was that the Directive imposed no minimum safeguards for the protection of personal data from unlawful access or abuse nor did it contain adequate provisions governing its scope and application. In effect, therefore, the Directive extended to all data generated by electronic communications systems, and to all subscribers thereto in the entire continent of Europe. In addition, it allowed the retention of data held by persons having no connection with criminal activity. Nor was any connection required between the data retained and any interest of public security. Such all-embracing powers, the Court felt, could not be regarded as 'strictly necessary even in the pursuit of crime prevention'.

The Data Retention Directive was implemented in the UK by the Data Retention Directive Regulations 2007 and 2009. Following the striking down of the EU Directive in *Digital Ireland*, the Westminster Parliament responded with the Data Retention Investigatory Powers Act 2014 ('DRIPA'). This sought to give effect to the *Digital Ireland* decision and thereby remove any uncertainty concerning the legality of the UK's data retention laws. It did not succeed.

In *R (on application of Davis and Others) v Secretary of State for the Home Department* [2015] EWHC 2092 (Admin), two prominent Members of Parliament, David Davies (Conservative) and Tom Watson (Labour), successfully persuaded the Divisional Court that the Act fell short of the requirements laid down in the CJEU *Digital Ireland* judgment and like the Directive itself, was, therefore, incompatible with EU law. The court's reasons were that despite the detailed findings in that judgment, s 1 of the Act still fell short of EU law in that it:

1 failed to restrict access to, and use of, communications data to the prevention of precisely defined criminal offences;

2 failed to provide adequate safeguards for access to communications data by making this dependent on prior approval by an independent judicial or administrative authority.

The 2014 Act was repealed at the end of December, 2016. Its replacement legislation, the Investigatory Powers Act 2016, received the Royal Assent on 29 November, 2016.

Sovereignty and the Rule of Law: a new hypothesis of constitutionalism

Change in the wind

Objective 4

The doctrine of the unlimited legislative authority of the Westminster Parliament remains in place as the legal and political cornerstone of the British constitution. Signs are emerging, however, that some amongst the judiciary may at least be prepared to contemplate whether the time is approaching when the doctrine should be recast to take account of changed political and constitutional realities, particularly the ever-growing power of an executive dominated House of Commons and the limited restraining powers of the upper House.

The decision in *Jackson* v *Attorney-General* [2006] 1 AC 262

Facts

The seminal case in this context is the House of Lords decision in *Jackson* v *Attorney-General* [2006] 1 AC 262.

On its face the case concerned a challenge to the validity of the Hunting Act 2004. The claimants argued that the authority conferred on Parliament by the Parliament Act 1911 did not include a power to use that same procedure to amend the 1911 Act itself. It followed, they said, that Parliament had no authority to enact the Parliament Act 1949, which reduced the 'delaying power' in the 1911 Act from two years to one year, and that the 1949 Act, and all those measures 'enacted' under it, had no legislative validity. The claimants did not seek to challenge 'head on' the well-established principle that courts could not question an Act of Parliament, but contended that this did not apply in the particular circumstances of the case. This was because, in their view, statutes enacted under the 1911 Act should be regarded as delegated rather than primary legislation and, therefore, open to judicial scrutiny. In other words, according to this analysis, what in effect happened in 1911 was that Parliament in its sovereign entirety (Monarch, Lords and Commons) conferred limited legislative authority on the Monarch and Commons only. The subordinate and limited authority so conferred was intended to allow subsequent Parliaments to enact 'ordinary' legislation without the consent of the Lords, but, absent such consent, the 1911 Act did not delegate to or empower subsequent Parliaments to alter its own 'sovereign' provisions.

Judgment

(a) In the circumstance of the case, but not for the reasons they had advanced, the complainants were right to argue that the rule excluding courts from questioning Acts of Parliament did not apply. Cases such as *Pickin* and others established that the courts had no jurisdiction to inquire into the process or procedure by which a legislative proposal had passed through its parliamentary stages. This, however, was not the issue in *Jackson*. The complainants were not challenging the Hunting Act on the basis of anything that had transpired as it passed through Parliament, but on the ground that the 'enactment' of the Parliament Act 1949 was founded on a fundamental misconstruction of the intention behind the Act of 1911. The essence of the case was, therefore, a matter of statutory construction and, as such, something which was properly within the sphere of judicial competence.

> These proceedings are highly unusual. At first sight a challenge in court to the validity of a statute seems to offend the fundamental constitutional principle that courts will not look behind an Act of Parliament and investigate the process by which it was enacted . . . In the present case the claimants do not dispute this constitutional principle . . . Their challenge to the lawfulness of the 1949 Act is founded on a different and prior ground the proper interpretation of . . . the 1911 Act. On this issue the court's jurisdiction cannot be doubted. This question of statutory interpretation is properly cognisable by a court of law. The proper interpretation of a statute is a matter for the courts, not Parliament. This principle is as fundamental in this country's Constitution as the principle that Parliament has exclusive cognisance . . . over its own affairs (*per* Lord Nicholls).

(b) The 1911 Act stated clearly and unequivocally that that which passed through Parliament according to those provisions allowing for a Bill to be presented for the Royal Assent after being rejected by the House of Lords constituted an 'Act of Parliament'.

> The meaning of the expression 'Act of Parliament' is not doubtful, ambiguous or obscure. It is as clear and well-understood as any expression in the lexicon of the law. The 1911 Act did, of course, effect an important constitutional change, but the change lay not in authorising a new form of sub-primary parliamentary legislation but in creating a new form of enacting primary legislation (*per* Lord Bingham).

In general terms, therefore, the 1911 law should not be understood as having delegated limited legislative power to the Monarch and Commons, but rather as recognising that ultimate legislative authority lay in the elected lower chamber and as providing a means whereby disputes between the upper and lower chambers could be determined without embroiling the Monarch in political matters.

> The overall objective of the 1911 Act was not to delegate power: it was to restrict, subject to compliance with the specified statutory conditions, the power of the Lords to defeat measures supported by a majority of the Commons, and thereby obviate the need for the

Monarch to create (or for any threat to be made that the Monarch would create) peers to carry the government's programme in the Lords. This was a procedure unwelcome to a constitutional Monarch, rightly anxious to avoid any appearance of participation in politics, and one which constitutionally-minded politicians were accordingly reluctant to misuse (*per* Lord Bingham).

That Parliament had so intended legislation passed according to the provisions of the 1911 Act to have full legislative status and validity was evidenced by the fact that a number of equally controversial measures have been placed on the statute book, without the consent of the House of Lords, yet on no such occasion had the legislative status of any such measure, whether primary or secondary in nature, even been raised (see the War Crimes Act 1991, the European Elections (Amendment) Act 2000, and the Sexual Offences (Amendment) Act 2000).

(c) 1911 Act could not be understood as intending that the power to enact legislation without the consent of the House of Lords should not be applicable to Bills seeking to amend the 1911 Act itself. In this the Law Lords expressed agreement with the Court of Appeal that there is:

no constitutional principle or principle of statutory construction which prevents a legislature from altering its own constitution by enacting alterations to the very instrument by virtue of powers in that same instrument if the powers, properly understood, extend that far (Lord Bingham).

Oppressive and wholly undemocratic legislation

As indicated, however, and apart from these various findings concerning the validity and status of the 1949 Parliament Act, the opinions delivered by the House of Lords in *Jackson* provide some interesting pointers concerning current or emerging judicial attitudes towards the doctrine of sovereignty in its traditional form, i.e. the view that as Parliament is sovereign its legislative power is continuing and permits of no limitations of any kind. Of particular significance in this context are the comments of Lord Steyn in which he canvassed the view that the time might not be far distant when certain constitutional fundamentals, at the very cultural and political heart of the British system of government, should be regarded as beyond Parliament's ordinary legislative competence. Such are the long-term implications of these ideas and their possible impact for the doctrine of legislative sovereignty in place at least since the time of A.V. Dicey (in the late nineteenth century), that Lord Steyn's words are worth quoting in full.

The Attorney-General said . . . that the government might wish to use the 1949 Act to bring about constitutional changes such as the altering of the composition of the House of Lords. The logic of this proposition is that the procedure of the 1949 Act could be used by the government to abolish the House of Lords. Strict legalism suggests that the Attorney-General might be right. But I am deeply troubled about assenting to such an exorbitant assertion of government power in our bicameral system. It may be that such an issue would test the relative merits of strict legalism and constitutional legal principle in the courts at the most fundamental level.

But the implications are much wider. If the Attorney-General is right, the 1949 Act could also be used to introduce oppressive and wholly undemocratic legislation. For example, it could theoretically be used to abolish judicial review of flagrant abuse of power by a government or even the role of the ordinary courts in standing between the executive and citizens. This is where we have to come back to the point about the supremacy of Parliament. We do not in the United Kingdom have an uncontrolled constitution as the Attorney-General implausibly asserts. In the European context, the second *Factortame* decision made that clear. The settlement contained in the Scotland Act 1998 also points to a divided sovereignty. Moreover, the European Convention on Human Rights as incorporated into our law by the Human Rights Act 1998, created a new legal order. One must not assimilate the European Convention . . . with multilateral treaties of the traditional type. Instead it is a legal order in which the United Kingdom assumes obligations to protect fundamental rights, not in relation to other states, but to all other individuals within its jurisdiction. The classic theory given by Dicey of the supremacy of Parliament is still the general principle of our Constitution. It is a construct of the common law. The judges created this principle. If that is so it is not unthinkable that circumstances may arise where the court may have to qualify a principle established on a different hypothesis of constitutionalism. In exceptional circumstances involving an attempt to abolish judicial review or the ordinary role of the courts, the Appellate Committee of the House of Lords or a new Supreme Court may have to consider whether this is a constitutional fundamental which even a sovereign Parliament acting at the behest of a compliant House of Commons cannot abolish.

Traces of similar revisionist proclivities were also evident in Lord Hope's judgment.

> . . . it is of the supremacy of the law that the courts shall regard as unauthorised and void the acts of any organ of government, whether legislative or administrative, which exceed the limits of the power that organ derives from the law. In its modern form now reinforced by the European Convention on Human Rights and the enactment by Parliament of the Human Rights Act 1998, the principle protects the individual from arbitrary government. The Rule of Law enforced by the courts is the ultimate controlling factor on which our constitution is based.

That in extreme circumstances the sovereignty of Parliament might have to give way to the Rule of Law and the fundamental values of the constitution was repeated by Lord Hope in *AXA General Insurance v Lord Advocate (Scotland) [2012] 1 AC 868, supra*:

> The question whether the principle of the sovereignty of the United Kingdom Parliament is absolute or may be subject to limitation in exceptional circumstance is still under discussion. For Lord Bingham, writing extra-judicially, the principle is fundamental and not open to change. Lord Steyn, on the other hand, recalled in Jackson the warning Lord Hailsham gave in 'The Dilemma of Democracy' (1978) about the dominance of a government elected with a large majority over Parliament. This, he said, had continued and strengthened inexorably since Lord Hailsham warned of its dangers. This was the context in which he said that the Supreme Court might have to consider whether judicial review or the ordinary role of the courts was a constitutional fundamental which even a sovereign Parliament acting at the behest of a complaisant House of Commons could not abolish.

All of this suggests that the judges may be in the early stages of developing an alternative and less absolute version of the original conception of parliamentary sovereignty according to which, in high constitutional matters at least, the doctrine would give way to demands of the Rule of Law. Such notions would appear to be premised on mounting judicial unease relating to dangers posed to constitutional fundamentals by the short-term party-political caprice of those 'in power' from time to time and perhaps possessing an electoral mandate from no more than 30 per cent of the enfranchised adult population.

Should it come to pass that the doctrine of sovereignty were to be recast in the way outlined, this would clearly effect a radical alteration, not only in the role of the judiciary, but in the distribution of power in constitutional matters between the judiciary and Parliament.

Lest, however, this should be thought to be something entirely new or unprecedented, it is perhaps worth recalling the sentiment expressed by Coke CJ as long ago as 1610 in *Dr Bonham's Case* (1610) 8 Co Rep 114, to the effect that even an Act of Parliament could be declared void if it offended 'common right and reason'. This, in itself, merely serves to reinforce, as reiterated by the House of Lords in *Jackson*, that just as the judges were responsible for formulating and articulating the doctrine of parliamentary sovereignty in its original form, it would appear to lie within their competence to restate the doctrine in response to changed political circumstances and that which Lord Steyn described as 'a different hypothesis of constitutionalism'.

Summary

The chapter explains the extent of the legislative power of Parliament and, in the absence of a written constitution, considers whether the power is subject to any meaningful legal or political restraints. Detailed comment is also devoted to the implications for Parliament's legislative power of British membership in the EU. The chapter concludes with a consideration of recent judicial indications that the time may be approaching when certain constitutional 'fundamentals' should receive a greater degree of protection from politically motivated legislative intrusions.

References

Bogdanor (2011) *Imprisoned by a doctrine: the modern defence of parliamentary sovereignty*, OJLS 179.

De Smith and Brazier (1998) *Constitutional and Administrative Law* (8th edn), Penguin.

Dixson (1935) *The Rule of Law and the Constitution*, 51 LQR 590.

Goldsworthy (2012) *Parliamentary Sovereignty's Premature Obituary*, http://ukconstitutionallaw.org (9 March 2012).

Jennings (1959) *The Law of the Constitution* (5th edn), London: University of London Press.

Wade (1955) *The Legal Basis of Sovereignty*, CLJ 172.

Further reading

Allen and Thompson (2014) *Cases and Materials on Constitutional and Administrative Law* (11th edn), Oxford University Press, Ch. 2.

Gordon (2015) *Parliamentary Sovereignty in the UK Constitution*, Oregon: Hart Publishing.

Heuston (1964) *Essays in Constitutional Law* (2nd edn), London: Stevens, Ch. 1.

Loveland (2015) *Constitutional Law, Administrative Law and Human Rights* (7th edn), Oxford: Oxford University Press, Ch. 2.

Steiner and Woods (2014) *EU Law* (12th edn), Oxford: Oxford University Press, Ch. 4.

Part 3

The composition and workings of Parliament

6

The franchise and the electorate

Objectives

After reading this chapter you should:

1. Understand the legal requirements of the right to vote in general, local and European elections, the meaning of the principal statutory provisions regulating the right to vote and the leading judicial decisions in which these provisions have been interpreted and applied.

2. Be aware of the reasons why certain categories of persons are not allowed to vote.

3. Recognise the meaning and difference between 'absent' voters and 'overseas' voters.

Introduction

The composition of the House of Commons is determined by the electorate voting in General Elections at least once every five years according to the terms of the Fixed Term Parliaments Act 2011 and, during such periods, in by-elections when a particular commons seat needs to be filled. Subject to certain restrictions explained below, every British citizen of 18 years and over resident in the United Kingdom has the right to vote. This is often referred to as 'universal adult suffrage'.

It has not always been thus. Until 1918 the right to vote was restricted to adult males (21 years and over) who owned property of a certain rateable value. The property qualification had been lowered incrementally in the nineteenth century (principally by the Reform Acts of 1832, 1867 and 1884) so that by the end of the century virtually all male householders had the vote. The property qualification was abolished by the Representation of the People Act 1918. The Act also extended the franchise to women of 30 years and over. Henceforth the only qualifications for the vote were in terms of age, citizenship and residence. Women of 21 years and over were enfranchised by the Representation of the People (Equal Franchise) Act 1928. The age qualification was reduced to 18 years by the Family Law Reform Act 1969. The current law in relation to these matters is contained in the Representation of the People Act 1983 as amended and supplemented by the Representation of the People Act (RPA) 2000.

The exact requirements of the citizenship and residence qualifications require some further explanation.

Qualifications

Citizenship

Objective
1

The following categories of persons, if resident in the United Kingdom and of voting age, have the right to vote:

(a) British citizens;

(b) citizens of British dependent territories;

(c) British overseas citizens;

(d) qualifying Commonwealth citizens (i.e. Commonwealth citizens who did/do not require leave under the Immigration Act 1971 to enter or remain in the UK;

(e) citizens of the Irish Republic.

Citizens of other states may not vote in the United Kingdom regardless of how long they may have been resident here. Citizens of European Union states may vote in elections for the European Parliament and local government elections. They may not vote, however, in elections for the Westminster Parliament.

Residence

Prior to 1948 it was necessary to prove residence in the constituency for three months prior to the 'qualifying date' (the date by which completed electoral registration forms were to be returned). Until the Representation of the People Act 2000, the rule was that the person must have been registered on the qualifying date (10 October) in the constituency in which they wished to vote (Representation of the People Act 1983, s 1).

The requirement to show residence on a particular 'qualifying' date was removed by the Representation of the People Act 2000, s 1. The position now is that a person who does not suffer from any legal incapacity (see disqualifications below) and who satisfies the nationality and age requirements is entitled to be registered in the constituency in which they are resident at the time the application is made (RPA 1983, s 1, as amended by RPA 2000, s 1).

Section 3 of the RPA 2000, which inserted a new s 5 into the 1983 Act, sets out the matters to be taken into account or recognised by Electoral Registration Officers when determining whether a person should be regarded as resident in a particular constituency. A key factor to be considered is the reason for the person's presence at the address given. Simple absence from the address on the date of the application will not operate as a disqualification if it results from the 'performance of any duty arising from or incidental to any office, service or employment' or by reason of attendance at an academic institution, providing that the person intends to resume residence at the given address within six months or that address serves as their permanent address and is where they would be living but for the performance of the duty.

Where a person is staying at an address other than on a permanent basis, he/she may be regarded as resident there 'if he has no home elsewhere'.

The meaning of the residence qualification has also been considered in a number of judicial decisions (see *Fox* v *Stirk* [1970]).

In a number of other cases in which challenges have been made to exclusion from electoral registers it has been suggested that whether a person's residence is sufficient for the purposes of registration should be determined not only by the degree of permanence but also by reference to the nature, quality and purpose of the residence in issue.

Hence in *Scott* v *Phillips* 1974 SLT 32, it was held that residence in a holiday home for three-and-a-half months per annum, although reasonably permanent, was residence for leisure and relaxation only and was, therefore, for functional purposes merely incidental to the place where the complainant lived for the rest of the year. This was consistent with the approach taken in *Ferris* v *Wallace*, 1936 SC 561, where it was decided that residence in a holiday home every weekend from April to September, and throughout the months of July and August, did not qualify. By contrast, in **Dumble** v **Electoral Registration Officer for the Borders** 1980 SLT 60, it was held that weekend residence in a constituency to enable the complainant to fulfil his duties as a prospective Conservative party candidate was of a type which qualified him to be registered. Also, in **Hipperson** v **Newbury Electoral Registration Officer** [1985] QB 1060, the court was prepared to accept that women living in the Greenham Common Peace Camp were resident there for electoral purposes. Their presence in the camp was reasonably permanent, it was for a purpose not merely incidental to their other residences, and the fact that their residence in the camp might be illegal did not matter for electoral purposes: '. . . we reject the submission that the franchise is affected by the fact that the qualifying residence is illegal' (per Sir John Donaldson MR).

Fox v Stirk [1970] 2 QB 463

In this case, the question arose as to whether students in halls of residence at Bristol University could register to vote in the constituency where the halls were situated as well as in the constituencies where they otherwise lived. The Court of Appeal gave an affirmative answer and held that a person could register in any place where they were 'ordinarily resident' which included any constituency where they dwelt 'permanently or for a considerable time'. Therefore it was possible to have the right to vote in more than one place providing the person resided with a 'reasonable degree of permanence' in each.

Note, however, that although a person may be eligible to vote in two or perhaps more constituencies, only one vote may be cast. Hence the person must decide in which constituency they wish to exercise the right. It is an offence to vote in more than one constituency.

Declarations of local connection

Certain categories of persons who may not be able to satisfy the normal requirements of 'residence' may still become entitled to vote by making a declaration of local connection. This applies to:

(a) persons in mental hospitals and remand prisoners who are unable to satisfy the criteria of residence for any place other than the one in which they are detained;

(b) homeless persons;

(c) persons living on boats without a permanent mooring.

Such declarations must include:

● the person's name;

● an address for correspondence or an undertaking to collect such correspondence from the electoral registration office;

● a statement that the person falls within one of the categories in (a) or (b) and which one;

- in the case of mental patients and remand prisoners, the name of the institution where the person is detained and where the person would be living if not detained;

- in the case of homeless persons, an address where, or near to, the person spends most of the time.

A person who has made a declaration of local connection may apply to be registered by being treated as if resident at the address given in the normal sense (RPA 1983, ss 7B and 7C, inserted by RPA 2000, s 6).

A declaration of local connection is valid for 12 months.

The electoral register

Purpose and importance

The keeping of electoral registers for the United Kingdom dates back to the Great Reform Act 1832. In the United Kingdom there is no single central register of those eligible to vote. Rather, there are separate registers for each local electoral district. The register is an essential element of the practice of democracy and, in the United Kingdom, inclusion in it is treated as conclusive of the right to vote. Hence, although a person may satisfy all of the more substantive essentials of eligibility, viz. age, nationality and residence, no vote may be cast if the person's name does not appear on the register for the constituency in which the vote is to be cast (Representation of the People Act 1983, s 1). In addition, the practical importance of the register is such that a person whose name appears in it, albeit by mistake, may not be prevented from voting. The same would appear to be applicable to a person whose name has been entered into the register but who has subsequently become disqualified, e.g. by receiving a prison sentence. All of this notwithstanding, a person who casts a vote while under a disqualification commits an offence and the vote itself may be discounted.

Electoral registration officers

The Representation of the People Act 1983, s 8, requires each local district council and London borough to appoint an Electoral Registration Officer ('ERO'). Each ERO is cast with the duty of drawing up an electoral register for the local government district for which he/she acts. Prior to 2002, the obligation on EROs was to compile a single register each year. However, contrary to public conceptions and understanding, the content of these (names, addresses, national insurance numbers, nationalities, ages), was not protected by law and could be sold to private interests for a prescribed fee. Mounting concern over the use of such personal and private information lead eventually, therefore, to the making of the Representation of the People (England and Wales) Regulations 2001. These provided that, henceforth, two registers should be compiled: a 'full' register, as previously, for electoral purposes, and an 'edited' register for other uses (see below).

Acting Returning Officers

In addition to an Electoral Registration Officer each district and London borough is under a duty to appoint an **Acting Returning Officer** (1983 Act, s35).

The modern practice is for both offices to be held by the same person. The principal responsibilities of the Acting Returning Officer are to ensure that elections are conducted lawfully and efficiently.

The Returning Officer's more specific tasks include:

- overseeing the nomination process for candidates and political parties;

- provision and notification of polling stations;

- appointment of presiding officers and polling clerks;
- staffing, administration and security of polling stations;
- preparation and distribution of ballot papers;
- issue, receipt and counting of postal ballot papers;
- checking candidates' election expenses returns;
- compilation and publication of full and final election accounts (i.e. the cost of the election process).

Each constituency also has a full (ie non 'acting') Returning Officer. The position is, however, honorary only and is conferred usually on a local Mayor or Sheriff.

Full and open electoral registers

The full register

The full register should contain the names and addresses of all those qualified to vote in the particular electoral district, i.e. the information necessary to enable EROs to ensure that persons so qualified and wishing to appear in the register are able to use their vote without interference or obstruction.

The full register may be used also for such other governmental purposes as may be specified in existing legislation (see below). It is a public document and is open for inspection in council offices, post offices, public libraries and other public buildings. With two stated exceptions, it is not available for sale (see below). Any use of the information found in it for a purpose other than those stipulated in the relevant legislation is an offence.

Access to the full register is regulated by the Representation of the People (England and Wales) Regulations 2001. This requires EROs to supply copies of it to:

- elected representatives including MPs, local councillors and MEPs;
- candidates for election including candidates seeking election to the Westminster Parliament or to local councils;
- local constituency parties;
- registered political parties;
- police forces;
- the security and intelligence services;
- the councils which appoint Electoral Registration Officers; and
- by virtue of the Juries Act 1974, the courts system for the compilation of lists of jurors.

In addition, the 2001 regulations make provision for copies of the full register to be sold to certain identified organisations for payment of a 'prescribed' fee. Currently, the principal organisations so specified include:

- government departments and 'any body which carries out the vetting of any person for the purpose of safeguarding national security';
- credit reference agencies registered under the Consumer Credit Act 1984.

The open register

The open register is formulated on the information contained in the full register. It is not intended for electoral purposes. That contained in it may sold for the prescribed fee and used for private commercial purposes. Persons not wishing for their private details to be use in this way have the right not to be included in it.

To a considerable extent, the introduction of the open register in 2002 dealt with judicial concerns expressed in *R (on application of Robertson* v *Wakefield Metropolitan Council* [2001] EWHC (Admin) 915, where the power permitting the unregulated sale and dissemination of private information from the full register, without allowing those affected any right of objection, was found to contravene existing data protection legislation and the European Convention on Human Rights in Article 8(1) (right to respect for private life) and Protocol 1 Art 3 (right to free elections).

Compiling the register

Registration by householder

For many years this was done by requiring one person, the 'householder', at each residential premises to complete the appropriate electoral registration form identifying all those residents there at 15 October (the 'qualifying date') and who might be eligible to vote at the next local or general election. This was done in the course of the annual electoral canvass conducted in each local government district during the period September–October in order to have the new register ready for publication on 1 December. Any failure by the householder to supply the required information was and remains an electoral offence (Representation of the People Act 1983, s 130).

According to this system, no provision existed for separate registration by individuals. It was, however, possible for a person to apply for a register to be 'corrected' where, in any respect, it could be shown 'not to have carried out the registration officer's intentions', i.e. it did not represent the information provided by householders in the annual canvass. Such intention could have included an intention 'to include the name of any person shown in the electors' lists as a person entitled to be registered' (Representation of the People Act 1983, s11).

This notwithstanding, and in more recent times, arguments were made that entrusting voter registration to a particular individual in each household was premised on the outdated social and cultural assumption that most people lived in families for which one person had overall responsibility. Nor was it acceptable that a person's right to vote should be entirely dependent on the actions of a third party.

The rolling register

All of this led initially to the passing of the Representation of the People Act 2000. This retained the traditional process of registration by householders but enabled persons whose names did not appear in the register, but yet claimed to be eligible to vote, to make an individual application at any time up to and until eleven working days before an election. This more flexible approach, allowing registration on an ongoing basis, was referred to as the 'rolling register'. In effect, and for so long as the system remained in operation, it allowed the traditional practice of registration by householders and the more modern idea of registration by individuals to be used side-by-side.

Individual electoral registration

Further progress towards a simple and uniform electoral registration system (individual electoral registration or 'IER') came with the Political Parties and Elections Act 2009. This provided the legal framework for the phased introduction of IER moving towards full national implementation by the end of 2016. In 2010, however, the incoming coalition government decided on greater expedition. To achieve this the Electoral Registration and Administration Act 2013 provided that the long-standing system of householder registration would come to an end and be replaced by a single system of individual electoral registration by the end of December 2015. The last full process of registration by householders was conducted in the autumn of 2011.

According to the new system, ERO's remain under a duty to conduct an electoral canvass of residential properties in their respective districts on a yearly basis. This is effected through 'household inquiry forms'. Completion and return of such forms does not, however, of itself, represent an application for registration to vote on behalf of the persons whose details are included. It is then for each individual to make such application on the forms supplied or downloaded on-line. Failure to do so may result in the imposition of a civil penalty.

Anonymous registration

Persons who fear that inclusion of their names and addresses on the Register could put their safety at risk may apply to be registered anonymously (Electoral Administration Act 2006, s 10). In such cases the person's place in the Register will be represented by their electoral number and the letter 'N'. An application for anonymous registration should include, *inter alia*:

1 the reasons for the person not wishing their details to appear in the Register;
2 support for the application by way of any relevant court order or by attestation (see below);
3 a declaration that the evidence submitted in support of the application is accurate and reliable and that the person is an EU or Commonwealth citizen.

Examples of the types of court order which may be relied upon would include injunctions, restraining orders, and non-harassment orders under the Protection from Harassment Act 1997, and non-molestation orders under the Family Law Act 1996. For the purposes of providing attestations, the qualifying public officials include police officers of the rank of Superintendent and above, and Directors of Social Services.

An anonymous registration remains valid for twelve months.

Casting the vote

A person may vote in person, by post or by proxy. Detained mental patients and remand prisoners must vote by post or proxy.

The RPA 2000 abolished most of the pre-existing restrictions on eligibility to vote by post. Hence, any person may now use a postal vote providing the application to do so is received on time, contains the required information and is genuine. The provision of false information is an offence. Where a proxy is used that person must be a British, Commonwealth or Irish citizen of voting age who is not subject to any electoral disqualifications (RPA 2000, Sched 4).

The person appointed to cast a proxy vote must also be a qualified elector. It is an offence for someone who has appointed a proxy to vote in person. Applications for proxy votes should be received at least six weeks before the election in which they are to be used except where medical evidence can be provided. A person refused a postal or proxy vote may appeal to the Electoral Registration Officer who must forward this to the local County Court.

Disqualifications

Objective 2

Any person falling into any of the following categories is disqualified from voting in parliamentary and local elections in the United Kingdom.

(a) *Aliens* (RPA 1983, s 1 as inserted by RPA 2000, s 1).

(b) *Minors.* A person who is under eighteen years when the register is compiled or when the application to register is made, but who will reach the age of eighteen during the next twelve months, has the right to be registered and to vote in any election which occurs after the qualifying age has been attained (*ibid*).

(c) *Excepted hereditary peers and peeresses.* Until the House of Lords Act 1999, hereditary peers and peeresses could register and vote in European and local elections but were disqualified from voting in parliamentary elections. The 1999 Act, section 3 removes this disqualification save in the case of 'excepted' peers, i.e. those 92 hereditary peers who may sit in the House of Lords by virtue of the 1999 Act, section 2.

(d) *Persons serving a sentence of imprisonment for a criminal offence.* The disqualification does not apply to remand prisoners. Remand prisoners may be registered in the constituency where the prison is situated if they are likely to be there for a period sufficient for them to be regarded as resident in that place or, alternatively, at the address they would have been living at but for the fact of the remand (RPA 1983, section 7A inserted by RPA 2000, s 5). In ***Hirst* v *United Kingdom*** [2005] ECHR 681 and ***Greens and MT* v *United Kingdom*** [2010] ECHR 1826 the blanket ban on prisoners voting, i.e. without any reference to the nature and gravity of their offences, was found to be incompatible with the right to free elections in ECHR Protocol 1, Art 3. In a later decision, however, the British government's protracted failure to legislate in response to these decisions was said to be not actionable in damages (***Tovey* v *Minister of Justice*** [2011] EWHC 271 (QB)).

(e) *Persons in mental hospitals.* Any person detained in a mental hospital as a result of criminal activity is disqualified from voting (RPA 1983, s 3A inserted by RPA 2000, s 2). Otherwise both compulsory and voluntary patients are entitled to be registered. The patient may be registered in the constituency in which the hospital is situated if likely to be resident there for an extended period or, alternatively, at some other place, usually the person's normal place of abode (RPA 1989, s 7 inserted by RPA 2000, s 4). Blanket bans on voting by compulsory patients contravene ECHR Protocol 1, Article 3 (right to vote in free elections (***Kiss* v *Hungary***, app no 38832/06, 20.5.10).

Special categories of voters

Absent voters

Objective 3

Since 1949 various categories of persons, including those suffering from blindness or other physical incapacity or those who could not reasonably be expected to be present during an election due to the nature of their occupation, service or employment, were entitled to register as absent voters and to vote by post or proxy. The Representation of the People Act 1985 added to these any person 'whose circumstances on the date of the poll will be or are likely to be such that he cannot reasonably be expected to vote in person' (e.g. those on holiday) (RPA 1983, Pt 1 as amended by RPA 2000, Sched 4).

Overseas voters

An overseas voter is:

(i) a person who is resident overseas but who was resident and registered to vote in the United Kingdom at any time within the previous fifteen years (the 'fifteen-year rule'); or,

(ii) a person who lived in the United Kingdom in the previous fifteen years when too young to vote with a parent or guardian who was a registered voter (RPA 1985, ss 1–3 as inserted by RPA 2000, Sched 2 and amended by the Representation of the People (Amendment) Regulations 2002).

A person who satisfies the above conditions will be placed on the overseas electors list. He/she is entitled to vote in elections to the Westminster or European parliaments but not in local elections or elections to the devolved assemblies. The 'fifteen-year rule' would appear to be 'too indirect and uncertain' to amount to an unjustifiable interference with the freedom of movement guaranteed by EU law (*R (on application of Preston)* v *Wandsworth Borough Council* [2011] EWHC (Admin)).

It is also within the margin of appreciation permitted to states in respect of restrictions on the right to vote as guaranteed by ECHR Protocol 1, Art 3 (*Schindler* v *United Kingdom* [2013] ECHR 423).

For the right to vote in free elections, see pp. 520–21.

In *Doyle* v *United Kingdom* [2007] ECHR 165, the applicant, a British national resident in Brussels, claimed that he should not be denied the right to vote in the UK unless and until he had registered to vote in the country of his residence and that such denial was a breach of Protocol 1, Art 3 of the ECHR. The decision of the ECtHR was that the right to vote is not absolute. In the particular matter of the need for, and the length of, qualifying residence requirements, these were felt to fall within the state's margin of appreciation and could be justified on the grounds that:

- 'a non-resident is less directly or less continually concerned with his country's day-to-day problems and has less knowledge of them';
- 'it is impractical for parliamentary candidates to present the different electoral issues to its citizens abroad';
- 'non-resident citizens have no influence on the selection of candidates or on the formulation of their electoral programmes';
- 'the close connection between the right to vote in parliamentary elections and the fact of being directly affected by the political bodies so elected';
- 'the legitimate concern that the legislature may have to limit the influence of citizens living abroad in elections on issues which . . . primarily affect persons living in the country'.

Service voters

Members of the armed forces, their spouses or civil partners may register to vote as ordinary voters through the normal registration process or, if outside, or likely to be outside, the UK, by completing a Service Declaration. A Service Declaration should state the address where the applicant is or would have been living in the United Kingdom or, if he/she cannot give any such address, an address in the United Kingdom at which he/she has lived (Representation of the People Act 1983, ss 14–16).

Service personnel who are qualifying Commonwealth citizens who were recruited in their country of origin or outside the United Kingdom without previously being resident in the United Kingdom but who were trained there, may register at:

1 the barracks where they were enlisted or trained;

2 the barracks at which they would be resident if not posted overseas;

3 the regimental headquarters where they may have been resident;

4 an address in the UK where they would be resident if not required to be in barracks or no longer in the armed forces.

A Service Declaration is valid for five years. It should be sent to the Electoral Registration Officer for the constituency in which the serving member is, would have been, or was, resident.

Services voters not able to attend at the constituency in which they are registered may vote by post or proxy.

Crown servants

Similar provisions for electoral registration apply to Crown servants working overseas and to the staff of the British Council (Representation of the People Act 1998, s 14). Such persons may register as ordinary voters in the constituency in which they are normally resident or by submitting a Crown Servant Declaration. The declaration should contain the address where the person is or would be residing in the United Kingdom or, if such cannot be given, an address where he/she has resided previously. A Crown Servant Declaration remains valid for 12 months only. Persons in this category of voter, out of the United Kingdom, may vote by post or proxy.

EU citizens

European Union citizens resident in the UK have the right to vote in:

(i)   European parliamentary elections;

(ii) UK local government elections.

Summary

The chapter explains the qualifications required to exercise the right to vote in UK parliamentary and local elections.

Further reading

House of Commons Research Paper, 97/26, *Voting Systems – The Alternatives*.

House of Commons Briefing Paper SN 04458, 2014, *Background to Voting Systems in the UK*.

House of Common Library, *Individual Electoral Registration*, Briefing Paper no 6764, 1711.15.

Rawlings (1988) *Law and the Electoral Process*, London: Sweet & Maxwell, Ch. 3.

Renwick (2011) *A Citizen's Guide to Electoral Reform*, Biteback Publishing.

7

The House of Commons: Members of Parliament

Objectives

After reading this chapter you should:

1. Know which categories of persons may and may not sit in the House of Commons and the reasons why certain categories of persons are disqualified from membership.

2. Be aware of the role of MPs and their principal functions and the nature of the relationship between MPs and their constituencies.

3. Understand the nature of the relationship between MPs and their political parties and the reasons for party discipline.

4. Know the conditions under which an electorate may recall their MP.

5. Be aware of gender, ethnicity, background and matters relating to the composition of MPs.

Disqualifications

Objective 1

The following categories of persons may not sit in the House of Commons.

Minors

For the purposes of membership of the House of Commons persons under 18 years are minors (Parliamentary Elections Act 1965, s 7) and are thus not eligible to take a seat in the House.

In *W, X, Y and Z v Belgium* (1975) 18 Yearbook 244, the European Commission of Human Rights concluded that Protocol 1, Art 3 of the Convention guarantees the right to stand for election, but did not consider that the minimum age of 25 years for candidacy of the Belgium Parliament was 'unreasonable or arbitrary . . . or . . . likely to interfere with the free expression of the people in the choice of legislature'.

Aliens

This exclusion does not apply to Commonwealth and Irish citizens, thus creating the anomalous situation in which Commonwealth citizens have no right of abode, but may be Members of the United Kingdom Parliament. European Union nationals do have the right of abode but may not sit in the Westminster Parliament (British Nationality Act 1981, Sched 7).

Peers

Prior to the House of Lords Act 1999 all hereditary and life peers were excluded from the House of Commons. This prohibition continues to apply to all life peers but in relation to hereditary peers now affects only those who remain Members of the transitional upper House, viz. the 90 'elected' hereditary peers (75 from within the different party groupings, according to the scheme adopted in 1999, and 15 by the whole House. The current party allocation of the 75 seats is Conservatives 42, Crossbench 29, Liberal Democrats 3, Labour 2) and the holders of the offices of Earl Marshall and Lord Chamberlain (1999 Act, s 3).

Clerics

The 26 senior bishops of the Church of England who comprise the spiritual element of the House of Lords (spiritual peers) are disqualified from membership of the House of Commons (House of Commons (Disqualification) Act 1975).

Prior to the House of Commons (Removal of Clergy Disqualification) Act 2001 clerical exclusions from the lower chamber extended also to the:

(a) priests and ministers of the Churches of England and Ireland (Anglican) and of the Church of Scotland (Presbyterian) (House of Commons (Disqualification) Act 1801);

(b) priests of the Catholic Church (Roman Catholic Relief Act 1829).

No such restrictions applied, however, to the priests of the Anglican Church in Wales (Welsh Church Act 1914), to the ministers of other Christian churches or to the priests and teachers of other faiths.

This anomalous situation was rectified by the 2001 Act. The Act removed the disqualifications on the Anglican priests of England and Ireland, ministers of the Presbyterian Church in Scotland and on Catholic priests (s 1). Eligibility for the House of Commons now extends to the clergy of all Christian churches and of all other faiths.

Psychiatric patients

Under the Mental Health 1983, section 141, if a Member is ordered to be detained on the grounds of mental illness, the detention must be reported to the Speaker. If the Member is still detained six months later (after a second medical report to the Speaker), the Member's seat is declared vacant.

Bankrupts

A person may not sit in the House of Commons if they are subject to a bankruptcy restriction order (in England and Wales) or are adjudged bankrupt in Northern Ireland, or if their estate has been sequestrated in Scotland (Insolvency Act 1986, section 247, Enterprise Act 2002, s 266).

It appears, however, that, although declared bankrupt, a Member is under no duty to make this known to the Speaker and may continue to sit until ordered to withdraw.

Persons convicted of corrupt or illegal electoral practices

A person convicted of a corrupt electoral practice (the more serious type of electoral offence) is disqualified from election for five years and from election in the constituency in relation to which the offence was committed for ten years (seven years if not personally guilty but guilty through their agent). A person guilty of an illegal electoral practice is disqualified from election for the constituency concerned for seven years (reduced to the duration of the Parliament for which the election was held if guilt is through their agent), but not, therefore, from election for an alternative constituency. The election of a successful candidate, guilty personally or through their agent is void (Representation of the People Act 1983, ss 159, 160, 173 and 174).

Following the General Election of 2010, an Election Court (usually two High Court judges) in the Oldham East and Saddleworth constituency found the winning candidate (Philip Woolas, Labour) guilty of making false statements against one of his competitors (Robert Watkins, Liberal Democrat) contrary to the Representation of the People Act 1983, s 106. Mr Woolas's election was, accordingly, declared void. The offending words in question were to the effect that Mr Watkins had sought to 'woo' certain extremist elements in the constituency and that he had received undeclared financial support from a wealthy Saudi Arabian Sheikh (*Watkins* v *Woolas*) [2010] EWHC 2702 (QB)).

Prisoners

Persons sentenced to imprisonment for more than one year or any indefinite sentence are disqualified during their term of imprisonment. Further, any nomination or election of such person as a candidate is void (Representation of the People Act 1981, s 1). If a sitting Member is so imprisoned their seat is vacated. These provisions were introduced as a response to the election of Bobby Sands in Fermanagh–South Tyrone in 1981. At the time Sands was a republican prisoner on hunger strike in the Maze prison near Belfast. His nomination and election aroused great passions and controversy on both sides of the Irish Sea. Subsequently Sands died after two months without food. Previously, if a Member was sentenced to imprisonment for any period, the Speaker was informed of the offence and sentence, but the prisoner remained a Member unless a motion was passed to exclude him.

If a sitting Member is imprisoned for less than twelve months, unless for treason, he/she is not automatically disqualified but the House could vote for expulsion. A prisoner serving a sentence of less than twelve months is not disqualified from nomination or election but, of course, could not sit until the sentence has been served. Persons convicted of treason (Treason Forfeiture Act 1870) and sentenced to less than twelve months would be disqualified. Whatever the period of sentence, such persons remain disqualified until pardoned or their sentence expires.

Excess Ministers

Not more than 95 holders of paid Ministerial office may sit and vote in the House of Commons (House of Commons (Disqualification) Act 1975, s 2(1) and Sched 2). Hence if an MP is given a Ministerial post in excess of the 95 they are disqualified unless and until another Minister is removed or put into the House of Lords.

Members of other legislatures

This disqualification applies to the members of the legislative assemblies of all states outside the Commonwealth with the exception of the Irish Republic (House of Commons (Disqualification) Act 1975 as amended by the Disqualification Act 2000). Although not dealt with in the 1975 Act, by a decision of the European Union in 2002, members of national legislatures may not, at the same time, take a seat in the European Parliament.

Holders of public office

This restriction extends to those who must be seen to be politically impartial, e.g. judges (but not lay magistrates), police, members of the armed forces. It also applies to those paid and appointed by the Crown (government) and therefore susceptible to government influence or pressure – for example, civil servants, members of boards of public corporations and those with positions incompatible with attendance at Westminster such as members of foreign legislatures, ambassadors and high commissioners (House of Commons (Disqualification) Act 1975, Pt II, Sched 1).

Self-disqualification

Members of Parliament may also disqualify themselves by applying for any of the ancient offices of bailiff or steward of the Chiltern Hundreds or the Manor of Northstead. This is the method by which MPs resign (1975 Act, s 4).

Expulsion

The House may declare a disqualified Member's seat vacant or may expel a Member for whatever reason it pleases. Tony Benn's Bristol South-East seat was declared vacant after he succeeded to his father's peerage in 1961. In the subsequent by-election Benn (by now Lord Stansgate) was re-elected. The beaten Conservative then presented a successful election petition (*Re Parliamentary Election for Bristol South-East* [1964] 2 QB 257) and was subsequently declared to have been elected. Benn later resigned his peerage under the provisions of the 1963 Peerage Act and regained the Bristol seat in a by-election in 1963.

The power of expulsion is very rarely exercised. Only three MPs were expelled from the House during the whole of the twentieth century. These were:

1 Horatio Bottomley, expelled in 1922 after being convicted of fraud;

2 Gary Allinghan, expelled in 1947 after making false allegations of corruption and drunkenness against fellow Members and lying to a parliamentary committee;

3 Peter Baker, expelled in 1954 after being convicted of uttering forged documents.

Effects of disqualification

(a) The House may declare the Member's seat vacant (Benn case, 1963).

(b) The House may request an advisory opinion from the Privy Council on the law relating to a particular issue of disqualification (Judicial Committee Act 1833, section 4; see *Re MacManaway* [1951] AC 161).

(c) The House may declare the seat vacant pursuant to the findings of an Election Court (two High Court judges) after consideration by the latter of an election petition (i.e. complaint by person aggrieved). This jurisdiction was given to the courts by virtue of the Parliamentary Elections Act 1868 and Parliamentary Elections and Corrupt Practices Act 1879. It is assumed that the House will comply with the court's findings.

(d) The House may declare the seat vacant pursuant to a successful determination of an application alleging disqualification to the Privy Council (House of Commons (Disqualification) Act 1975, s 7).

Role and functions of MPs

Role

Objective
2

Members of Parliament each have at least four constituencies: their conscience, the party, their geographical constituency and, usually, an interest group. Perhaps a fifth constituency could be said to be in the public interest. Most MPs now appear to accept that their principal loyalty is to the party, but opinions have long differed concerning the extent to which (and how often) MPs should be free to voice their own opinions. It was once generally believed, prior to the advent of organised political parties (post-1832) that an MP's principal function was to speak for their constituents.

> In the days when Parliament (or at least the Commons) existed largely to grant taxes to the monarch and occasionally, to present petitions for the redress of grievances, the primary loyalty of members was to those whom they represented. Members were seen as local representatives, living in the constituencies and often being maintained by them (Radice, Vallence and Willis, *Members of Parliament*).

Later views, however, sought to reject the opinion that MPs should see themselves as mere delegates of their constituency electorate.

> It ought to be the happiness and glory of a representative to live in the strictest union, the closest correspondence, and the most unreserved communication with his constituents. Their wishes ought to have great weight with him, their opinion high respect, their business unremitting attention. It is his duty to sacrifice his repose, his pleasures, his satisfaction to theirs; and above all, in all cases to prefer their interest to his own. But his unbiased opinion, his mature judgement, his enlightened conscience, he ought not to sacrifice to you, to any man, or to any set of men living . . . Your representative owes you not his industry only, but his judgement, and he betrays instead of serving you, if he sacrifices it to your opinion (Edmund Burke, Speech to the Electors of Bristol (1774) – see Bell, *The Works of Edmund Burke*, 1889).

Burke perceived MPs to be a socially and intellectually superior group of people, well qualified to perform the functions of government.

> Parliament is not a congress of ambassadors from different and hostile interests, which interests each must maintain as an agent and advocate against other agents and advocates; but Parliament is a deliberative assembly of one nation, with one interest, that of the whole, where not local purposes, not local prejudices ought to guide, but the general good resulting from the general reason of the whole. You chose a member indeed but when you have chosen him he is not the member for Bristol, but he is a member of Parliament (ibid).

Sentiments of the Burkean tradition were evident in Churchill's famous exposition on the role of MPs.

> What is the use of sending members to the House of Commons who say just the popular things of the moment and merely endeavour to give satisfaction to the government whips by walking through the lobbies oblivious to the criticism they hear. People talk about our parliamentary institutions and parliamentary democracy, but if these are to survive it will not be because the constituencies return tame, docile, subservient members, and try to stamp out every form of independent judgment.

For all this, even today, it could be dangerous for an MP to neglect the interests, views and problems of his constituents.

Indeed the more an MP takes an independent line at Westminster, the more he may need his local base, which must be both by rallying the troops against the political enemy and by pursuing local interests and solving local problems (Radice, Vallence and Willis, op. cit.).

Today, however, with a mass electorate, few MPs are elected because of their distinctive qualities or opinions. Most people vote for a party not for an individual and may be unaware, indeed may not even care, about the particular attributes of the individual for whom they vote. This, of course, strengthens the argument that MPs should sublimate the demands of conscience and constituency to those of the party.

Burke's claim to individual autonomy for the member is perhaps rather less compelling when put in the modern context of tight party discipline, where MPs owe their seats largely to their adoption by the particular party (ibid).

Particular functions

(a) To provide a check on the power of governments. Perhaps the most effective constraint is the government's own MPs and not those of the opposition whose criticism is more ritualistic and less damaging.

> . . . the real opposition of the present day sit behind the Treasury bench. (Lord Palmerston, 1827)
>
> A government is more concerned to retain the loyalty and support of its own backbenchers than to placate the opposition. If disaffection should break out among its backbenchers the government's management of the House becomes difficult, the signs of disunity affect its reputation in the country, and it may suffer defeats in the House in circumstances of maximum publicity (Turpin, *British Government and the Constitution*).

(b) To represent interests and grievances of constituents. Most MPs hold local 'clinics' and remain 'in touch' with local issues and concerns. These may be dealt with by asking questions in Parliament, by reference to the Parliamentary Commissioner or, more often, by informal contacts and lobbying.

(c) To represent interest groups, i.e. professional bodies and associations, trade unions, 'cause' groups (e.g. League Against Cruel Sports, etc.), charities, business organisations (e.g. CBI, Institute of Directors).

(d) To represent and support the party thus preserving party unity, enhancing party credibility and thereby making it more effective in either government or opposition.

(e) To contribute to the effective working of Parliament (e.g. by working in public bill and select committees, etc.).

(f) To prefer the interests of the nation to more narrow sectional causes in times of emergency (e.g. bipartisan approach during the Falklands War, towards Northern Ireland, the Gulf War, the wars in Iraq, and in Afghanistan and in Syria).

The relationship between MP and party

Some general comments

Objective 3

The least conspicuous but most important role of the MP is that of party loyalist. Nearly all MPs are party loyalists when the whips are on. The typical loyalist supports the party position without argument, saying little in the Commons and attracting no attention to himself or herself. Loyalists see their role as maintaining party unity . . . An MP soon learns that his or her personal views are subject to the iron cage of party discipline. Because of the iron cage of party discipline, the government does not need to respond to MPs; it is confident of the outcome of votes in the Commons . . . The effectiveness of government in securing its legislation is virtually one hundred per cent. It is far higher than what is normal in other democratic countries and qualitatively much greater than what a President achieves in Congress. (Rose, *Politics in England*)

Factors contributing to party discipline

These include the following.

Benefits of party unity

It is accepted by most MPs that they were elected primarily to sustain the party and not to pursue their own or their constituency interest in preference to that of the party. Too many displays of independence may produce a disunited party which may damage the party's reputation and public confidence in it. Disunited parties tend not to win General Elections, and MPs, particularly those in marginal seats, risk losing their seats.

In addition, government backbenchers do not wish to make it difficult for Ministers to manage the business of the Commons or to impede implementation of the government's legislative programme.

Danger of deselection

Too many incidents of disloyalty may result in an MP being deselected, i.e. the local constituency party may refuse to select the MP as its candidate for the next General Election. Note that it is a convention in the Tory party for sitting members to be reselected. Since 1981, however, all Labour MPs have had to go through the selection process each time a General Election is called.

> All I say is watch it. Every dog is allowed one bite, but a different view is taken of a dog that goes on biting all the time. If there are doubts that the dog is biting not because of the dictates of conscience but because he is considered vicious, then things happen to that dog. He may not get his licence renewed when it falls due. (Harold Wilson, *The Times*, 5 March 1967)
>
> An MP has to be very incompetent, quite exceptionally brave, or extremely lucky to be denied renomination. If he is rejected his exit is more likely to be caused by scandal, drink, unusual indolence, or some other personal disability, than by political differences with his local party (Gilmore, *The Body Politic*).

Desire for promotion

> . . . a body acting together must have the rewards of ambition, patronage and place always before their eyes and within their expectation and belief of grasping, as well as the fine expressions of love of their country and the patriotism which is a virtue (Lord Londonderry, 1837).

With the principal exception of Winston Churchill, very few politicians with a reputation for attacking the party leadership have achieved high political office.

Debt to party leader

If, as it is alleged, elections are widely perceived as contests between party leaders, it could be argued that many MPs on the government side may owe their seats to the popularity of their leader and are, therefore, honour bound to give him/her their support.

Loss of party whip

This is the ultimate disciplinary sanction and is seldom used as it is controversial and suggests party disharmony. An MP who suffers this fate may no longer be regarded as a member of the parliamentary party and, if not reinstated, would probably be deselected at the next General Election.

Threat of dissolution

Prior to the passing of the Fixed Term Parliaments Act 2011 the discretion to advise the Monarch to dissolve Parliament, thereby precipitating a General Election, lay with the Prime Minister. This, some argued, provided the Prime Minister with a very powerful weapon in relation to dissident MPs. Thus, the argument ran, since such MPs would not wish to lose their parliamentary seats, which might occur were a General Election to be held, the threat to call an election could prove very effective in terms of bringing such persons 'into line' and securing their support for government policy.

For the Fixed Term Parliaments Act 2011, see p. 33.

Others argued, however, that a Prime Minister who precipitated an election simply to secure his/her own position, and who, therefore, led a divided party into the electoral contest, would have been unlikely to secure sufficient electoral support for a further term in office.

Any such Prime Ministerial power, and all arguments relating to its effectiveness, must, however, remain in abeyance for so long as the 2011 Act remains in force.

The Recall of MPs Act 2015

Introduction

Objective 4

The Act was the result of dissatisfaction in recent years with the conduct of some MPs, and with the ways in which these were said to be performing their parliamentary functions. The Act provides an electoral process, not hitherto available in relation to the Westminster Parliament, whereby the electorate in any constituency may 'recall' their local MP – i.e. decide that they no longer wish that individual to be their parliamentary representative.

The recall conditions

A local poll to determine whether an MP should be recalled from Parliament, thereby triggering a by-election, may be held in any of three circumstances:

1 the MP has been convicted of an offence in the courts of the UK;

2 pursuant to a report of the Committee on Standards, the House has ordered an MP to be suspended:

- for 10 or more 'sitting' days or
- where the period of suspension was not specified, for a period of at least 14 days;

3 an MP has been convicted under the Parliamentary Standards Act 2009 section 10 (providing false or misleading information for expenses claims).

The recall procedure

Where any of the above conditions are met, the recall procedure is set in train. The key elements of this are as follows:

(a) the sentencing court notifies the Speaker of the MP's conviction;

(b) the Speaker notifies the relevant Petitions Officer (usually the Returning Officer for the constituency involved) that a recall petition should be opened in the constituency as soon as reasonably practicable to remain open for six weeks;

(c) a recall petition may not be opened where a General Election is to be held within the next six months.

A recall petition will be successful if it is signed by at least ten per cent of the local electorate, i.e. all those registered to vote. The MP's seat then becomes vacant and a by-election called to elect a new Member. The 'recalled' Member is not prohibited from standing in the by-election.

Gender, ethnicity, background, and related matters

Gender

Objective 5

Following from the 2015 General Election, the gender balance in the House of Commons was 459 male MPs (down from 510 in the 2010 Parliament) (71 per cent of all MPs) and 191 females (up from 92) (29 per cent). The first female to be elected to the House of Commons was the Countess Markievicz. She was returned as a member for Dublin in the General Election of 1918. However, as a member of Sinn Fein, the Irish Republican party, she refused to take her seat at Westminster. The first female to be elected to Parliament and to take her seat was Nancy Astor who served as MP for Plymouth from 1919 to 1945. The first black female to win a parliamentary seat was Diane Abbott who was first elected in 1987.

Ethnicity

The 2015 General Election returned 41 MPs of non-European origins, an increase of 14 over the previous Parliament. This constituted 6 per cent of all Members with 13 per cent of the total UK population being from a non-white background.

The first non-white MP is generally believed to have been David Ochterlony Dyce, returned for Sudbury in 1841. He was of Anglo-Indian descent. The first MPs of African descent were Bernie Grant (Tottenham), Paul Boateng (Brent South), and Diane Abbott (Haringey, South), all elected in 1987.

Education

A total of 32 per cent of all MPs in the 2015 Parliament went to fee-paying schools; 47 per cent attended state comprehensives with 19 per cent attending state selectives. Almost

90 per cent were university educated, with 150 or 23 per cent having studied at Oxford or Cambridge.

Occupation

194 MPs or 31 per cent in 2015 had a 'professional' background (lawyer, doctor, teacher/ lecturer, civil service/local government); 192 or 30 per cent came from the business sector; and 19 or 3 per cent had been manual workers.

Age

The average age of those elected in 2015 was 50.

Payment

As from May 2015, MPs were paid £74,000 per annum. The Prime Minister received £142,000 (since April, 2013). Cabinet Ministers received £134,000 (also since April 2013).

Summary

The chapter identifies and defines the categories of persons not eligible to sit as Members of the House of Commons and explains the role and functions of MPs in the British model of representative, parliamentary democracy.

References

Burke (1889) *The Works of Edmund Burke,* London: Bell.

Gilmore (1971) *The Body Politic,* London: Hutchinson.

Radice, Vallence and Willis (1987) *Members of Parliament,* London: Macmillan.

Leach, Coxall and Robins (2011) *British Politics,* London: Palgrave Foundation.

Rose (1986) *Politics in England* (4th edn), London: Faber and Faber.

Turpin (2011) *British Government and the Constitution* (7th edn), London: Butterworths.

Wilson, *The Times,* 5 March 1967.

Further reading

Crewe (2015) *The House of Commons: An anthology of MPs at work,* London: Bloomsbury.

Flynn (2012) *How to be an MP,* London: Biteback.

Hudson and Campbell (2015), The Constitution Unit, *UK elects most diverse Parliament but it's still not representative,* http://constitution-unit.com/2015/05/14

Rogers and Walters (2015) *How Parliament Works* (2nd edn), London: Routledge.

Rush (2001) *The Role of the Member of Parliament since 1868,* Oxford: Oxford University Press.

8

The House of Commons: principal functions

Objectives

After reading this chapter you should:

1. Understand the role of the House of Commons in the British system of responsible parliamentary democracy and its various functions and powers.

2. Appreciate the workings of the legislative process and the differences between Public Bills, Private Members' Bills, Private Bills and Hybrid Bills.

3. Recognise the importance and reasons for subordinate legislation and the effectiveness of related parliamentary and judicial controls.

4. Be aware of the various procedures, and their effectiveness, for the scrutiny of Ministerial decisions and government policy in general.

5. Understand the reasons for and workings of the procedures for dealing with financial legislation.

Introduction

Objective 1

The House of Commons consists of 650 Members of diverse political opinions and allegiances. It does not 'govern' the United Kingdom in the sense of being responsible for the formulation and implementation of policy nor did it evolve for that purpose. The function of government is performed by the Prime Minister and Cabinet, central government departments and local authorities acting, in the main, through powers given to them by Act of Parliament.

Nor is it the function of the House of Commons to 'control' the government of the day by dictating to it how the nation's affairs should be managed or inflicting regular defeats upon it. Were it otherwise the process of government and administration would become unstable and unpredictable as a result of frequent changes of government personnel and policy.

The principal function of the House of Commons is to subject the entire conduct of government to a continuous process of rigorous, critical inquiry.

> The only means of parliamentary control worth considering are those which do not threaten the . . . defeat of the government, but which help to keep it responsive to the underlying current and the more important drifts of public opinion. All others are purely antiquarian shufflings . . . Parliamentary control should not mislead anyone into asking for a situation in which governments can have their legislation changed or their lives terminated . . . Control

means influence, but not direct power; advice not command; criticism not obstruction; scrutiny not initiation; and publicity of secrecy (Crick, *The Reform of Parliament*).

Academic analyses of the workings of the House of Commons often deal with its functions under the separate headings of legislation, scrutiny of the executive and financial proceedings (i.e. the voting of taxing and spending powers) and with the procedures through which each of these activities is conducted. It is important, however, that such categorisation and concentration on procedural detail should not be allowed to obscure the common or central theme with which all of these activities are concerned – the ability of the House of Commons to identify executive inadequacies and wrongdoings and to expose these to the light of day. Providing this is done effectively then the House can genuinely claim to be both a practical, democratic safeguard against the abuse of government power and an essential vehicle for conveying to the electorate the necessary material to make an informed judgement on the government's competence and fitness to continue in office.

The principal responsibility for laying bare the flaws of government lies, of course, with the parties in opposition. Thus the particular importance of 'Her Majesty's Loyal Opposition' (the main or 'official' opposition party) in parliamentary and democratic processes. To some extent parliamentary procedures are only as effective as the use that is made of them. Hence a well-led and organised opposition may do much within the existing system to insist on government accountability to the elected chamber. By the same token, however, an opposition in disarray, perhaps after a particularly heavy election defeat, may be of little more than nuisance value as the government asserts its numerical majority in the business of the House.

Other more nebulous and covert political factors may also have their part to play in determining what is essentially a fluctuating relationship between government and Parliament. Hence even a government with a substantial majority may be affected and damaged by 'leaks', 'splits' over party policy, and challenges for the leadership of the party. Factors such as these may exacerbate discontent amongst the government's own backbenchers so that criticism comes from all sides of the House. Little wonder then that in Lord Palmerston's opinion the real opposition lay 'behind the Treasury bench'; an opinion with which, in the late twentieth century, both Margaret Thatcher and her successor, Mr Major, might have readily agreed.

On a more basic day-to-day functional level, the normal daily sitting times of the House of Commons are Monday, 2.30–10-30 pm; Tuesday and Wednesday, 11.30–7.30 pm; Thursday, 9.30–5.30 pm; and Friday, 9.30–3.30 pm. The House sits on Saturdays only on very rare occasions. This has occurred just three times since 1845. The last instance was on 3 April, 1982, when the House met to debate the invasion of the Falkland Islands. By way of illustration of the work of the House of Commons, in the parliamentary session 2015–16, the House met on 149 days at an average sitting time of 6.48 hours per day. The session lasted from 18 May, 2015 to 12 May, 2016 with the average daily attendance being 497.

Legislation

Some basic definitions

Objective 2

Parliament legislates both directly and indirectly. It legislates directly in the form of Acts of Parliament. It legislates indirectly in the form of delegated or subordinate legislation. That which Parliament does directly is sometimes referred to as 'primary' legislation. That which it does indirectly may be referred to as 'secondary' legislation.

Primary legislation

During its procedural stages through Parliament a legislative proposal is known as a 'Bill'. In terms of its intended scope of application and the procedure for its enactment, a Bill may be:

(a) a Public Bill;

(b) a Private Member's Bill;

(c) a Private Bill;

(d) a Hybrid Bill.

A Public Bill is a legislative proposal intended to be of general application, i.e. one which will alter the law applicable throughout the realm and to all persons within it. In most cases it will have been formulated and put before Parliament by the government as part of its legislative programme for the session. A good example of the same would be the annual Finance Bill which gives the government the authority it needs to collect the revenues required in order to provide the moneys for defence, public services, etc. A Public Bill may begin its parliamentary process in either the House of Commons or House of Lords. By convention, however, a Bill with significant financial or political implications will be introduced in the House of Commons.

A Private Member's Bill will, in most cases, also be 'public' or of general application in character. However, such a Bill will have been put before Parliament by an ordinary backbench MP and not by a government Minister. Also, in some respects, the procedure for introducing and enacting a Private Member's Bill differs from that used for a Public Bill proposed by the government. For these two reasons, therefore, a Private Member's Bill is often treated as a distinct type of legislative proposal. A good and relatively recent example of a legislative enactment of this type would be the Holocaust (Return of Cultural Objects) Act 2009.

A Private Bill is a legislative proposal of more limited application or scope. It will seek to have effect in a particular local government area or may relate to the activities of a particular statutory undertaker or company (e.g. a Water Co.). Where such a Bill is promoted by a local authority this will usually be to provide it with a power not available under general enabling legislation (e.g. education Acts, highways Acts, etc.). An example of this type of Bill would be the Greater Nottingham Light Rapid Transit Act 1994. It is common for such Bills to be referred to as Local Bills.

Where a Private Bill is promoted by a private company this will usually be for the purpose of enabling it to do that which may involve interference with private or public rights (see Lloyds Bank (Merger) Act 1985). On occasion, legislative changes relating to personal issues such as marriage or nationality may also be effected by this type of legislation (see Valerie Mary Hill and Alan Monk (Marriage Enabling) Act 1985; James Hugh Maxwell (Naturalisation) Act 1975). Private Bills of this type are sometimes referred to as Personal Bills. Two further marriage enabling Acts were passed in 1987. No other Personal Bills have been enacted since that time.

A Hybrid Bill is, as it suggests, a legislative proposal which contains both public and private elements. Hence, it will contain provisions which affect the public generally, alongside those which are more limited in application and relate to a particular locality or person(s) only. Two modern, well-published examples would include the Crossrail Bill 2005, to authorise the building of the Trans-Metropolis East-West rail link, and the High Speed Rail (London-Midlands) Bill 2013.

Secondary legislation

This is the general term used to describe legislation made by a subordinate authority (e.g. government Minister or local authority) pursuant to a law-making power given to it by an

Act of Parliament. As already indicated, such legislation may also be referred to as delegated or subordinate legislation. Secondary legislation made by a Minister will usually be in the form of a **statutory instrument**. This will contain a set of regulations applicable to the particular subject area (e.g. road traffic regulations). Secondary legislation made by a local authority will usually be in the form of by-laws (e.g. those which regulate the use of public parks and amenities).

Public Bills

Formation

As already explained, the vast majority are formulated by the government. These are drafted by a team of lawyers in the Parliamentary Counsel Office, a part of the Cabinet Office. A Cabinet committee (Legislation Committee) will be responsible for managing the government's legislative programme for each session – i.e. for ensuring that Bills scheduled for a particular session pass through their required Commons stages within the time available. Providing the government has a sufficient majority, few such Bills will be lost (i.e. defeated by votes) or withdrawn. Figures show that in the period since the end of the Second World War some 97 per cent of all Public Bills successfully passed their Second Reading stages in the House of Commons. This has much to do with the United Kingdom's two-party system and method of voting. The Shops Bill 1986 was the last government Bill of any significance to be lost on the floor of the House (196 votes to 282). Depending on various factors – particularly the significance and complexity of the Bills proposed, the amount of opposition, and whether an election is pending – the number of Bills introduced in a particular session may be anything from 20 to 70. In more recent years, the number of Public Bills put before the House of Commons and proceeding to Royal Assent have been as follows: 2012–13, 35; 2013–14, 30; 2014–15, 26; 2015–16, 29.

In the Parliaments of 2005 to 2010, the average number of Public Bills enacted per session was 33. In the Parliaments of 2010 to 2016, the figure was 28.4.

Reasons for introduction

(a) implementation of party manifesto;

(b) response to lobbying by pressure/**interest groups**;

(c) mental inquiries/committees, **Law Commissions** or parliamentary select committees;

(d) response to economic, social, industrial, public order or security problems perhaps not predicted in manifesto;

(e) response to political or other emergency (e.g. emergency legislation in wartime or used in Northern Ireland);

(f) implementation of treaty obligations (e.g. EU (Amendment) Act 2008).

Publication in draft

There is no general requirement that a Bill should be published in draft prior to being committed to its final form and submitted to Parliament. The practice does, however, have its benefits and found favour with the Select Committee on Modernisation of the House of Commons in its first report (1997–98, HC 190). In particular, it gives MPs the opportunity to comment on a Bill at its formative stage and at a time when the Minister may be more amenable to suggested amendments or alterations.

Once Bills are formally introduced they are largely set in concrete. There has been a distinct culture prevalent through Whitehall that the standing and reputation of Ministers has been dependent on their Bills getting through largely unchanged. As a result there has been an inevitable disposition to resist alteration not only in the main issues of substance, but also in matters of detail (para 7).

Bills published in draft will usually be examined by a parliamentary committee, often the appropriate **Departmental Select Committee**. For example, the Identity Cards Bill 2004 was considered by the Select Committee on Home Affairs. This practice enables a brief report to be issued, which may help inform debate and scrutiny as a Bill progresses through its parliamentary stages.

The numbers of Public Bills published in draft in recent parliamentary sessions has been as follows: 2011–12, 5; 2012–13, 3; 2013–14, 5; 2014–15, 3; 2015–16, 3.

Parliamentary procedure

(1) First Reading

Parliamentary Counsel submits the final text of the Bill with its Explanatory Notes to the House of Commons Public Bill Office. On the day appointed for the Bill's introduction to Parliament, a 'dummy' copy, containing only its short and long title, is laid on the Table of the House. At the completion of Question Time, the Speaker calls the sponsoring Minister or government Whip acting on the Minister's behalf. The Clerk of the Table reads out the short title of the Bill. The Minister or Whip stands and nods his/her assent. The Bill is thus deemed to have been given its First Reading. The proceedings are concluded by the Minister or Whip giving the date for the Bill's Second Reading. As this will usually not yet have been fixed, the practice is to give a purely nominal date, e.g. 'tomorrow'. The Bill is then ordered to be printed and published. No debate or division takes place at this stage. The House has, however, been given notice that the Bill has begun its parliamentary stages.

The actual text of the Bill is then presented to the Public Bill Office. There, the Clerk of Public Bills is responsible for ensuring that, *inter alia*, its text and content comply with the rules of the House; that its title adequately describes its content; that financial provisions requiring additional expenditure are printed in italics to indicate that financial resolutions will be required; and that it is genuinely a Public and not a Hybrid Bill (one which, in addition to its public general provisions, contains clauses which have a particular effect on some private or local interests).

(2) Second Reading

On the day scheduled, and at the appointed time during public business, the order of the day for the Second Reading of the Bill is read out by the Clerk. The responsible Minister then moves that the Bill now be read for a second time and whether the government deems its content to be compatible with the requirements of the Human Rights Act 1998. He/she then speaks in favour of its general policy and content. Opposition spokespersons then respond, followed by a general debate by the whole House.

For the Human Rights Act 1998, see pp. 498–544.

Detailed amendments may be suggested but not formally proposed at this stage. However, procedural amendments – e.g. that the Bill be read for a second time six months hence – may be taken. If carried, an amendment of this type would effectively defeat the Bill. At the conclusion of the debate, the House votes ('divides') on the question of whether the Bill should be read a second time or not. Should the vote be in favour, as will normally be the case, the Bill is deemed to have passed its Second Reading stage and may proceed to

Committee, Report, and Third Reading. Should the Bill be defeated it is deemed lost and may proceed no further.

Since 1967 it has been possible for a Minister to propose that a Bill be committed for its Second Reading debate to a Second Reading Committee (16–50 Members) providing not more than 19 Members object (usually non-controversial measures – on average about five per session). Albeit that a Second Reading debate has taken place in Committee, the actual vote or division on the Bill is taken in the whole House. Should a Bill contain financial clauses these must be further authorised by resolutions pursuant to motions introduced by the responsible Minister between Second Reading and Committee stage. These may be Money Resolutions or Ways and Means Resolutions. Money Resolutions authorise any part of a Bill which makes a significant charge on government funds. Ways and Means Resolutions provide specific parliamentary authority for the levying of any tax or other financial charge. Such financial resolutions are not debated if taken immediately after the Bill's Second Reading. If not, a debate of up to 45 minutes may be scheduled.

A Bill relating exclusively to Scottish affairs, generally those not devolved to the Scottish Parliament, may be referred for its Second Reading debate to the Scottish Grand Committee – providing not more than nine Members object. The Committee is composed of all Scottish Members. In addition to conducting such Second Reading debates, the functions of the Committee include the following:

(a) hearing oral questions to Scottish Office Ministers and law officers;

(b) conducting general debates on Scottish issues;

(c) hearing Ministerial statements relating to the same.

Similarly, a Bill dealing with Welsh affairs may be referred for its Second Reading to the Welsh Grand Committee. This consists of all Welsh Members and five others. The Committee may also conduct general debates on Welsh affairs, hear oral questions to Ministers and receive Ministerial statements.

(3) Committee stage

After Second Reading most Bills will be referred to a 'Public Bill Committee' for detailed consideration and amendment. Some Bills may, however, by resolution be referred to a Committee of the Whole House or, more occasionally, to a Select Committee of the House or Joint Select Committee consisting of Members from both Houses (e.g. House of Lords Reform Bill 2011). Consolidated Fund Bills (i.e. those authorising expenditure) will be dealt with in Committee of the Whole House as may minor Bills for which the Committee stage is a pure formality, and, from time to time, Bills of major public importance (e.g. European Union (Amendment) Bills 1992 and 2007 to give effect, respectively, to the Maastricht and Lisbon Treaties and the Bill which preceded the Terrorism Act 2006). The figures show that in recent times the committee stages of some five or six Bills per session have been dealt with in this way. For a Committee of the Whole House the Speaker vacates the chair. His/her place is then taken by the Chairman of Ways and Means (or deputy of same). The annual Finance Bill is, for purposes of expedition, considered partially on the floor of the House and partially in Public Bill Committee.

At any one time, up to ten Public Bill Committees may be at work in the House of Commons. These are identified numerically, i.e. Committees A to H with a further two committees dedicated to examining Scottish legislation. Private Members' Bills are usually referred to a Committee C.

Public Bill Committees consist of 16 to 25 Members chosen by the Committee of Selection. The composition of each committee should reflect party strengths in the House of Commons itself. The Committee of Selection will also be guided by representations from individual MPs, party whips, and the government department which drafted the Bill in question.

Originally such committees were appointed to serve for the whole **parliamentary session** and were referred to as Standing Committees. Thus their membership 'stood' or remained the same for Bills dealt with during that period. Currently, however, such committees are reconstituted for the purposes of each Bill according to Members' interests and qualifications. Ministers from the sponsoring department and opposition spokespersons will be represented. Given the composition of Public Bill Committees it is unlikely that major changes – amendments to clauses affecting the substance of the Bill or its policy objectives – will be made. Many other amendments may be made, however, and it is not unusual for the majority of these to be moved by the government – in response to pressure from within the party, views of interest groups, legal advice, etc.

The chairperson has a key role in expediting the business of the committee. He/she may eliminate amendments or proposals which are out of order or which are of a trivial or minor nature. The chair may also arrange for amendments of a similar content or intent to be considered collectively, and decide which amendments may be debated prior to a vote and which may be voted upon without debate.

For European Union Legislation, see pp. 166–7.
A Bill dealing exclusively with Scottish affairs may be referred to one of two Scottish Public Bill Committees. Legislation emanating from the European Union may be considered by a European Standing Committee. There are no Welsh Public Bill Committees.

(4) Report stage

A Bill considered by Public Bill Committee is then reported back to the House as amended or unamended. The House may accept or reject the amendments made but without further debate. New amendments and clauses may be proposed and considered. The Speaker will be careful to ensure that this stage is not used to rehearse arguments dealt with in committee.

Bills referred to a Committee of the Whole House or the Scottish Grand Committee for their Second Reading may remain in committee for their Report stage.

Unamended Bills from Committees of the Whole House go straight to Third Reading – i.e. there is no Report stage.

(5) Third Reading

By the time they have completed Committee and Report stages, most Bills will be different from those which were approved by the House at Second Reading. Important new provisions may have been inserted, or the original principles or ambit of the Bill may have been modified significantly. In these circumstances, the Third Reading stage gives an opportunity for any such changes to be debated and for the House to decide whether the Bill should be allowed to proceed in this altered form.

The usual practice is for the Third Reading to be taken, and to extend for approximately one hour, after the Bill has completed its Report stage. No further amendments may be put and, unless the Bill is of major political or constitutional importance, or has been altered radically since its Second Reading, the debate is likely to be short, often not extending for the full hour.

(6) Proceedings in the House of Lords

All Bills pass through similar procedural stages in the House of Lords, save that the Lords has no Public Bill committees. The Committee stage will usually be dealt with by

Committees of the Whole House. Should the Lords amend a Bill, the amendments must be referred to and accepted, rejected or amended by the House of Commons. If there is disagreement the disputed amendments, with reasons, are referred back to the House of Lords. This exchanging of amendments, usually only in relation to controversial measures, may go on until agreement is reached. In the event of no such agreement and in very rare instances, the government may feel obliged to invoke the Parliament Acts 1911–49 which allow for Bills rejected by the Lords to go for the Royal Assent after at least one year has elapsed.

The upper House has no power to amend **Money Bills** (i.e. those concerned wholly with finance). If such a Bill has not been passed by the Lords within one month of its receipt, it may proceed for the Royal Assent (Parliament Act 1911, s 1).

(7) The Royal Assent

By virtue of the Royal Assent Act 1967 this final stage of enacting a Bill may be either:

(a) announced by the Speakers in the House of Commons and the House of Lords pursuant to authority granted to both by the Monarch in letters patent; or

(b) given by Members of the upper House appointed as Lords Commissioners by the Monarch for the purposes of giving assent to a particular Bill or, more usually, a number of Bills.

Unless with the agreement of the House, a Public Bill must receive the Royal Assent in the session it is put before Parliament. If not the Bill fails and will have to be reintroduced in the next session.

'Carrying over'

The Select Committee on Modernisation of the House of Commons in its third report for 1997–98 (HC 543), whilst recognising that the above rule acted as an important discipline on the government in terms of the effective disposal of its legislative programme, felt that it should be applied flexibly so that, in appropriate cases, and in the interests of more effective scrutiny, a Bill might be 'carried over' from one session to another. This might be preferable, it was thought, to rushing important legislation through its final stages simply to meet the end of session deadline. The system was introduced on an experimental basis in the 2001–02 parliamentary session, and on a permanent basis in the session 2004–05.

The numbers of bills carried over in recent sessions have been as follows: 2010–12, 4 carried over to 2012–13; 2012–13, 5 carried over to 2013–14; 2013–14, 6 carried over to 2014–15; 2014–15, 4 carried over to 2015–16.

For the carrying over of a Public Bill a motion of the House in favour is required. This does not apply to Private or Hybrid Bills. These may be carried over as a matter of course and, in some cases, may take several years to complete their passage through Parliament.

Legislative Consent Orders

Notwithstanding the creation of legislative assemblies in Northern Ireland, Scotland and Wales, the Westminster Parliament remains sovereign to legislate on all matters relating to these parts of the United Kingdom. This includes enactments which affect matters within the areas of legislative authority conferred on the devolved assemblies. Any such use of the sovereign power is, however, regulated by the convention that no such legislation will be enacted unless and until a Legislative Consent Order has been approved by the devolved assembly in question.

English votes for English laws ('EVEL')

A new procedure for Public Bills applying to England or to England and Wales, but not to other parts of the United Kingdom, was adopted by the House of Commons in October, 2015. In the main, this was a reaction to the devolution settlement of 1998 and, in particular, the creation of a Scottish Parliament with control over Scotland's internal affairs. For those dissatisfied with the devolution arrangements, this produced an unacceptable imbalance between the powers of MPs from Scotland and those from England, i.e. that while all MPs from Scotland could still vote at Westminster on purely 'English legislation', English MPs no longer had any similar opportunity to vote on matters relating primarily to Scotland – most of these having been put within the legislative authority of the new Parliament in Edinburgh.

The EVEL requirements explained below were an attempt to remedy this perceived imperfect state of affairs. This was done by introducing a number of additional procedural elements into the parliamentary process for dealing with 'English' or 'English and Welsh' Public Bills. These are designed primarily to enable MPs representing English or English and Welsh constituencies to 'have the last say' and, if necessary, exercise a power of veto, over English or English and Welsh legislation.

The EVEL process

Certification

After First Reading, the Speaker is charged to 'certify' any Public Bill or part or clause of it which should be dealt with according to the EVEL process. In making his/her decision, the Speaker may consult with two MPs of his/her choosing – presumably two of the more senior Members of the House. Two tests must be applied to the Bill. Both of these must be satisfied. These are: does the Bill or any part or clause of it:

(a) apply exclusively to either England or to England and Wales;

(b) relate to a matter(s) put within the legislative authority given to one or more of the devolved assemblies set up in 1998.

The first Bill certified as satisfying these requirements was the Housing and Planning Bill 2015–16.

Bills certified as applying to England only

The First and Second Reading of Bills of this type remain as before, i.e. as for all Public Bills. The first change occurs at Committee Stage. The EVEL requirement here is that the Committee should consist entirely of MPs from English constituencies. The party balance in the Committee should reflect the party composition in the House of Commons as a whole. Following Committee, the Bill has its Report Stage before all MPs on the floor of the House. Further amendments may be made with all Members able to speak and vote.

From Report, the Bill goes to a Legislative Grand Committee (LGC), perhaps the principal innovation of the EVEL reforms. An LGC may give or refuse consent ('veto') to any certified Bill, part or clause of it. No detailed amendment of content may be made. All MPs may attend and speak but only those from English constituencies are allowed to vote.

Should the LGC give its consent to the Bill in its entirety, it may, without more, proceed to Third Reading. If consent to the Bill or any part or clause of it is refused, the Bill goes back before the whole House. Here it must pass through a further EVEL procedural element referred to as a Reconsideration Stage. The purpose of Reconsideration is to resolve those contentious elements of the Bill vetoed in the LGC. Amendments to the Bill for this purpose may be made. Other parts of the Bill are not considered. All MPs are eligible to speak and vote.

After Reconsideration, and if amended, the Bill is returned to the LGC. Again, the LGC may give or refuse consent to it in its amended form. If consent is given, the Bill may proceed to Third Reading. If consent to it is refused, the Bill is lost. If consent is refused to any part or clause of the Bill, the Bill may proceed to Third Reading with those elements omitted.

In those instances where, as a result of provisions having been removed from the Bill, other minor or technical changes are needed in order to ensure that the legislation remains workable, the Bill is referred to the whole House for Consequential Consideration. At completion of this stage, the Bill passes to Third Reading.

Given all of the above, the process for a Certified Bill required to pass through all elements of the EVEL procedure would be:

1 First Reading

2 Certification

3 Second Reading

4 Committee Stage

5 Report Stage

6 Legislative Grand Committee

7 Reconsideration Stage

8 Legislative Grand Committee

9 Consequential Consideration Stage

10 Third Reading.

Changes made to a certified Bill or elements of it in the House of Lords must go back to the House of Commons for approval by a 'double majority', viz. a majority of all MPs and a majority of all English MPs cast in a single vote on the floor of the House.

Bills certified as applying to England and Wales only

The legislative process for such Bills remains the same as for all other Bills up to and including Report Stage. In particular, therefore, the composition of the committee for this stage of the Bill is not prescribed by geographical factors, i.e. restricted to English and Welsh MPs only.

From Committee Stage the Bill moves to a Legislative Grand Committee where geographical limitations are imposed, i.e. although all Members may attend, only those from England and Wales are eligible to vote. Should consent be given, the Bill moves to Third Reading. If refused, the process described above is followed, i.e. Reconsideration, Legislative Grand Committee, in this case consisting of English and Welsh MPs, followed, if necessary, by Consequential Consideration.

Bill certified as including clauses applying to England or England and Wales only

As with Bills applying to England and Wales, a Bill of general application but with English or English and Welsh clauses in it, proceeds through all stages up to and including Report according to the normal process. Beyond this, however, any certified clauses must gain the consent of the appropriate Legislative Grand Committee passing them and if necessary to Reconsideration, Legislative Grand Committee and Consequential Consideration of the certified elements are to be included in the Bill that goes for Third Reading.

Public Bills not affected by EVEL

(i) Appropriation and Consolidation Bills; (ii) Private Members' Bills.

Private Members' Bills

Nature and subject-matter

Private Members' legislation represents one of the few remaining processes through which the House and its Members may exercise a truly creative and independent law-making function, i.e. one not dominated by the government.

Such Bills tend to relate to social, ethical, environmental or constitutional issues which the government may not have the time or – for a variety of reasons – the inclination to include in its legislative programme. Such reticence may be because:

(a) the matter is too sensitive and controversial (e.g. termination of pregnancy);

(b) it does not relate to party policy (e.g. animal research);

(c) there is no political gain to be made from the issues (family law reform, divorce, etc.);

(d) there is no clear party or public consensus relating thereto (e.g. pornography).

Example

Some famous examples of Private Members' Bills would include the Obscene Publications Act 1959, the Murder (Abolition of the Death Penalty) Act 1965, the Sexual Offences Act 1967 (legalisation of homosexual acts), and the Termination of Pregnancy Act 1968. Some interesting and more recent examples would include the Still-Birth (Definition) Act 1992, the Children and Young Persons (Protection from Tobacco) Act 1991, the Welfare of Animals at Slaughter Act 1991, Female Genital Mutilation Act 2003, the Human Fertilisation and Embryology Act 2004, the Forced Marriage (Civil Protection) Act 2007, the Holocaust (Return of Cultural Objects) Act 2009 and the Sunbed (Regulation) Act 2010.

Types of Private Members' Bills and procedure for enactment

(a) Ballot Bills

Thirteen Fridays (9.30 –2.30 pm) of each parliamentary session are dedicated to the consideration of Private Members' Bills and any other private Members' business. On the second Thursday of each session a ballot is held to decide which Members should be able to use the time available for the legislative measures of their choice. This is a matter of considerable interest to the majority of Members. Four to five hundred will usually participate in the ballot. Ministers and government whips may not participate, nor, by convention, do opposition leaders and spokespersons. Twenty names only are drawn. Of these only the first six to ten have any realistic possibility of securing the passage of a Bill. Successful Members may nominate a particular Friday for the Second Reading of their Bill (the first seven being set aside for this purpose). Hence the MP who came first in the ballot may claim precedence on the first Friday and so on. These same Bills then have precedence for their remaining procedural stages and Lords amendments on the remaining Fridays set aside for Private Members' legislation.

It is interesting to note that many Members may not have a particular Bill in mind when they enter the ballot. When, as often happens, an 'undecided' Member is drawn in the first

20 they will then be the subject of considerable lobbying from interest groups and other organisations – in the hope that they may introduce a Bill on their behalf. Also, the government may suggest a Bill to a successful MP. These will usually, but not uniformly, be minor measures which the government has been unable to fit into its legislative programme for that session. They are often referred to as 'handout' or 'whips' Bills (for a not insignificant handout Bill see the EU Referendum Bill 2013).

Some Members will decide, or may be persuaded, to introduce Bills which have little chance of success. They may do this simply to secure a debate and some publicity for a particular issue about which they have strong feelings. In recent years Bills of this type have raised such issues as abortion, embryo research, constitutional reform (freedom of information and the introduction of a Bill of Rights), smoking in public places, blood sports, etc.

A Bill given a Second Reading will then proceed to Public Bill Committee in the usual way. This will be a committee set up primarily to deal with Private Members' Bills. Some Bills, however, could be committed to other Public Bill Committees if these are not busy with government legislation. Having progressed through committee, Private Members' Bills return to the floor of the House for the Report and Third Reading stages.

In order to secure the success of a Bill the sponsoring MP will have to negotiate a number of major procedural obstacles. First, the Bill may be defeated at Second Reading by hostile Members. This will usually be the case if the Bill is opposed by the government. Although it is not usual for the government to formally oppose a Private Member's Bill (by imposing the 'whip'), communication to its backbenchers of government 'unease' about a particular measure will normally be sufficient to ensure its defeat. Second, a Private Member's Bill may simply be 'talked out'. In other words, Members opposed to the Bill will ensure that a particular procedural stage (usually Second Reading) has not been completed within the time available. Should this appear likely, the sponsoring Member may propose the 'closure' (see below). This, of course, must be supported by a majority of Members present. A simple majority, however (e.g. 26 for, 24 against), is not sufficient as, for the closure to be carried, at least 100 Members must vote in favour. Since attendance at the House on Fridays is often low, this is only likely in relation to those measures for which there is a considerable degree of backbench support. Also note that, as with all other proceedings on the floor of the House, a quorum of 40 is necessary if a vote is to take place.

The number of Ballot Bills passing into law in recent sessions were: 2014–15, 7; 2015–16, 4.

(b) Ten-minute Rule Bills

After Question Time on Tuesdays or Wednesdays, a Member who has given at least five sitting days' notice may propose and speak for ten minutes in favour of a particular Bill. Any Member opposed may have a similar period of time to speak against. There is no further debate. The House then divides on whether to give leave to introduce the Bill. If leave is given the Bill is deemed to have been read for the first time.

Ten-minute Rule Bills have only a limited chance of being enacted save in those rare cases where they are not opposed and sufficient time for their further procedural stages is either provided by the government – an unlikely event given the amount of government business to be conducted in each session of Parliament – or can be found during those Fridays dedicated to balloted Private Members' legislation. Only 7 such Bills were enacted in the period 1997–2017.

The purpose of introducing such a Bill is often to suggest a change in the law or to promote a particular cause. It also provides a Member with the opportunity to test parliamentary opinion on a matter concerning which the Member may wish to legislate in the future.

Two Ten-minute Rule Bills passed into law in 2015–16 and one in 2014–15. These included the Driving Instructors Registration Act 2016. A much publicised example of a Ten-Minute Rule Bill was the Cannabis (Legislation and Regulation) Bill 2015–16. The Bill was not successful.

(c) Presentation Bills

Apart from using the ballot or Ten-minute Rule procedures, any Member (having given notice) may put down a Bill for Second Reading on the day of their choice. Leave is not required. At least one day's notice must be given and the Bill then presented to the Clerk of the House. The Clerk reads out the short title of the Bill which is then deemed to have had its First Reading. No further procedure is possible unless, that is, time for the further stages of the Bill can be found on those Fridays devoted to Private Members' Bills (when Ballot Bills have precedence) or the government is prepared to make time available.

5 Presentation Bills were enacted in the period 2016–17.

Some general comments

A Private Member's Bill may not be introduced if its primary objective is to require additional government expenditure. Where such expenditure is necessarily incidental to the main purposes of a Bill, a financial resolution or resolutions moved by a government Minister would be required before the financial clauses could be considered in Public Bill committee. Hence, without government support a Bill of this type could not proceed.

The sponsoring Member is responsible for the drafting of a Bill. Parliamentary counsel are not normally available for this task – that is, unless the Bill has attracted government support. Financial and other assistance may, however, be provided by any supporting interest group. Also, since 1971, the MPs responsible for the first ten balloted Bills have been able to claim a small amount in expenses from public funds (£200).

Private Members' Bills may also be introduced in the House of Lords. Where this occurs the Bill must then be sponsored by an MP to guide it through its Commons stages. As with other non-balloted Bills, unless government or Private Members' time can be found, there is little hope of such Bills progressing through the House.

In the twelve years from session 2003–04 to that of session 2015–16, 63 Private Members' Bills of all types passed into law – an average of just over five per session.

Private Bills

Nature and subject-matter

Reference has already been made to the fact that such Bills do not attempt to make any change to the general law of the land but seek instead to make law for a particular local area, organisation (public or private), or individual.

In the eighteenth and nineteenth centuries, Bills of this type tended to dominate the legislative work of Parliament. They were used particularly for such purposes as land enclosure (by extinguishing rights of common) and to acquire land for the construction of railways and canals. The role of the Private Bill in this context has been revived in recent years as local authorities have sought statutory authorisation for the construction of rapid light transport systems (tramways) to relieve urban congestion. In the future, however, such projects will receive the necessary authorisation by Ministerial Orders made under the Transport and Works Act 1992. Sixty-five Private Bills were enacted in the period 2000–16 at an average of just less than four per session. Six were enacted in 2015–16. These included the Faversham Oyster Fishery Bill and the Southgate Cemetery Bill.

Procedure

As a general rule, notice of the intention to promote a Private Bill should be given by public advertisement in newspapers and the *London Gazette*, and in writing to all persons whose rights or interests may be directly affected. When this has been done a petition signed by the promoters and a copy of the Bill must be presented at the Private Bill Office of the House of Commons on 27 November each year. This is to allow time for the Examiners of Private Bills to ensure that standing orders relating to the pre-parliamentary stages of private legislation have been complied with.

The Bill is presented to the House of Commons by being placed on the Order Table by a clerk from the Private Bill Office. This also operates as the Bill's First Reading. At Second Reading a debate and division will occur only if a Member has given notification of opposition. A Bill requiring government expenditure or imposing a tax will require the appropriate financial resolutions to be moved by a Minister before it can proceed to its Committee stage.

If a Bill has not been opposed it will be sent to an Unopposed Private Bill Committee (four Members). An opposed Bill will go to an Opposed Private Bill Committee (seven Members). Proceedings in the latter are 'quasi-judicial'. The promoters and their opponents argue their cases, often represented by counsel. Witnesses are examined on oath. Members of the committee should have no particular interest in the Bill's subject-matter. In addition to considering individual clauses and suggested amendments, the committee will be concerned to see that the facts stated in the Bill's preamble (i.e. the introductory statement setting out the need for the Bill) are accurate and that the Bill is both in the local and national interest.

If the Bill is approved in committee it is reported to the House and then proceeds to its Third Reading (usually a formality) and thence to the House of Lords where it goes through much the same process.

Hybrid Bills

The procedure for enacting a Hybrid Bill is similar to that for Public Bills save that after Second Reading, if opposed, a Hybrid Bill is referred to a small Select Committee of MPs. This deals with the 'private' aspects of the Bill. Those persons whose legal interests are affected by the clauses in question may place their objections before the Committee. At this stage the general principle of the Bill is not in issue nor does the Committee concern itself with the Bill's public or general provisions.

The Bill then proceeds as normal to a Public Bill Committee and through its subsequent stages as if it were an ordinary Public Bill.

For discussion of the High Speed Rail Bill 2013–14 see pp. 109–10.

Such Bills are not commonplace. Probably the most publicised in recent times would be the High Speed Rail (London–West Midlands) Bill 2013–14.

Methods of curtailing debate

Reasons

If procedures for limiting discussion of particular Bills, particularly at Second Reading or in committee, were not available, it would be open for MPs to keep proceedings going for as long as possible thus interfering with the progress of Bills to which they were opposed and causing problems for the whole of the government's legislative programme. Hence standing orders provide a number of procedural devices which may be used to expedite the business of the House. These devices were adopted at the end of the nineteenth century when Irish Nationalist MPs, in pursuit of Home Rule for Ireland, sought to put pressure on the government by disrupting the parliamentary process. Prior to these events proceedings in the House continued so long as any Member had something relevant to say.

There is a danger, of course, that the devices mentioned below could be used to stifle informed debate and criticism and not simply as a means of ensuring parliamentary efficiency.

The closure

Any Member either in the House or in committee may move that 'the question be now put' (e.g. that the Bill be read for a second time). The Speaker may or may not accept the motion depending on whether they think that the various interested opinions represented in the House have been given a fair opportunity to contribute to the debate. If the motion is accepted the House then divides. The motion is carried and the debate ended providing at least 100 MPs vote for the closure. The question which the House has been debating is then put to the vote – i.e. whether the Bill should be given a Second Reading. Eighteen Public Bills were subjected to the closure in 2015–16.

The guillotine

This is properly known as the 'allocation of time motion' and is a procedure available to the government to secure the passage of legislation which it is anticipated may be vigorously opposed in the House. The motion, usually moved by a Member of the government, seeks either to set a date by which the particular Bill must have completed its Committee stage or to allocate a specific number of days to the Bill's various stages. Given the government's majority in the House such motions will normally be carried notwithstanding the expected protests of opposition Members. As the Bill proceeds through the House and the time or times set for the completion of its various stages are reached, further debate is 'guillotined' or brought to an end with the Bill then proceeding to its next stage.

> They may be regarded as the extreme limit to which procedure goes in affirming the rights of the majority at the expense of the minorities of the House and it cannot be denied that they are capable of being used in such a way as to upset the balance – between the claims of business and the rights of debate. But the harshness of this procedure is to some extent mitigated either by consultation between the party leaders or in the Business Committee in order to establish the greatest possible measure of agreement as to the most satisfactory disposal of the time available (May, *Parliamentary Practice*, p. 409).

The guillotine was used on three occasions in the parliamentary session 2015–16.

Programme motions

Both the closure and the guillotine are regarded as rather blunt instruments which are usually imposed on a resistant House of Commons. In more recent times, and particularly as a result of the urgings of the Select Committee on Modernisation of the House, greater emphasis has been placed on agreed programming whereby a timetable for a Bill's progress is agreed between party whips. When formulated, a programme motion will be put before the House after the Bill has been given its Second Reading. The motion will stipulate the date by which the Bill should complete its passage through committee and will state the time available for further discussion of the Bill during its Report and Third Reading stages.

Once a programme motion has been carried, a Programming Committee is appointed to determine the exact amount of time to be allocated to the Bill's subsequent parliamentary stages. This will consist of the Chairman of Ways and Means and up to eight other Members nominated by the Speaker.

Programming is said to have the dual advantages of enabling the government to dispose effectively of its legislative agenda for the session at the same time as allowing opposition parties a greater opportunity of ensuring that important elements of a Bill are subjected to some genuine parliamentary scrutiny.

> In short, the government gets its legislation, the Opposition chooses what areas get the focus of debate, and individual members get some greater certainty about the progress of business and the timing of votes (1999–2000, HC 589).

Nineteen Bills were subjected to this procedure in the parliamentary session 2014–15 and 23 in the parliamentary session 2015–16.

European legislation

Much of the law made by the European Union takes effect automatically in the United Kingdom. In the language of the TEU Treaty it is 'directly applicable' in member states. This applies to regulations made by the Council of the EU.

Directives, however, are binding only as to the result to be achieved. Hence they are not directly applicable as and when made. Domestic legislation is required to give effect to them. In the United Kingdom this is done by Act of Parliament or, as in the majority of cases, by subordinate legislation made under s 2(2) of the European Communities Act 1972.

Directives are discussed in Chapter 4.

The system for scrutinising EU legislation and other proposals is based on the principle that Ministers should not accede to such EU initiatives unless and until these have been considered according to the appropriate parliamentary procedures. This is known as the 'scrutiny reserve' and is formally embodied in a number of parliamentary resolutions.

Such parliamentary scrutiny of EU legislation and other affairs in general is exercised in a number of ways. First, government Ministers – particularly in their capacity as Members of the Council of Ministers – are answerable to Parliament in respect of matters relating to the EU. Such matters may be raised by written questions or – on the floor of the House – by oral questions or in debates concerning EU policy or the future development of the European Union. The House is assisted in these functions by six-monthly White Papers relating to European issues.

From 1974 detailed scrutiny of legislative proposals emanating from the EU was the responsibility of the Select Committee on European Legislation. Following the recommendations of the House of Commons Modernisation Committee in 1998, the Select Committee was given wider terms of reference and renamed the European Scrutiny Committee. This is an all-party Select Committee of 16 Members. It meets usually on a weekly basis when Parliament is in session. The Committee's primary function is to receive and consider all documentation and legislative proposals emanating from the EU. In relation to any such document or proposal, the Committee may:

● recommend no further action need be taken;

● recommend that the matter be considered by one of the three European Committees detailed below;

● recommend that the matter be referred for further debate on the floor of the House itself.

The number of EU documents considered by the European Scrutiny Committee for the session 2015–16 was 822. Of these, 33 were debated on the floor of the House.

European Union documents recommended by the European Committee for further consideration by the House are, as a general rule, referred to one of three European Standing Committees. Each has 13 members nominated by the Committee of Selection. The committees do not have a fixed membership and are reconstituted on a regular basis depending on the subject-matter of the particular EU documents they may be dealing with at any particular time. Other MPs may attend and speak but not vote. The three committees and their areas of responsibility, expressed in departmental terms, are as follows:

Committee A

Energy and Climate Change, Environment, Food and Rural Affairs, Transport, Communities and Local Government, Forestry, and similar responsibilities of the Scotland, Wales and Northern Ireland offices.

Committee B

HM Treasury, Work and Pensions, Foreign and Commonwealth Office, International Development, Home Office, Justice. Matters not otherwise allocated.

Committee C

Business, Innovation and Skills, Children, Schools and Families, Culture, Media, Sport and Health.

Delegated legislation

Objective 3

Numerous spheres of human activity are now regulated by various types of rules and orders made by subordinate authorities acting under legislative powers delegated to them by Act of Parliament. Indeed such is the volume of law made in this way, particularly by government departments, that this has become the most prolific source of legal rules operating in the United Kingdom. In historical terms the increase in the importance and use of delegated legislation is a relatively recent phenomenon and has been a feature of the development of the regulatory state.

Reasons for increased use

The particular reasons for this type of legislation are usually explained by reference to the following factors.

(a) Lack of parliamentary time

During the latter half of the nineteenth century as the state began to involve itself in such matters as public health, housing, education and safety at work, it became increasingly apparent that Parliament had neither the time nor the energy to enact all the legislation necessary for the detailed regulation of these activities. As a result, more frequent resort was made to the enactment of Bills setting out general policy objectives and standards, but which left the more detailed rule-making to government, both central and local.

The purpose and value of such delegation for the efficient functioning both of Parliament and of the process of administration was expressed thus in 1877:

> The adoption of the system of confining the attention of Parliament to material provisions only, and leaving details to be settled departmentally, is probably the only mode in which

parliamentary government can . . . be carried on. The province of Parliament is to decide material questions affecting the public interest, and the more procedural and subordinate matters can be withdrawn from their cognisance the greater will be the time afforded for the consideration of the more serious questions involved in legislation (Lord Thring, *Practical Legislation*, 1902).

As the twentieth century progressed and the amount of delegated legislation – or executive law-making – increased, some began to point to the dangers this posed for the preservation of the separation of powers. Fears were expressed that the legislative role of Parliament was being taken over by the executive:

For the doctrine of the Separation of Powers, see Chapter 2, pp. 40–8.

That there is in existence, and in certain quarters in the ascendant, a genuine belief that parliamentary institutions have been tried and found wanting, and that the time has come for the departmental despot, who shall be . . . a law to himself, needs no demonstration (Lord Hewart, *The New Despotism*, 1929).

This was one of the reasons for the creation of the Committee on Ministers' Powers (the Donoughmore Committee) which reported in 1932. In relation to delegated legislation its conclusion was that without it the legislative process would cease to function effectively but that the use of such law-making powers should be subject to effective parliamentary and judicial controls.

(b) Complexity of subject-matter

Parliament does not possess the expertise required to legislate effectively on many of the complex and technical issues which require legal regulation. Thus, for example, while many MPs might have general views on the risks associated with, say, the storage of dangerous chemicals or nuclear waste, it is not likely that these same persons would be possessed of sufficient relevant knowledge to be able to formulate a set of safety laws which would have sufficient practical utility in these particular contexts.

The preparation of legislation on such issues requires detailed discussions between the relevant government department and experts in the field. There is little use in Parliament attempting to legislate specifically on matters which MPs do not understand, nor would the public interest be well served by legal rules which related only imperfectly to the matters to which they were directed.

The details of such technical legislation need the assistance of experts and can be regulated after a Bill passes into an Act by delegated legislation with greater care and minuteness and with a better adaption to local and other special circumstances than they can be in the passage of a Bill through Parliament (Select Committee on Procedure, Sixth Report, 1966–67).

(c) Speed

Regulations may be made more quickly than Acts of Parliament. The use of delegated legislation, therefore, enables the executive to act quickly and appropriately in terms of the legal rules needed to deal with pressing and unforeseen circumstances:

for example, an increase in import duties would lose some of its effect if prior notice was given and importers were able to import large quantities of goods at the old lower rate of duty (ibid).

(d) Flexibility

Acts of Parliament will frequently introduce schemes, particularly in the context of social welfare, which need updating from time to time. It would, for example, be extremely impractical and time-consuming if Parliament had to pass an Act every time it was decided to make a minor alteration to the levels of prescription charges, eligibility for legal aid, or any of the other numerous charges and benefits which the state administers. Such minor changes – providing these are consistent with the overall objectives of the enabling Act – are regarded, therefore, as the function of delegated legislation.

(e) Times of emergency

Despite the normative requirements of the rule of law and the separation of powers, it is generally accepted that a substantial degree of law-making authority should be entrusted to the executive when the state or the community is threatened by, *inter alia*, war, terrorism or natural disasters. The assumption here is that in such times those in government, who may have to act quickly, are best placed to judge what is required in terms of legislation for the protection of the state and its populace.

Dangers of delegated legislation

Delegated legislation may be an established and essential part of an efficient legislative and administrative process but, as its detractors in the early part of the twentieth century made clear, it has its dangers, particularly if no effective restraints on its abuse are in place. Some of the dangers to constitutional propriety sometimes associated with it are listed below.

(a) Government by decree

The fear is that a government could use its majority in Parliament to enact enabling legislation which authorised it to make law on matters of general principle or policy – i.e. not on matters of detail as is believed to be the proper domain of government law-making power. There is no formal control to prevent this nor are there any clear rules as to what is policy and what is detail.

(b) Imposition of taxation.

It has been said that the use of delegated legislation to impose or alter rates of taxation is inconsistent with the requirement in the Bill of Rights 1689 that 'levying money for . . . the Crown . . . without consent of Parliament . . . is illegal'. This prescription is still adhered to in general terms. Hence the requirement of an annual Finance Act to effect major changes in matters relating to revenue and particularly to direct taxation.

Changes to indirect taxation of various types, including VAT, are now effected by virtue of delegated legislative powers. This would appear to be necessitated by the volume and complexity of the legislative rules operating in this context and by the need to have in place a system of law-making which permits ready application of the fiscal policies of the European Union.

(c) Alteration of Acts of Parliament

It is not unknown for an enabling Act to contain a clause which gives to the subordinate law-maker – usually a Minister – the power to make legal rules which alter either the terms of the enabling Act itself or those in other Acts of Parliament. A provision of this type is sometimes referred to as a 'Henry VIII clause', so named because 'that King is regarded popularly as the impersonation of executive autocracy' (Donoughmore Committee, above).

Delegated legislation which permits Ministers to amend primary legislation – that which has been enacted by Parliament – may be acceptable, so long as this is confined to matters of details. Cause for concern may arise, however, where such delegated power is used in relation to matters of substance.

It would appear that if the legal changes necessary to facilitate the Uk's departure from the EU are to be effected with the required expedition and clarity, this may have to be done by the way of Henry VIII process, ie through primary legislation allowing Ministers to make the preponderance of such changes in the form of statutory instruments.

(d) Retrospective effect

As a general rule retrospective legislation is contrary to the rule of law. The expectation is likely, therefore, that any retrospective provisions in a Bill will be the subject of adverse comment and debate in the House before the measure is enacted. However, not all delegated legislation is subject to such close parliamentary scrutiny, nor does it attract great public awareness. The risk of retrospective legislation being introduced in this way, and going unnoticed or unchallenged is, therefore, increased.

(e) Exclusion of judicial review

The importance of this type of legislation, and the potential for abuse of such delegated powers, suggests that at all times it should be open to judicial review on both substantive and procedural grounds.

The availability and effectiveness of judicial control may be negatively affected, however, by:

- wide, subjectively worded enabling provisions – e.g. 'the Minister may make such regulations as he thinks fit';
- the inclusion of an express **ouster clause** (i.e. a clause stating that the validity of regulations made under the Act may not be questioned in the courts).

Principal categories of delegated legislation

(a) Statutory instruments

Statutes which confer legislative powers on specific Ministers will usually provide that the Minister in question may make law in the form of a statutory instrument. Some 2,000 or more of these emanate from government departments annually. Each will contain regulations dealing with the subject-matter of the enabling Act (e.g. Road Traffic).

(b) Orders in Council

Where it is the intention of an enabling Act to confer a legislative power on the government as a whole as distinct from an individual Minister, the Act will usually provide that the power should be exercised by 'the Queen in Council'. Hence the famous provision in the Emergency Powers Act 1920 that, following the making of a proclamation of emergency, it was lawful for His Majesty in Council, by Order, to make regulations for securing the essentials of life to the community.

As with Acts of Parliament, the Monarch's role in making such legislation is purely formal. The legislation will be formulated by the government. The Lord President of the Council (a senior Cabinet Minister) then summons three or four other Ministers to a meeting of the Privy Council presided over by the Monarch. The consent of the Monarch and the Council to the proposed legislation is automatic.

The Order in Council will contain a set of regulations relating to the matter covered by the enabling power. Delegated legislation by Order in Council tends to be reserved for matters of greater importance or constitutional significance than that which is thought to be the proper subject-matter of Ministerial regulations. Hence, for example, Orders in Council may be used to stipulate the date when an Act will take effect, to make changes to the boundaries of parliamentary constituencies (Parliamentary Constituencies Act 1986) or, as indicated, to effect emergency regulations, as under the Civil Contingencies Act 2004. It is also possible for legislative authority conferred in this way to be exercised by whichever Minister(s) appears to be appropriate.

For procedural purposes, Orders in Council are treated as statutory instruments and are, therefore, subject to the Statutory Instruments Act 1946.

Orders in Council made under an Act of Parliament should be distinguished from those issued under the royal prerogative. The latter are a type of primary legislation and are examples of the Monarch's remaining original legislative authority (nowadays limited to certain matters relating to the civil service and armed forces).

(c) By-laws

This is the name given to laws made by local authorities, public corporations or other companies vested with statutory powers.

The enabling power for by-laws made by local authorities is the Local Government Act 1972, s 235. This authorised district councils to 'make byelaws for the good rule and government' of the areas under their control. Such by-laws must be approved by a Secretary of State, usually the Secretary of State for the Environment, Food and Rural Affairs.

(d) Legislative Reform and Remedial Orders

Legislative Reform Orders are made under the Legislative and Regulatory Reform Act 2006. This developed from the earlier provisions in the Deregulation and Contracting Out Act 1994 and the Regulatory Reform Act 2001. The Act allows Ministers to alter or repeal any primary legislation in order to remove any 'burden' imposed on a person or organisation which is disproportionate to the public good achieved. A burden is defined as any:

- financial cost;
- administrative inconvenience;
- obstacle to efficiency, productivity or profitability;
- criminal or other sanction which affects the carrying out of a lawful activity.

Use of the power is limited to circumstances where:

(i)   no non-legislative solution is available;

(ii) the Order is proportionate to the policy objective;

(iii) it strikes a fair balance between the public interest and those directly affected by it;

(iv) it does not remove any protection in provisions relating to health, safety or commercial interests.

Before making an Order, the Minister should consult with appropriate persons or bodies depending on the subject-matter, e.g. the Welsh Assembly or one of the Law Commissions. A draft order with explanatory documentation should then be laid before both Houses of Parliament. The explanatory material should include the Minister's recommendation concerning the appropriate parliamentary procedure for the Order's confirmation. This could be:

For general principles and procedures for parliamentary control of subordinate legislation, see pp. 172–3.

(a) the negative resolution procedure;

(b) the affirmative resolution procedure;

(c) the super-affirmative resolution procedure.

Either House by resolution may require that the procedure to be adopted should be one of the more onerous options than that recommended by the Minister, e.g. the affirmative rather than the negative resolution procedure.

Draft legislative reform orders are scrutinised by dedicated Select Committees in each House. A draft order subject to negative resolution must be laid before both Houses for 40 days. It will not be proceeded with if so recommended by either committee. The House in question may, however, resolve not to follow its committee's recommendation. In this case, the Order may be made after the 40-day period has elapsed.

An Order subject to affirmative resolution must also be laid before both Houses for 40 days. In this case, however, it may not be made unless approved by resolutions. If either Select Committee recommends against approval, no such affirmative resolutions should be passed unless it is resolved not to follow the committee's recommendation.

For the super-affirmative resolution procedure, the Order is laid in draft before both Houses for 60 days. During this period, it will be considered by the Select Committees. Either may recommend that it should not proceed. In this case, no further action will be taken unless the particular committee's recommendation is overruled by resolution. Alternatively, each committee may compile a report on the draft order. This, plus any resolutions passed by either House, and any other representations, must be considered by the Minister before any final version of the Order is made. The Order must then be approved by both Houses.

A Legislative Reform Order may not be used to:

- impose, abolish or vary any tax;
- create any new criminal offence;
- provide any new powers of entry, search or seizure or the giving of evidence under compulsion;
- amend the Legislative and Regulatory Reform Act 2006 itself;
- amend the Human Rights Act 1998;
- remove burdens arising solely from the common law.

A Remedial Order is an Order made under the Human Rights Act 1998 to amend a statutory provision which a court of law has declared to be incompatible with the requirements of the European Convention on Human Rights. Such orders are subject to a detailed process of parliamentary scrutiny similar to that used in the making of Legislative Reform Orders.

Administrative and parliamentary controls

(a) Consultations

A frequent requirement in enabling Acts, particularly those giving the power to make law by statutory instrument, is that when formulating the regulations the Minister responsible should consult with specified organisations and/or other organisations likely to be affected by the same.

The nature of the obligation imposed by a requirement to consult was explained in *R* v *Secretary of State for Social Services, ex parte Association of Metropolitan Authorities* [1986] 1 All ER 164:

> . . . the essence of consultation is the communication of a genuine invitation to give advice and a genuine receipt of that advice. In my view it must go without saying that to achieve consultation sufficient information must be supplied by the consulting to the consulted party to enable it to tender helpful advice. Sufficient time must be given . . . to enable it to do that, and sufficient time must be available for such advice to be considered. (per Webster J)

Even if an Act contains no obligation to consult it is usual administrative practice to consult those who may be involved in, or affected by, its implementation.

> No Minister in his right senses with the fear of Parliament before his eyes would even think of making regulations without . . . giving the persons who will be affected thereby . . . an opportunity of saying what they think about the proposal (Sir W.G. Harrison, *Evidence to the Committee on Ministers' Powers*, 1932).

(b) Publicity

The Statutory Instruments Act 1946, s 2(1), as amended by the Statutory Instruments (Production and Sale) Act 1996, provides that every statutory instrument (which definition includes Orders in Council) must be printed and sold by, or under the authority of, the King's printers of Acts of Parliament.

Where the contravention of a statutory instrument amounts to a criminal offence, it is a defence to prove that the instrument, or any relevant part of it, was not published and that no other reasonable steps had been taken to bring its content to the defendant's notice (s 3(2)).

(c) Parliamentary scrutiny

Most enabling Acts will require that statutory instruments made pursuant to them should be laid before Parliament (i.e. presented to the Votes and Proceedings Office in the House of Commons and the Office of the Clerk of the Parliaments in the House of Lords) according to one of the following procedures.

1 Laying subject to the negative resolution procedure

This is the procedure most commonly required by enabling Acts and is used for in excess of some 70 per cent of all statutory instruments.

The procedure's exact requirements are set out in the Statutory Instruments Act 1946, s 5. The instrument should be laid before Parliament for a period of 40 days. If either House passes an annulment or negative resolution in that period, the instrument ceases to have effect.

Note that (although there is some uncertainty on this point) a statutory instrument made according to this procedure probably takes effect at the time it is laid before Parliament. Thus it does not take effect as soon as it is made by the Minister (i.e. before it is laid), nor does it have to wait to become effective until the 40-day laying period has expired.

This is the most favoured procedure as it preserves parliamentary control without any unnecessary wastage of time. This is because a debate and vote in either House is only necessary in relation to that small minority of instruments to which particular objection has been taken.

Where a Member gives notice of intention to pray for the annulment of a particular resolution, the subsequent debate may take place in a Public Bill Committee. This was a new procedure introduced in the 1996–97 session.

2 Laying subject to the affirmative resolution procedure

This tends to be used for instruments which may relate to a matter of principle or possible political controversy – e.g. those which contain emergency regulations under the Civil Contingencies Act 2004 or which give effect to legislation for Northern Ireland under the Northern Ireland Act 1974.

The enabling Act will specify the period for which the instrument must be laid before one or both Houses. An affirmative resolution or resolutions must then be passed within that period if the instrument is to take effect.

While this procedure preserves effective parliamentary control over the delegated legislation subject to it, its use involves the allocation of precious parliamentary time to each instrument laid in this way.

3 Laying in draft subject to negative or affirmative resolutions

An instrument laid in draft, subject to the negative resolution procedure, cannot be made or become effective until the draft has been laid before Parliament and fortyx days have elapsed without an annulment resolution having been passed by either House.

An instrument laid in draft, subject to the affirmative resolution procedure, cannot be made or become effective until the required affirmative resolutions have been passed within the specified period.

All instruments laid before Parliament are subject to scrutiny by the Joint Committee on Statutory Instruments (seven Members from each House). The committee is charged with deciding whether a particular instrument should be drawn to the attention of the House on any of the following grounds:

- it imposes a tax or charge on public revenues;
- the enabling Act seeks to exclude it from judicial review;
- it purports to have retrospective effect without clear authority in the enabling Act;
- there appears to have been unjustifiable delay in its publication or laying before Parliament;
- it may be *ultra vires* or appears to make an unusual or unexpected use of the enabling power;
- it appears to have been drafted defectively;
- it requires elucidation on any other ground.

For the Merits of Statutory Instruments Committee, see p. 211.

Subordinate legislation required to be laid before Parliament may also be considered by the House of Lords Merits of Statutory Instruments Committee.

Delegated legislation and English votes for English laws

The EVEL procedure reforms of 2015 apply to the following types of statutory instruments and orders certified as affecting England only or England and Wales only:

(a) instruments laid before the House of Commons subject to an affirmative resolution;

(b) instruments laid before the House subject to a negative resolution;

(c) draft orders made under the Regulatory Reform Act 2001 or the Localism Act 2011 and laid subject to affirmative resolution.

The principal EVEL prescription here is that the parliamentary resolutions required to bring into effect instruments of types (a) and (c) above, and those required to nullify instruments of type (b), must all be supported by double majorities (ie majorities of all MPs and of English MPs in the same votes) when a vote is taken on the floor of the House.

Judicial supervision

A court may find a statutory instrument to be *ultra vires* and invalid on either substantive or procedural grounds.

An instrument will be *ultra vires* in the substantive sense if it deals with matters beyond the scope of the legislative authority conferred by the enabling Act. Particularly important in this context are certain judicial presumptions as to the intentions of Parliament when it confers delegated legislative powers. Thus it is presumed that, unless clear authority (by express words or necessary implication) is contained in the enabling Act, Parliament does not intend such powers to be used to:

- impose a tax (*Attorney-General* v *Wilts United Dairies Ltd* (1921) 37 TLR 884);
- deny or restrict the citizen's right of access to the courts (*Chester* v *Bateson* [1920] 1 KB 829);
- make law having retrospective effect (*Malloch* v *Aberdeen Corporation* 1974 SLT 253);
- restrict basic civil liberties or human rights (*Raymond* v *Honey* [1983] 1 AC 1).

A number of the above principles were applied by the Supreme Court in *Ahmed* v *HM Treasury* [2010] UKSC 2. The case involved a challenge to the validity of the Terrorism (United Nations Measures) Order 2006. The Order had been made under the United Nations Act 1946, s 1. This authorised the making of such orders to give domestic effect to UN resolutions. In this instance, the UN resolution required member states to take steps to 'freeze' or otherwise deny access to any financial assets in their jurisdiction belonging to persons who 'commit or attempt to commit acts of terrorism'. The 2006 Order had sought to implement the UN's objectives by enabling the British authorities to take the prescribed action against any funds held in the United Kingdom by persons the government had reasonable grounds for suspecting of the type of activity referred to in the resolution. The Supreme Court took the view that the UK government could not use a statutory power to make subordinate legislation giving effect to UN resolutions in order to:

(a) achieve a wider purpose than that contemplated by the resolution in issue, i.e. in this case to authorise action against the assets of those merely suspected of terrorist involvement;

(b) to curtail the rights of the individual where the enabling Act provided no express or implied authority to do so and where this was not absolutely necessary to implement the requirements contained in the UN resolution.

A statutory instrument may also be struck down for unreasonableness if it represents a use of the enabling power which is so outrageous or extraordinary that it could not have been intended by Parliament (*Sparks* v *Edward Ash* [1943] KB 223).

In the past courts have generally shown considerable reluctance to question instruments which have been laid before and approved by Parliament except in cases of extreme bad faith, improper purpose or manifest absurdity (*R* v *Secretary of State for the Environment, ex parte Hammersmith and Fulham LBC* [1991] 1 AC 521).

A statutory instrument may be *ultra vires* on procedural grounds if made in breach of a mandatory procedural requirement. Whether Parliament intended such requirement to be mandatory or merely directory is a matter of statutory construction. The preponderance of judicial and academic opinion suggests that a requirement to consult should be construed to be mandatory. Hence a failure to consult may result in the instrument in question being ruled to be invalid (*Agricultural, Horticultural and Forestry Industry Training Board* v *Aylesbury Mushrooms Ltd* [1972] 1 WLR 190).

For distinction between mandatory and directory procedural requirements see Chapter 15.

The consequences of a failure to publish a statutory instrument or to lay it before Parliament, where so required, are not entirely clear. Judicial comment suggests that where an instrument is not published according to the Statutory Instruments Act 1946, s 2(1), and no other reasonable steps are taken to make its content known, the instrument is probably invalid or at least ineffective (*Johnson* v *Sargant* [1918] 1 KB 101). This implies, however, that if such reasonable steps have been taken then the instrument may be effective notwithstanding the failure to publish in the statutory or formal sense (*R* v *Sheer Metalcraft* [1954] 1 QB 586). It would appear, therefore, that the publication requirement imposed by the 1946 Act should be understood as directory only.

In relation to a requirement to lay an instrument before Parliament, there is judicial authority for the view that this also should be regarded as directory only (*Bailey* v *Williamson* (1873) LR 8 QBD 118). Such a view does not, however, sit particularly easily with the provision in the Statutory Instruments Act 1946, s 4 that an instrument which is required to be laid before Parliament does not come into effect until this has been done.

The above grounds of review apply particularly to statutory instruments. The validity of a by-law may be challenged if:

(a) in its terms and application it goes beyond the ambit of the delegated law-making power (*R* v *Reading Crown Court, ex parte Hutchinson* [1988] QB 384);

(b) it was made in breach of a mandatory procedural requirement, e.g. lack of Ministerial consent (no case directly on this point);

(c) it is inconsistent with a provision in an Act of Parliament (*Powell* v *May* [1946] KB 330), or repugnant to a basic tenet of the common law (*London Passenger Transport Board* v *Sumner* (1935) 99 JP 387);

(d) it is unreasonable in the sense explained in *Kruse* v *Johnson* [1898] 2 QB 91, i.e. it is 'partial and unequal . . . as between different classes . . . manifestly unjust . . . disclosed bad faith . . . [or] involved such oppressive or gratuitous interference with the rights of those subject to them as could find no justification in the minds of reasonable men' (per Lord Russell CJ);

(e) it is so vague in its terminology that its exact meaning or scope of application cannot be readily ascertained (*Scott* v *Pilliner* [1904] 2 KB 855; *Percy* v *Hall* [1997] 3 WLR 573);

(f) it is inconsistent with European Union law (*Johnston* v *Chief Constable of the Royal Ulster Constabulary* [1987] QB 129 (ECJ)).

Scrutiny of executive action

Introduction

Objective 4

In addition to debating and amending the government's legislative proposals, the House of Commons is also concerned with the efficiency and propriety of the day-to-day working of the process of administration. Through a variety of procedures, therefore, the House seeks to examine the activities of those who are responsible for the making and implementation of government policy. The principal procedural devices used for this purpose are:

(a) Question Time;

(b) debates;

(c) select committees.

There were 40,696 questions of all types tabled in the parliamentary session for 2015–16.

Parliamentary questions

These allow Members to question Ministers on a topic of their own choosing. Most of these are answered in written form. There are four categories of parliamentary questions:

(a) Questions for oral answers.

(b) Questions for written answers.

(c) Urgent questions.

(d) Cross-cutting questions.

(a) Questions for oral answers ('starred' questions)

Oral questions provide Members with a rare, and much valued, opportunity to question Ministers on the floor of the House. This occurs at Question Time which occupies 50 to 60 minutes at the beginning of public business on Mondays to Thursdays inclusive. Questions are dealt with at 2.30–3.30 pm on Mondays and Tuesdays, 11.30 am–12.30 pm on Wednesdays, and 9.30–11.30 am on Thursdays. There were 4,742 questions for oral answers tabled in the session 2015–16.

A Member gives notice of a question either by handing it to the Clerks in the Table Office (the place where, in addition to questions, motions and amendments are formally presented to the House) or to the Clerk at the Table of the House directly in front of the Speaker's chair. The Clerks ensure that questions comply with the rules of the House and advise on amendment where this is not the case. Three days' notice must be given.

No more than eight starred questions may be posed by any one Member in any ten-day period and no more than two may be tabled for any one day. These latter two cannot be put to the same Minister. A Member may ask one 'supplementary' question for each question posed. Further supplementaries may be put by other Members at the discretion of the Speaker.

Around 15 to 20 oral starred questions may be answered although it is not uncommon for many more to be tabled. Starred questions not answered orally receive written answers unless the MP wishes a question to be deferred for later oral answer. Questions to particular Ministers are 'grouped' so that they may all be dealt with on the same day.

The order in which a particular day's questions are put is determined in a formal ballot known in Parliamentary language as the 'shuffle'. This is held three days in advance of the Question Time to which it relates. The questions are shuffled electronically. The number of questions which may be put to a particular Minister will depend on the length of time they are scheduled to appear at the despatch box. Since 2003, this has been fixed as shown in Table 8.1.

Prime Minister's questions were introduced in 1961. From 1997 to 2003 these were taken on Wednesdays from 3.00 to 3.30 pm. Following a change made in 2003, the time for 'PMQs' was moved to Wednesdays, from 12.00 to 12.35 pm.

There is no requirement to provide notice of the questions to be asked. The majority of MPs merely ask the PM to list his engagements for the day. Supplementary questions may relate to any aspect of government business or national affairs – very often pertaining to some issue of immediate concern. The Leader of the Opposition is permitted up to six supplementaries to any question he may have posed.

Until 1962, there was no limit on the duration of Question Time, no rota of Ministers, and no limit on the number of questions a Member could ask. Due, however, to the popularity of the procedure and the steady increase in the number of questions being asked, this position became untenable. The rules regulating the procedure, outlined above, were the result.

The conduct of any Question Time owes much to the influence of the Speaker. If too many supplementaries are allowed the Minister may be put under close scrutiny but many questions lower down in the priority list may go unanswered (in oral form at least). On the other hand, if too few supplementaries are called, the Minister may not really be extended.

Since 2007, and following a recommendation by the House of Commons Modernisation Committee, Members have been permitted to ask questions on current issues of public interest without having to give the usual period of notice. These are known as 'Topical Questions' and in any Question Time are taken during the last 15 minutes for those departments that answer questions for 60 minutes, and the last 10 minutes for those that answer for 40 minutes.

Table 8.1 Number of questions allowed

Time in despatch box	Number of questions
55 minutes	25 questions
50 minutes	20 questions
45 minutes	20 questions
30 minutes	15 questions
15 minutes	10 questions
10 minutes	8 questions

(b) Questions for written answers

These may be divided into three types:

(i) Ordinary written questions. These normally request an answer for two days after the day on which they are tabled. There is a convention that such questions should be answered within seven days but there is no absolute rule requiring an answer within a specified period.

(ii) Named day questions. It is expected that these will be answered on the date specified when the question is tabled. A minimum of two days' notice must be given. No more than five such questions may be tabled for any one day.

(iii) Questions for oral answers not dealt with at the Question Time for which they were tabled.

Written questions should be submitted at the Table Office, sent by post or tabled electronically by the parliamentary intranet.

There were 35,956 questions for written answers tabled in the session 2015–16.

(c) Urgent questions

These raise matters requiring an immediate Ministerial response. Advance notice is not required. Applications to ask such questions are made to the speaker on the day they are to be put (Mondays and Tuesdays, before 12 pm; Wednesdays, before 10.30 am; Thursdays, before 9.30 am). Such questions must relate to an urgent matter of public importance. Urgent questions were known previously as Private Notice Questions.

The Speaker will consider the MPs' representations and will take into account the Minister's views concerning the urgency of the matter before making his/her decision.

There were 77 urgent questions accepted by the Speaker in 2015–16.

(d) Cross-cutting questions

This is a new form of question first used in **Westminster Hall** in 2003. They enable Members to raise matters which affect more than one government department, i.e. they cut across the boundaries of departmental responsibilities.

Out of order questions

Questions may be ruled out of order on the following grounds:

- they do not relate to the exercise of the Minister's statutory or prerogative powers;
- they involve discussion of the role or reputation of the sovereign;
- they request a statement of opinion of law;
- they constitute statements and not questions;
- they refer to issues dealt with during a debate in the current session;
- they refer to a matter which is *sub judice*;
- the questions were asked in the previous three months;
- they relate to the date for dissolution;
- they relate to a matter pending in committee;
- they relate to a matter devolved to the Scottish, Irish or Welsh Assemblies.

Other grounds for refusing to answer

Answers have been withheld on the following grounds:

- the cost of finding information would be excessive;
- providing the information could be damaging to national security;
- the question relates to confidential exchanges between governments;
- the question relates to matters of commercial or contractual confidentiality;
- the question relates to the details of arms sales;
- the question seeks to elicit details of budgetary proposals;
- the question relates to the private affairs of an individual (except where these are the cause of public mischief);
- the question seeks to elicit information concerning the existence of particular Cabinet committees.

In the parliamentary session 2015–16, a total of 40,698 questions and 77 urgent questions were tabled; 4,742 of these were for oral answer and 35,956 for written answer only; 3,603 of the oral questions were given an answer on the floor of the House.

Merits of Question Time

(a) It is the only regular occasion upon which the government is formally and constitutionally required and obliged to account to Parliament for its management of the nation's affairs.

(b) It provides an opportunity for the opposition to select issues which may embarrass and discredit the government.

(c) It represents a formal manifestation and reinforcement of the convention of Ministerial responsibility.

If it were not for Question Time Ministerial responsibility would be even more difficult to enforce. It represents the only procedural device which ensures that Ministers appear regularly before the whole House to answer specific questions about current local, national and departmental affairs.

(d) It provides a rare opportunity for backbench MPs to question Ministers on issues of their own choosing. Other proceedings are dominated by the front benches.

(e) It allows MPs to raise local and regional issues in full parliamentary session with the government present.

(f) It provides a test of Ministerial competence and an opportunity for junior Ministers to impress.

(g) It makes Ministers aware of issues which otherwise might not have attracted their attention.

(h) It provides MPs with an opportunity to publicise incidents of government deceit.

The preparation of parliamentary answers takes precedence over all other departmental business. Permanent Secretaries check and must approve all answers before submission to Ministers. These prepared answers and statistical information will be studied by Ministers to ensure that they are able to 'field' and deal competently with whatever supplementary questions may be put.

Demerits

(a) It lasts for 50–60 minutes only, four times a week. Prime Minister's questions on Wednesday is just 35 minutes' duration.

(b) The operation of the rota limits the opportunities to question senior Ministers.

(c) The restraints on time and the number of questions and supplementaries which may be asked makes 'in depth' questioning impossible.

(d) Questions on a wide range of sensitive issues may be ruled out of order. Frequently, the spectre of national security or the *sub judice* rule will be invoked to avoid having to give answers.

(e) Government backbenchers often 'feed' questions to Ministers in order to:
- reduce the time for opposition questions;
- enable a Minister to make an announcement or to provide information which may flatter the government (e.g. a fall in unemployment);
- enable a Minister to defend or explain a decision or policy initiative.

(f) Questions must relate to topics within the parameters of Ministerial responsibility. Thus, for example, the 'day-to-day' activities of local authorities, public authorities and the police may not be raised.

Debates

The following constitute the major opportunities for the House to debate aspects of government policy.

- The Second Reading stage of the legislative process.
- Substantive motions for debate moved by the government where approval is sought for some aspect of government policy.

- Substantive motions for debate moved by the opposition, usually critical of some aspect of government policy, in the 20 Opposition Days (17 for topics chosen by the main opposition party and 3 for the topics selected by the second largest opposition party).

- The address in Reply to the Queen's Speech. The topics for debate are chosen by the opposition. This may go on for five or six days.

- The debate following the Budget proposals. This may also continue for four to six days.

- The three Estimates Days. The particular estimates to be debated are chosen by the Liaison Committee. Such debates tend to concentrate on the general areas of government policy and expenditure to which the estimates in question relate. Restraints of time and complexity militate against any more detailed analysis of whether the envisaged return or objective of the expenditure represents value for money. The debates may, however, be informed by reports from the relevant Select Committees.

- Adjournment debates immediately following the passage of Consolidated Fund Bills. Topics are chosen by backbenchers through ballot. These may entail all-night sittings.

- Recess adjournment debates. These debates take place on the last day before the House goes into recess. Topics are chosen by backbenchers subject to the discretion of the Speaker.

- Daily adjournment debates. These take place during the last half hour of each day's proceedings (Monday 10.00–10.30; Tuesday and Wednesday, 7.00–7.30; Thursday, 5.00–5.30). Topics for debate are chosen by backbenchers through ballot or at the discretion of the Speaker in the case of the Thursday adjournment debate.

- Emergency adjournment debates under Standing Order (SO) 9. These are moved by any Member after Questions and must raise specific and important matters that should have urgent consideration. If accepted by the Speaker the debate takes place on the same or following day. Should 40 or more MPs support the motion the debate must take place. If supported by between 10 and 40 MPs, the House may decide by division.

- Motions of censure to which the government has submitted or which are forced upon it by defeat in the House.

- Government adjournment debates. A Member of the government may move the adjournment of the House to facilitate a more wide-ranging general debate than is possible with a substantive motion.

- Private Members' motions. These usually take place on eight Fridays per session and four other half-days (usually Mondays). The opportunity to table such motions is determined by ballot among MPs.

For the Liaison Committee see p. 184 below.

Merits

(a) They force Ministers to explain and justify policy initiatives to the House.

> They may want to reveal as little as possible, but the government cannot afford to hold back too much for fear of letting the opposition appear to have the better argument. (Norton, *The Commons in Perspective*)

(b) They provide an opportunity for the opposition to expose flaws in government policy/ decisions and to present counter-arguments and suggestions for dealing with particular aspects of national affairs.

(c) They help to educate public opinion by presenting a variety of opinions and remedies for dealing with national concerns, e.g. the arguments for and against the UK's position in the EU, Scottish independence, etc.

(d) They provide an opportunity for disaffected Members on the government side to display dissent, thus embarrassing the government and perhaps causing policy concessions to be made.

(e) They provide a platform for the enhancement and making of parliamentary reputations.

(f) They give MPs an opportunity to present the views of constituents and interest groups.

Demerits

(a) The parliamentary timetable is arranged by government in consultation with the opposition. In the main, therefore, it is the government, not Parliament, that decides what will be debated and when. Otherwise, the opposition has the 20 Opposition Days and 3 days for the Estimates when it is able to choose the subject for debate. Again, however, this is largely a matter for the Shadow Cabinet and not for Opposition backbenchers.

(b) Most debates are dominated by frontbench speakers. Often MPs who wish to speak will not be called.

(c) Parliament lacks the time in any one session to:
- fully debate all issues of public concern;
- debate all crises or controversies as and when they arise;
- debate in detail all aspects and elements of new legislative measures.

(d) Legislative debates may be curtailed by the use of the 'guillotine' (allocation of time motion). The strange paradox is that the more significant and controversial a Bill is, the more likely it is to be guillotined.

(e) Debates appear to have very little immediate effect in terms of influencing government thinking or action.

(f) The content of debates appears to have very little effect on the way MPs vote. Most MPs will vote according to the 'whip', notwithstanding the quality of opposing arguments.

(g) They are often poorly attended as, in addition to the above:
- in any division or vote the government's majority will usually prevail;
- the primary role of backbench MPs, from the party's perspective, is to vote rather than speak – hence it is not unusual for MPs absent during debate to appear and vote when division bells ring;
- the quality of debate may be adversely affected by the practice of MPs reading prepared speeches rather than listening and responding to the different arguments used.

(h) They attract little public attention. Most people are largely unaware of what is happening in Parliament on a day-to-day basis. Only a minority of the electorate read the 'serious' newspapers which contain coverage of parliamentary proceedings. Also television coverage is limited and regulated by a strict code of conduct (imposed by both Houses) which restricts what programme makers may broadcast or record.

(i) Policy is formed and decisions are made before parliamentary debates take place. The government's perceived responsibility and role in debate is to defend its policies and decisions regardless of the merits of alternative proposals or the exposure of any defects in its own case. Hence, due to this adversarial approach, debates are not generally regarded as 'seminars' from which governments could learn and incorporate useful ideas into their own plans.

(j) It has been suggested that lobbying by interest groups may have greater impact on governments than views expressed during parliamentary debates.

Westminster Hall

In recent years the House of Commons has also held meetings in an additional chamber known as Westminster Hall. This followed a recommendation of the Select Committee on Modernisation of the House in its 1998–99 report (HC 194) that a new parallel chamber would relieve pressure on the floor of the House and give ordinary MPs an increased opportunity to contribute to debates.

The first sitting of Westminster Hall took place on Tuesday 30 November 1999. Current sitting hours are 4.30–7.30 pm (Mondays); 9.30–11.30 am and 2.30–5.30 pm, Tuesdays and Wednesdays; 1.30–4.30 pm, Thursdays. Business on Tuesdays and Thursdays is usually devoted to Private Members' debates while Thursday is generally used for discussion of Select Committee reports.

The Hall is laid out in an elongated horseshoe shape as part of a deliberate attempt to encourage a less partisan atmosphere than that prevailing in the House of Commons. Meetings in Westminster Hall are chaired by a deputy Speaker.

Select Committees

Nature

These are smaller than Public Bill Committees and usually consist of up to 15 MPs with the various parties being represented according to their proportion of seats in the House of Commons. They are given specific terms of reference (frequently to perform some type of inquiry or fact-finding exercise) and such other powers as the House considers appropriate. Such committees may be appointed from and by either House, or joint committees from both Houses may be formed.

Types

(a) Ad hoc Select Committees

These are appointed to investigate and report on specific topics, e.g. the Select Committees on political and constitutional reform 2010, and Members' expenses 2011.

(b) Regular or permanent Select Committees

The House of Commons has some 15 such committees which are appointed for every session. These include the **Public Accounts Committee**, the Select Committee on European Legislation, the Statutory Instruments Committee, the Select Committee on the Parliamentary Commissioner and the Select Committees for Standards and for Privileges.

Also falling within this category would be a variety of committees concerned with the internal affairs of the House, e.g. the Select Committees on Finance and Services, Selection, and Procedure.

(c) Departmental Select Committees

These scrutinise the activities of central government departments, each department being 'shadowed' by the appropriate Select Committee.

Usually in the region of 15 to 20 of these will be in operation at any one time. The exact number will vary as new government departments are established and others merged, etc.

Membership and workings of departmental Select Committees

The current Select Committees have between 11 and 16 members. Select Committee chairmen/women are elected by the House at the start of every Parliament. Other members of Select Committees are chosen by their parliamentary parties in secret ballot. In party-political terms, the composition of each committee must represent the different strengths of the parties in terms of Commons seats. The Chairs of Select Committees are elected by the whole House. The choice is made within the parameters of an overall inter-party agreement distributing chairs between the main parties – again, according to their strengths on the floor of the House. Each chair receives an additional parliamentary salary (currently £15,025 pa). By convention all committee members will be backbench MPs.

The committees investigate matters of their own choosing. They issue annual and special reports. Evidence and information is obtained from a wide range of sources, e.g. from Ministers, civil servants, representatives of interest groups and public authorities, academics, members of the public, etc. Hearings are usually open to the public and sometimes away from Westminster (occasionally abroad). Hearings may be broadcast on radio or television.

Government departments are expected to reply to committee reports within 60 days unless a longer period has been agreed with the committee. Some reports will be debated on the floor of the House. Two will normally be debated on each of the three annual Estimates days. Select Committee reports may also be debated on Thursday afternoons in Westminster Hall.

The chairpersons of all the Select Committees meet as the Liaison Committee. This decides which reports may be debated on the floor of the House, approves expenditure or oversees visits and considers any other matters relating to the workings and composition of the various committees. Since 2002, the Prime Minister has attended the committee twice yearly to discuss international and domestic affairs. Any person who refuses to comply with an order from a Select Committee may be referred to the full House which may decide whether a contempt of parliament has been committed and, if so, what, if any, sanction should be imposed.

As of summer 2016, there were 20 such committees. These were: Business, Innovation and Skills; Communities and Local Government; Culture, Media and Sport; Defence; Education; Energy and Climate Change; Environment, Food and Rural Affairs; Foreign Affairs; Health; Home Affairs; International Development; Justice; Northern Ireland; Science and Technology; Scottish Affairs; Transport; Treasury; Welsh Affairs; Women and Equality; Work and Pensions.

For more on the senior sessional Select Committees, see pp. 193, 243 and 167.

In addition to the above there was also a significant number of 'domestic' and other non-departmental Select Committees, some representing joint committees with the House of Lords.

In general terms, these fell into three categories:

(i) senior sessional Select Committees including the Public Accounts Committee, the Committee on Standards, the Select Committee for Privileges, and the European Scrutiny Committee;

(ii) ad hoc Select Committees set up to report on particular issues of current public concern, e.g. the Committee on Issues of Privilege (Police Searches on the Parliamentary Estate) – the Damien Green case, the Members' Allowances Committee and the Political and Constitutional Reform Committee;

(iii) internal committees dealing with the internal management and administration of the House, and with the functions and activities of backbench Members, e.g. Finance and Services Committee (budget and expenditure of the House); Backbench Committee (matters for debate in time allocated to backbench MPs).

Merits

(a) They provide a systematic infrastructure of committees for the detailed scrutiny of the conduct of government departments.

(b) They are the only parliamentary forum in which Ministers and other public servants (including civil servants) may be questioned 'in depth' by backbench MPs on topics not predetermined by party leaders.

(c) To a greater extent than during proceedings on the floor of the House, MPs in Select Committees regard themselves as working for Parliament and not just for their party. Hence in committee the adversarial party-political atmosphere that pervades the House of Commons is not so evident. In Select Committees, MPs are more prepared to act collectively across party lines, and thus to pursue a more objective and, therefore, credible approach in their investigations.

(d) Departmental Select Committees are able to elicit information which otherwise would not have been made available to MPs. The information thus acquired enables MPs to be more informed during debates and to ask more incisive questions.

(e) The committees enable backbench MPs to develop expertise in a particular sphere of public policy which would otherwise have been difficult for them to acquire.

(f) Interest groups concentrate considerable attention on the numerous advisory committees working for government departments and, prior to the introduction of departmental Select Committees in 1979, had decreasing confidence in the ability of Parliament to influence government policy. However, increased lobbying of Select Committees suggests that many interest groups now regard the same as being a useful means of transmitting views and ideas to the policy-makers.

(g) Through their investigations and related research the committees have produced useful 'banks' of information for future reference by MPs, interest groups and the government itself. Thus the 1981 Defence Committee Report on Polaris replacement options (Trident) is regarded as a classic appraisal of the arguments for and against the nuclear deterrent.

(h) Many MPs appear to regard membership of Select Committees as a springboard to promotion. Accordingly, membership is sought after and attendance is high.

(i) The reports attract a considerable amount of media attention particularly when, as is often the case, they are critical of the government.

Demerits

(a) Select Committees cannot impose any sanctions or other direct pressures on government as in the United States where Congressional Committees may withhold finance from Departments of State if dissatisfied with their conduct. It has been suggested that they should be empowered to reduce departmental estimates. At present, however, the report and its attendant publicity is their only weapon.

(b) Few of their reports are debated in Parliament.

(c) The Conservative administrations in power until 1997 did not accept that Select Committees could:

    (i) demand attendance of Ministers;

    (ii) question the civil service about 'conduct' (i.e. individual actions and decisions), or about:

- interdepartmental exchanges
- discussions in Cabinet committees
- advice given by law officers
- confidential information concerning private affairs of individuals or institutions
- national security.

(d) Civil servants have also been told 'to avoid giving written evidence about or discussion of the following matters':

- 'questions in the field of political controversy';
- 'sensitive information of a commercial or economic character';
- 'matters which may be the subject of sensitive negotiations';
- 'matters which are *sub judice*'.

(See Guidance for Officials Appearing Before Select Committees, 1980 – the 'Osmotherly Rules'.)

(e) They have inadequate numbers of research staff, resources and facilities. Parliament does not, like the US Congress, possess a 'counter-bureaucracy'.

Other relevant parliamentary procedures

Written petitions

The right of the people to petition the King, and later Parliament, is of ancient origins and is generally believed to have originated in Anglo-Saxon times. It is known to have been used after the Conquest (1066) to enable causes and grievances to be brought before the King in Council (*Curia Regis*). In Magna Carta it was recognised as an important right of all 'free men'. Later, in 1689, its essential constitutional value was boldly asserted in the articles of the Bill of Rights.

> That it is the right of the subjects to petition the King, and all commitments and prosecutions for such petitioning are illegal.

As time progressed, and in a society in which most people were not eligible to vote, the practice of petitioning Parliament became accepted as a readily available and not entirely ineffective means of transmitting grievances and causes to the highest levels of government and decision-making.

Simply in terms of the number of petitions presented, this method of bringing popular grievances and causes before the nation's representative assembly reached its zenith in the nineteenth century. The highest figure for a single parliamentary session, recorded in 1843, was 22,898. Some of the great issues brought before Parliament in this way included: slavery (100 petitions in 1788); parliamentary reform (24,492 petitions between 1825 and 1831); and votes for women (first women's suffrage petition 1865, 1,550 signatures). Perhaps the most famous of all such petitions was that presented to Parliament by the Chartist Movement in 1842. The petition contained over three million signatures and is believed to have exceeded six miles in length.

By the end of the 1800s, however, and with the extensions of the franchise in 1832, 1867 and 1884, the volume of petitions began to decline – a trend which continued apace in the early years of the twentieth century. Following the 1912–13 parliamentary session, in which nearly 10,000 petitions were presented against the Established Church (Wales) Bill (disestablishment of the Anglican Church in Wales), the number of petitions presented in a single session in Parliament exceeded 1,000 only once. Indeed, at some times during the 1900s, the petitioning of Parliament fell to its lowest level for centuries. The number of written petitions in session 2014–15 was 166.

E-petitions

The process of petitioning Parliament staged a revival in the period towards the end of the twentieth century. The average number submitted per session in the 1990s was just over 392. In the first ten years of the present century the figure was 175. The apparent inconsistency between the two figures is explained by the submission of 2,651 petitions in a single session in 1992–93.

In 2008 the Procedure Committee recommended the adoption of a modern e-petitions system which would retain and enhance the relationship between petitioners and constituency MPs.

Implementation of the scheme was announced by the Leader of the House of Commons on 29 July 2011. The website for the submission of e-petitions to the House of Commons (http://epetitions.direct.gov.uk/) went live on 4 August 2011.

Once submitted, an e-petition may stay 'open' for up to twelve months but may be closed by the petitioner at any time. Should an e-petition receive more than 100,000 signatures, it will be sent to the House of Commons where it will be remitted to the House of Commons Backbench Business Committee. The Committee will decide if it is to be debated on the floor of the House.

By the end of 2016, a total of 86,335 e-petitions had been submitted under the scheme. Of these, 41,880 had been accepted for publication, 2,377 had received 1,000 or more signatories, and 45 had been debated in Parliament.

Private correspondence

Members' letters are dealt with at the highest levels within government departments. Ministers are aware that their answers may appear in the media or may be raised in the House. There is no limit on the number of supplementaries. It has been claimed that this is a more effective means of eliciting information than Question Time. Major public service departments may receive thousands of questions per month from MPs.

Scottish and Welsh affairs at Westminster

The creation of the Scottish Parliament, and the devolution to it of wide legislative competence, has not entirely removed the Westminster Parliament from involvement in Scottish affairs. It remains responsible for 'reserved' matters and for the broad oversight of all the other legislative and policy issues outside the devolved areas.

For 'reserved' matters, see pp. 24–31.

Scottish business in the House is currently disposed of as follows:

(a) Parliamentary questions may be put to the Secretary of State for Scotland in the normal way. The Minister will appear at Question Time every four weeks, approximately for 15 minutes – a reduction from the full hour prior to devolution.

(b) Short general debates, the Second Reading of exclusively Scottish Bills, and further questions, may be dealt with by the Scottish Grand Committee, consisting of all 59 Scottish MPs.

(c) The Committee stage of exclusively Scottish legislation will be referred to one of two Scottish Public Bill Committees.

(d) The workings and estimates of the Scotland Office are scrutinised by the Scottish Affairs Select Committee.

The arrangements for Welsh business are not radically different. As with Scottish matters, questions may be put on the floor of the House to the Welsh Secretary when he/she appears at Question Time. Other questions, short debates and the Second Reading of Welsh Bills may also be dealt with in the Welsh Grand Committee (all Welsh MPs and five others). There are no Welsh Public Bill Committees.

Northern Irish affairs at Westminster

As with the Scottish Assembly, the devolution of legislative power to Northern Ireland was partial only. The Westminster Parliament retains the right to legislate for Northern Ireland in 'reserved' matters and to debate and consider Northern Irish matters in general outside the devolved areas.

Northern Irish business at Westminster is conducted in the following ways:

(a) The Secretary of State for Northern Ireland will appear at Question Time every four weeks approximately.

(b) Northern Ireland affairs may be debated in the Northern Ireland Grand Committee consisting of all 18 Northern Irish MPs and not more than 25 others. The Committee may also deal with Northern Irish Questions and the Second Reading of Northern Irish bills.

(c) The activities and workings of the Northern Ireland Office are scrutinised by the Select Committee for Northern Ireland Affairs.

Financial proceedings

History and significance

Governments cannot function without raising and spending money.

Objective 5

Parliament came into existence in the thirteenth century. From these earliest days one of its most important functions – indeed its *raison d'être* – was the granting of supply (money) to the executive ('the king'). Even then, when monarchs were still immensely powerful, it had been realised that moneys might more easily be obtained from subjects with their consent rather than on demand.

Traditionally redress of grievances always preceded supply, thus symbolising the contract between government and the governed. According to this, the latter would only provide the financial needs of the executive in return for government assurances that national and local grievances would receive attention. The executive's need to seek supply through Parliament provides the historical explanation and justification for Parliament's constitutional right to scrutinise and criticise government policy and action.

Financial proceedings in the House of Commons now provide a series of major opportunities for the opposition to debate and criticise the government's stewardship of the nation's affairs. These occasions include debates on the Estimates (spending proposals), the annual Budget (taxing proposals), the parliamentary stages of the Finance Bill, Consolidated Fund Bills (i.e. those authorising expenditure), and financial resolutions authorising expenditure arising out of other general legislative measures (health, education, etc.).

In none of these proceedings is it possible for Members to consider taxing or expenditure proposals in detail nor to amend the substance of any financial proposals. The Commons lacks the time and expertise to undertake meticulous scrutiny of government finance. Members are limited to debate of the general policy proposals to which the taxing and spending plans relate. Hence the idea that the Commons 'controls' government finance is somewhat notional. Note also that since 1911 the House of Lords has had no veto or delaying power in relation to financial measures.

In the unlikely event that a government failed to get its financial measures through the House it would be forced to resign. Hence the resignation of the Liberal government in 1909 following the House of Lords defeat of the Finance Bill.

Article 4 of the Bill of Rights 1689 provides that taxation without parliamentary consent is illegal. This is enforced by the courts.

See:

Attorney-General Wilts United Dairies, above;

- *Congreve Home Office* [1976] 1 All ER 697;
- *Bowles Bank of England* [1913] 1 Ch 57;
- *Dyson Attorney-General (No. 2)* (1912) 1 Ch 158;
- *Customs and Excise Commissioners Cure and Deeley Ltd* (1962) 1 QB 340.

Some basic rules

(a) Spending and taxing proposals may not be implemented without legislative approval.

(b) Spending and taxing proposals must be moved or supported by the Crown (i.e. by a Minister).

(c) Spending and taxing proposals must originate in the Commons.

(d) Estimates and related supply must be voted in the same session.

(e) Spending and taxing proposals must be approved by resolutions of the House of Commons. These are in addition to the normal stages in the legislative process. Such financial resolutions are usually taken after the Second Reading stage of the Bill containing the proposal in question.

Supply: procedure and scrutiny

The process for legitimising expenditure

Departmental estimates are prepared annually from autumn onwards for submission to the Treasury in December. Each government department submits its own 'estimate'. Each will contain, at least, the following elements:

- the net amount of money sought for the coming financial year;
- the services to be financed by the estimate;
- the department which will account for the estimate;
- any amounts already allocated to the department in votes on account.

After negotiation within the department and revision by the Treasury the estimates are submitted to the House of Commons in February or March. Since 1982 three days have annually been set aside for their debate. These debates must be concluded by 5 August.

When approved the Estimates are embodied in the Annual Appropriation Bill; one in March and one in July. This gives the government legal authority to withdraw sums of money from the Consolidated Fund to finance its obligations and activities.

Terminology and particular procedures

(a) Votes on account

Prior to the beginning of the financial year, and in order to keep the government in supply pending enactment of the Appropriation Bill (some time in July), the House will pass votes on account, to be embodied in Consolidation Fund Bills for enactment before 31 March, authorising withdrawals from the Consolidation Fund. These amounts will then be deducted from the main appropriation grant (Appropriation Act) in the following July or August.

(b) Excess votes

Where departments have overspent in the previous financial year the House may grant an excess vote which will then be included in a Consolidated Fund Bill to be enacted in the financial year immediately following the year in which the overspending occurred.

(c) Supplementary estimates

If departments have underestimated expenditure in any financial year, or if unforeseen causes of additional expenditure have arisen, supplementary estimates may be approved. These will be embodied in the main Appropriation Bill, if voted before July or, if later, then in subsequent Consolidation Bills.

(d) Consolidated Fund Standing Services

These are services financed out of the Consolidated Fund under the continuing authority of Acts of Parliament other than the Appropriation Act or Consolidated Fund Acts. For these purposes, therefore, annual grant of finance is not necessary. These services include payments to the National Loans Fund to service the national debt, most payments to the European Union, the Civil List and the salaries and pensions of certain people who are required constitutionally to be independent of the executive. These include members of the judiciary, Members of the European Parliament, the Speaker of the House of Commons, the Comptroller and Auditor-General, and the Parliamentary Commissioner for Administration.

(e) Supply services

These include the bulk of government supported **public sector** services. For these an annual submission of estimates and grant of supply is required. This applies, *inter alia*, to defence, health, social services, education, housing, etc.

Problems for parliamentary control

- The estimates are too detailed, complex, and voluminous to be fully comprehended by most MPs.
- There is insufficient time to consider the estimates item by item.
- MPs have no access to departmental documentation showing how the estimates were compiled.
- Most MPs do not have the expertise to identify or predict wastage, particularly where moneys are dedicated to complicated technical research and development projects.

Taxation: procedure and scrutiny

The Budget

The House must vote on the means by which the executive may acquire the amount of money needed to finance supply, i.e. its expenditure. The process through which this is done is usually referred to as the Budget.

The Budget cycle

The Budget cycle really begins with a pre-Budget Report published every November or December (the 'Autumn Statement'). The Report provides an outline of the government's view of the state of the national economy and shows how its taxing and spending plans fit into its broader economic strategy.

The Budget, itself, containing the government's taxation policy for the next 12 months, is formulated by the Treasury under the political supervision of the Chancellor of the Exchequer and the Prime Minister. This is not a Cabinet function. Other Ministers will be consulted but not actually informed of exact Budget details until, at the earliest, the day before the Chancellor delivers the Budget speech to the House of Commons. This is usually in March or April, just before, or at the beginning of, the new financial year. As soon as the Chancellor's Budget speech is concluded, the House passes a series of financial resolutions authorising immediate alteration of existing rates of taxation. Pending enactment of the main Finance Bill, these are given legitimacy by the Provisional Collection of Taxes Act 1968. The House then passes on to debate the government's taxing and economic proposals in general. The debate may continue for up to four days. Proposals for any new taxes which are to be levied before the annual Finance Act takes effect and authorisation for the renewal of any annual taxes (e.g. income tax, corporation tax) must be approved by special finance votes, known as Ways and Means Resolutions. These must be taken within ten sitting days of the Budget speech. Such resolutions remain effective until 5 August (Provisional Collection of Taxes Act 1968, s 1(2)). Effectively, therefore, this means that the Finance Bill must pass into law by this time.

The Budget proposals in their entirety form the basis of the annual Finance Bill. This proceeds through Parliament in the normal way except that at the Committee stage major or controversial items may be dealt with in a Committee of the Whole House while the rest of the Bill goes in the normal way to a Public Bill Committee. Until 1967 the entire Committee stage was taken on the floor of the House. This proved too time consuming, hence the procedural change.

After the Bill has been given its Third Reading in the House of Commons it is sent to the House of Lords. The financial privileges of the House of Commons require that all such financial measures be instituted in the lower House. The Lords will debate the Bill at Second Reading, but may not reject or amend it. Report and Third Reading are then mere formalities with the Bill going through these stages 'on the nod'. The Bill will usually complete its Lords stages within one sitting day. The Bill may then proceed for the Royal Assent in the normal way.

In September 2010, the government announced that future parliamentary sessions would run from May to May rather than November to November as was the tradition. This was intended as part of its wider reform to establish fixed-term Parliaments. As a consequence, and in order that it may complete its passage through the Commons, it is now necessary for the Finance Bill to be 'carried over' to the session after that in which it was introduced.

Late in 2016, the Chancellor of the Exchequer announced a change to the annual Budget timetable. This was that, from 2017 onwards, the Budget would be delivered to the House of Commons in November or December with the pre-existing Autumn Statement being replaced a the 'Spring Statement' to be given a few months later. This latter would not be concerned with significant tax changes thus avoiding the current uncertainty in financial dealings resulting from from such changes being made on a bi-annual basis.

Government finance and Select Committees

Various Select Committees are involved in scrutinising the government's financial policies and the use of public moneys. Thus, for example, the remit of the departmental Select Committees discussed above extends to the estimates and spending plans of the government departments falling within their jurisdiction. Scrutiny of Treasury affairs falls within the competence of the Treasury and Civil Service Committee.

Reference has already been made to the fact, however, that such committees have their limitations – particularly in terms of time and resources. Inevitably, therefore, their analysis and reporting of how spending decisions have been made, and whether public moneys are being used efficiently, is seldom sufficiently detailed or comprehensive to give the House of Commons an absolutely clear picture of how the government is managing the nation's financial affairs.

The Public Accounts Committee

This is one of the most important and prestigious of the House of Commons' sessional Select Committees. It was first appointed in 1861. Its principal functions are:

- to monitor and scrutinise government expenditure;
- to discover if public moneys have been used for unauthorised purposes (i.e. those for which there is no legislative authority);
- to highlight overspending and wastage of public funds.

The Committee consists of 15 MPs. By tradition it is chaired by a senior member of the opposition. It conducts its investigations through examination of the reports and information laid before it by the Comptroller and Auditor General (see below). The Comptroller's reports are based on their perusal of the accounts of each government department. In this way the Committee is given a relatively detailed insight into the financial workings of government. The Committee is not concerned with the merits of government policy. Its sole concern is the legality and efficiency in the use of public funds. Due to lack of time, the Committee will normally direct its attention to a limited number of issues raised in the Comptroller's report. As a general rule the Committee produces unanimous reports. Most of these are debated on the floor of the House and will be responded to by the government.

It should be pointed out, however, that the Committee provides only an *ex post facto* method of control and is generally concerned with actions and decisions taken some 18 months previously. Hence the Committee may only identify and condemn what has already occurred. It cannot prevent overspending or wastage from taking place – save to the extent that the Committee's very existence may have some precautionary effects. Also, not all of its members will be financial experts and, as ordinary backbench MPs, have many other calls on their time both in their constituencies and in Parliament.

The Comptroller and Auditor General

The Comptroller is an officer of the House of Commons. Holders of the office are appointed by the Crown upon a resolution of the House of Commons. The resolution is moved by the Prime Minister with the approval of the chair of the Public Accounts Committee (National Audit Act 1983, s 1). The Comptroller's salary is paid by an annual charge on the

Consolidated Fund. His or her security of tenure and independence is guaranteed by the provision that she or he may only be dismissed pursuant to resolutions of both Houses of Parliament (Exchequer Departments and Audit Act 1866, s 3).

The Comptroller is responsible for ensuring that all revenue raised by the government is lodged in the Consolidated Fund or the National Loans Fund at the Bank of England. Moneys cannot be withdrawn from either fund without his or her authorisation. This enables the Comptroller to monitor government expenditure as it occurs and to see that the government remains within the overall spending limits granted to it by Parliament. In his or her other capacity as Auditor General he or she also audits the accounts of each government department on an annual basis and is thus able to discern whether public moneys have been wasted or used for purposes other than those for which there is statutory authorisation.

By virtue of the National Audit Act 1983, the Comptroller is head of the National Audit Office (NAO). Those employed by the NAO are appointed by the Comptroller and are answerable to him/her. As such they are not civil servants and are not in any way subject to the control or influence of government Ministers or departments. The NAO provides the Comptroller with the expertise and administrative support necessary for the effective exercise of his/her functions.

The work of the NAO has two main elements. The first involves the audit of the estimates or financial statements of all central government departments, agencies and other public bodies. The NAO's second major area activity is the carrying out of value-for-money studies across the whole gamut of government projects, programmes and initiatives. In the region of sixty such studies are undertaken and published each year.

Although the Comptroller may not question the merits of departmental policies, the 1983 Act provides that she or he may pass comment on the 'economy, effectiveness and efficiency' with which a department has discharged its functions (s 6). This has been referred to as 'value for money' auditing.

The Comptroller's powers are not limited to central government departments. She or he may also audit the accounts of the National Health Service and any other body which receives 'more than half of its income from public funds' (s 7).

Problems for parliamentary control

- 'Although the tablets of stone on which the Finance Bill is written can be amended, in practice the government's reputation is at stake and so major substantive amendments are rare' (Treasury and Civil Service Committee, 6th Report, 1981–2, Budgetary Reform, HC 137).

- The government's principal spending and taxing proposals (i.e. the estimates and the Budget) are put to the House separately and at different times of the year. This militates against effective evaluation and criticism of the relationship between taxation and expenditure.

- Government borrowing is not subject to any form of control in the House of Commons. Nor has the House any direct involvement in the spending proposals of local authorities or public bodies other than government departments.

Financial legislation and English votes for English laws

Tax-raising Bills and measures

Those Bills certified as limited to England or England and Wales only may take effect with the consent of the appropriate Legislative Grand Committee, i.e. depending on the geographical application of the Bill, with the consent of an 'English' Legislative Grand Committee or that of an 'English and Welsh' Legislative Grand Committee.

Certified Budget resolutions made under the Provisional Collection of Taxes Act 1968 require approval by double majorities with all Members eligible to vote.

Public spending measures

In the matter of public spending, and regardless of the geographical application of particular measures, MPs from all parts of the United Kingdom will continue to be eligible to vote on:

(i) Appropriation Bills;

(ii) Consolidation Bills;

(iii) The Estimates;

(iv) Money resolutions (authority to spend and tax).

Other functions of the House of Commons

Provides personnel of government

It is a convention that the Prime Minister and most senior Ministers have seats in the Commons.

The Commons does not choose Members of the government. This is the function of the Prime Minister. It does, however, provide the people from which the choice is made.

The Commons may also influence the choice of Ministers since those MPs who show competence in parliamentary proceedings are more likely to be chosen.

Provides personnel of alternative governments

Her Majesty's Official or Loyal Opposition forms a 'Shadow Cabinet' which, through its activities in the House, attempts to establish itself as a credible and responsible alternative for which the electorate may decide to vote when a General Election occurs.

Should it be necessary in time of national emergency to form an alternative administration, without resort to the divisiveness of a General Election, the House can usually be relied upon to ensure the continuity of government. Alternative administrations (in both cases coalitions) were formed without elections in 1931, during a serious economic crisis, and in 1940 in the early years of the Second World War (after Chamberlain's resignation).

Legitimation

By convention the government's constitutional authority is dependent on maintaining the support of a majority of Members. Should the House pass a resolution of no confidence, the government must resign from office. This happened only three times in the twentieth century and only to minority governments, i.e. governments which did not have an overall majority of seats in the Commons. Hence on no occasion in the twentieth century was a majority government forced to resign. March 1979 was the last instance of a government being put out of office by an adverse confidence vote in the House of Commons. James Callaghan's minority Labour government lost the confidence motion by just one vote but, accepting the convention, resigned forthwith.

Also, through the legislative process, the House of Commons is an essential element in providing legitimacy – i.e. providing the necessary statutory authority – for government policies. The rule of law rejects government by decree, hence specific legislative authority must precede the implementation of particular policies. Very occasionally this authority may be withheld (see the Shops Bill 1986, which was intended to reduce restrictions on Sunday trading).

Note, however, that not all legitimacy for government action and decision is derived from Acts of Parliament. In certain contexts – particularly foreign affairs, defence, the maintenance of law and order and emergency powers – the royal prerogative remains an important source of authority for executive action.

Judicial powers

These include the following:

(a) The power to adjudicate and punish in matters of breach of privilege and contempt.

(b) The power to adjudicate between private and public interests during the Committee stage of Private Bills – particularly where these are opposed.

(c) The power of impeachment. Although perhaps now obsolete, this refers to the power of the Commons to bring judicial proceedings against any person 'accused of state offences beyond the reach of the law, or which no other authority in the state would prosecute' (Hood Phillips and Jackson, *Constitutional and Administrative Law*, 5th edn). The power was last used in 1801. The Commons act as accusers and the Lords as judges of both fact and law. Trial by Parliament might still be used to deal with incidents of corruption or subversion of the constitution by MPs. It is now far more likely, however, that such misdemeanours would be dealt with through the ordinary criminal law and/or, in the case of Ministers, by enforcement of the conventions of collective and individual Ministerial responsibility.

(d) Act of Attainder. These were strictly legislative and not judicial acts.

It was an Act of Parliament finding a person guilty of an offence, usually a political one of a rather substantial kind, and inflicting a punishment on him. The subject of the proceedings was allowed to defend himself . . . before both Houses. (ibid.)

This method of dealing with political offenders has not been used since the early eighteenth century.

Disciplinary powers

The House may suspend a Member for any period or expel a Member for life. As decisions of the House of Commons are not justiciable, a Member so treated has no legal redress. While suspension for a specified, and usually relatively short, period is not uncommon, in the twentieth century only three Members were excluded for life. These were:

- Horatio William Bottomley (Conservative, Worcester East), 1922, convicted of fraudulent conversion;

- Gary Allighan (Labour, Gravesend), 1947, alleging corruption and drunkenness amongst MPs and lying to the House of Commons committee set up to look into his allegations;

- Peter Arthur David Baker (Conservative, Norfolk South) 1954, convicted of uttering forged documents.

In the 2015–16 session, one member was ordered to withdraw.

Summary

The chapter explains the principal powers and functions of the House of Commons and concentrates in detail on:

- the workings of the legislative process;
- the effectiveness of the various parliamentary processes and procedures through which the government is held to account, viz. debates, Question Time, and departmental Select Committees.

References

Crick (1970) *The Reform of Parliament* (2nd edn), London: Weidenfeld & Nicolson.

Hewart (1975) *The New Despotism,* London: Greenwood Publication Group.

Hood Phillips and Jackson (1997) *Constitutional and Administrative Law* (5th edn), London: Sweet & Maxwell.

May (2011) *Parliamentary Practice* (24th edn), London: Butterworths.

Norton (1981) *The Commons in Perspective,* Oxford: Robertson.

Select Committee on Modernisation of the House, 1997–98, HC 90

Select Committee on Modernisation of the House, 1997–98, HC 543

Select Committee on Modernisation of the House, 1998–99, HC 194

Select Committee on Modernisation of the House, 1999–2000, HC 589

Select Committee on Procedure, 6th Report, HC 539

Thring (1902) *Practical Legislation:* London: John Murray.

Treasury and Civil Service Committee, 6th Report, 1981–82, Budgetary Reform, HC 137

Further reading

Griffith and Ryle (2002) *Parliament: Functions, Practice and Procedures,* London: Sweet & Maxwell, Chs 6, 7, 8, 9, 10 and 11.

House of Commons Library (2015) *Prime Minister's Questions,* Standard Note, SN/PL/05183.

House of Commons Library (2015) *English Votes for English laws,* Briefing Paper, no 7339, 2.12.15.

House of Commons Library (2012) *Public Bills in Parliament,* Standard Note, SN/PL/06507, 17.12.12.

Norton (2013) *Parliament in British Politics,* Basingstoke: Palgrave Macmillan.

Rogers and Walters (2015) *How Parliament Works* (7th edn), London: Routledge.

Rush (2005) *Parliament Today,* Manchester: Manchester University Press.

Seldon and Meekin (2016) *The Cabinet Office, 1916-1016: The Birth of Modern Government,* London: Biteback Publishing.

9

The House of Lords

Objectives

After reading this chapter you should:

1. Be aware of the current composition of the House of Lords.

2. Understand the remaining powers of the House of Lords.

3. Recognise the main functions of the House of Lords, its role in the legislative process and its relationship with the House of Commons.

4. Appreciate the major historical and contemporary developments relating to reform of the composition and powers of the House of Commons.

Origins and composition

Objective
1

The Westminster Parliament, consisting of assemblies of Lords (bishops, aristocracy and nobility), and Commons (local country squires and burgesses from the towns), is believed to have first convened towards the end of the thirteenth century. Some put the date at 1295. In these early times, and for many centuries that followed, the House of Lords was composed mainly of persons who had been 'ennobled' by the Monarch, usually for favours or services rendered, and who were therefore entitled to be known as peers or Lords of the realm. The peerages so created were, in legal terms, hereditary which meant that they survived their original holders and passed to their successors in the male line. From the beginning, therefore, the legitimacy and authority of the House of Lords was not, as in the case of the House of Commons, founded on any electoral franchise or related embryonic concept of representation, however narrow. The 'right' of the Lords or nobility to be involved in the process of government was widely accepted to be a natural adjunct of their social and economic status. The Lords were understood to belong to an educated, propertied élite who could be entrusted with political responsibility and who, more specifically, could be expected to use their political power in ways which would underpin and guarantee the nation's traditional social and political order.

Paradoxically, the idea that a relatively small, educated group from the upper echelons of society had an inherent role to play in the parliamentary process was strengthened, rather than weakened, by the extensions of the franchise from 1832 onwards (the Great Reform Act), as many took the view that the unelected chamber provided much needed continuity and operated as an important check on the ephemeral whims and ambitions of popular-ist politicians. This belief survived well into the twentieth century and goes some way to explaining why the introduction of life peers in 1958 was the only significant reform made to the composition of the House of Lords during that period. As time went on, however, it became increasingly difficult to reconcile the hereditary principle with rapidly developing concepts of social and liberal democracy. This was particularly so as, even after the 1958 reform, the newly introduced life peers were significantly outnumbered by the hereditary element. As a result, the question of the composition of the House of Lords remained an issue of concern throughout the last century. It was not until the General Election of 1997, how-ever, that it found its way towards the top of the political agenda as a part of New Labour's programme of constitutional reform and culminated in the House of Lords Act 1999.

For more on life peers, see pp. 199–200.

The New Labour government's stated intention was that reform of the second chamber would be achieved in two stages. The first stage, effected by the 1999 Act, would be the radi-cal reduction of the number of hereditary peers and the creation of a 'transitional' House of Lords consisting largely of life peers and with no one political party having an overall majority. This was to be followed by a wide-ranging process of consultation and debate leading to some sort of general political consensus for the proper composition and powers of a second chamber equipped for the demands of government in the twenty-first century.

For more detail on this debate, see pp. 213–23.

Prior to the 1999 Act taking effect, the composition of the House of Lords was as set out below.

Hereditary peers	759	(59%)
Life peers	505	(39%)
Archbishops/bishops	26	(2%)
Total	1290	

Source: House of Lords Annual Report 1999/2000.

Immediately after the Act took effect the composition was as follows:

Life peers	578	(83%)
Hereditary peers	91	(13%)
Archbishops/bishops	26	(4%)
Total	695	

Source: House of Lords Research Paper 00/61.

The composition of the House of Lords as of September 2016 was:

Life peers	693	(85.5%)
Hereditary peers	91	(11.2%)
Archbishops/bishops	26	(3.12%)
Total	810	

Source: House of Lords Information Office.

The declared political affiliations of the members of the House were:

Labour	205	(25.3%)
Conservative	205	(25.3%)
Liberal Democrat	110	(13.6%)
Crossbench	145	(17.9%)

Source: House of Lords Information Office.

The hereditary element in the unreformed House gave the Conservative party a substantial 'in-built' numerical advantage over all other political groups. In its final days some 40 per cent of its members accepted the Conservative whip. The second largest group was the Crossbenchers with nearly 30 per cent of members. The Labour party and Liberal Democrats could call on 15 per cent and 9 per cent of members, respectively.

Types of peers

Hereditary peers

All peers are created by the Monarch. For the creation of hereditary peerages the prerogative is exercised through the issue of a Writ of Summons or by Letters Patent. The Writ of Summons has, however, fallen into disuse. In modern times, therefore, all hereditary peerages have been created by Letters Patent issued on the advice of the Prime Minister. A peerage by writ descends to the heirs general, i.e. either male or female. A peerage created by Letters Patent – the more usual method in modern times – descends according to any limitations expressed in the patent which normally, but not invariably, restricts succession to male heirs.

No new hereditary peerages were created between 1964 and 1983 and it appeared that a convention against further appointments might be emerging. During Mrs Thatcher's premiership, however, the practice was revived. Hereditary peerages were conferred on William Whitelaw, the Conservative ex-Cabinet Minister (Viscount Whitelaw 1983); George Thomas, ex-Labour MP and Speaker (Viscount Tonypandy 1983); Harold Macmillan, Conservative Prime Minister 1957–63 (Earl of Stockton 1984); and the Duke of York (1986).

Hereditary peers may be divided into:

(a) holders of English peerages created before the Act of Union with Scotland 1707;

(b) holders of peerages of Great Britain created between 1707 and 1801;

(c) holders of peerages of the United Kingdom created since 1801;

(d) holders of Scottish peerages created prior to 1707 – originally limited by the Acts of Union to 16 elected by all Scottish peers, until the Peerage Act 1963 gave all such peers the right to sit.

Life peers

The Life Peerages Act 1958 permitted peerages to be conferred on persons of either sex for life. These attach to the particular individual only and do not pass to their heirs or successors.

Life peers are created by the Monarch on the advice of the Prime Minister (Life Peerages Act 1958, s 1). Appointment is by Letters Patent. Persons may be recommended as follows:

(a) as 'working' peers in the political sense from a list drawn up annually by the Prime Minister in consultation with other party leaders;

(b) by inclusion in the Queen's Birthday, and New Year Honours, Lists again on the advice of the Prime Minister primarily for the purpose of recognising the achievements of those named rather than for any party-political reason;

(c) by inclusion in a dissolution of Parliament Honours List, normally drawn up at the beginning of each new Parliament on the Prime Minister's advice principally for the purpose of giving seats in the House of Lords to former Ministers and MPs who did not seek re-election;

(d) by inclusion in a Resignation Honours List compiled by a Prime Minister who is resigning for reasons other than defeat in a General Election and who wishes to reward those to whom they feel some debt of gratitude;

(e) on the Prime Minister's advice so that those named may acquire a seat in Parliament and thus become eligible for Ministerial office.

Although the 1958 Act was enacted during a period of Conservative government, its objective was to facilitate increased Labour representation in the upper chamber. This may, at first sight, appear somewhat paradoxical. It was done, however, to preserve the credibility of the House and thus reduce the case for abolition or major reform. Given that Labour had been one of the two main parties since the early 1920s, and had held a large majority in the House of Commons between 1945 and 1951, its level of representation in the Lords had become increasingly untenable. In 1955, shortly before the Act was passed, the Labour presence in the House of Lords was just 55. Of the rest, 507 were in receipt of the Conservative whip and 42 were Liberals (there was a further crossbench element of 251). Labour's position in the House of Lords was also improved by the parliamentary resolutions of 1957 permitting peers to claim expenses in respect of daily attendance. Prior to this time they received no recompense whatsoever for their parliamentary activities and to this day receive expenses only, unlike MPs who receive an annual salary. The provision of expenses has, however, been of some assistance to those peers unable to finance their political careers from other sources of income.

Until October 2009 and the formation of the Supreme Court, life peerages were also awarded to 12 senior members of the judiciary to enable them to perform the judicial functions of the House. These appointments have now ceased. The existing 'Law Lords' were transferred to the Supreme Court at the time of its creation.

By convention, lay peers, i.e. those not qualified or appointed to the House for judicial purposes, did not sit or attempt to participate in its judicial work. The convention could be traced back to *O'Connell* v *R* (1844) 11 CL & F 115, when several lay peers who wished to vote against Daniel O'Connell's conviction for conspiracy were persuaded to withdraw. The last occasion when a lay peer attempted to take part in a case before the House of Lords was in *Bradlaugh* v *Gossett* (1883) LR 8 App Cas 354. His vote was ignored.

Spiritual peers

These consist of three groups:

(a) the Archbishops of Canterbury and York;

(b) the Bishops of London, Durham and Winchester;

(c) the next 21 diocesan bishops of the Church of England in order of seniority of appointment.

These numbers were fixed by the Bishoprics Act 1847. A spiritual peer's entitlement to sit ceases on resignation or retirement (at 70 years) from the qualifying office.

It will be noted that such guaranteed religious representation extends only to the Church of England. No similar entitlement extends to other Christian denominations or other religious faiths. Leaders of such denominations and faiths may be given life peerages but this is entirely at the discretion of the Prime Minister.

Those holding the qualifying offices will, like all bishops, have been appointed by the Crown on the advice of the Prime Minister. The Prime Minister makes his recommendations from names submitted to him by the Church Commissioners (the two Archbishops, three clerics, three laypersons and four representatives of the diocese concerned).

Disclaimer and disqualifications

Disclaimer

By virtue of the Peerage Act 1963, hereditary peers only (other than those of first creation), were enabled to disclaim their titles for life and thus become eligible for membership of the House of Commons. Such disclaimer is irrevocable and must be made within twelve months of succession or of coming of age (21 years). If the successor is already a member of the House of Commons the period for disclaimer is limited to one month only. The House of Lords Act 1999 does not prevent a hereditary peer who has disclaimed their title from being granted a life peerage and thus becoming eligible for membership of the upper House. As the disclaimer is for life only, the peerage is not extinguished and, on the death of the disclaimer, passes to the heir in the normal way.

As a general rule the facility to disclaim was left unaltered by the House of Lords Act 1999. It is, however, no longer a prerequisite of a hereditary peer's eligibility for membership of the House of Commons. The first hereditary peer to be elected to the House of Commons was the Earl of Caithness who was returned for Caithness, Sutherland and Easter Ross in the General Election of 2001. The 1999 Act does, however, appear to remove the right of disclaimer from those hereditary peers who remain in the House of Lords by virtue of election under s 2.

One of the principal reasons for the 1963 Act was the determination of the then Anthony Wedgwood-Benn not to become disqualified from membership of the House of Commons. A hereditary peerage (Lord Stansgate) had been conferred on Benn's father in 1940. This was done to increase Labour representation in the House of Lords during the period in office of the wartime coalition. Benn was aware, therefore, that on his father's death he would succeed to the title and be forced to vacate the Commons seat for Bristol South-East which he had won in 1951. To avoid this he attempted to secure the passage of a Personal Bill enabling him to renounce the unwanted title. All of this came to nought, however, and in 1960 Benn became Lord Stansgate. His nature being of the type not to give up readily, he then contested the subsequent by-election which he won with a massive and increased majority. Due to his disqualification, however, the second-placed candidate (the Conservative) was declared to have been elected. In effect, therefore, Bristol South-East had to be content with the candidate who had 'lost' the election. It was to avoid any repetition of these events that the 1963 Act was passed. Its passage enabled Lords Home and Hailsham to contest the 1963 Conservative leadership election. Benn also renounced his title and was re-elected to the House of Commons in the 1964 General Election. The number of hereditary peers taking advantage of the facility provided by the 1963 Act has not been as great as expected. Only 18 have done so to date.

Disqualifications

The following may not sit or vote in the House of Lords:

(a) aliens;

(b) bankrupts;

(c) persons under 21 years of age;

(d) persons sentenced to imprisonment for treason.

Attendance

Leave of absence

For each new Parliament a Writ of Summons will be issued to each person entitled to sit in the House. Any peer who does not intend or is unable to participate in the work of the House is expected to apply for leave of absence (to the Lord Chancellor) – a practice introduced in 1958.

Leave of absence may be granted for a session, for the remainder of a session, or for the remainder of the particular Parliament. At the beginning of each new session, peers given leave of absence for the session which has just come to an end will be asked if they wish the grant of leave to be renewed. The same question will also be put to those peers not granted leave for that session but who still failed to attend.

A peer granted leave of absence is expected not to attend proceedings in the period covered. This expectation is, however, binding in honour only. Hence a peer who is in receipt of a Writ of Summons and who has not become disqualified may not be prevented from attending. Leave of absence may be ended on one month's notice. The original purpose behind the leave of absence procedure was to discourage attendance by 'backwoodsmen' – i.e. hereditary peers who used their privilege of membership to enable them to attend and vote on major and (usually) controversial issues but who did not contribute to the work of the House on a regular basis.

Attendance figures

The average daily attendance of members of the House of Lords during the session 1951–52 was just 86. The House sat on 96 days and for a total of 292 hours. In the 1959–60 session, after the introduction of life peers, the figures increased to an average daily attendance of

Table 9.1 Average daily attendance, House of Lords

Session	Sitting days	Average length	Average attendance
1959–60	113	3 hrs 59 mins	136
1985–6	165	7 hrs 21 mins	317
1999–2000	157	7 hrs 35 mins	434
2006–7	146	6 hrs 42 mins	411
2012–13	137	6 hrs 36 mins	484
2013–14	149	6 hrs 47 mins	487
2014–15	126	6 hrs 32 mins	483
2015–16	149	6 hrs 48 mins	497

Source: House of Lords Information Office.

136 with the House sitting on 113 days for 450 hours. Since then, as Table 9.1 indicates, the figures have shown further improvement thereby creating a picture of a more active and well-patronised second chamber.

Powers

The nineteenth century

Objective
2

Throughout the nineteenth century the House of Lords retained legislative powers which were coterminous with those of the House of Commons. Consequently, any Bill which the Lords rejected at Second Reading could not pass into law. This power was, however, subject to the understanding that the Lords would refrain from defeating those measures for which the government had a clear electoral mandate.

In relation to financial measures the conventional understanding was that, while these should be introduced in the Commons and could not be amended by the House of Lords, the Lords could reject them outright.

The Parliament Act 1911

The Liberal administration which took office in 1906 was committed to a radical programme of social reform. Conflict with the House of Lords and the vested interests it represented was probably inevitable.

Matters came to a head when the Lords voted against the Finance Bill of 1909. This had proposed tax increases on income and property in order to finance the social legislation (including the introduction of old-age pensions and unemployment insurance) to which the government was committed. At the time, the government had a huge majority in the House of Commons. The figures for the seats won by the main parties in 1906 were as laid out in Table 9.2 (for a House of Commons consisting of 671 members).

As the Irish Nationalists and the Labour members generally supported the Liberals, this meant that the government had an effective Commons majority of some 356.

Despite this the Conservative party at large sought to justify the Lords' action on the ground that the government had no precise mandate for the financial proposals in issue. There was in this an obvious paradox in that an unelected second chamber was claiming to defend democratic principles by refusing to consent to measures supported by just over 76 per cent of the Members of the elected House of Commons.

The immediate consequence of the 1909 Budget crisis was a General Election early in 1910. The Liberals were returned to power, although with a reduced majority (with Labour and Irish Nationalist support this was in the region of 162 or 65 per cent of all MPs). The previously rejected Finance Bill was then enacted. Reducing the powers of the House of

Table 9.2 Seats won by main parties, 1906 General Election

Party	Seats won
Liberal	400
Conservative	157
Irish Nationalist	83
Labour	30

Source: House of Lords Information Office.

Lords and removing their legislative veto now became a government priority. Clearly it was unlikely that the Lords would readily accede to any legislative measure with this objective. The Prime Minister (**Herbert Asquith**) decided, therefore, to ask the King (**George V**) to create a sufficient number of peers to produce an overall majority in favour of reform (about 400 in total). The King agreed to do so, providing the Liberal government could secure direct electoral support for their proposals. Accordingly a further General Election was held (December 1910) and the Liberals were again returned to power (with an effective majority of 141). Faced with this apparent public support for a reduction in its powers and the threat of the creation of a large number of peers with Liberal sympathies – thereby eradicating its permanent Conservative majority – the House decided to 'cut its losses' and not to oppose the Parliament Bill which was enacted in 1911.

The 1911 Act had three main consequences. First, it removed the Lords' power of veto in respect of all Public Bills with the exception of any Bill introduced to extend the life of a Parliament beyond the prescribed maximum period of duration (reduced from seven to five years by s 7). The House also retained its power of veto in relation to Private Bills and subordinate legislation. Second, it replaced the Lords' veto in respect of Public Bills with a delaying power of two years. Thereafter, any Bill passed by the House of Commons but rejected by the Lords in three successive sessions could be presented for the Royal Assent providing two years had elapsed between the Bill's Second Reading in the Commons in the first of those sessions and its third Commons reading in the third session. Third, it allowed Bills certified by the Speaker to be 'Money Bills' to be presented for the Royal Assent if not passed by the House of Lords without amendment within one month of having been sent there from the House of Commons.

For distinction between Public and Private Bills, see Chapter 8.

The Parliament Act 1949

Despite the removal of its veto, the 1911 provisions still left the Lords with the facility to seriously disrupt a government's legislative programme – particularly in the last two years of a Parliament when any Bill rejected by the Lords could not become law until after a General Election. The Labour government which came into power in 1945 with a radical programme of industrial and social reform feared that, unless the delaying power was reduced, difficulties with the House of Lords might seriously interfere with the implementation of its policies.

The Parliament Act 1949 sought to deal with this problem. The Act reduced the delaying power to one year. The current position is that any Bill passed by the House of Commons but rejected by the House of Lords in two successive sessions may be presented for the Royal Assent providing one year has elapsed between its Commons Second Reading in the first session and its Third Reading in the same House in the following session.

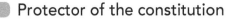

Functions

Protector of the constitution

Objective 3

It has been said that the powers of the Lords to reject any Bill to extend the life of a Parliament and to delay other controversial legislation represent the ultimate guarantees against executive exploitation of the unwritten constitution.

The life of Parliament was extended beyond the normal term of years on two occasions in the twentieth century. The Parliament elected in January 1910 continued until 1918 and that elected in 1935 continued until 1945. For obvious reasons it was thought unwise to divide the country for electoral purposes during time of war. Naturally, therefore, on these two occasions the question of the Lords vetoing the necessary statutory provisions did not arise. No other attempts to enact legislation for this purpose have been made.

Since it was introduced in 1911 the delaying power has been used on seven occasions in relation to Bills emanating from the House of Commons. These were the Irish Home Rule Bill 1912 (enacted 1914); the Welsh Church Bill 1913 (enacted 1914); the Parliament Bill 1947 (enacted 1949); the War Crimes Bill 1990 (enacted 1991); the European Parliamentary Elections Bill 1998 (enacted 1999); the Sexual Offences Bill 1999 (enacted 2000); and the Hunting Bill 2003 (enacted 2004).

It is generally accepted that the unreformed House was deterred from more extensive use of the delaying power due to continuing reservations over the political propriety of overruling the elected chamber and from the realisation that this would be likely to precipitate even more strident calls for abolition or radical change to the upper chamber's composition.

The purpose of the delaying power is to cause governments to 'think again' and to facilitate greater public debate about controversial legislative proposals. This may be seen to be of particular value in a political system in which the elected chamber is usually dominated by a political party which is supported by less than half of the electorate.

Initiation of legislation

In discussing the legislative process it is usual to talk of Bills passing through the House of Commons and then going to the House of Lords. Both Public and Private Bills may, however, be introduced into the House of Lords. The idea is that such Bills, having been fully debated and amended in the Lords, may then pass relatively quickly through the House of Commons, thus providing the latter with more time for consideration of the government's main legislative proposals. There is, however, a convention that Bills which may be politically controversial should go to the Commons first and, if approved, should not be voted down in the House of Lords.

Although most Private Members' Bills proposed in the Lords do not pass into law, the vast majority of government and Consolidation Bills introduced there will proceed to receive the Royal Assent. Consolidation Bills are those for which the Lord Chancellor has special responsibility and are usually dealt with by the Lords first. These re-enact existing legislation in a consolidated form, perhaps with changes recommended by the appropriate Law Commission, or may be Bills to repeal obsolete enactments. Perhaps of greatest significance, however, is the number and proportion of government Bills introduced in the upper chamber. In recent sessions this has been 10–15 per cent of the government's legislative programme. Eight government Bills were introduced in the Lords in the 2015–16 session.

By convention, major government Bills approved by the House of Commons are not voted down by the House of Lords. The convention has particular force in relation to Bills referred to in the government's election manifesto.

Revision of legislation

This is regarded by many as the most important function of the House of Lords and in any session will take up about half of its time. Taking into account all types of legislation, 4,788 amendments were proposed to Bills passed through the House of Lords from the House of Commons in 2015–16.

The procedural stages by which a Public Bill goes through the House of Lords are broadly similar to those in the House of Commons – see Table 9.3.

There are, however, a number of significant differences between the procedures of the two Houses. First, the Lords has no procedural mechanisms for curtailing debate (the Guillotine and Closure Motions are not used). Second, there is no provision, as in the House of Commons, for the selection of amendments to be debated. Thus all amendments which have been tabled may be discussed. Third, as indicated above, further amendments may be made at the Third Reading stage.

Some comment should also be made about the various methods according to which the Lords Committee stage of a Bill may be conducted. These are as follows.

(a) Committee of the Whole House

For the majority of Public Bills the House transforms itself into a committee so that the proceedings are conducted on the floor of the chamber. The House does not have a system of Public Bill Committees equivalent to that used in the House of Commons.

(b) Committee of the floor

This is a relatively recent innovation and was first used for the Children (Scotland) Bill in the 1994–95 session. All Lords are free to attend and participate. The use of this type of committee allows the House to proceed with other business on the floor of the chamber.

(c) Public Bill Committee

This type of committee is used relatively infrequently. Four Bills were dealt with in this way in session 2015–16. A limited number of peers are selected to constitute the committee. Measures dealt with in this way are usually government Bills of a technical and non-controversial nature. Lords not selected for such a committee may attend and speak but may not vote.

(d) Special Public Bill Committee

This new type of committee was first used in 1994–95 for the Law of Property (Miscellaneous Provisions) Bill. A committee of this type may be selected for a Bill where it is felt that effective scrutiny and revision will be best effected by a limited number of members possessing relevant expertise. The committee is empowered to take written and oral evidence from interested parties prior to making any amendments. The procedure has been described as 'well suited to the proposals put forward by the Lord Chancellor to facilitate the introduction of certain legal and technical Bills, for example, certain Bills proposed by the two Law Commissions' (House of Lords Procedure Committee, Third Report, 1993–94).

Table 9.3 Procedural stages of Public Bill, House of Lords

Procedural stage	Progress
First Reading	Purely formal and no debate.
Second Reading	General debate on the Bill's main principles.
Committee stage	Detailed consideration and amendment of individual clauses.
Report stage	Opportunity for further amendments to be moved.
Third Reading	Opportunity for further brief debate and last-minute amendments.

(e) Select Committee

A Bill may be committed to a Select Committee at any stage between its Second and Third Readings. This type of committee is used most frequently for controversial Private Members' Bills (e.g. Laboratory Animals Protection Bill 1978–79; Infant Life (Preservation) Bill 1986–87; Dangerous Dogs (Amendment) Bill 1995–96). The committee may take evidence and recommends to the House whether the Bill should proceed or not. It may also amend the Bill prior to recommitting it to a Committee of the Whole House.

(f) Scottish Select Committee

This is another new procedure which allows a Select Committee to take evidence on a Scottish Bill before the Bill is committed to any of the above types of committee for possible amendment. The committee may sit in Scotland. Peers who are not members may attend and participate in its proceedings. Recent legislative proposals dealt with in this way included the Deer (Amendment) (Scotland) Bill and the Education (Scotland) Bill (both in 1995–96).

The incidence of Bills revised in the House of Lords would tend to indicate that simple abolition of the second chamber is not a realistic option. If this were done without radical reform of the existing parliamentary system – and perhaps even of the entire constitutional structure (e.g. by creation of regional legislative assemblies) – there is an obvious case for suggesting that the House of Commons would no longer be able to function effectively and certainly would not be able to produce legislation of the desired utility and clarity of purpose.

Forum for debate

For various reasons it has been claimed that debates in the House of Lords are of a higher standard, less politically partisan, and more informative than those in the Commons.

(a) The parliamentary responsibilities of the House of Lords are not so great as those laid upon the lower chamber, hence there is more time for full discussion of legislative proposals and other issues of public concern (as stated, the guillotine and closure procedures are not used in the upper House). Also the convention that a government should resign if defeated in a vote of confidence or on a major issue does not apply to proceedings in the House of Lords. Hence, although adverse votes and criticism may cause the government some embarrassment, it will not be so concerned with the enforcement of party unity and discipline as is the case in the lower House. This and the crossbench element make, it is said, for a more open and less partisan approach.

(b) In addition, reference is usually made to the fact that many members of the House, particularly the life peers, will be persons of achievement and experience in politics, business, the professions, the church, etc. who are able to use these attributes to enhance the quality of proceedings.

Purely in terms of the time allocated to it, this function takes second place only to the Lords' consideration of Public Bills. The figures show that in any given session debates will account for some 20 to 25 per cent of the business of the House.

It is, of course, extremely difficult to assess the effect such debates may have either on the government or on public opinion generally. At one level this may appear to be negligible as most members of the public probably have little idea of, or interest in, the daily business of the upper House. However, this may be missing the point, in the sense that in the short term it is not the public which makes policy. The House of Lords, on the other hand, operates in what has been called the 'rarified' political atmosphere of Westminster and Whitehall. The working members of the House will have close contacts with those in power. They are all part of the political élite. Therefore – within that select group – the opinions and deliberations of the House of Lords may assume a greater degree of significance than is sometimes recognised.

Scrutiny of government policy

All of the above functions may be regarded as mechanisms through which the second chamber seeks to check on the activities of the executive. This is also true of some of the House of Lords Select Committees which are considered below.

Another method of scrutiny used extensively by the Lords, as in the Commons, is the parliamentary question. At the beginning of each day's business (Monday–Thursday) in the House up to four oral ('starred') questions may be put to government spokespersons. A member may not pose more than two questions on the same day. Supplementaries may be asked by any member but there is no general debate.

Question Time in the House of Lords is shorter than in the Commons and lasts for about 30 minutes. Note that questions are put to the government (requiring information) rather than to individual Ministers. Unstarred questions may be put at the end of the day's business. There is no time limit. The questions usually take the form of a speech and may be debated.

As with the House of Commons, peers may ask any number of written questions. Ministerial replies are normally given within two weeks.

The House of Lords also hears Private Notice Questions. As in the Commons these are oral questions on matters of urgency and must be submitted to the Leader of the House (a government Minister with a seat in Cabinet and who is responsible for the arrangement of business) before noon on the day they are to be asked. Usually, no more than two or three are posed per session.

Parliamentary questions are part of the general process whereby governments are made aware of the concerns of both those who support them and those who do not. They also help to elicit individual pieces of information from an executive prone to secrecy, all of which contributes to a broader impression of the government's competence and credibility.

Investigation by Select Committee

The House of Lords acquires information through a variety of sessional and ad hoc Select Committees. It does not, however, operate a system of departmental select committees equivalent to that established by the House of Commons in 1979.

Sessional Select Committees

Currently the House of Lords has five principal permanent or sessional Select Committees. There are the Constitution Committee, the Economic Affairs Committee, the European Union Committee, the Science and Technology Committee, the Communications Committee.

(a) The Constitution Committee

This was first appointed in 2001. It has twelve members. Its brief is to investigate and report on general matters of constitutional significance and on legislative proposals which may have constitutional implications. To date, the matters it has considered include: Parliament and the Legislative Process, 2004; Devolution – Its Effect on Legislative Practice at

Westminster, 2004; The Regulatory State – Ensuring Its Accountability, 2004; War-Making Powers and the Royal Prerogative, 2006; the Constitutional Reform Bill, 2005; the Identity Cards Bill, 2005; Terrorism Bill, 2005; Surveillance: Citizens and the State, 2008; Referendums in the UK, 2010; and English votes for English laws, 2016.

(b) The Economic Affairs Committee

This was established in 2001 and has thirteen members. It has a wide-ranging remit to 'consider economic affairs'. In addition to scrutinising economic policy (e.g. the annual Finance Bill), the committee initiates in-depth inquiries into a broad range of issues having economic implications. Recent reports have dealt with such diverse topics as climate change (2005) and the banking crisis (2009), financial devolution to Scotland (2015), the cost of HS2 (2015), and reforming the electricity market (2017).

(c) The European Union Committee

The committee was created in 1974. Its formal terms of reference are to 'consider European Union documents and other matters relating to the European Union'. Within this wide brief its principal function is to examine and report on all EU legislative proposals and the government's response to them.

The committee has a membership of twenty. The detailed work of the committee is conducted through a number of sub-committees to which other peers may be co-opted. As of 2010, these sub-committees were: Economic and Financial Affairs; Internal Market; External Affairs; Justice Institutions and Consumer Protection; Agriculture, Fisheries, Environment and Energy; Home Affairs; Health and Education.

The committee produces twenty reports per annum in the region, of which on average over half are debated on the floor of the House. Due to the time and expertise at its disposal, the committee's reports are regarded by many as being of a higher quality than those produced by the equivalent committee in the House of Commons. Matters considered in recent reports have extended to 'Brexit', 2016–17, and Brexit: UK–Irish relations, 2016–17.

(d) The Science and Technology Committee

Set up in 1980, the committee has the power to consider scientific and technological issues of particular social, political and environmental significance. The committee usually has fifteen to twenty members and will include members with scientific and other relevant backgrounds. In recent years its reports have included 'Waste or Resource?', 'Stimulating a Bioeconomy 2014', 'Priorities for Scientific Research' 2014, 'Genetically Modified Insects' 2015, 'EU membership and UK Science After the REferendum'.

(e) The Communications Committee

The Committee has between ten and fifteeny members. It was set up in 2006 to look at issues relating to communications, the media and creative industries. It has published reports dealing with the future of public service broadcasting 2009 and the digital switchover of television and radio 2010 the BBC licence fee (2016), and children and the internet (2017).

Other House of Lords Committees

Ad hoc sessional Select Committees are set up in the House of Lords for a variety of other purposes. As explained above, this may be to consider a piece of proposed legislation. Alternatively, as in the Commons, a Select Committee may be established to inquire into a particular matter of public interest. Such committees usually have between ten and fifteen members and, in the past, have often taken at least two sessions to produce their reports. Recent examples of such committees would include the 'Long-Term Sustainability of the NHS Committee 2016, and the 'HS2 Bill Select Committee' 2016.

Members of the House of Lords also staff a number of crucial 'domestic' sessional Select Committees and participate with MPs in the work of both sessional and ad hoc 'joint' Select Committees. The main domestic committees in the House of Lords are: the Committee for Privileges, the Select Committee of Procedure and the Select Committee of Selection. Current joint Select Committees include the Joint Committee on Human Rights, the Joint Committee on Statutory Instruments and the Joint Committee on Consolidation (of Bills, etc.).

Two other prominent Select Committees in the House of Lords are the Delegated Power and Regulated Reform Committee and the Secondary Legislation Committee. These are dealt with in the following section relating to House of Lords scrutiny of delegated legislation.

Scrutiny of subordinate legislation

Enabling or parent Acts which permit the making of subordinate legislation by Ministers may often provide for the 'laying' of such legislation before both Houses of Parliament subject to either the negative or affirmative resolution procedures. Negative resolution procedure, which is more frequently required, involves laying the instrument in which the regulations are contained for a prescribed period, usually 40 days. Should either House vote against the legislation within that period, it ceases to have effect. Where the affirmative resolution procedure is prescribed, the regulation may not take effect until approved by resolutions in both Houses. Both procedures, therefore, enable the House of Lords to veto any subordinate legislation laid before it.

Members of the House of Lords also participate in the work of the Joint Select Committee on Statutory Instruments. This considers all statutory instruments laid before Parliament and is empowered to draw Parliament's attention to any regulations which, *inter alia*, impose a tax, purport to have retrospective effect or which may appear to be *ultra vires*.

The powers of the House of Lords over subordinate legislation are not limited by the Parliament Acts. The convention is, however, that the Lords will not vote down an instrument which has the support of the House of Commons except in rare circumstances.

Until the end of 2016 there had been just four occasions on which the House had not approved statutory instruments laid subject to the affirmative resolution procedure. These were the:

- Southern Rhodesia (United Nations Sanctions) Order 1968;
- Greater London Authority Elections Order 2000;
- Gambling (Geographical Distribution of Casino Licences) Order 2007;
- Legal Aid, Sentencing and Punishment of Offenders Act 2012 Amendment Order 2012;
- Tax Credits (Income Tax Thresholds and Determination of Rates Amendment) Regulations 2015.

In the 1992–93 session the House set up the Delegated Powers Scrutiny Committee. The Committee was charged with examining Bills to see if they delegated legislative power to a Minister which appeared to be more extensive than justified by the circumstances. In 2001 it was redesigned as the Delegated Powers and Regulatory Reform Committee with a remit to 'report whether the provisions of any bill inappropriately delegate legislative power or whether they subject legislative power to an inappropriate level of parliamentary scrutiny' and to 'report on documents . . . laid before Parliament under the Regulatory Reform Act 2001'.

This happens very rarely and on only five occasions since the end of World War II. In 2006, the Joint Committee on Conventions (HL Paper 265, HL 2012, 2005–06) concluded that such action by the House of Lords should be contemplated only where:

(i) special attention has been drawn to the instrument by either the Joint Committee on Statutory Instruments or the Lords Select Committee on the Merits of Statutory Instruments;

(ii) the parent Act was a 'skeleton Bill' and the regulations in question are of a kind normally found in primary legislation;

(iii) the instrument is made under the Regulation Reform Act 2002 or is a remedial order under the Human Rights Act 1998;

(iv) the instrument is an Order in Council for Northern Ireland and is effectively primary legislation made by the government at a time when the Northern Ireland Assembly is not functioning;

(v) the instrument is an order to devolve further legislative competence to any of the devolved assemblies;

(vi) the instrument devolves further primary legislation competence to a devolved assembly;

(vii) Parliament was persuaded to delegate the power on the condition that any instrument made could be rejected by it.

The Secondary Legislation Committee was first appointed in 2003. Its primary task is to draw the attention of the House to any statutory instrument it considers:

- to be politically or legally important or to give rise to issues of public policy likely to be of interest;
- may inappropriately implement EU legislation;
- may imperfectly achieve its policy objectives.

Proposals for reform

The problem

Objective 4

Despite the changes made by the Parliament Acts and the slight modifications effected by the Life Peerages Act 1958 and the Peerage Act 1963, the existence and composition of the House of Lords continued to attract controversy throughout much of the last century. The question was not so much whether the second chamber should continue to exist, but whether it should continue in its traditional form – particularly whether it should continue to be dominated by a hereditary, unelected element. It was clear, however, that the House of Lords still performed some important parliamentary functions and provided a useful complement to the work of the House of Commons. Were it to be abolished, radical reform of the functions and procedures of the House of Commons would be essential to maintain parliamentary efficiency. The real issue was, therefore, and remains, whether it would be possible for the work of the House of Lords to be undertaken by a reformed and more representative chamber without doing any undue damage to existing constitutional arrangements and to the capacity of Parliament to discharge its functions effectively. Throughout the twentieth century, and up to the present time, the legal and conventional rules which have regulated the relationship between the two Houses, and on which the primacy of the House of Commons has been founded, have been as follows.

- The Prime Minister and the majority of all senior Ministers should have seats in, and be answerable to the House of Commons (convention).

- The government must resign if defeated in a vote of confidence in the House of Commons (convention).

For Parliament Act 1949, see above.

- Bills approved by the House of Commons but defeated in the House of Lords may go for the Royal Assent after one year has elapsed (Parliament Act 1949).

For Parliament Act 1911, see above.

- Money Bills may be presented for the Royal Assent if not passed by the House of Lords without amendment within one month of being sent there from the House of Commons (Parliament Act 1911).

- The Lords may not amend Finance Bills, Consolidated Fund Bills, or Appropriation Bills (convention).

- The Lords should not reject Bills approved by the House of Commons for which the government has an electoral mandate, i.e. in general, those Bills in the government's election manifesto (convention).

- The House of Lords should consider and dispose of government business within a reasonable time (convention).

- The Lords should not normally reject secondary legislation proposed by the government.

- Money Bills should originate in the House of Commons and should not be amended in the House of Lords.

Much of the debate on reform in recent times has tended to focus on these rules and the extent to which they may be adequate to maintain the established balance of power between the two houses, particularly with the enhanced legitimacy which might appear to attach to a reformed House of Lords with an elected element. Failure to achieve any substantial cross-party consensus on this central issue has been one of the main reasons for the protracted nature of the reform process and helps to explain why, to date, it has yet to be resolved.

Progress towards reform has also been complicated by fears that:

- a reformed House with a substantial elected element might feel justified in using its powers more assertively;

- if only on occasions, a reformed House might attempt to challenge the authority of the House of Commons leading to possible conflict and deadlock between the two Houses;

- governments with majorities in both Houses might not be subject to adequate parliamentary scrutiny and control;

- the election of members of the second chamber from geographical constituencies could lead to members of the House of Lords undertaking constituency responsibilities and a possible blurring of the representative obligations of members of the upper and lower chambers.

Controversy concerning the above and, more particularly the powers of the House of Lords in relation to subordinate legislation, broke out in late 2015. This was a result of the Lords voting against the Tax Credits (Income Thresholds and Determination of Rate) (Amendment) Regulations 2015. The intended effect of these was to reduce the number of persons eligible to claim working tax credits. The Parliament Acts 1911 and 1949 left the power of veto of the House of Lords over subordinate legislation. In this case, therefore, the effect of the vote was to prevent the regulations from proceeding through Parliament and from coming into effect. This led, in turn, to allegations that the Lords had acted unconstitutionally and in breach of convention.

Faced with such opposing views, the government initiated a review into 'Secondary Legislation and the Primacy of the House of Commons' (the Strathclyde Review, Cm 9177). In its report of December 2015 this proposed that the powers of the House of Lords to refuse to approve statutory instruments laid before Parliament subject to the affirmative resolution procedure or to vote against instruments laid subject to annulment should be replaced by a power of delay with instruments and regulations affected taking effect only if and when a vote in the House of Lords was overruled by the House of Commons.

The review further recommended that the House of Commons should look again at the procedure for making subordinate legislation relating to financial matters with consideration being given to adopting a procedure for dealing with those in the House of Lords not dissimilar to that used for the passage of 'Money Bills'.

The Bryce Conference 1917–18

This was established in the aftermath of the controversy surrounding the enactment of the Parliament Act 1911. The group convened had 15 members (seven from each House) and was chaired by Viscount Bryce, a senior politician and eminent academic lawyer. Its report was issued in 1918 (*Report of the Second Chamber Conference*, Cd 9038). This contained the following principal recommendations.

(a) The House should consist of 246 members elected by panels of MPs representing different regions of the country and a further 81 members consisting of hereditary peers and bishops elected by a joint Standing Committee of both Houses. The Law Lords would sit.

(b) With the exception of the Law Lords, all members would hold their seats for up to 12 years with one-third retiring every four years.

(c) The reformed chamber would have a power of veto over non-financial legislation with disputes between the two Houses being referred to a free conference committee consisting of up to 30 members of both Houses.

Perhaps inevitably, however, in a period of post-war reconstruction, parliamentary reform was not treated as an issue of great immediacy. It has also been suggested that the rise of the Labour party – which, by the 1920s had replaced the Liberals as the second major party – made the Conservative party increasingly uneasy about any diminution of their position in the Lords. Therefore, despite debates on the issue in 1922 and 1927, the Bryce proposals were never implemented.

The 1948 Conference of Party Leaders

When the House of Lords rejected the Parliament Bill 1947, the Labour government attempted to resolve the issue and secure some measure of agreement for reform by convening all-party talks. No consensus could be reached, however, on the powers to be left with the second chamber. As already explained, the government then pressed ahead with the Bill and secured its passage under the provisions of the Parliament Act 1911. The Conference did, however, manage to agree a number of general propositions relating to the questions of membership and composition.

(a) No single party should have a permanent majority.

(b) The right to attend and vote should not depend on possession of a hereditary title.

(c) Members of the upper House should be termed Lords of Parliament and should be appointed on the basis of personal distinction or public service.

(d) Hereditary peers, other than those appointed Lords of Parliament, should be eligible to become MPs.

(e) Women should be eligible for membership of the upper chamber.

(f) Remuneration should be paid in order to avoid exclusion of those without private means.

The Parliament Bill 1968

With Labour out of power from 1951 to 1964 reform of the second chamber did not have a prominent place on the political agenda. In 1967, however, the Wilson government initiated further all-party talks which led to the Parliament Bill 1968. The measure was supported by the Conservative leadership at the time. Its principal objectives were the phasing out of the hereditary element of the House's composition and a reduction in its powers.

The composition of the House was to consist of voting and non-voting peers. Voting peers would be 230 life peers (created on the advice of the Prime Minister) and the first holders of new hereditary peerages. Other hereditary peers would make up the non-voting element – they would have the right to sit and speak but not vote. This right would not pass to their successors. The party in power was to be given a 10 per cent majority over all other parties represented in the House but, by inclusion of a crossbench element, would not be permitted an overall majority. The reformed House would have been left with a delaying power of six months in relation to non-financial Public Bills. Its power over financial Bills was to remain unchanged.

Owing, however, to substantial opposition in the House of Commons and the government's fears for the rest of its legislative programme, the Bill was eventually withdrawn during its Committee stage. It was opposed by Labour MPs in favour of more radical change (including outright abolition) and by Conservatives who felt that the Bill went too far in terms of reducing the rights and powers of the hereditary element thereby weakening the party's position in the upper House. There was also a more general feeling that the composition of the principal element of the House (i.e. the life peers) should not be simply a matter of Prime Ministerial patronage.

The House of Lords Act 1999

In May 1997 the newly elected Labour government came into power with the stated intention of replacing the House of Lords with an elected second chamber with reduced powers. The delaying power was to be restricted to Bills relating to 'fundamental individual and constitutional rights'. The Lords would be able to delay these until the next election. In relation to other types of legislation, the power of the House would be limited to debate and revision. Public Bills would no longer be introduced in the second chamber.

The guiding principles and objectives behind the government's case for reform were explained in the White Paper, 'Modernising Parliament: Reforming the House of Lords' (Cm 4183, 1999). These were as follows:

(a) The United Kingdom needed a two-chamber legislature with a distinct role for the second chamber 'which must neither usurp, nor threaten, the supremacy of the first chamber' (Ch. 2, para 6).

(b) The institutions of government should 'reflect and serve the society which supports them' (Ch. 2, para 10).

(c) Modernising the parliamentary system would enhance Britain's democracy and improve the connections between the people of Britain and those they put in place to represent them.

(d) The continued question of the fate of the hereditary peers had in practice provided a distraction from full dispassionate consideration of what the United Kingdom actually wants and needs in terms of the functions and power of its second chamber (Ch. 2, para 2).

In essence the proposal was for a two-stage process of reform. Stage one would involve the creation of a transitional House of Lords from which the hereditary element would be removed and consisting, therefore, almost entirely of life peers. Stage two would be the creation of a new and permanent second chamber with its composition and powers based on the options presented by a Royal Commission.

The Bill to implement stage one was introduced in the parliamentary session of 1998–99. It passed into law with one amendment in November 1999. The main provisions of the Act were:

(a) the removal of the right of any person to be a member of the House of Lords by virtue of a hereditary peerage (s 1);

(b) the exemption from the above of 90 hereditary peers and the holders of the offices of Earl Marshal and Lord Chamberlain (s 2).

Such 'excepted' peers were to remain members of the House of Lords for life or until such time as Parliament enacted otherwise (*ibid*). House of Lords Standing Order 9 (Election of Hereditary Peers) provided for 75 of the 90 excepted peers to be elected by and in proportion to the four main party groups into which the peers were divided at the time the transitional House came into existence, i.e. Conservative, Labour, Liberal Democrat and Crossbench. The election took place in October and November 1999. The number of excepted peers elected by party was Conservative 42, Crossbench 28, Liberal Democrat 3, Labour 2.

The remaining 15 excepted peers were to be elected by the whole House to serve as Deputy Speakers and other office holders. The distribution of seats produced by this election was Conservative 9, Labour 2, Liberal Democrat 2, Crossbench 2.

Recommendations to the Monarch concerning the granting of non-political peerages in the transitional House were to be made by an independent Appointments Commission and not by the Prime Minister. The Prime Minister would, however, determine the number of non-party appointments to be made. The Commission is a non-statutory body and was established in May 2000.

The Royal Commission on Reform of the House of Lords 1999

The Royal Commission under the chairmanship of Lord Wakeham was established on 1 January 1999. Its terms of reference were:

- 'having regard to the need to maintain the position of the House as a pre-eminent chamber of Parliament and taking particular account of the constitutional settlement, including the newly devolved institutions, the impact of the Human Rights Act and developing relations with the European Union';
- 'to consider and make recommendations on the role and functions of a second chamber';
- 'to make recommendations on the method or combination of methods of composition required to constitute a second chamber fit for that role and those functions'.

The Royal Commission's report, *A House for the Future* (the 'Wakeham Report', Cm 4534) was published on 20 January 2000. Its principal proposals were:

(a) the new second chamber to consist of around 550 members;

(b) an as yet unspecified minority of these would be elected (see below) with the rest appointed by an independent Appointments Commission;

(c) the distribution of seats by political allegiance should reflect the votes cast for each party at the last General Election;

(d) a significant minority of members should be chosen on a regional basis which reflects the balance of political opinion within each of the nations and regions of the United Kingdom;

(e) the House to include a strong crossbench element of at least 20 per cent;

(f) at least 30 per cent of members to be women;

(g) the membership should represent a fair ethnic and regional balance;

(h) the Law Lords to remain in the upper chamber but the Church of England representation to be reduced from 26 to 16 with 15 seats for the representatives of other faiths (five for non-Anglican denominations in England; five for non-Anglican denominations in Scotland, Wales and Northern Ireland; five for non-Christian faith communities);

(i) members of the chamber would no longer be known as peers, and qualification for membership would no longer be dependent on the grant of a peerage.

The Commission presented three possible models for determining the elected element.

Model A

A total of 65 regional members chosen at the time of each General Election by a system of 'complementary election'. The proportion of the vote cast for the candidates of each party in each region would determine the number of seats from the overall total of 65 to be allocated to each party in the second chamber.

Model B

A total of 87 regional members to be elected by a system of proportional representation. These elections would take place at the same time as elections to the European Parliament with one-third (29) being elected on each occasion.

Model C

A total of 195 regional members to be elected by thirds using a 'partially open' system of proportional representation at the time of each European parliamentary election.

As to the powers of the second chamber, the Royal Commission proposed that, in relation to Public Bills and financial legislation, these should remain the same as those possessed by the unreformed House. The House should, however, lose its power of veto over subordinate legislation and be left with a delaying power of three months. New Select Committees should also be established dealing with the constitution, human rights and devolution.

The Commission's report was not received with universal acclaim. Principal criticisms were that it fell a long way short of providing the basis for a second chamber constituted on genuinely democratic principles and that it said little about ways in which a second chamber might be equipped to exercise a restraining influence over the excesses of a government-controlled House of Commons without challenging that chamber's primacy. Adverse comment was also made on the recommendation that the nation's most senior court should continue to be so closely linked to the legislature.

The government's response to the Commission's proposals was explained to the House of Lords in a debate on the Wakeham Report on 7 March 2000. It accepted 'the principles underlying the main elements' of the Commission's suggestions, in particular 'that the second chamber should clearly be subordinate, largely nominated, but with a minority elected element and with a particular responsibility to represent the regions'. It was also made clear that an attempt would be made to base any final proposals on cross-party consensus.

The White Paper of 2001: The House of Lords – completing the reform

In its manifesto for the 2001 General Election the government made the following pledge:

> We are committed to completing House of Lords Reform, including removal of the remaining hereditary peers, to make it more representative and democratic while maintaining the House of Commons traditional primacy. We have given our support to the report and conclusions of the Wakeham Commission, and will seek to implement them in the most effective way possible.

Six months later the White Paper 'The House of Lords – Completing the Reform' was produced (Cm 5291). As indicated in the government's manifesto, the White Paper was based largely on the findings of the Royal Commission but with a number of significant, detailed, departures.

The main proposals in the White Paper were as follows:

(a) no major changes should be made to the powers of the second chamber save as recommended by the Royal Commission in relation to subordinate legislation (see above);

(b) the reformed House should consist of no more than 600 members;

(c) a majority of the reformed House, and no more than 332, should be nominated by the main political parties in proportion to their shares of the national vote in the last General Election;

(d) there would be 'about' 120 appointed members with no particular political affiliations;

(e) a further 120 members should be elected by a party list system in large multi-member constituencies identical to those used for elections to the European Parliament;

(f) after the elapse of ten years from the enactment of reforming legislation, the size of the House would be 'capped' at 600, 'with an interim House as close as may be to 750 members to accommodate existing life peers' (para 2);

(g) an Independent Appointments Commission would be created to appoint the 120 independent members and to decide the number of 'political' seats to which each party was entitled;

(h) no group should have privileged access to the House based on the right of birth;

(i) the Church of England's representation would be reduced to 16 but these would not be supplemented by a further 15 religious members as recommended by the Royal Commission;

(j) judicial membership of the House would continue largely as before, with 12 full-time Lords of Appeal in Ordinary with an entitlement to remain members until the age of 75, whether or not still fully active judicially;

(k) members of the new House would be designated 'Members of the Lords' (ML).

The government's case against a mainly elected second chamber was that this could rival and 'usurp' the functions of the House of Commons and could be a recipe for damaging conflict in relation to which House had the final authority for determining the political legitimacy of the national government and the delivery of its legislative programme.

Parliament would lose the contribution of those independent, non-professional members, who bring to the House 'the expertise and experience of those who are leaders in a wider range of national endeavours, including commerce, the voluntary sector, education, health, the armed forces and the faith communities' (para 4).

The parliamentary response 2002

Two parliamentary reports on the matter were published in 2002. The first of these, in February, was published by the Public Administration Select Committee (*The Second Chamber: Continuing the Reform*, 2002, HC 494–1). Perhaps not surprisingly this appeared to seek some sort of middle way between the government's ideas and those of the opposition parties, particularly in the vexed matters of the size of the elected element and the overall complement of members. The committee favoured:

- a maximum membership of 350;
- 60 per cent of these to be elected, 20 per cent to be nominated by the political parties, with a further 20 per cent of non-aligned members appointed by an Independent Appointments Commission;
- members to serve for two Parliaments, i.e. a maximum period of ten years;
- elections based on the same constituencies as used for elections to the European Parliament;
- elections to be by a system of proportional representation;
- the bishops of the Church of England to have no *ex-officio* right of membership;
- hereditary peers to have no right of membership;
- members of the reformed House to be known as Members of the Second Chamber (MSC).

This report was followed in December 2002, by a report from the Joint Select Committee on House of Lords Reform (*House of Lords Reform: First Report*, HL 17 and HC 171).

In its view, and based on the reports and deliberations to that date, the choice lay between seven options:

1 a fully appointed second chamber;

2 a fully elected second chamber;

3 80 per cent appointed with 20 per cent elected;

4 80 per cent elected with 20 per cent appointed;

5 60 per cent appointed with 40 per cent elected;

6 60 per cent elected with 40 per cent appointed;

7 50 per cent elected with 50 per cent appointed.

In a series of House of Commons votes on the above, options 5, 3, 7, and 2 received the most support – 281, 272, 253, and 245 votes, respectively. No single option was, however, supported by a majority of Members.

As to the total complement of members, the Select Committee felt that this should be in the region of 600 with members serving for terms of ten years.

The White Paper of 2007

The next major attempt to break the deadlock and move the matter forward came in the form of a Cross-Party Working Group White Paper in February 2007 (The House of Lords Reform, Cm 7027). This drew heavily on certain general principles of all-party agreement formulated by the Cross-Party Working Group on Lords Reform convened in early 2006. The agreed principles were:

- the House of Lords should complement but not rival the House of Commons;
- it should have both an elected and non-elected element;
- at least 20 per cent of members should be non party-political;
- no single party should have an overall majority;
- membership should reflect the population's gender and racial diversity;
- a range of religious opinions should be represented;
- the remaining hereditary element should be removed;
- members should serve long, single terms of office;
- a form of direct popular election should be used to determine the composition of the elected element.

No agreement was reached, however, on two key issues:

- the proportion of members to be determined by direct election;
- the form of direct election to be used.

After a wide-ranging discussion of the various options, and consistent with the above general principles, the White Paper set out the government's favoured scheme for reform. Its main provisions were:

- a 'hybrid' House of 540 members;
- no single party to have an overall majority;
- 50 per cent to be elected with 50 per cent appointed (20 per cent of non-party and 30 per cent party-political);
- the elected element to be returned by a partially 'open' list system (i.e. votes could be cast for individuals as well as party-lists);
- members to serve for single terms of 15 years maximum;

- elections to be conducted in constituencies coterminous with those used for elections to the European Parliament and at the same time as European elections;
- the remaining hereditary element to be removed;
- the number of *ex-officio* seats for the bishops to be reduced.

The House of Commons debated the White Paper proposals on 6 and 7 March 2007, and was given the opportunity to vote on a series of options including the government's favoured 50/50 recommendation. The results of the various divisions were as follows:

Option	For	Against
1. Full 100% appointed	196	375
2. 20% elected	No division	
3. 30% elected	No division	
4. 50% elected	155	418
5. 60% elected	178	392
6. 80% elected	305	267
7. 100% elected	337	224

It will be seen that the government's preferred 50/50 option was rejected and that a majority of Members indicated a preference for a wholly directly elected second chamber.

The White Paper of 2008

Following these events, and on the basis of further discussion with the Cross-Party Working Group, the government published a further White Paper in July 2008 (An Elected Second Chamber: Further Reform of the House of Lords, Cm 7438).

In a lengthy analysis (running to 176 pages) of the issues raised by reform, the White Paper contained the following general propositions:

- Members of the reformed House should serve for periods of 12–15 years.
- Elections should take place at the same time as General Elections to the House of Commons with each election returning one-third of the second chamber's total membership.
- Members should be returned from large multi-member constituencies.
- The total number of members should be less than that in the House of Commons and should be set at between 400 and 450.
- The elected element of the House should be directly elected using any of the First Past the Post, Single Transferable Vote (STV), Alternative Vote or Semi or Open List systems.
- An appointed element in a reformed House would provide the continued presence of an independent element qualified by expertise and experience rather than party affiliation and loyalty and could ensure parliamentary representation of the various sections and interests within British society, ethnic, professional, etc.

The size of any appointed element should be set at the level of 20 per cent as approved by the House of Commons in the vote of March 2007 (see above).

- Appointments to the House should be by the Monarch following the recommendation of a statutory Appointments Commission. This would consist of seven members recruited on a 'non-party basis'.

- Should the reformed House contain an appointed element, a number of seats should be allocated to the bishops of the Church of England. These would not count towards the 20 per cent of members appointed by the Appointments Commission.

Reform of the House of Lords should not affect its powers. These should remain unchanged. House of Lords Reform Bill 2012 (Cm 8077)

Four Labour administrations having been unable to take the matter forward and following the inconclusive General Election of 2010, House of Lords reform was one of the primary commitments sought by the Liberal Democratic party as part of the overall 'package' of agreed policies necessary for their participation in the coalition government which took office in May of that year. The Bill was put before Parliament on 27 June 2012.

The content of the Bill was as outlined below.

Composition and nomenclature

The second chamber should retain its title as the House of Lords. It should consist of 450 members plus ministerial and clerical members (see below): 360 of its members or 80 per cent should be directly elected; 90 members or 20 per cent should be nominated by a Statutory Appointments Commission. Over and above the 450 full-time members, whether elected or appointed by the Appointments Commission, the Prime Minister should be able to appoint a further limited number of persons to serve as government Ministers with seats in the House of Lords. Such persons would remain members for only so long as their terms of office in government. In addition there would be 12 clerical members drawn from the bishops of the Church of England. The Archbishops of Canterbury and York and the Bishops of London, Durham, and Winchester hold office as of right under the Bishoprics Act 1878. These five would remain. The other seven clerical members would be selected by the Church of England. Clerical members would serve for one electoral period of five years. The link between membership of the House of Lords and the hereditary peerage would be broken. In the reformed House, no hereditary peers would be eligible to sit as of right or by statutory dispensation. Members would not have the title 'Lord'. A new name or title would be chosen by Parliament.

Tenure and terms of office

Elected and appointed members would serve for single, non-renewable terms of up to 15 years. Each would retain their seats for 'three electoral periods', i.e. the time periods between the date of their election/appointment and the next three House of Lords elections – usually amounting to approximately 15 years. The first election to the House of Lords took place in 2015.

Election 1	Election 2	Election 3	Election 4
(2015)	(2020)	(2025)	(2030)
(Member elected)		(Member's term comes to an end)	
Electoral period	Electoral period	Electoral period	
1	2	3	
5 years	5 years	5 years	

Members of the reformed House would be eligible to vote in elections for both the House of Commons and the House of Lords.

Taxable salaries would be paid to both elected and appointed members. These would be set and reviewed by the Independent Parliamentary Standards Authority.

Elections

Elections would take place at the same time as elections to the House of Commons. The franchise would be the same as that for General Elections to the House of Commons. For the sake of continuity, each election for the House of Lords would be for a third of the members only i.e. 120 members would be returned to the House on each occasion. Elections to the reformed House would be by Open List system for England, Scotland and Wales and by the Single Transferable Vote in Northern Ireland. The Open List allows voters to cast their vote for a party list, for an individual candidate within any party list, or for an individual candidate. Large multi-member electoral districts would be used. These would be the same as for elections to the Parliament of the European Union.

The process of creation and 'transitional periods'

First transitional period

The reformed House would be created incrementally through two transitional periods. The first transitional period would begin with the first election to the reformed House. At this stage, 120 members would be elected and 30 would be appointed by the Appointments Commission.

In addition to these, two-thirds of the existing members of the House (excluding hereditary members) would be eligible to serve and would be selected as 'transitional members'. As the total complement of the House in summer 2012 was 825, the figure for the transitional members during period one, had the proposals been implemented, would have been in the region of 550.

The clerical element would consist of the 5 *ex-officio* clerical members and 16 other bishops selected by the Church of England.

Up to eight additional members would consist of Ministerial appointments made by the Prime Minister.

First election

120 elected members

30 appointed members

550 (approx) transitional members

21 clerical members

8 (approx) Ministerial members

Second transitional period

The second transitional period would begin at the time of the second election to the House of Lords (presumably five years later according to the Fixed Term Parliaments Act).

On this occasion a further 120 members would be elected and another 30 appointed. In addition to these, one half of the existing transitional members would be eligible for selection to continue to serve as transitional members for the second transitional period.

The number of clerical members would be reduced to 16 (5 *ex officio* and 11 chosen by the Church).

Second election

240 elected members

60 appointed members

225 (approx) transitional members

16 clerical members

9 (approx) Ministerial members

The reformed House

At the time of the third election, the process of creating the reformed House would be completed. The remaining 120 elected peers would be returned to the House and 30 more appointed thus giving the House its full complement of 450+. At this time all transitional members would stand down.

In addition to the 450 elected and appointed members, there would be 12 clerical members (5 *ex officio* and 7 chosen by the Church) plus the Ministerial appointments.

Third election

360 elected members

90 appointed members

12 clerical members

8 (approx) Ministerial members

Powers and functions

No major changes in these matters were proposed and it was confirmed that the relationship between the Commons and the Lords would continue to be regulated by the Parliament Acts 1911 and 1947. The Bill contained no provisions amending or altering the role or functions of the House of Lords or seeking to confer any additional responsibilities upon it. The delaying power of one year for 'ordinary' Public Bills, and, up to one month, in the case of 'Money Bills', were, therefore, to remain in place.

Much ado about nothing

The Bill received its Second Reading in the House of Commons on 9 and 10 July 2012. The voting figures were 452 to 124. Problems for the Bill's future implementation were, however, immediately apparent in that 91 Conservative MPs felt unable to give it their support. Faced with this remaining level of dissension, the Bill was withdrawn from Parliament after eight weeks (3 September 2012).

Immediately following these events, some of the reasons given for this sizeable 'rebellion', and for the continuing unease amongst some MPs concerning the entire House of Lords reform agenda, included:

1 Significant numbers of MPs remained fearful that a reformed and more democratic second chamber could challenge the traditional supremacy of the House of Commons.

2 An unreformed and largely appointed second chamber provided a ready opportunity for MPs to remain in Parliament should they lose their Commons seats or, with the passing of time, begin to find the work and responsibilities of an MP too demanding.

3   The progress of House of Lords reform had long been held back by an 'unholy alliance' of those opposed to radical change of any kind and those more progressive elements which had long tended to view most reform proposals as not going far enough.

4   In the vote against the Reform Bill of July 2012, there was a significant number of MPs who were unable to resist the opportunity to inflict political damage on the leading advocate of Lords reform, i.e. the Liberal Democratic Deputy Prime Minister, Nick Clegg.

Summary

The chapter sets out the composition, powers and functions of the House of Lords paying particular attention to:

● The role of the House in the law-making process and that of scrutinising the activities of government.

● The process of reforming the House of Lords beginning in 1911 and explaining in detail the changes made, and the proposals for change, following the passing of the House of Lords Act 1999.

References

Bradley and Ewing (2006) *Constitutional and Administrative Law*, London: Longman.

Griffith and Ryle (2002) *Parliament: Functions, Practice and Procedures*, London: Sweet & Maxwell.

Report of the Second Chamber Conference [Bryce Conference] (1918) Cd 9038.

Modernising Parliament: Reforming the House of Lords (1999) Cm 4183.

A House for the Future [Wakeham Report] (2000) Cm 4534.

House of Lords: Completing the Reform (2002) Cm 5291.

Joint Committee on House of Lords Reform, First Report (2002) HC 171, HL 17.

Joint Committee on House of Lords Reform, Second Report (2003) HC 668, HL 97.

Public Administration Select Committee: The Second Chamber: Continuing the Reform (2002) HC 494–1.

The House of Lords Reform (2007) Cm 7027.

An Elected Second Chamber: Further Reform of the House of Lords (2008) Cm 7438.

Further reading

Brazier (2008) *Constitutional Reform* (3rd edn), Oxford: Clarendon Press, Ch. 5.

Bollinger (2012) *The House of Lords 1911–2011: A Century of Non-Reform*, Oxford: Hart.

Dorey and Kelso (2011) *House of Lords Reform since 1911*, London: Palgrave Macmillan.

House of Commons Library (2016) *The Parliament Acts*, Briefing Paper 00675, 25.2.16.

House of Commons Debate Pack (2016) *Summary of House of Lords Reform Since 2015*, 13.1.16.

House of Commons Briefing Paper no 5996, *Conventions on the Relationship Between the Commons and the Lords*, 4.11.15.

Raine (2015) *House of Lords Reform: a History: 1971-2014*, Berne.

Russell (2015) The Constitution Unit, *The Lords and tax credits: fact and myth*, http://constitution-unit.com/2015/10/22

Russell (2013) *House of Lords: Westminster Bicameralism Revised*, Oxford: Oxford University Press.

Shell (2013) *The House of Lords*, Manchester: Manchester University Press.

10

Parliamentary privilege

Objectives

After reading this chapter you should:

1. Have an understanding of the various parliamentary privileges and the reasons for their development.

2. Recognise the meaning of contempt of Parliament and the extent of Parliament's powers to punish for breaches of privilege and contempt.

3. Appreciate the role of the courts in determining the existence and extent of particular privileges.

4. Understand the extent of the judicial power to supervise the use of the parliamentary power to punish for contempt.

Nature and sources

Definition

Objective 1

This consists of a body of rules which identify those special rights and legal immunities which are essential, it is claimed, if individual MPs and Parliament collectively are to be able to perform their functions fearlessly, independently and without outside interference: the sum of the peculiar rights enjoyed by each House collectively as a constitutional part of the High Court of Parliament and by Members of each House individually, without which they could not discharge their functions, and which exceed those possessed by other bodies or individuals (May, *Parliamentary Practice*).

Origins

Both Houses of Parliament constitute the High Court of Parliament. As such, in addition to legislating and scrutinising government activity, both have long claimed judicial and disciplinary powers in relation to their own Members and other persons whose activities impinge on the workings of either House or a Member of the same.

Particular sources

Parliamentary privilege is part of the 'law and custom of Parliament' and is found in:

1 written and unwritten parliamentary practices;

2 statute, e.g. Bill of Rights 1689, Parliamentary Papers Act 1840, Broadcasting Act 1990;

3 precedent, including judicial decisions in which particular privileges have been recognised or their extent considered (principal examples would include *Stockdale v Hansard* (1839) 9 Ad & E 1; *Prebble v Television New Zealand Ltd* [1995] 1 AC 321; and *Chaytor and Others v R* [2010] UKSC 52); and the various parliamentary resolutions adopted when issues of privilege have come before either House (see below, e.g. *Sandy's Case* (1938); *Browne's Case* (1947); the *Strauss Case* (1958)).

The various privileges

These are divided traditionally into two categories.

(a) Those claimed by the Speaker at the beginning of each new Parliament (the ancient and undoubted rights and privileges of the Commons):
   ● freedom of speech;
   ● freedom from arrest;
   ● freedom of access to the Crown through the Speaker;
   ● that the Crown will place the most favourable interpretation on deliberations in the House.

(b) Those not claimed expressly but now accepted as part of the law and custom of Parliament:
   ● the right of the House to regulate its own internal composition;
   ● the right of the House to regulate its own internal proceedings;
   ● the right to punish for breach of privilege and contempt;
   ● the right of impeachment;
   ● control of government finance and the right to initiate all financial legislation.

Freedom of speech

History

During the conflict between the King and Parliament in the seventeenth century there were a number of celebrated incidents of royal interference in the business of the House of Commons. In 1629 three MPs who had criticised the King's government (Charles I), and who were prominent advocates of imposing limits on the royal prerogative, were arrested and sentenced to imprisonment for using 'seditious words' and causing 'tumult' in the House (*R v Eliot, Hollis and Valentine* (1629) 3 St Tr 294).

Charles I governed for the next 11 years without calling a Parliament. When Parliament was recalled in 1640 (in an attempt to raise money for defence purposes) he was once again subjected to determined opposition and criticism. His response was to march into the chamber of the House of Commons with 400 armed men in an attempt to arrest the leading anti-royalists (including John Hampden of the *Ship Money Case*).

For the *Ship Money Case*, see Chapter 12, p. 279.

The House refused to identify the objects of the King's anger and the Speaker informed Charles: 'May it please Your Majesty, I have neither eyes to see or tongue to speak, in this place but as this House is pleased to direct, whose servant I am here.' The Civil War began in 1642.

After the Glorious Revolution in 1688, and as part of the redefinition of the royal prerogative and the relationship between King and Parliament, Parliament decided to embody its right to conduct its deliberations free from outside interference in the Bill of Rights 1689. Article 9 provided that 'the freedom of speech or debates in Parliament ought not to be impeached or questioned in any court or place out of Parliament'.

General scope of the privilege

It is generally understood to mean that no criminal or civil proceedings may be brought against a Member of Parliament or any other person in respect of words used in parliamentary proceedings. Thus MPs and those giving evidence before Select Committees have complete legal immunity in respect of actions for defamation or prosecutions for criminal libel, sedition, breaches of the Official Secrets Acts, contempt of court, incitement to racial hatred, incitement to disaffection, etc.

Thus in *Dillon v Balfour* (1887) 20 Ir LR 600, the court refused to entertain an action for defamation in respect of a Ministerial statement made during a parliamentary debate that the plaintiff, a midwife, had deliberately refused to attend a pregnant woman. Likewise, in *Goffin v Donnelly* (1881) LR 6 QBD 307, it was held that statements made to a parliamentary committee could not form the basis of an action for slander.

Even to attempt to institute legal proceedings in response to words used in Parliament would appear to amount to an interference with these protected parliamentary rights. In *Duncan Sandy's Case* (1937–38 HC Deb 146), an MP was informed that he might be prosecuted under the Official Secrets Acts after he had asked a parliamentary question which revealed a knowledge of sensitive defence information concerning the perilous state of the United Kingdom's air defence systems. The matter was considered by the House, which resolved that the threat to prosecute was a breach of privilege.

The inability of members of the public to sue for defamation arising from what an MP has said in the House was challenged before the ECtHR in *A v United Kingdom* [2002] ECHR 811. The Court found that to the extent that the privilege interfered with the applicant's rights under the Convention, it was justified as a proportionate means of promoting the legitimate aim and public interest in free and open debate in the nation's representative assembly and of regulating the relationship between Parliament and the judiciary.

The privilege is absolute, which means it remains effective notwithstanding that the parliamentary statement in question was made maliciously, i.e. with intent to damage or with reckless disregard for the truth.

Absolute privilege also applies to statements made in judicial proceedings. It should be distinguished from qualified privilege which applies to a variety of communications providing these are made without malice. Qualified privilege is a defence to actions in defamation only. An oft quoted definition of the circumstances in which it applies is that given by Lord Atkinson in *Adam v Ward* [1917] AC 309.

> A privileged occasion is an occasion where the person who makes a communication has an interest, or duty, legal, social or moral, to make it to the person to whom it is made, and the person to whom it is made has a corresponding interest or duty to receive it.

Proceedings in Parliament

The term has never been precisely defined either by statute, the Commons or the courts but clearly applies to debates, speeches and questions in the House, deliberations and evidence given in committee, and actions taken by officers of the House in pursuance of its orders (see below, *Bradlaugh* v *Gossett* (1884) LR 12 QBD 271). It may apply also to the preparation of such materials (Joint Committee on Parliamentary Privilege, HC 214-1, 1998/99).

The making and the content of a parliamentary resolution is, of course, a parliamentary proceeding for the purposes of legal immunity. Not everything done, however, in the pursuit or application of such resolution may be so automatically classified. Thus, in an opinion given by the Clerk to the House in 2009, it was argued that, although a resolution authorising building work in the House would, of itself, be a parliamentary proceeding, that done for the purpose of carrying out the work would not. This was the approach taken in *Chaytor* v *R* [2010] UKSC 52, where the Supreme Court found that, while the resolution setting out the rules for the claiming of expenses by MPs should be regarded as a parliamentary privilege, this did not apply to all aspects of administration and execution of the scheme and did not, therefore, give MPs any immunity from the criminal law in respect of the submission of potentially fraudulent claim forms.

In terms of what is said on the floor of the House, absolute privilege clearly prevails over judicial injunctions, including so-called 'super-injunctions' seeking to protect the privacy of an individual. Less certain, however, is whether the defence of fair or honest comment extends to media reporting of any such proceedings in Parliament in which a breach of an injunction occurs.

The extent to which other communications between Members of Parliament, Ministers and members of the public relating to parliamentary or public business are privileged remains a matter of some uncertainty. In this context the following findings and propositions are worthy of note:

(a) A letter from an MP to a Minister relating to a matter of public concern within the Minister's area of competence is not a proceeding in Parliament and, therefore, not absolutely privileged (*Strauss Case*, 1958 HC Deb 430). The common law defence of qualified privilege would, however, probably apply – but, as explained, this would give protection for actions in defamation only, providing such communication was not malicious.

Strauss Case 1958 HC Deb 430

This case arose out of correspondence between George Strauss, a Labour MP, and the Minister responsible for the electricity industry. The correspondence contained comments which were potentially defamatory of members of the London Electricity Board (a public corporation). After the Minister had communicated these complaints to the Board's chairman, Strauss was informed that the Board intended to sue for libel unless the offending comments were withdrawn.

Strauss raised the matter in the House and claimed that the threat to sue constituted a direct infringement of his privileges as a Member. The Committee of Privileges accepted his argument and recommended that such communications should be treated as parliamentary proceedings and, therefore, as absolutely privileged. Perhaps surprisingly, however, the full House rejected the Committee's conclusions (by 218 to 213) – the majority view being that the defence of qualified privilege provided sufficient protection for communications of this type.

Opinions on the *Strauss* decision differ. The Select Committee on Parliamentary Privilege (1966–67 HC Deb 34) felt that due to the amount of essential parliamentary and public business conducted by correspondence between Members and Ministers this should be covered by absolute privilege. The *Strauss* decision, it recommended, should be overruled by legislation. A different view, however, was taken by the Joint Committee on Parliamentary Privilege (1998/99 HL 43-I/HC 214-J) some 30 years later. Its opinion was that the 'exceptional protection' provided by the Bill of Rights, Art 9, 'should remain confined to the core activities of Parliament, unless a pressing need is shown for an extension'.

The Committee pointed out that, in the forty years since the *Strauss* decision, the qualified privilege attaching to Members' correspondence seemed 'to have enabled Members of both Houses to carry their functions out satisfactorily'. There was, therefore 'insufficient evidence of difficulty, at least at present, to justify so substantial an increase in the amount of parliamentary material protected by absolute privilege'. Given that the boundaries of privilege had 'to be drawn somewhere . . . the present boundary [was] clear and defensible' (1998–1999 Report, paras 108–110).

(b) According to a Speaker's ruling of 1958, the definition of a parliamentary proceeding would extend to a communication between an MP and a Minister following an invitation given by the Minister in Parliament perhaps at Question Time or during a debate (1958 HC Deb 591).

Other communications between Members or a Member and a Minister may be covered and, therefore, absolutely privileged if they are immediately related to a current, or imminent and scheduled, proceeding in the House. There is, however, no specific authority for this.

(c) By definition, therefore, communications and actions not related to current or imminent parliamentary business probably do not amount to proceedings in Parliament. Hence the ruling by the Select Committee of Privileges in 1987 that the showing of a film about the government's secret spy satellite project (Zircon) within the precincts of the House did not qualify. Those Members responsible, therefore, were not immune from judicial sanction. Although an issue of public concern, the subject-matter of the film did not relate to any item of parliamentary business being considered or about to be considered by the House.

This makes it clear that the term 'parliamentary proceedings' has no essential connection with the bricks and mortar of the Parliament buildings. Thus, if a Select Committee travels overseas to conduct an investigation and take evidence, its formal sessions (wherever conducted) would, for the purposes of English law, be absolutely privileged.

(d) A Member who, for his/her own purposes, repeats or publishes outside of Parliament what he/she has said within its walls has no claim to the protection of Article 9 (*R v Lord Abingdon* (1794) 170 ER 337; *R v Creevey* (1813) 105 ER 102). This, however, is a general rule only, and does not apply where:

(i) there is a clear public interest in repetition of the parliamentary words which the Member ought to serve;

(ii) there is a close nexus between the use of the words in and out of Parliament so that 'the prospect of his obligation to speak on the second occasion (or the expectation or promise that he would do so) is reasonably foreseeable at the time of the first and his purpose of speaking on both occasions is the same or very closely related' (Laws LJ, *Makudi v Baron Triesman of Tottenham* [2014] EWCA Civ 179).

Thus, in the *Triesman* case itself, a defamatory allegation made by a Member of the House of Lords (Lord Triesman) to the House of Commons Select Committee on Culture, Media and Sport, and repeated before an extra-parliamentary inquiry set up to look into it, was classified as a proceeding in Parliament for the purposes of Art 9 and, accordingly, immune from civil proceedings. The allegation was to the effect that members of football's world governing body (FIFA) were prepared to accept financial payments and other incentives in exchange for using their votes to support England's 2018 World Cup bid.

(e) As indicated in relation to the *Strauss Case*, communications about public affairs between MPs and between an MP and a Minister, if made without malice, would probably attract qualified privilege in relation to proceedings for defamation. Qualified privilege also applies to a letter from a constituent to an MP about a matter of public concern, local or national, or that which might reasonably be said to relate to the MP's functions and responsibilities as a constituency representative (*R v Rule* [1937] 2 KB 375; *Beach v Freeson* [1972] 1 QB 14).

Given the likelihood that the term 'matters of public concern' would generally be understood as applying to the workings of the courts, qualified privilege would appear to extend to communications and complaints relating to the same between constituents and MPs. Whether this remains the case if the legal proceedings in question, or some aspect of them, are subject to an injunction, i.e. a judicial order prohibiting dissemination of any information relating thereto, is somewhat less clear. The comment of the parliamentary Joint Committee on Injunctions and Privacy in 2011 was:

> it seems probable that the same privilege would be extended to a person who wished to communicate to an MP information which was otherwise precluded from dissemination by an injunction. However, Erskine May appears to suggest that such a communication would only be protected if it was connected with proceedings in Parliament and was not communicated by the constituent in a personal capacity.

If the constituent's letter raises a purely personal matter having nothing to do with any public business or Member of the House (e.g. a private person's alleged infidelity), it attracts no privilege whatsoever and it matters not that the letter was posted within the precincts of Parliament (*Rivlin v Bilankin* [1953] 1 QB 485).

(f) Although the absolute privilege attending parliamentary words gives an MP immunity from legal proceedings, it does not give any exemption from the penal powers of the House itself. A Member could, therefore, be subjected to parliamentary sanctions (e.g. suspension) if it was felt that he or she was abusing the privilege of freedom of speech or using unparliamentary expressions.

Parliamentary papers

It had for long been accepted at common law that parliamentary privilege extended to papers circulated amongst MPs by order of the House. However, in *Stockdale v Hansard* (1839) A & E 1, it was held that privilege did not extend to such papers (in this case a report from the Inspectors of Prisons) when published generally outside the precincts of Westminster.

This led to the enactment of the Parliamentary Papers Act 1840. The Act conferred:

(a) absolute privilege on the publication of reports, papers, votes or proceedings printed by order of, or under the authority of either House (s 1);

(b) absolute privilege on correct copies of such authorised reports, papers, etc. (s 2);

(c) qualified privilege on extracts from or abstracts of the above (s 3) – in this case it is for the defendant to show that publication of such extracts or abstract was bona fide and without malice (***Dingle* v *Associated Newspapers Ltd*** [1960] 2 QB 405).

None of the above, however, applies to the type of reporting of events in Parliament which regularly appears in newspapers. Such reports are, however, protected by the common law defence of qualified privilege providing that they represent a fair and accurate record of what was said or done. This was made clear in ***Wason* v *Walter*** (1868) LR 4 QB 73, in which the plaintiff brought an action against the editor of after it published a report of a debate in the House of Lords during which the plaintiff had been called a liar. It was felt that as the reporting of debates in Parliament was in the public interest, those responsible should be entitled to a degree of legal immunity:

> it is of paramount public and national importance that the proceedings of the Houses of Parliament should be communicated to the public, who have the deepest interest in knowing what passes within their walls, seeing that on what is then said and done, the welfare of the community depends (*per* Lord Cockburn CJ).

The defence has been given statutory reinforcement by the Defamation Act 1996, s 15 which gives qualified privilege to 'a fair and accurate report of proceedings in public of a legislature anywhere in the world'.

This does not mean that the report must simply précis the contents of the particular proceeding. It is sufficient that the report was 'fairly and honestly made' and is a 'fair presentation of what took place so as to convey to the reader the impression which the debate itself would have made on a hearer of it' (*per* Lord Denning MR, ***Cook* v *Alexander*** [1974] QB 279). Hence, if a newspaper were to report just one speech from a debate or concentrate entirely on one side of the argument only, the privilege would be unlikely to apply.

Beyond this, honest journalistic comment in the form of opinion on parliamentary and political affairs in general, founded on a reasonable and accurate basis of fact, and published without malice, may attract the common law defence of fair or honest comment on a matter of public interest. It matters not that the comment may be exaggerated or appear prejudiced. The key factors are the existence of the facts and the honesty or genuine nature of the opinion (***Waterson* v *Lloyd*** [2013] EWCA Civ 136; no libel to publish a statement that an MP's claims of £70,000 in expenses over a period of four years for the upkeep of his family home was 'a scandal').

In relation to allegations and statements of fact, as distinct from opinions, made by the press and media about matters of public affairs generally, and found subsequently to be inaccurate, a degree of protection is given by the defence sometimes referred to as 'Reynolds' privilege'. This is of comparatively recent origins and is generally attributed to the judgment of the House of Lords, and particularly that of Lord Nicholls, in ***Reynolds* v *Times Newspapers Ltd*** [1990] 3 WLR 1010. Reliance on the defence depends on the existence of three prerequisites:

(a) the public interest was such that there was a duty to publish the material in question;

(b) those to whom the material was directed had an interest in receiving it;

(c) in deciding whether to publish the information, the particular press or media outlet had behaved responsibly.

Should an MP disclose information in Parliament, the publication of which has been prohibited by a judicial injunction, it is not clear whether any newspaper report of those proceedings in which the information in question is repeated would be covered by the qualified privilege just described. There are strong indications to the effect that this would not be the case.

> The press must rely on the protection of the common law. The common law affords protection against claims for defamation. It is doubtful whether the common law affords protection against a contempt of court claim, or against prosecution for a breach of the official secrets legislation when a newspaper carries a report of statements made in Parliament in breach of a court 'no publicity' injunction or in breach of the Official Secrets Act (Joint Committee on Parliamentary Privilege, HL 214–2, 1999).

Broadcast parliamentary proceedings

Qualified privilege extends to the use of extracts from, or abstracts of, a parliamentary paper in the making and broadcasting of radio or television programmes (Defamation Act 1952, s 9; Broadcasting Act 1990, s 203).

The protection is, however, confined to parliamentary papers – it does not appear to extend to live or recorded broadcasts of verbal exchanges during the conduct of general parliamentary proceedings, e.g. debates, Question Time, Public Bill and Select Committees, etc. It is generally assumed, however, that a court would regard the qualified privilege extended to fair and accurate newspaper reports of parliamentary business to be also applicable to the broadcasting of similar material.

It should be emphasised again, however, that, as a general rule, qualified privilege is a defence to actions in defamation only. Hence television or radio networks which broadcast a parliamentary statement which amounted to a crime, e.g. a breach of the Official Secrets Act, would not be protected.

Parliamentary proceedings as evidence in court

As a general principle, official parliamentary records may be cited in legal proceedings for the following limited purposes only:

(a) 'as a guide to the construction of ambiguous legislation' (*Pepper* v *Hart* [1992] 3 WLR 1032);

(b) to clarify a statute's general or overall purpose (*Three Rivers District Council* v *Bank of England (No. 2)* [1996] 2 All ER 363);

(c) 'to prove what was done and said in Parliament as a matter of history' (*Prebble* v *Television New Zealand Ltd* [1995] 1 AC 321);

(d) in judicial review proceedings, for the purpose of citing a decision or policy statements announced in Parliament preparatory to challenging it or their validity (Joint Committee on Parliamentary Privilege, 1998–99 Report, paras 48 and 49);

(e) to explain motivation for executive action outside of Parliament (*Toussaint* v *Attorney General St Vincent and the Grenadines* [2007] UKPC 48).

This is based on the judicial acceptance that 'parties to litigation . . . cannot bring into question anything said or done in the House by suggesting that the actions or words were inspired by improper motives, or were untrue or misleading' (Lord Browne-Wilkinson,

Prebble v *Television New Zealand Ltd, supra*). By way of balance, however, it has also been recognised that, if it is not possible to question parliamentary words or actions in court, it would be unfair, if only purely on procedural grounds, to allow such words to be relied on either by a court or tribunal or any party to a dispute (*Office of Government Commerce* v *Information Commissioner* [2008] EWHC 774 (Admin)).

Hence, subject to what is said below, official parliamentary records or oral testimony as to what occurred during parliamentary proceedings should not be used to initiate or support:

(a) any civil cause of action (*Church of Scientology* v *Johnson-Smith* [1972] 1 QB 522; *Rost* v *Edwards* [1990] 2 All ER 641);

(b) any application for judicial review (*R* v *Secretary of State for Trade, ex parte Anderson-Strathclyde plc* [1983] 2 All ER 233);

(c) any criminal prosecution (*ex parte Wason* (1869) LR 4 QB 573).

A major exception to the above was effected by the Defamation Act 1996, s 13. This qualified Art 9 of the Bill of Rights and allows an MP to waive the absolute immunity attending their words and actions in Parliament so that these may be used in any libel proceedings in which the Member may be involved. The Act was precipitated, *inter alia*, by the decision in *Allason* v *Haines*, *The Times*, 25 July 1995, where the court struck out a libel action brought by an MP when it became apparent that the defence was based on the alleged impropriety of actions taken by the plaintiff in the course of a parliamentary proceeding. The view of the court was that under such circumstances, it would be manifestly unfair to allow the action to proceed. As a result, however, the MP was deprived of the opportunity to 'clear his name'.

The prohibition on the admission in legal proceedings of testimony touching on what was said, done or decided in Parliament was confirmed by the House of Lords in *Hamilton* v *Al Fayed* [2000] 2 All ER 224. It was made clear, however, that such prohibition does not apply in proceedings for defamation involving an MP who has waived the protection of privilege.

The present law relating to the use of parliamentary proceedings before the courts of law was the subject of a Green Paper published in April 2012 (Parliamentary Privilege, Cm 8318).

The general position taken was that, for the purpose of civil proceedings, the absolute privilege attaching to that which has been said in Parliament should remain in place. In relation, however, to criminal proceedings, and following from the MPs' expenses scandal of 2009, the Green Paper expressed unease about the continuing possibility of MPs seeking to use parliamentary privilege to avoid prosecution for criminal offences.

By way of an attempt to limit this less desirable use of the privilege, the Green Paper proposed legislative amendment of the Bill of Rights 1689, Art 9, to the following effect.

(a) As a general rule, and other than in specific and limited circumstances, MPs charged with criminal offences should no longer be able, as a matter of course, to rely on absolute privilege to prevent what had been said or done in Parliament being used in evidence against them.

(b) This would be subject to an exception applying to the so-called 'speech offences' which MPs might, on occasions, feel obliged to transgress the prohibitions of, in order to contribute as effectively as possible to the fulfilment of Parliament's most essential functions – in particular the full and unhindered debate of matters of public and national interests. Words amounting to the commission of such offences would, therefore, continue to be privileged.

Criminal behaviour covered by the exception would include offences under the following:

- Incitement to Disaffection Act 1934;
- Official Secrets Act 1989 (disclosure of information relating to defence, security and intelligence, etc.);
- Terrorism Acts 2000 and 2006 (support of a proscribed organisation, incitement of terrorism, encouragement of terrorism);
- Public Order Act 1986 (using threatening words or behaviour, words causing harassment, alarm or distress, etc.);

For the relevant Acts, see pp. 634–8, 654–61, 607–10.

- common law rules relating to contempt of court and misconduct in public office.

Freedom from arrest

Arrest for a civil offence

An MP may not be arrested for a civil offence. The extent of the immunity thus afforded is, however, minimal as the only civil offence which remains generally 'arrestable' is that of civil contempt of court (see *Stourton* v *Stourton* [1963] P 302). Civil contempt is committed by disobedience to an order of a court imposing a civil obligation (e.g. to pay damages). The protection provided by the privilege comes into effect 40 days before the beginning of each parliamentary session, continuous during the session, and for a further 40 days after the session has ended. It is a privilege of ancient origins, the purpose of which was to ensure that legal impediments could not be used to prevent an MP travelling to and from Parliament, after this had been summoned by the King.

Since the Debtors Act 1869 and the abolition of the power to arrest and imprison for failure to repay a debt, the privilege has ceased to provide MPs with any meaningful or necessary protection.

In 1967 and 1977 the Select Committee of Privileges recommended its abolition. Its abolition was also recommended by the Joint Committee on Parliamentary Privilege in its 1998–99 Report and more recently in the 2012 Green Paper on Parliamentary Privilege (Cm 8318).

Arrest for a criminal offence

An MP may be arrested for a criminal offence, at any time or place, in the normal way. This would appear to include arrest within the precincts of Parliament subject only to the provisos that:

- the permission of the Speaker should be sought if the arrest is to be effected at a time when the House was sitting;
- the arrest operation should be conducted in a way which causes minimal interference with the business or proceedings of the House (*Lord Cochrane's Case*, 1815).

An MP may not be arrested, however, in those rare circumstances where the offence could be regarded as integral to, or permissible for, the proper fulfilment of one of Parliament's 'core' functions (see *Duncan Sandy's Case*, *supra*).

The extent to which parliamentary privilege limits the power of the police to enter parliamentary premises to search for evidence of offences committed by MPs or others remains a 'matter of some uncertainty'. The matter was brought into the public eye in 2008 by the search of an MP's office in the House of Commons by members of the Metropolitan Police Force. The police action was conducted without notice, without warrant, and when Parliament was in recess. At the time, the Speaker expressed the view that, whilst the actions of the police might not have been incompatible with Parliament's established privileges *per se*, it would be preferable if further such operations were not conducted within the Palace of Westminster without:

- the existence of a warrant specifying the material or articles to be searched for;
- the Speaker's consent.

Prosecution for a criminal offence

An MP who is suspected of a criminal offence may, like any other person, be prosecuted in the courts of law. This remains the case albeit that the offence may have been committed within the confines of the Palace of Westminster. As, however, with the power of arrest, this is subject to those rare circumstances in which the offence may be regarded as essential or permissible for the carrying out of one of Parliament's more important functions. Thus, MPs had no immunity from prosecution under the Theft Act 1968, s 17 (false accounting) in respect of the submission of allegedly fraudulent claims for expenses.

> It can confidently be stated that parliamentary privilege or immunity from criminal prosecution has never ever attached to ordinary criminal activities by Members of Parliament. With the necessary exception in relation to the exercise of freedom of speech, it is difficult to envisage the circumstances in which the performance of the 'core' responsibilities for a Member of Parliament might require or permit him or her to commit a crime, or in which the commission of a crime could form part of the proceedings in the House for the purpose of Article 9 of the Bill of Rights. Equally we cannot discern from principle or authority that privilege or immunity in relation to such conduct may arise merely because the allegations are based on activities which have taken place within the 'walls' of Parliament (*per* Lord Judge LCJ, ***Chaytor v R*** [2010] EWCA Crim 1910).

In similar fashion, no immunity extends to any Members of Parliament who has been detained without trial under emergency or special powers legislation (***Captain Ramsey's Case*** (1940)).

MPs in prison

The House has the right to be informed of the arrest of an MP or their remand in custody or sentence to imprisonment and the reasons therefore. Such an MP could be expelled.

A convicted MP has no right to any special privileges while in prison. However, an MP merely remanded in custody should be allowed to fulfil as many of their representative functions as practicable (see Committee of Privileges Report, 1970).

MPs and legal proceedings

(a) Service of a writ within the precincts of the House is a contempt.

(b) A subpoena for an MP to give evidence during a parliamentary session is probably not enforceable when the House is in session.

(c) MPs are exempt from jury duty (Juries Act 1974).

Right of the House to regulate its own composition

History

Until the middle of the nineteenth century the House of Commons took the view that it had an exclusive right to adjudicate on all claims arising out of disputed elections (i.e. whether a particular candidate was disqualified or an individual was entitled to vote) and was not just restricted to deciding the competence or fitness of a particular Member to sit. The right was conceded by James I after the events surrounding the election of Sir Francis Goodwin, an alleged outlaw (*Goodwin* v *Fortescue* (1604) 2 St Tr 91), and recognised by the House of Lords in *Barnardiston* v *Soame* (1674) 6 St Tr 1063; (1689) 6 St Tr 1119. In the nineteenth century, however, this jurisdiction was delegated to the courts (Parliamentary Elections Act 1868).

Present scope

The privilege now extends to the following:

(a) the right of the House to determine by resolution when the writ should be issued for the holding of a by-election;

(b) the right to determine whether a particular Member is disqualified;

(c) the expulsion of a Member deemed unfit to serve, for whatever reasons – e.g. conviction for a serious criminal offence (*Peter Baker's Case*, 1954) or contempt of Parliament (*Gary Allighan's Case*, 1947).

An MP aggrieved by such decision may not seek judicial redress. A decision to exclude constitutes a proceeding in Parliament and, as such, may not be questioned in a court of law. The House does not, however, have the power to prevent an excluded Member from seeking re-election but could resolve that such person, if elected, should not be allowed to take their seat (*Wilkes' Case*, 1769–74; *Bradlaugh* v *Gossett* (1884) LR 12 QBD 271).

Right of the House to regulate its internal proceedings

Scope

The House of Commons claims the exclusive and conclusive right to:

(a) decide what it will discuss or consider;

(b) settle or make rules for its own proceedings and determine whether such rules have been complied with.

Role of the courts

For details of the *Pickin* case, see Chapter 5, p. 109.

The courts must presume that the House discharges its functions 'properly and with due regard to the law' (Stephen J, *Bradlaugh* v *Gossett*, *supra*) and, therefore, will not investigate or adjudicate upon alleged breaches of parliamentary procedure.

In the past the courts have refused to inquire into:

(a) alleged procedural defects in the passage of a Bill through Parliament (*Pickin* v *British Railways Board* [1974] AC 765);

(b) the conduct of proceedings in Select Committee (*Dingle* v *Associated Newspapers*, *supra*);

(c) the validity of reports laid before the House (*Harper* v *Secretary of State for the Home Department* [1955] Ch 238).

Nor will the courts entertain proceedings in which it is claimed that the government must comply with a Ministerial promise to put a Bill before Parliament prior to taking a particular course of action, e.g. a Bill providing for the holding of a referendum before taking a decision to sign the Treaty of Lisbon (*R (on the application of Wheeler)* v *Office of the Prime Minister* [2008] EWHC 1409 (Admin)).

> . . . It is clear that the introduction of a Bill into Parliament forms part of the proceedings within Parliament. It is governed by the Standing Orders of the House of Commons . . . It is done by a Member of Parliament in his capacity as such, not in any capacity he may have as a Secretary of State or other member of the Government . . . To order the defendants to introduce a Bill into Parliament would therefore be to order them to do an act within Parliament in their capacity as Members of Parliament and would plainly be to trespass impermissibly on the province of Parliament (*per* Richards LJ).

The courts also lack the competence to question the merits or procedural propriety of the House's disciplinary and domestic activities. In the famous case of *Bradlaugh* v *Gossett* (*supra*), the House took the view that Charles Bradlaugh, who had been elected for Northampton, was disabled from swearing the required oath of allegiance because of his religious views (he was an atheist). It was resolved, therefore, that he should be excluded. The House would not accept the argument that the Parliamentary Oaths Act 1866 gave Bradlaugh the option of making a non-religious affirmation. Although it appeared that the House might have misconstrued the relevant statutory provisions, Bradlaugh's attempt to have the decision set aside was unsuccessful. The court was adamant that it could not question a parliamentary decision notwithstanding that it might be wrong in law:

> It seems to follow that the House of Commons has the exclusive power of interpreting the statute so far as the regulation of its own proceedings within its own walls is concerned; and that, even if that interpretation should be erroneous this Court has no power to interfere with it directly or indirectly (*per* Stephen J).

The same principle was applied in *R* v *Graham-Campbell, ex parte Herbert* [1935] 1 KB 594, where the court held that it had no jurisdiction to inquire into alleged breaches of the licensing laws by the House of Commons Kitchen Committee.

Beyond its immediate and relatively mundane facts, the *Herbert* decision directed attention to a question of related but wider constitutional significance, viz. the extent to which the general law of the land and, in particular, Acts of Parliament, were applicable within the precincts of Westminster.

In the years following the case, two views were put forward. The first was that legislation does not apply to Parliament unless this is stated expressly. The second approach was to argue that, where it is silent on the point, statute applies to Parliament except where it interferes with or could inhibit the essential internal affairs of either House.

In more recent times, it has been the second of these views which has attached the greater level of support. Hence, in the *Chaytor* case in 2010, the opinion of the Supreme Court was:

> Following *Ex parte Herbert* there appears to have been a presumption in Parliament that statutes do not apply to activities within the Palace of Westminster unless they expressly provide to the contrary. That presumption is open to question.

Following from this, and relying on the *Chaytor* judgment, the position taken by the 2012 Green Paper on Parliamentary Privilege was:

> In the light of the *Chaytor* judgment, the likely line to be taken by the courts in the future appears to be reasonably clear. Courts remain respectful of parliamentary privilege and exclusive cognizance, but, statute law and the courts' jurisdiction will only be excluded if the activities in question are core to Parliament's functions as a legislative and deliberative body.

Exclusion of strangers

The Commons has always claimed the right to exclude non-members ('strangers') in order to ensure freedom of speech and to prevent interruption of proceedings. The procedure for exclusion is for a Member to move 'I spy strangers'. The Speaker then puts to the vote the question that 'strangers do withdraw'. There is no debate on this issue. If carried the resolution operates for the remainder of that day. Further, the Speaker may, of their own volition, order strangers to withdraw.

Proceedings in camera

The House may also resolve to move into secret session for the remainder of a day's sitting. It would then be a contempt for a Member to disclose anything said or done in that secret session unless the House otherwise resolved. The publication of any such matter would be a breach of privilege.

Right of the House to punish for breach of privilege and contempt of Parliament

Objective 2

Breach of privilege is committed by abuse of, or interference with, any of the established privileges of the House. Any breach of privilege amounts to a contempt.

Contempt of Parliament is a more open-ended concept and consists of any act or omission which obstructs the House or its Members or offends against the House or its dignity. Hence a contempt may be committed without any breach of privilege. Erskine May defines contempt as follows:

> any act or omission which obstructs or impedes either House of Parliament in the performance of its functions, or which obstructs or impedes any Member or officer of such House in the discharge of his duty, or which has a tendency directly or indirectly, to produce such result may be treated as a contempt even though there is no precedent for the offence (May, *Parliamentary Practice*).

Examples of contempt

- Disorderly conduct in the presence of the House.
- Refusal to give, or giving false, evidence to the House or any of its committees.
- Interference with witnesses giving evidence to the House or its committees.
- Obstruction of MPs going to or from the House.
- Inclusion of falsehoods in any personal statement made to the House.
- Actual or attempted bribery and corruption by or of any Member.

- Disobedience to the orders of the House or interference with officers, witnesses or proceedings before the House.
- False, perverted or unauthorised reports of parliamentary proceedings.
- Revealing details of confidential proceedings.

Improper pressure on an MP to perform their duty in a particular way (see below, *Browne's Case*, etc.).

- Molestation of an MP in relation to their conduct in the House (*Sunday Graphic Case*, 1956: contempt by national newspaper to print an MP's telephone number so that readers could contact him directly to protest against his views on the Suez Crisis – the MP was inundated with calls).
- Derogatory or contemptuous imputations damaging to the dignity of the House or any of its Members (*Duffy's Case*, 1965: contempt to suggest that MPs had been 'half-drunk' during debates; *Junior's Case*, 1956: contempt to suggest that proposed petrol-rationing restrictions were unduly favourable to MPs; *Protestant Telegraph Case*, 1966: contempt to suggest that an MP was a traitor; *Ashton's Case*, 1974: contempt to suggest that MPs were prepared to surrender their independence for financial gain).

Phone 'hacking'

The matter was considered in 2011 by the Select Committee on Standards and Privileges. Its opinion was that a contempt could be committed by:

(a) 'a specific act of hacking which could be shown to have interfered with a proceeding in Parliament or to have impeded or obstructed a Member from taking part in such a proceeding';

(b) 'a series of acts of hacking which, by creating a climate of insecurity either generally in the House or in one of the committees or for a Member or group of Members or officers of the House, can be shown to have interfered with proceedings in Parliament'.

In the matter of purely legal restrictions, the Committee felt the most relevant criminal sanction to be that contained in the Regulation of Investigatory Powers Act 2001 s 1, viz. intentionally and without lawful authority intercepting any communication in the course of transmission by means of a public or private telecommunications system.

Other possibly applicable criminal offences identified by the Committee were:

- The Computer Misuse Act 1990, s 1 (knowingly to cause a computer to perform any function with intent to secure unauthorised access to any program or data held in a computer);
- The Data Protection Act 1998, s 55 (knowingly or recklessly obtaining personal data without the consent of the data controller).

Possible civil remedies considered by the Committee were:

- breach of confidence;
- breach of data protection;
- breach of copyright.

The first finding of contempt of Parliament relating to phone hacking was that of September, 2016, when two former journalists were found to have misled a parliamentary Select

Committee in 2009 concerning the extent of the practice at the now defunct newspaper *The News of the World*. The recommended punishment was that the pair be admonished by the Speaker at the bar of the House.

Procedure for dealing with alleged breaches of privilege or contempt

In 1978 the House resolved that henceforth it would only entertain complaints about actions which threatened 'substantial damage' to the workings of the House or its Members. An allegation of breach of privilege or contempt must be referred to the Speaker, in writing, as soon as is reasonably possible after the incident complained of. The Speaker must then decide whether the complaint:

(a) raises a matter of privilege or contempt;

(b) suggests that there has been substantial interference or damage;

(c) has been made as soon as reasonably practicable.

If these criteria are satisfied, the Member who made the complaint will, as a matter of urgency, be allowed to move that the issue be referred to the Select Committee on Privileges. The resulting debate and vote will be given precedence over other business and will usually take place on the day following the Speaker's ruling.

The Select Committee is chaired by the Leader of the House. Other members will include the law officers and senior backbenchers from the government and main opposition parties. It has power to send for all persons, papers and records relevant to its inquiries. The committee, however, is not obliged to act judicially. Hence those against whom complaints have been made are not entitled to be heard or to be legally represented.

The Committee reports to the House that a breach or contempt has or has not been committed. The report will then be debated in the House and its findings and recommendations may be accepted or rejected.

Financial inducements

There are no legal or parliamentary rules prohibiting MPs from engaging in 'outside' employment or from receiving fees or payments for such extra-parliamentary activities. Members are forbidden, however, from entering into any contractual or other arrangements, or from accepting any financial or other material benefit, which restricts their freedom of action in Parliament or as a constituency representative. Following from this, it is a contempt to attempt to bribe an MP in order to influence his/her conduct in the House or to offer any payment, reward or financial inducement to persuade an MP to advocate any matter in the House or take any other action including:

- speaking in debate;
- voting in the chamber or committee;
- asking a parliamentary question;
- tabling a motion;
- introducing or proposing amendments to a Bill.

It is also a contempt for an MP to accept any such payment.

The above rules are founded on a long process of parliamentary development. In 1695 the House resolved that 'the offer of money, or other advantage to a Member of Parliament for promoting any matter whatsoever pending or to be transacted in Parliament is a high crime and misdemeanour'. Later, in 1858, the House resolved that it was improper for a Member to promote any matter or cause in the House for which they had or were acting for any pecuniary reward. In 1945 the Committee of Privileges concluded that it would be a breach of privilege for money to be offered to a Member or donated to any charity or local political party for the purpose of inducing a Member to ask or pursue a particular question with a Minister.

No contempt is committed, however, if an MP is offered or receives payment to represent the general interests of a particular organisation or concern group – so long as no pressure is put on the MP to act, speak or vote in the House in a particular way and the arrangement or relationship between the MP and the 'outside' interest does not seek in any way to limit the MP's freedom of action in parliamentary matters.

> ... this House declares that it is inconsistent with the dignity of the House, with the duty of a Member to his constituents, and with the maintenance of the privilege of freedom of speech, for any Member to enter into any contractual arrangement with an outside body, controlling or limiting the Member's complete independence and freedom of action in Parliament or stipulating that he shall act in any way as the representative of such outside body in regard to any matters to be transacted in Parliament (Resolution of the House, 15 July 1947).

Thus a decision by a trade union or professional association to terminate its relationship and financial support of any MP due to dissatisfaction with his/her general conduct or effectiveness as a Member would not be a contempt (*Browne's Case*, 1947). However, a contempt would be committed by such an organisation were it to seek to use its financial relationship with a Member to influence his/her actions in the House in a specific or direct way, e.g. by threatening to withdraw financial support unless the MP speaks or votes in accordance with organisation's objectives (*Scargill's Case*, 1975).

Pressure from party whips does not amount to a breach of privilege or contempt (Speaker's rulings 1956 and 1975). Attempts by local political parties similarly to influence a Member's actions in the House could, however, be contemptuous.

In 1975, the Commons adopted a resolution requiring MPs to disclose relevant pecuniary interests or benefits, whether direct or indirect, in any debate of the House or its committees. Failure to disclose is a contempt.

The modern history of the detailed parliamentary system for the regulation of the 'outside' activities of MPs and, in particular, the receipt of related payments or benefits, began with the introduction of the Register of Members' Financial Interests in 1975. More recently, following a series of public controversies relating to 'cash for questions' and MPs' expenses, the rules and procedures were extended in a further effort to ensure that MPs conduct their public and private affairs in ways which better accord with the public view of constitutional propriety.

The resulting and existing framework of such rules and procedures is as follows.

The Register of Members' Financial Interests

The main purpose of the Register is to 'provide information of any pecuniary interest or other material benefit which a Member receives which might reasonably be thought by others to influence his or her actions, speeches or votes in Parliament, or action taken in his or her capacity as a Member of Parliament' (Select Committee on Members' Interests, First Report, 1991–92, HC 236). The current Register specifies twelve classes of financial interest or other material benefits which should be entered in the Register:

1 remunerated directorships of public or private companies;

2 remunerated offices, professions, trades or employment;

3 services rendered to clients of any organisation falling within 1 or 2 above with which the Member has any paid position or relationship;

4 financial sponsorships, support or other material benefit in relation to a Member's election expenses or any other form of financial support;

5 gifts, benefits or hospitality which relate in any way to an MP's membership of the House and exceeds 1 per cent of his/her annual parliamentary salary;

6 overseas visits arising out of membership of the House, where the cost exceeds 1 per cent of the MP's salary and which are not made for the purposes of the government or Parliament;

7 overseas benefits or gifts related to membership of the House in excess of 1 per cent of the MP's parliamentary salary;

8 land or property of substantial value, i.e. greater than the MP's parliamentary salary, or from which a substantial income is received, i.e. greater than 10 per cent of the Member's salary;

9 shareholdings greater than 15 per cent of the issued capital of the company or 15 per cent or less than the issued capital, but greater in value than the Member's salary;

10 loans and credit arrangements as specified by the Political Parties, Elections and Referendums Act 2000, Sched 7A;

11 any other financial interests or material benefits which might be thought to influence the Member's conduct both in the House or as a Member generally;

12 any family members remunerated through parliamentary allowances.

By resolution of the House in 2009 it was provided that mere registration of an interest under any of the above heads was no longer of itself sufficient and that henceforth Members should be required, and on a monthly basis, to register the full and exact amount of each payment received and, with limited exceptions, the name of the person, organisation or company from whom or which the payment was made.

Registration is regarded as sufficient disclosure for the purpose of voting on matters to which the interest relates. However, should a Member wish to speak in the antecedent proceedings – either in the House or in committee – the interest should be declared.

Failure to comply with the rules for registration may be regarded as a contempt. In 2000 Teresa Gorman, Conservative MP for Billericay, was suspended from the House for two months for failing to register three rented properties in south London and two rented-out properties in Portugal.

The Parliamentary Commissioner for Standards

The office was created in 1995 following from the first report of the Committee for Standards in Public Life (Cm 2850). The Commissioner has responsibility for:

- the compilation and maintenance of the Register of Members' Financial Interests;
- advising Members on matters relating to the registration of individual interests;
- advising the Select Committee on Standards on the interpretation of the Members' Code of Conduct (see below);
- receiving and investigating complaints from MPs and members of the public concerning the registration of interests or other issues relating to the propriety of a Member's conduct and reporting his/her findings to the Select Committee for Standards.

In the parliamentary session 2015–16, a total of 1,174 complaints were received of which 1,161 were not taken further. Most of these (989) were beyond the Commissioner's remit. Twelve were accepted for further inquiry.

The Commissioner for Standards is appointed by resolution of the House of Commons and is an independent officer of the House. As such his/her decisions are not susceptible to judicial review (*R* v *Parliamentary Commissioner for Standards and Privileges, ex parte Al-Fayed* [1998] 1 WLR 669).

The Select Committee for Standards

The Committee was established by resolution of the House on 12 March 2012. The Committee's jurisdiction and functions were exercised previously by the Select Committee on Standards and Privileges. The remit of the Committee is to:

- oversee the work of the Parliamentary Commissioner for Standards;
- examine the arrangements proposed by the Commissioner for the compilation of the Register of Members' Financial Interests;
- consider complaints made in relation to the registering or declaring of interests referred to it by the Commissioner;
- consider any matter relating to the conduct of Members including specific complaints of alleged breaches of any code of conduct which the House has agreed as referred to it by the Commissioner for Standards.

The Select Committee for Standards should not be confused with the Committee for Standards in Public Life. The latter is not a parliamentary Select Committee. It was created by the government of the then Prime Minister, John Major, in 1994 and charged with making such recommendations as might be required 'to ensure the highest standards of propriety in public life'. The Committee has ten members, all appointed by the Prime Minister. It is funded by, but independent of, the Cabinet office and has been referred to as an 'advisory, non-departmental, public body'. The Committee reports directly to the Prime Minister.

The Members' Code of Conduct

This was first adopted by the House of Commons in 1996. Like the office of Parliamentary Commissioner for Standards, the introduction of the Code resulted from the first report of the Committee for Standards in Public Life (Cm 2850). The Code complements the rules relating to the registration and declaration of Members' interests. The primary concern of the Code is to regulate those activities which could damage the reputation or standing of the House or of MPs generally. The detailed rules are founded on a set of general principles of public propriety formulated by the Committee for Standards in Public Life. These are applicable to all persons holding public office and seek to impose some basic general standards in terms of 'selflessness', 'integrity', 'objectivity', 'accountability', 'openness', 'honesty', and 'leadership'.

The rules provide, *inter alia*:

- Members should serve the public interest and give this precedence over private or personal concerns.
- Members should not act as paid advocates in any proceedings before the House.
- The acceptance of a bribe including any fee in connection with the promotion of any Bill or other matter before Parliament is contrary to the law of Parliament.

- Members should be open and frank in providing information for the Register of Members' Financial Interests.

- Information received in confidence in the course of fulfilling an MP's parliamentary duties should be used for purposes related to those duties and never for any financial gain.

- The use of allowances and/or expenses provided from the public purse should be related to a Members' parliamentary duties and not to the gaining of any undue personal or financial benefit.

Complaints of breach of the Code, whether from MPs or members of the public, are made to the Parliamentary Commissioner for Standards. After investigation, the Commissioner's findings are reported to the Select Committee for Standards which, in turn, may report the matter to the full House.

The Independent Parliamentary Standards Authority

The Authority was created by the Parliamentary Standards Act 2009. The Act was passed by way of reaction to the revelations and controversy relating to MPs' expenses and allowances which began in the spring of 2009. The Authority is a body corporate and consists of five Members. These are appointed by the Monarch on the advice of a Speaker's Committee consisting of the Speaker, the Leader of the House of Commons, the Chair of the Committee on Standards with five backbench MPs.

The 2009 Act gave the Authority a number of administrative and regulatory functions including determining and overseeing the payment of Members' salaries and allowances, and formulating the rules according to which such allowances and expenses may be claimed.

The Compliance Officer

The Parliamentary Standards Act, as amended by the Constitutional Reform and Governance Act 2010, provided for the creation of a Compliance Officer to be appointed by the Parliamentary Standards Authority. The Compliance Officer is charged with investigating complaints that an MP has been overpaid in the matter of allowances or expenses. Such investigations may be initiated:

- by the Compliance Officer of his own volition;

- at the request of an MP;

- at the request of the Independent Parliamentary Standards Authority;

- as a result of a complaint from a member of the public.

For more on the First Tier Tribunal, see pp. 696–97.

Where it is found that an MP has been paid an amount to which he/she is not entitled, the Compliance Officer may serve the MP in question with a 'repayment direction'. Where this occurs, the Independent Standards Authority may recover the amount specified by deducting this from the MP's salary. Such repayment directions are appealable to the First Tier Tribunal.

Punishments

(a) *Expulsion* – the ultimate sanction which may be imposed upon an MP for contempt or for general unfitness to serve. As indicated above, this penalty has only been imposed on two occasions since 1945. Only in **Allighan's Case**, however, was the punishment used to deal with an incident of contempt (false allegations by Allighan that MPs would provide confidential information to the press either for money or under the influence of drink). In **Baker's Case** expulsion was ordered after the MP was imprisoned for seven years for fraud.

(b) *Suspension* – The Speaker may order any MP who behaves in a gross disorderly manner to be suspended for the rest of the day's sitting. In more serious cases, or where the MP refuses to submit to the Speaker's ruling, an MP may be 'named'. The House then decides whether the MP should be suspended. If the motion is carried, the Member is suspended for five days. Where a Member is 'named' for a second time in the same session, the period of suspension is twenty days. If named again, i.e. for a third time, suspension is for the rest of the session.

(c) *Censure by the Speaker* – The offender, if not an MP, is summoned to the Bar of the House to receive the 'dressing down'. A Member is reprimanded or admonished in their seat. Since 1945 only two Members and one journalist have been dealt with in this way.

(d) *Imprisonment* – Members are imprisoned in the Clock Tower while strangers are handed to the Sergeant-at-Arms who takes them to one of HM's prisons. Imprisonment is during the House's pleasure but cannot last beyond the end of the Parliamentary session. It has been suggested that this power is obsolete as it was last used in 1880. An alternative view is that imprisonment might still be imposed 'in extreme cases of disobedience if the general political sense so allowed' (Griffith and Ryle, *Parliament*).

For the *Allighan* and *Baker Cases*, see Chapter 8.

(e) *Fine* – The House last imposed a fine in **White's Case** (1666). The power was denied by Lord Mansfield in the latter half of the eighteenth century (**R v Pitt**; **R v Mead** (1763) 3 Burr 1335). It has also been suggested that at common law the House may have no power to fine as it is not a court of record.

(f) *Non-payment of salary* – The Parliamentary Standards Authority Act 2009 provides that the duty to pay an MP's salary is subject to anything done in the exercise of the disciplinary powers of the House of Commons so that a salary may be withheld or deductions made from it.

Arrangements in the House of Lords

Allegations of breach of the Code of Conduct for the House of Lords and of misconduct generally are made to the House of Lords Commissioner for Standards. Like his/her counterpart in the House of Commons, the Commissioner is an independent officer of the House.

The Commissioner reports his/her findings to the Sub-Committee on Lords Conduct. The Committee reviews the Commissioner's findings and may recommend whether and what sanction may be imposed or other action taken. The reports of both the Commissioner and the Sub-Committee are presented to the House of Lords Committee for Privileges and Conduct to which the impugned Member has a right of appeal. Having heard any appeal, the Committee reports the matter to the full House, which has the final say in the making of any decision or imposition of penalty. The most severe penalty which may be imposed is suspension for the rest of the relevant parliamentary session. The House of Lords does not possess the power to expel a Member for any longer period or for life.

The courts and parliamentary privilege

Established principles

Objective 3

The House has exclusive jurisdiction to determine whether a breach of privilege has been committed. It cannot, however, create new privileges by resolution. This can only be done by Act of Parliament (see Parliamentary Papers Act 1840, above; Parliamentary Commissioner Act 1967 – extended absolute privilege to communications between an MP and the Commissioner).

The courts and contempt

Established principles

It is for the House, not the courts, to decide what constitutes contempt. The courts also recognise the right of the House to punish for contempt.

Matters of uncertainty

Doubt remains concerning the power of the courts to grant relief to a person committed to prison for contempt of the House. Where a person is so committed, but no reasons are given in the Speaker's warrant, it is unlikely that a court would grant habeas corpus (***Burdett v Abbott*** (1814) 14 East 1; ***Sheriff of Middlesex Case*** (1840) Ad & E 273). Where, however, reasons are given and these show no just cause for the committal, then – according to Holt CJ in ***Paty's Case*** (1704) *2 Ld Raym*–habeas corpus could be issued.

Parliamentary privilege and the European Convention of Human Rights

Karacsony v *Hungary* and *Szel* v *Hungary*, App Nos 43461/13 and 44357/13, 17.5.16, represent the first occasions on which the Court of Human Rights has been called upon to consider the extent to which a national parliament is entitled to regulate its own internal affairs, and to restrict the freedom of expression of Members of Parliament in debate, without fear of judicial interference.

In *Karacsony*, the applicants were members of the 'Dialogue for Hungary' party, an opposition group in the Hungarian parliament. The applicants in *Szel* were members of the 'Politics Can Be Different' party. In both cases the Hungarian parliament had imposed fines on the various applicants for disrupting its proceedings. In *Karacsony* this had amounted to placing a large placard in the parliamentary chamber, directed at the party in government which stated: 'You steal, you cheat and you lie.' A few weeks later, during a debate about smoking and the tobacco industry, a further placard was displayed by the same party saying: 'Here operates the national tobacco mafia.' In *Szel* the case revolved around the display of a banner in the parliamentary chamber which contained the words 'land distribution instead of land robbery'. It was claimed that the imposition of fines on the MPs involved amounted to a breach of their right to freedom of expression as guaranteed by the Convention in Article 10(1)).

Clearly, apart from the particular facts of the case, the application raised a number of interesting questions and, in particular, the extent to which the ECtHR may be prepared to intrude upon the activities of national parliaments and to thereby impose the Convention's requirements on their internal workings and procedures. The guiding principles elucidated by the court are set out below. These recognise the importance and rationale of the principle of 'parliamentary autonomy' (sovereignty), but make clear that, for ECHR purposes at least, this should not be regarded as absolute:

(i) In any democratic system, the freedom of parliamentary debate was of fundamental importance deserving a 'very high level of protection'.

(ii) Accordingly, the conduct of parliamentary affairs was a matter in which states should be allowed a wide margin of appreciation and freedom of action.

(iii) This notwithstanding, 'the universally recognised principle of parliamentary immunity offered enhanced but not unlimited protection to speech in parliament'.

The exercise of free speech in parliament had to yield on occasions to the legitimate interests of protecting the orderly conduct of parliamentary business as well as the protection of the rights of other members of parliament.

(iv) Parliamentary autonomy should not be used to suppress expression by minority MPs or as a basis for the majority to abuse its dominant position.

(v) Nor could it be relied upon 'to justify imposing a sanction which was clearly in excess of parliament's powers, arbitrary or *male fide'*.

Despite the broad margin of appreciation given to the principle of parliamentary autonomy, certain minimum procedural safeguards should be available to ensure:

- in disciplinary proceedings, the right of an MP to be heard and to know reasons for any sanction imposed;

- fair and proper treatment of minorities;

- the independence and impartiality of the Speaker.

In finding a breach of Article 10, and on the particular facts of the dispute, the court accepted the view that the sanctions imposed on the MPs were disproportionate to maintain order in Parliament.

The court's decision was heavily influenced by a number of key considerations, viz.:

- the importance of orderly conduct in parliament did 'not mean that the freedom of expression rights of Members of Parliament in the political debate lose the highest protection that is required for the free expression of ideas';

- in the matter of 'the need to protect speech in Parliament it should be borne in mind that not only authorised speech constitutes communication contributing to the public debate of eminently political issues in society. In the Court's view, other communicative acts in Parliament (including votes, walk-outs and other informal expression of agreement and disagreement) are also constitutive elements of the broader social communication originating from Parliament';

- the actions taken by the applicants did not create a significant disturbance, did not delay or prevent the taking of a vote, and did not, therefore, disturb the actual functioning of Parliament;

- the need to 'maintain decorum' in parliamentary functions fell short of a convincing justification for substantial retribution on 'expressive political speech of relevant importance';

- the applicant's accusations, however controversial, did not challenge or undermine the authority of Parliament nor did these expose Parliament to ridicule or disrespect.

Summary

The chapter identifies and explains the extent of the legal privileges or exemptions from the ordinary law given to Parliament as a whole, and to MPs individually, to enable them to fulfil their functions as effectively as possible. It deals with the parliamentary processes and procedures for protecting and enforcing these privileges and for maintaining acceptable standards for behaviour in public life by MPs and those involved in the process of government.

References

Committee on Standards in Public Life, CM 2850.

Erskine May's Treatise on the Law, Privilege, Procedures and Usages of Parliament (2011), London: Butterworths.

Griffith and Ryle (2002) *Parliament: Functions, Practice and Procedures,* London: Sweet & Maxwell.

Joint Committee on Parliamentary Privilege, First Report (1999) HL 214–2.

May (1989) *Parliamentary Practice* (21st edn), London: Butterworths.

Parliamentary Privilege, CM 8318. Select Committee on Members' Interests, First Report (1991–2) HC 236.

Further reading

Bradley and Ewing (2014) *Constitutional and Administrative Law* (16th edn), London: Pearson, Ch. 11.

Erskine May (2011), ibid., Chs 5–9, 11.

Gordon and Jack (2013), *Parliamentary Privilege: Evolution or Codification,* London: The Constitution Society.

House of Commons (2012), *Parliamentary Privilege,* Cm 8313.

House of Commons Library (2012) *Disciplinary and Penal Powers of the House of Commons,* Standard Note, SN/PL/06487.

House of Commons Library (2010) *Parliamentary privilege and individual Members,* Standard Note, SN/PL/04905.

Lakin, *Parliamentary Privilege, Parliamentary Sovereignty, and Constitutional Principle,* UK Const.L.Blog, 11.2.13.

Monro (1999) *Studies in Constitutional Law* (4th edn), London: Butterworths, Ch. 7.

Part 4

The Executive

11

The Prime Minister and Cabinet

Objectives

After reading this chapter you should:

1. Understand the role of the Monarch and of political parties in determining who becomes Prime Minister.

2. Appreciate the constitutional and political roles of the Prime Minister and the extent of the prerogative and political powers available to the Prime Minister in Cabinet and in Parliament.

3. Recognise the limits on Prime Ministerial powers and their effectiveness.

4. Be able to identify the role of the Cabinet in decision- and policy-making and the case for, and the effectiveness of, the doctrine of Cabinet confidentiality.

5. Understand the nature, purpose and main requirements of the Ministerial Code relating to conduct.

Introduction

Style and substance

Personality and style

Not all Prime Ministers possess or even attempt to exercise the same degree of political and constitutional power. Prime ministerial power is a varied rather than a fixed commodity. Much depends on a particular incumbent's personality and style of leadership, and on a range of largely external factors over which the Prime Minister may have little direct or immediate control, e.g. the size of his/her party's majority in Parliament, the state of the international economy, political or personal scandals affecting his/her party or ministerial team, etc.

Conviction politics

Some Prime Ministers have been referred to as 'conviction' politicians, i.e. as persons who have a deep belief in a particular set of political ideals and whose time in political office is devoted to their realisation.

In modern political and constitutional history perhaps the most celebrated of such was the Conservative Prime Minister, Mrs Margaret Thatcher, in office from 1979 to 1990.

Mrs Thatcher became widely known for her resolute and single-minded style of leadership and for her apparently unqualified commitment to neo-liberal economic values, i.e. individualism, private rather than public enterprise, the free market, deregulation of the economy and the reduction of the welfare and regulatory state – all of which in time were elevated to a political ideology in its own right, i.e. 'Thatcherism'. Her unwavering dedication to this was such that her style of leadership was sometimes described by use of the acronym 'TINA' – there is no alternative.

> It must be a conviction government. As Prime Minister I cannot waste time having any internal arguments. (The Observer, 25 February 1979)

Although perhaps less strident in his style of presentation, Mr Blair's political general political approach, was also widely be regarded as having displayed tendencies of deep personal commitment towards certain dearly-held ideals and the same desire to promote these above all else. This was encapsulated in his much vaunted 'Third Way' of addressing the nation's needs and which proved to be something of an amalgam of Thatcherite free market economics combined with a less sceptical approach towards the role of the state in matters of social and economic improvement, hence such political initiatives as the minimum wage, expansion of the NHS, and 'education, education, education'. It is self-evident also that Mr Blair was a leading proponent of, and, some would say, the intellectual authority behind, the policy of UN and NATO intervention overseas towards eradication of political tyranny and of its substitution with regimes committed to western political values. This overall approach was reflected domestically in his determined pursuit of more liberal social policies and of the drive for the better protection of human rights.

Like Mrs Thatcher, Mr Blair is said to have preferred making major decisions outside of Cabinet with small groups of favoured Ministers, official and advisers. The informal 'first names only' tone of these meetings led to Mr Blair's style of premiership being referred to as 'couch' or 'sofa' government rather than Cabinet government. And again, as with Mrs Thatcher, Mr Blair's preference was for Cabinet meetings to be held only once a week and these, reputedly, often for less than an hour.

Consensus Prime Ministers

Prime Ministers such as Harold MacMillan (1957–63), Harold Wilson (1964–70 and 1974–76), James Callaghan (1976–79) and John Major (1992–97) are generally said to have been good 'chairmen' and conciliators rather than charismatic evangelical leaders. Wilson described the Prime Minister as being like the conductor of an orchestra, trying to ensure that all the instruments, i.e. the government Ministers, played together and harmoniously for the collective good. Mr MacMillan, reportedly, had a quote from 'The Gondoliers', a Gilbert and Sullivan opera, pinned over the Cabinet door. This read: 'Quiet calm deliberation disentangles every knot.'

Serendipity

It has sometimes been said that the power and popularity of any Prime Minister depends to a considerable extent on nothing more than a good run of luck – particularly in relation to those matters which are generally outside any of the Prime Minister's direct spheres of influence. Thus the premierships of Ted Heath (Conservative) 1970–74, and Jim Callaghan (1976–79) were 'dogged', and their reputations seriously damaged, by industrial unrest and disruptive labour relations disputes in the public utilities and services. Although blamed on government policies, these had as much to do with the demise of the old, labour-intensive, heavy industries as they did with any errors of prime ministerial judgment or too rigid adherence to narrow and inflexible political or economic dogmas. In more recent times, of course, it is generally accepted that, for all his other alleged deficiencies, Gordon Brown (Labour) (2007–10), was unfortunate to have only recently assumed office when the international banking crisis hit in 2008 following the collapse of the American bank Lehman Brothers and the failure of the American 'sub-prime' lending market.

Parliamentary support

Other than such unpredictable domestic and international events, which could almost be described as twists of political fate, the authority of any of those holding the post of Prime Minister will be affected directly, to their detriment or benefit, by the size of the governing party's majority in Parliament. Thus, in addition to their personalities and committed beliefs, it is probably no accident that the degree of power both Mrs Thatcher and Mr Blair were able to exercise was related directly to the firm parliamentary foundations on which their administrations were based. The various parliamentary majorities secured by them were as follows:

Mrs Thatcher	
1979	43
1983	144
1987	102

Mr Blair	
1997	179
2001	167
2005	65

Recent Prime Ministers

Gordon Brown

Mr Blair resigned as Prime Minister in June 2005. Gordon Brown was elected as leader of the New Labour party unopposed and succeeded Mr Blair as Prime Minister. Mr Brown's relatively short period in office was dogged by rumours of party splits and possible challenges to his leadership. Such dissension, to the extent it existed, was said to have been attributable to Mr Brown's rather forceful personal manner with his colleagues, micromanagement coupled with his reluctance to delegate, and to his generally remote and aloof style of leadership. Nine Cabinet Ministers resigned during Mr Brown's three years in office.

The General Election of 2010 (7 May) produced a 'hung' Parliament – i.e. a Parliament in which no single party had an overall majority in the House of Commons. The state of the parties immediately following the national vote was Conservatives 307, Labour 258, Liberal Democrats 57, others 28. After five days' delay, during which negotiations took place between the three main parties, a coalition government was formed between the Conservatives and Liberal Democratic parties. At this stage (11 May), Gordon Brown, the incumbent Prime Minister, resigned the premiership.

David Cameron

Following Mr Brown's resignation, David Cameron, the Conservative leader, was appointed Prime Minister. His coalition government had an overall majority of 78 seats. Nick Clegg, the leader of the Liberal Democrats, was given the post of deputy Prime Minister. Mr Cameron's Cabinet of May 2010 had 23 members. Eighteen of these were Conservative, and five Liberal Democrats. This was the first coalition government to take office in the United Kingdom since the Con–Lab wartime administration of 1940–45. By summer 2014, six Cabinet Ministers had resigned from Mr Cameron's administration.

The 2015 General Election saw Mr Cameron returned to office as the head of a Conservative government with an overall majority of 12 seats. This was 66 seats less than the Con–Lib Dem Coalition of 2010–15.

Assessments of the effectiveness of Mr Cameron as Prime Minister have tended to emphasise that at no stage did he set out to achieve any grand, far-reaching political design or ideology and that his approach tended to be generally more low-key and pragmatic than some of his predecessors, particularly Mrs Thatcher.

> Cameron can hardly be said to have provided the sort of radical policy vision and driving sense of mission that Margaret Thatcher did in the 1980's . . . 'I don't like grand plans and great visions,' he once said, accepting that having clear principles was important but criticising leaders who had 'too much of a mission' or who were driven by 'some sort of messianic cause' (Theakston, Evaluating David Cameron as Prime Minister, British Politics).

It has been argued also that Mr Cameron's ability to effect any significant programme of national reform or change of political direction was from the beginning affected prejudicially by a range of matters beyond his control. These would include:

(i)   the after-effects of the 2007–08 banking crisis and the consequent economic depression;

(ii)   the re-emergence of the Conservative party divisions over membership of the European Union;

(iii)   the various EU debt crises;

(iv)   increasing instability of the constitutional settlement based on the Acts of Union with Scotland 1707 (see the Scottish Referendum vote and debate 2014);

(v)   the growing general discontent with the 'establishment' and its elites, e.g. continuing problems with 'the city' (corporate tax avoidance, excessive salaries, manipulation of Libor rates, etc.), disillusionment with established political parties (demise of Labour party and rise of SNP in Scotland, rise of UKIP in England), loss of belief in integrity of the press (phone hacking, Levenson inquiry, etc.), undermining of public confidence in the police (Hillsborough, 'Plebgate', Rotherham child abuse, etc.).

As to Mr Cameron's personal style of leadership, attention has been drawn to the following attributes and characteristics which are said to have typified his approach:

● media 'savvy' with good presentation and communication skills and the ability to present himself and his policies to the media and public with considerable effect;

● favoured collective policy- and decision-making;

● like Mr Blair, preferred working in small informal groups and to rely on personal charm and social dexterity rather than confrontation to get his way;

- tended to avoid micro-management, preferring to let Cabinet colleagues get on with the job;
- appeared statesmanlike and 'prime-ministerial' on big occasions;
- gave impression of being confident, relaxed and of being cool and calm under pressure.

In more negative terms, it has been said of Mr Cameron that he:

- sometimes appeared detached and 'out-of-touch' with the needs and concerns of 'ordinary people';
- could appear casual and easy-going to the point of indifference;
- was politically competent but not inspiring;
- lacked real depth of conviction, believing in much but nothing too much;
- could be 'caught out', e.g. in the House of Commons, through 'broad-brush' rather than detailed knowledge of issues.

(For above, see Byrne, Randall and Theakston, *Evaluating Prime Ministerial Performance: David Cameron in Political Time.*)

Choosing a Prime Minister

The role of the Crown

Objective
1

According to convention the Monarch must appoint as Prime Minister the person who commands a majority in the House of Commons or who is in the best position to form and sustain a government in office. Hence, in theory, the Monarch's role is purely formal. She appoints but does not choose.

It has been suggested, however, that in certain circumstances the Monarch might still have to become involved in the decision-making process. This would be most likely to occur where an election produced a 'hung' Parliament, i.e. a Parliament in which no single party had an overall majority in the House of Commons.

The workings of the British electoral system render such indecisive results unlikely. Only five 'hung' Parliaments were returned in the twentieth century (January 1910, December 1910, December 1923, May 1929, February 1974). Of the four general elections held in this century, only one, that of 2015, has produced an indecisive result. There are no specific rules that regulate how the Monarch should act in these circumstances. History and practice, however, indicate that the following approach might be thought appropriate.

(a) For the Monarch to allow the incumbent PM, now no longer with a majority, to be given an opportunity to form a further administration. This might be a minority government if the Prime Minister still leads the largest single party, or a government with cross-party support – perhaps a coalition (see 1931 National Coalition).

(b) If this proves impossible, for the Monarch to invite the leader of the largest single party, if not the Prime Minister, to see if he or she is able to form a viable minority or cross-party majority administration (e.g. 2010 Conservative–Liberal Democrat Coalition).

(c) If this fails, for the Monarch, on advice, to invite any other party leader, or person capable of forming a government, to see if an alternative administration may be formed.

(d) All of these possibilities having been considered or exhausted, to dissolve Parliament so that a further election may be held.

Party procedures for choosing a leader

Labour party

Elections for the Labour leader take place:

(a) where the incumbent leader dies, resigns or loses his/her parliamentary seat;

(b) where the party is in opposition at least each annual session of the party conference;

(c) where the party is in government if requested by a majority of a party conference.

If a leadership vote occurs to fill a vacancy, e.g. because the leader has died or resigned, a candidate MP must be nominated by 15 other Labour MPs if he/she is to stand. Where, however, a challenge to an incumbent leader is precipitated the requirement is for nomination by 20 Labour MPs. The voting is by all members of the Labour party and its affiliated organisations nationally. The voting system used is the single transferable vote (STV). Labour leadership elections took place in September 2015 and in the same month of 2016. The votes cast were as follows:

2015		2016	
Jeremy Corbyn	251,417 (59.5%)	Jeremy Corbyn	313,209 (61.8%)
Andy Burnham	80,462 (19%)	Owen Smith	193,229 (38.2%)
Yvette Cooper	71,928 (17%)		
Liz Kendall	18,857 (4.5)		

Five candidates contested the Labour leadership election of 2010. After three rounds and three eliminations, two candidates remained – the brothers David and Ed Milliband. The voting in the fourth and last round of the ballot was as shown below.

Candidate	MPs & MEPs	Members of Constituency Labour Parties	Members of affiliated Unions
David Miliband	140 (17.81%)	66,814 (18.13%)	80,266 (13.40%)
Ed Miliband	122 (15.52%)	55,992 (15.20%)	119,455 (19.93%)
Total			
David Miliband 49.35%			
Ed Miliband 50.65%			

Conservative party

The Conservative party did not adopt a procedure for electing its leaders until 1965. When a leader died or resigned it was assumed that a potential successor would automatically 'emerge' and be appointed on the basis of consensus following internal deliberations amongst party members. This system worked well enough but was found wanting after the resignations of Sir Anthony Eden in 1957 and Harold Macmillan in 1963. When Eden resigned after the Suez Crisis two possible successors 'emerged': R.A. Butler and Harold Macmillan. The Queen was forced to consult with senior Conservatives (including Churchill), and eventually opted for Macmillan. When Macmillan resigned in 1963 six possible successors 'emerged': Butler, Lord Hailsham, Lord Home, Reginald Maudling, Edward Heath and Ian McLeod. Once again the Queen was 'dragged' into the internal machinations of a divided Conservative party.

Sir Alec Douglas (Lord) Home was the eventual 'choice'. To avoid any repetition it was decided in 1965 that future leaders would be chosen by ballot amongst all members of the parliamentary party. In 1998 the franchise was extended to include both the parliamentary Conservative party and members of local Conservative constituency associations. According to this system a leadership election may be triggered in two circumstances:

(a) resignation of the incumbent;

(b) a motion of no confidence by the parliamentary Conservative party.

Where this occurs, the leading two candidates are identified by a series of ballots amongst Conservative MPs – the candidate with the least votes in each ballot dropping out until only two are left. The successful candidate is then chosen by simple majority in a ballot of all Conservative party members.

The results of the Conservative leadership election following the resignation of David Cameron in 1916 was as follows:

Candidate	First ballot 5 July 2016		Second ballot 7 July 2016		Members'vote (Cancelled)
	Votes	%	Votes	%	
Theresa May	165	58.2	199	60.5	Unopposed
Andrea Leadsom	66	20.1	84	25.5	Withdrew
Michael Gove	48	14.6	46	14	Eliminated
Stephen Crabb	34	10.3	Withdrew and endorsed May		
Liam Fox	16	4.9	Withdrew and endorsed May		

Accordingly Theresa May became the new leader of the Conservative party and, therefore, Prime Minister.

Liberal Democrats

The constitution of the Liberal Democratic party provides for leadership election where the incumbent party leader:

(a) resigns;

(b) dies or becomes too ill to continue;

(c) loses his/her parliamentary seat;

(d) loses a vote of confidence amongst all Lib Dem MPs;

(e) is asked to resign by at least 75 local Lib Dem constituency associations.

All members of the Lib Dem party nationally are eligible to vote. The voting system used is the single transferable vote (STV). The last Lib Dem leadership election was in July, 2015. Tim Farron was elected. The 'turnout' was 56 per cent of Lib Dem members. Mr Farron received 56.6 per cent of the votes cast.

The status, standing and tenure of the Prime Minister

The Prime Minister is the nation's political leader and head of government. He/she is not the head of state. That office is reserved to the Monarch and the Monarch alone. The Prime Minister is not directly elected or elected by a different process other than the periodic General Elections for the House of Commons as a whole. Rather, he/she is appointed to the office by the Monarch acting under the royal prerogative. The conventional qualifications are that he/she should:

(a) be a member of the House of Commons;

(b) be able to command a working majority in the House of Commons – either as the leader by the biggest party overall or of a coalition of parties.

The Prime Minister is not appointed for a fixed term of a period of years. Accordingly, the Prime Minister remains in office until:

(i) he/she no longer commands a majority in the House of Commons either as a result of a General Election (e.g. John Major 1997, Gordon Brown 2010) or a vote of no confidence on the floor of the House (James Callaghan 1978);

(ii) he/she loses the leadership of the majority party in the House of Commons (Margaret Thatcher 1990);

(iii) he/she resigns for reasons of:

- age (Winston Churchill 1954);
- ill-health (Harold Macmillan 1962);
- a wish to retire from rigours of political life (Harold Wilson 1976);
- fulfilment of agreement with senior Cabinet colleague (Tony Blair 2007);
- loss of political credibility (David Cameron 2016).

The powers of the Prime Minister

The conventional power of patronage

Objective 2

Although in strictly legal terms it is the Monarch who appoints all Members of the government and who makes many other appointments in both church and state, convention requires that all of these are made on the advice of the Prime Minister. Hence, the real power to 'hire and fire' belongs to the Prime Minister alone. But the power is not unlimited. In forming a government the Prime Minister must be aware of the need to preserve party unity and public confidence. Hence he/she may be constrained by the need to include persons of ability, experience and stature from the various 'wings' of the party (hence the survival of prominent figures from the more liberal faction of the party in Mrs Thatcher's governments).

Excessive use of the power of dismissal may also have prejudicial effects on public confidence and the government's standing in Parliament. 'The electorate instinctively neglects any party which cannot form a government, and tends to despise a party that cannot form a united government' (Coote, *The Government We Deserve*). In total there were 129 Ministerial resignations (for many types of reason) during Mrs Thatcher's period in office. By mid-1996 Mr Major's record appeared to be little better, 76 resignations occurring since he became Prime Minister in 1990. In general, however, Mr Major's losses tended to be less high profile and acrimonious than some of those suffered by his predecessor. The bare figures also hide the fact that, in comparison to Mrs Thatcher, Mr Major often displayed a marked reluctance to sack Ministerial colleagues and had little enthusiasm for large-scale Cabinet 'reshuffles'.

Whatever other criticisms may be made of it, Mr Blair's premiership was not typified by high-profile Ministerial dismissals or resignations and certainly not to the extent, as in the latter years of the Thatcher era, that his government was destabilised. His Cabinet reshuffles tended to be less controversial and motivated, in the main, by primarily pragmatic political reasons. Also, like Mr Major, Mr Blair showed no great enthusiasm for 'sacking' Cabinet colleagues. The most prominent resignations from Mr Blair's governments were those of Robin Cook, Leader of the House and Former Foreign Secretary, and Claire Short, International Development Secretary, both of whom resigned over the 2003 war against Iraq. Four senior Cabinet Ministers resigned during the tenure of the coalition government 2010–15 and one from Mr Cameron's majority Conservative administration 2015–16.

The conventional powers in relation to the Cabinet

The Prime Minister determines the size and composition of the Cabinet and the number, subject-matter and composition of Cabinet committees. He/she also determines when the Cabinet meets, the agenda for discussion, chairs Cabinet meetings and sums up whatever conclusions have been reached.

Traditionally the Cabinet meets twice a week. Mrs Thatcher, however, seldom called more than one Cabinet meeting per week. She also reduced the number of Cabinet committees and the number of occasions on which such committees met.

The Prime Minister has almost exclusive control over Cabinet agenda. It is not possible for Ministers to insist on an item being included.

> . . . the Prime Minister arranges the order of business, and can keep any item off the agenda indefinitely. It is regarded as quite improper for a Minister to raise any matter which has not previously been accepted for the agenda by the Prime Minister (King, *The British Prime Minister*).

But any persistent attempt to stifle debate of significant issues can lead to dissent and ultimately resignations. Thus Michael Heseltine resigned as Secretary of State for Defence in 1986 when Mrs Thatcher refused to permit further discussion of the decision to allow Westland Helicopters to be sold to Sikorski, an American enterprise, rather than a European consortium favoured by Heseltine.

The Cabinet rarely, if ever, votes. The sense of the meeting is 'summed up' by the Prime Minister.

> Ex Prime Ministers have confirmed – as I can – that in reaching a decision Cabinet does not vote, except to save time on minor procedural matters. On many issues, discussion is confined to one or two, or very few ministers, and, perhaps after suggesting a formula which appears to command assent, the Prime Minister asks 'Cabinet agree?' – technically a voice vote, sometimes a murmur. On a major issue, it is important not only to give the major protagonists their heads, but to ensure that everyone expresses an opinion, by going round the table to collect the voices. The Prime Minister usually keeps a tally of those for and against after which he records his assessment of the dominant view – or occasionally puts forward a suggestion of his own which all or nearly all, can support (Wilson, *The Governance of Britain*).

Most Prime Ministers use the devices of partial and inner Cabinets to make decisions, thus avoiding full Cabinet discussion. Such decisions are then usually referred to Cabinet for approval or presented as a *fait accompli*. A partial Cabinet refers to a group of Ministers selected to direct and coordinate government actions usually in relation to an urgent situation or national crisis (e.g. Falklands War). An inner Cabinet refers to an informal and fluctuating group of senior Ministers whom the Prime Minister trusts and favours and with whom major issues will often be discussed – and a common view formed – prior to Cabinet proceedings.

Other prime ministerial powers

These include:

(i) heading the formation and presentation of government policy to Parliament and the nation;

(ii) determining the size and structure of the central government – how many and which government departments and agencies and the allocation of functions between them, etc.;

(iii) managing the working relationship between government, Parliament and the opposition;

(iv) advising the Monarch as to the calling of elections according to the terms of the Fixed Parliaments Act 2011;

(v) representing the government on the international stage and conducting foreign relations generally with other heads of government;

(vi) negotiating and signing treaties with foreign governments;

(vii) use of the royal prerogative to deploy armed forces overseas;

(viii) leading the state in times of emergency;

(ix) control of matters relating to national security and to the security and intelligence services;

(x) management of the civil service;

(xi) management of the relationship between the Westminster Parliament and the devolved assemblies of Scotland, Northern Ireland and Wales.

Factors contributing to the power of the Prime Minister

Support of the Cabinet Office

The Cabinet Office consists of some 200 or more senior civil servants and other advisers. Its primary role is 'to support the Prime Minister, the Deputy Prime Minister and Cabinet Office Ministers in organising and coordinating government business' (Cabinet Office Annual Report 2010–11). The Office is headed by the Cabinet Secretary, who is the Prime Minister's principal adviser on issues of major importance. The office may be represented in the Cabinet itself by a Minister appointed specifically for that purpose.

The Office was created in 1916 to provide the Cabinet with administrative and secretarial support. Surprisingly enough, prior to this, no machinery existed for preparing Cabinet agenda or recording its decisions. It has been said that, as a result, Ministers were sometimes unclear about what had been decided and the policy priorities they were required to pursue in their departments.

In this, its original dimension, the Secretariat's main concerns were related to the efficient functioning of the Cabinet system and included:

- notifying Ministers of Cabinet meetings;
- preparing and circulating Cabinet agenda and papers;
- recording Cabinet proceedings;

- transmitting Cabinet decisions to the relevant government departments;
- attending to Cabinet correspondence;
- maintaining Cabinet papers and records.

Further functions were added to the above as the process of Cabinet government developed. Amongst the more important of these were the responsibilities of the Cabinet Office in relation to Cabinet committees – also a development of the twentieth century. The support of the Cabinet Office here includes the compiling and circulating of Cabinet committee minutes and agenda, and the drafting of reports of Cabinet committee proposals for full Cabinet consideration.

For Cabinet committees, see pp. 269–70.

The modern Cabinet Office also includes specialist policy units to assist the Prime Minister and Cabinet in the formation and implementation of specific government policies and responsibilities. This is particularly valuable for the Prime Minister who, unlike other senior Cabinet Ministers, does not preside over and, therefore, cannot rely upon the extensive research facilities provided by large government departments. Also, the actual number and particular responsibilities of such Cabinet Office units may vary from time to time depending on the Prime Minister's preferences, the prevailing political circumstances, and the policy priorities of the moment. At the beginning of the time in office of the government elected in 2015, the different elements of the Cabinet Office were as below.

- The Economic and Domestic Affairs Secretariat.
- The European and Global Issues Secretariat.
- The National Security Secretariat.
- The Joint Intelligence Organisation.
- The Office for Political and Constitutional Reform.
- The Office for Propriety and Ethics.

The Prime Minister's Office

Despite his/her pre-eminent position, the Prime Minister has one obvious weakness in relation to other Cabinet ministers. This is that he/she does not have a large government department to provide information, advice and all-round support. To remedy this, a number of devices have been used to improve the Prime Minister's effectiveness.

Paramount amongst these is Prime Minister's Office. This consists of a relatively small body (usually in the region of 200) of senior civil servants and other expert political advisers. The PM's office has often been described as being just another element within the larger Cabinet Office which supports the Cabinet as a whole. This view is not, however, universal with others arguing that, in a practical functional sense at least, the primary purpose of the Office is to sustain the Prime Minister in office against all from within or outside the government and its party who might seek to challenge his/her position.

The Office consists of a number of different sections or units. These are not fixed or permanent, their number, size and remit being entirely at the behest of the Prime Minister him or herself. This notwithstanding, in modern times, these would normally include the following.

The Private Office

The major responsibility of this small group of civil servants (usually five or six) is to help the Prime Minister manage and prioritise the mass of paperwork and communications with which they have to deal. The Private Office also coordinates the Prime Minister's diary, helps with the preparation of speeches and generally ensures that the Prime Minister is adequately briefed and prepared for both official and parliamentary business.

The No. 10 policy unit

This body was established by Harold Wilson in 1974 and has been retained by his successors. Its members are political appointees (usually nine or ten). They are particularly concerned with the analysis and evaluation of policy proposals and with projecting the practical and political consequences of such proposals.

During Mrs Thatcher's tenure in office there occurred a number of much publicised inconsistencies between views emanating from such special advisers and those of members of the Cabinet. The most controversial of these were the differences of opinion between Nigel Lawson (then Chancellor of the Exchequer) and Professor Alan Walters over economic policy, which contributed to Lawson's eventual resignation.

The political office

Its principal function is to keep the Prime Minister in touch with opinion in the governing party and its organisations at both national and local level. It is composed of party members and not civil servants.

The No. 10 press office

This has the important role of handling the Prime Minister's relationship and arrangements with the media. Normally its members are civil servants. This caused some controversy during the Thatcher years due to the allegedly proactive political role played by her Press Office Chief, Bernard Ingham.

Specialist advisers (the 'Kitchen Cabinet')

The term refers to a group of advisers, usually experts in a particular field and who are neither MPs nor permanent members of the civil service. These may be appointed by the Prime Minister or by other Ministers. At the end of the first Blair administration there were alleged to be some 77 of these in Whitehall as a whole, of whom 28 were directly attached to **No. 10**. Also during the Blair administration an Order in Council was made allowing the political advisers Alastair Campbell and Jonathan Powell to give instructions to civil servants. The Order was revoked by the Brown government in 2007. There were 97 such advisers or 'spads' engaged by Mr Cameron after he was returned to No. 10 in May, 2015. Reliance on such experts has been alleged to be at odds with underlying constitutional values since it may appear to diminish the role of the Cabinet and allow national policy to be influenced unduly by persons with no democratic mandate or direct accountability.

Think-tanks

Prime Minsters can look outside for advice and support. Thatcher maintained contact with a number of right-wing intellectual groups, including the Centre for Policy Studies, the Institute for Economic Affairs and the Adam Smith Institute. Blair turned to bodies such as the Fabian Society, the Policy Studies Institute and Demos, often placing New Labour wrapping around Thatcherite policies. Cameron favoured the right wing Policy Exchange (Pilger, 1998).

Party loyalty and party discipline

The majority of government and party members will have no wish to antagonise the Prime Minister. Most will realise that their hopes of advancement are dependent on their favour, and that the Prime Minister will be able to claim some of the credit for the party's success in the last General Election. It is also well appreciated that dissent and disunity do little for a party's public image and may adversely affect future electoral prospects.

Paradoxically, however, large parliamentary majorities – as Mrs Thatcher had after 1983, and as Mr Blair had after the 1997 and 2001 elections – tend to give MPs greater latitude for backbench revolts. 'A smallish working majority tends to keep a party *and* a government on its toes, a landslide is bad for party discipline, enabling rebellion with impunity' (Jenkins, *Mrs Thatcher's Revolution*). Note, however, that small majorities are no absolute guarantee of party unity – particularly where party managers have failed to convince backbenchers of the political or economic necessity of an unpopular proposal. Hence the failure of the Conservative government in December 1994 to defeat an opposition motion condemning increased VAT on domestic fuel.

The voting and two-party systems

Almost invariably the British 'first past the post' voting system works to give the party which has secured the largest percentage of the popular vote (usually well below an absolute majority of 50+ per cent) an exaggerated proportion of the seats in the House of Commons thus accentuating the extent of that party's dominance of parliamentary activity. This was illustrated most graphically by the General Election result of 1997 where Mr Blair's New Labour party was rewarded with 416 or 63.5 per cent of the available parliamentary seats for just 43.2 per cent of the popular vote. The result of the 2015 election paid testimony to the same trend – albeit not quite so dramatically. On this occasion Mr Cameron's Conservative party secured 331 or 50.9 per cent of the seats (650) for a return of 30.4 per cent of the votes cast.

Media exposure

In recent times coverage of political events has increasingly tended to concentrate on personalities rather than on the details of party policy. In all of this the Prime Minister is given the limelight. The PM's activities and utterances on both the domestic and international scenes are brought into people's homes on a daily basis. More than any other politician, the Prime Minister has the opportunity to convey her or his views to the electorate and to project and develop an image which will enhance his or her popularity.

The effect of two World Wars

Some have argued that the central and crucial role played by Lloyd-George in the First World War and Churchill in the Second World War enhanced the prestige and power of the office. Powers assumed during these crises were not all surrendered during peacetime. It is generally agreed that Mrs Thatcher became more dominant after the Falklands War and the successful General Election campaign which followed it.

Limits on Prime Ministerial power

The Cabinet

Objective 3

Despite the Prime Minister's pre-eminent position in relation to other Ministers, insistence on policies not fully supported in Cabinet tends to result in dissent and dissatisfaction (often revealed by 'leaks') and, possibly, in Ministerial resignations – all of which damage the image of both the government and the Prime Minister. Towards the end of her premiership, it is generally accepted that Mrs Thatcher's power-base within the Conservative party and her image nationally were seriously damaged by her policy differences with, and the eventual resignations of, Sir Geoffrey Howe (Leader of the House of Commons and previously Foreign Secretary and Chancellor of the Exchequer) and with Nigel Lawson (Chancellor of the Exchequer).

As indicated, although the Prime Minister has the power to deal with Ministerial opposition by 'sacking' members of the Cabinet, too many sackings may give the impression of a divided government. There is also the danger that 'sacked' Ministers may become the focus of discontent on the backbenches.

From time to time the Cabinet may be able to persuade the Prime Minister to change his or her stance in relation to a particular issue. In 1969, for example, the Cabinet combined to force Harold Wilson to abandon plans to place additional legal restraints on the activities of trade unions. It has also been claimed that the pro-European element in Mrs Thatcher's Cabinet successfully persuaded her to take a less sceptical attitude towards membership of the European Monetary System and to the general question of entrusting further and greater powers to the European Community.

Parliament

Government defeats, or the withdrawal of proposals because of parliamentary opposition, tend to damage the credibility of the Prime Minister and may create suspicions that they are no longer in effective control of the nation's affairs, i.e. that the government has 'lost its way'.

In the final analysis, of course, governments and Prime Ministers may be put out of office by adverse confidence votes in the House of Commons. The Labour Prime Minister (James Callaghan) and government were forced to resign in 1979 after losing a confidence motion by just one vote. Also note that in 1940, although a vote of no confidence in the Prime Minister's handling of the war was defeated (by 80 votes), the then Conservative premier, Neville Chamberlain, still felt compelled to resign. The fact that 33 of his own MPs voted against him and 40 abstained demonstrated a widespread and cross-party absence of support.

The parliamentary party

Lord Palmerston (Prime Minister 1855–58 and 1859–65) once said that the real opposition sat 'behind the Treasury bench'. Criticism from opposition MPs is to be expected. It is almost ritualistic and, in the normal course of events, does little to damage either Prime Minister or government. Dissent on the government's own benches, however, can be far more detrimental. Backbench 'revolts' undermine the Prime Minister's authority and may cause difficulties for implementation of the government's legislative programme. In late 1994, for example, John Major's embarrassment was considerable when Conservative backbenchers opposed a number of key government initiatives. Due to overt backbench disaffection the Second Reading of the Bill increasing the UK's European budgetary contribution was made a matter of confidence (i.e. the government said it would resign if defeated) and shortly afterwards, as already mentioned, the government was defeated by an opposition motion condemning its planned increase in VAT on domestic fuel (15 Conservative MPs failed to obey the party whip). In addition, persistent backbench unrest concerning the government's attitude towards the European Union did little to enhance Mr Major's standing.

As indicated above, the Prime Minister's power of patronage in relation to Ministerial appointments is constrained by the need to preserve party unity. It is generally accepted that such appointments should recognise the existence of different views and factions within the party. A prudent Prime Minister will seek, therefore, to choose a government around which all the party can unite. A government chosen purely from the Prime Minister's particular persuasion or faction would inevitably have to deal with dissent from those elements of the party aggrieved by their exclusion.

The media

The growth of the importance of the media in scrutinising and constraining the exercise of prime-ministerial power has been paralleled in modern politics by the correlative increase in the amount of time spent by the Prime Minister in broadcasting and television studios rather than in the chamber of the House of Commons itself – a trend given considerable impetus by the decision of the Blair government in 2003 to reduce the number of sessions of prime-ministerial questions from two to one per week.

> The mass media have gained much of the power to check the executive that has traditionally vested with Parliament, and recent Prime Ministers have responded to the challenge by a host of media-related activities. As in many other parliamentary democracies, managing the media has become an important new task of Prime Ministers seeking to keep control of the public agenda to the greatest possible extent (Professor Ludgen Helms, University of Innsbruck, evidence to House of Commons Political and Constitutional Reform Committee, 2014).

The Monarch

In strict constitutional terms the Monarch still reserves the residual prerogative right to dismiss the Prime Minister. The power has not been used since 1783. As a result of the unwritten nature of the British constitution, no other formal legal procedure exists for removing a Prime Minister from office (the rule that a Prime Minister must tender his/her resignation if defeated in a vote of confidence or at a General Election being a purely conventional requirement). This being so, the prerogative power of the Monarch remains the only legal remedy for dealing with a premier who ignores conventional restraints or who, in some other way, behaves unconstitutionally or in a manner seriously damaging to the national interest. It is conceivable, for example, that the Monarch might be forced to act should a Prime Minister refuse to resign after losing the confidence of a majority in the House of Commons. Clearly, however, it is a royal power which would have to be reserved for the most extreme circumstances.

For the Monarch's influence in modern government, see Chapter 2.

> The power is said to survive for use if a government should act to destroy the democratic or parliamentary bases of the constitution. But unless the Sovereign's judgment of the necessity to dismiss her ministers on these grounds should be generally supported by public opinion, the monarchy itself would be placed in jeopardy (Turpin, *British Government and the Constitution*).

The civil service

It has been suggested that those in the senior echelons of the civil service regard themselves as the custodians of certain traditional views and values concerning the British system of government and that such attitudes, coupled with civil service responsibility for the implementation of policy, may be used to thwart Prime Ministerial and Cabinet intentions – particularly where these are of a radical nature. Such covert opposition to government policy may manifest itself in a number of ways including, *inter alia*, delay (both in terms of action and the provision of necessary information), the organisation of resistance amongst and within the departments of state involved, and the leaking of information to the media. Mrs Thatcher, on a number of occasions, made clear her displeasure concerning alleged civil service resistance to some of her policy objectives. One example was her concern about the 'Whitehall' ethos in relation to cuts in public expenditure. She is also said to have suspected pro-European elements in various departments, but particularly in the Foreign Office, Ministry of Defence, and the Department of Trade and Industry. This may explain why Mrs Thatcher was accused of attempting to 'politicise' the civil service, i.e. insisting on the appointment and preferment of persons likely to be sympathetic to her particular perspective.

Interest groups

The standing of a Prime Minister may also be damaged by determined and widespread opposition from those representing major interests within society. In the long term, for example, Mrs Thatcher's reputation was not helped by criticism from churches and charities concerning some of the alleged social consequences of monetarist policies. Nor would the fortunes of any Conservative government be well served by opposition from any of those organisations traditionally regarded as supportive of Conservative ideology, e.g. the CBI, Institute of Directors, National Farmers' Union, etc. In the same vein, a Labour premier and government at odds with traditional bastions of Labour support would be unlikely to prosper. Industrial unrest and trade union agitation in the winter of 1978–79 ('the winter of discontent'), for example, is generally agreed to have been a significant factor in Labour's defeat in the 1979 General Election.

Leaks

These have become an increasingly common tactical device to embarrass the Prime Minister and government. They are used by Ministers to generate opposition to policy proposals to which they are opposed but cannot criticise due to the convention of collective Ministerial responsibility.

> The unattributable leak involves the disclosure of matters that are secret only because of the doctrine of collective responsibility – such as the subject of Cabinet discussion, Cabinet decisions, views assigned to different Ministers, and the like. The leak gives information known only by Ministers. The main motives for leaks . . . became the desire to inform – or mislead – their followers in the parliamentary party about the stand they had taken in the Cabinet on a particular issue. Thus the doctrine of collective responsibility and the unattributable leak grew up side by side as an inevitable feature of the Cabinet in a mass two-party system. In every Cabinet the leak will be deplored and condemned, but it is paradoxically necessary to the preservation of the doctrine of collective responsibility. It is the mechanism by which the doctrine of collective responsibility is reconciled with political reality. The unattributable leak itself is a recognition and acceptance of the doctrine that members of a Cabinet do not disagree in public (Walker, *The Cabinet*).

By-election defeats

Sometimes these may be put down to a government's mid-term unpopularity (a frequent but not necessarily unavoidable feature of modern British politics). However, a succession of defeats – particularly if these continue after the mid-term period – will tend to have a detrimental effect on the Prime Minister's domestic standing and may cause backbench concern about the Prime Minister's suitability to lead the governing party into the next

General Election. Mrs Thatcher's position was considerably weakened by by-election defeats in the autumn of 1990 (Eastbourne and Bradford). The Eastbourne defeat was particularly damaging as this had previously been regarded as an absolutely safe Conservative seat.

The Major government of 1990–7 was also adversely affected by a series of by-election losses. These not only had consequences for Mr Major's image, but by 1996 had reduced his majority from 21 to just 1. Twenty-one by-elections took place during the Parliament of 2010–15. The results by party were as follows: Labour, 14; Sinn Fein, 2; UKIP, 2; Conservatives, 1; Liberal Democrats, 1; Respect 1. At the time of writing (January, 2017), eight had taken place in the Parliament of 2015–20. The results were: Labour, 5; Conservatives, 2; Liberal Democrats, 1.

Public opinion polls

These contain regular assessments of the extent of the Prime Minister's popularity and, notwithstanding doubts as to their accuracy, may (if consistently detrimental) help to destabilise their position. It has been alleged, for example, that public opinion polls create an electoral momentum of their own. Put another way, they help to mould public opinion rather than simply measure it. Thus, if such polls repeatedly tell the electorate that the Prime Minister is unpopular and not regarded as a competent leader capable of winning the next election, this may further diminish his/her standing and influence electors to vote for an alternative party and leader. Gloomy public opinion polls may also be factors in creating backbench unease – possibly resulting in a leadership challenge, particularly once a government has passed its mid-term point and MPs begin to concentrate on the spectre of the next election.

External political and economic pressures

National governments are no longer able to exercise such exclusive control over their domestic economic affairs as once was the case. Changes in US or EU interest rates, for example, may have immediate and not necessarily beneficial consequences for the United Kingdom's economy. Rates of taxation, particularly VAT, may be affected by membership of the European Union. Decisions by OPEC affecting the price of oil may have 'knock-on' effects for costs and inflation. The economy in general may be damaged by worldwide recession (e.g. the banking crisis of 2008). These are just a few examples but they clearly illustrate the sort of external forces which, although not directly of its own making, can diminish public confidence in an administration and its leader. Little wonder, then, that sheer good luck is said to be one of the factors which Prime Ministers must have if they are to survive.

Party conferences

The extent to which MPs are affected or influenced by the votes and opinions of party conferences is a matter of some uncertainty. This is not usually a problem for Conservative premiers as the Conservative party conference has no policy-making powers. Conservative conferences seldom vote and usually try to avoid open controversy or criticism of the party leadership. It follows, however, that when dissent is shown, this is something which the leadership would be unwise to ignore. The position is rather different in the Labour party. According to the formal rules of the Labour Constitution, the annual party conference is the party's primary policy-making body. Thus it is provided that 'the work of the party shall be under the direction and control of the party conference' and that 'no proposal shall be included in the party programme unless it has been adopted by conference by a majority of not less than two-thirds'. Successive Labour governments have, however, adopted the position that they should not be bound rigidly and absolutely by conference decisions and that Labour in power is under a constitutional obligation to conduct national affairs in the best interests of the entire community – also that, as the problems facing the nation will often change rapidly and unpredictably, the government must be free to adapt policy and action to the demands of the moment.

The Cabinet

Composition

Objective 4

Appointment to and allocation of portfolios within the Cabinet is entirely within the grant of the Prime Minister. These days the Cabinet will usually consist of 20–25 Ministers, but again this is a matter for the Prime Minister. The heads of the major departments will be included, as will the Leader of the House of Commons (responsible for expedition of government business in the House), the Leader of the House of Lords (responsible for government business in the upper House), the Chancellor of the Duchy of Lancaster (responsibilities determined by Prime Minister – sometimes party chairperson in Conservative governments), and the Chief Secretary to the Treasury (Chancellor of the Exchequer's 'No. 2').

Note that not all Ministers will be members of the Cabinet. Within each department there will be a 'team' of Ministers junior to the departmental head or Secretary of State. Next in order of seniority are Ministers of State and, beneath them, Under Secretaries of State and parliamentary private secretaries. The total number of Ministers in a government, therefore, may be well in excess of 100. Only 95 paid Ministers may have seats in the House of Commons (House of Commons (Disqualification) Act 1975). This is to minimise exploitation of the 'pay-roll vote', i.e. the number of MPs bound by the convention of collective Ministerial responsibility and, therefore, obliged to support the government.

Functions

According to the 1918 Haldane Committee on the Machinery of Government (Cmnd 9230) the Cabinet has three major responsibilities:

> . . . the final determination of policy to be submitted to Parliament;

> . . . the supreme control of the national executive in accordance with the policy prescribed by Parliament;

> . . . the continuous co-ordination and delimitation of the interests of the several departments of state.

The final determination of policy

Clearly the majority of major decisions concerning the management of parliamentary and national affairs are considered within Cabinet. However, due to reasons of time, and the size and complexity of modern government, it is not possible for the Cabinet in twice-weekly meetings to give its full attention to all issues relating to the formation and implementation of policy and to the multifarious other matters with which the government must deal. Inevitably, therefore, other mechanisms and procedures have been developed to expedite the process of policy and decision-making.

(a) Cabinet committees

Until 1992 the exact number, designation and composition of these was not made public. Mrs Thatcher reportedly had some 25 such standing committees and another 110 ad hoc working parties. In May 1992 premier Major allowed the existence and composition of these committees to be made known. They are usually chaired by a Cabinet Minister and will consist of other Ministers, mostly not of Cabinet rank, from those departments with an interest in a particular committee's area of responsibility. For the purposes of the Coalition which took office in 2010, each committee had a Chair from one party and a Deputy Chair from the other. Most are permanent but ad hoc committees may be set up to deal with or oversee a particular problem.

Their principal functions are to coordinate the activities of the various departments of state, to formulate policy suggestions or proposed courses of executive action (or oversee the same) for Cabinet consideration, and to deal with and make recommendations related to any other matter referred to them.

The full list of Cabinet committees released by the Cabinet Office early in 2016 identified 30 committees and sub-committees. The full list was with numbers of Ministers attending was:

- Constitutional Reform Committee (12)
- Economic Affairs Committee (23)
  - Airport Sub-Committee (10)
  - Reducing Regulations Sub-Committee (17)
- European Committee
- European Affairs Committee (16)
- European Referendum Committee (6)
- Home Affairs Committee (20)
  - Armed Forces Sub-Committee (15)
- National Security Council (10)
  - Nuclear Deterrence and Security Sub-Committee (6)
  - Threats, Hazards, Resilience and Contingencies Sub-Committee (18)
  - Cyber Sub-Committee (8)
  - Syria and Iraq Sub-Committee (8)
  - Strategic Defence and Security Review Sub-Committee (10)
  - Counter-Terrorism Sub-Committee (13)
- Parliamentary Business and Legislation Committee (12)
- Social Justice Committee (10)
- Public Expenditure Committee (5)
  - Efficiency Sub-Committee (9)

In addition to the above, during Mr Cameron's premiership, and for the first time, a new type of Ministerial committee was created to be concerned more with the implementation of government policy rather than with its function. These are described as 'Implementation Task Forces'. As of 2016, these and the number of ministers involved were:

- Childcare (11);
- Child Protection (12);
- Digital Infrastructure and Inclusion (8);

- Earn or Learn (9);
- Exports (8);
- Health and Social Care (6);
- Housing (11);
- Immigration (12);
- Tackling Extremism in Communities (16);
- Troubled Families (8);
- Syrian Returns (6).

Source: Cabinet Office

(b) Inner and partial Cabinets

As already explained, the term 'partial Cabinet' refers to a group of Cabinet Ministers selected by the Prime Minister to direct and coordinate some aspect of government action, often in relation to a matter of urgency or where expedition is needed to deal with an immediate and serious threat to the national interest. Note, for example, such use by Mrs Thatcher during the Falklands War (1982) and the periodic convening of a group of senior Ministers (the 'Star Chamber') to mediate in the annual public expenditure negotiations between the Treasury and the main spending departments.

Such informal Ministerial groups can be used to thwart or obstruct the plans of particular Ministers. For example, after the inner city riots of 1981 Michael Heseltine (Minister for the Environment) proposed a major spending programme to deal with inner city dereliction.

> Mrs Thatcher convened an informal ministerial group, with a majority of members chosen by the Prime Minister who would be unsympathetic to Mr Heseltine's proposals. The extra spending which was ultimately authorised was on nothing like the scale urged by Mr Heseltine.
> (Brazier, *Constitutional Practice*)

The 'inner Cabinet', also referred to above, consists of that small group of particularly trusted senior Ministers, usually holding key Cabinet posts, to whom the Prime Minister may refer for advice and support on an informal and confidential level. Although outnumbered by the rest of the Cabinet, decisions and courses of action proposed by such powerful groupings are unlikely to be defeated when and if put before a Cabinet meeting.

It has been claimed, for example, that no full Cabinet discussion took place before Neville Chamberlain's decision to meet Hitler in Munich in 1938 ('peace in our time') and, similarly, that the full Cabinet was not party to the decision to invade Egypt in 1956 (Suez Crisis).

(c) Matters outside Cabinet control

For more on conventions of Cabinet government, see Chapter 3.

It appears to be accepted that, due to their special nature, certain specific government responsibilities are not subject to direct Cabinet control. Such matters would appear to include:

For more on the power of Prime Ministerial patronage see p. 258.

- the power of Prime Ministerial patronage;
- the **prerogative of mercy** (largely a matter for the Secretary of State for the Home Department but note suggestions that the political sensitivity sometimes attaching to decisions to commute sentences or pardon or release persons in custody is such that some level of Ministerial discussion would appear appropriate);

For this prerogative in general, see Chapter 11.

- the formation of the Budget (although most Ministers will have some awareness of general budgetary policy and intentions, the details of the entire package are largely a

For Budget
procedure in the
House of Commons,
see Chapter 8.

matter for the Chancellor and the Chief Secretary to the Treasury in consultation with the Prime Minister and, perhaps, those Ministers directly affected by a particular proposal – otherwise most Members of the government receive notification of the Budget only hours before it is put before the House).

Control of the national executive

Although in strict constitutional theory this remains a primary function of the Cabinet, for practical reasons the degree of control which it is actually able to exercise over the extensive machinery of central government is somewhat limited.

It is not possible for a body of some 20 to 25 persons which meets only once or twice per week to be fully appraised of, or make decisions in relation to, all those concerns of the various government departments. More detailed consideration and supervision of departmental activity and policy tends to be undertaken by Cabinet committees and sub-committees and in negotiations between Prime Minister, Chancellor, Cabinet Secretary and individual Ministers.

As the size of government increased in the twentieth century, doubts began to emerge concerning the validity of the theory that Ministers 'control' their departments and that collectively, in Cabinet, they exercise effective authority over the entire central government bureaucracy. Indeed, in more recent times, arguments relating to the size and complexity of government appear to have affected executive interpretation of the convention of Ministerial responsibility. Hence it is now not uncommon for Ministers to plead that they should not be expected to take the blame for the actions and decisions of civil servants which they had not directly sanctioned or were not aware of. This type of sentiment was evident in Ministerial submissions to the 1995 Scott Inquiry which dealt with the extent of government knowledge concerning arms sales to Iraq immediately prior to the Gulf War of 1991–92.

Such concerns about the effectiveness of Cabinet and Ministerial control of government departments (and the civil servants within them), and the extent to which Ministers are able to account to Parliament for what goes on within them, has led in recent times to the introduction of mechanisms for the more rigorous scrutiny of executive activity. These include the appointments of the Parliamentary Commissioner (1967) and the Health Service Commissioner (1974), the creation of the system of departmental parliamentary select committees, and the setting up of the National Audit Office (1983) to give assistance to the work of the Comptroller and Auditor General.

Continuous coordination of the several departments of state

To a considerable extent, in day-to-day practical terms, this is one of the primary functions of Cabinet committees and sub-committees. The process of coordination is also assisted by the work of the Cabinet Office (see above).

From time to time Prime Ministers have attempted to improve the extent of coordination by restructuring the departmental composition of central government. Departments may disappear altogether with their functions being transferred elsewhere or may be amalgamated into single 'giant' departments with Ministers of State responsible for the previously separate areas of responsibility. Hence the Department of the Environment (established in 1971, now known as DEFRA) encompassed local government, housing and planning, all of which (at various times) had the responsibilities of separate ministries.

The Ministerial Code of conduct

Introduction

Objective 5

A set of general standards for the regulation of ministerial conduct and activities is generally accepted to have been in existence for many decades and at least since the close of World War II. The broad content of this was first published in 1992. The version in use at the time of writing was that of 2016. This begins with the general admonition that 'Ministers of the Crown are expected to behave in a way that upholds the highest standards of propriety'.

The seven principles of public life

The Code sets out seven basic precepts of public morality which should infuse and typify the discharge of all ministerial functions:

1. 'selflessness' (Ministers should act solely in the public interest);
2. 'integrity' (Ministers should avoid relationships which could influence their conduct and not act for personal gain);
3. objectivity (Ministers should exercise their powers and make decisions impartially, fairly, on merits avoiding any discrimination or bias);
4. accountability (ministerial actions and decisions should be submitted to parliamentary and public scrutiny);
5. openness (Ministers should act transparently and should not withhold information unnecessarily);
6. honesty (Ministers should be truthful);
7. leadership (Ministers should exhibit the standards required in public life and in their own behaviour).

Practical application

The Code goes on to specify how such general standards should impact on the performance of a Minister's duties:

- Ministers should act in compliance with the law;
- Ministers should abide by the rules of collective and individual ministerial responsibility;
- Important policy announcements should be made to Parliament first, and not to the media;
- Ministers should not mislead Parliament and should resign if found to have done so;
- Ministers should avoid all conflicts between their public and private obligations;
- Ministerial facilities should not be used for party political purposes;
- Ministers should not accept gifts or favours which could cloud their obligation to act in the public interest.

Ministers' interests

In addition to the House of Commons Register of Members' Interests, those who are government Ministers are required to complete a form giving information about:

- their financial affairs, including both assets and liabilities;
- their tax affairs;

- directorships or shareholdings;
- investment properties;
- other public appointments;
- links with charities as a patron, trustee or member;
- blind trusts;
- other relevant interests;
- interests of their spouse, partner or close family members.

Compliance with Code and Register of Ministers' Interests

These do not impose any legally binding obligations but are not entirely unenforceable. Hence, and according to the Code itself, where a breach is alleged, and after taking the advice of the Cabinet Secretary, the Prime Minister may refer the case to the Independent Adviser on Ministers' Interests – a post created in 2006. After consideration, the Independent Adviser reports his/her findings, i.e. breach or no breach, back to the Prime Minister upon which further action may be taken at a political level. In addition, it should be remembered, that Ministers are not exempt in any way from the requirements of both the civil and criminal law which, in respect of their public or private conduct, may be enforced against them in the normal way (see conviction and imprisonment of Geoff Huhne, former Secretary of State for the Environment for perverting course of justice, 2013).

Reasons for Cabinet confidentiality

This is supported by a variety of political, conventional and legal rules. In the narrow party-political sense it is clearly something which helps to preserve an image of a united and focused administration. Or, to put it more bluntly, it helps to hide mistakes and ineptitude. It also underpins various public interests including the need for candour and plain-speaking in Ministerial deliberations, and the obvious benefits of a certain amount of secrecy in relation to defence, counter-subversion and sensitive aspects of foreign policy.

The principal conventional rules operating in this context are, of course, those of collective and individual Ministerial responsibility which force Ministers to either 'close ranks' and give unreserved support to all government actions and decisions or to relinquish office through resignation or dismissal. When faced with this choice of job or conscience, the trend in recent times has been for Ministers to remain in office. This is something of a compromise which enables particular policy preferences to be pursued from within and, of course, does less immediate damage to hopes of political advancement.

For the doctrine of confidentiality, see Chapter 22.

For the doctrine of public interest immunity, see Chapter 13.

The legal rules of most obvious relevance in this context are those relating to the equitable doctrine of confidentiality and to the common law concept of public interest immunity.

At the moment, suffice to say that Ministers (or ex-Ministers) may be restrained from publishing information entrusted to them in the course of their Ministerial responsibilities if this would damage the public interest in government confidentiality or adversely affect national security (*Attorney-General* v *Jonathan Cape* [1976] QB 752). The rules of public interest immunity prevent the use of Cabinet papers in legal proceedings except in very limited circumstances (*Burmah Oil Co Ltd* v *Bank of England* [1980] AC 1090).

Nevertheless, as explained above, Ministerial 'leaks' have become an accepted part of the British political process, and the written and broadcast media regularly publish information which could only have been gained from a source within government. How, then, is it possible to reconcile the incidence of leaks with the existence of rules designed to preserve confidentiality? This may be possible if the leak is understood as a tempering expedient which infuses the conventional and legal rules with a degree of flexibility and political efficacy without which meaningful extra-parliamentary debate of controversial issues would be inhibited to a degree not entirely compatible with the norms of democracy. The ideal, therefore, is a balance which preserves the integrity and effectiveness of Cabinet government without imposing undue fetters on the day-to-day functioning of the political process.

Summary

The chapter considers the principal factors contributing to the power of the Prime Minister and their pre-eminent position within the British constitution and its system of government. It then proceeds to assess the effectiveness of the various parliamentary and political techniques through which these powers are controlled. The chapter concludes with an explanation of the powers and functions of the Cabinet and the workings of the Cabinet system in the United Kingdom.

References

Blake (1975) *The Office of Prime Minister*, Oxford: Oxford University Press.

Brazier (1994) *Constitutional Practice*, Oxford: Clarendon Press.

Coote (1969) *The Government We Deserve*, London: Eyre and Spottiswood.

Jenkins (1989) *Mrs Thatcher's Revolution: The Ending of the Socialist Era*, London: Jonathan Cape.

King (1969) *The British Prime Minister*, London: Macmillan.

Report of the Machinery of Government Committee [Haldane Committee] (1918) Cmnd 9230.

Turpin (2002) *British Government and the Constitution* (5th edn), London: Butterworths.

Walker (1970) *The Cabinet*, London: Jonathan Cape.

Wilson (1976) *The Governance of Britain*, London: Weidenfeld and Nicolson.

Further reading

Black and Jones (2010) Premiership: *The Development, Nature and Powers of the Office of Prime Minister* (Societas), Exeter: Imprint Academic.

Buckley (2006) *The Prime Minister and Cabinet*, Edinburgh: Edinburgh University Press.

Diamond (2013) *Governing Britain: Power, Politics and the Prime Minister*, London: Palgrave Macmillan.

Kavanagh and Seldon (2008) *The Powers Behind the Prime Minister*, London: HarperCollins.

Hennessy (1986) *The Cabinet*, Oxford: Blackwell.

House of Commons Political and Constitutional Reform Committee, *The Role and Powers of the Prime Minister*, 24.6.14, HC 351.

House of Lords Select Constitution Committee, *The Cabinet Office and the Centre of Government*, 4th Report, HL 30, 2009–10.

Jenkins (2006) *Thatcher and Sons*, London: Allen Lane.

Jennings (1969) *Cabinet Government*, London: Cambridge University Press.

Wilson (1977) *A Prime Minister on Prime Ministers*, London: Weidenfeld and Nicolson.

12

The royal prerogative

Objectives

After reading this chapter you should:

1. Have an understanding of the nature and extent of the royal prerogative and its relationship with constitutional convention.

2. Appreciate the history and development of the royal prerogative.

3. Recognise the remaining importance of the royal prerogative as a source of government power and its relationship with the principles of representative democracy and Acts of Parliament.

Nature and significance

Terminology

Objective
1

For more on the definitions of the Monarch and the Crown, see Chapter 1.

In discussing the royal prerogative it will be necessary to make frequent reference both to the Monarch and to the Crown. In common parlance these terms tend to be used interchangeably. For students of the constitution, however, this can lead to confusion as, for all practical political purposes, the two terms have significantly different meanings. Hence when reference is made to the Monarch this is usually understood to mean the person who, through the formal ceremony of coronation has, for the time being, been recognised as the titular head of state. The concept of the Crown is, however, not so limited, transient or personal and is generally used to describe the sum of central government departments, forces and agencies, presided over by the Prime Minister and Cabinet, through which the nation's national and international affairs are conducted.

In the context of the royal prerogative, the significance of this distinction lies in the fact that a limited number of prerogatives are, in formal terms at least, still exercised by the Monarch in person (principally appointment of the Prime Minister and the summoning and dissolution of Parliament), while most of the remainder are exercised by the Crown according to its impersonal and institutional identity as just defined.

Some definitions

The term royal prerogative applies to those ancient powers and immunities – once exercised or influenced by the Monarch personally and thought to be a natural attribute of the Monarch's constitutional and political pre-eminence – which were left untouched by the conflicts and political restructuring which occurred during the seventeenth century.

In the late nineteenth century Dicey described the prerogative as follows:

> The prerogative appears to be historically and as a matter of fact nothing else than the residue of discretionary or arbitrary authority which at any given time is legally left in the hands of the Crown . . . From the time of the Norman Conquest down to the Revolution of 1688, the Crown possessed in reality many of the attributes of sovereignty. The prerogative is the name of the remaining portion of the Crown's original authority . . . Every act which the executive government can lawfully do without the authority of an Act of Parliament is done in virtue of the prerogative (Dicey, *An Introduction to the Law of the Constitution*).

A century earlier, another frequently cited definition had been provided by the eminent judge and jurist, Sir William Blackstone:

> By the word prerogative we usually understand that special pre-eminence, which the King hath, over and above all other persons, and out of the ordinary course of common law, in right of his regal dignity . . . It can only be applied to those rights and capacities which the King enjoys alone, in contradiction to others and not to those which he enjoys in common with any of his subjects, for if once any prerogative of the Crown could be held in common with the subject, it would cease to be a prerogative any longer (Blackstone, *Commentaries on the Laws of England*).

These two definitions are not coterminous. The definition provided by Dicey is clearly, in two important respects, less specific and therefore potentially more generous in terms of the amount of executive power it permits. First, it appears to suggest that if the Crown takes an action for which it has no specific authority, it may be presumed to be acting under the prerogative. This being so, the precise content of the prerogative must remain beyond definition and, in its starkest terms, would appear to mean that the prerogative allows the Crown to do whatever it likes providing it does not act illegally (i.e. in ways forbidden by existing common law or statute). Second, and by definition, it appears to infer that the prerogative is not limited, as Blackstone proposed, to the special rights and immunities peculiar to the Crown, but also extends to all that which it may do in common with ordinary citizens, e.g. the making of contracts. What might be called 'the Blackstone view' was supported by the Court of Appeal in *R v Secretary of State for Health, ex parte C* [2000] 1 FLR 627:

> Prerogative is, properly speaking, legal power which appertains to the Crown but not to its subjects. Blackstone explained the current use of the term . . . Although the courts may use the term prerogative in this sense, they have fallen into the habit of describing as prerogative every power of the Crown which is not statutory, without discriminating between powers which are unique to the Crown such as the power of pardon, from powers which the Crown shares equally with its subjects because of its legal personality, such as the power to make contracts, employ servants and convey land (Hale LJ).

This 'third' species of Crown 'powers', i.e. those other than statutory and prerogative powers proper, have been referred to, simply, as the Crown's common law powers (*R (on application of Hooper) v Secretary of State for Work and Pensions* [2005] 1 WLR 1681). As such, they do not operate in any sphere of government action already regulated by statute and may not be used to interfere with the rights of the subject. Also, although the Crown has the legal capacity to do that which a private person or corporation may do, 'as an organ of government, it can only exercise those powers for the public benefit and for identifiably government purposes within limits set by the law' (Carnwath LJ, *Shrewsbury and Atcham Borough Council* v *Secretary of State for Communities and Local Government* [2008] EWCA Civ 148).

Source

The royal prerogative is part of the common law. It represents those powers which, over the centuries, the courts have recognised as attaching to and emanating from the Monarch. The prerogative is available for use, therefore, without any grant of parliamentary authority or approval.

Much of the legal authority for modern government is, of course, now provided in legislation. However, the significance of these common law or prerogative powers should not be underestimated. Nor is it difficult to find modern examples of the courts referring to the prerogative as the source of power for executive action – sometimes controversial – not authorised by statute.

Examples

In 1984, when Mrs Thatcher decided that those employed at the government's intelligence gathering and communications headquarters at Cheltenham should be required to terminate their membership of trade unions and professional associations, the decision was said to be authorised by the prerogative in relation to the management and conduct of the civil service (*Council of Civil Service Unions* v *Minister for the Civil Service* [1985] AC 374). Shortly afterwards the Secretary of State for the Home Department's decision to supply police forces with CS gas and plastic bullets was also justified by reference to the prerogative – this time the miscellaneous and indeterminate array of powers contained within the power to keep the Queen's peace (*R* v *Secretary of State for the Home Department, ex parte Northumbria Police Authority* [1988] 2 WLR 590).

For further discussion of the case, see below.

The prerogative and convention

The use of all the major prerogatives is regulated by constitutional convention. Principal amongst these is the rule that the prerogative to appoint the Prime Minister must be exercised in favour of the person who commands a majority in the House of Commons. Those other prerogatives in which the Monarch is still personally involved – for example, the appointment of Ministers – should then be exercised on the Prime Minister's advice. Others – for example, the prerogative in foreign affairs and to maintain the Queen's peace – are exercised by the government ('the Crown') on the Monarch's behalf. In this way conventions ensure that the prerogative is exercised by persons who are answerable ultimately to the electorate.

Importance

As already indicated, the prerogative – despite its ancient origins – remains an important source of governmental power. It extends, *inter alia,* to the conduct of foreign affairs (including the making of treaties and declaring war and peace), the power of patronage, command of the armed forces, the summoning and dissolving of Parliament, giving the

Royal Assent to legislation and the prerogative of mercy. Clearly, without it the process of government would be unable to function effectively and many of those powers currently provided by the prerogative would have to exist in statutory form.

History

The King, the prerogative and Parliament

Objective
2

After the Norman Conquest an effective system of central government in England was established by William the Conqueror and his immediate successors. From this time onwards, as head of state and feudal lord, the Monarch exercised extensive political, administrative and legal power. The King had the right to demand military service, to impose and receive revenues and taxes, to make law and to dispense justice as well as exercising all those other powers necessary to defend the realm and preserve the peace.

Even in Norman times, however, it was customary for the Monarch to exercise these powers in consultation with the *Curia Regis* (the King's council) rather than in an entirely autocratic fashion. Also, from the thirteenth century onwards, it became common practice for the Monarch, from time to time, to summon Parliaments which, in return for granting the additional revenues required by the King ('supply'), claimed the right to debate and criticise the Monarch's stewardship of the nation's affairs. It is generally accepted, therefore, that although extensive, the powers of English monarchs were never despotic.

In the sixteenth century, under the Tudors, English monarchy probably reached its zenith in terms of power and prestige. For all this, however, the Tudors – particularly Henry VIII and Elizabeth I – tended to govern through and with Parliament rather than in conflict with it.

In 1603 Elizabeth I was succeeded by the first of the Stuart kings, James I. The views of the Stuarts concerning, in particular, the divine right of kings and the sympathies of James' successors (principally Charles I and James II) for Roman Catholicism – with all that that implied for the established Protestant church and England's relations with other Protestant states of Europe – soon led to domestic discontent and unease. What followed was a century punctuated by conflict concerning the proper constitutional relationship and balance of power between Monarch and Parliament and the extent of the royal prerogative.

The attitudes of the courts

Many of the disputes concerning the extent of the prerogative produced litigation in which individuals challenged the validity of royal actions and decisions. In other cases questions concerning the remaining scope of prerogatives were referred to the judges for their opinions. As (in those days) the King had the power both to appoint and dismiss members of the judiciary, it was perhaps not surprising that these decisions and opinions often favoured the royal perspective. However, some judges – particularly Coke CJ during the reign of James I – were prepared to resist Stuart claims and, in a number of famous cases, attempted to impose parameters to the use and content of royal power.

Cases decided for the King

Case of Impositions (Bates' Case) (1606) 2 St Tr 371 (*held* that the King could impose taxes in the form of customs duties without parliamentary consent where this was done not for the purpose of raising revenue simpliciter but for the regulation of trade, and that the court could not question the King's assertion that this was the purpose of his actions).

Case of Ship Money (*R v Hampden*) (1637) 3 St Tr 825 (*held* that the King could tax in time of emergency, without parliamentary consent, for the purposes of defending the realm; in this case increasing the navy – note, however, the Crown's concession that, in times of peace, Parliament's consent would be necessary).

Darnel's Case (*The Five Knights' Case*) (1627) 3 St Tr 1 (*held* that the writ of habeas corpus was not sufficient to secure the release of a person imprisoned under the prerogative for failure to pay tax imposed without parliamentary consent).

Godden v Hales (1686) 11 St Tr 1165 (*held* that the prerogative empowered the King to suspend or dispense with the operation of penal laws, including those contained in statute, where this was believed to be necessary in the interests of the state – belief which could not be questioned by the courts).

Cases decided against the King

Prohibitions del Roy (1607) 12 Co Rep 63 (Coke CJ, supported by all the common law judges, declared that the King could no longer dispense justice personally and that this could only be done through and by his judges).

Case of Proclamations (1611) 12 Co Rep 74 (Coke CJ again, supported by three other senior judges – in response to a request for clarification from the King's council – declared that the King could no longer change any part of the common law, statute or custom or create new offences by royal proclamation).

The Civil War and the Glorious Revolution

Charles I (1625–49) was unable to reach any effective understanding with an increasingly restless Parliament concerning the amount of influence it should have over the direction of the nation's affairs. The rift was exacerbated by the fact that by this time the House of Commons was dominated by Protestant fundamentalists or 'puritans' who were opposed not only to the King's style of government but also to the dogma and government of the established Anglican Church (i.e. the bishops) of which the King was the head.

Weary of obstruction and parliamentary criticism, Charles governed for 11 years (1629–40) without summoning Parliament at all. It was eventually recalled in 1640 when additional revenues were needed to deal with insurrection in Scotland. By now, however, the extent of its demands for reform of church and state were far beyond anything Charles was prepared to contemplate. In an attempt to reassert the authority of the monarchy he resorted to arms. The Civil War lasted from 1642 to 1647. Charles was defeated and executed in 1649. England then became, in effect, a republic. The dominant figure in its government was Oliver Cromwell, who was given the title Lord Protector. So long as he was alive and supported by the military, this radical alternative to monarchy remained viable. On his death, however, in 1658, and in the absence of any other revolutionary leader of similar stature, the country began to drift into disorder as the government lost much of its authority and sense of direction.

Order and stability were preserved by the restoration of the monarchy in 1660 (Charles II 1660–85). The country then passed through a relatively settled period until Charles II was succeeded by his brother James II in 1685. James was autocratic in style and a Roman Catholic. His attempts to place Catholics in prominent positions in the army and the government caused immediate resentment. However, as both his daughters from his first marriage (Mary and Anne) were practising members of the established Protestant church, it was felt that in the long term the Protestant succession and existing constitution were probably secure. This prospect was removed, however, in 1688 when James' second wife gave birth to a son and Catholic heir.

Events then gathered pace. In November 1688 the Protestant Dutch prince, William of Orange – husband of Mary Stuart, James's eldest daughter – landed with an armed force on the south coast. His purpose, he claimed, was to preserve the existing constitution and established church, not to drive James from the throne. James was, however, forced to abdicate after parts of his army defected to William. Parliament then offered the throne to William and Mary as joint monarchs. This was done on the understanding that they would concede to the restrictions on royal power contained in the Bill of Rights, formulated by Parliament early in 1689.

The Bill of Rights 1689

This remains in force today and, as already indicated, is one of the founding documents of the British constitution. The principal objective of the Bill was not to remove all royal power and influence but to radically reduce the Monarch's capacity to act in contravention of the wishes of Parliament. The Bill provided that the Monarch could not tax, make law, or maintain a standing army in peacetime without parliamentary consent.

The Bill of Rights did not deal directly with the question of the Monarch's religious affiliation. This was left to the Act of Settlement 1700, which limited the succession to protestant heirs and expressly excluded Roman Catholics.

The demise of royal power

More than three centuries have passed since these dramatic events. Since then, however, the prerogative has remained largely intact. The most significant change has been the evolution of those constitutional conventions already described which have minimised the extent of the Monarch's personal involvement in its use.

The extension of the franchise in the nineteenth century began the process of genuinely democratising the British constitution. This was reflected by the emergence of the central convention that the government should be formed from the elected majority in the House of Commons and that a government unable to maintain that majority had lost the right to remain in office. Royal influence over the formation, tenure and composition of governments was, thereby, radically reduced. Autocratic royal use of the prerogative in such changed political circumstances could not have been reconciled with the emerging expectations of responsible and representative parliamentary government. That this was accepted by the British monarchy was instrumental in securing its survival. Henceforth, therefore, the use of the prerogative was to be a matter for the Crown in the form of the elected government rather than for the Monarch in person.

Principal remaining prerogatives

Introduction

Objective
3

The prerogative remains an extensive mixture of rights, powers, duties and immunities operating in all three spheres of government (executive, legislative and judicial). An exhaustive coverage of its entire content is beyond the scope of this text. An exhaustive list of all remaining prerogatives may be found in the *Review of the Executive's Royal Prerogative*

Powers: Final Report, Ministry of Justice, 2009. The following classification will serve, however, to provide some appreciation of its remaining utility in the modern state.

Executive prerogatives

Patronage

Elevation to most senior positions in church and state, including Ministerial and judicial appointments and those in the armed forces, are made in the name of the Monarch – as are the granting of peerages and preferment of honours. By convention this is now done on the advice of the Prime Minister or other Ministers (e.g. Lord Chancellor in the case of certain judicial offices). Certain honours, however, remain within the Monarch's personal grant. These are the Order of the Garter, the Order of the Thistle, the Order of Merit and the Royal Victoria Order (for personal service to the Sovereign).

Command and deployment of the armed forces

The Sovereign is Commander-in-Chief of the armed forces. Although some matters relating to the same are regulated by statute (e.g. military discipline), the authority for decisions concerning the use and deployment of such forces is still derived from the prerogative and not from Act of Parliament. Such matters may be raised and criticised during the course of parliamentary debate, but no prior parliamentary authority or subsequent ratification is necessary for the commitment of British forces. The prerogative is also the authority for decisions relating to military recruitment, procurement and weaponry. Hence whether or not British forces are armed with the nuclear deterrent is a matter for Her Majesty's Government in the exercise of Her prerogative and not something done under the authority of legislation. Also, decisions in these matters will clearly and frequently be of a sensitive political and security nature and, as such, beyond the scope of judicial review.

> The disposition, armament and direction of the defence forces of the State are matters decided upon by the Crown and are within its jurisdiction as the executive power of State . . . If the methods of arming the defence forces and the disposition of those forces are at the decision of Her Majesty's Ministers for the time being, as we know that they are, it is not within the competence of a court to try the issue whether it would be better for the country that that armament or those dispositions should be different (**Chandler v Director of Public Prosecutions** [1964] AC 763, *per* Viscount Radcliffe).

Keeping the Queen's peace

The Court of Appeal in **R v Secretary of State for the Home Department, ex parte Northumbria Police Authority** (supra), recognised the existence of an executive prerogative 'to take all reasonable steps to preserve the Queen's peace' (per Purchas LJ). Hence, as explained above, the Secretary of State for the Home Department was empowered – whether or not so authorised by statute – to supply police forces with CS gas and plastic bullets. This prerogative is also the source of the authority exercised by police officers to do all that is reasonably necessary to prevent breaches of the peace.

Defence of the realm and emergency powers

The House of Lords in **Burmah Oil v Lord Advocate** [1965] AC 75 concluded that the prerogative 'certainly covers doing all those things in an emergency which are necessary for the conduct of the war' (per Lord Reid). In most modern wars or emergencies, however, the state has usually armed itself with an extensive array of special statutory powers (e.g. Defence of the Realm Act 1914; Emergency Powers (Defence) Act 1939; Prevention and Investigation Act 2011 and the Civil Service Contingencies Act 2004 for serious contingencies in peacetime). As a result, resort to the emergency prerogatives has been limited and, in the absence of usage, some doubt has arisen as to the exact content of the Crown's remaining powers in this context. At various times the following powers have been claimed:

(a) the right to requisition and destroy property;

(b) the right to enter upon land and construct fortifications;

(c) the right to demand personal service within the realm;

(d) the right to intern aliens.

It has been suggested that, strictly speaking, the first two of these should not be classified as prerogatives. This is based on the proposition that in a genuine emergency such actions would probably not be illegal if taken by a private citizen. If so, and adopting Blackstone's general definition, they may not belong to 'those rights and capacities which the King enjoys alone'.

The conduct of foreign and colonial affairs

Most of that which is done by the government in the execution of British foreign policy or for the maintenance of British interests abroad receives its legitimacy from the prerogative. More specifically, and principally, the prerogative in foreign affairs encompasses the following:

(a) declaring war and peace;

(b) making treaties;

(c) recognition of foreign states and government;

(d) sending and receiving diplomatic representatives;

(e) annexation and cessation of territory.

State immunity

Consistent with the above jurisprudence relating to the Crown, British courts are also generally resistant to question the actions and decisions of foreign sovereigns (i.e. foreign sovereign states) within their own jurisdictions. This would appear to be not so much an extension of the prerogative, but rather the domestic application of a long established principle of international law.

> An English court will not sit in judgment on the sovereign acts of a foreign government or state. It will not adjudicate upon the legality, validity or acceptability of such acts, either under domestic or international law. For a court to do so would offend against the principle that courts will not adjudicate upon the transactions of foreign sovereign states (Lord Nicholls, *Kuwait Airways Corporation v Iraqi Airways Corporation (Nos 4 and 5)* [2002] AC 883).

The principle is founded on the comity of nations.

> The principle that the conduct of one independent government cannot be successfully questioned in the courts of another . . . rests at last upon the highest considerations of

international comity and expediency. To permit the validity of the acts of one sovereign state to be re-examined and perhaps condemned by the court of another would very certainly imperil the amicable relations between governments and vex the peace of nations (Clarke J, *Oetjen* v *Central Leather Co* 246 US 297 (1918)).

As with the immunity relating to the Crown's activities overseas, the rule relating to foreign sovereigns is not absolute and permits of a number of exceptions. Thus it is generally accepted as permissible for British courts to entertain proceedings relating to a foreign state where it can be shown that no effective judicial remedy, or other means of securing justice, exists in the state in issue (*AK Investment CJSC* v *Kyrgyz Mobil Tel Ltd* [2011] UKPC 7). Also, and beyond this, the domestic courts have made clear that not everything done or occurring within a foreign jurisdiction should qualify as a fully-fledged act of, or by, a foreign government. Areas of activity and other matters not falling within the meaning of the term have been held to include the following.

(a) As a general rule, that which was not done within the territory of the state (*Kuwait Airways*, supra).

(b) Acts which are in breach of clearly established rules of international law, British domestic public policy or which amount to grave infringements of human rights (*Behaj* v *Straw* [2014] EWCA Civ 1594).

(c) Judicial decisions.

(d) Commercial activities.

(e) Questions of whether a particular act or event took place but without any examination of its legality (*Yukos Capital SARL* v *OJSC Rosneft Oil Co.* [2012] EWCA Civ 855).

Statutory ratification of treaties

An element of statutory regulation of the prerogative in foreign affairs was introduced by the Constitutional Reform and Governance Act 2010. This provided a statutory system whereby Parliament may prevent government ratification of any treaty of which it (Parliament) does not approve. The Act does not, however, affect the decision to enter into, to negotiate, to determine the content of, or to conclude any such international agreement. The royal prerogative remains, therefore, the legal authority for the conduct of these aspects of the treaty-making process.

The system of negative parliamentary approval introduced by the Act provides that, as a general rule, a treaty to which the United Kingdom intends to accede should not proceed to ratification unless it has been laid before Parliament and no resolution of the House of Commons has been passed to the effect that such ratification should not take place.

The final ratification of a treaty remains a government power acting under the royal prerogative.

Neither Parliament nor the government may amend a treaty once it has been concluded. Any desired changes would normally be effected by a further treaty agreement.

For further discussion of the concept of justiciability, see Chapter 15.

Management and regulation of the civil service

Prior to the passing of the Constitutional Reform and Governance Act 2010, decisions in this context were still, in the main, made under the authority of the prerogative – this included matters relating to civil servants' pay and conditions of service. It was generally accepted that civil servants were employed at the Crown's 'pleasure' and that the Crown had the prerogative to dismiss them at will without incurring any common law liability (e.g. for breach of contract). The Crown was, however, bound by the Employment Rights Act 1996 and could, therefore, be liable for unfair dismissal.

The principal effect of the 2010 Act in this context was to replace the prerogative powers with a detailed system of statutory regulation. The overall legal authority for the management and control of the civil service, including the power to hire and dismiss individual civil servants, was thereby vested in the Minister for the Civil Service (normally the Prime Minister) (s 3). Note, however, that s 3 does not apply to the process of national security vetting. This will, therefore, continue to be carried out under existing prerogative powers.

The pre-existing prerogative in this area was the authority for the controversial decision taken by Prime Minister Thatcher in denying employees at the government's communications centre at Cheltenham (GCHQ) the right to be members of trade unions or professional associations. On that occasion the Prime Minister acted under an Order in Council (Civil Service Order in Council 1982) made, not under any statutory power, but in the exercise of the prerogative – thus illustrating that the Crown retains certain primary law-making powers.

> The Order in Council was not issued under powers conferred by any Act of Parliament. Like the provisions in Orders in Council on the same subject it was issued by the sovereign by virtue of her prerogative, but of course on the advice of the government of the day (***Council of Civil Service Unions v Minister for Civil Service*** [1985] AC 374, *per* Lord Fraser).

Legislative prerogatives

Summoning, proroguing and dissolving Parliament

Historically, monarchs summoned and dissolved Parliaments as they saw fit. As explained above, the determination of Charles I to govern without Parliament, and his resentment of the criticisms made therein, was one of the principal causes of the Civil War in the seventeenth century. Towards the end of the Stuart period, the Meeting of Parliament Act 1694 provided that Parliament should be summoned at least once every three years. Until the passing of the Fixed Term Parliaments Act 2011, the position was that the Monarch dissolved Parliament on the advice of the Prime Minister. The proclamation effecting the dissolution also specifies the date for the meeting of the new Parliament. For the future, it would appear that the prerogative to dissolve Parliament will be exercised subject to the requirements of the 2011 Act.

The prerogative of prorogation, also exercised on Prime Ministerial advice, is used to terminate each parliamentary session. The prorogation usually lasts for only a few days – usually from a Thursday in late November until the opening of the new session the following Tuesday or Wednesday.

The Royal Assent

The Royal Assent by Commission Act 1541 authorised the giving of the Royal Assent by commissioners appointed for that purpose. This is the usual practice. The Royal Assent was last given by the Monarch personally in 1854. It was last refused by Queen Anne in 1707 (Scottish Militia Bill). It is known that in 1913 George V contemplated and took advice concerning the constitutional propriety of refusing his assent to the Irish Home Rule Bill 1912, but eventually conceded that he was bound to act, i.e. to consent, as advised by the Prime Minister (Asquith). Notification that the assent has been given to particular Bills is given to the House by the Speaker (Royal Assent Act 1967).

Legislation does not bind the Crown

Acts of Parliament do not apply to or bind the Crown in any way unless a contrary intention is clearly stated or is necessarily implicit from the words used.

> The modern rule of construction of statutes is that the Crown, which today personifies the executive government of the country and is also a party to all legislation, is not bound by a statute which imposes obligations or restraints on persons or in respect of property, unless the statute says so expressly or by necessary implication (*BBC* v *Johns* [1965] Ch 32, per Lord Diplock).

Note, however, the opinion expressed in the Scottish courts in *Dumbarton District Council* v *Lord Advocate*, *The Times*, 18 March 1988, later overruled by the House of Lords (*Lord Advocate* v *Dumbarton District Council* [1990] 2 AC 580), that the Crown should be regarded as bound by legislation except where this might prejudicially affect the Crown's existing rights, privileges, immunities or interests. This was consistent with the comment in Hood Phillips and Jackson (*Constitutional and Administrative Law*):

> The question of whether the Crown is bound by statutes is a matter of interpretation, but there is a presumption in favour of the prerogative of immunity. The general rule is subject to criticism. It has been suggested that the presumption should be reversed by legislation so that the Crown would be bound by statute unless it was expressly declared not to be bound, or public policy required the exemption of the Crown in a particular case.

Law making

There remain a limited number of contexts in which legislation, usually in the form of an Order in Council, may be made under the royal prerogative and without parliamentary approval. The most significant of these relate to the government of Crown colonies and the regulation and management of the civil service. Legislative acts of the sovereign are classified as 'primary' legislation, but do not have equivalent status as Acts of Parliament and are not beyond the scope of judicial review (*R (on application of Bancoult)* v *Foreign Secretary* [2008] UKHL 61).

Also note that, as a general principle, and since the *Case of Proclamations* (1611) 12 Co Rep 74, the Crown has no power to legislate domestically without the consent of Parliament.

Judicial prerogatives

The administration of justice

Although justice is still dispensed in the Queen's name, it has long been accepted (at least since the *Prohibitions del Roy* (1607) 12 Co Rep 63) that the Monarch may no longer participate personally in the exercise of judicial power. It is also generally accepted that the Monarch has no remaining prerogative to create new courts, particularly if these are to be involved in the application of statutory rules. It has been suggested, however, that the prerogative might still extend to the creation of courts or tribunals concerned purely with the interpretation of rules emanating from the common law or the prerogative. Some support for this may be derived from *R v Criminal Injuries Compensation Board, ex parte Lain* [1967] 2 QB 864, where the Court of Appeal assumed that the Commission, which had not been established under any statute, must have been created under, and its authority derived from, the royal prerogative.

The prerogative of mercy

The power is exercised by the Secretary of State for Justice. It extends to the granting of full or conditional pardons and to the reprieve or remission of sentences. A pardon removes all those 'pains, penalties and punishments' which have resulted from a conviction. It does not, however, extinguish the conviction itself. This can only be quashed by a court (*R v Foster* [1985] QB 115). A conditional pardon usually involves the substitution of a lesser form of punishment (e.g. life imprisonment for the death penalty). A reprieve or remission is effected by the reduction of the whole or part of the sentence but again does not expunge the original conviction.

The need for the granting of full or 'free' pardons was reduced significantly by the creation of the Criminal Cases Review Commission under the Criminal Appeals Act 1995. The Commission has powers to refer possibly unsafe convictions to the Court of Appeal. In December, 2013, a free pardon was granted posthumously to Alan Turing who committed suicide in 1954 after being convicted of gross indecency with another man. During World War II, Turing, a mathematician, had played a leading role in 'cracking' the German High Command's military code system ('Enigma').

The last conditional pardon was granted to Derek Bentley, also posthumously, in 1993. Bentley had been executed 41 years previously for the murder of a policeman in 1952 notwithstanding that it was his accomplice (Christopher Craig) who had carried the gun and fired the fatal shot.

Protecting the public interest

At any time, the Crown, acting through the Attorney-General, may commence legal proceedings for the general public benefit – usually to restrain illegalities which could damage the public interest. The power may be used, for example, to initiate proceedings against a public body or statutory undertaker which is believed to be abusing its powers. A private citizen may only bring civil proceedings in respect of such abuse if they have sufficient interest or legal standing (*locus standi*), i.e. the individual's interests have been particularly and detrimentally affected by the alleged abuse (see *Gouriet v Union of Post Office Workers* [1978] AC 435): 'the Crown always has standing for this purpose, whereas a private individual might be refused relief on the ground that he had no more interest in the matter than any other member of the public' (Wade and Forsyth, *Administrative Law*).

Frequently the Attorney-General will become involved in such proceedings at the instigation or 'relation' of an individual who may lack sufficient standing to bring proceedings in their own name. This is known as a relator action. In practice, the case is brought and conducted by the concerned individual but the Attorney-General's consent and the lending of their name to the proceeding removes any problems of standing (see *McWhirter v IBA* [1973] QB 629).

The prerogative also empowers the Attorney-General to discontinue indictable proceedings by entering a plea of *nolle prosequi* (to be unwilling to prosecute).

The prerogative and statute

Since statute has supreme legal force and the prerogative is part of the common law, it is axiomatic that Parliament may abolish or modify the prerogative by express words or 'necessary intendment' (*De Morgan* v *Director General of Social Welfare* [1998] 2 WLR 427).

Where statute and the prerogative are coterminous or deal with the same subject-matter – e.g. both provide a power to requisition property – the general principle is that the prerogative goes into abeyance. Therefore, and so long as the relevant statute remains in existence, the Crown is bound to use the power provided by Parliament.

This was established in the following case.

Attorney-General v *De Keyser's Royal Hotel* [1920] AC 508

During the First World War the Crown requisitioned the plaintiff's hotel for use by the Royal Flying Corps during the First World War. After the war the plaintiff sued for compensation. A statutory power to requisition property had been provided by the Defence of the Realm Act 1914. The Act gave those affected a right to claim compensation. The Crown argued, however, that in requisitioning the hotel it had merely been exercising its prerogative for the defence of the realm and that it had not sought to use the power in the 1914 Act. Had the court accepted this, the plaintiff's action would have failed as it had never been established that the Crown was obliged to provide recompense for property requisitioned under the prerogative.

The House of Lords, however, was not prepared to accept that the Crown could 'pick and choose' a statutory or prerogative power depending on which one put it in the most advantageous position *vis-à-vis* the rights of the individual. What was to become known subsequently as the '*De Keyser's* principle' was summed up by Lord Atkinson:

> ... when such a statute, expressing the will and intention of the King and of the three estates of the realm, is passed, it abridges the royal prerogative while it is in force to this extent: that the Crown can only do the particular thing under and in accordance with the statutory provisions and that the prerogative power to do that thing is in abeyance.

More recent authority has suggested that the principle as thus articulated may be subject to the qualification that if the prerogative in question gives the citizen some positive benefit or protection it does not go into abeyance unless this is the clear intention of the statute with which the prerogative coincides.

In *R* v *Secretary of State for the Home Department, ex parte Northumbria Police Authority* (supra), the Secretary of State for the Home Department decided to use the prerogative to maintain the Queen's peace to supply the police with CS gas and plastic bullets. In an application for judicial review it was argued that the power to decide how to equip police forces had been entrusted to individual police authorities by the Police Act 1964. Hence, by virtue of the *De Keyser*'s principle, any ancient prerogative to do this had been displaced.

The judgment of Purchas LJ contained the proposed limitation to the *De Keyser*'s principle mentioned above.

> Where the executive action is directed towards the benefit or protection of the individual, it is unlikely that its use will attract the intervention of the courts. In my judgment before the

courts will hold that such executive action is contrary to legislation, express and unequivocal terms must be found in the statute which deprive the individual from receiving the benefit or protection intended by the exercise of executive power.

Since no such 'unequivocal' terms could be found in the 1964 Act, the court assumed that it could not have been Parliament's intention to put the prerogative into abeyance.

If a statute which has put a prerogative into abeyance is eventually repealed, the restriction on the use of the prerogative is thereby removed. Being no longer in abeyance or a state of suspension, the particular prerogative may be resorted to once again. It has been suggested, however, that this should not apply in the case of minor prerogatives which are no longer necessary for the practice of effective modern government.

It is implicit in what has been said that the prerogative must not be used to thwart the exercise of a statutory power. Despite its importance, the prerogative is not something which the executive may use to avoid the wishes of Parliament (***Laker Airways* v *Department of Trade*** [1977] QB 643). This was made abundantly clear by the House of Lords in ***R* v *Secretary of State for the Home Department, ex parte Fire Brigades Union*** [1995] 2 AC 513. This concerned the criminal injuries compensation scheme which had been established in 1964 using powers contained in the royal prerogative. Nearly a quarter of a century later it was decided to put the scheme into statutory form. The necessary authority was provided by the Criminal Justice Act 1988. The Act provided that the relevant sections were to be brought into effect on a day appointed by the Secretary of State for the Home Department (s 171). Five years later, when this had still not been done, the Minister decided to make changes to the original scheme which, it was believed, was proving too expensive. These changes were again to be effected under the authority of the royal prerogative.

For judicial prerogatives, see p. 285.

Following an application for judicial review of the Secretary of State for the Home Department's actions, the House of Lords made the following findings:

(a) Where an Act of Parliament allows a Minister a discretion as to when its provisions should come into operation, this does not permit the Minister to decide that the Act, or any such provisions, should not take effect at all. It simply gives the Minister the freedom to determine when the time is right, perhaps in terms of the availability of resources and facilities, for effective implementation of the legislation in issue.

(b) In the period after a statute has been enacted and before its coming into effect, it is not lawful for the Minister to use the prerogative in a way which obviates the need for the statute to be implemented. It is for Parliament to repeal legislation and not the government under the royal prerogative.

The prerogative and the courts

Limited judicial control

Reference has already been made to Coke CJ's assertion in the ***Case of Proclamations*** (1611) that the 'king hath no prerogative but what the law of the land allows'. This established the basic principle that it is for the courts and the courts alone to determine the powers contained within the prerogative. The courts have also long claimed the authority to determine the scope or limits of the prerogatives so identified. These principles made it clear that the judiciary was not prepared to allow the Crown to be the final arbiter as to the content and extent of its common law powers of government.

This was well illustrated by the decision in *Burmah Oil* v *Lord Advocate* (below).

Burmah Oil v Lord Advocate [1965] AC 75

During the Second World War the plaintiff's oil installations in Rangoon had been destroyed by British forces as they evacuated the city and retreated from the Japanese. After the war the plaintiff claimed compensation. The Crown argued that its prerogative right to destroy property in time of war for the defence of the realm was not qualified by any liability to provide financial reparation. This argument was not accepted by the House of Lords. In its view the Crown was only exempt from paying compensation where the damage was done during the course of a battle ('battle damage'). No such exemption applied, however, where the property had been destroyed purely to prevent it falling into enemy hands ('denial damage').

However, until the watershed decision in the GCHQ case, such delineation of the content and scope of the prerogative was believed to represent the full extent of judicial authority in this context. The courts were not prepared, therefore, to review or question the prerogative's mode of exercise. The common law rules devised for judicial supervision of statutory powers (contained in the *Wednesbury* principles and the rules of natural justice) did not apply, therefore, to the use of the prerogative. The resulting position appeared somewhat incongruous. An individual aggrieved by alleged government abuse of a statutory power could apply for judicial review and perhaps have the offending decision overturned. If, however, the complaint related to the manner of use of a prerogative, then no such redress was available.

Hence in *Gouriet* v *Attorney-General*, above, the Court of Appeal (Lord Denning MR dissenting) felt that it was unable to question the decision of the then Labour Attorney-General not to commence legal proceedings to prevent what appeared to be illegal industrial action by the Post Office Workers Union. The allegation that the Attorney had reneged on his duty to protect the public interest for purely party-political interests (i.e. a desire not to antagonise the Trade Unions) was not something on which the court was prepared to comment. The Attorney-General had exercised a prerogative power and the propriety of his actions was not susceptible, therefore, to judicial inquiry.

Such refusal to inquire into the prerogative's mode of exercise reflected a deeply ingrained judicial deference towards the Monarch which continued to influence English law long after the revolutionary settlement of the late seventeenth century. The assumption was that, although the King was bound by law, he had to be trusted to act according to it (*Darnel's Case* (1627) 3 St Tr 1). Therefore, it was not for those subordinates to whom his judicial power had been entrusted to use that power against its source. The problem was, however, that this judicial temerity towards the prerogative continued in existence long after the Monarch had ceased to have any genuine influence over its use. As a result a whole range of powers now exercised by the government 'on the Monarch's behalf' remained exempt from judicial control – a state of affairs hardly consistent with some of the principal imperatives of Dicey's version of the rule of law.

Indications of a growing judicial awareness of what was becoming an increasingly anomalous and anachronistic state of affairs at last began to emerge in the 1970s. In particular, the then Master of the Rolls, Lord Denning, urged a change of approach.

Seeing that the prerogative is a discretionary power to be exercised for the public good, it follows that its exercise can be examined by the courts just as any other discretionary power that is vested in the executive (*Laker Airways* v *Department of Trade*, *supra*).

GCHQ: judicial control extended

These sentiments were finally given effect by the House of Lords in *Council of Civil Service Unions* v *Minister for the Civil Service* [1985] AC 374, above, where the House of Lords articulated the general principle that henceforth the way in which a particular prerogative had been used should be regarded as reviewable providing the subject-matter of the decision in issue could be treated as 'justiciable' or 'amenable to the judicial process'. In effect, this meant that the courts could entertain challenges to the exercise of a prerogative where this did not relate to matters of 'high state policy' or to other matters so politically sensitive or contentious as to be outside the proper sphere of judicial inquiry:

> The courts are not the proper place wherein to determine whether a treaty should be concluded or the armed forces disposed in a particular manner or Parliament dissolved on one day rather than another (*per* Lord Roskill).

For the sake of greater clarification, Lord Roskill went on to provide a list of those particular prerogatives, the subject-matter of which, would continue to be regarded generally as 'non-justiciable'. These were the making of treaties, the defence of the realm, the prerogative of mercy, the grant of honours, the dissolution of Parliament and the appointment of Ministers.

That the treaty-making power was unsuitable for review was confirmed shortly afterwards in *ex parte Molyneaux* [1986] 1 WLR 331, where the court felt unable to question the validity of the 1985 Anglo-Irish Agreement, and later in *R* v *Secretary of State for Foreign and Commonwealth Affairs, ex parte Lord Rees-Mogg* [1994] 1 All ER 457, in which the court declined any jurisdiction to question the government's decision to ratify the 1992 Treaty on European Union.

For the Treaty on European Union, see Chapter 4.

'Reviewable' prerogatives

Cases subsequent to GCHQ have made clear that the justiciable or reviewable exercises of prerogatives are those which have minimal political or policy content and which tend to be concerned with the regulation of individual rights, interests or legitimate expectations. The following are the prerogatives which, to date, have been held to be amenable to the judicial process.

(a) The refusal of a passport (*R* v *Secretary of State for Foreign and Commonwealth Affairs, ex parte Everett* [1989] QB 811).

(b) The regulation and management of the civil service (*Council of Civil Service Unions* v *Minister for the Civil Service*, supra).

(c) The issuing of warrants to 'tap' telephones (*R* v *Secretary of State for the Home Department, ex parte Ruddock* [1987] 1 WLR 1482). This is now done under the authority of the Interception of Communications Act 1985 and not under the prerogative.

(d) The Secretary of State for the Home Department's residual common law powers in the sphere of immigration, including the power to expel friendly aliens (*R* v *Secretary of State for the Home Department, ex parte Beedassee* [1989] COD 525).

(e) The power to make *ex gratia* payment for criminal injuries compensation (*R v Criminal Injuries Compensation Board, ex parte Lain* [1967] 2 QB 864).

(f) The prerogative of mercy (*R v Secretary of State for the Home Department, ex parte Bentley* [1993] 4 All ER 442; *R (on application of B) v Secretary of State for the Home Department* [2002] EWHC Admin 587).

(g) Exclusions of members from the armed forces where this is done primarily in the interests of maintaining good order and discipline and not for reasons of national security *simpliciter* (*R Ministry of Defence, ex parte Smith* [1996] All ER 257).

An interesting example of this revised judicial approach to the prerogative occurred in the following case.

R (on applications of Abassi) v *Secretary of State for Foreign and Commonwealth Affairs* [2002] EWCA Civ 1598

> The case arose out of an allegation that the Secretary of State had not done sufficient to safeguard the rights of British subjects detained by the US military authorities at Guantanamo Bay, Cuba. In the event it was held that the UK government was not under any judicially enforceable legal duty to protect its citizens overseas. In the course of so finding, however, the Court of Appeal made clear that the government's remaining discretion whether or not to act on behalf of its subjects should not be regarded as entirely beyond judicial scrutiny simply because it was exercised under the prerogative in the sphere of foreign affairs.
>
> It is not an answer to a claim for judicial review to say that the source of the power of the Foreign Office is the prerogative (*per* Lord Phillips MR).

'Unreviewable' prerogatives

Time moves on and it is now clear that Lord Roskill's list of unreviewable or 'non-justiciable' prerogatives should no longer be regarded as absolutely sacrosanct.

The first major judicial incursion into these 'protected' categories of government action came in the *Bentley* case (point (f) *supra*); a case concerned with the prerogative of mercy. On this occasion, the Court's view was that, in terms of its susceptibility to review, there was no good reason for treating the prerogative in penal affairs any different from a whole range of related statutory powers operating in the same context (e.g. the granting of parole), all of which, it was felt, raised similar issues of policy and public safety.

The judicial move away from the rigid distinction between justiciable and non-justiciable prerogatives was also evident in *R (on application of Bancoult) v Secretary of State for Foreign and Commonwealth Affairs* [2007] EWCA Civ 498, where the Court of Appeal quashed a prerogative Order in Council operating in the sphere of foreign affairs and touching on the UK's military relationship with one of its closest allies (the USA).

The particular effect of the Order in Council had been to prevent the inhabitants of the Chagos islands from returning to their native territory. This was a British colony from which the islanders had been excluded in 1971 in order that an American military base could be sited there. The Court of Appeal felt that, although 'considerable latitude' had to be extended to the executive government in deciding what made for 'the peace and good government of a colony', this did not extend to the permanent exclusion of the colony's entire population from its homeland. Going further, and commenting on Lord Roskill's 'would be' non-justiciable prerogatives, Sedley LJ stated that the existence of such predetermined blanket exclusions of whole areas of government power from judicial review could not be regarded as entirely compatible with the modern emphasis on 'subject-matter' as the primary criterion for determining whether a particular exercise of power could be questioned in the courts.

It would appear, therefore, that the time has now come when it would be right to consign Lord Roskill's list of excluded powers to the annals of history and to regard the 'subject-matter' criterion for judicial review as the sole, and equally applicable test, for the use of all government powers, whether these emanate from the prerogative or from statute. This was the position taken by Lords Carnwath and Mance when giving the judgment of the Supreme Court in *R (on application of Sandiford)* v *Secretary of State for Foreign and Commonwealth Affairs* [2014] 1 WLR 2697), where the Court felt able to review a prerogative decision of the Minister not to supply the applicant with the necessary finances to allow her to try to reopen a decision of the Indonesian Supreme Court sentencing her to death for drugs offences.

> Since the decision in *Council of Civil Service Unions* v *Minister for the Civil Service* . . . the principles of public law applicable to the exercise of common law [i.e. prerogative] and statutory powers have been assimilated.

It has been made clear, however, that any judicial inquiry into claims relating to actions taken under any of the hitherto 'protected' or 'unreviewable' prerogative powers should be conducted with great caution and should avoid judicial incursions into what should remain non-justiciable aspects of executive power (*Youssef* v *Secretary of State for Foreign and Commonwealth Affairs* [2016] UKSC 3: Minister's decision to refuse to recommend removal of appellant's name from United Nation's list of persons associated with Al Quaida was not outside the power of review).

The prerogative and Parliament

As has been stated, that which is done by the government under the royal prerogative does not require prior parliamentary consent or subsequent approval. This gives the government of the United Kingdom great freedom of action and the ability to take major, and sometimes controversial decisions, e.g. to go to war, without reference to the nation's elected representatives. The government did agree to a vote before the 2003 war in Iraq, but this was not constitutionally obligatory, either legally or in terms of conventional practice.

In recent times this lack of any direct or systematic control over such key prerogatives has become an issue of increasing concern, and particularly so because of events in Iraq and Afghanistan. These conflicts brought into sharp relief the realisation that the prerogative to wage war is, in effect, vested in the personal discretion of the Prime Minister and that most of the modern conflicts in which the United Kingdom has been involved appear to have been 'wars of choice', based on political and moral priorities, rather than 'wars of necessity' in the sense of immediate self-defence (see House of Lords Constitution Committee, Fifteenth Report, 2005–6, 'Waging War: Parliament's Role and Responsibility', HL 236).

In 2004, a report by the House of Commons Select Committee on Public Administration recommended that 'any decision to engage in armed conflict should be approved by Parliament, if not before the military action, then as soon as possible afterwards' (Fourth Report, 2003–4, HC 422). The government's initial response both to this and other like suggestions for reform was to argue that, as with all the prerogatives, the power to deploy the armed forces remained within the democratic spectrum and that Ministers were accountable to Parliament for all such and related decisions.

This, however, did little to mollify parliamentary 'unease'. Far from it indeed, as, in a related report, the House of Lords Constitution Committee expressed the view that 'the ability of UK governments to engage in conflict is paradoxically less democratic than when the Monarch exercised the power personally'.

> In the past, the Monarch's power to make law and deploy the armed forces was checked by Parliament's control of the resources necessary for the exercise of the power. Now the government of the day not only exercises the royal prerogative but also generally controls the House of Commons and its power over finance – through parliamentary majorities, use of the whips and control of the parliamentary timetable – thereby undermining the brake on executive power (HL 236, *supra*).

The Committee went on to recommend a significantly increased role for Parliament but felt that this would be better achieved by the development of a relevant constitutional convention rather than any resort to regulation by statute.

> Our conclusion is that the exercise of the royal prerogative by the government to deploy armed forces oversees is outdated and should not be allowed to continue as the basis for legitimate law-making in our 21st century democracy. Parliament's ability to challenge the executive must be protected and strengthened. There is a need to set out here precisely the extent of the government's deployment powers and the role Parliament can, and should, play in their exercise . . . We recommend that there should be a parliamentary convention determining the role Parliament should play in making decisions to deploy force or forces outside the United Kingdom to war, intervention in an existing conflict, or to environments where there is a risk that the forces will be engaged in conflict.

Such convention, the Committee felt, should encompass the following obligations:

- the government should seek parliamentary approval if proposing deployment of British forces outside the UK into an actual or potential armed conflict;
- when seeking such approval, the government should indicate the deployment's objectives, its legal basis, likely duration and give an estimate of its size;
- if for reasons of emergency and security, such prior application is impossible, information about the deployment should be provided within seven days of its commencement or as soon as possible and parliamentary approval sought at this stage;
- where British troops have been committed, Parliament should be kept informed of the deployment's progress and approval should be sought for any change in its nature or objectives.

Subsequent to the change of Prime Minister in June 2007, these matters were addressed in a Green Paper released by the government in the following July ('The Governance of Britain', Cm 7170). This conceded the case for greater parliamentary involvement in the exercise of a wide range of major government powers currently vested in the prerogative (deployment of the armed forces, satisfying treaties, dissolving and recalling Parliament, prerogative of mercy, appointing bishops and judges, control and management of the civil service).

> The government believe that, in general, the prerogative power should be put onto a statutory basis and brought under thorough parliamentary control and scrutiny.

As to the deployment of troops outside the United Kingdom, the issue which largely sparked the debate, the Green Paper acknowledged that 'the government should seek the approval of the representatives of the people in the House of Commons for significant non-routine deployments of the armed forces into armed conflict'. This, it was proposed, should be done through the formulation of a convention or the adoption of legislation 'taking into account the need to preserve the flexibility and security of the armed forces'.

> More generally, the Green Paper concluded with the commitment that government will consider and consult around the question 'whether all the prerogative powers should, in the

long term, be codified and brought under statutory control'. The prerogatives identified for particular consideration were the prerogatives of mercy and the power to issue and revoke passports, both of which 'can have a profound effect on the lives of individuals'.

To date, these good intentions have resulted in limited but not insignificant reforms. Of the changes made, and the reduction of the prerogative effected, the following would appear to be the most noteworthy:

● The regulation of the prerogative relating to the dissolution of Parliament by the Fixed Term Parliaments Act 2011.

● The replacement of the prerogative powers dealing with the management and control of the civil service with statutory powers provided by the Constitutional Reform and Governance Act 2010.

● The introduction, also by the Constitutional Reform Act, of a statutory system for the approval of treaties prior to ratification.

For more on the Constitutional Reform and Governance Act 2010, see p. 283.

Beyond this, however, the major question of whether, how, and to what extent, statutory limits should be placed on the prerogative relating to military actions overseas remains unresolved.

For the Constitutional Reform Act, see pp. 47–8.

Summary

The chapter explains the difference between the Monarchy and the Crown within the British constitution and considers the extent of the remaining common law powers of both institutions. Detailed comment and analysis is directed also towards effectiveness of the parliamentary and judicial control over the exercise of these powers.

References

Blackstone (1873) *Commentaries on the Laws of England,* London: Macmillan.

Blake (1999) *Royal Prerogative,* London: HarperCollins.

Dicey (1959) *An Introduction to the Law of the Constitution* (10th edn), ed. Wade, E.C.S., London: Macmillan.

Hood Phillips and Jackson (2001) *Constitutional and Administrative Law,* London: Sweet & Maxwell.

House of Commons Select Committee on Public Administration (2003–4), Fourth Report, HC 422.

House of Lords Constitution Committee (2005–6), Fifteenth Report, *Waging War: Parliament's Role and Responsibility,* HL 236.

The Governance of Britain (2008) Cm 7170.

Wade and Forsyth (2004) *Administrative Law* (9th edn), Oxford: Oxford University Press.

Further reading

Bogdanor (1997) *The Monarch and the Constitution,* Oxford, Oxford University Press.

Loveland (2015) *Constitutional Law, Administrative Law and Human Rights* (7th edn), Oxford: Oxford University Press.

Monro (1999) *Studies in Constitutional Law* (2nd edn), Oxford: Oxford University Press, Ch. 8.

Payne and Sunkin (1999) *The Nature of the Crown: A Legal and Political Analysis,* London: Clarendon.

Vincenzi (1998) *Crown Powers, Subjects and Citizens,* London: Continuum Publishing.

13

Legal liability of the Crown and public authorities

After reading this chapter you should:

1. Understand the traditional legal status of the Crown.

2. Appreciate the extent to which the Crown was subject to the law prior to the Crown Proceedings Act 1947.

3. Understand the reasons for the enactment and main provisions of the 1947 Act and the law of contract and tort as currently applicable to the Crown and central government.

4. Appreciate the elements of the tort of breach of statutory duty.

5. Know the circumstances in which a public authority may be liable for the use of, or failure to use, a statutory power.

6. Be aware of the application of the law of negligence to the actions of the police.

7. Understand the meaning and application of the doctrine of public interest immunity.

8. Be aware of the issues surrounding public interest immunity and national security.

Introduction: the Crown

The Crown's protected legal status

Objective 1

For many centuries it has been accepted that the Monarch in his/her personal capacity is completely immune from civil or criminal proceedings. This facet of the constitution found expression in such ancient legal maxims and principles as 'the King can do no wrong' and 'the King cannot be sued in his own courts'. Unfortunately, however, as the distinction between the Monarch in his/her personal and public capacities – i.e. between the Monarch and the Crown as the central government – became increasingly apparent, neither Parliament nor the courts changed the law accordingly. As a result, many of the immunities and privileges designed originally to protect the dignity and status of the person of Monarch became attached to the Crown as an institution. This meant that the ordinary private law dealings of the Crown with its subjects (e.g. in contract and tort) were not regulated solely by the generally applicable rules and procedures, but were subject to a set of principles – highly disadvantageous to the private litigant – designed for a political order which had ceased to exist.

The position remained the same until the Crown Proceedings Act 1947. By this time, of course, the Crown had become a major employer and contractor. The likelihood of other organisations or individuals having grievances against the Crown and wishing to seek legal redress was thus greatly increased. In such circumstances the Crown's special and protected legal position represented a major weakness in the British constitution. Once again, ancient legal principles had been allowed to survive into an age in which they had no practical relevance. The legal relationship between the Crown and its 'subjects' was thus clearly inconsistent with the rule of law and contained an obvious potential for injustice.

The Crown in contract and tort

Historical background

Objective
2

The legal liability of the Crown in these matters is governed currently by the Crown Proceedings Act 1947. In the years prior to the Act, and due to its pre-eminent constitutional status, the Crown, in formal legal terms, was immune from suit in either of these most fundamental elements of the English common law. Put in a somewhat starker form, this meant that neither the Crown as an institution, nor any of the government departments or agencies through which it acted, could be sued in either contract or tort as a matter of legal right.

In contract, the Crown, being an institution, could only make contracts through its agents or employees. In turn, therefore, and according to the law of agency, this meant that any liability for breach rested with the Crown only, as principal, and not with the individual Crown employee through which the contract had been made. But as the Crown could not be sued directly, this appeared to leave the aggrieved person without any legally enforceable remedies.

In the law of tort the situation of the individual litigant in dispute with the Crown was equally difficult. Here, due to its immunity, the Crown could not be sued either for the tortious acts authorised by it or vicariously for such acts committed by its employees acting in its service.

The potential for injustice in this state of affairs did not, of course, go unnoticed. Accordingly, and over time, a number of procedural devices were evolved designed to give those aggrieved by the Crown's civil wrongs some possibility of a measure of redress in the ordinary courts of law.

In the contractual context the device relied upon became known as the Petition of Right – a process whereby the aggrieved individual sought permission from the Crown, through the Attorney-General – to pursue a judicial judgment against it. Depending on the facts of the case, this would take the form of a declaration or statement of the contractual rights to which the complainant was entitled. The most normal course was for such Petitions of Right to be granted and for any judgments given, although not legally binding, to be complied with.

In cases in which the allegations against the Crown raised questions in tort, it remained open for the complainant to bring the case against the individual Crown employee believed to have been responsible for the injury or damage in issue. Accordingly, and where this occurred, the practice was for the Crown to 'stand behind' the individual concerned and thus to bear any financial burden imposed. Otherwise, in those circumstances where the individual tortfeasor could not be identified, the expectation was, first, for the Crown to 'nominate' a person against whom the case could be brought – normally the Crown employee with particular management or other responsibility for the Crown function in the course of which the damage or injury occurred – and, second, once again, to supply any damages or costs which the nominated person might be required to pay.

And so the position remained until the mid-1940s. At this time, however, a number of senior judges began to express unease about being required to preside over cases founded on the fiction that the individual appearing before them as the defendant actually was the person responsible for the damage or injury alleged. The principal cases in question were actions for damages in tort in which the Crown put forward nominated defendants i.e. persons who it was known had not personally committed the act complained of (see *Adams v Naylor* [1946] AC 543; *Royster v Cavey* [1947] 1KB 204). This judicial unease, in turn, led directly to the passing of the 1947 Act.

The Crown Proceedings Act 1947

Liability in contract

Objective 3

Section 1 of the Act provided:

> Where any person has a claim against the Crown . . . and, if this Act had not been passed, the claim might have been enforced, subject to His Majesty's fiat, by petition of right . . . then, subject to the provisions of this Act, the claim may be enforced as of right . . .

In effect this meant that thereafter, and subject to certain remaining exceptions and immunities, the Crown could be sued in contract in the normal way.

The old Petition of Right procedure was thereby abolished and the Crown thus bound by law to submit itself to the relevant jurisdiction of the courts.

It was not, however, the 1947 Act's intention to put the Crown in exactly the same position in terms of its contractual capacity as that of a private individual. There remained circumstances in which it was felt the public interest might still not be best served by holding the Crown or government to all of its contractual obligations. These public policy exceptions to the Crown's capacity in contract had already been recognised by the law developed under the old Petition of Right procedure. Therefore, by providing that litigants could sue 'as of right' only in circumstances where an action could have been pursued under a Petition of Right, the 1947 Act made clear Parliament's intent that these pre-existing exceptions, considered below, should continue to operate in the Crown's favour.

Contracts that fetter future executive action

In *Rederiaktiebolaget Amphitrite v R* [1921] 3 KB 500, the owners of a neutral Swedish ship brought a petition of right action for breach of contract and damages after it had been detained in a British port in breach of an undertaking given by the government. The incident occurred during the First World War when all 'foreign' ships required official clearance before being allowed to leave the United Kingdom. The owners had been given an assurance that the necessary clearance would be given if the ship brought a certain type of cargo to this country.

The action was rejected for the following reasons:

> It is not competent for the government to fetter its future executive action, which must necessarily be determined by the needs of the community when the question arises. It cannot by contract hamper its freedom of action in matters which concern the welfare of the state (*per* Rowlatt J).

A similar approach was taken to a contractual fetter on emergency legislative powers entrusted to the Crown in the Second World War. Hence, in *Crown Lands Commissioners v Page* [1960] 2 QB 274, it was held that the Crown was entitled to requisition land which it had previously leased to the complainant if it was of the opinion that the land was needed for the purposes of defending the realm.

> When the Crown, or any other person, is entrusted by virtue of the prerogative or statute, with discretionary power to be exercised for the public good, it does not, when making a private contract . . . undertake . . . to fetter itself in the use of those powers, and in the exercise of its discretion.

Thus it was recognised that the Crown's contractual obligations might sometimes be inconsistent with its prerogative to protect the public interest. However, the notion that the Crown may not fetter its future executive action to act in the public good is both vague and problematical. Taken literally it could be understood to mean that the Crown could avoid any contract it chose, since any agreement it has entered into will, perforce, have limited its freedom of action to the extent of the obligations thereby incurred.

This, presumably, is not what was intended when the *Amphitrite* case was decided – otherwise persons and organisations might be discouraged from contracting with the Crown at all, particularly if large sums of money were involved. This, in turn, might prejudice the Crown's efficiency by affecting its ability to acquire the goods and services needed to perform its functions. It is generally accepted, therefore, that the *Amphitrite* rule does not apply to the Crown's ordinary commercial transactions and may only give exemption from liability where the contrary demands of the public interest are both immediate and substantial.

An alternative view is that the case should be regarded as having been wrongly decided and that the only immunity the Crown requires in order to satisfy the public interest is immunity from the remedies of specific performance and injunction (i.e. those which would hold the Crown to fulfil a contract) – but that the Crown should always be liable to pay damages where a contractual obligation was sacrificed for public interest reasons.

> The liability to pay damages would not prevent the Crown from taking action which was required in the public interest; it would simply require the Crown to pay the true cost of the action taken. In order to preserve its freedom of action, only one immunity is needed by the Crown, and that is immunity from the remedies of specific performance and injunction (Hogg, *The Liability of the Crown*).

If accepted in future cases this would mean that legal remedies would not be available to hold the Crown to a contractual undertaking if this would be damaging to the public interest, but would allow the other contracting parties to secure financial reparation in respect of the breach. In this way both the public and private interests would be protected.

Contracts dependent on votes of money by Parliament

In those circumstances in which the Crown enters into an agreement which states expressly that the Crown's performance of it, for example by way of payment, is dependent on a vote of supply of finance by Parliament, authority suggests any refusal by Parliament to grant the moneys required renders the contract to be unenforceable. In such incidences it would appear, therefore, that parliamentary supply of the moneys stipulated operates as a condition – precedent to the Crown's fulfilment of its obligations (*Churchward v R* (1865) LRS QB 173). In modern circumstances this type of situation could arise, for example, if a government decided to enter into an agreement to purchase a new and controversial weapons system but found later that, on this issue at least, it did not command sufficient support in the House of Commons to vote the moneys to pay for it.

Where, however, as is often the case, a government contract appears to fall within the broad ambit of the Crown's normal day-to-day financial dealings, i.e. it has little direct

For financial proceedings in the House of Commons, see Chapter 8.

connection with major aspects of political policy, and makes no reference to any specific supply of money by Parliament, it appears generally accepted that the Crown is liable to pay for the performance of its obligations using those sums voted annually to enable government departments to fulfil their functions generally (*New South Wales* v *Bardolph* (1934) 52 CLR 455).

In the extremely unlikely circumstances that such moneys were inadequate to pay for a contract when it fell due, the probability is that the court would regard the contract as unenforceable. In financial terms the Crown can only do that which it has been enabled to do by Parliament. The enforcement of contracts outside the Crown's financial capacity would, therefore, be inconsistent with this principle.

The Crown and its employees

The Crown may not be sued in contract in respect of the summary dismissal of a civil servant. Civil servants hold office at the Crown's pleasure and their services may be dispensed with as and when the Crown sees fit: 'Such employment being for the public good, it is essential for the public good that it should be capable of being determined at the pleasure of the Crown . . .'(*per Lord Herschell*, *Dunn* v *R* [1896] QB 116).

Note, however, that civil servants may bring proceedings in respect of alleged unfair dismissal under the modern employment protection legislation. This is, however, a statutory and not a common law remedy (see the Employment Rights Act 1996, s 191).

At one time the existence of a power to dismiss at pleasure was, in some quarters, taken to mean that civil servants did not have any sort of contract with the Crown whatsoever and, therefore, could not sue in respect of other types of dispute arising out of their relationship with their employer (see *Lucas* v *Lucas and High Commissioner for India* [1943] P 68).

The case-law was, however, uncertain. Other decisions suggested that the existence of a power to dismiss at pleasure was not necessarily inconsistent with the existence of a contractual relationship and that aggrieved civil servants should at least be able to recover arrears of pay (see *Sutton* v *Attorney-General* (1923) 39 TLR 294; *Terrell* v *Secretary of State for the Colonies* [1953] 2 QB 482; *Kodeeswaran* v *Attorney-General of Ceylon* [1970] AC 1111).

The latter view has been supported by more modern authority. The courts now appear to accept that a contractual employer–employee relationship may exist between the Crown and its civil servants unless, in a particular case, it can be shown that this was not the Crown's intention. Hence, while for public interest reasons the Crown may still have the common law (i.e. prerogative) right to dismiss at pleasure, other grievances arising out of its legal relationship with its employees may be pursued by way of actions for breach of contract (see *R* v *Lord Chancellor's Department, ex parte Nangle* [1992] 1 All ER 897; *McClaren* v *Home Office* [1990] ICR 824; *R* v *Civil Service Appeal Board, ex parte Bruce* [1988] 3 All ER 686, per May LJ).

The Crown and the law of agency

Under the common law the Crown has unlimited contractual authority. The view that it may only enter into contracts incidental to the usual functions of government is not supported by authority. It is not open to the Crown, therefore, to seek to avoid a contract on the ground that it was beyond its powers. If, however, its contractual capacity in any particular context has been limited by statute, a contract made outside those limitations would be *ultra vires* and invalid.

Since the Crown is an institution and not an individual it cannot enter into contracts personally. This is done by Ministers or civil servants on its behalf. To a considerable extent such contracts are regulated by the normal private law rules of agency. This means that the person who acted for the Crown is not personally liable for the contract's performance. It is the Crown as principal against whom the contract is actionable. This will be the case providing that the person who made the contract was acting within their actual, ostensible or usual authority. An agent's actual authority is that which was conferred on him or her by the principal (in this case a Minister or other empowered superior). Ostensible authority is that which the principal by word or deed has represented ('held out') the agent to have, but which is beyond the latter's actual authority. Usual authority is that which an agent of the type in question would usually be expected to have but which, in a particular case, is greater than the actual authority conferred. This may arise where, for whatever reasons, a principal has imposed restrictions on the scope of authority normally conferred on agents operating in a particular sphere of trade and failed to take reasonable steps to make these known to those with whom the agent might be expected to deal.

Robertson v Minister of Pensions [1949] 1 KB 227

In this case, a disabled ex-army officer made written enquiries about his eligibility for a pension to the government department which might usually have been expected to have dealt with such matters, viz. the War Office. He received a letter in return saying that he qualified for the type of pension in issue. Strictly speaking, however, he had applied to the wrong department as the authority to decide matters of this type had been vested in the Ministry of Pensions. When, however, the Ministry of Pensions sought to deny his eligibility, it was held that the Ministry could not change the decision and that the plaintiff was entitled to rely on the War Office having the authority which it had both assumed and which he might reasonably have expected it to have.

If, however, a Crown agent's authority is limited by legislation, the above common law rules cannot clothe the agent with a degree of authority in excess of such statutory restrictions. In these circumstances any contract entered into beyond the statutory restraints would be invalid and unenforceable (*Attorney-General of Ceylon v Silva* [1953] AC 461).

In *Silva* a Crown agent had legislative authority to sell any goods, except those belonging to the Crown, left unclaimed in a customs warehouse. A quantity of steel which had been stored in the warehouse and which belonged to the Crown was 'sold' to the plaintiff. When the steel was not delivered he sued for breach of contract. It was held that the contract was clearly outside the authority granted and that no concept of agency could give legitimacy to that which had been prohibited by legislation.

The normal rule is that an agent who makes a contract outside the scope of his/her authority may be sued for breach of warranty of authority. The person who has been misled into making an unenforceable contract is, therefore, provided some means of redress. It would appear, however, that such right of action is not available against Crown agents (*Dunn v MacDonald* [1897] 1 QB 401). This was said to be in the interests of public policy, otherwise 'no man would accept any office of trust under government'.

Liability in tort

Section 2 of the 1947 Act removed most of the Crown's immunity in tort and rendered it liable:

(a) vicariously, for the torts of its employees;

(b) in respect of those common law duties owed by an employer to its employees;

(c) in respect of those common law duties owed by the owners or occupiers of property (e.g. the rule in *Rylands* v *Fletcher* (1868) LR 3 HL 330).

Section 2(2) provided that the Crown could be sued in tort for failure to comply with any statutory duties imposed by statutes binding upon the Crown as well as upon other persons, e.g. Occupiers' Liability Act 1957.

The categories of persons coming within the definition of Crown servant or employee were defined by s 2(6). The definition extends to persons appointed directly or indirectly by the Crown and who are paid wholly out of the Consolidated Fund or other moneys provided by Parliament or from any other fund certified by the Treasury. The Crown is not vicariously liable, therefore, for the torts of police officers, or the employees of local authorities or of other statutory or public corporations.

Liability for judicial actions and decisions

Section 2(5) retained the Crown's immunity in tort in respect of anything done or omitted to be done by those exercising responsibilities of a judicial nature or any responsibility 'in connection with the execution of judicial process'. Hence, were a judge to impose a sentence of imprisonment for an offence carrying a maximum penalty of a fine, no liability for false imprisonment could be imposed on the Crown.

The immunity was applied in *Quinland* v *Governor of Belmarsh Prison* [2002] EWCA Civ 174, where a Crown Court clerk mistakenly drew up an order of imprisonment for two years six months instead of two years three months. The Court of Appeal was satisfied that the clerk was acting in the execution of the judicial process and was thus immune from damages for false imprisonment.

Note also that judges in the superior courts (Crown Court in indictable cases, High Court and above) may not be made liable for anything said or done in the exercise of their judicial functions however malicious, corrupt or oppressive those actions or decisions might be (*Anderson* v *Gorrie* [1895] 1 QB 668). This remains the case even if the act or decision in question represented an excess of jurisdiction, provided this was an honest mistake. Liability may attach, however, to that done outside jurisdiction and in bad faith (*Re McC* [1985] AC 528).

Judges of inferior courts, e.g. county courts, also enjoy immunity for that done while acting judicially and in the honest belief that jurisdiction existed (*Sirros* v *Moore* [1975] QB 118).

Some uncertainty has surrounded the position of magistrates. Relatively recent authority suggests that a magistrate could be personally liable in respect of acts done in innocent excess of jurisdiction. Hence if a magistrate, acting bona fide, imprisoned a person where no power to impose a custodial sentence existed, liability for unlawful imprisonment could have been imposed. The position of magistrates is, however, now covered by the Justices of the Peace Act 1997, ss 51–57. These provide that a magistrate will not be liable for that done within jurisdiction or for that done without jurisdiction unless, in the latter case, the plaintiff can prove bad faith.

Liability for actions of members of the armed forces

The reforms introduced by the 1947 Act did not extend to the relationship between the Crown and members of the armed forces. Here, the general pre-existing immunity of the Crown in tort was expressly preserved by the 1947 Act in s 10. Although couched in rather convoluted terms, the overall effect of the section may be summarised as follows. Where a serviceman was injured as a result of the acts of any of his fellows while both were 'on duty', or, while not on duty, he suffered such injury 'on any land, premises, ship, aircraft or vehicle' being used for Crown purposes, or the injury was suffered 'in consequence of the nature or condition' of any such land, premises, ship etc., and the Minister of Defence certifies that the injuries were 'attributable' to his military service and, therefore, pensionable, no right of action for damages lies against the Crown or, where identifiable, the particular serviceman who caused the injury.

Over the years, however, and after a number of high-profile cases in which badly injured service personnel so precluded from taking legal action were awarded pensions well below the value of any damages they might otherwise have been awarded, a campaign was launched, led by the media and supported by numbers of MPs, for a change in the law. This led to the Crown Proceedings (Armed Forces) Act 1987 which 'suspended', rather than repealed section 10 and left the Minister with the power to re-activate the section 'in case of imminent national danger, great emergency or warlike operations outside the United Kingdom' (s 2).

Absent such re-activation, the 1987 Act enabled service personnel to sue for damages in the previously excluded categories of circumstances specified, as outlined above in the 1947 Act. The 1987 Act, however, was not expressed to have retrospective effect, with the result that it did not apply to incidents arising before it came into effect. In other words, service personnel who might still have wished to sue in respect of injuries or damage incurred in the year before the 1987 Act remained precluded from any judicial process.

These matters came to the fore in *Matthews* v *Minister of Defence* [2003] UKHL 4. The case concerned an ex Royal Navy electrical engineer who claimed that in later life he had become ill as a result of coming into contact with asbestos when working on naval ships in the period 1955–68. He argued that, in so far as section 10 precluded him from legal redress, it was incompatible with the fair trial and judicial process guarantees in Art 6 of the European Convention of Human Rights.

In response, the House of Lords delivered a wide-ranging analysis of the purposes and exact requirements of said article. It did not, their Lordships said, create substantive rights independent of domestic legal systems. Where, however, such rights had been created, Art 6 was concerned to ensure that the full realisation of such rights was not inhibited by the imposition of procedural fetters – except where these could be justified on proportional public interest grounds.

It followed that Art 6 could only avail the complainant of a remedy if section 10 could be understood as imposing a purely procedural impediment to the enforcement of a hitherto existing substantive right – in this instance, the right to sue for damages for personal injuries. The House felt, however, that the section could not be so construed. Section 10, it was felt, was primarily concerned with matters of substantive law rather than procedure. Its principal effect was to make clear that the reforms introduced in 1947 had not removed the Crown's long-standing immunity in tort in respect of service personnel. The House added that to the extent that this may have been thought to be unfair, section 10 had, in effect, instituted a 'no-fault' system of compensation to ensure that financial recompense for this special category of Crown servants should not be subject to the uncertainties of the adversarial legal process.

Providing section 10 has not been revived, it will be for the plaintiff service personnel in any action for negligence to establish the normal principles of liability – i.e. foresight, proximity and the existence of a duty of care.

In *Mulcahy* v *Minister of Defence* [1996] 2 WLR 474, the plaintiff sued for damages in respect of deafness caused by the alleged negligence of a fellow soldier when firing a howitzer during the Gulf War. The tests of foresight and proximity were satisfied but the Court of Appeal would not accept that it was just, fair and reasonable to impose a duty of care on one service person towards another while a battle was in progress or, in those circumstances, a duty on the Crown to maintain a safe system of work.

Crown liability for acts done overseas

Act of state

As a general rule, that done overseas by the Crown (i.e. the British government), its agents, employees or armed forces is, for legal purposes, classified as an 'act of state'. The traditional doctrine associated with this was that the domestic courts of the United Kingdom would not grant a legal remedy to a foreign national who claimed to have been injured or suffered some form of loss or damage as a result of such activities. The doctrine was of some considerable utility in the days of the British Empire when British government officials and military personnel tended to be active in most parts of the known world. In effect the doctrine granted legal and financial immunity to the process of imperial expansion without which, given the scale on which it occurred, and according to the methods used, could have proved extremely costly.

With the demise of Britain's imperial status in the quarter of a century following World War II, and the various grants of independence to former colonies during that period, the practical relevance of the doctrine appeared to be on the wane – so much so, in fact, that numbers of respected academic voices were prepared to suggest that the time was fast approaching when the doctrine would be seen as merely a legal relic of the nation's imperial past.

Such proposals have, however, proved to be somewhat premature and this particularly in the light both of more recent British involvement in a series of major overseas military engagements (Kosovo 1999, Afghanistan 2001, Iraq 2003) and the readiness of the British authorities to fall back on the act of state defence when faced with the potential legal consequences of what may have been done in these conflicts in the name of the state. This, in turn, has required the domestic courts to look again at the doctrine's specific requirements and to adapt these for service in the context of the United Kingdom's political and military competence in the modern world.

Elements of the doctrine

In modern judicial parlance it is not uncommon for the doctrine to be described as having two major elements or 'limbs' – either of which may be used to avoid national liability for that done outside of the state's territory.

The first of these takes the form that those acts of Crown agents or armed forces overseas in alleged pursuance of British foreign policy interests are not actionable in the law of tort if the effect of this would be contrary to British public policy or other national interests (*Serder Mohammed* v *Secretary of State for Defence* [2016] 2 WLR 247). The second limb is founded on the principle that the subject-matter of certain types of actions and decisions taken by the state should be regarded as 'non-justiciable', i.e. as belonging to that sphere of executive responsibility upon which the courts are not qualified to comment, i.e. foreign affairs and other international relations, the making of public policy in domestic and financial affairs, national security, and the defence of the realm.

The first limb: a defence in tort

Although not a topic-area replete with case law, the act of state defence in tort would appear to be applicable in the following circumstances:

(i)   The claimant was a foreign national (see ***Walker v Baird*** [1892] AC 491, seizure of claimant's lobster factory on the coast of Newfoundland in fulfilment of fisheries agreement with France – defence not available – claimant a British national);

(ii)   The act was not committed outside of British territory (see ***Johnstone v Pedlar*** [1921] 2 AC 262, search and seizure of claimant's personal property during Irish War of Independence 1919–21 – defence not available – although the claimant was an American, the act took place in British territory);

(iii)   The act was not related to the exercise of British foreign policy (see ***Nissan v Attorney-General*** [1970] AC 178, claim for damage to hotel occupied by British troops in Cyprus as part of peace-keeping mission – defence not applicable – trivial acts of vandalism could not be related to an act of state);

(iv)   In the circumstances of the case, allowing the individual to sue in tort would not be contrary to British public policy (***Serdar Mohammed***, *supra*, detention of suspected insurgent by British troops in Afghanistan in contravention of Afghan law, act of state not applicable – no compelling public policy reasons for allowing the troops to break the local law with impunity).

The first reported example of the tort defence being applied judicially would appear to be ***Buron v Denman*** (1848) 2 Ex 167. Here the claimant was the owner of a slave-trading station on the west coast of Africa. His property had been destroyed by a British naval vessel under the defendant's command. This was at a time when the British government was committed to the suppression of the slave trade. The slave-trader's action failed. The court was confident that in the circumstances prevailing it would clearly have been against British interests to have granted him a remedy.

The second limb: non-justiciable executive actions

During the hey-day of British imperialism, the courts were required to deal with a series of claims arising out of the seizure of goods, property and territory by those acting for the Crown in places far beyond the United Kingdom's traditional boundaries. Acts of this nature being so closely related to issues of foreign policy, such cases clearly illustrated the types of subject-matter the courts felt disinclined to inquire into or make judgments upon.

A striking example of this was provided by the decision of the Privy Council in ***Secretary of State for India v Kamachee Boye Sahabe*** (1859) 13 Moore 22.

Following the death of the Rajah of Tanjore without male heir, and the seizure of his property by the East India Company, the Rajah's widow sued the British government for compensation. The court's view was that the seizure of the territory was made by the company 'acting in the exercise of the sovereign power of the Crown in the state's sovereign affairs' and was, therefore, too close to matters of government policy to fall within the court's normal sphere of competence.

In more modern times the question of the justiciability of actions taken by the government overseas was raised again in the ***Serdar Mohammed*** decision. In this instance the act complained of was the arrest and detention of Afghan civilians suspected of terrorist activity. The court's view here was that the legality of a person's arrest was not sufficiently closely related to issues of foreign policy or to any other non-justiciable subject-matter so as to be beyond its area of jurisdictional competence.

We consider that claims challenging whether HM forces acted lawfully under the local law are clearly justiciable. The court will not be required to rule on the legality or otherwise of high policy decisions such as whether to participate in 'the multi-national force . . . from which the complaints made in these proceedings are remote. On the contrary, the court is well-equipped to deal with such issues albeit arising under the law of a foreign state. Determining whether an individual has been unlawfully deprived of his liberty is quintessentially a matter for a court.

Act of state and the Human Rights Act 1998

Whether pleaded under either of the above limbs of the doctrine, act of state does not provide a defence to claims alleging violations of the Human Rights Act 1998. This is founded on two main principles:

(i) the Act binds all domestic public bodies to act in accordance with it in all circumstances other than those in relation to which a valid derogation from its requirements has been made (ss 6 and 14);

(ii) as part of the common law, the act of state doctrine cannot override the requirements of an Act of Parliament.

Public authorities generally

Statutory duties and powers: private law liability

Public authorities generally

Some basic principles

The Crown Proceedings Act 1947 does not apply to public authorities other than the Crown. It has no application, therefore, to local authorities or to other public corporations or bodies engaged either in the process of government and administration or in the provision or regulation of public services. As a general rule, therefore, such bodies may be held legally accountable in the direct sense for their activities and to a similar extent as any private entities operating in the commercial sphere of the economy or in the provision of public utilities.

It would be misleading, however, to convey the impression that the law treats such public authorities in exactly the same way as private organisations. Hence, in any study of constitutional and administrative law, it is necessary to identify those elements of the common law which have been developed to take particular account of the distinctive nature of public authorities, their statutory foundations and those extensive legal responsibilities conferred upon them. Such rules, as set out below, are premised on a series of broad constitutional and related principles which include the following:

1 in whatever they do, public authorities must, at all times, act for the public benefit and the protection of the public interest;

2 the contractual capacity of public bodies, other than the Crown, is limited to agreements compatible with the powers conferred upon them by Parliament;

3 neither the courts nor the common law should attempt to impose legal liabilities or obligations upon public authorities which were not intended by Parliament, or . . . which may impose excessive financial burdens upon them;

4 functions entrusted to public authorities by statute should be legally enforceable and actionable in private law only to the extent as is consistent with the nature of the function in issue and the intentions of the empowering legislation.

Public authorities in contract

For further details on contracts beyond the powers of public authorities see Chapter 15.

As a general rule, public authorities are not bound by contracts which fetter the full and free exercise of their statutory powers. Such powers having been given for the protection of the public interest, it is axiomatic that no contractual or other limits should be imposed on the extent of the discretion conferred by Parliament for that purpose.

The principle was well illustrated by the decision in *William Cory* v *London Corporation* [1951] 2 KB 476. Here the plaintiffs entered into a contract with the Corporation to ship sewage down the Thames for disposal at sea. The contract imposed certain obligation in terms of the way the sewage was to be covered and contained during shipment. Some years later, and while the contract was still in operation, the Corporation introduced new by-laws which laid down even stricter requirements for the carriage of sewage by barge. The plaintiffs sought rescission of the contract and argued that it contained an implied term that the authority would not use its powers in ways inconsistent with its pre-existing contractual obligations. The Court of Appeal held that the Corporation, as a public authority, was not competent to enter into agreements which fettered the future exercise of its powers. When making by-laws it was bound, therefore, to regard the protection of the public interest as the paramount and overriding consideration.

Public authorities in tort

As explained, the overall effect of the Crown Proceedings Act was to approximate the position of the Crown in tort to that of other public authorities. Both are now subject to the ordinary law as it applies between private citizens. Unlike private citizens, however, public authorities have been entrusted by Parliament with a wide range of legal powers and duties, the exercise of which may result in damage or interference with the rights of others. This has necessitated the development of additional tortious rules which are peculiar to those who exercise statutory functions.

Breach of statutory duty

Objective
4

This is a distinct tort with its own requirements. It is not simply a particular aspect of negligence or nuisance. In essence it requires the plaintiff to show:

(a) that a public body or statutory undertaking was under a statutory duty to take a certain course of action;

(b) that the duty to act was not fulfilled;

(c) that the failure caused damage to the plaintiff.

No carelessness or negligence need be established. Nor does the plaintiff have to prove any interference with a common law right: 'It is a general rule of law that, when a Ministerial duty is imposed, an action lies for breach of it without malice or negligence' (*per* Bovill CJ, *Pickering* v *Jones* (1873) LR 8 CP).

Similar sentiments were expressed in *Wilkinson* v *City of York* [2011] EWCA 209, a case concerned with the duty to maintain the highway placed on highway authorities by the Highways Act 1980, s 41.

So if a highway is out of repair, there is a failure to maintain, even though the highway authority has not been negligent at all.

This should not be understood, however, as a simplistic assertion that every breach of statutory duty is actionable in tort. Other factors must be established to the court's satisfaction. Of crucial importance will be the intention of the legislation in which the duty is contained. Some duties – such as the obligation lying on the Minister for Education 'to promote education in England and Wales' – may be regarded, primarily, as broad statements of political intent more suitable to parliamentary scrutiny and criticism than to judicial enforcement:

> Parliament has recently become fond of imposing duties of a kind which, since they are of a general and indefinite character, are perhaps to be considered as political duties rather than as legal duties which a court could enforce (Wade and Forsyth, *Administrative Law*).

In those cases where, given the nature of the duty and the resource constraints on the authority, exact or absolute compliance is probably impossible – e.g. the duty in the Highways Act 1980, s 41 to keep the roads clear of water, snow and ice. Here the obligation on the authorities to do all that it reasonably could under the circumstances (*Cross v Kirklees Metropolitan Borough Council* [1998] 1 All ER 564).

Thus in *R v Camden and Islington Health Authority, ex parte K* [2001] EWCA Civ 240, the Court of Appeal found the duty on health authorities to provide after-care services for patients discharged from mental hospitals was not an absolute obligation but a requirement to use their best endeavours to secure treatment in the community which was adequate for the needs of particular patients.

Other duties may be contained in statutory rules which are construed to be merely directory and, therefore, not intended to create legally enforceable rights. Hence, the prison rules made under the Prison Act 1952 (which regulate the government of prisons and the entitlement of inmates), have been held not to provide prisoners with any rights enforceable either in public or private law (*R v Deputy Governor of Parkhurst Prison, ex parte Hague* [1992] 1 AC 58). Also, even if it can be shown that the duty was intended to be legally enforceable, the court must be satisfied that this was meant to include private law actions for damages as well as public law proceedings for judicial review (*R v ILEA, ex parte Ali*, *The Times,* 21 February 1990).

If the statute which imposes the duty also provides a remedy for its enforcement, this may be understood as evincing a parliamentary intention that other remedies, including actions for damages, should be deemed to have been excluded. In *Atkinson v Newcastle Waterworks Co* (1877) 2 Ex D 441, the defendants failed in their statutory duty to maintain a certain pressure in the water mains. As a result the local fire brigade were unable to extinguish a fire at the plaintiff's premises. The plaintiff's action for damages was, however, unsuccessful. This was because the statute in question (the Waterworks Clauses Act 1847) provided that, for breaches of the duties it imposed, a Waterworks Company could be prosecuted and fined to a maximum of £10. This was assumed to be an exclusive remedy precluding any right of action for damages. This is, however, not a rigid rule and there are examples of courts departing from it where it was felt that the degree and type of damage suffered was not that which the legislature could have had in mind when the statutory remedy was included. Thus the statutory remedy in the Waterworks Clauses Act, which operated against the plaintiff in the *Atkinson* case, was held not to be absolutely exclusive in *Read v Croydon Corporation* [1938] 4 All ER 631. On this occasion a water authority failed to fulfil its duty in the 1847 Act to provide a clean and wholesome water supply. This caused an outbreak of typhoid in Croydon which killed 38 people and affected hundreds of others. Stable J held that:

> While there is no doubt that for some of the statutory duties imposed . . . the penalty provided in the Act is exclusive, it is difficult to believe that the legislature intended that it should be exclusive in the case of each breach of every duty under the Act. I find it impossible to hold . . . that the legislature intended that there should be one remedy . . . equally applicable

to so trivial a breach as the failure to maintain a certain pressure of water . . . and to a deliberate dereliction of duty resulting in the destruction of a large community by the supply of poisonous water.

Liability for breach of statutory duty will also not be imposed unless the plaintiff can show that they belong to the particular category of persons that the statute was designed to protect (*Cutler* v *Wandsworth Stadium Ltd* [1949] AC 398) and, similarly, that the damage suffered was of a type which it was passed to guard against (*Gorris* v *Scott* (1874) LR 9 Ex 125).

It should also be remembered that, in the case of the Crown, liability under this head may only be imposed in respect of duties contained in statutes which bind the Crown expressly or by necessary implication.

Negligence and statutory powers

Objective
5

Due to its attendant complexities, much of that which is done by public authorities in the process of modern government is effected under the legal auspices of statutory powers rather than the more rigid and prescriptive rubric of statutory duties. The vesting of authorities with powers rather than duties permits of discretion and flexibility in terms of whether and how a particular power should be used. This, in turn, enables such authorities to act appropriately in the wide variety of circumstances with which they may have to deal or to which they may have to respond. It also takes account of the fact that decisions relating to the use of powers, and the provision of public services, may often be heavily influenced by considerations of public policy and the availability of resources.

The question whether public authorities should be under a common law duty of care (i.e. should be liable in negligence) in respect of the way statutory powers are exercised has proved to be extremely complex and remains fraught with uncertainty. In *Gorringe* v *Calderdale Metropolitan Borough Council* [2004] 1 WLR 1057, Lord Steyn's comment was that 'this is a subject of great complexity and very much an evolving area of the law . . . no single decision is capable of providing a comprehensive analysis'.

The reason for this uncertainty and for what, in effect, is an 'on-going' judicial debate in this area, may be summarised as follows. First, while there may often be a natural and understandable tendency to wish to provide relief for those who claim to have suffered injury or damage arising out of the way a statutory power has been used, judges are very much aware that converting statutory powers into common law duties, i.e. by requiring that these should be exercised in certain ways, may not always be consistent with the wishes of Parliament, i.e. if Parliament had wished to place an authority under a duty to act in a certain way, it would no doubt have done so. Second, as mentioned above, the extent to which an authority may be able to exercise a certain power, may be heavily influenced, and indeed constrained, by the finance available to it at any particular time. On occasions, therefore, alleged inadequacies in the use of a power may be more a matter of lack of resources rather than any discernible lack of will or care on the authority's part. Third, there is an obvious danger that the imposition of duties of care in negligence could have adverse effects in terms of the way powers are exercised – thereby frustrating the public policy objectives of the enabling legislation. Thus, in the making and implementing of decisions, authorities might be influenced towards greater caution and a general 'safety-first' approach eschewing bolder, more imaginative courses of action, which might carry with them an increased risk of litigation.

Notwithstanding Lord Steyn's cautionary sentiments quoted above, the modern history of judicial decision-making in this area of the law suggests that a number of general principles may be extrapolated.

Thus a court may be prepared to impose a duty of care where the exercise of a power involves a heavy 'operational' element and the authority has moved beyond the purely discretionary element of the process, i.e. whether the power should be exercised at all and, if so, how, and is actually in the process of implementing its decision or chosen course of action. Hence, it has been held that a duty of care could arise in respect of the way a child has been treated after being taken into care under the relevant Children's Acts (*Barrett* v *Enfield London Borough Council* [2001] 2 AC 550). Also in *Phelps* v *Hillingdon London Borough Council* [2001] 2 AC 619, liability was imposed where a child psychologist, employed by a local education authority, negligently failed to diagnose the complainant's dyslexia.

The complexities and uncertainties really begin, however, where the alleged negligence relates mainly to the exercise of discretion (see Dyson LJ in *Carty* v *London Borough of Croydon* [2005] EWCA Civ 19), i.e. the process through which the authority 'made up its mind' about how the power in question should be used or particular statutory function should be carried out. Here, there has been a general judicial tendency against intervention particularly where, as is often the case, the exercise of discretion has been influenced by political and policy considerations unsuitable for judicial analysis.

One of the leading cases in this matter is *X (minors)* v *Bedfordshire County Council* [1995] 2 AC 633. On this occasion Lord Browne-Wilkinson expressed the view that while it would not generally be appropriate to impose a duty of care for the doing of that which had been authorised by Parliament, liability could still conceivably arise where an authority's decision about the use of a power was so absurd or irrational as to be beyond the legal remit conferred by the enabling legislation.

> Most statutes which impose a statutory duty on local authorities confer a discretion as to the extent to which, and the methods by which, such duty is to be performed . . . It is clear both in principle and from the decided cases that the local authority cannot be liable in damages for doing that which Parliament has authorised. Therefore, if the decisions complained of fall within the ambit of such statutory discretion they cannot be actionable in common law. However, if the decision complained of is so unreasonable that it falls outside the ambit of the discretion conferred on a local authority, there is no a priori reason for excluding all common law liability.

Similar views were expressed by Hale LJ in *A* v *Essex County Council* [2003] EWCA Civ 1848.

This approach was not, however, given unequivocal approval by a majority of their Lordships in *Stovin* v *Wise* [1996] AC 923, where the court seemed reluctant to give any greater credence to the postulated link between abuse of discretion (i.e. irrationality) in the public law sense and a recognition of a private law duty of care in negligence. Similar sentiments were expressed in *Gorringe* (*supra*), where Lord Hoffmann opined that 'the suggestion that there might exceptionally be a case in which a breach of a public law could found a private law right of action has proved controversial and it may have been ill-advised to speculate on such matters'.

All of this appeared to suggest that if irrationality in the exercise of statutory discretion was to be no longer regarded as a precondition to the imposition of common law liability in negligence, it remained conceivable that such common law liability could be held to exist in respect of a decision clearly falling within the boundaries of an authority's lawful powers. This was recognised by Lord Slynn in *Phelps* (*supra*).

It does not follow that the local authority can never be liable in common law negligence for damage resulting from acts done in the course of performance of a statutory duty. This House decided – *Barrett v Enfield Borough Council* – that the fact that acts which are claimed to be negligent are carried out within the ambit of a statutory discretion is not in itself a reason why it should be held that no claim for negligence can be brought in respect of them. It is only when what is done has involved the weighing of competing public interests or has been dictated by considerations on which Parliament could not have intended that the courts would substitute their views for ministers or officials that the courts would hold that the issue is non-justiciable on the ground that the decision was made in the exercise of a statutory discretion.

It could be argued, however, that in many of the cases in which such sentiments were expressed, the authority's use of the power in issue had moved beyond the purely discretionary stage and had reached the point discussed above (the decisions in *Barrett* and *Phelps*) where the authority was in the process of implementing decisions already taken. Few cases could be cited, therefore, in which the exercise of discretion alone, within an authority's powers, was held to be actionable in negligence.

Amidst all this remaining uncertainty it is clear at least that judicial resistance towards the notion that a public authority may be liable in negligence for simple inactivity, i.e. for not exercising a power at all, has hardened considerably. The circumstances in which such complaints may arise were well illustrated by the facts in *Gorringe*, mentioned above. Here the complainant alleged that the local authority's failure to paint warning signs on a particular and potentially dangerous stretch of road was the main cause of a road traffic accident in which she suffered serious injuries.

That liability might arise from such scenarios had been contemplated by Lord Hoffmann in *Stovin v Wise* (*supra*). The case was also related to issues of road safety and involved a complaint that a stretch of road could have been rendered less dangerous had the responsible local authority chosen to use its powers to improve visibility at certain road junctions. Lord Hoffmann made further reference to the possible link between irrational exercise or 'non-exercises' of power and liability in negligence.

> I think that the minimum pre-conditions for basing a duty of care upon the existence of a statutory power, if it can be done at all, are first that it would in the circumstance have been irrational not to have exercised the power, so that there was in effect a public law duty to act, and secondly, that there are exceptional grounds for holding that the policy of the statute requires compensation to be paid to persons who suffer loss because the power was not exercised.

This approach found favour with the Court of Appeal in *Larner v Solihull Metropolitan Borough Council* [2000] EWCA Civ 359, another case involving an alleged failure by a local authority to provide adequate warning signs on a dangerous part of the highway. Dealing with the question whether liability could even arise in such circumstances, Lord Woolf's comment was:

> If a statutory duty does not give rise to a private right to sue for breach, it would be unusual if it nevertheless gave rise to a duty of care at common law . . . to pay compensation for foreseeable loss caused by the duty not being performed . . . However . . . we would accept that there can be circumstances of an exceptional nature where common law liability can arise. For that to happen it would have to be shown that the default of the authority falls outside the ambit of discretion given to the authority by the [statute]. This would happen if an authority acted wholly unreasonably . . . As long as any common law duty is confirmed in this way, there are no policy reasons which are sufficient to exclude the duty. An authority could rely on lack of resources for not taking action and then it would not be in breach. These difficulties in the way

of claimants mean that the existence of a residual common law duty should not give rise to a flood of litigation.

Later, however, in the *Gorringe* case, the House of Lords displayed a distinct unease about the further development of this particular line of reasoning and baulked at the idea of constructing a firm legal principle that a public authority could be put under a common law duty to do that which it had not been given a statutory duty to do – and this notwithstanding that the failure to act might have appeared to have been unreasonable. Hence Lord Hoffmann's comment that 'speaking for myself, I find it difficult to imagine a case in which a common law duty can be founded simply upon the failure (however irrational) to provide some benefit which a public authority has power . . . to provide'. To support this view he also made reference to the decision of the Court of Appeal in *Capital and Counties plc* v *Hampshire County Council* [1997] QB 1004, to the effect that the statutory obligation on fire brigades to provide efficient fire-fighting services did not place them under a common law duty to answer a call for help.

> In our judgment the fire brigade are not under a common law duty to answer a call for help . . . If, therefore, they fail to turn up in time because they have carelessly misunderstood the message, got lost on the way, or run into a tree, they are not liable.

The current understanding of the law in these matters was summarised by the Court of Appeal in *Connor* v *Surrey County Council* [2011] QB 429. Given the various nuances of opinion to be found in the relevant case-law, as discussed above, it is perhaps worth quoting in full the key passage in which this summary was contained.

> These following states of affairs may be discerned in the succession of authority. (1) Where it is sought to impugn, as the cause of injury, a pure choice of policy under a statute which provides for such a choice to be made, the court will not ascribe a duty of care to the policy-maker. So much is owed to the authority of Parliament and, in that sense, to the rule of law. (2) If a decision, albeit a choice of policy, is so unreasonable that it cannot be said to have been taken under the statute, it will (for the purpose of the law of negligence) lose the protection of the statute . . . but the claimant must still show a self-standing case for the imposition of a duty of care [viz. that it would be fair, just and reasonable to do so]. (3) There will be a mix of cases involving policy and practice, and operations, where the court's conclusion as to the duty of care will be sensitive as to the particular facts: 'the greater the element of policy involved, the wider the area of discretion accorded, the more likely it is that the matter is not justiciable so that no action in negligence can be brought (Lord Slynn in *Barrett*). This is likely to be so in a large class of cases. (4) There will be purely operational cases . . . where liability for negligence is likely to attach without controversy (*per* Laws LJ).

Given the formative and developing state of the law in this area, it would perhaps be sensible to understand the above statement as setting out a framework of general rules only. Hence the *Connor* case itself may be regarded as authority for the proposition that failure to exercise a statutory discretion may yet be regarded as forming the basis for a private law action for damages in at least one, albeit rare and very distinct circumstance. This would appear to be where:

(a) exercise of the statutory discretion in issue is the only way of the authority complying with a pre-existing common law obligation, e.g. a duty of care in tort; and

(b) the particular exercise of discretion contended for would not infringe any of the essentially public-law prescriptions within which, for the most part, public authorities are bound to operate.

The facts of *Connor* were that a head teacher of a local primary school sued the authority for the damage to her mental health caused by a campaign of unfounded allegations and criticisms mounted against her by some of the school's governors. There appeared to have been only one way in which the authority could have acted in accordance with its pre-existing duty of care towards her (i.e., as her employer, to take reasonable steps to protect her physical and mental health). This would have been to have used its powers in the Education Acts to suspend the governing body in its entirety and replace it with an 'interim executive board'. As, in all the circumstances, it appeared that this could have been done without infringing or contravening any of the authority's public law obligations, the Court of Appeal was unable to discern any good reason for rejecting the argument that, on the particular facts of the case, the authority's failure to exercise the relevant statutory discretion constituted an actionable breach of the duty of care owed to the complainant.

Justiciability

Questions of policy

As a precondition to an action in tort for carelessness in the exercise of discretion, it must be shown that the decision in issue was justiciable, i.e. it fell within the type of matter judges are competent to decide. The difference between justiciable and non-justiciable discretionary powers was explained by Lord Browne-Wilkinson in the *Bedfordshire* case. The case involved actions for damages relating to the way the local authority had used its childcare powers in relation to a number of children who appeared to have been seriously neglected by their parents.

> The first question is whether the determination by the court of the question whether there has been a breach of duty will involve unjusticiable policy questions. The alleged breaches of that duty relate for the most part to the failure to take reasonable practical steps, e.g. to remove the children, to allocate a suitable social worker or to make proper investigations. The assessment by the court of such allegations would not require the court to consider policy matters which are not justiciable. They do not necessarily involve any question of the allocation of resources or the determination of general policy. There are other allegations the investigation of which by a court might require the weighing of policy factors, e.g. allegations that the county council failed to provide a level of service appropriate to the plaintiff's needs (*ibid*).

It should be noted, however, that any blanket and rigid exclusion of liability in tort on these grounds may be inconsistent with the right to a fair trial guaranteed by Art 6 of the European Convention on Human Rights (see *JD and Another* v *East Berkshire Community Health NHS Trust* [2003] EWCA Civ 1151).

Intentions of Parliament and the public interest

Even though it may be decided that a particular exercise of a decision-making power is justiciable, its careless exercise may still not be actionable if the court feels that the imposition of a common law duty of care would be inconsistent with the wishes of Parliament or the public interest. The question and impact of Parliament's intentions was considered in *Clunis* v *Camden and Islington Health Authority* [1998] QB 978.

Clunis v *Camden and Islington Health Authority* [1998] QB 978

In this case, the plaintiff had been discharged from a mental hospital into the care of the defendants. He subsequently committed an unprovoked and fatal attack as a result of which he was convicted of manslaughter. He sued for negligence and alleged that had he been properly assessed by the defendants he would have been returned to hospital, either compulsorily or consensually, and would, therefore, have been unable to commit the offence. His action failed. The Court of Appeal felt that although the Mental Health Act 1983, s 117, imposed a duty on health authorities to provide after-care for mentally disordered persons discharged from hospital, there was nothing in the section to suggest that Parliament intended any alleged failures of the duty to be actionable in damages.

Similar reasoning lay behind the decision in *Philcox* v *Civil Aviation Authority*.

Philcox v *Civil Aviation Authority, The Times,* 8 June 1995

The plaintiff sued for damages in respect of his aeroplane which had crashed just one month after being inspected and given a certificate of airworthiness by the defendants. The Court of Appeal held, however, that the Civil Aviation Authority's regulatory functions in this context had been cast upon it by Parliament primarily for the purposes of protecting the public. Hence it could not be just and reasonable to impose a duty of care on the Authority towards individual owners.

The law relating to the circumstances and extent to which policy considerations may exclude a public authority's liability in negligence is currently in a state of reappraisal and development and must be approached, therefore, with a degree of caution. In the *Bedfordshire* case, as already indicated, the court felt that for a variety of reasons it would not be appropriate to impose a duty of care in respect of the exercise of statutory childcare functions by local authorities. The principal reasons for this were:

(a) that decisions in this context were multi-disciplinary involving police, educational bodies, doctors and others, and 'to impose such liability on all the participant bodies would lead to almost impossible problems of disentangling as between the respective bodies the liability. . . of each for reaching a decision found to be negligent';

(b) that the spectre of litigation could lead to excessive caution and delay in decision-making to the detriment of children at risk.

The court went on to reach the more general conclusion that it had probably never been Parliament's intention that regulatory or welfare legislation passed for the benefit of society in general should be actionable in tort by individuals: 'In my judgment . . . the courts should hesitate long before imposing a common law duty of care in the exercise of common law powers or duties conferred by Parliament for social welfare purposes' (*ibid*).

This aspect of the decision in the *Bedfordshire* case attracted a degree of comment and criticism and it was not long before the wisdom of granting local authorities such extensive legal immunity in social welfare matters was revisited.

In *Barrett* v *Enfield London Borough Council* [1999] 3 WLR 79, Lord Steyn expressed the view that while 'it was no doubt right for the courts to restrain within reasonable bounds claims against public authorities exercising statutory powers in the social welfare context' it was 'equally important to set reasonable bounds to the immunity such authorities may assert'. This, in turn, appeared to presage a move towards a more fact-based, and case-by-case approach, for determining the extent to which effective fulfilment of this genus of powers might be prejudiced by private legal proceedings. A similar process of judicial thought also appeared to influence the finding of the House of Lords in *Phelps* v *Hillingdon London Borough Council* [2000] 3 WLR 776, where the court concluded that public policy considerations did not operate as a complete barrier to actions for negligence against local authorities in respect of alleged failures by educational psychologists employed by them.

It would also appear to be the case that a rule of law which provides that the public interest in the effective performance of public law powers should, in all cases, prevail over the right of the individual to seek legal redress in cases of alleged negligence, may well be at odds with the right to a fair trial in Art 6 of the European Convention on Human Rights. In particular, denial of the right to legal process appears to preclude consideration of such matters as the gravity of the negligence and the seriousness of the injury sustained in particular cases (see *Osman* v *United Kingdom* (1998) 29 EHRR 245).

The implementation of the decision

As to the implementation of decisions after a statutory discretion has been exercised, the House of Lords in the *Bedfordshire* case felt that the ordinary principles of negligence should apply.

> If the plaintiff's complaint alleges carelessness, not in the taking of a discretionary decision to do some act, but in the practical manner in which that act has been performed (e.g. the running of a school), the question whether or not there was a common law duty of care falls to be decided by applying the usual principles, i.e. those laid down in *Caparo Industries plc* v *Dickman* [1990] 2 AC 605. Was the damage to the plaintiff reasonably foreseeable? Was the relationship between the plaintiff and the defendant sufficiently proximate? Is it just and reasonable to impose a duty of care?

This was subject to the proviso, however, that the imposition of a duty of care should not be 'inconsistent with, or have a tendency to discourage, the due performance by the local authority of its statutory duties'.

Negligence and the police

Objective 6

As a general rule, actions against the police alleging common law negligence in the investigation and prevention of crime and those other related core police functions are unlikely to succeed. This would appear to remain the case no matter how far below the normally expected standards of competence and efficiency the police conduct in issue may have fallen.

That such extensive legal immunity has been granted to the police is generally attributed to the decision of the House of Lords in *Hill* v *Chief Constable of West Yorkshire* [1989] AC 53.

The claimant was the mother of Jacqueline Hill, the last of the 13 victims of Peter Sutcliffe, the 'Yorkshire Ripper'. Her case was that had the police conducted their investigation into the killings more efficiently and expeditiously it would have been possible for them to have arrested Sutcliffe before he murdered her daughter.

Mrs Hill's claim was unsuccessful. There were two main reasons for this.

(a) The claimant's daughter had not been at any greater or 'special and distinctive' risk from Sutcliffe than any of the other young women in the part of the country (i.e. west Yorkshire and south-east Lancashire) where the attacks had been carried out. No sufficient relationship of proximity had existed, therefore, between the police and any of the women who had been murdered.

(b) Hard though it might seem, the imposition of a duty of care in this and related circumstances would not be in the best interests of effective policing and, therefore, of the general public. This was justified as follows.

  (i) Were it otherwise, disproportionate amounts of police resources, time, and effort would have to be directed towards responding to those types of criminality most likely to result in actionable claims for damages should any mistakes be made.

  (ii) 'Playing safe' or defensive policing would become the norm with police officers less inclined to 'take a chance' by doing something which might speed up the possibility of a successful 'result', but which, at the same time, might increase the risk of something going wrong, e.g. by leaving a known suspect at large in the hope that he/she might lead the police to other offenders.

  (iii) The police would become embroiled in an ever-increasing incidence of on-going civil legal proceedings to the detriment of their effectiveness in the fight against crime.

Application of the *Hill* principle

Notwithstanding the controversy attracted by it, the essence of the *Hill* principle has remained unchanged and in place for over 30 years. Some of the more prominent examples of its application are set out below.

Osman v Ferguson [1999] 4 All ER 444

The claimant's father was shot dead and the claimant (a 15-year-old schoolboy) was shot and wounded by one of the claimant's schoolteachers who had developed an unhealthy obsession towards him. The claim in negligence was based on the police failure to arrest the schoolteacher before the shooting took place not with standing that, over a period of time, he had, pursued and harassed the claimant and committed acts of criminal damage against his family's property. Held: *Hill* applied. Regardless of what the police had or had not done, no duty of care was owed.

Brooks v Commissioner of Police of the Metropolis [2005] 2 All ER 289

In 1993 Stephen Lawrence was murdered by a white racist gang in London. The claimant was a friend of Stephen's and was with him when the attack took place. He alleged that the police had failed to treat him as a victim of the crime and, in its aftermath, to give him the support and protection he required. Held: *Hill* applied. No duty of care was owed by the police in their treatment of the witnesses or the victims of crime.

Robinson v Chief Constable of West Yorkshire Police [2014] EWCA Civ 15

The police arrested a suspected drugs dealer in the street. The drugs dealer resisted arrest and injury was caused to the claimant, a passer-by. Held: *Hill* applied. No duty of care was owed to public in respect of the conduct of arrest operations.

CLG v Chief Constable of Merseyside [2015] EWCA Civ 36

The claim followed a failure by the police to ensure names and addresses of witnesses to a gang-related shooting did not leak out into the public domain. Held: *Hill* applied. No duty of care of confidentiality lay on the police in the conduct of their investigations.

Michael v Chief Constable of South Wales [2015] UKSC 2

Despite two 999 calls the police failed to arrive at the claimant's daughter's premises in time to prevent her being murdered by her ex-partner. Held: *Hill* applied. No duty of care rested on the police to respond to 999 calls.

Smith v Chief Constable of Sussex [2008] EWCA Civ 39

The police failed to arrest the claimant's ex-partner who had made a series of threats against him and who eventually attacked the claimant with a hammer causing serious and permanent injuries. who Held: *Hill* applied. The police were not under a duty of care to arrest suspects at any particular time in the process of preventing crime.

Rathband v Chief Constable of Northumbria Constabulary [2016] EWHC 181 QB

The claimant police officer was shot in the face and seriously wounded by a dangerous armed criminal who had set out to kill members of the police force. He claimed in respect of the failure of his superior officers to warn him that the offender armed and dangerous was in his immediate vicinity. Held: *Hill* applied. No duty of care existed in relation to the persuit of an offender.

The Hill principle applies also to the conduct of internal police investigations (e.g. into the way a particular operation or investigation was carried out) and to police disciplinary proceedings (***Connelly v Police Service of Northern Ireland*** [2006] NIQB 98).

Exceptions to the Hill principle

Not a core function

Where the allegedly careless act by the police occurred in the performance of a function not relating directly to the investigation and prosecution of crime, the *Hill* principle, by virtue of its own terms, does not apply. The judicial view here is that, in such less critical or sensitive matters, it would not be credible to argue that the imposition of a duty of care would be likely to compromise any of the key public interests which the *Hill* principle seeks to protect.

Examples of police activities not falling within the ambit of their core functions would include careless driving of police cars (***Smith v Chief Constable of Nottinghamshire*** [2012] EWCA Civ 161), and inadequate traffic management, ie (failure to close lanes on the carriageway after a road traffic accident (***Knightly v Johns*** [1982] 1 WLR 348)).

Causing the injury or damage

No protection in negligence is given to the police where the injury or damage complained of was the direct, immediate, and foreseeable, and direct result of any police action or failure to act.

In ***Reeves v Metropolitan Police*** [2000] 1 AC 360, the police were held liable in negligence for failing to do everything reasonably necessary to prevent the suicide of a person held in police custody. The person had made a suicide attempt earlier in the day and had made other attempts previously. A duty of care was also owed to a female police officer when a fellow officer, without warning of cause, discharged a firearm in her presence (***Schofield v Chief Constable of West Yorkshire*** [1998] EWCA Civ 838).

See also ***Donachie v Chief Constable of Greater Manchester Police*** [2004] EWCA Civ 405 in which the defendant was found to be under a duty of care to provide his officers with the equipment necessary to protect them from those types of injuries which might be inflicted by violent criminals.

Creation of new or additional danger

In *Rigby* v *Chief Constable of Northumberland* [1985] 1 All ER 1242, the police attended a break-in at a gunsmith's shop. By way of attempt to 'flush out' the offender, a senior officer at the scene ordered gas canisters to be fired through one of the shop's windows. No fire-fighting equipment was summoned. The shop was burnt to the ground. The Court felt that the actions of the police had, in the circumstances prevailing, significantly exacerbated the damage which the claimant, the owner of the shop, might otherwise have been expected to suffer. The claimant's action for damages was upheld.

Assumption of responsibility

Based on the concept of proximity, and notwithstanding that the police may be acting in the course of investigation or prevention of crime, a duty of care may be found to exist where:

(a) As part of the investigative process, the police have assumed a degree of responsibility for the safety and welfare of an individual, perhaps in return for information;

(b) Assurances to this effect have been given to the individual concerned;

(c) Such assurances have been accepted and relied upon.

The above was articulated in detail in *An Informer* v *A Chief Constable* [2012] EWCA Civ 197. Here, relying on promises of protection and confidentiality, the claimant gave information to the police about business associates who, he alleged, had engaged in criminal activities. Subsequently, however, in the course of the police investigation, the claimant himself was arrested and, as a result, suffered financial loss. The court took the view that, although the police were under a duty of care to the claimant who was an authorised covert human intelligence source, the duty did not extend to economic loss.

Exceptional circumstances

In the years since the *Hill* decision, a number of judgments have conceded, albeit in rather general terms, that in certain extreme circumstances the full scope of the principle of police immunity in negligence might not always be applicable and that this was so even in the context of the investigation and prevention of crime. Special or exceptional circumstances could be conceived of, therefore, where the police failings were so severe as to 'compel the conclusion that the absence of a remedy in damages would be an affront to the principles which underlie the common law', e.g. where the conduct in question amounted to 'outrageous negligence' (Lord Nicholls, *Brooks* v *Commissioner of Police of the Metropolis* [2005] UKHL 24).

In *Rush* v *Police Service of Northern Ireland* [2011] NIQB 28 the claimant was the widower of one of the 28 people killed by the Real IRA bomb which exploded in the centre of Omagh, County Tyrone in August, 1998. His claim for negligence was based on the contention that the police had been given prior notice that an attack of this type might occur and that they could have done more to have minimised the risk. An attempt to have the case struck out on the basis of the *Hill* principle was not successful. Gillan J in the Northern Ireland High Court took the view that the 'precision of the knowledge and the exactitude of the information put this claim within the brackets of outrageous negligence'. In the event, however, the case did not proceed beyond this stage due to the untimely death of the claimant.

Judicial dicta

Beyond those generally acknowledged exceptions to the rule, dicta may be cited from a number of cases in which modifications to the *Hill* principle have been urged. In the main, these have been founded on the principle of proximity.

One of the most authoritative of these was that proposed by Lord Kerr in *Michael* v *Chief Constable of South Wales* (*supra*) in the Supreme Court. The elements of Lord Kerr's exception to *Hill* were:

(i) information has been given to the police;

(ii) this conveys to them that serious harm is likely to be inflicted on an intended victim if urgent action is not taken;

(iii) in the circumstances, the police might reasonably have been expected to provide the required protection;

(iv) the protection could have been provided without any undue danger to the police themselves.

A not dissimilar judicial suggestion for modification of *Hill* had been made previously by Lord Bingham in *Smith* v *Chief Constable of Sussex Police* (*supra*) and has since been referred to generally as Lord Bingham's 'liability principle'.

> If a member of the public, A, furnishes a police officer, B, with apparently credible evidence that a third party whose identity and characteristics are known, presents a specific and immediate threat to his life and physical safety, B owes a duty to take reasonable steps to prevent it being executed.

Police investigations and the Human Rights Act

Like all public authorities, the police are obliged to carry out their functions in accordance with the Human Rights Act 1998 and the European Convention on Human Rights 1953 to which it gives effect in English law (HRA s 6(1)). Legal proceedings against the police under the Human Rights Act are not precluded or inhibited in any direct way by the decision in *Hill*. Violations of the 1998 Act may result, therefore, in awards of damages to the victim(s) of the police actions in question (ss 7 and 8).

In the context of alleged police failings in the investigation and prevention of crime, the most salient elements of the European Convention on Human Rights would appear to be:

(i) as first recognised in *Osman* v *United Kingdom* (1998) EHRR 245, the implied obligation in Art 2(1) (the right to life) to take reasonable steps to protect any person whose life is known or should have been known to be at real and immediate risk from the criminal acts of another;

(ii) the implied obligation, also found in Art 2(1), and explained originally in *McCann* v *United Kingdom* [1995] 21 EHRR 97, to conduct an effective investigation into any violent, unusual or unexplained deaths or death for which the state might appear to bear a degree of responsibility;

(iii) the implied obligation in Art 3 (the prohibition of torture, inhuman or degrading treatment) to conduct an effective investigation into credible allegations of violations of the state's requirements and particularly, for police purposes, acts amounting to serious crimes of violence against the person committed by either 'state agents' or ordinary individuals (see *DSD and NVD* v *Commissioner of Police for the Metropolis* [2014]

EWHC 436 (QB), failure to detect and arrest the London 'black cab rapist' who committed in excess of 105 sexual assaults on female passengers in the period 2002–09);

(iv) the implied obligation in Art 4 (the prohibition of forced labour, servitude or slavery), applied in *OOO* v *Commissioner of Police of the Metropolis* [2011] 1246 (QB) to conduct an effective investigation into credible allegations of prohibited activities (see *OOO* above, failure to investigate claimants' allegations that they had been subjected to forced labour since they entered the UK as children).

It follows from all of this that, providing an individual claim against the police relates to one or more of the above types of human rights violations, proceedings for damages under the Human Rights Act may sometimes succeed, where, in similar circumstances, a claim for damages alleging common law negligence would not. Lest, however, this should lead to any firm conclusion that the restrictions of the *Hill* principle may now be easily circumvented, the following matters should be taken into consideration:

(a) The courts have set a high evidential threshold for those seeking to prove that the police knew or should have known that a person's life was at real and immediate risk. Thus it has been said that 'only those claims which would fall within "outrageous negligence" will pass the so-called *Osman* test' (McIvor, 'Getting Defensive about Police Negligence', *Cambridge Law Journal,* Vol 69, No 1, 133–150).

(b) The obligation in the *Osman* test is not absolute. It is 'merely to take reasonable measures to avoid the risk'. It was made clear in *Osman* itself that what is or is not reasonable to expect the police to do in these cases is to be judged by reference to a number of public interest concerns not greatly dissimilar to those underlying the *Hill* principle, viz.:

- the need to avoid irresponsible and disproportionate burdens on the police and state;
- the difficulties in policing a modern society;
- the unpredictability of human conduct;
- the operational choices which have to be made in relation to police resources and priorities.

(c) The primary purpose of the ECHR was to establish a legally enforceable framework of basic human rights standards for the exercise of powers by European states and which could be used to bring any human rights violations to an end – this being a worthwhile remedy in itself. It was not intended, therefore, as an alternative means of allowing aggrieved private citizens to make claims for financial compensation for any effects which such violations may have had upon them.

Where an infringement of an individual's human rights has occurred, the concern will usually be to bring the infringement to an end and any question of compensation will be of secondary, if any, importance (Lord Woolf, *Anufrijeva* v *Southwark London Borough Council* [2004] QB 1124).

- Awards of damages under the Human Rights Act are discretionary only (s 8) and not, as at common law, as of right once the alleged wrong has been established.

- The power in section 8 to make such awards is phrased in negative terms and is restricted to those circumstances in which, without more, the established public law remedies would appear inadequate to provide redress. No award of damages is to be made unless, taking into account the availability of other remedies, the court is satisfied that the award is necessary to afford just satisfaction to the person in whose favour it is made.

- Awards of damages in human rights cases are to be viewed, therefore, as additional to the primary remedial objective of having the human rights breach terminated, e.g. by the granting of a public law remedy, and are, therefore, not awarded in every case.

- Given the secondary importance of awards of damages in human rights cases, the awards made tend to be lower than that expected in proceedings at common law. In *OOO* v *Commissioner of Police for the Metropolis*, *supra*, the awards made for failure to investigate thoroughly breaches of Art 4 were just £5,000 for each of the claimants.

Negligence and the emergency services

Police, fire and coastguard services

None of the above are under a common law duty to respond to a '999' call. Accordingly, no liability in negligence arises should they fail or be late in doing so (*Capital and Counties plc* v *Hampshire County Council* [1997] QB 1004). Nor may any of such services be sued in respect of the way an emergency has been dealt with unless, that is, the actions of the emergency service in question have caused damage which might otherwise not have occurred (*ibid*).

Ambulance service

Here the position is different. Once a '999' call has been made, the ambulance service is under a duty to the ill or injured person to respond to it and to do so in a reasonably timely manner. In *Kent* v *Griffiths* [2000] QB 36, a doctor attended a patient who was suffering from a serious attack of asthma. Two phone calls for an ambulance were made. This took 40 rather than the expected 15 minutes to arrive. The patient went into respiratory arrest which could have been avoided had the ambulance arrived more quickly. The Court of Appeal ruled that the ambulance service should be regarded as providing services equivalent to those delivered by hospitals and not those provided by the police and fire services. This meant that staff of the ambulance service owed a duty of care to those who sought their help not dissimilar to that owed to patients by doctors and nurses.

For further discussion of state liability under ECHR Art 2 (the right to life), see Chapter 16 and Chapter 17.

Attempts to explain this different approach to the ambulance service tend to have been based on the rules of proximity, i.e. while the functions of the police, fire and coastguard services are directed towards the welfare of the public at large, the ambulance service owes a more specific and distinct duty of care to the particular person(s) it has chosen to help.

Breach of European Union obligations

Government bodies are also subject to obligations laid on them by EU law, and a body of legal rules is currently being developed to determine the extent to which such obligations may be enforced by way of actions for damages in the domestic courts of member states.

The fundamental principle, now firmly established, is that the state may be made liable in damages for all executive, legislative and judicial acts in breach of EU law (*Brasserie du Pêcheur SA* v *Germany* [1996] 2 WLR 506). The conditions for successful enforcement of state liability are:

(a) there has been a sufficiently serious breach of EU law;

(b) the rule of law infringed was intended to confer legal rights on individuals;

(c) a causal link existed between the breach and the damage suffered by individuals.

On the basis of the above principles the rule of state liability has been held to be applicable where:

- A member state has failed to implement an EU directive (*Francovich* v *Italy* [1993] 2 CMLR 66).

- The legislature of a member state has adopted legislation which is inconsistent with EU law (*R* v *Secretary of State for Transport, ex parte Factortame Ltd (No. 4)* [1996] QB 404).

- There has been a serious breach of EU law by a national court of final appeal including misinterpretation or application of relevant legal provisions or error in the assessment of facts and evidence (*Köbler* v *Republik Österreich* [2004] All ER (EC) 23), *Traghetti del Mediterraneo SpA* v *Italy* [2006] All ER (EC) 983.

In relation to courts of final appeal, and to protect the need for legal certainty the view of the CJEU was that:

> State liability for an infringement of Community law . . . can be incurred only in the exceptional case where the court has manifestly infringed the applicable law. In order to determine whether that condition is satisfied, the national courts hearing a claim for reparation must take account of . . . the degree of clarity and precision of the rule infringed, whether the infringement was intentional, whether the error of law was excusable or inexcusable . . . In any event, an infringement of Community law will be sufficiently serious where the decision concerned was made in manifest breach of the case-law of the Court of Justice in the matter.

State liability will usually arise in respect of directly effective obligations imposed by Treaty Articles or regulations – provided that, in both cases, the obligation was imposed in clear and unconditional terms.

In certain circumstances, however, a directly effective right of action against the state may also be found in a directive. This will be the case where, in addition to (a)–(c) above:

(i) the directive imposes an obligation on the state (*Faccini Dori* v *Recreb Srl* [1995] 1 CMLR 665);

(ii) the obligation contained therein has the necessary degree of specificity, i.e. it is possible to discern from it the exact nature of the directive's requirements;

(iii) the time allowed for implementation of the directive by national legislation has elapsed (*Marshall* v *Southampton and South West Hampshire Area Health Authority (No. 1)* [1986] QB 401).

A directive which seeks to create rights which are legally enforceable between individuals but not against the state would, by definition, not appear to give rise to any issue of state liability. A state may be made liable, however, in respect of its failure to give effect to such a directive. Here it would be the state's failure to ensure the directive's proper implementation in accordance with EC Treaty Art 249 which would be the basis of the cause of action and not its breach of any directly effective EU law (*Francovich* v *Italy*, *supra*).

The requisite conditions for this species of liability are:

(a) there has been a sufficiently serious breach of EU law;

(b) the result prescribed by the directive entails the granting of rights to individuals;

(c) the content of those rights can be readily identified from the provisions of the directive;

(d) there is a causal link between the breach of the obligation imposed on the state and the loss suffered by individuals.

Dillenkofer v *Federal Republic of Germany* [1997] 2 WLR 253

The German government had failed to give effect to a directive which sought to impose on the suppliers of package holidays an obligation to ensure that funds were available to compensate those whose holiday plans might be disrupted by the insolvency of a holiday company. As a result the plaintiffs were unable to recover recompense after suffering the type of loss and inconvenience to which the directive related. On a reference under EC Art 234 by a German court, the European Court of Justice ruled that:

(a) a failure to implement a European directive was, *ipso facto*, a sufficiently serious breach of EU law;

(b) the directive had clearly been intended to confer legally enforceable rights on individuals;

(c) the content of those rights was readily discernible;

(d) there was an obvious causal link between the German government's failure and the loss suffered by the plaintiffs.

The right to damages for breach of EU law extends to compensatory damages only and does not include any right to claim punitive damages (*R* v *Secretary of State for Transport, ex parte Factortame (No. 5)* [1999] 3WLR 1062.

It is for each member state to ensure that individuals obtain reparation for loss and damages caused to them by non-compliance with EU law whichever public authority may be liable for the breach and/or for the making of reparation (*Konle* v *Austria* [1999] ECR 1–3099). There is no absolute rule, however, that such reparation must be provided by the member state itself in order for its obligations under EU law to be fulfilled. Hence EU law does not preclude a public law body, in addition to the state itself, from incurring liability for loss or damage caused to individuals as a result of measures it took in breach of EU law. Where the criteria for state liability exist such claims should be determined on the basis of the relevant national legal rules for the award of reparation for such loss or damage (*Haim* v *Kassenzahnarztliche Vereinigung Nordrhein* [2000] All ER (D) 916).

Misfeasance or misconduct in public office

A government official who causes injury through a deliberate misuse of power commits the tort of misfeasance in public office. Some conscious or malicious element of abuse must be present. Also, the perpetrator must have intended to inflict injury or have been aware that it would be the likely consequence of their actions. In *Three Rivers District Council* v *Bank of England (No. 3)* [1996] 3 All ER 558, the tort was said to be committed where a public officer:

(a) performed or omitted to perform an act with the object of injuring the plaintiff (i.e. where there was targeted malice);

(b) performed an act which he knew or ought to have known he had no power to perform and which he knew would or could injure the plaintiff.

That which was done *ultra vires* but innocently, or as a result of mere incompetence, is, therefore, not actionable (*Dunlop* v *Woollahra Municipal Council* [1982] AC 158). Damages would also appear to be available for deliberate government abuse of EU law (*Bourgoin SA* v *Ministry of Agriculture, Fisheries and Food* [1986] QB 716).

The tort was found to have been committed in *Elliott* v *Chief Constable of Wiltshire*, *The Times*, 5 December 1996 where a police officer made false allegations to a newspaper editor. These were that one of the newspaper's reporters was guilty of various criminal offences. The officer's objective was to get the reporter 'sacked' so that he would be unable to continue investigating and reporting on corruption in the police.

Whether the employing authority would be vicariously liable for actions of this type is a matter of some uncertainty. One opinion is that vicarious liability should exist providing the act was done in pursuance of the authority's authorised functions. There is, however, *obiter* judicial opinion that a public authority should not be made liable for the deliberate excesses of its employees (*R* v *Deputy Governor of Parkhurst Prison, ex parte Hague* (*supra*)).

The tort is not actionable *per se*, i.e. without proof of financial loss or physical or mental injury (*Watkins* v *Home Office* [2006] UKHL 17).

In *Karagozlu* v *Metropolitan Police Commissioner* [2006] EWCA Civ 1691, loss of liberty resulting from false and malicious allegations by a police officer was held to be sufficiently akin to physical injury to give a cause of action.

The defence of statutory authority

Where the fulfilment of a statutory function is impossible without some level of interference with private rights, it is not actionable so long as the interference caused is inevitable and is the minimum necessary to secure the function's proper discharge. Hence, in *Allen* v *Gulf Oil Refining* [1981] AC 1001, those living in the vicinity of an oil refinery were unable to recover redress in respect of the smell, vibration and noise which was emitted. As the location and operation of the refinery were authorised by statute, no action could lie in respect of its inevitable consequences.

> ... it is well settled that where Parliament by express direction or by necessary implication has authorised the construction and use of an undertaking or works, that carries with it an authority to do what is authorised with immunity from action based on nuisance (*Dobson* v *Thames Water Utilities Ltd (No. 2)* [2011] EWHC 3253).

The requirement of inevitability is crucial if the defence is to be accepted. In *Manchester Corporation* v *Farnworth* [1930] AC 171, the existence of statutory authority did not exempt the Corporation from liability for the damage caused by noxious fumes and gases emitted by an electricity power station as the court was not satisfied that all due care had been taken to keep the emissions to a minimum. In *Metropolitan Asylum District Managers* v *Hill* (1881) 6 App Cas 193, the authority were liable in nuisance for building a smallpox hospital in a residential area. Although the authority had the statutory power to build hospitals, the siting of them was a matter for its discretion. Since the hospital could have been built in a place where less interference and nuisance would have been caused, the extent of transgression of private rights could not be said to be the inevitable minimum.

Remedies

The trial of an action against the Crown will be conducted according to the ordinary procedures of the High Court or County Court. The action will normally be taken against the particular government department concerned or against the Attorney-General.

A judgment obtained against a public authority other than the Crown may be enforced in the normal way. By virtue of the Crown Proceedings Act 1947, however, the Crown retains a number of important immunities in this context. These would appear to be based on the premise that the issuing of compulsory orders against the Crown could be prejudicial to its dignity and, in certain circumstances, to the public interest.

Section 25(3) of the 1947 Act provides that the Crown, through the appropriate department, shall make payment of damages and costs awarded against it in civil proceedings (see ***Davidson* v *Scottish Ministers (No. 2)*** [2004] UKHL 34). Such awards may not be enforced, however, by the ordinary methods: '. . . no execution or attachment or process in the nature thereof shall be issued out of any court for enforcing payment by the Crown of any such money . . . ' (s 25(4)). Since, however, the duty to make payment is contained in statute, it would appear that – in the extremely unlikely event of non-payment – it could be enforced by way of a Mandatory Order against the responsible government department.

For Mandatory Order, see Chapter 16.

Section 21 of the 1947 Act has caused some problems of interpretation. Section 21(1) precludes a court from issuing any injunction, order for specific performance or order for the delivery up of property against the Crown. Section 21(2) contains the further prohibition against the granting of any injunction or order against an officer of the Crown 'if the effect of granting the injunction or making the order would be to give relief against the Crown which could not have been obtained in proceedings against the Crown'. After a period of some uncertainty this has now been interpreted to mean that an injunction may be issued against a Minister in respect of powers conferred on them by name (e.g. 'the Secretary of State for Education'), but not where the powers or duties are conferred on the Crown itself (***M* v *Home Office*** [1993] All ER 537).

The prerogative orders of mandamus, certiorari and prohibition (now mandatory, quashing and prohibitory orders) do not issue against the Crown. They may be used, however, against a Minister of the Crown in respect of powers conferred on the Minister by name.

Crown privilege and public interest immunity

Background

Objective 7

The doctrines of Crown privilege and its derivative, that of public interest immunity ('PII'), deal with the legal rules and procedures which determine the circumstances in which relevant material (evidence) may be withheld from legal proceedings on grounds that its disclosure and use for such purposes could in some way damage an important aspect of the public interest, e.g. the maintenance of defence and national security, the effectiveness of the police in the prevention of crime, diplomatic relations, etc.

Civil proceedings

Prior to the trial of a civil claim, the parties are required to exchange lists of, and be prepared to disclose, documents relevant to the issue in dispute and containing material information. Until the Crown Proceedings Act 1947, however, this duty did not apply to the Crown. It was also accepted that the Crown had the right to assert that documents should not be used in evidence if revelation of the contents would be damaging to the public interest. This was referred to as a plea of Crown privilege.

Section 28 of the 1947 Act removed the Crown's general immunity from the duty of disclosure but reserved to it the right to continue to plead privilege in certain limited circumstances:

... this section shall be without prejudice to any rule of law which authorises the withholding of any document or the refusal to answer any question on the ground that the disclosure of the document or the answering of the question would be injurious to the public interest (s 28(l)(b)).

Few would argue against the need to do what is required to protect key elements of the public interest. However, this notwithstanding, it remains the case that the withholding of relevant material from legal proceedings can have significant consequences for the quality of justice dispensed to individuals and on public attitudes towards the fairness of the judicial system. It also raises concerns about the extent to which Ministers and officials are able to 'cover up' their allegedly illegal or disreputable conduct when their actions and decisions are challenged in the courts.

Duncan v *Cammell Laird and Co* [1972] AC 624: big brother knows best

In this historical context, and in terms of the development of the law of Crown privilege, one of the more prominent decisions in the twentieth century was that of the House of Lords in *Duncan* v *Cammell Laird* – decided at the height of World War II.

The case involve a claim for privilege in respect of the design specifications of a new type of naval submarine, the prototype of which had sunk in the Irish Sea on its maiden voyage. The claim arose out of an action for negligence by the widow of one of the 99 members of the crew – the total ship's complement – who had been lost in the accident.

That the documents should be treated as privileged was accepted by the court. This came as no great surprise at a time when few would have agreed that allowing information of this nature to enter the public domain, and thereby become available to the enemy, could have been regarded as a particularly good idea. At the same time, however, the House of Lords took it upon itself to extend the law of Crown privilege in ways which were to prove more than a little controversial long after the war years had passed.

(a) It was for the Crown (i.e. the government) and not for the courts to decide whether the protection and use of material as evidence would or would not cause any damage to a particular public interest. Hence, where and when a plea of privilege was entered in any case, it was to be regarded as conclusive of the matter and was not a result which could be examined, questioned or overruled by the court dealing with the case.

(b) Pleas of Crown privilege could be of two types:
   (i) That the content of the particular document(s) in issue included information which could be damaging to the public interest (a 'contents' claim);
   (ii) That the document(s) sought belonged to a particular interrelated group or 'class', e.g. those dealing with the work of the Cabinet or confidential exchanges between government ministers, which should remain immune from disclosure in its entirety regardless of the fact that not all of the documents in the class contained sensitive material (a 'class' claim).

In the years that followed *Cammell Laird*, concerns with the decision tended to concentrate on the extent to which it permitted secrecy to be maintained in respect of whole rafts of official documents merely at the 'say so' of a government Minister and with little hope of any meaningful legal redress even in those cases where there were strong indications that material was being withheld, not for the public benefit, but for reasons of a somewhat more dubious nature, e.g. to deflect criticism from the government.

Examples from the 1950's of Crown privilege being pleaded in relation to classes of documents which appeared to have little to do with any of the nation's key public interests or needs would include *Ellis* v *Home Office* [1953] 2QB 135 (prison medical records) and *Broome* v *Broome* [1955] P190 (marriage and relationship counselling for members of the armed forces).

Discontent and criticism resulted eventually in executive concessions. In 1956 the Lord Chancellor announced that privilege would no longer be claimed in respect of certain classes of documents including: witness statements of accidents on the road, or on government premises, or involving government employers; ordinary medical reports on the health of civilian employees; medical reports where the Crown was sued in negligence; papers needed for defence against a criminal charge; witnesses' ordinary statements to the police; and reports on matters of fact relating to liability in contract.

Conway v Rimmer [1968] AC 910: a change of course

The law of Crown privilege as enumerated in the *Cammell Laird* case remained in place for over 20 years and until the decision of the House of Lords in *Conway* v *Rimmer* in 1968.

The case resulted from a claim for malicious prosecution by a young ex-police constable who had lost his job after being accused of stealing a torch from one of his colleagues.

The claimant sought disclosure of documents held by the police containing reports made about him by senior officers when he was undergoing his probationary training. He alleged that these contained material showing that the officer who had made the accusation of theft, was already maliciously disposed towards him.

The House of Lords was in no doubt that the *Cammell Laird* decision had been correct on its facts, i.e. in time of war it would have been against the public interest to have allowed the designs of naval submarines to be discussed in open court. The House was not prepared, however, to give full endorsement to those other aspects of the judgment outlined above preferring instead to set out a new set of ground rules for the use of Crown privilege. These remain the basis of the modern law in this area:

(a) Ministers were no longer to be regarded as the final arbiters between the competing public interests of government confidentiality and the needs of justice. Full weight should be given to Ministerial opinions, but these were not to be understood as absolutely binding or as precluding judicial scrutiny or inspection of the documents in issue.

(b) The judicial discretion to scrutinise documents should, however, be used particularly sparingly where privilege was claimed in relation to the content of a specific document.

(c) In other cases, especially where privilege was claimed, not because of the contents of particular documents, but due to the class to which they belonged, and Ministerial reasons for privilege appeared inadequate or unclear, courts should be prepared to exercise their power of inspection to decide whether the need to do justice was outweighed by the public interest in concealment.

(d) Judges should treat with caution the argument that classes of documents should be regarded as privileged for no better reason than this was necessary to secure 'freedom and candour of communication with and within the public service, so that government decisions can be taken on the best advice and the fullest information'.

(e) Despite this, however, certain specific classes of documents should continue to be regarded as unsuitable for use in judicial proceedings. These included Cabinet papers, Foreign Office dispatches, documents relating to national security, high level inter-departmental minutes, and correspondence and documents pertaining to the general administration of the armed forces or high level personnel in the service of the Crown.

Class claims after *Conway* v *Rimmer* – the continuing controversy

Candour

Notwithstanding the views expressed in the *Conway* case, the argument that the frankness of views and advice tendered within organisations (both public and private) could be inhibited by the knowledge that such communications might be used as evidence has continued to be argued as a ground for claims of immunity from production. This approach was relied on successfully in *Gaskin* v *Liverpool Corporation* [1980] 1 WLR 1549, where the plaintiff sought damages for negligence arising out of his treatment while in a children's home run by the defendants. His attempt to secure documents and files relating to the time spent in care failed. The court was of the opinion that these belonged to a class of documents – i.e. those concerned with the proper functioning of the child care service – which should remain confidential.

Claims based on the candour argument were, and are, of course, no longer conclusive and binding. In each case, therefore, it remains possible for the court to balance the public interest in concealment against the competing interests of justice. Hence the argument was rejected in both *Campbell* v *Tameside Metropolitan Borough Council* [1982] QB 1065, and *Williams* v *Home Office (No. 1)* [1981] 1 All ER 1151.

Examples

In *Campbell* a teacher sued for negligence arising out of injuries caused to her by a disruptive pupil, whom, she argued, the defendants had not taken reasonable steps to protect her against. The Court of Appeal's view was that any public interest in concealing psychiatric and other reports of evidential value to the plaintiff was not sufficient to justify a possible injustice. Some guidance was also given in terms of the considerations to be used in the balancing of interests. Hence, where documents are clearly of considerable significance for the success of a litigant's case, this casts a greater burden upon the party pleading immunity to establish a countervailing and overriding public interest in concealment. Conversely, where documents might appear to be of minimal evidential value, a court might be persuaded more easily of the public interest in concealment.

> In these cases the court should and can consider the significance of the documents in relation to the decision of the case. If they are of such significance that they might well affect the very decision of the case, then justice may require them to be disclosed ... But if they are of little significance, so that they are very unlikely to affect the decision ... then the greater public interest may be to keep them confidential (*per* Lord Denning MR).

The *Williams* case involved a challenge by a prisoner to the legality of his detention in an experimental 'special control unit' at Wakefield prison. The Home Office again used the proper functioning of the public service argument to plead immunity for a whole variety of documents containing records of communications between civil servants and between the latter and government Ministers concerning the Wakefield experiment. After inspection of the documents in issue, 6 out of 23 were ordered to be produced. There was, said McNeill J, a 'reasonable probability that the documents were likely to contain material in support of the plaintiff's case'.

The merits of the candour argument were also considered by the House of Lords in *Burmah Oil* v *Bank of England* [1980] AC 1090. It was not something which impressed Lord Keith:

> The notion that any conscientious public servant would be inhibited at all in the candour of his writings by consideration of the off-chance they might have to be produced in litigation

is, in my opinion, grotesque. To represent that the possibility of it might significantly impair the public service is even more so . . . [T]he candour argument is an utterly insubstantial ground for denying access to relevant documents.

Lord Fraser in **Air Canada v Secretary of State for Trade** [1963] 2 AC 394, expressed a similarly sceptical view: 'I do not think that even Cabinet minutes are completely immune from disclosure in a case where, for example, the issue involves serious misconduct by a Cabinet Minister.' Lord Wilberforce, however, also in **Burmah Oil**, above, was more circumspect and was clearly still prepared to regard the need for candour as a matter to be considered in balancing the public interests involved:

It seems now rather fashionable to decry this [candour] but if as a ground it may once have been exaggerated it has now, in my opinion, received an excessive dose of cold water. I am certainly not prepared – against the view of the Minister – to discount the need, in the formation of such very controversial policy . . . for frank and uninhibited advice . . . from and between Ministers.

Confidentiality

Closely related to the candour argument, this consists of the claim that organisations whose effectiveness depends on the receipt of information given in confidence should not be required to reveal that information or its sources as to do so might run the risk of these 'drying up', thus prejudicing future inquiries. As with the candour argument, the extent of the damage to the public interest resulting from a breach of confidentiality must be weighed against the public interest in the dispensation of justice.

Two of the most frequently cited cases in which confidentiality was accepted as a justification for public interest immunity are **Alfred Crompton Amusement Machines Ltd v Customs and Excise Commissioners (No. 2)** [1974] AC 405, and **D v NSPCC** [1978] AC 171. In the first case the Commissioners acquired information from customers and other sources concerning the value of machines supplied by an amusement company. This was done in the course of assessing the company's liability for purchase tax. In the opinion of the House of Lords, production of documents containing this information could have damaged the public interest in the effective execution of one of the Commissioners' principal functions, viz. the collection of revenue as authorised by Parliament.

Here . . . one can well see that the third parties who have supplied this information to the commissioners because of the existence of their statutory powers would very much resent its disclosure by the commissioners . . . and it is not fanciful to say that the knowledge that the commissioners cannot keep such information secret may be harmful to the efficient working of the Act (*per Lord Cross*).

Similarly, in the **NSPCC** case it was felt that the Society should not be required to produce the source of an allegation of child abuse.

I would extend to those who give information about neglect or ill-treatment of children to a local authority or the NSPCC a similar immunity from disclosure of their identity in legal proceedings to that which the law accords to police informers. The public interests served by preserving the anonymity of both classes of informants are analogous; they are of no less weight in the case of the former than in the latter class, and in my judgment are of greater weight than in the case of informers to the Gaming Board to whom immunity from disclosure of their identity has recently been extended by this House (*per* Lord Diplock).

Subsequently, in **Bookbinder v Tebbit** [1992] 1 WLR 217, public interest immunity was held to extend to information supplied to the Audit Commission in the course of investigating alleged irregularities in the financial affairs of a local authority. The court felt that the efficiency of the Commission – particularly its functions of inquiring into possible illegal usage of public finances – could be impaired if the identities of its informants were to be disclosed.

The case for confidentiality must, however, be convincing. In *Norwich Pharmacal Co Ltd* v *Customs and Excise Commissioners* [1974] AC 133, no public interest was found in permitting the Commissioners to withhold information received from traders concerning the identities of companies importing chemical compounds manufactured in breach of the plaintiff's patent. The House of Lords was not convinced that fear of disclosure would deter honest traders from supplying information exposing the activities of those seeking to obtain an unfair commercial advantage.

The courts are reluctant to concede any absolute rule that certain types of communication should always be regarded as protected by confidentiality. This was made clear in *R (on application of Binyam Mohamed)* v *Secretary of State for Foreign and Commonwealth Affairs* [2011] QB 218, where the government argued that, for the purposes of national security and the maintenance of the special relationship between the intelligence services of the United Kingdom and the United States, it was essential that information passed over by US agencies should not be used in legal proceedings or otherwise put into the public domain. The then Lord Chief Justice's response was:

> the confidentiality principle is . . . subject to the clear limitation that the government and intelligence services can never provide the country which provides intelligence with an unconditional guarantee that the confidentiality principle will never be set aside if the courts conclude that their interests make it necessary and appropriate to do so (*per* Lord Judge).

The end of class immunity?

In December 1996 the Attorney-General made a statement to the House of Commons concerning the future use of public interest immunity (PII) certificates in both civil and criminal proceedings. The main principles of the statement were as follows:

> Under the new approach, Ministers will focus directly on the damage that disclosure would cause. The former division into class and contents claims will no longer be applied. Ministers will claim public interest immunity only when it is believed that disclosure of a document would cause real damage or harm to the public interest . . . The new emphasis on the test of serious harm means that Ministers will not, for example, claim PII to protect either internal advice or national security material merely by pointing to the general nature of the document. The only basis for claiming PII will be a belief that disclosure will cause real harm.

This appeared to presage the end of class claims by central government. The statement was, however, not legally binding and could not affect the practice of other persons and bodies, whether public or private. It was inevitable, therefore, that class claims would continue to be asserted by bodies such as the police, local councils and health authorities. It would soon become apparent, however, that judicial unease with the entire concept of class immunities was hardening into the state of a general policy in whatever the context. This was consistent with the jurisprudence of the European Convention on Human Rights, which prefers concessions to the public interest to be considered on a case-by-case basis rather than applied as inflexible blanket immunities (see *Osman* v *United Kingdom* (2000) 29 EHRR 245). Hence in a number of cases claims to class or blanket immunities for information relating to police informers were rejected in favour of a balancing exercise by the court (see *Savage* v *Chief Constable of Hampshire* [1997] 1 WLR 1061; *Powell* v *Chief Constable of North Wales*

Constabulary, The Times, 11 February 2002; ***Whitmarsh v Chief Constable of Avon and Somerset***, unreported). The judicial reluctance to simply accept a class immunity in one of the most well established contexts was approved by the Court of Appeal in ***Chief Constable of Greater Manchester Police v McNally*** [2002] EWCA Civ 14. There Auld LJ spoke of the need to 'soften' the rigidity of the pre-existing class system:

> so as to permit a balance of competing interest in a case specific manner [as] part of a wider jurisprudential move away from near absolute protection of various categories of public interest in non disclosure . . . Now with the advent of Human Rights to our law, this move has the force of European jurisprudence behind it.

From Crown privilege to public interest immunity

Crown privilege a misnomer

In 1972 the House of Lords expressed disapproval of the term 'Crown privilege' and said that the right to assert that documents should be withheld in order to protect the public interest should not be confined to the Crown. This was in the case of ***R v Lewes Justices, ex parte Secretary of State for the Home Department*** [1973] AC 388 (***sub nom Rogers v Secretary of State for the Home Department***), which concerned the functions of the Gaming Board. Rogers applied for a certificate of consent to apply to the magistrates for licences for certain bingo clubs. The Board asked the police for information about Rogers. The police reply was prejudicial to his application and consent was refused. Rogers commenced proceedings for criminal libel against the Chief Constable of Sussex and sought production of the police report containing the information which had been submitted to the Board. The Secretary of State for the Home Department and the Board claimed the document was privileged.

The House of Lords disposed of the case as follows.

(a) The term 'Crown privilege' was a misnomer and it should be open to any person or organisation, public or private, to question the benefit to be gained by allowing the production of particular documents or types of information.

(b) The dangers of disclosure outweighed the risk of injustice to Rogers, as a breach of confidentiality could have damaged the effectiveness of the Board.

In the event, therefore, the claims of the Minister and that of the Board concerning the privileged nature of the documents were upheld. The court's view was that performance of the Board's statutory functions – i.e. the regulation and control of gaming establishments – could be seriously prejudiced if persons became reluctant or refused to supply the Board with relevant information out of fear that such might be revealed in legal proceedings. This, it was felt, posed a greater risk to the public interest than did the danger of individual applicants for licences feeling that they had been dealt with unfairly through not being made fully aware of the case against them.

Public interest immunity: General principles

Although the basic rules relating to the withholding of documents and materials from legal cases developed originally in the context of civil claims, it is now accepted that pleas of PII may be made in both civil and criminal proceedings. For civil cases the guiding rules are as follows:

(a) Pleas of PII should be restricted to relevant material which has some significance for the issues to be decided.

(b) Due weight should be given to the views of the party claiming immunity particularly where this was a government Minister or other senior officer of state. Accordingly, a court should confine its discretion to inspecting the material in question, i.e. by taking a look at it, to those instances where it was satisfied that this could give 'substantial support' to the case of the party seeking production and where it had doubts about the public interest need for non-disclosure (*Air Canada* v *Secretary of State for Trade* [1983] 2AC 394).

(c) Having inspected the material, and answered the question above in the affirmative, it was for the court to carry out the 'balancing exercise' or the weighing of the competing demands of the public interests involved, e.g. whether the need to protect national security or, perhaps, the confidentiality of diplomatic exchanges, should be allowed to prevail over the requirements of openness and fairness in judicial proceedings.

(d) Matters to be taken into account in the balancing exercise should include:
   (i)   how pressing and important is the public interest in non-disclosure;
   (ii) to what extent would this be damaged by the degree of disclosure sought;
   (iii) the nature, context, and gravity of the claimant's case;
   (iv) to what extent would this be prejudiced by non-disclosure;
   (v)   could sufficient information be disclosed to enable justice to be done, e.g. by 'gisting', without undue damage to the public interest pleaded.

(e) A person holding documents in an immune class is under a duty to plead PII in respect of them. It is not for the individual to decide to what extent disclosure might damage the public interest – that is the function of the court. Beyond this general rule, however, dicta suggest that a court would be unlikely to interfere with a decision to disclose immune material if this had been made by a person in a position to, and practised in, making judgments of that type, e.g. a government Minister or other high-ranking public official (*Makanjuola* v *Commissioner of Police of the Metropolis* [1992] 3All ER 617; *R* v *Chief Constable of West Midlands, ex parte Wiley* [1995] 1 AC 247).

(f) Where sensitive material may be relevant to a case, but neither of the parties to the dispute have claimed PII in respect of it, it remains open to the court to inspect the material and, of its own volition, order against disclosure should this be deemed to be where the balance of interest lies (*Conway v Rimmer*, supra; *R v Lewes Justices, ex parte Home Secretary*, *supra*).

Public interest immunity and criminal proceedings

Disclosure of evidence: general principles

According to the Criminal Procedure and Investigations Act 1996, as amended by the Criminal Justice Act 2003, s 32, the prosecution in a trial on indictment or contested summary trial should disclose to the defence that which they intend to use as evidence in court and any other material which might tend to undermine the prosecution's case or assist the case for the accused. Therefore, it is only in respect of a refusal to disclose such material that a court may be asked to rule on a plea of public interest immunity.

Background

It was towards the end of the twentieth century before it was finally and unequivocally concluded that PII could be pleaded in criminal cases.

The cases in regard to public interest immunity do not refer to criminal proceedings, but the principles are expressed in general terms. Asking myself why those general expositions should not apply to criminal proceedings, I can see no answer but that they do. It seems correct in principle that they should apply. The reasons for the development of the doctrine seem equally equivalent to criminal as to civil proceedings (*per* Mann LJ, *R* v *Governor of Brixton Prison, ex parte Osman (No. 1)* [1992] 1 All ER 108).

Its use in this context is, therefore, of relatively recent origins.

Principles of application

The balancing exercise

(a) If the prosecution believes that the public interest lies in not disclosing documents in their possession, this should be made known to the defence. It is not open to the prosecution to remain silent about the existence of possibly significant documents on the grounds of public interest immunity.

As indicated, it is crucial in criminal cases – in relation to both class and contents claims – that the court should be the final arbiter of whether the public interest lies in concealment or disclosure. Hence, in every case in which the prosecution feels that material documents are covered by immunity they should, after giving notice to the defence and identifying the particular protected class to which the documents belong, apply to the court for an appropriate ruling. In general this should be dealt with *inter partes* with the defence being given the opportunity to make any related representations.

This is not, however, an absolute rule and a number of exceptions to it were identified by the Court of Criminal Appeal in *R* v *Davis, Johnson and Rowe* (1993) 97 Cr App R 110. Lord Taylor CJ said that where even to disclose the category of the material in question could cause damage to the public interest, the defence should still be notified that an application to the court was to be made (i.e. for a ruling whether public interest immunity applies) 'but the category of the material need not be specified and the application will be *ex parte*'. More controversially, it was also his opinion that in a 'highly exceptional case' where even to reveal an intention to apply for such a ruling would 'let the cat out of the bag' (i.e. indirectly put into the public domain information normally covered by immunity), 'the prosecution should apply to the court, without notice to the defence'. In *R* v *H* [2004] 2 AC 134, the House of Lords approved, in exceptional circumstances, consideration of evidence by a court without notice to the defendant and, if necessary, the appointment of special counsel to protect the interests of the defendant. It held, however, that disclosure must be ordered if the effect of non-disclosure was to render the trial process, viewed as a whole, unfair to the defendant.

> The problem of reconciling an individual's right to a fair trial with such secrecy as is necessary in a democratic society in the interests of national security or the prevention or investigation of crime is inevitably difficult to resolve in a free society governed by the rule of law. It is not very surprising that complaints of violation have been made against member states including the United Kingdom; some of which have exposed flaws in, and malfunctioning of, our domestic procedures. The 'European Court' has, however, long accepted that some operations must be conducted secretly if they are to be conducted effectively (Lord Bingham).

(b) In performing the balancing exercise in criminal cases courts should give additional weight to the public interest in the administration of justice. Here, given the potentially grave consequences for the defendant of a guilty verdict, it is crucial that justice is both done and seen to be done.

> I acknowledge that the application of the public interest immunity doctrine in criminal proceedings will involve a different balancing exercise to that in civil proceedings . . . Suffice it to say for the moment that a judge is balancing on the one hand the desirability of preserving the public interest in the absence of disclosure against, on the other hand, the interests of justice. Where the interests of justice arise in a criminal case touching on or concerning liberty or conceivably on occasion life, the weight to be attached to the interests of justice is plainly very great indeed (*ibid*).

The *Air Canada* test that the party seeking production is able to show that the information for which immunity is pleaded is likely to contain 'material of real importance', does not appear to apply to criminal proceedings. Hence, subject to a possible exception in relation to highly sensitive security material, it appears that inspection must follow automatically from any plea of immunity.

Closed material procedure (see below) may not be used in criminal proceedings. Accordingly, should the prosecution wish to withhold material for reasons of national security, it must do so by pleading PII and even in these circumstances it remains obliged to disclose as much material as is required to allow the charge to be defended. Should it feel unable to do so, it should abandon the prosecution altogether.

(c) Public interest immunity hearings from which the defendant and his representatives are excluded may not be offensive to the Convention on Human Rights, and particularly the fair trial guarantees in Art 6, providing that the defendant's interests are safeguarded adequately (*Edwards and Lewis v United Kingdom* (2004) 40 EHRR 24). As to the practice of such 'closed' hearings, note, however, the unease expressed by the House of Lords in *R v H*, [2004] 2 AC 134.

> There will be very few cases indeed in which some measure of disclosure to the defence will not be possible, even if this is to be confined to the fact that an *ex parte* application is to be made. If even that information is withheld and if the information to be withheld is of significant help to the defendant, there must be a very serious question whether the prosecution should proceed, since special counsel, even if appointed, cannot then receive any instructions from the defence at all.

Should the prosecution be so concerned about the disclosure of documents that they are unwilling to entrust the balancing exercise to the court, they should – rather than risk injustice – abandon the prosecution.

In *Jasper v United Kingdom* [2000] 30 EHRR 441, the above procedure was found to be in general compliance with the requirements of Art 6 of the European Convention on Human Rights. The Court of Human Rights was, however, at pains to emphasise the need for *ex parte* applications to be subject to proper and adequate safeguards and, in particular, that the defence be kept informed and permitted both to make submissions and generally participate in the process so far as might be possible without revealing the material in question.

Denial of the existence of potentially public interest immunity material at the trial stage is a breach of Art 6 and is not cured by an *ex parte* application in respect of such material on appeal (*Atlan v United Kingdom* (2002) 34 EHRR 33).

Public interest immunity and national security

Security versus justice

Objective 8

Case law suggests that, as a general rule, where PII is pleaded on grounds of national security and/or the defence of the realm, these will be given considerable weight in the balancing exercise and, in a great many cases, will be found to prevail over an application for disclosure in order to do justice in a particular case. This, however, brings with it the harsh legal reality that in, certain circumstances, where a compelling plea of PII is accepted in relation to sensitive material directly relevant and central to a claimant's case, the effect may be to make it almost impossible for the case to be heard according to the normally applicable standards of procedural justice or, occasionally, and at worst, for it to be tried at all.

The way in which this may occur may be illustrated by reference to the decision in *Carnduff* v *Rock* [2001] EWCA Civ 683. Here, a police informant sued for damages alleging a failure by the police to pay monies promised to him for providing information which had led to the arrest and conviction of certain criminal suspects. The police, however, were granted PII for those parts of their records containing details of the informant's dealings with his 'police handlers' – it being accepted by the court that such materials belonged to a well-established class of immune materials. In such circumstances, therefore, the court felt it had no option but to 'strike out' the claimant's action as having no realistic prospect of success.

Confidence in the absolute fairness of the PII process was further affected by the decision in *Tariq* v *Home Office* [2011] UKSC 35. This appeared to qualify the decision of the House of Lords in *Secretary of State for the Home Department* v *AF* [2009] UKHL 28, viz. that in all circumstances the party seeking to withhold sensitive information should be obliged to disclose at least a non-damaging summary or the 'gist' of it. The Supreme Court in *Tariq*, however, leaned towards a more flexible and perhaps less demanding requirement. This was that the extent of disclosure in any case should be regarded as 'fact sensitive' and that any absolute duty to disclose even the gist of relevant national security material should be limited to cases in which the liberty of the subject or some such other fundamental right might appear to be directly and immediately at stake.

This state of affairs caused widespread concern in both legal and political circles – a great deal of unease being felt at the prospect of valid and meritorious legal claims against the state being repeatedly 'trumped' by the ace of national security and the perceived need to accede to its demands at all times and whatever the cost to the administration of justice.

Closed material procedure

A possible means of reconciling such key public interests was provided by the Special Immigration Appeals Commission Act 1997. This allowed for appeals against immigration and deportation decisions on grounds of national security to be heard in 'closed sessions, i.e. in the absence both of the person making the appeal and his/her legal representatives; his/her 'interests' being safeguarded by the presence in the closed hearing of a 'Special Advocate' drawn from a panel of security-cleared barristers appointed by the Attorney-General. This enabled the Commission to hear evidence which might otherwise have been excluded on grounds of public interest immunity but without the risk of this becoming public knowledge.

This 'closed material procedure' (CMP), as it became known, for dealing with sensitive evidence was later extended, *inter alia*, to hearings before the Investigatory Powers Tribunal

(Regulation of Investigatory Powers Act 2000, s 18); Employment Tribunals dealing with cases involving government employees (Employment Relations Act 2004, s 36); and appeals in the High Court against Terrorism Prevention and Investigation Measures ('TPIMs') (Terrorism Prevention and Investigation Measures Act 2011, ss 6–8). The process became an established part of the English legal system in general by virtue of the Justice and Security Act 2013. This authorised the use of closed material proceedings in any civil case involving sensitive security material being heard before the High Court, the Court of Appeal or the Supreme Court.

Summary

The chapter explains the circumstance in which the Crown and other public authorities in the United Kingdom may be sued in the ordinary courts in respect of the way they have used any of the powers and duties entrusted to them in order to fulfil their governmental functions. It also explains the law relating to 'Crown privilege' and 'public interest immunity', i.e. the particular circumstances in which evidence that might, in some way, prejudice the process of government or the public interest, may be withheld from legal proceedings.

References

Allen (1993) 'Public Interest Immunity and Ministers' Responsibilities' [1993] Crim LR 660.

Calvert (1985) *An Introduction to British Constitutional Law*, London: Financial Training.

Hogg (1989) *The Liability of the Crown* (2nd edn), Australia: Law Book Co. Ltd.

Keane (1996) *The Modern Law of Evidence* (4th edn), London: Butterworths.

Wade and Forsyth (1994) *Administrative Law* (7th edn), Oxford: Clarendon Press.

Further reading

Craig (2016) *Administrative Law* (8th edn), London: Sweet & Maxwell, Ch. 20.

Cripps (1994) *The Legal Implications of Disclosure in the Public Interest* (2nd edn), London: Sweet & Maxwell, Ch. 8.

Cross and Tapper (2010) *Cross and Tapper on Evidence* (12th edn), Oxford: Oxford University Press, Chs 9 and 10.

Keane and McKeown (2014) *The Modern Law of Evidence* (10th edn), Oxford: Oxford University Press.

Mitchell (1984) *The Contracts of Public Authorities*, London: London School of Economics.

Turpin (1989) *Government Procurement and Contracts*, London: Longman.

Wade and Forsyth (2014) *Administrative Law* (11th edn), Oxford: Oxford University Press.

Part 5

Judicial supervision of executive power

14

Judicial review: nature and grounds for

Objectives

After reading this chapter you should:

1. Understand the nature of judicial review as a distinct legal process and its place in the workings of the modern British constitution.

2. Appreciate the principal common law grounds for judicial review contained in the doctrine of *ultra vires* and the rules of natural justice or procedural fairness.

3. Recognise modern developments in the law of judicial review including the doctrines of irrationality, proportionality and legitimate expectation.

The nature of judicial review

Purpose and essence

Objective 1

In order to enable them to fulfil their governmental functions, public authorities are vested with a wide range and variety of legal powers and duties. Most of these are derived from Acts of Parliament. Some may still be found in the common law, particularly the royal prerogative. Judicial review is the legal process through which an individual may challenge the legality of the way in which any of these powers has been used. An application for judicial review is made to the Administrative Court of the Queen's Bench Division of the High Court.

This new and burgeoning dimension of judicial review is dealt with in Chapter 17 which is devoted specifically to the overall impact of the 1998 legislation.

Traditionally applications for judicial review were founded on allegations that an authority had acted either *ultra vires* (i.e. beyond its powers) or in breach of the rules of natural justice (the common law rules of procedural fairness). In more modern times, however, the enactment of the Human Rights Act 1998 has provided a further fertile ground for allegations of abuse of power and it is probably true to say that the majority of applications for review are now founded under some alleged contraventions of one or more of the human rights provisions encompassed by the Act.

A public body acts *ultra vires* if it does that for which it had no legal authority either in statute or common law. It acts in breach of the rules of natural justice if, in making a decision, it contravenes any of the procedural rights the common law accords to a person affected by the exercise of a decision-making power. In either case such misuse of power will result in a finding that the body's actions were void *ab initio*, i.e. of no legal effect from the beginning.

The modern tendency is to deal with the specific rules contained within the doctrines of *ultra vires* and natural justice under the headings of illegality, irrationality, and procedural impropriety. This classification was first proposed by Lord Diplock in the *GCHQ* case and will be considered in more detail below.

Suffice it to say, at present, that a decision is void for illegality if the decision-making body stepped outside the legal limits of its authority or failed to exercise its discretion consistent with the intentions of Parliament or the underlying values of the English legal system. A decision is irrational and of no legal effect if it is so extraordinary or perverse that no reasonable decision-maker could have arrived at it. Procedural impropriety occurs where the decision-maker fails to comply with any relevant procedural requirements imposed by the enabling statute (i.e. the one in which the decision-making power is contained) or the common law rules of natural justice (i.e. the right to a fair hearing and the rule against bias).

In applying these tests to determine the legality and validity of government action, the High Court is exercising its ancient supervisory jurisdiction over 'subordinate' government officials and bodies – in effect, all those vested by law with the authority of government. This jurisdiction is said to be inherent; in other words, it is derived from centuries of constitutional development and not from any formal grant of authority by Parliament. It is through the exercise of this jurisdiction that the British constitution gives practical effect to its most fundamental underlying values and to the imperatives contained in the doctrines of the sovereignty of Parliament, the rule of law and the separation of powers.

Judicial review and constitutional fundamentals

Acts of Parliament are the source of most of the powers exercised by administrative and judicial bodies. These are the commands of the sovereign body which lay down the nature and extent of the authority so granted. It is logical, therefore, for the courts to assume and insist that the repositories of such authority do that and only that which has been commissioned by Parliament. At its simplest level, therefore, a public body acts lawfully (*intra vires*) so long as it uses its powers within and according to the grant of authority given to it by Parliament. If not, it has exceeded its lawful authority and acted *ultra vires*.

Judicial review is given further justification and definition by the requirements of the rule of law. As already explained, the rule of law is a doctrine of political morality. It seeks to impose certain minimum standards of conduct on those responsible for the process of government. These are the standards which are perceived to be commensurate with the practice of good government in a liberal democracy. In the language of judicial review they are encapsulated in words such as legality, reasonableness, rationality, fairness and in the rejection of such concepts as arbitrary and unrestricted discretionary power (i.e. that without any legal foundation or discernible legal limits).

Judicial review is concerned with the enforcement of these standards and with the application of legal rules, enshrined in the doctrines of *ultra vires* and natural justice, which have been developed for this purpose. Thus, if a decision-maker makes a finding on the basis of wholly irrelevant considerations, this may be condemned as unreasonable in law and *ultra vires* the ambit of the power used. If the decision is one which may have a seriously detrimental effect on an individual's legal rights, and that individual has been given no opportunity to be heard orally or through written representations, the decision-maker may be said to have acted unfairly so that again the validity of the decision may be challenged in proceedings for judicial review.

Judicial review may be further understood as an expression of, and as being underpinned by, the doctrine of the separation of powers. It is an expression of the doctrine in that it represents one of the principal 'checks and balances' developed by the constitution to guard against abuse of power. Judicial review is underpinned by the separation of powers in that its effectiveness and credibility depends on the existence of an independent and impartial judiciary. A judiciary subject to executive influence could not be relied upon to act as an impartial arbiter in disputes involving the individual and the state.

The legal and conventional rules which seek to guarantee judicial independence and impartiality have already been considered. These presume that, for meaningful legal control of power, judges must be able to find against government officials without fear of sanction or retribution and that they must be seen to be exercising their supervisory jurisdiction without political favour or bias.

The scope of judicial review

Government bodies exercise both public and private law powers. It is in relation to the former that an application for judicial review may be made. The distinction between the two is somewhat blurred and is considered in more detail below. For introductory purposes, however, a public law power may be described as one which will usually be authorised by statute or the royal prerogative and is concerned with the regulation or protection of some aspect of the public interest. The exercise of a public law power will often involve the restriction of private law rights where this is perceived to be for the public benefit – e.g. the compulsory purchase of land for the provision of public amenities.

Authority for the private law actions of a public body will be derived usually from the contract with, or from the consent of, those in relation to whom the function is exercised. It will be a function which is not integral to the usually understood meanings of the words 'government' or 'public administration'. An example would be the authority of a public body to dismiss an employee for incompetence or misconduct. This authority will be drawn from the contract of employment agreed between that body and the particular employee. It is a contractual right which will be claimed and exercised in the appropriate circumstances by all employers whether in the public or private sector. The exercise of the right is not directly related to any of the usually understood functions of government. It is a private legal arrangement between the public body in its role as an employer and the individual affected. It does not create any powers or obligations in which the public have a direct interest. If the body has done something not permitted by the contract, the individual's remedy is to sue in respect of the breach, not to apply for judicial review.

Power and jurisdiction

These words appear frequently in the language of judicial review. They are generally used to demarcate the boundaries of decision-making authority within which a public body is free to act without judicial interference. Although the terms are often treated as synonymous, it is more accurate to confine the word 'power' to the administrative and secondary legislative authority conferred on executive bodies, both central and local. Thus the Secretary of State for the Home Department may be said to have the 'power' to deport from the

United Kingdom any person whose presence here is not conducive to the public good (Immigration Act 1971). Where, however, it is the extent of the decision-making competence of a judicial body (e.g. an inferior court or administrative tribunal) which is in issue, the concept of 'jurisdiction' is generally to be preferred. Here, as a general rule, the word refers to the matters upon which the court or tribunal has been given the authority to make decisions and to the law which it has been empowered to apply for that purpose.

The existence of power or jurisdiction as so explained was once assumed to be discernible at the outset of the decision-maker's inquiry and could be determined by asking certain fundamental questions – principally, was the body properly constituted and was it dealing with a matter upon which it was legally entitled to decide? If such questions were answered in the affirmative then the decision-maker had power or jurisdiction to proceed safe from risk of judicial review. It was, therefore, not open to a court to question the sufficiency of evidence for a particular decision or its reasonableness (i.e. whether there were reasonable grounds for it or whether any irrelevant matter had been taken into account). Nor would a court say that a decision-maker had gone outside its lawful jurisdiction if it misinterpreted any of the legal rules which it had the authority to apply to the matters remitted to it. As a general principle, questions of fact, discretion and law were all assumed to lie within the decision-maker's jurisdiction or power. Errors relating thereto did not justify any finding that the decision-maker had acted *ultra vires*: 'Where a court has jurisdiction to entertain an application, it does not lose its jurisdiction by coming to a wrong conclusion, whether it was wrong in law or in fact' (per Lord Coleridge CJ, *R* v *Central Criminal Court JJ* (1886) 17 QBD 598).

As understood in this sense, the concepts of jurisdiction and power permitted only a limited role for judicial review.

> Although the courts would insist on compliance with statutory requirements as to form and procedure, it was extremely difficult to persuade them that a Minister had acted *ultra vires* by erring in law or fact, or that he was under an implied obligation to observe the rules of natural justice, or that in exercising a discretionary power he had been influenced by legally improper considerations (De Smith, *Judicial Review of Administrative Action*).

It is generally accepted that the position remained largely thus until the 1960s. By this time, however, pro-executive judicial tendencies – so evident during the Second World War and its immediate aftermath – had begun to diminish. A change in judicial policy became evident. Although not so articulated, this was no doubt in response to what was perceived to be the ever-increasing power of the state – particularly the wide discretionary powers being vested in Ministers and other public officials. It became apparent from a number of key decisions that judicial understanding of the concepts of power and jurisdiction was being revised in order to permit more extensive and effective legal control of the powers of government. These were no longer to be questions determinable primarily at the outset of the inquiry. Henceforth, errors such as lack or insufficiency of evidence, abuse of discretion (e.g. irrelevancy) and mistake of law committed during the inquiry, were to be regarded as 'going to jurisdiction'. Lack or insufficiency of evidence was asserted as a jurisdictional matter in *Ashbridge Investments Ltd* v *Minister of Housing and Local Government* [1965] 1 WLR 1320: '. . . the court can interfere with the Minister's decision if he has acted on no evidence, or if he has come to a conclusion to which on the evidence he could not reasonably have come' (per Lord Denning MR).

The same was said of abuse of discretion by the House of Lords in *Padfield* v *Minister of Agriculture* [1968] AC 997:

> Parliament must have conferred the discretion with the intention that it should be used to promote the policy and objects of the Act . . . [I]f the Minister . . . so uses his discretion as to thwart or run counter to the policy and objects of the Act . . . the law would be very defective if persons aggrieved were not entitled to the protection of the courts (*per* Lord Reid).

Perhaps the most important case in the 1960s in terms of extending the scope of judicial review was *Anisminic v Foreign Compensation Commission (No. 2)* [1969] 2 AC 147. On that occasion the House of Lords, in deciding that a tribunal could lose jurisdiction if it made a mistake of law, made it abundantly clear that jurisdictional errors could occur during, as well as at the beginning of, any inquiry.

> Lack of jurisdiction may arise in many ways. There may be an absence of those formalities or things which are conditions precedent to the tribunal having any jurisdiction to embark on an inquiry. Or at the end the tribunal may make an order that it has no jurisdiction to make. Or in the interviewing stage, while engaged on a proper inquiry, the tribunal may depart from the rules of natural justice; or may ask itself the wrong questions; or it may take into account matters which it was not directed to take into account. Thereby it would step outside its jurisdiction. It would turn its inquiry into something not directed by Parliament and fail to make the inquiry which Parliament did direct. Any of these things would cause its purported decision to be a nullity (*per* Lord Pearce).

All of this tends to suggest that the meaning of power or jurisdiction is a matter of judicial policy which may be adjusted from time to time in accordance with the judges' view of their relationship with the executive and the need to maintain the effectiveness of the constitutional balance inherent in the separation of powers.

Review and appeal contrasted

In exercising the power of review the court's inquiry should be directed solely to the legality of the decision in issue – i.e. whether the decision-maker acted illegally, irrationally or improperly in a procedural sense. The merits of the decision are not in issue. It matters not, for example, that the body appears to have made the 'right' decision – i.e. one which, given the relevant factual and policy considerations, most objective observers would have agreed with. If it has acted unlawfully – e.g. the decision was not one that it was empowered to make – the matter is subject to judicial review. By the same token, if the body appears to have made the 'wrong' decision, but has done so without any abuse of power, its findings of fact are not a matter for judicial inquiry.

Where an individual feels that a decision made by a public body in relation to them was simply 'wrong', the appropriate remedy is to appeal. Whether a right of appeal exists will depend on the enabling Act (i.e. the statute which conferred the particular decision-making power). If such right has been granted, the person or body vested with the appellate jurisdiction may then reconsider the facts and either approve the original decision or superimpose its own. The issue of legality does not arise. The question for the appellate body is whether the original decision was right or wrong given the factual and, perhaps, policy considerations on which it was made.

This distinction between review and appeal is of fundamental constitutional importance and, as the following example will illustrate, is directly relevant to proper observance of the doctrines of the sovereignty of Parliament and the separation of powers.

R v Cambridge Health Authority, ex parte B [1995] 1 WLR 898

This case concerned a young girl who appeared to be terminally ill. The only treatment available which might have prolonged her life was extremely expensive and had only a remote chance of success. It was decided, therefore, that as this would not represent a prudent use of scarce public resources, the treatment would not be given.

This caused considerable public outcry. Many thought the decision not only 'wrong' but morally indefensible. This may have weighed heavily on members of the judiciary for, although the Health Authority did not appear to have acted beyond the ambit of its powers, the High Court granted an application for judicial review. *Certiorari* was issued to quash the decision and the Health Authority was ordered to reconsider the issue.

An appeal against the grant of review was then made to the Court of Appeal. Its members were also clearly in great sympathy with the girl's plight. Sir Thomas Bingham MR said that 'in a perfect world any treatment which a patient . . . sought would be provided if doctors were willing to give it'. He also recognised, however, that judicial review should not be granted simply because a court had misgivings about an administrative body's findings on a particular matter which fell within the jurisdictional limits given to it. It would be an abuse of the court's proper constitutional function to exercise a power of appeal in the guise of judicial review:

> . . . the courts are not, contrary to what is sometimes believed, arbiters as to the merits of cases of this kind. Were we to express opinions as to the likelihood of the effectiveness of medical treatment, or as to the merits of medical judgment, then we would be straying far from the sphere which, under our constitution, is accorded to us. We have one function only which is to rule upon the lawfulness of decisions. That is a function to which we should strictly confine ourselves.

Thus the Court of Appeal was emphasising that it was not for a court to question decisions on matters of fact and policy which Parliament has entrusted to a particular administrative authority. So to do would subvert the will of Parliament and transgress the separation of powers by taking the court into the realms of public policy. In this case the question of how best to use the limited resources made available to the Health Service was a matter which clearly fell within the domain of the executive branch of government.

Review and appeal may also be contrasted by reference to their legal origins. The right to judicial review emanates from the common law. It is the fundamental right of any person aggrieved by an act of government. It is not something which is derived from, or dependent on, an Act of Parliament.

As already indicated, however, there is no inherent common law right to appeal against the merits of a public body's decision. In some instances, where Parliament confers a power to decide, that power will be made subject to a right of appeal. In others it may not. All will depend on the enabling legislation and whether those responsible for its enactment felt that a right of appeal would be detrimental to administrative efficiency or any other public interest (e.g. national security). This has produced a somewhat haphazard system of appeals in which some powers to decide are appealable and others are not.

Grounds for judicial review

Development and classification

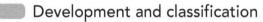
Objective
2

The latter half of the twentieth century witnessed a major expansion of the law relating to judicial supervision of state power, i.e. judicial review. This was founded on, and resulted in, a detailed and rapid development of the traditional common law doctrines of *ultra vires* and the rules of natural justice. As indicated above, these were the two principal elements of the common law long relied upon by the courts to give practical expression to the sovereignty of Parliament and the underlying values of the rule of law, viz. that the agencies of government and the state should not exceed or abuse the powers conferred upon them, nor should they take decisions or actions affecting an individual's rights without giving that person a fair and unbiased hearing.

The extension of the legal framework for the supervision and control of state power during this period is widely attributed to mounting judicial concerns relating to party-political control of the parliamentary and democratic processes and the resulting use of the sovereign body to confer evermore and greater powers on to the executive branch of government and this, often, for purely short-term party-political ends.

As the process continued and in an attempt to give this newly developed area of law greater accessibility and clarity, attempts were made to isolate and clarify the various rules into different 'heads' or types of judicial review – these depending on the different varieties of abuse of power to which particular rules were directed. Perhaps the most authoritative of such classifications was provided by the House of Lords in the well-known case of **Council for Civil Service Unions v Minister for the Civil Service** [1985] AC 374. Here it was suggested that the rules for judicial review should henceforth be understood as falling into three broad categories – those of 'illegality', 'irrationality', and 'procedural impropriety'. These encompassed, respectively, the doctrine of *ultra vires,* i.e. excess and abuse of power; the concept of reasonableness as explained originally in **Associated Provincial Picture Houses v Wednesbury Corporation** (*supra*), sometimes referred to as the 'Wednesbury test'; and the requirements of both procedural *ultra vires* and the rules of natural justice.

Illegality

This head of judicial review is concerned with the control of:

(i) *power* (the type of legal authority exercised by administrative and government bodies) and *jurisdiction* (they type of legal authority exercised by courts and tribunals), and ensuring that the body acts within, and according to, the legal authority conferred on it (jurisdictional control);

(ii) *discretion*, i.e. ensuring that when dealing with a matter within its power or jurisdiction the body uses its power to decide and does so according to the full extent of the discretionary remit entrusted to it (control of discretion).

A body acts outside its power or jurisdiction if it:

1 takes a decision or action which was beyond the limits of its statutory or common law powers (simple *ultra vires*);

2 fails to take a decision or action which it was legally obliged to do (failure to fulfil a statutory or other legal duty);

3 takes any decision or action for which it had legal authority but in relation to the wrong subject-matter (error of jurisdictional fact);

4 bases a decision on a wholly inadequate or erroneous basis of fact (no-evidence rule);

5 applies a mistaken or extraneous legal rule to the matter to be decided (error of law).

A body acts *ultra vires* by failing to exercise or abusing a discretionary power when it:

1 delegates its power to decide to a subordinate without the statutory authority to do so (unlawful delegation);

2 allows its power to be exercised by another and unauthorised body (surrender or abdication of discretion);

3 limits the exercise of its discretion by applying rigid policy rules (fettering of discretion by policy);

4 limits the exercise of its discretion by inconsistent contractual obligations or other undertakings (fettering of discretion by contract);

5 allows the exercise of its discretion to be influenced unduly by an unauthorised body (acting under dictation or improper pressure);

6 exercises its discretion on the basis of irrelevant considerations (irrelevancy);

7 uses its power for an improper or unauthorised purpose (improper purpose).

Jurisdictional control

Simple *ultra vires*

One of the most famous examples of the principle may be illustrated by reference to the decision in ***Attorney-General* v *Wilts United Dairies***.

Attorney-General v *Wilts United Dairies* (1921) TLR 884

On this occasion the House of Lords enforced the basic constitutional principle that a public authority should not impose any tax or financial charge without clear statutory authorisation. The facts were that under emergency wartime legislation the government had been given the power to control the production and supply of food. In a purported exercise of this power the Minister of Food granted the Dairy Company a licence to buy and distribute milk in the southwest of England. This was subject to a condition that the company pay a 2d charge to the government for every gallon of milk purchased. When the government brought proceedings for arrears of such payments, the court found that the imposition of the charge offended the ancient rule, embodied in the Bill of Rights 1689, that no tax should be levied without the approval and authority of Parliament. No such express or implied authority could be construed from the enabling legislation:

> . . . if an officer of the executive seeks to justify a charge upon the subject made for the use of the Crown he must show in clear terms that Parliament has authorised the particular charge. I am clearly of the opinion that no such powers . . . are given to the Minister of Food by the statutory provisions on which he relies (*per* Atkin LJ).

It should not be assumed from the above that there is any rigid principle confining a body solely to that which has been expressly authorised by statute. A body may also do that which is reasonably incidental to the fulfilment of specific express powers:

> . . . whatever may be fairly regarded as incidental to, or consequential upon, those things which the legislative has authorised, ought not . . . to be held, by judicial construction, to be *ultra vires* (*per* Lord Selborne, ***Attorney-General* v *Great Eastern Railway Co*** (1880) 4 App Cas 473).

Failure to fulfil a statutory duty

The difficulties associated with the legal enforcement of statutory duties have already been considered in the context of private actions for damages for breaches of the same. Where, however, such duty is sufficiently specific as to enable a court to identify its requirements with reasonable precision, it will be *ultra vires* and illegal for a public body to fail to give effect to it.

In most cases, however, a statutory duty will be couched in language which allows some flexibility and discretion in terms of what is required to fulfil it. Hence, if a local authority is under a statutory duty to ensure that its streets are lit adequately, this does not impose any exact obligation as the word 'adequately' permits different interpretations. Clearly, if an authority failed to provide any lighting whatsoever, it would act *ultra vires*. If it were to provide some lighting but less than that which could reasonably be regarded as adequate, this also would not be sufficient to bring its actions within the boundaries of legality.

R v Camden London Borough Council, ex parte Gillan (1988) 21 HLR 114

In this case, the Council was under a duty in the Housing Act 1985 to hear and decide whether persons were homeless intentionally or unintentionally and to secure the provision of accommodation as appropriate. Due to a lack of resources, however, the authority's homeless persons unit was open between 9.30 am and 12.30 pm on weekdays only, during which time its staff were available to deal with applications and enquiries made by telephone but not in person. This was held to be less than the acceptable minimum in terms of fulfilment of the duty and, therefore, *ultra vires*.

Error of jurisdictional fact

It is not uncommon for enabling legislation to provide that a power or jurisdiction to decide may be exercised only when a particular fact or state of fact is in existence. Hence if a local council has the statutory authority to seize and destroy all black dogs the lawful use of the power to seize and destroy is dependent on the existence of two questions of fact, viz. is the animal in question (a) black, and (b) a dog. Use of the power to seize and destroy a brown dog or a black cat would therefore be *ultra vires*.

Such facts have been variously defined as jurisdictional facts, precedent facts, preconditional facts and collateral facts. The particular terminology favoured is not of great significance providing it is understood that their function is to delineate the subject-matter or factual context in relation to which the power should be exercised.

The principle is sometimes traced to the decision in the following case.

White and Collins v Minister of Health [1939] 2 KB 838

The case concerned the validity of a compulsory purchase order. This was made in the course of a local authority's statutory power to acquire land compulsorily for the purpose of building houses providing that the land in question did not form part of any 'park, garden or pleasure ground'. According to the Court of Appeal this made the *vires* of any such order dependent on the existence of a certain state of fact, i.e. that the land to be acquired did not fall into any of the proscribed categories.

> The first and most important matter to bear in mind is that the jurisdiction to make the order is dependent on a finding of fact; for, unless the land can be held not to be part of a park . . . there is no jurisdiction in the borough council to make, or in the Minister to confirm, the order (*per* Luxmoore LJ).

The principle was also articulated in *R v Secretary of State for the Home Department, ex parte Khawaja* [1984] AC 74, where it was held that the statutory power to arrest, detain and exclude illegal entrants from the United Kingdom could be exercised only against those who were, in fact, illegal entrants. It could not be used, therefore, against persons whom the Home Office simply believed to be illegal entrants, no matter how reasonable that belief may have been: 'That is a "precedent fact" which has to be established. It is not enough that the immigration officer reasonably believes him to be an illegal entrant if the evidence does not justify his belief' (per Lord Fraser).

Similarly, in *Tan Te Lam v Superintendent of Tai a Chau Detention Centre* [1996] 4 All ER 256, the Privy Council held that a power to detain an illegal migrant to Hong Kong 'pending' that person's removal and return to Vietnam could be exercised lawfully only where such removal was actually pending, i.e. as a matter of fact was likely to occur within a reasonable time.

The no-evidence rule

Where the necessary jurisdictional facts are in existence so that a body enters upon its jurisdiction lawfully, its findings of fact therein are not subject to review. Findings of fact within jurisdiction are, as a general rule, a matter for appeal and not judicial review.

However, this is subject to one major qualification, sometimes referred to as the 'no-evidence rule'. According to this a decision may be *ultra vires* if:

(a) it was based on no evidence whatsoever;

(b) the evidence available was so minimal that no reasonable decision-maker could have based a decision of any kind upon it;

(c) it was based on a wholly mistaken understanding of the facts.

> On judicial review, a court may not only quash the authority's decision if it is held to be initiated by legal misdirection or procedural impropriety or unfairness or bias or irrationality or bad faith, but also if there is no evidence to support factual findings made or they are plainly untenable or if the decision-maker is shown to have misunderstood or been ignorant of an established, and relevant fact . . . (Lord Bingham, *Runa Begum v Tower Hamlets London Borough Council* [2003] 2 AC 430)

Coleen Properties Ltd v Minister of Housing and Local Government [1971] 1 WLR 433

In this case, a local authority had power to compulsorily acquire slum properties for the purpose of redevelopment and, as part of such scheme, to acquire other properties (i.e. those which were not slums) where this was 'reasonably necessary for the satisfactory development' of the area in question (Housing Act 1957, s 43). A compulsory purchase order was served on a property of this type belonging to Coleen Properties Ltd. They appealed against it. A local public inquiry was convened. At the inquiry the local housing authority offered no evidence relating to the need to acquire the property in question. The compulsory purchase order was later confirmed by the Minister after he had considered the report of the inspector who had presided over the inquiry.

In the instant proceedings the Court of Appeal held that the Minister could not have reached any valid conclusion that it was 'reasonably necessary' to acquire the property for the proper development of the area concerned. In the absence of evidence to this effect having been put to the local inquiry, no such evidence was contained in the inspector's report. Therefore, there was no factual material before the Minister on which he could have based his decision.

Error of law

This occurs where a public body, more often a court or tribunal, misconstrues or gives an incorrect meaning to a legal rule which it has been empowered to apply to the facts of cases coming before it for decision.

The traditional view was that where a decision-maker erred in law this did not 'go to jurisdiction'; that is, the decision-maker did not act *ultra vires*. Mistakes of law within jurisdiction could only be remedied through an appeal (where such right existed) or by applying for review for what was known as 'error of law on the face of the record'. The latter was an ancient ground of relief, popular until the mid-nineteenth century, and was used to challenge the validity of decisions where a mistake of law or procedure could be found in the written record of the particular proceedings. It was a useful remedy in the days before the present hierarchy of courts was established (Judicature Acts 1873–75) when rights of appeal from inferior courts and tribunals did not always exist, and was typical of an age in which procedural correctness and the keeping of accurate records was sometimes accorded a higher priority than justice itself. As a result, however, of the Summary Jurisdiction Act 1848, after which petty sessions or magistrates' courts were no longer required to keep detailed records of decisions, and the Judicature Acts (above) which provided for appeals on matters of fact and law from inferior courts, the remedy lost much of its significance.

Where an official or body committed this type of abuse the resulting decision was 'voidable' (i.e. valid unless and until challenged), and not *ultra vires* and void *ab initio* (i.e. of no legal effect from the beginning).

The remedy of error of law on the fact of the record staged something of a revival as a result of the decision in *R v Northumberland Compensation Appeal Tribunal, ex parte Shaw* [1952] 1 KB 338, where the Appeal Tribunal misapplied a regulation which determined the amount of compensation payable to persons who became redundant as a result of the health service reorganisation in 1946. The complainant had no right of appeal from the tribunal's decision and resort to this ancient remedy was the only means by which the court could relieve an obvious injustice:

> ... the court of King's Bench has an inherent jurisdiction to control all inferior tribunals, not in an appellate capacity, but in a supervisory capacity. This control extends not only to seeing that the inferior tribunals keep within their jurisdiction, but also to seeing that they observe the law ... the Lord Chief Justice has, in the present case, restored *certiorari* to its rightful place and shown that it can be used to correct errors of law which appear on the fact of the record, even though they do not go to jurisdiction ... With the advent of many new tribunals, and the plain need for supervision over them, recourse must once again be had to this well-tried means of control (*per* Lord Denning).

The law remained thus until the landmark decision in *Anisminic v Foreign Compensation Commission (No. 2)* [1969] 2 AC 47, wherein the House of Lords expressed the view that henceforth an error of law which affected the decision of a tribunal or official should be regarded as 'going to jurisdiction', i.e. as rendering the decision *ultra vires* and void.

> The breakthrough that *Anisminic* made was the recognition ... that if a tribunal whose jurisdiction was limited by statute or subordinate legislation mistook the law applicable to the facts as it had found them, it must have asked itself the wrong question, i.e. one into which it was not empowered to inquire and so had no jurisdiction to determine (*per* Lord Diplock, *O'Reilly v Mackman* [1983] 2 AC 237).

The facts of the ***Anisminic*** case were as follows. After the Suez Crisis 1956–57, the United Kingdom received a payment of £27.5 million from Egypt to be distributed among British nationals and companies whose property had been seized or destroyed by the Egyptian authorities during the crisis. The task of determining which persons and companies so qualified was given to the Foreign Compensation Commission (established under the Foreign Compensation Act 1950). The Commission was to decide individual claims according to the terms of eligibility set out in the Foreign Compensation (Egypt) (Determination and Registration of Claims) Order 1959. These provided, *inter alia*, that any claimant or 'successor in title' to the same had to be of British nationality.

Anisminic was a British company whose claim appeared to fall within the necessary criteria. The company claimed compensation in respect of one of their subsidiaries (Sinai Mining) which had been seized during the hostilities and subsequently given over to an Egyptian company, which operated under the name TEDO. Anisminic's claim was, however, rejected. The Foreign Compensation Commission based its decision on the ground that although Anisminic had British nationality, its successor in title, TEDO, did not.

When Anisminic challenged the validity of this conclusion, the House of Lords held that the Foreign Compensation Commission had misconstrued the Order in Council. In particular, the Commission had been wrong to concern itself with the nationality of Anisminic's successor in title. This only became a relevant issue where a successor in title was making the claim. Where a claim was made by the original owner, as in this case, the question of any successor's nationality did not arise and was not something that the Commission was empowered to consider. The Commission had, therefore, 'asked itself the wrong question' or, put another way, had applied an element of the Order in Council which did not relate to the facts before it.

The judgment appeared to suggest, however, that it remained possible for an error of law to be made which did not affect a tribunal's findings and that, if and when this lesser type of error occurred, the mistake would not render the decision to be *ultra vires* and void. In later cases, however, both the Court of Appeal and the House of Lords cast doubt upon the view that it was possible to draw any rational or workable distinction between jurisdictional and non-jurisdictional errors in the sense explained above (see Lord Denning MR, ***Pearlman v Keepers and Governors of Harrow School*** [1979] QB 56; ***Re Racal Communications Ltd*** [1981] AC 374). Gradually the view began to emerge that any error of law made by administrative tribunals, officials or inferior courts (e.g. magistrates' and county courts) should be regarded as jurisdictional. The rationale for this was that Parliament could not have intended such bodies to possess the authority to make conclusive findings as to the correct meaning of the law (i.e. the rules and regulations such bodies had been empowered to apply to cases coming before them). Hence, where it was claimed that an administrative tribunal, etc. had 'erred in law', this was a proper matter to be brought before the High Court by way of judicial review.

The present attitude of the courts in this matter has been summarised as follows:

> The concept of error of law within jurisdiction is rapidly becoming obsolete. As a result of a series of judgments the courts now assume that Parliament does not intend to confer jurisdiction or power on inferior courts or public authorities to determine questions of law. All errors of law by public authorities except superior courts are now regarded (or may easily be turned into) jurisdictional errors (*Lewis, Judicial Remedies in Public Law*).

This approach was confirmed by the House of Lords in ***Page v Hull University Visitor*** [1993] 1 All ER 97, and in ***Williams v Bedwellty Justices*** [1996] 3 All ER 737. In the latter case Lord Cooke said that 'the authorities now establish that the Queen's Bench Division of the High

Court has now in judicial review proceedings jurisdiction to quash a decision of an inferior court, tribunal or other statutory body for error of law'.

Control of discretion

Unlawful delegation

This occurs where a statute has given power or jurisdiction to body A, and body A, without express or implied authority, delegates the exercise of that power or jurisdiction to body B. This is unlawful delegation. Any decision or action by body B is *ultra vires* and unlawful.

Barnard v *National Dock Labour Board* [1953] 2 QB 18

In this case, the Dock Workers (Regulation of Employment) Order 1947 had conferred disciplinary powers over dock workers on to the National Dock Labour Board with authority to delegate the exercise of the same to Local Dock Labour Boards. No authority for further delegation of the power could be construed from the legislation. The delegation to, and the exercise of, the disciplinary power by a Port Manager was, therefore, *ultra vires* and unlawful.

The principle was also applied in the following case.

R v *Liverpool City Council, ex parte Professional Association of Teachers, The Times,* 22 March 1984

The Education Act 1944 stipulated that a local education authority should consider a report from its education committee before exercising any of its powers. This made it clear that any report was to be formulated by the education committee collectively and not by any other person or body. It was unlawful, therefore, both for an education committee (as in this case) to delegate the formulation of such report to its chairman and for the education authority to act on the basis of the same.

In the interests of administrative efficiency the rule is applied with a degree of flexibility to those exercising administrative powers. A more strict approach is adopted, however, in relation to judicial functions. Thus, where an administrative body is empowered to decide, its decision remains valid albeit that the body has relied upon the recommendations or advice of a committee or an executive official. Where, however, the function is judicial in nature, it would appear that the decision-maker may not rely on reports or recommendations and must consider all the relevant materials before reaching a decision.

> Every member of a judicial body must have access to all the evidence and papers in the case, he must have heard all the arguments and he must come to his own conclusion. The maxim *delegatus non potest delegare* applies strictly to judicial functions (*per* Denning MR, *R* v *Race Relations Board, ex parte Selvarajaran* [1975] 1 WLR 1686).

Even an administrative body must, however, have something before it more than a mere recommendation. There must be some sort of report, albeit brief, which explains the reasons for the recommendation (see *R* v *Chester Borough Council, ex parte Quietlynn Ltd* (1985) 83 LGR 308).

The rule against delegation does not mean that all the decision-making powers conferred by statute on specific government Ministers have to be exercised by those Ministers personally. If it were so the efficient disposal of administrative business would become impossible. Hence it is permissible for such powers to be exercised by a civil servant on the Minister's behalf. This is consistent with the constitutional convention that the Minister is politically answerable for all the actions and decisions of their civil servants. 'Constitutionally, the decision of such an official is, of course, the decision of the Minister. The Minister is responsible. It is he who must answer before Parliament' (*per* Lord Greene MR, *Carltona Ltd* v *Commissioners of Works* [1943] 2 All ER 560).

R v *Skinner* [1968] 2 QB 700

In this case, S appealed against a conviction for drink-driving. The Road Traffic Act 1967, s 7 required the Secretary of State for the Home Department's consent for the use of any particular breathalyser device. S argued that the device used in his case had been approved by a senior civil servant but not by the Minister personally. His appeal was rejected. Widgery LJ explained that: 'It is not strictly a matter of delegation, it is that the official acts as the Minister himself and the official's decision is the Minister's decision.'

The rule, however, has its limits and would appear to extend only to those for whose actions the Minister is directly accountable. In *R (on application Bourgass)* v *Secretary of State for Justice* [2015] UKSC 54, a person serving a prison sentence successfully challenged a decision to extend a period of solitary confinement beyond the initial 72 hours permitted. The power to make such a decision had been conferred on the Minister (Prison Rule 45), but, as was the usual practice, had been exercised by a prison manager, i.e. a person working in the prison service and, therefore, not within the Ministry of Justice. The court emphasised that the relationship between prison governors, officers, and the Minister 'bear no resemblance to that governing the relationship between a Minister and his departmental officials' (Lord Reed).

Surrender or abdication of discretion

This occurs where a public body without any formal or conscious act of delegation to a subordinate, allows, or agrees to, the exercise of its power by another body or official or, without due consideration, simply applies the views or recommendations of another body or official to the issues before it. The principle may be illustrated by reference to two well-known cases.

Ellis v *Dubowski* [1921] 3 KB 621

In this case, a local authority had statutory power to license premises to be used as cinemas and to attach to such licences conditions regulating the types of material which could be shown, i.e. as to good taste, public decency, etc. (Cinematograph Act 1909). This was, in effect, a power of censorship. In purported exercise of the power an authority granted a licence subject to the condition that no film be shown which had not been granted a certificate by the British Board of Film Censors. This condition was held to be invalid. It was clear that the authority, instead of exercising and retaining the discretion entrusted to it, had decided to defer, in all cases, to the views of the Board of Film Censors. The Board was, however, a domestic body without any statutory powers whatsoever. Its certificates were intended to be regarded as advisory only. In each case, therefore, the final decision as to the fitness of a particular film for public exhibition was to be taken by the local authority to which Parliament had given the appropriate statutory power (cf. *Mills* v *London County Council* [1925] 1 KB 213).

Lavender v Minister of Housing and Local Government [1970] 1 WLR 1231

This case concerned the minister's power to determine appeals against refusals of planning permission by local planning authorities. Lavender appealed against a refusal to allow him to mine gravel deposits in an area of prime agricultural land. It was the Minister's policy not to grant appeals in such cases unless so advised by the Minister of Agriculture. In effect, therefore, the discretion to grant or refuse an appeal in this context was being exercised by the Minister of Agriculture and not by the Minister to whom the power had been given: 'by applying and acting on his stated policy I think the Minister had fettered himself in such a way that in this case it was not he who made the decision for which Parliament had made him responsible' (*per* Willis J).

Acting under dictation

This could be regarded as a more extreme species of surrender or abdication of discretion. It occurs where a public body allows its decision to be dictated or influenced unduly by an unauthorised person or body so that it cannot be said that its discretion has been exercised lawfully. Subject to what has been said already, a public body must remain free to exercise its discretion on both the merits of the particular issue to be decided and the requirements of any relevant public interests. The body acts *ultra vires,* therefore, if, for example, it decides on the basis of instructions of some unauthorised superior in the constitutional hierarchy. Nor must it allow itself to be influenced by threats of what may occur (e.g. public disorder), unless it reaches a particular decision.

For many years there were few proven examples of this type of abuse in English law and it was generally illustrated by reference to the Canadian case of *Roncarelli* v *Duplessis.*

Roncarelli v Duplessis (1959) 16 DLR (2d) 689

This case concerned a decision of a statutory body (the Quebec Licensing Commission) to revoke R's liquor licence after being instructed to do so by the state's Prime Minister and its Attorney-General. R had apparently incurred the state government's displeasure by standing as surety for certain Jehovah's Witnesses charged with distributing literature – some of which was believed to be seditious – without a licence. The licensing commission's decision was quashed. It had not applied itself objectively to the case against R. It had simply done as it was told.

In more recent times, however, allegations of such flawed decision-making have been raised in English courts.

R v Waltham Forest LBC, ex parte Baxter [1988] QB 419

In this case, the Court of Appeal was asked to consider whether the practice of local councillors to vote in accordance with party policy as determined by a local party caucus could be regarded as a failure by them to exercise their individual discretion according to the particular merits of questions put before them. The court's view was that, while councillors were entitled to be influenced and guided by party policy, it would be unlawful for them to behave as if bound by it so absolutely and rigidly as to disable them from making up their own minds.

The exercise of discretion on the basis of a threat of public disorder was in issue in the following case.

R v *Coventry City Council, ex parte Phoenix Aviation* [1995] 3 All ER 37

On this occasion, to avoid the danger of further disorder and disruption by animal rights protestors, the council decided to suspend the permission, previously granted to applicants, to export livestock from Coventry City Airport. The Divisional Court's view was that the rule of law did not allow a public body to act as directed by unlawful protests and threats from a particular pressure group. According to the legislative scheme under which the authority had acted, it was not empowered to discriminate between lawful traders except in emergency circumstances. In the absence of such emergency the authority was bound, with the assistance of the police, to keep the airport open to all lawful users.

Fettering of discretion by policy

This occurs where a public body, perhaps a local council, adopts a particular policy – e.g. not to give any discretionary grants to students – and then applies that policy so rigidly and dogmatically that the merits of individual cases are not considered. A body may adopt a general policy to guide and give consistency to the exercise of its decision-making powers. It is still bound, however, to apply its mind to each case or application which comes before it and must be prepared to make exceptions where this would appear to be deserved or appropriate.

The rule is sometimes traced to the decision in *R* v *Port of London Authority, ex parte Kynoch Ltd* [1919] 1 KB 176 and, in particular, to the dictum of Bankes LJ:

> There are on the one hand, cases in which a tribunal in the honest exercise of its discretion has adopted a policy, and, without refusing to hear an applicant, indicates to him what its policy is, and that after hearing him it will in accordance with its policy decide against him, unless there is something exceptional in his case.

The principle was applied in the following case.

British Oxygen Co Ltd v *Minister of Technology* [1971] AC 610

The Industrial Development Act 1966 had given the Minister a power to give grants to companies investing in new plant and machinery. The Minister's policy was, however, not to award such grants for items costing less than £25. British Oxygen applied for a grant to assist in the purchase of new gas cylinders each costing about £20. Their application was refused. They then challenged the Minister's decision claiming that his policy had precluded proper consideration of their application. It was held that the policy was perfectly lawful providing that the Minister, through his officials, considered each application with a genuine readiness to make exceptions to it. The rule was articulated with eminent clarity by Lord Reid:

> The general rule is that anyone who has to exercise a statutory discretion must not 'shut his ears to an application' . . . [A] ministry or large authority may have had already to deal with a multitude of similar applications and they will almost certainly have evolved a policy . . . There can be no objection to that providing the authority is always willing to listen to anyone with something new to say.

On the facts it was held that Ministry officials had 'listened to all that the applicant . . . had to say'. Thus there had been a valid exercise of discretion and there was no ground for regarding the refusal of British Oxygen's application as being unlawful.

A change of policy may sometimes operate to an individual's detriment and may mean, for example, that a person may no longer qualify for some benefit or advantage that they might otherwise have expected to receive. This might occur, for example, if lack of funds caused a local education authority to reduce the number of discretionary awards it had hitherto decided to make available to persons seeking to pursue postgraduate studies.

The cases show that a public body cannot be prevented from changing its policies and must be free to do so as is required by the public interest. Judicial review may only be granted in the context of policy changes in the following circumstances.

(a) Where the policy adopted or the decision to depart from a particular policy or policy rule(s) was wholly irrational (*R v Secretary of State for Health, ex parte US Tobacco International Inc* [1992] QB 353; *R v Secretary of State for the Home Department, ex parte Gangadeen; R v Secretary of State for the Home Department, ex parte Khan* [1998] 1 FLR 762).

(b) Where a refusal to exempt an individual from the new policy can be shown to have been unreasonable in the *Wednesbury* sense (*Associated Provincial Picture Houses Ltd v Wednesbury Corporation* [1948] 1 KB 223), i.e. the policy-maker 'took into account matters he ought not to have taken into account or neglected to take matters into account which he ought to have taken into account' and 'has come to a conclusion so unreasonable that no reasonable Secretary of State could have come to it' (per Pill LJ, *R v Secretary of State for the Home Department, ex parte Hargreaves* [1997] 1 All ER 397).

(c) Where the decision in question was based on a change of policy which was undisclosed or was 'kept hidden' (see *Lumba (WL) v Secretary of State for the Home Department* [2011] UKSC 12, in which the Home Office operated a secret or hidden policy that, after serving their sentences, foreign national prisoners would continue to be detained with a view to deportation. This was at variance with the published policy that such persons would be released when their sentences had been completed unless good grounds existed for their continued detention).

(d) Where the changed policy was applied in a 'blanket' fashion so as to preclude the discretion to make exceptions where this might appear to have been justified by the circumstances (*Lumba (WL) v Secretary of State for the Home Department*, *supra*).

(e) Where the policy decision or change prevents or inhibits a decision-making body from exercising its powers in accordance with the rules of procedural fairness, e.g. the government decision to henceforth deny legal aid to persons in custody affected by certain prison disciplinary decisions and by proceedings of the Parole Board (*R (on application of Howard League for Penal Reform) v Lord Chancellor* [2015] EWCA Civ 819).

Fettering of discretion by contract or agreement

A public body abuses its discretion if by contract or agreement it undertakes not to exercise a power to decide or to limit the range of decisions otherwise available to it. As stated, Parliament intends the discretionary powers it confers on public bodies to be exercised in accordance with the public interest. Hence, those entrusted with this task should avoid private arrangements which inhibit the fulfilment of such intention.

If a person or body is entrusted by the legislature with certain powers or duties expressly or impliedly for public purposes, those persons cannot divest themselves of those powers or duties. They cannot enter into any contracts or take any action incompatible with the due exercise of their powers or duties. (*per* Earl of Birkenhead, **Birkdale District Supply Co** v **Southport Corporation** [1926] AC 355)

Stringer v *Minister of Housing and Local Government* [1970] 1 WLR 1281

In this case, S applied for planning permission to build houses near the Jodrell Bank telescope in Cheshire. His application was, however, refused pursuant to an agreement between the University of Manchester (the owners of the telescope) and the local planning authority to the effect that no development would be permitted in the telescope's immediate environs. This agreement, and the refusal of planning permission in execution of it, was held to be *ultra vires* and void. The local planning authority had been entrusted with a statutory power to grant or refuse applications for planning permission (Town and Country Planning Act 1971). It was obliged, therefore, to consider each and every application on its merits and not to disable itself from doing so by inconsistent undertakings.

The rule is sometimes attributed to the decision in **Ayr Harbour Trustees** v **Oswald** (below).

Ayr Harbour Trustees v *Oswald* (1883) 8 App Cas 623

In this case, the Harbour Trustees had a statutory power to acquire land compulsorily for the purpose of developing the harbour. A piece of land was acquired from Oswald for this purpose. In order to reduce the cost of compensation by way of severance payments to him in respect of that part of his land which had not been acquired, the Harbour Trustees agreed to a perpetual covenant in which they promised not to use the land acquired in any way which would restrict Oswald's access to the harbour. This agreement was held to be *ultra vires* and illegal. It was clearly inconsistent with the objectives of the enabling Act, i.e. that land acquired under it would be used as the public interest in the proper development of the harbour might from time to time require.

This principle should not be understood as giving a public body the freedom to avoid any contract which, at some later stage, may be found to be incompatible with the unfettered use of a statutory power. Hence, in *R* v *Hammersmith and Fulham Borough Council, ex parte Beddowes* [1987] QB 1050, the Conservative-controlled council decided to sell a number of blocks of flats which were in need of refurbishment. They did this so that the cost of making the flats habitable and returning them to the local housing stock could be borne by the private sector. Concerned, however, by the imminence of local elections, a scheme was devised to try to prevent the decision being reversed should the council 'change hands'. The device used was the inclusion of a restrictive covenant in the contract of sale for the first block which prevented the council from re-letting any of the flats in the remaining blocks if and when these (the flats) became vacant. This, it was hoped, would make the sale of the other blocks unavoidable since their utility for public sector housing would be increasingly diminished. It was accepted that the council had both the statutory power to sell the flats and to include restrictive covenants in the contracts of sale.

It was clear, however, that this particular covenant operated as a major restriction on the ways in which any subsequent council might wish to use its housing powers in relation to these properties. According to the Court of Appeal, however, this did not render the covenant to be unlawful *per se*. What mattered was whether the insertion of the covenant could be regarded as a reasonable method of achieving the authority's 'primary purpose' in the use of its housing powers, viz. 'the provision of housing accommodation in the district' – which the court felt it could:

> if the purpose for which the power to create restrictive covenants is being exercised can reason-ably be regarded as the furtherance of the statutory object, then the creation of the covenant is not an unlawful fetter. All the powers are exercisable for the achieving of the statutory objects in relation to the land, and the honest and reasonable exercise of a power for that purpose cannot properly be regarded as a fetter upon another power given for that same purpose.

Therefore, not every contract which fetters discretion will be unlawful. All will depend on whether the contract in issue may be seen as a reasonable way of achieving the objectives of the statute in which the particular contractual power was contained. If it may, then the contract is *intra vires* and effective notwithstanding that the use of other powers to achieve that same objective has thereby been inhibited (*per* Fox LJ).

Fettering of discretion by estoppel

Closely allied to fettering of discretion by contract is that of fettering of discretion by estoppel. In private law the doctrine of equitable estoppel holds a person to a promise or assurance which has been relied and acted upon to their detriment by the person to whom it was made (***Central London Property Trust Ltd* v *High Trees House Ltd*** [1947] KB 130).

Attempts have been made to utilise the doctrine in public law. In particular it has been argued that if an official or employee of a public body gives an assurance that the body will exercise a power to decide in a person's favour or misleads a person into believing that something may be done without the body's consent (e.g. that a pro-posed building development may be commenced without planning permission), the body is then bound by that assurance – providing, of course, that it has been relied and acted upon.

The use of the doctrine in public law has its attractions as it would give protection to an individual who had acted in good faith on the basis of what had been said by a public offi-cial. On the other hand, this might often result in a public body being bound to exercise a power in a way which did not best serve the requirements of the public interest (as in the above example, if the proposed building development had injurious consequences for the local community).

For some time judicial comment on the relevance of estoppel in public law was marked by a lack of clarity and uniformity. It now appears to be established, however, that estoppel cannot be pleaded if this would result in a public body being unable to use its discretion or decision-making power as the public interest demands.

This basic principle may be attributed to two cases in both of which a local government officer gave an unauthorised assurance that a particular development or use of land could be commenced without a grant of planning permission by the local planning authority (i.e. the local council).

Southend Corporation v *Hodgson (Wickford) Ltd* [1962] 1 QB 416

In this case, H was considering buying a piece of land for use as a builder's yard. He contacted the authority's borough engineer and asked whether planning permission was required. The borough engineer, without any authorisation or reference to the local council, told H that it was not. H bought the land and began to use it for the purpose stated. Complaints were then received from nearby residents. As a result, the local planning authority served H with an enforcement notice under the Town and Country Planning Act 1947 (i.e. an order to discontinue a use of land for which planning permission has not been granted). H claimed that the assurance he had received disabled the council from using its enforcement power in respect of the land in issue.

This was not something the court was prepared to accept. In its view power to issue enforcement notices had been conferred on local planning authorities to enable them to protect their local communities against unauthorised development, particularly where such might cause unwarranted interference with the rights or interests of others. An unauthorised and erroneous statement of a local official could not prevent the authority from using its discretion as intended by Parliament.

> After all, in a case of discretion there is a duty under the statute to exercise a free and unhindered discretion. There is a long line of cases . . . which lay down that a public authority cannot by contract fetter the exercise of its discretion. Similarly . . . an estoppel cannot be raised to prevent or hinder the exercise of the discretion (*per* Lord Parker CJ).

A similar decision was reached in the following case.

Western Fish Products Ltd v *Penwith District Council* [1981] 2 All ER 204

On this occasion conversations with local planning officers misled the complainants into believing that they could use premises as a fish processing factory without applying for planning permission. When an enforcement notice was served by the local planning authority they argued that the authority was bound by its officers' statements. The Court of Appeal's decision was summarised in the following comment by Megaw LJ:

> The defendant council's officers, even when acting within the apparent scope of their authority, could not do what the 1971 Act [Town and Country Planning Act] required the . . . council to do and if their officers did or said anything which purported to determine in advance what the . . . council would have to determine in pursuance of their statutory duties, they would not be inhibited from doing what they had to do.

Also see *R* v *East Sussex County Council, ex parte Reprotech (Pebsham) Ltd* [2003] 1 WLR 348, where, once again, the court refused to accept that a misleading statement by a planning officer that planning permission was not needed was binding on the authority.

In addition to the above, it has long been established that estoppel cannot be used:

(a) to prevent a public body performing a statutory duty (*Maritime Electric Co Ltd* v *General Dairies Ltd* [1937] 1 All ER 248);

(b) to bind a public body to a decision or course of action which is beyond its powers (*Rhyl UDC* v *Rhyl Amusements Ltd* [1959] 1 All ER 257).

However, there appear to be just two circumstances in which an estoppel may hold a public body to a statement or decision it wishes to avoid. The first of these is where the decision or statement is made by an official in the exercise of a power to decide validly delegated to them (***Lever Finance Ltd v Westminster Corporation*** [1971] 1 QB 222). The second occurs where the public body claims that a decision or action is not valid due to minor procedural irregularities (***Wells v Minister of Housing and Local Government*** [1967] 2 All ER 104).

Before leaving this topic, it should be pointed out that attempts to use estoppel in public law, such as the above, were made at a time when the concept of legitimate expectation and abuse of power had not been fully developed. It may be, therefore, that now the concept is recognised, such claims would be dealt with within its terms. If so, there is probably 'no longer a place for the private law doctrine of estoppel in public law or for the attendant difficulties which it brings with it' (***Flanagan v South Buckinghamshire District Council*** [2002] EWCA Civ 690).

> It is true that in early cases such as the ***Wells*** case and ***Lever Finance*** Lord Denning used the language of estoppel in relation to planning law. At that time the public law concepts of abuse of power and legitimate expectation were very undeveloped and no doubt the analogy of estoppel seemed useful. In ***Western Fish*** the Court of Appeal did its best to reconcile these invocations of estoppel, with the general principle that a public authority cannot be stopped from exercising a statutory discretion or performing a public duty. But the result did not give universal satisfaction . . . It seems to me that in this area public law has already absorbed whatever is useful from the moral values which underlie the private law concepts of estoppel and the time has come for it to stand upon its own two feet (*per* Lord Hoffmann, *ex parte Reprotech*, *supra*).

It should be noted also that bad or misleading advice by public servants may give cause for an action in negligence where it falls within the principles set out in ***Hedley Byrne and Co v Heller*** [1964] AC 465. Hence in ***Lambert v West Devon BC***, *The Times*, 27 March 1997, damages were awarded to the plaintiff after he had been wrongly informed by a senior local government officer that he could commence building work pending a related application for a variation in planning permission.

Irrelevancy

The above discussion of judicial supervision of discretionary power has concentrated on the various ways in which a public body may be said to have failed to exercise the decision-making power conferred upon it. Under the head of irrelevancy and the one that follows (improper purpose) the concentration changes to those situations in which the discretion is exercised but in ways which contravene the intentions of Parliament.

Except where the enabling power has specified the matters to be considered when a power to decide is used, or a legitimate expectation has been created that some matters will or will not be taken into account (see ***R v Secretary of State for the Home Department, ex parte Findlay*** [1985] AC 318), the repository of the power has a wide discretion in terms of the factors which may be relied upon. The court will intervene, however, if it feels that matters clearly pertinent to a particular inquiry have been ignored or that other factors which had no relevance were considered.

Hence, in the famous case of ***Roberts v Hopwood*** [1925] AC 578, a local council (Poplar) had statutory authority to pay its employees such wages as it thought fit. The council decided to pay its employees a minimum wage of £4 per week. This was to apply to both men and women. When the reasonableness and legality of the council's actions was challenged the House of Lords held that the council had been influenced by such irrelevances as 'eccentric principles of socialist philanthropy' and a 'feminist ambition to secure the equality of the sexes in the matter of wages' (*per* Lord Atkinson), and that it had failed to take into account the falling cost of living and the level of wages nationally.

It would appear that if a judge wishes to interfere with a particular decision it will seldom be beyond their powers of intellect to identify some matter which should or should not have been considered and to use this as a justification for judicial review. Hence, this is a ground of review which gives the judges themselves a considerable degree of discretion in terms of whether to invalidate a particular action or decision. It has even been alleged that a judge's view of what is or is not relevant to the making of a decision may sometimes be influenced by political or other values. Clearly, for example, in *Roberts* (*supra*), the court was uneasy about the council allowing itself to be influenced by egalitarian concepts of social engineering and the equality of men and women in the labour market. Also, in ***Bromley Borough Council* v *Greater London Council*** [1983] 1 AC 768, where the council in Bromley decided to provide cheap and subsidised public transport in the metropolis, their Lordships felt that the statutory requirement to run London Transport 'economically and efficiently' (London Transport Act 1969) meant that fares should be fixed 'in accordance with ordinary business principles' (*per* Lord Keith). This appeared to exclude the wider social and environmental considerations which had influenced the council. In both this and the *Roberts* case – in what were, arguably, as much political as legal opinions – their Lordships felt that the councils involved should have given greater attention to their fiduciary duty to their ratepayers, now council tax payers, (i.e. to control public spending) and rather less to the political mandates which the councils claimed they were fulfilling (the relevance of a political mandate to the exercise of discretion was also discounted in ***Secretary of State for Education and Science* v *Metropolitan Borough of Tameside*** [1977] AC 1014).

The cases suggest that judges are particularly concerned to see that authorities give careful attention to the financial consequences of their actions. In other words, at least from the judicial perspective, financial considerations would appear to be of a higher priority than other factors which may have influenced a decision, e.g. social policy or an electoral mandate. The judicial prioritisation of financial considerations obvious in the *Roberts* and *Bromley* cases was also evident in ***Prescott* v *Birmingham Corporation*** [1955] Ch 210, where it was felt that a decision to grant concessionary public transport to old-age pensioners had also been affected by a failure to give sufficient consideration to the extra costs that this might impose upon ratepayers (see also earlier cases such as ***Price* v *Rhondda UDC*** [1923] 2 Ch 372; ***Short* v *Poole Corporation*** [1926] Ch 66).

Where an allegation of irrelevancy is made, it is for the applicant to identify the issues which should or should not have been considered. It is not open to the applicant to suggest that a decision appears to be so illogical that it could not have been reached without consideration of some unspecified irrelevant material. In ***R* v *Lancashire County Council, ex parte Huddleston*** [1986] 2 All ER 941, an unsuccessful allegation of irrelevancy was made by a prospective student who was refused a discretionary maintenance award. As she had an excellent academic and personal record she could not understand why her application had been unsuccessful. However, although she suspected something extraneous may have influenced the authority's thinking, she was unable to specify what this might have been (see also ***Cannock Chase UDC* v *Kelly*** [1978] 1 WLR 1).

Improper purpose

Statutory powers must be used for the express or implied purposes for which they were given. If a power is used for some ulterior purpose, or in a way which is clearly inconsistent with the objectives of the enabling Act, then it has been used illegally. Where a power is used to achieve more than one purpose – e.g. as in ***Webb* v *Minister of Housing and Local***

Government [1965] 2 WLR 755, where a power to build sea defences was used to build both a sea wall and a promenade – the court has to identify the authority's main purpose or objective and determine whether this was consistent with the dominant purpose for which the power was given:

> If Parliament grants power to a government department to be used for an authorised purpose, then the power is only validly exercised when it is used by the department genuinely for that purpose as its dominant purpose. If that purpose is not the main purpose but is subordinated to some other purpose which is not authorised by law, then the department exceeds its powers and the action is invalid (*per* Lord Denning LJ, *Earl Fitzwilliams Wentworth Estates Co Ltd* v *Minister of Town and Country Planning* [1951] 2 KB 284).

The fact that other purposes are achieved is not fatal so long as these are reasonably incidental to the main and authorised purpose. Hence, in *Hanks v Minister of Housing and Local Government* [1963] 1 QB 999, alterations to the pattern of roads in an area compulsorily acquired for housing redevelopment, being secondary and reasonably consistent with the development process, were found to be permissible. Also, in *Westminster Corporation* v *London and North Western Railway Co Ltd* [1905] AC 426, the court took no objection to a power to provide public conveniences being used to build the same under a road with accesses on either side thereby creating a subway. Again it was felt that the authorised purpose – the provision of a public convenience – had been the authority's main concern and that the creation of a subway was merely secondary and reasonably incidental to this purpose.

What is an authorised purpose may not always be easily discernible from the statutory language used. In these circumstances, as with irrelevancy, the decision as to whether to intervene or not is largely a matter of judicial discretion which, it has been alleged, may occasionally be influenced by values rather than law. In *R* v *Inner London Education Authority, ex parte Westminster City Council* [1986] 1 WLR 28, for example, a power to use public moneys to provide information about the services provided by local authorities was found to have been used for an unauthorised purpose when moneys were spent on a campaign explaining how those services were being adversely affected by reductions in central government funding.

It has also been held that local councils should not use their powers for the purpose of penalising those of opposing political opinions (see *Wheeler* v *Leicester City Council* [1985] AC 1054; *R* v *Lewisham Borough Council, ex parte Shell UK Ltd* [1988] 1 All ER 938; *R* v *Derbyshire County Council, ex parte Times Supplements Ltd* (1990) 3 Admin LR 241; *R* v *Somerset County Council, ex parte Fewings* [1995] 3 All ER 20).

Similarly, powers should not be used for purely party-political gains without any reference to public interest which the power was designed to serve. This was the essence of the decision in *Porter* v *Magill* [2002] UKHL 67, where a local Conservative-controlled authority adopted a policy of increasing the numbers of council houses made available for sale in the marginal wards of its district. This was not primarily done for the house objectives of the enabling Act but to increase the number of owner-occupiers and, therefore, potential Conservative voters in the wards affected. In *R (on application Core Issues Trust)* v *Transport for London* [2014] EWCA Civ 34, Transport for London (TFL) refused to display advertising propounding the applicant's views that homosexuality was both unnatural and reversible. The Court of Appeal's view was this was lawful providing it had been done in pursuance of the authority's statutory obligation not to perform its functions in a discriminatory fashion, but not if it was done for the purpose of advancing the Mayor of London's popularity in the gay community thereby improving his prospects in the next London mayoral elections.

For the sake of convenience and similarity, using power in ways which frustrate the objectives of the enabling Act may also be dealt with in the general context of improper purpose. The two leading cases on this point are *Padfield* v *Minister of Agriculture* [1968] AC 997, and *Laker Airways* v *Department of Trade* [1977] QB 643. In *Padfield* the Minister acted illegally when, without good reason, he refused to refer a complaint made by a milk producer to a complaints procedure which had been set up to deal with problems arising out of the national milk marketing scheme. According to the House of Lords, the complaints procedure had been included in the Act (the Agricultural Marketing Act 1958) as a means of dealing with all reasonable and relevant concerns raised by producers and, absent good reasons, it was not open to the Minister to use his power of referral in a way which thwarted this objective. In the *Laker* case it was held that the Minister could not seek to protect British Airways' dominant position on the transatlantic route by using powers contained in an Act designed, *inter alia,* to ensure competition on all long-distance passenger routes.

Reasonableness

Wednesbury unreasonableness

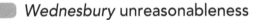

Objective 3

The concept of reasonableness in *Associated Provincial Picture Houses Ltd* v *Wednesbury Corporation*, [1948] 1 KB 223, the Court of Appeal explained that unreasonableness as a species of *ultra vires* could be understood in two senses. First, the term could be used as a general heading for those types of error usually dealt with under the heading of abuse of discretion.

> Lawyers familiar with the phraseology commonly used in relation to the exercise of statutory discretion often use the word unreasonable in a rather comprehensive sense. It has frequently been used and is frequently used as a general description of things that must not be done. For instance, a person entrusted with discretion must . . . direct himself properly in law. He must call his attention to matters he is bound to consider. If he does not obey these rules he may truly be said . . . to be acting unreasonably (*per* Lord Greene MR).

Second, it was said that unreasonableness could be used as a separate and distinct head of review. In this sense it would apply to that type of decision which it might not be possible to impugn for the more usual causes of abuse of discretion, e.g. irrelevancy, improper purpose, but which might appear to be 'so unreasonable that no reasonable authority could even have come to it' (*ibid.*). As Lord Greene admitted, however, 'to prove a case of that kind would require something overwhelming'.

Irrationality

The test of irrationality is generally regarded as a reformulation of the *Wednesbury* principle. It is usually attributed to Lord Diplock in the *GCHQ* case, where he said:

> By irrationality I mean what can now be succinctly referred to as '*Wednesbury* unreasonableness' . . . It applies to a decision which is so outrageous in its defiance of logic or of accepted moral standards that no sensible person who had applied his mind to the question to be decided could have arrived at it.

It is clear from the statements of both Lord Greene and Lord Diplock that this ground of review may only be used to attack that which is completely perverse or extraordinary.

Hence, it would be unconstitutional for a judge to intervene for unreasonableness or irrationality merely because they might not agree with, or approve of, a particular decision. The test is therefore pitched at a particularly high level to avoid any danger or accusations of judges using the unreasonableness/irrationality test as a means of substituting their own opinions for those vested with the power of government.

Examples of cases in which decisions of public authorities have been struck down for *irrationality simpliciter* are limited in number. This may be for two principal reasons. First the requirements of the test, as explained above, are not easy to satisfy. Second, for a decision to approach the required threshold, set as high as it is, it will, in most cases, be almost inevitable that one of the more specific types of abuse which are easier to establish, e.g. irrelevancy or improper purpose, will be present.

Irrelevancy did, however, play a large part in the court's findings in *R (on application of Gurung) v Ministry of Defence* and *R (on application of Rogers) v Swindon NHS Primary Care Trust*.

R (on application of Gurung) v Ministry of Defence [2002] EWHC 2463 (Admin)

This case concerned a scheme introduced by the government to provide compensation for members of the armed forces interned by the Japanese during the Second World War. McCombe J felt it was irrational of the Ministry of Defence to have refused such compensation to a member of the Gurkha regiment on the ground that, at the material time, the Gurkhas had been subject to Indian rather than British military law and discipline.

R (on application of Rogers) v Swindon NHS Primary Care Trust [2006] EWCA Civ 392

The application for judicial review in this case resulted from the PCT's refusal to fund a medical recommendation that the applicant's breast cancer be treated with the drug Herceptin. The Court of Appeal felt it was not rational to refuse such funding where:

- the treatment had been recommended by the responsible consultant clinician;
- the authority had the necessary finance to do so;
- this would not have opened the financial 'floodgates', as only 13 other women in the PCT's catchment area fulfilled the specified medical criteria for prescription of the drug;
- no exceptional circumstances or reasons had been shown for the decision.

Proportionality

The doctrine of proportionality favours a standard of judicial review which causes no significant impediment to efficient public administration but which, at the same time, seeks to prohibit the use of powers in ways which cause greater levels of interference with the rights of others than is required to achieve the legitimate objective pursued. The doctrine was formulated originally within the domestic legal systems of France and Germany. From this, it was later accepted as the appropriate test of judicial review to be applied to the acts of government by both the law of the European Union and that of the European Convention on Human Rights. In these contexts the test became directly applicable to cases before the courts of England and Wales as a result of the European Communities Act 1972 and the

Human Rights Act 1998. These gave domestic effect, respectively, to the two pan-European bodies of law.

Modern examples of the doctrine of proportionality being applied to those matters regulated by EU law and to those falling within the remit of the ECHR would include, respectively, *Digital Rights Ireland Ltd* v *Minister for Communications, Marine and Natural Resources* [2015] QB 127, and *Beghal* v *Director of Public Prosecutions* [2013] UKSC 49.

The *Digital Rights Ireland* case concerned the legality of EU Data Retention Directive 2006/24/EC which required providers of publicly available electronic communications networks to retain communications data for periods of six months to two years. This was primarily in order to harmonise data protection rules across Europe to better facilitate the fight against crime. The directive was found to be disproportionate to that end in that it applied to data of all types held by any and all persons without, in either case, the need to show any direct connection between either the person holding it, or the data itself, and criminal activity.

The issue in *Beghal* was the extent to which those powers in the Terrorism Act 2000 permitting persons entering the UK to be detained for questioning and search for up to nine hours without the need for reasonable suspicion, and to be prosecuted for failing to provide information sought, could be regarded as achieving a proportionate balance between the need to prevent terrorism and the individual's rights in ECHR Art 5 (personal liberty), Art 6 (rule against self-incrimination), and Art 8 (respect for private and family life).

The Court was not persuaded that in the special security circumstances prevailing that the state's clearly legitimate objectives could have been addressed effectively by less intrusive measures or by making use of the powers in question dependent on the existence of reasonable suspicion.

> Given the current very real and immediate threat of terrorism in the state, the level of intrusion into the privacy of the individual is comparatively light and not beyond the reasonable expectations of those who travel across the UK's international boundaries. It is not an unreasonable burden to expect citizens to bear in mind the interests of improving the prospects of preventing or detecting terrorist outrages. In these circumstances the port questioning and associated search powers represent a fair balance between the rights of the individual and the interests of the community at large.

Following the arrival of proportionality review onto the English side of the Channel, it was generally assumed that the two tests would operate 'side-by-side' but separately in the distinctive spheres indicated. Any further advance of proportionality, and certainly its use beyond the remit of EU and ECHR law, was not widely supported during this early period. This was due largely to fears that it permitted a standard of review unfamiliar to English law and one which involved an unacceptable degree of judicial scrutiny of the factual basis and merits of particular decisions, thereby confusing the proper roles and remits of the judicial and executive branches of government.

> There are three good reasons why this is so. First, there exists a constitutional imperative: if Parliament confers decision-making power on a particular agency, the courts would frustrate Parliament's sovereign will if they arrogated that power to themselves. Secondly, there is the pragmatic imperative: the courts, particularly on substantive matters of policy, have considerably less expertise than the designated authority . . . And, thirdly, there exists a democratic imperative: the electoral system operates as an important safeguard against abuse of public power by requiring many public authorities to submit themselves to the verdict of the electorate at periodic intervals. If this system of political accountability is to function, it is important that the decision-making role of these agencies is not usurped by the courts (Sixth Annual Lecture to the Singapore Academy of Law, 1999).

The first real 'chinks' in the defence of traditional English common law review began to appear in the last year of the twentieth and the early years of the current century. Perhaps influenced by the European jurisprudence of proportionality, members of the British judiciary began to embark on a process of redefining the requirements of 'the *Wednesbury* test' and to developing a more calibrated and less inflexible version of Lord Greene's famous doctrine. The generally favoured way forward in any given case was that the long-standing 'one test fits all' version of *Wednesbury* reasonableness should give way to a case by case approach which allowed the standard of review to be determined by facts, nature, and context of the case in issue. In practical terms this meant a more demanding test being applied to decisions affecting 'important' or fundamental rights with a less rigorous or intense approach being used for decisions not having such serious 'rights' consequences for those affected and those made in relation to one of these areas of executive responsibility close to the very limits of judicial competence, i.e. matters to do with government policy, public finance and national security.

The first clear indication of a move in this direction is generally attributed to the House of Lords decision in *R* v *Secretary of State for Home Affairs, ex parte Bugdaycay* [1987] AC 514. The case came from a decision of the Home Secretary to deport the applicant to a country where, it was alleged, his life might be in danger. The view of Lord Bridge on this was:

> The most fundamental of all human rights is the individual's right to life and when an administrative decision under challenge is said to be one which may put the applicant's life at risk, the basis of the decision must surely call for the most anxious scrutiny.

The nature and rationale for this more nuanced understanding of the reasonableness test was later explained by the then Lord Chancellor, Lord Irvine, in 1999:

> It is already a well-established principle in English public law that judicial review does not constitute a monolithic standard of supervision. Rather, the intensity of review in any particular case is determined by its facts and context. For example, the courts accept that it is appropriate to adopt a relatively deferential attitude to decisions concerning national economic policy. In contrast, the courts certainly subject executive action of what engages human law rights to much more thorough-going scrutiny (Sixth Annual Lecture to the Singapore Academy of Law, 1999).

See also *R* v *Secretary of State for Department of Education and Employment, ex parte Begbie* [1999] EWCA Civ 2100, where Laws LJ spoke of 'a sliding scale of review more or less intrusive according to the nature and gravity of what is at stake'.

During the process of redefining the requirements of reasonableness, it became apparent that elements of the doctrine of proportionality had begun to infuse the theory and language of those involved. In a case concerning the legality of the policy prohibiting gay men and women from membership of the armed forces, the Court of Appeal's view was:

> The Court may not interfere with the exercise of an administrative discretion on substantive grounds save where the court is satisfied that the decision is unreasonable in the sense that it is beyond the range of responses open to a reasonable decision-maker. But in judging whether the decision-maker has exceeded this high measure of appreciation the human rights context is important. The more substantial the interference with human rights, the more the court will require by way of justification before it is satisfied that the decision is reasonable in the sense outlined above (*Lustig-Prean v United Kingdom* [2000] 29 EHRR 548).

It was at this point that some amongst the judiciary began to speak of the congruity of seeking to maintain two tests of review within a single legal system. This was very much the sentiment of Dyson LJ in *Association of British Civilian Internees – Far East Region* v

Secretary of State for Defence [2003] EWCA Civ 473. The case concerned the legality of rules laid down by the government for deciding which of those persons interned by the Japanese during the World War II were entitled to compensation.

> Trying to keep the *Wednesbury* principle and proportionality in separate compartments is unnecessary and confusing. It is true that sometimes proportionality may require the reviewing court to assess for itself the balance that has to be struck by the decision-maker, and that would be arrived at on an application of the '*Wednesbury* test', has been relaxed in recent years. Even in cases which have nothing to do with fundamental rights, the '*Wednesbury* test' is moving closer to proportionality and, in some cases, it is not possible to see daylight between the two tests. Although we did not hear argument on the point, we have difficulty in seeing what justification there now is for retaining the '*Wednesbury* test'. But we consider that it is not for the Court to perform its burial rites.

For similar comment, see Lord Slynn in *R v Secretary of State for the Environment, Transport and the Regions, ex parte Holding and Barnes* [2001] UKHL 23.

English proportionality

Bank Mellat v Her Majesty's Treasury (No. 2) [2013] UKSC 39, was concerned with the validity of a direction made under the Iran (Financial Sanctions) Order 2007 which restricted the complainant's access to British financial markets and services. The purpose of the Order and directions made under it was to inhibit the progress of Iran's nuclear development programme. The direction was found to be disproportionate to that aim in so far as, and for no obvious reason, the government had not found it necessary to impose any similar sanctions of equal severity on other major Iranian financial institutions.

In the course of so finding the court was minded also to grasp the 'proportionality nettle' and give consideration to the possible adoption by English law of a test of review fashioned on both this and the post-*Bugdaycay* case-law of reasonableness. According to this, the exercise would involve 'an exacting analysis of the factual case advanced in defence of the measure, in order to determine:

(i) whether its objective is sufficiently important to justify the limitation of a fundamental right;

(ii) whether it is rationally connected to the objective;

(iii) whether a less intrusive measure could have been used;

(iv) whether, having regard to these measures and to the severity of the consequences, a fair balance has been struck between the rights of the individual and the interests of the community' (Lord Sumption).

In the same case, but in a dissenting judgment, Lord Reed proposed a similarly structured test. This was so, save for the last element, which in Lord Reed's version was

> whether, balancing the severity of the measure's effects on the rights of the persons to whom it applies against the importance of the objective, to the extent that the measure will contribute to its achievement, the former outweighs the latter.

This general approach to the exercise of English proportionality was approved, again by the Supreme Court, in both *Kennedy v The Charity Commission* [2014] UKSC 20 and *Keyu v Secretary of State for Foreign and Commonwealth Affairs* [2015] UKSC 69. *Kennedy* involved an unsuccessful claim by a journalist that a refusal by the Charity Commission to reveal details of an inquiry into alleged misuse of charitable funds was a disproportionate restriction on his right of access to information under ECHR Art 10 (freedom of speech). Lord Mance expressed the court's view of the proportionality test as follows:

> The advantage of the terminology of proportionality is that it introduces an element of structure into the exercise, by directing attention to factors such as suitability or appropriateness, and the balance or imbalance of benefits and disadvantages. There seems no reason why such factors should not be relevant to judicial review even outside the scope of Convention and EU law.

Also in *Kennedy* it was made clear that, as with the redefined meaning of reasonableness, proportionality should not be regarded as imposing a monolithic test and that the intensity of its demands should be determined by the context in which it is being applied, i.e. that greater or lesser intensity of scrutiny and strictness in the application of its requirement might be appropriate depending on the type of rights in issue, e.g. whether 'fundamental' or not and the nature of the administrative action being challenged, e.g. whether relating to public policy, national security, or finance.

In *Keyu* the court rejected the complainant's contention that the government's failure to hold a public inquiry into the killing of 26 unarmed civilians by British troops in a former colony (Malaysia, then Malaya) was disproportionate to the need to do justice and right a long-standing and well-founded grievance.

In *Bank Mellat*, however, the question of whether any such test should replace that of reasonableness, and for all purposes, although posed, was left unanswered; it being felt that such a major change in the country's constitutional law should not be made except with the approval of a full bench of the court, i.e. nine or more Supreme Court Justices.

Any such remaining judicial reticence concerning full commitment to the proportionality test appears to have to do with concerns (held by some but not all) that it does, or could, facilitate an intensity of judicial inquiry not felt hitherto as being within the proper remit of English judges or entirely compatible with the doctrine of the Separation of Powers. The foremost amongst these is the view that while *Wednesbury* unreasonableness allows the decision-maker a wide area of decision-making autonomy and authorises judicial interference only where an authority has gone beyond this to an extent that a reasonable decision-maker could not have contemplated, proportionality review allows, indeed requires, the court to look more closely at both the facts and reasoning underlying the decision in question and so to determine whether any misunderstanding or flawed assessment of these could have caused an unnecessary or disproportionate use of powers.

Procedural impropriety

Albeit a public body acts within its powers or jurisdiction and uses its discretion according to law, the validity of its decisions may still be questioned on grounds of procedural impropriety. The complaint may allege procedural *ultra vires* or a breach of the rules of natural justice.

Procedural *ultra vires*

It is commonplace for enabling statutes to require the powers they confer to be exercised in accordance with specified procedural requirements. Thus, where an Act gives a Minister the power to legislate by way of statutory instrument, it will often stipulate that he/she should consult with interests affected and that the instrument should be laid before Parliament according to one of the procedures set out in the Statutory Instruments Act 1946.

As a matter of statutory construction, the courts draw a distinction between procedural requirements which should be treated as mandatory and those which may be regarded as directory.

A mandatory procedural requirement must be complied with if the action or decision taken is to be valid in law. As a general principle such a requirement will be regarded as mandatory if non-compliance with it might cause substantial prejudice to the person or persons affected by the exercise of the power. The requirement will usually have been imposed to improve the quality of the decision-making process, i.e. by providing for greater public participation and more openness than might otherwise have been the case. Hence a requirement to consult those likely to be affected by administrative or legislative action will usually be treated as mandatory, as will a requirement to hear objections from those who may be affected detrimentally. Thus, in *Bradbury* v *Enfield Borough Council* [1967] 1 WLR 1311, a local education authority acted procedurally *ultra vires* when it failed, as required by the Education Act 1944, to give adequate public notice of and opportunity to object to its plan to change the status of a number of its secondary schools from selective to comprehensive. In *R* v *Camden London Borough Council, ex parte Cran* [1995] RTR 346, a local council failed to comply with a statutory obligation to consult with local residents before making an order designating an area as a controlled traffic zone. This was held to be fatal to the validity of its scheme.

Failure to comply with a directory requirement does not have such drastic consequences. A public body is expected to act in accordance with the same but should it fail to do so this does not affect the validity of the action or decision in question. By definition, therefore, directory requirements tend to be concerned with matters of procedural detail rather than substance. Non-compliance is, therefore, unlikely to result in any serious prejudice or disadvantage.

Coney v *Choyce* [1975] 1 All ER 979

This was another case in which a local education authority had decided to change from a selective to a comprehensive system of education. In accordance with the 1944 Education Act, the authority gave public notice of its intentions in local newspapers and public buildings. It failed, however, to post the required notices outside all the schools affected. It was held that the principal objective of the relevant provisions in the 1944 Act was that adequate publicity should be given to such intended changes and that those affected should be notified both of the right to object and how that right should be exercised. The court felt that, in substance, this had been done. The requirement to put up notices outside the particular schools was treated, therefore, as directory only.

A procedural requirement may also be regarded as being merely directory for reasons of public policy.

Williams v *Home Office (No. 1)* [1981] 1 All ER 1151

W was serving a long term of imprisonment. He was believed to be a difficult prisoner and was put in solitary confinement for six months. This decision was not reviewed every 28 days as required by Prison Rule 43 (made under the Prison Act 1952). Accordingly, W challenged the validity of his treatment. The court conceded that the prison authorities had not acted as required but felt that the system of prison government would be undermined if prisoners were allowed to mount legal challenges to the implementation of the prison rules.

The rules of natural justice

The essence of natural justice

The rules of natural justice or procedural fairness, also sometimes referred to as the duty to act fairly, represent the English common law's minimum procedural standards for the legitimate exercise of decision-making powers of government. The rules should be observed by any public body or official making a decision which could have significant adverse consequences for the rights, interests, or other material concerns of the person or persons affected (*Ridge* v *Baldwin (No. 1)* [1964] AC 46; *Re Pergamon Press* [1971] Ch 388). Such procedural standards find practical expression in two main principles:

(a) the right to a fair hearing (*audi alteram partem*);

(b) the rule against bias (*nemo judex in causa sua*).

The primary purpose of the rules is to ensure that those legally empowered to make decisions affecting others do so according to an open and even-handed process capable of properly identifying and balancing the various interests involved, both public and private. More specifically, it has been said that the observance of natural justice serves to:

(a) ensure that the decision-maker receives all the information relevant to the issue in hand and that it is properly tested;

(b) avoid the feelings of resentment aroused if a party affected by a decision-making process is not given an opportunity to influence its result;

(c) minimise the suspicions associated with decisions made 'behind closed doors' and, particularly, the taint of self-serving partiality;

(d) underpin the Rule of Law by promoting 'congruence between the actions of decision-makers and the law which should govern their actions' (*Osborn* v *Parole Board* [2013] UKSC 61).

All of this helps to explain why the body of procedural rules has been said to encapsulate the 'principles of fair play' (Maugham J, *Maclean* v *The Workers' Union* [1929] 1 Ch 602) and the remarks of Jackson J in the US Supreme Court that even 'severe substantive laws can be better endured if they are fairly and impartially applied' (*Shaughnessy* v *United States* (1953) 345 US 26).

Whether a decision-making power should be exercised according to the rules of natural justice, and to what standard, tends to be determined by the seriousness of the consequences for the person or persons affected rather than by any conceptual analysis of the nature or type of decision-making process employed, i.e. whether it might be described as being akin to the form of decision-making typified by the procedure used in courts and tribunals (i.e. the 'judicial process') or whether it is purely of the administrative genus employed by executive officials when implementing the rules and requirements of public policy. As indicated above, however, the nature and form of the decision-making process does have some relevance to the particular standard of natural justice or fairness to be observed. As a general rule, therefore, a higher standard of natural or procedural justice will tend to be expected in the conduct of judicial and like proceedings with rather less demanding requirements, subject always to an irreducible minimum, being applicable to those administrative processes in which considerations of public policy and the wider community inherent may also play their part (see *McInnes* v *Onslow-Fane* [1978] 1 WLR 1520).

The view of the Court of Appeal in *R* v *Board of Visitors of Hull Prison, ex parte St Germain* (see below) was to the effect that every power to decide may be placed on a notional decision-making spectrum which ranges between that which is wholly judicial to that which is purely administrative. Those processes with characteristics which require them to be placed nearer the judicial end of the spectrum should be accepted as attracting and requiring higher standards of natural justice, with the rigour of such requirements diminishing incrementally the nearer to the administrative end of the spectrum a process might be placed.

Natural justice and the Human Rights Act

In addition to the protection of the rules of natural justice, and since the enactment of the Human Rights Act, individuals with procedural grievances also have a right of recourse to the procedural guarantees in Arts 5 and 6 of the European Convention on Human Rights. In many cases the various elements of these articles now provide the principal grounds on which such complaints are founded. For a variety of reasons, however, this does not mean that the rules of natural justice have thereby been rendered redundant. This is particularly so because the requirements of Arts 5 and 6 do not extend to all of the decision-making procedures within the process of government by which an individual may be affected. Thus, for example, Art 6, the Convention's principal procedural guarantee, deals primarily with those procedures for determining civil rights/obligations and criminal charges and would appear, therefore, to have no express application to a whole range of decision-making, investigative and advisory functions which may, in some way, affect an individual's interests or prospects, but do not impinge directly on any specific legal right/obligation or criminal liability. Thus it has been held that while Art 6 does not apply to the functions of the Parole Board, the Board is nevertheless bound to act in accordance with the common law principles of procedural fairness (***Roberts v Parole Board*** [2005] UKHL 45). In these and related circumstances, therefore, resort to the rules of natural justice and the requirements of fairness will remain a valuable legal basis for redress of procedural irregularity.

A flexible concept

Depending on the circumstances, a fair hearing may involve any or all of the following elements:

- the right to be informed in advance of the case to be met – i.e. the factual basis on which the decision-maker may act;
- the right to a reasonable time in which to prepare a response;
- the right to be heard verbally or in writing;
- the right to cross-examine persons who may have made prejudicial statements to the decision-maker;
- the right to be legally represented;
- the right to reasons for the decision.

As has been indicated, however, the right to a fair hearing is a flexible concept. This means that its requirements are not fixed or constant – i.e. it is not possible to state that whenever the rule applies its content must always consist of all the elements listed above. The case-law illustrates that the requirements of a fair hearing will vary from case to case depending on the circumstances:

> it is important to bear in mind that the recognition of an obligation to observe procedural fairness does not call into play a body of rigid procedural rules which must be observed

regardless of circumstances. Where the obligation exists its precise content varies to reflect the common law's perception of what is necessary for procedural fairness in the circumstances of the particular case (*per* Deane J, *Haoucher* v *Minister of State for Immigration and Ethnic Affairs (1990) 93 ALR 51*).

To determine the precise procedural obligations resting on the decision-maker in any given case the courts apply a number of criteria. Paramount amongst these are:

- the nature of the decision-making power;
- the consequences of its exercise for the person affected;
- the demands of the wider public interest;
- the intentions of Parliament.

Hence if it is concluded that the decision-making power in issue has the tripartite structure so typical of the judicial process and requires the decision-maker to determine a dispute between two parties, it will generally be assumed that this imposes an obligation to act in accordance with a high standard of procedural fairness which might, for example, include the right to be heard personally. If, added to this, it is clear that the decision may have very serious consequences for the person affected then the procedural expectations may be further increased so as to extend perhaps to rights of cross-examination and legal representation.

Applying the same rationale, if the power to decide is classified as being purely administrative or bureaucratic – e.g. a bipartite decision by a local authority to refuse an application for a discretionary student grant – the decision-maker will still be expected to act fairly but the requirements of fairness in this situation will be less demanding. Proper consideration of the individual's written application would probably suffice.

This type of approach was evident in the following case.

R v Board of Visitors Hull Prison, ex parte St Germain (No. 2) [1979] 3 All ER 545

The applicant, a prisoner, was accused of breaches of the prison code of discipline arising out of a riot in Hull prison in 1976. The prison rules provided that prisoners charged with less serious offences against the code should be dealt with by prison governors. The cases of those charged with more serious matters were to be referred to the prison's board of visitors. The allegations against St Germain fell into the latter category.

Each prison has a board of visitors. These perform a variety of functions including acting as disciplinary tribunals. By way of punishment a board of visitors could award loss of remission for up to six months or loss of privileges for each charge proved. When the applicant appeared before the board the evidence against him was presented by the prison governor. Much of this consisted of statements which had been collected from prison officers who had been on duty at the material times. None of these officers was present at the hearing. The charges against the applicant were found proved and, by way of punishment, he suffered a substantial loss of remission. He applied for judicial review on the ground that he had not been given a fair hearing, i.e. he had not been given an opportunity to cross-examine those officers whose prejudicial statements had been put to the board.

It was held that the facility to cross-examine was not an inevitable element of the right to a fair hearing. The proceedings were, however, clearly judicial in nature and had resulted in further loss of liberty for the applicant – the most serious penalty of all under English law. Also, some of the evidence in question had included eyewitness accounts of the applicant's alleged wrongdoing. It followed from all this that the board was bound to observe a fairly rigorous standard of procedural fairness which, in the circumstances, extended to a right of cross-examination. The board's refusal to permit this meant that the applicant had been treated unfairly.

Note that in April 1992 the disciplinary powers of boards of prison visitors were removed under powers contained in the Criminal Justice Act 1991.

This may be contrasted with the decision in the following case.

R v Manchester Metropolitan University, ex parte Nolan [1994] ELR 380

The applicant was a law student who was alleged to have committed a serious breach of the University's examination regulations (by having lecture notes on his desk during two examinations). The examination board which considered his case resolved that he should be deemed to have failed his examinations and should not be given an opportunity to resit them. The board took into account the applicant's written submissions but did not permit him to appear in person.

The applicant applied for judicial review on the ground, *inter alia*, that he had not been given a fair hearing. In the circumstances, however, it was held that the board had done enough to satisfy the requirement of procedural fairness. It had not exercised a judicial power and the consequences of its decision were not so serious as to warrant observance of the type of procedural rights claimed by the applicant. In particular, the court pointed out, the exam board's decision did not preclude the applicant from pursuing the same qualification at an alternative institution of higher education.

In determining the appropriate standard of procedural fairness in any given situation a court will also be aware that the decision-making power in issue will have been entrusted to the body for a particular statutory purpose, usually related to the protection of some aspect of the public interest. While it is important that the individual is treated fairly, it is not the function of the court to impose procedural requirements on the decision-maker which would inhibit the proper exercise of the power as intended by Parliament.

Where a power has been given to a public body to deal with matters of urgency or it is necessary to use a power immediately to avoid public danger, insistence on procedural exactitude – i.e. the need to give advance notice, hearings, etc. before taking action – would clearly not accord with either the wishes of Parliament or the obvious and overriding demands of the public interest. In **R v Secretary of State for Transport, ex parte Pegasus Holdings Ltd** [1988] 1 WLR 990, the Minister did not act unfairly when he summarily suspended permits to fly aircraft in and out of the United Kingdom previously granted to certain Romanian pilots. This was after they had failed flying tests conducted by the Civil Aviation Authority. Schiemann J's comment was that 'the rules of natural justice do apply but . . . in such an emergency as the present, with a provisional suspension being all that one is concerned with, one is at the low end of the duties of fairness'.

Application of the rules of natural justice may also have potentially negative implications for a variety of other key public interests including those relating to the efficient expedition of public administration (e.g. by causing delays in decision-making) and the need for confidentiality in relation to certain types of information (e.g. that relating to national security and the investigation of crime).

All of these are matters which the court must be cognisant of when determining the procedural demands appropriate to the circumstances of any particular case.

Elements of the right to a fair hearing: potential elements

The right to be informed of the case to be met

In most circumstances a person who may be affected prejudicially by the decision of a public body will be entitled in advance to know at least the substance of the case on which that decision will be based: 'If the right to be heard is to be a real right which is worth anything it must carry with it a right in the accused man to know the case which is made against him' (per Lord Denning, *Kanda* v *Government of Malaya* [1962] AC 322).

The rule was applied in the following case.

R v Hampshire County Council, ex parte K [1990] 2 All ER 129

The local authority had reason to suspect that the applicant had been sexually abusing his daughter. These suspicions were given added credence by certain medical examinations and reports commissioned by the authority to which the applicant was not given access. In the ensuing application for judicial review, the Divisional Court ordered the suspension of care proceedings initiated by the authority. The applicant had been treated unfairly. Prior to the commencement of such proceedings he should have been allowed access to the medical reports so that he might have had a realistic opportunity to contest their contents.

Disclosure of the public body's information in detail and its precise sources may be required in the exercise of judicial or disciplinary powers, particularly where these may intrude upon a legal right or other substantial interest (*R* v *Army Board of the Defence Council, ex parte Anderson* [1992] 1 QB 169). Otherwise, in the interests of administrative efficiency, 'chapter and verse' may not be required and, as indicated, the general 'gist' of the case to be answered may be sufficient. Other public interests may also limit the extent of the right. Thus it has been held that natural justice does not require disclosure of information which would be injurious to national security (*R* v *Secretary of State for the Home Department, ex parte Hosenball* [1977] 1 WLR 766), or prejudicial to the fight against crime (*R* v *Gaming Board for Great Britain, ex parte Benaim* [1970] 2 QB 417).

The right to reasonable time to prepare a response

Giving a person the substance of the case to be answered will provide only minimal procedural benefit if that occurs only a short time before the actual decision is to be made. Save what has been said above about the possible effects of any countervailing public interests, the person affected will usually be entitled to sufficient time in which to digest that information and formulate a response.

R v Thames Magistrates, ex parte Polemis [1974] 1 WLR 1371

In this case, a cargo ship docked in the Thames and shortly afterwards an oil slick appeared beside it. A summons to answer a charge under the Control of Pollution Act 1971 was served on the ship's master. This required him to appear in the local magistrates' court in the afternoon of the same day on which the summons was served. His subsequent conviction was quashed for unfairness. Lord Widgery CJ concluded that 'any suggestion that he had been given a reasonable chance to prepare his defence [was] completely unarguable'.

See also *R (on the application of Clark-Darby)* v *Highbury Magistrates Court* [2001] EWHC Admin 959, where a magistrates' order in respect of unpaid council tax was quashed due to failure to give the applicant adequate notice of the proceedings.

The right to be heard

Due to the wording of this central element of the fair hearing rule, it is often assumed that it implies a right to be heard orally before the decision-maker. This is not the case. The essence of the rule is that the individual must be given a reasonable opportunity of conveying their views to the decision-maker whether this be orally or by written representations. The giving of oral hearings may often cause serious delays in administrative decision-making generally. The recognition of such a right will occur, therefore, only in the context of the exercise of powers which, according to the criteria already considered, attract the highest standards of procedural fairness. Hence, in *R v Army Board of the Defence Council, ex parte Anderson*, above, notwithstanding the court's view that in dealing with the applicant's allegations of racial abuse by his fellow soldiers the Board was bound to act judicially, this did not mean that the applicant should have been given an oral hearing. The flexible nature of the right was summarised by Taylor LJ:

> Whether an oral hearing is necessary will depend upon the circumstances of the particular case and upon the nature of the decision to be made. It will also depend upon whether there are substantial issues of fact which cannot be satisfactorily resolved on the available written evidence. This does not mean that whenever there is a conflict of evidence in the statements taken, an oral hearing must be held to resolve it. Sometimes such a conflict can be resolved merely by the inherent unlikelihood of one version or the other. Sometimes the issue is not central to the issue for determination and would not justify an oral hearing.

Cross-examination

Inevitably, the question whether procedural fairness requires cross-examination will only arise in those circumstances where the individual is entitled to an oral hearing. Where this is required it has been suggested that it carries with it an automatic right to question those who give evidence to the decision-maker (*R v Deputy Industrial Injuries Commissioner, ex parte Moore* [1965] 1 QB 456). This is, however, probably too great a generalisation. In *Bushell v Secretary of State for the Environment* [1981] AC 75, the House of Lords was not prepared to conclude that objectors to a new road scheme had any absolute right to question government experts when these appeared before the ensuing public inquiry. The House was mindful of the need not to 'over-judicialise' the procedure and was not convinced that, even in judicial proceedings, cross-examination was the only fair way of ascertaining relevant factual material. All depended on the circumstances of the particular case and whether, in that specific context, a fair hearing could be provided without 'insisting on observance of the procedures of a court of justice which professional lawyers alone are competent to operate effectively' (*per* Lord Diplock). The House concluded, therefore, that 'refusal by an inspector to allow a party to cross-examine orally at a local inquiry a person who had made statements of fact or expressed expert opinions is not unfair *per se*' (*ibid*).

Legal representation

The existence of a right to be legally represented before the decision-maker will be recognised only where the individual has a right to be heard orally and all the surrounding circumstances indicate that the hearing cannot be conducted fairly unless legal representation is allowed.

In *R v Board of Visitors Maze Prison, ex parte Hone and McCartan* [1988] 1 AC 379, it was argued that the right should extend to all prisoners appearing before Boards of Prison Visitors. The House of Lords rejected any such rigid rule. In its view the matter lay within the discretion of the decision-maker. The criteria to be taken into account in exercising this discretion had been explained previously in *R v Secretary of State for the Home Department, ex parte Tarrant* [1985] QB 251. These were as follows:

(a) the seriousness of the charge and the potential penalty;

(b) where any points of law were likely to arise;

(c) the capacity of the prisoner to present their own case;

(d) the complexity of the procedure;

(e) the need for reasonable speed in decision-making;

(f) the need for fairness between prisoners and between prisoners and prison officers.

With the exception of (f), these criteria would appear to be of relevance to decision-makers generally when the question of allowing legal representation or not falls to be decided. Hence, in those circumstances where a severe penalty may be imposed and difficult questions of law or procedure may be involved, the decision-maker should ponder carefully before refusing a request for representation. Any refusal must be based on careful consideration of the above criteria and their proper application to the facts of the case.

Reasons

Statutory requirements

A duty to give reasons may be imposed by statute. Such duty is imposed by the Tribunals and Inquiries Act 1992, s 10 on all those tribunals listed in Sched 1 to the Act. Where this is the case the reasons given should be 'proper, intelligible and adequate' (per Megaw J, *Re Poyser and Mills' Arbitration* [1964] 2 QB 467). If the reasons given are 'improper' they will 'reveal some flaw in the decision-making process which will be open to challenge on some ground other than the failure to give reasons' (e.g. irrelevancy) (per Lord Bridge, *Save Britain's Heritage v No. 1 Poultry Ltd* [1991] 1 WLR 153). If they are unintelligible 'this will be equivalent to giving no reasons at all' (*ibid*). Where the function is purely administrative, a relatively brief outline of the basis for the decision may suffice. Thus an immigration officer satisfied the obligation with the words 'I am not satisfied that you are genuinely seeking entry only for this limited period' (*R v Secretary of State for the Home Department, ex parte Swati* [1986] 1 WLR 477). Tribunals exercising judicial functions may be expected to give greater detail. Hence, in *R v Immigration Appeal Tribunal, ex parte Khan* [1983] QB 790, the view was that the tribunal should provide parties with sufficient information to show that the matter remitted to it had been duly considered and that this should be accompanied by the evidence for its conclusions.

Deficiency of reasons may not be a ground for judicial review *per se*. In the context of refusals of planning permission it has been held that such deficiency 'will only afford a ground for quashing the decision if the court is satisfied that the interests of the applicant have been substantially prejudiced by it' (*Save Britain's Heritage, supra*).

The requirements of fairness

Where there is no statutory obligation, the giving of reasons may be required by the duty to act fairly. The following cases provide some indication of the circumstances in which this may apply.

In *R v Civil Service Appeals Board, ex parte Cunningham* [1991] 4 All ER 310, the Board awarded the applicant £6,500 by way of compensation for his dismissal from the prison service. On the facts this was some £9,000 less than he might have expected from an industrial tribunal. No reasons for awarding the lower amount were given. All three members of the Court of Appeal felt that the Board had acted unfairly but reached this conclusion by different 'routes'. Lord Donaldson MR felt that the failure to give reasons contravened the applicant's legitimate expectation that, in a procedural sense, he would not be treated less fairly than those whose employment disputes would be dealt with before an industrial tribunal to which the statutory duty to give reasons in the Tribunals and Inquiries Act 1992 applied. McCowan LJ's view was that an obligation to give reasons followed from the fact that the Board had exercised a judicial function which was not subject to appeal. Leggett LJ also emphasised that the Board had made a judicial decision which affected the applicant's livelihood but which, in the absence of reasons, could not be subjected to judicial review: 'For it is only by judicial review that the board's award can be challenged; and without reasons neither the person dismissed nor the court can tell whether to apply for or to grant judicial review'. He further pointed out that the 'unexplained meagreness' of the award compelled an inference that the decision was irrational.

The issue of the right to reasons was considered subsequently by the House of Lords in ***R v Secretary of State for the Home Department, ex parte Doody*** [1993] 3 WLR 154, where it was decided that a mandatory life prisoner was entitled to reasons if the Minister decided to depart from the 'tariff' (the minimum term to be served) recommended by the trial judge. It was felt to be unfair that a prisoner given a mandatory life term should be treated any less favourably than a person sentenced to a specific term for which reasons would be given by the trial judge when the sentence was imposed. Other considerations which appeared to influence the decision in *Doody* were that 'tariff' decisions affected a fundamental freedom and that the giving of reasons would have no major adverse consequences on the functioning of the penal system or other public interest. It was also pointed out that the giving of reasons would provide the only 'means of detecting the kind of error which would entitle the court to intervene' (*per* Lord Mustill).

An attempt to extract some broader principles from *Cunningham* and *Doody* was made by the Divisional Court in ***R v Higher Education Funding Council, ex parte Institute of Dental Surgery*** [1994] 1 WLR 242. The applicants were aggrieved by the research rating given to them by the Council. This was lower than they had expected and, it was estimated, would result in a loss of research funding in the region of £270,000. No reasons had been given for the decision.

Sedley J felt that *Cunningham* and *Doody* could be used as authorities for the following two principal categories of cases in which fairness required the giving of reasons:

(a) where this was an obvious consequence of 'the nature of the process' and its effect on the person concerned – e.g. as in *Doody*, where the subject-matter was 'an interest so highly regarded by the law (for example, personal liberty) that fairness requires that reasons be given as of right' (see *R (on application Bourgass* v *Secretary for Justice, supra,* prisoner entitled to outline explanation for continued solitary confinement beyond the initial period of 72 hours);

(b) where there was 'something peculiar' or 'aberrant' about the decision which operated as a 'trigger factor' for the giving of reasons – e.g. as in *Cunningham* where the amount of compensation awarded appeared to be excessively low.

It was not felt, however, that the Funding Council's decision fell into either of these categories. Academic judgments were not such that their very 'nature and impact' called for reasons 'as a routine aspect of procedural fairness'.

The court felt it could not intervene simply because the decision had serious consequences for the applicants as this would have been tantamount to imposing a general duty to give reasons on all administrators ('a point to which the court . . . cannot go'). Nor was there anything so peculiar or aberrant about the decision so as to 'trigger' the reasons requirement.

Full protection of the rule may not be afforded, however, if the complainant has been engaged in work relating to the security or intelligence services (*R (on application of Tucker)* v *Director General of the National Crime Squad* [2003] EWCA Civ 2).

The rule is a recognised element of ECHR Art 6 (right to a fair trial) and was applied in *Glas Nadezhda EOOD v Bulgaria* (2007) 48 EHRR 817, where a public authority failed to give reasons for their refusal to grant a broadcasting licence.

The rule against bias

The general rule

A person empowered by law to make decisions having potentially detrimental consequences for the rights, interests or legitimate expectations of others should not act if they have any actual, financial or apparent interest in the subject-matter of the issue to be determined. Should this occur the decision will be tainted by bias and may be held to be void or of no legal effect. The law in this context is presaged on the maxims that 'no man should be judge in his own cause' (*Dr Bonham's Case, supra*) and that 'justice should not only be done but should manifestly and undoubtedly be seen to be done' (*R v Sussex Justices, ex parte McCarthy* [1924] 1 KB 256).

Actual bias

If the decision-maker has a preconceived personal bias in the outcome of the decision or consciously favours or disfavours one of the parties who may be affected by it, this may well amount to bad faith in addition to representing a blatant contravention of natural justice. Examples of this type of abuse are rare. 'It is necessary . . . to put on one side the very rare case where actual bias is shown to exist. Of course, if actual bias is proved, that is an end of the case; the person concerned must be disqualified' (*per* Lord Goff, *R v Gough* [1993] AC 646).

Financial bias

A decision-maker with a direct financial interest is disqualified and decisions made by the same are thereby rendered void. Actual bias need not be shown. The existence of the financial interest is sufficient. In *Dimes v Grand Junction Canal Proprietors* (1852) 3 HL Cas 759, a decision of the Lord Chancellor was set aside for bias because he had a financial shareholding in the canal company. It was emphasised that the finding of bias contained no inference that the Lord Chancellor had been 'in the remotest degree influenced by the interest that he had in this concern'. It was, however, 'of the last importance that the maxim no man is to be judge in his own cause should be held sacred' (*per* Lord Campbell).

The vitiating financial interest need not be substantial but it must be direct.

R v Hendon Rural District Council, ex parte Chorley [1933] 2 KB 696

In this case, a council granted planning permission for the development of a certain piece of land. Their decision was held to be invalid on the ground that one of the councillors who voted for the resolution was also an estate agent acting for the owners of the land in a prospective sale which was contingent on planning permission being granted.

A financial interest will not operate as a vitiating factor, therefore, if it is too remote. Hence two justices who were trustees of institutions (a hospital and a friendly society) which held bonds in Bradford Corporation were not disqualified from acting in a case in which the Corporation was involved (*R v Rand* (1866) LR 1 WB 230). In these circumstances a finding in favour of the Corporation could not have resulted in any discernible or tangible benefit for the justices.

The decision of the House of Lords in *R v Bow Street Stipendiary Magistrate, ex parte Pinochet Ugarte (No. 2)* [1999] 1 All ER 577, illustrated that a decision might also be quashed for bias where a decision-maker, although not shown to be actually biased or to have a direct stake in the decision, has some other direct interest in its outcome.

In November 1998, a five-member appellate committee of the House of Lords, including Lord Hoffmann, ruled that General Pinochet enjoyed no continuing immunity in respect of alleged crimes against humanity committed while Head of State of Chile and that it was open to the Secretary of State for the Home Department, therefore, to decide whether the General should be extradited to Spain under the Extradition Act 1989 for alleged offences against Spanish nationals during the period he was in office. During the proceedings leading to this decision, Amnesty International was given leave to put written and oral testimony to the House which was of significant prejudice to the General's case.

Within a matter of days, however, it emerged that Amnesty had close and long-standing links with both Lord and Lady Hoffmann. Lady Hoffmann had been in Amnesty's employ in an administrative capacity for over 20 years while Lord Hoffmann was currently a director of Amnesty International Charity Ltd. General Pinochet's lawyers responded by petitioning the House of Lords that the decision should be set aside or Lord Hoffmann's judgment be discounted.

Held:

(a) The House had jurisdiction to rescind or vary any of its earlier decisions where a party had been dealt with unfairly. A decision could not be reopened, however, simply because it was alleged to be wrong:

> In principle it must be that your Lordships, as the ultimate court of appeal, have power to correct any injustice caused by an earlier order of this House. There is no relevant statutory limitation on the jurisdiction of the House in this regard and therefore its inherent jurisdiction remains unfettered . . . However, it should be made clear that the House will not reopen any appeal save in circumstances where, through no fault of a party, he or she has been subjected to an unfair procedure . . . [T]here can be no question of [a] decision being varied or rescinded . . . just because it is thought that [it] is wrong (*per* Lord Browne-Wilkinson).

(b) A judge, including a member of the House of Lords, who had a direct interest, albeit non-pecuniary, in the outcome of a case was disqualified for bias:

> . . . although the cases have all dealt with automatic disqualification on grounds of pecuniary bias, there is no good reason in principle for so limiting automatic disqualification. The rationale of the whole rule is that a man cannot be a judge in his own cause. [I]f, as in the present case, the matter at issue does not relate to money or economic advantage but is concerned with the promotion of the cause, the rationale of disqualifying a judge applies just as much if the judge's decision will lead to the promotion of a cause in which the judge is involved together with one of the parties (*ibid*.).

(c) The decision of November 1999 should, therefore, be set aside and the issue reheard before a differently constituted House.

Apparent bias

The test of bias generally accepted as applicable in English law prior to the coming into effect of the Human Rights Act 1988 was that laid down by Lord Goff in *R v Gough* (*supra*).

[H]aving ascertained the relevant circumstances the court should ask itself whether . . . there was a real danger of bias on the part of the relevant member of the tribunal in question, in the sense that he might unfairly regard (or have unfairly regarded) with favour, or disfavour, the case of a party to the issue under consideration by him (*per* Lord Goff).

This was the test used to invalidate the controversial decision not to resume the inquest into the *Marchioness* disaster (*R* v *Inner West London Coroner, ex parte Dallaglio* [1994] 4 All ER 139). The coroner had described some of the relatives seeking the resumption as 'mentally unwell' and 'unhinged'. This led the Court of Appeal to conclude that 'there was a real danger that the coroner might have unfairly regarded with disfavour' the cases of those towards whom he had expressed these negative sentiments.

A real danger of bias required 'more than a minimal risk' but 'less than a probability'. To 'unfairly regard with disfavour' required that the decision-maker 'was predisposed or prejudiced against one party's case for reasons unconnected with the merits of the issue' (*per* Simon Brown LJ, *ex parte Dallaglio*).

The real danger test has been held to be applicable to the exercise of administrative as well as judicial powers (*R* v *Secretary of State for the Environment, ex parte Kirkstall Valley Campaign Ltd* [1996] 3 All ER 304). The test should, however, be applied more or less rigorously depending on the circumstances: 'what amounts to bias is not a fixed quantity but a function of the procedure under scrutiny and the events occurring in the course of it' (per Sedley J, *R* v *Manchester Metropolitan University, ex parte Nolan, supra*). Hence it was held that the decision of a local council could not be impugned for bias simply because a majority of councillors were predisposed to take a particular view by virtue of their party-political affiliations. It was inevitable in a pluralist democracy that party policy will influence the decisions of those elected to positions of authority. Parliament must have had this in its contemplation, therefore, when it conferred the powers in issue. Judicial intervention for bias in these circumstances would thus be incompatible with the intentions of the sovereign body and inimical to the process of decision-making in a democratic system of government (*R* v *Amber Valley District Council, ex parte Jackson* [1985] 1 WLR 298).

With the advent of the Human Rights Act 1998, and the requirement that domestic public authorities, including courts, should exercise their functions in accordance with the European Convention on Human Rights, the test of bias as explained in *Gough* has been subjected to a degree of linguistic modification. Domestic courts have sought to stress its strictly objective nature and compatibility with the test preferred by the Court of Human Rights in its jurisprudence relating to Art 6 (right to a fair trial), i.e. was there an objectively justified and legitimate reason for fearing a lack of partiality in the decision-maker (*McGonnell* v *United Kingdom* (2000) 30 EHRR 289).

The reconstructed 'real danger' test was set out by Chadwick LJ in *Taylor* v *Lawrence* [2001] EWCA Civ 119:

> Where actual bias has not been established the personal impartiality of the judge is to be presumed. The court then has to decide whether, on an objective appraisal, the material facts give rise to a legitimate fear that the judge might not have been impartial. If they do, the decision must be set aside. The court must ask itself whether the circumstances – and that includes all the circumstances which a fair minded and informed observer would have properly regarded as material, whether known to the appellants or not – would leave a fair minded and informed observer to conclude that there was a real danger that the judge was biased.

The *Gough* test as so modified has been approved by the House of Lords in a number of cases (see *Porter* v *Magill* [2001] UKHL 67 and *R (on application of Al Hasan)* v *Secretary of State for the Home Department* [2005] UKHL 13), and was applied in *Helow v Secretary of State for the Home Department* [2008] UKHL 62. Here the petitioner (claimant), a Palestinian activist, alleged bias against a judge who had refused to set aside an immigration decision not to grant her political asylum in the United Kingdom. The allegation of bias was founded on the judge's membership of the International Association of Jewish Lawyers and Jurists, whose magazine, circulated to all members, had published a series of anti-Palestinian articles. It was argued that a fair-minded and informed observer might have thought that the views put forward by the Association represented those of the judge or, alternatively, that the judge might, subconsciously, have been influenced by the magazine's content.

The House of Lords dismissed both contentions.

> It is no doubt possible to conceive of circumstances involving words or conduct so extreme that members might be expected to become aware of them and disassociate themselves by resignation if they did not approve or did not wish to approve of them. But the present material falls far short of involving such circumstances . . . Judges read a great deal of material which is designed to influence them, but which they are trained to analyse and to accept, reject, or use as appropriate. A person may well subscribe to or read publications in order to inform him or herself about views different to his or hers. The suggestion that mere membership gives rise in the eyes of a fair minded observer to a real possibility of unconscious influence, through some form of osmosis, by materials in the relevant association's periodical which would be available to a member is a blanket proposition of great potential width that I reject without hesitation (*per* Lord Mance).

The doctrine of legitimate expectation

Procedural expectations

As already indicated, it is now well established that the rules of natural justice should be observed in the exercise of a decision-making power which could have serious detrimental consequences for the rights or interests of the person affected. In more recent times the courts have refined this to mean that natural justice should be observed in circumstances where the individual has a legitimate expectation that this will be so. A legitimate expectation in this sense may be defined, therefore, as a legally enforceable procedural right. Such legitimate expectations or right may arise in a variety of ways.

First, this may result from an assurance given by the decision-maker that no decision will be made without prior consultation with, or hearing the representations of, the person affected. This element of the doctrine was applied in the following case.

Attorney-General for Hong Kong v Ng Yuen Shiu [1983] 2 AC 629

The complainant had entered Hong Kong illegally. Prior to being served with a deportation order he had been questioned by the authorities but had been given no proper opportunity to present his case in full. Previously, however, the Hong Kong authorities had given an undertaking that such persons would be 'interviewed' personally and that 'each case will be treated on its merits'. The Privy Council quashed the deportation order on the ground that the complainant had been given a legitimate expectation of a fair hearing and that this had not been honoured:

> when a public authority has promised to follow a certain procedure, it is in the interests of good administration that it should act fairly and should implement its promise, so long as implementation does not interfere with its statutory duty.

Second, a legitimate expectation may arise from the previous practice of the decision-maker. Thus, if it has been usual practice to give the person affected a hearing before exercising a particular power to decide, this may give an individual a legally enforceable expectation that they will be treated in the same way. Hence in *R v British Coal Corporation, ex parte Vardy* [1993] ICR 720, a decision to close several coal mines was quashed due to the corporation's failure to consult with miners and trade unions affected in accordance with established practice.

> The above two methods of creating procedural legitimate expectations were recognised by the House of Lords in the *GCHQ* case: 'Legitimate, or reasonable, expectation may arise either from an express promise given on behalf of a public authority or from the existence of a regular practice which the claimant can reasonably expect to continue' (*per* Lord Fraser).

Third, there are plentiful dicta to the effect that an expectation of being treated in accordance with natural justice may flow from the nature of the interest or benefit enjoyed by the individual.

The benefit or interest enjoyed must be one of substance so that it would be unfair to remove it without procedural fairness. Thus the holder of a licence on which a livelihood depends has a legitimate expectation of a hearing before any decision may be made not to renew or to revoke it (*McInnes v Onslow-Fane, supra*). In *R v Brent London Borough Council, ex parte Gunning* (1985) 84 LGR 168, it was held that the interest of parents in the provision of local education was sufficient to create a legitimate expectation that they would be consulted by the local education authority before it made any recommendations for the closure and amalgamation of any of its schools.

It should be noted also that a procedural legitimate expectation may be lost because of the behaviour of the person on whom the benefit has been bestowed. In *Cinnamond v British Airports Authority* [1980] 1 WLR 582, the Court of Appeal held that a number of private hire car drivers had no right to a hearing prior to a decision by the authority denying them access to Heathrow airport. They had repeatedly ignored airport by-laws by 'jumping' the queue of licensed hackney cabs to pick up passengers at the arrivals terminus and had charged such passengers exorbitant fares. Repeated warnings and prosecutions had failed to achieve any change of conduct. Shaw LJ concluded that 'the drivers had put themselves so far outside the limits of tolerable conduct as to disentitle themselves to expect any further representations on their part could have any influence or relevance'.

Substantive expectations

It is now also well established that assurances or the past practice of a public authority may create legitimate expectations which would appear to be more of a substantive rather than a procedural nature. Such substantive legitimate expectations may arise in the following circumstances:

(a) where a public body gives an assurance that it will not withdraw a certain substantive benefit but then seeks to resile on the assurance after it has been relied upon;

(b) where a public body seeks to depart from an existing policy which has guided its actions and decisions in a certain context.

Assurances

The leading case here is as follows.

R v North and East Devon Health Authority, ex parte Coughlan [1999] LGR 703

The case centred around an assurance given to a group of disabled persons living in local authority accommodation that they would not be moved from that accommodation and would be allowed to remain there 'for as long as they chose'. The Court of Appeal held that the assurance bound the authority. It was, however, at pains to point out that this did not set aside the general rule that an authority must be free to change a decision where it is in the public interest to do so. Rather, it represented the recognition of an exception where, on the facts of a particular case, the requirements of fairness clearly overrode the authority's public policy concerns. The crucial facts in the case before them which persuaded the Court of Appeal that the authority should honour its assurance were:

(i) the promise had been given on a number of occasions and in precise terms to a group of severely disabled people and related to what would be their home for the rest of their lives;

(ii) the representation was unqualified and had been relied on by those to whom it had been made;

(iii) a decision not to honour the promise would be equivalent to a breach of promise in private law;

(iv) no overriding public policy reasons for departing from the promise had been provided by the authority;

(v) requiring the authority to honour its promise would not place it in breach of other statutory or common law duties.

The extent of the protection offered by this aspect of the doctrine was further developed by the decision in *R (on application of Bibi and Al-Nashed)* v *Newham London Borough Council* [2001] EWCA Civ 607, where it was stated that, although detrimental reliance on a promise would normally be required for legal enforcement of a substantive expectation, this was not an absolute rule. In appropriate circumstances fairness could render an assurance binding on an authority despite the absence of such reliance.

Policy

Most decision-making powers entrusted to central and local government authorities are exercised in accordance with the policy rules formulated to give effect to national and local political priorities in those areas of government activity in which the powers operate. Ignoring for the moment the political background and merits of such policies, this has the obvious advantage of minimising arbitrariness and uncertainty in the administrative process. Accordingly, albeit that an individual may not support the policy being implemented in a particular matter, he/she is at least ensured of being treated in the same way as those others in similar circumstances. Thus, for example, if a person appears to fall within the criteria laid down by policy rules in order to qualify for a particular government benefit, and all others in a similar position have been successful in their applications, he/she has a legitimate expectation that his/her application will also succeed and that only a good and convincing explanation from the authority will prevent this from being so. Such standards of good practice in decision-making have, in this way, come to be regarded as an integral part of the duty to act fairly.

> The individual has a public law right to have his or her case considered under whatever policy the executive sees fit to adopt . . . a decision-maker must follow this published policy unless there are good reasons for not doing so (Lord Dyson, *R (on application of Lumba)* v *Secretary of State for the Home Department* [2011] UKSC 12).

The doctrine was applied in *R (on application of Rashid)* v *Secretary of State for the Home Department* [2005] EWCA Civ 744 in which it was found that the applicant had a legitimate expectation that his application for refugee status would be dealt with according to the appropriate Home Office policy and in the same way as those of other applicants whose circumstances were identical to his own.

The above rule was thought originally to extend also to decisions made in breach of policy rules of which the complainant had no knowledge when the error was made. For some, however, the idea that a legally enforceable expectation could be based on policy rules which the individual concerned had never heard of went to the very boundaries of legal logicality. This, in turn, led to a change of approach for cases such as these. Accordingly, the current position appears to be that, while such decisions remain subject to judicial review, this is better understood as being based on the rule of law principle that, in the public interest of the highest standards of public administration, decision-making powers should be exercised in compliance with the requirements of certainty and consistency (*R (on application Mandalia* v *Secretary of State for the Home Department* [2015] UKSC 59).

Beyond this it is unlikely that the doctrine may be used to enforce general political commitments or promises made by politicians or made by political parties in their election manifestos.

> Even if we accepted that the relevant ministerial statements had the effect of a promise to hold a referendum in respect of the Lisbon Treaty, such a promise would not in our view give rise to a legitimate expectation enforceable in public law, such that the courts could intervene to prevent the expectation being defeated by a change of mind concerning the holding of a referendum. The subject-matter, nature and context of a promise of this kind place it in the realm of politics, not of the courts, and the question whether the government should be held to such a promise is a political rather than a legal matter *(per* Richards LJ, *R (on application of Wheeler)* v *Office of the Prime Minister [2008] EWHC 1409 (Admin))*.

The public interest

Albeit that the criterion for the recognition of a substantive legitimate expectation would appear to be satisfied, it may not be given effect if outweighed by substantial countervailing considerations of public policy.

In *R (on application of Naik)* v *Secretary of State for the Home Department* [2011] EWCA Civ 1546, the claimant was a prominent Muslim academic who had been refused permission to enter the United Kingdom to fulfil a number of public speaking engagements. The decision was taken in the exercise of the Minister's statutory power to refuse entry permission to any person whose presence in the state was deemed not to be conducive to the public good.

The claimant's argument was that, as he had previously, and on a number of occasions, been allowed to enter the United Kingdom for similar purposes, this gave him a legitimate expectation that the issue of whether he posed any threat to public safety and security had been concluded in his favour and that he would, therefore, continue to be allowed into the country to fulfil his public speaking activities. The Court of Appeal's view was that:

(a) the mere fact that the claimant had been allowed to enter the United Kingdom on a number of occasions did not mean it had been decided once and for all that he posed no threat to public safety and order;

(b) the Home Secretary could not be constrained by the doctrine of legitimate expectation or any other common law doctrine from exercising his/her power to protect public safety as appeared to be required from time to time by the circumstances and exigencies of the moment.

Beyond this, no legitimate expectation of a particular benefit may be founded on a government policy which has been revoked and which the claimant was unaware of when it existed and, therefore, could not have relied upon. In *Rahman v Secretary of State for the Home Department* [2011] EWCA Civ 814, the claimant, who had no leave to remain in the United Kingdom, challenged the Home Secretary's decision to deport him, his wife, and their two children to their 'home' state of Bangladesh. The challenge was based on the right to family life in ECHR Art 8 and particularly on the government policy, operated between 1999 and 2008, that, as a general rule, the power of deportation should not be used against families with young children who had lived in the United Kingdom for seven years or more. The claimant's challenge was rejected on the grounds that:

- although the claimant and his family had lived in the United Kingdom for more than seven years, his application for leave to remain had not been made until 2009;
- the seven-year policy rule had been revoked in 2008;
- the claimant had not been aware of the policy when it existed.

Outrageous unfairness

Modern case-law suggests unfairness, although normally concerned with procedural failings, may amount to an abuse of power in the substantive sense, and without any significant procedural error or breach of legitimate expectation, where a decision 'is so outrageously unfair that it should not be allowed to stand' (Simon Brown LJ, *R v Inland Revenue Commissioners, ex parte Unilever* [1996] STC 681). Some political uncertainty exists, however, as to whether the principle represents a free-standing ground of judicial review or is merely a euphemism for a particular species of irrationality.

In the *Unilever* case itself the abuse was found to have been committed where the Inland Revenue over a period of 20 years, and on some 30 occasions, decided not to enforce time-limits on claims by Unilever for tax relief. On a subsequent occasion, and without warning or explanation, and in circumstances where relief would normally have been granted for a timely application, the time limit was enforced. The abuse may also be seen from the facts of *R (on application of Rashid) v Secretary of State for the Home Department* [2005] EWCA Civ 744, where the claimant asked for his refusal of political asylum to be reconsidered. The initial refusal was found to have been due to the department's failure to apply the correct policy rules. The department then delayed so long in dealing with the reconsideration claim that, by the time the decision was made (three years later), the claimant no longer qualified as the rules had been changed.

Summary

The chapter explains the relationship between the power of judicial review and those other fundamental legal doctrines of the British constitution. It also sets out the more detailed legal rules developed in the ordinary courts of law for the regulation of the exercise of powers by government departments, bodies, agencies and officials.

References

Lewis (2004) *Judicial Remedies in Public Law* (2nd edn), London: Sweet & Maxwell.

De Smith (1995) *Judicial Review of Administrative Action* (5th edn), London: Stevens.

De Smith, Woolf and Jowell (2002) *Principles of Judicial Review* (6th edn), London: Sweet & Maxwell.

Wade and Forsyth (2004) *Administrative Law* (7th edn), Oxford University Press.

Further reading

Cane (2011) *Administrative Law* (8th edn), Oxford: Oxford University Press, Ch. 1.

Elliot (2016) *From Heresy to Orthodoxy: Substantive Legitimate Expectations in English Public Law,* Legal Studies Research Paper, Series Paper No 5/2016, University of Cambridge Faculty of Law.

Fenwick and Phillipson (2016) *Text Cases and Materials on Public Law and Human Rights (4th edn),* London: Routledge-Cavendish, Ch. 1.

Leyland and Anthony (2016) *Administrative Law* (8th edn), Oxford: Oxford University Press.

15

Judicial review: applications for, exclusion of, and exclusivity

Objectives

After reading this chapter you should:

1. Know the process and requirements for making an application for judicial review.

2. Be aware of the remedies available to an applicant and the abuses of power to which these are applicable.

3. Appreciate the meaning, purpose and effect of the statutory devices for the exclusion of judicial review.

4. Understand the principle of exclusivity and the restriction of applications for judicial review to abuses of power in the public regulatory sphere of government activity.

Applying for judicial review

Introduction

Objective 1

With judicial review, the party bringing the proceedings is the applicant. The main purpose of the proceedings will be to ask the court to consider the legal validity (*vires*) of the actions or decisions of a public authority so that, if any of these are found to be unlawful, they may have no detrimental consequences, legal or otherwise, for the person(s) affected.

The procedure

The main procedural principles for applying for judicial review are contained in the Senior Courts Act 1981, s 31, Pt 54 of the Civil Procedure Rules 2016, and in the accompanying Practice Directions. Such applications are heard generally in the Administrative Court which forms part of the Queen's Bench Division of the High Court.

Pre-Action Protocol

This was introduced in 2002. The purpose of the Protocol process and its requirements is to encourage both claimants and defendants to consider whether the dispute can be dealt with by a means other than formal litigation.

The parties should consider whether some form of alternative dispute resolution would be more suitable than litigation, and if so to endeavour to agree which form to adopt . . . The courts take the view that litigation should be a last resort and that claims should not be issued prematurely when a settlement is still actively being explored. Parties are warned if the Protocol is not followed . . . then the court must have regard to such conduct when determining costs (Ministry of Justice, Pre-Action Protocol, 2008, para 3.1).

For this purpose, and the assistance of the parties, the Protocol sets out a code of good practice and the steps which should normally be taken before making a claim. No prescriptions are laid down as to how such alternative settlement should be pursued. The Protocol does, however, identify a number of procedures which could be used. These include the various ombudsman schemes, 'early neutral evaluation' by an independent third party, and mediation.

The Protocol does not apply in urgent situations as, for example, in asylum and deportation cases, where the claimant may be about to be removed from the United Kingdom.

Applying for leave

Should no alternative to legal proceedings be possible, the applicant begins by applying for 'permission' (previously referred to as 'leave') to apply for judicial review (r 54(1)) to a single High Court judge. The decision is taken on the basis of written submissions from both parties. Where permission is refused, the applicant may request that the decision be reconsidered at a later oral hearing of which the respondent should be given notice and opportunity to appear. An application must be made 'promptly' and within three months from the date when the grounds for the application first arose (s 31(7)). The court has a discretion to accept out-of-time applications where there is 'good reason' for doing so (per Lord Goff, *R v Dairy Produce Quotas Tribunal, ex parte Caswell* [1990] 2 AC 738). Thus an out-of-time application involving a 'strong public interest', i.e. the legality of selling copies of electoral registers to commercial enterprises, was accepted in *R (on application of Robertson) v City of Wakefield Metropolitan Borough Council* [2001] EWCA Admin 915. Applications made within three months but not promptly may also be rejected (*R v Independent Television Commission, ex parte TV Ltd The Times,* 30 December 1991). An appeal against a refusal of an application for leave may be made to the Court of Appeal.

Standing or sufficient interest

Permission will not be granted unless the applicant can show that he/she has 'sufficient interest' in the subject-matter of the complaint (s 31(3)). The test appears to have two elements.

First the applicant must establish that he/she has an 'arguable case', i.e. that an abuse of power is a 'real as opposed to theoretical possibility' (per Lord Donaldson MR, *R v Secretary of State for the Home Department, ex parte Swati* [1986] 1 WLR 477). This excludes 'obviously hopeless cases' but does not impose a particularly demanding evidential threshold. Thus it is not necessary that a *prima facie* case of abuse must be established: 'The threshold, if one excludes hopeless cases, is fairly low' (per Nolan J, *R v Inspector of Taxes, ex parte Kissane* [1986] 2 All ER 37).

Second, the applicant must be able to show that they have 'standing' or *locus standi* in relation to the alleged abuse of power, i.e. that some right, interest or legitimate expectation deserving of legal protection has been detrimentally affected or that the alleged abuse of power appears to be of such severity or substance that any member of the public or community served by the public body in question is justified in bringing it before the courts.

If permission is granted, the sufficiency of the applicant's interest may be considered again when the full application for judicial review goes for trial. At this stage the proceedings are *inter partes* (literally 'between the parties') with the result that the court is in possession of all the relevant facts and submissions of law. It thus has a fuller and clearer perspective of the nature and extent both of the alleged abuse and the extent of the applicant's interest in it.

> There may be simple cases in which it can be seen at the earliest stage that the person applying for judicial review has no interest at all or no sufficient interest to support the application . . . But in other cases this will not be so. In these it will be necessary to consider the powers or duties in law of those against whom the relief is asked, the position of the applicants in relation to those powers and duties and to the breach of those said to have been committed. In other words, the question of sufficient interest, in such cases, cannot be considered in the abstract . . . it must be taken together with the legal and factual context (*per* Lord Wilberforce, *R v Inland Revenue Commissioners, ex parte National Federation of Self-Employed and Small Businesses Ltd* [1982] AC 617).

Thus an applicant who has been accorded standing at the *ex parte* leave stage may find that recognition withdrawn when the substantive application for review is made.

Clearly, where an application shows that a party's interests have been particularly affected (i.e. more than the interest of others), this will probably be sufficient to satisfy the standing requirement. The test is, however, not so strict. Hence, there are many examples of ratepayers and community charge payers being held to have standing to challenge spending decisions which affected entire communities (*R v Waltham Forest London Borough Council, ex parte Baxter* [1988] QB 419: decision to impose general rate increase; *Prescott v Birmingham Corporation* [1955] Ch 210: decision to grant old-age pension concessionary travel on local public transport).

There are also numerous dicta to the effect that a person no more affected by an abuse than any other member of the general public 'may be allowed to seek judicial review where there is a serious issue of public importance which the court should examine' (Lewis, *Judicial Remedies in Public Law*). Were it not so, then an individual would be unable to challenge an abuse of power with national rather than purely individual or local implications.

> I regard it as a matter of high constitutional principle that if there is good grounds for supposing that a government department or public authority is transgressing the law . . . in a way which offends or injures thousands of Her Majesty's subjects, then any one of those offended or injured can draw to it the attention of the courts of law and seek to have the law enforced (*per* Lord Denning MR, *R v Greater London Council, ex parte Blackburn* [1976] 1 WLR 550).

Thus, in *R v HM Treasury, ex parte Smedley* [1985] QB 657, a taxpayer had standing to challenge the validity of an Order in Council approving a supplementary budget for the European Community.

In line with this flexible and liberal approach towards standing, it is now clear that interest or cause groups have standing to represent or protect their particular sectional concerns. This remains the case notwithstanding that the group is an unincorporated association which cannot sue or be sued in private law as it has no private rights to defend (*R v North West Traffic Commissioners, ex parte Brake* [1995] NPC 167). Both the Child Poverty Action Group and the National Association of Citizens' Advice Bureaux have been held to have standing to challenge social security regulations (*R v Secretary of State for Social Services, ex parte Child Poverty Action Group* [1989] 3 WLR 1116). In another case, a public sector union was held to have sufficient interest to challenge a decision of a local authority not to pay those employees who had taken part in a 'day of action' (*R v Liverpool City Corporation, ex parte Ferguson* [1985] IRLR 501).

The approach of the courts appears to be that if a substantial issue of public law is raised by an established, genuine and respected interest group, it should be accorded standing. This was the view expressed in *R v Inspectorate of Pollution, ex parte Greenpeace Ltd (No. 2)* [1994] 4 All ER 329, where Greenpeace was given standing to challenge a decision authorising British Nuclear Fuels to discharge radioactive waste from its plant at Sellafield in order to test its new thermal oxide reprocessing plant (THORP). In recognising the sufficiency of Greenpeace's interest, Otton J said:

> I have not the slightest reservation that Greenpeace is an entirely responsible and respected body with a genuine concern for the environment . . . It seems to me that if I were to deny standing to Greenpeace, those it represents would not have an effective way to bring issues before the court.

A similar rationale for according standing to an interest group was given by Rose LJ in *R v Secretary of State for Foreign and Commonwealth Affairs, ex parte World Development Movement Ltd* [1995] 1 All ER 611. The court felt that the applicants were an internationally recognised and widely supported group which for over 20 years had been campaigning 'by democratic means to improve the quantity and quality of British Aid to other countries'. As such they had sufficient interest to seek review of a government decision to fund the Pergau dam project in Malaysia.

> It cannot be said that the applicants are 'busybodies', 'cranks' or 'mischief-makers'. They are a non-partisan pressure group concerned with misuse of aid money. If there is a public law error, it is difficult to see how else it could be challenged and corrected except by such an applicant.

Substantial difference test

For many years the common law position was that a court could refuse an application for judicial review where the facts were such that the outcome for the application would almost *inevitably* have been the same regardless of whether or not the authority had abused its powers in some way. This was changed by the Criminal Justice and Courts Act 2015, section 84 which amended section 31 of the Senior Courts Act 1981. This created a less demanding test, allowing, as it does, the High Court to refuse judicial review if it considers it *highly likely* 'that the outcome for the applicant would not have been substantially different if the conduct complained of had not occurred'. In the main, this requires the court to determine whether the authority's action or decision would *most probably* have been exactly the same even if the abuse, e.g. failure to give the person a fair hearing, had not been committed.

> for example, a public authority might fail to notify a person of the existence of a consultation where they should have, and that person does not provide a response where they otherwise might have. If, however, that person's likely arguments had been raised by others and the public authority had taken a decision properly in the light of those arguments, then the court might conclude that the failure was highly unlikely to have affected the outcome (Criminal Justice and Courts Act 2015, Explanatory Notes, para 632).

This is, however, qualified by the exception that even in those circumstances an application for judicial review may still be permitted or granted where the court considers it appropriate to do so 'for reasons of exceptional public interest'.

The changes apply also to the review jurisdiction of the Upper Tribunal. The principle justification advanced for them was to reduce the amount of public finance devoted to the judicial process.

Also required by the 2015 Act is that 'no application for judicial review will be granted leave unless the applicant has . . . provided the court with any information about . . . the service, nature and extent of financial resources available, or likely to be available, to the applicant to meet liabilities arising in connection with the application' (s 85(1) amending s 31(3) of the Senior Courts Act 1981).

The effect of this is to remove the discretion from both the High Court and the Upper Tier Tribunal to grant leave to apply for judicial review unless and until such financial information as may be specified has been produced.

Such further barrier to open access to justice would appear to engage both the right to a fair hearing (ECHR, Art 6) and the right to privacy of personal information (ECHR, Art 8). It would appear also to be inconsistent with traditional common law requirements in these matters. For these reasons, the requirement has not been met with universal approval amongst those involved in the workings of the legal process.

> The requirement to disclose personal information in order to secure access to the court has been expressly recognised by the Court of Appeal as having a chilling effect on claimants' willingness to bring judicial review proceedings precisely because it is so invasive of privacy (*R (on application of Garner)* [2010] EWCA Civ 1006, Sullivan LJ).

Discovery of documents

An applicant for judicial review may apply for, but has no right to, discovery of documents. Where an application for discovery is made the matter lies within the discretion of the court:

> . . . discovery should not be ordered unless and until the court is satisfied that the evidence reveals reasonable grounds for believing that there has been a breach of public duty: and it should be limited to documents strictly relevant to the issue which emerges from the affidavits (*per* Lord Scarman, the *IRC* case).

Discovery will not be ordered to test the accuracy of an affidavit unless there is evidence before the court to suggest that the affidavit is unreliable or misleading (*R v Secretary of State for the Environment, ex parte Doncaster Borough Council* [1990] COD 441). Nor will it be ordered merely 'in the hope that something might turn up' (*ibid.*).

Cross-examination

Most of the evidence in review proceedings is submitted to the court in the form of affidavits (sworn written statements) and not through oral testimony. Cross-examination may be permitted, however, for the purpose of clarification or for disposing of factual inconsistencies between the parties. This will be the exception rather than the rule and should only occur 'where the justice of the particular case so requires' (*per* Lord Diplock, *O'Reilly* v *Mackman* [1983] 2 AC 237).

Remedies

Objective 2

A successful applicant for judicial review may be awarded any one or a combination of the following remedies: a quashing order (previously *certiorari*), a mandatory order (previously *mandamus*) or a prohibiting order (prohibition) (the prerogative orders), or an injunction or declaration. An award of damages may be made in conjunction with one of the above in appropriate circumstances (see below). The prerogative orders are entirely public law remedies and may only be awarded through an application for judicial review. Both the injunction and the declaration are, however, also private law remedies and may be awarded in ordinary civil proceedings (i.e. other than applications for judicial review).

In review proceedings the award of a remedy is entirely at the discretion of the court. This means that even though a ground for judicial review may be established, the applicant may still not be awarded a remedy. Thus relief may be refused because of, *inter alia,* the applicant's unmeritorious or unreasonable behaviour (***Cinnamond v British Airports Authority*** [1980] 1 WLR 582), delay in commencing proceedings (*R v Aston University, ex parte Roffey* [1969] 2 QB 538) or because of the damage that might be done to the public interest in administrative efficiency. Hence, in *R v Secretary of State for Social Services, ex parte Association of Metropolitan Authorities* [1986] 1 All ER 164, the court refused to quash social security regulations which were procedurally *ultra vires* following the Minister's failure to consult with certain prescribed organisations (i.e. those representative of local authorities). To have granted relief, it was felt, would have caused serious administrative problems for the majority of authorities which had already implemented the regulations, not least because all applications for benefit decided under them would have had to be reconsidered.

Quashing and prohibiting orders

A quashing order quashes, i.e. renders void from the outset, a decision which was *ultra vires* the power of the decision-making body or made in breach of the rules of natural justice. A prohibiting order prevents a public body or official from taking any *ultra vires* action or decision.

Although authority exists for the view that such orders were restricted to judicial decisions affecting the 'rights of subjects' (*R v Electricity Commissioners, ex parte London Electricity Joint Committee* [1924] 1 KB 171), it is now generally accepted that the remedies go to both administrative and judicial decisions having detrimental consequences for an individual's rights, interests or legitimate expectations (*R v Hillingdon Borough Council, ex parte Royco Homes* [1974] 1 QB 720).

The remedies will not issue against the Crown specifically but are available against Ministers of the Crown. This is not a serious limitation since most statutory powers of government are conferred on Secretaries of State rather than on the Crown by name. It was generally believed that *certiorari* did not lie in relation to *ultra vires* subordinate legislation (*R v Hastings Board of Health* (1865) 6 B& S 401). There is, however, some uncertainty on this point as the remedy was used to quash regulations in *R v Secretary of State for Health, ex parte United States Tobacco International Inc* [1992] QB 353.

Mandatory orders

A mandatory order (*mandamus*) lies to compel a body to perform or fulfil a public law duty which has been imposed upon it by statute or common law. The remedy will issue where there has been a refusal or unreasonable delay in performing the duty in question (*R v Secretary of State for the Home Department, ex parte Phansopkar* [1976] QB 606). As a general rule the applicant should have requested performance before the order is applied. However, both the request and refusal may be construed from the circumstances.

The duty in question must be reasonably specific. Hence, where the extent and mode of compliance with a duty is a matter of policy and the availability of resources, a mandatory order would appear to be inappropriate. Alleged failures in such cases may be remedied at the political level, e.g. criticism in Parliament and media. Such 'political' duties would include that laid on the Secretary of State for Education by the Education Act 1944, s 1:

> to promote the education of the people of England and Wales and to progressive development of institutions devoted to that purpose and to secure the effective execution by local authorities . . . of the national policy for providing a varied and comprehensive educational service in each area.

The need for specificity does not mean that the duty must be express. Hence, while the mandatory order does not lie to order the performance of a power, it may issue to require that the discretionary element of a decision-making power be exercised according to law (e.g. on the basis of relevant considerations and for authorised purposes). This may be seen from the facts of the following case.

R v Hounslow London Borough Council, ex parte Pizzey [1977] 1 WLR 58

The applicant had applied to the Borough Council to have premises registered under the Public Health Act 1936 as a common lodging house. The authority, however, refused to consider her application. *Mandamus* then issued on the basis that it was implicit in the grant of a power to decide that the body would apply its discretion to the facts of each case.

A mandatory order does not lie against the Crown but, as with the other prerogative orders, may be used where the duty is cast upon a named Minister or official. In its discretion the court may also refuse the order where the 'authority is doing all that it honestly and honourably can to meet the statutory obligation, and that its failure . . . arises really out of circumstances over which it has no control' (*R v Bristol Corporation, ex parte Hendry* [1974] 1 WLR 498). Albeit that a breach of duty is established, *mandamus* may also be refused if the court feels that a more appropriate alternative remedy is available – e.g. a default power whereby the enabling statute enables the appropriate minister to give 'such directions as to the exercise . . . of the duty as appear to him to be expedient' (Education Act 1944, s 68).

Failure to comply with a mandatory order amounts to a contempt of court for which the offending body, e.g. local authority, may be fined (*Re Cook's Application* (1986) 1 NIJB 64) or its members imprisoned (*R v Poplar Municipal Borough Council (No. 2)* [1922] 1 KB 95).

Injunction

Injunctions may be mandatory or prohibitory. A mandatory injunction requires the party to whom it is addressed to take some action to redress an unlawful act. In *Attorney-General v Bastow* [1957] 1 QB 514, a mandatory injunction was issued to remove caravans from land which had been put there without planning permission. A prohibitory injunction may issue to:

- restrain *ultra vires* actions;
- restrain breaches of statutory duties;
- restrain repeated breaches of the criminal law (*Attorney-General v Sharp*, see below);
- restrain a public nuisance, e.g. repeated obstruction of the highway.

Where a party seeks an injunction against a public body other than in an application for judicial review, it must be shown that there has been interference with a public right 'such that some private right of his is at the same time interfered with' or 'where no private right is interfered with . . . the plaintiff, in respect of his public right, suffers special damage peculiar to himself from the interference with the public right' (*per* Buckley J, *Boyce* v *Paddington Borough Council* [1903] 1 Ch 109). A party seeking an injunction in an application for judicial review must satisfy the test of sufficient interest.

An injunction may not issue against the Crown in civil proceedings or against an officer of the Crown 'if the effect . . . would be to give any relief against the Crown which could not have been obtained in proceedings against the Crown' (Crown Proceedings Act 1947, s 21(2)). This does not impose any barrier to the use of injunctions against a Minister where the power, usually in statutory form, is conferred on them by name (*M* v *Home Office* [1994] 1 AC 377).

Declaratory judgments

In its present form the declaration is a statutory remedy introduced by the Rules of Court of 1883 made under the Judicature Acts 1873–75. Like the injunction, it is not a purely public law remedy and is used extensively in some areas of private law.

The perhaps peculiar feature of the declaration is that it has no coercive force but simply defines and states the legal rights and obligations of the parties to the proceedings. This, however, has proved to be a great advantage as it means that the remedy is available not just against Ministers named in empowering statutes but against the Crown itself. As a result of the Crown's traditional legal immunity, the coercive remedies already mentioned do not issue. Hence, in review proceedings against the Crown, the declaration is the appropriate remedy.

The declaration's lack of coercive force has not had detrimental consequences for its effectiveness. If an action or decision of a public body is declared to be unlawful this is normally sufficient to ensure that the offending act is rectified. There are few modern examples of a public body refusing to comply with terms of a declaratory judgment (*Webster* v *Southwark Borough Council* [1983] QB 698).

The declaration is available for review of all types of decision and action, whether taken in the exercise of administrative, judicial or legislative powers.

As a general rule, a court (in its discretion) will refuse to make a declaration where the complaint raises a purely hypothetical issue. Hence, it was refused in *Blackburn* v *Attorney-General* [1971] 1 WLR 1037, where it was alleged that it would be unlawful for the government to sign the Treaty of Rome as this would involve an irreversible surrender of the sovereignty of the Westminster Parliament.

Damages

An award of damages may be made to an applicant for judicial review but only in conjunction with one of the other remedies. Also, the applicant must be able to show that 'such damages could have been awarded to him in an action begun by him by writ at the time of the making of the application' (Senior Courts Act 1981, s 31(4)) – i.e. where the abuse of power by the authority interfered with a private or actionable public law right of the applicant.

Also, where an application for judicial review is misconceived because it is concerned with the enforcement of private rather than public law rights, the court has a discretion to allow the proceedings to continue as if they had been begun by writ. For the applicant, who then becomes the plaintiff, this avoids the expense and delay which would be occasioned if the review proceedings were struck out and had to be recommenced by ordinary private law procedure.

Habeas corpus

The prerogative writ of habeas corpus issues to secure the release of a person who has been detained unlawfully. It has its own special procedure and is not sought, therefore, through an application for judicial review.

An application for the writ may be made by the detainee or, if this is not possible, by some other person on their behalf. The application is made to the Divisional Court *ex parte* (i.e. without notice to the other side) supported by the grounds in the form of an affidavit. If a *prima facie* case is shown notice will be served on the 'gaoler' (in modern times usually the Secretary of State for the Home Department or a prison governor) specifying the date and place where the merits of the case will be heard. It is for the gaoler to prove the lawfulness of the detention. If this is not done the writ issues *ex debito justiciae,* i.e. as of right and not as a matter of judicial discretion.

Habeas corpus will issue for jurisdictional errors only – in particular:

- simple *ultra vires* (see *ex parte Hopkins* (1891) 61 LJ QB 640);
- non-existence of a jurisdictional fact or preconditional circumstances (see *R v Secretary of State for the Home Department, ex parte Khawaja* [1984] AC 74);
- no evidence;
- error of law.

It will not issue, therefore, for alleged procedural unfairness, abuse of discretion (e.g. irrelevancy) or unreasonableness. The sole concern of the court is the existence of a power to detain.

It follows from this that habeas corpus may not be used to question the validity of a decision which preceded the exercise of the power to detain. Hence, if a prospective immigrant is refused leave to enter the United Kingdom and is then detained pending deportation, the validity of the refusal of leave may be tested in an application for judicial review but not by way of habeas corpus (*R v Secretary of State for the Home Department, ex parte Muboyayi* [1991] 3 WLR 442).

In relatively modern times the writ has been used to determine the validity of detention:

- pending extradition (*Oskar v Australia* [1988] AC 366);
- pending the removal of illegal immigrants (*Azam v Secretary of State for the Home Department* [1974] AC 18);
- pending deportation (*R v Governor of Brixton Prison, ex parte Soblen* [1963] 2 QB 243);
- pending the return of fugitive offenders (*R v Governor of Pentonville Prison, ex parte Osman* [1990] 1 WLR 277);
- on remand in custody (*R v Governor of Armly Prison, ex parte Ward, The Times,* 23 November 1990);
- by the police for questioning (*R v Holmes, ex parte Sherman* [1981] 2 All ER 612);
- under the mental health legislation (*TTM v London Borough of Hackney* [2011] EWCA Civ 4).

In those cases in which an application for habeas corpus is resisted on grounds that the person or authority against whom the writ is sought no longer has control over the detainee, the writ may still be issued where this is felt justified on the material before the court 'to test the truth' of such claims (*Barnardo v Ford* (1892) AC 326; *R v Secretary of State for Home*

Affairs, ex parte O'Brien [1923] 2 KB 361), 'or that there are reasonable grounds on which it may be concluded that the respondent will be able to exert that control' (Lord Kerr, *Rahmatullah* v *Secretary of State for Foreign and Commonwealth Affairs* [2012] UKSC 48). Here, the Minister attempted to resist the issue of a writ sought in respect of a British national who had been arrested by British forces in Iraq but later handed over to the Americans and transferred to their detention facility at Begram Airbase in Afghanistan. The court accepted the applicant's contention that the British Secretary of State either retained a sufficient degree of control over him to bring about his release or at least the circumstances were such that there must be some doubt and uncertainty concerning the Minister's claims that this was not the case.

As to the legality of the applicant's detention, and for a period of seven years after the war in Iraq had ended, the court was particularly exercised by considerations that:

- the American military authorities did not appear to have complied with some important aspects of the Geneva Convention;

- the British government had not been formally consulted about the transfer to Afghanistan;

- in 2010 an American Detainee Review Board had decided that the applicant was not an 'enduring security threat' and that his continued detention was no longer necessary.

Relator proceedings

The Attorney-General has the prerogative power to commence private or public law proceedings against any person or body whose unlawful activities would appear to be injurious to the public interest. Since the Crown is responsible for ensuring that the law is obeyed and that power is not abused, the question of standing does not arise. The Attorney always has standing to litigate for the general public benefit.

Example

An example of the Attorney-General enforcing the public interest occurred in *Attorney-General* v *Sharp* [1931] 1 Ch 121. The defendant had been prosecuted 48 times for operating bus services without a licence. The business was so profitable he had carried on regardless in flagrant breach of the relevant regulations which sought to impose certain minimum standards for the protection of the public. Eventually proceedings for an injunction were brought by the Attorney-General to enforce compliance with the law on pain of imprisonment for contempt of court.

The Attorney-General may also give leave for his name to be joined in proceedings instigated by an individual. This will tend to occur where proceedings are believed to be in the public interest but the individual's personal standing may be insufficient to bring the alleged abuse before the court. In theory the proceedings are then brought by the Attorney-General 'at the relation' or request of the individual. The Attorney has a discretion whether to give such leave. There is authority for the view that his decisions in this context are non-justiciable (*Gouriet* v *Union of Post Office Workers* [1978] AC 435). The use of the Attorney's name avoids all problems of standing albeit that for all practical purposes, 'the actual conduct of proceedings is entirely in the hands of the relator who is responsible for the costs of the action' (*per* Lord Denning MR, *McWhirteR* v *IBA* [1973] QB 629).

The remedies sought in a relator action will be the injunction or the declaration. Where such proceedings are brought to enforce a public right or duty, it remains to be decided whether the rule in *O'Reilly* v *Mackman* applies. According to Lewis in *Judicial Remedies in Public Law,* it 'is likely that the courts will allow the Attorney-General to proceed by ordinary action'.

For details of this case, see pp. 406–7.

Although the facility to commence relator actions remains, it may be that the current willingness of the courts to grant standing both to individuals and interest groups where the public rather than an individual interest may be at stake will reduce the need for the Attorney-General's involvement.

Exclusion of judicial review and ouster clauses

 ### Meaning and explanation

Objective 3

Just as Parliament may use its sovereign legislative authority to confer legislative, executive and judicial powers on its subordinates, it may also exert that same authority to protect the exercise of such powers from judicial interference. This may be done as follows:

(a) by inserting an exclusion or 'ouster' clause in the enabling Act which seeks, in express terms, to exclude or 'oust' the power of judicial review;

(b) by phrasing the powers so conferred in such wide subjective terms as to minimise the grounds on which the exercise of the power may be questioned;

(c) by providing a statutory remedy to deal with any alleged abuses of powers or duties in the enabling Act.

The courts also assume that Parliament intends certain powers to be regarded as 'non-justiciable', i.e. as matters beyond the scope of judicial review. These tend to be discretionary powers which relate to sensitive political or security issues. The view here is that judicial intervention would be inimical to the public interests which such powers seek to protect.

This illustrates that the effectiveness of judicial review and of the functioning of the separation of powers in the British constitution are, at all times, subject to the sovereignty of Parliament. In a strictly legal sense, there is nothing inevitable about the 'balanced' relationship between the legislative, executive and judicial powers of government. Parliament's sovereign legislative will is, after all, little more than a constitutional euphemism for the wishes of the executive or those who control the House of Commons. Moreover, it is probably naive to believe that those in power gain any great satisfaction or comfort from the knowledge that their excesses may be corrected by judicial intervention.

There is a danger, therefore, that judicial review could be rendered nugatory by the executive control of the drafting of enabling legislation. Wholesale use of this tactic would, however, be regarded as a flagrant breach of British constitutional traditions and would no doubt attract considerable political opprobrium. The courts have also made it clear that the citizen's access to the courts to challenge alleged abuses of power is to be regarded as a crucial and fundamental constitutional right. It is also now protected by the Human Rights Act 1998. Accordingly restriction of it will only be given judicial recognition if couched in the clearest of express terms without any uncertainty or ambiguity. Thus, where the Lord

Chancellor sought to radically increase the fee for issuing a writ (i.e. for commencing civil proceedings), the order purporting to implement his decision was declared to be *ultra vires* the powers conferred on him by the Supreme Court Act 1981 (*R v Lord Chancellor, ex parte Witham* [1997] 2 All ER 779). Laws J said that access to the courts was 'as near to an absolute right as any which could be envisaged' and that he would find 'great difficulty in conceiving a form of words capable of making it plain beyond doubt to the reader of a statute that the provision in question prevented him from going to court'. Therefore, since the radically increased fee would have seriously prejudiced the right for the less affluent, it could not be allowed to stand.

Given these restraining factors, legislative attempts to render the use of powers 'judge proof' have generally been restricted to those circumstances where this appears to be justified by what is perceived to be an overriding public interest.

Ouster clauses

Shall not be questioned in any legal proceedings
Smith v *East Elloe* RDC [1956] AC 736

Mrs Smith sought to challenge the validity of a compulsory purchase order by virtue of which 8½ acres of her property had been acquired by the local authority. The order had been made in 1948 and confirmed in the same year by the Minister of Health after a local public inquiry. The procedure for making compulsory purchase orders was contained in the Acquisition of Land (Authorisation Procedure) Act 1946. This provided that 'if any person aggrieved by a compulsory purchase order desires to question the validity thereof . . . he may within six weeks from the date on which notice of the confirmation or making of the order . . . is first published . . . make an application to the High Court'. The Act went on to provide that once this period had elapsed 'a compulsory purchase order . . . shall not . . . be questioned in any legal proceedings whatsoever'.

Mrs Smith commenced her proceedings in 1954 alleging, *inter alia*, that the order had been 'wrongfully made and in bad faith'. The court felt that the action could not be entertained and that it was bound to accept and apply the will of Parliament as clearly expressed in the ouster clause. It was cognisant of both the deep-rooted principle that the legislature cannot be assumed to oust the jurisdiction of the court – particularly where fraud is alleged – except by clear words and the view that 'a statute is, if possible . . . to be construed as to avoid injustice'. Nevertheless, as there was nothing ambiguous about the language or the intent of the ouster, the court felt bound to apply the 'first of all principles of construction that plain words must be given their plain meaning'. Thus the court accepted that once the six-week period had elapsed no judicial redress was available in respect of a compulsory purchase order, no matter that it was made in bad faith or in blatant abuse of the prescribed procedures.

The effectiveness of such 'partial' ousters – i.e. those which restrict legal proceedings to a prescribed period – was later confirmed in *R v Secretary of State for the Environment, ex parte Ostler* [1976] 3 WLR 288. Such clauses are found typically in Acts which permit the compulsory acquisition of land for public works, housing, highways, etc. The policy behind them is to protect public bodies against the complications, particularly the financial costs, which might accrue if, after such works had been completed, the legal process for acquiring the land necessary was found to have been defective.

The meaning of a similarly worded clause was considered by the House of Lords in the following case.

Anisminic v Foreign Compensation Commission (No. 2) [1969] 2 AC 147

On this occasion the ouster clause in question provided that any 'determination by the Commission . . . shall not be questioned in any court of law' (Foreign Compensation Act 1950, s 4). Unlike the clause in issue in the *Smith v East Elloe* case, this was an absolute ouster – i.e. no limited period was provided in which a legal challenge to the Commission's decisions could be made.

In its judgment the House of Lords displayed a clear reluctance to accept that a decision-making power could be put completely beyond the scope of judicial scrutiny so that not even blatant abuses of power could be rendered *ultra vires* and of no effect. Hence the conclusion that if the Commission made a decision which was outside its jurisdiction, so as to be null and void, this could not in law be regarded as any sort of determination at all. Therefore, since the express language of the ouster limited its application to 'determinations' of the Commission, it could not give any protection to that which did not qualify to be so described.

Any apparent inconsistency between this and the approach taken in the *Smith* case was explained in *Ostler* on the grounds that in the *Anisminic* case:

(a) there was a complete or absolute ouster which 'precluded the court from entertaining a complaint at any time about the determination';

(b) 'the House was considering a determination by a truly judicial body';

(c) 'the House had to consider the actual determination of the tribunal, whereas in the *Smith* v *East Elloe* case the House had to consider the validity of the process by which the decision was reached' (*per* Denning MR).

However convincing this attempt to distinguish the two cases may be, it leaves the conclusion that a court will give full effect to the intended meaning of a partial ouster clause but may resort to the *Anisminic* approach to avoid compliance with an absolute or complete ouster. This was confirmed by the Court of Appeal in *R v Cornwall County Council, ex parte Huntington* [1994] 1 All ER 694, where Simon Brown LJ quoted with approval the following statement made when the case was before the Divisional Court:

The intention of Parliament when it uses an *Anisminic* clause is that questions as to validity are not excluded . . . When paragraphs such as those considered in *ex parte Ostler* are used, then the legislative intention is that the question as to validity may be raised . . . in the prescribed time . . . but that otherwise the jurisdiction of the court is excluded in the interest of certainty (*per* Mann LJ).

The *Anisminic* decision was followed and applied by the Court of Appeal in *R v Secretary of State for the Home Department, ex parte Al-Fayed* [1997] 1 All ER 228, where the applicant was allowed to apply for judicial review of the Minister's decision to refuse him British nationality despite the existence in the enabling Act (British Nationality Act 1981, s 44) of a clause stating that 'the decision of the Secretary of State . . . shall not be subject to appeal . . . or review in any court of law'. Lord Woolf quoted from the Privy Council decision in *Attorney-General v Ryan* [1980] AC 718, to the effect that 'to come within the prohibition of appeal or review by an ouster clause of this type, the decision must be one which the decision-making authority . . . had jurisdiction to make'.

Shall be final

The effect of clauses which state that exercise of a particular decision-making power shall be regarded as 'final' was summed up with eminent clarity by Denning LJ, *R v Medical Appeal Tribunal, ex parte Gilmore* [1975] 1 QB 574:

I find it very well settled that the remedy by *certiorari* is never to be taken away except by the most clear and explicit words. The word final is not enough. That only means 'without appeal'. It does not mean 'without recourse to *certiorari*' [i.e. judicial review]. It makes the decision final on the facts but not final on the law.

Such clauses do not, therefore, exclude judicial review. They merely protect exercises of the decision-making power from any statutory right of appeal that might otherwise have been available. Whether such clauses are effective to exclude a right of appeal on a point of law is a matter of uncertainty. Lord Denning MR in *Pearlman v Keepers and Governors of Harrow School*, above, thought they did not. His view was not supported, however, by the House of Lords in *Re Racal Communications*, above, where the House felt that if a power was to be treated as not subject to appeal this rendered it non-appealable on any ground.

It has also been held that, if the effect of a finality clause is to prevent any challenge to the factual merits of a decision, this also precludes any right of action in negligence against the decision-maker since such action would inevitably bring into question the quality of the decision-maker's conclusions (*Jones v Department of Employment* [1989] QB 1).

'As if enacted in this act'

This form of words has been used in enabling Acts which have conferred subordinate law-making powers on Ministers and other public bodies. The apparent objective of the formula is to give the subordinate legislation so made the sovereign legal status of the enabling Act itself, thus rendering it immune from judicial review.

Once again, however, the exclusive effect of such attempted ouster has been minimised by judicial interpretation. Thus it has been held that as Parliament could not have intended subordinate law-makers to act unlawfully it must be assumed that the clause could relate only to that which had been made according to and, therefore, *intra vires* the Act containing the law-making power (*R v Minister of Health, ex parte Yaffe* [1930] 2 KB 98).

Subjectively worded powers

It is not uncommon for an Act to provide that a power may be exercised where the repository is 'satisfied' or 'of the opinion' that certain facts or conditions exist. Alternatively the Act may provide that the repository may do whatever is thought 'fit' or 'necessary and expedient' to deal with particular circumstances.

Such terminology was presumably intended, and in the past has been held to mean, that any honest, albeit subjective, belief in the existence of the prerequisite facts or circumstances, or the need for a certain course of action, must be accepted as sufficient for a valid exercise of the power. Hence, in *Robinson v Minister of Town and Country Planning* [1947] KB 702, the Minister had a statutory power to compulsorily acquire bomb-damaged property 'where . . . satisfied that it is requisite for . . . dealing satisfactorily with extensive war damage' that an area should be 'laid out afresh and developed as a whole'. In answer to a challenge to the validity of a particular compulsory purchase order the response of the Court of Appeal was:

> How can this Minister, who is entrusted by Parliament to make or not to make an executive order according to his judgment and acts bona fide (as he must be assumed to do in the absence of evidence to the contrary) be called upon to justify his decision by proving that he had before him materials sufficient to support it (*per* Lord Greene MR).

Consistent with the approach already explained towards express ousters, the modern judicial attitude towards such subjectively worded powers is to insist that, in so far as the subject-matter of a particular decision is justiciable – e.g. is not a matter of political opinion or judgment – it is reviewable for **Wednesbury** unreasonableness. Thus, in **Secretary of State for Education and Science v Metropolitan Borough of Tameside** [1977] AC 1014, the House of Lords refused to accept that the Minister's power to issue directives to a local education authority 'if satisfied' that such authority had acted unreasonably in the exercise of its statutory functions was beyond the scope of judicial scrutiny.

> The section is framed in subjective form – if the Secretary of State 'is satisfied'. This form of section is quite well known, and at first sight might seem to exclude judicial review. Sections in this form may, no doubt, exclude judicial review on what is . . . a matter of pure judgment. But I do not think that they go further than that. If a judgment requires, before it can be made, the existence of some facts, then, although the evaluation of those facts is for the Secretary of State alone, the court must inquire whether those facts exist, and have been taken into account, whether the judgment has been made upon a proper self-direction as to those facts, whether the judgment has not been made upon other facts which ought not to have been taken into account (*per* Lord Wilberforce).

Alternative remedies

A statute which confers a power on a public authority may, at the same time, provide a remedy for dealing with alleged abuses of that power. Hence, as already explained, statutes which authorise the compulsory acquisition of land and property will normally provide a right of appeal on a point of law (to the High Court) against a compulsory purchase order, which right should be exercised within six weeks of the order's confirmation by the Secretary of State (usually the Minister for the Environment, Food and Rural Affairs).

Such statutory remedy may be regarded as exclusive by the courts if this appears to have been the intention of Parliament. If the statutory remedy is so regarded this means that the validity of the administrative action or decision in question cannot be challenged by judicial review or any other procedure.

Where the statutory remedy provided is a right of appeal to a court of law – frequently the High Court – this will usually be assumed to exclude resort to judicial review 'save in exceptional circumstances' (*per* Sir John Donaldson MR, **R v Secretary of State for the Home Department, ex parte Swati**, *supra*).

R v Cornwall County Council, ex parte Huntington [1994] 1 All ER 694

In this case, the applicants sought judicial review of an order made by the local authority under the Wildlife and Countryside Act 1981 recognising a newly established right of way. The Act provided a right of appeal to the High Court against any such order to be exercised within six weeks of its confirmation by the Minister. In this case, however, the application for judicial review was made prior to the order being confirmed. Thus, the applicants argued, as they were not challenging a confirmed order, they were not bound by the statutory procedure and remained free to commence proceedings for judicial review.

This argument was firmly rejected. Parliament had provided a scheme for making, confirming and challenging the order in question and it was clearly Parliament's intention that all related legal proceedings should be conducted thereby. All other methods of challenge – whether before, during, or after the six-week period allowed – had therefore been excluded:

> it seems clear as a matter of construction that Parliament intended – and, indeed, to my mind intended for good reason – that the remedy by way of statutory application . . . should be the exclusive avenue of address available to those aggrieved by . . . orders of this kind if and when such orders come to be confirmed (*per* Simon Brown LJ).

Note, however, the decision in *R* v *Wiltshire County Council, ex parte Lazard Brothers and Co Ltd*, *The Times*, 13 January 1998, which held that, where a local council had resolved to make an order under the Wildlife and Countryside Act 1981 (in this case designating a road through a village as a byway open to all traffic), the decision remained open to review until the consequent order had actually been made. In the opinion of the court, judicial review was not excluded by the existence of the statutory remedy mentioned above, i.e. appeal to the High Court against a confirmed order. Rather, this was just one of the many matters which a court could take into account in exercising its discretion whether or not to grant review.

Where a statute provides an administrative remedy only – e.g. by way of complaint to the relevant Minister – the courts are less likely to accept that this is intended to exclude judicial review where it is alleged that the body invested with the power or duty has acted *ultra vires*. This would appear to be the ratio of the Court of Appeal decision in the following case.

Meade v *Haringey London Borough Council* [1979] 1 WLR 637

> The authority had closed a number of schools after their caretakers had taken strike action. The Education Act 1944, s 99 provided that if the Minister was satisfied 'upon complaint by any person . . . that any local authority . . . have failed to discharge any duty imposed on them by . . . this Act, the Minister may make an order declaring the authority . . . to be in default . . . and giving such directions for enforcing the execution thereof as appear . . . to be expedient . . . ' Despite the existence of such statutory remedy, legal proceedings were brought for, *inter alia*, a declaration that the authority was in breach of its statutory duty in s 8 of the 1944 Act to provide adequate schools and education for the needs of the community. To the argument that any such proceedings were excluded by the statutory remedy, Lord Denning MR replied:
>
> > Now although that section does give a remedy – by complaint to a Minister – it does not exclude any other remedy. To my mind it leaves open all the established remedies which the law provides in cases where a public authority fails to perform its statutory duty either by an act of commission or omission.

Justiciability

Meaning and explanation

The courts regard certain types of decision-making powers as being unsuitable for judicial review. These are generally matters relating to sensitive issues of public policy or the allocation of financial resources. The general judicial opinion appears to be that the scrutiny and control of decision-making in these contexts is essentially a matter for the parliamentary and political processes. Hence, although not excluded from questioning the exercise of such powers, the courts tend to treat such subjects as being 'non-justiciable'.

> The graver a matter of State and the more widespread its possible effects the more respect will be given, within the framework of the constitution, to the democracy to decide its outcome . . . Of course, they [the electorate], may or may not be satisfied and their satisfaction, or otherwise, will sound in the ballot box. There is, and cannot be, any expectation that the unelected judiciary will play any role in such questions, remotely comparable to that of government . . . (*per* Lord Hoffmann in *Secretary of State for the Home Department* v *Rehman* [2001] 3 WLR 877)

The following represent some of the most significant of these areas of government activity.

The formation of legislation

In the case of most legislation, the decision whether to place a particular Bill before Parliament is part of the political process and, therefore, not suitable for judicial scrutiny. Also, once the decision to do so has been made, the procedure is governed by parliamentary standing orders. It is, therefore, covered by parliamentary privilege (*R (on application of Wheeler)* v *Office of the Prime Minister* [2008] EWHC 1409 (Admin)).

The content of primary legislation is, of course, not subject to judicial scrutiny except in so far as it contravenes the law of the European Union. Subordinate legislation, however, may be reviewed for both simple and procedural *ultra vires*. The formulation of both types of legislation is, however, regarded as part of the political process which may be questioned and debated in Parliament but not in the courts. Hence it is extremely unlikely that a court would entertain an application for judicial review which alleged abuse of discretion by a Minister in the formulation of a regulation – e.g. failure to consider relevant considerations. Also, it has been held that a person likely to be affected by a piece of subordinate legislation has no right to be heard as its content is being determined unless it is so provided in the enabling Act (*Bates* v *Lord Hailsham* [1972] 1 WLR 1373).

Government policy and finance

The judiciary have displayed a marked reluctance to entertain disputes dealing with the reasonableness or rationality of government policy or decisions relating to the allocation of public finances.

R v *Secretary of State for the Environment, ex parte Hammersmith and Fulham London Borough Councils* [1991] 1 AC 521

This case concerned the Minister's power in the Local Government Act 1988, s 100 to 'cap' the spending plans of any local council if these were 'in his opinion . . . excessive'. The applicants argued that a local council should be free to spend what a 'sensible' authority in the particular circumstances obtaining in its area might reasonably decide was appropriate and that the Minister was entitled to form the opinion that projected expenditure was 'excessive' only where it was so 'profligate and extravagant that no sensible authority could have approved it'.

In rejecting this argument the House of Lords held that there were no 'objective criteria' by which spending decisions could be judged to be excessive or unreasonable. This was entirely a matter of political opinion to be determined on the basis of what would best serve the public interest. The Minister's discretion in this matter was, therefore, non-justiciable.

> The formulation and implementation of national economic policy are matters depending essentially on political judgment. The decisions which shape them are for politicians to take and it is in the political forum of the House of Commons that these are to be properly debated and approved or disapproved on their merits (*per* Lord Bridge).

Similarly, in *R (on application Rotherham Metropolitan Borough Council)* v *Secretary of State for Business, Innovation and Skills* [2014] UKSC 6, the Supreme Court felt unable to question a ministerial decision concerning the distribution of EU structural funds amongst the regions.

> The Secretary of State's allocation is a discretionary decision of a kind which the courts have traditionally been reluctant to disturb. There is no right answer prescribed by the EU Treaty to

the question how EU structural funds should be distributed within a member state. There is not even any clear principle on which this should be done. Instead, the Secretary of State was required to make a complex evaluation of a wide range of overlapping criteria, all of which involved difficult and sensitive technical judgments about matters of social and economic policy (Lord Sumption).

This should not be understood as an all embracing exclusion of judicial review in each and every policy-related matters and would appear not to have full application to policy decisions or changes which prevent or inhibit a decision-making body from conducting its proceedings in accordance with the principles of legality and those of procedural fairness. Accordingly the courts have shown a preparedness to question decisions based on policy which appears to be:

(a) unreasonable or irrational;

(b) undisclosed;

(c) so rigid as to not permit of exceptions;

(d) to undermine the rules of procedural fairness.

National security

The basic premise

English judges have long been reticent about upsetting executive decisions relating to the defence of the realm or the protection of national security. An impressive litany of cases attests to this judicial preference and sympathy for the maxim *salus populi suprema lex* (the safety of the people is the highest law).

Two wartime decisions provide classic illustration of this tendency. In *R v Halliday* [1917] AC 260, the House of Lords refused to quash a regulation authorising internment without trial. No specific authority for this ultimate restriction on personal freedom could be found in the enabling Act (Defence of the Realm Act 1914). Their Lordships felt, however, that the traditional canon of interpretation forbidding denial of basic freedoms except with express parliamentary authority, i.e. unrestricted access to the courts, should not be applied during wartime.

> It appears to me to be sufficient answer to this argument that it may be necessary in time of great public danger to entrust great powers to His Majesty in Council and Parliament may do so feeling certain that such powers will be reasonably exercised (*per* Lord Finlay LC).

Similarly, in *Liversidge v Anderson* [1942] AC 206, during the World War II, the Secretary of State for the Home Department's power to intern without trial any person he had 'reasonable cause to believe . . . to be of hostile origins or associations' was construed by the House of Lords to mean that he could intern any person he *honestly* believed to be of such origins or associations whether such belief was reasonable or not. Obvious judicial reluctance to question the actions of government in time of war was also apparent in *Campaign for Nuclear Disarmament v Prime Minister* [2002] EWHC 2777 (Admin), where the court felt unable to inquire into the legality of the invasion of Iraq.

Other modern decisions cases attest to the continuing judicial reluctance to question either the use of discretion or the procedure employed when executive officials make decisions in this context. The non-justiciable nature of discretionary powers in the sphere of national security was restated by the Court of Appeal in the following case.

R v *Secretary of State for the Home Department, ex parte Chahal* [1995] 1 All ER 658

The applicant challenged a deportation order served on him under the power contained in the Immigration Act 1971 to remove from this country any person whose presence in the United Kingdom is deemed 'not to be conducive to the public good'. The particular reason for the Secretary of State for the Home Department's decision was that the applicant was believed to be involved in Sikh terrorism. In response to the applicant's argument that the decision was irrational because any such involvement would be no threat to the United Kingdom, the court concluded that in matters of national security it was not competent to review or question the basis on which the Minister had based his decision.

In *R (on application of Carlile)* v *Secretary of State for the Home Department* UKSC 60, the Supreme Court felt unable to question the Home Secretary's decision to refuse UK entry to a 'dissident Iranian politician'. The Minister's reasons were that the Iranian politician's presence in the UK would 'not be conducive to the public good for reasons of foreign policy (relations with Iran) and in the light of the need to take a firm stance against terrorism'.

The case for a degree of judicial deference to the executive government in such matters was explained by Lord Sumption.

> We have no experience and no material which could justify us in rejecting the Foreign Office assessment in favour of a more optimistic assessment of our own. To do so would not only usurp the proper function of the Secretary of State. It would be contrary to long established principle which this court has repeatedly and recently confirmed. It would step beyond the proper function of a court of review. And it would involve rejecting by far the strongest and best qualified evidence before us. In my opinion it would be a wholly inappropriate course for us to take.

National security and procedural justice

Many of the other more important cases concerning the justiciability of issues relating to national security have involved alleged breaches of the rules of natural justice – particularly the right to a fair hearing. In the most famous of these, the *GCHQ* case, the House of Lords conceded that for the effective protection of the public interest in national security, it was for the executive and not the courts to determine the degree of procedural justice which could properly or safely be afforded to those detrimentally affected by related decisions.

> The decision on whether the requirements of national security outweigh the duty of fairness in any particular case is for the Government and not for the courts. The Government alone has access to the necessary information, and in any event, the judicial process is unsuitable for reaching decisions on national security (*per* Lord Fraser).

A number of the cases in this context have concerned the Home Secretary's power to make deportation orders against persons whose presence in the UK was deemed 'not to be conducive to the public good' (Immigration Act 1971, s 3). Contravention of the right to a fair hearing and the failure to give reasons for decisions have been the principal complaints. On each occasion, however, the courts have refused to intervene and have preferred the public interest in national security to that of procedural fairness:

> Great as is the public interest in the freedom of the individual and the doing of justice to him, nevertheless, in the last resort, it must take second place to the security of the country itself (*per* Lord Denning MR, *R* v *Secretary of State for the Home Department, ex parte Hosenball* [1977] 1 WLR 766).

Cogent evidence

Notwithstanding all of the above a court is unlikely to submit to Ministerial claims to be acting in the interests of national security unless it can be shown that there is some plausible connection between the action taken and the alleged security demands.

> Once the factual basis is established by evidence so that the court is satisfied that the interest of national security is a relevant factor, the court will accept the opinion of the Crown . . . as to what is required to meet it (*per* Lord Scarman, the *GCHQ* case).

In *R* v *Secretary of State for the Home Department, ex parte Ruddock* [1987] 1 WLR 1482, Taylor J's opinion was that 'cogent evidence' was required to justify a plea of national security for the purpose of excluding judicial review. In *R* v *Secretary of State for the Home Department, ex parte Stitt* (1987) *The Times*, 3 February, Watkins LJ felt that the Minister's decision could not be questioned 'once there was bona fide evidence that national security was involved'. Similar sentiments may be found in the judgment of Lord Hoffmann in *Secretary of State for the Home Department* v *Rehman* (*supra*).

Forbidden areas and proportionality

In more recent years increased resort to proportionality as an instrument for judicial review, particularly for cases in which the decision to protect national security has infringed a human right, has paved the way for a more nuanced and, it would appear, less deferential judicial approach to these more policy-sensitive areas of executive responsibility. The idea here is that courts should not simply take a 'black and white' attitude to the issue and regard this type of executive decision-making as being a completely 'forbidden area' (see Lord Phillips, *R (on application of Abani)* v *Secretary of State for Foreign and Commonwealth Affairs* [2002] EWCA Civ 1598). Rather, although significant, the executive's superior knowledge and expertise in these areas should be regarded as one of the various matters to be taken into account in the proportionality balancing exercise, i.e. whether the level of interference with the rights of those affected went beyond the bounds of that which was required to achieve the national security objective.

> I have no doubt that it is for the court to make the proportionality assessment, but I have equally no doubt that in some parts of that assessment, the court should be very slow indeed to disagree with the assessment made by the government. (Lady Hale, *R (on application of Carlile)* v *Secretary of State for Home Department*, *supra* exclusion of dissident Iranian from UK not disproportionate to fight against terrorism and need to maintain good relations with Iranian government).

Exclusivity

Meaning and explanation

Objective 4

For Senior Courts Act 1981, s 31, see p. 386.

A person alleging an abuse of power by a public authority, i.e. that the authority has acted *ultra vires*, in breach of the rules of natural justice or the requirement of the Human Rights Act 1998, and who wishes to bring the claim before the courts, should commence those proceedings by way of an application for judicial review. This is a distinct type of legal process and should be conducted according to the prescriptions in the Senior Courts Act 1981, section 31.

The rule in *O'Reilly* v *Mackman*

As a general rule, this is the sole procedure by which any such public law matter may be brought before a court of law. Any attempt to do so by an alternative means, e.g. an action for damages, would be rejected as an **abuse of process** regardless of the merits of the claim. Such procedural 'exclusivity' for public law cases is usually attributed to the House of Lords decision in *O'Reilly* v *Mackman* [1983] AC 237. Here, Lord Diplock stated that, henceforth, it would be regarded as 'contrary to public policy and, as such, an abuse of the court, to permit a person seeking to establish that a decision of a public authority infringed rights to which he was entitled to protection under public law by ordinary action'.

In the case itself, a group of prisoners alleged that disciplinary decisions affecting them had been made in breach of the rules of natural justice. Since the decisions in question had been made years before the event, each of the claimants had sought to commence their legal proceedings by way of an ordinary private law writ – as would be used, for example, when claiming damages in contract or tort – and thus to avoid the rule that applications for judicial review should be brought within three months of the alleged abuse.

For rules on applying for leave, see p. 387.

The House of Lords justified its finding of abuse of process by reference to the following.

(a) The application for judicial review procedure as contained in the Senior Courts Act 1981 was designed specifically for disposing of public law cases, i.e. allegations of abuse of power made by a private individual against a public authority.

(b) The primary purpose of such proceedings was to ensure that public authorities acted according to law rather than to provide persons aggrieved with some sort of personal redress, financial or otherwise.

(c) The procedure was introduced, initially, to respond to the potentially adverse consequences for the public interest, both social and financial, of allowing the decisions of public bodies to be ruled unlawful and invalid years after these had been made, e.g. a decision to commence some major scheme of public works.

(d) It could not have been intended, therefore, that those with a public law grievance against an authority should be allowed a choice of legal process, including those devised and developed over hundreds of years for dealing with purely private law disputes.

As explained, the rule in *O'Reilly* v *Mackman* has been construed to be of general effect only. It is subject, therefore, to a number of exceptions. These are as set out below.

Abuse of power as a collateral issue

This occurs where an allegation of abuse of power is made in a case concerned primarily with the assertion or challenging of a private law. Thus in *Roy* v *Kensington, Chelsea and Westminster Family Practitioner Committee* [1992] 2 WLR 239 the plaintiff, a doctor, sued the Family Practitioner Committee in respect of payments withheld from him due to his alleged failure to devote sufficient time to general practice. The powers relied on by the Committee were derived from statutory rules concerned with the effective provision of public services generally. This notwithstanding, and since the primary objective of the action was the enforcement of the doctor's private and contractual rights, the court found no abuse of process in allowing the action to proceed.

Abuse of power as a defence

An abuse of public power may be pleaded as a defence in ordinary civil or criminal proceedings.

Wandsworth London Borough Council v Winder [1985] AC 461

A council tenant, when sued for arrears of rent, was allowed to plead that the rent charged by the authority amounted to an unreasonable and *ultra vires* use of its powers. Lord Fraser said that despite the inconvenience which might be caused to public authorities by the avoidance of the rules relating to applications for judicial review – particularly that applications should be made promptly – the substantive right of every individual to raise public or private law principles in their defence could not be relegated by an essentially procedural rule to a matter of judicial discretion (i.e. confined to review procedure which commences not as of right by a judicial leave). Only clear words in an Act of Parliament could so proscribe this right.

Statutory remedy provided

In some instances a statute or 'enabling Act' may provide its own alternative remedy for dealing with alleged abuses of the powers conferred by it.

Buckley v The Law Society [1983] 2 All ER 1039

In this case, the defendants, acting under the Solicitors Act 1957, took control of the plaintiff's business finance pending inquiry into allegations of dishonesty. According to the same Act, solicitors so affected could contest the Law Society's decisions in the Chancery Division, proceeding by way of originating summons. The plaintiff solicitor abided by these procedural dictates. The Law Society, however – apparently in an attempt to avoid his subsequent requests for discovery – argued that, since their disciplinary and supervisory powers over the legal profession emanated from statute, they were in nature and origin manifestly public law powers so that the plaintiff should have proceeded by way of judicial review. According to this procedure, it was argued, he would have been unlikely to secure discovery since this is seldom awarded against bodies exercising judicial or disciplinary functions. Sir Robert McGarry VC, in the Chancery Division, said it would be 'remarkable indeed' if the Law Society could resort to a specific statutory power to discipline a solicitor but the solicitor could not rely on the remedies in that same statute to seek redress. Hence, although the power used by the Law Society was of a public nature, the complainant was not disqualified from using the statutory remedy. Discovery was ordered against the Law Society to establish whether or not they had adequate information in their possession on which to base a finding of dishonesty against the plaintiff.

Judicial review and contractual powers

Public law procedure is not the appropriate method for challenging the decisions of government agencies when exercising contractual powers.

R v British Broadcasting Corporation, ex parte Lavelle [1983] 1 WLR 23

The applicant was suspected of theft from her employers. She was given only one hour's notice of the disciplinary hearing to which she was entitled according to the BBC's disciplinary code, after which she was dismissed from their employ. She applied for judicial review on the ground that she had not been given a fair hearing. Woolf J in the High Court said that Ord 53 made it clear that applications for judicial review should be confined 'to reviewing activities of a public nature as opposed to those of purely private or domestic character'. Since the BBC's disciplinary appeals procedure derived its authority from the contract of employment, and was not underpinned or regulated by statute in any way, it should be classified as essentially domestic. *A fortiori*, the correct procedure was by writ and not by application for review.

In *McClaren* **v** *Home Office* [1990] ICR 824, Lord Woolf explained:

an employee of a public body is normally in exactly the same situation as other employees. If he has a cause of action and he wishes to assert or establish his rights in relation to his employment he can bring proceedings for damages, a declaration or an injunction . . . in the High Court or County Court in the ordinary way. The fact that a person is employed by the Crown may limit his rights against the Crown but otherwise his position is very much the same as any other employee. However, he may, instead of having an ordinary master and servant relationship with the Crown, hold office under the Crown and may have been appointed to that office as a result of the Crown exercising a prerogative or . . . a statutory power. If he holds such an appointment then it will almost invariably be terminable at will . . . but whatever rights the employee has will be enforceable normally by an ordinary action.

Disputes between a public sector employer and an employee may, however, be susceptible to judicial review where:

(a) the decision in question (i.e. to dismiss or otherwise), was made for reasons of public policy – e.g. 'the public interest that the civil service should be administered in a way which is free from political bias and other improper motive' (*per* Roche J, *R v Civil Service Appeal Board, ex parte Bruce* [1988] 3 All ER 686);

(b) the power to dismiss or otherwise is regulated by statute (*McClaren* **v** *Home Office*, *supra*);

(c) the power to dismiss or otherwise is subject to a right of appeal to a body created under statute or the prerogative (*ex parte Bruce*, *supra*).

Judicial review beyond statutory or prerogative powers

Although judicial review is normally concerned with the abuse of power by bodies established by, and deriving their authority from, statute or the prerogative, it is now firmly established that it is also the appropriate remedy for the abuse of power by bodies having no such origins but which perform monopolistic regulatory functions which would otherwise – for the better protection of the public interest – have to be exercised by a government agency. This was decided by the Court of Appeal in *R v Panel on Takeovers and Mergers, ex parte Datafin plc* [1987] QB 815. Neither the facts of the case nor the eventual decision that no abuse of power had been committed by the Panel are of any great significance. Of crucial importance, however, was the Court of Appeal's view that the Panel fell within the scope of judicial review notwithstanding that it possessed no formal legal foundations or powers, whether from statute, the prerogative or otherwise. The reasons given for this finding were as follows.

(a) There is no absolute rule restricting judicial review to powers emanating from statute or the prerogative only (see *R v Criminal Injuries Compensation Board, ex parte Lain* [1967] 2 QB 864).

(b) The Panel performed functions of national importance as the body through which self-regulation of the City was effected.

(c) Although possessing no legal power *de jure*, it exercised 'immense power' *de facto* by:
- 'devising, promulgating, amending and interpreting the City Code on Take-overs and Mergers';
- investigating and determining through quasi-judicial procedures whether breaches of the Code had been committed;
- the imposition or threat of sanctions relating thereto.

(d) The government had accepted that the City should be subject to effective regulation and control. As a matter of policy, however, it had been decided that this regulatory function should not, at least for the time being, be undertaken by a government agency armed with legislative powers. The favoured approach was for self-regulation through application by the Panel of the aforementioned Code. Therefore, although not backed by legislation, the Panel could be said to be fulfilling government policy in this context. Were these functions not performed by the Panel, it was highly likely that an alternative body would have to be created either by statute or under the royal prerogative.

Subsequently, in *R v Insurance Ombudsman, ex parte Aegon Life Assurance Ltd* [1994] COD 426, the principle established by the *Datafin* decision was summarised as follows:

> . . . a body whose birth and constitution owed nothing to any exercise of governmental power may be subject to judicial review if it had been woven into a system of governmental control or was integrated into a system of statutory regulation or was a surrogate organ of government or, but for its existence, a government body would assume control.

To date there would appear to be a judicial preference for confining the legal supervision of other such regulatory bodies – i.e. those without *de jure* legal powers or origins – to those concerned with the maintenance of ethical standards in the commercial and professional spheres. Hence the following have been held to fall within the scope of judicial review:

- the Advertising Standards Authority Ltd (*R v Advertising Standards Authority, ex parte Insurance Service plc* (1990) 2 Admin LR 77): 'a body clearly exercising a public function which, if the Authority did not exist, would no doubt be exercised by the Director-General of Fair Trading';

- the Code of Practice Committee of the British Pharmaceutical Industry (*R v Codeof Practice Committee of the British Pharmaceutical Industry, ex parte Professional Counselling Aids Committee* (1991) 3 Admin LR 697);

- LAUTRO (*R v Life Assurance and Unit Trusts Regulatory Organisation, ex parte Ross* [1993] QB 17);

- FIMBRA (*R v Financial Intermediaries Managers and Brokers Regulatory Association, ex parte Cochrane* [1990] COD 33);

- hospital ethics committees (*R v Ethical Committee of St Mary's Hospital, ex parte Harriott* [1988] 1 FLR 512);

- the professional conduct committee for barristers (*R* v *General Council of the Bar, ex parte Percival* [1991] 1 QB 212);

- the disciplinary process of the London Metal Exchange (*R* v *London Metal Exchange Ltd, ex parte Albatros Warehousing BV* (unreported, 30 March 2000).

For the present, however, this is as far as the courts have been prepared to go in the development of this new dimension of judicial review. Thus there have been repeated refusals to extend judicial review to bodies responsible for the administration and conduct of various sporting activities (see *R* v *Jockey Club, ex parte RAM Racecourses Ltd* [1993] 2 All ER 225; *R* v *Disciplinary Committee of the Jockey Club, ex parte Massingberd-Mundy* [1993] 2 All ER 207; *R* v *Football Association of Wales, ex parte Flint Town United Football Club* [1991] COD 44). Attempts to seek judicial review of the decisions of those responsible for the 'government' of religious communities have also been held to be an abuse of process (see *R* v *Chief Rabbi, ex parte Wachmann* [1991] COD 309; *R* v *Imam of Bury Park Mosque, Luton, ex parte Sulaiman Ali*, *The Independent,* 13 September 1991).

Other cases in which the *Datafin* principle has been applied include *Hampshire County Council* v *Hammer Trout Farm* [2003] EWCA Civ 1056 (private company entrusted with regulation and control of local farmers' markets); *Donaghue* v *Poplar Housing and Regeneration Community Association* [2001] EWCA Civ 595 (housing association entrusted with management of public housing stock); and *Wylie* (*Re an application for Judicial Review*) [2005] NIQB 2 (registered friendly society exercising fisheries licensing powers on Lough Neagh).

Summary

The chapter explains the modern procedure for applying for judicial review and the remedies that may be awarded to successful applicants. The narrative then moves on to explain the legislative techniques ('ouster clauses') sometimes used to limit the scope of judicial intrusion into the exercise of government power. The chapter closes with the topic of exclusivity. This deals with the difference between 'public' and 'private' law powers thereby enabling readers to understand and identify those types of government activity which fall within the scope of judicial inquiry and review, i.e. public law powers, and which do not, i.e. private law powers. Explanation is given also to the development of those modern legal principles permitting judicial review of the decisions of 'private' bodies or organisations (i.e. in general, those not created by statute) where these perform functions or provide services which would otherwise fall to be provided by some type of government body or agency.

Reference

Lewis (2014) *Judicial Remedies in Public Law* (5nd edn), London: Sweet & Maxwell.

Further reading

Beatson, Matthews and Elliot (2011) *Administrative Law: Text and Materials* (4th edn), Oxford: Oxford University Press, Ch. 15.

Craig (2016) *Administrative Law* (8th edn), London: Sweet & Maxwell, Ch. 15.

Fordham (2012) *Judicial Review Handbook* (6th edn), London: Hart Publishing, Ch. 4.

Wade and Forsyth (2014) *Administrative Law* (11th edn), Oxford: Oxford University Press

Part 6

Human rights

16

The European Convention on Human Rights

Objectives

After reading this chapter you should:

1. Appreciate the historical and political background to the European Convention on Human Rights.

2. Understand the relationship between the European Convention on Human Rights and EU law.

3. Recognise the background to, and main provisions of, the European Charter of Fundamental Rights and the relationship between the Charter and the ECHR.

4. Have an understanding of the composition and workings of the European Court of Human Rights.

5. Be able to understand the general principles of European Human Rights law of the content of the rights protected by the Convention.

6. Understand the principle of derogation.

7. Understand the extent of the Convention's extra-territorial application.

Introduction

Objective 1

By virtue of the Human Rights Act 1998, the principal provisions of the Convention are enforceable directly in the English legal system to the extent that these are compatible with the unambiguous requirements of domestic legislation. The Convention and its jurisprudence has thus become the basis of any detailed analysis of the source and extent of civil and human rights within the United Kingdom and of the reciprocal duties of the state in ensuring the necessary conditions in which such rights may be enjoyed. This is widely regarded as the most significant development in English law since the passing of the European Economic Communities Act in 1972 and gives citizens of the United Kingdom the direct protection of a range of rights hitherto either not recognised by, or developed fully within, the English common law.

The European Convention on Human Rights has now been given effect in the domestic systems of nearly all of its contracting members, thus providing a common basis to the human rights law of 47 European states.

Formulation

The Convention was formulated in 1949 by the Council of Europe. It was signed in Rome by the Council's original members in November 1950 and took effect in September 1953. Its objective was to avoid the sort of atrocities and abuses of human rights witnessed in Europe in World War II.

The Council of Europe pre-dates the European Community/Union and is a separate organisation. It was established to secure greater understanding and cooperation between European states and, in particular, to promote the ideals of parliamentary government, social and economic development, and to advance the cause and protection of human rights. The Council is the widest association of European states. It acts through a Committee of Ministers (usually foreign secretaries) advised by a Parliamentary Assembly consisting of members from national legislatures.

At its inception the Council consisted of representatives from the United Kingdom, the Republic of Ireland, France, Italy, Holland, Belgium, Sweden, Denmark, Luxembourg, Greece and Turkey. Most other European states have since become members including some from the former 'communist bloc'.

The primary aim of the European Convention was to promote uniform protection of certain fundamental human rights among the member states of the Council of Europe. In its original preamble, as ratified by the United Kingdom in 1951, the ECHR could receive a petition from an individual or group of individuals claiming to be victims of a violation of the Convention by a member state only if the state had declared that it recognised the competence of the Commission to receive such individual applications (Art 25). A member state was not obliged to accept the compulsory jurisdiction of the Court (Art 46) and only a member state or the Commission had the right to bring a case before the Court (Art 44). The United Kingdom did not accept the competence of the Commission to receive petitions from individuals until 1966. Articles 25, 44 and 46 have now all been repealed and no longer form any part of the Convention. The jurisdiction of the Court is now accepted as compulsory over all member states, and individuals have the right to apply to the Court directly. Such member states are bound by Art 46 to abide by the judgments of the Court in any cases to which they are parties.

Member states are obliged to furnish all the necessary materials and facilities to enable an effective complaint to be made (Art 28). Refusal to disclose relevant documents is, therefore, a breach of the Convention (*Kukayev* v *Russia* [2007] ECHR 729). Other means of hindering applications are proscribed by Art 34 (*Colibaba* v *Moldova* [2007] ECHR 847; threat of criminal investigation of applicant's lawyer).

The ECHR and EU law

Objective
2

The European Convention on Human Rights was not part of the law of the European Union. As indicated above, it was instituted and developed as a separate system of jurisprudence with its own institutions and procedures. However, as European Union law began to develop its own conception of human rights, it became increasingly apparent that this would be influenced by the standards and ideals to which the Convention is directed. Thus, in a number of cases in which the interpretation and application of European Union law has touched on issues of human rights, the Court of Justice indicated its willingness to be guided by the jurisprudence of the Convention and to give recognition to the rights protected thereby: 'international treaties for the protection of human rights on which the member states have collaborated or of which they are signatories, can supply guidelines which should be followed within the framework of community law' (*Nold v Commission* [1974] ECR 491). In addition the Treaty of the European Union provides a degree of protection to those aspects of human rights related to its central economic and social objectives including equal treatment of women and freedom from discrimination generally in the workplace and the freedoms attaching to EU citizenship, particularly the freedoms of movement and labour between member states.

As a result, although prior to 2000 the Convention did not have direct legal force in the United Kingdom, elements of its jurisprudence had already begun to be assimilated into the domestic legal system to the extent that these had influenced the law of the European Union: 'Through the jurisprudence of the Court of Justice the principles, though not the text, of the Convention now inform the law of the European Union' (per Sedley J, *R v Secretary of State for the Home Department, ex parte McQuillan* [1995] 4 All ER 400).

The close relationship between EU law and the Convention on Human Rights was given formal recognition in the Treaty of European Union 1992 which provided that the Union 'shall respect fundamental rights as guaranteed by the European Convention' (EC Art 6). This did not amount, however, to a formal incorporation of the Convention into EU law. The EU's commitment to human rights was, however, taken a step further by the Treaty of Amsterdam 1997 which conferred powers on the Council of Ministers, acting with the consent of the European Parliament, to suspend the voting and other rights of member states found to be guilty of 'serious and persistent breaches' of Convention rights.

The European Court of Justice has emphasised that its jurisdiction in matters of human rights, and its competence to be guided by the jurisprudence of the European Convention on Human Rights, applies only where it is seized of a question relating to the meaning of EU law. It is not the appropriate forum, therefore, for raising issues of compatibility between the Convention on Human Rights and national law if no question of EU law is directly involved (*Kremzow v Austria* [1997] ECR I-2629).

The expansion of the EU's human rights jurisdiction has led, inevitably, to a situation in which the fundamental rights of EU citizens receive protection from both of the pan-European systems of law. Whatever advantages this may have had, it has meant also that the content of the rights to be enforced could be interpreted differently within the two systems – thus undermining the maintenance of legal clarity and certainty. Accordingly, and in an attempt to minimise such eventualities, the ECtHR has engaged in the development of the doctrine of equivalent protection – often attributed originally to the Court's decision in *Bosphorus v Ireland*, app no 45036/98, 30.6.2005.

This is to the effect that each of the two pan-European legal systems is assumed to provide equally effective protection of human rights. Hence, in practical terms, an allegation of a breach of human rights by a contracting state in its application of EU law should be, and may be safely, entrusted to the courts of that jurisdiction thus obviating the need for any involvement by the ECtHR.

> The approach that became known as the doctrine of equivalent protection, basically brought the Strasbourg Court to acknowledge that the EU human rights regime is equivalently protective as that of the Council of Europe. This 'finding' allowed the Strasbourg Court not to engage in the review of cases involving the EU. As long as the EU human rights regime is equivalently protective with that of the Council of Europe, there is no need for a Strasbourg review (De Hert and Korenica, The Doctrine of Equivalent Protection, *German Law Journal*, vol. 13, no. 07).

The doctrine represents a prime example of necessary pragmatic improvisation by the Strasbourg judiciary and is not founded on any legally binding treaty provisions. For all this, however, and notwithstanding its success in reducing the incidence of conflict between the two systems, the doctrine was not left unaffected by the Treaty of Lisbon 2007 and, in particular, the treaty's provisions authorising EU accession to the ECHR. If and when this occurs, the obvious and immediate result would be that any alleged breaches of the Convention by an EU institution could be raised before and ruled upon by the ECtHR – the very thing that the doctrine of equivalent protection appeared to be predicated against. It would also be possible for the EU to be joined in proceedings at Strasbourg in which a contracting state may be alleged to have acted in breach of the Convention in its implementation of its EU obligations. It remains to be seen, however, whether the ECtHR would be prepared to go so far as to question, and possibly condemn, a decision of the ECJ itself for human rights inadequacies, and especially so where the human rights issue in dispute results from the ECJ's interpretation of EU law, a matter in which it has long claimed to be the ultimate authority. In the long term, however, pragmatic good sense may well prevail and an approach adopted which would be founded on a recognition of the particular but distinct areas of expertise of the two courts and of their primary authority within the legal systems for which they were devised.

> In the event of accession, the tasks of the Luxembourg and Strasbourg Courts will be complementary. The ECJ will continue to take the final decisions on all questions of Union law, in particular the distribution of competences between the Union and its member states. If the ECtHR were to find incompatibilities between the Convention and EC or EU law, the relevant EU institutions would be responsible for taking the action needed to bring the corresponding regulations, and their application in specific cases, into line with the Convention's requirements. Like other parties, the EU institutions would . . . have a measure of discretion in executing the Strasbourg Court's judgments. In other words external scrutiny in the field of fundamental and human rights in no way conflicts with the ECJ's role as the court of last instance for the interpretation of Union law (Polakiewicz, 'EU Law and the ECHR').

The competence of the EU to ratify the Convention was given detailed consideration by the European Court of Justice in *Opinion 2/94*, *The Times*, 16 April 1996. It was felt that such a radical extension of the scope and content of EU law could not be affected without substantial amendment of the TEU itself. No provision could be found in the existing Treaty which conferred on EU institutions any general power to enact rules on human rights or to conclude international conventions in that context.

The matter was taken forward by TEU Art 6(2), as amended by the Treaty of Lisbon.

> The Union shall accede to the Convention for the Protection of Human Rights and Fundamental Freedoms.

For the purposes of the ECHR itself, the legal basis for the accession of the Union is found in Art 59(2).

Official talks on the EU's accession to the ECHR began in July 2010. The required draft legal instruments were agreed in October 2010. For any final accession agreement to take effect, this would require approval, for the ECHR, by the Committee of Ministers of the European Council and the Parliamentary Assembly (see above) and, for the EU, by the European Council and Parliament, and by the 28 member states.

The European Charter of Fundamental Rights

The formulation of a charter of basic human rights, if only of the status of a political declaration, was one of the major priorities of the German presidency of 1999 and led to the commissioning of a Draft Charter of Fundamental Human Rights of the European Union by the Cologne European Council in June of that year. The Charter was formulated by a specially appointed convention consisting of the European Commission, representatives of the 15 national governments, 30 representatives from national legislatures, and 16 MEPs. It was completed in October 2000 and 'welcomed' by the Nice European Council in the following December. By the Treaty of Lisbon 2007, the Charter was accorded the same legal status as the treaties on which the EU is founded. With full ratification of the Treaty in 2009, it became part of the EU's legal system. The Charter does not seek to give direct effect to the ECHR in EU law. It does not, therefore, endow EU citizens with the facility to pursue their particular human rights grievances through the EU's law and legal system in matters having nothing to do with the actions of the EU or its institutions of government. The Charter does, however, require that the EU will exercise its legislative and other powers in ways which accord with the Convention, and that member states will do likewise when implementing EU law in their own jurisdictions.

As to its content, the Charter has 54 articles divided into seven chapters. These are: Human Dignity (Ch I); Freedom (Ch II); Equality (Ch III); Solidarity (Ch IV); Citizens' Rights (Ch V); Justice (Ch VI); General Provisions and Interpretation (Ch VII).

The principal rights and guarantees contained within the first six chapters are as follows.

(I)   Human Dignity: right to life; integrity of the person; prohibition of torture, inhuman or degrading treatment or punishment; prohibition of slavery and forced labour.

(II)   Freedoms: right to liberty and security of the person; respect for private life; protection of personal data; right to marry and found a family; freedom of thought, conscience and religion; freedom of expression and information; freedom of assembly and association; freedom of the arts and sciences; academic freedom; right to education; freedom to work and choose an occupation; freedom to conduct a business; right to property; right to political asylum; protection in the event of removal, expulsion, or extradition.

(III)   Equality: equality before the law; non-discrimination; cultural, religious and linguistic diversity; equality between men and women; the rights of children; the rights of the elderly; the rights of the disabled.

(IV)   Solidarity: workers' rights to information and consultation; right of collective bargaining; right of access to placement services; protection from unfair dismissal; fair working conditions; prohibition of child labour; right to maternity and paternity leave; right to social security and assistance; right to health care; access to services of general economic interest; right to environmental protection; right to consumer protection.

(V)   Citizens' Rights: right to vote and stand in EU and national elections; right to be treated fairly, impartially and within a reasonable time by the institutions of the EU; right of access to the documents; right to complain to the EU Ombudsman; right to petition EU Parliament; freedom of movement and residence; right to diplomatic protection.

(VI)   Justice: right to a fair trial; presumption of innocence; right to protection from principles of legality and proportionality; right not to be tried twice for same offence.

Protocol 30 to the Charter contains what has been popularly referred to by the domestic media as the United Kingdom's 'opt-out'. It also applies to Poland and the Czech Republic. Its effect is to preclude the domestic courts in these countries from invalidating any 'laws, regulations, or administrative provisions, practices or action' which are inconsistent with the Charter or from finding that the social and economic rights contained in Chapter IV create 'justiciable' or autonomous legally enforceable rights.

Otherwise, EU citizens will be able to use the Charter as a basis for legal proceedings in both national courts and the EU General Court (previously the Court of First Instance) relating to the way EU law has been interpreted or the powers of the EU institutions of government have been exercised.

The Charter represents a more ambitious and wide-ranging statement of human rights than that currently provided by the Convention. To avoid incompatibility between the two, Art 52(3) of the Charter states that to the extent that it 'contains rights which correspond to rights guaranteed by the Convention for the Protection of Human Rights and Fundamental Freedoms, the meaning and scope of those rights shall be the same as those laid down by the said Convention . . .' The Charter is intended, therefore, to complement, rather than to compete with, Europe's existing human rights legal system.

The European Court of Human Rights

Composition

The current provisions relating to the composition and working of the ECtHR are contained in Articles 19–51 of the Convention. Judges of the Court are elected by the Parliamentary Assembly from lists of three nominees proposed by each member state (Art 22). The number of judges elected is equivalent to the number of contracting states at any one time (Art 20). They are appointed for non-renewable terms of nine years. The age of retirement is 65 (Protocol 15). Those appointed are required to be persons of high moral character and of recognised juristic competence (Art 21). Judges sit in their individual capacity. They do not represent any state and must not engage in any activity which is incompatible with their independence or with the demands of full-time office (Art 23). A judge may not be removed from office unless the other judges decide by a two-thirds majority that he/she has ceased to fulfil the required obligations (Art 24).

Organisation and operation

Objective
4

The Court functions through Committees, Chambers and a Grand Chamber (Art 27). Committees consist of three judges and deal primarily with questions of admissibility relating to individual applications under Art 34. The principal grounds for admission are that:

(a) all domestic remedies whether judicial or administrative have been exhausted (*McCaughey* v *United Kingdom* [2013] ECHR 682, killings of civilians in N Ireland by security forces – not open to ECtHR to consider alleged breaches of Art 2 while related civil proceedings ongoing);

(b) the complaint was properly made within four months of such exhaustion (*Ngendakuamana* v *Netherlands* 116380/11 [2013] ECHR 421, application made within six months containing all required information and documents, not properly presented without signature of applicant or representative);

(c) the complaint does not amount to an abuse of the right to complain, i.e. it raises a genuine rather than frivolous or vexatious grievance and is not made for any improper purpose, e.g. political propaganda;

(d) it relates to a right protected by the Convention;

(e) it does not attempt to assert a right in a way which extinguishes another, e.g. by assertion of the right of assembly to an extent incompatible with the freedom of expression;

(f) it is substantially the same as a matter already examined by the Court or by another procedure of international investigation.

Where a Committee concludes that an application 'is not considered inadmissible', the application will be transferred to a Chamber (Art 29). Chambers consist of seven judges and are empowered to decide on both the admissibility and merits of individual and inter-state applications (ibid.). Chamber decisions will normally be final save for any case which raises 'a serious question affecting the interpretation of the Convention or where the resolution of the questions . . . might have a result inconsistent with a judgment previously delivered by the Court' (Art 30). In these circumstances a Chamber may 'relinquish jurisdiction in favour of the Grand Chamber' (ibid.). The Grand Chamber consists of 17 judges. In addition to that just described, its jurisdiction extends at the request of one of the parties and 'in exceptional circumstances' to the re-examination of a Chamber decision where this 'raises a serious question affecting the interpretation or application of the Convention . . . on a serious issue of general importance' (Art 43). Such application for re-examination should be made within three months of the Chamber decision complained of (Art 44). Except in these circumstances, i.e. those provided for in Art 30 and 43, Chamber decisions are to be regarded as final.

Further changes to the organisation and workings of the Court were effected by Protocol 14, which entered into force in June 2010. These include the provisions that:

- plainly inadmissible decisions may be rejected by a single judge with cases of doubt being referred to a Committee or a Chamber;

- Committees of three judges will be able to declare applications admissible and reach decisions on their merits in clearly well-founded cases and those in which there is well-established case-law.

Procedure

Applications may be made by one contracting state against another (state application, Art 33) or by an individual against any such state (individual application, Art 34). The procedure before the Court is adversarial and in public unless, 'in exceptional circumstances' it decides otherwise (Art 40). Much of the Court's work, however, is based on consideration of written submissions which are also accessible to the public (*ibid.*). Oral proceedings are conducted through legal representation for which legal aid is available.

Once a case has been admitted and before proceeding to a decision on the merits, the Court will attempt to achieve a 'friendly settlement' between the parties (Art 38). Negotiations to this end are confidential and may result, for example, in the payment of compensation, the changing of an offending government decision or a commitment to a change of law or administrative practice. In *Faulkner* v *United Kingdom*, *The Times*, 11 January 2000, the applicant complained that legal aid was not available in Guernsey to enable him to sue the authorities there for false imprisonment – an alleged breach of Art 6 (right to a fair trial). The matter was resolved by friendly settlement involving an undertaking by the United Kingdom to reform the legal aid system in Guernsey to bring it into compliance with Convention requirements and by payment to the applicant of £6,000 compensation and £14,000 costs. A friendly settlement also disposed of the application in *Tsavachidis* v *Greece* [1999] ECHR 4, 21 January 1999, Hudoc, alleging breaches of Arts 8, 9 and 10 as a result of government interference with the activities of Jehovah's Witnesses. The Greek government undertook to pay compensation to the applicant and, more significantly, to discontinue the practices complained of, in particular that of secret surveillance.

If no such settlement can be reached, the Court will proceed to judgment. Findings on the merits are by majority vote (Art 44) and are binding on contracting states in international law (Art 46).

Workload

The number of cases dealt with by the Court has increased dramatically in recent years. In 2000 the number of applications considered was 10,500. By 2015 this had increased to 56,300 with 64,850 cases pending. Over half of these related to just four contracting states – Ukraine, 21.4 per cent, Russia, 16.7 per cent, Turkey, 13 per cent and Italy 11.36 per cent.

The vast bulk of cases do not proceed to final judgment. Most are either declared inadmissible or are struck out. The number of cases proceeding to judgment in 2015 was 823; 24.4 per cent of these concerned the right to a fair trial (Art 6), 23.02 per cent the prohibition of torture and inhuman or degrading treatment (Art 2) and 15.7 per cent the right to liberty and security (Art 5).

General principles of European human rights law

Matters of interpretation

As the Convention was originally conceived as a treaty between its signatory or contracting states, it is to be interpreted in accordance with the international rules governing such matters contained in the Vienna Convention on the Law of Treaties 1969, 'other principles of international law of which it forms a part', and in the fulfilment of treaty commitments entered into after the Convention was signed (*Al-Saadoon and Mufdhi* v *United Kingdom* [2010] ECHR 285).

In particular, this requires that a treaty 'be interpreted in good faith in accordance with the ordinary meaning to be given to the terms of the treaty in their context and in the light of its object and purpose' (Art 31).

This may be seen as the foundation of the Court's assertion that pursuit of the Convention's objectives should not be hindered by pedantic literalism or rigid adherence to outdated precedent. Rather, the Convention should be understood as a 'living instrument' to be given a meaning consistent with prevailing social, cultural and political tendencies in a contracting state (*Tyrer* v *United Kingdom* (1978) 2 EHRR 1, see p. 444).

The general objectives of the Convention have been defined as the 'protection of individual rights' (*Soering* v *United Kingdom* (1989) 11 EHRR 439) and the 'promotion of the ideals and values of a democratic society', to wit, 'pluralism, tolerance and broad-mindedness' (*Kjeldsen, Busk Madsen and Pedersen* v *Denmark* (1979–80) 1 EHRR 711); *Handyside* v *United Kingdom* (1979–80) 1 EHRR 737). Hence the Court's continued emphasis on the importance of Art 10 (freedom of expression), as underpinned by Art 11 (association and assembly), as one of the 'basic conditions for the foundation and progress of a democratic society' (*Piermont v France* (1995) 20 EHRR 301).

Consistent with the above, the Court does not recognise the doctrine of precedent beyond that necessary to ensure a reasonable degree of 'legal certainty and the orderly development of the Convention's case-law' (*Cossey v United Kingdom* (1990) 13 EHRR 622). The Court therefore preserves the right to depart from previous decisions where there are 'cogent reasons for doing so' (ibid.).

For the obligation to investigate deaths occurring before a state ratified the Convention, see pp. 435–6.

As a general rule, the Convention does not have retrospective effect and cannot be used to remedy abuses committed before it came into operation (1953) or was signed by a particular state (*Thiermann v Norway* app no 18712/03, 13.0.07). It cannot be relied on, therefore, in respect of atrocities committed in World War II (*Associazione Reduci Dalla Prigionia Dalla 'Internamento E Dalla Guerra Di Liberazione' v Germany*, app no 45563/01, 4.9.07).

The Convention may be amended by the uniform and established practice of signatory states (*Soering v United Kingdom* (1989) 11 EHRR 439; *Ocalan v Turkey* (2005) 41 EHRR 45). Such constructive amendment would appear to have taken place in relation to those circumstances in which the Convention, in its original form, permitted the use of the death penalty, i.e. (Art 2(i)) 'in the execution of a sentence of a court following conviction of a crime for which this penalty is provided by law':

> all but two member states have now signed Protocol 13 and all but three of the states which have signed it have ratified it. These figures, together with consistent state practice in observing the moratorium on capital punishment, are strongly indicative that Art 2 has been amended so as to prohibit the death penalty in all circumstances (*Al-Saadoon and Mufdhi v United Kingdom*, *supra*).

Negative and positive obligations

When first instigated the Convention seems generally to have been understood as imposing a series of negative obligations on states by identifying those human rights with which they should not interfere. According to this approach, the state was not under any clear duty to act as guarantor of such rights by seeking to ensure that the activities of one individual did not impinge on the rights of another. It was enough that the state simply 'stood back' and refrained from any unwarranted transgression either by itself or those under its direction.

In more recent times, however, the Court has begun to develop a theory of state obligation which requires more than mere negative compliance. This has been premised to a considerable extent on the general but positive duty in Art 1 which requires contracting states 'to secure to everyone within that jurisdiction the rights and freedoms defined in . . . this Convention'.

Making the requirement effective and meaningful, it has been argued, requires the state to go beyond negative compliance and to do so by providing a system of laws, law enforcement and public administration which enable the individual to enjoy Convention rights free from interference whatever the source, i.e. whether from a state or the individual citizens.

This was the approach adopted by the Court in *Plattform 'Artze für das Leben' v Austria* (1991) 13 EHRR 204, where it found that the state's obligation in relation to the right of assembly (Art 11) was not discharged simply by allowing marches and demonstrations to take place within its jurisdiction. The state was obliged to go further by taking reasonable steps to ensure that any person or group wishing to exercise the right peacefully was able to do so notwithstanding the opposition of others. This, and cases like it, form the basis of the emerging principle that although the Convention was not designed to have 'horizontal effect', i.e. to be enforceable by one individual against another, an individual whose right is infringed by another private person may have a cause of action, albeit against the state, if the breach of the Convention right can be attributed to the state's failure to guarantee adequately the right in question.

This principle was applied in *Z v United Kingdom* (2001) 34 EHRR 97, where it was held that serious parental neglect could amount to inhuman and degrading treatment and that a failure by a local authority to use its powers to protect a child from being treated in this way constituted an actionable breach of its rights in Art 3.

The margin of appreciation

In securing the rights articulated by the Convention, each state is permitted a 'margin of appreciation' or independent national judgment. The Convention thus concedes a degree of flexibility and discretion in the way it is interpreted and applied in the national context. No attempt is made, therefore, to set rigid and absolute standards. Were it otherwise the potential for political tensions between member states, and between such states and the court, would be greatly increased to the detriment of the consensual basis on which the effective operation of the Convention depends. What is required, therefore, is that member states achieve the maximum degree of compliance with the Convention's general standards as is compatible with particular national interests, circumstances and traditions. The doctrine of the margin of appreciation reflects the conception on which the Convention was originally based, i.e. that the primary obligation for the protection of human rights lies with the state. According to this view, the Convention should be seen as imposing general standards of official conduct and a right to challenge state action where there has been less than substantial compliance.

It is apparent that the extent of the margin of appreciation permitted to states varies depending on the particular legitimate aim pursued and the nature of the right alleged to have been infringed. A considerable margin appears to be permitted to states, for example, in relation to measures dealing with public morality. Hence the Court's view in *Handyside v United Kingdom* (1976) 1 EHRR 737, that 'the view taken . . . of the requirements of morals varies from time to time and from place to place, especially in our era' and that 'by reason of their direct and continuous contact with the vital forces of their countries, state authorities are in principle in a better position than the international judge to give an opinion on the exact content of those requirements'. A similar tendency to give considerable deference to the judgment of state authorities also appears to apply to measures dealing with national security and with social and economic policies.

Despite surrounding controversy, the law regulating *in vitro* fertilisation (IVF) in the UK (Human Fertilisation and Embryology Act 1990) was held to fall within the state's margin of appreciation in *Evans v United Kingdom* [2007] ECHR 264. The Act gives both parties to a marriage/relationship the right to withdraw consent from treatment at any time before the embryos are implanted. The applicant argued that her husband's withdrawal of consent after their relationship had ended effectively denied her the Art 8 right to give birth and form a genetically related family. Her ex-husband's case was that Art 8 gave him the right not to have a family or to do so with the person of his choice.

The ECtHR's decision was that the case raised issues of 'great moral and ethical delicacy' on which there was no European consensus or common approach either to the question whether the practice should be used at all or in what circumstances. It was, therefore, a matter in relation to which all contracting states should be allowed the widest possible margin in determining the appropriate legal rules.

The nature and subject-matter of the right in issue are further factors to be considered. Thus, for example, greater flexibility appears to be afforded to states in matters affecting Arts 8 and 9 (respect for family life and the freedom of religion), than is permitted in relation to Art 10 (freedom of expression) which the Court has repeatedly stressed has an irreducible minimum if the standards of liberal democracy on which the Convention is founded are to be maintained.

Unqualified, limited and qualified rights

The Convention contains what has been referred to as a hierarchy of rights which fall into three broad categories distinguished by the grounds and the extent to which the rights therein may be restricted by the state.

The first category contains the unqualified or absolute rights. It encompasses Arts 3 (prohibition of torture), 4 (prohibition of slavery), and 7 (no punishment without law) and elements of Art 9 (thought, conscience and religion). These rights may not be restricted or interfered with by the state whatever the circumstances or however pressing the state may perceive the public or social interest to be.

Articles 2, 5 and 6 fall into the second category, the limited rights. These deal with the right to life, the right to liberty and security of the person and the right to a fair trial. Such rights may be subject to restrictions but only in accordance with the specific and strictly limited circumstances as prescribed by the Articles.

The third category consists of the Convention's qualified rights. The exact circumstances in which these may be subject to state interference are not so precisely defined as with the limited rights, but any restriction must be based on clear legal authority ('according to' or 'prescribed by law') and must be proportionate ('reasonably necessary in a democratic society') to the achievement of any of the Convention's legitimate aims, e.g. the prevention of crime or the protection of public order or health. The principal rights in this category are those contained in Arts 8 (private and family life), 9 (freedom to manifest one's religion), 10 (expression) and 11 (assembly and association).

The principle of certainty (according to or prescribed by law)

The requirement that restrictions imposed on Convention rights should be according to or prescribed by law (see in particular, Arts 8, 9, 10 and 11) has three principal, related elements all inherent in the doctrine of the Rule of Law and its insistence that that which is to qualify as law must have a certain minimum form and quality. Hence, according to the case-law of the European Court of Human Rights, any attempted restriction of a Convention right will be legally valid and effective only if it is:

(a) founded on and in full compliance with an established form of law, i.e. in the United Kingdom context, legislation or common law, rather than mere policy rules or administrative guidelines;

(b) readily accessible and available to members of the general public;

(c) phrased in sufficiently clear terms to enable individuals affected to adjust their conduct as required.

The principle is well illustrated in the domestic context by the decisions in *Steel and Others* v *United Kingdom* and *Hashman and Harrup* v *United Kingdom*. Both were concerned with the common law powers of police and magistrates in the United Kingdom to deal with alleged breaches of the peace at public demonstrations and the compatibility of such powers with the requirement in Art 10(2) that any interference with the right of assembly should be 'prescribed by law'.

Steel and Others v United Kingdom (1999) 28 EHRR 603

In this case, exception was taken to the common law power of police officers to arrest and detain any person behaving in a way likely to cause such breach of the peace. This, it was argued, did not achieve the necessary degree of legal certainty since neither the meaning of what constituted a breach of the peace or amounted to behaviour likely to cause the same had ever been adequately defined. After careful consideration of the common law in issue, the Court came to the conclusion that this hitherto rather vague aspect of English police powers had been addressed to its satisfaction by the English courts in a number of decisions during the 1980s and 1990s. It was thereby 'sufficiently established that a breach of the peace is only committed when an individual causes harm, or appears likely to cause harm, to persons or property or acts in a manner the natural consequence of which would be to provoke others to violence'.

Hashman and Harrup v United Kingdom (2000) 30 EHRR 241

The application in this case was rather more successful. The case arose out of a demonstration against fox hunting and was concerned with the power of magistrates to bind persons over to keep the peace and to be of good behaviour as entrusted to them as long ago as the Justice of the Peace Act 1361. In this instance the Court accepted the complaint that the prescription 'to be of good behaviour' did not make clear exactly what it was 'that the subject of the order may or may not lawfully do'. Nor could the Court, as in the *Steel* case, find any previous judicial decisions in which the exact meaning of the phrase had been adequately defined. It amounted, therefore, to the very type of vague and imprecise restriction on the right of assembly which Art 10(2) sought to proscribe.

The above principles and requirements are also applicable to statutory provisions. In **Liberty v United Kingdom** [2008] ECHR 568 the applicants alleged that, during the 1990s, all tele-communications between Dublin, London and the continent of Europe had been monitored and intercepted by the British government. Some of the intercepted material, it was argued, must inevitably have included communications between the applicants and clients in Ireland, which the applicants had assumed were subject to legal privilege. The applicants claimed breach of Art 8 (right to privacy), and in particular the right to respect for private correspondence in that, while the actions of the state may have been for a legitimate aim within the meaning of Art 8(2), the statutory scheme in the Interception of Communications Act 1985 for the authorising and regulation of intercepts did not contain any clear rules setting out the criteria for determining, *inter alia*, the types of such communications which could be subject to further examination and which, if any, could be disseminated to other members of the government and intelligence services and possibly stored for further security or criminal investigation purposes.

In finding for the applicants the ECtHR concluded that the relevant provisions in the 1985 Act failed to indicate 'with sufficient clarity, so as to provide adequate protection against abuse of power, the scope or manner of exercise of the very wide discretion conferred on the state to intercept and examine external communications' and, in particular, 'it did not, as required by the Court's case-law, set out in a form accessible to the public any indication of the procedure to be followed for selecting for examination, sharing, storing and destroying, intercepted material'. See also ***Bykov v Russia*** [2009] ECHR 441 (police use of remote radio transmitting device to listen to applicant's conversations in his private premises – no effective and accessible legal rules regulating this type of surveillance).

Proportionality

The concept of proportionality as a means of testing whether municipal action is compatible with Convention standards is well established in the jurisprudence of the Court of Human Rights. Hence where a state claims that a particular action represented an exercise of a lawful power to protect a legitimate public interest, the test applied will be whether the action taken was proportionate to the aims pursued and whether the reasons for it given by the state were both relevant and sufficient.

Bowman v United Kingdom (1998) 26 EHRR 1

In this case, the applicant distributed literature in a parliamentary constituency (Halifax) during the 1997 General Election which contained information explaining the views of the main candidates concerning abortion. This was alleged to be an offence under the Representation of the People Act 1983, s 75, which prohibited expenditure of over £5 in a particular constituency during an election campaign by any unauthorised person (i.e. a person not authorised by an election agent) for the purpose of promoting or disparaging a specific candidate or candidates.

The applicant argued that the offence represented a constraint on her freedom of expression contrary to Art 10 of the Convention. Article 10 permits restrictions on the right only to the extent that these are 'necessary in the interests of a democratic society' for the protection of certain public interests. The Court recognised that some limits on election expenditure during General Election campaigns might be legitimate for the purpose of preserving equality between candidates and, therefore, ensuring fair elections as required by Protocol 1, Art 3. The provision of the 1983 Act, s 75, however, operated as an unnecessarily severe restriction on the dissemination of opinions during such elections. The Court found difficulty in understanding how, in a society which imposed no limits on the amount of money political parties could spend on their national publicity campaigns, it could be thought 'necessary' to restrict the expenditure of individuals seeking to disseminate views in particular constituencies to just £5.

The concept was also applied in ***Steel v United Kingdom*** which, as already explained, dealt with the power of police in the United Kingdom to arrest and detain demonstrators for behaviour likely to cause a breach of the peace.

The case was a composite of three separate applications under Art 10, all raising similar issues. In the first a demonstrator had walked in front of a member of a grouse shoot to prevent him discharging his gun. The applicant in the second case had placed herself in front of construction machinery to prevent it from being used to clear the ground for the construction of a motorway. In both instances the Court felt the behaviour in issue posed a real danger to public order to the extent that the arrest and detention of the applicants could not be regarded as disproportionate to the legitimate aim pursued by the police, viz. 'the prevention of disorder' (Art 10(2)).

The third application was made by a group of demonstrators who had assembled outside a conference centre where a meeting of the arms industry was taking place. The demonstrators carried placards and distributed leaflets. No disruption was caused nor was anything said or done which was particularly an offence to those entering the building. In these very different circumstances the court was unable to discern any acceptable degree of proportionality between the actions of the police and the needs of public order.

Legitimate aims

Restrictions placed on the Convention's qualified rights must be directed towards the promotion of one or more of the public interests or 'legitimate aims' recognised by the Article in question. The legitimate aims common to Arts 8–11 are public safety, the protection of public order, health or morals and the rights of others. Other legitimate aims include the protection of national security and the prevention of crime (Arts 8(2), 10(2) and 11(2)), the economic well-being of the country (Art 8(2)), territorial integrity, confidentiality and the reputation of the judiciary (Art 10(2)).

Imposition of a restriction for any other purpose or public concern, however laudable this may appear to be, would breach the Convention article to which it related.

Piermont v *France* (1995) 20 EHRR 301

In this case, the applicant, a German 'green' MEP went to a French administered island in the South Pacific where a general election was about to be held. The applicant spoke at a number of political rallies and was extremely critical of the French government's reluctance to discontinue nuclear tests in that part of the world. Despite the fact that no recorded incidents of violence had occurred on such occasions and that she had not advocated any such violence or disorder, the applicant was ordered to be deported for what was described as 'an attack on French policy'. The Court found a breach of Art 10(1) on the ground that the action taken against her had been taken for largely political reasons none of which fell within the legitimate aims for which restrictions of freedom of expression could be imposed according to Art 10(2).

The rights protected by the Convention

Objective 5

Article 1 requires the contracting states to secure adequate protection for the following rights and freedoms.

Right to life (Art 2)

Content

Article 2 imposes two express obligations on the state. These are:

(a) the duty to protect life ('everyone's right to life shall be protected by law') (Art 2(1)); and

(b) the duty not to use potentially lethal force except where this is 'absolutely necessary' to:
- defend a person from unlawful violence;
- effect an arrest or prevent a prisoner from escaping;
- quell a riot or insurrection (Art 2(2)).

Beyond these express requirements, and in the years since the inception of the Convention, the ECtHR has interpreted Art 2(1) as containing a number of further obligations of an implied nature. These are:

(a) a duty to put in place effective legal, administrative, and law enforcement systems, sufficient to protect against:
- offences against the person;
- the use of excessive force by the state;
- hazardous or dangerous activities and events;
- inadequate health services;

(b) a duty to take appropriate preventative operational measures to safeguard the lives of:
- those who may be at risk from the criminal acts of others;
- those belonging to certain vulnerable categories of individuals under the control of the state, viz. prisoners, compulsory psychiatric patients and military conscripts;

(c) a duty to investigate thoroughly the causes of all deaths (other than those from natural causes) and life-threatening events – particularly those in which the state or its agents may appear to have been involved.

The justification for the development of these implied elements of Art 2(1) derives from the assumed founding intention that the Convention should remain an effective living instrument relevant to the times and circumstances in which it is being applied.

The crucial nature of the rights contained in Art 2 is self-evident. Without these, the rights in the Articles that follow could be rendered meaningless. As a result, the obligations imposed on the state by Art 2 cannot be derogated or departed from whatever the circumstances whether during peace, war or national emergency.

The phrase 'protected by law' in Art 2(1) means that, although there is no fixed obligation on contracting states to incorporate the Convention into their domestic legal systems, they are nevertheless under a binding expectation to ensure that they have laws in place which give substantial effect to it.

The ECHR and the meaning of life

The meaning of the word 'life' is, of course, central to Art 2's scope and application. As the Article provides protection for 'everybody's' life, it has no application to any species of life other than human life. No protection is given, therefore, to animals or to artificial legal persons, e.g. private companies or public authorities. This should not be understood, however, as meaning that all such non-human entities are completely beyond the Convention's scope and its safeguards in their entirety. Indeed, the law of the Convention is replete with examples of successful applications by companies, trade unions, and religious bodies, seeking the protection of Convention articles not similarly restricted to human beings (e.g. Art 6, right to a fair trial; Art 9, freedom of religion; Art 10, freedom of expression; Art 11, freedom of association and assembly).

No clearly definitive statement can be found in the jurisprudence of the ECtHR indicating when, at least for Convention purposes human life begins, i.e. whether this should be understood as being at conception, birth, or at some time between these two events as when, for example, the foetus might be considered to be viable. Nor is any such guidance offered by the terms of the Convention itself which contains no reference to the matter whatsoever. This alone provides ample testimony to the degree of controversy which the matter engenders and the strength of feeling which the different opinions attract.

Against this background, the modern approach of the ECtHR has been to recognise and accept the vexed nature of the moral, theological and scientific issues in play, the lack of any consensus related to the rights of the unborn amongst contracting states, and on this basis to acknowledge that this should be one of those aspects of European human rights law in which states should be allowed a generous margin or appreciation, i.e. the ability to develop national law in ways consistent with the general precepts of the Convention but which also reflect national values and traditions.

The interpretation of Article 2 in this connection has been informed by a clear desire to strike a balance, and the Convention institutions' position in relation to the legal, medical, philosophical, ethical or religious dimensions of defining the human being has taken into account the various approaches to the matter at national level. This has been reflected in the consideration of the diversity of views on the point at which life begins, of legal cultures and national standards of protection, and the state has been left with considerable discretion in the matter (*Vo v France* [2004] ECHR 326).

While it remained in existence, the matter was considered on a number of occasions by the European Commission of Human Rights. The Commission's remit, as explained previously, was concerned primarily with establishing the facts of cases and determining questions of admissibility. Its findings and opinions, therefore, may not be regarded as being of the same force or status as those of the ECtHR itself.

The cases in issue were concerned with various aspects of abortion, i.e. the deliberate and artificial termination of the development of the foetus. Overall, the Commission tended to err in favour of the view that, for Convention purposes, human life should be understood as beginning at the time of birth. Otherwise, the Commission's general approach may be summarised as follows:

(a) Article 2(1) should not be perceived as vesting the unborn child with any absolute right to life;

(b) the termination of pregnancy was not, therefore, in all circumstances contrary to the Convention's requirements;

(c) any rights which might be conferred on the unborn child should be regarded as of limited effect only;

(d) if and when such rights were to be identified, these should be balanced with, and should not prevail over, the rights and interests of the mother;

(e) given the complexity and emotive nature of the issues involved, and the diverse ways in which these are dealt with by the legal systems of member states, this was not an area in which the ECHR's institutions should attempt to lay down any rigidly prescriptive rules.

The life of the foetus is intimately connected with, and cannot be regarded in isolation of, the life of the pregnant woman. If Article 2 were to be held to cover the foetus and its protection under the Article were, in the absence of an express limitation, seen as absolute, an abortion would have to be considered as prohibited even where the continuance of the pregnancy would involve a serious risk to the pregnant woman. This would mean that the unborn life of the foetus would be regarded as having a higher value than the life of the pregnant woman (*X v United Kingdom* (1980) app no 8416/79).

Of the few cases in which the rights of the unborn child under Article 2 have been contemplated in any detail by the ECtHR, *Vo v France*, cited above, may be regarded as one of the most prominent. As will be seen, however, such were the particular contentions raised in the case, that it was possible for these to be disposed of without the Court having to express any unequivocal view as to whether or not the unborn attract any rights under Article 2 and, if so, what these might be.

The applicant in *Vo* was a pregnant woman who attended a hospital in France for a related and routine examination. Whilst there, she was mistaken for another patient of the same name who was in the hospital to have a coil removed. As a result of this error, the doctor who examined the application unintentionally pierced the applicant's amniotic sac. This, in turn, led to her having to undergo a 'therapeutic' abortion and the loss of her six-month-old foetus.

In the French courts, the applicant sought unsuccessfully to have the doctor responsible convicted of the crime of unintentional homicide – the finding of the Court of Cassation being that the offence did not apply to the unborn child. In her subsequent application to the ECtHR, the applicant argued that, absent any appropriate criminal process through which the matter could be disposed of, the French legal system was unable to provide protection for the right to life of the foetus as required by Article 2(1). The Court's principal findings were:

(a) in respect of unintentional deaths in the sphere of public health, the Article 2 requirement that the domestic legal system provide protection for the right to life could be satisfied by the availability of effective civil procedures and did not necessitate the existence of criminal law sanctions;

(b) it followed that, in the French system, the state's Article 2 obligation for unintentional deaths arising from medical treatment was fulfilled by the right of the individual to sue for damages for negligence by way of an adversarial procedure;

(c) even in the event that Article 2 were to be construed as directly applicable to the unborn child, the civil process thus provided was sufficient to protect the rights of both the mother and the foetus;

(d) without anything approaching European consensus in the matter, the issue of when life begins was better left to be decided at state level.

Two further cases of interest and relevance in this context would be **Boso v Italy** [2002] ECHR 846 and **Evans v United Kingdom** [2006] ECHR 200. Neither decision, however, may be regarded as having any substantial effects on the principles explained above.

Boso concerned a complaint that the Italian law, which permitted the applicant's wife to have their child aborted against his wishes, did not provide adequate protection either for his rights or for the right to life of the unborn child. The law in question (Law no. 194, 1978), allowed for termination within twelve weeks, where the pregnancy put the woman's physical or mental health at risk, or, after that, where the continuance of the pregnancy would, inter alia, pose a real danger to the mother's life.

According to the ECtHR, and given the context, such provisions fell within the state's margin of appreciation and struck a 'fair balance between, on the one hand, the need to ensure protection of the foetus and, on the other, the woman's interests'. The Court thus concluded that the Italian state could not be found to have 'gone beyond its discretion in such a sensitive area'.

The issue in **Evans** was whether any legal rights could be regarded as attaching to the applicant's fertilised embryos. The case arose after the applicant's partner, whose sperm had been used to fertilise the applicant's eggs *in vitro*, withdrew his consent to their further use, i.e. to the fertilised eggs being implanted into the applicant's uterus. This withdrawal of consent resulted from the break-up of their relationship. According to the terms of the Human Fertilisation and Embryology Act 1990, in these circumstances, the fertilised eggs were required to be destroyed. In response to the applicant's contention that the requirements of the Act violated the embryo's right to life, the ECtHR, as in both *Vo* and *Boso*, fell back on the argument that 'in the absence of any European consensus on the scientific and legal definition of the beginning of life, the issue of when the right to life begins comes within the margin of appreciation which the Court generally considers that states should enjoy in this sphere'.

From the above it remains clear that existing ECHR jurisprudence may not be relied upon as forming the basis of any firm principle to the effect that certain minimum rights should be regarded as attaching to the unborn child and that these should be recognised and guaranteed by domestic legal systems. At the same time, however, it is not possible to interpret the relevant statements expressed by the ECtHR to date as unequivocally and categorically ruling out any such developments at some time ahead. The matter, therefore, remains open, thereby allowing the Court to change its position if and when the circumstances might change, e.g. as when any greater and related consensus might seem to be emerging amongst contracting states.

The ECHR and the death penalty

Article 2(1) expressly concedes to contracting states the right to administer capital punishment pursuant to 'the sentence of a court following . . . conviction of a crime for which this penalty is provided by law'. This is, however, now subject to Protocol 2, Art 6, and Protocol 13, Art 1, by which all contracting states, bar one (43 out of 44), have abolished its use. Such collective approach and practice would also appear to have been sufficient to effect a constructive amendment to Art 2(1), rendering the words permitting the death penalty to be no longer effective (*Al-Saadoon and Mufdhi* v *United Kingdom* [2010] ECHR 285).

Duty to protect life (Art 2(1))

(a) Effective legal, administrative, and law enforcement systems

The positive duty in Art 2(1) requiring states to take steps to protect the lives of those within their jurisdiction and to 'prevent life from being put avoidably at risk' was first recognised in *LCB* v *United Kingdom* (1998) 27 EHRR 212. Initially, the detailed content of this obligation was believed to be limited to the deterrence of crimes against the person – particularly crimes of violence.

> This involves a primary duty on the state to secure the right to life by putting in place an appropriate legal and administrative framework to deter the commission of offences against the person, backed up by law enforcement machinery for the prevention, suppression, and the punishment of breaches of such provisions (*Makaratzis* v *Greece* [2004] ECHR 694).

The need for 'appropriate legal, administrative and law enforcement systems' would appear to extend to the following:

- an adequate system of civil and criminal courts;
- adequate criminal and civil laws prohibiting crimes against the person;
- competent criminal investigative and prosecution processes;
- proper regulation of the use of force by the state, the security and armed forces.

(i) Protection against crimes of violence

In any state, an obvious threat to the right to life is that posed by the aggressive and violent tendencies of some members of the community. Clearly, no state can ensure conditions of absolute safety. As indicated, however, the obligation is to provide a degree of security generally commensurate with the normative expectations of European societies.

Opuz v *Turkey* [2009] ECHR 870 was a case of extreme domestic violence in which the applicant's mother was shot dead by the applicant's husband and the applicant herself was subject to a series of brutal assaults and beatings. This caused the applicant to become so fearful of her husband that she felt unable to press charges against him. An Article in the Turkish Criminal Code provided that, in such circumstances, the public prosecutor was not under an obligation to proceed against the person allegedly responsible for the criminal act in question. It was also apparent, from the evidence in the case, that the Turkish authorities were generally reluctant to bring criminal charges in relation to what they perceived to be 'domestic disputes'. The ECtHR concluded that all of this produced a situation in which the Turkish legal system was not competent to ensure either that the criminal law was brought to bear in all cases of serious violence against the person or that this was done with sufficient rigour and expedition to deter further related incidents of physical aggression.

> However, the Court regrets to note that the criminal investigations in the instant case were strictly dependent on the pursuance of complaints by the applicant and her mother . . . it observes that the application of the aforementioned provisions and the cumulative failure of the domestic authorities to pursue criminal proceedings . . . deprived the applicant's mother of her life and safety. In other words, the legislative framework then in force . . . fell short of the requirements inherent in the state's positive obligation to establish and apply effectively a system punishing all forms of domestic violence and providing sufficient safeguards for the victims.

(ii) Protection against unlawful violence and the use of excessive force by the state

In relation to the police, the basic requirement is that the use of force, when effecting an arrest or exercising any other lawful power, should be subject to a clear framework of law and regulations sufficient to ensure that the conduct of police officers accords with the relevant standards of international law and with the 'pre-eminence of human life as a fundamental value' (*Nachova* v *Bulgaria* [2005] ECHR 465).

The above requirements remain applicable in the terrorist context. Hence, notwithstanding the severity of the threat posed to the state, anti-terrorist operations should be conducted within a legal and administrative framework which ensures proper regard for the right to life and in particular:

- adequate legal protection for the lives of ordinary people in areas where anti-terrorist operations are being carried out (*Kiliç* v *Turkey* [2000] ECHR 128);
- proper accountability of those responsible for, and involved in, such operations (ibid.);
- clear understanding amongst the state forces of the limited circumstances in which it is lawful to use lethal force (*Suleymanova* v *Russia* [2010] ECHR 663).

> In addition to setting out the circumstances when deprivation of life may be justified, Art 2 implies a primary duty on the state to secure the right to life by putting in place an appropriate legal and administrative framework defining the limited circumstances in which the law enforcement officials may use force and firearms, in the light of relevant international standards. Furthermore, the national law regulating police operations must secure a system of adequate and effective safeguards against arbitrariness and abuse of force and even against avoidable accident (*ibid.*).

(iii) Protection against dangerous activities or events

The extension of the duty to protect life to the risks posed by hazardous activities was recognised in *Öneryildiz* v *Turkey* [2004] ECHR 657.

In the case itself, 39 people, including 9 members of the applicant's family, were killed by a methane gas explosion in a rubbish dump near their home. The ECtHR was in no doubt that the accident was largely attributable to an inadequate regulatory system applicable to the disposal of rubbish, and to the failure of the relevant local authorities to enforce such regulatory powers as did exist.

> The obligation indisputably applies in the particular context of dangerous activities where, in addition, special emphasis must be placed on regulations geared to the special features of the activity in question, particularly with regard to the level of the potential risk to human lives. They must govern the licensing, setting up, operation, security and supervision of the activity, and must make it compulsory for all those concerned to take practical measures to ensure the effective protection of citizens whose lives may be endangered by the inherent risks . . . In any event, the relevant regulations must also provide for appropriate procedures, taking into account the technical aspects of the activity in question, for identifying shortcomings in the processes concerned, and any errors committed by those responsible at different levels.

In certain circumstances, the duty requires the state to have rules and systems in place designed 'to protect individuals from risks to their lives resulting from their own activity or behaviour' and have in place 'an appropriate regulatory system for rescuing people in distress and to ensure the availability of emergency services where it has been brought to the notice of the authorities that the life or health of an individual is at risk on account of injuries sustained as a result of an accident' (*Furdik v Slovakia* [2008] ECHR 1767). In the same case, it was made clear that 'the duty may go beyond the provision of essential emergency services such as fire brigade and ambulances . . . and include the provision of air-mountain or air-sea rescue facilities to assist those in distress'.

The duty to protect life has also been applied to the dangers posed by natural and environmental disasters. In *Budayeva v Russia* [2008] ECHR 216, eight people were drowned in a mud slide. The state was found liable through its failure to ensure the existence of a local government and regulatory system adequate to provide effective flood protection facilities and evacuation arrangements for those in immediate danger. The issue on *Ozel v Turkey*, app no 14350/05, 17.11.2015, was the application of Art 2 to loss of life caused by an earthquake. While conceding that the state had no control over earthquakes, the court observed that, in an area prone to this type of natural hazard, Art 2 required the authorities to adopt measures to reduce the scale of damage and any injury which might be caused. Appropriate planning and building regulations in a seismic-risk area were found to be essential anticipatory measures.

Also see *Albekov v Russia* [2008] ECHR 1029 (breach of Art 2(1) as a result of failure to have in place a regulatory system requiring areas used by the military to be fenced off, clearly signposted, and cleared of mines and other dangerous materials) and *Kalender v Turkey*, app no 4314/02, 15.12.09 (breach of Art 2 as a result of inadequate safety regulations and precautions leading to a fatal railway accident).

(iv) Protection against inadequate health care and medical services

After some uncertainty, it now appears to be established that the duty to protect life requires states to adopt a system of administrative processes and regulation sufficient to ensure 'high standards in the provision of health care and medical services' (*Powell v United Kingdom* [2000] ECHR 703). The duty does not extend, however, to individual errors of medical judgement or mistakes in clinical practice.

> The Court accepts that it cannot be excluded that acts and omissions of the authorities in the field of health care policy may, in certain circumstances, engage their responsibility under the positive limb of Article 2. However, where a contracting state has made adequate provision for securing high professional standards and the protection of lives of patients, it cannot accept that such matters as an error of judgment . . . in the treatment of a particular patient are sufficient of themselves to call a contracting state to account . . . under Article 2 of the Convention . . .

In this context, therefore, the primary concern of the ECtHR has been the general or overall standards and with ensuring that systemic failures do not lead to lives being lost or put at unnecessary risk. In practical terms, this means that health authorities should employ competent and well-qualified staff working with adequate resources and facilities according to accepted practices designed to protect the lives of patients.

This general duty is underpinned by the requirements:

1 to ensure the existence of an effective and independent judicial system so that the causes of deaths of patients in the care of the medical profession can be determined and those responsible made accountable (***Byrzykowski v Poland*** [2006] ECHR 648);

2 to ensure that inquiries into patient deaths take place promptly and that any failures of health care provision are communicated to others 'so as to prevent the repetition of similar errors and thereby contribute to the safety of users of all health services' (ibid.).

Inability to pay fees does not provide the state with a justification for failure to provide a patient with urgently needed treatment (***Senturk v Turkey*** [2013] ECHR 295).

(b) The operational duty of prevention

(i) Persons at risk from crimes of violence

The existence of a more 'targeted' duty to take specific measures to safeguard the life of a particular individual was first recognised in ***Osman v United Kingdom*** (1998) 29 EHRR 245. Here, the ECtHR laid down what has become known as the ***Osman*** duty or principle. This was that the state is under an obligation to take 'preventative operational measures' to protect an individual whose life was known, or ought to have been known, to be at 'real and immediate risk' from the criminal acts of another. In these circumstances, and if a breach of Art 2 is to be avoided, the relevant state authorities should 'take measures within the scope of their powers which, judged reasonably, might have been expected to avoid that risk'. The Court added that any such obligation should be applied in ways which avoided placing an impossible or disproportionate burden on the state and police bearing in mind 'the difficulties involved in policing a modern society, the unpredictability of human conduct and the operational choices which must be made in terms of priorities and resources'.

Subject to the above, it is also clear that the ***Osman*** duty applies to police or military operations in circumstances where it is known, or ought to have been known, that the lives of innocent individuals may be at risk. Accordingly, those involved in the planning, control and execution, of such operations should take 'all reasonable measures available to them in order to prevent a real and immediate risk of unnecessary and innocent loss of life' (***Abdurashidova v Russia*** [2010] ECHR 495).

(ii) Prisoners

As indicated above, and since the ***Osman*** decision, the case-law of the European Convention on Human Rights has extended the scope of the preventative operational duty in order to give additional protection to various categories of vulnerable individuals who, rather than controlling their own destinies, are completely dependent on the state for all decisions relating to their treatment and welfare.

The peculiar vulnerability of prisoners and detainees has been recognised in a series of cases since ***Keenan v United Kingdom*** (2001) 33 EHRR 38. Particular attention has been drawn to their susceptibility to violence, bullying, blackmail, sexual abuse by fellow inmates, self-harm and suicide, and to the fact that many prisoners suffer from mental disorders which may prejudice their ability to care for and protect themselves. The rule is, therefore, that if a prison authority knows, or ought to have known, that the life of a particular person in custody is under enhanced threat from self-harm, suicidal tendencies, or the violent propensities of other inmates, it is under a duty to do all that could reasonably be expected to safeguard the prisoner's right to life.

In *Renolde v France* [2008] ECHR 1085, a mentally disturbed young prisoner hung himself in his cell from a rope made from knotted sheets. This followed several incidents of self-harm and other suicide attempts. A breach of Art 2(1) was found in that, despite full knowledge of the prisoner's condition, the prison authorities had failed to ensure that he was provided with appropriate psychiatric treatment and that he was actually taking the medication which had been prescribed for him.

> In the light of the state's positive obligation to take preventative operational measures to protect an individual whose life is at risk it might have been expected that the authorities, faced with a prisoner known to be suffering from serious mental disturbance and to pose a suicide risk, would take special measures geared to his condition to ensure its compatibility with continued detention.

In these, as in other circumstances, if a breach of Art 2 is to be established, both elements of the *Osman* duty must be satisfied, i.e. the risk of suicide must be both real and immediate. Hence, where a prisoner who was being monitored regularly, and whose behaviour and mental state gave no indication of an imminent likelihood of suicide, managed to hang himself from the bars of his cell, no breach of Art 2(1) was committed. In these circumstances, the ECtHR concluded, although the risk of suicide may have been 'real', it could not have been judged to have been sufficiently immediate or imminent to have imported the *Osman* duty (*Keenan v United Kingdom*). Also see *Gagiu v Romania*, app no 63258/00, 24.2.09 (failure to provide medical care necessary to prevent prisoner's death where it was known or should have been known that he was suffering from a life-threatening disease).

The *Osman* duty applies to both sentenced prisoners and those detained under executive powers, e.g. pending deportation or held under anti-terrorist or special powers legislation (*Slimani v France* [2004] ECHR 396). It does not, however, require a state to intervene, either by release or force feeding, to prevent a prisoner or detainee from starving him- or herself to death – provided, that is, that the appropriate medical treatment has been administered or made available (*Horoz v Turkey*, app no 1639/03, 31.3.09).

(iii) Compulsory psychiatric patients

In terms of the protection offered by the *Osman* duty, comparison has inevitably been drawn between the position of sentenced prisoners and persons detained in mental hospitals. Clearly, psychiatric patients are similarly vulnerable to bullying, intimidation and violence from other patients, and have an enhanced susceptibility to self-harm and suicide. In addition, there will be those amongst such patients who, because of their mental condition, may be incapable of making decisions for themselves and who may be required to undergo courses of medical treatment or medication without their consent and with little or no knowledge of its purpose or effects.

Hence, for all these reasons, and because the state is entirely responsible for their safety and welfare, it is now accepted that the duty to protect life at the targeted operational level applies to any compulsory psychiatric patient whose life the state knows, or ought to have known, is at risk of self-harm, suicide or other immediate threat (*Herczegfalvy v Austria* (1992) 15 EHRR 437).

The case of *Nencheva v Bulgaria* app no 48609/06, 18.6.13; concerned the deaths of 15 mentally disordered and vulnerable children and young persons in a state-run institution. These occurred during the winter of 1996–97. Despite being aware of the poor conditions under which those affected were being kept, and that these had already cost lives, the state had failed to take any effective remedial action. Those conditions extended to insufficient food, medicines, clothes, bedding and heating.

(iv) Military conscripts

Persons conscripted into the armed forces are, like prisoners and compulsory patients, under the comprehensive control of the state and, at the same time, may be exposed to numerous dangers, risks, and pressures, seldom experienced by ordinary members of the civilian population. Since, as the evidence shows, such factors tend to increase the risk of suicide, they have, in a number of cases, been accepted as providing sufficient justification for including conscripts within the ambit of the *Osman* principle.

Kilinc v *Turkey* [2005] ECHR 367, *Ataman* v *Turkey* [2006] ECHR 481 and *Demirci* v *Turkey* [2008] ECHR 477 were all cases in which young military conscripts, with known psychiatric disorders, shot themselves after being provided with loaded guns for the purpose of guard duties. In each case it was held that the state had failed in its duty towards the soldiers, and that persons of this type, who were known to be at risk, should, in general, not be allocated to duties which involved the use of firearms, nor should they be allowed access to weapons of any type.

(c) Duty to investigate

The positive duty to protect life has been held to be infringed where no 'thorough and adequate investigation' has been conducted into deaths in police custody or as a result of the operations of security forces (*Aksoy* v *Turkey* (1997) 27 EHRR 553). It is now clear that the duty applies to any death caused by use of force or in circumstances where it appears that agents of the state may have been implicated. The state should act of its own volition and not leave it to next of kin to press for an explanation. Failure to investigate properly the lethal shooting of IRA suspects at a time when it was alleged that the security forces in Northern Ireland were engaged in a shoot-to-kill policy was, according to this principle, held to be a breach of Art 2 in *Jordan and Others* v *United Kingdom* (2001) 11 BHRC 1.

Also, in the Northern Ireland context, the ECtHR reached similar findings in a series of later decisions concerned with complaints of alleged security force involvement in a number of paramilitary killings (*Bracknell* v *United Kingdom* [2007] ECHR 989; *McCartney* v *United Kingdom* [2007] ECHR 994; *O'Dowd* v *United Kingdom* [2007] ECHR 990). The full facts of these killings were never brought to light. The need for proper scrutiny and explanation was explained in *Bracknell* as follows:

> . . . it must be remembered that the essential purpose of such investigations is to secure the effective implementation of the domestic laws which protect the right to life and, in those cases involving state agents or bodies, to ensure their accountability for deaths occurring under their responsibility.

To date, the most extensive application of the various requirements of the Article 2 investigative duty was that provided by the ECtHR in *Armani de Silva* v *United Kingdom* [2016] ECHR 314. The case arose from the death of Jean Charles de Menezes, a young Brazilian man, who was mistakenly shot dead by a police officer in the immediate aftermath of the London tube bombings in 2005. No breach of Article 2, whether in relation to the actions of the police on the day in question or to subsequent inquiries into what had happened, was found – the court being satisfied with the thoroughness of the way in which the authorities had looked into the tragic incident. The key elements of the duty lying on the state in such circumstances was said to be as follows:

(i) the persons responsible for and carrying out the investigation should be independent from those implicated in the events;

(ii) the investigation should be capable of leading to the establishment of the facts, of determining whether the force used was or was not justified, and of identifying and punishing those responsible;

(iii) reasonable steps should be taken to secure all the relevant evidence including, *inter alia*, eye-witness testimony, forensics, and, where appropriate, an autopsy which provided a complete and accurate record of injury and an objective analysis of clinical findings including the cause of death;

(iv) the investigation's conclusions must be based on thorough objective and impartial analysis of all relevant elements;

(v) the nature and degree of scrutiny required to satisfy the minimum threshold of the investigation's effectiveness should depend on the circumstances of each case and the practicalities of the related investigative work;

(vi) particularly stringent scrutiny should be applied to suspicious deaths in which state agents are implicated;

(vii) the investigation should be accessible to the deceased's family to the extent necessary to safeguard their legitimate interests;

(viii) there should be an appropriate element of public scrutiny;

(ix) the investigation should be conducted with all due promptness and expedition;

(x) should the investigation involve or lead to legal proceedings, these should satisfy the obligation to protect the right to life by law and ensure that life-threatening offences do not go unpunished.

Where an application under Art 2 arising from alleged killings by state forces has been lodged, any failure to provide documents and papers requested by the Court may, of itself, amount to a failure to conduct a proper investigation (*Musayev v Russia* [2007] ECHR 643). Any investigation that is initiated should be concluded with reasonable expedition (*McCaughey v United Kingdom* [2013] ECHR 682 – inquest into killing of applicant's relatives in 1990 in Northern Ireland by members of security forces not held until 2012, breach of Art 2).

In *Tanis v Turkey* [2005] ECHR 561, the relatives of two persons believed to have been taken into police custody, and who subsequently disappeared, made a successful application under Art 3 in respect of the increased psychological suffering inflicted on them by the slow, obstructive and ineffective nature of the subsequent, unsuccessful inquiry into the 'mystery'. From this and other cases, it is apparent that the duty to investigate alleged breaches of the Convention by state officials also arises in relation to the possible infliction of inhuman or degrading treatment.

In two particular circumstances, the duty to investigate may be invoked in relation to deaths in which a state or its agents may be alleged to have been involved but which took place before the date on which the state in question ratified the Convention (the 'critical' date). As will be explained, these should not be understood as overt exceptions to the rule that the Convention does not apply retrospectively.

The circumstances referred to may arise where:

(a) a 'genuine connection' could be found between the death and the investigative obligation resting on the state;

or

(b) the normal requirements for such connection might not be present but the alleged abuse of human rights was so heinous as to challenge the essential human rights values on which the Convention was founded.

In both situations, the obligations under Article 2 arise from what was done or should have been done in relation to deaths after the state in question ratified the Convention – thus preserving the rule that proceedings may not be brought against the state in respect of deaths occurring before that date.

The elements of a genuine connection have been said to include:

1 the death(s) occurred 'shortly', and not more than ten years, before the 'critical date' for the state in question, but elements of the investigation into it/them were carried out after that date;

or

2 a 'plausible' piece of new and relevant evidence came to light after the 'critical date' which was 'sufficiently weighty and compelling' to warrant a new round of proceedings (*Janowiec* v *Russia* [2013] ECHR 1003).

The 'fall back' requirement of a breach of Convention values, i.e. where the above 'genuine connection' criteria appear not be satisfied, may be found to exist in those unusual and, therefore, rare circumstances in which the post-ratification obligations were related to an earlier incident of killing or loss of life which was 'of a larger dimension than an ordinary criminal offence and amounted to the negation of the very foundations of the Convention' (*Janowiec*). Examples given included war crimes, genocide and crimes against humanity.

Neither the 'genuine connection' nor the Convention values tests may be used as the basis of proceedings relating to events, however serious, which occurred before the Convention came into existence. Thus the Grand Chamber's decision in *Janowiec* that no Convention obligation lay on the Russia Federation to investigate the events surrounding the Katyn Massacre of 1940 – i.e. the 'extra-judicial executions' of over 20,000 Polish military personnel by officers of the Russian secret police (the NKVD).

The use of lethal force (Article 2(2))

General principles

Article 2(2) permits the state to use force that may result in loss of life but only in certain limited circumstances (see above) and where this is 'absolutely necessary' for the end pursued. To secure compliance with these restrictions, the ECtHR has insisted that states put in place a clear and adequate framework of laws and administrative rules 'defining the limited circumstances in which law-enforcement officers may use force and firearms' (*Nachova* v *Bulgaria*, *supra*).

An actual death is not an absolute precondition for the application of this part of the Article. It is sufficient that the individual was the 'victim of conduct which by its very nature put [his/her] life at risk' (*Kolyadenko* v *Russia* [2012] ECHR 338).

Perhaps, inevitably, and to ensure, as the Convention directs, that potentially lethal force is resorted to only as a weapon of last resort, and in extremis, considerable attention has been paid to the requirements of the concept of absolute necessity. Thus, the ECtHR has stressed repeatedly that the term 'absolutely necessary': 'indicates a stricter and more compelling test of necessity must be employed from that normally applicable when determining whether state action is necessary in a democratic society under para 2 of Arts 8–11 of the Convention' (**Bubbins v United Kingdom** [2005] ECHR 159). In this context, therefore, the level of force used must be strictly proportionate to the achievement of the aims pursued. Applied practically, this means, for example, that when exercising the power of arrest – the second of the permitted circumstances in which lethal force may be used:

> there can be no such necessity where it is shown that the person to be arrested poses no threat to life or limb and is not suspected of having committed a violent offence even if the failure to use lethal force may result in the opportunity to arrest the fugitive being lost (**Nachova**, *supra*).

The precondition of absolute necessity is not, however, insisted upon without some degree of flexibility and it has been recognised that some extra latitude should be allowed to a state where it is dealing with sudden life-threatening situations, over which its agencies have only minimal control and, of which, its police and security forces may have little experience, e.g. acts of terrorism.

> That being said, the Court may occasionally depart from that rigorous standard of 'absolute necessity'. As the cases show, its application may be simply impossible where certain aspects of the situation be far beyond the Court's expertise and where the authorities had to act under tremendous time pressure and where their control of the situation was minimal (**Finogenov v Russia** [2011] ECHR 2234).

In similar vein, it has been accepted that 'exceptional measures' may be taken by the state where this appears necessary to deal with 'illegal armed insurgency' and that, at the extremes, these may include the deployment of armed combat troops and the use of strikes by military aircraft. Such actions should, however, be carefully planned, taking into account the risk posed to the lives of civilians, and directed as precisely as possible against the insurgents. It follows that such exceptional measures do not extend to the indiscriminate bombing of areas in which it is expected there may be civilians (**Kerimova v Russia** [2011] ECHR 744).

Controlling public demonstrations

The ECtHR has expressed particular concern about the use of lethal force to deal with public demonstrations and has stressed both the need for proportionality and that such force should be resorted to only as a last resort as part of carefully controlled operations (**Koshiyev v Russia** [2005] ECHR 132 (needless killing of civilians in Chechen War)). See also **Erdogan v Turkey** [2005] app no 19807/92, 13.9.06 (opening fire on violent but unarmed protestors without any attempt to use less-threatening methods – tear gas, water cannon, rubber bullets, etc.). In all such cases, the state authorities must ensure that 'the public order operation was planned, organised, and carried out in such a way as to minimise as so far as possible the use of lethal force'. Providing this is done, an honest but reasonable mistake by one of the state's agents trying to restore the peace, does not amount to a breach of Art 2.

> The court reiterates that the use of force by agents of the state in pursuit of the aims of Article 2 . . . may be justified under this provision where it is based on an honest belief which is perceived for good reasons to be valid at the time but which subsequently turns out to be mistaken (**Giuliani and Gaggio v Italy** [2009] ECHR 1271).

Members of the police and security forces are expected to possess the appropriate moral and physical qualities for the effective exercise of their functions. It was, therefore, no answer to an alleged breach of Article 2(2) by an officer who opened fire on a rowdy demonstration to argue that he had acted in an 'excusable state of emotion, fear or panic' (*Aydan* v *Turkey* app no 16281/10, 12.3.13).

Rescuing hostages

The requirements of Art 2 extend, in addition, to rescue operations by police and security forces where lives may be at risk, e.g. operations mounted to free persons being held hostage by terrorists. The requirement here is that the planning and implementation of such operations should be such that the risk of loss of life is reduced to a minimum. This was found not to have been the case in *Finogenov* v *Russia* (2011) ECHR 295, where a decision was taken to pump a little used narcotic gas into a Moscow theatre where over 900 people were being held by members of the Chechen separatist movement. Some of the failings of the operation listed by the Court included: no centralised coordination of the various emergency services involved; no directions as to how information about the victims' conditions and the medication administered to them should be recorded and exchanged; and no clear plan for their distribution to the available hospitals in order to avoid overcrowding.

Apprehending criminals and suspected terrorists

The need for proportionality and for careful planning applies also to the arrest of potentially dangerous and violent criminal suspects (*Saoud* v *France*, app no 9375/02, 9.10.07) and to operations to intercept suspected terrorists. The case of *McCann, Farrell and Savage* v *United Kingdom* (1995) 21 EHRR 97 concerned the attempted arrest and shooting dead of three IRA suspects in Gibraltar. It was held that, although it might not be a breach of the Convention to take the lives of terrorists believed to be about to detonate a bomb, the lack of proper planning or exercise of effective control over the arrest operation itself precluded those in charge of it from ensuring that lethal force was resorted to only in those circumstances permitted by Art 2(2), viz. that which was absolutely necessary to effect a lawful arrest.

Disappearances

In relation to what has been referred to as the 'disappearance cases', it has been made clear that a breach of Art 2 may be construed from the facts, i.e. a person is taken into custody, is not seen or heard of for years, and the state is unable to provide a plausible explanation for these events (*Shakhabova* v *Russia* [2010] ECHR 661).

Assisted dying

The right to life in Art 2, as interpreted by the Court of Human Rights, does not give a person the right to have their life ended or to be assisted in taking the necessary steps to achieve this result at the time of their own choosing. This remains the case notwithstanding that the person is terminally ill or that, through illness, their life has become intolerable (*Pretty* v *United Kingdom* [2002] 35 EHRR 1). It does, however, appear to permit both the withdrawal of treatment in appropriate cases (*Widner* v *Switzerland* 1993, unreported) (see below) and the termination of pregnancy for legitimate medical or social reasons (*H* v *Norway* (1992) 73 DR 155).

The decision in *Pretty* should not be understood as imposing on the state any positive obligation to prevent persons from ending their own lives. The sole clear requirement in this matter is to 'prevent an individual from taking his or her own life if the decision has not been taken freely and with full understanding of what is involved' (**Haas v Switzerland**, app no 31332/07, 20.1.11). Beyond this the ECtHR has taken the view that personal choices about when and how an individual's life should be ended are entitled to a measure of protection from the right to respect for private life contained in Art 8(1).

> The Court considers that an individual's right to decide by what means and at what point his or her life will end, provided he or she is capable of freely reaching a decision on this question and acting in consequence, is one of the aspects of the right to respect for private life within the meaning of Article 8 of the Convention (**Haas**, *supra*).

In practical terms this would appear to put states under a duty to take all necessary measures to enable persons to end their own lives with as much dignity as possible where:

(a) this is the free and fully informed wish of the person concerned;

(b) the person has the physical capacity to take the appropriate action.

To ensure these requirements are fulfilled, the state is under a further collateral duty 'to establish a procedure capable of ensuring that a decision to end one's life does indeed correspond to the free wish of the individual concerned' (**Haas**, *supra*). As with all elements of the right to respect for private life, however, states may impose restrictions on the right of the individual to end their life where these are, *inter alia*, in the interests of the legitimate aims of protecting persons in general from hasty decisions, preventing abuse, and ensuring that patients lacking discernment do not obtain access to lethal medication.

Any such rules adopted towards these ends should be sufficiently clear to enable those involved to have some reasonable awareness of the legal consequences of their actions. Hence, notwithstanding Switzerland's legalisation of assisted dying, save where any of those involved acted for selfish motives, the Swiss state remained in breach of Article 8 where medical guidelines provided information concerning the prescription of lethal drugs for persons near to death, but said nothing about similar prescriptions for those not terminally ill but who were unwilling to endure the extremes of mental and physical deterioration to which old age might subject them (**Nencheva v Bulgaria**, app no 48609/06, 18.6.13).

Withdrawal of treatment

In **Lambert v France** [2015] ECHR 185, the ECtHR Grand Chamber made clear that the withdrawal of artificial life-saving treatment was not, *per se*, incompatible with the right to life. This notwithstanding, the court conceded that the matter of whether or not to permit the withdrawal of such treatment, the arrangements governing this, and the appropriate decision-making processes for striking a balance between the patient's rights, those of close relatives, and relevant medical opinions, remained something about which there was no clear consensus amongst ECHR regulatory states. Inevitably, therefore, each state was permitted a wide margin of appreciation in terms of how the matter should be regulated within its own jurisdiction. Key components in ensuring that decisions fell within such margin and so accorded with Article 2 were:

- the wishes of the patient him/herself if known or possible to deduce;
- the wishes of close family members;
- the opinions of medical personnel involved and other experts in the field;
- the effectiveness of the process for assessing and measuring all of the above.

The case of **Lambert** itself involved a 32-year-old man who had suffered serious head injuries in a road traffic accident in September 2008. This left him tetraplegic, in complete dependency, and in a vegetative or minimally conscious condition being kept alive by artificial nutrition and hydration administered through a gastric tube.

In April 2013, in line with the wishes of his wife and six of his eight brothers and sisters, and the view of his medical team that his condition was irreversible, Mr Lambert's source of nutrition was withdrawn and hydration reduced so that he might be allowed to die.

His family was, however, divided over the issue and, within weeks, a judicial order, requiring the hospital to resume treatment, was issued in favour of Mr Lambert's mother, father, and half-brother and half-sister. Over the ensuing 12 months the matter was kept under detailed and constant review and remitted again to the French court. The view of the Conseil d'Etat, France's highest court, given in June 2014, was that under all the circumstances, and with full account being taken of all the wishes and opinions of those involved or consulted, the withdrawal of treatment from Mr Lambert would not be unlawful.

The last resort for those of Mr Lambert's family opposed to ending his treatment was to take the case to the ECtHR in Strasbourg – the contention being that to withdraw treatment would amount to a breach of Mr Lambert's Article 2 right to life.

Here, the Court felt unable to condemn the overall approach adopted by the French legal and medical authorities. It was content that the domestic legal framework for dealing with questions of this type was compatible with the demands of the Convention and that the rules had been applied with a degree of care which exceeded all basic requirements. Every aspect of Mr Lambert's case had been considered, as had the wishes of his family, and the views of the medical team immediately responsible for his case. Other medical opinions had been sought as had the expert general observations of France's highest ranking medical and ethical bodies. Accordingly the contention that the matter had not been dealt with according to the requirements of Article 2 was found to be 'manifestly ill founded'.

Rights after death

The human quality is extinguished upon death. The right to life does not, therefore, give any guarantees in respect of the treatment of, and respect for, the dead. Thus, in one case, mutilation of a corpse was held not admissible as an application under Art 2 (*Akpinar* v *Turkey* [2007] ECHR 183). It did form the basis, however, of an application under Art 3 (degrading treatment) following from the distress and suffering caused by the return of the mutilated bodies to the deceaseds' families.

This is also a further aspect of the right to life where some support is given by the right to respect for private and family life in Article 8(1). Hence in *Sabanchiyeva* v *Russia* [2013] ECHR 757 the state was in breach of Article 8 after the bodies of a number of armed insurgents killed in a gun battle with the security forces were cremated and disposed of without reference to their families.

As indicated in *Akinpar*, rights relating to the dead may attach to the deceased person's relatives. This is so under both Article 3 (prohibition of torture, inhuman or degrading treatment) and Article 8(1) (right to respect for private and family life).

All of this was well exemplified by the decision in *Elberte* v *Latvia* [2015] ECHR 1, where, without knowledge or consent, tissue was removed from the body of the applicant's husband who had been killed in a car crash. Breach of Article 3 and a finding that she had been subjected to distress and suffering was founded on the facts that:

- she had not found out about the removal of the tissue until two years after the event and only after an inquiry had been launched into the illegal removal of organs and tissues from dead persons;
- the circumstances of the removal in her husband's case had not been explained to her;

● she had not been told why her husband's body had been returned to her with his legs tied together.

In relation to Article 8(1), the court further accepted her contention that the taking of tissue from her husband's body without her knowledge or consent was not compatible with her right to respect for private and family life.

Prohibition of torture, inhuman and degrading treatment (Art 3)

Basic rules and definitions

Article 3 permits of no exceptions and is **non-derogable** (see below, Art 15). Thus no matter how pressing a particular public interest may be, departure from the Article's requirements is not permitted. Such treatment or punishment is not justified, therefore, in the fight against terrorism (***Ireland* v *United Kingdom***, below).

The Article has both a positive and a negative element. The negative requirement prohibits the state's use of the types of activity to which the Article is directed. The positive element is that the state should seek to take all reasonable measures to 'properly address' any activities falling within the prohibited categories and prevent the continuing resort to such activities where the risk is 'real and foreseeable' (***Dordevic* v *Croatia*** [2012] ECHR 309).

For breach of Art 3, no deliberate intent to hurt, damage, degrade, distress, or humiliate need be shown. It is enough that the actions complained of, whatever their motivation, had any of these effects. Thus, for example, a long line of ECtHR cases has found violations of the Article's requirements in the way state authorities have dealt with requests to provide information about the whereabouts and fate of missing relatives and causing, thereby, heightened feelings of distress and anxiety (***Kulayev* v *Russia***, app no 29361/02, 15.11.07).

Example

A degrading punishment was held to have been inflicted in ***Tyrer* v *United Kingdom*** (1978) 2 EHRR 1, where an Isle of Man court sentenced a 15-year-old boy to three strokes of the birch after he had been found guilty of an assault. On the same basis, a decision to deport a woman to her country of origin where she was accused of adultery and where stoning remained one of the penalties which could be imposed, was found to be potentially offensive to Art 3 in ***Jabari* v *Turkey*** (2001) 29 EHRR CD 178. For other examples of degrading treatment, see ***Wiktorko* v *Poland*** [2009] ECHR 531 (female in sobering-up centre stripped naked and put in restraining belts by one female and two male attendants), ***Slyusarev* v *Russia*** [2010] ECHR 619 (failure to provide spectacles for prisoner with defective eyesight), ***Bouyid* v *Belgium***, app no 234280/09, 28.9.15 (person being interrogated in custody slapped in the face by police officers), and ***Lyalyakin* v *Russia*** [2015] ECHR 293 (Russian soldier forced to undress and stand in front of unit on parade ground in his briefs while receiving reprimand).

Torture

Torture constitutes 'deliberate inhuman treatment causing very serious and cruel suffering' (***Dordevic* v *Croatia*** [2012] ECHR 309).

In ***Chitayev* v *Russia*** [2007] ECHR 60, a finding of torture resulted from electrocution, beatings, strangulation with adhesive tape, suffocation with polythene bags, and skin being torn away with pliers. This occurred while the applicants were being interrogated by Russian troops about suspected involvement with Chechen rebel fighters.

Other examples of torture resulting from excessive physical violence against suspects in state custody would include **Savin v Ukraine**, app no 34725/08, 16.2.12, where the applicant was so badly beaten during his interrogation that he was left disabled, suffering from sensory and motor impairment and from convulsive disorder. Acts of sexual violence, e.g. the rape of prisoners or detainees by state personnel, may also constitute torture. The ECtHR has described rape as a 'particularly abhorrent form of physical and mental violence' which:

- exploits the vulnerability and weakened resistance of the victim;
- leaves deep psychological scars which may not respond to the passage of time as other forms of violence; and
- was capable of causing acute physical pain (**Aydin v Turkey** [2005] ECHR 325).

In **Cestaro v Italy**, app no 6884/11, 7.4.15, the court confirmed that torture could attach to the actions of state agents outside the context of interrogation in custody. Here the applicants who had taken part in the violent protests which accompanied the 2001 G8 summit in Italy were found hiding in a school. Although they offered no resistance, they were subjected to premeditated, systematic, and prolonged beatings by the police.

Inhuman treatment

Treatment has been held by the Court to be 'inhuman' because, *inter alia*, it was premeditated, and was applied for hours at a stretch and caused either actual bodily injury or intense physical and mental suffering. Inhuman treatment was found in **Kucheruk v Ukraine** [2007] ECHR 712 where a prisoner was denied appropriate psychiatric treatment, beaten with truncheons and kept handcuffed and locked in solitary confinement for long periods and in an ordinary criminal prison.

For treatment to be 'inhuman', actual 'hands on' physical abuse is not essential. Accordingly, in **Gafgen v Germany** [2010] ECHR 759, the threat of imminent considerable pain by police officers seeking a confession was found sufficient.

The distinction between torture and inhuman treatment is intended to 'attach a special stigma to inhuman deliberate treatment causing very serious and cruel suffering' (**Ciorap v Moldova** [2016] ECHR 265).

Treatment has been considered 'degrading' where it was such as to arouse in its victims feelings of fear, anguish and inferiority capable of humiliating and debasing them and possibly breaking their physical and moral resistance (**Dordevic v Croatia**, supra).

Inhuman treatment is not limited to incidents of violence or other types of physical abuse and may, for example, be committed by medical procedures imposed without consent. Such was the finding in **Bataliny v Russia**, app no 10060/07, 23.7.15, where the applicant was subjected to drug trials including treatment with a new antipsychotic medication.

Alleged breaches of Article 3 are subject to the duty of effective investigation. In **M and M v Croatia** [2015] ECHR 759, the applicant alleged domestic abuse by her father. Four-and-a-half years later, while the applicant remained in her father's custody, criminal proceedings were still pending against him. From the length of time taken by the criminal proceedings, it was concluded that the requirements of promptness and reasonable expedition had not been complied with.

Examples

Other examples of breaches of Art 3 relating to the treatment of prisoners include: *Melnik v Ukraine* [2006] ECHR 258 (inadequate medical care resulting in failure to diagnose TB); *Neverzhitsky v Ukraine* [2005] ECHR 210 (force feeding without clear evidence of medical necessity in a way which caused unnecessary physical and psychological suffering); *Yildiz v Turkey*, app no 22913/04, 5.12.06 (imprisonment of person too ill to endure incarceration); *Tarariyeva v Russia* [2009] 48 EHRR 26 (inadequate facilities in prison operating theatre); *Yakovenko v Ukraine* [2007] ECHR 877 (failure to provide treatment specified in prison regulations for HIV/Aids); *Grori v Albania* [2009] ECHR 1076 (prisoner suffering from multiple sclerosis prescribed interferon beta but given multi-vitamins and antidepressants instead); *Elafteriadis v Romania*, app no 38427/05, 25.1.11 (failure to protect prisoner with serious lung disease from exposure to passive smoking); *Julin v Estonia*, app no 16563/08, 29.5.12 (confinement to 'restraint' bed for nine hours); *Vladimir Vasilyev v Russia*, app no 28370/05, 10.1.12 (failure to provide necessary orthopaedic footwear).

Prisoners and detainees

Disproportionate sentences

As a general rule, a sentence of imprisonment imposed by a competent court, according to a fair procedure, and for a legitimate end, may not, of itself, constitute a violation of Art 3, and this notwithstanding the normal degree of degradation and humiliation resulting from such enforced incarceration. Such violation could only occur if the sentence imposed were to be grossly disproportionate to the crime(s) committed. This is a strict test so that contravention is likely only on 'rare and unique occasions' (*Vinter v United Kingdom* [2012] ECHR 66069/09) where the sentence would appear to be 'grossly disproportionate etc.' (*Willcox and Hurford v United Kingdom* [2013] ECHR 292). No breach occurred, therefore, where a person was sentenced to life imprisonment for murder accompanied by an order that, other than in exceptional circumstances, e.g. terminal illness or serious incapacity, life should mean life as the crimes involved were particularly heinous (*Vinter*, *supra*).

Physical force

Violations of the Article would be occasioned, however, by any recourse to physical force against a detainee not made 'strictly necessary' by his own conduct (*Tomasi v France* (1993) 15 EHRR 1). Even the use of handcuffs may offend Art 3 if not reasonably necessary in the prevailing circumstances (*Raninen v Finland* (1998) 26 EHRR 563). Where a healthy person is taken into custody but, on release, is found to have suffered injuries, the state must provide a plausible explanation (*Menesheva v Russia* [2006] ECHR 222).

Poor prison conditions

Poor conditions, for example overcrowding, inadequate food, toilet facilities, heating, etc., may amount to degrading treatment (*Sulejmanovic v Italy* [2002] ECHR 727, six prisoners held in cell of 16.2 square metres), as may the denial of medical treatment (*Hurtado v Switzerland*, 28 January 1994, Hudoc). Detention of a severely disabled person in physical conditions completely unsuitable to their needs was found to amount to degrading treatment in *Price v United Kingdom* [2002] 34 EHRR 53. A finding of degrading treatment was also made in *MS v United Kingdom* [2012] ECHR 804, resulting from the extended detention of a vulnerable mentally disordered patient in a police cell. The state is not liable under Art 3, however, where a prisoner is kept in poor conditions of their own making. Hence the failure of the application in *McFeeley* v *United Kingdom* (1981) 3 EHRR 161, a case arising out of the 'dirty protest' in the Maze Prison, Belfast, where prisoners daubed their cells with excrement and refused to wear prison clothes as a protest against the withdrawal of their status as political prisoners.

Solitary confinement

Solitary confinement of a prisoner in harsh conditions has been held to be within the margin of appreciation applicable to Art 3 even to the extent of rigorous programmes of isolation devised for terrorist suspects (*(Kröcher and Müller* v *Switzerland* 34 (1984) 6 EHRR 345). The line of acceptability is crossed, however, by 'complete sensory isolation coupled with complete social isolation' such as could 'destroy the personality' (*Ennslin, Baader and Raspe* v *FRG* (1978) 14 DR 64).

Internees in Northern Ireland

Ireland v *United Kingdom* (1978) 2 EHRR 25 represents the most controversial and well-known case brought under Art 3 involving the domestic government. The case arose out of the interrogation techniques and general treatment used against suspected republican activists and sympathisers arrested in the internment operation of August 1971. The principal allegation was that suspects had been hooded and forced to lean against a wall supported only by their fingertips and on tip-toe while being subjected to white noise and continuous questioning for long periods. Those who collapsed were subject to beatings and all were deprived of food, drink and sleep. The Court's conclusion was that this constituted inhuman and degrading treatment but not torture.

This illustrates that the threshold for torture is high. Deliberately inhuman treatment causing serious and cruel suffering appears to be required as in *Cakici* v *Turkey* (2001) 31 EHRR 133, in which the applicant's brother was beaten, one of his ribs broken, his head split open, and he was subjected to electric shock treatment while in police custody.

Effects of ill-treatment on prisoners' relatives

Serious ill-treatment of a prisoner may also amount to a violation of the Article 3 rights of his/her relations. This was the decision in *Salakhov and Islyamova* v *Ukraine*, app no 28005/08, 14.3.13 in respect of the psychological impact on a mother of having to watch her son dying from aids, without medical care, while in pre-trial detention.

Force-feeding

Article 3 imposes no absolute prohibition on the force-feeding of prisoners. All depends on the health and condition of the prisoner, the methods used, and the degree of force applied. In *Ciorap* v *Moldova* (*supra*) the applicant complained that:

- some of the other prisoners in his cell suffered from infectious diseases including TB;
- there were no windows in the cells and no access to natural light;
- the rudimentary sanitary conditions allowed no privacy.

His complaints having fallen on deaf ears, the applicant went on hunger-strike. He also cut his wrists and attempted to set fire to himself.

The applicant's hunger-strike lasted for 24 days. During this period he was fed against his will. Prison staff forced him to open his mouth by pulling his hair, gripping his neck, and standing on his feet until he could no longer bear the pain and opened his mouth to cry out.

This was held open by insertion of a metal mouth-widener and his tongue held out of his mouth with a pair of pliers. A hard tube was pushed down into his stomach through which liquidised food was poured into him.

In these circumstances, the court had no doubt that the treatment of the applicant amounted to torture. A number of particular factors were identified:

- at the time the force-feeding began, no medical evidence existed to show that the applicant's life was in immediate or serious danger;
- less intrusive methods, e.g. intravenous drips, could have been used;
- the amount of force used had subjected him to great physical pain and humiliation;
- the authority's primary objective had been to bring his protest to an end rather than to safeguard his health and welfare.

Compulsory psychiatric patients

Other than in clear-cut cases of physical or mental abuse, the issue of whether a person ordered to be detained in hospital has been dealt with in accordance with Article 3 depends on the cumulative effect of a series of considerations:

- the nature, severity and immediacy of the person's medical needs and requirements;
- the need to respect the person's right to respect for human dignity;
- whether the person has been properly diagnosed and has been/is being provided with the appropriate medical needs;
- the stringency of the detention regime;
- the length of time for which the person has or may be detained;
- the need to avoid suffering beyond that inevitably associated with forced incarceration;
- the extent to which continued detention is compatible with the person's ongoing medical needs.

These were the findings in **Rybeku v Albania** [2007] ECHR 1109, which dealt with the case of a chronic paranoid schizophrenic who had been committed to an ordinary criminal prison after being sentenced for murder. While there, his mental condition was not regularly assessed nor were any changes made to his medication or treatment when his condition began to deteriorate.

> Although Article 3 of the Convention cannot be construed as laying down a general obligation to release detainees on health grounds, it nonetheless imposes an obligation on the state to protect the well being of such persons, for example, by providing them with the requisite medical assistance. There are three particular elements to be considered:
>
> (a) the medical condition of the detainee;
> (b) the adequacy of the medical assistance and care provided;
> (c) the advisability of maintaining the detention measure in view of the state of health of the applicant.

The treatment of children

In individual cases the state does not bear any direct responsibility under the ECHR in respect of the way a child is treated by its parents. Article 3 may be engaged, however, if the state does not have in place an adequate legal and law enforcement system sufficient to provide effective deterrence against ill-treatment or abuse of children from whatever source. Thus the finding of a breach of Article 3 in *A v United Kingdom*, app no 25599/94, 23.9.98, in relation to a case in the domestic courts, where the defence of reasonable parental chastisement, then available in English law, was pleaded successfully to secure the acquittal on a charge of assault of a person charged with caning his 9-year-old stepson. Other circumstances in which the ill-treatment of a child might be attributable to the state would include:

(a) the child is under the state's direct care or supervision (*Scozzari and Giunte v Italy*, app no 39331/98, 13.7.02);

(b) the state has placed a child in its care in, or failed to remove the child from, an abusive situation (*Z v United Kingdom* (2001) 34 EHRR 97).

In *O'Keefe v Ireland*, app no 35810/09, 28.1.14, the applicant successfully alleged a breach of Art 3 in that she had been subjected to sexual abuse when a pupil in a state funded National School owned and managed by the Catholic Church. In this overall educational context, the Court identified an inherent obligation on governments to ensure the protection of children from ill-treatment, especially when in primary education. It emphasised that the nature of child abuse was such, particularly when the abuser was in a position of authority, that the existence of effective detection and reporting mechanisms were fundamental to the proper implementation of the criminal law designed to deter such abuse. Nor could the state absolve itself from its responsibilities by transferring there to a non-state body or organisation, such as a Church, regardless of how authoritative and respected this might be.

Deportation and exclusion

Albeit that a contracting state has not itself been guilty of the type of treatment forbidden by Art 3, it may still act in breach of the Article if it expels a person to another state where that individual could face a real risk of being subjected to such treatment either by the receiving state or non-state agents in that state (*Soering v United Kingdom* (1989) 11 EHRR 439; *Ahmed v Austria* (1996) 24 EHRR 278). This remains the case notwithstanding that the person's presence is believed to be prejudicial to national security (*Chahal v United Kingdom* (1997) 23 EHRR 413). The death penalty has been abolished in 46 of the Convention's 47 signatory states, and suspended in Russia. It would appear to be a breach of Art 3 for a Convention state to hand over a person suspected of crimes to a non-Convention state where there is a real possibility that the suspect may be executed (*Al-Saadoon and Mufdhi v United Kingdom* [2010] ECHR 285).

The rule against deporting persons to states where their rights under Art 3 may be abused is not limited to what might be referred to as 'formal' acts of removal, i.e. according to a rule-based process with right of appeal. It applies also to ad hoc incidents of summary repatriation as in the immediate return to their country of origin of migrants intercepted at sea (*Hirsi Jamaa v Italy*, app no 27765/09, 23.02.12).

A particularly difficult issue which has arisen in relation to Art 3 and the power of deportation has been the extent to which, if at all, the Article's guarantees may be relied upon by persons who are seriously ill to prevent their being sent to a state in which appropriate or adequate medical treatment may not be available to them. To date, the general principles laid down to dispose of such cases are as follows:

(i) Albeit that advances in medical science, together with social and economic differences between states, have meant that the level of treatment available in a contracting state and a particular person's country of origin might vary considerably, Art 3 does not place an obligation on the contracting state to alleviate such disparities through the provision of free and unlimited health care to non-nationals who have no legal right to remain within its jurisdiction. Any findings to the contrary would be to place too great a burden on contracting states in general.

(ii)   This being so, a non-national who is subject to expulsion has no general entitlement to remain in the territory of a contracting state purely to continue to benefit from that state's medical and social services systems.

(iii) This remains the case even though it may be apparent that the person's condition, circumstances, and possibly life expectancy, might be significantly reduced should the deportation proceed.

(iv)   It will only be in these 'very exceptional cases' where there are 'compelling humanitarian considerations' that the deportation of a seriously ill person might contravene Art 3 (*N* v *United Kingdom* [2008] ECHR 453).

D v *United Kingdom* (1997) 24 EHRR 423 remains one of the very few examples in which the requirements for the prevention of deportation of a seriously ill person were found to have been satisfied. This was another case in which a contracting state, in this instance the United Kingdom, sought to deport a person in the advanced stages of HIV. The evidence before the Court was that the person affected had already suffered severe and irreparable damage to his immune system and that he was close to death. It was accepted also that the medical services in his 'home' state did not have the capacity to provide him with the palliative care and treatment he required and that he had no family or close friends there able to look after him.

> In view of these exceptional circumstances and bearing in mind the critical stage now reached in the appellant's fatal illness, the implementation of the decision to remove him . . . would amount to inhuman treatment . . . in violation of Article 3.

Freedom from slavery, servitude and forced or compulsory labour (Art 4)

This prohibition does not extend to work done in the ordinary course of detention, to military service or to any service exacted in time of emergency or calamity threatening the life or well-being of the community.

Slavery has been defined as 'the status or condition of a person over whom any or all of the powers attaching to the right of ownership are exercised' (1926 Slavery Convention).

It has been held that forced or compulsory labour does not extend to: a requirement that a lawyer give his services free to impecunious defendants (*Van der Mussele* v *Belgium* (1984) 6 EHRR 163); a requirement that a notary charge less for work done for non-profit-making organisations (*X* v *Federal Republic of Germany* (1979) 18 DR 216); or to a rule that unemployed persons who refuse to accept work could be denied unemployment benefit (*X* v *Netherlands* (1976) 7 DR 161).

The right is non-derogable.

In comparison to other elements of the Convention, Art 4 has not, to date, generated a similar volume of case-law. In relatively recent times some of the more significant cases would include *Saliadin* v *France* [2005] ECHR 545, and *Rantzev* v *Cyprus and Russia*, app no 25965/04, 7.1.10). In *Saliadin* an under-aged illegal immigrant living with relatives was required to undertake domestic duties for 15 hours per day without pay over a period of years. The state was engaged through a failure of the positive obligation to ensure effective implementation of the domestic laws designed to protect against this type of abuse. The complaint in **Rantzer** related to the trafficking of young girls from the Russian Federation to Cyprus. The ECtHR had no doubt that such activities fell within the ambit of the types of conduct prohibited by Art 4.

> The Court considers that trafficking in human beings, by its very nature and aim of exploitation, is based on the exercise of powers attaching to the right of ownership. It treats human beings as commodities to be bought and sold and put to forced labour, often for little or no payment, usually in the sex industry, but also elsewhere.

Right to liberty and security of the person (Art 5)

Deprivation of liberty

Article 5(1) of the Convention provides that no one should be deprived of their liberty except in those situations provided for, in the Article's paragraphs (a)–(f) (see below). The jurisprudence of the ECtHR makes clear that the meaning of deprivation of liberty is not limited to the confinement of persons behind prison walls. According to the Court, and for Convention purposes, the concept has three principal elements:

(1) the objective element of a person's confinement to a certain limited place for a not negligible amount of time;

(2) the additional subjective element that they have not validly consented to the confinement in question;

(3) the confinement must be imputable to the state (**Storck v Germany** (2005) 43 EHRR 96).

In determining whether the particular measures or constraints imposed on an individual are sufficient to amount to a deprivation of liberty, the Court should consider his/her 'concrete' situation, i.e. the entirety of the facts and circumstances relating and contributing to the position in which the person finds him/herself. Among the various factors to be considered will be the nature, severity and duration of the constraints imposed and the manner in which these were implemented (**Guzzardi v Italy** (1981) EHRR 333). Some examples of deprivations of liberty other than by confinement behind prison walls would include:

- placing a voluntary psychiatric patient in a closed mental hospital subject to severe restrictions (**HL v United Kingdom** [2004] ECHR 471);
- holding a 5-year-old foreign national without his family in a centre for adult illegal immigrants (**Leger v France** [2006] ECHR 380);
- confinement of crew on board ship after it had been arrested on suspicion of carrying drugs (**Medvedyev v France** [2010] ECHR 1671);
- house arrest in excess of 24 hours (**Mancini v Italy** [2001] ECHR 502; **Vachev v Bulgaria** [2004] ECHR 325).

Limitations

The right, as articulated by the Convention, is subject to various exceptions. These permit that a person's liberty may be denied:

(a) following a sentence of imprisonment imposed by a competent court;

(b) for non-compliance with a court order or an obligation imposed by law;

(c) following a lawful arrest on suspicion of commission of a criminal offence and preparatory to being brought before a competent legal authority;

(d) in the case of a minor, for the purpose of educational supervision or bringing them before a competent legal authority;

(e) in the case of persons of unsound mind, alcoholics, drug addicts or vagrants, and for preventing the spread of infectious diseases;

(f) to prevent a person entering a state unlawfully or prior to extradition or **deportation**.

Article 5 also provides that everyone who has been arrested has the right:

- to be informed promptly of the reasons for the arrest and any charge(s) to be made;
- to be brought promptly before a court and to release on bail or to be tried within a reasonable time;
- to challenge the legality of the detention before a competent and independent legal authority.

Detention following conviction by a competent court

The Convention may not be used to challenge a conviction (***Krzycki v Federal Republic of Germany*** (1978) 13 DR 57) or sentence (***Weeks v United Kingdom***) imposed in accordance with municipal law. The Court of Human Rights might, however, be prepared to consider the legality of a period of detention resulting from a purely administrative decision, i.e. a decision to recall a prisoner who had been released on licence.

Weeks v United Kingdom (1988) 10 EHRR 293

The applicant had been released on licence after serving ten years of a life sentence. He was then recalled to prison a year later. The Court's opinion was that there was sufficient causal link between the Home Office's recall decision and the municipal court's original sentence. Both the original sentence and the recall decision had been made in the interests of social protection and the rehabilitation of the applicant based on his record. Also, the trial court had imposed a life sentence in the full knowledge that it lay within the discretion of the Secretary of State for the Home Department to release and recall life prisoners.

This may be contrasted with the decision in ***Stafford v United Kingdom*** (2002) *The Times*, 31 May. On this occasion, Art 5 was found to have been violated by continuing to hold a life prisoner after the tariff element (deterrence and retribution) had been served on the ground that, if released, he might commit other non-violent offences unconnected with the original reason for his imprisonment. This, in effect, amounted to imprisonment by executive decree. A conviction as a result of proceedings conducted in 'flagrant denial of justice' does not amount to a conviction by a competent court (***Stoichtov v Bulgaria*** (2005) ECHR 189).

Non-compliance with a court order or an obligation imposed by law

This exception recognises the legality of imprisonment for matters such as civil contempt, refusal to pay a fine or maintenance order, or failure to comply with specific legal obligations, e.g. refusal to do military service (***Johansen v Norway*** (1985) 44 DR 155). In this type of case the imprisonment usually follows the act of non-compliance. It has also been held, however, that this provision gives the state the right to detain a person where there is an immediate and pressing need to ensure that a significant legal obligation *is* actually complied with. Hence, no breach of the Convention was committed where three persons entering Great Britain from Ireland were detained for 45 hours to ensure compliance with the obligation in the Prevention of Terrorism Order 1976 that such persons submit themselves to 'further interrogation' if required (*McVeigh, O'Neill and Evans v United Kingdom* (1983) 5 EHRR 71).

Detention on suspicion of commission of a criminal offence

It appears to be sufficient that the suspect is arrested on suspicion of the type of activity which presupposes or necessarily involves the commission of a specific offence albeit that the particular offence or offences with which the suspect may be charged have not yet been identified.

Brogan v United Kingdom (1988) 11 EHRR 117

In this case, the applicant had been arrested on suspicion of being 'concerned in the commission . . . of acts of terrorism' (viz. the use of violence for political ends). This does not constitute a specific offence. The Court was satisfied, however, that the above statutory definition of terrorism was sufficiently clear and 'in keeping with the idea of an offence' as to satisfy the Convention's requirements.

The initial arrest must be for the purpose of enforcing the criminal law. It matters not that no charges are eventually brought or that, at the time of arrest, the police do not have sufficient evidence for that purpose (*Brogan*, *supra*). There must be, however, reasonable suspicion that an offence has been committed which supposes 'the existence of facts or information which would satisfy an objective observer that the person concerned may have committed the offence' (*Fox, Campbell and Hartley v United Kingdom* (1990) 13 EHRR 157).

Article 5(2) requires that the suspect shall be 'informed promptly . . . of the reasons for his arrest and any charge against him'. 'Promptly' need not necessarily be at the time of the arrest and it appears to be sufficient that reasons are revealed or may be deduced during the subsequent interrogation (*Fox*, *supra*). The reasons must be given in language which the suspect can understand and must be sufficient to enable the legality of the arrest to be challenged in a municipal court (Art 5(4)).

After arrest the suspect should be brought 'promptly' before a judge or competent legal authority (Art 5(3)) for review of 'the circumstances for and against detention and of ordering release if there are no such reasons' (*Schiesser v Switzerland* (1979) 2 EHRR 417). Such judge or legal authority must not be a person or body having any connection with the bringing, defending or determining any charges which may be brought against the person detained. The maximum period for which a person may be held in police or state detention without appearing before a judicial authority should not exceed four days (*McKay v United Kingdom* [2006] ECHR 820). Where detention pending trial is ordered, this should be for specific and limited periods (*Tymoshenko v Ukraine* [2013] ECHR 389).

In *Hood v United Kingdom* (2000) 29 EHRR 365, Art 5(3) was found to have been violated by domestic court martial procedures particularly in terms of the role of commanding officers and their involvement in decisions relating both to the need for continued detention of particular suspects and the charges to be brought against them. In *Brogan v United Kingdom* (supra) the requirement that review of the need for detention take place promptly was held to have been offended by the applicant's detention for four days pursuant to the Prevention of Terrorism Act (Temporary Provisions) 1984, s 12. This remained the case notwithstanding the particular conditions prevailing in Northern Ireland. Rather than amend the 1984 Act, the United Kingdom government opted to enter a derogation from Art 5 according to the terms of Art 15 (see below). The circumstances applying in Northern Ireland were later found to be within the permitted grounds for such departure from normal Convention standards (***Brannigan and McBride v United Kingdom*** (1993) 17 EHRR 539).

The suspect has a right to be tried within a reasonable time. What is reasonable will depend on the circumstances and the complexity of each case. This does mean, however, that preparation of the case against the suspect must be conducted with all due expedition. The suspect may be kept in detention during this period providing there are 'relevant and sufficient reasons' (***Wemhoff*** v ***Germany*** (1980) 1 EHRR 55). These have been held to include the dangers of flight and interference with the course of justice, the prevention of crime, and the maintenance of public order. Strong suspicion of guilt, in the absence of one of the above dangers, is not sufficient for continued pre-trial detention (***Morganti v France*** (1996) 21 EHRR 34). Periods of pre-trial detention for seven years (***Mansur v Turkey*** (1995) 20 EHRR 535), and four years (***Yagie and Sargin v Turkey*** (1995) 20 EHRR 505) have both been held to contravene Art 5.

The automatic refusal of bail pursuant to the Criminal Justice and Public Order Act 1994, s 25, without reference to the defendant's particular circumstances, was condemned in ***Caballero v United Kingdom*** (2000) 30 EHRR 643. In its original form the section stipulated that bail could not be granted to defendants charged with homicide or rape having previously been convicted for such offences.

A person deprived of their liberty for an indefinite period should also be allowed access to a court or competent independent tribunal at reasonable intervals to test the legality of their detention. The court or tribunal should be possessed of the power to order the person's release if such legality is lacking and should make such decisions 'speedily' (Art 54). This has been the basis of successful challenges to the length of time between Parole Board reviews of the need for further detention of a person recalled from parole after serving a life sentence (***Oldham v United Kingdom*** (2001) 31 EHRR 34) and of a young offender detained 'at her Majesty's pleasure' (***Hussain v United Kingdom*** (1996) 21 EHRR 1). The Parole Board's powers and procedures were also found to be at fault under Art 5(4) in ***Curley v United Kingdom*** (2001) 31 EHRR 14. The breach on this occasion was the Board's inability to order the release of a life prisoner once the tariff period of his sentence, i.e. that for deterrence and punishment, had been served; the Board's powers at that time being limited to the making of recommendations subject to the approval of the Secretary of State for the Home Department.

Article 5(4) imports a number of procedural requirements and standards similar to some of those imposed by Article 6 (right to a fair hearing). Hence, albeit that the case against the 'suspect' is based on particularly sensitive, security-laden information, he/she is entitled to the gist of the allegations to be answered. This remains so, notwithstanding the modification of the individual's procedural rights by special legislation, e.g. that enacted to deal with terrorism (***Sher v United Kingdom***, app no 5201/11, 20.10.15).

Detention of minors

For the purposes of the Convention a minor is a person under 18 years of age. A minor may be detained for educational supervision, e.g. to ensure attendance at school, or in order to be brought before a court so that they may be removed from harmful surroundings. Detention for educational supervision should be in an institution designed for that purpose and not in a remand or other prison except for a short period as a preliminary to allocation to the former (***Bouamer v Belgium*** (1988) 11 EHRR 1). None of the exceptions to the right in Article 5(1) permit the preventative detention of a young person who has committed offences but who is below the age of criminal responsibility (***Blokhin v Russia***, app no 47152/06, 14.11.13, 12-year-old boy committed to 30 days' detention to 'correct his behaviour').

Detention of a minor prior to a court appearance is permitted if this is in the child's interests, e.g. for the preparation of psychiatric reports or pending a judicial order placing them in care. Detention of a minor for three days and nine hours without access to a judge or legal advice has been held to be excessive even in cases of suspected terrorism (*Ipek* v *Turkey* [2009] ECHR 188).

Detention of persons of unsound mind and to prevent the spread of infectious diseases

The terms 'alcoholics', 'drug addicts' and 'infectious diseases' have not yet been interpreted by either the Commission or the Court of Human Rights. Persons of unsound mind are those who, according to reliable and objective medical expertise, are suffering from the kind or degree of mental disorder warranting confinement (*Winterwerp* v *Netherlands* (1980) 2 EHRR 387). Vagrants have been defined as persons 'who have no fixed abode, no means of subsistence and no regular trade or profession' (*De Wilde, Ooms and Versyp* v *Belgium* (1979–80) 1 EHRR 373). Detention to prevent the spread of HIV/Aids may fall within Art 5 providing it is used as a tactic of last resort (*Enhorn* v *Sweden* [2005] ECHR 34). An order of a court that a person be committed to a psychiatric unit should be implemented with reasonable expedition (*Mocarska* v *Poland* [2007] ECHR 894).

Whether or not a person admitted to a psychiatric unit 'voluntarily' has been deprived of their liberty under Art 5, would appear to depend on the degree of supervision and control to which the person is subject and whether they would have been allowed to leave the hospital had they so wished (*HL* v *United Kingdom* [2004] ECHR 720). The *HL* decision cast doubt on the previously held view that voluntary patients could be prevented from discharging themselves on grounds of common law necessity, i.e. that they might have posed a threat to themselves or others.

Persons having served a term of imprisonment for a criminal offence and any further period permitted for preventative detention should not be denied release on purely psychiatric grounds – particularly where no such justification for the detention was previously relied upon (*Glien* v *Germany* [2013] ECHR 1206).

Detention of persons in private psychiatric clinics, without sufficient subjective element of consent, clearly falls outside the categories of detention recognised by Art 5. Where this occurs, the breach may be attributable to the state through its failure to provide adequate protection against such excesses.

Article 5(1) requires the provision of legal assistance for persons of 'unsound mind' who wish to challenge involuntary incarceration.

> Effective legal representation of persons with disabilities requires an enhanced duty of supervision of their legal representatives by the competent domestic courts (*Constancia* v *The Netherlands* [2015] ECHR 397).

Detention of an illegal entrant pending deportation or extradition

Such detention is lawful providing it occurs in relation to the exercise of a valid power to exclude, deport or extradite according to the municipal law of the state concerned (*Bozano* v *France* (1987) 9 EHRR 297). The subsequent deportation in extradition proceedings must be expedited with 'requisite diligence' (*Lynas* v *Switzerland* (1976) 6 DR 141).

> Any deprivation of liberty . . . will be justified . . . only for so long as deportation or extradition procedures are in progress. If such proceedings are not prosecuted with due diligence, the detention will cease to be permissible (*A* v *United Kingdom* [2009] ECHR 301).

Persons in pre-trial detention being considered for expulsion should be informed of this possibility and allowed access to the relevant documentation in order to mount a challenge should they so wish (**Shamayev v Georgia** [2005] ECHR 233).

Executive detention

Except where a state has entered a valid derogation of an obligation under Article 5, as where the 'very life of the national is threatened' (ECHR Art 15, see pp. 493), executive detention or internment without trial is clearly incompatible with the entire purpose behind the right conferred by it. Nor is it mentioned or even alluded to in the Article's permitted exceptions. Obviously, were it otherwise, Article 5 would be rendered almost meaningless.

As, however, the ECtHR has made clear many times, the Convention should not be viewed as imposing a set of absolutely rigid obligations incapable of being interpreted in ways which respond to changing circumstances and possibly unforeseen but legitimate national commitments, e.g. recent involvement of European nations in armed insurrection and conflicts in the Middle East.

Such judicial expediency in relation to the Convention's requirements was particularly evident in the Grand Chamber decision in **Hassan v United Kingdom** [2014] ECHR 936 where the Court, in effect, articulated a further and implied exception to the Article 5 right.

> The Court is mindful of the fact that internment in peacetime does not fall within the scheme of deprivation of liberty governed by Article 5 of the Convention without the exercise of the power of derogation under Article 15. It can only be in cases of international armed conflict where the taking of prisoners of war and the detention of civilians who pose a threat to security are accepted features of international humanitarian law, that Article 5 could be interpreted as permitting the exercise of such broad powers.

Note that this contemplates the use of such powers according to a very specific set of pre-conditions:

(i) the existence of an international armed conflict – an internal national conflict or an internal 'internationalised' armed conflict (e.g. Afghanistan) will not do;

(ii) the observance and application of relevant international humanitarian law, including effective procedural safeguards including, e.g. regular periodic and not infrequent reviews, by a body competent to provide 'sufficient guarantees of impartiality and fair procedure to protect against arbitrariness' (**Mohammed**, *supra*).

Right to a fair trial (Art 6)

General content and scope

Article 6 gives every person the right to a fair and public hearing within a reasonable time by an independent and impartial tribunal 'in the determination of his civil rights and obligations or any criminal charge'. It further provides that each person charged with a criminal offence shall be presumed innocent until proved guilty and shall have the right to:

(a) be informed promptly of the nature of the charge against him in language he understands;

(b) adequate time and facilities to prepare a defence including the right to appoint and communicate with a legal adviser;

(c) defend the case personally or through legal representation;

(d) obtain the attendance of and examine witnesses on his behalf;

(e) be assisted by an interpreter if he cannot understand the language used in the court.

Civil rights and obligations

Since the fair trial guarantees in the Article extend to the 'determination of civil rights and obligations' generally, their application is not confined solely to the proceedings of courts of law in the traditionally understood sense. The decision-making powers of administrative tribunals are clearly covered as is the exercise of powers to decide by public authorities and officials, providing civil rights and obligations are affected.

What amounts to a 'civil right or obligation' has never been given a precise definition. Originally, the term was generally understood as encompassing the rights and obligations of private persons in their relationships with each other and with the state other than in the exercise of its public law functions, i.e. those relating to the process of government and administration. For the purposes of Art 6, therefore, a relatively sharp distinction was drawn between what have been referred to as 'private law rights' and those falling within the comparatively more recent concept of 'public law rights', e.g. welfare state benefits.

With the passage of time, however, the ECtHR began to adopt a more expansive view of Art 6's proper sphere of operation. As it did so, the distinction between private and public law rights, as previously applied in this context, began to become less distinct and decisive. Thus, in a number of cases, it was held that Art 6 could be applied to disputes between states and civil servants relating, for example, to matters such as conditions of service/employment and to pension entitlements, in which context it was felt issues of public policy or the 'state's sovereign functions' (see *Pellegrin* v *France* [1999] ECHR 140) were only remotely involved (see, for example, *Satonnet* v *France* [2000] ECHR 415, termination of employment, *Lambourdiere* v *France* [2000] ECHR 413, pension entitlement).

Out of this has developed a train of authority which has attempted to give clearer definition of the types of public law rights which do, and which do not, fall within the ambit of Art 6. This, in turn, has led to the current position whereby Art 6 may be taken as applying to a public law right, and to disputes and decisions relating to it, where the right in question derives from the application of specific rules or regulations laid down by legislation but does not involve the exercise of wide official discretion or the application of the general interests of public policy. Decisions affecting housing payments, tax liabilities, and welfare benefits would appear to fall within these criteria (*Tsfayo* v *United Kingdom* (2009) 48 EHRR 18). This process of reasoning also appears to explain why Art 6 has no application to decisions to deport or remove foreign nationals from a particular contracting state.

> In general . . . proceedings which exclusively concern decisions of administrative authorities to refuse leave to an alien to enter . . . or to deport or expel an alien, do not involve the determination of the civil rights and obligations of the alien. In this regard, I can see no reason to depart from the case-law . . . that because of the substantial discretionary and public policy element in such decisions, proceedings relating to them ought not to be seen as determining the civil rights of the person concerned even if they . . . have major repercussions on his private and family life, prospects of employment, financial position and the like . . . (*Maaouia* v *France* [2000] ECHR 455)

Despite these developments the ECtHR has made clear its insistence that tax disputes should not be regarded as falling within the ambit of Art 6 (*Ferrazini* v *Italy* (2002) 24 EHRR 45).

Criminal charges

In this context the Court of Human Rights has taken the view that Art 6 is engaged where a person has been informed by a competent legal authority that an allegation of a criminal act has been made against him (*Corigliano* v *Italy* (1983) 5 EHRR 334). It is applicable, therefore, before any charge is made in the formal and official sense and, therefore, at least from the time of arrest on suspicion (*Wemhoff* v *Germany* (1980) 1 EHRR 55).

Key factors in determining what amounts to a criminal charge are the nature of the act itself (see *Steel* v *United Kingdom* (supra), where a breach of the peace was found to constitute a criminal offence for the purposes of Art 5(1)); its classification in the domestic law of the state involved; and the severity of the penalty which could be imposed (*Ezeh and Conners* v *United Kingdom* [2003] ECHR 1485). Hence disciplinary charges have been held to be 'criminal' for the purposes of Art 6 where these may result in loss of liberty (*Bell* v *United Kingdom* [2007] ECHR 47, summary proceedings before commanding officers in armed forces; *Campbell and Fell* v *United Kingdom* (1984) 7 EHRR 165, *Black* v *United Kingdom* [2007] ECHR 54, summary proceedings before prison governors).

The criminal 'limb' of Art 6 would appear to have no application to procedures which fall short of actual charge or prosecution for a specific offence (*R* v *United Kingdom* [2007] ECHR 87, not applicable to formal warning under the Crime and Disorder Act 1998).

The ECtHR has held that, in certain circumstances, a breach of Art 6 may be 'cured' by the opportunity to have the matter considered again on appeal (*Adolf* v *Austria* (1982) ECHR 2).

> It is possible for a higher tribunal, in certain circumstances to make reparation for an initial violation of the Convention (*Kyprianou* v *Cyprus* [2004] ECHR 43).

Such facility is more likely to be recognised where the initial decision was made by an administrative or disciplinary body, rather than by a court of law in the full sense (*Dory* v *Sweden*, unreported, 2003). As to disciplinary decisions in general, these may be subject to Art 6, providing that in any particular case the decision is determinative of, or has a substantial effect on, a significant civil right, e.g. as where it causes a person to lose their employment.

Where a body exercising powers which engage Art 6 fails to act fairly, no breach will be committed if its decisions are subject to an effective process of review, i.e. one which enables the complainant to have the defective decision set aside and remade subject to the Article's requirements (*Bryan* v *United Kingdom* (1996) 21 EHRR 342).

Kingsley v *United Kingdom* (2001) 33 EHRR 13

The decision in this case illustrates that the domestic process of judicial review may sometimes be inadequate to ensure that such redress is available in domestic courts. The applicant had applied for judicial review of a decision of the Gaming Board to revoke his Certificate of Approval as a person fit to hold a management position in the gaming industry (Gaming Act 1968, s 19). Despite the Court of Appeal's acceptance that the applicant had shown an arguable case of bias, it was felt that the Gaming Board's decision could not be set aside. This was premised on the 'doctrine of necessity', i.e. that since the allegation of bias affected all of the Board's members it was not possible for the matter to be remitted to it for a fresh decision. Moreover, since, according to English law, issues relating to the merits of a decision could not be considered in an application for judicial review, the Court was also precluded from making any findings or superimposing its views concerning the applicant's fitness to manage gaming clubs or businesses. In these circumstances, therefore, English judicial review offered no process through which the offending decision could be corrected and remade in accordance with the Convention's procedural standards.

As a general rule, Article 6 does not apply to the making of decisions which are of temporary or interim effect only and which are not, therefore, finally determinative of the right(s) in issue. This, however, is subject to the exception that Art 6 may be engaged where the decision in the relevant proceedings has a substantial effect on the later vindication or denial of the claimant's Convention right (*Ringeisen* v *Austria (No. 1)* (1971) 1 EHRR 455).

The right to a fair trial for the determination of a person's civil rights is not offended by the legal immunity often granted by the legal systems of contracting states to members of their national legislatures. Such immunity from suit will normally be of a temporary nature only, and will continue only for so long as the person remains an elected representative. It does not, therefore, deny the right completely and exists for a legitimate aim of public policy, i.e. the freedom of speech and actions in parliamentary assemblies (*Kart* v *Turkey* [2009] ECHR 1981).

Right of access to a court

In *Golder* v *United Kingdom* (1975) 1 EHRR 524, it was held that the right to a fair trial presupposed an individual's unimpeded right of access to the appropriate court. Golder was a prisoner who wished to commence proceedings for defamation against a prison officer. According to the Prison Rules then in force he could not be prevented from bringing such action to trial but could be denied access to a solicitor in the preparation of his case. This was held to be sufficient impediment to contravene Art 6. The refusal to grant legal aid to an impecunious indigent was also found to amount to an unlawful impediment in *Airey* v *Ireland (No. 2)* (1981) 3 EHRR 592.

For more on derogation under Art 15, see pp. 493–4.

Inevitably, and without proper derogation under Art 15, the complete closure of the courts in any part of the state, without provision of any valid alternative judicial process, amounts to a breach of Art 6 (*Khamidov* v *Russia* [2007] ECHR 928, closure of courts in Chechnya 1998–2001).

Right to a fair hearing

This has been interpreted to include the following.

(a) The right to know the case to be answered and the evidence relating thereto (*McMichael* v *United Kingdom* (1995) 20 EHRR 205). The withholding of evidence to protect the public interest is permissible only after careful weighing of the public interests involved by a competent judicial authority (*Rowe* v *United Kingdom* (2000) 30 EHRR 1).

> The entitlement to disclosure of relevant evidence is not, however, an absolute right. In any criminal proceedings there may be competing interests such as national security and the need to protect witnesses at risk of reprisal . . . which must be weighed against the rights of the accused. In some cases it may be necessary to withhold certain information from the defence so as to preserve the rights of another individual or to safeguard an important public interest. (*Edwards and Lewis* v *United Kingdom* (2004) 40 EHRR 24)

(b) In criminal cases and in civil cases involving an assessment of the person's conduct, character or lifestyle, the right to an oral hearing before the court or tribunal. Trial *in absentia* may be permitted where the right to a hearing has been waived or where every effort has been made to secure the person's presence (*Colozza* v *Italy* (1985) 7 EHRR 516).

(c) The right to 'equality of arms'. This has been held to mean that everyone who is a party to proceedings subject to Art 6 shall have a reasonable opportunity of presenting their case under conditions which do not cause any substantial disadvantage *vis-à-vis* their opponent (*Kaufman* v *Belgium* (1986) 50 DR 98). The principle was offended by conducting the trial of the two juvenile defendants in the Jamie Bulger case in a Crown Court before a judge and jury with all the formality of adult proceedings 'which must at times have seemed incomprehensible and intimidating for a child of 11' (*T and V* v *United Kingdom* (2000) 30 EHRR 121).

(d) The existence of rules of evidence regulating the use of unfairly or illegally obtained evidence, hearsay testimony and providing for adequate pre-trial disclosure of relevant materials (*Schenk* v *Switzerland* (1988) 13 EHRR 242). These should, in particular, enforce the basic principle, that statements obtained by force or threats should not be used in legal proceedings (*Harutyunyan* v *Armenia* [2007] ECHR 541). Evidence which is obtained illegally but not in a way which affects its credibility or accuracy, e.g. in the course of an illegal search, may be admitted provided this does not prejudice the overall fairness of the proceedings (*Lee Davies* v *Belgium*, app no 18704/05, 28.7.09).

In criminal cases the admission of evidence from absent witnesses does not, of itself, defeat the fairness of the proceedings providing this depends on:
- whether there was good reason for a witness's absence;
- whether it was the totality of the evidence for the prosecution or appeared decisive of the accused's guilt;
- whether there were sufficient contributing factors including effective procedural safeguards to ensure that the trial as a whole was fair (*Al-Kawaja and Tahery* v *United Kingdom* [2011] ECHR 2127, *Schatschaschwili* v *Germany* [2015] ECHR 1113.

Recent case-law shows that fair trial guarantees may be given added effect by Article 8(1), i.e. the right to respect for 'personal integrity' as an integral element of the right to respect for privacy. Hence in the context of rape, the ECtHR has made clear that, although the defence should be allowed to challenge the credibility of the accuser, this should not be allowed to go to the point of causing deliberate distress and humiliation (*Y* v *Slovenia* [2015] ECHR 519).

(e) The freedom from self-incrimination. This right was held to have been infringed in *Saunders* v *United Kingdom* (1996) 23 EHRR 313, where, in the course of a Department of Trade and Industry investigation into a company takeover, the applicant was obliged to answer questions on pain of criminal sanctions, including imprisonment, according to powers given to DTI inspectors by the Companies Act 1985, ss 434–36. A further violation was found to be apparent in the requirement in the Irish Republic's anti-terrorist legislation that a person in custody who failed to provide a full account of their movements during any specified period was liable to summary conviction and imprisonment for up to six months (*Heaney and McGuinness* v *Ireland* (2001) 33 EHRR 12).

(f) Reasons for the decision. These must be given with sufficient clarity to enable the individual to 'usefully exercise the right of appeal available to him' (*Hadjianastassiou* v *Greece* (1993) 16 EHRR 219). Lack of reasons for a criminal conviction where the verdict is pronounced by a jury is not, per se, unfair. This is providing that it is clear from the charges laid, together with the questions put to the jury, which piece of evidence and factual circumstances the jurors had ultimately based their answers to the questions on (*Agnelet* v *France* [2013] ECHR 276).

(g) The right to legal representation and to legal aid where necessary for the administration of justice. These are express rights in criminal cases and extend to pre-trial proceedings including questioning in police custody (*Magee* v *United Kingdom* (2001) 31 EHRR 35; *Averill* v *United Kingdom* (2001) 31 EHRR 36). If a lawyer is requested and, unless in the particular circumstances, there are 'compelling reasons' for a refusal, the questioning should not begin until the lawyer is present (**Salduz v Turkey** [2008] ECHR 1542). A valid waiver of these rights should not be construed from the fact that the person answers questions prior to the lawyer's arrival (**Pishchalnikov v Russia** [2009] ECHR 1357). Any attempt to use statements or admissions given in breach of these rules as evidence contravenes Article 6(3). Also see **Ocalan v Turkey** [2005] 41 EHRR 45 (denial of access to lawyer for seven days while in pre-trial custody followed by restrictions on number and length of consultations and lack of any opportunity to conduct these out of hearing of prison guards). In **Benham v United Kingdom** (1996) 22 EHRR 293, the applicant had been tried without legal representation and committed to prison for three months for non-payment of the community charge. The Court of Human Rights held that although the proceedings were civil, the potential severity of the sentence meant that he should have been allowed access to legal aid and thus enabled to be legally represented at his trial. In other cases relating to civil proceedings, the Court has held that whether provision of legal aid is necessary for a fair trial depends on the facts and circumstances of each case, including the importance of the issues at stake, the complexity of the proceedings and the ability of those involved to present their own case effectively. In **Steel and Morris v United Kingdom** [2005] ECHR 103, a breach of Article 6 was found to have resulted from a refusal of legal aid to the defendants in a complex and controversial action for defamation. The ECtHR noted that the proceedings at first instance had lasted 313 days, had involved 130 oral witnesses and 40,000 papers of documentation. In addition, a degree of difficulty had attended some of the legal issues raised. The right to legal representation and advice at all stages of the criminal process has been strictly enforced where the suspect is a minor (**Güveç v Turkey** [2009] ECHR 88). If suspected of 'offences' and questioned by the police, the right to legal representation applies to persons below the age of criminal responsibility (**Blokhin v Russia**, supra).

A comprehensive explanation of the suspect's Article 6 right of access to a lawyer was provided by the Grand Chamber in **Ibrahim v United Kingdom** [2016] ECHR 750, a case in which the police conducted 'safety interviews' of persons suspected of planting bombs on the London underground, just two weeks after the attacks of 21 July, 2005, but which failed to detonate. The main guiding principles were as set out below:

(i)   given the privilege against self-incrimination and the right to silence, there could be no justification for a failure to inform a suspect of these rights;

(ii)   having regard to the fundamental nature and importance of early access to legal advice, restriction of the right could be permitted only for compelling reasons and in exceptional circumstances;

(iii)   where the state demonstrated convincingly the existence of an urgent need to avert serious adverse consequences for life, liberty, or physical integrity, this could amount to a compelling reason for restriction of access;

(iv)   a 'non-specific' fear that access to a solicitor could result in a leak of information potentially damaging to police inquiries was not sufficient of itself.

In refusing the application for breach of Article 6, the court's findings were:

- the government had demonstrated an urgent need for the 'safety interviews', viz. the danger to life and limb;
- the perpetrators of the 21 July attack had still been at liberty;
- the police, quite properly, were seeking, as a matter of urgency, to obtain information about any further planned attacks and the identities of those involved;
- there was a clear legislative framework for the restrictions in domestic law;

- these contained strict limits on the amount of time such restrictions of access could be imposed for (48 hours maximum);
- the principal legal safeguards for those taken into custody and dealt with in criminal procedures had been observed, i.e. they had been informed of their right to silence and legal advice; during their trial and on appeal they had been given the opportunity to challenge the police version of the 'safety interview'; their evidence had been put to the jury and carefully summarised by the trial judge and the jury reminded that they had been denied legal advice at the safety interview. All in all, it could not be said that the applicant had been treated unfairly.

(h) The right to sufficient time to prepare a case or submission (***Galstyan*** v ***Armenia*** [2007] ECHR 936). For such purposes, the individual has the right to consult in private, or at least out of hearing of police and state personnel, with a legal adviser. This extends to video conferences (***Zagaria*** v ***Italy*** app no 58295/00, 27.11.07).

Right to a public hearing

This right exists to protect litigants from the dangers of 'justice in secret with no public scrutiny' (***Pretto*** v ***Italy*** (1984) 6 EHRR 182). The press and public may, however, be excluded from all or part of a trial where this is in the interests of 'morals, public order or national security . . . where the interests of juveniles or the private life of the parties so require, or . . . where publicity would prejudice the interests of justice' (Art 6(1)). This proviso was held to justify excluding the press and public from prison disciplinary proceedings in ***Campbell and Fell*** v ***United Kingdom*** (1984) 7 EHRR 165. The Court felt that such proceedings could be conducted *in camera* for reasons of 'public order and security' and that public hearings would impose a disproportionate burden on the state in terms of the risks to security which would have to be guarded against.

The giving of evidence *in camera* or out of view of the court and public in legal proceedings generally may be permissible if this is necessary to ensure a witness's safety (*X* v ***United Kingdom*** 2 Digests 456 (1980)).

Right to trial within a reasonable time

In criminal cases 'time' for this requirement starts to run from the time a person has been notified that they have been accused of an offence. In civil cases time begins to run from the initiation of legal proceedings.

What is a reasonable time will depend on the circumstances of each case. The case should be prepared as expeditiously as is permitted by the complexity of the issues involved and any difficulties in gathering evidence or securing the attendance of witnesses. Greater expedition is expected in criminal cases so that the suspect should not 'remain too long in a state of uncertainty about his fate' (***Stogmuller*** v ***Austria*** (1980) 1 EHRR 155). This requirement was breached in ***Zimmermann and Steiner*** v ***Switzerland*** (1984) 6 EHRR 17, where, because of a backlog of cases, an appeal was pending before the Swiss Supreme Court for three and a half years. The obligation applies also to the determination of matters arising out of the litigation in question. Thus, a breach of Art 6 was committed where it took over four years to determine a particular litigant's liability for costs (***Robins*** v ***United Kingdom*** (1998) 26 EHRR 527).

In certain circumstances, delays in legal proceedings may impact on other Convention rights. ***Silih*** v ***Slovenia*** [2007] ECHR 537 arose out of an action for medical negligence following the death of a hospital patient. Commenced in 1993, the action did not come to trial until 2006. The protracted delay meant that there had been no effective inquiry into the death as required by Art 2.

For more on Art 2 requirements, see pp. 514–9.

Right to an independent and impartial tribunal

An independent tribunal is one which is free from any outside influences, particularly from the executive branch of government. The crucial requirement here is that those exercising judicial functions must have genuine security of tenure. This need not be protected by law but must exist in fact (*Eccles, McPhillips and McShane v Ireland* (1988) 59 DR 212).

An impartial tribunal is one which is free of prejudice or bias. Impartiality may result from actual personal bias or a sufficient appearance of bias to cast 'legitimate doubt' on a particular judicial officer's fitness to dispose of the proceedings (*Hauschildt v Denmark* (1990) 12 EHRR 266). In criminal cases the need for impartiality extends to members of the jury where one is used (*Sander v United Kingdom* (2001) 31 EHRR 44, breach of Art 6 where juror made racist remarks in considering case against Asian defendant).

The United Kingdom's courts martial procedures were held to be inadequate to satisfy this element of Art 6 in a series of cases decided during the 1990s. This was in addition to their deficiencies under Art 5(4) as explained above. The Court took particular exception to the overriding powers exercised by the 'convening officer' (often the relevant commanding officer) according to the terms of the Army and Air Force Acts 1955. Such powers extended to determining the charges to be brought, appointing members of the court, its prosecuting officer, and confirming its findings before these could be given effect – all of which fell far short of the requirements of independence and impartiality (see *Findlay v United Kingdom*, 6 June 2000, Hudoc; *McDaid v United Kingdom*, 10 October 2000, Hudoc; *Cable v United Kingdom* (1999) 30 EHRR 1032). The procedures for domestic courts martial were amended by the Armed Forces Act 1996 which, *inter alia*, abolished the position of convening officer. The changes effected by the 1996 Act were found to be Convention compatible in *R v Spear; R v Hastie; R v Boyd* [2001] 2 WLR 1692.

Executive involvement in the sentencing process by the fixing of tariffs for persons sentenced to indeterminate terms of imprisonment (i.e. the period for punishment and deterrence) was condemned in *T v United Kingdom*, 14 December 1998, Hudoc. Although a long-standing procedure in the United Kingdom, its effect was to minimise judicial involvement in determining the actual form to be served.

Amongst the rights guaranteed specifically for the conduct of criminal cases, the right to an independent and impartial tribunal is perhaps the most significant.

Presumption of innocence

The requirement is that 'when carrying out their duties, the members of a court should not start with the preconceived idea that the accused has committed the offence charged; the burden of proof is on the prosecution, and any doubt should benefit the accused' (*Barberà, Messegué and Jabardo v Spain* (1989) 11 EHRR 360).

To avoid such misconceptions it has been held that public officials should not make statements to the effect that they believe a suspect to be guilty of a particular offence before that person has been tried by a competent court. 'Article 6(2) . . . may be violated by public officials if they declare that somebody is responsible for criminal acts without a court having found so' (*Krause v Switzerland* (1978) 13 DR 73).

Violation was held to have occurred in *Allenet de Ribemont v France* (1995) 20 EHRR 557, where, during a press conference, the French Minister of the Interior and other high-ranking police officials made clear their belief that the applicant had been involved in the murder of a French MP. It was held that the French authorities had encouraged the public to believe that the applicant was guilty and had thus prejudiced the outcome of any subsequent judicial proceedings. In the event the applicant was never brought to trial.

The presumption applies to appeal as well to the first instance proceedings. So far as appeal proceedings are concerned, this does not prevent a first instance conviction being referred to, but this should be done with 'all the discretion and circumspection necessary [for] the presumption of innocence to be respected' (*Konstas* v *Greece*, app no 53466/07, 24.5.11).

The presumption of innocence does not imply any absolute right to silence. It is, therefore, permissible for a court to place reasonable adverse inferences on a suspect's refusal to answer police questions so long as this is done in the context of all the evidence (*Murray* v *United Kingdom* (1996) 22 EHRR 29).

A court should not convict a person on the basis of their silence alone (*Averill* v *United Kingdom* (supra)) and should hesitate to use such silence against a suspect where a plausible excuse for it has been offered, e.g. where the suspect was advised to remain silent by his solicitor who believed him to be suffering from the symptoms of heroin withdrawal (*Condron* v *United Kingdom* (2001) 31 EHRR 1). Although not absolute, the right to silence has an irreducible 'essence' or minimum. In order to determine whether a particular act or measure has transgressed upon it unduly, it is necessary for the court to consider the nature and degree of compulsion used or authorised to secure the evidence; the existence and effectiveness of any relevant procedural safeguards; and the use(s) to which the information may be put (*Jalloh* v *Germany* (2006) 44 EHRR 667).

O'Halloran and Francis v *United Kingdom*, app nos 15809/02 and 25624/02, 29.6.07, involved a challenge to s 172 of the Road Traffic Act 1988. This requires the registered keeper of a motor vehicle believed to have been involved in certain types of road traffic offences (e.g. speeding), to provide information concerning the identity of the driver. Failure to provide such information is an offence unless it can be shown that the person did not know and could not reasonably have been expected to have obtained that information. Finding against the applicants, the Court held that:

(i) Although the compulsion in s 172 was direct, it was specific and limited in scope. It applied only when a motoring offence was suspected and was confined to the name of the driver.

(ii) Conviction could be avoided if the person did not know and could not reasonably have been expected to have ascertained the information required.

(iii) The information could not, of itself, be sufficient evidence of the commission of a road traffic offence. This would still have to be proved beyond reasonable doubt giving the person concerned the opportunity to give evidence and call witnesses.

The decision was, however, not unanimous. In a dissenting judgment, Judge Pavlovschi (Moldova) felt unable to avoid the conclusion that where a car was believed to have been involved in an alleged speeding offence, a compulsory statement by a person that they had been driving the car could not be regarded as anything other than a significant act of self-incrimination. On this basis, he felt constrained to issue the cogent warning that 'if one begins seeking to justify departures from the basic principles of modern criminal procedure and the very essence of the notion of a fair trial for reasons of public policy, and if the Court starts accepting such reasons, we will have a real threat to the European order as protected by the Convention'.

Right to be informed of the charge

The right of the defendant in criminal proceedings to be informed promptly of the case to be answered does not duplicate the requirement relating to the giving of reasons for arrest in Art 5(2). The obligation in Art 6 is to provide sufficient information to enable a suspect to prepare an adequate defence. The suspect is also entitled to sufficient time and means, particularly through access to legal advice, for that purpose. This is a particularly important guarantee for those in custody on remand. If the suspect does not wish to conduct their own defence, they have the right to be legally represented. There is also a right for this to be paid for by legal aid where the suspect does not have sufficient means and where the interests of justice so require.

Extradition and deportation

Article 6 is a factor to be taken into account when states are exercising powers of extradition or deportation. A person should not be sent or returned to a state in which he/she may be required to stand trial in 'flagrant denial' of any of the Article's principal procedural requirements, e.g. as in ***Othman (Abu Qatada)* v *United Kingdom*** [2012] ECHR 56, by the admission of evidence obtained by torture.

> The right to a fair trial in criminal proceedings, as embodied in Article 6, holds a prominent place in a democratic society. The court does not exclude that an issue might exceptionally be raised under Article 6 by an extradition decision in circumstances where the fugitive has suffered or risks suffering a flagrant denial of a fair trial in the requesting state (***Soering* v *United Kingdom***, supra).

A flagrant denial of justice goes beyond mere irregularities or lack of safeguards in the trial procedures such as might result in a breach of Art 6 if occurring within the contracting state itself. What is required is a breach of the principles of fair trial guaranteed by Art 6 which is so fundamental as to completely nullify or destroy the very essence of fair procedure.

No punishment without law (Art 7)

This article provides that no one should be convicted of an offence or subjected to a penalty which did not exist at the time the allegedly criminal act was committed. This prohibition applies both to the creation of new offences having retrospective effect and to the reinterpretation of pre-existing laws 'to cover facts which previously clearly did not constitute a criminal offence' (***X Ltd and Y* v *United Kingdom*** (1982) 28 DR 77). Nor should a person be subjected to a penalty if he/she has not been found to have transgressed a lawful restriction (***Varvara* v *Italy***, app no 17475/09, 29.10.13, confiscation of applicant's property after criminal proceedings became time-barred and were discontinued).

It is permissible, however, for an existing offence to be given judicial clarification and 'adapted to new circumstances which can reasonably be brought under the original conception of the offence' (***X Ltd and Y***, supra). Hence, no breach of Art 7 was committed by two decisions in the United Kingdom courts that a husband could be guilty of raping his wife. It was held that this development in the common law was reasonably foreseeable given changing social attitudes and the contingent dismantling by the courts of the husband's legal immunity (***SW* v *United Kingdom; CR* v *United Kingdom*** (1996) 21 EHRR 363).

The rule against retrospective penalties was held to have been contravened in ***Welch* v *United Kingdom*** (1995) 20 EHRR 247. In 1988 the applicant was convicted of drugs offences committed in 1986. The judge made a confiscation order against him (for £59,000) under the Drug Trafficking Offences Act 1986. The provisions of the Act did not become effective, however, until 1987, well after the offences had been committed. The Article requires a minimum level of legal certainty in legal rules, whether statute or judge-made, to ensure that those subject to them know in advance when their actions may attract criminal sanctions. In ***Jorgic* v *Germany*** [2007] ECHR 583, a case arising out of the conflict in Bosnia, Art 7 was used to challenge the German law's definition of the offence of genocide, i.e. 'destruction of a group'. The applicant had been convicted of the offence in respect of the mass killings of Muslim civilians. Since the same definition, although not universal, had been adopted in other legal codes, the Court felt that, with proper legal advice, it would have been reasonably possible for him to have foreseen that his conduct might fall within it.

Right to respect for private, family life, home and correspondence (Art 8)

Private life

Meaning and scope

Respect for private life has been held to extend to such matters as personal and sexual identity, i.e. personal preferences in terms of name or gender, to matters of sexual orientation and lifestyle and to the safeguarding of physical and moral identity.

> As the Court has had previous occasion to remark, the concept of 'private life' is a broad term not susceptible to exhaustive definition. It covers the physical and psychological integrity of a person. It can sometimes embrace aspects of an individual's physical or social identity. Elements such as, for example, gender identification, name and sexual orientation and sexual life fall within the personal sphere protected by Article 8. Article 8 also protects a right to personal development, and the right to establish and develop relationships with other human beings and the world outside (*Pretty* v *United Kingdom* (2002) 35 EHRR 1).

Those who seek publicity, often for personal kudos and/or financial gain, e.g. entertainers and 'celebrities,' enjoy a lesser degree of protection for their private lives. Accordingly, although Article 8 may be used to protect a person's name and identity, the full extent of that protection did not apply to the use of a pop star's name and to satirical and humorous references to a book he had written, contained in an advertisement for cigarettes. The court was exercised by the need for freedom of speech in relation to people who willingly court the attention of the media and put themselves in the public eye (*Bohlen* v *Germany* [2015] ECHR 194).

Identity, gender and sexual orientation

The right to define oneself as male or female is one of the most basic essentials of self-determination (*Van Kuck* v *Germany* [2003] ECHR 285). The link between gender and identity is particularly relevant to those who have undergone gender reassignment therapy. Until relatively recent times the Court had refused to interpret the Convention as guaranteeing full legal recognition to post-operative gender and had not been prepared to accept that Art 8 gives any absolute right to alteration of birth certificates (*Sheffield and Horsham* v *United Kingdom* (1998) 27 EHRR 163). The position appeared to be that a refusal to allow birth certificates and other personal documents to be altered could constitute a breach where the use and need for such documentation was a regular feature of daily life (*B* v *France* (1993) 16 EHRR 1). Otherwise, however, in states where this did not appertain and where, accordingly, the administrative burden imposed on the state would be out of proportion to the advantages to be gained by the individual, no breach of Art 8 was committed.

Whatever the contemporary validity of this distinction, and in a classic manifestation of the 'living' nature of the Convention, the Grand Chamber in *Goodwin* v *United Kingdom*

(2002) 35 EHRR 18, decided that the time had come to give full legal recognition to post-operative transsexuals, and that this included the right to have their chosen gender recorded on birth certificates and other official documents:

> In the twenty-first century the right of transsexuals to personal development and to physical and moral security in the full sense enjoyed by others in society cannot be regarded as a matter of controversy requiring the lapse of time to cast clearer light on the issues involved.

The Court's principal reasons for this major development were:

- the conflict between social reality and law which exposed transsexuals to feelings of vulnerability, humiliation and anxiety was a serious interference with private life;
- it was anomalous that the state authorised gender reassignment treatment but did not recognise its full legal implications;
- there was clear evidence of a continuing international trend in favour of full legal recognition of the new sexual identity of post-operative transsexuals;
- while the Court did not underestimate the important repercussions any major change would have both in the sphere of birth registration and other official documentation, it did not regard these as insuperable;
- it had not been shown that any such change would cause disproportionate damage to any related public interest.

Following the *Goodwin* decision, it has been held that post-operative male to female transsexuals should be granted the pension entitlements accorded to women (*Grant* v *United Kingdom* [2006] ECHR 548).

State compliance with this aspect of gender recognition is not fulfilled merely by granting a legal right to gender reassignment therapy. It is also necessary to have rules in place which make clear the necessary legal conditions and administrative processes for such courses of treatment. Without these, doctors might be reluctant to act, thereby rendering the right nugatory (*L* v *Lithuania* [2007] ECHR 725).

Whether gender reassignment therapy could legitimately be refused because the person requesting it, a female to male transsexual, might not be permanently unable to procreate, was considered in *Y.Y.* v *Turkey*, app no 14739/08, 10.3.15. Notwithstanding the complexity of the issue the Court's clear view was that the principle of respect for the applicant's physical integrity precluded any obligation on him to undergo permanent sterilisation as part of the reassignment process. The Court made clear also that the developing law in this context should be guided by certain general precepts:

(a) ensuring transsexuals have full enjoyment of the right to personal development and physical and moral integrity should no longer be regarded as a controversial question;

(b) as recognised at an international level, transsexualism was a medical condition requiring treatment to enable the persons concerned to realise their full human potential.

In the matter of sexual orientation and the practice of same between consenting adults, the Convention gives each individual the freedom to follow their personal inclinations and to protection from discrimination relating thereto. An individual's sexuality has been described as a most 'intimate aspect' of private life which should not be restricted except for 'serious reasons having to do with the preservation of public order and decency and the need to protect the citizen from what is offensive and injurious' (see *Dudgeon* v *United Kingdom (No. 2)* (1982) 4 EHRR 149; Art 8 violated by legal rules in Northern Ireland which made intercourse between men a criminal offence). The Article has been used successfully to challenge the ban on gays in the British armed forces (*Lustig-Prean* v *United Kingdom*; *Smith and O'Grady* v *United Kingdom* (2000) 29 EHRR 548), and the conviction for gross indecency of a group of males who engaged in group sex which was wholly consensual and non-violent (*ADT* v *United Kingdom* (2001) 31 EHRR 33). No breach of Art 8 was committed, therefore, by the criminalisation of sadomasochistic sexual activity where this was violent and caused injury (*Laskey* v *United Kingdom* (1997) 24 EHRR 39).

Personal physical and moral integrity

The right to private life guarantees respect for each person's personal, physical, moral and psychological integrity (*X and Y* v *Netherlands* (1986) 8 EHRR 235). In this sense Art 8 may be engaged by such matters as the taking of compulsory blood tests in paternity proceedings (*X* v *Austria* (1979) 18 DR 154) or by compulsory testing for various medical purposes (*Acmanne* v *Belgium* (1984) 40 DR 252). In both cases the interference in question was found to be legitimate under Art 8(2) as being in the interests of the protection of health generally and the rights and freedoms of others. See also *Association X* v *United Kingdom* (1978) 14 DR 31, where the Commission again accepted the same Art 8(2) justification for a national vaccination programme.

Other physical integrity cases engaging Art 8 have included compulsory urine tests for road traffic purposes (*Peters* v *Netherlands* (1994) 77-A DR 75); persistent loud noise caused by aeroplanes (*Rayner* v *United Kingdom* (1986) 47 DR 5); offensive smells (*Lopez-Ostra* v *Italy* (1994) 20 EHRR 277); the use of corporal punishment in schools (*Costello-Roberts* v *United Kingdom* (1993) 19 EHRR 112); the failure to protect against chemical pollution (*Guerra* v *Italy* (1998) 26 EHRR 357); the sterilisation of a female Roma without her full consent (*VC* v *Slovakia* [2011] ECHR 1888); taking photographs of a person without their consent (*Reklos and Davourlis* v *Greece* [2009] ECHR 200); covert intimate filming of a 14-year-old girl by her stepfather (*Soderman* v *Sweden*, app no 5786/08, 4.4.13). Ill health as a result of prolonged exposure to noxious fumes from a large steel works and failure to provide alternative accommodation was raised in *Fadeyeva* v *Russia* [2005] ECHR 376. Albeit that the works had been privatised in 1993, the state was found responsible through its failure to introduce sufficient environmental controls.

The right to physical and moral integrity does not give any unqualified entitlement to termination of pregnancy as this is a matter in which states are vested with a wide margin of appreciation. It does, however, confer rights of access to information and guidance about termination, to travel to other jurisdictions where terminations may be performed, and to adequate after-care services where this has occurred (*A, B and C* v *Ireland* [2010] ECHR 2032). The mother-to-be would also appear to have the right to determine where the baby will be born (whether at home, etc., or in hospital) and the procedure to be used (*Ternovsky* v *Hungary*, app no 67545/09, 14.12.10).

Access to information

A further development in this context has been the recognition of a right to be provided with information to enable those engaged in certain types of potentially hazardous activities to assess the full extent of the risks involved. Hence in *Vilnes* v *Norway*, app no 52806/10,

5.12.13 the Court found that the state had failed to ensure that the applicants, who were deep-sea divers, had received essential information on the risks associated with a certain type of rapid decompression tablets.

Article 8 also has relevance for the protection of personal data and information. It may be engaged, therefore, by refusals of access to such information (*Gaskin* v *United Kingdom*, supra) and by keeping and storing such materials without consent (*Hewitt and Harman* v *United Kingdom* (1989) 14 EHRR 657).

Private life and the police

The power in the Police and Criminal Evidence Act 1984, s 64 permitting the indefinite retention of fingerprints, cellular samples, and DNA taken from the persons who may have been suspected, but who later were not convicted of any offence, was condemned as a breach of Art 8 in *S and Marper* v *United Kingdom* [2008] ECHR 1581. The ECtHR felt that the relevant law in this matter failed to maintain a proper balance between the private rights and public interests involved, i.e. the right to privacy and the protection against crime, and was particularly concerned that:

- the data in question could be retained indefinitely irrespective of the nature or gravity of the offence with which the person might originally have been suspected;
- persons entitled to the presumption of innocence were being treated in the same way as convicted persons;
- many of the persons whose samples had been retained were minors.

In the UK, legislation regulating the use and retention of DNA and other samples taken in the course of a criminal investigation may now be found in the Protection of Freedoms Act 2012.

Family life

Meaning and scope

For the Convention's purposes, the concept of family life extends considerably beyond the formal relationships created by marriage or cohabitation and any offspring created thereby. In this wider sense the concept has been held to extend to the relationship between a child and her grandparents with whom she had lived in her early years (*Bronda* v *Italy*, 9 June 1998, Hudoc) and that between a child in care and his uncle following allegations of sexual abuse against the child's mother (*Boyle* v *United Kingdom* (1994) 19 EHRR 179). It has also proved of considerable utility for those affected by relationships created outside wedlock and those which have become dysfunctional. Thus Art 8 was violated by the failure to consult a child's natural father before its adoption was arranged (*Keegan* v *Ireland* (1994) 18 EHRR 342). Other violations have resulted from denials of parental access to a child in care (*Johansen* v *Norway* (1996) 23 EHRR 33; *Glaser* v *United Kingdom*, 19 September 2000, Hudoc) and by an authority's failure to consult the natural parents when making decisions affecting the well-being of a child also in care (*W* v *United Kingdom* (1983) 10 EHRR 29).

Rights to respect for family life do not depend entirely on the existence of biological connection factors. Hence a legal rule denying any family rights to a person who had played a major part in the bringing up of a child he believed to be his but who later failed a paternity test, could not be regarded as consistent with his Article 8 rights (*Nazarentov* v *Russia* [2015] ECHR 686).

In order to preserve the conventional concept of family life, the ECtHR has made clear that state authorities should only use their powers to remove a child from its natural parents in 'very exceptional circumstances' and, even then, if and when appropriate, should do what was possible to 'rebuild the family'. The fact that a child could be placed in a more beneficial environment for his or her upbringing does not, on its own, justify removal from the care of the child's biological parents (*Amanalachioai v Romania*, app no 4023/04, 26.5.09).

Fathers-to-be do not have any right to be consulted or to apply to a court before their child is aborted. In this context their rights are superseded by those of the mother (*Evans v United Kingdom* [2007] ECHR 264). Fathers do, however, have the right to withdraw their consent from the creation of a pregnancy by IVF using embryos developed from eggs using their sperm (*Evans v United Kingdom*, supra).

After a period of some uncertainty (see *Estevez v Spain*, app no 58752/00, 15.5.01), the ECtHR has recognised that the 'relationships of same-sex couples living in stable *de facto* partnerships' should be accepted as falling within the meaning of family life (*PB and JS v Austria* [2010] ECHR 1146). For all practical purposes, therefore, this establishes that the legal protection and benefits accruing to families in the traditional sense, and to those in family relationships, should be equally applicable to those living in permanent and close social bonds based on, or deriving from, same-sex unions or arrangements. This same approach was applied in *Vallianatos v Greece*, app no 29381/09, 7.11.13, where a law giving a degree of legal recognition and protection to unmarried different-sex couples, and to their children, was found in violation of Articles 8 and 14 through its failure to apply the same provisions to couples in same-sex relationships.

The matter was taken further in *Oliari v Italy* [2015] ECHR 716, where the Grand Chamber found a breach of Article 8(1) in the failure of Italian law to provide for same-sex civil unions, or some other official recognition of such relationships, from which legal benefits might flow.

The court was particularly exercised by the following factors:

(i)   the continual international movement towards legal recognition of same-sex unions;

(ii) the inability of the Italian authorities to point to any countervailing public interest;

(iii) evidence of popular support amongst Italian people for recognition of such unions;

(iv) recognition of same-sex unions would not place any undue burden on the Italian state and would bring the law into line with social reality;

(v)   such recognition had been called for by the Italian courts.

Imprisonment

If family life has been disrupted by a sentence of imprisonment the state is under an obligation to seek to maintain the prisoner's family ties (*McCotter v United Kingdom* (1993) 15 EHRR CD 98). This was not done where a person sentenced to life imprisonment was permitted two family visits per year (*Khoroshenko v Russia* [2015] ECHR637). The obligation to preserve family ties does not give a sentenced person a right to be held in the prison nearest or most convenient to his place of abode. On the other hand, in *Khodorkovsky and Lebeder v Russia* [2011] ECHR 5829/04, the court was not satisfied that placing a convict in a prison thousands of kilometres from his home could be regarded as proportionate to the needs of prisoner safety and the avoidance of prison overcrowding.

Notwithstanding the disruption to a prisoner's Art 8 entitlements caused by separation and distance, a long-term prisoner would appear to have the right to have a family by means of artificial insemination (*Dickson v United Kingdom* [2007] ECHR 1051).

Deportation

Family life may also be affected prejudicially by deportation. Hence it was a breach of Art 8 for the Dutch government to deport an alien male after his marriage to a person with the right of abode in Holland had come to an end. In particular, this severed his links with his son in circumstances where the deportee had committed no offence and posed no obvious threat to any of the legitimate interests for which, according to Article 8(2), restrictions on family life may be imposed (*Clitz v Netherlands* (1988) 11 EHRR 360). Even where deportation is for a legitimate aim, e.g. prevention of disorder or crime, it may still be disproportionate to the aim's achievement if its effect is the potential destruction of a family (*Beldjoudi v France* (1992) 14 EHRR 801; breach of Art 8 to deport Algerian male married to a French female albeit he had a criminal record and had served over ten years in prison).

Issues to be taken into account in determining whether a person convicted of offences should be returned to his/her country of origin include:

- the nature and seriousness of the offences committed;
- the length of time the person has been in the country;
- how long it has been since the offence was committed;
- whether the person is married, how long for, and whether he/she has any children;
- if the person is married, whether the spouse knew of the offences when the marriage took place;
- the difficulties the spouse might encounter in the country to which the person is to be expelled;
- the nationalities of the various persons involved (*Boultif v Switzerland* (2001) 33 EHRR 1179; and *Uner v Netherlands* (2007) 45 EHRR 14.

None of these factors should be regarded as conclusive of the rectitude of the decision whether or not to expel, but are important criteria in determining whether any expulsion was a proportionate response to the legitimate aim pursued (*Maslov v Austria* [2008] ECHR 546). Their application may be illustrated by reference to the decision in *A W Khan v United Kingdom*, app no 47486/06, 12.1.10. The applicant had entered the country from Pakistan at the age of three. He had been educated here and had spent most of his formative years here also. When he was 27, he was sentenced to seven years for drugs offences. Following his release, the decision was taken to deport him. The ECtHR held that, although the severity of his offences must weigh heavily in the balance, it would be a disproportionate response to expel him from the United Kingdom. This was the case, the Court felt:

> having regard to the length of time the applicant has been in the United Kingdom, his very young age at the time of entry, the lack of any continuing ties with Pakistan, and the fact that [he] has not re-offended since his release from prison.

In a quite different context, an interesting extension to the rights of family life occurred in *Foxley v United Kingdom* (2001) 31 EHRR 25. Here, it was held to be a breach of Art 8 to withhold from a 'widowed' father a state benefit (i.e. widowed mother's allowance) which would have accrued to him had he been a widowed mother.

Home

Legal right or social aspiration

The right to respect for an individual's home does not imply an absolute right to be provided with a place to live.

> It is important to recall that Article 8 does not in terms recognise a right to be provided with a home. While it is clearly desirable that every human being have a place where he or she can live with dignity and which he or she can call home, there are unfortunately in the contracting states many persons who have no home. Whether the state provides funds to enable everyone to have a home is a matter for political not judicial decision (***Chapman v United Kingdom*** [2001] ECHR 43).

Peaceful enjoyment

This notwithstanding, for those who have a home, Article 8(1) does give a right to peaceful enjoyment of it.

Article 8 is clearly engaged, therefore, by unjustified entry into an individual's premises (see ***McLeod v United Kingdom*** (1999) 27 EHRR 493) or by the use of covert surveillance techniques other than in accordance with Art 8(2) (***Govell v United Kingdom***, 14 January 1998, Hudoc; ***Khan v United Kingdom*** (2001) 31 EHRR 45).

The right to peaceful enjoyment may also be at issue in cases involving environmental intrusions into property rights.

Hatton v United Kingdom (2002) 34 EHRR 1

This case was concerned with the noise made by aeroplanes taking off and landing at Heathrow Airport during the night and the consequent sleep disturbance caused to nearby residents. It was held that, although the state had not actually caused the noise, it remained in breach of Art 8 in not ensuring that adequate research was carried out into the merits of the competing interests to enable a fair and proportionate balance to be drawn in terms of the amount of night-time use of the airport.

Eviction, demolition, and refusal of planning permission

While Article 8(1) may not be used to assert that the state is legally obliged to provide each person with a house, this is not to say that the Article has no part to play at all in the proper exercise of central or local government powers in this context. Hence, Article 8(1) has been used as the basis for development of the principle that any use of a statutory power to deprive a person of their home should not proceed without informed consideration of the extent to which any such action may be regarded as a proportionate response to the difficulty or conflict of private and public interests with which the authorities may be attempting to deal. It might normally be expected that this process would be conducted by some sort of lower level court or tribunal. It is, however, for each individual state to determine how exactly the obligation should be fulfilled in their particular jurisdictions. From this general principle, it becomes apparent that the obligation imposed by Article 8(1) in this context should be regarded as primarily procedural rather than substantive in form. It is interesting to note also that the obligation remains applicable notwithstanding that the person claiming its protection appears to have no firm legal right to remain in the property concerned.

The principle has been applied in a variety of housing-related contexts. These would include the following:

(i) The removal or 'moving on' of travellers from sites on which they had been settled for long periods (***Connors*** v ***United Kingdom*** [2004] ECHR 223, 'the eviction of the applicant and his family from the local authority site was not attended by the requisite procedural safeguards, namely, the requirement to establish proper justification for the serious interference with his rights and consequently cannot be regarded as justified by a pressing social need proportionate to the legitimate aim being pursued').

(ii) The termination of leases belonging to person living in housing association or council properties (***Kay*** v ***United Kingdom*** [2010] ECHR 223, 'The loss of one's home is the most serious form of interference with the right to respect for the home. Any person at risk of an interference of his magnitude should in principle be able to have the proportionality of the measure determined by an independent tribunal in the light of the relevant principles under Article 8 of the Convention').

(iii) An order to demolish a house built without planning permission (***Ivanova and Cherkazo*** v ***Bulgaria*** [2016] ECHR 373, 'the applicants had not had at their disposal a procedure enabling them to obtain a proper review of the proportionality of the intended demolition of the house in which they lived and in the light of their personal circumstances').

Domestic cases involving applications brought by travellers refused planning permission for the use of land as caravan sites have, to date, been unsuccessful. Here the ECtHR has been content that the procedures in the relevant legislation providing a right of appeal against refusal of planning permission, first to an inspector and from there to a Minister, is generally sufficient to satisfy the procedural requirement for assessing issues of proportionality (see ***Buckley*** v ***United Kingdom*** [1996] ECHR 39, 'the court considers that proper regard was had to the applicant's predicament both under the terms of the regulatory framework, which contained adequate procedural safeguards protecting her interests under Article 8 and by the responsible planning authorities when exercising their discretion in relation to the particular circumstances of her case').

Correspondence

The right to respect for correspondence seeks to protect the confidentiality of private communications and uninterrupted and uncensored communication with others. The term 'correspondence' extends to all modern techniques of electronic communication as well as to the more traditional modes of conveying information common at the time of the Convention's inception. Hence, the term has been held to encompass:

- telephone conversations at home or at work (***Malone*** v ***United Kingdom*** (1985) 7 EHRR 14; ***Halford*** v ***United Kingdom*** (1997) 24 EHRR 523);
- letters and other paper communications (***Taylor-Sabori*** v ***United Kingdom*** (2002) 36 EHRR 248);
- telex messages (***Christie*** v ***United Kingdom*** [2007] ECHR 253);
- emails and internet communications (***Copland*** v ***United Kingdom*** [2007] ECHR 253);
- communications in the course of business (***Halford*** v ***United Kingdom***, supra);
- private radio communications (***BC*** v ***Switzerland***, app no 21353/93, 21.11.95).

Two well-known cases in which the British government was held to be in breach of the right to privacy of correspondence were *Malone v United Kingdom*, *supra*, and *Halford v United Kingdom*, *supra*. *Malone* is dealt with in more detail below. *Halford* was the case which established that the right to privacy of correspondence may apply to telephone conversations in the workplace. The particular facts of the case were that the applicant's office phone was being monitored by her employers. This was not being done, however, according to the law, as there was no proper legal authority for such action and, by definition, no adequate legal regulation of the circumstances in which this could and could not be done.

The right to respect for the privacy of correspondence extends to the right not to receive unsolicited information or information which is offensive or pornographic. The state is not answerable, however, for the receipt of random emails or other internet communications sent out by persons unknown (*Muscio v Italy*, app no 31358/03, 13.11.07).

To the extent that secret surveillance activities involve interference with an individual's correspondence or electronic communications, this further element of Art 8 may also be engaged. Breaches may result, therefore, from telephone-tapping of domestic phone calls (*Malone v United Kingdom* (1985) 7 EHRR 14) and those made and received at the workplace (*Halford v United Kingdom* (1997) 24 EHRR 523).

In those instances in which the state adopts secret surveillance powers which might potentially be used against any and all members of the population, e.g. the monitoring of telecommunications, each individual may claim victim status for the purpose of challenging the overall compatibility of the measures with the right to respect for privacy. Where, however, an individual alleges a specific act of surveillance interfered with his Art 8 rights, but because of the covert nature of the acts involved, cannot prove what was done, it is enough for him to show that there was a 'reasonable likelihood' that the interference did actually happen (*Kennedy v United Kingdom* [2010] ECHR 682).

> The Court therefore accepts that an individual may, in certain circumstances, claim to be the victim of a violation occasioned by the mere existence of secret measures or of legislation permitting secret measures without having to allege that such measures were in fact applied to him ... Where an actual interception was alleged, the Court has held that in order for there to be an interference it has to be satisfied that there was a reasonable likelihood that the surveillance measures were applied to the applicant.

The Court's reasons for adopting this approach have been explained as follows:

> Sight should not be lost of the special reasons justifying the Court's departure from its general approach which denies individuals the right to challenge a law *in abstractio*. The principal reason was to ensure that the secrecy of such measures did not result in the measures being effectively unchallengeable and outside the supervision of the national judicial authorities and the Court ... Where there is no possibility of challenging the alleged application of secret surveillance measures at the domestic level, widespread suspicion and concern among the general public that secret surveillance powers are being abused cannot be said to be unjustified. In such cases, even where the risk of surveillance is low, there is a greater need for scrutiny by the Court (*Kennedy v United Kingdom*, *supra*).

The *in abstractio* approach to intrusive legislation, as explained in *Kennedy*, was applied in *Roman Sakarov v Russia* [2015] ECHR 1068 to Russian secret surveillance laws which required mobile network operators to install equipment which enabled to authorities to access any and all mobile telephone conversations as was thought fit. This could be done without any sort of judicial authorisation or supervision and without remedy for abuse or excess.

Correspondence in the traditional sense, i.e. letters etc., is, of course, also protected. Breaches here have included interceptions of a bankrupt's mail pursuant to a court order redirecting this to a trustee in bankruptcy (Insolvency Act 1986, s 371) after the order had expired (*Foxley* v *United Kingdom* (2001) 31 EHRR 25) and official interference with prisoners' correspondence where this was not based on any significant public interest justification (*Campbell* v *United Kingdom* (1993) 15 EHRR 137). Thus, in a case involving a prisoner who had suffered a brain haemorrhage, no public interest justification existed for monitoring his correspondence with the hospital consultant who was treating him (*Szuluk* v *United Kingdom* [2009] ECHR 845).

Interference with privacy and family life

The state may not interfere with the rights in Art 8 except where any restriction imposed is 'in accordance with the law and is necessary in a democratic society in the interests of national security, public safety or the economic well-being of the country, for the prevention of disorder or crime, for the protection of health or morals, or for the protection of the rights and freedoms of others'.

As explained above, to be 'in accordance with the law' a restriction must be founded on and regulated by clearly expressed and accessible legal rules. Mere administrative guidelines are not enough (*Malone* v *United Kingdom* (*supra*), authority and criteria for telephone-tapping Home Office guidelines only; *Khan* v *United Kingdom* (*supra*), similarly for use of covert listening devices). The monitoring of emails by public bodies, without clear legal authority and specification, has also been held not to be in 'accordance with the law' (*Copland* v *United Kingdom* [2007] ECHR 253).

In order to be 'necessary' a restraint must relate to a 'pressing social need' and be proportionate to the aims pursued (*Olsson* v *Sweden* (1989) 11 EHRR 259). In *Dudgeon* v *United Kingdom* (*supra*) it was held that interference with private life and privacy could be justified only for 'particularly serious reasons'. Such reasons were found to exist in *Klass* v *Federal Republic of Germany* (1980) 2 EHRR 214, where the tapping of telephones was done in the interests of counter-terrorism operations. Also in *Leander* v *Sweden* (1987) 9 EHRR 443, the national security interest was held to be sufficient to justify the collection of information and the keeping of secret police files on candidates for sensitive postings within the armed services.

To be proportionate the restriction should be no more than is necessary to deal effectively with the issue in question. Entry into private premises to prevent a breach of the peace was, therefore, not 'necessary' in this sense where the apprehended breach was not imminent (*McLeod* v *United Kingdom* (*supra*)).

Freedom of religion (Art 9)

The essence of the right

Each individual has the right to freedom of thought, conscience and religion, alone or in community with others, in private or in public and the right to manifest that religion or belief in worship, teaching, practice and observance (Art 9(1)). 'A healthy democratic society needs to tolerate and sustain pluralism and diversity' (*Eweida* v *United Kingdom* [2013] ECHR 37).

Accordingly the state is under a positive duty to ensure that the holders of a particular belief can enjoy it safe from interference, impediment or discrimination (*Otto-Preminger Institut* v *Austria* (1994) 19 EHRR 34). This does not extend, however, to guaranteeing a right of absence from employment on particular religious holy days or days of worship (*X v United Kingdom* (1981) 22 DR 27). The right protects both religious and non-religious beliefs.

> It is in its religious dimensions, one of the most vital elements that go to make up the identity of believers and their conception of life, but it is also a precious asset for atheists, agnostics, sceptics and the unconcerned (*Kokkinakis v Greece* (1994) 17 EHRR 397).

In *Arrowsmith v United Kingdom* (1978) 19 DR 5, the Commission of Human Rights felt that the Article extended to pacificism but did not accept that this gave the applicant the right to attempt to subvert others from their legal and military duty (the applicant had been convicted under the Incitement to Disaffection Act 1934 after she had distributed leaflets at an army barracks urging soldiers not to serve in Northern Ireland).

The state is not entitled to prevent the practice of a religion or other belief, nor must it attempt to enforce the same on those within its jurisdiction (*Angelini v Sweden* (1986) 51 DR 41). Nor, as a general rule, is it open to the state to assess the value or credibility of a particular belief. The state's role is that of neutral and impartial organiser of the exercise of such beliefs. Accordingly, other than limited assessment of such matters as the level of agency, seriousness, cohesion and relative importance of a belief, this excluded the state from exercising any discretion in determining whether any beliefs, religious or otherwise, should be regarded as acceptable and, therefore, legitimate. It has been said that the right in Article 9 would be 'highly theoretical and illusory if the degree of discretion granted to states allowed them to interpret the nature of religious denomination so restrictively as to deprive non-traditional and minority forms of religion of legal protection' (*Izzetin Dogan v Turkey* [2016] ECHR 387, failure of the Turkish authorities to give full recognition to the Alevi faith).

In the same case it was made clear that the corollary of the obligation of neutrality and impartiality was the 'principle of autonomy of religious communities according to which it was the task of the highest spiritual authorities . . . to determine to which faith that community belonged'. This meant that 'only the most serious and compelling reasons could justify state intervention' (ibid.). The Article is, therefore, a protection against state discrimination or indoctrination, whether for religious or atheistic purposes.

While the Article seeks to protect the individual's right of belief, it does not preclude the existence of laws which have been influenced by the state's dominant religion. Hence the now repealed prohibition of divorce in the Irish Constitution did not offend the Convention (*Johnston v Ireland* (1987) 9 EHRR 203).

Breaches of Art 9 have been committed by the imposition of criminal penalties on evangelical Christian sects in respect of their proselytising activities (*Kokkinakis v Greece* (1994) 17 EHRR 397); by dismissal from military service due to sympathies with Muslim fundamentalists (*Kalac v Turkey* (1999) 27 EHRR 552); by requiring incoming members of a national legislative assembly to take a religious oath of allegiance (*Buscarini v San Marino* (2000) 30 EHRR 208); and by state refusal to recognise and allow a church to practise its faith where this posed no realistic danger to the public interest (*Church of Bessarabia v Moldova*, 13 December 2001, Hudoc).

Interference with the freedom of thought and religion

The first element of Art 9(1), the right to freedom of thought, conscience and religion, is an absolute right and is not subject to the types of restrictions permitted by Art 9(2). Article 9(2) applies to the right to manifest one's religion or belief only. Restrictions may be imposed such as are 'prescribed by law and are necessary in a democratic society in the interests of public safety, for the protection of public order, health or morals, or for the protection of the rights and freedoms of others'.

Article 9 provides no absolute right to wear or display religious dress, emblems or symbols. The wearing or displaying of such items is a way of manifesting a religious or other belief. It is, therefore, subject to such restrictions as may be imposed under Art 9(2). In respect of the wearing of religious dress or symbols, it has been held that, while Art 9 may provide some protection where this is done in 'public areas open to all', restrictions could be imposed 'in public establishments where religious neutrality should take precedence over the right to manifest one's religion' (*Arslan* v *Turkey*, app no 41135/98, 23.2.10).

It is also apparent that Art 9 offers little protection for the display of religious symbols or icons in state schools or other public buildings in which secular activities may be conducted and in which persons from all sections of the community may be engaged. Such displays, it has been held, could be disturbing for members of other religious groups, or for those not having any religious belief or who object to such beliefs. This was the approach taken in *Lautsi* v *Italy* [2009] ECHR 1901, where the applicant successfully objected to the presence of crucifixes on the walls of the classrooms in the school in which her children were being educated.

> This could be encouraging for religious pupils, but also disturbing for children who practised other religions or were atheists, particularly if they belonged to religious minorities. The freedom to believe in any religion . . . was not limited to the absence of religious services or religious education: it extended to practices and symbols which expressed a belief, religion or atheism . . . The state was to refrain from imposing beliefs in premises where individuals were dependent on it. In particular it was required to observe confessional neutrality in the context of public education, where attending classes was compulsory irrespective of religion, and where the aim was to foster critical thinking in pupils . . . The compulsory display of a symbol of a given confession in premises used by the public authorities, and especially in classrooms, restricted the right of parents to educate their children in conformity with their convictions, and the right of the children to believe or not to believe.

In all such religious symbols cases, much depends on the circumstances and, therefore, the nature and extent of the 'manifestation', and its potential impact on those to whom the particular symbol has been displayed. Hence, for British Airways to sack a female employee for wearing a crucifix at work was found disproportionate to the company's aim of maintaining a certain corporate image of corporate neutrality. The cross had been worn discreetly and had not detracted in any way from the employee's professional image. Conversely, forbidding a nurse to wear a crucifix and chain at work was a proportionate restriction where there were fears that the cross might come into contact with an open wound or that a disturbed patient might seize and pull the chain causing injury (*Eweida*, supra).

Given the lack of national consensus in these matters, the state's margin of appreciation here is wide. Thus the French law prohibiting wearing of the burca and niqab was found to be within the policy choices open to a state committed to secularism and felt necessary in order to enable diverse ethnic communities and religious groups to live together with the minimum of friction. As such the measure could be regarded as contributing to the legitimate aim of protecting the rights and freedoms of others (*SAS* v *France* [2014] ECHR 43835/11).

A similar approach was adopted in *Ebrahamian* v *France* [2015] ECHR 1041 where no breach of Article 9 was found in the state's refusal to allow the applicant to wear a veil at work in the psychiatric ward of a hospital. It was felt that, given the nature of her employment, the state could require her to refrain from making known her religious affiliations. This was so the patients would not doubt the impartiality of her care and was consistent with the French state's 'overarching values of secularism and neutrality'.

Types of interference with the right to manifest one's religion or beliefs which have fallen within that permitted by Art 9(2) have included requiring conscientious objectors to undertake alternative public duties extending beyond the standard period of compulsory military service (*Autio v Finland* (1991) 72 DR 245: necessary for the protection of public safety) and refusal to grant religious exemptions from legislation requiring the wearing of crash-helmets by motorcyclists (*X v United Kingdom* (1978) 14 DR 243: necessary in the interests of public safety).

As Art 9(2) does not identify the needs of national security as one of the grounds for imposing restrictions on the right to manifest a religion or belief, such concerns alone cannot be pleaded as justification for actions taken for this purpose (*Nolan v Russia* [2009] ECHR 262).

Freedom of expression (Art 10)

The purpose and content of the right

This includes the freedom 'to hold opinions and to receive and impart information and ideas without interference by public authority and regardless of frontiers'. The jurisprudence of the Convention recognises this as one of the most important freedoms protected thereby – particularly so because it underpins and is essential for the realisation of many of the Convention's other guarantees. Feldman, *Civil Liberties and Human Rights in England and Wales* (2002), gives four principal reasons for the special position of this right:

(a) it is a 'significant instrument of freedom of conscience and self-fulfilment';

(b) it enables peoples 'to contribute to debates about social and moral issues';

(c) it allows the 'political discourse which is necessary in any country which aspires to democracy';

(d) it 'facilitates artistic and scholastic endeavour of all sorts'.

It is also clear that the freedom of expression is at constant and considerable risk of political interference. This is because those who pursue power may, having achieved it, find difficulty in resisting the temptation to use it against critics and opponents.

The Article, in essence, contains two related but distinct rights. These are the rights to impart and disseminate information and the right to receive it. Article 10 does not create a general right of freedom of, and access to, information albeit that this may relate to an individual or to a matter of public concern (*Guerra v Italy*, supra). It does, however, prohibit a government from restricting the flow of information to a person from those willing to impart it (*Open Door Counselling and Dublin Well Woman Clinic v Ireland* (1992) 15 EHRR 244; breach by court injunction prohibiting dissemination of information concerning access to abortion).

In *Kalda v Estonia* [2016] ECHR 92 (restriction of access by prisoners to internet sites containing legal information) note that the case did not recognise any general right of prisoners to be given access to the internet, only that, where such access was permitted, Article 10 may be violated by attempts to regulate the choice of sites a prisoner may wish to use.

The freedom extends to the spoken word and to radio and television broadcasting, pictures, images, print, films, plays, works of art and to computer information systems. It also implies the negative freedom not to speak (*Goodwin* v *United Kingdom* (1996) 22 EHRR 123).

While the Article would appear to be directed principally at the activities of the state, it would also appear to contain an obligation requiring the state to provide conditions in which the individual may exercise the right free from oppressive interference by others, e.g. groups opposed to the view in issue (*Plattform 'Ärzte für das Leben '* v *Austria*, *supra*).

The types of speech protected

The protection of the Article extends to that which shocks, offends or which is regarded as distasteful as well as that which may be received with equanimity (*Sunday Times* v *United Kingdom* (1979) 2 EHRR 245). It is unlikely, however, that it protects that which is racist in content (*Glimmerveen and Hagenbeck* v *Netherlands* (1979) 18 DR 187), or which is openly sympathetic to terrorism activities (*Purcell* v *Ireland* (1991) 70 DR 262). It was, therefore, a breach of Article 10 to prosecute a person for sending letters which expressed respect for a terrorist leader but which did not seek to support or praise terrorist activities or acts of violence (*Yaçinkaya* v *Turkey*, app no 25764/09, 1.10.13). The principle is also well established that no breach is committed by the public espousal of controversial views at a demonstration or protest meeting albeit that such views may be profoundly disturbing to others (*Perincek* v *Switzerland*, app no 27510/08, 17.12.13). The Convention does not seek to protect, however, that which is merely abusive and which does not contribute in any meaningful way to the open discussion of matters of public concern or legitimate interest (*Janowski* v *Poland* (2000) 29 EHRR 705). It follows that the positive duty on the state to guarantee freedom of expression obliges it to give protection to those elements of the media which may be critical of, or even ideologically opposed to, the government itself (*Ozgur* v *Turkey*, 16 March 2000, Hudoc).

Democracy and political debate

Although the Court has, on occasions, stressed that it does not attribute greater or lesser importance to freedom of speech in particular contexts (*Muller* v *Switzerland* (1991) 13 EHRR 212), the case-law does suggest a recognition of the democratic advantages in allowing a considerable degree of latitude to the press and media generally in relation to matters of public interest and the activities of those in political and public life. Article 10 was breached, therefore, by a finding of criminal defamation against the editor of a magazine after the publication of an article attributing neo-Nazi views to a prominent politician (*Oberschlick* v *Austria* (1991) 19 EHRR 389). The Court was clearly of the opinion that those engaged in the hurly-burly of political life must expect to be subjected to a more rigorous degree of criticism than is appropriate in comment on the activities and integrity of private citizens.

> The limits of acceptable criticism are accordingly wider in regard to the politician acting in his public capacity than in relation to a private individual. The former inevitably and knowingly lays himself open to close scrutiny of his every word and deed by both journalists and the public at large and he must display a greater degree of tolerance, especially when he himself makes statements that are susceptible to criticism. A politician is certainly entitled to have his reputation protected even when he is not acting in his private capacity, but the requirements of that protection have to be weighed against the interests of open discussion of political issues.

Ukrainian Media Group v *Ukraine* [2005] ECHR 198, involved a conviction of a newspaper owner for publishing sarcastic 'value judgments' in the course of a vigorous 'polemic' against certain prominent politicians engaged in the 1999 Ukrainian presidential election. It was found, however, that no breach of Art 10 had been committed, notwithstanding that the complainant may have been greatly offended, or even shocked, by the tone and strength of the language used. The ECtHR felt that those who had freely engaged in politics 'held themselves open to robust scrutiny and criticism'.

Other cases in which judicial restrictions on material critical of those in public life were held to offend Art 10 would include *Krone Verlag GmbH* v *Austria*, 26 February 2002, Hudoc; and *Feldek* v *Slovakia*, 12 August 2001, Hudoc. In the latter case, a breach of Art 10 was committed by a court's decision that it was defamatory to refer to a politician's 'fascist past'.

Judicial sanctions for defamation were also found to violate Art 10 following allegations in a Norwegian newspaper of the use of cruel and illegal methods by some of those engaged in seal hunting. On this occasion the Court's view was that the private interest in the protection of reputations was 'outweighed by the vital public interest' in ensuring an informed public debate over a matter of local and national as well as international interest (*Bladet Tromso* v *Norway* (1999) 29 EHRR 125). The Court added, however, that journalistic freedom in relation to matters of public concern generally was 'subject to the provision that they are acting in good faith in order to provide accurate and reliable information in accordance with the ethics of journalism'. Thus, to assert that the controversial French politician Jean-Marie Le Pen had advocated racial murder and to describe him as the 'chief of a gang of killers' and 'a vampire who thrives on the bitterness of his electorate but sometimes on their blood', overstepped the mark.

> Wording that expresses the intention of stigmatising an opponent and which is capable of stirring up violence and hatred goes beyond that which is tolerable in political debate, even in respect of a figure who occupies an extremist position in the political spectrum (*Lindon Otcharkovsky-Laurens and July* v *France* [2007] ECHR 836).

Given all of the above, and the ECtHR's emphasis on the importance of the media in the democratic process, attempts by states to prohibit the publication of particular newspapers, albeit for temporary periods only, due to their political sympathies, are unlikely to be found compatible with the Convention's requirements (*Urper* v *Turkey* [2010] ECHR 61).

Accordingly, and despite the importance given by the ECtHR to the unhindered dissemination of material relating to public affairs, no absolute protection attaches to internet news or other similar outlet portals which invite and permit publication of comments from readers made anonymously and without pre-registration. This remained the case notwithstanding the operation of a 'notice and take down' system unless where that was sufficient to enable clearly unlawful comments to be removed without delay and without notice from an alleged victim or third party (*Delfi AS* v *Estonia* [2015] ECHR 586).

Freedom of expression and advertising

Privately owned newspapers and other media outlets are free to exercise editorial discretion in deciding whether to publish articles, comments and letters submitted by private individuals and have similar discretion in relation to that produced by their own staff and reporters. The state's obligation to ensure freedom of expression does not give private citizens or organisations any unfettered right of access to the media in order to put forward opinions. An effective exercise of freedom of the press presupposes the right of newspapers to establish and apply their own policies in the matter of the content of advertisements (*Remuszko v Poland*, app no 1562/10, 16.7.13).

Freedom of expression and the internet

Article 10 applies to the internet in its role as one of the most important mechanisms for the dissemination and communication of information. To the extent that the internet deals with comment on matters of political and public affairs generally, the margin of appreciation permitted to states in seeking to regulate the content of web material is likely to be very narrow (*Axel Springer AG v Germany [GC]* [2013] ECHR 227). This was illustrated by the decision in *Cengiz v Turkey* [2015] ECHR 1052, where the court found a breach of Article 10 in the decision of the Turkish authorities to prohibit access to an internet website which had published material believed to insult the memory of Kemal Ataturk (the 'father' of the modern Turkish state) – an offence under Turkish law. A further factor weighing on the court was that, while the relevant Turkish legal provisions could be construed as allowing interference with this type of material, nothing could be found which specifically authorised the extent of the interference in this instance, i.e. the closing down of an entire website. Accordingly, such action did not appear to be 'prescribed by law'. A somewhat less strict approach may, however, be applied in other contexts, e.g. where commercial speech is concerned (*Mouvement Raelien Suisse v Switzerland* [2012] ECHR 1595).

To the limited extent that state regulation of the internet may be permitted, this should not be *ad hoc* or subject to wide legislative or executive discretion. Hence, as in other contexts, any veto powers in this area should be subject to an appropriate, widely accessible regulatory framework showing clearly when regulation may occur and the process for doing so (*Editorial Board of Pravoye Delo and Shtekel v Ukraine* [2011] ECHR 748). Failing this, any attempt to interfere with internet communications or content is likely to be condemned as not 'prescribed by law'.

The ECtHR has recognised that due to the factual realities of ease of immediate access, many internet websites may not be able to exercise the same level of control over potentially illegal content as may be possible within the more traditional types of media outlets. This does not mean, however, that the internet may be regarded as a 'law free zone'.

Hence in *Delfi AS v Estonia* (*supra*), the right to freedom of expression was held not to extend to an internet news portal's publication of offensive comments, including threats of violence, against a prominent Estonian businessman. Nor was the court swayed by the arguments that the applicants (who had been fined in the Estonian courts) had little or no control over the comments uploaded by the site's users, that the website operated a 'notice and take down' policy, and that the comment had some connection with a matter of public concern. It was exercised, however, by the fact that, although the offensive comments were eventually removed from the site, this was not until six weeks after these had been posted and not until the applicants had been contacted by the legal representatives of those at whom the threats and abuse had been aimed.

> If accompanied by effective procedures allowing for rapid response, 'notice and take down' systems can function in many cases as an appropriate tool for balancing the rights and interests of all those involved. However, in cases where third-party user comments are in the form of hate speech and direct threats to the physical integrity of individuals . . . the rights and interests of others and of society as a whole may entitle contracting states to impose liability on internet news portals, without contravening Article 10 of the Convention, if they fail to take measures to remove clearly unlawful comments without delay, even without notice from the alleged victim or from third parties.

Some domestic applications

One of the most controversial cases in which the law of the United Kingdom was measured against the requirements of Art 10 was *Sunday Times* v *United Kingdom*.

Sunday Times v *United Kingdom* (1979) 2 EHRR 245

The case concerned a series of articles which the newspaper wished to publish about the drug thalidomide. This had been prescribed for pregnant mothers and had resulted in numbers of children being born with various degrees of deformity. A writ had been issued alleging negligence against Distillers Ltd, the company responsible for manufacturing the drug. The proceedings had, however, been dormant for some time while the parties negotiated a possible settlement. This notwithstanding, an injunction was granted to prevent the *Sunday Times* articles being published. The Court felt that the information contained therein could be contemptuous in that it might prejudice the trial of the action if and when it took place.

The view of the Court of Human Rights was that the English law of contempt did not achieve an acceptable balance between the freedom of expression and the proper administration of justice and was weighted too heavily in favour of the latter. This was so because it prevented the publication of information concerning an issue of public concern once a writ had been issued albeit that, in the particular circumstances, it was unlikely that the matter would come to trial for some considerable time, if at all.

This decision resulted in the enactment of the Contempt of Court Act 1981. The Act permits the publication of material relating to legal proceedings up and until the time those proceedings have become 'active', viz. when the case has been set down for a hearing.

Other significant cases in which the domestic law has been alleged to be incompatible with Article 10 have included *Tolstoy Miloslavsky* v *United Kingdom*.

Tolstoy Miloslavsky v *United Kingdom* (1995) 20 EHRR 442

The applicant complained about an award of damages of £1.5 million which had been made against him by a jury in a libel action. The Court of Human Rights felt this to be excessive and not proportionate to the damage suffered by the person who had been defamed. It was also of opinion that the rule in English law which restricted judicial interference with such awards to circumstances where the jury's decision could be said to be capricious, unconscionable or irrational prevented appellate courts from ensuring that damages were reasonably commensurate with the loss which they were designed to compensate.

Here, section 32(1) of the Communications Act 2003 which prohibits political advertising on TV and radio was found not disproportionate to the protection of free and open debate on matters of public interest. The specific aim of the ban was to regulate the extent to which wealthy individuals and organisations might otherwise be enabled to use the broadcast media to propagate their particular points of view. The ECtHR was influenced by the following considerations:

1 the power of the media to influence public opinion;

2 the limitation of the ban to paid advertising;

3 the provision of broadcasting time to the major political parties by way of party political broadcasts;

4 the lack of any European consensus in the matter of political advertising widened the margin of discretion available to individual contracting states;

5 the ban had not been opposed in Parliament and not been found incompatible with the ECHR by the domestic courts.

Interference with the freedom of expression

As with the preceding two Articles, Art 10 may be departed from for a variety of public concerns. These include national security, territorial integrity, public safety, the prevention of disorder or crime, the protection of health or morals, the reputation or rights of others, the impartiality of the judiciary and the safeguarding of information received in confidence (Art 10(2)). Any interference must be proportionate to the aim pursued and 'be prescribed by law'. In *Prager and Oberschlick v Austria* (1996) 21 EHRR 1, it was held that law which restricted criticism of the judiciary did not amount to a breach of the right to freedom of expression. It was necessary in a democratic society to maintain confidence in the judicial system. Reasonable restrictions proportionate to this objective were, therefore, consistent with the public interest exceptions in Art 10(2).

It is clear that the Court of Human Rights will only accept interference with the freedom of the press where, in the circumstances, the needs of a competing public interest appear to be particularly pressing. Thus, in *Goodwin v United Kingdom* (1996) 22 EHRR 123, a court order requiring a journalist to reveal his sources, in order to prevent further disclosures of confidential information concerning a company's financial difficulties, was found to be incompatible with Art 10. The journalist was already subject to an interim injunction in respect of the publication of information believed to have been extracted from a stolen copy of the company's business plan. This, it was felt, was sufficient to protect the legitimate interests of the company concerned. The further order relating to the production of sources amounted, therefore, to an unnecessary and disproportionate response to the needs of the situation. Clearly imprisonment of a journalist for refusal to reveal his sources will rarely be acceptable under Art 10 (*Voskuil v Netherlands* [2007] ECHR 965).

Other disproportionate interferences with the right have been committed by the total prohibition of comment on matters pending before the courts (not 'necessary' for maintaining the authority and impartiality of the judiciary (*Worm v Austria* (1998) 25 EHRR 454)); refusing to lift interlocutory injunctions restraining the publication of information relating to the security services after such information had become otherwise widely available – not 'necessary' in the interests of national security (*Observer and Guardian v United Kingdom* (1991) 14 EHRR 153); the arrest and detention of demonstrators not using or provoking violence – not 'necessary' for the prevention of disorder (*Steel v United Kingdom*, *supra*); without specific legal authority, and preventing a journalist from travelling to a public demonstration at which disorder was suspected – not according to law (*Gsell v Switzerland* [2009] ECHR 1465).

Criminalisation of speech which seeks to deny genocide and related atrocities, but which is unlikely to cause public disorder or be intrusive of the rights of others, is unlikely to fall within that permitted by Article 10(2). Accordingly in *Perincek v Switzerland* [2015], ECHR 907, the applicant's conviction in a Swiss court in respect of his claim at a public meeting that the Armenian genocide was an 'international lie' could not be justified. The Grand Chamber was content that the statement related to a matter of public interest and did not amount to a call to disorder. Nor could it be regarded as affecting the rights or dignity of the Armenian community in Switzerland.

Restrictions held to be compatible with Art 10(2) as proportionate responses in the circumstances to legitimate public concerns have included prohibiting children's literature due to its sexual content – 'necessary' for the protection of morals (*Handyside* v *United Kingdom*, *supra*); the seizure of an allegedly blasphemous film to prevent its exhibition in a predominately Roman Catholic community – 'necessary' for the protection of the rights of others (*Otto-Preminger Institut* v *Austria*, *supra*); the prohibition of the verbatim publication of statements by terrorist organisations (*Falakaoglu* v *Turkey* [2005] ECHR 258); and the prosecution of a French mayor for the calling of a boycott of Israeli products (*Willem* v *France*, app no 10883/05, 16.07.09).

Freedom of assembly and association (Art 11)

Article 11 protects the right of the individual to organise and meet peacefully with others for the propagation of ideas and the furtherance of political, social, cultural or economic interests. It expressly guarantees the right to join a trade union.

Freedom of assembly

The individual is given the right to meet with others in public or in private and to engage in peaceful marches and demonstrations. The right extends to peaceful assemblies only. It does not apply to 'a demonstration where the organisers and participants have violent intentions which result in public disorder' (*G* v *Federal Republic of Germany* (1989) 60 DR 256). The danger that an otherwise peaceful demonstration may meet with opposition is not, therefore, of itself, a sufficient reason for imposing restrictions or refusing to allow it to proceed (*Christians Against Fascism and Racism* v *United Kingdom* (1980) 21 DR 138). If it were, the freedom could be completely negated by the aggressive tactics of those prepared to take direct action to obstruct the promotion of causes to which they were opposed. In these circumstances, therefore, the state is under a positive obligation to do that which is reasonable to ensure that the right to assemble peacefully can be exercised free from disruption and intimidation (*Plattform*, *supra*). The state is also under an obligation to recognise and accept that any demonstration in a public place is likely to cause some degree of disruption. A certain level of tolerance is thus to be expected of the authorities. This need not extend, however, to that which is beyond what is 'inherent in any demonstration'. Article 11, therefore, gave no protection to French lorry drivers who completely blocked a motorway whilst taking part in a national day of protest organised by the French trade union movement (*Barraco* v *France*, app no 31684/05, 5.3.09).

It is unlikely that Art 11(1) guarantees the freedom to assemble for purely social purposes. No breach was committed, therefore, by the owners of a shopping centre who, after a series of incidents of vandalism, excluded a group of young adult males from the centre's common areas. According to the European Commission of Human Rights there was no indication in existing European human rights case-law 'that freedom of assembly is intended to guarantee a right . . . to assemble for purely social purposes anywhere one wishes' (*Anderson* v *United Kingdom*, 27 October 1997, Hudoc).

An assembly which is peaceful but not lawful, e.g. is trespassory, would appear to fall within the protective compass of the right with the result that any interference must be in accordance with the criteria prescribed in Art 11(2), i.e. be prescribed by law and be proportionate to the securing of a legitimate aim (*G* v *Federal Republic of Germany*, *supra*).

State legislation requiring a grant of permission before an assembly may be held does not constitute a violation of the right providing again the discretion is exercised in accordance with the requirements of Art 11(2) (*Rassemblement Jurasien Unité v Suisse* (1978) 17 DR 93). The ultimate state power is, of course, that which could be used to prevent an assembly from taking place at all, thus extinguishing the right entirely for those affected. Such drastic action may be justified, therefore, only if its object, e.g. the prevention of disorder, cannot be achieved by other means (*Christians Against Fascism and Racism*, *supra*). The banning of a march may also be legitimate, albeit that no immediate violence may result from it, if this is done in the overall context of seeking to diffuse a politically tense or volatile situation (*Milan Rai v United Kingdom*, 6 April 1995, Hudoc).

Failure to provide prior notification of a meeting or protest where this is required, is, therefore, not, of itself, sufficient legal justification for dispersing a lawful gathering (*Bukta v Hungary* [2007] ECHR 610).

An assembly should not be banned merely because it is feared that it may be used to express controversial views unless, of course, it can be shown that this could lead to disorder or other undue damage to a legitimate public interest (*Stankov v Bulgaria*, 2 October 2001, Hudoc). It is a violation of Art 11 to arrest and detain a person to prevent them from attending a public demonstration on the basis of vague, general allegations, e.g. 'offences of an extremist nature', and without genuine and reasonable suspicion of 'specific and concrete' offences (*Shimovolos v Russia*, app no 30194/09, 21.6.11; *Schwabe and MG v Germany*, app no 8080/08, 1.12.11).

Once a demonstration has begun, it is incumbent on the authorities to engage with the leaders of it in order to 'communicate their position openly, clearly and promptly' before any action is taken to disperse or seriously restrict it (*Frunkin v Russia* [2016] ECHR 64).

Although the restrictions on the right of assembly may often be imposed prior to or during the march or demonstration concerned, Art 11 may also be infringed by resort to post-demonstration penalties or sanctions. In *Ezelin v France* (1991) 14 EHRR 362, the applicant, a French lawyer, suffered a violation of his Art 11 rights when he was subjected to the disciplinary processes of the French legal profession after participating in a public protest against the imprisonment of members of the Guadeloupe independence movement.

In recent years, as already explained, police regulation of public protest in the United Kingdom by use of the ancient common law power to prevent breaches of the peace has been referred to the Court of Human Rights on a number of occasions. The overall result of these applications appears to be that although the meaning of the breach of the peace power is now sufficiently well defined in case-law to be 'according to law', this level of certainty and legitimacy does not extend to the related judicial power to bind over persons to keep the peace and to be of good behaviour (*Steel v United Kingdom*, *supra*; *Hashman and Harrup v United Kingdom*, *supra*).

In addition to a breach of Article 11, a state's failure to prevent interference with a lawful and peaceful demonstration may have consequences under other elements of the Convention.

The case of *Identoba v Georgia* [2015] ECHR 474, concerned a peaceful demonstration by a group seeking greater protection for the rights of gay, bisexual, lesbian and transgender persons. Despite having notified the authorities of their intentions and their perfectly peaceful behaviour, the 30 demonstrators were surrounded by a much larger crowd by which they were physically and verbally abused. This, the court felt, had subjected the applicants to a level of fear and insecurity as to 'reach the threshold of severity' required under Article 3 (the rule against degrading treatment). Moreover, the fact the authorities had known or ought to have known of the risk of homophobic and transphobic attacks, but had not done sufficient to prevent such, could be seen as 'tantamount to official indifference of even connivance on the part of the law-enforcement authorities in the commission of hate crimes, and, for Convention purposes, a breach of Article 14, i.e. a discriminatory application of its obligations in Article 3'.

Freedom of association

This element of the Article guarantees the right of the individual to form and join organisations for the purpose of advancing a particular cause or interest. In *Vogt* v *Germany* (1996) 2 EHRR 205, it was applied to the dismissal of a teacher because she was a member of the Communist party. The individual is given a degree of choice in terms of whether they join or refuse to join an interest group or other collective entity. The Article does not guarantee the right to membership of any organisation of a person's choosing nor does it contain a right not to be expelled from the same. In the case of trade union membership, however, it has been suggested that expulsion might be contrary to Art 11 if it was not done 'in accordance with union rules or where the results were wholly arbitrary or where the consequences of exclusion . . . resulted in exceptional hardship such as job loss because of a closed shop' (*Cheall* v *United Kingdom* (1985) 42 DR 178). The right of a trade union to determine its own membership extends to excluding those whose political views would appear to be incompatible with the traditions of the union (*Associated Society of Locomotive Engineers and Firemen* v *United Kingdom* [2007] ECHR 184, exclusion of member of British National Party).

Closed shop agreements were considered in *Young, James and Webster* v *United Kingdom* (1982) 4 EHRR 38. Such agreements were prohibited if they struck 'at the very substance of the freedom guaranteed by Article 11' as would be the case if they required the dismissal of persons already in employment. The substance of Art 11 was found to have been infringed in *Sigurjonssen* v *Iceland* (1993) 16 EHRR 462. The offending provision was a legal requirement that licensed taxi-drivers be members of a particular drivers' association. Persons who felt unable to join would not be given a licence and would thus be denied the opportunity to earn a living as a taxi-driver.

The positive duty on the state to ensure that persons are able to enjoy the right and protection offered by Art 11 was in issue in *Wilson* v *United Kingdom* (2002) 35 EHRR 20. The duty was not fulfilled, the Court found, in circumstances, as in the United Kingdom, where it was possible for an employer to offer employees financial incentives to give up trade union membership.

Public bodies and organisations are not regarded as 'associations' for the purposes of Art 11(1). Hence, no right to membership or to participate in their activities is given. The Article is not infringed, therefore, by rules requiring compulsory membership of professional regulatory bodies providing these qualify as 'public bodies' according to the applicable legal criteria (*Le Compte, Van Leuven and De Meyere* v *Belgium* (1981) 4 EHRR 1).

Interference with the right of assembly and association (Art 11(2))

Interference with the rights in Art 11 is permitted for reasons of national security, public order, the prevention of crime, the protection of health, morals or for the protection of the rights and freedoms of others (Art 11(2)). The rights may also be restricted in terms of the extent to which they may be relied upon by members of the armed forces, the police and government employees (ibid.). In *Council of Civil Service Unions* v *United Kingdom* (1988) 10 EHRR 269, the European Commission considered the extent to which the government could invoke Art 11(2) to interfere with the right of its employees to enjoy trade union

For more on the
GCHQ case, see
Chapter 12.

membership. The view was that the Prime Minister's order excluding trade union members from employment at the Government Communications Headquarters at Cheltenham fell within the permitted restrictions. This was so because the institution (GCHQ) dealt with highly sensitive information having to do with national security and which could be related to the activities of the police and armed forces.

As with the Convention's other qualified rights, any such interference must be 'prescribed by law' and 'necessary in a democratic society'. These requirements were not breached by an order preventing Druids from holding a service at Stonehenge to celebrate the summer solstice (*Pendragon v United Kingdom*, 19 October 1998, Hudoc). The order was made under the Public Order Act 1986, s 14A (power to ban trespassory assemblies) which was phrased with sufficient precision and clarity to be 'prescribed by law'. The Commission was also satisfied that the action was 'necessary in a democratic society', as proportionate to the legitimate aim of preventing disorder 'as there had been considerable disorder at Stonehenge in previous years and more recently'. Other factors noted by the Commission were that the ban was limited to four days only, did not apply to gatherings of 20 or fewer and did not prevent the applicants from conducting their service somewhere else.

Restrictions should not be imposed on the basis of nothing more than groundless suspicions or prejudices. Thus it was not necessary, or for a legitimate aim, to ban a march concerned with the rights of minorities simply because the local Mayor believed that 'propaganda about homosexuality' was not a proper subject for the exercise of the Art 11 right (*Baczkowski v Poland* [2007] ECHR 370). Nor was the state justified in refusing to register an anti-Mafia organisation because of speculation that it might attempt to usurp the functions of police and courts in the fight against crime (*Bozgan v Romania*, app 35097/02, 11.10.07).

In matters relating to the political process, and given the essential role played by political parties in the proper functioning of democratic societies, it would appear that very convincing and compelling reasons should exist for the imposition of restrictions on the activities of such organisations and that the state's margin of appreciation in this context should be regarded as particularly narrow (*Christian Democratic People's Party v Moldova* [2006] ECHR 132). Such prerequisites to the banning of a political party may, however, be satisfied where the party is sympathetic to terrorism and opposed to democracy. In such circumstances, it may well be that its prohibition can be regarded as proportionate to the maintenance of democratic values (*Batasuna v Spain*, app no 25803/04, 30.6.09).

Right to marry and found a family (Art 12)

Marriage

The right to marry has been described as a 'strong right'. Hence, although not absolute, and subject to national laws, both in the manner of its exercise and substance, the right may not be restricted to an extent which impairs its essential character and purpose or which unduly inhibits its exercise (*Hamer v United Kingdom* [1977] ECHR 2; *Draper v United Kingdom* (1980) 24 DR 72). In the main, the types of restrictions found to be permissible have been those relating to age and capacity, bigamy, and the relationships within which it is generally believed marriages should not be conducted (the rules of consanguinity). In the matter of such relationships, the general view of the ECtHR appears to be that, while national laws may rightly restrict marriages between close 'blood' relatives, such restrictions should not be applied to those other family members who may be described as 'in-laws' (*B and L v United Kingdom* [2005] ECHR 584). Other types of restrictions also found to be permissible have been those concerned with the use of marriage as a means of avoiding immigration control. Nor does any breach of Art 12 result from delay in the exercise of the right while the appropriate investigations are being conducted (*Sanders v France*, app no 31401/96, 5.12.96).

As Art 12 confers the right to marry on 'men and women of marriageable age', it has generally been assumed that the guarantee was originally intended to protect marriage between heterosexuals and does not apply to same-sex couples (*W v United Kingdom* (1989) 63 DR 4). Also, to date, the ECtHR has retained the position that contracting states have not, as yet, developed sufficient consensus in the matter to justify significant change and has held that, in such circumstances, 'the national authorities are best placed to assess and respond to the needs of society in the field given that marriage has deep-rooted social and cultural connotations differing largely from one society to another' (*Schalk and Kopf v Austria*, app no 30141/04, 24.6.10). The right has, however, been extended to post-operative transsexuals. This followed from the finding that such persons were entitled to full legal recognition of their changed gender (*Goodwin v United Kingdom, supra; I v United Kingdom* [2002] ECHR 592).

The right applies to prisoners and persons in executive custody. Prison authorities are, therefore, required to act in accordance with the Article's requirements except where there are 'overriding security considerations' for not doing so (*Frasik v Poland*, app no 22933/02, 5.1.10).

The right has been held not to include any implicit right to divorce (*Johnston v Ireland* (1987) 9 EHRR 203).

Founding a family

This limb of the Article precludes compulsory but not voluntary sterilisation or abortion. The right to family life would also appear to be incompatible with the imposition of excessive restrictions on the opportunity available for adoption. It is unlikely, however, that Art 12 imposes any obligations on the state in terms of providing the social and economic conditions which could be said to reinforce the stability of marriage.

Although Art 12 does not state expressly that the right to marry and found a family is subject to the types of public interest considerations articulated elsewhere in the Convention (see, for example, Arts 8 to 11) the ECtHR has been at pains to emphasise that it cannot be regarded as enforceable in all circumstances. Thus it cannot be relied on by persons serving sentences of imprisonment to assert their conjugal rights.

> Although the right to found a family is an absolute right in the sense that no restrictions similar to those in para (2) of Art 8 of the convention are expressly provided for, it does not mean that a person must at all times be given the actual possibility to procreate his descendants. It would seem that the position of a lawfully committed person detained in the prison in which the applicant finds himself falls under his own responsibilities and that his right to found a family has not otherwise been infringed (*X v United Kingdom* (1975) 2 DR 105).

The state may not, however, operate a blanket-ban on prisoners having children by means of artificial insemination, nor should states adopt policies which only prohibit artificial insemination in the most exceptional circumstances. Each request should be considered on its own merits and should involve 'a real weighing of the competing individual and public interests' (*Dickson v United Kingdom* [2007] ECHR 1051).

The protocols

Nature and general content

These represent further agreements between the contracting states which have supplemented the rights originally guaranteed. The protocols seek to require or guarantee:

- the right to peaceful enjoyment of property (Protocol 1, Art 1);
- the right to education in conformity with religious or philosophical convictions (Protocol 1, Art 2);
- the right to free elections at reasonable intervals by secret ballot (Protocol 1, Art 3);
- the right not to be imprisoned for breach of a contractual obligation (Protocol 4, Art 1);
- freedom of movement and residence (Protocol 4, Art 2);
- the right not to be expelled or refused entry to the contracting state of which an individual is a citizen (Protocol 4, Art 3);
- the prohibition of collective expulsions of aliens and stateless persons (Protocol 4, Art 4);
- the abolition of the death penalty (Protocols 6 and 13);
- the right of aliens not to be expelled from a contracting state except in accordance with legal procedures which require the giving of reasons accompanied by right to have the decision reviewed and to be legally represented at such review (Protocol 7, Art 1);
- the right to a review of criminal convictions and sentences (Protocol 7, Art 2);
- the right to compensation for miscarriages of justice (Protocol 7, Art 3);
- the right not to be tried twice for the same offence (Protocol 7, Art 4);
- the right of spouses to equal legal treatment (Protocol 7, Art 5).

To date the United Kingdom is not a party to Protocols 4, 6 or 7. The Human Rights Act 1998 gives legal effect in the United Kingdom to the right to peaceful enjoyment of property (Protocol 1, Art 1), the right to education (Protocol 1, Art 2), and the abolition of the death penalty (Protocol 6).

The right to property (Protocol 1, Art 1)

The right is conferred on both natural and legal persons. A person has the right to 'peaceful enjoyment of his possessions' and should not be deprived of these 'except in the public interest and subject to the conditions provided for by law and by the general principles of international law'. The Convention recognises, however, that the state has the right 'to enforce such laws as it deems necessary to control the use of property in accordance with the general interest or to secure the payment of taxes or other contributions or penalties'.

The case-law to date demonstrates a preference for the term 'possessions' to be given a liberal interpretation thus allowing the protocol an extensive sphere of application. Accordingly its protection covers both tangible and intangible assets and has been held to encompass, *inter alia*, contractual rights, shares, leases, licences, business goodwill, patents, debts, entitlements to rents and rights under contributory pensions.

The state's *judgment* as to what is in the public interest will be respected unless that judgement is 'manifestly without reasonable foundation' (***Handyside v United Kingdom**, supra*). This is particularly so in social and economic matters where a wide margin of appreciation is allowed (***James v United Kingdom*** (1986) 8 EHRR 123). In this case the aim of social justice in housing was accepted as a legitimate public interest for legislation permitting the compulsory transfer of ownership of property from one individual to another. Protocol 1, Art 1 was, therefore, no impediment to the implementation of the Leasehold Reform Act 1967 which allowed the tenants of residential properties in central London held on long leases to acquire the ownership of those properties notwithstanding the claims of the original lessors.

Social justice in housing and the need to prevent a large number of persons becoming homeless at the same time has also been accepted as a legitimate public interest for laws suspending tenant eviction orders (*Spadea v Italy* (1995) 21 EHRR 482) provided such suspensions were not continued for such long periods as effectively to deprive the landlord of their property (*Palumbo v Italy*, 4 September 1996, Hudoc).

An obvious public interest justifying proportionate interference with property rights is the investigation and prevention of crime. No breach of the protocol was committed, therefore, by the seizure and destruction of property found to be obscene under the Obscene Publications Act 1959, s 3 (*Handyside v United Kingdom*, *supra*).

Any interference with property or possessions must be 'provided for by law'. This imports the test of certainty as considered above. It was satisfied in *James v United Kingdom* (*supra*), as the authority for the interference complained of was the Leasehold Reform Act 1967.

In order to prove a violation it must be shown that the state has interfered with the applicant's peaceful possession of their property or has deprived the applicant of their possessions or has subjected those possessions to some unacceptable degree of control (*Sporrong v Sweden* (1982) 5 EHRR 35).

Any act of interference should be proportionate to the aim pursued and must secure a fair balance between the competing public and private interests involved (ibid.). This balance was not achieved in the *Sporrong* case where the applicant's property was subjected to lengthy 'expropriation permits' and prohibitions on construction pending the redevelopment of the centre of Stockholm. No domestic procedure existed through which these restrictions could be challenged and their length of application possibly reduced. The result was that the applicant's property was effectively placed under planning 'blight' for the considerable period of years during which the restrictions applied.

Although the protocol does not give an express right to compensation for invasion of property rights, whether and to what extent compensation is paid is relevant to the question of the proportionality of the action in question. It is probable that the taking of property without compensation would satisfy the proportionality test only where this was done for the purposes of the most urgent and weighty of public interest needs:

> ... the taking of property without payment of an amount reasonably related to its value will normally constitute a disproportionate interference and a total lack of compensation can be considered justifiable ... only in exceptional circumstances. Article 1 does not, however, guarantee a right to full compensation in all circumstances, since legitimate objectives of public interest may call for reimbursement of less than the full market value (*Holy Monasteries v Greece* (1994) 20 EHRR 1).

These principles were recognised and applied in *Lithgow v United Kingdom* (1986) 8 EHRR 239, where the court found no violation in the United Kingdom government's method of assessing compensation for the purposes of nationalising the aircraft and shipbuilding industries. The method was based on a valuation of individual shareholdings at the particular date prior to the decision to nationalise and not on the market value of the assets affected. It was permissible, the court said, in determining compensation, to take into account 'the nature of the property taken and the circumstances of the taking', i.e. the political and economic background for the state's actions.

The standard of compensation for a whole industry may differ, therefore, from the standard required in other cases (*ibid.*).

The protocol concludes by preserving expressly the right of the state to resort to seizure and other measures against an individual's property in order to enforce liabilities for non-payment of taxes or 'other contributions and penalties', e.g. national insurance payments and judgment debts. As a general rule state laws for these purposes will be accepted by the court unless they are devoid of reasonable foundation (*Gasus Dosier-und Fordertechnik GmbH v Netherlands* (1995) 20 EHRR 403).

The right to education (Protocol 1, Art 2)

The protocol is phrased in the negative and provides that no one 'shall be denied the right to education'. The state is also enjoined to 'respect the rights of parents to ensure such education and teaching in conformity with their own religious and philosophical convictions'.

The duty on the state, therefore, is not to finance and provide a universally available educational system, but to the extent that educational facilities are available, whether publicly or privately funded, to avoid restriction and regulation of them to a degree which undermines the substance of the right (*Belgium Linguistics Case* (1979–80) 1 EHRR 241). If state-funded education is available, but the parents wish their child to be educated outside that system, no obligation lies on the state to finance their choice (*Family H v United Kingdom* (1984) 37 DR 10J). The protocol does not provide an absolute guarantee of access to the school of the parents' choosing (*X v United Kingdom*, app no 11644/87, unreported) nor does it prevent the suspension and possible expulsion of a disruptive child if that is a proportionate response to the difficulties caused (*X v United Kingdom*, app no 13477/87, unreported).

The right is generally accepted as being concerned mainly with primary and secondary education. The state is permitted to restrict access to third level education to those with appropriate academic qualifications (*Patel v United Kingdom* (1980) 4 EHRR 256).

The need to show respect for the rights of parents requires the state to consider whether and to what extent those wishes may be accommodated. It is not enough that these are simply 'noted' or 'taken into account' (*Campbell and Cosans v United Kingdom* (1982) 4 EHRR 293). It was a breach of this requirement to suspend a pupil for almost a year because his parents disagreed with the school's policy towards corporal punishment. This made the pupil's access to education conditional on agreeing to accept the risk of that which was contrary to their philosophical convictions.

Including studies of religious, philosophical or ethical nature in a school's curriculum does not offend the requirement to respect parents' wishes providing the material is delivered in an objective fashion and is not employed for the purposes of indoctrination (*Kjeldsen, Busk Madsen and Pedersen v Denmark, supra*).

If a child is adopted, the rights conferred by the protocol pass from the natural to the adoptive parents (*X v United Kingdom* (1977) 11 DR 160). Where one parent is granted custody of a child, the other parent's Convention's education rights cease to exist (*X v Sweden* (1977) 12 DR 192).

That element of Protocol 1, Art 2 dealing with the wishes of parents is subject to a reservation by the United Kingdom to the effect that it is accepted 'only as far as is compatible with the provision of efficient instruction and training and the avoidance of unreasonable public expenditure'.

The right to free elections (Protocol 1, Art 3)

States which have signed the European Convention on Human Rights 'undertake to hold free elections at reasonable intervals by secret ballot under conditions which will ensure the free expression of the will of the people in the choice of legislation'. This confers an individual right of action as exercised in **Matthews v United Kingdom** (1999) 28 EHRR 361, where an EU citizen resident in Gibraltar challenged successfully his exclusion from the franchise for the European Parliament. The Court of Human Rights felt it was axiomatic that as Gibraltar was subject to EU law, EU citizens resident there should be able to participate in elections for the European Parliament.

The rights guaranteed by the Protocol apply to the conduct of elections for national assemblies only and have no application to local elections, presidential elections or to referendums (**McLean and Cole v United Kingdom** [2013] ECHR 1368.

Implicit in the obligation to hold free elections are the rights to vote and stand as a candidate in elections for national legislatures (**Mathieu-Mohin v Belgium** (1987) 10 EHRR 1), but not according to a particular electoral system (**Liberal Party v United Kingdom** (1980) 21 DR 211).

The state is not precluded from imposing conditions on candidature, e.g. requirements for nomination papers to be endorsed by a minimum number of signatures (**Association X, Y and Z v Federal Republic of Germany** (1986) 5 DR 90) or from restricting the election of persons who have, for example, seriously abused a public position or whose conduct has threatened to undermine the rule of law or the state's democratic foundations.

Any attempts, however, to remove the right to vote from whole categories of persons, e.g. convicted prisoners, will require considerable justification. This follows from the ECtHR's view of the importance of the democratic process (see **Frodl v Austria** [2010] ECHR 508, 'the foundations of an effective and meaningful democracy'), and, in the case of prisoners, its oft repeated position that a sentence of imprisonment removes the right to personal liberty and attendant freedoms but not all other rights guaranteed by the Convention (see **Scoppola v Italy (No. 3)**, app no 126/05, 22.5.2012.

Following this general position, the all-embracing ban on voting by sentenced prisoners in the United Kingdom (imposed under the Representation of the People Act 1983, s 3) was found in violation of the Convention's requirements in a series of well-publicised cases (see **Hirst v United Kingdom (No. 2)** [2005] ECHR 681; **Greens and MT v United Kingdom** [2010] ECHR 1826; **Firth v United Kingdom** [2014] ECHR 874.

Contrary to contemporary claims in certain sections of the British media, in none of these cases did the ECtHR suggest that Protocol 1, Art 3 gave any and all sentenced prisoners the unfettered right to vote – only that states should avoid blanket bans and should be open to allowing certain categories of prisoners to exercise the franchise depending on the nature and seriousness of the crime(s) committed and the length of sentence imposed, etc.

The entire issue of votes for prisoners represents one of the few occasions in modern legal and political history upon which the British government, supported by a considerable body of opinion in the Westminster Parliament, has actively contemplated refusing to comply with a ruling of the ECtHR and of thereby putting the United Kingdom in breach of its international obligations as a signatory of the Convention.

Abolition of the death penalty (Protocols 6 and 13)

The first major step towards the abolition of the death penalty in contracting states was effected by the adoption of Protocol 6 in 1982. Protocol 6, Art 1, provided that 'the death penalty shall be abolished' and that 'no person shall be condemned to such penalty or executed'. The requirement was, therefore, for the repeal of any legal provisions authorising judicial execution. It was not enough that the authority is available but is not used.

While phrased in the form of a prohibition, the protocol gave the individual the positive right not to be subjected to the ultimate sanction. The absolute nature of the prohibition was, however, limited to peacetime; Art 2 permitting provisions authorising the death penalty to be introduced in time of war.

The matter was taken further by Protocol 13, adopted in 2002. This prohibited the use of the death penalty in all circumstances, including in time of war.

The state may not derogue from or enter a reservation in respect of its obligations under Protocol 13.

Expelling a person to another state in which they are under sentence of death may amount to a breach of Art 3 (*Bader* v *Sweden*, app no 13284/04, 8.11.05).

In the United Kingdom use of the death penalty was suspended in 1959. The legal authority for it was removed by the Abolition of the Death Penalty Act 1965.

Collateral rights

The substantive rights and guarantees in Arts 2–12 and the subsequent protocols are underpinned by Arts 13 and 14. Art 13 provides that each contracting state must have systems or procedures in place through which these rights may be pursued by the individual. This should not be interpreted as meaning that national remedies must exist for enforcement of the guarantees contained in the Convention. It does require, however, that procedures should be available to allow arguments related to the Convention to be raised. In the context of the United Kingdom, and prior to the enactment of the Human Rights Act 1998, judicial review on grounds of irrationality and abuse of discretion were held to provide an effective remedy where executive power was exercised in ways which appeared substantially at odds with the standards required by the Convention (*Soering* v *United Kingdom* (1989) 11 EHRR 439).

The European Court of Human Rights has, however, passed adverse comment on the reluctance of English courts to question executive decisions made in the alleged interests of national security. In *Chahal* v *United Kingdom* (1997) 23 EHRR 413, the applicant had been ordered to be deported from the United Kingdom for reasons of national security. Deportation decisions made on this ground were, at the time, not subject to a right of appeal to the Immigration Appeals Tribunal (Immigration Act 1971, s 15(3)). Nor did the applicant achieve any satisfaction from an application for judicial review, as the court felt unable to question the Minister's reasons due to the national security implications (*R v Secretary of State for the Home Department, ex parte Chahal* [1995] 1 All ER 658). In effect, therefore, English law provided no competent procedure through which the applicant could pursue rights protected by the Convention.

In the context of immigration and deportation the United Kingdom's response to this was the creation of the Special Immigration Appeals Commission (Special Immigration Appeals Commission Act 1997). The Commission may hear appeals against deportation orders where the Home Secretary's decision was taken wholly or partly in reliance on information which the Minister feels should not be made public for reasons of national security because of the relationship between the United Kingdom and another state, or for other public interest concerns.

A complaint made under Art 13 is not dependent on showing a breach of any of the Convention's primary rights in Arts 2–12. It is enough to show an 'arguable case' of such breach can be made but that no appropriate procedure leading to an effective remedy appears to exist.

Article 14 places the state under an obligation to ensure that Convention rights are secured without discrimination on grounds of sex, race, colour, language, religion, political or other opinion, national or social origin, association with a national minority, property, birth or other status. The prohibition of discrimination, although wide, is not exhaustive or all-embracing. It follows that the Article will be engaged only if the alleged discrimination affects one or more of the personal characteristics specified. In order to constitute discrimination on any such ground, there must be a difference in treatment of persons in analogous situations without any objective and reasonable justification (*Kjeldsen Madsen and Pedersen v Denmark* (1976) 1 EHRR 371).

Article 14 does not contain a free-standing right against discrimination whatever the context. It may be pleaded only in relation to the way the state has acted in the observance of any one of the primary rights covered by the Articles of the Convention and its protocols, e.g. freedom of the person, freedom of speech, etc. Note though, that for discrimination under Article 14 to be found, the applicant does not have to show any direct infringement of the primary right affected.

> Article 14 is not a free-standing right: it applies only where the act in question 'falls within the ambit of' another Convention right, although there need be no infringement of that right as such (*Petrovic v Austria* (2001) 33 EHRR 13).

Some useful applications of Article 14 would include the following.

Cobzaru v Romania [2007] ECHR 669. The applicant claimed the police had not properly investigated a complaint of police violence as required by Art 3 (see p. 519) and that this was related to his racial origins. The court found discrimination under Article 14 in that relevant documents showed that the state investigations had described the applicant as 'a twenty-five year old gypsy well known for causing scandals and always getting into fights'.

Baczkawski v Poland [2007] ECHR 370. The applicant applied for permission to hold a march to protest against homosexual discrimination. This brought into play his rights under ECHR, Article 11. Permission to march was refused but it was apparent from the reasons given the minds of the authorities had been influenced by 'apparent homophobia' in breach of Article 14.

Abdalaziz, Cabales and Balkanali v United Kingdom (1985) EHRR 471. At the time, the United Kingdom's immigration rules permitted the wives of resident non-national males to enter the state in order to live with their husbands. The same facility did not extend to the husbands of resident non-national women. The court felt that this was not inconsistent with Article 8 (the right to respect for private and family life) as this did not give a right to establish a home in a country of a couple's choosing. There was, however, a breach of Article 14 in that the immigration rules in issue gave greater protection to the family life of non-national men than that accorded to their female counterparts.

In an entirely different context, a breach of Article 14 concerning the right to education (Protocol 1, Art 2) was found to have occurred where a visually impaired student was refused access to a music school (*Cam v Turkey* [2016] ECHR 206). In reaching its decision the court drew on the United Nations Convention on the Rights of Persons with Disabilities thereby demonstrating its readiness to take into account relevant international law developments in interpreting the scope of the Convention's various elements.

Derogation in times of national emergency (Art 15)

Objective
6

Article 15 permits contracting states to take measures which interfere with the rights protected by the Convention 'in time of war or other public emergency threatening the life of the nation'. These measures should be no more than that which is 'strictly required by the exigencies of the situation'. The right of derogation does not apply to Arts 2 (except for death resulting from lawful acts of war), 3, 4 or 7. A state wishing to take advantage of this facility should inform the Secretary-General of the Council of Europe of the measures it has taken and the reasons for them. The fact that a derogation has been made does not prevent an individual petition in respect of the Article to which the derogation relates. It would be necessary, however, for the applicant to show that the derogation was not justified by the circumstances or that the action taken went beyond that which was necessary to deal with the danger to the public.

One of the clearest and most specific judicial expositions of the requirements of a public emergency for the purposes of Article 15, was provided by the *Greek Case* (1969) 12 YB 1:

> Such public emergency may then be seen to have, in particular, the following characteristics:
>
> 1 It must be actual or imminent;
> 2 Its effects must involve the whole nation;
> 3 The continuance of the organised life of the community must be threatened;
> 4 The crisis or danger must be exceptional, in that the normal measures or restrictions permitted by the Convention for the maintenance of public safety, health and order, are plainly inadequate.

For UK purposes, the first domestic emergency to be recognised as of sufficient severity to meet the requirements of Art 15 was the IRA Border Campaign 1956–62. At no stage did the level of violence and disorder reach that witnessed in the later Northern Ireland 'Troubles' from 1968 to 1998. This notwithstanding, the ECtHR felt that:

> the existence at the time of a public emergency threatening the life of the nation was reasonably deduced by the Irish government from a combination of several factors, namely: . . . the existence in the territory of the Republic of Ireland of a secret army engaged in unconstitutional activities and using violence to attain its purposes; . . . the fact that this army was also operating outside the territory of the state thus seriously jeopardising the relations of the Republic with its neighbour; . . . the steady and alarming increase of terrorist activities from the autumn of 1956 and throughout the first half of 1957 (*Lawless v Ireland (No. 3)* (1961) 1 EHRR 15).

The qualifying threshold for derogation from Art 5 was crossed by the violence in Northern Ireland post-1968 (*Ireland v United Kingdom* (1978) 2 EHRR 25; *Brannigan and McBride v United Kingdom* (1993) 17 EHRR 539). This allowed the United Kingdom to derogue from the requirement in ECHR Art 5(3) that arrested or detained persons should be brought promptly before a judge (see Prevention of Terrorism Acts 1974 and 1989). This was also the case in respect of the threat of international terrorism and the derogation from Art 5 made by the United Kingdom following the events of '9/11'.

> Although when the derogation was made no al Qaeda attack had taken place within the territory of the UK, the Court does not consider that the national authorities can be criticised, in the light of the evidence available to them at the time, for fearing that such an attack was 'imminent', in that an atrocity might be committed without warning at any time.

> The requirement of imminence cannot be interpreted so narrowly as to require a state to wait for a disaster to strike before taking measures to deal with it. Moreover, the danger of a terrorist attack was tragically shown by the bombings and attempted bombings in London in July 2005 to have been very real. Since the purpose of Article 15 is to permit states to take derogating measures to protect their populations . . . the existence of the threat must be assessed primarily with reference to those facts which were known at the time of the derogation.

States are allowed a wide margin of appreciation as to if and when the Art 15 requirements have been met.

> By reason of their directed continuous contact with the pressing need of the moment, the national authorities are in principle in a better position than the international judge to decide both on the presence of such an emergency and the nature and scope of derogations necessary to avert it. In this matter, Art 15(1), leaves those authorities with a wide margin of appreciation (*Ireland* v *United Kingdom*, *supra*).

The margin is, however, not unlimited. It is for the court to rule whether, *inter alia*, the states have gone beyond the extent strictly required by the exigencies of the crisis. The domestic margin of application is thus accompanied by a European supervision (*A* v *United Kingdom* (2009) 49 EHRR 625).

Reservations (Art 57)

Article 57 allows that at the time of signing the Convention or any of its protocols a contracting state may 'make a reservation in respect of any particular provision of the Convention to the extent that any particular law then in force in its territory is not in conformity with the provision'.

The United Kingdom took advantage of Art 57 when signing Protocol 1, Art 2 (right to education) by declaring:

> in view of certain provisions in the Education Acts . . . the principle affirmed in the second sentence in Article 2 [requirement to respect the wishes of parents] is accepted by the United Kingdom only so far as it is compatible with the provision of efficient instruction and training, and the avoidance of unreasonable public expenditure.

The Convention's extra-territorial competence

Objective
7

The original draft of the ECHR provided that the contracting states were bound by it in relation 'to all persons residing within their territories'. In the Convention's final version this had, however, been abandoned in favour of the requirement that states should observe the Convention in their dealings with 'all those within their jurisdiction'.

Although continuing to emphasise that the Convention should be understood primarily as a regional document, the ECtHR has interpreted this less restrictive formulation to mean that a contracting state may be bound by its requirements extra-territorially in a number of limited circumstances. These were explained most recently by the Grand Chamber in *Al Skeini* v *United Kingdom* [2011] ECHR 1093.

(a) Effective control of an area

> This may exist where, as a result of lawful or unlawful military action a contracting state has control of a territorial area sufficient to allow it to give effect to the Convention in that place. This may be through its own military presence and administration or by the

provision of military, political or economic support to an insurgent regime. Whether, in any situation, the effective control principle is satisfied is a question of fact depending mainly on the extent of the military and/or other types of support provided.

(b) State agency authority

This test may be satisfied in the following situations

(i)   where the acts of diplomatic and consular agents, present in a foreign territory in accordance with international law, exert authority and control over others;
(ii) where a contracting state, through the consent, invitation or acquiescence of the government of a foreign territory, exercises all or some of the public powers normally exercised by that government;
(iii) where persons are brought within a contracting state's jurisdiction and control through the use of force by the state's agents acting outside of its territory.

(c) The Convention's 'legal space'

The ECtHR has emphasised that where the territory of one Convention state has been occupied by the armed forces of another, the occupying state should, in principle, be held accountable under the Convention for breaches of human rights within that territory. To argue otherwise, it has been said, would deprive the population of that territory of the rights and freedoms they had hitherto enjoyed thus placing them 'in a vacuum of protection within the Convention legal space' (*Al Skeini*, *supra*).

The effective control of an area test was found to have been satisfied in *Loizidon v Turkey* [1996] ECHR 70, by the presence of 30,000 Turkish troops in northern Cyprus (breach of Art 1, Protocol 1 by denial of access to property) and in *Ivantoc v Moldova and Russia* [2011] ECHR 191, through the extensive military, political and financial support provided by the Russian Federation to the insurgent regime in Transdnistria – part of the sovereign territory of Moldova (breach of Arts 3 and 5; ill-treatment and extended detention of civilians).

Examples of state actions falling within the criterion of state agency authority include an arrest by Turkish officials on a Turkish aircraft at a Kenyan airport (*Ocalan v Turkey* (2005) 41 EHRR 45), and the handing over of a suspect by police in Costa Rica to agents of the Italian government (*Freda v Italy* (1980) 21 DR 250).

Responsibility for the actions of state agents against persons under their control in the territory of a foreign state was illustrated by a number of cases resulting from the activities of British forces in Iraq during and following the war there in 2003. Prominent amongst these would be *Al-Skeini v United Kingdom* [2011] ECHR 1093 and *Al-Jedda v United Kingdom* [2011] ECHR 1092. Hence in *Al-Skeini*, the UK government was found in breach of Art 2 for failing to conduct an independent investigation into the deaths of Iraqi civilians in British military custody. In *Al-Jedda*, a breach of Art 5 was found to have been committed by the indefinite detention of such persons in the British military base at Basra.

In those circumstances in which a state has lost control over part of its territory, either as a result of insurgency or the incursions of another sovereign power, this does not mean that it is absolved automatically and entirely of all responsibility for activities there which are in breach of the Convention. Hence, even in this situation and as an expression of its jurisdictional responsibility, the state remains under a positive obligation to take all those diplomatic, economic and political measures that are within its power to take, and are in accordance with international law, to secure compliance with the Convention. This includes 'those measures at its disposal for re-establishing control over that territory' (*Ivantoc v Moldova and Russia*, supra, *Catan v Moldova and Russia*, app no 18454/04, 19.10.12).

In *Mozer* v *Republic of Moldova and Russia* [2016] ECHR 213, the applicant had been arrested by the authorities of the self-proclaimed 'Moldovian Republic of Transdniestra' (MRT) where he was suspected of defrauding the company he worked for. The facts showed that the insurgent regime was supported directly by the Russian Federation and could not have existed without it. Nor was the 'MRT' recognised by the international community.

The applicant complained about his treatment while in custody awaiting trial by the 'Tiraspol People's Court'. His principal allegations were that he had been arrested and imprisoned unlawfully in breach of ECHR Art 5 and that while in custody had been subjected to inhuman and degrading treatment contrary to the Convention, Article 3, i.e. held in a damp, overcrowded, cigarette smoke-filled cell and denied essential medical treatment.

No violations of the Convention were found to have been committed by the Moldovan government.

> As regards the obligation to re-establish control, there was nothing to indicate that the Moldovan government had not taken all measures within its power to re-establish control over Transdniestrian territory. As to the obligation to secure respect for the applicant's rights, the Moldovan government had made considerable efforts to support the applicant, in particular through appeals to various inter-governmental organisations and foreign countries including Russia, a decision of the Moldovan Supreme Court quashing the applicant's conviction and an investigation into the allegations of unlawful detention.

Violations were attributed, however, to the Russian Federation.

> While there was no evidence that persons acting on behalf of the Russian Federation had directly participated in the measures taken against the applicant, Russian responsibility under the Convention was nevertheless engaged by virtue of its continued military, economic and political support for the 'MRT' which could not otherwise survive.
>
> The Convention may also apply extra-territorially to actions taken by a contracting state on the high seas. This may be the case where, for example, one of its naval vessels intercepts and takes possession of a merchant ship, and its crew into custody, in the course of suppression of the international trade in drugs (*Medmedyer, supra*).

The ECtHR will not entertain applications from nationals of non-contracting states, resident in those states, in respect of actions of a contracting state committed within its own territory (*Ben El Mahi* v *Denmark*, app no 5853/06, 11.12.06; complaint by Moroccan nationals not living in Denmark about Danish papers publishing caricatures of the Prophet Mohammed).

Multi-national military operations, national liability and the United Nations

In modern times the commitment of European armed forces overseas has tended to be in the context of multi-national operations (Kuwait, Kosovo, Iraq, Afghanistan) either mandated by the United Nations or with its acquiescence. In terms of legal responsibility for the actions of such forces, the general principle applicable is that nation states remain liable in law for what their troops may have done except in those situations where the UN retained 'ultimate authority and control' for such national forces so that 'operational command only' was delegated to them (see *Behrami* v *France* (2007) 45 EHRR SE10).

In a series of decisions arising out of the modern conflicts already referred to in which European troops were engaged, the ECtHR took the view that the UN retained ultimate control and authority during the war in Kosovo (*Behrami, supra*) but not during the currency of the later armed interventions in Iraq or Afghanistan (see *Al-Jedda* v *United Kingdom* [2011] ECHR 1092).

Accordingly, therefore, in these Middle-Eastern conflicts, the European nations involved, including the United Kingdom, remained directly answerable in the courts for alleged illegalities committed by their armed forces (but see the doctrine of act of state, pp. 303).

Summary

The following are amongst the principal matters addressed by the chapter:

- the formation and objectives of the European Convention on Human Rights;
- the jurisdiction, powers and workings of the European Court of Human Rights;
- the general principles of European human rights law including the principles of certainty and proportionality;
- the content of the Convention's principal articles of human rights;
- the force of the Convention in the United Kingdom prior to the Human Rights Act 1998.

References

De Hert and Korenica [2002] *The Doctrine of Equivalent Protection*, German Law Journal 13(7).

Feldman (2002) *Civil Liberties and Human Rights in England and Wales* (2nd edn), Oxford: Oxford University Press.

Polakiewicz (2002) *EU Law and the ECHR*, Social Science Research Network.

Further reading

Dickson (2012) *The European Convention on Human Rights and the Conflict in Northern Ireland*, Oxford: Oxford University Press.

Harris, O'Boyle and Warbrick (2016) *Law of the European Convention on Human Rights* (3rd edn), Oxford: Oxford University Press.

Jacobs, White and Ovey (2010) *The European Convention on Human Rights* (5th edn), Oxford: Oxford University Press.

Janis, Kay and Bradley (2008) *European Human Rights Law: Text and Materials* (3rd edn), Oxford: Oxford University Press.

Mowbray (2012) *Case Materials and Commentary on the European Convention on Human Rights* (3rd edn), Oxford: Oxford University Press.

Schabas (2015) *The European Convention on Human Rights: A Commentary*, Oxford, Oxford University Press.

The human rights act 1998

After reading this chapter you should:

1. Recognise the distinction between rights and freedoms and the extent and effectiveness of legal protection of individual freedoms in the domestic jurisdiction prior to the Human Rights Act.

2. Understand the reasons for the enactment of the Human Rights Act and the relationship between the HRA and the law of the European Convention on Human Rights.

3. Be aware of the statutory framework for implementing the Act in the United Kingdom. Have a knowledge of the general principles of human rights law developed in the UK since the Act came into effect.

4. Appreciate the extent to which the HRA applies extra-territorially.

5. Have an understanding of the test of judicial review for alleged abuses of human rights.

6. Recognise the impact of the HRA for the protection of human rights in the United Kingdom.

7. Be aware of the HRA and the principle of derogation.

Freedom versus rights

Introduction

Objective 1

Prior to 1998, the British constitution contained no positive statement of basic human rights similar to those found in the constitutional provisions of many other liberal democracies. According to the traditional domestic approach, the citizen was possessed of a range of 'freedoms' or civil liberties, the principal of these being the freedoms of expression, association and assembly and of the person. In these contexts, and beyond certain minimal legal restrictions, the belief was that the individual should be free to do or say as they wished without fear of interference by officialdom or the forces of law and order. Freedom in this negative sense was founded on certain generally held assumptions concerning the proper distribution of power and liberty in the relationship between the state and the individual and on the contingent expectation that in a free society certain aspects of human conduct should be restricted only to the extent strictly necessary for the effective protection of certain essential public interests, viz. the prevention of crime and disorder; defence and national security; and the maintenance of public morality. In domestic terms, therefore, freedom was understood as a natural and residual attribute of citizenship which, for many, was so ingrained in the nation's political culture as to obviate the need for any express articulation of 'fundamental rights' or the need to protect the same through legislative entrenchment or other procedures.

The role of Parliament and the courts

Throughout the greater part of the twentieth century it was widely assumed that the maintenance of these individual freedoms could be safely entrusted to Parliament and the judiciary. Parliament, it was widely believed, with its representative credentials and history of resistance to the untrammelled expansion of executive power, could be relied upon to resist pressure from governments to enact legislation which violated unduly generally held expectations concerning the proper boundaries of executive authority.

Similar assumptions tended to pervade popular views and rhetoric concerning the role and responsibilities of the judiciary in its related tasks of interpreting Parliament's will and the development of the common law. Generations of judicial independence and the judiciary's oft-stated preference for effective legal control of executive discretion were, in many quarters, accepted as providing a sufficient structural and ideological basis for a sustained and reliable judicial policy of identifying and insisting upon a sacrosanct and irreducible minimum of individual freedoms which the judges would be vigilant to protect.

As the century progressed, however, developments within and external to the United Kingdom began to cast doubt on some of these old certainties and on the continuing viability of the traditional model for securing individual freedom in modern political circumstances.

In particular, the role of Parliament began to be questioned as increasingly effective party-political control of the House of Commons made it possible for governments to use compliant parliamentary majorities to support illiberal legislative provisions for short-term political gain. This led to expressions of unease concerning the ability of Parliament in this political sense to defend the citizen's traditional freedoms against the cumulative effects of such incremental infringement and the apparently entirely piecemeal and ad hoc process of subjecting established freedoms to minor legislative 'modifications' in order to respond to what, at any particular time, was perceived to be a justified public need.

All too often this proved too tempting for governments to resist as it enabled those in power to assuage media and public criticism by being seen to have acted decisively to deal with the political or social issue of the moment. In the last quarter of the twentieth century legislation of this type encompassed a range of anti-terrorist provisions authorising extended periods of detention, restrictions on movement within the United Kingdom (exclusion orders) and stop and search without reasonable suspicion (Prevention of Terrorism Acts); measures increasing the powers of the police to detain and question suspects in 'ordinary' criminal investigations (Police and Criminal Evidence Act 1984), to regulate the conduct of public protest (Public Order Acts), to intercept communications (Interception of Communications Act 1985); and those effecting changes to criminal procedure including the reduction of the right to silence (Criminal Justice and Public Order Act 1994) and restriction of the accused's right of access to material collected by the prosecution in the course of formulating the case to be answered (Criminal Procedure and Investigations Act 1996).

For each measure of this type a rational justification could be advanced. Those not so concerned with the immediate politics of such matters began, however, to draw attention to the long-term consequences of such continuing 'one-off' acts of political expediency and to the danger that, perhaps almost imperceptibly, the substance of civil liberties in the

United Kingdom might be reduced to a level below that necessary for the maintenance of a genuinely free and democratic society.

Also, despite the confidence often reposed in the judiciary in these matters, it became increasingly apparent that while judges might usually attempt to interpret legislation in ways which minimised its impact on individual freedoms, they could not resist provisions enacted for the unambiguous purpose of increasing executive power to the cost of such freedoms. Hence, despite judicial assertions that certain 'fundamental values are part of the common law's priorities' (*per* Sedley J, *R* v *Secretary of State for the Home Department, ex parte McQuillan* [1995] 4 All ER 400), judges have long been powerless to defend these against the clear intent of the sovereign body.

> Within the British Constitution, it has traditionally been assumed that every social value is constantly prey to the vicissitudes of political controversy; that no moral principles are beyond the reach of majorities; that no constituent concept enjoys protection from the outcome of parliamentary elections (Loveland, *Constitutional Law: A Critical Introduction*).

At the same time as concerns were being expressed about the domestic state of affairs in these matters, extensive liberal statements of human rights, often modelled or based directly on the International Declaration of Human Rights 1948 and the European Convention on Human Rights 1953, were becoming the norm in the constitutions of other European states, a trend which extended to those states in the eastern part of the continent just emerging from the Soviet era. Against this background, the rather narrow and negative conception of individual freedoms still pertaining in the United Kingdom appeared increasingly outdated and inadequate particularly in terms of the lack of any developed jurisprudence in relation to such matters as rights to privacy, thought, conscience, religion and family life.

As the twentieth century drew to a close, and after nearly twenty uninterrupted years of Conservative administrations, the public mood in the United Kingdom appeared to be ready for change in a variety of contexts including matters relating to the constitution. In the run-up to the 1997 General Election the Labour party sought to take advantage of this by promising reform of the House of Lords, the creation of regional parliaments and, most significantly in the present context, the enactment of legislation to enable citizens of the United Kingdom to rely on the European Convention on Human Rights for the purpose of initiating and defending legal proceedings involving the state in domestic courts and tribunals.

Labour's resounding victory in the election of May 1997 is now a matter of political history. Having gained power with a massive parliamentary majority, legislation to give effect to the above manifesto proposals was duly enacted.

Objectives of the 1998 Act

Enactment and constitutional implications

Objective 2

The Human Rights Act received the Royal Assent on 9 November 1998. It came into effect in England and Wales on 2 October 2000. From that date the rights and freedoms guaranteed by the European Convention on Human Rights (ECHR) became directly enforceable in the courts of the United Kingdom to the extent that is compatible with primary legislation and the ultimate sovereignty of Parliament. The Act imposed a duty on all public bodies to act in accordance with Convention rights in all their doings and required courts and tribunals to take into account the jurisprudence of both the European Court and Commission of

Human Rights where these touch on a case before them. It is also required that all legislation should be interpreted in accordance with the Convention in so far as this is possible.

The Act was a legislative instrument of great significance and has been described as the most important domestic legal development for a generation. For the first time in the history of English law, individuals were provided with a charter of positive human rights which the state was obliged to respect and observe. Some of these rights, particularly the rights to life, religion and privacy, had not hitherto enjoyed direct legal protection in the United Kingdom.

The Act inevitably enhanced the role of the judiciary as guardian of individual rights and gave judges a more specific and firm legal basis on which to measure the correct balance of power and rights between individual and the state. Some critical voices have argued that, because of the rather general terms in which the rights in the European Convention are expressed, the Act opened the way for increased judicial law-making in the most sensitive of contexts with minimal political and democratic supervision. Whatever the truth of these sentiments, they would appear to understate, whether consciously or not, the role which English judges had already played in the formation of English law, particularly the common law, where, in the absence of immediate legislative parameters, the judges' perceptions of underlying social and moral values have long exercised a powerful influence.

In the English legal system, the Act's effects have been felt far beyond the narrow confines of those matters traditionally regarded as falling within the compass of public law and have impacted on all those legal disciplines where the interpretation and application of the rules therein may have any direct or indirect consequences for any of the rights guaranteed by the Convention.

Principal provisions

Application of ECHR jurisprudence (s 2)

Objective 3

In deciding any matter to which the Convention relates, courts and tribunals in the United Kingdom 'must take into account' any relevant decisions of the European Court of Human Rights, the European Commission of Human Rights or the European Committee of Ministers (s 2(1)). 'The judgments of the European Court are . . . not binding on domestic courts. They constitute material, very important material, that must be taken into account' (Lord Scott, *R (on application of Animal Defenders International)* v *Secretary of State for Culture, Media and Sport* [2008] UKHL 15).

For the distinction between primary and secondary legislation, see Chapter 8, pp. 152–4.

Given such phraseology, the extent to which English courts may feel able to depart from ECtHR judgments remains uncertain. Under international law, the Strasbourg Court is the final arbiter of the Convention's meaning. International law, however, is not binding directly on, or enforceable by, the courts of the United Kingdom.

This, in turn, premises the possible development of two separate meanings of the Convention, i.e. that formulated by the domestic courts for application in a UK context, and that of the ECtHR, based on a more wide-ranging perspective, and, pursuant to the UK's signature of the Convention, for the purposes of the English legal system, having effect in international law only.

The 1998 Act incorporated into domestic law the articles of the Convention . . . But the incorporated articles are not merely part of domestic law. They remain, as they were before the 1998 Act, articles of a Convention binding on the United Kingdom under international law. In so far as the articles are part of domestic law, this House is . . . the court of final appeal whose interpretation of the incorporated articles will, subject only to legislative intervention, be binding in domestic law. In so far as the articles are part of international law they are binding on the United Kingdom as a signatory of the Convention and the European Court is, for the purposes of international law, the final arbiter of their meaning and effect (Lord Scott, *ibid.*).

Given, however, the existence of such international obligations and, within the permitted margin of discretion, the general empathy of the domestic courts to the evolution of common European principles, it would appear highly unlikely that two seriously divergent bodies of jurisprudence will emerge.

The force of Strasbourg judgments in domestic courts was evidenced by the comments of Lord Hoffmann in *Secretary of State for the Home Department* v *MB and AF* [2009] UKHL 28. On this occasion, the House of Lords was asked to consider a case to which, all were agreed, a decision of the ECtHR was directly applicable. Lord Hoffmann was, however, clearly ill at ease with the European Court's findings, i.e. that Control Order proceedings under the Prevention of Terrorism Act 2005 were subject to an 'irreducible minimum' of procedural justice. Notwithstanding these misgivings, and as the following quote illustrates, he felt he had little option but to defer to the Strasbourg decision.

> I think that the decision of the ECtHR was wrong and that it may well destroy the system of Control Orders which is a significant part of this country's defences against terrorism. Nevertheless, I think that your Lordships have no choice but to submit to it. It is true that s 2(1)(a) of the Human Rights Act 1998 requires us only 'to take into account' decisions of the European Court of Human Rights. As a matter of domestic law, we could take the decision in *A* v *United Kingdom* into account but nevertheless prefer our own view. But the United Kingdom is bound by the Convention, as a matter of international law, to accept the decisions of the European Court of Human Rights or its interpretation. To reject such a decision would almost certainly put this country in breach of the international law obligation which it accepted when it acceded to the Convention. I can see no advantage in your Lordships doing so.

Even this, however, should not be understood as meaning that the courts of England and Wales are under an absolutely binding obligation to apply ECHR law exactly as pronounced by the European Court of Justice. Neither the House of Lords nor the Supreme Court have been prepared to go quite that far and appear to prefer the preserving of a residual right to depart from a European decision in what have been referred to as 'rare occasions'.

> The requirement to 'take into account' the Strasbourg jurisprudence will normally result in this Court applying principles that are clearly established by the Strasbourg Court. There will, however, be rare occasions when this Court has concerns as to whether the decision of the Strasbourg Court sufficiently appreciates or accommodates aspects of our domestic process. In such circumstances, it is open to this Court to decline to follow the Strasbourg decision giving reasons for adopting this course. This is likely to give the Strasbourg Court the opportunity to reconsider the particular aspect of the decision which is in issue so that there takes place what may prove to be a valuable dialogue between this Court and the Strasbourg Court (*per* Lord Phillips, *R* v *Horncastle* [2009] UKSC 14).

Following from these rather general strictures, a more specific set of rules for the regulation of the relationship between the domestic courts and the ECHR was proposed by the Court of Appeal in *R (on application of Hicks)* v *Commissioner of Police of the Metropolis* [2014] EWCA Civ 3.

> We think that the following principles are clear: (1) It is the duty of domestic courts to enforce domestically enacted Convention rights. (2) The ECtHR is the Court that must ultimately

interpret the meaning of the Convention. (3) The UK courts will be bound to follow an interpretation of a provision of the Convention if given by the Grand Chamber as authoritative, unless it is apparent that it has misunderstood or overlooked some significant feature of English law or practice which, properly explained, would lead to that interpretation being reviewed by the ECtHR when its interpretation was being applied to English circumstances. (4) The same principle and qualification applies to a clear and constant line of decisions made by the ECtHR other than one of the Grand Chamber. (5) Convention rights have to be given effect in the light of the domestic law which implements in detail the 'high level rights' set out in the ECHR. (6) Where there are 'mixed messages' in the existing Strasbourg case-law, a real judicial choice will have to be made about the scope and application of the relevant provision of the Convention (Maurice Kay LJ).

In *R v McLoughlin* [2014] EWCA Crim 188, the issue before the Court was whether whole life sentences for murder were compatible with the rule against inhuman and degrading punishment in ECHR Article 3. The Grand Chamber's view, as previously expressed in *Vinter v United Kingdom* [2013] ECHR 786, was that such sentences were ECHR compatible providing that the domestic rules applicable to their use 'retained sufficient element of flexibility to allow such sentences to be reduced where this appeared to be justified by relevant compassionate considerations'. In the UK context, however, the ECtHR went on to find that this requirement was not satisfied due to the relevant policy rules set out in the Prison Service Order 4700, ch 12, which sought to limit the power of the Minister of Justice to release life prisoners (Crime (Sentences) Act 1997, s 30) to grounds of terminal illness or other serious physical or mental incapacity only.

This led inevitably to a 'raft' of applications by whole life prisoners in the UK seeking to challenge the sentences imposed upon them. Despite, however, the ECtHR's findings in *Vinter*, and for the following reasons, these were found to be misconceived.

(a) The ECtHR had failed to fully appreciate the common law rule to the effect that administrative policy rules, i.e. in this case, the Prison Service Order, were not effective to limit the exercise of a discretionary power as conferred by an Act of Parliament, viz. the 1997 Crime (Sentences) Act.

(b) Accordingly, and in compliance with a proper understanding of the legislative scheme applicable to whole life sentences in the UK, the Minister, in exercising his section 30 power, had, at all times, as required by the ECtHR interpretation of Article 3, remained free to take into account any of those matters, compassionate or otherwise, which appeared relevant to the case before him/her.

Interpretation of domestic legislation

Primary and secondary legislation, passed or to be passed, is to be interpreted in accordance with Convention rights 'in so far as it is possible to do so' (s 3(1)). Legislation, therefore, should be given a purposive meaning but to an extent which falls short of that which would 'contort the meaning of words to produce implausible or incredible meanings' (Secretary of State for the Home Department, Jack Straw, *Hansard* HC, 3 June 1998, col 422).

In some senses, therefore, the interpretative function of the domestic courts may often be directed towards, not only the intentions of Parliament, as has traditionally been the case, but also to the intended meaning of the Convention – at least, that is, in those many cases to which the Convention will no doubt have some relevance. To this extent, therefore, reference to *Hansard* for purposes of statutory interpretations as permitted by *Pepper v Hart*

[1992] 3 WLR 1032 would appear to be otiose for the purpose of rendering statute to be Convention compatible.

No attempt was made to repeal or amend expressly or by necessary implication the provisions of previous primary legislation inconsistent with the Convention. Where the meaning of a statute is sufficiently clear that it is not possible for it to be given an interpretation which complies with the Convention, the court remains, therefore, under a duty to abide by and to apply that clear intent. Nor did the 1998 Act attempt to diminish the legal competence of future parliaments to legislate in ways which might offend the Convention. It did, however, as will be explained below, introduce a procedural device into the legislative process designed to limit the tendency of governments to promote such incompatible legislation to circumstances where public needs would appear to be compulsive.

The extent of the interpretive obligation imposed by s 3 was considered by the House of Lords in *R v A (No. 2)* [2001] UKHL 25. Lord Steyn was of the opinion that to carry out 'the will of Parliament as reflected in section 3 it might sometimes be necessary to adopt an interpretation which linguistically may appear strained' and that 'the techniques to be used will not only involve the reading down of express language . . . but also the implication of provisions'. Lord Hope was similarly robust. His view was that where words in a statute were incapable of standing up to the test of compatibility, s 3 permitted a court to 'modify, alter or supplement' the words used to achieve the desired result.

For all this, s 3 should not be understood as authorising judges to amend or rewrite legislative provisions simply because these might appear to be at odds with the Convention. That there are clearly limits beyond which the judges should not go in this regard was recognised by the Court of Appeal in *R (on application of Chester) v Secretary of State for Justice* [2010] EWCA Civ 1439. Here, the court was asked to consider the meaning and effect of s 3 of the Representation of the People Act 1983. The apparent object of the section was to prohibit any exercise of the right to vote in any parliamentary, local or European elections by all those serving sentences of imprisonment in the United Kingdom. By the time of the *Chester* decision, the section had already been condemned by the ECtHR on two occasions (*Hirst v United Kingdom (No. 2)* [2005] ECHR 681 and *Greens and MT v United Kingdom* [2010] ECHR 1862). The court's opinion was that the section's 'blanket and indiscriminate' nature, i.e. its removal of the right to vote from all prisoners without reference to the types or gravity of the offences committed, put the section well beyond the margin of appreciation permitted to the United Kingdom for proper implementation of Protocol 1, Art 3, the right to vote in free elections. For all this, however, and given the indisputable clarity of the words used, the Court of Appeal felt it had little option but to give effect to the section as written and that even to attempt to reach a meaning compatible with the Convention would constitute an unacceptable transgression upon Parliament's legislative competence. This approach was confirmed by the Supreme Court *in R (on application of Chester) v Secretary of State for Justice* [2013] UKSC 63.

Secondary legislation which is incompatible with the Convention may be regarded as invalid unless 'primary legislation prevents the removal of the incompatibility' (s 3(2)(c)), for example, where the enabling Act ousts any judicial jurisdiction to quash any secondary legislation made under it.

Although the obligation to read and give effect to legislation in ways which are compatible with the Convention would appear to be directed primarily at courts and tribunals, it is not so expressly restricted and would appear to apply, therefore, to any person or body in whatever capacity charged with interpretation and application of the Act.

Declarations of incompatibility (ss 4 and 5)

When it is not possible to interpret a provision in primary legislation in accordance with the Convention, or where a piece of incompatible subordinate legislation cannot be quashed due to the wording of its enabling Act, a court at the level of the High Court or above may make a 'declaration of incompatibility' (s 4(1)–(4)). Such declaration will not affect the validity, continued operation or enforcement of the legislation in question.

On those occasions where the making of such declaration is contemplated by a court, notice should be given to the Crown in order that it may be able to exercise its entitlement to be joined in the proceedings (s 5). This will enable the Crown, usually through the Attorney-General, to plead the legislation's compatibility with the Convention should it so wish and, in any case, prepare itself for the possibility of a declaration of incompatibility being made.

While no power to make such declarations of incompatibility is given to lower courts and tribunals, it should be remembered that such bodies, in addition to being obliged to give effect to the Convention so far as domestic legislation permits, are subject to a further duty to give reasons for their decisions. Hence, where such inferior court or tribunal is unable to arrive at a Convention compatible decision because of the clear and contrary intent of a legislative provision applicable to the case before it, this will inevitably appear in, and form an important element of, its statement of reasons. In effect, therefore, where this occurs, the inferior body in question will be making what amounts to a statement of incompatibility albeit not of the type, or with the consequences, of those falling within the express terms of the Act.

Following the making of a declaration of incompatibility under s 4, and upon determination of any right of appeal, a Minister of the Crown, to be determined presumably by the subject-matter of the legislation, may 'by order make such amendment to the legislation as he considers necessary to remove the incompatibility' (s 10). Such Remedial Orders may also be made following a finding of incompatibility by the European Court of Human Rights in a case in which the United Kingdom is involved (s 10(1)–(4)) or where, also for reasons of incompatibility, a provision of domestic legislation has been quashed by a domestic court and such remedial action is deemed to be a matter of urgency (s 10(4) and Sched, para 2(b)).

Use of this 'fast-track' procedure should not be resorted to as a matter of course but should be confined to circumstances where there are compelling reasons for proceeding in this way (s 10(2)). In the normal course of events, therefore, remedial action should be by way of primary legislation.

Remedial Orders made under s 10 must be laid before Parliament for 60 days and approved by resolutions of both Houses (Sched 2, para 2). The draft orders should be accompanied by an explanation of the incompatibility and the reasons for proceeding by way of remedial order rather than by primary legislation (Sched 2, para 3). An order may come into effect before being laid before Parliament 'because of the urgency of the matter' (Sched 2, para 2). The order should then be laid before Parliament in the normal way and will cease to have effect unless approved by resolutions of both Houses within 120 days (Sched 2, para 4).

The first declaration of incompatibility to be confirmed by the Court of Appeal occurred in the following case.

Wilson v First County Trust Ltd *(No. 2)* [2001] 3 WLR 42

The case concerned the provision in the Consumer Credit Act 1974 that a contract for the loan of money was not enforceable by the money-lender unless made in a certain prescribed form and, in particular, included a term correctly stating the amount of credit involved (s 127(3)). The effect of the provision was to deny a money-lender access to the courts to enforce such agreement regardless of the circumstances including those in which the contract may have been made in good faith and have genuinely reflected the agreement made. The court accepted that the impugned provision could be said to have been enacted for a legitimate policy aim, i.e. protection against unscrupulous lenders, but felt that the blanket exclusion of all rights of action by money-lenders, other than in the circumstances permitted by s 127(3), and regardless of the facts of particular cases, was disproportionate to its achievement and incompatible, therefore, with the fair trial requirements in Art 6.

A v Secretary of State is discussed in greater detail below.

A controversial and 'newsworthy' use of s 4 occurred in *A and Others* v *Secretary of State for the Home Department* [2004] UKHL 56. Here, the House of Lords declared the power of executive detention in s 23 of the Anti-Terrorism Crime and Security Act 2001 to be incompatible with the right to liberty of the person in Art 5.

New legislation and statements of compatibility (s 19)

A Minister introducing new legislation into either House of Parliament is required to make a statement of compatibility declaring that 'in his view' the Bill is compatible with the Convention rights (s 19(1)(a)). Where any doubt exists, a statement should be made declaring that, although the Minister is not able to make a statement of compatibility, it remains the government's intention to proceed with the Bill in question (s 19(1)(b)). Such statement should be in writing and should be submitted to whichever House is appropriate prior to the Bill's second reading (s 19(2)).

The purpose of this requirement is to ensure that a government wishing to legislate inconsistently with the Convention does so openly making it plain that this is its conscious objective, thereby subjecting its intention to debate in Parliament and to wider scrutiny and analysis by the media and public at large.

> Parliament would expect the Minister to explain his or her reasons during the normal course of the proceedings on the Bill. This would ensure that the human rights implications are debated at the earliest opportunity (Cmd 3782 , above, para 3.3).

Section 19 does not apply to Private Members' Bills or to secondary legislation. The government has said, however, that 'as a matter of good practice, a minister inviting Parliament to approve a draft statutory instrument or statutory instrument subject to affirmative resolutions should volunteer his or her view concerning its compatibility with the Convention rights' and that 'such a statement should always be made regarding secondary legislation which amends primary legislation' (*The Human Rights Act 1998: Guidance for Departments*, 2nd edn, February 2000).

The duty on public authorities (s 6)

The Act requires public authorities to act in accordance with Convention rights in the discharge of any of their functions or powers. The obligation is contained in the negative pronouncement that 'it is unlawful for a public authority to act in a way which is incompatible with a Convention right' (s 6(1)). Section 6(6) provides that an act for these purposes includes a failure to act. The obligation does not apply where the authority could not have acted differently because of the requirements of relevant primary legislation (s 6(2)).

The definition of public authority preferred by the Act is wide and extends to:

(a) government bodies in the usually understood or 'obvious' sense, e.g. Ministers, government departments, local and health authorities, the police, prison and immigration authorities and the armed forces but not Parliament itself or those executing its functions (s 6(3));

(b) courts and tribunals;

(c) any other person or body to the extent that it has been entrusted with functions of a public nature, i.e. those which contribute to the fulfilment of government powers, functions or responsibilities.

The third element of the above definition was intended to put within the ambit of the Act's requirements those many private utilities and companies now responsible for areas of activity which were previously performed by nationalised industries or by government departments. The term 'functions of a public nature' has, however, proved difficult to define. As a matter of general principle, it would appear that it was not intended to have an identical meaning to that developed in the common law for the purposes of judicial review, but rather to be limited to those types of activities for which Her Majesty's Government may be held directly answerable before the ECtHR.

> Section 6(3)(b) is a domestic law provision which has no direct parallel in European rights or domestic jurisprudence. Various guides to its interpretation have been suggested . . . Lord Woolf CJ considered that section 6 was clearly inspired by the approach developed by the courts in identifying the bodies and activities subject to judicial review. Several recent authorities have indeed assimilated the tests. However, it is clear . . . that while authorities on judicial review can be helpful, section 6 has a different rationale, linked to the scope of state responsibility in Strasbourg (Lord Mance, *YL* v *Birmingham City Council* [2007] UKHL 27).

This is based on the assumption that the Act was intended to do no more than provide an alternative and more convenient venue for human rights proceedings, i.e. the courts of the United Kingdom rather than that at Strasbourg and not to impose English common law principles onto ECtHR jurisprudence.

Problems have arisen, however, in relation to the term's more specific application. Thus, in *YL* v *Birmingham City Council* (*supra*), the House of Lords divided three to two on the question whether it encompassed the activities of a privately run care home for the elderly. Most of the residents in the home had been placed there by the local authority in performance of its obligations under the National Assistance Act 1948.

The majority of the House could not accept that a body with no direct statutory powers or duties, not democratically accountable, and which acted purely for profit rather than the public interest, could be said to be exercising a public function.

> Southern Cross is a company carrying on a socially useful business for profit. It is neither a charity nor a philanthropist. It enters into private law contracts with the residents in care homes and with the local authorities with whom it does business. It accepts no public funding, enjoys no special statutory powers, and is at liberty to accept or reject residents as it chooses . . . and to charge whatever fees in its commercial judgment it thinks suitable. It is operating in a commercial market with commercial competitors (Lord Scott).

Those in the minority, however, emphasised the primary role played by this, and other like companies, in the performance of a publicly funded service instituted by Parliament to fulfil the public interest in protecting a particularly vulnerable section of the population.

> This was a function performed for the appellant pursuant to statutory arrangements, at public expense in the public interest (Baroness Hale).

Given the importance of the issue, and this very obvious lack of judicial unanimity, further analysis of the question may be expected as the case-law develops.

Enforcing Convention rights (ss 7–9)

An individual may use a breach of a Convention right as a sword or a shield. Hence such breach may be relied upon to found an action for damages, as a ground for judicial review, or may be used by way of defence in any civil or criminal proceedings (s 7(1)). Subject to any pre-existing and more restrictive limitation period, proceedings against an authority should be commenced within 12 months of the act complained of or such longer period as the court may consider equitable having regard to all the circumstances (s 7(5)).

A person who relies on a breach of Convention rights in legal proceedings must be a 'victim' of the unlawful act for the purposes of the Convention in Art 34, i.e. a person who has been affected by a violation of the Convention rights in question to his/her detriment. The victim may be an individual, a company (***Pine Valley Developments v Ireland*** (1991) 14 EHRR 319), or the relative of a victim who is dead providing the complaint relates to the cause of death or the relative has sufficient legitimate moral or pecuniary interest in pursuing the deceased person's claim (***Sadik v Greece*** (1997) 24 EHRR 323). A person who has not yet been affected by a breach of a Convention right may also be a victim within the meaning of Art 34 if there is a reasonable likelihood that they may be at imminent risk of such a breach, i.e. the application or consequences of Convention intrusive legislation (***Norris v Ireland*** (1991) 13 EHRR 186). This generally liberal judicial approach to the victim test was well illustrated by the findings of the Supreme Court in ***AXA General Insurance Ltd v Lord Advocate*** [2011] UKSC 46. Here the insurance company was recognised as having victim status to challenge the validity of an Act of the Scottish Parliament (Damages (Asbestos-related Conditions) Scotland Act 2009). The Act required employers to insure employees against the risk of certain conditions caused by contact with asbestos. The court accepted that the claimants were thus 'directly affected' by the Act as it exposed their funds to an increased likelihood of asbestos-related claims. Going from this, the claimants argued that since the Act touched on matters protected by the ECHR, viz. Protocol 1, Art 1, the right to property, it was beyond the Scottish Parliament's legislative competence.

As a general rule, a person ceases to be a victim for the purposes of the European Convention if he/she has been awarded adequate compensation or redress through some alternative domestic process, for example, an action for damages for personal injury, and the public authority against which the proceedings were brought has acknowledged the alleged breach of the Convention (***Rabone v Pennine Care NHS Trust*** [2010] EWCA Civ 698).

Where the victim is a member of a trade union or interest group, such organisation has no standing to bring the proceedings on the person's behalf (***Greenpeace v Switzerland*** (1996) 23 EHRR 116). It may bring a case, however, if a breach of a Convention right has affected its collective interests, e.g. its right to act on behalf of its members or to demonstrate in favour of its cause (***Plattform 'Ärtze für das Leben' v Austria*** (1991) 13 EHRR 204). Similarly, churches (***Church of Scientology v Sweden*** (1980) 21 DR 109), professional associations (***Hodgson v United Kingdom*** (1988) 10 EHRR 503) and political parties (***Liberal Party v***

United Kingdom (1982) 4 EHRR 106) have all qualified as victims in respect of prejudicial government decisions.

The Convention's victim test would appear to be narrower than that developed domestically for the purposes of judicial review and would appear to exclude an applicant having no greater interest than any other member of the community. Such *actio popularis* have been permitted in review proceedings generally in respect of serious abuses of power or where no other means existed of testing the legality of the allegedly unlawful act.

For sufficient interest see pp. 444–6.

To enforce a Convention right a court or tribunal may grant any remedy within its jurisdiction as appears to be 'just and appropriate' (s 8(1)). Where the complaint relates to a judicial act, it should proceed by way of:

(a) a right of appeal;

(b) an application for judicial review;

(c) any other forum as may be prescribed (s 9(1)).

Where a breach of an individual's rights under the Act is established, a court may 'grant such relief or remedy or make such order within its powers as it considers just and appropriate' (s 8(1)). Damages may also be awarded by a court with authority to do so if it is 'satisfied that the award is necessary to achieve just satisfaction to the person in whose favour it is made' (s 8(3)).

As, in most cases, the object of the complaint will be to bring the breach to an end, the remedy of choice will often be one, or a combination of, the various orders used traditionally to deal with abuses of power by public authorities. Although damages may also be awarded, it has been made clear that, under the Human Rights Act, such awards have a different purpose to that of damages in private law. The following points of distinction should be noted. Under the Human Rights Act:

- the court has a discretion of whether to make an award, unlike in the common law where a successful claimant has a right to financial recompense;

- the purpose of the award is to achieve 'just satisfaction' and not, as in the common law, to restore the complainant to the position he would have been in had the wrong not been committed;

- in determining whether an award should be made, and how much it should be, the court is obliged to take into account the approach of the ECtHR;

- the court should be mindful of the need to seek a balance between the interests of the victim and those of the public as a whole.

Key factors to be considered in awarding damages under the Act should be the seriousness, scale and manner of the violation. Following the jurisprudence of the ECtHR, awards should not be excessive, but should be sufficient to ensure national 'respect for Convention rights' and to provide the necessary degree of encouragement to public authorities 'while not unduly depleting welfare funds' (*Anufrijeva v London Borough of Southwark* [2003] EWCA Civ 1406; *Barnard v London Borough of Enfield* [2002] EWHC 2282 (Admin)).

In order to preserve the principle of judicial immunity, the right to damages for judicial acts done in good faith 'may not be awarded otherwise than to compensate a person to the extent required by Article 5(5) of the Convention', i.e. for arrest and detention in contravention of any of Art 5's provisions (s 9(3)). Judicial acts not in good faith and in breach of Convention rights will be actionable under s 8(1). Awards of damages under s 9(3) should be against the Crown and not the judicial officer responsible (s 9(4)).

Human rights under the 1998 Act apply to anyone who is actively present in the country, whether on a short-term basis or even illegitimately (*R (on application of Baiai)* v *Secretary of State for the Home Department* [2007] EWCA Civ 478).

Extra-territorial effect

Objective 4

For the Convention's extra-territorial competence, see pp. 494–7.

In relation to British public authorities, the Human Rights Act has extra-territorial effect coterminous with that of the ECHR. This has been held to arise in three circumstances:

(i) Effective control of an area ('ECA')

(ii) State agent authorised control

(iii) Convention legal space.

R (on application Al Skeini and others) v *Secretary of State for Defence* [2007] UKHL 26 was one of a number of cases brought under the HRA relating to events arising from the Iraq war of 2003 and the subsequent occupation of Iraq by troops from the US, the UK and other allied nations. Inevitably, in all such cases, a key issue was the extent to which the UK authorities remained bound by the Act when acting outside of the state's national boundaries.

The proceedings in *Al Skeini* arose as a result of the fatal shootings of a number of Iraqi civilians by British soldiers and the violent death of another while in British military custody. All of the deaths occurred in the southern part of Iraq for which the British military contingent had been given responsibility. The particular complaint of the applicants was that the British authorities had not conducted a thorough and effective investigation into the killings according to the requirements of ECHR Art 2(1).

The majority view in the House of Lords was that the degree of military and administrative control exercised in southern Iraq had not been sufficient to satisfy the ECA test.

> In my opinion, it would require a high degree of control by agents of the state of an area of another state before it could be said that that area was within the jurisdiction of the former. The test for establishing that is and should be stringent, and in my judgment the British presence in Iraq [fell] well short of that degree of control (Lord Roger).

In the same case, however, the British authorities were held to be in breach of Article 2(1) and, in particular, the investigative duty in relation to the complaint alleging abuse of Iraqi prisoners. In this instance though, the principle relied upon was agency authority and control, i.e. the British military's assumption of authority and control over the person(s) concerned in a British base. In very limited circumstances, British government liability for the actions of British troops overseas under Article 2's investigative duty may extend to events occurring before the rights of individual petition to the ECtHR was granted (1966). These 'limited circumstances' arise where:

(i) the event was of particular gravity (e.g. multiple loss of life) and no proper inquiry was conducted;

(ii) the lapse of time between the deaths triggering the investigative duty and the 'critical date', i.e. 1966, was reasonably short and, as a general rule, not in excess of ten years (*Keyu* v *Secretary of State for Foreign Affairs* [2015] UKSC 69).

Accordingly and after a period of uncertainty, it would appear to be established that within the circumstances outlined above, the Convention should be regarded as generally applicable to the actions of members of the armed forces serving abroad. Allegations of violations of Article 2 (the right to life) are, however, unlikely to succeed where these arise from deaths of properly equipped soldiers killed in 'military operations conducted in the face of the enemy' (*Smith* v *Ministry of Defence* [2013] UKSC 41). Possible breaches could arise, however, from, for example, the deaths of soldiers from friendly fire or because of inadequate equipment or planning in training exercises.

The full implications of modern case-law in this context were summarised succinctly by the Court of Appeal in *Mohammed* v *Secretary of State for Defence* [2015] EWCA Civ 843:

> Whenever or wherever a state which is a contracting party to the ECHR purports to exercise legal authority or uses physical force abroad, it must do so in a way that does not violate ECHR rights.

Further significant extensions of the principles of extra-territorial application would appear to be unlikely. Both the ECtHR and the Supreme Court have emphasised that the ECHR should be understood primarily as a 'regional' document, i.e. that the obligations contained within it were designed for European states with kindred political cultures and, therefore, expectations, in terms of the process and conduct of government. Other than in the limited circumstances prescribed, therefore, it would appear unrealistic and inappropriate to insist on its application in entirely different political and cultural environments. This approach was evident in the decision of *R (on application of Smith)* v *Secretary of State for Defence* [2010] UKSC 29, where the right to rely on the protection given by the Act was held not to be applicable to members of the armed forces serving abroad when outside of or away from a British military base or other military facility.

Human rights and judicial review

Objective 5

Where it is alleged that a public authority has acted in breach of the Human Rights Act, the court will be asked to consider one or more of the following questions:

(i)   Did the authority interfere with any of the rights guaranteed by the Act?

(ii) Was the act/decision in question taken in accordance with or as prescribed by law, i.e. was there clear and accessible legal authority for that which was done or decided and did this enable those subject to the Act to foresee the consequences of their actions?

(iii) Was the act/decision directed towards one of the broad and legitimate aims of public policy recognised by the ECHR?

(iv) Within any of those broad policy aims, was the act/decision necessary in a democratic society, i.e. was it proportionate to the achievement of the authority's particular purpose?

Of these, and due to its relative subjectivity and imprecision, by far the most judicial attention has been paid to the requirements of the test of proportionality and , as discussed above, the differences between these and the elements of the traditional common law test of reasonableness. Fortunately for students and practitioners of English law, a particularly clear definition of these matters was given in *SS (Nigeria)* v *Secretary of State for the Home Department* [2013] EWCA Civ 550, where Laws LJ explained how the test of proportionality, when properly understood and applied, imposes both a more demanding standard of judicial review while, at the same time, preserving the required and established separation of powers between the executive and the judiciary.

> There is no doubt that proportionality imposes a more demanding standard of public decision-making than conventional *Wednesbury* review, whose essence is simply an appeal

to the rule of reason. But the true innovation effected by proportionality is not . . . to be defined in terms of judicial intrusion or activism. Rather it consists of the introduction into judicial review and like form of process of a principle which might be a child of the common law itself: it may be (and often has been) called the principle of minimal interference. It is that every intrusion by the state upon the freedom of the individual stands in need of justification. Accordingly, any interference which is greater than required for the state's proper purposes cannot be justified.

This exposition of the test does not mean that the court, in effect, looks at the options which were open to the authority for dealing with a problem and, applying the requirement of minimal interference, identifies which of these should have been chosen. Rather, it restricts judicial interference to those circumstances in which it could not have been rationally concluded that the choice taken by the authority fell within the range of proportionate responses available to it (*R (on application of Lord Carlile of Berriew) v Secretary of State for the Home Department* [2013] EWCA Civ 199).

An example of the United Kingdom adopting measures which were found to be disproportionate to the legitimate aim pursued, on this occasion the prevention of crime, may be found in *R (on application of JF) v Secretary of State for the Home Department* [2009] EWCA Civ 792. The offending provisions in this instance were those in the Sex Offenders Act 2003, requiring persons sentenced under the Act to more than 30 months' imprisonment to report any change of address or travel plans to the police and to do so for the rest of their lives without any prospect of review or remission.

> Parliament's objective in establishing the Sex Offenders Register, was to assist the police to detect and prevent sexual offending. This is an objective which all right-minded people would applaud without hesitation or qualification. But . . . a scheme which obliges offenders who are sentenced to 30 months' detention or more to remain on the Register for the rest of their lives without any possibility of review, even if they can demonstrate that they are no longer a risk, does nothing to promote that lawful objection and, in our view, is disproportionate for that reason (*per* Dyson LJ).

In determining whether an authority has acted proportionately, it has been made clear that the courts should allow the decision-maker a margin of discretion or judgment, the extent of which should be determined principally by the status of the decision-maker and the context in which the particular decision was made. This it has been made clear, is not the same as applying the Strasbourg concept of the margin of discretion allowed by the ECtHR to individual states in terms of the ways in which thought most appropriate, in their own particular circumstances, for honouring their obligations under the Convention.

> We do not apply the Strasbourg margin of appreciation because we are a domestic not an international tribunal . . . Being a domestic tribunal, our judgments as to the deference owed to the democratic powers will reflect the culture and traditions of the British state (Laws LJ, *International Transport Roth GmbH, and others v Secretary of State for the Home Department* [2002] EWCA Civ 158).

Note should also be taken of the comments of Laws LJ in *SS (Nigeria)* (*supra*).

> But the principle does not tell us that when a challenge is brought on the ground of its violation, the court must always be the primary judge of the principle's fulfilment or otherwise. The court insists that the decision-maker respect the principle; but this is perfectly consonant with the decision-maker's discretion as to what constitutes minimal interference. As the cases show, the breadth of the margin is conditioned by context and, in particular, driven by two factors: (1) the nature of the public decision, and (2) its context. The importance of these

considerations of proportionality is as follows. The principle of minimal interference means that the fundamental right in question in the case can never, lawfully, be treated as a token or a ritual.

But the margin of discretionary judgment enjoyed by the primary decision-maker, though variable, means that the court's role is kept in balance with that of the elected arms of government; and this serves to quieten the constitutional anxieties that the Human Rights Act draws the judges into ground they should not occupy.

Further useful explanation of the margin of discretion principle, and its method of application may be found in **R *(on application of Wilson)* v *Wychavon District Council*** [2007] EWCA Civ 52.

When reviewing legislative provisions pursuant to its obligations under the Human Rights Act 1998, the Court accords Parliament a discretionary area of judgment which is the domestic counterpart of the margin of appreciation accorded at international level, by the Strasbourg court, to the state. The extent or scope of that discretionary area of judgment depends on the circumstances, the subject-matter, and the background. On one hand, a wide margin of appreciation or discretionary area of judgment is usually allowed in matters of social or economic policy . . . on the other hand, the margin or discretionary area is generally much smaller in relation to discrimination on particularly sensitive grounds such as gender or race . . . Further the margin will tend to be narrower where the right at stake is crucial to the individual's enjoyment of intimate or key rights . . . particular significance attaching to the extent of the intrusion into the personal sphere . . . (*per* Richards LJ).

The application of the concept was well illustrated by the Court of Appeal in the following case.

R (on application of Farrakhan) v *Secretary of State for the Home Department* [2002] EWCA Civ 606

The case concerned the Secretary of State for the Home Department's refusal to admit to the United Kingdom the black Muslim leader, Louis Farrakhan. The decision was taken on the basis of the applicant's previously expressed racial views and the fear that if he was allowed to speak in the United Kingdom disorder could occur. The Court was in no doubt that Art 10 was engaged by the Secretary of State for the Home Department's decision but felt that, for the following reasons, the decision lay within the margin of discretion which should be allowed to him without judicial interference:

1   the Strasbourg Court attaches considerable weight to the right under international law of a state to control immigration into its territory;
2   the decision was the personal decision of the Minister;
3   the Minister was far better placed than the court to assess the consequences of the applicant's entrance to the United Kingdom;
4   the Minister was democratically answerable for his decision.

Application of the Human Rights Act

Objective 6

At the time of writing, many other cases had been decided domestically on the basis of the requirements of the 1998 Act. Some of the more significant are set out below and arranged by reference to the particular Convention right which was in issue.

Article 2: Right to life

Scope and content

The general extent of the obligations imposed by Art 2 in English law were explained by Wilson J in *R (on application of Plymouth City Council) v County of Devon Coroner* [2005] EWHC 1014 (Admin):

> Article 2 read in conjunction with section 16(1) and (6) of the Human Rights Act 1998, imposes three distinct duties on the state:
>
> (a) a negative duty, namely, by its agents not to intentionally take a person's life save in the circumstances specified in the article . . . ;
>
> (b) a positive duty to take all reasonable steps to protect a person's life . . . In some situations this duty ('the protective duty') requires the state to do more than effectively to operate a criminal justice system designed to deter the taking of life. One example is that the state is required to take all reasonable care to protect the life of a person involuntarily in its custody . . . Another example is that the state is required to seek to protect a person from death as a result of incompetent medical treatment or care . . . ;
>
> (c) a second positive duty, collateral to the first, namely the investigative duty. Art 2 requires the state to furnish an appropriate investigation into the cause of a death which has been, or may have been, caused or contributed to . . . by a breach of the state's protective duty under Art 2 . . .

To date these obligations have been considered and applied to a variety of sensitive and controversial topics including the separation of conjoined twins, withdrawal of medical treatment and deaths in executive custody.

Medical treatment

In *Re A (Children)* [2001] 2 WLR 480, the Court of Appeal ruled that Art 2 did not render unlawful an operation to separate conjoined twins when both could not be saved and where both would die if the operation was not performed. The court's view was that the requirement that 'no one should be deprived of his/her life intentionally' must be given its natural and ordinary meaning and, construed in that way, applied only to cases where the prohibited act was the cause of death. Hence, in the medical circumstances in issue, it did not import any prohibition to an operation, other than those already contained in the common law of necessity, which were satisfied by the facts of the case.

The issue of withdrawal of treatment from a person in a permanent vegetative state was raised in *NHS Trust A v M; NHS Trust B v H* [2001] 1 All ER 801. This was also found not to be an intentional deprivation of life for the purposes of Art 2 since the real cause of the person's death would be the original illness or injury and not the decision to cease to administer treatment. The court was also satisfied that such decision would not violate the state's positive duty to protect life providing it was made in accordance with the law and, in the view of a respectable body of medical opinion, was in the patient's best interests.

Assisted suicide

Withdrawal of medical treatment is not the same as recognising a right to die or to be assisted to die at the time of one's own choosing. Art 2 protects the right to live with as much dignity as possible until life reaches its natural end. The position appears to be that it may be lawful, under certain circumstances, to allow a person to die, but it is not lawful to kill regardless of the individual's wishes (*R (on application of Pretty)* v *DPP* [2001] UKHL 61). It is unlikely, therefore, that the prohibition of assisted suicide (Suicide Act 1961, s 2(1)) is incompatible with the Convention.

In *R (on application of Purdy)* v *DPP* [2009] UKHL 45, the complainant successfully challenged the DPP's refusal to state whether her husband would be prosecuted if he helped her travel to Switzerland to have her life terminated. On this occasion, however, the case was decided by reference to the general principles of certainty and legality rather than breach of any of the Convention's substantive articles. The offending material was the DPP's unpublished criteria for deciding when, and whether, to bring proceedings under the 1961 Act. These, it was felt, were not sufficiently accessible or clearly expressed to provide concerned individuals with any reasonable prospect of predicting whether or not their actions would attract criminal sanction.

For further comment on related issues and the protection afforded to the wishes of those who are dying by Art 8, see pp. 532–4.

The operational duty to prevent deaths

The implied positive element of Art 2 articulated by the ECtHR in *Osman* v *United Kingdom* (1998) 29 EHRR 245, i.e. to provide protection for the life of a specific individual where this is threatened by 'a real and immediate risk from the criminal acts of a third party', was considered by the House of Lords in *Chief Constable of Hertfordshire* v *Van Colle* [2008] UKHL 50. Mr Van Colle, an optician, had been murdered by an ex-employee. This occurred while the latter was awaiting trial on charges of theft from Mr Van Colle's business premises. During that period, the eventual murderer made a number of threatening phone calls to Mr Van Colle. These told Mr Van Colle that he would be 'in danger' if he did not withdraw the above criminal charges. The police were notified of the phone calls and were, therefore, aware of the threat. Mr Van Colle's parents brought proceedings under the 1998 Act. Applying *Re Officer L* [2007] 1 WLR 2135 it was held that:

(a) 'the test of real and immediate risk is one not easily satisfied, the threshold being high and . . . a court should not lightly find that a public authority has violated . . . an individual's rights or freedoms, thereby ruling . . . that the United Kingdom has violated an important international convention';

(b) 'the Strasbourg court in *Osman* roundly rejected the submission . . . that the failure to perceive the risk to life . . . to take preventative measures to avoid that risk, must be tantamount to gross negligence or wilful disregard of the duty to protect life';

(c) the real and immediate test should be applied according to the circumstances which were known or ought to have been known at the time of the event and not on the basis of the wisdom of hindsight;

(d) it was not appropriate, as suggested by the Court of Appeal, to apply a lower test where the risk had been contributed to by the actions of the state itself, e.g. as in the instant case, by the bringing of criminal charges;

(e) in all such cases, the central question was should the police 'making a reasonable and informed judgment on the facts known . . . at the time, have appreciated there was a real and immediate risk to life' of the person affected (Lord Bingham).

The requirement that the risk to a person's life must be shown to be immediate does not mean that the operational duty will apply only where the threat would appear to be imminent in the sense of being about to happen. It is sufficient that the facts suggest it is 'present and continuing', for example, where there is a risk of a psychiatric patient taking his/her own life but the likelihood of the risk being realised may increase and decrease on an almost daily basis (see *Rabone, supra*).

According to these principles, and on a careful analysis of the facts, particularly that the murderer had not committed any serious offences previously, that he was charged with theft to the value of £4,000 only, and that he had made no express threat of death or violence to Mr Van Colle, it was the court's opinion that it could not be concluded that the police had failed to make 'a reasonable and informed judgment on the facts known to them at the time'.

In addition to protecting those whose lives are threatened by the criminal activities of others, the *Osman* duty has been held applicable to various groups of vulnerable people, under the control of the state or for whom the state has assumed responsibility, whose lives are at real and immediate risk from self-harm or suicide. To date, these groups have been held to include: prisoners and detainees, compulsory psychiatric patients, and military conscripts (*Savage* v *South Essex Partnership NHS Foundation Trust* [2008] UKHL 74). Later cases establish that a single death threat is probably not, of itself, sufficient to trigger the preventative obligation and that further evidence supportive of the threat will normally be required (*JR20's Application* [2010] NIQB 11).

In relation to psychiatric patients, the duty was understood initially as applying to compulsory patents only and not, therefore to those admitted to hospital voluntarily. The logic of this distinction was, however, questioned by the Supreme Court in *Rabone* v *Pennine Care NHS Trust*, *supra*. Here the court felt that the key distinctions between the two types of patients in terms of such factors as vulnerability, the ability to make rational decisions and the degree of control exercised by the state, were often more apparent than real. On the facts of the case, therefore, it followed that the duty had been owed to a severely depressed, voluntary psychiatric patient who, after a number of failed attempts, had managed to take her own life.

In those circumstances where the police have been informed that an incident of violence has or is about to take place, the *Osman* duty may arise regardless of whether they have been made aware of the identities of those at risk. Here, it is sufficient that the police knew or ought to have known such victims existed. Nor is it enough for the police to rely on the wisdom of hindsight and to argue that, given the way the events transpired, a more timely or apposite mode of intervention on their part would have made little difference to the outcome (*Sarjantson* v *Humberside Police Chief Constable* [2013] EWCA Civ 1252).

The duty to investigate

The requirement to hold an investigation should be viewed as an integral element of the state's duty to protect the lives of those within its jurisdiction. It may be activated, therefore, by an unusual death, near death, or 'life threatening' incident as part of the process of 'learning lessons' by which the state's performance of the duty is informed and made more effective. This remains the case even though there has been no obvious breach or suspected breach of Art 2 or direct state involvement in the incident complained of. 'Many activities today carry with them so great a risk to life that the duty of the state . . . will include a duty to require investigations of one form or another to be carried out in the event of a mishap, even if this does not actually result in loss of life.' The above marks a development from the duty's original conception as a purely secondary and procedural obligation, only to be deployed contingent to an alleged breach of the Article's substantive requirements, i.e. not to take and protect the lives of those within its jurisdiction (*R (on the application of JL)* v *Secretary of State for the Home Department* [2008] UKHL 68).

Some of the more important rules identified in the many domestic cases dealing with the duty to investigate deaths in which the state may have been involved, including that element of it applying to Art 3, would include the following.

(i)   The duty is not fixed or constant. Its requirements will depend on the circumstances of each case and are 'highly fact sensitive'. Hence, a more demanding approach may be expected in cases involving children or members of other vulnerable groups *(R (on the application of Mousa)* v *Secretary of State for the Home Department* [2010] EWHC 3304 (Admin)).

(ii)   A more stringent approach might also be expected to be the norm in cases where the only persons with knowledge of the relevant events are 'officers of the state' (*Banks* v *United Kingdom* (2007) 45 EHRR SE 15.

(iii) In the normal course of events, where acts of unlawful violence are involved, the duty would be satisfied by a criminal trial, with an adversarial procedure, before an independent and impartial judge (*R (on the application of P)* v *Secretary of State for Home Affairs* [2010] QB 317).

(iv)   Where the allegations are not of intentional violence, but raise issues of negligence, a civil or disciplinary process and remedy may be sufficient (*R (on the application of P), supra*).

(v)   Because death is always treated as a matter of major concern, and because the victims in Art 3 cases will normally be alive and able to pursue their own claims, investigations under Art 2 would normally be expected to be more rigorous (*R (on application of AM)* v *Secretary of State for the Home Department* [2009] EWCA Civ 219).

(vi)   While internal or 'in-house' inquiries may not always be sufficient for Convention purposes, these should not be discounted entirely. In certain circumstances a combination of procedures, e.g. an in-house investigation and a civil action for damages might be enough (*AM, supra*).

(vii) Whatever the process used, the Convention imposes a minimum requirement that it is effective to the extent of enabling 'the facts to become known' (*Banks, supra*).

(viii) The general extent of the investigative obligations imposed on the state under Arts 2 and 3 should not become so onerous that 'the financial cost would be wholly disproportionate to the benefits'. This is a matter in which the responsible authority must be allowed a wide margin of discretion (*AM, supra*).

(ix)   While the investigative duty imposes requirements of 'promptness and reasonable expedition', these should be applied with 'a sensible degree of flexibility' (*Mousa, supra*).

(x)   As a general rule investigations under Arts 2 or 3 should concentrate on the alleged breaches of the Convention and not be drawn into wider matters of 'public and political debate', e.g. the general atmosphere and conditions inside the nation's prisons (*R (on application of MM and AO)* v *Secretary of State for the Home Department* [2012] EWCA Civ 668).

As a general rule, and as the Human Rights Act does not have retrospective effect, the Art 2 investigative duty does not apply to deaths which occurred before the Act came into force (October 2000) (*Re McKerr* [2004] UKHL 12). A major exception to this is that, in limited circumstances, the duty may apply to 'historic deaths' where some further event or procedure relating to the death occurred or continued after the Act's implementation, e.g. 'where the event occurred and an investigation was initiated before the entry into force of the Convention but a significant part of that investigation was only carried out after that date' (Lady Hale, *Re McCaughey and Quinn* [2011] UKSC 20). In these circumstances, therefore, the investigative requirement imposed by Art 2 should be seen as an autonomous, free-standing obligation which was triggered by the new event or proceedings rather than by the original death.

Of the cases in which Art 2 has been pleaded in the English courts, most have resulted from concerns relating to deaths in executive custody. It has been repeated that an inquest will 'normally' be the appropriate way of discharging the state's obligations in these matters but that this may not be sufficient where the circumstances surrounding a particular incident show the possible existence of a systemic problem rather than an individual and isolated failing or inadequacy (see *R (on application of Scholes)* v *Secretary of State for the Home Department* [2006] EWHC 1 (Admin). In *R (on application of Amin)* v *Secretary of State for the Home Department* [2003] UKHL 51, Lord Bingham outlined the main elements of the investigative duty.

> The purposes of such an investigation are clear: to ensure as far as possible that the full facts are brought to light: that culpable and discreditable conduct is exposed and brought to public notice: that suspicion of deliberate wrongdoings . . . is allayed: that dangerous practices and procedures are rectified: and that those who have lost their relatives may at least have the satisfaction of knowing that lessons learned from his death may save the lives of others.

Other such cases in which the rule has been applied include *R (on application of D)* v *Secretary of State for the Home Department* [2006] EWCA Civ 143 (attempted suicide in prison – no proper public inquiry and no opportunity for family members to question prison staff); *Amin* (supra) (prisoner murdered by cell-mate, internal inquiry only from which family members excluded); *R (on application of Middleton)* v *Coroner of West Somerset* [2004] UKHL 10 (suicide in prison – no findings made by inquest as to whether the deceased suicide risk was known and whether appropriate precautions taken).

Where the death is of a person in custody, it is not necessary for the complainant to show that the authorities knew or should have known of the risk and its imminence. The death alone is sufficient to trigger the obligation (*R (on application of JL)* v *Secretary of State for the Home Department* [2007] EWCA Civ 767).

A further extension of the investigative duty in the prison context has been its application to 'attempted' as well as 'successful' suicides. For these purposes, an attempted suicide is one which has 'near death' consequences or which causes serious injury (*R (on application of JL)* v *Secretary of State for the Home Department* [2008] UKHL 68). The duty is not applicable, therefore, to injuries resulting from acts of self-harm (*R (on application of P)* v *Secretary of State for Justice* [2009] EWCA Civ 701).

The right to life and the armed forces

It is unlikely that a violation of Article 2 could arise from the death of a properly trained and equipped member of the armed forces engaged in armed conflict as commanded by the state. A violation could occur, however, where for example, a soldier was killed by 'friendly fire', or because of the inadequacies of training, planning or equipment.

> The guarantee in the first sentence of Article 2(1) is not violated simply by deploying servicemen and women on active service overseas as part of an organised military force which is properly equipped and capable of defending itself, even though the risk of their being killed is inherent in what they are being asked to do. On the other side of the coin, there is nothing that makes the Convention impossible or inappropriate of application to the relationship between the state and its armed forces as it exists in relation to overseas operations in matters, such as, for example, the adequacy of equipment, planning or training (Lord Hope, *Smith* v *the Minister of Defence* [2013] UKSC 41).

As stated, however, state liability under Article 2 will seldom arise out of 'military operations conducted in the face of the enemy' (*ibid.*). A further limitation is that while a violation could otherwise be related to lack of proper equipment etc., procurement decisions taken at a high policy level may fall within the parameters of the types of decisions, which the courts feel reluctant to question – i.e. political assessments of defence requirements and what is financially possible.

The right to life does not require Her Majesty's Government to conduct a full inquiry into the lawfulness of its actions before committing troops to an armed conflict (*R (on the application of Gentle)* v *The Prime Minister* [2008] UKHL 20). The House of Lords decision was based on the following considerations:

(i)   ECHR Art 2 could not be interpreted as precluding the state from entering into an unlawful war. The legal status of a war did not make it more or less likely that those involved in it would be killed.

(ii) Courts should be reluctant to interpret the Convention in ways which would require scrutiny of matters of 'high policy'. Decisions of this type, in this case to go to war against Iraq, were questions of 'political judgment' for which Ministers were 'answerable to Parliament and ultimately the electorate' (Lord Hope).

(iii) It was not open to domestic courts to make conclusive findings of international law.

The right to life and the media

In a separate development relating to the activities of the media, it is now clear that the *Osman* duty may be used to prevent the publication of information which might expose a person to a real risk of being killed as, for example, where this might reveal the person's whereabouts or any change of identity (*King* v *Sunday Newspapers Ltd* [2010] NIQB 107; *Venables* v *Mirror Group Newspapers*, *The Times*, 9 December 1998).

Article 3: Prohibition of torture, inhuman or degrading treatment

Positive and negative elements

In applying Art 3, the English courts have been careful to emphasise the distinction between the Article's express negative duty not to inflict ill-treatment and the implied positive duty, recognised by the ECtHR, to protect persons against such treatment from whatever the source (*Lumbuela* v *Secretary of State for the Home Department* [2004] 3 WLR 561), and have made clear that while the negative duty is absolute, i.e. permits of no exceptions regardless of the circumstances, the implied positive duty is less rigid and, in the interests of practicality, obliges the state only to do that which is reasonable, i.e. relevant and proportionate to the threat (*Gezer* v *Secretary of State for the Home Department* [2004] EWCA Civ 1730). Hence, no breach of Art 3 was committed by the police and army in Belfast who escorted groups of Catholic children to school through an angry loyalist mob. The defence services managed to protect the children from violence and the throwing of missiles, but were unable to shield them completely from the threats and abuse directed at them. Although the mob's behaviour amounted to inhuman or degrading treatment, the House of Lords was satisfied that, in the difficult circumstances prevailing, the police and army personnel had done all that could reasonably have been expected of them (*E* v *Chief Constable of the Royal Ulster Constabulary* [2008] UKHL 66).

Extradition, deportation and asylum

A significant number of domestic cases have been concerned with the circumstances in which a breach of the Article may result from an executive decision to expel a person from the United Kingdom. As explained above, the jurisprudence of the ECtHR establishes that this may occur where there are strong grounds for believing that the person affected would face a real risk of torture, or inhuman or degrading treatment in the state to which they are to be returned. The general principles to be applied in determining whether such belief is well founded were set out by the Court of Appeal in *J* v *Secretary of State for the Home Department* [2005] EWCA Civ 629.

> First, the test requires an assessment to be made of the severity of the treatment which it is said that the applicant will suffer if removed. This must attain a minimal level of severity. The court has said on a number of occasions that the assessment of its severity depends on all the circumstances of the case. But the ill treatment must necessarily be serious such that it is an affront to fundamental humanitarian principles to remove an individual to a country where he is at risk of serious ill treatment.
>
> Secondly, a causal link must be shown to exist between the act or threatened act of removal . . . and the inhuman treatment relied on as violating the applicant's Article 3 right . . .
>
> Thirdly, in the context of foreign cases, the Article 3 threshold is particularly high, simply because it is a foreign case. And it is even higher when the alleged inhuman treatment is not the direct or indirect responsibility of the public authorities of the receiving state, but recurs from some naturally occurring illness, whether physical or mental.
>
> Fourthly, an Article 3 case can, in principle, succeed in a suicide case.
>
> Fifthly, in deciding whether there is a real risk of a breach of Article 3 in a suicide case, a question of importance is whether the applicant's fear of ill treatment in the receiving state . . . is objectively well founded.
>
> Sixthly, a further question of considerable relevance is whether the removing and/or receiving state has effective mechanisms to reduce the risk of suicide.

In a great many of these deportation cases, the claims tend to relate to fear of persecution or ill-treatment for political or religious reasons. The application of Art 3 is, however, not so limited and extends, in addition, to those with realistic fears of death, torture or imprisonment on grounds of sexual orientation (*HJ (Iran) and HT (Cameroon)* v *Secretary of State for the Home Department* [2010] UKSC 31).

It is no answer to claims for protection against persecution to argue that, if and when deported, any such risks could be avoided were the person involved simply to keep quiet about their beliefs or sexual orientation, or were to behave in a way which suggested different beliefs or orientations from those actually held (*RT (Zimbabwe)* v *Secretary of State for the Home Department* [2012] UKSC 38).

The existence of domestic laws and accession to treaties guaranteeing respect for fundamental rights in the receiving state are not, in themselves, sufficient for Convention purposes if the evidence shows a history of abuse of human rights being resorted to or tolerated by the authorities. Nor do assurances from the receiving state absolve domestic authorities from examining whether, in their practical application, they provide an adequate level of protection to persons returned there. The weight to be given to such assurances is a question of fact to be determined, in each case, by the circumstances prevailing in the state in question at the material time and by the application of the following tests:

- were the assurances sufficient to ensure that the person would not be subjected to treatment contrary to Art 3;

- had they been given in good faith;

- was there a sound objective basis for believing that the assurances would be fulfilled, i.e. a 'settled political will' to fulfil them, an 'objective national interest' in doing so, and adequate state control of the state's security agencies to ensure compliance;

● was fulfilment of the assurances capable of being verified *(RB (Algeria)* v *Secretary of State for the Home Department* [2009] UKHL 10).

In the matter of the treatment of 'late' asylum seekers (i.e. those who failed to apply for refugee status immediately on entry and are, therefore, not entitled to support under the Immigration and Asylum Act 1999 and Nationality, Immigration and Asylum Act 2002), the duty imposed by Art 3 is limited to protecting the applicants 'against an imminent prospect of serious suffering caused by denial of shelter, food, or the most basic necessities of life' (*R (on application of Adams)* v *Secretary of State for the Home Department* [2005] UKHL 66).

Other than in the most exceptional circumstances, seriously ill failed asylum seekers may not rely on Article 3 to prevent their removal and return to a state which lacks the medical facilities to provide them with appropriate treatment. Accordingly, no exception could be made in favour of six terminally ill patients who were 'not on their deathbed' (*GS (India)* v *Secretary of State for the Home Department* [2015] EWCA Civ 40).

Articles other than Art 3 may be engaged by the proposed removal of an individual from the United Kingdom. The threshold test is high and it will usually be necessary for the complainant to show the likelihood of serious and flagrant abuse of the right concerned to the extent that it is completely denied or nullified (*E M (Lebanon)* v *Secretary of State for the Home Department* [2008] UKHL 64).

Article 5: Right to liberty and security of the person

Deprivation of liberty: general principles

Following the jurisprudence of the ECtHR, the domestic courts have made clear that what amounts to a deprivation of liberty for the purposes of Art 5 is heavily dependent on the particular facts and circumstances of each case. Hence in *Cheshire West and Chester County Council* v *P* [2011] EWCA Civ 1257, the Court of Appeal was asked to consider the case of a seriously mentally disabled 39-year-old male, who was unable to care for himself or make reasoned decisions about his care and place of residence and who lived in accommodation provided by the local authority according to an intensive care regime often involving one-to-one attention and, at times, a measure of physical restraint. The court felt that to have subjected a person of full capacity to equivalent controls and constraints could well have amounted to a deprivation of liberty. This was not so, however, in the case of the person in issue due to the special circumstances prevailing and the consequent 'reason, purpose and motive' behind the constraints applied to him.

Fairness in the penal system

In the relatively short time it has been directly enforceable in the United Kingdom, Art 5 has proved to be of particular utility for those aggrieved by the workings of the penal system and the related processes for determining whether, and when, prisoners may be released on licence or recalled from such release. The case-law in this context, both from Strasbourg and the domestic courts, has resulted in major changes to the rules regulating the penal system's disciplinary and decision-making procedures providing, in turn, greater openness, fairness and independence for those affected.

An important case in this context was *R (on application of Brooke)* v *Parole Board* [2008] EWCA Civ 29. Amongst other things, the Parole Board decides whether life and long-term prisoners should be released from detention before their sentences have been served. Board members are appointed, and may be dismissed, by the government (Minister of Justice). The

Minister also makes significant contributions to the materials to be considered by the Board in each case. This degree of executive involvement in the composition and workings of the Board was felt to be inconsistent with the Art 5(4) requirement that prisoners should have access to an independent and impartial tribunal to test the legality of their detention. Other significant decisions in this context include:

- *Girling* v *Parole Board* [2005] EWHC 546 (Admin) (mandatory life prisoner who had served the punitive or tariff element of his sentence had the right to be released or given access to legal proceedings through which any refusal to release could be challenged);

- *R* v *Lichniak* [2002] UKHL 47 (risk to life or limb should be regarded as the only valid ground for continued detention after a tariff period had been served);

- *R (on application of West)* v *Parole Board* [2005] UKHL 45 (although a 'court' for the purposes of Art 6, and determining criminal charges for the purposes of Art 8, the Parole Board should not be expected to follow the exact procedures expect in a criminal court of law);

- *R (on application of Smith)* v *Secretary of State for the Home Department* [2005] UKHL 51 (length of time to be served by a person sentenced to be detained at Her Majesty's pleasure to be determined by an independent tribunal, not by the Minister);

- *R (on application of Noorkiev)* v *Secretary of State for the Home Department* [2002] EWCA Civ 770 (lapse of two months between the end of the tariff period and consideration by the Parole Board of the prisoner's eligibility for release was an excessive delay);

- *Hirst* v *Secretary of State for the Home Department* [2006] EWCA Civ 945 (reasons for recall from parole should be given promptly).

Individual freedom and the terrorist threat

A perhaps more controversial domestic application of Art 5 has been its use to test the human rights compatibility of the UK's anti-terrorist legislation.

A and Others v Secretary of State for the Home Department [2004] UKHL 56

In this case, the House of Lords was concerned with section 23 of the Anti-Terrorism, Crime and Security Act 2001, which permitted the continued and indefinite detention of foreign terrorists who could not be deported from the UK by reason of Art 3, i.e., if removed they faced a real and imminent threat of ill-treatment in the country to which they might be returned. The House of Lords found the section to be directly incompatible with Art 5 and that it could not be sustained by the government's use of the derogation provisions in the 1998 Act (see s 14). Whilst being prepared to concede that post '9/11' the UK was facing a 'public emergency threatening the life of the nation', the court could not accept that the detention of foreign nationals could be regarded as 'strictly required by the exigencies of the situation', particularly when British nationals were also known to pose a threat but no similar measures had been thought necessary in their case.

The decision in *A* was one of the main contributing factors to the enactment of the Prevention of Terrorism Act 2005, since repealed by the Terrorism Prevention and Investigation Measures Act 2011. The 2005 Act empowered the government to make 'control orders', restricting the liberty and movements of terrorist suspects, but did not involve actual detention in prison. Such orders provided fertile grounds for litigation and complaints that the restrictions imposed exceeded that permitted by Art 5 (see *Secretary of State for the Home*

Department v *JJ and Others* [2007] UKHL 45; *Secretary of State for the Home Department* v *AF* [2007] UKHL 46; *Secretary of State for the Home Department* v *E* [2007] UKHL 47). The Act of 2011 replaced Control Orders with Terrorism Prevention and Investigation Measures ('TPIMs').

These matters are dealt with in detail, see pp. 663–4.

Political asylum and deportation of foreign nationals

In this context Art 5 has proved to be of considerable utility in challenging exercises of the power of executive detention contained in the Immigration Act 1971, Schedule 3 – viz., the power to detain any person liable to be deported from the United Kingdom pending a decision whether to proceed with their removal and for so ever long as such removal may take and the power in the UK Borders Act 2007 to detain those foreign national prisoners sentenced to a period of imprisonment of a least twelve months who have completed their sentence and who are subject to the Act's automatic deportation provisions. The section represents one of the few remaining powers of detention without trial available to the British government. It is an important weapon in the legal armoury for effecting immigration control and is resorted to with considerable frequency. No express limits are imposed by the Act in terms of the length of time for which such detainees may be held in custody.

Given all of this, there have been occasions when the potential for abuse in s 5(3) has attracted a degree of judicial unease. This, accompanied by a determination to subject the exercise of the power it contains to a body of effective legal constraints, has led to the formulation of a set of rules, directed towards the proper use of the power, and founded on both ECHR Art 5 and the relevant elements of the traditional common law. Some of the more important of these rules would include:

(i) The Minister must intend to deport the person and can only use the power to detain for that purpose (*R (on application of Lumba)* v *Secretary of State for the Home Department* [2011] UKSC 12).

(ii) The deportee can only be detained for a period that is reasonable in all the circumstances to effect the deportation process (*Bizimana* v *Secretary of State for the Home Department* [2012] EWCA Civ 414, detention for 21 months caused by unnecessary and protracted delay in processing the claimant's case).

(iii) Before the expiry of the reasonable period, if it becomes apparent that the Minister will not be able to effect the deportation within a reasonable time, he/she should not proceed with it (*Bizimana, supra*: serious and unresolved complications in determining the claimant's nationality and country of origin).

(iv) When it is decided to proceed with the removal, the Minister should act with reasonable diligence and expedition to effect that decision.

(v) Continued detention can only be justified where there is a sufficient and realistic prospect of removal but it is not necessary for the Minister to identify a finite time or period within which removal can reasonably be expected to be effected (*R (on application of MH)* v *Secretary of State for the Home Department* [2010] EWCA Civ 1112).

(vi) As the period of detention gets longer, the greater the degree of certainty and proximity of removal that will be required in order to justify continued detention (*R (on application of MH)*, *supra*).

(vii) The power should be exercised in accordance with published public policy rules and without other serious errors in the conduct of the deportation process. Failure to do so renders the detention unlawful at common law, i.e. the tort of false imprisonment, and a breach of Art 5 (*R (on application of Lumba)* v *Secretary of State for the Home Department* [2011] UKSC 12: application of unpublished policy favouring continued detention of foreign national prisoners recommended to be deported at the conclusion of their prison sentences; *R (on application of Kambadzi)* v *Secretary of State for the Home Department* [2011] UKSC 23: failure to apply policy rule requiring regular reviews of the need for detention).

(viii) The policy rule that, other than in exceptional circumstances, the mentally ill should not be detained pending deportation should be understood as subject to a threshold requirement relating to the seriousness of the illness and as applicable primarily to those suffering from a serious condition (*R (on application of LE (on application of Jamaica)* v *Secretary of State for the Home Department* [2012] EWCA Civ 597).

The mentally disordered or incapacitated

A person suffering from a mental disorder which makes it appropriate for him to receive medical treatments necessary for his/her health or safety or for the protection of other persons may be admitted to hospital compulsorily (Mental Health Act 1983, s 3). Given that this is, effectively, a power of extra-judicial detention, the courts have taken the view that the powers in the 1983 Act should be interpreted strictly and that any deviation from the procedures prescribed by the Act for such compulsory admissions should result in the subsequent detention being regarded as incompatible with the requirements of Art 5 (*TTM* v *London Borough of Hackney* [2011] EWCA Civ 4).

Persons otherwise mentally incapacitated, but not subject to any related legal restrictions, have the same rights under Article 5 as anyone else. Accordingly, if their daily living arrangements would amount to a deprivation of liberty for a person of full capacity, these are also a loss of liberty for the incapacitated person. Such persons were entitled, therefore, to independent periodic assessment of any arrangements made for their care to ensure that these remained compliant with Article 5 and in their best interests (*Surrey County Council* v *P and Others* [2014] UKSC 19).

Children, the disabled and persons in care

The imposition of moderate constraints on children or young persons in the course of reasonable parental discipline and control will seldom amount to an Article 5 deprivation of liberty. This would cover, for example, sending a child to his/her room for bad behaviour and for a short period, or 'grounding' a rebellious teenager, i.e. refusing to allow him/her to leave the family home to meet with friends and acquaintances (*Cheshire West and Chester Council* v *P* [2011] ECWA Civ 1257). Article 5 could, however, be engaged by constraints which are more severe both in time and intensity and whether or not for a good cause.

The general principles of ECHR jurisprudence relating to the deprivation of liberty of persons with mental disorders or disabilities are as follows:

(i) The issue of what might be 'best' for such persons in terms of care and treatment should not be confused or conflated with the concept of deprivation of liberty.

(ii) The meaning and requirements of physical liberty are the same for everyone. Simply because a person suffers from a mental disorder or disability does not mean that his/her freedom may be subjected to restraints which would not be regarded as acceptable if applied to a person not similarly disordered or disabled.

(iii) The key feature is whether the person concerned is under continuous supervision and control and is not free to leave.

(iv)   The person's acquiescence towards a controlled regime or to restriction of movement is not relevant.

In relation to those in care, the requirement to live in a particular place, whether in local authority accommodation or a foster home will not, of itself, be a deprivation of liberty (*G v E, A Local Authority and F* [2010] EWHC 621 (Fam)). In terms of the regime in a care home, or the constraints imposed upon a particular individual living there, all will depend on the overall 'concrete' situation, i.e. an assessment of all the factors affecting the way that the person is living and being treated.

Individual freedom and public order

For exceptions to the Art 5 right to liberty and security of the person, see pp. 449–50.

The right to liberty and security of the person is, of course, subject to certain express exceptions. Surprisingly perhaps, none of these makes any express reference to the needs of public order and the safety of the community, i.e. to the effect that the right may be restricted to maintain the peace. This uncertainty or perhaps 'omission' was considered by the House of Lords in *Austin* v *Metropolitan Police Commissioner* [2009] UKHL 5. Here, the House was not prepared to accept that the right in Art 5(1) should be applied or enforced so rigidly that this:

For the facts of *Austin*, see pp. 605–6.

(a)   exposed the community to the dangers of public disorder;

(b)   impacted negatively on the ability of the state to fulfil its obligations under other elements of the Convention, e.g. the duty to protect life under Art 2.

For more about 'absolute' articles, see p. 422 above.

With this process of reasoning, the court, in effect, went on to recognise a further and, in this instance, implied exception to Art 5(1) allowing the state to restrict the right for the purposes of maintaining peace and order and protecting those who might be put at risk by it. The Convention, it was felt, including those articles generally regarded as 'absolute', should be interpreted in a way which achieved a meaningful and constructive balance between the requirements of the different obligations imposed.

A somewhat different approach to the absence of any public order exception in Art 5 was taken by the Court of Appeal in *Cheshire West and Chester County Council* v *P* [2011] EWCA Civ 1257. This was to the effect that the omission should be understood as a matter of deliberate intent and as meaning that those who formulated the Convention did not believe that the types of police tactics used by states to preserve public order amounted to a deprivation of liberty for Convention purposes – therefore no exemption was needed to permit them.

> Whatever their country's particular historical experiences, the framers of the Convention can hardly have forgotten the problem of public disorder, or intended to deny the authorities the conventional means of coping with it. Yet it finds no reference in Article 5. The conclusion can only be that the framers did not see the exercise of police power in such circumstances as involving deprivation as opposed to restriction of liberty (Munby LJ).

Breach of Article 5 and damages

Article 5(5) vests the courts with a discretion to award damages to those who have been arrested or detained in breach of the Article's various guarantees. Awards of financial compensation for other types of loss or damage resulting from breaches of Art 5, e.g. for anxiety or distress, while not prohibited, are less likely to be made. This is founded on the view that the main purpose of the Convention is the prevention of violations of human rights rather than the provision of compensation when such breach may be found to have occurred and that a mere finding of a violation, with all of the attendant publicity, may often be sufficient for that purpose (***Sturnham*** v ***Secretary of State for Justice*** [2012] EWCA Civ 452).

Article 6: right to a fair trial

Limits on fair trial guarantees

To date it has been aspects of this Convention right, more than any other, which have been at issue in any of the proceedings which have been commenced under the terms of the 1998 Act.

A number of cases have dealt with some of the various and well-documented limitations on fair trial rights, including limitations placed on the presumption of innocence and the rule against self-incrimination which have been imposed by Parliament in recent years to deal with the threats caused by such matters as drink-driving and the increase in drug-related offences.

The general approach taken by the domestic courts has been founded on the principle, often stated by the Strasbourg Court, that the rights in Art 6 are not absolute and may be subjected to moderate and proportionate restrictions in pursuit of clear legitimate aims. Thus in relation to drink-driving legislation it has been held that the rule against self-incrimination is not violated by the requirement that the owner of a vehicle should provide information concerning the identity of its driver at the time of an alleged offence. A legislative obligation to answer a simple question, on pain of a moderate non-custodial penalty, particularly where this was not part of the process of interrogation and could not lead to incrimination for the original offence, could not be regarded, it was felt, as a disproportionate response to the public danger caused by drinking and driving (***Brown*** v ***Scott (Procurator Fiscal, Dunfermline)*** [2001] 2 All ER 97).

A similar approach was taken to the irrebuttable presumption in the road traffic legislation to the effect that the amount of alcohol in a person's blood at the time the specimen was taken was no less than that present at the time of the offences. Since the legislation existed to control the amount of alcohol consumed before a vehicle was driven the court could find no serious intrusion upon the presumption of innocence in an assumption which, being based on a test taken some time after the alleged offence had been committed, would often operate in the suspect's favour (***Parker*** v ***Director of Public Prosecutions***, *The Times*, 26 January 2001).

Questions on presumption of innocence have also been raised in the context of anti-drugs legislation. In ***HM Advocate*** v ***McIntosh*** 2001 SCCR 191, the Privy Council considered the provision which allows a court to assume, in the absence of viable explanation, that any discrepancy between the income and assets of a person convicted of a drug-trafficking offence was the product of that offence, thus empowering it to make a confiscation order. The approach taken by the court was that, as the making of such order did not involve any fresh accusation and followed from the original offence, it was something which should properly be regarded as a part of the sentencing process. Hence, although the proceedings were to be conducted in accordance with the requirements for determinations affecting civil rights, they did not import the elements of Art 6 relating to the trial of criminal charges including the presumption of innocence in Art 6(2). The willingness of domestic courts to read Art 6 as subject to crucial public interests was again apparent in ***Secretary of State for the Home Department*** v ***MB*** [2006] EWCA 1140, where the Court of Appeal confirmed that those involved in decision-making proceedings subject to Art 6 requirements do not have an absolute right to be informed of all the evidence against them if this could seriously prejudice national security or the prevention of crime and that, in appropriate circumstances, the withholding of information would not vitiate the making of a Control Order under the Prevention of Terrorism Act 2005.

Article 6 was in issue again in the controversial case involving the government's attempts to reduce the number of illegal immigrants gaining entry to the country by concealing themselves in lorries and containers (***International Transport Roth GmbH v Secretary of State for the Home Department*** [2002] EWCA Civ 158). The government's attempt to deal with the problem was contained in the Immigration and Asylum Act 1999. This consisted of a legislative scheme whereby a carrier found to be carrying an illegal immigrant was liable to pay a fixed penalty of £2,000 for each such individual. According to Lord Simon Brown LJ, the scheme was criminal in nature and offended Art 6(1), (2) and (3). This was because:

(a) it imposed a reverse burden of proof, in that the carrier could only avoid such penalty by showing that he did not know or could not reasonably have been expected to know of the person's presence;

(b) the lorry in question could be detained pending determination of these issues;

(c) the penalty was fixed, therefore precluding the imposition of penalties proportionate to the facts.

> The hallowed principle that the punishment must fit the crime is irreconcilable with the notion of a substantial fixed penalty . . . the fixed penalty cannot stand unless it can be judged proportionate in all cases having regard to the culpability involved.

Similar issues were at the basis of the complaint in ***R v Keogh*** [2007] EWCA Crim 528. This concerned the provisions in ss 1–4 of the Official Secrets Act 1989 whereby it is a defence for a person charged with revealing official information to show that they did not know that this would be damaging or harmful to the state. Again, the court felt, putting onto the defendant the burden of disproving a substantial element of the offence, i.e. guilty knowledge, rather than requiring the prosecution to prove it, was not wholly consistent with the requirements of a fair trial.

For more on the reverse onus of proof in ss 1–4 of the Official Secrets Act, see p. 637.

Judicial review

Further significant developments in domestic procedural standards have resulted from the application of Art 6 to the law relating to applications for judicial review. In particular this has led to the adoption of the Convention's jurisprudence concerning the test of bias. The test would appear to be similar to that of reasonable suspicion of bias, frequently referred to in domestic courts, at least until the decision in ***R v Gough*** [1993] AC 646, and is satisfied where there is a legitimate reason to fear lack of impartiality in the decision-maker (***Director General of Fair Trading v Proprietary Association of Great Britain*** [2001] 1 WLR 700).

Disciplinary and interim decisions

Disciplinary decisions, too, have been recognised as potentially falling within the protective ambit of Art 6's procedural guarantees. This would appear to be the case where such proceedings are determinative or substantially determinative of a significant civil right, e.g. a contractual right to employment. Hence, a teacher dismissed for improper conduct (sexual contact with a 15-year-old male pupil) should have been allowed legal representation before the school governors, when the decision was made, and should not have been told that his right of representation was limited to the support of a union official (***R (on application of G) v Governors of X School*** [2010] EWCA Civ 1).

As a general rule, the procedural prescriptions in Art 6 do not apply to purely interim or provisional decisions made prior to any final determination of the matter in hand. This is, however, not an absolute rule and may not be followed if the interim decision has a major impact on the final outcome. Thus it has been held that the consequences of a provisional listing of a care worker as unfit to work with vulnerable adults (Care Standards Act 2000) could be such as to justify the application of Art 6 to the decision-making process – particularly where, as is often the case, any such decision impacts directly on the care worker's established civil right to remain in the employment in which he/she is engaged.

It was, therefore, a breach of Art 6 for the Minister to provisionally list a care worker without first having given her a full opportunity to make representations to him/her (*R (on application of Wright) v Secretary of State for Health* [2009] UKHL 3).

Decision-making in the penal system

As with the salient elements of Art 5, the fair trial guarantees in Art 6 have proved to be a substantial benefit to those aggrieved by the workings of the decision-making processes in the United Kingdom's penal system. Particularly significant decisions in this context include:

- *R (on application of Anderson) v Secretary of State for the Home Department* [2002] UKHL 46 (the punitive or tariff period of a life sentence should be fixed by the trial judge and not the Minister);

- *R (on application of Greenfield) v Secretary of State for the Home Department* [2005] UKHL 14 (prison disciplinary proceedings which engage civil rights should be conducted in accordance with the Convention's fair trial guarantees).

The fair trial guarantees in Art 6 have also been held to be applicable to the process for making and serving anti-social behaviour orders (ASBOs) (*R (on application of M) v Secretary of State for Constitutional Affairs* [2004] EWCA Civ 312; *R (on application of McCann) v Manchester Crown Court* [2003] 1 AC 787).

> . . . the making of a full ASBO is a civil proceeding which can involve the determination of civil rights within the meaning of Article 6(c) (Kennedy LJ).

Fairness and the control of terrorism

In the context of anti-terrorist legislation, Art 6 was relied on in a significant number of cases to ensure minimum standards of procedural fairness, particularly in the making of Control Orders under the Prevention of Terrorism Act 2005. Persons involved in Control Order hearings were thus held to have the right to be informed of at least 'the gist' of the suspicions

For further details of Control Orders, see Chapter 21, pp. 663–4.

against them. This remained the case even though it might have appeared that disclosure of the material would make little difference to the outcome of the proceedings (*Secretary of State for the Home Department v AF* [2009] UKHL 28).

Fairness, deportation and expulsion

In the sphere of deportation and removal from the United Kingdom, Art 6 has been relied on to give added protection to foreign nationals who fear that they may face an unfair trial if returned to their country of origin. To avoid being returned there, the requirement, in this context, appears to be that the person is able to show that, in addition to being subjected to an unfair trial, there is a real likelihood that this could lead, for example, by way of punishment, to a breach of one or more of the person's substantive rights also protected by the Convention.

If an alien is to avoid deportation because he faces unfair legal process in the receiving state, he must show that there are potential grounds for believing that there is a real risk, not merely that he will suffer a flagrant breach of his Art 6 rights, but that the consequence will be a serious violation of a substantive right or rights (*RB (Algeria)* v *Secretary of State for the Home Department* [2009] UKHL 10).

Fair hearings, open justice and national security

The introduction into the English legal system in recent times of specially adapted 'closed' procedures for evidence relating to matters of national security represents one of the most significant challenges to the ideals of open justice experienced in modern legal history. Such proceedings, often referred to as 'closed material procedures' (CMPs), are so described as they are conducted in the absence of the party bringing or defending the claim. This, it has been argued, flies in the face of the age-old assumption that the quality of justice, and public confidence in it, may be maintained only if courts and tribunals are openly accessible to press, media and public alike and are, therefore, at all times, subject to public scrutiny and comments.

The theory behind closed material proceedings is that:

(i)   they permit courts and tribunals to consider the sort of sensitive evidence which might otherwise have been excluded for reasons of public interest immunity;

(ii) this facilitates the making of decisions on the basis of all material evidence relevant to particular cases;

(iii) the closed nature of the proceedings provides an effective guarantee that sensitive security-related material will not find its way into the public domain.

> The power is a seductive one for the government and even for the courts. It enables the government to place material before them without risk of public exposure or scrutiny and with the knowledge that it is shielded from challenge because evidence cannot be adduced to respond to it (the other parties not knowing what it is). Judges will be attracted by the fact that it enables them to see all the evidence relevant to the decisions they have to make (Lord Brown, 26.3.13, HL Col 1032).

The procedure was first authorised for use by the Special Immigration Appeals Commission Act 1997. The Act created the Special Immigration Appeals Commission with jurisdiction to hear appeals against immigration and deportation decisions taken in 'the interests of national security' (Immigration Act 1971, s 3). It also allowed for relevant security-sensitive evidence to be heard by the Commission in closed sessions.

In the years that followed 1997, and despite widespread unease about its implications, the use of closed proceedings was extended to other court and tribunal jurisdictions in which sensitive material might be in issue:

(i)   claims before the Investigatory Powers Tribunal alleging human rights violations by the intelligence and security forces (Regulation of Investigatory Powers Act 2000, s 65);

(ii) appeals against proscription decisions made by the Proscribed Organisations Appeals Commission (Terrorism Act 2000, s 2, Scheds 3 and 4), i.e. decisions to ban organisations believed to be involved in terrorist activities;

(iii) claims of racial discrimination in the delivery of services (Race Relations (Amendment) Act 2000, ss 7 and 8;

(iv) appeals against expulsions and banning from premises where dangerous explosives are stored heard by the Pathogens Access Appeal Commission (Anti-Terrorism, Crime and Security Act 2001, s 70);

(v)   appeals against referral or refusals of planning permission (Planning and Compulsory Purchase Act 2004, s 80);

(vi) hearings before Employment Tribunals involving claims by Crown employees (Employment Relations Act 2004, s 36);

(vii) appeals to the High Court against the imposition of Control Orders (Terrorism Act 2005, ss 2 and 10 and Sched 1) and, later, against their replacements, Terrorism Prevention Investigation Measures (TPIMs) under the Terrorism Prevention and Investigation Measures Act 2011, ss 6–8;

(viii) County Court proceedings dealing with allegations of sex discrimination (Equality Act 2006, s 87);

(ix) appeals against the imposition of financial restrictions on persons suspected of terrorist-related activities (Counter-terrorism Act 2008, s 67);

(x)   disability discrimination claims in County Courts (Equality Act 2010, s 117);

(xi) hearings before the various elements of the First and Upper Tier Tribunals (First Tier Tribunal (General Regulatory Chamber) Rules 2009).

After this piecemeal incremental process of development, full recognition of the utility of the CMP process in the British legal system was effected by the Justice and Security Act 2013. This allowed for sensitive evidence to be heard in closed proceedings in any civil case being heard before the High Court, Court of Appeal, or Supreme Court. The court may proceed in this way on application by any of the parties to a case or of its own volition providing it is satisfied that:

(a) open disclosure of the material in question would pose a real risk of harm to national security;

(b) consideration has been given to applying for PII but, in all the circumstances, it was felt that the interests of justice would be better served by consideration of the sensitive material in closed session, e.g. because of the amount of sensitive material in issue or its relevance to the proceedings.

The Act requires also that the person holding the material, often a government Minister, should consider whether it may be possible to provide the claimant or other party with at least a non-damaging summary of its content.

On those occasions when a court or tribunal goes into closed session, the 'interests' of the excluded parties will be represented by a 'Special Advocate'. These are security-cleared barristers selected from a panel appointed by the Attorney-General. Such advocate may not reveal any of the security-related material put before the closed court to any of the excluded parties whose interests he/she is seeking to protect.

A Minister may apply for a case or parts of it to be heard in CMP even though he/she is a party to the case in question.

In *McGartland* v *Secretary of State for Home Office* [2015] EWCA Civ 686, the Court of Appeal described the CMP process as 'a serious departure from the fundamental principles of open justice and natural justice'. Despite this, however, and other widespread criticism of it, attempts to challenge the validity of the process against European human rights standards have, to date, met with little success. Thus, in a series of cases, the view has been taken that the failure to disclose at least a summary of the sensitive material heard in closed proceedings does not, of itself, fall short of the minimum procedural standards imposed by Article 6 (*Tariq* v *Home Office* [2011] UKSC 35; *CF* v *The Security Service* [2013] EWHC 3402

(QB); *Mohammed v Foreign and Commonwealth Office* [2013] WLR (D) 439; *Kiani v Secretary of State for the Home Department* [2015] EWCA Civ 776). Examples of the types of material dealt with in closed proceedings under the 2013 Act would include:

- information relating to ministerial reasons for imposing financial restrictions on persons believed to be involved in, or giving support to, Iran's nuclear development programme (*Q (on application of Sarkandi) v Secretary of State for Foreign and Commonwealth Affairs* [2015] EWCA Civ 687;

- information relating to the police protection programme provided for a secret agent who had provided the security forces in Northern Ireland with information about IRA operations (*McGartland v Secretary of State for Home Affairs, supra*).

The advent of closed proceedings for dealing with sensitive material in civil cases has not altered or replaced the principles of public interest immunity as a means of deciding whether sensitive material may be used as evidence. It remains possible, therefore, for cases touching on sensitive matters to be tried in open court and on the basis of the evidence available for use, i.e. which is not affected by a judicial ruling that in respect of the evidence at issue, the interests of state security should take precedence over the exactitudes of procedural fairness in a particular case.

For the state, however, the inception and extended role of the CMP process has some very clear advantages. These include:

(a) if an application to proceed in this way is accepted by the trial court, this obviates the risk, always present with a plea of PII, that the court might feel minded not to accept the Minister's argument for withholding the information in question and, therefore, permit it to be used in open proceedings;

(b) it avoids the state being put into the type of dilemma with which it was faced in *Binyam Mohammed v Secretary of State for Foreign and Commonwealth Affairs* [2010] EWCA Civ 65; i.e. of having a choice between producing sensitive material in open court to defend itself against allegations of complicity in the imprisonment and ill-treatment of British nationals at Guantanamo Ban or – as was the final choice – simply abandoning the proceedings and paying out large sums in compensation to the claimants.

Breach of Article 6 and damages

Breaches of Art 6 are actionable in damages according to the principles developed at Strasbourg. The complainant must show 'loss of procedural opportunity' (i.e. that procedural defects may have affected the outcome of the trial), or 'anxiety and frustration' caused by, for example, delays in the trial process (*R (on application of Greenfield) v Secretary of State for the Home Department* [2005] UKHL 14).

Some other applications

Other findings of note in relation to domestic applications of Art 6 have included decisions that a fair trial may be prejudiced through gross incompetence by legal advisers (*R v Nangle, The Independent*, 8 November 2000); that although trial *in absentia* is generally compatible with Art 6, a defendant may waive their right to be present if, aware of the trial date, they knowingly and deliberately absent themselves from the proceedings (*R v Hayward; R v Jones; R v Purvis* [2001] 3 WLR 125); that, providing the balancing exercise between the private and public interests was carried out by a judge, no breach of Art 6 was committed where, in a criminal trial, the lawfulness of the defendant's arrest was established on the basis of material put to the judge in an *ex parte* public interest immunity application (*R* v *Smith* [2001] 1 WLR 1031); no adequate independence and impartiality in the hearing of appeals against refusals of housing benefit by Housing Benefit Review Boards composed of councillors from the local authorities whose officers had made the impugned decisions (*R (on application of Bewry)* v *Norwich City Council* [2001] EWHC Admin 657, *Runa Begum FC* v *Tower Hamlets LBC* [2003] UKHL 5).

Article 7: no punishment without law

The wider implications of Art 7 for English law were considered by the Court of Appeal in *R* v *Misra and Srivastava* [2004] EWCA Crim 2375.

> In our view the central thrust of the Article is to prohibit the creation of offence, whether by legislation or the incremental development of the common law, which have retrospective effect. It reflects a well understood principle of domestic law, that conduct which did not contravene the criminal law when it took place should not retrospectively be stigmatised as criminal, or expose the perpetrator to punishment (Judge LJ).

In *R* v *Rimmington* [2005] UKHL 63, the Lords articulated the Article's requirements:

> There are two guiding principles: no one should be punished under a law unless it is sufficiently clear and certain to enable him to know what conduct is forbidden before he does it; and no one should be punished for an act which is not clearly and ascertainably punishable when the act was done. (Lord Bingham)

To date, the test of certainty as applied by both the ECtHR and the domestic courts does not appear to be excessively demanding. Hence in *Rimmington*, *supra*, the Court of Appeal found sufficient precision for Art 7 purposes, in the definition of the old common law offence of public nuisance. The approved version of the offence is quoted below.

For more on public nuisance, see p. 612.

Article 8: right to respect for private and family life

General scope and content

Since the 1998 Act came into effect, the House of Lords, and later the Supreme Court, have been at pains to emphasise that the central obligation imposed on the state by Art 8 was to conduct its affairs in ways which give respect to the 'rights' it articulates but that the Article does not impose an absolute duty on the state to provide a political and social system which guarantees the delivery of these 'rights' in their purest form (see *Secretary of State for Work and Pensions* v *M* [2006] UKHL 11). Also, it has been made clear that, while the right extends protection to such broad and unspecific concepts as 'personal autonomy' and 'physical integrity', it should not be understood as conferring a degree of individual freedom coterminous with that advocated by J.S. Mill, i.e. the right to do as one wishes provided no harm is done to others nor does it confer any absolute freedom to do as an individual may wish in the privacy of his/her own home. Persons detained, and, therefore, effectively resident in mental hospitals, could not rely on Art 8 as giving them a right to smoke in or on hospital premises *(R (on application of N)* v *Secretary of State for Health* [2009] EWCA Civ 795).

Like other articles in the Convention, Art 8 imposes both negative and positive obligations on the state (see above). The negative obligation is to avoid arbitrary interference with an individual's Art 8 rights. The positive obligation is to adopt measures which will create the circumstances in which these rights may be enjoyed.

Where the ECtHR identifies a positive obligation on the state in the context of Art 8, it often has two aspects: (1) to require the introduction of a legislative or administrative scheme to protect the right to private and family life; and (2) to require the scheme to be operated competently so it is capable of achieving its aim (*Anufrijeva, supra*).

It has been held, therefore, that in limited circumstances, Art 8 could be infringed by a state's failure to provide basic levels of income support and housing, where this results in hardship 'sufficiently severe to engage Art 3' or where family life involving children is 'seriously inhibited' (*ibid.*).

The general scope and intended sphere of operation of the right to private and family life was considered in detail by the House of Lords in *R (on application of Countryside Alliance and Others)* v *Attorney-General* [2007] UKHL 52. The case arose from a challenge to the ban on hunting imposed by the Hunting Act 2004. Here Baroness Hale identified two categories of expression or enjoyment of private life – the first embracing the privacy of the person's home and personal communications and, the second, the personal and psychological space for developing his/her sense of self and making relationships with other people. In the context of the particular facts of the case itself the House identified the central purpose of Art 8 as being 'to protect the individual against the intrusions of the state, unless for good reason, into the private sphere within which individuals expect to be left alone to conduct their personal affairs and live their personal lives as they choose' (Lord Bingham). Hunting, however, was felt to be far too public an activity to fall within this or any other recognised conception of Art 8. The House also felt unable to draw any analogy with the cases in which Art 8 had been relied on to protect the traditional ways of life of particular ethnic groups (see *G and E* v *Norway* (1983) 35 DR 30, Lapps living in the far north of Norway; *Buckley* v *United Kingdom* (1996) 23 EHRR 101, *Chapman* v *United Kingdom* (2001) 33 EHRR 399, gypsy caravan-dwellers):

> The hunting fraternity cannot plausibly be portrayed in such a way. The social and occupational diversity of this fraternity . . . leaves no room for such an analogy (*ibid.*).

The meaning of 'the family' for Convention purposes was considered in *R* v *Secretary of State for Health, ex parte L (M)* (2001) 1 FLR 406. The case involved a challenge to the policy of restricting child visits to patients in secure hospitals to circumstances where the visit was deemed to be in the child's best interests and, in the case of patients convicted of very serious offences, where a close family relationship existed between the prisoner and the child. In the instant case this had been relied on to prohibit the applicant, a convicted murderer detained in Rampton Hospital, from being visited by his niece. The challenge failed on two grounds. First, the court felt that the policy was not disproportionate to the legitimate aims of protecting children from the danger of exposure to certain types of serious offenders. Second, as a general principle, it was not prepared to accept that Art 8 extended to the normal relationship between uncle and the niece.

It is clear from this that expectations of privacy are not limited to those activities which take place out of the public gaze. Hence, for example, private life considerations come into play when any systematic or permanent record is kept, perhaps by the police or a local authority, arising from that done in the public domain, e.g. CCTV footage, police files etc. Accordingly Article 8(1) was engaged when a local newspaper, at the instigation of the police, published photographic images of a 14-year-old boy allegedly participating in serious incidents of public disorder. No breach was committed, however, due to the publication falling within the legitimate aims or public policy objectives permitted by Article 8 (2), i.e. in this instance, the prevention of crime and disorder (*Re application for Judicial Review, J38 (Northern Ireland)* [2015] UKSC 42).

Assisted suicide

The law relating to assisted suicide in the UK is contained currently in the Suicide Act 1961, section 2. This prohibits and criminalises the provision of such assistance in all circumstances and makes no exception, therefore, in the case of persons of full mental competence.

That the right to respect for private life in Article 8(1) applies to the process of dying, and to the wishes of the persons concerned, was recognised by the House of Lords in *R (on application of Purdy)* v *Director of Public Prosecutions* [2009] UKHL 45. Here the House concluded also that, in these circumstances, any restriction of the right was, therefore, justifiable only if a necessary and proportionate means of achieving one or more of the legitimate aims articulated by Article 8(2) – usually, in this context, the protection of health and the rights of others or, more specifically, the safeguarding of the vulnerable including those who were gravely ill and often elderly.

The question of whether section 2 of the 1961 Act might be so regarded was given some lengthy consideration in *R (on application of Nicklinson and another)* v *Ministry of Justice* [2014] UKSC 38 – to date the leading case on the extent to which, if at all, English law should draw limits to the freedom of the individual to decide when and by what means they wish to die.

In the case itself, both the applicants were almost completely paralysed, one from stroke and the other from spinal injury. Both were unable to care for themselves and wished to bring their lives to an end. Neither, however, was capable of doing so without a considerable degree of help and assistance.

Concerned about the implications for their friends and relatives, and in order to take matters forward, they sought declarations (see above, HRA, s 4) that, in so far as the prohibition in section 2 of the Suicide Act extended to those who were mentally fully competent, and not just to the more vulnerable, it could not be regarded as a necessary and proportionate restriction for the purposes of ECHR Article 2(2).

A Supreme Court of nine members dismissed the applications unanimously. The following views were expressed.

(a) Given the sensitive medical, moral, and social issues involved, the question of the extent to which assisted suicide should be restricted by law was better left for Parliament to decide (Lords Sumption, Hughes, Reed and Clarke) or, at least, remitted for consideration by Parliament before any judicial intervention would be justified (Lords Neuberger, Mance and Wilson).

(b) The all-embracing nature of the ban in section 2 was such that the Court would be justified in making a declaration of incompatibility without more and without waiting for any parliamentary involvement. Any such declaration would not, however, affect the validity of the 1961 Act, nor would it affect Parliament's sovereign authority, rather it would merely draw its attention to the gravity of the human rights issues involved.

Matters of sexual orientation and gender

In *R (on application of Wood)* v *Metropolitan Police Commissioner* [2009] EWCA Civ 414, Laws LJ expressed the view that 'an individual's personal autonomy makes him . . . the master of all those facts about his identity, such as his name, health, sexuality, ethnicity, his own image of which the cases speak; and also of the zone of interaction between himself and others'. Predictably, therefore, Art 8 has proved useful in giving greater legal security and recognition to same-sex couples. Thus it has been said that same-sex couples living with children of former marriages should be regarded as families for Art 8 purposes (see *Secretary of State for Work and Pensions* v *M, supra*). Other cases contain findings that same-sex couples should have the same rights as heterosexual couples in matters of landlord and tenant (*Fitzpatrick* v *Sterling Housing Association* [2001] 1 AC 27) and succession to shared property (*Ghaidan* v *Godin-Mendoza* [2004] 2 AC 557).

The right to respect for family life does not give same-sex couples any right of sexual cohabitation in prison (*R (on application of Hopkins)* v *Secretary of State for Justice* [2016] EWHC 606 (Admin)), nor to be provided with details of exactly what types of behaviour may be engaged in freely and without sanction (*Bright* v *Secretary of State for Justice* [2014] EWCA Civ 1628). That this needed to be said is consistent with the rule that a sentence of imprisonment removes only those rights inconsistent with a period of lawful incarceration.

In terms of marriage, and without need for direct reference to the requirements of the Human Rights Act, the rights of lesbian, gay and trans-sexual partners were changed dramatically by the Marriage (Same Sex Couples) Act 2013 and the Gender Recognition Act 2004. These, for all general purposes, equated the marital rights of persons in the above categories of persons to those available traditionally to heterosexuals.

Private and family life, deportation and expulsion

Other state powers having the potential for dramatic interference with private and family life would include those relating to deportation for the commission of criminal offences and removal from the United Kingdom for breaches of the immigration rules.

Some of the more significant decisions made under Art 8 in this context would appear to include:

- The power to deport or remove a person from the United Kingdom should be exercised on the basis of the criteria set out in *Boultif* v *Switzerland* (2001) 33 EHRR 1179, *Uner* v *The Netherlands* (2007) 45 EHRR 14, *Maslov* v *Austria* [2008] ECHR 546 and *JO (Uganda) Secretary of State for the Home Department* [2010] EWCA Civ 10.

- Although the consequences for the family lives of those affected, in both cases of deportation for criminal behaviour and removal for immigration reasons, might often be similar, in the balancing exercise for determining the proportionality of the state's actions, as a general rule, greater weight should be given to the public interest in preventing crime and disorder than to that of maintaining an effective immigration system (*JO (Uganda)* v *Secretary of State for the Home Department, supra*).

- In exercising the power to deport a foreign national from the United Kingdom for committing criminal offences, the principal public interests to be taken into account are:
  (a) the risk of re-offending;
  (b) leading other foreign nationals to understand that, whatever their particular circumstances may be, similar consequences may follow if they break the criminal law;
  (c) 'demonstrating the role of deportation orders as an expression of society's revulsion at serious crimes and building public confidence in the treatment of foreign citizens who have committed serious crimes' (*OH (Serbia)* v *Secretary of State for the Home Department* [2008] EWCA Civ 694, *Reid* v *Secretary of State for the Home Department* [2010] EWCA Civ 138).

- In considering the position of family members in both deportation and removal cases, the material question is not whether there are insuperable objects to them following the person to the country to which he has been sent, but whether they cannot reasonably be expected to follow him there (*VW (Uganda) and AB (Somalia)* v *Secretary of State for the Home Department* [2009] EWCA Civ 5, *EB (Kosovo)* v *Secretary of State for the Home Department* [2008] UKHL 41).

● In deciding whether to remove a person from the United Kingdom, the impact and consequences for all of that person's immediate family members should be considered and not just the effects on the person subject to the decision (*R (on application of Razgar)* v *Secretary of State for the Home Department* [2004] UKHL 27). Should children be involved, particular regard must be had to their best interests (*ZH (Tanzania)* v *Secretary of State for the Home Department* [2011] UKSC 4). This is an important consideration, but should not necessarily prevail over all other public interests including the need to protect the community against the activities of criminals (*SS (Nigeria)* v *Secretary of State for the Home Department* [2013] EWCA Civ 550).

Privacy and the law of confidence

Although Art 8 gives express protection against intrusions into privacy by the state, English law does not recognise, nor has it ever developed, any common law tort of privacy on which individuals could rely in respect of similar intrusions by other private actors. The increased awareness of the value of a legal right to privacy, following the enactment of the Human Rights Act, particularly in an age of aggressive media determined to pry into the lives of both public and private individuals, has, however, provided the impetus for the domestic judiciary to develop the law of confidence to the extent that this may be used to provide redress for abuses of private information, whether written or pictorial.

> The time has come to recognise that the values enshrined in Articles 8 and 10 are now part of the cause of action of confidence . . . the courts have been able to achieve this by absorbing the rights protected by Articles 8 and 10 into this cause of action . . . The values embodied in Articles 8 and 10 are as much applicable in disputes between individuals or between an individual and a non-government body as they are in disputes between an individual and a public authority (Lord Nicholls, *Campbell* v *MGM* [2004] 2 WLR 1232).

Similar sentiments were expressed by the Court of Appeal in *Douglas* v *Hello! Ltd* [2005] EWCA Civ 595:

> We conclude that in so far as private information is concerned, we are required to adopt . . . the cause of action formerly described as breach of confidence (Lord Phillips, MR).

The position now appears to be that it is the nature of the information itself, rather than the existence of a confidential relationship between the parties, which is the primary factor in giving the information legal protection (*Venables and Thompson* v *News Group Newspapers Ltd* [2001] Fam 430). The duty will arise 'whenever the party subject to the duty is in a situation where he knows, or ought to know that the other person can reasonably expect his privacy to be protected' (ibid.). In *Campbell* v *MGM* (*supra*), this was held to apply to the details of a celebrity's attendance at Narcotics Anonymous.

> Now the law imposes a duty of confidence whenever a person receives information he ought to know is fairly and reasonably to be regarded as confidential. Even this formulation is awkward. The continuing use of the phrase 'duty of confidence' and the description of the information as 'confidential' is not altogether comfortable. Information about an individual's private life would not, in ordinary usage, be called 'confidential'. The more accurate natural description today is that such information is private (Lord Nicholls).

Linguistically, at least, the law was taken a step further in *Browne* v *Associated Newspapers* [2007] EWCA Civ 295, where the Court of Appeal confirmed the existence of a tort of 'private information, not dependent on the existence of a confidential relationship'.

> The first question under Art 8 is whether the claimant has a reasonable expectation of privacy in the particular circumstances of the case. That is the relevant question in determining whether there was previous confidential relationship between the parties or not . . . The cause of action . . . has now thrown off the need for an initial confidential relationship (Clarke MR).

Although no longer a precondition to the legal protection of information, the significance of a previous confidential relationship between the parties should not be discounted entirely. It remains a relevant circumstance in determining the sensitivity of information and may well add weight to the claimant's case for a reasonable expectation of privacy.

Article 9: freedom of religion

The extent of the protection

The benefits of religious freedom in a democratic society were explained with great clarity by the House of Lords in *R (on application of Williamson)* v *Secretary of State for Education and Employment* [2005] UKHL 15.

> Religious and other beliefs and convictions are part of the humanity of every individual. They are an integral part of his personality and individuality. In a civilized society individuals respect each other's beliefs. This enables them to live in harmony. This is one of the hallmarks of a civilized society. Unhappily, all too often, this hallmark has been noticeable by its absence. Mutual tolerance has had a checkered history even in recent times. The history of most countries, if not all, has been marred by the evil consequences of religious and other intolerance (Lord Bingham).

In dealing with a complaint under Art 9, it would appear to be open to a domestic court to conduct a factual inquiry into whether the particular belief is honestly held as a matter of good faith and is not 'just an artifice' (Lord Bingham, *supra*). Beyond this, however, courts should be reluctant to embark upon any inquiry into the validity of the particular religion or other belief being pleaded.

> Each individual is at liberty to hold his own religious beliefs however irrational or inconsistent they appear to some (Lord Bingham).

The judges do appear, however, to be ready to exercise a greater degree of supervision over the actual practice and manifestation of religious or other beliefs. The belief may be atheistic, agnostic or sceptic, but 'must relate to the aspect of human life or behaviour of comparable importance to that normally found within religious beliefs' and must be 'consistent with basic standards of human dignity or integrity'. Hence 'manifestation of a religious belief which involved subjecting others to torture or inhuman punishment would not qualify for protection'. The belief should also be 'coherent in the sense of being intelligible and capable of being understood' (Lord Bingham).

The complaint in the *Williamson* case was that the ban on corporal punishment in schools imposed in 1998 violated the belief that 'part of the duty of education in the Christian context that teachers should be able to stand in the place of parents and administer physical punishment to children who are guilty of indiscipline'. The House of Lords found that corporal punishment which violated a child's physical and moral integrity to a degree incomparable with ECHR Arts 3 or 8 could not be sustained under any other element of the Convention. The objective of the 'blanket' ban in question which, by definition, prohibited milder forms of punishment had been 'to protect children against the distress, pain, and other harmful effects the infliction of physical violence may cause'. This, the court felt, was a legitimate aim, and the means chosen to achieve it were not disproportionate in their adverse effects on parents who believed that the controlled administration of corporal punishment 'to a mild degree' could be beneficial (Lord Bingham).

> Parliament was entitled to take this course because this issue is one of broad social policy. As such, it is predominantly well-suited for decision by Parliament. The legislature is to be accorded a considerable degree of latitude in deciding which course should be selected as the best course in the interests of school children as a whole (Lord Bingham).

Freedom of religion and public interest

A much publicised case brought under Art 9 related to a school's refusal to allow a female pupil a particular type of religious dress (the 'jilbab') (*R (on application of Begum) v Denbigh High School* [2006] UKHL 15. The majority of the House of Lords felt that, as the complainant had a free choice whether to attend the school in question or transfer to an alternative establishment where her particular religious preferences could be accommodated, it could not be said that her religious rights had been denied. The minority view was that, to the extent that her rights may have been infringed, this fell within the area of judgment afforded to the state by Art 9(2) and that the ban was not disproportionate to the legitimate aim of trying to achieve social cohesion and promoting the ability of young people of diverse races and religions to live together in peace and harmony.

Great publicity also attended a decision of the Welsh Assembly Government to order the slaughter of a sacred bullock belonging to the 'Community of the Many Names of God'. It was suspected that the bullock had been exposed to bovine TB. The Court of Appeal accepted, therefore, that the interference with the Community's religious rights could be justified by the public policy grounds specified in Art 9(2) – in this case, the danger of the disease spreading (*Surayanda v Welsh Assembly Minister* [2007] EWCA Civ 893).

As explained above, Art 9, in effect, contains two related but distinct rights. These are, first, the right to hold a particular religion or belief and, second, the right to manifest whichever religion or belief is held. The second is a qualified right only and may not be conducted or insisted upon in a way which offends certain key public interests including the rights and freedoms of others (Art 9(2)). It was open, therefore, for a local authority to terminate the contract of employment of a registrar who, because of her religious beliefs, felt unable to celebrate civil partnerships between gay and lesbian couples. The claimant's desire to manifest her religion in this way in the course of her employment could not be asserted or upheld to the extent that it overrode the majority commitment to equality of treatment for members of the gay and lesbian communities (*Ladele v London Borough of Islington* [2009] EWCA Civ 1357). A similar approach was adopted in *Bull and Bull v Hall and Preddy* [2012] EWCA Civ 83. This was the case, again well publicised, in which the owners of a guesthouse were found in breach of the Equality Act (Sexual Orientation) Regulations 2007, through their refusal to accept a booking from a male gay couple. According to the owners of the guesthouse, the effect of the regulations was to require them to act in ways which contravened their religious rights under Art 9 and that the exercise of these rights could not, therefore, be penalised as discriminatory. As in the *Ladele* case, however, the court's response was that the right to act in accordance with or to manifest a particular belief was qualified rather than absolute and that the 2007 Regulations were a proportionate way of ensuring that the right in Art 9(2) was not applied in a way which always 'trumped' the protection of the rights and freedoms of others, e.g., as in this case, the general right of all members of the community to be free from discrimination on grounds of their sexual orientation.

Article 10: right to freedom of expression

Freedom of expression and democracy

The extent to which the values of a democratic society are underpinned by the right to freedom of expression and, particularly, its essential utility in the political context was recognised by the House of Lords in *Rushbridger* v *Attorney-General* [2003] UKHL 38.

> Freedom of political speech is a core value of our legal system. Without it the Rule of Law cannot be maintained. Whatever may have been the position before the Human Rights Act . . . it is difficult to think of a rational argument justifying the criminalisation of a citizen who wishes to argue for a different form of government (Lord Steyn).

In the same case, it was made clear that judges would 'not hesitate to use the strong interpretative obligation' in the HRA, s 3(1) to 'read down' statutory provisions seeking to inhibit free political discourse.

In this general context, i.e. the freedom of debate in relation to matters of public concern, the relevant principles to be considered where it is alleged that a person's Art 10 rights have been unnecessarily restricted by a national court or tribunal, were explained by the Court of Appeal in *R (on application of Gaunt)* v *Office of Communications* [2011] EWCA Civ 692:

(i)   the need for the restriction must be established convincingly;

(ii)   regard should be had to the particular words used and to the context in which they were made public;

(iii) the latitude to be accorded to someone who insults another in public is greater if the insulting words are used in the context of an open discussion of matters of public concern or in the context of the freedom of the press;

(iv)   there is a distinction to be drawn between harsh words which constitute a gratuitous personal attack, and those which form part of a political debate;

(v)   the inherent risk in live broadcasting is that there is no possibility of reformulating, perfecting, or retracting the statement before publication (e.g. in live broadcast debates);

(vi)   in the context of religious opinions and beliefs, it is legitimate to insist on an obligation to avoid as far as possible expressions that are gratuitously offensive to others and which do not contribute to any forum of public debate capable of furthering progress in human affairs;

(vii) the interference with the person's Art 10 rights should be proportionate to the legitimate aim pursued;

(viii) for the purpose of determining the proportionality of the interference in issue, a margin of discretion is to be accorded to the national authorities;

(ix)   in deciding whether or not the court or tribunal went beyond the margin of discretion, the severity of the sanction imposed is potentially relevant.

The case in *Gaunt* arose out of a decision by Ofcom that the treatment of a 'guest' on a public affairs radio broadcast, during which the guest, a local councillor, was referred to as a 'Nazi', 'health Nazi', and an 'ignorant pig', constituted a breach of s 2 of the 2010 Broadcasting Code. The topic of the interview was the decision of Redbridge London Borough Council to ban smokers from becoming foster parents. Ofcom's finding was found to be a reasonable and proportionate response to the broadcast on the grounds of:

For the Broadcasting Code, see pp. 616–8.

(a) the nature of the language used;

(b) the 'hectoring' tone and 'bullying' manner of the interview overall;

(c) the interviewer's persistent interruptions;

(d) the shouting down of the guest's responses;

(e) the categorisation of the guest's responses as 'insults';

(f) the fact that Ofcom had imposed no sanction other than the finding itself.

The court was at pains to emphasise that in deciding cases of this type, it was important to consider the overall picture that, as in the instant case, its decision was founded on a combination of the factors, particularly those in points (a) to (e) above, rather than any one of them, and the conclusion that the cumulative effect of the combination was to prevent any meaningful and useful debate on the issue in question from taking place.

Freedom of expression and contempt of court

Article 10 will clearly have a considerable role in preserving the freedom of the press and will be a factor to be considered in the application of the Contempt of Court Act, s 10, viz. the power of the court to reveal their sources of information where this is deemed to be necessary in the interests of justice, national security or the prevention of crime. In *Ashworth Security Hospital* v *MGN Ltd* [2001] 1 WLR 515, the Court of Appeal felt that no breach of Art 10 had occurred where the power was used to order disclosure of the identity of the person responsible for passing to a journalist material derived from the medical records of Ian Brady (the 'Moors Murderer'). In the court's view, the disclosure of highly confidential medical information to the press was 'an attack on an area of confidentiality which should be safeguarded in any democratic society' and of sufficient severity to override the competing public interest in the protection of journalistic sources. In *John* v *Express Newspapers* [2000] 3 All ER 257, it was also emphasised that the proportionality of any such order for disclosure, i.e. whether it was 'necessary in a democratic society', would depend, *inter alia*, on whether the party seeking disclosure had shown that all other reasonable means had been taken to identify the source.

Freedom of expression and prisoners

The rights of prisoners under Art 10 were again in issue in *R (on application of Nilsen)* v *Full Sutton Prison* [2004] EWCA Civ 1540. Here the decision was that no breach of Art 10 had been committed by prohibiting the publication of a prisoner's memoirs when these included details of his notorious crimes including the murders of his homosexual lovers. The ban imposed by the prison's authorities was found to be a proportionate means of pursuing a relevant legitimate aim, i.e. to prevent a prisoner from glorifying, and profiting from, his crimes.

Freedom of expression and privacy

A recurring theme in the domestic Art 10 cases decided to date has been the potential for conflict between the freedom of expression and information and the individual's right to argue that the revelation of certain information would damage his/her right to privacy as protected by Art 8. One such case was *Attorney-General's Reference (No. 3 of 1999), Re BBC* [2009] UKHL 34, where the House of Lords felt that the requirements of Art 10 were sufficient to override a court order that the identity of a person acquitted of rape should not be revealed in any publication or broadcast. The proper approach in such 'conflict' cases was explained in *McKennitt* v *Ash* [2006] EWCA Civ 1714:

> . . . in such a case where the complaint is of the wrongful publication of private information, the court has to decide two things. First, is the information private in the sense that it is in

principle protected by Article 8. If 'no', that is the end of the case. If 'yes', the second question arises: in all the circumstances, must the interest of the owner of the private information yield to the right of freedom of expression conferred on the publisher by Article 10. The latter enquiry is commonly referred to as the balancing exercise (*per* Buxton LJ).

Where the balancing exercise has been carried out by a judge at first instance, an appellate court should not intervene unless it is clear that the judge erred in principle, reached a decision which was clearly wrong or, on the facts, was outside the ambit of conclusions which could be reached (*AAA* v *Associated Newspapers* [2013] EWCA Civ 554).

In *PJS* v *News Group Newspapers* [2016] UKSC 26, the claimant, a well-known show business personality, sought to prevent the *Sun on Sunday* from publishing details of his sex-life. The claimant was married with two young children.

The newspaper's case was that publication of the material was in the public interest. This was so, it was argued, because, while the claimant had often courted publicity in order to further his career, he had not been open about his extra-marital activities.

The findings of the Court were:

(i)   there was no recognised public interest to be served by the publication of the details of a person's sexual infidelity;

(ii) the mere reporting of a person's sexual encounters outside of marriage did not fall within the meaning of freedom of expression as protected by ECHR Article 10;

(iii) the couple's children had 'independent privacy interests of their own' which would clearly have been damaged by publication of accounts of their parents' sex-lives.

Freedom of expression and advertising

Article 10 does not give an unfettered right for 'public space' to be used for particular expressions of opinion or commercial promotions. This was the decision of the Court of Appeal in *R (on application Core Issues Trust)* v *Transport for London* [2014] EWCA Civ 34, in which it was held that Transport for London had acted lawfully in refusing to allow advertising space to be used to publicise the applicant's views that homosexuality was unnatural and reversible.

> Individuals do not have an unconditional or unlimited right to the extended use of public space especially in relation to facilities intended for advertising or information campaigns. The ECtHR has clearly established that it is permissible for public bodies to restrict advertising on the basis of content provided that any restrictions are prescribed by law and necessary in the pursuit of a legitimate aim [and] that the exercise of the right of freedom of expression carried with it duties and responsibilities including a duty to avoid as far as possible an expression that is, in regard to objects of veneration, gratuitously offensive to others and profane.

Article 11: right to freedom of assembly and association

Freedom of assembly and expression of public feeling

The types of gathering covered by Art 11, and the extent to which it applies to meetings and assemblies not directly concerned with political issues or matters of public concern, was considered by the House of Lords in *R (on application of Countryside Alliance)* v *Attorney-General* [2007] UKHL 52.

As explained above, the case arose out of the ban on fox-hunting imposed by the Hunting Act 2004. The general opinion of the House of Lords was that the jurisprudence of Art 11 had not yet been developed to the point where the right could be regarded as applicable to assemblies held for purely sporting, recreational or social purposes. In combination with

Art 10 (freedom of expression), the right was said to be essential to the process of democracy and the demonstration of public feeling, but, beyond this, its protection did not go.

> There is a threshold which must be crossed before the Article becomes applicable. The purpose of the activity provides the key to its application. It covers meetings in private as well as in public, but it does not guarantee a right to assemble for purely social purposes. The right of assembly that the claimants seek to assert is no more than a right to gather together for pleasure and recreation . . . It falls well outside that the kind of assembly where protection is fundamental to the purpose and functioning of a modern democracy (Lord Hope).

Freedom of assembly, public order and national security

The common law's sometimes controversial powers to prevent breaches of the peace (see below), and particularly to take preventative action against wholly innocent persons (e.g. peaceful protesters and 'innocent bystanders') have also been considered in the context of Art 11. In *R (on application of Laporte)* v *Chief Constable* [2007] AC 105, the decision of the House of Lords was that the powers should not be used to prevent or restrict protests and demonstrations except where a breach of the peace was reasonably apprehended and 'imminent' in the sense of there being an immediate, pressing, threat and that, although the powers might be used against 'innocent' persons, this should only be done in 'extreme and exceptional circumstances' and as a measure of 'last resort'.

For more on this, and its application by the Court of Appeal in *Austin* v *Metropolitan Police Commissioner* [2007] EWCA Civ 989, see the discussion in Chapter 19, pp. 605–6.

The banning of protests and demonstrations for reasons of national security was at issue in *Tabernacle* v *Secretary of State for Defence* [2009] EWCA Civ 23. The case involved a challenge to the validity of the Atomic Weapons Establishment (AWE) Aldermaston Byelaws 2007. The byelaws had been made to prohibit the Women's Peace Camp situated close to the Aldermaston site. The view of the Court of Appeal was that if, for the purposes of Art 11(2), the byelaws were to be regarded as a justifiable interference with the protestors' freedom of assembly, it would be necessary for the government to show that they had been made for genuine security-related concerns and not just because the continued presence of the protesters was felt to be irritating or a nuisance – a requirement which the government was unable to satisfy.

> Rights worth having are unruly things. Demonstrations and protests are likely to be a nuisance. They are liable to be inconvenient and tiresome or at least perceived as such by those who are out of sympathy with them. Sometimes they are wrong-headed and misconceived. Sometimes they portray a type of arrogance which assumes that spreading the word is always more important than the mess which, often literally, the exercise leaves behind. As for the test, whether or not the [women's] cause is wrong-headed or misconceived is neither here nor there and, if their activities are inconvenient or tiresome, the Secretary of State's shoulders are surely broad enough to cope (*per* Laws LJ).

As indicated by the above comment, the courts would generally appear to accept that a certain level of 'nuisance' and/or 'inconvenience' may be an inherent and inevitable consequence of most, if not all, exercises of the right of peaceful assembly – particularly so if these take place in public places. Such nuisance and inconvenience may not always, therefore, be regarded as amounting to a 'pressing social need' justifying government intervention as this would render the right to be almost meaningless. It follows that only nuisance and inconvenience at the more serious end of the scale may be likely to be accepted as satisfying the pressing social need test.

This more serious type of disruption was evident in the facts of the *City of London Corporation* v *Samede* [2012] EWHC 34 (QB) – the case arising out of the creation of an anti-capitalism protest camp in the immediate environs of St Paul's Cathedral, London. In reaching its decision that there had been 'substantial objective justification' for the issuing of injunctions ordering the dispersal of the camp, the court was clearly much exercised by the extent of the camp's impact on a wide range of private and public interests and relevant legal proscriptions, viz. interference with the property rights of the Church and City of London, obstruction of the highway, breach of planning laws, interference with the Art 9 rights of those visiting to worship in the Cathedral, damage to local businesses and to the work and morale of Cathedral staff, overloading of the local drainage system, and an increase in local criminal activity and anti-social behaviour.

Article 12: right to marry and found a family

Article 12 does not give an absolute right to marry and procreate in all circumstances. It is expressed to be subject to the laws of the state and may also be required to give way to rational and legitimate public policy considerations (*R (on application of Mellor)* v *Secretary of State for the Home Department* [2001] EWCA Civ 472).

> But from the earliest days the right to marry has been described as fundamental, it has been clear that the scope afforded to national law is not unlimited and it has been emphasised that national laws . . . must never injure or impair the substance of the right and must not deprive a person or category of person of full legal capacity of the right to marry or substantially interfere with the exercise of the right (Lord Bingham, *R (on application of Baiai)* v *Home Secretary* [2008] UKHL 53).

Hence it has been held that a person serving a prison sentence could not rely on Art 12 as the basis of a claim that prison policy prohibiting inmates to start families through artificial insemination contravened the ECHR as this was irrational in the common law sense.

> The purpose of imprisonment . . . is to punish the criminal by depriving him of certain rights and pleasures which he can only enjoy when at liberty. Those rights and pleasures include the enjoyment of family life, the exercise of conjugal rights and the right to found a family . . . a prisoner cannot procreate by the medium of artificial insemination without the positive assistance of the prison authorities. In the absence of exceptional circumstances, they commit no infringement of Art 12 if they decline to provide that assistance (Lord Phillips MR, *Mellor*, *supra*).

In *R (on application of Baiai)* v *Home Secretary* (supra), the requirement that persons subject to immigration control be granted ministerial consent, as a precondition to entering into a marriage recognised by domestic law (Asylum and Immigration (Treatment of Claimants) Act 2004) was held not incompatible with Art 12 providing it was read subject to the proviso that permission should be refused only in cases of 'marriages of convenience', i.e. those entered into for immigration purposes. Article 12 was pleaded successfully in *R (on application of Aqyular Quila* v *Secretary of State for the Home Department* [2010] EWCA Civ 1482 – a case concerned with r 277 of the Immigration Rules then in force. This prohibited foreign nationals between the ages of 18 and 21 from entering the United Kingdom to live with married partners with the right to reside here, and also aged between 18 and 21. Such blanket prohibition, it was felt, without reference to the facts and circumstances of individual cases, could not be regarded as a proportionate way of attempting to deal with the government's particular objective, i.e. the increased incidence of forced marriages and associated criminal activities.

Derogation from the Human Rights Act

Objective 7

Section 14 of the 1998 Act allows the UK government to derogate from the full force of Convention requirements in those circumstances identified by the Convention in Art 15 – i.e. in a 'public emergency threatening the life of the nation' and to an extent 'strictly required by the exigencies of the situation'.

The first use of s 14 was made in 2001. The Human Rights Act 1998 (Designated Deroga-tion) Order 2001 was introduced by the government in an attempt to prevent judicial attacks on s 23 of the Anti-Terrorism Crime and Security Act 2001, viz. the power to detain foreign 'terrorist suspects for indefinite periods'. The Order was, however, challenged suc-cessfully in *A and Others* v *Secretary of State for the Home Department* (*supra*) where, for the reason explained on p. 522, the House of Lords took the view that the powers in s 23 could not be regarded as 'strictly required by the exigencies of the situation' and that there was, therefore, no legal basis for the Derogation Order.

The House did accept, however, that post '9/11' it was not unreasonable for the govern-ment to take the view that the United Kingdom was facing a public emergency threaten-ing the life of the nation. In more general terms, their Lordships went on to say that the existence or otherwise of such emergency was largely a political question in which the executive should be allowed a wide, if not wholly unlimited, margin of discretion. Lord Hope's view was that 'there was ample evidence to show that the government was fully justified in taking the view in November 2001 that there was an emergency threatening the life of the nation' and that this was 'pre-eminently for the executive and Parliament' to decide.

Summary

The chapter explains the reasons for the passing of the Human Rights Act 1998 and further encompasses:

- the powers given to domestic courts to deal with inconsistencies and conflicts between statutes and human rights requirements;
- whether, and in what circumstances, the 1998 Act may be applied retrospectively;
- judicial review of government decisions alleged to contravene human rights obligations;
- application of the Act in the United Kingdom since it took effect in October 2000.

References

Amos (2014) *Human Rights Law: A Textbook for UK Lawyers,* London: Hart Publishing.

Labour Party (1996) *Bringing Rights Home.*

Loveland (1996) *Constitutional Law: A Critical Introduction,* London: Butterworths.

Rights Brought Home: The Human Rights Bill (1997) Cm 3782

Further reading

Amos (2014) *Human Rights Law (2nd edn),* Oregon: Hart Publishing.

Clayton and Tomlinson (2009) *The Law of Human Rights* (2nd edn), Oxford: Oxford University Press.

Dickson (2012) *Human Rights and the United Kingdom Supreme Court,* Oxford: Oxford University Press.

Rowe and Hoffman (2013) *Human Rights in the United Kingdom (4th edn),* Harlow : Pearson.

Wadham and Mountfield (2015) *Blackstone's Guide to the Human Rights Act 1998* (7th edn), Oxford: Oxford University Press.

18

Police powers, personal liberty and privacy

Objectives

After reading this chapter you should:

1. Understand the extent of the police power of stop and search.

2. Be aware of the extent of the police power of arrest without warrant.

3. Recognise the extent of the citizen's power of arrest.

4. Know the rules regulating the process of questioning and detention in custody.

5. Understand the extent of the police powers of entry and search with and without warrant.

6. Appreciate the content of the rules regulating police access to 'privileged', 'excluded' and 'special procedure' material.

7. Understand the scope of, and limitations on, the rules relating to state access and use of communications and communications data.

8. Be aware of the remedies for police malpractice or abuse of power.

9. Have an understanding of the power of Police Community Support Officers.

Personal freedom

In a free society it is generally assumed that the individuals should be able to go about their business without fear of arbitrary arrest and detention or other forms of capricious interference with their personal liberty or privacy. Impositions on personal liberty should have a clear legal foundation, should not be a matter of wide executive discretion and, in normal circumstances, should exist only where this is reasonably necessary for the prevention of crime and the preservation of public order.

Personal freedom in the United Kingdom is restricted by a variety of statutory and common law rules. The principal statutory provision operating in this context is the Police and Criminal Evidence Act 1984 (PACE). This confers power on the police to stop and search, to arrest without warrant, to detain for questioning, to enter private premises to arrest suspects and persons unlawfully at large, and to search both persons and premises for evidence of offences. The 1984 Act also provides the individual with various safeguards and rights (e.g. the right to legal advice) which the police are required to observe in the exercise of these powers. Further extensive powers were conferred on the police by the Serious Organised Crime and Police Act 2005, and by the Terrorism Acts 2000, 2006 and 2011.

The principal rules empowering and regulating police conduct in the Police and Criminal Evidence Act 1984 are supplemented by eight Codes of Practice (CoP) made under ss 60 and 66. These are Code A, stop and search; Code B, entry and search of premises; Code C, detention and questioning; Code D, identification of suspects; Code E, audio-recording of interviews; Code F, visual recording of interviews; Code G, arrest; and Code H detention and questioning of terrorist suspects. These may be revised from time to time and provide a detailed practical framework for the exercise of the powers already referred to. The Codes are not, however, directly enforceable. Hence no civil or criminal proceedings may be founded solely on a police officer's failure to comply with them (s 67). This should not be taken as meaning that the Codes are purely advisory or that they can be ignored with impunity. Hence, abuse of the Codes is made an express ground of police disciplinary proceedings (s 67(8)). A further pressure for compliance is the power of the trial court to rule that evidence gained in breach of Code requirements may be regarded as inadmissible.

Stop and search

Before PACE

The position at common law

Objective 1

No common law power exists allowing a police officer to physically stop and detain an individual, even for a short period, either for the purpose of search or questioning. Hence, short of arrest, or where the statutory powers of stop–search are available, a police officer may stop, search and/or question only with the individual's consent. In *Rice* v *Connolly* [1966] 2 QB 414, it was held that, although every citizen had a moral duty to assist the police, there was no legal duty to that effect. It follows that a failure to stop and answer police questions does not, *per se*, amount to an obstruction of a police officer in the execution of their duty. It is also no obstruction to tell a person not to answer police questions (*Green* v *DPP* [1991] Crim LR 782).

Technically, therefore, every non-consensual physical contact between a police officer and a member of the public would appear to amount to a trespass. It has been held, however, that a police officer, in order to do their duty, may do that which is reasonable in the circumstances to attract a person's attention and that this may include physical touching such as a tap on the shoulder (*Donnelly* v *Jackman* [1970] 1 All ER 987). In *Collins* v *Wilcock* [1984] 3 All ER 374, however, it was held that a police officer who wished to talk to a woman had no power to take hold of her arm to prevent her walking away. The court expressed the view that in each case the test must be 'whether the physical conduct so persisted in has, in the circumstances, gone beyond generally accepted standards of conduct; and the answer to that question will depend on the facts of the particular case' (per Goff LJ). In *Mepstead* v *DPP* [1996] Crim LR 111, therefore, taking hold of a person's arm in order to get him to calm down and listen to what was being said to him did not take the police officer outside his course of duty. In this instance a limited degree of physical force was justified in order to enable the officer involved to gain control of the situation and convey information to the individual about the nature and consequences of his behaviour. This may be further contrasted with *Bentley* v *Brudzinski* (1982) 75 Crim App Rep 217, where the unlawful physical taking hold of the individual to prevent his departure, took place after he had stopped and, in a calm and orderly way, answered the questions which had been put to him.

Stop and search in PACE

Who may be searched and for what

Section 1 of the Act confers a general power to stop and search 'any person or vehicle' for 'stolen or prohibited articles' (s 1(2)). Prohibited articles include anything made or adapted for use in connection with certain offences (burglary, theft, taking and driving away, obtaining by deception, criminal damage) or intended for use in relation to these offences. Hence, providing the article was made or adapted for any of the prescribed purposes, the power exists, even though the possession is 'innocent' in the sense that there is no intention to use the thing for an illegal purpose. Also, the possession of ostensibly innocent articles (e.g. a screwdriver), if intended for use in connection with any of the specified offences, would also provide grounds for lawful exercise of the power.

In addition to the above, the term 'prohibited articles' also applies to 'offensive weapons'. These include any article made or adapted for causing injury to persons (therefore, presumably, not animals) or intended for such use by the person in possession or any other person (e.g. an accomplice).

Hence, as with articles related to the commission of offences, stop–search would be justified even though the person in possession did not intend to use the thing to cause injury. Thus, for example, possession of an item of World War II memorabilia (i.e. bayonet, grenade and pistol) would probably provide grounds for search. In similar fashion, use of the power would also appear to be justified where the article would normally be regarded as harmless (e.g. knitting needles), but the person in possession intends to cause injury with it.

The Serious Organised Crime and Police Act, s 15, amended PACE, s 1, to give police officers an additional power to stop and search for display fireworks.

According to the Code of Practice introduced in 2014, powers to stop and search should be used 'fairly, responsibly, and with respect for people being searched and without unlawful discrimination'. The Race Relations (Amendment) Act 2000 makes it unlawful for police officers to discriminate on the grounds of race, colour, ethnic origin, nationality or national origins when using their powers.

Where the power may be used

The power may be used in any place to which members of the public have a right of access 'on payment or otherwise' or by express or implied permission. This would include, therefore, pubs, cinemas, sports stadia, etc. The power may also be exercised in 'any place to which people have a ready access . . . and which is not a dwelling'. This includes places where members of the public have no right to go but to which it is easy for them to gain access – e.g. private premises and buildings, but not dwellings – without fear of interference, and open spaces such as playing fields where no significant effort is made to keep the public out.

If the person is in the garden or yard of an occupied dwelling, the power may not be used unless the police officer reasonably believes that the person does not live there or does not have express or implied permission to be there.

Reasonable grounds

There must be reasonable grounds for suspecting that stolen or prohibited articles will be revealed by the search. It would appear that reasonable grounds may exist even though the person was in 'innocent' possession – i.e. did not know that they were in possession or did know but was not aware that the item was stolen or prohibited. Reasonable grounds should not be based on purely 'personal factors', e.g. colour, hairstyle, dress, age, previous convictions or stereotyped images of certain persons.

The Code of Practice states that:

> Reasonable suspicion cannot be supported on the basis of personal, racial, cultural or religious factors alone. Rather, it should be supported by accurate and current information which relates to the possession of an article for which there is a power to stop and search.

Prior to the search

The person may be detained for as long as is reasonably necessary for the purposes of the search (s 2). The grounds for suspicion must exist before this is done. In the absence of such pre-existing grounds there is no power to stop and question to see if any can be found. Where grounds to stop and search do exist, the person may be questioned to see if they have a satisfactory explanation sufficient to remove the officer's suspicion. If so the search should not take place.

Before any search, reasonable steps should be taken to inform the person to be searched (or in charge of the vehicle) of the following:

(a) the officer's name (except in terrorist investigations) and the station to which they are attached and, if not in uniform, their warrant card;

(b) the object of the search;

(c) the right to a copy of the written record of the search;

(d) the reason for the stop and search (*R v Fennelley* [1989] Crim LR 142).

Failure to provide the information in (a) has been held to render the search unlawful (*Osman v DPP* (1999) 163 JP 725; *R v Bristol* [2007] EWCA Crim 3214).

Conduct of the search

The search should be carried out at the place where the person or vehicle was detained or 'nearby'. The meaning of 'nearby' is not defined by the Act but the following may be a reasonable representation of Parliament's intention:

> it is submitted that it should be interpreted quite narrowly. To move a vehicle from a congested spot into a side street, or a person from the public gaze into an alley, would be a reasonable action to take and would not prevent the search from being 'nearby' (Card and English, *Butterworths' Police Law*).

The person or vehicle should not be detained for longer than is reasonably necessary to complete the search. The extent of the search should be determined by what is reasonably necessary to achieve its objective – i.e. if the person is reasonably believed to have put a stolen or prohibited article into his pocket then the search should be limited to that pocket.

If the search is conducted in public it should be restricted to a superficial examination of outer clothing. Other garments such as an outer coat, gloves and jacket may not be required to be removed, although this may be requested. Where reasonable grounds exist for a more thorough search (e.g. removal of shirt), this should be done out of public view – in a police van, for example – and by an officer of the same sex without an officer of the other sex being present unless the person to be searched so requests. A search in an empty street is in public.

In every case the police should seek to carry out the search with the individual's cooperation. A forcible search may be made only where the person refuses to cooperate or resists. In this case reasonable force may be used.

PACE, s 1, does not give police officers any express power to require persons to 'stop and account' for their activities, nor is there any other explicit statutory basis for this.

Voluntary searches

Code of Practice A, states that 'an officer must not search a person, even with his or her consent, where no power to search is applicable' and that:

> even where a person is prepared to submit to a search voluntarily, the person must not be searched unless the necessary legal power exists and the search must be in accordance with the relevant power and the provisions of this Code. The only exception, where an officer does not require a specific power, applies to searches of persons entering sports grounds or other premises carried out with their consent as a condition of entry.

This would appear to be a self-imposed, practical limitation, rather than a statement of law as, where a person fully and freely consents to be searched, it is unlikely that a trespass would be committed. Thus, the Code of Practice in force until 2006 expressly contemplated 'voluntary searches', providing it was made clear to the person affected that they were not under legal compulsion.

After the search

A written record must be completed on the spot or as soon as reasonably practicable afterwards. This should include the person's ethnic type, the officer's identity, the object and grounds for the search, the date, time and place it occurred and whether or not the action led to anyone being arrested.

Note that there is no power to require the person to reveal their name or other personal details (it is a power to search not to question).

Searching vehicles

The power extends to anything which is in or on the vehicle, the contents of a roof rack or containers or packages on the back of an open lorry.

If the vehicle is in a yard or garden attached to and used in connection with an occupied dwelling, the officer may not search unless they reasonably believe that the person in charge of the vehicle does not live in the dwelling or the vehicle is there without the occupier's permission.

After searching an unattended vehicle the officer should leave a notice stating that they have searched it, the name of the police station to which they are attached, that an application may be made for compensation for any damage caused and where a copy of the search record may be obtained. The notice should be left inside the vehicle if reasonably practicable without causing damage. Where practicable the vehicle should be left secure.

Stopping vehicles

Note that the provisions in the 1984 Act relating to the searching of vehicles do not contain any express power to stop a vehicle for this purpose. There is, of course, nothing to prevent an officer signalling or requesting that a vehicle be brought to rest preparatory to using the stop–search power.

Otherwise, powers to stop vehicles may be found elsewhere in both statute and the common law. The most significant statutory power is contained in the Road Traffic Act 1988 (RTA), s 163(1). This provides that a person driving a motor vehicle must stop when ordered to do so by a police officer in uniform. Section 163(2) makes similar provision in relation to cyclists. It is an offence to disobey (s 163(3)). It would appear that this power may be used to facilitate performance of any of the officer's legitimate duties. Hence, if after using the power, the officer formed reasonable grounds for searching either the vehicle or the driver they could proceed to exercise the stop–search power. It would, however, probably be an abuse of s 163 for the officer to stop a vehicle for no better reason than to discover if grounds for a search could be found.

Section 163 is generally regarded as containing an implied obligation on the driver to remain at rest for a reasonable period to enable the officer to carry out their duty but confers no power to detain either the vehicle or the driver unless some specific suspicion of an offence exists (e.g. that the vehicle is stolen) or arises immediately after the vehicle has been brought to rest (see *Lodwick* v *Saunders* [1985] 1 WLR 382).

There would also appear to be a common law power to stop a vehicle as part of the officer's duty to investigate and prevent crime (see *Steel* v *Goacher* [1983] RTR 98).

A vehicle or vehicles may also be stopped where this is reasonably believed to be necessary to prevent a breach of the peace (see *Moss* v *McLachlan* (1984) 149 JP 167).

Road checks

The 1984 Act also seeks to regulate the use of RTA, s 163 for general road checks – i.e. where, for the period of the check, all or selected vehicles in a particular locality are stopped. Section 4 provides that such general checks may be authorised by a superintendent or above where the police:

- are investigating an indictable offence which has been or may be committed and have reasonable grounds for suspecting the suspect to be in the locality;
- are looking for a witness to such an offence;
- are looking for a person unlawfully at large.

A road check may be authorised by an officer below the rank of superintendent where this 'appears to him' (subjective) to be a matter of urgency for any of the above purposes.

A road check should not continue beyond seven days. This is a power to stop at random without any particular suspicion relating to the vehicle in question or its occupants.

Stop and search in the Criminal Justice and Public Order Act 1994

The power in the 1994 Act is contained in s 60. This allows a police officer of the rank of superintendent or above to authorise the stopping and searching of persons and vehicles for offensive weapons or dangerous instruments where they reasonably believe that incidents of serious violence will take place in their police area and it is necessary to use the power to prevent their occurrence. If it is reasonably believed that incidents of serious violence are imminent and no superintendent is available, the power may be exercised by a chief inspector or inspector. Such authorisation may be for any period up to 15 hours and may be extended for a further six hours by a superintendent or the officer responsible for the original authorisation.

It will be noted that this section permits the searching of any person or vehicle even though no specific suspicion exists relating thereto.

> A constable may, in the exercise of those powers, stop any person or vehicle and make any search he thinks fit whether or not he has any reasonable grounds for suspecting that the person or vehicle is carrying weapons or articles of that kind. (s 60(5))
>
> Notwithstanding the lack of need for reasonable suspicion, section 60 should not be understood as conferring an unlimited power to stop and search any person or vehicle as and when an office may wish. In particular, the power must be exercised for the purposes for which the authorisation was given only, i.e. to prevent reasonably apprehended incidents of serious violence. It may not be relied upon, therefore, to stop and search persons or vehicles for reasons unconnected with the authorisation (*R on application of Roberts* v *Commissioner of Police of the Metropolis Commissioner* [2014] EWCA Civ 69).

The 'suspicion-less' stop–search power in s 60 is not incompatible with the right to respect to private life enshrined in the European Convention on Human Rights, Art 8(1). This is so because, whatever its scope, it must still be exercised in accordance with all the human rights requirements imposed by the Convention and without discrimination. This, together with the disciplinary sanctions which may be imposed on officers who abuse their powers, 'guard against the risk that the section 60 power will be exercised when the officer does not in fact have good reasons for the decision' (*R (on application of Roberts)* v *Commissioner of Police for the Metropolis* [2015] UKSC 79).

Violent Crime Reduction Act 2006

Sections 45 and 46 of the Act permit authorised members of staff to stop and search any school pupil or college student reasonably suspected of possessing a knife or other offensive weapon on school or college premises.

Other stop–search powers for the purpose of controlling specific types of illegal activity may be found in the Crossbows Act 1987, the Deer Act 1991, the Protection of Badgers Act 1992 (also see, in the context of wildlife preservation, the stop–search powers in the Poaching Prevention Act 1862, the Conservation of Seals Act 1970 and the Wildlife and Countryside Act 1981), the Prevention of Terrorism Acts 1989, 1996, the Terrorism Act 2000 and the Terrorism Prevention and Investigatory Measures Act 2011.

Arrest

Some general comments

Powers of arrest in the United Kingdom may be found in a variety of statutory and common law provisions. A statute may authorise an individual's arrest:

- only after a warrant has been issued by a magistrate;
- without a warrant in specified circumstances – usually for the apprehension of someone suspected of one of the more serious types of criminal offence (i.e. an 'indictable offence').

A person may also be arrested without warrant under a number of surviving common law powers – principally to prevent breaches of the peace and, in certain circumstances, for obstruction of a police officer in the course of their duty.

In practice, most arrests are now effected under statutory powers and without warrant – the principal powers being those contained in PACE, s 24. One of the objectives of the Act was to introduce some order and clarity into the wide range of statutory and common law powers of arrest hitherto existing. Hence, subject to certain exceptions listed in Sched 2, all such previous powers were repealed (see s 26) and replaced by the general powers of arrest in the above sections.

The purpose of an arrest

Until relatively recent times it was assumed that the power of arrest existed principally to allow the authorities to bring a person before a court to answer charges of a criminal nature. It is now accepted, however, that a person who is suspected of an offence may be arrested and brought into custody for the purpose of questioning related thereto (*Holgate-Mohammed* v *Duke* [1984] AC 437). Also, an arrest is probably not unlawful if the requisite suspicion exists and the correct reasons for it are given albeit that the arrest has been effected in the course of the investigation of other more serious offences, i.e. as a 'holding charge', and does not represent, therefore, the primary motivation for taking the suspect into custody (*R* v *Chalkley*; *R* v *Jeffries* [1998] 2 All ER 155).

In most circumstances police officers have a *power* rather than a *duty* to arrest. This should be exercised according to conventional public law principles of reasonableness and rationality (*Holgate-Mohammed* v *Duke, supra*). The intensity of this domestic standard of review would appear to have been increased by the passing of the Human Rights Act.

> Although Art 5 of the ECHR does not require the court to evaluate the exercise of discretion in any different way than it evaluates the exercise of any other discretion, it must do so in the light of the important liberty which is at stake (Brooke LJ, *Paul* v *Chief Constable Humberside Police* [2004] EWCA Civ 308, approving the views of Latham LJ in *Cummings* v *Chief Constable of Northumbria Police* [2003] EWCA Civ 1844).

Related guidance for police officers in the relevant Code of Practice includes:

> The use of the power must be fully justified and officers exercising the power should consider if the necessary objectives can be met by other, less intrusive means. Arrest must never be used simply because it can be used (CoP G, para 1.3).

Arrest without warrant

Objective 2

Prior to the Serious Organised Crime and Police Act (SOCPA), PACE contained two major powers of arrest without warrant. These were to be found in ss 24 and 25. Section 24 gave police officers a power to arrest without warrant any person reasonably suspected of committing, being about to commit, or having committed an arrestable offence; generally defined as an offence for which a person could be sentenced to a term of imprisonment of five years or more. In practical operational terms, this was the main power of arrest available to police officers from the time PACE came into effect at the beginning of 1986.

Section 25 allowed a police officer to arrest without warrant any person reasonably suspected of committing or having committed a 'non-arrestable offence', i.e. an offence not carrying a term of imprisonment of five years or more, where one of the 'arrest conditions' had been satisfied. These included that the person was suspected of having given a false name and/or address or that it was necessary to make an arrest to prevent physical harm or damage being done.

Major amendments to s 24 were affected by SOCPA, s 110, which also repealed s 25 entirely. The amended version of s 24 provides that a police officer may arrest without warrant any person who:

- is about to commit an offence;
- is committing an offence;
- they have reasonable grounds for suspecting is about to commit an offence;
- they have reasonable grounds for suspecting is committing an offence;
- they have reasonable grounds for suspecting has committed an offence.

It will be noted that the concepts of arrestable and non-arrestable offences have been abolished. The revised power allows police officers to arrest without warrant in respect of the commission or intent to commit *any* crime and facilitates arrest, therefore, for relatively minor offences in circumstances not hitherto permitted by PACE, s 25.

Ingredients of a valid arrest

An arrest is not lawful simply because a police officer is executing a power vested in him/her by statute or the common law. A number of other important requirements may have to be satisfied if such an intrusion into a person's personal liberty is to be regarded as justifiable. Thus, in many circumstances, for example, valid exercise of the power in s 24 will depend on the existence of reasonable suspicion, and fulfilling the test of 'necessity' introduced by SOCPA, s 110. Also PACE s 28 provides that an arrest is not valid unless the person is told that they are under arrest and given the reasons for it.

Reasonable suspicion

The existence of sufficient grounds for an arrest rests on the answers to three questions. These were set out by Sir Anthony Clarke MR in *Raissi* v *Metropolitan Police Commissioner* [2008] EWCA 2842 and repeated by Richards LJ in *Alford* v *Chief Constable of Cambridgeshire Police* [2009] EWCA Civ 100.

1 Did the arresting officer suspect that the person who was arrested was guilty of the offence? The answer to this question depends entirely on the findings of fact as to the officer's state of mind.

2 Assuming the officer had the necessary suspicion, was there reasonable cause for suspicion? This is purely an objective requirement to be determined by the judge if necessary on the facts found by a jury.

3 If the answer to the two previous questions is in the affirmative, then the officer has a discretion which entitles him to make an arrest and that . . . discretion has to be exercised in accordance with the principles laid down by Lord Greene MR in *Associated Provincial Picture Houses Ltd* v *Wednesbury Corporation* [1948] 1 KB 223, i.e. the test of reasonableness.

Powers of arrest unqualified by the need for reasonable suspicion are not compatible with the European Convention on Human Rights, Art 5 (*Fox, Campbell and Hartley* v *United Kingdom* (1990) 13 EHRR 157; *Stepuleac* v *Moldova*, app no 8207/06, 6.11.07). Reasonable suspicion must be based on something more than a person's previous record or the officer's personal prejudices in matters of personal appearance, lifestyle, race, etc.

The cases indicate, however, that – in terms of the amount of relevant evidence or information which a police officer must possess in order to justify an arrest – this is not a particularly demanding requirement. The test is satisfied if a police officer acts on the basis of evidence or information which enables a plausible connection to be made between the suspect and a particular offence. Simply being 'uncooperative and truculent' in response to police questions does not, of itself, give sufficient basis for a reasonable suspicion (*Alanov* v *Chief Constable of Sussex Police* [2012] EWCA 234). Nor is it necessary that sufficient evidence exists to charge the person with an offence or that the information on which the suspicion is based is something which could be put before a court as evidence (*Holtham* v *Commissioner of Police of the Metropolis*, *The Times*, 8 January 1987).

Note that other powers in PACE may be used only where there is a reasonable *belief* in the existence of certain facts. Hence the power to enter private premises without warrant for the purpose of effecting an arrest exists where it is reasonably believed, *inter alia*, that a person who has committed an indictable offence may be found there (s 17). It is generally accepted that 'reasonable belief' denotes a state of mind which has progressed well beyond mere suspicion to a point which approaches certainty or conviction. Such state of conviction is not, therefore, a prerequisite of a valid arrest. It is enough that sufficient evidence exists to raise sufficient doubt in the officer's mind to justify further inquiries.

In *Castorina* v *Chief Constable of Surrey* [1988] NLJR 180, police officers went to investigate a burglary at the premises of the plaintiff's former employer. The plaintiff had been 'sacked' a short time before the offence was committed. The evidence suggested that it was an 'inside job' and may have been the work of someone bearing a grudge. On this basis the plaintiff was arrested and detained for questioning in police custody for nearly four hours. She was then released without charge.

Her action for false arrest and imprisonment was upheld in the County Court. The arrest could not have been lawful, it was held, unless the officers 'had an honest belief founded on a reasonable suspicion leading an ordinary cautious man to the conclusion that the person arrested was guilty of the offence'. The court did not accept that on the small amount of evidence available to the officers they could have reached such a conclusion. On appeal, however, the Court of Appeal rejected this test as being too severe. It was not necessary that the arresting officers had evidence which led them to believe or conclude that the suspect was guilty. All that was required was that they had acted on evidence which would have caused a reasonable person to *suspect* the plaintiff (see also *Bull* v *Chief Constable of Sussex* (1995) 159 LG Rev 893).

The reasonable grounds for an arrest must be in the mind of the officer who effects it. These need not, however, be based on their own observations or inquiries but may, for example, be founded on information supplied by other officers or informers (*O'Hara* v *Chief Constable of Royal Ulster Constabulary* [1997] 1 All ER 129) or on that supplied by police computer records (*Hough* v *Chief Constable of Staffordshire Police* [2001] EWCA Civ 39).

A suspicion is not reasonable if it is based solely on a person's friends or associates. Hence, no reasonable grounds for arresting a person exist simply because a person is closely related to or on close terms with a person or persons whom the police do reasonably suspect to have committed offences (*Raissi* v *Metropolitan Police Commissioner* [2008] EWCA Civ 1237; *Buckley* v *Chief Constable of Thames Valley Police* [2009] EWCA Civ 356).

Necessity

Although a relatively recent new test introduced by SOCPA 2005, the requirement appears not wholly unrelated to the more long-standing common law principles of reasonableness and rationality as applied in the context of police powers (see above). The precise statutory obligation is that the powers of arrest conferred by PACE, s 24, should not be exercised unless the officer in question has reasonable grounds for believing that 'it is necessary to arrest the person in question' for any of the following reasons:

(a) to enable the name or address of the person . . . to be ascertained . . . ;

(b) to prevent the person in question:
    (i) causing physical injury to themselves or another person,
    (ii) suffering physical injury,
    (iii) causing loss of or damage to property,
    (iv) committing an offence against public decency,
    (v) causing an unlawful obstruction of the highway;

(c) to protect a vulnerable child from the person in question;

(d) to allow the prompt and effective investigation of the offence or of the conduct of the person in question;

(e) to prevent any prosecution for the offence being hindered by the person's disappearance.

The requirement that a police officer should not effect an arrest unless this is believed to be 'necessary' does not mean that he/she must consider and reject all possible alternative courses of action before the arrest is made. It has been recognised that any such obligation would prejudice the officer's ability to respond quickly, appropriately, and proportionately, to the situations with which he/she may be confronted.

> To require of a policeman that he pass through particular thought processes each time he considers an arrest and in all circumstances no matter what urgency or danger may attend a decision, and to subject that decision to the test of whether he has considered every material matter and excluded every immaterial matter, is to impose an unrealistic and unattainable burden. The officer ought to apply his mind to alternatives short of arrest, and if he does not do so he is open to challenge . . . But the challenge, if it comes, is not one which requires the officer's decision to be subjected to a full-blown reasons challenge. It is one which requires it to be shown that on the information known to the officer he had reasonable grounds for believing arrest to be necessary for an identified section 25(5) reason (Hughes LJ, *Hayes v Chief Constable of Merseyside Police* [2011] EWCA 911).

In *Lord Hanningford of Chelmsford v Chief Constable of Essex* [2013] EWHC (QB) 243, the claimant was a 72-year-old member of the House of Lords. He was suffering from high blood pressure and depression and had just been released from prison where he had been serving a sentence for fraudulent expenses claims relating to his parliamentary duties. The police went to his house at 6.45 am and arrested him on suspicion of further fraudulent expenses claims arising from the time when he was leader of Essex County Council. In upholding his claim for false arrest and imprisonment, the court could find no reasonable grounds on which it could have been believed that any of the arrest conditions for the test of necessity had been satisfied and particularly so, as in all previous dealings with the police, the claimant had not been obstructive in any way. Similar findings were made in *B and Others (Former Soldiers) v Police Service of Northern Ireland* [2015] EWHC 369, a case involving a number of ex-soldiers who had been part of the military operation which led to the killing of 13 civilians and the serious wounding of 14 others, in the city of Derry in the north of Ireland in January 1972 ('Bloody Sunday'). Here the decision was that, although there might have been reasonable grounds for suspicion on which to have arrested the soldiers, such action could not be deemed to have been necessary. This was so as the ex-soldiers had co-operated fully with current and previous inquiries into the events in question and remained ready to meet with, and be interviewed by, the Northern Irish police (PSNI) in any designated police station in England and Wales.

Fact of arrest

Section 28(1) of PACE provides that an arrest is not lawful unless the person is told that they are under arrest at the time of the arrest or as soon as reasonably practicable afterwards. No precise linguistic formula is required but the words and/or actions of the officer must be such that an ordinary reasonable person would be in no doubt that an arrest has taken place (*Wheatley v Lodge* [1971] 1 All ER 173). Statements such as 'I shall have to ask you to come to the police station' would appear to be inadequate to convey the necessary degree of compulsion (*Alderson v Booth* [1969] 3 QB 216). In another case, the words 'you must come with me' were held to be sufficient (*Tims v John Lewis and Co Ltd* [1952] AC 676).

When dealing with a person with serious hearing difficulties, it is not enough for the officers involved to make whatever adjustments to their usual practice they feel at the time to be appropriate. Rather, the police in general should adopt clear anticipatory policies and procedures for persons with different types of disability (*Finnigan v Chief Constable of Northumbria Police* [2013] EWCA Civ 1191).

Reasons for arrest

An arrest is also not lawful unless the person is informed of the grounds for arrest. Again this information should be given at the time of the arrest or as soon as reasonably practicable afterwards (PACE, s 28(3)). The arresting officer must give the grounds or reason even though this may be obvious. He or she need not, however, explain the reason in the precise legal terminology of the particular statute or common law offence. In *Abassy v Commissioner of Police of the Metropolis* [1990] 1 WLR 385, telling a person he had been arrested for 'unlawful possession' of a motor car was sufficient reason to support a valid arrest for taking a motor vehicle without consent under the Theft Act 1968.

Gelberg v Miller [1961] 1 All ER 291

In this case, G parked his car in a narrow street where parking was restricted. He was asked to move it by a police officer. When G refused, he was told he was being arrested for obstructing the officer by not moving his car. The officer's intention was to arrest G for obstructing him in the course of his duty. On the facts no power of arrest without warrant for this offence existed. G could have been arrested, however, for obstructing the highway. The court decided that the officer had not acted unlawfully. In the circumstances an offence arrestable without warrant had been committed, and the words used by the officer were sufficient to convey the general nature of that offence to G. It did not matter that the officer had an alternative offence in his mind nor that he had failed to use the precise terminology of obstruction of the highway.

> The whole point of the law is that the citizen must be told what the constable suspects he has done wrong. It does not have to be done in any technically precise way but . . . it must convey to the individual enough to show that the arrest is lawful. I have no difficulty with the proposition that technical or formal words are unnecessary. Although no constable ever admits to saying 'You're knicked for handling this gear' or 'I'm having you for twocing this motor', either will do and, I have no doubt, frequently does (Sedley LJ, *Clarke v Chief Constable of North Wales* [2000] All ER 477).

If reasons are not given at the time of arrest when it would have been reasonable to do so, the arrest is unlawful and the person affected has a right of action for unlawful arrest and imprisonment. If, however, reasons are given at some later stage, the arrest becomes lawful from that time onwards (*Lewis* v *Chief Constable of South Wales* [1991] 2 All ER 206). Similarly, if reasons are not given at the time of arrest because this would not have been reasonably practicable, and are still not given when it becomes reasonably practicable, the arrest becomes unlawful from that moment but again becomes lawful if and when the reasons are given (*DPP* v *Hawkins* [1988] 1 WLR 1166).

The requirements of s 28(3) would appear to be sufficient to comply with the obligations imposed by ECHR Art 5(2) (*Taylor* v *Chief Constable of Thames Valley Police* [2004] EWCA Civ 858).

Purpose of arrest

Article 5(1)(c) of the European Convention on Human Rights allows the police to arrest or detain a person 'for the purpose of bringing him before the competent legal authority on reasonable suspicion of having committed an offence or when it is reasonably considered necessary to prevent him committing an offence'. Clearly, therefore, the required 'purpose' for the arrest or detention need not be that of bringing the person before a court for the determination of his/her guilt or innocence. Rather, the primary reason for the requirement is to enable the 'competent legal authority' to inquire into the legality of the actions of the police and of the person's detention and thus to avoid the incidence of 'internment without trial' (*R (on application Hicks)* v *Commissioner of Police for the Metropolis* [2014] EWCA Civ 3).

The use of force

The Criminal Law Act 1967, s 3 permits as much force as is reasonable in the making of an arrest. PACE, s 117 permits the use of similar force in the exercise of other powers conferred by the Act. The use of excessive force does not invalidate an arrest but may be the cause of a civil action or criminal prosecution for assault (*Simpson* v *Chief Constable of South Yorkshire* (1991) 135 SLJ 383).

Search after arrest

Under PACE, s 32 a person who has been arrested may be searched if a police officer has reasonable grounds for believing that he/she:

● may present a danger to themselves or others;

● may be in possession of something which may be used to effect an escape;

● may be in possession of something which might be evidence of an offence.

Section 32 also empowers the police to search any premises where the arrested person was immediately before, or at the time of, the arrest for an indictable offence. Section 18 provides a further power to search any premises occupied or controlled by a person under arrest for an indictable offence.

As with other powers which interfere with private rights, the powers of search in PACE have been interpreted both literally and restrictively. Hence, in the exercise of the power in s 32, the premises to be searched must actually be occupied by the person under arrest. It was, therefore, a trespass for the police to enter and search premises which a person under arrest did not occupy, but had falsely given as his address. It did not matter that the police had acted reasonably and in good faith on the basis of the information given (***Khan v Metropolitan Police Commissioner*** [2008] EWCA Civ 723).

Citizen's arrest

Objective
3

PACE, s 24, as amended by SOCPA, s 110, allows a private citizen to arrest without warrant anyone who:

- is committing an indictable offence;
- he/she has reasonable grounds for suspecting to be committing an indictable offence;
- has committed an indictable offence;
- he/she has reasonable grounds for suspecting to have committed an indictable offence and that offence has been committed.

The person making the arrest must have reasonable grounds for believing that the arrest is necessary to prevent the suspected offender:

- causing physical injury to themselves or another person;
- suffering physical injury;
- causing loss or damage to property;
- making off before a constable can assume responsibility for them.

It must also be apparent to the person making the arrest that 'it is not reasonably practicable for a constable to make it instead'.

The citizen's power of arrest is narrower than that of the police officer in the following respects. First, the private citizen's power is limited to indictable offences. These are offences which should be tried by judge and jury and tend to be the more serious types of criminal activity. The concept is wider than that of 'arrestable offence' and would encompass some crimes which would not have fallen within the power of arrest found in the original version of s 24. Second, the private citizen has no power to arrest any person who is, or who is reasonably suspected to be, about to commit an indictable offence. Third, the private citizen has no power to arrest a person who is reasonably suspected of being guilty of an indictable offence if that offence has not been committed.

Hence, if A, a private citizen, reasonably suspects B of theft, and the particular theft has been committed by B or some other person, the arrest of B is lawful. If, however, A reasonably suspects B of theft but the particular theft has not been committed, either by B or anyone else, the arrest of B would be unlawful. Note that in the latter situation the arrest of B by a police officer with the requisite suspicion would be perfectly lawful. As explained above, a police officer may arrest without warrant any person reasonably suspected of having committed an indictable offence. The legality of the arrest is not affected in any way by the fact that the offence has not been committed.

R v Self [1992] 1 WLR 657

In this case, S was suspected of the theft of a bar of chocolate. He was followed from the shop and challenged by a shop assistant and store detective. They accused him of theft and told him he would have to return to the shop. A scuffle ensued and S ran away. A bystander who had witnessed all of this gave chase. After some resistance he managed to arrest S. S was then charged with theft and two counts of assault with intent to resist arrest. He was found not guilty of the theft. This meant that, although the shop assistant, store detective and bystander may have had reasonable grounds for suspecting S of being guilty of an arrestable offence, no such offence had been committed. In these circumstances, therefore, no citizen's power of arrest existed. From this it followed that S had been justified in acting as he did and could not be guilty of trying to resist a lawful arrest:

> section 24(5) makes it abundantly clear that the powers of arrest without warrant where an arrestable offence has been committed require as a condition precedent an offence committed. The power of arrest is confined to the person guilty of the offence or anyone who the person making the arrest has reasonable grounds for suspecting to be guilty of it (*per* Garland J).

The procedural requirements for a valid citizen's arrest are similar to those for arrest by a police officer. Hence, both the fact of and the grounds for the arrest must be communicated to the arrested person at the time of the arrest or as soon as is reasonably practicable afterwards. In the case of a citizen's arrest, however, the reasons or grounds for the arrest need not be given if these are obvious.

Arrest with warrant

There are a variety of statutory powers of arrest with warrant. Of these the most significant is the power contained in the Magistrates' Court Act 1980, s 1. The procedure commences by the person seeking the warrant – usually a police officer – laying information before a magistrate. This is a sworn statement identifying the particular offence a person is suspected of having committed. A warrant may only be issued in respect of a person over 17 years of age suspected of having committed an indictable offence or an offence punishable by imprisonment or whose particulars are insufficiently well known to enable a summons to be served.

To be valid the warrant must contain the name of the person to be arrested and the offence of which they are suspected. Where a police officer executes a warrant which the magistrate had no power to issue, the officer is protected from civil action by the Constables' Protection Act 1750 provided they acted in good faith.

The officer effecting the arrest need not have the warrant in their possession at the time but the arrested person has the right to see the warrant on demand as soon as possible (Magistrates' Courts Act 1980, s 125(3)).

A magistrate may also issue a warrant under the 1980 Act for the arrest of a person believed likely to give material evidence in a case before the court.

Arrest at common law

Any person may arrest without warrant:

- a person whom they have reasonable cause to believe will commit a breach of the peace if not apprehended;
- a person who is committing a breach of the peace in their presence;
- any person who it is reasonably suspected has committed a breach of the peace which, unless the person is arrested, will reoccur in the immediate future.

A breach of the peace is committed 'when harm is done or is likely to be done to a person or, in his presence, to his property or a person is put in fear of being harmed through an assault, an affray, a riot, unlawful assembly or other disturbance' (*R v Howell* [1982] QB 416). This is the only remaining common law power of arrest.

Detention and questioning

Designated and non-designated police stations

Objective
4

For the purpose of the reception and detention of persons who have been arrested, the 1984 Act distinguishes between designated and non-designated police stations. A designated police station is one which has the necessary facilities for the detention and interviewing of suspects. Stations without these facilities are non-designated police stations. Designation is a function of the chief constable for the police district in question (s 35).

An arrested person should be taken to a designated police station as soon as practicable unless:

(a) there is none in the locality;

(b) the arrest has been effected without assistance and it appears to the officer that they will be unable to take the arrested person to a designated police station without that person causing injury to themselves, the officer or some other person (s 30).

In either case, if the police wish to detain a person beyond six hours from the time of their arrival at a non-designated police station, that person should be taken to a designated station.

Arrival at the police station

When the arrested person arrives at the police station they should be taken before the custody officer as soon as practicable. This will usually be an officer of the rank of sergeant (s 35). The custody officer is responsible for ensuring that persons in detention are treated in accordance with the Act and its Codes of Practice and, in particular, that due observance is given to the rights and safeguards intended for those in police custody. The custody officer will decide whether there is sufficient evidence to charge the person with an offence. If so, the arrested person should be:

(a) released without charge and on bail;

(b) kept in police detention to enable the Crown Prosecution Service to decide whether to charge or not;

(c) released without charge and without bail; or

(d) charged.

If the custody officer is not so convinced, he/she may order that the person be released or detained for questioning. A decision to detain for questioning may be made only if the custody officer has reasonable grounds for believing that this is 'necessary to secure or preserve evidence relating to an offence for which [the suspect] is under arrest or to obtain such evidence by questioning him' (s 37). The suspect should be informed of:

- the grounds for detention;
- the right to have a friend, relative or other interested person know of their arrest;
- the right to consult privately with a solicitor;
- the right to see the Codes of Practice (s 38).

The first 24 hours

The arrested person may then be detained for questioning for up to 24 hours calculated from the time they first arrived at the police station (s 41). The custody officer's decision authorising such detention must be reviewed within six hours of its making and thereafter at intervals of not less than nine hours. If this is not done the detention becomes unlawful (*Roberts* v *Jones* [1999] 1 WLR 662). The questioning should cease, however, once the investigating officer believes that enough evidence has been obtained to charge the person with an offence. The person should then be taken before the custody officer for that purpose (CoP C, para 11.4).

After 24 hours (continued detention)

If at the expiry of 24 hours the person has not been charged, he/she should be released unless an officer of the rank of superintendent or above has reasonable grounds for believing that the person may have committed an indictable offence and that the person's continued detention for questioning for any period of up to 12 hours is necessary to secure evidence relating thereto (s 42). The person should be given the grounds for continued detention and be given the opportunity to make representations personally or through a solicitor. Failure to do so may result in the continued detention being held to be illegal (*Re an Application for a Warrant of Further Detention* [1988] Crim LR 296). In effect, therefore, the police are authorised to keep a person suspected of a serious offence in custody without charge for up to 36 hours.

After 36 hours (further detention)

Should the police wish to hold the person in custody for longer than 36 hours they must apply to a magistrate for a warrant of further detention (s 43). The application must be made before the 36 hours has elapsed unless it is not practicable for the court to which the application is to be made to sit before the expiry time. In this case, a further 6 hours is permitted within which the application can be made. The police must satisfy the magistrate that they are investigating an indictable offence and that further questioning of the detained person is necessary to secure, preserve or obtain relevant evidence. If so satisfied a warrant may be issued authorising the police to keep the person in detention for whatever further period the court deems fit, up to a maximum of 36 hours. This could bring the total period for which the person has been held since arriving at the police station up to 72 hours. The detained person has the right to be present at the hearing and to be legally represented. Should an application of a warrant of further detention be made after the elapse of 36 hours in circumstances where it would have been practicable to deal with the matter within the specified time, the warrant is invalid and the person's further detention is unlawful (*R* v *Slough Justices, ex parte Stirling* [1987] Crim LR 576; *R* v *Sedgefield Justices, ex parte Milne* (1981) unreported).

Extension of further detention

Prior to the expiry of the warrant of further detention the police may apply for an extension of the permitted time (s 44). The grounds and procedure for making such application are the same as those for granting further detention. The period of extension may be for any time the magistrates deem appropriate provided that this does not take the total period for which the person has been in detention to above 96 hours. This, therefore, is the maximum period for which a person may be held in custody without charge (save, that is, for the special provision in the Prevention of Terrorism Acts).

Detention and bail

Where a person who has been arrested and detained is then released on bail, but is rearrested for failing to answer the bail or to comply with any of the conditions attached to it (see PACE, s 46A), the time already spent in detention should be counted in calculating how much longer he/she may be detained for and when the periodic reviews of detention, and any applications for continued or further detention, should be made (Police (Detention and Bail) Act 2011, s 1).

Interviewing suspects

The Police and Criminal Evidence Act 1984 and Code of Practice C provide a number of key safeguards designed to minimise the possibility of malpractice during the process of questioning. The use of improper methods which are calculated to 'make the suspect talk' may often seek to achieve this by undermining his/her free will. However, this often serves only to cast doubt on the absolute credibility of any statement or confession the suspect may have made. Such material is, therefore, of little use as evidence.

The principal safeguards are:

- that a contemporaneous electronically recorded or written record must be kept of the conduct and content of the interview;
- that the suspect should be cautioned before being questioned about any offence they are suspected of committing;
- that the suspect should be given access to legal advice;
- that the suspect should not be subjected to continuous questioning without breaks for rest and refreshment.

Code of Practice C, provides that 'an interview is the questioning of a person regarding his involvement or suspected involvement in a criminal offence'. The Code further provides that such interview should take place at a police station unless the consequent delay would be likely to lead to:

- interference with or harm to relevant evidence;
- interference with, or peripheral harm to, other people;
- serious loss or damage to property;
- other suspects being arrested;
- hindrance in the recovery of property related to an offence.

The detained person should be told or reminded of their rights before the interview begins (see below, the caution and the rights contained in ss 56 and 58). He/she should have put to them any 'significant statement or silence' for which they were responsible in the period prior to the beginning of the interview. The interview should cease as soon as the investigating officer is satisfied that all relevant questions have been put to the suspect and believes that there is enough evidence to enable a prosecution to succeed.

As stated, an accurate written or electronically recorded record should be kept. This should be made during the course of the interview unless this is not practicable or would interfere with the course of the interview. If the record is not made contemporaneously, it should be compiled as soon as is practicable afterwards. These requirements apply to all interviews whether conducted at the police station or elsewhere.

Where a written record is kept, the detained person should be given the opportunity to read and sign it thus verifying that it represents a true record of what took place. If the interview was recorded, the recording should be sealed in the detained person's presence and the detained person should be asked to sign the seal.

Compliance with these requirements gives the trial court a reasonable degree of assurance that statements and confessions given during police questioning may be relied upon. By definition, therefore, statements and confessions acquired in breach of these requirements have reduced credibility and may not be admitted as evidence (*R* v *Chung* [1991] Crim LR 622).

The caution

A person who refuses to answer police questions does not commit an offence, e.g. obstruction of a police officer in the course of their duty. A trial court may, however, place an 'adverse inference' on a suspect's silence if he/she seeks to rely on any facts by way of defence which were not mentioned during questioning by the police (Criminal Justice and Public Order Act 1994, ss 34–37, applied in *R* v *Argent* [1997] 2 Crim App Rep 27).

The wording of the caution reflects these basic principles: 'You do not have to say anything. But it may harm your defence if you do not mention when questioned something which you later rely on in court. Anything you do say may be given in evidence.'

Where a police officer is questioning a person merely for the purpose of acquiring information and does not suspect that person of an offence, the caution need not be administered (*R* v *Shah* [1994] Crim LR 125; *R* v *Marsh* [1992] Crim LR 455). Otherwise, the caution should be administered:

- as soon as there is a ground for suspecting that a person may have committed an offence (*R* v *Rouf*, Smith Bernal Casetrack, 13 May 1999);
- at the time of a person's arrest unless it is impracticable to do so because of the person's behaviour or because the person has already been questioned immediately before the arrest took place;
- if and when the person is charged with an offence.

The person should be reminded that he/she is under caution before being interviewed and after any breaks in the interview process.

Failure to administer the caution as required may result in any statements the suspect has made being ruled to be inadmissible as evidence (*R* v *Saunders* [1988] Crim LR 521; *R* v *Hunt* [1992] Crim LR 582).

Right to contact a friend or relative

A person being held in police custody has the right to have a friend or relative informed as to their whereabouts as soon as is practicable (s 56). The exercise of this right may be delayed for up to 36 hours where the person is suspected of an indictable offence and an officer of the rank of inspector or above reasonably believes that such contact would lead to:

- interference with relevant evidence;
- interference with or physical injury to other persons;

- the alerting of other suspects;
- the recovery of property obtained as the result of such offence being hindered or the suspect benefiting from their criminal conduct.

The right to legal advice

Every person in police custody must be informed of their right to consult a solicitor in private and must be allowed to exercise such right unless its delay for up to 36 hours is authorised according to the same criteria as for delay in informing a friend or relative of the person's whereabouts (s 56, see above) – i.e. the person is suspected of an indictable offence and a superintendent or higher rank has reasonable grounds for believing that contact with a solicitor might lead to interference with evidence, harm being done to other persons, the alerting of suspects or the 'fruits of the crime' not being recovered.

The courts regard the right articulated by s 58 as fundamental. Clear words must be used when informing the suspect of their entitlement in this regard (*R v Beycan* [1990] Crim LR 185). Also, although the right of access to legal advice may be delayed, fulfilment of the obligation to tell the suspect that the right exists may not (*R v Absolam* (1989) 88 Crim App Rep 332).

Delay of access may not be authorised simply because it is believed that contact with any legal adviser whatsoever might lead to any of the negative consequences specified. The officer authorising the delay must have reasonable grounds to believe that access to the *particular* solicitor named would result in such consequence(s) (*R v Samuel* [1988] 2 All ER 135). In *R v Davison* [1988] Crim LR 442, a detained person asked to see a solicitor but did not name one. Permission was refused as others involved in the crime under investigation were still at large. This was a breach of s 58. The suspect having failed to specify which solicitor he wished to see, the authorising officer could not, at this stage, have had any grounds for believing that allowing access to a particular legal adviser would have had any of the consequences justifying delay.

> In the light of *R v Samuel* . . . it is clear that the police must be near certain that a solicitor granted access to the defendant would warn off an inside man or get rid of the proceeds of the robbery. No solicitor having been nominated by the defendant, the police could have no reasonable fear relating to an individual solicitor passing a message on from the defendant (*R v Davison, supra*).

Where delay is justified, the detained person should be given reasons for it and should be informed forthwith if and when those reasons have ceased to exist (*R v Cochrane* [1988] Crim LR 449).

The general rule is that if a detained person has asked for legal advice the interview should not begin until they have received it. The detained person must also be allowed to have their solicitor present while the interview takes place.

Given the importance attached to this right by the courts, improper refusal of it will often be treated as sufficient ground for refusing to admit the detained person's statement as evidence. Where urgent needs of public safety require that a person be interviewed without the presence of a solicitor, e.g. to find weapons or explosives (a 'safety' or 'emergency' interview), any statements made by the suspect may be admitted as evidence against them. This remains the case notwithstanding that the primary purpose of the interview was to protect the public and not to secure evidence against the interviewee (*R v Ibrahim and Others* [2008] EWCA Crim 880).

It is unlikely, however, that wrongful refusal of access to a solicitor is actionable in damages at common law. In *Cullen* v *Chief Constable RUC* [2003] UKHL 39, the House of Lords was content that, to date, such breaches of statutory access requirements had been dealt with satisfactorily by way of judicial review and, therefore, felt unable to accept any general principle that damages for breach of statutory duty could be awarded where no specific harm had been occasioned. The right of access to a solicitor was said to be 'a public law right incapable of forming the basis of a common law right of action for breach of statutory duty' (Lord Millett). Note, however, that this was a majority decision and that Lords Bingham and Steyn took the opposite view.

It should be noted also that failure to allow a suspect access to a solicitor may amount to a breach of the requirements of Article 6 (the right to a fair trial) for which damages may be recoverable (see *Salduz* v *Turkey*, supra (suspect's right to presence of lawyer during interrogation save where 'compelling reasons for refusal'); *Dovorski* v *Croatia* [2015] ECHR 927 (suspect's right to lawyer of choice not merely one permitted by police save where 'relevant and sufficient reasons').

Albeit that the right in s 58 has been said to be of a 'fundamental' nature, the effectiveness of it would appear to be subject to one major limitation. As explained by the House of Lords in *Re McE* [2009] UKHL 15, this was to the effect that covert surveillance of private conversations between solicitors and persons in custody was permissible providing this was done according to the terms of the Regulation of Investigatory Powers Act 2000, i.e. where this had been authorised by the Home Secretary or a senior designated police officer on the grounds that it was believed necessary in the interests of national security, preventing or detecting serious crime, or the economic well-being of the state (s 32).

Notwithstanding some obvious unease about being 'driven to this unpalatable conclusion', the House felt that, given the wording of the relevant provisions in the 2000 Act and, in particular, s 27 ('the conduct to which the Act applies shall be lawful for all purposes'), it had little option but to interpret the legislation in this way.

> The answer to the question must depend on the parliamentary intention that is to be derived from the terms of the statute, and I do not think that is capable of further deliberation. I would hold that . . . conversations between a detainee and his solicitor that are taking place in private in the exercise of a statutory right may be subjected to intrusive surveillance that has been duly authorised under section 32 of RIPA so long as it is conducted strictly in accordance with the conditions which the authorisation lays down. In all other respects the statutory right to privacy must be respected (*per* Lord Hope).

While not rejecting the practice as wholly inimical to the right of privacy in ECHR Art 8(1), the ECtHR has made clear that the surveillance of a legal consultation constitutes an 'extremely high degree of intrusion into the right to respect for private life and correspondence' and that, as such, its practice must be subject to the most 'stringent safeguards' (*R.E.* v *United Kingdom* [2013] ECHR 852. For the purposes of domestic law, these are contained currently in the Codes of Practice for Property and Covert Surveillance.

Search of detained persons

The custody officer is under a duty to ascertain, and keep a record of, what property the detained person had with them when brought into the police station and may conduct a search of the person for that purpose (s 54). The search should be carried out by an officer of the same sex as the person to be searched. Clothes and personal effects may be seized if the custody officer believes any of these may be used by the detainee to cause physical harm, to damage property, to interfere with evidence or to assist an escape. The extent of the search is limited to that which is necessary to enable the custody officer to carry out his duty. This may be a strip search, i.e. a search which may involve the removal of shoes socks, and outer clothing, if the custody officer reasonably considers that the person has concealed an article which they would otherwise not be allowed to keep.

A more thorough or intimate search of a person in custody may be conducted if an officer of at least the rank of inspector has reasonable grounds for believing that the person may have concealed on him/her either an item which could be used to cause physical injury, or is a Class A drug (s 55). An intimate search is a physical examination of body orifices other than the mouth. Such search should normally be carried out by a registered nurse but may be effected by a police officer of the same sex as the detainee where an officer of the rank of inspector reasonably believes that the person is concealing something which could be used to cause injury and that it would be impracticable to wait for a nurse or a doctor to attend.

Fingerprints, footprints, DNA and other databases

The pre-existing practice relating to the above under PACE, s 64, whereby such materials could be retained indefinitely without reference to the type of offence or offender, and whether or not the person had been tried for, or convicted of, any offence was found incompatible with ECHR Art 8 (right to respect for private life) in both *S and Marper* v *United Kingdom* [2008] ECHR 1581 and *R (on application of GC)* v *Metropolitan Police Commissioner* [2011] UKSC 21.

The current provisions regulating the use, retention and destruction of the types of materials referred to were inserted into PACE by the Protection of Freedoms Act 2012, s 63. As required by the ECtHR, these seek to relate the length of times for which such material may be retained to the age of the offender and type of offence in issue.

The broad effect of the Act is that fingerprints and DNA profiles:

(i) taken from persons arrested for, or charged with, a minor offence will be destroyed following a decision not to charge or acquittal;

(ii) taken from persons charged with, but not convicted of, a serious offence may be retained for up to three years – with possible extension up to a further two years on application to a District Judge;

(iii) taken from persons arrested on suspicion of, but not charged with, a serious offence may be retained for similar periods, i.e. three years with a possible two years extension, on application to the Commissioner for the Retention and Use of Biometric Materials.

The formulation and holding of databases or other types of information concerning a person or persons on no occasion charged or convicted of any offence(s) may also amount to a breach of Article 8 if disproportionate to any relevant public policy need, e.g. prevention of crime or the maintenance of public order (*R (on application of Catt)* v *Association of Chief Police Officers* [2013] EWCA Civ 192; database on person who regularly attended a public demonstration against the armaments industry but who had not been convicted of any related offences).

DNA material, whether taken from an individual or otherwise acquired, e.g. in the search or examination of a crime scene, should be used for criminal law enforcement purposes only (PACE, Part II). Such material was not available for use in determining questions of paternity for the purpose of care proceedings (*X and the Commissioner of Police of the Metropolis* v *Z and a Local Authority* [2015] EWCA Civ 34).

Treatment of detainees

Various elements of Code of Practice C seek to ensure that persons detained in police custody are not subjected to any unacceptable degree of physical and psychological discomfort during the inquiry and interview process. It provides that in any period of 24 hours the detained person must be allowed a continuous period of rest for at least eight hours. This should normally be at night and free from any unnecessary interruption. Interviews should be conducted in rooms which are adequately heated, lit and ventilated. The detained person should be allowed to sit while being questioned. Breaks from questioning should be allowed at meal times and short breaks should be allowed at intervals of approximately two hours. The requirements that the detained person be allowed eight hours of rest and breaks from questioning may be departed from if there are reasonable grounds for believing that such delay would:

- involve a risk of harm to any person or serious damage to, or a loss of, property;
- delay unnecessarily the detained person's release;
- otherwise prejudice the outcome of the investigation.

Cells should be adequately lit, heated, ventilated and cleaned. Clean bedding of a reasonable standard should be provided. Access to washing and toilet facilities should be provided. Detainees should also be given at least two light meals and one main meal every 24 hours. They should be visited regularly and receive prompt clinical attention when necessary.

Detention under the common law

The above detention regime in PACE does not apply to persons detained under common law power, e.g. for breaches of the peace. The common law requirements that such persons should be taken before a magistrate as soon as is reasonably practicable or otherwise released unconditionally would appear to meet the standards imposed by the ECHR Art 5 (*Williamson* v *Chief Constable of West Midlands* [2003] EWCA Civ 337).

Inadmissible evidence

The rules in PACE

As already indicated, ill-treatment or malpractice in relation to those in detention or breach of the rules regulating the process of questioning may lead to any confession or statements made by the detained person being ruled to be inadmissible by the trial court. This issue is regulated by PACE, ss 76 and 78.

The effect of PACE s 76 is to place the trial court under a legal duty to exclude any confession which has been obtained by oppression or any other means which makes it unreliable. Oppression includes torture, inhuman or degrading treatment or the use of threats of violence. If oppression is alleged, it is for the prosecution to prove beyond reasonable doubt that such techniques were not used. One of the most frequent reasons for confessions being held to be unreliable is that they were made in response to some kind of inducement – i.e. a holding out to the suspected person that, in return for a confession, they will be given some sort of advantage, benefit or concession. Thus, in *R v Howden-Simpson* [1991] Crim LR 49, the defendant's confession was ruled inadmissible because it had been given in response to a promise that if he confessed to two offences he would not be charged with others which he was also suspected of having committed.

Note that where oppression or unreliability is established under s 76, the court has no discretion: it must exclude the confession. Also note that the section applies to confessions only and not to other statements.

PACE s 78 gives the trial court a discretion to exclude both confessions and other statements if 'having regard to all the circumstances, including the circumstances in which the evidence was obtained, the admission of the evidence would have . . . an adverse effect on the fairness of the proceedings'. Although worded obscurely, its practical effect is to allow the court to exclude:

- confessions obtained by improper means not covered by s 76 (*R v Mason* [1987] 3 All ER 481);
- other statements which may have been obtained by force, pressure, threats, inducements or where some other improper act has been committed.

The cases suggest a general judicial opinion that evidence obtained from a person in police custody whose treatment was in 'significant and substantial' breach of the rules regulating detention and questioning should not be admitted (*R v Walsh* [1988] Crim LR 449). Evidence has been excluded under this provision in the following circumstances:

- no contemporaneous record made of interview (*R v Maloney and Doherty* [1988] Crim LR 523);
- access to solicitor refused improperly (*R v Davison, supra; R v Samuel, supra; R v Alladice* (1988) 87 Crim App Rep 380);
- continuous questioning without adequate rest or breaks (*R v Trussler* [1988] Crim LR 446);
- breach of the suspect's human rights.

In many cases, evidence has been excluded because a variety of the relevant rules have been transgressed and the cumulative effects of this for maintaining standards of fairness (e.g. *R v Saunders* (*supra*): suspect not cautioned properly and no contemporaneous record kept; *R v Walsh* (*supra*): suspect improperly refused access to solicitor and no contemporaneous record kept). Indeed, in one case it was suggested that an accumulation of serious breaches of the rules could amount to oppression within the meaning of s 76 (*R v Davison*, *supra*).

Admissibility and the European Court of Human Rights

Whether evidence, particularly unlawfully obtained evidence, is admissible or not is a matter which may also engage Art 6 (right to a fair trial). The position taken by the European Court of Human Rights on this issue has not differed greatly from that of the domestic law, i.e. that the crucial test is not the legality of the way the evidence was obtained but the overall effect its admission would have on the fairness of the proceedings. In *R v Mason* [2002] EWCA Crim 385, police officers placed listening devices in prisoners' cells without legal authority and, thus not 'according to law'. This was found to be a breach of Art 8 (right to privacy). This did not mean, however, that the evidence gained thereby was automatically inadmissible under Art 6. The Court of Appeal quoted from the judgement of the Court of Human Rights in *PG and JH v United Kingdom*, *The Times*, 19 October 2001:

> Whilst Art 6 guarantees the right to a fair hearing, it does not lay down any rules on the admissibility of evidence as such which is, therefore, primarily a matter for regulation under national

law . . . It is not the role of the court to determine . . . whether particular types of evidence – for example, unlawfully obtained evidence – may be admissible . . . The question which must be answered is whether the proceedings as a whole, including the way in which the evidence was obtained, were fair.

In *Mason*, the defendants not having been tricked or induced into making statements, the covertly obtained evidence was found to be admissible. If aggrieved, it remained open to them to seek a remedy for breach of Art 8 (see also *R v Bailey* [2001] EWCA Crim 733).

This may be contrasted with the decision in *Sepil v Turkey* app no 21313/05, 12.1.10, where the Court found that the police had obtained evidence by deliberately inciting the applicant to commit a crime. Here, the police contacted the applicant by phone and offered to buy heroin. After the transaction had been completed, the applicant was arrested. The Court's view was that the public interest could not justify the use of evidence obtained as a result of police incitement, i.e. in this case to induce the commission of an offence which would otherwise not have been committed. This, it was felt, would have exposed the applicant 'to the risk of being definitively deprived of a fair trial from the outset'.

Entry, search and seizure

Introduction

Objective
5

The Police and Criminal Evidence Act 1984 left untouched those powers to search premises for evidence of specific offences contained in previous enactments (e.g. Misuse of Drugs Act 1971, s 23(3); Obscene Publications Act 1959, s 3). In addition to these, PACE created two general powers of entry and search to assist the police with the investigation of more serious criminal offences. The principal powers of search conferred by the Act are found in ss 8 and 9. Further general powers of entry for a variety of purposes are contained in s 17.

Search with warrant

Section 8 of the 1984 Act permits a magistrate to issue a warrant authorising the search of premises if he/she is satisfied, pursuant to an application by a constable, that there are reasonable grounds for believing that an indictable offence has been committed and that there is material in the specified premises which is likely to be admissible evidence of substantial value to the investigation of that offence(s). In addition, one of the following further conditions must be satisfied:

- it is not practicable to communicate with any person entitled to grant access to the premises;
- although it is practicable to communicate with someone entitled to grant access to the premises, it is not practicable to communicate with any person entitled to grant access to the evidence;
- entry to the premises will not be granted without a warrant;
- the purpose of the search may be frustrated or seriously prejudiced unless the police can gain immediate access to the premises.

The police officer applying for a warrant must state: the ground for making the application; the enactment under which the application is made; the premises to be searched; the object of the search (s 15); and whether the warrant for one or more searches and, in the latter case, the grounds for this, are whether the desired number of entries to be authorised is unlimited or a specific maximum (s 15). If the application is refused, no further application may be made for a warrant to search the same premises unless supported by fresh evidence.

A warrant may not be issued under s 8 to search for material which is subject to legal privilege, excluded material or special procedure material (see below). The procedure both for applying for a search warrant and executing the same is contained in PACE, ss 15 and 16.

The same procedure governs the issuing of warrants under any other enactment.

Content of the warrant

A valid search warrant must contain the following information:

- the name of the applicant;
- the date of issue;
- the statute under which it is issued;
- the premises to be searched;
- as far as is practicable, the articles or persons sought.

A warrant which fails to specify any of the above, or does not do so adequately, or which purports to authorise the seizure of materials not permitted by the enabling Act, is invalid (*R v Reading Justices, ex parte South West Meat Ltd* [1992] Crim LR 672; *R v Hunt* [1992] Crim LR 747; *Darbo v DPP* [1992] Crim LR 56). If the building to be searched is divided into flats or separate dwellings, the warrant should specify which flat is to be searched (*R v South Western Magistrates' Court, ex parte Cofie* [1997] 1 WLR 885).

An exception to the above was effected by the Serious Organised Crime and Police Act 2005, s 113, which amended PACE, s 8. This provides that police may apply for an 'all premises warrant' when it is felt necessary to search all the premises occupied or controlled by a particular person but it is 'not reasonably practicable' to specify all of those premises at the time of applying for the warrant. Warrants for particular or named premises are to be referred to as 'specific premises warrants'.

Execution of the warrant

A warrant to enter and search remains valid for three months from the date of issue (s 16(3)). It may be executed by any police officer and may authorise them to be accompanied by other persons who may or may not be other police officers (s 16(1) and (2)). Most warrants authorise one entry only. Multiple entries may be permitted providing the magistrates who grant it are satisfied that this is necessary 'to achieve the purpose for which the warrant is issued'. Execution of the warrant should be at a 'reasonable hour' unless this would frustrate the purpose of the search (s 16(4)).

The occupier's consent to entry should be sought unless: the premises are known to be unoccupied; there is no person present authorised to grant entry; or there are reasonable grounds for believing that such communication would frustrate the objects of the search or endanger the officers. Reasonable force may be used to effect entry where any of the above conditions apply or access has been refused. Reasons for resort to the use of force should be given if the owner/occupier is present (*Linehan v DPP* [1999] All ER 1080). Where the occupier of the premises is present, the officer executing the warrant should identify him/herself and produce their warrant card if not in uniform. The officer should also produce the warrant and supply the occupier with a copy (ibid.). If the occupier is not present, the same rules apply to any person who appears to be in charge of the premises. If no such person is present, a copy of the warrant must be left in a prominent place on the premises.

A failure to show the original warrant or any part of it to the occupier or other person present, or a failure to provide a correct copy of the same, will render the entry and search to be unlawful and deprive the police of any lawful authority to retain possession of any items which were seized (*R v Chief Constable of Lancashire, ex parte Parker* [1992] 2 All ER 56). Code of Practice B provides that the officer should also produce a notice specifying, *inter alia*, whether the search is made with warrant or with consent, the extent of the powers of search and seizure in the authorising Act, and the rights of both the occupier and the owner of any property seized.

As a general rule the officer should provide the necessary identification, the warrant, and the above notice before the search begins. This is not necessary, however, if to do so would frustrate the object of the search (Code B, para 5.8, as confirmed by the Court of Appeal in *R v Longman* [1988] 1 WLR 619).

Premises should be searched only to the extent which is necessary to secure the items specified in the warrant 'having regard to the size and nature of whatever is sought'. The search should be conducted 'with due consideration for the property and privacy of the occupier . . . and with no more disturbance than necessary'. Reasonable force may be used to implement the search where the 'co-operation of the occupier cannot be obtained or is insufficient for the purpose' (Code B). The officer may seize any items covered by the warrant (s 8(2)) and other items which they have reasonable grounds for believing to be evidence of any offence or to have been obtained in consequence of such offence (s 19). This includes information in a computer (s 20). The search should end once all the items specified in the warrant have been found or the officer in charge is satisfied that these are not on the premises. For the effectiveness of the search, and where necessary to ensure the safety both of those carrying it out and any persons found on the premises, e.g. as in a search for firearms or explosives, the latter may be detained for the minimum period required (*Connor v Chief Constable of Merseyside* [2006] EWCA Civ 1549).

> Where, in addition to looking for the items specified in the warrant relied upon, the entry into the specified premises enables the police to pursue other objectives having nothing to do with offences related to those items, e.g. the acquisition of information concerning other criminal activities, the function of the court is to determine whether the purpose for which the warrant was sought was the primary purpose for entering the premises in question (*R (on application Pearce) v Commissioner of Police of the Metropolis* [2013] EWCA Civ 866).

Proceedings for abuse of powers provided by a search warrant should be pursued by an action for trespass and not by way of judicial review (*R v Chief Constable of Warwickshire* [1999] 1 WLR 564).

Legally privileged, excluded and special procedure materials

General comment

Objective
6

Sections 9–14 of PACE deal with the procedure for and the extent of police access to various types of confidential information held, for example, by solicitors, doctors, accountants, banks, social workers, etc. The general rule is that legally privileged material is never obtainable. Access to excluded and special procedure materials (defined below) cannot be given by the issue of a warrant by a magistrate under s 8. Under s 9, however, those in possession of such material may, in specified circumstances, be required to deliver them up to the police pursuant to an order of a circuit judge. The procedure for issue of the same is found in PACE, Sched 1.

Legally privileged material

This consists of:

(a) communications in the form of legal advice between professional legal adviser and client whether or not related to legal proceedings;

(b) other communications between professional legal adviser and client and between the latter and any other person which do relate to actual or contemplated legal proceedings.

As already indicated, no warrant or other order may be issued authorising premises to be searched for the same unless the materials are held for a criminal purpose (s 10(2)).

The general purpose of the provision is to ensure that the individual is able to speak freely to their legal adviser without the danger of incriminating themselves by records of such conversations falling into the hands of the police. This does not mean, however, that everything held in a solicitor's office is privileged and unobtainable. The privilege applies only to that related to legal advice or legal proceedings. Hence, in *R v Inner London Crown Court, ex parte Baines and Baines* [1987] 3 All ER 1025, it was held that documents held by a solicitor which related purely to certain commercial activities (i.e. the financing and purchasing of a house), were not legally privileged.

Material held for a criminal purpose is excluded from the privilege (s 10(2)). The criminal purpose may be that of the solicitor, the client, or some other person and it matters not that the person in possession – usually the solicitor – is innocent of that purpose.

R v Central Criminal Court, ex parte Francis and Francis [1988] 3 All ER 77

In this case, access was sought to information held by a solicitor relating to certain property transactions. The police believed that the moneys to finance the same had been supplied by a relative of the client and were derived from drug-trafficking. Both the solicitor and the client were thought to be unaware of the moneys' dubious origins. By a majority, the House of Lords decided that otherwise legally privileged materials could be held for a criminal purpose albeit that such purpose could not be attributed to the person in possession of them. Hence, in the case itself, the criminal purpose of a third party was sufficient to negate any privilege which might otherwise have attached to the material in question, thereby rendering it subject to production according to the procedure in PACE, Sched 1 (see below).

Excluded material

This is defined as:

(a) personal records acquired or created in a trade, business, profession, or other occupation or for the purposes of diagnosis or medical treatment; or

(b) human tissue or tissue fluid taken for the purpose of diagnosis or medical treatment; or

(c) journalistic materials consisting of documents or records held in confidence.

Special procedure material

This consists of:

(a) any journalistic material which does not fall within the definition of excluded material – i.e. documents and records not held in confidence or other materials, held in confidence or not, compiled or acquired for the purpose of journalism;

(b) material which is neither legally privileged nor excluded material acquired or created in any trade, business, profession or occupation which is held in confidence, i.e. subject to an express or implied undertaking or statutory requirement to restrict disclosure or maintain secrecy. Examples of this category of special procedure materials would include the accounts of a Youth Association (*R v Central Criminal Court, ex parte Adegbesan* [1986] 3 All ER 113); conveyancing documents held by a solicitor (*R v Inner London Crown Court, ex parte Baines and Baines*, supra); bank accounts (*R v Leicester Crown Court, ex parte DPP* [1987] 3 All ER 654).

Journalistic materials are protected in the interests of a free press. Hence journalists are enabled to collect information about criminal activities without having to worry that – save in exceptional circumstances – their premises may be searched by the police (see Contempt of Court Act 1981, s 10).

Procedure for access

The process begins by the police making an *inter partes* application to a circuit judge. Notice of application for production should be served on the person believed to be in possession of the requisite materials. Notice need not be served on the person under investigation if they are in possession (*R v Leicester Crown Court, ex parte DPP*, supra). The notice should specify the premises where the material is believed to be and the nature of the offence being investigated – e.g. 'robbery', 'fraud' (*R v Central Criminal Court, ex parte Carr*, The Independent, 5 March 1987). The material sought should also be identified to avoid contravention of Sched 1, para 11 to the effect that it should not be concealed, destroyed, altered or disposed of.

At the hearing the police must satisfy the judge that one of the two sets of access conditions has been met. The person in possession has a right to be heard and to know the evidence on which the application is based (*R (on application British Sky Broadcasting* v *Commissioner of the Police of the Metropolis* [2014] UKSC 17). The court has an additional discretion to hear also the person under investigation (*R v Lewes Crown Court, ex parte Hill* (1990) 93 Crim App Rep 60).

The first set of access conditions applies to special procedure material only. These are that there are reasonable grounds for believing that:

- an indictable offence has been committed;
- there is special procedure material in the specified premises;
- the material is likely to be of substantial evidential value to the offence being investigated;

and that:

- other methods of obtaining the material have been tried without success or have not been tried because they were likely to fail;
- because of the material's likely benefit to the investigation the public interest in its production outweighs the public interest in confidentiality.

The second set of access conditions applies to both excluded and special procedure material. These are that:

- a warrant to search for the material could have been granted under a pre-PACE enactment (all such powers having been repealed by PACE, s 9(2));
- there are reasonable grounds for believing that excluded or special procedure material may be found in the premises specified.

If either set of access conditions is satisfied, the judge may order that the materials sought be delivered up to the police within seven days or that they be allowed access to them. Failure to comply constitutes contempt of court. In the event of such failure, a warrant may be issued authorising the police to enter and search. A search warrant may also be issued by a circuit judge in respect of excluded or special procedure material where either set of access conditions is satisfied and:

- it is not practicable to communicate with any person entitled to grant access to the premises in question;
- the above is practicable but it is not practicable to communicate with any person entitled to grant access to the materials;
- disclosure of, or access to, the material is restricted by statute and is, therefore, unlikely to be given unless in compliance with a warrant;
- notice of an application for an order is likely to seriously prejudice the investigation.

Such warrants are subject to the general provisions applying to search with warrant considered above.

Other statutory powers of entry

Section 17 of PACE specifies the circumstances in which a police officer may enter premises without a search warrant. All pre-existing powers of entry without warrant were repealed (s 17(5)). The specified circumstances are:

(a) to execute a warrant of arrest;

(b) to arrest a person for an indictable offence;

(c) to arrest a person under section 1 of the Public Order Act 1936 (wearing a uniform denoting membership of a political organisation in a public place) or s 4 of the Public Order Act 1986 (causing fear or provocation of violence);

(d) to arrest for any offence under ss 6–10 of the Criminal Law Act 1977 (squatting);

(e) to recapture a person unlawfully at large whom the officer is pursuing (i.e. in 'hot-pursuit' of, see *De Souza* v *DPP* [1992] 4 All ER 545);

(f) to save life or limb or prevent serious damage to property.

Except in the case of (f), the officer must have reasonable grounds for believing that the person is in the property.

Entry at common law

In addition to the above, the common law power to enter private premises without warrant to deal with actual or apprehended breaches of the peace is preserved expressly by s 17(6).

In *McLeod* v *Metropolitan Police Commissioner* [1994] 4 All ER 553, the Court of Appeal's view was that this 'was a power to enter premises to prevent a breach of the peace as a form of preventative justice' where there is 'a real and imminent risk' of such breach being committed.

Note that the above are principally powers of entry only. Section 17 confers no general power of search beyond that of effecting the purpose for which entry was made – i.e. to find the person to be arrested or recaptured or to deal with the danger specified in (f). As explained above, however, s 32 allows a police officer to search any premises where a person was immediately before or at the time of arrest (for evidence of the offence for which they were arrested). Section 18 permits the officer to search any premises occupied or controlled by a person under arrest (for evidence of the offence or any other offences that person may have committed).

Consensual entry

As a general rule, a consensual entry and search of premises, i.e. with the permission of the occupier, does not amount to a trespass at common law or to a breach of the right to respect for private life (ECHR, Art 8). This remains the case, notwithstanding that the entry and search was repeated at regular intervals, e.g. as in *R (on application of M)* v *Chief Constable of Hampshire* [2014] EWCA Civ 1651, in which the police regularly attended and searched the premises of a registered sex offender. On each occasion, the occupier of the premises was asked for and gave permission to enter. The visits were made in order to monitor his activities and assess any continuing risk he posed to the community. The fact that if refused entry it would have been open to the police to apply for a warrant under the Sex Offenders Act 2003, did not, the court felt, unless supported by further evidence that the occupier of the premises felt he had no real choice, prevent the consent he gave from being regarded as truly consensual.

Seizure

The extent of the power of seizure available to a police officer who is lawfully in private premises is governed by PACE, s 19. The power is to seize anything the officer has reasonable grounds for believing to have been obtained through the commission of an offence or to be evidence of any offence and, in either case, which it is necessary to seize in order to prevent it being concealed, lost, damaged, altered or destroyed. This is a power of seizure only and confers no authority to enter and search for such items. However, used in conjunction with the powers of entry and search discussed above, s 19 has the following practical consequences:

- a police officer lawfully on premises in order to execute a search warrant may seize any items covered by section 19 which they 'happen upon' in search for the articles specified in the warrant (*R* v *Southwark Crown Court and HM Customs, ex parte Sorsky Defries* [1996] Crim LR 195);

- a police officer lawfully on premises to effect an arrest or recapture a person unlawfully at large whom they are pursuing may seize any items covered by section 19 which they 'happen upon' while looking for the person in question;

- a police officer on premises with the occupier's consent may seize any items covered by section 19 which they happen to see there while acting within that consent.

Goods seized lawfully may be retained for use at a trial, for forensic, and for other investigative purposes, or 'for so long as is necessary in all the circumstances' (s 22). Where, however, no such evidential or law enforcement purpose exists, or has ceased to exist, police have no power to retain such goods simply because they continue to suspect that the goods may have been stolen or are connected to some criminal activity (*Gough* v *Chief Constable West Midlands* [2004] EWCA Civ 206: successful action by garage owner for return of car parts police believed to have been stolen but after decision not to prosecute). See also: *Wells* v *Chief Constable Merseyside Police* [2000] QB 427 (£36,000 believed to be proceeds of drug trafficking ordered to be returned after decision not to prosecute and notwithstanding a genuine belief that the money had been derived from crime); *Costello* v *Chief Constable Derbyshire Constabulary* [2001] 1 WLR 1437 (successful action for return of car believed to have been stolen after decision not to prosecute).

The fact that police have been ordered to return lawfully seized goods does not mean that such goods are exempt from being 're-seized' under the Proceeds of Crime Act 2002 (*Merseyside Police* v *Hickman* [2006] EWHC 451). The power of seizure under the 2002 Act applies to property or cash obtained through unlawful conduct which includes 'property into which the proceeds of criminal conduct can be traced' (Mitting J, *Hickman, supra*).

For practical operational reasons, the power of seizure in section 19 was extended by the Criminal Justice and Police Act 2001, section 50. This allows that a person lawfully on premises may seize:

(a) anything he/she has reasonable grounds for believing may be contained in something for which they are authorised to search the premises;

(b) anything he/she would be entitled to seize 'but for its being comprised in something else that [they have] no power to seize'.

These powers may be used where, in all the circumstances, ascertaining the seizable property on the premises would not be reasonably practicable due to constraints of time, the number of persons needed, or technology.

Such difficulties may arise for the law enforcement agencies perhaps because of the bulk of the material or because it is contained within a set of documents which may also contain privileged material. It may also be the case that the material is held on computer. Hence it may be impossible to establish which material is relevant and seizable unless all the information stored is examined forensically. This may require removing the computer and/or imaging the entire contents of its hard disks and/or removing CD ROMs or memory sticks.

The provision gives the police and law enforcement agencies a choice of how to deal with these problems. First, they may remove entire collections of documents or information, however stored, so that these can be examined elsewhere. Second, it is recognised, that with the advance of technology, it may be perfectly possible to keep material for which there may be a power of seizure within the same physical object as perfectly innocent material or that which may be privileged.

A power of seizure from the person in similar circumstances is given by s 51. The explanatory notes to the Act say that this is necessary because, for example, individuals might have on them hand-held computers or computer disks which might contain electronic data which the police might wish to seize. Alternatively, they could be carrying a suitcase containing a bulk of correspondence which could not be examined in the street (para 165).

Force

Section 117 of PACE permits an officer to use reasonable force, where necessary, in order to exercise any of the powers conferred by the Act.

In the case of powers of entry, the general principle is that force should only be used 'if need be' (per Waller LJ, *Lunt v DPP* [1993] Crim LR 534). Otherwise, the officer should take all reasonable steps to secure the occupier's consent (subject to the exceptions dealt with above in the context of search with warrant). Where that consent is refused, unless circumstances make it 'impossible and impracticable or undesirable', the occupant should be given reasons for any forced entry (*O'Loughlin v Chief Constable of Essex* [1998] 1 WLR 374).

Surveillance

Introduction

Objective 7

Effective policing and the protection of national security depends on information and intelligence. Much useful material can be gained by listening to or intercepting communications between individuals, by accessing information systems and by the more traditional means of watching and listening to people in their domestic and working environments. Any such activities by law enforcement agencies have, however, serious implications for the rights of individuals, particularly those relating to respect for private life, home and correspondence as contained in Art 8 of the European Convention on Human Rights.

For most of the twentieth century, the law in the United Kingdom paid little heed to these aspects of criminal investigations. Hence, to the extent these sorts of activities were engaged in by the police and intelligence services, this was not based on any clear legal foundation.

Legislation to provide for and to regulate the interception of communications by post and telephone was finally introduced by the Interception of Communications Act 1985. This followed the decision in *Malone v United Kingdom* (1985) 7 EHRR 14 where the European Court of Human Rights decided that the previous practice in the United Kingdom, whereby telephone tapping was regulated by the Home Office guidelines only, did not comply with the Convention requirement that interference with the right to privacy (Art 8) should be:

(i) 'in accordance with the law', i.e. founded on easily accessible and comprehensible legal rules; and,

(ii) limited to circumstances where this could be related to one of the Convention's 'legitimate aims' or permissible public interests, e.g. the prevention of disorder or crime.

Prior to 1985, interception of postal communications was already subject to the rather minimal requirements of the Post Office Act 1953. This provided that the opening of a postal packet was an offence unless pursuant to a warrant issued by the Home Secretary. The procedure and criteria for grant of such warrants were again, however, found only in Home Office rules which had no formal basis in law.

The first modern pieces of legislation to authorise and regulate interference with private property rights for the purposes of electronic and other methods of surveillance were, for the police, the Police Act 1997, and for the security and intelligence services (MI5 and MI6 and GCHQ), the Intelligence Services Act 1994.

Despite the relative modernity of much of the above legislation, continuing and rapid developments in both information and communications technology and in surveillance techniques meant that, for certain purposes, the legal framework it provided soon proved no longer adequate, either as a sufficient legal basis for the activities of the law enforcement agencies, or for the proper protection of the rights of the individual. In particular, none of the legislation mentioned contained any specific provisions relating to private telecommunications systems nor was any of it designed to deal with such developments as pagers, mobile phones, emails, the internet or the protection of information by encryption. Parliament's response to these difficulties, and its attempt to modernise the law in this context for both law enforcement and human rights purposes, was provided by the Regulation of Investigatory Powers Act (RIPA) 2000.

The stated purpose of the Act was to consolidate the law relating to the use of investigatory powers and to ensure that these were used in compliance with the Human Rights Act 1998. The activities to which the Act was directed are:

(i) 'directed surveillance' of persons and activities in public;

(ii) 'intrusive surveillance' of persons and activities in residential premises;

(iii) 'covert human intelligence sources' ('CHIS') (i.e. informants);

(iv) interception of communications;

(v) acquisition of communications data;

(vi) access to information protected by encryption.

By the end of the first decade of the current century, the ruthless rapidity in the development of electronic communications and information technology had been such that the legal framework provided by the Act of 2000 was already becoming inadequate for either:

(a) its use and application by the police, security, and intelligence services;

(b) provision of the level of protection against abuse required by the European Convention on Human Rights.

Property interference

The Police Act 1997 permits the police to interfere with rights over private property for the purpose of installing surveillance devices for the detection of serious crime. Serious crime is any offence which involves, *inter alia*, the use of violence or results in substantial financial gain for which a person could be sentenced to a term of imprisonment of three years or more. Authorisation for such activities should be granted by a chief officer of police or equivalent of the National Crime Agency and should be approved by a Judicial Commissioner where the property in question is a dwelling house or office premises. In the case of MI5, MI6 or GCHQ, the authority for property interference should be in the form of a warrant issued by the Home Secretary. The action permitted thereby should relate to any of the functions of the agency. The stated functions of MI5 include the protection of national security from threats of espionage, terrorism or sabotage by foreign agents or powers or from other acts intended to undermine parliamentary democracy by political, industrial or violent means, and the support of the police in dealing with serious crime. The functions of MI6 are to obtain information and to perform other tasks in relation to persons outside the United Kingdom in the interests of national security with particular reference to defence and foreign policy and the prevention or detection of serious crime. The principal stated function of GCHQ is to monitor and to process communication signals and to use the information for similar purposes.

The Investigatory Powers Act 2016 changed these existing provisions to enable the security and intelligence services to be granted a property warrant for the prevention and detection of serious crime where the property is within the UK.

Directed surveillance

This is covert surveillance which is likely to result in the obtaining of private information about any person. It would include, for example, following, listening to or filming suspects in public or places to which the public have access. Directed surveillance may not be employed in relation to anything taking place in residential premises or a private vehicle and may not involve any surveillance activity which requires the presence in any such premises or vehicle of any person or surveillance device. Authorisation is by police officers of the rank of superintendent or above and in other organisations (see below) by such persons as are designated by the Home Secretary (s 30). Grounds on which such authorisations may be issued include the prevention and detection of crime or disorder, public safety, and the needs of national security. The current legislation permits 43 different types of public bodies to engage in such surveillance. This includes many which would not ordinarily be regarded as primary law enforcement agencies, e.g. all local authorities, various government departments, the NHS and the Royal Mail. No such authorisation is needed for an immediate response to a recent event or development or where it would be impracticable for this to be sought.

The person granting the authorisation must believe that the conduct which they have sanctioned is necessary for, and proportionate to, that which is sought to be achieved.

Intrusive surveillance

Intrusive surveillance is that which is carried out covertly in relation to anything taking place in any residential premises or private vehicle or any facility in a police station, court or prison being used for the purpose of legal consultations. It may be undertaken by placing a person or device inside the place or premises or outside the same in a way which produces information of equivalent quality.

Authority for intrusive surveillance must be given by a chief officer of police or by the head of the National Crime Agency. As with directed surveillance, this should be for the purposes of, *inter alia*, preventing or detecting crime, public safety or national security. Except in urgent cases, any such authorisation will not take effect until approved by a Judicial Commissioner.

Authorisation for intrusive surveillance by the security or intelligence services (MI5 or MI6) must be given by the Home Secretary in the form of a warrant. For the purposes of MI5, such warrants may be granted, *inter alia*, on grounds of the prevention or detection of serious crime or the interests of national security. Warrants granted to MI6 or to GCHQ (the Government Communications Headquarters) should be limited primarily to matters of national security.

Covert human intelligence sources

The use of covert human intelligence sources occurs where a member of a law enforcement agency or other public authority permitted to engage in such activities establishes a personal or other relationship with another for the covert purpose of persuading that person to obtain or provide information.

Authorisation for the use of such sources may be given by a police officer of the rank of superintendent or above and for other public bodies by such persons as may be designated by the Home Secretary. Where authorisation is sought for the use of a CHIS for a period extending beyond 12 months, this should be given by a chief constable of police only. Such authorisation may be given for, *inter alia*, CHIS activities relating to the prevention or detection of crime or in the interests of public safety or national security.

The personal relationships police officers may enter into in order to acquire information include those of an intimate sexual nature (***AJA and Others* v *Commissioner of Police for the Metropolis*** [2013] EWCA Civ 285).

Surveillance by local authorities

Local authorities may access communications data and employ both the use of directed surveillance and covert human intelligence sources by virtue of, and according to the requirements in, RIPA ss 21–25 (communications data), ss 28–29 (directed surveillance) and Sched 1. Local authorities, however, are not entrusted with powers of intrusive surveillance. Authorisation for the accessing of communications data or for surveillance activities must be granted by a senior ranking local government official and must be for the purpose of detecting or preventing the commission of any criminal offence punishable by a sentence of imprisonment for six months or more or offences relating to the sale of alcohol to children. Any such authorisation comes into effect only after approval by a justice of the peace (JP). The Justice must be satisfied that there are reasonable grounds on which the person giving the authorisation could reasonably have believed that resort to the RIPA procedures was 'necessary and proportionate'. The types of matters investigated by local authorities would include benefit fraud, environmental crime, trading standards violations, employment of minors fly tipping, anti-social behaviour, sale of alcohol or tobacco to minors and loan 'sharking'.

The use of closed circuit television and automatic number plate recognition by local authorities and the police should accord with a code of practice issued by the Home Secretary. This may relate, *inter alia*, to the circumstances in which deployment of these methods of acquiring information is appropriate, the use and retention of any images gained, information to be provided to the public and provision of complaint procedures (Protection of Freedoms Act 2012, s 29). Responsibility for overseeing compliance with the code lies with the Surveillance Camera Commissioner to be appointed by the Minister (s 34). The Commissioner is required to produce an annual report for submission to the Prime Minister and Parliament.

Access to communications and communication data

General

Much of the relevant law here is contained currently in the Investigatory Powers Act 2016. The Act repealed and replaced the relevant elements of the Regulation of Investigatory Powers Act 2000, the Data Retention and Investigatory Powers Act 2014, and the Anti-Terrorism, Crime and Security Act 2001.

Interception of communications

Targeted interception

This involves accessing and making available the content of an electronic or postal communication, e.g. listening to a phone call or reading an email during the course of its transmission. The 2016 Act conferred powers on nine agencies. These are GCHQ, the Security and Intelligence Services, the Ministry of Defence, HMRC, the National Police Agency, the Police Service of Northern Ireland, Police Scotland and the Metropolitan Police.

Any such interception is lawful only if effected pursuant to a warrant. Interception warrants are issued by the Secretary of State for Home Affairs on application by the head of any of the above services.

A warrant that relates to a particular person, organisation or set of premises, should name the person, organisation or premises in question. A warrant that relates to a group of persons who have a common purpose, e.g. a particular terrorist group or movement, should describe that common purpose or activity and name or describe as many of the persons involved as is reasonably practicable.

To become effective and available for use an interception warrant must be approved by a Judicial Commissioner, i.e. a senior judicial office holder of High Court rank or equivalent. An interception warrant remains valid for six months.

The conditions required for the grant and approval of an interception warrant are that: it is considered necessary and proportionate for the protection of national security, the prevention and detention of serious crime or the economic well-being of the state where this has implications for national security and the information sought cannot be obtained by any less intrusive means.

In those instances where an interception warrant is requested in order to access the communications of a Member of Parliament, this should not be granted without the Prime Minister's consent.

A warrant to intercept communications subject to legal privilege, e.g. those between lawyer and client relating to legal proceedings, should not be granted unless there are 'exceptional compelling circumstances' which make the interception necessary and arrangements are in place to determine how the material will be 'handled, retained, used and destroyed'.

The government's case for the interception power was put as follows:

> Interception is a vital tool that allows law enforcement and the security and intelligence agencies to identify and understand serious crime and national security threats facing the UK. It provides the intelligence to support operational activity which leads to arrests and prosecutions. Terrorists increasingly use a range of communications services to radicalise, recruit and plan their attacks. Criminals use these services to commit crime and evade detection. Law enforcement and the security and intelligence agencies must be able to continue to access terrorists' and criminals' communications to counter these threats and protect the public (Home Office Factsheet, Interception of Communications, www.gov.uk).

Unlawful use of the above powers is a criminal offence. Nor may the product of an interception be used as evidence in legal proceedings.

Bulk interceptions

This is concerned with the collection of communications sent and received by unspecified persons outside of the United Kingdom whether or not the persons whose communications are affected are suspected of any activity prejudicial to the well-being of the domestic state. The collection of any such volume of communications will be followed normally by a process of selection to determine which of these should be read, looked at or listened to.

The power is available to the intelligence and security agencies only. It is not, therefore, a power which may be used by the police. The legality of any such bulk interception is dependent on the grant of a warrant to the head of the agency concerned by the Secretary of State for Home Affairs and approval by a Judicial Commissioner.

A bulk interception warrant may be granted where considered necessary for purposes of national security, the prevention or detection of crime or the economic well-being of the state where this has implications for national security. Its issue, and the actions permitted by it, should be proportionate to the pursuit of any of these purposes.

The warrant need not specify the name or names of any persons or their addresses. Such warrant should, however, contain some general statements of the type of particular threat or activity in connection with which it is to be used, e.g. planned attacks by Isis.

A bulk interception warrant should not be granted or used if the desired information could have been obtained by a less intrusive means. Bulk interception of communications without a warrant is a criminal offence.

The government's case

Due to the nature of the global internet, the route a particular communication will travel is largely unpredictable. Access to large volumes of data is essential to enable communications relating to subjects of interest to be identified and subsequently pieced together in the course of an investigation (Home Office Factsheet, Bulk Interception, www.gov.uk).

Communications data

Definitions

This consists of information relating to the use of a communications system, but not the content of the communications, transmitted through it. Communications data would, therefore, include data showing certain communications had taken place between whom, when and how often. This might be details of numbers of phone calls, the numbers called and when, or similar material relating to sending, receiving, etc., of texts or emails.

The definition of communications data extends also to internet connection records. These are records held by internet service providers or wi-fi operators. Full web addresses are not included as these could be defined as 'content' rather than 'data'. Thus a connection to 'google.co.uk' or perhaps 'facebook.com' would constitute data. Records of searches made, and for what, would be content.

For the purposes of authorised access to it, communications data is divided into two categories:

(a) Targeted data communications.

(b) Bulk data communications data.

Targeted data communications consists of those made by a particular target or device and passing between such targets or devices. Bulk data communications are those not so targeted consisting, accordingly, of communications between members of the public generally.

Targeted data communications: access and retention

Communications data may be acquired and accessed by those public authorities specified by Parliament. Currently these include the police, the intelligence services, the NHS, local authorities, the Financial Service Authority, the Serious Fraud Office and both the ambulance and fire services.

This data should be obtained on a case-by-case basis as authorised by a senior officer of the authority at a rank determined by Parliament. Generally, in the police, this would be an officer of the rank of Superintendent or above. Communications data may be acquired where this is believed to be reasonable and proportionate for the preservation of national security, the prevention or detection of crime or disorder, the economic well-being of the country where this has implications for national security, the interests of public health, public safety, the collection of revenue, financial regulation, the investigation of miscarriages of justice, the prevention of death or injury, the identification of someone who has died or to find next of kin. In these contexts, the acquisition which consists of internet connection records is limited to identifying the sender of a communication, the communications services a person is using, or to determine whether a person has been accessing or making illegal material available online.

The acquisition of data communications by a local authority is lawful only with the approval of a justice of the peace. Local authorities have no right of access to internet communication records.

In order to make communications data readily accessible to the government bodies and agencies specified, communications services providers may be ordered to retain any such materials as specified in a data retention notice for any period of up to twelve months.

A decision to serve a data retention notice should be made by the Secretary of State and approved by a Judicial Commissioner. A retention notice should specify the operation to which it applies, the data which is to be retained and the period for which it is to be detained.

Bulk communications data

Access to communications in bulk targeting particular individuals, devices or sources, is limited to the security and intelligence services. Such access must be authorised by warrant from the Secretary of State and approved by a Judicial Commissioner. The granting of such access is permissible only where it is necessary and proportionate to the protection of national security and to enable those services to carry out their statutory functions in that context. The data communications which may be accessed in bulk do not include internet connection records nor, as with targeted data, may any right of access be given to the content of such communications.

Provision is made for the Secretary of State to establish a 'Request Filter' system. This will be concerned primarily with the process for dealing with complex data communications requests. In essence this will be done by a specialised unit at the Home Office and will involve the filtering out of relevant from irrelevant data before this is supplied to the agency to which the warrant has been granted.

The government's view

Communications data is an essential tool for the full range of law enforcement activity and national security investigations. It can be used to investigate crime, to keep children safe, support of disprove alibis or tie suspects to a particular crime scene. Sometimes communications data is the only way to identify offenders, particularly where offences are committed on-line, such as child exploitation or fraud (Investigatory Powers Bill, Communications Data and Home Office Factsheet, www.gov.uk).

Equipment interference

Definition

Information given on the website of the Security Service (MI5) provides the following description:

This is the practice of gaining access to computers and like devices in order to monitor data and communications such as geolocation, texts and emails. The practice is known otherwise as computer network exploitation ('CNE'), cyber espionage or, perhaps most popularly, as 'hacking'.

Briefing material supplied to MPs during the passage of the Bill through Parliament explained the matter as follows:

> Equipment interference is not passive. It is more likely to involve activity breaking into an adversary's computer network in order to monitor, disrupt, deny or degrade their communications. This could be as straightforward as using someone's login credentials to gain access to data held on a computer. But there are more sophisticated means of gaining access to people's devices and computers such as through infecting them with malware.

Prior to the enactment of the current investigatory powers legislation, equipment interference was used primarily by military, security and intelligence agencies generally in order to 'exploit, attack and defend against adversarial entities or malicious users'. It consists of techniques and processes that use computers or computer networks to penetrate targeted systems or networks. In 2013, it was claimed that the National Security Agency of the United States had hacked into more than 50,000 computer networks around the world as part of its global intelligence-gathering operations.

Targeted equipment interference warrants

The Act provides that equipment interference is lawful in the United Kingdom only if done pursuant to a warrant. This should be issued by the Secretary of State and approved by a Judicial Commissioner.

The police may apply for an equipment interference warrant for the purpose of preventing or detecting serious crime. In the case of the security and intelligence agencies, a warrant may be applied for on grounds of national security, preventing or detecting serious crime, or in the economic well-being of the United Kingdom where this relates to security interests. Whichever service has applied for the warrant, it should be granted approval only if it is considered necessary for, and proportionate to, the particular use for which the warrant states it is required.

An equipment interference warrant remains valid for six months.

Bulk equipment interference

This refers to equipment interference in order to obtain overseas related communications, equipment data or 'other information'. The term extends, therefore, to that sent or received by unspecified persons outside of the 'British Islands'.

A warrant to obtain such material may be granted to the security and intelligence services only and should be considered necessary and proportionate to the fulfilment of their statutory function in the context of protecting national security, the prevention and detection of serious crime or the economic well-being of the nation where this relates to the protection of national security.

A bulk equipment interference warrant should be issued by the Secretary of State and, to become effective approved by a Judicial Commissioner. A warrant so issued and approved remains in effect for six months.

Should such bulk equipment interference yield material relating to persons in the United Kingdom this may not be examined save subject to the terms of a targeted equipment interference warrant as explained above.

The government's case

> Carefully directed searches of large volumes of data allow the agencies to identify patterns of activity that the agencies would otherwise be unable to discover. This significantly narrows

down the areas for investigation, prioritises intelligence leads, and provides valuable information that can be followed by MI5 or law enforcement agencies. Access to this data is crucial to monitor known and high-priority threats and uncover other identities or communications methods targets may be using. Access to large volumes of data is essential to enable fragments of communications or other data relating to subjects of interest to be identified and subsequently pieced together in the course of an investigation (Home Office Factsheet, Bulk Equipment Interference Warrants: www.gov.uk/government/publications/investigatory-powers-bill-fact-sheets).

Bulk personal datasets

A bulk personal dataset (BPD) is a dataset containing information about a wide range of people, most of whom are not of interest to the security and intelligence agencies (Interception of Investigatory Powers Bill, Draft Codes of Practice).

Examples of BDPs would include the electoral roll, driving licences, telephone directories, the land registry, national insurance numbers, tax returns, lists of persons holding passports, persons holding licensed firearms, etc.

BPDs may often include large amounts of personal information, most of which will relate to persons not on the 'security radar'.

Warrants authorising the retention and examination of BFDs may be granted to the security and intelligence agencies only. Warrants are of two types:

(a) class BPD warrants;

(b) specific BPD warrants.

A class BPD warrant authorises retention and examination of a particular category of datasets, e.g. those containing travel information, but may not include health records.

Specific dataset warrants relate to a particular dataset, i.e. one that does not fall within an existing class.

Whether class or specific, a BPD warrant may be granted by the Secretary of State where it is believed that this is necessary and proportionate for a stated operation conducted for the purposes of national security, the prevention or detection of crime or the economic well-being of the United Kingdom so far as this is relevant to the interests of national security. The warrant does not become effective until approved by a Judicial Commissioner.

The dataset or sets examined under a warrant should be limited to those needed for the operational purposes stated in it.

A bulk personal dataset should not be regarded as 'necessary' solely because it relates to the activities of a trade union.

Bulk personal datasets remain valid for six months.

The government's case

Bulk personal datasets are essential in helping the security and intelligence agencies identify subjects of interest or individuals who surface in the course of an investigation, to establish links between individuals and groups, to understand better a subject of interest's behaviour and connections and quickly to exclude the innocent. In short, they enable the agencies to join the dots in an investigation and to focus their attention on individuals or organisations that threaten our national security (Home Office Factsheet, Bulk Personal Datasets and www.gov.uk).

Encrypted data

Encryption refers to the process of turning computer data into a series of letters and/or numbers which cannot be deciphered or 'unscrambled' except with the correct password or key. The practice has developed for the purposes of confidentiality and transaction security in e-commerce.

Where encrypted information has been obtained by a law enforcement agency through the exercise of one of its powers, e.g. the execution of a warrant under this or other statutory provision, s 49 of the Regulation of Investigatory Powers Act 2000 enables a properly authorised person to serve a notice on a specified individual or organisation requiring such to deliver up the information in intelligible form or supply the key necessary to decrypt it. Failure to comply with such notice is an offence (s 53).

An encryption notice may be served in the interests of:

- national security;
- preventing or detecting crime;
- the economic well-being of the United Kingdom where this relates to national security.

The person serving the notice must have reasonable grounds for believing that:

(i) the protected information is in possession of the persons on whom the notice is served;

(ii) its service is necessary in any of the interests cited above;

(iii) its service is proportionate to what is sought to be achieved;

(iv) an intelligible version of the information cannot be obtained otherwise.

Permission to serve an encryption notice must be granted by a judge or by the Secretary of State for the Home Department in the case of an application by a member of the intelligence services (Sched 2).

The executive's powers in relation to encrypted data were extended by the Investigatory Powers Act. This included a provision to require a Communications Service Provider (CSP) by way of a 'technical capability notice' to have in place systems to allow authorised agencies ready and easy access to encrypted material held by it. A technical capability notice may be served by the Secretary of State where this is necessary and proportionate to the given statutory purpose of the investigation and where the notice has been approved by a Judicial Commissioner. The government has stated that such requirements should only be placed on those companies likely to be subject to data communications requests on a regular basis.

Scrutiny of the exercise and use of investigatory powers

A number of agencies and procedures have been created for the purpose of seeking to ensure that the powers of surveillance made available to the police and to the security and intelligence services are exercised efficiently, legally, and for the purposes laid down in the enabling legislation. Principal amongst these are the Investigatory Powers Commission (Investigatory Powers Act 2016), the Investigatory Powers Tribunal (Regulation of Investigatory Powers Act 2000, s 65) and the Intelligence and Security Committee of the House of Commons (Justice and Security Act 2013, s 1).

Two further Commissioners for the supervision and regulation of the use of investigatory powers were created by the Protection of Freedoms Act 2012.

(a) The Commissioner for the Retention and Use of Biometric Material (the 'Biometrics Commissioner'). The Commissioner's role is:

- to keep under review the retention and use by the police of DNA samples, DNA profiles and fingerprints;
- to decide applications by the police to retain DNA profiles and fingerprints;
- to review national security determinations made by the police for the purpose of retaining such materials.

(b) The Surveillance Camera Commissioner. The Commissioner's main areas of concern are to:

- encourage compliance with the surveillance camera code of practice;
- review how the code is working;
- provide the Minister with advice about whether the code should be amended.

The Investigatory Powers Commission (IPC)

This consists of a body of Judicial Commissioners headed by the Investigatory Powers Commissioner. It is tasked with scrutinising, investigating, and auditing the use of investigatory powers by those to whom these are entrusted. The IPC will exercise the functions previously carried out by the Interception of Communications Commissioner, the Intelligence Services Commissioner, and the Chief Surveillance Commissioner – all created by the Regulation of Investigatory Powers Act 2000.

Members of the Commission are appointed by the Prime Minister for renewable terms of three years. All must hold, or have held, high judicial office (High Court judge or equivalent or above). Within each three-year period a member of the Commission may be dismissed only by resolutions of both Houses of Parliament. As explained, individual members of the Commission, i.e. Judicial Commissioners, have responsibility for giving approval or otherwise to the various types of warrants needed for the exercise of powers relating to the interception of communications, access to communications data and equipment interference. The Investigatory Powers Commissioner is charged also with the submission of annual reports on the Commission's work to the Prime Minister. Such reports should then be laid before Parliament. Other reports on matters of particular concern may be issued by the Commissioner as and when this would appear to be appropriate.

The Investigatory Powers Tribunal (IPT)

The Tribunal is an independent court with the same status as the High Court. It decides complaints under the Investigatory Powers Act 2016, the Regulation of Investigatory Powers Act 2000, and the Human Rights Act 1998. Its main concern is to determine whether any of the investigatory powers entrusted to public authorities have been used unlawfully, i.e. in ways which were not necessary, proportionate, or for the purposes of any of the public interest objectives ('legitimate aims') provided for in statutes in which the powers are found.

> A complaint can be about any interference which the complainant believes has taken place against him, his property or communications. This includes interception, surveillance, and interference with property. The public authorities include security and intelligence agencies, military and law enforcement agencies, as well as a range of government departments, regulations and local authorities (Investigatory Powers Tribunal, www.ipt-uk.com/).

Members of the Tribunal are appointed by the Prime Minister but may be dismissed by resolutions of both Houses of Parliament only.

The Tribunal makes its decisions by applying the established principles of judicial review. It is the sole forum for dealing with allegations of illegality against any of the security or intelligence agencies. Such matters may not be brought before the ordinary courts of law.

As a result, it was not open to a former member of the intelligence services, who had been refused permission to publish his memoirs, to bring proceedings in the High Court for breach of Art 10 (freedom of expression) against the Security Services Director of Establishment (*R (on application of A)* v *Director of Establishment of the Security Services* [2009] UKSC 12).

An appeal on a point of law lies from the Tribunal to the Court of Appeal. There is no right of appeal from a decision of the Tribunal on its merits.

Criticisms of the Investigatory Powers Act

For some, the Investigatory Powers Act 2016 has been perceived as a 'snoopers' charter' and the legal basis for mass surveillance of people within and without the United Kingdom whether or not suspected of any criminal or terrorist activity. For others, it is a much needed modernisation of legal rules which have lagged behind the pace of communications technology and which will enable the police and intelligence services to respond more effectively and rapidly to the dangers posed by those who would use the cyber world to threaten the safety and security of all those within the domestic state.

Some of the following would be amongst the concerns voiced by those, not necessarily opposed to the Act in its entirety, but perhaps uneasy about the full extent and implications of some of the powers it contains.

(i)   It allows for access to private information and communications on the basis of executive warrant or authorisation, i.e. by a government Minister, or senior member of the security and intelligence services.

(ii)   Bulk authorisations, i.e. those not directed to a particular person(s), premises, or materials are incompatible with the long-established common law rule prohibiting executive use of 'general warrants' (see above p. 570).

(iii)   It enables the police and security and intelligence services to monitor, collect and analyse private information without the knowledge of those affected.

(iv)   It permits access to the personal information of persons not suspected of posing any risk to national security.

(v)   The 'request filter' enables the Home Office to sift through masses of data thereby facilitating the possible collation and correlation of information from a multiplicity of various sources, i.e. 'big data analysis'.

(vi)   The mass collection of data carries with it the temptation to base suspicion on stereotypes rather than 'hard', fact-based evidence.

(vii)   Bulk interception warrants, limited, allegedly, to overseas communications, are effected by tapping fibre optic cables. Since a large amount of domestic internet traffic is routed by the USA, such data may also be caught in the trawl.

(viii) As an IP address may be used by different people at the same time, this could lead to a person being investigated for internet use for which he/she was not responsible.

(ix)   Communications service providers may be required to retain masses of the communications data and internet connection records for up to twelve months.

(x) Warrants are not required for access to internet communications records – only for access to content.

(xi) While internet connection records do not show the content of a website visited, they do show the webpage address which will usually give some indication of the type of material being sought or looked at.

(xii) Authorisation of access to communications data and the issuing of data retention notices may be granted by a senior police officer without the need for judicial approval.

Parliamentary oversight of the Security and Intelligence Services

General parliamentary oversight of the activities of the 'secret services' is carried out by the Intelligence and Security Committee The current Committee was established pursuant to the requirements of the Justice and Security Act 2013, s 1. The Committee consists of nine members. These are selected by each House from its own number. The choice is, however, limited to those nominated by the Prime Minister in consultation with the Leader of the Opposition. Government Ministers are not eligible for membership. The Committee consists, therefore, of backbench MPs and peers only.

The Committee's remit is to examine and oversee the expenditure, administration, policy and operations of both the intelligence and security services, the General Communications Headquarters or 'GCHQ', the Joint Intelligence Organisation in the Cabinet Office, the Office of Security and Counter Terrorism in the Home Office, the Office of Defence Intelligence in the Ministry of Defence and those intelligence and security elements in other government departments or agencies.

Remedies for police malpractice

False arrest and imprisonment

Objective 8

A person arrested unlawfully, either because no power of arrest existed or because any of the requirements of a valid arrest was not complied with, may sue for the tort of false arrest and imprisonment. The tort of assault and battery might also apply both to the above and to abuse of the power of stop and search. An action for false imprisonment would also be available to a person who was detained for a longer period than that permitted by PACE, ss 41–43. The issue whether otherwise lawful detention may be rendered actionable by breaches of the rules relating to the treatment of detainees and the conditions of detention remains a matter of some uncertainty. The probability is that it is not rendered actionable (*Weldon* v *Home Office* [1991] 3 WLR 340; cf. *Middleweek* v *Chief Constable of Merseyside* [1990] 3 All ER 662). As discussed above, failure to comply with any requirement in the Codes of Practice in relation to a person in detention is not actionable in itself.

Habeas corpus

A person who believes he/she has been detained unlawfully – or another person on their behalf – may also apply to the Divisional Court of the Queen's Bench Division for a prerogative writ of habeas corpus. If the court accepts the allegation as set out in the applicant's affidavit, the writ is issued requiring the detained person to be brought before the

For details of habeas corpus proceedings, see above, pp. 394–5. court. The issue is then decided on its merits and, if those holding the detained person cannot provide satisfactory authority or justification, his/her release will be ordered.

Trespass

An action for **trespass** to land and/or goods may be used where a person's premises have been searched and perhaps items seized, if there was no legal authority for such intrusion or if any of the requirements for valid search were not complied with. An entry which is lawful initially (either with a warrant to search or under s 17) may be rendered unlawful *ab initio* and, therefore, a trespass from the beginning, if a police officer does something in the premises which exceeds the purpose for which the power of entry was given. In *Harrison and Hope* v *Chief Constable of Greater Manchester*, unreported, 14 August 1994, the police entered premises lawfully under s 17 to arrest a person believed to have committed an arrestable offence. The suspect was not there. However, the police searched the premises, including a wardrobe and drawers in a bedroom belonging to an 11-year-old boy. The plaintiffs were awarded £2,000 for trespass.

Malicious prosecution

Malice, in the sense of 'any motive other than a desire to bring a criminal to justice', must be shown to establish the tort of malicious procurement of a warrant. Incompetence or negligence is not enough (*Keegan* v *Chief Constable Merseyside* [2003] EWCA Civ 936).

Misconduct in public office

In particularly serious cases of police misconduct, the officer or officers involved may be charged with the common law offence of misconduct in public office. The offence is committed where a public officer, without reasonable excuse or justification, wilfully neglects to perform his/her duty or is guilty of wilful misconduct, to such a degree as to be so far below acceptable standards as to amount to an abuse of the public's trust (*Re Attorney-General's Reference No. 3 of 2004* [2004] EWCA Crim 868). The maximum sentence for the offence is life imprisonment.

Negligence

For reasons of public policy and the effective performance of their duties, the police may not be held liable in damages for negligent performance of their 'core' functions, viz. the investigation and prevention of crime and the maintenance of law and order (see *Hill* v *Chief Constable of West Yorkshire*, supra). Thus, no liability attached to the police for the shooting of a person believed to be about to commit a robbery. This was so despite the fact that the officer who fired the shot had been briefed, erroneously, that the suspect had fired on the police when carrying out previous offences (*Davis* v *Commissioner of Police for the Metropolis* [2016] EWHC 38 (QB)).

Human Rights Act 1998

No exemption from liability in damages attaches to the police for breaches of the 1998 Act. Accordingly, the police may be liable for:

- failure to protect any person from a real and immediate threat of death or serious violence resulting from the criminal acts of another (the *Osman* principle), e.g. late response to serious incident of violent disorder (beating of claimant with baseball bats) after receipt of a series of 999 calls (*Sarjantson* v *Humberside Police Chief Constable* [2013] EWCA Civ 1252);

- failure to properly investigate unexplained or violent deaths or serious crimes of violence or allegations of ill treatment (ECHR, Articles 2 and 3);

- incidents of unlawful arrest and/or detention (ECHR, Article 5);

- unlawful entry into private premises or breach of privacy by surveillance (ECHR, Article 8).

A person aggrieved by the actions of a police officer also has the option of making a complaint according to the police complaints procedure now contained in the Police Reform Act 2002, Pt 2. This may result in the officer being disciplined but does not provide the complainant with any right of legal redress or of financial compensation.

Police Community Support Officers

Objective
9

Police Community Support Officers (PCSOs) are civilian employees of police authorities designated by chief police officers to exercise a range of powers. Currently the process for such designation and the powers, to date, conferred on CSOs may be found in the Police Reform Act 2002, s 122 and Sched 8. These include power to:

- issue fixed penalty notices relating to various types of anti-social behaviour, truancy, and offences against local by-laws and to disperse and remove any person under 16 to their place of residence;

- request name and address of any persons committing a fixed penalty offence or offences that cause injury, alarm, distress or damage;

- detain for up to 30 minutes pending the arrival of a police officer, any person who, as required above, refused to give their name and address and to search such persons for items that might be used to cause injury or effect escape.

PCSOs may also be designated powers to:

- require a person not to consume alcohol in a specified public place and confiscate alcohol from persons under 18;
- seize tobacco from persons under 16;
- enter premises to save life and limb under PACE, section 17;
- remove abandoned vehicles;
- stop and direct traffic;
- carry out road checks under PACE, s 4;
- enforce cordons under the Terrorism Act 2000;
- stop and search persons and vehicles under the Terrorism Act 2000;
- require persons to stop begging in public places;
- seize controlled drugs unlawfully found in a person's possession.

Also, it should be remembered, that PCSOs have the powers of arrest in respect of indictable offences available to all private citizens.

Summary

The chapter provides comprehensive coverage of the extent of the principal police powers of search, arrest and detention found, in the main, in the Police and Criminal Evidence Act 1984, as amended and extended by the Serious and Organised Crime and Police Act 2005. The main principles of the Regulation of Investigatory Powers Act 2000, dealing with, *inter alia*, the legal rules applying to electronic and covert surveillance, are also set out and explained.

Reference

Card and English (1998) *Butterworths' Police Law* (5th edn), London: Butterworths.

Further reading

Card and English (2015) *Police Law* (14th edn), Oxford, Oxford University Press.

Ozin and Norton (2015) PACE: *A Practical Guide to the Police and Criminal Evidence Act 1984* (4th edn), Oxford: Oxford University Press.

Zander (2006) *The Police and Criminal Evidence Act 1984* (5th edn), London: Sweet & Maxwell.

19

Restrictions on the rights of freedom of assembly and association

Objectives

After reading this chapter you should:

1. Understand the distinction between the freedom of assembly and that of association.

2. Know the ingredients of the public order offences in the Public Order Act 1986.

3. Appreciate the extent of the common law restrictions on the freedom to march and demonstrate and the concept of breach of the peace.

4. Recognise the extent of the statutory restrictions on the freedom to march and demonstrate.

Introduction: the freedoms defined

Objective
1

The freedom of association and assembly encapsulates two related but not entirely identical concepts. The freedom of association refers to the right of the individual to join whichever organisations they wish (e.g. political parties, cause groups, etc.), and implies that the state shall not impose unjustified restrictions on the existence of such groups. The freedom of assembly deals with the right of the individual to meet with others in public or private and, in concert with them, to march or demonstrate in support of whichever cause they may wish to further.

Freedom of association

English law imposes few restrictions on the freedom to form and join organisations for political or other purposes. The freedom does not extend, however, to those groups which would seek to achieve their objectives by overtly violent means. Hence the Terrorism Act 2000 gives the Secretary of State for the Home Department the power to proscribe any organisation they believe 'commits, participates, prepares, promotes or is otherwise engaged in acts of terrorism' (s 3).

Freedom of assembly

This is subject to a wide range of statutory and common law restrictions. Most of the relevant statutory rules are to be found in the Public Order Act 1986 and the Criminal Justice and Public Order Act 1994. The common law power to do all that is reasonably necessary to prevent breaches of the peace is also of considerable practical significance in this context.

The Public Order Act 1986 gave the police extensive powers to regulate the conduct of both processions (i.e. gatherings which move from A to B) and public assemblies (i.e. gatherings which stay in one place). The Act also contains a range of offences with which those who endanger public order may be charged. The Criminal Justice and Public Order Act 1994 supplemented the 1986 Act, principally by providing additional preventative powers to deal with types of assemblies not covered by the latter.

Statutory restrictions and marches and assemblies

Marches

Objective 2

The 1986 Act contains three main powers or requirements in relation to the above. These are:

- the need to give advance notice;
- the power to impose conditions;
- the power to ban.

Advance notice

Section 11 requires that the organisers of certain types of public procession must give the police at least six days' advance notice of their intentions. The types of processions affected are those which are intended:

(a) to show 'support for or opposition to the views or actions of any person or body of persons';

(b) 'to publicise a cause or campaign';

(c) 'to mark or commemorate an event'.

The requirement does not apply to processions which are 'customarily held in the police area' or to funeral processions. Nor does it apply where it is not reasonably practicable for advance notice to be given – i.e. where the procession is an immediate response to a very recent event. In this case notice should be given as soon as is reasonably practicable.

Mass weekly cycle rides held in central London since 1995 at the same time and day of each month, could amount to processions 'commonly or customarily held' in the relevant police area for the purposes of exemption from the notice requirement notwithstanding that the route taken varied significantly from week to week (*Kay* v *Metropolitan Police Commissioner* [2008] UKHL 69).

The notice should specify the date, time and proposed route of the procession. The name and address of one of the organisers should also be included. It should be delivered to a police station in the district where the procession is to take place. Failure to comply with any of these requirements renders the organisers guilty of an offence.

Section 11 does not require that the police give consent to a proposed march. It is solely concerned with the giving of notice. It does, however, forewarn the police so that the powers in ss 12 and 13 may be exercised as is appropriate.

Conditions

Section 12 of the 1986 Act allows the police to impose conditions on the conduct of a procession where it is reasonably believed that:

(a) it may result in serious public disorder, serious damage to property or serious disruption to the life of the community; or

(b) the purpose of the organisers is to intimidate other persons so as to prevent them doing what they have a right to do or to make them do what they have a right not to do.

The power may be exercised in advance of the procession by the Chief Constable of the police district in question or 'on the spot' by the senior officer present (which could be an ordinary constable if no more senior officer is in the vicinity). Such conditions may be imposed as appear to be necessary to prevent any of the dangers listed above. On the spot conditions may be imposed verbally. Those imposed in advance should be in writing. These could relate to the route to be taken, the numbers taking part, the display of banners or emblems, etc.

Any person who organises or takes part in a procession and who knowingly fails to comply with such conditions – except where this is due to circumstances beyond the person's control – commits an offence and may be arrested without warrant.

In **Van El and Jukes v Director of Public Prosecutions** [2013] EWHC 195 (Admin), the claimants took part in a march in central London. This was to protest against the government's education policies. A condition was imposed requiring the marchers to follow a particular route and not to enter Trafalgar Square where an anti-capitalist camp had been set up. A police cordon had been put in place to prevent this from happening. This caused some of the marchers to become 'agitated'. Accordingly, and to avoid disorder, the police decided to let them through. Some, including the claimants, then went to Trafalgar Square and joined the camp. They were arrested and convicted of acting in breach of the s 12 condition. The court's findings were:

(i) the police 'on the spot' could let persons through a cordon but could not waive anticipatory conditions imposed by a senior officer;

(ii) where a person left a demonstration, it was a question of fact whether he/she was or was not still participating in the protest and, therefore, subject to any restrictions imposed upon it;

(iii) on the facts of the case, the trial judge had been right to decide that, although the claimants had left the main body of protesters, they were still involved in the protest and bound, therefore, by the condition in question.

Bans

Section 13 provides that if the Chief Constable for the police district where a procession is due to take place 'reasonably believes' that the powers in s 12 will not be sufficient to prevent 'serious public order', they may apply to the local council for an order prohibiting all public processions or any class of the same in the area for a period not exceeding three months. The council may make such order only after receiving the consent of the Secretary of State for the Home Department. In the Metropolitan Police District such bans may be imposed by the Metropolitan Police Commissioner with the Secretary of State for the Home Department's consent.

Any person who organises or takes part in a procession which they know is prohibited commits an offence and may be arrested without warrant.

Section 13 has attracted controversy because it does not permit the police to ban a specific march. Its terms make it clear that only 'blanket bans' (i.e. those affecting all or any class of procession) may be imposed. Inevitably, therefore, where such ban is made, as well as prohibiting those processions which might endanger public order, it will affect processions not thought to represent any such danger whatsoever. The validity of a s 13 ban will not be questioned by a court unless it is unreasonable or capricious (*Kent* v *Commissioner of Police of the Metropolis*, *The Times*, 15 May 1981). This is consistent with the general reluctance of the courts to interfere with the exercise of discretion conferred on chief officers of police except in the most extreme cases where a power is used in a way which could never have been within Parliament's contemplation.

Meetings and assemblies

A public assembly is a gathering of two or more persons in a public place which is wholly or partly open to the air (1986 Act, s 16, as amended by Anti-Social Behaviour Act 2003, s 57). The Public Order Act 1986 provided the police with a power to impose conditions on the holding of such gatherings but did not give any power to impose a ban. A power to ban trespassory assemblies was, however, inserted into the 1986 Act by the Criminal Justice and Public Order Act 1994.

Conditions

The power to impose conditions on a public assembly is contained in s 14 of the 1986 Act. The grounds on which such conditions may be imposed are exactly the same as those applying to processions (see above). The power may be exercised by the Chief Constable of the police district in which the assembly is to take place or by the senior officer 'on the spot'.

An offence is committed by any person who organises or participates in such assembly and who knowingly fails to comply with any condition(s) applying thereto. That person may be arrested without warrant.

A conviction for failure to comply with a s 14 condition cannot be upheld if, on the facts, the ground on which the condition(s) was imposed did not exist or the person accused did not know, and could not reasonably have been expected to know, that the condition had been imposed.

Police v *Reid* [1981] Crim LR 702

In this case, a crowd gathered outside the South African embassy in London to protest against apartheid. Some of the demonstrators shouted and made insulting gestures at persons who were gathering for a reception which was being held at the embassy. A police officer using a loud hailer told the demonstrators to move away from the front of the embassy building. In the officer's view this was justified on the ground of intimidation. The defendant and others who did not comply were arrested and charged with an offence under s 14. In the stipendiary magistrate's opinion, however, causing discomfort did not amount to intimidation.

Intimidation could only occur where a threat or violence was used to compel a person to act in a way inconsistent with their legal rights.

Brickley and Kitson v *The Police*, *unreported*, July 1988

This case was also concerned with a demonstration outside the South African embassy. Again the demonstrators were instructed to move away from the embassy and, on this occasion, to hold their protest in a nearby street. The appellants' conviction for failure to comply was reversed by the Crown Court as, given the noisy and disorderly conditions which prevailed, the Court was not satisfied that they were fully aware either that conditions had been imposed or what those conditions were.

Bans and trespassory assemblies

Section 14A of the 1986 Act contains a power to ban trespassory assemblies. A trespassory assembly is one held on land to which the public has no, or only a restricted, right of access without the permission of the occupier. The procedure for prohibiting such assemblies is the same as that in s 13 relating to processions. The appropriate Chief Constable may apply to the local council for an order banning all such assemblies 'in the district or a part of it' where they reasonably believe that a trespassory assembly is intended to be held which may lead to serious disruption of the life of the community or may do significant damage to land, or to a building or monument which is of historical, archaeological, architectural or scientific interest. Such ban may then be imposed with the consent of the Secretary of State for the Home Department. In the Metropolis the banning order is made by the Metropolitan Police Commissioner, again with the Secretary of State for the Home Department's consent.

Any person who takes part in such an assembly knowing that it has been prohibited commits an offence (s 14B).

The wording of s 14A makes it clear that a trespassory assembly may take place on a public highway since this is a place to which the public have 'only a limited right of access' (i.e. to pass and repass). Hence, should a gathering of 20 or more take place on a highway within an area to which a banning order applies, those knowingly assembled in contravention of it commit an offence under s 14B except where the assembly does not cause unreasonable interference to the public's primary right of passage (*DPP* v *Jones* [1997] 2 All ER 119).

Protests and demonstrations in the vicinity of Parliament

Additional powers to control demonstrations of one or more persons in the area surrounding the Palace of Westminster were conferred by the Serious Organised Crime and Police Act, 2005, ss 132–138. The objective of these provisions was explained by Sir Anthony Clarke MR, in *R (on application of Haw)* v *Secretary of State for the Home Department* [2006] EWCA Civ 532.

> The purpose of such control and regulation [is] not to suppress legitimate extra-parliamentary opposition, but because of Parliament's concern that the unrestricted exercise of freedom of expression so close to Parliament posed a threat to democratic freedom.

The Act does not contain any outright power to ban demonstrations in what is referred to as the 'designated area', viz. any area so specified by order of the Secretary of State for the Home Department within one kilometre of Parliament Square. It does provide, however, that it is an offence to hold a demonstration without 'authorisation'. Such authorisation must be granted providing it is sought according to the stipulated procedure. Conditions may, however, be imposed where in the 'reasonable opinion' of the Metropolitan Police Commissioner these are 'necessary' to prevent:

- hindrance to persons entering or leaving the Palace of Westminster;
- hindrance to the proper operation of Parliament;
- serious public disorder;
- serious damage to property;
- disruption to the life of the community;
- a security risk in any part of the designated area;
- risk to the safety of members of the public.

Conditions may relate to the time, place, size and duration of the demonstration, and to the items that may be carried (e.g. banner or placards), and to the 'maximum permissible noise levels'.

Persons seeking authorisation to hold a demonstration should, where reasonably practicable, give at least six days' written notice of their intentions. Failing this, notice should be given as soon as is reasonably practicable and, in all cases, not less than 24 hours preceding the planned event. It is an offence to hold a demonstration in contravention of any prescription imposed by the Commissioner.

The above provisions have been held compatible with Art 11 (the right to Association and Assembly) of the European Convention on Human Rights (*Blum* v *DPP* [2006] EWHC 3209 (Admin)).

The Police Reform and Social Responsibility Act 2011, sections 141–149 were enacted to prevent protesters from erecting tents or other structures to be used for the purposes of sleeping in the open area outside the Parliament buildings. The Act provides that a police officer who has reasonable grounds for believing that a person is engaging in such a 'prohibited activity on' the area of Parliament Square or the paths adjoining it may order that person to desist.

Failure to comply with such instruction is an arrestable offence. The restrictions imposed by the Act are not incompatible with the ECHR in Article 10 (freedom of speech) and Article 11 (freedom of assembly and association) (*R (on application Gallestegui* v *Westminster City Council and Others)* [2013] EWCA Civ 28).

Other statutory preventative powers

The above represent the principal statutory powers designed to prevent public processions and assemblies from becoming disorderly or disruptive. As the terms of the various provisions make clear, they have general application to the type of public demonstration often seen on the streets and in public places in the United Kingdom. Further relevant powers may be found in the Anti-Social Behaviour Act 2003 and the Criminal Justice and Public Order Act 1994. The powers in the 2003 Act are directed primarily towards general low-level, disorderly and offensive behaviour rather than, as with the above, public protests and demonstrations connected with a particular cause or expression of opinion, political or otherwise. The Criminal Justice and Public Order Act was passed to deal with public concerns relating to the activities and lifestyles of 'new-age' travellers, protests against fox-hunting and 'blood sports' and crowds of young people attending 'raves'. It contains a range of related restrictions and police powers which apply in private premises and property.

Powers to disperse disorderly groups

Section 30 of the 2003 Act enables a senior police officer to delineate an area in which there has been significant and persistent anti-social behaviour. The officer may then authorise the giving of 'dispersal directions' to groups of two or more whose behaviour in the area has resulted in, or is likely to result in, members of the public being harassed, alarmed or distressed. Such authorisation may be for a maximum period of six months.

Failure to comply with such directions is an offence. The power may not be used against persons engaged in a lawful demonstration taking place within the terms of the Public Order Act 1986, s 11. Persons under 16 and not under 'effective parental control' between 9 pm and 6 am may be 'removed' to their place of residence. Reasonable coercion may be used: (*R (on application of PW)* v *Metropolitan Police Commissioner* [2006] EWCA Civ 458). For the purposes of the Act, a public place includes highways and any other place to which, at the material time, the public have a right of access on payment or by express or implied permission.

Despite being concerned primarily with general, low-level, disruptive and unruly behaviour, the Act's dispersal power may be used to control the type of public protests and demonstrations which engage the rights in ECHR, Art 11. That this had never been Parliament's intention was rejected in *R (on application of Singh)* v *Chief Constable West Midlands* [2005] EWHC 2840 (Admin). There, the court took the view that the provisions in s 30(5)(b) preventing the use of the dispersal power against marches covered by the 1986 Act, s 11, clearly illustrated that Parliament had been mindful of the use of power in the disputed context and had thus taken care to limit that use but not to proscribe it absolutely.

Power to remove trespassers on land

Section 61 of the 1994 Act allows the police to order persons trespassing on land to leave if certain conditions are satisfied. These are that the senior officer present reasonably believes that two or more persons are trespassing on land with a common purpose to reside there for any period, that the occupier has taken reasonable steps to ask them to leave and:

(a) a damage has been caused to the land or property or threatening, abusive or insulting words have been used towards the occupier or anyone acting on their behalf; or

(b) there are six or more vehicles on the land.

The 1994 Act was amended by the Anti-Social Behaviour Act 2003, s 60, to include a further power to order persons to leave land and remove any vehicles or other property where they have 'at least one vehicle on the land', 'a common purpose of residing there for any period', the occupier has asked the police to remove the vehicle, and there is a suitable alternative caravan site in the locality (CJPO Act 1994, s 62A).

Where an order to leave has been given, any person who fails to comply with it as soon as is reasonably practicable may be arrested without warrant and charged with an offence. A conviction will only follow, however, if the court is satisfied that the trespassers knew or should have known that they had been requested to leave.

Krumpa and Anderson v *DPP* [1989] Crim LR 295

K and A were living in converted buses on land belonging to a Tesco store. A Tesco representative told them that bulldozers would soon be arriving on the site to prepare it for development. Three weeks later the police ordered K and A to leave the site. It was held that the information conveyed by the Tesco representative to K and A did not amount to a request to leave. The police were not empowered, therefore, to order them to leave the site. It followed that K and A committed no offence when they failed to comply with the instruction.

A further power to deal with trespasses not involving damage or the danger of disorder is contained in ss 77 and 78. This allows the appropriate local authority to direct persons residing in vehicles:

- on land forming part of a highway,
- on any unoccupied land, or
- on any occupied land without the occupier's permission,

to leave the land in question. Failure to comply constitutes an offence but is not arrestable without warrant. In addition, a magistrate's court may authorise the authority to take such steps as are reasonably necessary to ensure that the trespassers and their vehicles are removed (s 78).

Before issuing any such directions the local authority is under a duty to have regard to the individual circumstances of the persons affected and any duties which may be owed to them under any relevant Children, Education, Social Services and Housing Acts (*R v Lincolnshire County Council, ex parte Atkinson* [1996] Admin LR 529). Only those on the land when the directions are served are affected by them. Hence, such directions do not apply to those who arrive at a later date (*ibid.*).

Although the use of powers to remove travellers from private land may touch upon their ECHR Art 8 rights (to home, family life, etc.), no breach of the Convention is committed if the action is taken for legitimate aims of public policy, e.g. protection of the environment, the rights of others. Also, as in these circumstances it is probable that the 'home' was established illegally, it is more likely that removal will be regarded as a proportionate response to the original unlawful act (*R (on application of Fuller) v Chief Constable of Dorset* [2001] EWHC 1057 (Admin)).

Powers to deal with aggravated trespass

A trespass becomes an aggravated trespass if the intention of those involved is to intimidate those taking part in a lawful activity (e.g. hunting) on land (excluding highways) or to obstruct or disrupt that activity (s 68). Aggravated trespass is an offence and is arrestable without warrant. Where an aggravated trespass is committed the police may order those involved to leave the land as soon as is practicable and may arrest without warrant those who refuse to do so (s 69).

No section 68 offence is committed by a trespasser if he/she can produce credible evidence to suggest that the activity he/she went on to the land to disrupt was not lawful. In these circumstances it is for the Crown to establish the legality of the activity in question.

An activity is unlawful for the purposes of section 68 only if its primary purpose was the commission of a specific criminal offence against the law of England and Wales. It is not enough to show that it had some distant connection with an allegedly illegal activity in another jurisdiction. In *Richardson v Director of Public Prosecutions* [2014] UKSC 8, the accused had no defence when they went to disrupt the activities of a shop which was selling goods from an Israeli firm which was operating on the West Bank of the Jordan contrary to various resolutions of the United Nations.

Trespass into royal residencies and other designated sites

SOCPA 2005, s 128, introduced the above offence following a number of well-publicised intrusions into royal residencies. The offence may be committed at any site 'designated' by the Secretary of State for the Home Department. Such designation may be made in relation to:

- any Crown land;
- any land owned privately by the Monarch or her immediate heir;
- any land where designation would appear to be in the interests of national security.

Powers to deal with 'raves'

Section 63 of the 1994 Act, as amended by the Anti-Social Behaviour Act 2003, s 58, provides that a police officer of the rank of superintendent or above may direct persons who it is reasonably believed have come to prepare, wait for, or attend a 'rave', to leave the land in question and remove any vehicles or other property they have with them. A 'rave' is a gathering of twenty or more 'at which amplified music is played during the night . . . and is such as, by reason of its loudness and duration and the time at which it is played . . . likely to cause serious distress to the inhabitants of the locality'. Any person who fails to comply with such direction commits an offence and may be arrested without warrant.

Section 64 gives the police a power to enter upon land without warrant to ascertain if a rave is taking place there or to enforce a direction issued under s 63. The police may also stop persons proceeding to a rave providing the power is exercised within five miles of the site of the gathering. Disobedience of police instructions would amount to an obstruction of the particular officer in the course of their duty.

The position in Northern Ireland

For Northern Ireland different provisions for marches and processions were introduced by the Public Processions (Northern Ireland) Act 1998.

Persons organising public processions or protests are required to give the police at least 28 days' notice of their intentions (s 6). Conditions may then be imposed, not by the police, but by a body known as the Parades Commission for Northern Ireland (s 1). The members of the Commission are appointed by the Secretary of State for Northern Ireland. The Commission is, however, 'not to be regarded as the servant or agent of the Crown' (s 1 and Sched 1). The Commission will be empowered to impose such conditions as it 'considers necessary' (s 8). In so doing the Commission will be required 'to have regard to' *inter alia*:

- any public disorder or damage to property which may result from the procession or protest;
- any disruption to the life of the community which the procession or protest may cause;
- any impact which the procession or protest may have on relationships within the community; and
- the desirability of allowing a procession customarily held along a particular route to be held along that route.

Failure to comply with any such condition, unless because of circumstances beyond the person's control, will constitute an offence punishable by a maximum sentence of six months' imprisonment.

Note that the power to impose conditions on processions and protests in Northern Ireland is not dependent on the Commission having a *reasonable* belief that any of the above consequences might result from a particular procession. It is sufficient that the Commission has directed its attention towards these possibilities.

The power to ban processions and protests in Northern Ireland is vested in the Secretary of State. The power may be exercised where the Minister 'is of the opinion' that a ban is 'necessary in the public interest' having regard to the possible consequences of the procession in terms of serious public disorder; serious damage to property; serious disruption to the life of the community; serious impact on relationships within the community; or any undue demands which may be placed on the police or military forces (s 11). The Secretary of State is also empowered to ban all or any class of processions or protests in a particular area for a period not exceeding 28 days based on consideration of similar criteria.

Common law preventative powers

Breach of the peace

Objective
3

It is the duty of every police officer to do all that is reasonably necessary to prevent an actual or reasonably apprehended and imminent breach of the peace. The concept has already been defined in the context of common law powers of arrest (see *R v Howell* [1982] QB 416).

In relation to the preservation of order during processions and at public and private meetings, the obligation to prevent breaches of the peace provides the police with a variety of powers. These have been held to include the following.

Arrest

A police officer may arrest without warrant any person who:

(a) has committed a breach of the peace in their presence;

(b) they reasonably believe is about to commit a breach of the peace;

(c) they reasonably believe is about to renew a breach of the peace which has been committed or is reasonably believed to have been committed (*R v Howell*, *supra*; *Lain v Chief Constable of Cambridgeshire*, 14 October 1999, unreported). The essential principle that a breach of the peace must involve violence or the threat of it was confirmed in *Percy v DPP* [1995] 3 All ER 124. The appellant trespassed on a military base on a number of occasions and had been bound over to keep the peace. She did not commit or threaten any violence. The Divisional Court took the view that mere civil trespass does not amount to a breach of the peace. It followed that the magistrates had no power to bind her over.

Detention

The House of Lords, in *Albert v Lavin* [1982] AC 546, held that the reasonable steps which a police officer may take to prevent a person breaching the peace included the power to detain that person against their will without arresting them for so long as the necessity exists.

The power to detain to prevent a further breach of the peace is limited to circumstances where there is a real, rather than a fanciful, apprehension based on all the circumstances that if released the prisoner will commit or renew their breach of the peace within a short time (*McGrogan v Chief Constable of Cleveland* [2002] EWCA Civ 86).

Stop

A person may be stopped from proceeding to any place for the purpose of participating in any procession or assembly if it is reasonably believed that breaches of the peace will be occasioned by the same. The power to stop may be used in circumstances where 'there is a real risk of a breach of the peace in the sense that it is in close proximity both in place and time' (*per* Skinner J, *Moss v McLachlan* (1984) 149 JP 167). In this case, which arose out of the 1984 Miners' Strike, the power was held to provide sufficient justification for stopping a group of miners from travelling to various collieries to join fellow strikers on the picket lines. The miners in question were stopped as they left the motorway at a point within five miles of the pits to which they were travelling. Breaches of the peace had already occurred on the picket lines which they intended to join. The court was in no doubt that in these circumstances the police possessed the power to stop and that those miners who had refused to do so were guilty of obstruction.

Desist and disperse

Where a procession or meeting which it is reasonably believed may result in a breach of the peace is in progress or is about to commence, any person organising, conducting or addressing the meeting may be ordered to desist and those taking part may be ordered to disperse. Any person may be arrested for obstruction if such instruction is ignored. Two famous cases illustrate the point.

O'Kelly v *Harvey* (1883) 14 LR Ir 105

This case concerned a public meeting in Co. Fermanagh to protest about the rents imposed on Irish tenant farmers. The meeting was to be addressed by Parnell, then leader of the Irish Nationalist Party. It was believed that the meeting would be attended and disrupted by loyalists. The defendant, a justice of the peace, ordered the plaintiff, one of the organisers, to disperse the meeting. When the plaintiff refused, the defendant took hold of him and gave him into the custody of a police officer. The plaintiff's action for assault and battery was unsuccessful. The court's reasoning was as follows:

> even assuming that the danger to the public peace arose altogether from the threatened attack of another body on the plaintiff and his friends, still; if the defendant . . . had just grounds for believing that the peace could only be preserved by withdrawing the plaintiff and his friends from the attack with which they were threatened it was . . . the duty of the defendant to take that course (*per* Law CJ).

Duncan v *Jones* [1936] 1 KB 218

In this case, D was one of the organisers of the National Unemployed Workers Movement. She wished to hold and address a meeting outside a centre for unemployed persons. Disturbances had occurred at meetings she had conducted there in the past. Accordingly, she was instructed by J, a police officer, to move away from the centre and to hold the meeting in a street at a distance of some 175 yards. It was held that D had been rightly arrested for obstruction when she refused to do so.

It might also be appropriate to mention under this subheading the power of the police to order the numbers participating in a particular gathering to be reduced.

Piddington v *Bates* [1960] 3 All ER 660

In this case, 18 persons gathered to picket a works' premises where an industrial dispute was going on. Eight of the 24 employees were still working. It was held that the police were entitled to direct the number of pickets to be reduced and to arrest for obstruction those who did not comply. The court found that, although there had been no violence on the picket line, 'the police reasonably anticipated that a breach of the peace might occur' (*per* Parke CJ).

The common law powers of the police to disperse protest meetings were applied in ***La Porte and Christian v Commissioner of Police for the Metropolis*** [2014] EWHC 3574 (QB), where these were found sufficient to allow them to use reasonable force to eject disorderly protesters from a Town Hall. The protesters were trying to force their way into the council chamber to disrupt a council meeting called to consider making cuts to local government services.

Seizure of provocative emblems

Humphries v *Connor* (1864) 17 ICLR 1

> The defendant was a police officer in Co. Cavan, Ireland. He stopped the plaintiff and took from her an orange lily (a loyalist emblem) which she was wearing on her coat. The plaintiff's action for assault did not succeed. The court felt that the officer was entitled to believe that the wearing of the emblem might provoke a violent reaction from persons of a nationalist persuasion. It would have been 'absurd to hold that a constable may arrest a person whom he finds committing a breach of the peace but that he must not interfere with the individual who has provoked him . . .' (*per* Hayes J).

Entry without warrant

The authority for the police power to enter private premises where an imminent breach of the peace is reasonably anticipated, and to remain there until the danger has passed, is usually assumed to be *Thomas* v *Sawkins* [1935] 2 KB 249. It has already been mentioned in the context of PACE, s 17. The power may be used to deal with domestic disputes (*McLeod* v *Metropolitan Police Commissioner*, *supra*) or anticipated disorder at a meeting to be held in private premises (as was the case in *Thomas* v *Sawkins*, *supra*). The police may remain on the premises for so long as the danger exists.

The test of imminence

For a number of reasons, the above powers have proved controversial and, in an increasingly libertarian age, have been the subject of a considerable degree of adverse comment. The principal criticisms have been:

- they permit the restriction of important individual freedoms where no offence has been committed;
- they are unduly open-ended and unspecific;
- in some instances, they derive from authority decided in an age of different attitudes towards the correct relationship between the individual and the state.

These concerns go some way to explaining the modern judicial insistence that such powers become available to the police only when it is reasonably believed that a breach of the peace is imminent, in the sense of being about to happen. Reasonable apprehension that a breach may occur at some time in the relatively near future is not enough. A degree of pressing immediacy, sufficient to rule out consideration of alternative courses of action, is required.

The current test of 'imminence' was laid down by the House of Lords in *R (on application of Laporte)* v *Chief Constable of Gloucestershire* [2007] AC 105.

> The requirement of imminence is relatively clear-cut and appropriately identifies the common law power (or duty) of any citizen including the police, to take preventative action as a power of last resort catering for situations about to descend into violence (Lord Mance).

In the same case, other similar articulations of the test included: 'something which is about to happen' (Lord Rodger); 'will take place in the near future' (Lord Brown).

The test is not fixed or constant. There is, therefore, no 'sliding scale' of imminence justifying the use of increasingly restrictive powers as the degree of immediacy grows.

> . . . no power or duty arises to take any preventative action unless and until the constable or citizen reasonably apprehends that an actual breach of the peace is imminent (about to

happen) . . . the reasonable apprehension of an imminent breach of the peace is an important threshold requirement which must exist before any form of preventative action is permissible at common law (Lord Brown).

Until, therefore, the time at which the requisite degree of threat has been reached, none of the common law powers may be used. Note that the requirement for reasonable belief or apprehension in the imminence of threat means that an honest and genuine belief is not enough (*R (on application of McClure)* **v** *Metropolitan Police Commissioner* [2012] EWCA Civ 12).

In *Laporte* the test was not satisfied when the police turned back coachloads of demonstrators who were still five kilometres away from a planned protest meeting. At the time, no disorder had occurred, or appeared about to occur, either at the place where the coaches had been stopped or at the location of the meeting. It was held that the police apprehension of a breach may have been reasonable, but that no such breach was imminent.

Restricting lawful conduct

It has been suggested that the old breach of the peace case-law supports the proposition that the police in the United Kingdom have the authority to prevent a lawful and peaceful meeting from taking place if it is reasonably believed that the meeting would be opposed by those prepared to use violence or behave in a way which produced a risk of it. This, in turn, appeared to mean that, according to English law, the freedom of assembly must always give way to the perceived needs of public order and that the authorities were under no specific legal obligation to defend the freedom against those bent on using whatever means they deemed appropriate to prevent demonstrations of support for causes to which they were opposed.

All of this must now, however, be read subject to a series of decisions in the 1990s suggesting a clear judicial intent to limit the circumstances in which the police may interfere with and restrict lawful behaviour to situations where the conduct:

(a) interferes with the lawful rights of others; and

(b) its natural consequence would be to provoke violence which, in the circumstances, although unlawful, would not be entirely unreasonable.

> It is only if otherwise lawful conduct gives rise to a reasonable apprehension that it will, by interfering with the rights and liberties of others, provoke violence which, though unlawful, would not be entirely unreasonable that a constable is empowered to take steps to prevent. (Sedley LJ, *Redmond-Bate* **v** *DPP* [1999] All ER (D) 864)

The *Redmond-Bate* decision was approved by the Court of Appeal in *Bibby* **v** *Chief Constable of Essex* [2000] EWCA Civ 113. The effect is to bring English law in this context into closer compliance with the right to freedom of assembly as protected by the European Convention on Human Rights, Art 11.

This is achieved by:

(a) giving genuine legal protection to those wishing to meet or demonstrate peacefully and within the law;

(b) requiring the police, if the peace is to be kept, to direct their attentions to those who would oppose and disrupt the lawful conduct of others.

The legality of the use of breach of the peace powers against 'innocent bystanders' was considered by the Court of Appeal in *Austin* **v** *Metropolitan Police Commissioner* [2007] EWCA Civ 989.

In May 2001, a large-scale public demonstration took place in London's Oxford Circus. Those taking part wished to protest against 'globalisation'. Given events at previous similar gatherings, the police reasonably suspected an imminent and major breach of the peace. A police cordon was thrown around the area to prevent or contain the expected disorder. Innocent bystanders, i.e. those who had just happened to be in the vicinity at the time, and who were not part of the demonstration, were amongst those held within the cordon. Some were kept there for up to seven hours. In the circumstances, however, no false imprisonment had been committed.

> The appellants were 'imprisoned' for the purposes of the tort of false imprisonment but their imprisonment was lawful because, although the appellants did not themselves appear to be about to commit a breach of the peace, on . . . the findings of fact, the police had no alternative but to ask all those in Oxford Circus to remain inside the police cordon in order to avoid an imminent breach of the peace by others (Sir Anthony Clarke, MR).

In the course of deciding the case in *Austin*, the Court of Appeal also set out its interpretation of the exact findings of the House of Lords in *Laporte*, *supra*, on this issue. These were said to be:

(i) where a breach of the peace is taking place, or is reasonably thought to be imminent, before the police can take any steps which interfere with or curtail in any way the lawful exercise of rights by innocent third parties, they must ensure that they have taken all other practical steps to ensure that the breach, or imminent breach, is obviated and that the rights of innocent third parties are protected;

(ii) the taking of all other practical steps includes (where practicable), but is not limited to, ensuring that proper and advance preparations have been made to deal with such a breach, since failure to take such steps will render interference with the rights of innocent third parties unjustified or unjustifiable;

(iii) where and only where there is a reasonable belief that there are no other means whatever whereby a breach or imminent breach of the peace can be obviated, the lawful exercise by third parties of their rights may be curtailed by the police;

(iv) this is a test of necessity which it is to be expected can only be justified in truly extreme and exceptional circumstances; and

(v) the action taken must be both reasonably necessary and proportionate.

The events in Hyde Park of May 2001 were considered in two further cases and from a slightly different perspective. On both of these occasions, the question to be decided was whether the police tactics used on that day, and particularly the cordoning off or 'kettling' of such a large number of people, including those not involved in the demonstration, were compatible with the rights protected by Article 5 (the right to liberty and security of the person). In *Austin* v *Metropolitan Police Commissioner* [2009] UKHL 5, the general opinion of the House of Lords was that such use of the common law powers available to the police was unlikely to be offensive to the Convention provided that whatever steps were taken were 'resorted to in good faith' and were 'proportionate to the situation which has made the measures necessary' (Lord Hope). In *Austin* v *United Kingdom* [2012] ECHR 105, the view of the Grand Chamber of the ECtHR was that such commonly occurring restrictions could not properly be described as deprivations of liberty for Art 5 purposes so long as they were rendered unavoidable as a result of circumstances beyond the control of the authorities and were necessary to avert a real risk of injury or damage, and were kept to the minimum required for that purpose.

Subsequent case-law has made clear that no common law power exists to require persons held within a cordon to supply their names and addresses and/or to be photographed as conditions of being allowed to leave the area of containment (*R (on application of Megesha* v *Commissioner of Police of the Metropolis* [2013] EWHC 1695 (Admin)).

Statutory public order offences

Introduction

Objective 4

Should the above preventative powers prove inadequate to keep the peace at a public procession or assembly, those suspected of disorderly conduct may be charged with a range of public order offences. As with the preventative powers, the principal source of the relevant provisions is the Public Order Act 1986. It will be seen that these offences are worded in sufficiently expansive terms to encompass disorderly behaviour in public places which may not be related to any procession or assembly.

Riot

Section 1 of the 1986 Act provides that, where there are 12 or more persons present together using or threatening violence for a common purpose such as would cause a reasonably firm person present at the scene to fear for their safety, each person using violence intentionally is guilty of riot.

The offence may be committed in a public or private place. The common purpose requirement means that the offence cannot be used to deal with brawls or general mêlée. The common purpose need not be pre-arranged. Hence, in *R* v *Jefferson and Others* [1994] 1 All ER 271, riot was committed when a crowd of about 300 youths went 'on the rampage' in the centre of Bedford to celebrate a victory by the English football team. It is not necessary for the prosecution to prove that a reasonably firm person witnessed the defendants' actions and was put in fear by them. The test is objective. It is sufficient, therefore, to show that the behaviour of those involved would have had such effect on a reasonably firm person had one been present (*R* v *Davison* [1992] Crim LR 31). Note that only persons using violence may be charged with riot. Those merely threatening violence may be charged with one of the lesser offences dealt with below. Riot is the most serious of the public law offences. It is arrestable and carries a maximum sentence of ten years' imprisonment.

Violent disorder

This offence is contained in the 1986 Act, s 2. It is committed where three or more persons present together use or threaten unlawful violence intentionally such as would cause a reasonably firm person present to fear for their safety. Each person using or threatening violence is guilty of the offence.

No common purpose need be proved and it is enough for a conviction that the defendant was merely threatening violence.

> In order properly to understand the phrase 'present together' it is necessary to have regard to the mischief at which the section was aimed. Sections 1, 2 and 3 of the Act are all aimed at public disorder of a kind which could cause ordinary people at the scene to fear for their personal safety . . . That being so, we think the expression 'present together' means no more than being in the same place, at the same time. Three or more people using or threatening violence

in the same place or at the same time, whether for the same purpose or different purposes, are capable of creating a daunting prospect for those who may encounter them simply by reason of the fact that they represent a breakdown of law and order which has unpredictable consequences. We are unable to accept that the phrase requires any degree of co-operation between those who are using or threatening violence; all that is required is that they be present in the same place at the same time (*per Moore-Bick LJ, R v NW* [2010] EWCA Crim 404).

Where three or more persons are charged with violent disorder, fewer than three may be convicted provided 'there is evidence before the jury that there were three people involved in the criminal behaviour, though not necessarily those named in the indictment and the defence are apprised of what it is they have to meet' (*R v Mahroof* (1988) 88 Crim App Rep 317).

The offence is arrestable and may be committed in public or private. A person convicted of violent disorder may be sentenced to five years' imprisonment.

Affray

Section 3 of the 1986 Act created the statutory offence of affray. It is committed by any person who uses or threatens unlawful violence intentionally such as would cause a reasonably firm person present to fear for their safety.

The offence is directed at unlawful fighting. For the purposes of this offence the threat of unlawful violence cannot be made by words alone. Some threatening action must be used. In *R v Robinson* [1993] Crim LR 581, the defendant told the driver of a car that, unless he gave the defendant a lift, the defendant would simply take his car. It was held that affray had not been committed as the threat consisted entirely of words. Affray was committed, however, in *R v Dixon* [1993] Crim LR 579, where the defendant ordered his Alsatian dog to attack two police officers ('Go on, kill'). The Court of Appeal took the view that the dog had, in effect, been used as a weapon with which to threaten the officers. Affray was also committed in *R v Davison*, *supra*, where the defendant brandished a knife at police officers and said, 'I'll have you'.

A person who commits affray may be arrested without warrant. The offence may be committed in a public or private place and carries a maximum sentence of three years' imprisonment.

Fear or provocation of violence

By virtue of s 4 of the 1986 Act it is an offence to use threatening, abusive or insulting words or behaviour towards another person or to display any threatening, abusive or insulting writing, sign or other visual representation. The words, behaviour or display must be intended or be likely to provoke or cause fear of immediate violence (i.e. violence which is not necessarily instantaneous but which may occur in a short time: *Valentine v DPP, Current Law*, June 1997). The offence may be committed in a public or private place. A person may not be charged under s 4, however, if they used the words or behaviour, or displayed the sign, inside a dwelling house to another person inside that or another dwelling house. Hence, in *R v Va Kun Hau* [1990] Crim LR 518, where a bailiff and police officer were in the defendant's house to collect unpaid parking fines, no offence was committed when the defendant brandished a knife at them. The decision might have been different if the defendant had stood in his doorway brandishing the knife at the bailiff and police officers as they approached his premises. Given that the offence does not apply where both parties are in a dwelling house, it cannot be used in the context of domestic disputes.

The words, behaviour, or sign must be used or shown in the presence of the person who it is claimed was put in fear of violence.

R v Atkin [1989] Crim LR 581

In this case, customs officers and a bailiff went to the defendant's premises in connection with unpaid VAT. The bailiff remained in the car while the officers went inside to talk to the defendant. The defendant had a gun in his hand and said that if the bailiff got out of the car he was 'a dead 'un'. The customs officers relayed this message to the bailiff. The defendant was acquitted of the s 4 offence as words could not be threatening, etc. unless used in the presence of the person claimed to have been put in fear of immediate violence.

The words or behaviour must carry a threat of immediate violence. An allegation that they might lead or contribute to violence at some indeterminate time in the future is not enough. Hence, where a bookshop displayed a copy of the book *The Satanic Verses* in its window, no offence was committed. Although this might have contributed to a general climate of resentment which may have manifested itself in violence, the display itself was not something which was either intended or likely to cause or provoke an immediate violent reaction (*R v Horseferry Road Stipendiary Magistrate, ex parte Siadatan* [1991] 1 QB 260).

A person who commits the offence may be arrested without warrant and sentenced to six months' imprisonment.

Causing intentional harassment, alarm or distress

This offence is found in the 1986 Act, s 4A. It was inserted by the Criminal Justice and Public Order Act 1994, s 154. Its terminology is similar to the offence of causing fear or provocation of violence, save that the s 4A offence is committed by words, behaviour or signs (which are threatening, abusive or insulting) that cause a person 'harassment, alarm or distress' and were intended to have that effect. Hence, both the intent and the requisite consequences must be proved. As with the s 4 offence, it may be committed in public or private but not if the parties are in the same or different dwelling houses. It is a defence to show that the accused was inside a dwelling and had no reason to believe that what was said, done or displayed would be seen or heard by another person. It is also a defence if it can be shown that the accused's conduct was reasonable – e.g. that they intentionally harassed or caused alarm to another person to prevent the latter from committing a crime.

Any person reasonably suspected of committing the offence may be arrested without warrant and, if convicted, sentenced to a term of imprisonment of up to six months.

Causing harassment, alarm or distress

The offence in s 5 of the 1986 Act is linguistically very similar to that in s 4A. Here, however, it is sufficient if any threatening, abusive words, behaviour or display (sign, writing or other visual representation) were used 'within the hearing or sight of a person likely to be caused harassment, alarm or distress'. Hence it does not have to be shown that actual harassment, alarm or distress was caused. The defendant must intend their action to be harassing, alarming or distressing or be aware that it may be so interpreted. It appears to be enough that other persons were 'near enough' to hear the offensive words and, therefore, not necessary to show that someone actually did hear the words used (*Taylor v DPP* [2006] EWHC 1202 (Admin)).

The offence, unlike those in ss 4 and 4A, may also be committed by 'disorderly behaviour' which is likely to cause the specified reactions. The same defences are available as those in s 4A. In addition, it is a defence to show that the accused had no reason to believe that there was any person within hearing or sight likely to have been harassed, alarmed or distressed by their behaviour, thereby insulting behaviour is not, however, an offence under this section.

Whether any person felt harassed, alarmed or distressed by the words or behaviour in question is a matter of fact to be determined by evidence. It should not be inferred from the words above. In *Harvey* v *Director of Public Prosecutions* [2011] All ER (D) 143, 'the "f" word' was used several times against a police officer executing a stop-search for drugs. The court's view was that, although the word was capable of being threatening or abusive, the context in which it was used was crucial. It would be unlikely to have this effect, it was concluded, when, as in this instance, it had been used solely to experienced police officers. The offensive conduct need not be directed at the person likely to suffer from it. Hence the offence was committed by a person seen to be staggering about in the middle of a busy road (also shouting and gesticulating) thereby putting those nearby in fear that an accident would be caused (*Lodge* v *DPP*, *Times*, 26 October 1988). The offence may also be committed by threatening telephone calls and letters (*DPP* v *Mills* [1997] QB 300.

Note that the offence only becomes arrestable if the person carries on with the behaviour after being ordered to desist by a police officer. In *DPP* v *Hancock and Tuttle* [1995] Crim LR 139, the court was of the view that the power of arrest was limited to the officer who gave the warning. However, the Public Order (Amendment) Act 1996 makes it clear that the power of arrest extends to any officer and is not restricted as suggested above. In *Groom* v *DPP* [1991] Crim LR 711, G swore and made racist remarks at H. A police officer told G to apologise. G continued to be abusive and was arrested. The court's view was that to tell a person to apologise necessarily implied that the offensive behaviour should be discontinued. G's arrest was, therefore, lawful.

Despite its apparent width, s 5 should not be used to impinge upon the freedom of expression guaranteed by the European Convention on Human Rights.

> A peaceful protest will only come within the terms of section 5 and constitute an offence where the conduct goes beyond legitimate protest and moves into the realms of threatening, abusive or insulting behaviour, which is calculated to insult either intentionally or recklessly, and which is unreasonable (*per Hallett J, Percy* v *DPP* [2001] EWHC Admin 1125).

The concept of 'harassment' as a criminal offence was further extended by the Protection from Harassment Act 1997. This was Parliament's response to the type of activity generally referred to as 'stalking'. The Act makes it an offence for any person to pursue a course of conduct which they knew or ought to have known 'amounts to harassment of another' (ss 1 and 2). In *Huntingdon Life Sciences Ltd* v *Curtin*, *The Times*, 11 December 1997, the High Court decided, given its origins, that Parliament could not have intended the Act to be used to prosecute those engaged in protesting about a matter of public interest – in this case anti-vivisectionists protesting against the activities of a company engaged in the use of animals for research purposes.

The 1997 Act was subsequently amended, and its powers widened, by the Criminal Justice and Police Act 2001 and SOCPA 2005. The 2001 Act provided police with a power to direct protesters away from homes where their activities might cause harassment, alarm or distress (s 42). The prescriptions in the 2005 Act represented the government's response to, *inter alia*, the intimidation of those engaged in bio-medical research, i.e. the type of activity in the *Huntingdon Life Sciences* case. The Act prohibits conduct designed to stop persons going about their lawful business, creates a new offence of harassing a person in their home and empowers police to issue directions to deal with such incidents (ss 125–127).

The Crime and Disorder Act 1998 provides that sentences in excess of those provided for in the 1986 Act will be available to the courts in respect of offences under ss 4, 4A and 5 of the latter Act where such offences are shown to have been 'racially aggravated', i.e. where the offence was motivated by racial hostility or such hostility was demonstrated to the victim. Expressions of xenophobia and unspecific hostility to 'foreigners', in general, would appear to be enough. It is not necessary, therefore, to show that the racially aggravating behaviour was directed towards an identifiable racial or ethnic group (*R v Rogers* [2007] UKHL 8, s 4 offence racially aggravated by words 'bloody foreigners' and 'get back to your own country').

Stirring up hatred

Sections 18–29 of the 1986 Act, as amended by the Racial and Religious Hatred Act 2006 and the Criminal Justice and Immigration Act 2008, are concerned with actions, materials and representations which may be inflammatory on grounds of race, religion or sexual orientation. The following constitute an offence if likely or intended to stir up hatred on racial, religious or sexual grounds:

- the use of threatening, abusive or insulting words, behaviour or visual representations in a public or private place;
- the publication of threatening, abusive or insulting written materials;
- the public performance of any play which involves the use of threatening, abusive or insulting language;
- the distribution, showing or playing of any threatening, abusive or insulting recorded visual images or sounds;
- the broadcasting of any threatening, abusive or insulting materials.

It is also an offence to possess such inflammatory material. A warrant may be granted to search premises where it is reasonably suspected such materials may be found.

R v Sheppard [2010] EWCA Crim 65 was concerned with an internet publication, 'Tales of the Holohoax'. This sought to cast doubt on the truth of the Holocaust. By way of defence to the charges of publishing racially inflammatory written materials, the defendant contended that the material which was made available on the internet could not be described as 'written' and that, as the web server through which it had been disseminated was in California, no offence had been committed in the United Kingdom. These arguments were rejected by the Court of Appeal. Its view was:

(a) the meaning of 'written' material in the 1986 Act must have been intended to extend to new types of communication;

(b) the domestic courts had jurisdiction in the matter as a significant element of the offence, i.e. the preparation and uploading of the materials, had been committed in the United Kingdom.

Other relevant statutory offences

Obstruction of the highway

Prima facie the right of each individual on a public highway is to pass and repass along it in the course of their lawful business and to stop for rest or to make necessary repairs (*Hickman v Maisey* [1900] 1 QB 753). In theory, therefore, any other use – including public assemblies – represents a trespass against the highway authority and an offence against the Highways Act 1980, s 137. This section makes it an offence to wilfully obstruct free passage along the highway without lawful authority or excuse.

In practice, however, the courts have generally sought to strike a balance between the public right of passage and that of freedom of assembly. Hence, the cases suggest that a conviction under the 1980 Act is unlikely unless it can be shown that the defendant's use of the highway was unreasonable (*Hirst and Agu v Chief Constable of West Yorkshire* (1987) 85 Crim App Rep 143). This is a question of fact in each case and will depend on such matters as the duration of the obstruction, its purpose, the place where it occurred and its extent – i.e. whether the highway was totally or only partially obstructed (*Nagy v Weston* [1965] 1 All ER 78).

Obstruction of a police officer

The Police Act 1996, s 89(2), provides that it is an offence to resist or wilfully obstruct a police officer in the execution of their duty. The offence is arrestable without warrant where the person's behaviour interferes with a lawful arrest or may lead to a breach of the peace (*Wershof v Commissioner of Police of the Metropolis* [1978] 3 All ER 540).

The offence is of general application but has particular utility in the public order context. Given that police officers are under a common law obligation to preserve the peace, it is an arrestable obstruction to impede any reasonable course of action or any directions given for that purpose. Hence, should the police reasonably believe that an assembly may lead to disorder, they may do or direct that which is reasonably necessary to prevent that eventuality and arrest for obstruction those who refuse to cooperate.

Common law offences

Public nuisance

Obstruction of the highway as a result of a public assembly or otherwise may amount to the indictable common law offence of public nuisance. For a conviction to be sustained the obstruction must have constituted an 'unreasonable use' of the stretch of highway in issue (*R v Clark* [1964] 2 QB 315).

Public nuisance is also actionable in tort by a person who has suffered damage over and above that inflicted on the rest of the public (e.g. the road obstructed led to the plaintiff's premises).

Summary

The chapter identifies and explains the nature and extent of the statutory and common law powers available to magistrates and the police to regulate and control public demonstrations and processions. The various criminal offences relating to public disorder are also catalogued and defined.

In addition, the chapter contains coverage of relevant recent developments including the introduction of powers to deal with trespassers on private land, protests within the vicinity of Parliament, intrusions into royal palaces and residencies, and general 'anti-social behaviour' in public places.

Further reading

Allen and Thompson (2011) *Cases and Materials on Constitutional and Administrative Law* (10th edn), Oxford: Oxford University Press.

Bailey, Harris and Jones (2009) *Civil Liberties: Cases and Materials (6th edn),* Oxford: Oxford University Press.

Beggs, Thomas, Rickard and Messenger (2012) *Public Order: Law and Practice,* Oxford: Oxford University Press.

Thornton and Brandon (2010) *The Law of Public Order and Protest,* Oxford: Oxford University Press.

20

Restrictions on the rights of freedom of expression and information

Objectives

After reading this chapter you should:

1. Understand the relationship between the freedom of expression and representative democracy.

2. Recognise the extent of legal and other restrictions on the broadcast media.

3. Know the meaning of obscenity and pornography and related restrictions.

4. Be aware of the meaning and content of the common law offences of outraging public morals and outraging public decency.

5. Understand the relationship between freedom of expression and the needs of public order and national security.

6. Appreciate the concept of breach of confidence and extent of related restrictions.

7. Recognise the relationship between the freedom of expression and the needs of data protection.

8. Be aware of the extent to which the criminal law and the law of defamation may be used to regulate publication on the internet.

Introduction

Objective 1

The principal justifications for restraints operating in this context would appear to be that these are the minimum necessary to:

● preserve social harmony and public order;

● safeguard certain fundamental standards of public morality;

● ensure the proper administration of justice;

● enable the state to function effectively in the fulfilment of the various public interests for which it is responsible.

The restraints themselves consist of:

● statutory and non-statutory complaints procedures and codes of practice relating to the press and broadcast media;

- an extensive range of statutory and common law offences relating to, *inter alia*, sedition, blasphemy, obscene publications, contempt of court and official secrecy;
- civil wrongs such as breach of confidence and defamation.

Defamation is, of course, a significant restriction on the freedom of expression of both the individual and the media. Given, however, that it will be explained in detail in any standard textbook on the law of tort, defamation is not dealt with in the text that follows. Note in passing, however, that it is not possible to defame a local council (***Derbyshire County Council v Times Newspapers*** [1993] 1 All ER 1011) or a political party (***Goldsmith v Bhoyrul*** [1998] 2 WLR 435).

The freedom of expression is, of course, essential for the practice of democracy. Without it there can be no meaningful political debate and no effective monitoring and criticism of the activities of government. It is no coincidence that the burning of books and the prohibition of the free exchange of views has been one of the first steps taken by many of the most oppressive regimes which have held power in various parts of the world.

> It is unacceptable in our democratic society that there should be a restraint on the publication of information relating to government when the only vice of that information is that it enables the public to discuss, review and criticise government action (*per* Mason J, ***Commonwealth of Australia v John Fairfax and Sons Ltd*** (1980) 147 CLR 39).

In a democracy, therefore, the function of the law-maker must be to achieve a workable balance between the right to freedom of expression and such restrictions as are necessary for the protection and well-being of the whole community.

Freedom of expression and the mass media

The press

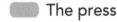

Objective 2

It is often claimed that the United Kingdom has a 'free' press. By this it is meant that the publication of newspapers and magazines is not subject to any direct political control. No prior official consent is needed for publication of the same nor does the government have any legal authority to influence editorial policy (i.e. the content of such publications). The law does not require press reporting to be fair or impartial or to achieve any sort of balance in the way particular topics, political or otherwise, are treated. As a result, great power and responsibility is left in the hands of newspaper editors and proprietors.

The Press Complaints Commission

This was created in 1991 following the recommendations of the Calcutt Committee (*Report of the Committee on Privacy and Related Matters*, Cm 1102, 1990). It replaced the much-criticised Press Council which had been in existence since 1953. The Press Council was a non-statutory body funded by the newspaper industry from which half of its members were drawn. It dealt with complaints from the public about press abuses (invasions of privacy, inaccuracy, etc.) and could censure editors and recommend the publication of apologies. It had no legal authority, however, to insist on compliance with its decisions and proved ineffective to prevent some sections of the press from indulging in the type of vulgarity and offensive intrusions into people's private lives which became a cause of increasing public concern in the 1970s and 1980s.

The Press Complaints Commission is also a non-statutory body. It has an independent chairperson and fifteen other members. Ten of these are from the newspaper industry.

It deals with complaints alleging violation of the Press Code of Practice. This contains detailed guidelines dealing with matters such as accuracy, privacy, misrepresentation, harassment, intrusion into grief or shock, and the interviewing of children and victims of crime.

Like its predecessor, however, the Commission has no coercive or preventive powers and cannot insist on the payment of compensation. It may censure an editor or recommend that an apology or right of reply be published but has no legal authority to ensure compliance with its decisions. It is widely held that it has had little obvious effect on the behaviour of the less scrupulous newspaper editors and reporters. It has been described as a 'confidence trick which has failed to inspire confidence' and a further example of the fact that press self-regulation is an 'oxymoron' (Robertson, *Freedom, the Individual and the Law*).

The inadequacies of press self-regulation and the apparent ineffectiveness of the Press Complaints Commission were brought into sharp relief by the Millie Dowler affair and the more general phone-hacking scandal which it precipitated. Following from this, and the further related allegations presented to the Leveson Inquiry (The Inquiry into the Culture, Practice and Ethics of the Press, 2011) it was decided that the continued existence of the Commission could not be justified but that it should remain in being until an alternative system for regulation of the press and printed media could be agreed upon.

The Independent Press Standards Organisation

The Press Complaints Commission was replaced by the Independent Press Standards Organisation (IPSO) in September, 2014. IPSO's remit extends to the editorial content of printed newspapers and magazines and to that published in the whole gamut of electronic communications, e.g. through websites, emails, texts, tweets, and blogs. 'Regulated entities', i.e. those producing or transmitting information in the above forms, are to comply with IPSO's editors' code of practice. This encompasses such matters as accuracy, opportunity to reply, privacy, harassment, intrusion into grief or shock, welfare of children, reporting of crime, subterfuge and victims of sexual assault; no reference is made in the order to such matters as good taste, decency or due impartiality.

IPSO operates primarily through The Regulation Board and a Complaints Committee. The Regulation Board has twelve members. These should not be employed by any regulated entity nor a member of the government or Parliament or a member of the executives or assemblies of Scotland, Wales or Northern Ireland. The specific functions of the Board include, *inter alia*, the monitoring of compliance with the order and to providing an effective complaints procedure for dealing with alleged contraventions of it.

Individual complaints are dealt with by the IPSO Complaints Committee. This is appointed by the Regulation Board and also has 12 'independent members'.

Where a breach of the editors' code is established, the perpetrator will be required to publish an apology or correction or submit to an adjudication.

Should a complaint raise a matter of particular gravity, an Investigatory Panel may be appointed to consider whether a 'serious and systemic breach of the code' may have been committed. Should this be established, a fine may be imposed.

Broadcasting

The BBC

Until 1954 broadcasting was the sole responsibility of the BBC. The BBC was established under Royal Charter in 1926 and broadcasts according to the terms of a licence granted to it by the government acting through the Secretary of State for the Home Department under the Wireless Telegraphy Acts. It is controlled by a Board of Governors who are appointed (and may be dismissed) by the Crown on the advice of the Prime Minister. It is a non-profit-making organisation and is financed by parliamentary grant equivalent to the net revenue from TV licence fees.

Despite its much vaunted and justified reputation for political independence, the licensing provisions under which the BBC operates give considerable powers of control to the Secretary of State for the Home Department. These include powers to:

- take over the BBC in times of emergency;
- direct that any material or class of material specified in a written notice should not be broadcast.

The BBC has also undertaken:

- not to broadcast that which could offend against good taste or decency, or be likely to encourage crime or disorder, or be offensive to public feeling;
- to comply with the statutory duties imposed on independent television including the obligation to observe due impartiality and balance in its coverage of political issues (see below); and
- to comply with the Ofcom broadcasting code set out below.

The Secretary of State for the Home Department is empowered to revoke the BBC's licence should the Corporation act in breach of it or any ministerial directions imposed thereunder.

Ofcom and independent broadcasters

Independent broadcasters operate under licences granted by the Office of Communications (Ofcom). Ofcom's powers derive from the Communications Act 2003. The licensing function was exercised previously, and until 2003, by the Independent Television Commission and the Radio Authority.

As the regulatory authority, Ofcom is under a duty to set basic standards for the content of TV and radio services (2003 Act, s 319; Broadcasting Act 1996, s 109). These are set out in a Code of Practice which should seek to secure the following objectives:

- that persons under the age of 18 are protected;
- that material likely to encourage the commission of crime or lead to disorder should not be included in TV or radio programmes;
- that news programmes are presented with 'due accuracy and impartiality' and without giving 'undue prominence . . . to the views and opinions of particular persons or bodies';
- observance of the 'proper degree of responsibility' with respect to the content of religious programmes;
- adequate protection for members of the public from the inclusion of 'harmful or offensive' materials.

Ofcom's first broadcasting code came into effect in July 2005. It was designed to unify and modernise the codes previously laid down by the Independent Television Commission, the Radio Authority, and the Broadcasting Standards Commission, to whose responsibilities and functions Ofcom succeeded. The Ofcom Code at the time of writing was that which took effect in May 2016.

As well as seeking to secure compliance with the legal requirements of the 2003 Act, the Broadcasting Act 1996, the Human Rights Act 1998, and relevant EU directives, the Code attempts to strike an acceptable balance between the freedom of expression and the interests of those felt to be in need of protection from full media coverage and exposure to all aspects of modern life (e.g. those under 18). The licences granted by Ofcom require broadcasters to adhere to the Code. In the case of the BBC, observance is required by the BBC Agreement 1996. Where a breach appears to have occurred, Ofcom will investigate and publish its findings. These are available on the Ofcom website. In the case of serious or repeated breaches, sanctions may be imposed. These include fines and the revocation or shortening of licences.

The Code applies to both independent television and radio. It is set out in ten sections with appropriate headings. In the main, the Code seeks to regulate and control the inclusion of programme material which might be damaging to the under-18s, cause harm and offence, encourage crime or which might offend the prescribed standards of impartiality, accuracy, fairness and privacy. Special restrictions apply to programmes broadcast before 9.00 pm (the 'watershed'), when young children might be expected to be watching. These restrictions relate, in particular, to programmes containing adult sexual material, nudity or offensive language and to that which might glamourise or encourage such activities as smoking or the abuse of drugs or alcohol.

In addition to the above, Ofcom has succeeded to the functions of the Broadcasting Complaints Commission established by the Broadcasting Act 1996 and is required to provide procedures for hearing complaints relating to the non-observance of the standards protected by the Codes of Practice.

As a general rule, the provisions of the Broadcasting Code do not fall foul of Art 10 of the European Convention on Human Rights (*R (on application of Gaunt)* v *Office of Communications* [2011] EWCA Civ 692).

Party election broadcasts

Both the BBC in its Charter and Agreement, and the main independent broadcasters by the Communications Act 2003, are required to devote broadcasting time to political parties during election times. The obligation extends only to those parties registered with the Electoral Commission (see Political Parties, Elections and Referendums Act 2000). The regulation of party political broadcasts in the independent sector is the function of Ofcom. The BBC is, of course, responsible for its own network. Both the BBC and Ofcom lay down general guidelines according to which such broadcasts should be conducted. These provide certain minimum requirements for determining the length, frequency, allocation and scheduling of the broadcasting time available. For as independent broadcasters the current Ofcom rules are that:

- each major party should be allowed two or more broadcasts;
- recognition as a major party should be based on previous election performance and trends in public opinion polling;
- other registered parties should qualify for a party election broadcast (PEB) if they are contesting one-sixth or more of the seats up for election;
- consideration should be given to making additional allocations to other parties 'if evidence of their past and/or current electoral support' means that it would be appropriate to do so.

Similar general provisions may be found in the elections section of the BBC's Producers' Guidelines. Because of the numbers of broadcasters involved, and in order to ensure some acceptable level of fairness and uniformity, the detailed rules governing particular elections are formulated by the Broadcasters' Liaison Group. This consists of representatives from the BBC, ITV, STV, UTV, Channel 4, Channel 5, Sky, S4/Croeso, and the Electoral Commission. The rules and qualifying criteria formulated by the Group for the 2010 and 2015 General Elections were based on the threshold criterion that parties contesting a minimum of one-sixth of the seats up for election in England, Wales, Scotland or Northern Ireland qualified for at least one PEB in that 'nation'. This meant that the qualifying numbers of seats for a PEB in the different parts of the United Kingdom were:

- England 89;
- Scotland 10;
- Wales 7;
- Northern Ireland 3.

For the 2015 General Election, the actual number of PEBs offered to the major parties in England was:

- In Great Britain, the Conservative Party, the Labour Party, the Liberal Democratic Party;
- In Scotland, the Scottish National Party;
- In Wales, Plaid Cymru;
- In Northern Ireland, the Alliance Party, the Democratic Unionist Party, Sinn Fein, the Social Democratic and Labour Party, the Ulster Unionist Party;
- In England and Wales, the United Kingdom Independence Party.

On this basis, and for the 2015 General Election, those parties found to be entitled a minimum of two party election broadcasts were:

- Labour 5;
- Conservatives 5;
- Liberal Democrats 4.

Ofcom is responsible also for the rules relating to general party political broadcasting (PPBs). The present dispensation is determined by the number of votes cast for each party at the most recent General Election. One broadcast is allocated for each two million votes and, in overall terms, a party is entitled to a maximum of five PPBs each year with a convention that the same number will be given to the government and main opposition party. A party excluded from 'air-time' through application of these rules has no legal remedy under ECHR, Art 10 (Freedom of Expression) unless the exclusion was 'discriminatory, arbitrary or unreasonable' (*R (on application of Pro Life Alliance) v BBC* [2003] UKHL 23).

Other than PPBs, general political 'advertising' is prohibited by the 2003 Act, ss 319 and 321(2). The purpose of such ban is to 'prevent the annexation of the political process by the rich and powerful' (Joint Committee on Human Rights, 9th Report, 2001–2, HL 149, HC 1102).

> In the United Kingdom we do not want our government or its policies to be decided by the highest spender. Our democracy is based on more than one person one vote. It is based on the view that each person has equal value . . . We want everyone to be able to make up their own minds on the important issues of the day. In this we need the free exchange of information and ideas. We have to accept that some people have greater resources than others with which to put their views across. But we want to avoid the gross distortions which unrestricted access to the broadcast media will bring (Baroness Hale, *R (on application of Animal Defenders International) v Secretary of State for Culture, Media and Sport* [2008] 3 All ER 193).

Political advertising

What constitutes 'political advertising' is widely defined in the 2003 Act and extends to anything directed towards influencing government policy or public opinion in the United Kingdom. The application of the ban may be compatible with ECHR Art 10, providing that, in each case, its use was based on 'relevant and sufficient reasons' and that it doesn't undermine the essence of open debate (*Vgt Verein gegen Tierfabriken* v *Switzerland* (2001) 34 EHRR 159).

No breach of Art 10 was committed by the Irish Radio and Television Commission in its refusal to allow a TV advert for a religious video. Given the context, the ECtHR felt this to be a matter in which the state had a wide margin of discretion and noted also that the ban applied to the audio-visual media only. The applicant had not been prevented, therefore, from placing adverts in newspapers and magazines (*Murphy* v *Ireland* (2003) 38 EHRR 212).

Whether the domestic ban on political advertising was compatible with Art 10 was considered by the House of Lords in the *Animal Defenders* case, *supra*. The case was precipitated by the applicant's failure to secure broadcasting time for an advertisement dealing with the abuse of animals. In refusing the application, and like the ECtHR in *Murphy*, the House was much influenced by the similar limited nature of the ban and its application to the audio-visual media only, and by the dangers of allowing the power of that media to be used for propagating financially well-supported sectional interests.

Whether an advert was directed towards political ends should be determined by its content and text alone without reference to the claimed intentions of the publisher (*R (on application of London Christian Radio)* v *Radio Advertising Clearance Centre* [2013] EWCA Civ 1495; advertisement stating that Christians were being '"marginalised" in the workplace' had political intent, i.e. the law should be changed).

The government and programme content

As to government control of programme content, the 1990 Act, s 10, provides that at any time the Secretary of State for the Home Department may direct any licensed network not to include any matter which may be specified by notice.

It is thus apparent that the Minister acting on behalf of the government has the legal authority to exert extensive control over both state and independent broadcasting. These powers are, however, seldom resorted to – probably because their use usually attracts considerable political controversy. Hence, the government was criticised when, in 1988, it directed both the BBC and the independent networks not to broadcast words being spoken by representatives of Sinn Fein and other paramilitary organisations proscribed under the emergency legislation in force in Northern Ireland. The directions were subsequently rescinded to allow Sinn Fein and spokespersons for loyalist organisations to participate in the Northern Ireland peace process.

Theatres

Censorship of the theatre was brought to an end by the Theatres Act 1968. Prior to that time a play could not be performed in public unless a licence had been granted by the Lord Chancellor.

A theatre cannot operate unless licensed by a local authority. An authority may attach conditions to the licence in relation to 'physical safety or health only'. It may not attach any conditions which seek to regulate 'the nature of plays which may be performed' (Theatres

Act 1968, s 1). The 1968 Act does, however, make it an offence to present or direct a performance of a play which is obscene or which contains threatening, abusive or insulting words or behaviour intended or likely to cause a breach of the peace (Theatres Act, ss 1 and 3).

As with the offence under the Obscene Publications Act 1959, dealt with below, a play is obscene if, taken as a whole, it would tend to deprave and corrupt those likely to see it (Theatres Act 1968, s 2). No offence is committed, however, if it can be proved that performing the play was for the public good in the interests of drama, opera, ballet, literature, learning or any other art (s 3). No prosecution under the 1968 Act may be commenced without the Attorney-General's consent.

It is an offence under the Public Order Act 1986 to present or direct any public performance of a play which is intended or likely to stir up racial hatred (s 20).

Cinema

Cinemas Act 1985

Premises may not be used for the showing of films unless licensed by the appropriate district council or borough council in London (Cinemas Act 1985, s 1). The Act gives district councils the power to attach conditions to the licence specifying the types of films which may be shown. It is the practice of local councils to view potentially controversial films and to instruct licence holders (i.e. cinema owners) whether the film contravenes the standards imposed by the council's licensing conditions. The showing of a film in breach of the licensing conditions could result in the licence being withdrawn.

British Board of Film Classification

In deciding whether to allow a film to be shown in its district a local council will usually place great reliance on the recommendations of the BBFC. This was established in 1912 and was originally known as the British Board of Film Censors. It is a non-statutory body that was created, and is financed, by the film industry itself. It is concerned principally with explicit portrayal of sexual and violent conduct, and classifies each film within a range of six categories ranging from 'U' (suitable for all) to '18R' (distribution restricted to specially licensed premises to which persons of under 18 years are not permitted).

As a result of its non-statutory nature, the Board's classifications are not legally enforceable, nor are they binding on local authorities. It is open, therefore, for a local council to ban a film which the BBFC has classified as fit for general distribution or, alternatively, to allow a film to be shown which the BBFC felt was unsuitable for classification even within the '18R' category.

The Obscene Publications Act 1959 did not apply to the public showing of films. This was changed by the Criminal Law Act 1977, s 53. The public showing of a film may amount, therefore, to the offence of publishing an obscene article contrary to the 1959 Act, s 2(1). It is a defence to prove that the showing of the film was for the public good in the interests of 'drama, opera, ballet, literature, learning or any other art' (*ibid*, s 4(1A)).

The Video Recordings Act 1984

This makes it an offence to supply or to be in possession of a video for the purposes of supply which has not been classified by the BBFC. It is also an offence to supply a video in breach of the terms of its classification. The 1984 Act does not apply to video games or video works:

- designed to 'inform, educate or instruct';
- 'concerned with sport, religion or music' (s 2).

In making a classification the BBFC is bound to consider the 'harm that may be caused to potential viewers, or through their behaviour, to society' by the manner in which the work deals with:

● criminal behaviour;

● drugs;

● violent behaviour or incidents;

● horrific behaviour or incidents; or

● human sexual activity (s 4A).

The meanings of the terms 'video work' and 'video recording' in the 1984 Act were amended by the Criminal Justice and Public Order Act 1994 to include 'any other device capable of storing data electronically' (Sched 9, para 22).

Freedom of expression, obscenity and pornography

Obscene publications

The Obscene Publications Act 1959

Objective 3

Section 2(1) of the 1959 Act made it an indictable offence to publish an obscene article whether for gain or not. The offence thus stated contains a number of key words which require further definition.

Publish

For the purposes of the Act this has a much wider meaning than the publication of books and magazines by publishing companies. The Act states that a person publishes an article if the person 'distributes, circulates, sells, lets on hire, gives, lends or offers it for sale or letting for hire' or, in the case of recorded material, 'shows, plays or projects it'. The 1959 Act has since been amended by the Criminal Justice and Public Order Act 1994, s 84 so that the definition of 'publishes' now extends to the transmission of data which is stored electronically. Hence, the transmission of material contained in a computer database, bulletin board or disk may constitute an obscene publication. *R v Fellows; R v Arnold* [1997] 2 All ER 548, was one of the first convictions under the 1959 Act resulting from the transmission of obscene material by computer. The defendants committed the offence by compiling a database of child pornography which they made available on the internet. *R v Perrin* [2002] EWCA Crim 747 makes clear that the mere uploading and transmission of material electronically constitutes publication.

Publication to one person is sufficient. In *R v GS* [2012] EWCA Crim 398, publication took place through the transmission of comments to a recipient in an internet chat room. These were part of an explicit conversation concerning incestuous and sadistic paedophile sex acts on young children.

Article

This term is defined by the Act as extending to anything 'containing or embodying matter to be read or looked at . . . any sound record, and any film or other record of a picture or pictures' (s 1(2)). Books, pictures, records, films, compact discs, video cassettes, tapes, television and sound broadcasts, and computer images have all been held to fall within the definition as have those articles from which the images are to be reproduced (e.g. photographic negatives and memory sticks).

Obscene

An article is obscene if, taken as a whole, it would tend to deprave and corrupt those likely to see, hear or read it. The phrase 'deprave and corrupt' was not defined by the Act. In *R v Penguin Books* [1961] Crim LR 176, Byrne J said that to deprave meant 'to make morally bad, to pervert, or debase, or corrupt morally'. To corrupt, he continued, meant 'to render morally unsound or rotten, to destroy the moral purity or chastity of, to pervert or ruin a good quality, to debase, to defile . . . '

Whether an article is obscene or not is a question of fact which should be left to the jury to decide. Expert evidence is admissible in exceptional circumstances only, as where obscene material relates to matters outside the experience of the ordinary jury member – e.g. evidence of child psychiatrists as to the possible effects on children of cards sold in chewing gum packets depicting graphic scenes of violence (*DPP v A and BC Chewing Gum Ltd* [1968] 1 QB 159) and medical evidence concerning the effects of taking cocaine (*R v Skirving* [1985] QB 819).

The requirement that the effect of the allegedly obscene article be judged 'as a whole' means that it is not open to the prosecution to base its case on particular parts or extracts drawn from it, e.g. those containing particularly graphic descriptions or depictions of sexual activity. Such material must not be considered, therefore, out of the context in which it is used. Hence, in the famous trial concerning D.H. Lawrence's book *Lady Chatterley's Lover*, jurors were told to read and base their decisions on the potential effects of the complete work and not to concentrate on, or be influenced unduly by, the 'purple passages' contained therein (*R v Penguin Books*).

If the article contains a number of distinct items, as might be the case with a magazine, then each item must be judged individually. If any one is found to be obscene, this taints the whole of the article or publication (*R v Anderson* [1972] 1 QB 304).

It does not have to be proved that the defendant intended to deprave and corrupt their potential audience. 'Obscenity depends on the article and not upon the author' (*Shaw v DPP* [1962] AC 220). Nor is it necessary to show that any overt, depraved or corrupt behaviour resulted from the publication. The intention to publish material which a reasonable person might have been expected to know could have a tendency to deprave and corrupt is sufficient.

An article is not obscene simply because it could have a tendency to deprave and corrupt a person or persons of a particularly sensitive or gullible disposition. If the article is published to one person only then it must be shown that that person was likely to be depraved and corrupted. Hence, in *R v Clayton and Halsey* [1963] 1 QB 163, no offence was committed when the only proved publication of allegedly obscene photographs was to two policemen experienced in dealing with this sort of material.

When the publication is more general or wide reaching the requirement is that the article would tend to have the stipulated effect on a 'significant proportion' of the audience to which it is directed (*R v Calder and Boyars Ltd* [1969] 1 QB 151). The Act imposes, therefore, a relative test. An article cannot be judged to be obscene without reference to its likely readers: 'in every case the magistrates or the jury is called upon to ascertain who are the likely readers and then to consider whether the article is likely to deprave and corrupt them' (*per* Lord Wilberforce, *DPP v Whyte* [1972] AC 849). A significant proportion of a particular audience means 'a part which is not numerically negligible but which may be less than half' (*ibid.*).

It is no defence to argue that the article is only likely to be seen or heard by those who have already been depraved and corrupted: 'The Act is not merely concerned with the once for all corruption of the wholly innocent; it equally protects the less innocent from further corruption, the addict from feeding or increasing his addiction' (*ibid.*).

Obscene material is not confined to that dealing with sexual conduct. In *Calder (John) Publications Ltd* v *Powell* [1965] 1 QB 509, it was held that a book could be obscene if it 'highlighted . . . the favourable effects of drug-taking' so that there was 'a real danger that those into whose hands the book came might be tempted to experiment with drugs'. This was confirmed in *R* v *Skirving*, above. It has also been held that that which has a tendency to induce violence may be regarded as obscene (*DPP* v *A and BC Chewing Gum Ltd*, *supra*).

The Obscene Publications Act 1964

Under the 1959 Act no offence is committed unless the obscene article was published. Hence, mere possession – albeit of large stocks of potentially obscene material for commercial purposes – was not rendered unlawful. Accordingly, the 1964 Act (s 1(1)) amended the 1959 Act and added to the offence of publishing an obscene article that of possessing an obscene article 'for publication for gain' (s 2(1)). This gives the police the power to search for and seize obscene material and to charge the possessor with an offence without having to wait for and prove publication. The offence thus phrased avoids the difficulties encountered in cases such as *Mella* v *Monahan* [1961] Crim LR 175, where the display of pornographic magazines in a shop window was held not to be a publication within the meaning of the 1959 Act. Although the Act specified that to offer an article for sale was to publish it, the court felt bound to apply the contractual rule that a display of goods in a shop window was merely an invitation to treat.

Forfeiture proceedings

If information is laid before a magistrate that there are reasonable grounds for believing that obscene materials are being kept on specified premises for publication for gain, a warrant may be issued authorising the police to search for and seize the same (1959 Act, s 3). Following such seizure the occupier may be summoned to show cause why the material should not be forfeited. The right to contest forfeiture proceedings also extends to any others responsible for producing the article (author, publisher, etc.) or 'through whose hands' it has passed prior to seizure.

Such proceedings do not involve bringing any charge against the person in possession. Accordingly, the only sanction they might suffer is the loss of the material in question and any profit that it might have returned. As, however, it has proved difficult to secure convictions for publishing or possessing obscene articles, there is statistical evidence to suggest that, for practical purposes, the police favour the forfeiture procedure. It is apparently easier to persuade a magistrate that a thing is obscene than it is to convince a jury.

Defences

(a) Aversion

In a number of cases it has been held that, if the likely effect of a particular article is to be so revolting as to turn its audience against the type of activity depicted, then it cannot be said to have any tendency to deprave and corrupt. Thus the conviction of the publishers of *Last Exit to Brooklyn*, a book which contained 'graphic descriptions of the depths of depravity and degradation in which life was lived in Brooklyn', was overturned by the Court of Appeal because the trial judge in summing up had failed to emphasise that, although the book was 'intentionally disgusting, shocking and outrageous, it made the reader share in the horror it described and thereby . . . being aware of the truth, he would do what he could to eradicate those evils' (*per* Salmon LJ, *R* v *Calder and Boyars*, *supra*). The overwhelmingly repulsive nature of the material in question was also held to be a ground for overturning a conviction for obscenity in *R* v *Anderson*, *supra*.

(b) Innocent publication

By virtue of s 2(5) of the 1959 Act it is a defence for a person charged with publishing or possessing an obscene article to prove that they had not examined the article and had no reason to suspect that it might be obscene. The defence is designed primarily to protect booksellers, newsagents, etc. in circumstances where there is nothing about a particular article – e.g. in the case of a magazine, its usual content or, if the article is a book, its title or the reputation of the author – which would have alerted a reasonable person to its possibly obscene content.

(c) Public good

The 1959 Act, s 4, provides that a person should not be convicted of publishing or possessing an obscene article, nor be subject to forfeiture proceedings under s 3, if it is proved that publication of the article in question is in the public good 'in the interests of science, litera-ture, art or learning, or of other objects of general concern'. The defence exists to ensure that the 1959 Act cannot be used to prevent the publication of that which has significant and obvious literary or artistic merit whether conventional or unconventional.

Where reliance is made on the defence, the function of the court is to determine, first, whether the article is obscene and second, and only if so, whether its publication is for the public good (*DPP* v *Jordan* [1976] 3 All ER 775). It has been held that the potentially open-ended phrase 'other objects of public concern' should be interpreted *ejusdem generis* or as relating to the type of subject-matter indicated by the words 'science, literature, art or learn-ing'. Thus, it was held in *Jordan*, *supra*, that the possible therapeutic effects of pornographic literature for those unable to satisfy their sexual desires within heterosexual or homosexual relationships could not be related to the objects of public concern with which s 4 was con-cerned. Nor have the courts been prepared to accept that sexually explicit material is pro-tected by s 4 because it may be expected to contribute to the 'learning' process of its audience. The type of learning meant by s 4 is that which has some conventional scholastic value (*Attorney-General's Reference (No. 3 of 1977)* [1978] 3 All ER 1166).

Other relevant statutory restrictions

Possessing extreme pornography

The offence of possessing extreme pornography was created by the Criminal Justice and Immigration Act 2008, s 63, as amended by the Criminal Justice and Courts Act 2015, s 37.

Under the Act, an image is pornographic if it can reasonably be assumed to have been produced solely or principally for purposes of sexual arousal. An image is 'extreme' if it is 'grossly offensive', 'disgusting' or 'otherwise of an extreme character' and portrays 'in an explicit and realistic way' any of the following:

- an act which threatens a person's life;
- an act which results, or is likely to result, in serious injury to a person's anus, breasts or genitals;

- an act which involves sexual intercourse with a human corpse;

- a person performing an act of intercourse or oral sex with an animal (whether dead or alive), see *R v Baddiel* [2016] EWCA Crim 474 (B convicted of receiving and keeping unsolicited extreme pornographic images on his iPhone for 27 days);

- rape or other non-consensual penetration by any part of the body or 'anything else'.

The offence does not apply to an otherwise pornographic image if it is an integral part of a 'classified film', i.e. one 'in respect of which a classification certificate has been issued by a designated authority' (e.g. the British Board of Film Classification).

A person charged under s 63 has a defence if he/she can show that:

- he/she had 'a legitimate reason for being in possession of the image concerned';

- he/she were 'sent the image without any prior request having been made' and 'did not keep it for an unreasonable time';

- he/she 'had not seen the image concerned and did not know, nor had any cause to suspect, it to be an extreme pornographic image' (s 65).

Sending indecent material through the post (Postal Services Act 2000)

Section 85 of the 2000 Act provides that it is an offence to send any 'indecent or obscene' material through the post. Unlike the Obscene Publications Act 1959, no definition of the word 'obscene' is provided. Hence it would appear that the ordinary dictionary meaning should be applied. The same goes for the word 'indecent'. In *R v Stanley* [1965] 2 QB 327, Lord Parker CJ said that 'the words "indecent or obscene" convey one idea, namely, offending against the recognised standards of propriety, indecent being at the lower end of the scale and obscene at the upper end of the scale'.

This is a summary offence and does not include any public good defence.

Sending unsolicited sexual publications (Unsolicited Goods and Services Act 1971)

It is an offence under this Act (s 4) to send to any person unsolicited matter describing human sexual techniques or material advertising such matter. The offence so defined is of sufficient scope to criminalise the sending of matter which might not be thought to be indecent or obscene for the purpose of the Postal Services Act 2000.

Publishing 'horror comics' (Children and Young Persons (Harmful Publications) Act 1955)

The Act was passed in response to the perceived dangers for children of reading 'horror comics'. The offence thereby created (s 1) has a number of elements which consist of the following:

- publishing, printing or selling any book, magazine or such work consisting wholly or mainly of stories told in pictures;

- portraying the commission of crimes, acts of violence or cruelty, or of a horrible or repulsive nature; and

- which is likely to fall into the hands of children, and to corrupt any child into whose hands it does fall.

The Act has rarely been invoked. Any prosecution requires the consent of the Attorney-General. No public good defence is made available. A person who sells the item has a defence, however, if he/she can prove that he/she had not examined the contents and had no reasonable cause to suspect it contained offensive material.

Taking indecent photographs of children (Protection of Children Act 1978)

The Act was passed in response to growing concerns about child pornography. It made it an offence to take, show or distribute any indecent photograph or film of a person under 16 years. Possession of such material was made an offence by the Criminal Justice Act 1988, s 160.

To keep pace with computer technology the meaning of 'photograph' in the 1978 Act, s 7, was extended by amendments contained in the Criminal Justice and Public Order Act 1994, s 84. As a result, the offence set out above now applies to any indecent 'pseudo-photograph', viz. 'an image whether made by computer graphics or otherwise howsoever which appears to be a photograph' and to any 'data stored on a computer disc or by other electronic means which is capable of conversion into a pseudo-photograph'.

In *R v Smith*, *The Times*, 23 April 2002, the Court of Appeal held that the act of voluntarily downloading an indecent image from a web page was an act of making a photograph or pseudo-photograph providing it was a deliberate and intentional act with the knowledge that the image was, or was likely to be, an indecent photograph or pseudo-photograph of a child.

No offence is committed by any person who, with legitimate reason, distributes, or is in possession of, such indecent photographs, but who has not seen them and does not know and has no reason to suspect that they are indecent (1978 Act, s 1(4)).

Where s 1(4) does not apply it is no defence for a person who has been charged with distribution or possession to plead that they did not know that the person depicted in the photographs was under 16 years of age (*R v Land* [1998] 1 All ER 403).

Importing indecent articles or publications (Customs Consolidation Act 1876 and Customs and Excise Management Act 1979)

The 1876 Act prohibits the importation of 'indecent or obscene prints, paintings, photographs, books, cards, lithographic and other engravings, or any other indecent or obscene articles'. The 1979 Act provides that any such 'goods . . . shall be liable to forfeiture'. No definition of the words indecent or obscene is given, nor are defendants able to plead a public good defence.

By virtue of EU law, import restrictions or trade with other EU states may not be imposed unless, *inter alia*, for the purpose of public morality and providing that the restrictions are not a means of 'arbitrary discrimination . . . between Member States' (Arts 30 and 36). It has been seen that English law regards that which is obscene as offensive to public morality and trading in such material is prohibited. To this extent, therefore, the import restrictions explained above would appear to be consistent with EU requirements. English law does not, however, impose similar restrictions on that which is merely indecent. Hence it could be argued that restricting its importation is not required to uphold public morality and discriminates against those wishing to send to and trade in such material in the United Kingdom.

Displaying indecent images in public
(Indecent Displays (Control) Act 1981)

Section 1 of the Act introduced the offence of displaying publicly any indecent material. The Act was passed in response to public concerns about the open display of pornography in sex shops and some newsagents. A display is public if it is visible from a place to which the public have access. No offence is committed if the display is accessible only on payment of a fee by an adult or is in a part of a shop to which access can be gained only after passing an adequate warning notice.

Sending indecent material electronically
(Communications Act 2003)

While the Postal Services Act 2000 deals with the sending of indecent material by post, the 2003 Act, s 127, contains the offence of sending any message by means of a public electronic communications network which is 'grossly offensive or of an indecent, obscene, or menacing character'.

In *DPP* v *Collins* [2006] UKHL 40, where, in a series of phone calls to his MP, the defendant expressed his views on immigration in extreme racist language.

Malicious Communications Act 1988
(sending material to cause distress or anxiety)

Section 1 of the Act created the offence of sending any letter or article or electronic communication which is indecent, grossly offensive, false or threatening for the 'purpose of causing distress or anxiety'.

In *Connolly* v *DPP* [2007] EWHC 237 (Admin) the defendant sent pictures of an aborted foetus to three pharmacists. The Court found the pictures so offensive as to be beyond the protection offered by ECHR Art 10.

Protection from Harassment Act 1997
(communications causing harassment)

The sending of threatening or malicious messages by electronic or other means would appear to be open to prosecution under the extensively worded provision in section 1 of the 1997 Act. This renders it an offence to pursue a course of action which the person knows amounts to harassment of another. Aggravated harassment occurs where the course of action, i.e. something which is done at least twice, causes fear of violence.

Sexting (Criminal Justice and Courts Act 2015)

Section 33 of the Act seeks to deal with what has become known popularly as 'sexting' and such activities.

The section makes it an offence to 'disclose' (give, show or make available) a 'private sexual photograph or film' without the consent of the person photographed and with the intent of causing distress to that person. A person charged with the offence has a defence if he/she can prove that he/she reasonably believed that the disclosure was:

(i) necessary for the prevention, detection or investigation of crime;

(ii) made for the publication of journalistic material which was in the public interest;

(iii) made for a financial or other reward by the person in the photograph or film.

A photograph is 'private' if it depicts something that 'is not normally shown in public'. It is 'sexual' if it shows all or part of a person's 'genitals or pubic area' or something which, because of its nature, 'a reasonable person would consider to be sexual'.

Possessing a paedophile manual (Serious Crime Act 2015)

The offence of possessing a paedophile manual was created by section 270 of the 2015 Act. A paedophile manual is defined as 'any item containing advice or guidance about abusing children sexually'. Defences to a charge under section 270 include the following:

- the person had a legitimate reason for having the item;
- the person did not know and had no reason to suspect the item contained the type of sexual material alleged;
- the item was unsolicited and was not kept for an unreasonable time.

Sexual communication with a child (Serious Crime Act 2015)

Section 67 of the above inserted section 15A into the Sexual Offences Act 2003 and included the offence of communicating with a person under 16 for the purpose of 'obtaining sexual gratification'. The offence is limited to persons of eighteen years or over.

Identifying victims of female genital mutilation (Serious Crime Act 2015)

Section 71 of the 2015 Act inserted section 4A into the Sexual Offences Act 2003 making it an offence to publish any matter likely to lead members of the public to identify a person as an alleged victim of female genital mutilation (FGM). No offence is committed if the defendant had no knowledge of the content of the publication or where the victim aged 16 or over 'freely' gave written consent to it.

Online pornography (Audiovisual Media Services Regulations 2014)

The Regulations implemented EU Directive 2007/65 and amended the Communications Act 2003. Their main effect is to require that paid-for video-on-demand ('VoD') should not contain a video that has been refused classification by the British Board of Film Classification. Also prohibited are videos given an R18 certificate or containing material that might be damaging to persons under eighteen unless made available in ways that ensure that such persons will not normally see it.

Relevant common law offences

Objective
4

Conspiracy to corrupt public morals
Shaw v DPP [1962] AC 220

S published a magazine entitled ***The Ladies Directory***. This contained telephone numbers and descriptions of the services offered by prostitutes. S was convicted of the offence of conspiracy to corrupt public morals. The case remains controversial because the offence was previously unknown. It represents, therefore, an example of judicial law-making. Lord Simons (in the House of Lords) justified this as follows:

In the sphere of criminal law I entertain no doubt that there remains in the courts a residual power to enforce the supreme and fundamental purpose of the law, to conserve not only the safety and order but

> also the moral welfare of the state and that it is their duty to guard it against attacks which may be the more insidious because they are novel and unprepared for.
>
> He went on to say that a conviction for the offence was appropriate only where the defendant's behaviour was 'destructive of the very fabric of society'.

Conspiracy to outrage public decency

Knuller v DPP [1973] AC 435

> K published a contact magazine for homosexuals. The House of Lords upheld a conviction for conspiracy to corrupt public morals. K's conviction for conspiracy to outrage public decency was quashed only on the grounds of a misdirection by the trial judge. This represented another example of judicial law-making in this controversial context. Lord Simon explained the nature of the offence as follows: 'Outraging public decency goes considerably beyond offending the standards, susceptibilities of, or even shocking reasonable people ... The offence is concerned with recognised minimum standards of decency, which are likely to vary from time to time.' The essence of the offence was said to be inserting outrageously indecent matter on the inside pages of magazines sold in public.

In *R v Gibson* [1990] 2 QB 619, the Court of Appeal confirmed that it was an indictable offence 'to do or exhibit anything in public which outrages public decency, whether or not it also tends to deprave and corrupt those who see or hear it'. The offence has also been said to be committed by that which 'outrages minimum standards of public decency as judged by the jury in a contemporary society' (Thomas LJ, *R v Hamilton* [2007] EWCA Crim 2062).

Where common law offences such as the above are used to found prosecutions in relation to obscene articles, no public good defence may be relied upon.

Also, note *R v Johnson* [1997] 1 WLR 367, where it was held that obscene telephone calls may amount to a public nuisance.

Freedom of expression and the administration of justice

General nature of contempt of court

Contempt of court may be either civil or criminal in nature. Civil contempt is committed by refusal to comply with an order of the court, e.g. failure to act in accordance with the terms of an injunction or a decree of specific performance. Although a civil obligation, a person who commits this type of contempt may be sentenced to up to two years' imprisonment (Contempt of Court Act 1981, s 14).

Criminal contempt is committed by words or actions which interfere with or obstruct the proper administration of justice or which bring the judicial system into disrepute. Obvious examples would include interference with jurors or witnesses, misbehaviour during judicial proceedings and refusal to give evidence or to attend court when ordered to do so.

Certain other types of criminal contempt are of more direct relevance to the issue of freedom of expression. These are:

- scandalising the court;
- publishing matter prejudicial to the course of justice.

Scandalising the court

It is a criminal contempt to utter or publish words which amount to scurrilous attacks on the integrity and impartiality of a judge or court of law. Reasoned criticism of the same made in good faith without abuse or malice is permissible. The line between this and criticism that is contemptuous is crossed where some improper purpose or motive in the exercise of the judicial function is alleged (*R v Commissioner of Police of the Metropolis, ex parte Blackburn (No. 2)* [1968] 2 QB 150).

Proceedings for this type of contempt are rare. One of the most famous cases is *R v New Statesman, ex parte DPP* (1928) 44 TLR 301. Criminal contempt was held to have been committed by the publication of an article which alleged that any person who believed in birth control would not receive a fair trial before Mr Justice Avery.

Publications prejudicial to the course of justice

Prima facie, the publication of material that might tend to affect the outcome of civil or criminal proceedings amounts to a contempt. Every person has the right to a fair trial regardless of past history, reputation or the allegations made against them and to a decision based solely on an objective and dispassionate assessment of the evidence given in court. It is thus a contempt, for example, to publish material which suggests that a person is guilty of an offence after that person has been charged but before the trial has begun.

The law of contempt in this context is now governed by the Contempt of Court Act 1981. This creates an offence of strict liability 'whereby conduct may be treated as a contempt of court as tending to interfere with the course of justice . . . regardless of intent to do so' (s 1).

The offence may be committed only when proceedings are 'active' (s 2). A criminal case becomes active when:

- a person is arrested without warrant;
- a warrant for arrest is issued;
- a summons is issued;
- a person is charged orally with an offence.

In the case of a civil matter the proceedings are active from the moment when the action is set down for trial ('from the time when arrangements for the hearing are made'). The serving of a writ, therefore, does not make a civil case active for the purpose of the law of contempt.

The content of the publication must be such that it creates 'a substantial risk that the course of justice in the proceedings in question will be seriously impeded or prejudiced' (s 2). The judicial view would appear to be that appellate courts are seldom likely to be affected in this way by media comment on particular proceedings:

> it is difficult to envisage circumstances in which any court in the United Kingdom exercising appellate jurisdiction would be in the least likely to be influenced by public discussions of the merits of a decision appealed against or of the parties' conduct in the proceedings (*Re Lonrho plc* [1980] 2 AC 154).

Many of the modern cases on contempt have been concerned with the type of publicity given by certain newspapers to trials which have attracted the public interest. *Attorney-General v Mirror Group Newspapers* [1997] 1 All ER 456, dealt with a newspaper's coverage of the trial of Mr Geoffrey Knight, who was charged with assault on a well-known actress. Schiemann LJ explained that in determining whether a publication has created a substantial risk of seriously affecting the course of justice, the following matters should be taken into consideration:

- the likelihood of the publication coming to the attention of a potential juror;
- the likely impact of the publication on an ordinary reader at the time of publication;
- the residual impact of the publication on a notional juror at the time of the trial.

Defences

The 1981 Act exempts three types of publication from the strict liability rule. Hence, in these circumstances, no contempt is committed without proof of intent:

- where the defendant, having taken all reasonable care, is unaware that the proceedings to which the publication relates have become 'active' within the meaning explained above (s 3);
- where the publication in question represents 'a fair and accurate report of legal proceedings held in public, published contemporaneously and in good faith' (s 4);
- where the publication represents 'a discussion in good faith of public affairs or other matters of general public interest' and the 'risk of . . . prejudice to particular legal proceedings is merely incidental to the discussion' (s 5).

Other relevant restrictions

In those rare circumstances where a court decides that justice will be best served by holding proceedings in private, publication of information relating thereto may amount to a contempt where, *inter alia*:

- the proceedings relate to the care, welfare or upbringing of an infant;
- the proceedings relate to national security;
- the publication of information relating to the proceedings has been prohibited by the court (Administration of Justice Act 1960, s 12).

Restrictions may also apply to proceedings held in public. Hence a court may order the postponement of the reporting of particular proceedings for such period as appears necessary to avoid 'a risk of substantial prejudice to the administration of justice' (1981 Act, s 4(2)). It is also a contempt:

- to publish the name of the complainant in a rape case without the court's consent (Sexual Offences (Amendment) Act 1976, s 4);
- to publish the name of any child involved in any legal proceedings contrary to a direction given by the court (Children and Young Persons Act 1933, s 39);
- to publish the name of any witness contrary to a direction by the court (this is a common law power).

Contempt and journalists' sources

Where a party seeks disclosure of a journalist's sources of information, perhaps for the purpose of bringing or defending legal proceedings or protecting a legal right (e.g. confidentiality), a court may make an order requiring production of that information only if satisfied that this is necessary in the interests of national security, the prevention of disorder, the prevention of crime or the administration of justice (Contempt of Court Act 1981, s 10). The justification for the protection of journalists' sources was explained by the European Court of Human Rights in *Goodwin* v *United Kingdom* (1996) 22 EHRR 123:

> Protection of journalistic sources is one of the basic conditions for press freedom . . .Without such freedom sources may be deterred from assisting the press in informing the public on matters of public interest. As a result the vital public watchdog role of the press may be undermined and the ability of the press to provide accurate and reliable information may be adversely affected.

The meaning of the word 'necessary' in section 10 was considered by the House of Lords in *Re an Inquiry under the Companies Securities (Insider Dealing) Act 1985* [1988] 1 All ER 203, where Lord Griffiths said:

> I doubt if it is possible to go further than to say that 'necessary' has a meaning that lies somewhere between 'indispensable', on the one hand, and 'useful' or 'expedient', on the other, and to leave it to the judge to decide which end of the scale of meaning he will place it on the facts of any particular case. The nearest paraphrase I can suggest is 'really needed'.

Disclosure in the interests of national security was ordered in the well-known case of *Secretary of State for Defence* v *Guardian Newspapers Ltd* [1985] AC 339, after a junior civil servant at the Ministry of Defence delivered highly confidential information to the *Guardian* newspaper detailing the schedule for the arrival of American nuclear missiles ('Cruise') at the Greenham Common airbase. The court's view was that to uphold journalistic privilege in these circumstances could have serious consequences for the ability of the UK government to enter into arrangements with friendly states which were essential for the preservation of national security and the proper defence of the realm. The civil servant in question was later convicted of offences against the Official Secrets Act 1911 and sentenced to six months' imprisonment (*R* v *Tisdall*, *The Times*, 26 March 1984).

A number of other well-publicised cases were concerned with attempts by private companies to discover the identities of employees allegedly responsible for 'leaking' confidential information which could have been damaging to the company concerned if published. In these cases it was established that information necessary for the administration of justice is not confined to that which is required for proper disposal of actual legal proceedings but extends to that which is needed to protect a legal right, e.g. confidentiality. Hence, in a number of instances, and not without adverse academic comment, journalists have been ordered to reveal their sources purely to preserve commercial confidentiality in circumstances where, the court felt, publication could have done substantial damage to commercial interests and was not justified by any countervailing public interest, e.g. the need to expose corruption or 'iniquity' (see *X Ltd* v *Morgan Grampian (Publishers) Ltd* [1990] 2 All ER 1; *Camelot Group plc* v *Centaur Communications Ltd* [1998] 1 All ER 251).

Freedom of expression, public order and national security

Introduction

Objective
5

The principal objectives of the provisions operating in this context are to restrict the utterance and dissemination of words that:

- could incite persons to violence or be seriously detrimental to the maintenance of social harmony and public order;

- could reveal information which might prejudice the competence of the state to protect vital national interests.

Note that the common law offences of blasphemy and blasphemous libel were abolished by the Criminal Justice and Immigration Act 2008, s 79. The offences of sedition and seditious libel were abolished by the Coroners and Justice Act 2009, s 73.

Incitement to disaffection

It is an offence to 'maliciously and advisedly . . . seduce any member of Her Majesty's Forces from his duty or allegiance to Her Majesty' (Incitement to Disaffection Act 1934, s 1) or to be in possession of any document for that purpose (s 2). It follows that a relatively trivial act, such as persuading a soldier to overstay their leave, would satisfy the requirements of the offence. Mere proof that the words were likely to have the above effect is not sufficient. The defendant must be shown to have acted 'wilfully and intentionally' for the above purposes (*R* v *Arrowsmith* [1975] QB 678).

Prosecutions for this offence are rare and require the consent of the Director of Public Prosecutions. In *Arrowsmith* the defendant was convicted of the offence in s 2 after she had distributed leaflets at army barracks urging soldiers billeted there not to serve in Northern Ireland if so ordered.

The Police Act 1997, s 91 contains a similar provision making it an offence to 'cause disaffection amongst members of any police force' or to induce any police officer to withhold their services or commit breaches of discipline (originally Police Act 1964, s 53).

Religious and racial hatred

For more on the 2006 Act, see Chapter 19, pp. 610–1.

The Racial and Religious Hatred Act 2006 created the offences of:

- using threatening words or behaviour, or,
- displaying any threatening written material, or,
- distributing or publishing any threatening material,

intended to stir up religious hatred.

The prohibitions apply also to the content of plays and films.

The Official Secrets Act

Reasons for official secrecy

Even a democratic government requires a measure of secrecy for some of its functions, as a means whereby it can better carry out its duties on behalf of the people. Among the primary tasks of the government are the defence of the nation from external threats, the maintenance of relations with the rest of the world and the preservation of law and order. Defence against external attack would be severely prejudiced if the potential enemies had access . . . to the details of our plans and weapons. It would be impossible to negotiate with other countries if all discussion, however delicate, was conducted completely in the open. Some measures for the prevention of crime would be ineffective if they were known to criminals. Some of the internal processes of government should be conducted in confidence if they are to result in effective policies. The presentation of clear issues to Parliament and the electorate depends upon ministers and administrators being able . . . to argue out all possibilities with complete frankness and free from the temptation to strike public attitudes (Departmental Committee on Section 2 of the Official Secrets Act 1911, Cmnd 5104 [the Franks Committee]).

More cynical commentators have suggested that official secrecy has had more to do with:

- the traditional 'establishment' view that the process of government is too important and complicated to be understood or appreciated by the general populace;
- the 'covering up' of mistakes made by civil servants and politicians and preserving the facade of government unity.

Official Secrets Act 1911

Section 1 provides that it is an offence if any person for a purpose prejudicial to the safety or interests of the state:

(a) obtains, publishes or communicates any information which might be useful to an enemy;

(b) enters, approaches or is found in the vicinity of a prohibited place (e.g. military establishment or property).

It would appear that it is not within the competence of a court to decide on the basis of evidence whether a particular act might be prejudicial to the interests of the state. This is a matter of political judgement falling within the Crown's non-justiciable prerogatives. Hence, once the prosecution has proved that the defendant intended the consequence of his/her actions, it is for the Crown to decide whether those consequences were prejudicial to its interests and to advise the court accordingly (*Chandler* v *DPP* [1964] AC 763).

Section 2 of the 1911 Act contained what was to become the Act's most controversial provision. This made it an offence to make any unauthorised communication of information gained in the service of the Crown to any unauthorised person. Hence the offence extended to relatively innocuous information having nothing to do with defence, national security, the investigation of crime, etc. It was also an offence to receive such information or to fail to take reasonable care of it. As a result of considerable criticism and political pressure from across the party divide, s 2 was eventually repealed and replaced by the Official Secrets Act 1989.

Official Secrets Act 1989

This limits the protection of the criminal law to certain specified classes of official information.

Security and intelligence

Section 1 deals with information relating to security and related intelligence. It provides that it is an offence for any member of the security forces or any person who has been notified that they are subject to the Act to disclose, without lawful authority, any information or document 'relating to security or intelligence which is or has been in his possession by virtue of his position as a member of . . . these services or in the course of his work' after being notified that this is subject to the section's requirements. It is a defence for the accused person to show that they 'did not know, and had no reasonable cause to believe, that the information . . . related to security or intelligence' (s 1(5)). Note that the section covers all information relating to the security forces. It matters not whether the information revealed is particularly sensitive or wholly innocuous.

The only exception to the prohibition of disclosure of this type of information is that it was made with 'lawful authority'. This was considered in *R v Shayler* [2002] UKHL 11 (see below).

> . . . it is open to a former member of the service to seek authorisation from his former superior or head of the service, who may no doubt seek authority from the secretary to the cabinet or a minister. Whoever is called upon to consider the grant of authority must consider with care the particular information or documentation and weigh the merits of that request bearing in mind . . . the object which the statutory ban or disclosure seeks to achieve and the harm (if any) which would be done by the disclosure . . . If the information . . . were liable to disclose the identity of agents or compromise the security of informers, one would not expect authorisation to be given. If, on the other hand, [it] revealed matters which, however scandalous or embarrassing, would not damage any security or intelligence interest . . . another decision might be appropriate (Lord Bingham).

Section 1(3) creates the offence of making a 'damaging disclosure of any information . . . relating to security or intelligence' without lawful authority. This applies to all past or present Crown servants, government contractors, and police officers. It is, therefore, a lifelong duty. The defence in s 1(5), explained above, is also available to any person charged with this offence. It is also a defence for the person to show that they did not know that the disclosure was damaging.

It is probable that a court would not be prepared to consider evidence as to whether the disclosure of particular information was 'damaging' to the interests of the state (i.e. the Crown). Again, it is likely that this would be viewed as a political question relating to that element of the royal prerogative remaining beyond the scope of judicial comment.

Defence

Section 2 deals with disclosures of information relating to the defence of the realm. The offence consists of making a 'damaging disclosure of any information . . . relating to defence without lawful authority'. A damaging disclosure is that which:

(a) 'damages the capability of . . . the armed forces . . . or leads to loss of life or injury to members of those forces or serious damage to the equipment or installations of those forces' (s 2(2)(a));

(b) 'damages the interests of the United Kingdom abroad, seriously obstructs the promotion or protection . . . of those interests or endangers the safety of British citizens abroad' (s 2(2)(b)).

It is a defence for the accused to show that they did not know and had no reasonable cause to believe that disclosure of the information would be damaging in any of the above senses (s 2(3)). For the reasons already given, however, the willingness of a court to hear evidence on what is or is not damaging to the state remains open to question.

International relations

Section 3 makes it an offence for any past or present Crown servant or government contractor, without lawful authority, to make a damaging disclosure of any information relating to international relations or any confidential information which was obtained from a state other than the United Kingdom. The meaning of damaging is that given in s 2(2). Again, it is a defence to show lack of knowledge or reasonable cause to believe that the disclosure was damaging.

Investigation of crime

Section 4 identifies the last principal category of protected information, viz. that relating to crime and its investigation. The relevant offence is committed by a past or present Crown servant without lawful authority disclosing information which is likely to or results in 'the commission of an offence or facilitates an escape from custody . . . or impedes the prevention or detection of offence or the apprehension or prosecution of suspected offenders'. As with the preceding two categories of information, the defence of innocent publication is available (s 4(4)).

Any further disclosure by the recipient of information falling into any of the above categories is an offence providing that the recipient knew or should have known that the information fell within one of the protected categories (s 5).

Lawful authority

The Act also creates the further offence of making, without lawful authority, a damaging disclosure of information relating to security, intelligence, defence or international relations which has been communicated in confidence to another state and which has come into the person's possession without that state's authority (s 6).

All of the above offences are committed only where the disclosure is made 'without lawful authority'. Such lawful authority to disclose information exists where:

- the disclosure is made by a Crown servant 'in accordance with his official duty';
- the disclosure is made by a government contractor 'in accordance with official authorisation' or for the purposes for which they are a government contractor 'without contravening an official restriction';
- the disclosure is made by a person who is neither of the above to a Crown servant or with official authorisation.

Defences

No public interest defence is included in the Act in respect of any of the categories of unlawful disclosure created by it. A defendant is not entitled to be acquitted, therefore, simply because they believed it was in the public interest to make the disclosure in question (*R v Shayler* [2002] UKHL 11). The same case also decided that the 1989 Act was not incompatible with the European Convention, Art 10 on the grounds that it:

(a) is directed towards legitimate aims;

(b) contains internal review mechanisms for those concerned by the work or actions of the security services;

(c) allows disclosures with appropriate authorisation, which decisions are subject to judicial review.

In *R v Keogh* [2007] EWCA Crim 528, the reverse onus of proof in the 1989 Act sections 1–4, i.e. requiring the person charged to show that they did not know and could not have been reasonably expected to have known that their disclosure of official information was damaging to the state, was found *prima facie* incompatible with the presumption of innocence in ECHR Art 6(2). The court's view was that it should be for the prosecution to prove, rather than the defence to disprove, the existence of guilty knowledge – a substantial element of the offence. In compliance with HRA 1998, s 3, the court chose to 'read down' the offending words so that the 1989 Act should be understood as requiring the state (the 'Crown') to prove both that the disclosure was damaging to its interests and that there was reasonable cause to believe the defendant knew this to be so.

For the Human Rights Act 1998, section 3, see Chapter 17, pp. 503–4.

DA-notices

The publication or broadcasting of material sensitive to national security may also be restrained by the issue of a DA-notice. These notices seek to prevent the dissemination of information relating to the following where this would be damaging to the public interest:

- defence plans, operational capability, state of readiness and training;
- defence equipment;
- nuclear weapons;
- defence communications technology;
- the security and intelligence services;
- contingency plans for war or national emergency;
- information relating to the defence and security establishments and installations.

DA-notices are issued by the Defence, Press and Broadcasting Advisory Committee, composed of representatives from the Ministry of Defence and the media. Such notices tend to be issued only after more informal methods of communication have failed to achieve the desired result. The material not to be published will be specified therein.

The Committee was not created by statute or under the royal prerogative. Hence, DA-notices have no legal force or sanctions attached to them. The system attempts to achieve a degree of self-regulation. There is always the possibility, however, that the publication of information in contravention of such notice may amount to a breach of the Official Secrets Acts.

Breach of confidence and abuse of private information

Objective
6

A person may also be under an obligation not to disclose information which has been given in confidence or acquired against the wishes of those to whom it relates by an invasion of their privacy. Until the Court of Appeal's decision in *Douglas* v *Hello! Ltd* [2001] 2 All ER 289, it was generally accepted that such duty of confidence was limited to that which derived from:

(a) express or implied contractual terms;

(b) the special nature of the relationship between the parties.

In general, equity required exchanges of information to be treated confidentially where:

(a) the particular relationship cannot function effectively without it;

(b) in all the circumstances, the public interest in protecting the relationship clearly outweighs any countervailing public interest(s), e.g. that of freedom of information and expression.

Thus it was established that an action for breach of confidence could be used to prevent an employee from revealing or exploiting trade secrets confided by an employer (*Seager* v *Copydex Ltd* [1967] 1 WLR 923), or to prevent the disclosure of personal secrets exchanged between husband and wife during marriage (*Argyll* v *Argyll* [1967] Ch 302). Other examples of relationships which have been recognised as giving rise to a duty of confidence would include doctor and patient, priest and penitent, solicitor and client, and banker and customer.

The *Hello!* case involved proceedings for an injunction to restrain the proprietors of a popular magazine from publishing unauthorised photographs taken at a celebrity wedding. No contractual or prior relationship of a type previously held to import a duty of confidentiality existed between the parties claiming breach of confidence and the magazine proprietors. This was not something, however, which the court felt should be fatal to the claimants' case. Sedley LJ's opinion was that 'the law no longer needs to construct an artificial relationship of confidentiality between intruder and victim; it can recognise privacy itself as a legal principle drawn from the fundamental value of human autonomy'. Such sentiments in the judgment in the *Hello!* case are generally regarded as marking the beginnings of the development of the modern tort of abuse of private information.

The restrictions on the freedom of expression discussed above have all been imposed by the criminal law. Hence the law is only brought to bear after the offensive words have been used or published. Breach of confidence or abuse of private information, however, is a civil concept with the remedy sought usually being an injunction to prevent the disclosure or publication in question. It is a valuable means, therefore, of stopping the dissemination of information before damage has been caused rather than simply punishing the perpetrator after it has been done.

It is also now clear that in certain contexts the duty applies to the relationship between the Crown and those who work in its service whether these be Ministers, civil servants or members of the intelligence and security services. This will be the case where the revelation of information could do serious damage to any of those public interests for which the government is directly responsible.

> In some instances disclosure of confidential information entrusted to a servant of the Crown may result in a financial loss to the public. In other instances such disclosure might tend to harm the public interest by impeding the efficient attainment of proper government ends and the revelation of defence or intelligence secrets certainly falls into that category (*per* Lord Keith, *Attorney-General v Guardian Newspapers Ltd (No. 2)* [1990] 1 AC 109).

Hence, an action for breach of confidence will lie to prevent an ex-member of the intelligence and security services from publishing memoirs which contain sensitive information about the activities of those services and the identities of their personnel (*ibid.*).

Where the Crown is the plaintiff in an action for breach of confidence this will involve the court in a delicate balancing exercise between the competing public interests:

> disclosure . . . will serve the public interest in keeping the community informed and in promoting discussion of public affairs. If, however, it appears that disclosure will be inimical to the public interest because national security, relations with foreign countries or the ordinary business of government will be prejudiced, disclosure will be restrained. There will be cases in which the conflicting considerations will be finely balanced, where it is difficult to decide whether the public's interest in knowing and expressing its opinion, outweighs the need to protect confidentiality (*per* Mason J, *Commonwealth of Australia v John Fairfax and Sons Ltd*, *supra*).

The requirement that disclosure must do substantial damage to a public interest for which the Crown is responsible means that an injunction will not be granted to prevent disclosure of any and all information entrusted to a Crown servant in confidence. It has been said that the 'court will not prevent the publication of information which merely throws light on the past workings of government, even if it be not public property, so long as it does not prejudice the community in other respects' (*ibid.*).

Attorney-General v *Jonathan Cape Ltd* [1976] QB 752

The government sought to prevent publication of an ex-Cabinet minister's memoirs. These contained details of Cabinet discussions some 10 to 12 years previously. The court accepted that, as a general principle, there was a public interest in maintaining confidentiality of Cabinet proceedings but that, given the nature of the proposed disclosures and the length of time which had passed since they were current, any damage they might do did not outweigh the public interest in the freedom of information.

It also follows, as a further general principle, that a court will be unlikely to injunct disclosure of information, whatever its source and nature, if this is already widely available. Hence, in the *Spycatcher* case the House of Lords felt that injunctions could not be used to prevent newspapers from publishing highly sensitive security-related information contained in a book written by an ex-spy which was not yet on sale in the United Kingdom. The publication of the book in other parts of the English-speaking world (e.g. Ireland and the United States) meant that the information in question was already in the public domain so that the damage had already been done (*Attorney-General* v *Guardian Newspapers, supra*).

There are dicta to the effect, however, that this should not apply to a member or ex-member of the security and intelligence services and that there is an overriding public interest in making such persons subject to a lifelong duty of confidence regardless of whether the public already has access to the information which they may wish to publish. Thus in *Attorney-General* v *Blake* [2000] 3 WLR 625, the House of Lords ruled that the Crown had a legitimate interest in preventing an ex-member of the Secret Intelligence Service who had defected to the Soviet Union from profiting from disclosure of official information, whether classified or not, acquired while a member of the secret service and thereafter. According to Lord Nichols the disclosure of such information undermined the morale and trust of those engaged in secret and dangerous operations. In his view 'an absolute rule against disclosure, visible to all, made good sense'. The Crown was, therefore, entitled to whatever profits had been derived from the breach of confidentiality owed to it.

It would also appear to be the case that even though information is of the type that could damage a vital public interest, no breach of confidence is committed by its disclosure if this reveals serious abuses of power by the government:

The press has a legitimate role in disclosing scandals by government. An open democratic society requires that that be so. If an allegation be made by an insider that, if true, would be a scandalous abuse by officers of the Crown of their powers and functions . . . the duty of the confidence . . . cannot be used to prevent the press from repeating the allegation (*per* Scott J, *Attorney-General* v *Guardian Newspapers, supra*).

In a democracy, in such circumstances, the public interest in the freedom of information would outweigh the public interest in confidentiality.

A significant consequence of the enactment of the Human Rights Act 1998 is that the requirements of Art 10 of the European Convention on Human Rights must now be considered where a government seeks to injunct information to prevent it coming into the public domain. It will be necessary, therefore, to show that the injunction serves a legitimate aim and is a proportionate response to the danger posed by publication. Where the injunction is sought by an individual to protect their privacy, Art 8 will also be brought into play. In these circumstances the court's function will be to reach a decision for or against publication which represents a fair and reasonable balance between the competing interests of privacy and the need for freedom of expression (*Campbell* v *Mirror Group Newspapers Ltd* [2002]

EWHC 499). Thus by 'absorbing the rights which Articles 8 and 10 protect into the long-established action for breach of confidence', the courts are able to develop the concept in a way which complies with their duty in the Human Rights Act, s 6, not to act in a way which is incompatible with a Convention right (see Lord Woolf CJ, *A v B plc* [2002] EWCA Civ 337). It is also clear that when a court is deciding where the balance lies between the Art 10 rights of the media and the Art 8 rights of any children likely to be affected by the publication, 'particular weight' must be given to the child's best interests (*ETK v News Group Newspapers Ltd* [2011] EWCA Civ 439).

The relationship between the law of confidence and abuse of private information, as it has developed, and the right of freedom of expression in ECHR Art 10, was the central issue in ***HRH Prince of Wales v Associated Newspapers*** [2006] EWHC 522 (Ch). The case arose out of newspaper publications of extracts from the Prince's 'Hong Kong Diaries'. These were made at the time of the handback of Hong Kong to China in 1997. Despite the very public nature of the role of the Prince in general, and the wide public interest surrounding his visit to Hong Kong, the court felt his diaries could not be regarded as part of the public record of his activities there and that he retained a reasonable expectation of confidence and privacy in relation to his personal 'musings' about this episode in his life.

> The fact that the Hong Kong Journal is not of a highly personal or private nature, in the sense that it does not deal with matters of an intimate or medical nature or about members of his family and that its contents are a very long way from the often salacious celebrity information that sometimes features in privacy claims, does not rob the claimant of a reasonable expectation of privacy in the matters to which in his Hong Kong Journal he refers (Blackburne J).

The court stressed that the public interest in 'the right to know' should not be confused with 'what it is in a newspaper's commercial interest to know', and that, although a public figure might expect that 'his actions will be more closely scrutinised by the media', he is still 'entitled to a private life'.

When the case was dealt with by the Court of Appeal, Phillips CJ said that while the Prince of Wales might be a figure of 'constant and intense media interest', this did not deny him the right to commit his private thoughts to writing and to keep them private as an aspect of his 'own human autonomy and dignity' (***HRH Prince of Wales v Associated Newspapers Ltd*** [2006] EWCA Civ 1776).

For development of the tort of 'private information', see Chapter 17, p. 536.

In this context the ECtHR has made clear that the public interest should not be equated with public curiosity or the 'public's thirst for information about the private life of others or the readers' wish for sensationalism or even voyeurism' (***Couderc and Hachette Filipacchi Associés v France*** [2015] ECHR 992). Article 10 was not intended primarily to protect the publication of the purely salacious and trivial. Hence the fact that published comment related to a public figure did not, of itself, render it immune from legal sanction or beyond the reach of the right to respect for privacy in ECHR Art 8(1).

Freedom of information and data protection

Introduction

Objective 7

The state in its various guises both central and local, collects and holds a mass of detailed information about, and relating to, the lives of most of its citizens. Until the Data Protection Act 1984, which was concerned with personal information held on computer, this was not a matter subject to any legal regulation either in terms of giving any right of access to such information or of regulating its use and disclosure to third parties.

In December 1997 the government issued a White Paper, 'Your Right to Know' (Cm 3818). This stated that 'unnecessary secrecy in government leads to arrogance . . . and defective decision-making' (para 1.1). The White Paper was followed by a draft Bill as part of a consultation exercise (Cm 4355, 1999). The stated intention of the Bill was to 'extend professionally the right of the public to have access to official information held by public authorities' and, in so doing, to promote:

(a) 'better informed discussion of public affairs';

(b) 'greater accountability of public authorities';

(c) 'more effective participation in the making and administration of laws and policies'.

Freedom of Information Act 2000

After considerable public and parliamentary debate (and amendment) this led to the Freedom of Information Act 2000. The Act provides a general right of access to information held by public authorities subject to a fairly lengthy catalogue of exemptions.

Any person applying for access to information is entitled to be informed whether the authority holds the information in question and, if it does, to have it communicated to them 'promptly' and within 20 working days (ss 1 and 10). The right to know whether certain information is held by a particular authority does not apply to, *inter alia:*

(i)   that relating to the formation of government policy;

(ii)   ministerial communications;

(iii)   advice given or requested by any of the Crown's law officers;

(iv)   the operation of any ministerial private office (s 35).

The principal classes of information exempt from the duty of disclosure are:

(a) that which is reasonably accessible by other means (s 21) or which is to be published (s 22);

(b) that which relates to the security or intelligence services (s 23) or to the royal household (s 37);

(c) personal information (s 40) or that provided to the authority in confidence (s 41);

(d) that to which legal or professional privilege applies (s 42);

(e) that which might prejudice:

- the safeguarding of national security (s 24), defence or the effectiveness of the armed forces (s 26);
- relations between the United Kingdom and any other state or international organisation (s 27) or between any two administrations in the United Kingdom (s 28);
- the United Kingdom's economic interests (s 28);
- criminal investigations or proceedings (s 30);
- law enforcement (s 31);
- the effective conduct of public affairs (s 36);
- the physical or mental health of any individual (s 38);
- trade secrets or commercial interests (s 43).

Where a request is made for information that is a dataset and the applicant requests that this should be communicated in electronic form, then the authority should, as far as is reasonably practicable, so provide the information in a reusable format (s 11).

The Act further provided for the creation of an Information Commissioner. His/her general functions were to include the promoting, disseminating, teaching, and assessment of good practice in connection with the provision of information by public authorities (s 147). The Commissioner was tasked also with investigating complaints relating to any failures by a public authority to act in accord with the Act's requirements (s 50). Upon receipt of a complaint, the Commissioner may:

(i)   serve an information notice on the authority requiring it to provide details of its handling of the matter to date (s 50);

(ii) serve a decision notice on the authority identifying what it should do to rectify any failure to declare whether it holds the information sought or to disclose it (s 50);

(iii) serve an enforcement notice requiring the authority to comply with any of its obligations under the Act (s 52).

Either the applicant or the public authority may appeal to the First Tier Tribunal against a decision notice (s 57). The public authority also has a further right of appeal against a decision notice and/or an enforcement notice (s 57). In certain circumstances an appeal may be referred directly to the Upper Tier? Tribunal (s 57). Cases heard before the First Tier Tribunal may be appealed to the Upper Tribunal on grounds of error of law (s 57). The Upper Tribunal is deemed to be a court of law with similar status to that of the High Court (s 3).

The Black Spider Case

Perhaps the most publicised case concerning the workings of the Act would be *R (on application Evans)* v *Attorney-General* [2015] UKSC 212. The case centred on a request by a journalist (Evans) for disclosure of correspondence between numbers of government departments and the heir to the throne, Prince Charles. Due to the allegedly rather dubious nature of the Prince's handwriting, the proceedings are often referred to as the 'Black Spider Case'.

The correspondence itself was said to contain the Prince's opinions on a number of environmental issues in which he was taking a keen interest.

The request was dealt with at seven different levels.

The initial request for information

This was made to the government departments concerned, under section 1 of the Act, and the Environmental Information Regulations 2004. The regulations gave effect to EU Council Directive 2003/4 EC which provided for public access to environmental information. Although conceding that the correspondence did exist, and only after some considerable prevarication, the government's response was that the correspondence was subject to the Act's exemptions from disclosure relating to:

(a) communications between the monarch, the royal family and royal family except where disclosure was outweighed by the public interest (s 37);

(b) personal information (s 40);

(c) information which would cause a breach of confidentiality except where the disclosure was in the public interest (s 41).

The complaint to the Information Commissioner

Not satisfied with this Mr Evans complained to the Information Commissioner. He was again unsuccessful. In explaining the refusal of disclosure, and relying very heavily on the exemption in section 37, the Commissioner cited the 'weighty public interest' in maintaining the conventional rules relating to the ability of the monarch to exercise the right to consult government Ministers, allowing the heir to the throne to learn the business of government, preserving the political neutrality of the royal family, and protecting its privacy and dignity.

The Upper Tribunal

Still not content, the applicant exercised his right of appeal (s 57). This was referred to the Upper Tribunal. Here, Mr Evans, at last got 'a result'. According to the Tribunal, the 'essential reason' for upholding the case for disclosure was that it would 'generally be in the overall public interest for there to be general transparency as to how and when Prince Charles seeks to influence government'. Other public interest factors cited were:

- increased public understanding of the influence of Prince Charles on matters of public policy and of the interaction between government and monarch generally;
- more effective public assessment of the accuracy of media claims concerning Prince Charles's 'inappropriate lobbying/interference';
- informing the 'broader general debate surrounding constitutional reform'.

The Attorney-General's certificate

The government's response to this was for the Attorney-General to issue an order overriding the Tribunal's decision (s 53). This was on the basis that the Attorney had 'on reasonable grounds formed the opinion that in respect of [Mr Evans's] request for disclosure there was no failure to comply with section 1', i.e. the Act's disclosure requirements.

The issue of the Attorney-General's certificate followed a Cabinet decision claimed to have been made in the 'exceptional circumstances' that:

- the correspondence consisted of private and confidential communication between the Prince and government Ministers;
- the correspondence formed part of the Prince's education for kingship;
- the potential damage disclosure would do to the Prince's neutrality and his ability to fulfil his duties when King;
- the 'ability of the monarch to engage with the government of the day whatever its political colour and maintain political neutrality as a cornerstone of the UK's constitutional framework'.

The application for judicial review

Mr Evans's next move was to take the case before the Administrative Court by way of an application for judicial review. He argued that, in the absence of fresh evidence or opinion, the Attorney could not claim to have had reasonable grounds for overriding the Tribunal's decision and that such grounds could not be said to exist simply because he disagreed with its findings. He further claimed that once a judicial body (i.e. the Upper Tribunal) had decided non-disclosure was not consistent with the requirements of EU law, in this instance EU Council Directive 2003/4 EC, that finding could not be rendered ineffective or overruled by a member of the executive government.

Both contentions were rejected by the court.

The appeal to the Court of Appeal

It was only at this point that the case appeared to have turned decisively in Mr Evans's favour. In the Court of Appeal's view the argument that section 53 allowed the Attorney-General to override the Upper Tribunal's decision for no better reason than that he disagreed with it was indeed a 'remarkable proposition'. As such, it was not something the court was prepared to uphold. The court was convinced also that the Attorney-General's intervention in the proceedings was at odds with the clear intent of the EU Environmental Information Directive.

The appeal to the Supreme Court

Like an ageing champion boxer 'slugging it out' to the end, the government decided to take the fight to the final round. It appealed to the Supreme Court.

The Court's 'final words' on the matter were as set out below.

- The citizen had a constitutional right to challenge decisions of the executive in the courts and to have any such, i.e. the refusal of disclosure, set aside if found not in accordance with relevant legal principles. Accordingly the power in s 53 enabling a member of the executive government to restore an executive decision which had been overruled by a court or tribunal was not compatible with normative constitutional expectations.

  > a statutory provision which entitles a member of the executive to overrule a decision of the judiciary merely because he does not agree with it would not merely be unique in the United Kingdom, it would cut across two fundamental constitutional principles (*the Separation of Powers and the Rule of Law*) (Lord Neuberger).

- It followed that the existence of any such power would be recognised by a court only where Parliament's intent to this effect could be found in express words or clear intent in the enabling statute. None such could be found in s 53.

- The Attorney-General could not claim to have reasonable grounds for overriding a judicial decision in favour of disclosure, where he had no fresh material on which to base his findings. His disagreement alone did not amount to reasonable grounds.

- The prerequisites for lawful use of s 53 to override a judicial decision were:

  - 'a material change of circumstances' since the judicial decision in issue;
  - the decision in question was 'demonstrably flawed in fact or in law'.

- The EU Directive provided that a government refusal to disclose environmental information should be subject to both an administrative review and a challenge in a court of law with any such judicial decision to be regarded as final. Clearly, therefore, in the instant proceedings, once the matter had been decided by the Upper Tribunal, it was no longer open to the government to revisit the issue and insist on a non-disclosure by resort to the Attorney-General's s 53 powers.

Data Protection Act 1998

The Freedom of Information Act operates alongside the Data Protection Act 1998. This provides the individual with rights in relation to 'personal data' against any person or body falling within the definition of a 'data controller'. Personal data is that which relates to a living individual and from which that individual may be identified (s 1). A data controller is a person who 'determines the purpose for which . . . any personal data . . . are to be processed' (*ibid.*).

The principal rights given to the individual are:

(a) to be informed whether any personal data relating to them is being processed by the data controller, the purposes for which it is to be used and the persons to whom it may be disclosed;

(b) to have the data communicated to them (s 7).

The rights are enforceable by court order where a valid request is not complied with (*ibid.*). They are not absolute rights, however, and do not apply where disclosure could, *inter alia*, prejudice national security, the prevention or detection of crime or the apprehension or prosecution of offenders (ss 28 and 29).

The Act applies to the details of expenses claims by MPs and is not excluded by the rules of parliamentary privilege (***Corporate Officer, House of Commons*** v ***Information Commissioner*** [2008] EWHC 1084 (Admin)).

The meaning of 'data' in the 1998 Act is wider than in the original Data Protection Act 1984 and extends beyond that held in computers to include that which is:

(i) recorded with the intention that it should be processed by means of such equipment;

(ii) recorded as part of a filing system (s 1).

The Act imposes a duty on a data controller to discharge their functions in relation to personal data in accordance with prescribed data protection principles; these are that the data shall be:

- processed lawfully and fairly and only with the individual's consent or in performance of a legal duty, the administration of justice, a statutory or other function of a public nature;
- obtained for specified and lawful purposes;
- adequate, relevant and not excessive to those purposes;
- kept accurate and up to date;
- kept only for so long as is necessary;
- processed in accordance with the rights of the data subject;
- protected against unauthorised processing, loss or damage;
- not transferred to a country outside the European Economic Area unless that country has adequate protection for the rights of data subjects (s 4 and Sched 1).

Overall supervision of the Act's requirements is given to the Data Protection Commissioner (s 51). The Commissioner may serve an enforcement notice on any data controller alleged not to be acting in accordance with the data protection principles (s 40). Failure to comply with such notice is an offence (s 47).

The Commissioner must lay an annual general report before Parliament on the exercise of their functions and such periodic specific reports as they think appropriate (s 52).

Freedom of expression, the internet, and the law of tort

Defamation

Objective 8

The sending, showing or publication of any message or other material which discredits or lowers a person's reputation, causes that person to be shunned, avoided, or subject to hatred, ridicule or contempt, constitutes the tort of defamation of character.

Unlike the USA, English law has no 'single publication rule', i.e. that only the first publication, whether electronically or in print, is legally actionable. For the domestic law, the result of this is that each and every further publication, constitutes a 'fresh' and actionable commission of the tort. This has been held not to be incompatible with the right to freedom of expression in the European Convention on Human Rights, Art 10 (*Times Newspapers Ltd (Nos. 1 and 2)* v *United Kingdom* [20009] ECHR 451).

Intentionally causing physical or psychological harm

The tort has three main elements:

(i)   words or conduct directed towards a person for which there is no justification;

(ii)   an intention to cause severe distress;

(iii)   that the person suffered physical harm or recognised psychiatric illness.

It is unlikely that the tort may be used to prevent an individual from publishing true information about themselves. Hence in *Rhodes* v *OPO* [2015] UKSC 32, it was not available to prevent the publication of a book which contained graphic and shocking accounts of the sexual abuse suffered by the author when a child. This was notwithstanding the claim that the book would be likely to cause psychological harm to the author's son.

Freedom of expression, the internet and the criminal law

The views of the House of Lords and the Crown Prosecution Service

The legal regulation of freedom of expression on the internet was considered by the House of Lords Communications Committee in its 2013–14 Report 'Social Media and Criminal Offences' (HL Paper 37, 29.7.14). This adopted the view that the main types of illegality which could be committed via the internet could be dealt with by way of the existing criminal law.

> There are two different ways to think about the harmful acts committed using social media: either they are new acts, or they are the acts already prohibited by the criminal law but committed in the new forum of social media as opposed to elsewhere. We have been persuaded that the latter is usually the case.

The Committee's principal recommendation was:

> There are aspects of the current statute law which might appropriately be adjusted and certain gaps which might be filled. We are not however persuaded that it is necessary to create a new set of offences specially for acts committed using the social media and other information technology.

CPS prosecution guidelines

In October 2016, the Crown Prosecution's new 'Guidelines on Prosecuting Cases Involving Communications Sent via Social Media' set out the range of offences which are available currently in cases of abuse of this form of expression. These included a range of pre-existing criminal acts and a number of more recent additions to the criminal law found mainly in the Criminal Justice and Courts Act and the Serious Crime Act, both of 2015. These latter two, in particular, may be viewed as the first pieces of domestic legislation to introduce offences directly tailored to wrongful online behaviour, e.g. 'sexting' and 'revenge porn'.

The principal offences, as identified by the CPS in this context, are as set out below. These were divided into four separate categories.

1 Threats

(i)   Messages or communications threatening to kill (Offences Against the Person Act 1861, s 16).

(ii)   Messages or communications putting a person in fear of violence (Protection from Harassment Act 1997, s 4).

(iii) Messages or communications to intimidate jurors or witnesses in legal proceedings (Criminal Justice and Public Order Act 1994, s 51).

(iv)   Messages or communications conveying any threat, false information or indecent or grossly offensive content, to cause distress or anxiety (Malicious Communications Act 1988, s 1).

(v)   Messages or other material sent by a 'public electronic communications network' which are grossly offensive, indecent, obscene or menacing or, containing false information for the purpose of causing annoyance, inconveniences or needless anxiety (Communications Act 2003, s 127).

2 Communications targeting specific individuals

(i)   Using social media to cause harassment to persuade a person not to do something he/ she was entitled to do or to do something which he or she was not under any obligation to do (Protection from Harassment Act 1997, ss 1 and 2).

(ii)   Conduct associated with stalking which constitutes harassment, including sending unwanted communications, attempting to make contact, publishing any material relating to the 'victim' or monitoring a person's use of the internet or social media (Protection from Harassment Act 1997, s 2A).

(iii) Messages or communications putting a person in fear of violence (Protection from Harassment Act 1997, s 4).

(iv)   Messages or communications putting a person in fear of stalking (*ibid*).

(v)   Communications amounting to controlling or coercive behaviour in an attempt to intimidate a person in an intimate or family relationship, e.g. those communications causing the victim to fear violence or serious alarm or distress.

(vi)   Showing or communicating a sexual image without consent of the individual depicted (Criminal Courts Act 2015, s 33).

   The offence is known colloquially as 'revenge pornography' . . . which usually refers to the actions of an ex-partner, who uploads onto the internet, or posts on a social networking site, or shares by text or email, intimate sexual images of the victim (CPS Guidelines).

(vii) Communications used to coerce a person into non-consensual sexual activity (Sexual Offences Act 2003, s 4).

(viii) Communications inciting a child to engage in sexual activity (Sexual Offences Act 2003, s 8).

(ix) Communications for meeting a child following sexual grooming (Sexual Offences Act 2003, s 15).

(x) Communications committing 'hate crimes'.

3 Breach of court orders or other legal restrictions

(i) Communications for the purpose of bribing or intimidating jurors or for otherwise interfering with the process of justice (common law offence of perverting the course of justice).

(ii) Disclosing information concerning jury deliberations (Juries Act 1974, s 20).

(iii) Publishing information which could lead to the identification of a complainant of a sexual offence (Sexual Offences (Amendment) Act 1992, s 1).

(iv) Communications in breach of reporting restrictions imposed by a court (Contempt of Court Act 1981, s 4).

4 Communications which are grossly offensive, indecent, obscene or false

(i) Electronic communications which are grossly offensive, indecent or false intended to cause distress or anxiety to the victim (Malicious Communications Act 1988, s 1).

(ii) Electronic communications which are grossly offensive, indecent, obscene, menacing, or false, intended to cause annoyance, inconvenience or needless anxiety (Communications Act 2003, s 127).

Those who encourage others to commit a communications offence may be charged with encouraging an offence under the Serious Crime Act 2007, s 44: for instance encouragement to tweet or re-tweet a grossly offensive message or the creation of a derogatory hashtag; or making available personal information ('doxing') so that individuals may be more easily targeted by others. Such encouragement may sometimes lead to a campaign of harassment or 'virtual mobbing' or 'dog-piling', whereby a number of individuals use social media or messaging to disparage another person, usually because they are opposed to that person's opinions (CPS Guidelines, 10.10.16).

Summary

The chapter provides understanding of the extent to which English law has imposed restrictions on the freedom of speech in the perceived interests of public decency, the administration of justice, public order and national security. It identifies and explains the principal statutory and common law offences relating to the spoken, recorded and broadcast word and comments on the other legal powers and extra-judicial mechanisms used to regulate the publication and dissemination of information and performance or portrayal of forms of art, literature and drama.

Particular attention is paid to the restrictions applying to radio and television broadcasting and to the development of the modern law of confidence dealing with the use and abuse of private information.

References

Departmental Committee on Section 2 of the Official Secrets Act 1911 (1972) [Franks Committee] Cmnd 5104.

Joint Committee on Human Rights, 9th Report (2001–2) HL 149, HC 1102.

Report of the Committee on Privacy and Related Matters [Calcutt Committee] (1990) Cm 1102.

Robertson (2006) *Freedom, the Individual and the Law* (8th edn), London: Penguin.

Your Right to Know (1997) Cm 3818.

Further reading

Bailey, Harris and Jones (2009) *Civil Liberties: Cases and Materials* (6th edn), Oxford: Oxford University Press, Chs 5–7.

Carey (2012) *Media Law* (5th edn), London: Sweet & Maxwell.

Melville-Brown (2016) *Internet publication and freedom of expression,* Law Society Gazette, 14.5.09.

21

Freedom and emergency powers

Objectives

After reading this chapter you should:

1. Have an understanding of the political circumstances in which emergency powers may be used in the United Kingdom.

2. Appreciate the extent and content of the powers used to deal with terrorism in Northern Ireland.

3. Understand the reasons for the enactment of the Terrorism Act 2000 and the nature and extent of the powers and offences in this Act.

4. Appreciate the reasons for the enactment of the Anti-terrorism, Crime and Security Act 2001 and the nature and extent of the powers and offences provided.

5. Recognise the reasons for the enactment of the Terrorism Act 2006 and the extent and requirements of the offences it contains.

6. Understand the reasons for the enactment of the Terrorism Prevention and Investigation Measures Act 2011.

7. Be able to describe the provisions of the Counter-Terrorism and Security Act 2015.

8. Be aware of the nature and extent of emergency powers available to the authorities to deal with civil contingencies.

Emergency powers in general

Objective 1

Emergency powers may be defined as those which give the state the legal competence to deal with extraordinary and immediate threats to political, social and economic stability. Such threats may come in the form of:

- external aggression by another state(s);
- political terrorism for the purpose of changing the domestic political order or that of a foreign state;
- widespread disruption to the normal life of the community resulting from natural disasters or other causes of serious civil disruption, e.g. strikes in essential services.

The powers to deal with such contingencies will be contained principally in Acts of Parliament. Relevant common law powers may also be found in the royal prerogative.

For the royal prerogative, see Chapter 12.

The existence of emergency powers on a more permanent basis, particularly when designed to deal with terrorism, may suggest a significant lack of social consensus concerning the legitimacy of the state. Such legislation will be likely to impose those restrictions on the liberties of the subject as are deemed appropriate to deal with the threat.

Emergency powers in wartime

On both occasions in the twentieth century when the very existence of the state was threatened by external aggression, Parliament responded by conferring extensive emergency powers on the executive. The principal enactments of this type were, for World War I, the Defence of the Realm Acts 1914–15 and the Military Service Act 1916, and, for the World War II, the Emergency Powers (Defence) Acts 1939–40. These gave the executive government the authority to control almost every aspect of national life and, in particular, to make such regulations as were deemed necessary for the defence of the realm, public safety and the successful prosecution of the war.

In both wars these Acts contained powers to, *inter alia*:

For judicial review of emergency and national security power, see Chapter 15, pp. 402–3.

- conscript persons into military and industrial service;
- intern enemy aliens without trial;
- regulate the supply and distribution of food (rationing).

Although access to the courts to challenge alleged abuses of such powers was not excluded expressly, reference has already been made to the obvious judicial reluctance to review the exercise of discretionary powers in such times of national difficulty (see *R v Halliday* [1917] AC 260; *Liversidge v Anderson* [1942] AC 206).

Emergency powers and terrorism

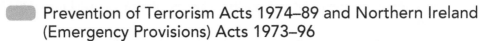

Prevention of Terrorism Acts 1974–89 and Northern Ireland (Emergency Provisions) Acts 1973–96

Objective 2

The Prevention of Terrorism Act (PTA) 1974 was the United Kingdom's first piece of modern, generally applicable, anti-terrorist legislation. It was introduced as a 'temporary' response to increased IRA activity on the mainland of the United Kingdom in the early 1970s. Its specific timing was a direct result of the Birmingham pub bombings of 1974 in which 21 people were killed and 162 injured. Such was the political mood at the time that the Act passed through nearly all its parliamentary stages in a single day notwithstanding that it contained a wide array of security powers beyond those normally available, or indeed generally held to be acceptable, for the investigation and prosecution of 'ordinary' criminal activities. Its provisions were directed principally at terrorism connected with Irish affairs. The Act was revised and re-enacted on a number of occasions, until its final version in 1989. Amongst its core provisions were powers authorising police to:

(a) stop and search vehicles, their occupants and pedestrians, for articles which could be used for the purposes of terrorism (ss 13A and 13B, inserted by the Criminal Justice and Public Order Act 1994, s 81 and the Prevention of Terrorism (Additional Powers) Act 1996);

(b) arrest and detain any person reasonably suspected of involvement in specified terrorist offences and to detain such persons for questioning for 48 hours and for a further five days with the Secretary of State for the Home Department's consent (s 14);

(c) enter and search premises, with warrant, reasonably believed to contain a terrorist suspect on evidence of substantial value to a terrorist investigation (s 14);

(d) conduct such searches without warrant on the authority of an officer of the rank of superintendent or above where the investigation was reasonably believed to be one of great urgency necessitating immediate action in the interests of the state (Sched 7, para 7).

These were in addition to the powers conferred on the Secretary of State for the Home Department to:

(a) proscribe any organisation appearing to be concerned in terrorism occurring in the United Kingdom in connection with affairs in Northern Ireland (s 1) (membership of such organisation being an offence under s 2);

(b) exclude from or prevent any person entering or remaining in any part of the United Kingdom if satisfied that such person had been concerned in acts of terrorism relating to Northern Ireland (ss 4–7).

For the purposes of the civil and military security forces on the ground in Northern Ireland itself, these powers were complemented by those contained in the Northern Ireland (Emergency Provisions) Acts, an important feature of which was that many of the powers found therein were exercisable by members of the armed forces as well as by police officers. The original Northern Ireland (Emergency Provisions) Act 1973, as with the first PTA, was also revised and re-enacted on several occasions. It was also subject to annual renewal by Parliament. At the time of the 1998 Good Friday Agreement, the version of the Act in force was the Northern Ireland (Emergency Provisions) Act 1996. In addition to authorising the Secretary of State for Northern Ireland to proscribe organisations appearing to be engaged in or promoting acts of terrorism and making membership of such organisations an offence (ss 30–31), the Act contained powers permitting:

(a) any member of the security forces (i.e. either police or army) to stop any person for as long as was necessary to obtain information concerning that person's identity, movements, and knowledge of any recent explosions or fatal or life-threatening incidents – all of this on pain of arrest without warrant (s 25);

(b) any member of the RUC to arrest without warrant any person they had reasonable grounds to suspect of any offence under the Act (s 18);

(c) any member of the armed forces to arrest without warrant any person they had reasonable grounds to suspect of 'any offence' (s 19);

(d) any member of the security forces to stop and search any person for possession of weapons, explosives or radio transmitters without need for reasonable suspicion (s 20(6));

(e) any member of the RUC to enter and search any premises without warrant where it was suspected on reasonable grounds that any person suspected of a terrorist offence might be found (s 18);

(f) any member of the security forces to enter and search any premises without warrant either for weapons or explosives (s 19); or where it was considered necessary to do so in the 'course of operations for the preservation of peace or the maintenance of order' (s 26).

In addition, and although not used since 1976, the Northern Ireland emergency powers legislation retained the power of indefinite detention without trial or internment available to the Northern Ireland Secretary in relation to any person they were 'satisfied' had been engaged in the planning or commission of acts of terrorism and whose detention was 'necessary for the protection of the public' (s 36 and Sched 3). The provisions containing this power were eventually repealed by the Northern Ireland (Emergency Provisions) Act 1998.

The Terrorism Act 2000

Background

Objective 3

The Act was based on the proposals contained in the government's consultation paper 'Legislation Against Terrorism' (Cm 4178, 1998) which, in turn, were influenced considerably by Lord Lloyd's report of the Inquiry into Legislation Against Terrorism (Cm 3420, 1996). It was intended to be a comprehensive, all-purpose instrument of anti-terrorist legislation applicable throughout the United Kingdom and to terrorism in general whatever its source or purpose. It thus repealed and replaced the Prevention of Terrorism Acts and the Northern Ireland (Emergency Provisions) Acts and is not subject to annual or periodic parliamentary renewal. According to the government's consultation paper, its aim was 'to create legislation which is both effective and proportionate to the threat which the United Kingdom faces from all forms of terrorism – Irish, international and domestic – which is sufficiently flexible to respond to a changing threat, which ensures that individual rights are protected and which fulfils the United Kingdom's international commitments' (above, para 8).

The case set out by Lord Lloyd in his 1996 report for maintaining a different legal framework for dealing with terrorism than that applicable to 'ordinary crime' included the following:

● terrorism frequently involves the use of lethal force directed at, or capable of, causing extensive and indiscriminate casualties and is designed to create fear amongst the civilian population generally;

● its purpose is to secure political or ideological objectives by violence or threat of violence and thus to subvert the democratic process;

● it is perpetrated by highly trained and committed individuals, usually well-armed, acting on behalf of well-resourced organisations;

● terrorists have proved particularly difficult to catch and convict without special offences and additional police powers;

● the overall decline of terrorist incidents in recent years has been more than offset by the trend towards more deadly weapons and higher casualties.

Such arguments have, however, not proved sufficient to stifle all criticism of the Act and, particularly, the allegation that legislation of this type should be regarded as an extraordinary and temporary expedient for dealing with a pressing emergency or threat to social and political stability and that the enactment of permanent 'special powers' legislation, particularly at a time when the principal cause of terrorism in the United Kingdom appeared to have diminished, threatens the credibility of the United Kingdom's claim to be a genuinely free, liberal democracy.

The definition of terrorism

For the purposes of the Prevention of Terrorism and the Northern Ireland (Emergency Provisions) Acts this meant 'the use of violence for political ends' and included 'any use of violence for the purpose of putting the public or section of the public in fear'. Application of the concept in the Prevention of Terrorism legislation was limited, in the case of some powers and offences (including proscription and exclusion) to action in connection with the affairs of Northern Ireland and, in relation to others (including stop and search, arrest, search and seizure), to terrorism directed towards either the affairs of Northern Ireland or those of states beyond the United Kingdom. It did not apply, therefore, to acts of political violence relating to the internal affairs of those parts of the United Kingdom other than Northern Ireland.

In the Terrorism Act 2000 terrorism is expressed as the use or threat of certain types of action in or outside the United Kingdom designed to influence the government of the United Kingdom or any government, and intimidate the public or section of the public, for the purpose of advancing a political, religious or ideological cause (s 1). The types of action referred to are those which:

(i) involve serious violence against a person;

(ii) involve serious damage to property;

(iii) endanger a person's life (other than that of the perpetrator of the act);

(iv) create a serious risk to the health or safety of the public;

(v) are designed to interfere with or seriously disrupt an electronic system (s 1(4)).

The contention that the Act's failure to stipulate any required intention or state of mind for causing any of the above consequences meant that terrorist acts could be committed by accident was considered in the *Miranda* case (p. 662). The implications of the suggestion was explained by the court, viz. a group of junior doctors erect a sign as part of a protest against government policy towards the NHS (i.e. for a political cause), but do so in a way which endangers the lives of passers-by (consequence (iv), above).

> They have taken an action designed to influence the government to advance a political cause which (even if entirely unknown to them) endangered the public or created a risk to health and safety (Dyson, MR).

The court's response to this was that Parliament could not have intended a definition so widely drawn that it could have such potentially absurd implications. The result is that the anti-terrorist powers contained in the 2000 Act, whether of stop–search, or arrest, may not be used unless it can be shown that the person actually intended his/her actions to cause any of the required consequences.

If firearms or explosives are used in the commission of any of (i) to (v) above, the action amounts to terrorism whether or not it is designed to influence the/a government or intimidate the public (s 1(3)).

Hence, although the new definition eschews the rather vague notion of 'violence for political ends', it seeks to extend the ambit and application of the term in a variety of ways and will apply to:

- acts falling within the definition wherever these are committed including those concerned purely with affairs in England, Scotland or Wales;
- acts directed to religious or ideological issues rather than overtly political causes;
- acts which may not cause or threaten any direct risk of personal violence or injury but which are directed towards property, or such matters as the workings of public services and utilities or telecommunications and computer systems.

As so phrased, therefore, it is conceivable that terrorism could now encompass, in pure legal terms at least, those forms of direct action or protest sometimes engaged in by, for example, environmental and animal rights groups and by trade unions where such activities might have an impact on public health or safety.

The definition extends to activities directed against regimes outside of the United Kingdom (*R* v *F* [2007] EWCA Crim 243). It is not confined, therefore, to that which is intended to destabilise or change the domestic system of government, its policies, or the constitution of the United Kingdom. It applies also to actions by non-state armed troops against foreign armed troops in their national territory (*R* v *Gul* [2013] UKSC 64).

Proscription and deproscription

The Act proscribes all organisations listed in Sched 2 and enables the Secretary of State for the Home Department to add or remove organisations to or from the Schedule (s 3(1)–(3)). The Minister may take such action 'only if he believes' that an organisation commits, participates, prepares, promotes or is otherwise concerned in acts of terrorism (s 3(4)–(5)). Unlike its predecessors this new power of proscription is not limited to organisations using violence in connection with the affairs of Northern Ireland. Note also the lack of any express requirement that the Minister's decision be based on reasonable grounds. As of late 2016, there were 59 different organisations listed in the Schedule.

A major new departure in the 2000 Act was the provision of a procedure enabling a proscribed organisation to appeal against the proscription decision. An application may be made to the Minister to exercise the power to remove an organisation from Sched 2 by the organisation or any person affected by its proscription (s 4(1)–(2)). Should such application be refused, a right of appeal is given to a Proscribed Organisation Appeals Commission (POAC) (s 5(1)–(2)). The Commission is to allow an appeal against a refusal of an application to deproscribe an organisation if it considers that the decision 'was flawed when considered in the light of the principles applicable on an application for judicial review' (s 5(3)). Where the Commission allows an appeal this determines that the Minister has acted in contravention of the Human Rights Act. He or she is required, therefore, either to lay a deproscription order before Parliament subject to the affirmative resolution procedure or, in more urgent cases, make an order removing the organisation from Sched 2 which will lapse within 40 days unless approved by resolution passed by both Houses within that period (ss 5(5), 123 and 124). Decisions of the Commission may be appealed on a point of law to the Court of Appeal (s 6) and remain open to judicial scrutiny notwithstanding the restrictive security consideration which may be involved. Any such decision may be set aside if not founded on reasonable grounds (*Secretary of State for the Home Department* v *Lord Alton of Liverpool* [2008] EWCA Civ 443).

Following the deproscription of an organisation, a right of appeal becomes available to any person convicted of any of the various offences in the Act relating to the membership or financing of it (s 7). These offences are contained in sections 11–13, 15–19 and 56 as set out below.

Members of the POAC are to be appointed by the Lord Chancellor who is also empowered to make rules regulating its procedure and workings (Sched 3). Three members must attend its proceedings one of whom must be a person who holds or has held high judicial office within the meaning of the Appellate Jurisdiction Act 1876 (*ibid*). The rules made by the Lord Chancellor for the conduct of the Commission's proceedings may provide that, in certain circumstances:

(i)   its business may be conducted without an oral hearing;

(ii) reasons for proscription may be withheld;

(iii) legal representatives may be excluded (*ibid*).

Terrorist and related offences

The principal offences contained in the Terrorism Act are:

- belonging or professing to belong to a proscribed organisation unless the person can prove that they did not take part in the activities of the organisation at any time during which it was proscribed (s 11);

- inviting support for a proscribed organisation or arranging a meeting to further that organisation's objectives or to be addressed by a person who belongs or professes to belong to a proscribed organisation (s 12);

- addressing a meeting for the purpose of encouraging support for a proscribed organisation (ibid.);

- wearing items of clothing or otherwise wearing, carrying or displaying any article in a public place in a way which arouses reasonable suspicion that they are a member or supporter of a proscribed organisation (s 13);

- raising or providing money or other property intended or reasonably suspected to be for the purposes of terrorism (s 15);

- possessing money intending it to be used for the purposes of terrorism or in circumstances where there is reasonable cause to suspect that it might be so used (s 16);

- entering into arrangements by which terrorist property is placed under the control of another for the purposes, *inter alia*, of concealment, removal from the jurisdiction or transfer to nominees (s 18, money 'laundering');

- failing to disclose as soon as reasonably practicable any belief or suspicion based on information gained in the course of employment or any trade, business or profession that a person has committed any of the offences in ss 15–18 (s 19);

- prejudicing a terrorist investigation either by disclosing information about it to another ('tipping off') or by concealing relevant material (s 39);

- giving, receiving, or inviting another to receive instruction or training in the making or use of firearms, explosives or chemical, biological or nuclear weapons (s 54);

- directing at any level the activities of an organisation concerned in terrorism (s 56);

- possessing an article in circumstances which give rise to a reasonable suspicion that it is possessed for a terrorist purpose (s 57);

- making or possessing records or documents containing information likely to be useful to a person committing or preparing an act of terrorism (s 58);

- inciting another person to commit an act of terrorism wholly or partly outside the United Kingdom (ss 59–61);

- doing anything outside the United Kingdom as an act of or for the purposes of terrorism where the action would have amounted to the commission of certain offences involving causing explosions, using biological or chemical weapons (s 62);

- doing anything outside the United Kingdom amounting to an offence under ss 15–18 of the Act if committed in the United Kingdom (s 63).

Fund-raising offences

Note that no offence is committed under sections 15–18 above (the fund-raising offences) if a person's involvement is with the express permission of a police officer or any suspicion that the money may be used for terrorist purposes is revealed to the police as soon as reasonably practicable (s 21). This provides protection for undercover agents and police informants.

The possession offences

In terms of the various offences created by the Act, by far the most prosecutions to date have been brought under section 57 (possession of an article for a terrorist purpose) and section 58 (possession of information likely to be useful to a terrorist).

Section 57 is wider in scope than section 58. Section 58 is concerned only with the possession of documents or records containing information of a particular type. Section 57, on the other hand, applies to the possession of any 'article' – an expression that extends to any substance or other thing (s 121).

The first ingredient the Crown has to establish under section 57(1) is that the defendant possessed the article. This means that the Crown must prove both that the defendant knew he had the article and that he had control of it. Possession may, however, be assumed where the article was on any premises at the same time as the defendant, or while the defendant was the occupier, or which he habitually used otherwise than as a member of the public (s 57(3)). Also, the Crown must prove beyond reasonable doubt that the circumstances of the defendant's possession gave rise to a reasonable suspicion that his possession was for a purpose connected with terrorism. There is, however, no obligation for the Crown to prove exactly what that terrorist purpose was (*R v G, R v J* [2009] UKHL 13).

Electronically stored documents and materials may amount to an 'article' within the meaning of section 57 (possession of an article for terrorist purposes) (*R v Rowe* [2007] EWCA Crim 635). Ideological propaganda is, however, not enough. Whatever the nature of the article, be it documentary or otherwise, there must be a 'direct connection between the object possessed and an act of terrorism' (*Zafa and Others v R* [2008] EWCA Crim 184).

Section 58(1) has three main elements. Thus, to secure a conviction, the Crown must prove beyond a reasonable doubt, that:

(i)   the defendant possessed the document or record in question in the sense that he had control of the material and was aware that he had it;

(ii) the document or record contained the kind of information likely to provide practical assistance to a person preparing or committing an act of terrorism;

(iii) the defendant knew the type of information it contained.

So far as possession is concerned, it is noticeable that section 58 does not contain any notion of 'assumed awareness', i.e. as in section 57(3) which, as explained, allows the court to assume knowledge of possession in certain circumstances.

> So in order to prove its case under section 58(1), the Crown must satisfy the jury . . . for instance, that a defendant who owned a flat was aware that her boyfriend had brought a document of the relevant kind into the flat, or else that, despite her claim that he had kept it locked away beyond her control, she not only knew that the document was in the flat, but she also had control over it (*per* Lord Rodger, *R v G, R v J, supra*).

Note too, that the offence in section 58 concentrates on possession rather than intent. It matters not, therefore, that the person in possession of the document or record does not intend to use the information to commit a terrorist act or for any terrorist purpose.

> So the offence is apt to catch someone who gathers the information and stores it with a view to passing it on to someone else who is preparing an act of terrorism or else the accused may

have gathered and stored the information without having any clear idea of what he intended to do with it. None of this matters, since the legislation makes it an offence simply to collect, record or possess information of this kind (*ibid*).

An entirely innocuous document (e.g. a map) does not constitute information likely to be useful to a terrorist purely because of the surrounding circumstances. The document itself must contain information of such a nature as to raise a reasonable suspicion that it is intended to be used to assist in the preparation or commission of an act of terrorism. It 'must be information that calls for an explanation'.

> What is not legitimate under section 58 is to seek to demonstrate by reference to intrinsic evidence that a document innocuous on its face is intended to be used for the purpose of committing or preparing a terrorist act (Lord Phillips CJ, *K* v *R* [2008] EWCA Crim 185).

Both section 57 and section 58 provide defences for persons charged with the offences they contain. Under section 57(2), it is a defence for the defendant to prove that his possession of the 'article' in question was not for a purpose connected with terrorism. It does not matter that the alternative purpose pleaded is unreasonable or unlawful – e.g. that the defendant was in possession of explosives because he planned to blow open a bank vault; provided the purpose was not related to terrorism, the defence remains valid.

The defence in section 58 requires the accused to show that he had a reasonable excuse for collecting or possessing the information likely to be of use to a terrorist. Here, therefore, an absurd or illegal purpose for the possession, e.g. to blow open a bank vault, is not good enough, as that which is absurd or illegal cannot be regard as reasonable (*R* v *G*, *R* v *J*, *supra*). What the Crown must do to destroy the defence of reasonable excuse is to disprove the explanation put forward by the defendant. It does not have to go further and prove what the defendant's actual reason was for possessing the information (*R* v *AY* [2010] EWCA Crim 762).

It is no defence to a charge under the Act that the defendant's designs were directed towards a tyrannical or oppressive regime.

> In our judgment the terrorist legislation applies to countries which are governed by tyrants and dictators. There is no exemption from criminal liability for terrorist activities which are motivated or said to be morally justified by the alleged nobility of the terrorist cause (*R* v *F*, *supra*).

The 'noble cause argument' was rejected also in ***Sarwar and Ahmed*** v *R* [2015] EWCA Crim 1886 – a case in which the defendants had gone to Syria to fight with Al-Nusra, a proscribed organisation, against the regime of President Assad. It follows that if, in any case, a defendant's conduct falls within the requirements of terrorism as provided by the Act, the offence is committed regardless of the merits of the defendant's particular beliefs.

Terrorist property

This is defined as money or other property which is:

(a) likely to be used for the purposes of terrorism;
(b) the proceeds of the commission of acts of terrorism or acts carried out for the purposes of terrorism (s 14).

The disclosure to a police officer of a belief or suspicion that money or other property is terrorist property or is derived from such property does not contravene any statutory or common law provision restricting the disclosure of information (s 20). A court which convicts a person of any of the offences in sections 15–18 (also ss 11–12 in Northern Ireland) may order forfeiture of any money or property in that person's possession or control which, at the time of the offence, was intended, or reasonably suspected as being for use, for terrorist purposes (ss 23 and 111). That which is reasonably suspected to be terrorist property and is being imported or exported from the United Kingdom or moved between Northern Ireland and Great Britain may be seized and detained for forty-eight hours by police, immigration or customs officers (section 25). Continued detention of the same for periods of up to three months to a maximum of two years may be authorised by a magistrate (section 26). An application to a magistrates' court for forfeiture of the property may be made under section 28.

The provisions in the 2000 Act, sections 24–31, relating to the seizure and detention of terrorist cash were replaced by extended provisions in the Anti-Terrorism, Crime and Security Act 2001, section 1 and Sched 1. The principal difference effected by these later provisions was to allow the power of seizure to be used anywhere in the United Kingdom and not just at border crossings as envisaged by section 25 of the 2000 Act.

Terrorist investigations and related powers

A terrorist investigation is one which is concerned with:

(a) the commission, instigation or preparation of acts of terrorism;

(b) an act which appears to have been done for a terrorist purpose;

(c) the resources of a terrorist organisation;

(d) the possibility of proscribing or deproscribing an organisation;

(e) the commission, preparation or instigation of an offence under the Act (s 32).

A terrorist is a person who has committed any of the offences in sections 11, 12, 15–18, 54 or 56–63 or who has been concerned in the commission, preparation or instigation of acts of terrorism (s 40).

For the purposes of such investigations and for preventing terrorist activities, the Act entrusts the police with an extensive array of powers of stop and search, arrest, detention, entry, search and seizure and restriction of movements. For Northern Ireland these powers are supplemented with powers to stop and question and generally to override private and public property rights where this is thought to be in the interests of peace and order.

Arrest and detention

A police officer may arrest without warrant any person whom he/she reasonably suspects to be a terrorist (s 41). The arrested person may be searched to discover if they have anything in their possession which might constitute evidence that they are a terrorist (s 43) and may be detained by the police for up to 48 hours (s 41). Further detention may be authorised by a judicial authority up to a maximum of 14 days from the time of the arrest providing there are reasonable grounds for believing that further detention is necessary to obtain or preserve relevant evidence and that the investigation is being conducted diligently and expeditiously (2000 Act, Sched 8, para 38). The detained person has the right to appear and be legally represented before the judicial authority to whom the application for the warrant of further detention is made (*ibid*). The judicial authority is, however, given powers to exclude both from any part of the hearing and to order that any information on which the application is based be withheld from them (*ibid*).

Given the need not to unduly inhibit the police in the fight against organised terrorism, such restrictions do not contravene the procedural requirements of ECHR Art 5(4) – the right of every person who has been arrested or detained to question the legality of this before a court of law (*Sher* v *United Kingdom* [2015] ECHR 920).

Stop and search

The Act contains three principal powers of stop and search. The first authorises any police officer to stop and search any person reasonably suspected to be a terrorist to discover whether the person is in possession of anything which could constitute evidence related to that suspicion (s 43). The police may also search any vehicle which is stopped for this purpose. The second power of stop-search in the 2000 Act (s 43A) was inserted by the Protection of Freedoms Act 2012, s 60(3). This allows a police officer to stop and search any vehicle, its driver, any passengers and anything in or on the vehicle, providing he/she reasonably suspects that the vehicle is being used for a terrorist purpose.

The third power of this type found in the 2000 Act (s 47A), also inserted by the Protection of Freedoms Act (s 61(1)), allows a police officer in uniform to stop and search any person, vehicle, passengers or pedestrians for anything that might show that the person is a terrorist or that the vehicle is being used for a terrorist purpose. So long as this is the police officer's reason for conducting the search, he or she need not have any reasonable suspicion that such material may be found. However, such power may only be exercised in a specific and limited area where this has been authorised by a senior officer. Such officer must reasonably suspect that a terrorist act may take place in the area specified and that the use of the extended stop-search power is necessary to prevent it.

Entry and search of premises

The powers of entry and search provided by the Act relate to both evidence of terrorism and those suspected of it. Section 37 authorises a police officer to enter and search premises with warrant from a magistrate for the purposes of a terrorist investigation and to seize and retain any relevant material found there likely to be of substantial value to any such investigation and not merely the one for which the warrant was granted. A further power is given to a circuit judge to order a person to provide an explanation for any articles found in the course of the search. In cases of urgency both the search warrant and any order for explanation may be issued by a superintendent of police (s 37 and Sched 5, paras 13–16). Entry and search of any premises with warrant may also be made where there are reasonable grounds for suspecting that a person who is or has been involved in acts of terrorism may be found there (s 42).

Cordons and parking restrictions

Sections 33–36 and 48–52 give police wide powers to regulate the movement and use of vehicles and the movement of persons in designated areas to further a terrorist investigation or for the purposes of preventing terrorism.

By virtue of sections 33 and 34 an area may be designated as a cordoned area for the conduct of a terrorist investigation. Pursuant to such designation movements of vehicles and persons in and out of that area, and within it, may be restricted. It is an offence to refuse to comply with police instructions (s 36). A designation under section 33 may not exceed 28 days (s 35).

Authorisation to restrict parking on a specified road or roads where this is expedient to prevent acts of terrorism may be given by an officer of the rank of Assistant Chief Constable or Commander in the City of London or Metropolitan area (s 48). Parking in contravention of the restrictions imposed without reasonable excuse is an offence (s 51). An authorisation under section 46 may be imposed for renewal periods of 28 days (s 50).

Powers at ports and borders

Persons entering the UK may be stopped, detained, searched and questioned for up to nine hours to determine whether they may be involved in terrorist activities (2000 Act ss 40, 53, and Schedule 7). No reasonable cause or suspicion is needed.

Due to the immediacy and gravity of the threat posed by international terrorism, and the need to protect national security, the power to stop and search without reasonable suspicion has been found to be proportionate to the problem, directed towards a legitimate aim, and, as such, not incompatible with ECHR Art 5 (the right to liberty and security of the person) (*Beghal* v *Director of Public Prosecutions* [2015] UKSC 49). The power is, however, at odds with the Convention in Art 10 (the right to freedom of expression). This is through the lack of adequate safeguards to restrict and regulate police access to confidential journalistic material including that relating to journalistic sources (*R (on application Miranda)* v *Secretary of State for the Home Department* [2016] EWCA Civ 6).

Following the *Miranda* decision the Home Office announced it had 'changed the code of practice for examining officers to instruct them not to examine journalistic material at all. This goes above and beyond the court's recommendations in this case'.

The Anti-Terrorism, Crime and Security Act 2001

Objective
4

The stated purpose of the Act was to build on existing anti-terrorist and related legislation 'to ensure that the Government, in the light of the new situation arising from the September 11 terrorist attacks on New York and Washington, have the necessary powers to counter the threat to the UK' (Explanatory Notes to 2001 Act, para 3). The Act contains a miscellany of powers directed towards the above objective. The following represent some of its major provisions:

- the power to seize terrorist cash or property found at any place in the United Kingdom (s 1 and Sched 1);

- the power to freeze any assets which might otherwise be made available to a person or government involved in actions threatening the life or property of UK nationals or residents or the United Kingdom's economy (ss 4–16);

- extension of the existing statutory powers authorising disclosure of information by public authorities to include that which may assist in criminal investigations or proceedings and, in relation to such proceedings, removing any obligation of secrecy, other than contained in the Data Protection Act 1998, otherwise falling on the Inland Revenue and Customs and Excise (ss 17–20);

- extensions of both the meaning of racial hatred in the Public Order Act 1986, s 17, to include hatred directed at a group outside the United Kingdom and of the provisions concerning increased sentences for racially aggravated offences to include religiously aggravated acts (ss 37–42);

- making it an offence to transfer any biological agent or toxin to another person if it is likely to be kept or used otherwise than for prophylactic, protective or other peaceful purposes (ss 43–44);

- making it an offence to knowingly cause a nuclear explosion or develop a nuclear device except where authorised by the Secretary of State (ss 47–48);

- extension of police powers of search of persons in detention for the purposes of ascertaining their identity including whether the person 'has any mark' that would tend to identify them as a person involved in the commission of an offence (s 90);
- the power to remove disguises if reasonably believed to be being worn to conceal a person's identity (s 94).

Terrorism Act 2006

Objective 5

In the aftermath of the London bombings in July 2005, it was decided to extend the security powers already contained in the 2000 Act. The Act of 2006 was passed also to give effect to the Convention on the Prevention of Terrorism introduced by the Council of Europe in 2005.

The following new offences were created:

- encouraging or glorifying acts of terrorism (s 1);
- disseminating information to encourage or glorify acts of terrorism, or which might be useful to terrorists (s 2);
- preparing acts of terrorism including possession of items which could be used to commit acts of terrorism (s 6);
- attending any place for the purpose of preparing or training for the commission of acts of terrorism (s 8);
- making or possessing a radioactive device for the purposes of terrorism (s 9);
- using such devices for the purposes of terrorism (s 10).

All of the above have extra-territorial effect (s 17).
Other significant additions to the 2000 Act powers included:

- a widening of the powers of proscription to include organisations whose activities include the glorification of terrorism (s 21);
- an extension of the period of detention for which terrorist suspects may be held without charge from 14 to 28 days (s 23);
- allowing magistrates to issue 'all premises warrants' to search for evidence of terrorist offences (s 26).

The offence in section 2 above has been held not to be incompatible with the right to freedom of expression (ECHR Art 10(1)). This is because Art 10 does not contain an absolute right and, given the nature of the terrorist threat, is proportionate to and consistent with the legitimate aims, i.e. the justifications for departure from it, found in Art 10(2) (*R v Iqbal* [2014] EWCA Crim 2650).

Terrorism Prevention and Investigation Measures Act 2011

Background

Objective 6

The Act gave the Home Secretary power to serve a Terrorism Prevention Investigation Measure (TPIM) imposing restrictions on the movements and activities of any person suspected of involvement in terrorist activities (s 2). It repeals entirely the Prevention of Terrorism Act 2005 and the Control Order regime which it introduced.

The 2005 Act was the then government's response to the London tube bombings of the same year. While the Act was in force, 48 Control Orders were served under it. In the main, these contained restrictions requiring persons to, *inter alia*, remain within their residence for long periods within each 24 hours and within a particular locality, and to refrain from contact or association with the other specified individuals.

Albeit that relatively few Control Orders were actually issued under the regime then in force, the very existence and nature of the powers involved, and the interpretation and application of them, attracted a considerable degree of adverse comment. Thus, in some quarters it was argued that such extensive curtailment of the individual freedoms of persons who had not been convicted of any offence could not easily be reconciled with the very essentials of the British system of justice. Also, and in similar vein, attention was drawn to the procedure for making Control Orders which allowed for much of the evidence against those affected to be withheld from them on grounds of national security or public safety. All of these concerns led, in turn, to a succession of legal challenges to the way in which the Control Order powers were being used and to a number of well-publicised judicial decisions in which it was held that either the particular restrictions imposed, or the process through which this had been effected, were unlawful and in violation of the ECHR. Some of the more important outcomes of such proceedings were as follows:

- in the absence of express words, powers to impose restrictions on persons subject to Control Orders did not include a power of personal search (**Secretary of State for the Home Department v GG** [2009] EWCA Civ 160);

- powers to require persons to remain within specified premises for particular periods of each day could not be used to effect a state of virtual house arrest and in no case for more than sixteen hours per day (**JJ v Secretary of State for the Home Department** [2007] UKHL 45);

- confinement to specified premises for fifteen hours per day, being electronically tagged, and required to live fifteen miles away from family and friends amounted to an unlawful degree of social isolation (**Secretary of State for the Home Department v AF** [2009] UKHL 28);

- notwithstanding the demands of national security, those subject to Control Orders were entitled to know at least the 'gist' of the evidence and suspicions against them (**Secretary of State for the Home Department v MB** [2007] UKHL 46);

- Control Orders should not be served on persons against whom there was sufficient evidence to bring criminal proceedings (**Bingham v Secretary of State for the Home Department** [2009] UKHL 47).

The incoming government of 2010 was committed to a review of the Control Order system and of anti-terrorist powers in general. The findings of the review were published in January 2011 (Review of Counter-Terrorism and Security Powers, Review Findings and Recommendations, Cm 8004). The review's principal findings were:

- For the foreseeable future it remained likely that there would continue to be a small number of people in the country who were assessed to pose an immediate and significant terrorist threat but who could not be prosecuted or deported.

- Notwithstanding advances in human and, particularly, technological surveillance, such techniques, on their own, did not constitute an adequate means of managing the risk posed by potential terrorists.

- Control regimes limited primarily to travel restrictions were also unlikely to provide sufficient protection. Five of the seven persons who absconded under the Control Order system had been subject to such restrictions.

- So far as the terrorist threat was concerned, the evidence did not support the conclusion that amendment of the rule against the use of communications intercept material in court would significantly increase the likelihood of successful prosecutions.

- While prosecution of people engaged in terrorist activity in the country should remain the priority, imposing restrictions on the actions of those believed to be engaging in terrorism would continue to be 'an imperfect if sometimes necessary alternative'.

Founded on the above, the review's overall conclusion was that the government should 'move to a system which will protect the public but will be less intrusive, more clearly and tightly defined and more comparable to restrictions imposed under other powers in the civil justice system' and in which there would be 'an end to the use of forced relocation and lengthy curfews that prevent individuals leading a normal daily life'.

TPIMs: making and content

The 2011 Act permits that a Terrorism Prevention Investigation Measure may be served on an individual where the Home Secretary reasonably believes:

- that the individual is, or has been, involved in 'terrorism-related activity';
- some, or all, of that activity is 'new terrorism-related activity';
- that the measures are 'necessary for purposes connected with preventing or restraining the individual's involvement with terrorism-related activity'.

Terrorism-related activity is defined as the 'commission, preparation, or instigation of acts of terrorism' or that which facilitates, instigates or encourages such conduct or is intended to do so (s 4). New terrorism-related activity is defined as terrorism occurring at any time, or, in the case of a person who has previously been served with a TPIM, terrorism occurring since that time.

The Minister may attach to a TPIM notice any or all of the types of measures specified in Sched 1 to the Act such as are considered reasonably necessary given the nature of the terrorist risk posed by the particular individual.

The principal restrictions, and the categories of measures to which they belong, are as set out below.

Overnight residence measures

- A requirement to reside at a specified residence which is either the individual's own residence or that provided by the Minister in an appropriate or agreed locality.
- A requirement to notify the Minister of the identities of others resident at the specified address.
- A requirement to remain overnight at the residence between specified hours.

Travel measures

- A requirement not to leave the United Kingdom without the Minister's permission.
- A requirement not to seek or obtain any passport or travel document without the Minister's permission.

Exclusion measures

- A requirement not to enter any specified area, place, premises or building including particular streets, localities or towns where the individual's associates may live or congregate.
- A requirement not to enter any such place without the Minister's permission, or without giving notice to the Minister, or without complying with any conditions which may be imposed.

Movements direction measures

- A requirement to act in accordance with any directions given by a police officer concerning the individual's movements where such directions are given to secure compliance with other specified measures.

Financial services measures

- A requirement not to hold more than one bank account without permission.
- A requirement not to hold more than a specified amount of cash without permission.

Property measures

- A requirement not to transfer money or other property to a person or place outside the United Kingdom without the permission of the Minister.
- A requirement to disclose to the Minister such details as may be specified relating to any property in which the individual has an interest or may exercise any right of access or use.

Electronic communications measures

- A requirement not to possess a mobile phone or other communications device without ministerial permission.
- A requirement that such device may only be possessed subject to specified conditions.

Association measures

- A requirement not to associate or communicate with specified persons or specified descriptions of persons without ministerial permission.
- A requirement to give notice to the Minister before associating or communicating with other persons and to comply with any conditions in connection with associating or communicating with others.

Work and studies measures

- A requirement not to carry out any specified work or studies without ministerial permission.
- A requirement to give notice to the Minister before carrying out any work or study and to comply with any conditions relating to the same.

Report measures

- A requirement to report to a specified police station at such times as may be required.
- A requirement to comply with any directions given by a police officer in relation to such reporting.

Photography measures

- A requirement to allow photographs to be taken of the individual at such times and places as may be required.

Monitoring measures

- A requirement to comply with arrangements for enabling the individual's movements to be monitored, e.g. by wearing an electronic tag.
- A requirement to maintain any such apparatus in a specified manner.
- A requirement to comply with any directions given by persons with responsibility for carrying out the monitoring arrangements.

Judicial supervision

Before imposing a TPIM on an individual, the Minister must secure the permission of the High Court (s 6). This applies except where it is reasonably believed that the urgency of the case requires immediate measures to be taken (s 7). The function of the court is to ensure that the required conditions for the making of the measures are in existence. The court may refuse permission if it finds that the Minister's conclusions in these matters were 'obviously flawed'.

An application for permission to make a TPIM may be made in the absence of the individual concerned and without any notice of the application being given. This is intended to avoid giving any advance notice of the Minister's intentions and to avoid any risk of the individual absconding before the measures can be imposed. Where, however, permission is granted, a directions hearing must be held within seven days (s 8) at which the individual has the right to be present. At the directions hearing the court must give directions for a further hearing (a 'review' hearing) in relation to the imposition of measures in question. This should be conducted 'as soon as practicable'. As was the case with Control Orders, the court in TPIM proceedings may have both 'open' and 'closed' elements. The individual concerned and his/her legal representatives have the right to be present at the open hearings. The individual will not be allowed to be present, however, at the closed parts of the proceedings or to see the closed material. Closed material is that which contains sensitive information which it would not be in the public interest to disclose, e.g. because of the demands of national security, international relations, or the detection and prevention of crime. Such proceedings must, however, be conducted with regard to the essentials of ECHR Art 6 (right to a fair trial). This means that however sensitive the material against the individual appears to be, the Minister should either disclose the 'gist' of the case against him/her or not continue with proceedings (see *Secretary of State for the Home Department* v *AF* [2009] UKHL 28; *A* v *United Kingdom* [2009] ECHR 301).

Consultation with police

Before applying for judicial permission to impose a TPIM, the Minister should consult with the relevant Chief of Police to determine whether there is sufficient evidence on which the person could be prosecuted (s 10). For the purpose of tendering such advice, the Chief

Officer should consult with the relevant prosecuting authority. This would be the Crown Prosecution Service in England and Wales, the appropriate Procurator Fiscal in Scotland, and the Director of Public Prosecutions in Northern Ireland.

Powers to serve TPIMs

The Act provides a wide range of powers of entry, search, and seizure, available without warrant, to enable the police to carry out the actual process of serving and enforcing a TPIM once it has been made (s 24). These include powers to:

- enter and search any premises where the individual is reasonably believed to be;
- search the individual to ascertain whether he/she is in possession of anything that contravenes the measures imposed or is in possession of anything which could be used to cause harm or injury;
- seize anything found in order to ascertain whether the measures imposed are being, or are about to be, contravened and anything which provides evidence of an offence.

Reasonable force may be used to effect these powers. Also, any person who an officer wishes to subject to the power of personal search, may be detained for that purpose (Sched 1, paras 3 and 4).

It is a criminal offence not to comply with any of the requirements contained in a TPIM. The maximum penalty is five years' imprisonment or a fine of £5,000 (s 23).

Appeals, review and renewal

Appeals against extension or variation of a TPIM may be made to the High Court (s 16). Grants of permission to impose a TPIM are appealable only on a point of law (s 18).

In addition to those sections of the Act containing powers for the making and serving of TPIM powers in general, detailed provision is also made for on-going executive and parliamentary scrutiny of their application and continued justification. Thus, in relation to each TPIM that has been served, the Minister should keep under review the issue of whether its continued application remains reasonably necessary to protect the public against terrorism or to prevent the individual's involvement in it (s 11). Also, and on a more general level, the Minister is required, every three months, to prepare a report on the exercise of his/her TPIM powers and to lay copies of the report before both Houses of Parliament (s 19). Further to this, an annual report on the workings of the Act is to be prepared by an 'independent reviewer' which is also to be laid before Parliament.

The Minister's TPIM powers were to remain in effect for five years only from the date of the Act coming into operation (14 December 2011), subject to renewable periods of five years by statutory continuation order, currently Terrorism Prevention and Investigation Measures Act 2011 (Continuation) Order 2016.

Enhanced TPIM powers

Mindful that in case of urgency and changed circumstances, the powers in the 2011 Act might not be sufficient to respond to an increased terrorist threat, the government holds in store an Enhanced Terrorism Prevention and Investigation Measures Bill ready to be put through Parliament should the need arise. This would permit the imposition of more stringent restrictions where the Minister is 'satisfied on the balance of probabilities' that the individual is or has been engaged in terrorist activities. The enhanced measures provided for in the Bill include:

- a requirement that the individual reside at a specific residence in any part of the United Kingdom;
- a requirement that no other persons be allowed to live at that residence without ministerial permission;
- a requirement to remain at the residence during specified times of the day;
- a requirement that the individual should not travel out of any specified area without ministerial permission;
- a requirement not to have access to any electronic communications device;
- a requirement not to communicate or associate with any other person except with ministerial approval.

These provisions are intended to supplement rather than supersede the existing TPIM regime. In other words, albeit that the Enhanced TPIM powers in the Bill have been passed into law, the existing or 'ordinary' TPIM provisions would remain in operation. Use of the enhanced powers would also be subject to similar controls as those found in the 2011 Act. Thus, an enhanced TPIM would remain in existence for two years, prior permission to impose the measures would have to be obtained from the High Court, and directions and full review hearings would be required once an enhanced TPIM had been made.

Should the need for enhanced TPIM powers arise at a time when Parliament is not in session, the 2011 Act, section 26, makes provision for the bringing into effect of enhanced powers equivalent to those in the Bill by virtue of an Enhanced TPIM Order. Such Order could remain in effect for up to ninety days and would have to be laid before Parliament as soon as practicable after it had been made.

TPIMs and Control Orders

Given the executive claims that the TPIM provisions in the 2011 Act would introduce a more specific, proportionate and less intrusive scheme for restricting the activities of those suspected of terrorist involvement than that provided by the 2005 Act, it would appear appropriate to set out the main differences between the two systems.

- The 2005 Act gave the Minister power to make Derogating and Non-Derogating Control Orders. A Derogating Control Order imposed restrictions of a severity which constituted a departure from the requirements of ECHR Art 5 (right to liberty and security of the person). Such Orders could not be made unless and until an instrument of derogation had been issued by the UK government in accordance with Art 15. No similar provision, i.e. for the imposition of TPIM restrictions so severe as to require a formal derogation from normative ECHR obligations, may be found in the 2011 Act.

- The power to make Control Orders could be used against any person the Minister reasonably *suspected* to be involved in terrorist-related activity. The 2011 Act imposes a more demanding test for the imposition of a TPIM, i.e. that the Minister has a reasonable *belief* of involvement in such activity.

- A Control Order remained effective for twelve months but could be renewed on unlimited occasions for further periods of twelve months at a time. A TPIM also has effect for twelve months but may be renewed for only one further twelve-month period.

● Some of the more intrusive restrictions which could be contained in a Control Order may not be imposed by an 'ordinary' TPIM, e.g. requirements to remain within a specified residence during the day time, to reside at any place specified by the Minister, whether or not that was a place with which the individual had a local connection, or to comply with a command to supply information to a specified person.

The provisions of the 2011 Act in relation to passports have not replaced the royal prerogative in the national security context, i.e. the power to withdraw a passport where this is perceived to be in the national interest (*R (on application of XH and ALT)* v *Secretary of State for the Home Department* [2016] EWHC 1898 (Admin)).

Counter-Terrorism and Security Act 2015

Introduction and background

Objective 7

On 29 August 2014, the Joint Terrorism Analysis Centre raised the level of the terrorist threat to the UK from 'substantial' to 'severe'. This meant that the threat of a terrorist attack was deemed to be 'highly likely'. On 14 September 2014, and in response to the above, the Prime Minister announced that legislative proposals would be introduced to enable the authorities to stop people travelling overseas for terrorist purposes, to stop terrorist suspects from returning to the UK, and to deal with similar persons already in the UK who posed a risk to national security.

The Act represented the fulfilment of those intentions.

Restrictions on the freedom to travel in and out of the UK

These are contained in two main powers.

(a) the power to search for, to seize and to retain, 'travel documents', i.e. passports, tickets and other travel permits, where a police officer has reasonable grounds to suspect that a person intends to leave Great Britain or Northern Ireland to become involved in terrorist activity outside of the UK (s 1);

(b) the power to impose a Temporary Exclusion Order ('TEO') on any person reasonably suspected of being, or having engaged in, terrorist activity outside of the UK (s 2).

Search, seizure and retention of travel documents

(i) The power may be exercised by a police officer or customs or immigration official so designated by the Home Secretary.

(ii) Following any such seizure, further retention should be authorised by an officer of the rank of superintendent or above.

(iii) Otherwise such documents should be returned as soon as possible except where:
   ● consideration is being given to revoking the person's passport;
   ● it is being decided whether to charge the person with an offence;
   ● consideration is being given to making the person subject to an order or measure connected with protecting the public from a risk of terrorism, e.g. a 'TPIM';
   ● steps are being taken to carry out any of the above.

(iv) The documents should not be detained beyond fourteen days without judicial authority (a district judge).

(v)   Reasons should be given for the exercise of the power and the reasons for the officer's suspicions.

(vi)   The ground(s) for retention should be made known to the person affected.

(vii) Any decision to retain documents should be reviewed by a senior police officer before the elapse of 72 hours from the time of seizure.

(viii) Following application to a district judge, the period of retention may be extended for any period up to 30 days (from the time of seizure) providing it is shown that those involved in considering whether further action should be taken have acted diligently and expeditiously.

(ix)   The person should be notified of the application and allowed to appear before the judicial authority.

(x)   The power of search, seizure and retention is reinforced by two offences in Sched 1, para 15. These are:
- failing to hand over documents without reasonable cause;
- obstructing or frustrating an authorised search.

Temporary exclusion orders

(i)   A TEO requires the person to which it applies not to return to the UK except in accordance with a 'permit to return' issued by the Home Secretary.

(ii)   A TEO may be made where the Home Secretary:
- reasonably suspects that the person has been engaged in terrorist-related activity outside the UK;
- reasonably considers that the making of the Order is necessary to protect the public in the UK from an act of terrorism.

(iii) The making of a TEO requires prior judicial consent save in cases of urgency where the consent should be sought after the Order has been made.

(iv)   A TEO remains in force for up to two years but may be revoked by the Minister at any time.

(v)   A person on whom a TEO has been served may be allowed back into the UK but only where a permit to return has been granted in accordance with the provisions attached to it. Breach of any such Order invalidates the permit.

(vi)   Offences relating to the TEO regime include:
- returning to the UK in contravention of the TEO without reasonable excuse;
- failure to comply with any obligations imposed by a TEO without reasonable excuse.

Amendments to the Terrorist Prevention Investigatory Measures Act 2011

Three principal amendments were made to the 2011 Act.

(a)   In the making of a TPIM, the Minister may agree with an individual the locality in which that person should live or, alternatively, an individual may be required to reside in a locality which the Minister deems appropriate.

(b)   A person subject to a travel restriction under the 2011 Act, and who travels outside the United Kingdom, will not be able to rely on the defence of reasonable excuse.

(c)   A TPIM may include provisions restricting an individual's freedom to leave a particular area in the UK unless with the Minister's permission.

Restrictions on the carriage of persons to and from the UK

The Act enables the Minister to make 'Authority to Carry Schemes' (s 22). These may apply to travel in and out of the UK by plane, train or ship.

The effect of such a scheme is to require ministerial consent for the carriage of passengers into or out of the UK. Any such scheme should specify:

- the types of carriers to which applies;
- the categories of passengers or crew for which permission to carry must be sought;
- providing it is in 'the public interest', the categories of passengers and crew for which permission may be refused.

Being drawn into terrorism

Section 26 of the 2015 Act imposes a duty on various specified authorities (see Sched 6) to have regard to the need to prevent persons from being drawn into terrorism. The specified authorities include the police, local authorities, heads of and governing bodies of schools, colleges and universities, NHS Trusts, and prison governors. Guidance may be issued to such by the Minister concerning the exercise of the duty imposed. In this, colleges and universities are to pay particular regard to the needs of academic freedom and the freedom of speech.

Monitoring authorities are to be appointed by the Minister to oversee the application of the duty by the educational authorities affected. Appropriate directions may be issued to any institution found to be falling short of relevant requirements.

Terrorism Act 2000

In this context, the principal changes made by the 2015 Act are contained in sections 42 and 43. These relate to insurance for the payment of ransom monies to terrorist groups and to existing provisions dealing with the search of goods entering or leaving the UK.

Section 42 makes it an offence to make an insurance payment to an insured person where the insurer knows or has reasonable cause to suspect that this relates to any money or property handed over in response to the demands of a terrorist organisation. The offence carries a maximum penalty on conviction of 14 years.

Section 43 provides that the power in the 2000 Act to search goods about to leave the UK for that which may be used for terrorist purposes extends to goods which are held by an air or sea cargo agent for the purposes of export but which are not about to leave the UK immediately.

Emergency powers in peacetime

Objective
8

The law in this context is contained primarily in the Civil Contingencies Act 2004. The Act resulted from a review of civil emergency planning arrangements prompted by the winter floods of 2000 and the foot and mouth outbreak of 2001. In addition, by this time, the existing legislation dealing with civil emergencies was widely felt to be out-of-date politically and not to make adequate provision for emergencies arising from environmental problems and terrorism. The Civil Defence Act 1948 was concerned mainly to enable local authorities and the emergency services to take defensive measures, short of actual combat, in response to 'hostile attack' by a 'foreign power'. Beyond this, the Emergency Powers Act 1920 empowered the government to make emergency regulations. The meaning of 'emergency' was, however, defined rather narrowly as being confined to events which deprived a substantial part of the community of the 'essentials of life' by interfering with the supply of food, water, light, fuel or transport.

The 2004 Act repealed and replaced the Civil Defence Act 1948, the Civil Defence (NI) Act 1950, the Emergency Powers Act 1920 and the Emergency Powers (NI) Act 1926. The Act is divided into two parts. Part 1 deals with 'local arrangements for civil protection' and sets out the powers and duties applicable to local authorities and other 'category one responders' in emergency circumstances. Category one responders include, *inter alia*, the police, fire brigades, ambulance services and health authorities.

For this part of the Act, an emergency is defined as an event or situation which causes 'serious damage' to human welfare or the environment in any 'place in the United Kingdom' or war or terrorism which threatens 'serious damage' to national security (s 1). Serious damage to human welfare is defined as that which includes:

- loss of human life;
- human illness or injury;
- homelessness;
- damage to property;
- disruption of supply of food, water, energy, fuel or money;
- disruption of a system of communication;
- disruption of transport;
- disruption of health services (s 1(2)).

The definition of serious damage to the environment extends to that which causes:

- contamination of land, water or air with biological, chemical or radioactive matter;
- disruption or destruction of plant or animal life (s 1(3)).

The principal duty cast on each category one provider is to 'from time to time, assess the risk of an emergency occurring and make provisions to ensure that:

(a) in the event it will continue to be able to fulfil its functions;

(b) it is able to respond to the exigencies of the threat or emergency as these occur' (s 2).

Also, if needs be, a category one provider may be ordered by a Minister to perform any of its functions, as considered appropriate, to prevent an emergency occurring or to deal with any emergency circumstances (ss 5 and 6).

Part 2 of the Act confers powers on Ministers to make emergency regulations. What amounts to an emergency, for the purposes of this power, is phrased in similar terms to the definition in Part 1 – save that here the events must threaten 'serious damage' in a 'part or region' of the United Kingdom rather than being confined or limited to a particular locality or 'place' (s 19).

Where such emergency has occurred or is about to occur, and there is an urgent and necessary need, regulations may be made by Her Majesty in Council to deal with it (s 20). Alternatively, in situations where any delay might cause 'serious damage', the necessary regulations may be made by a senior Minister.

Emergency regulations may make any provision considered appropriate in the particular circumstances and, *inter alia*, for the purposes of protecting human welfare and the environment (s 22(2)). Such regulations may:

(a) provide Ministers with further powers;

(b) provide for the requisition or confiscation of property;

(c) provide for the destruction of property, animal or plant life;

(d) prohibit or restrict the freedom of movement from or to a particular place;

(e) prohibit meetings in assemblies of particular kinds at specified places and times;

(f) prohibit travel at specified times;

(g) prohibit other specified activities;

(h) require a person to carry out any functions;

(i) amend any legislation;

(j) authorise the deployment of the armed forces (s 22).

The width of this law-making power is self-evident. The only express restrictions of any note to which it is subject are that it may not be used to require compulsory military service (**conscription**), to prohibit industrial action, to create new criminal offences other than in relation to non-compliance with emergency regulations, or to alter the Human Rights Act 1998. In addition, regulations made under the Act should not be disproportionate to the emergency circumstances with which they were intended to deal (s 23).

Emergency regulations may be made for renewable periods of 30 days (s 26). They must be laid before Parliament as soon as is reasonably practicable and lapse after seven days if not approved (s 27).

Emergencies and the common law

In addition to the prerogative powers which relate to the maintenance of law and order and the defence of the realm, the common law also appears to vest in the 'civil authority' (i.e. the Secretary of State for the Home Department) the power to use such force as is reasonably necessary to quell riots or insurrection. This may be effected by calling in the aid of military personnel providing that they remain under the civil authority's control. The taking of life by the police or the military may be justified in circumstances of grave disorder.

For prerogative powers, see Chapter 12.

In the most extreme circumstances of civil insurrection – as occurred in Ireland during the period 1919–21 – the courts may accept that the country is in a state of war sufficient to justify resort to martial law. In effect, this means that the ordinary process of law and government is suspended and that responsibility for the restoration of law and order is transferred to the military authorities. In these circumstances the military authorities may:

● make law by decree;

● take such action as is deemed fit to enforce the same;

● use military tribunals to try those alleged to be guilty of any transgressions.

Where the judiciary have accepted that the country is in a state of war or civil insurrection, it would appear that redress may not be given in an ordinary court of law in respect of the way in which the military authorities have exercised their responsibilities.

Summary

The chapter provides comprehensive coverage of the principal statutory and common law powers available to police and public authorities to deal with public emergencies and the threat of terrorism. It includes extensive comment on the legislation introduced to deal with terrorist activity arising out of the problems of Northern Ireland (the Northern Ireland (Emergency Provisions) Act and the Prevention of Terrorism Act) and the extensive, general, anti-terrorist powers contained in the Terrorism Acts 2000 and 2006 and the Counter-Terrorism and Security Act 2015.

References

Legislation Against Terrorism (1998) Cm 4178.

Inquiry into Legislation Against Terrorism (1996) Cm 3420.

Review of Counter-Terrorism and Security Powers, Review Findings and Recommendations (2011) Cm 8004.

Further reading

Bradley, Ewing and Knight (2014) *Constitutional and Administrative Law* (16th edn), Harlow: Pearson.

Dempsey and Cole (2006) *Terrorism and the Constitution,* London: New Press.

House of Commons Library (2012*) Justice and Security Bill,* Research Paper 12/80, 14.12.12.

House of Commons Library (2014) *Terrorism Prevention and Investigation Measures Act 2011,* Briefing Paper, SN 06799, 21.1.14.

Staniforth (2013) *Blackstone's Counter-Terrorism Handbook* (3rd edn), Oxford: Oxford University Press

Walker (2014) *Blackstone Guide to the Anti-Terrorism Legislation* (3rd edn), Oxford: Oxford University Press

Walker (2011) *Terrorism and the Law* (2nd edn), Oxford: Oxford University Press.

Part 7

Tribunals, inquiries and complaints procedures

22

Tribunals and inquiries

Objectives

After reading this chapter you should:

1. Understand the reason for the development of tribunals and inquiries.

2. Be aware of the principles underlying the composition and procedure of tribunals.

3. Appreciate the nature, role and conduct of public inquiries, particularly in the regulation of land use, and the procedural rights of objectors.

4. Have an understanding of the reasons for the Inquiries Act 2005 and the nature of the public inquiries held under it.

5. Be aware of the reasons for the creation of the Council on Tribunals in 1958.

6. Know the reasons for reform of the tribunals system.

7. Appreciate the nature, structure and workings of the new tribunals system under the Tribunals, Courts and Enforcement Act 2007.

8. Understand the role and functions of the Administrative Justice and Tribunals Council and the debate surrounding its abolition.

Introduction

Administrative tribunals

Although it might still be widely assumed that most formal disputes, and certainly those involving points of law, between individuals and between individuals and the state will be dealt with in the traditional courts of justice, this is no longer the case, and has not been for some considerable time. As the figures make abundantly clear, a person seeking formal adjudication of a dispute in the United Kingdom is now far more likely to have their case heard in an administrative tribunal than in a court of law. Contemporary figures show that some 300,000 cases are referred to tribunals annually. Those regularly dealing with the heaviest caseloads are the Social Security and Child Support Tribunals, Employment Tribunals and Immigration and Asylum Tribunals. It is clear from all this that the importance of tribunals in the English legal system, and particularly as an inexpensive and speedy means of dealing with grievances against government agencies, cannot be overstated.

Most tribunals are a product of the welfare state and have been established to deal with the myriad disputes arising out of decisions relating to eligibility for benefits, services, grants, licences, etc.

> The welfare state could not function without an elaborate judicial system of its own. Claims for benefit, applications for licences, disputes about controlled rents, planning appeals, compulsory purchase of land – there are a host of such matters which have to be adjudicated upon from day to day and which are, for the most part, unsuitable for the regular courts. In the background are the courts of law with supervisory and often, also, appellate functions. But the front line judicial authorities for administrative purposes are bodies created *ad hoc* (Schwartz and Wade, Legal Control of Government).

Many tribunals make decisions by applying legal rules to the facts of particular cases. To this extent, therefore, their function is not dissimilar to courts of law. On the other hand, tribunals are deliberately designed to provide a speedier and cheaper means of adjudication which is accessible and comprehensible to ordinary individuals.

Although some tribunals exercise an important first-instance jurisdiction (e.g. the licensing function of the Civil Aviation Authority), most are appellate bodies dealing with appeals against the decisions of central and local government officials. A tribunal of this type may overrule an official's decision and substitute its own findings where:

- there has been a mistake of fact;
- there has been a mistake of law;
- the official's discretion has been exercised in a way which is incompatible with the policy of the enabling legislation.

While tribunals typically deal with disputes between the individual and the state, it should be noted that some adjudicate between one individual and another. The most well known amongst these would be employment tribunals which have jurisdiction over, *inter alia*, claims for unfair dismissal, and rent assessment committees.

Public inquiries

These also may be attributed to the increase in the regulatory powers of the state, particularly in the context of land use. Their primary function is to gather information and allow individuals an opportunity to make representation before an executive decision is taken which may have adverse consequences for private rights and/or wider public concerns (e.g. whether to proceed with a slum clearance scheme).

In a general sense, inquiries may be distinguished from tribunals in that they were not designed primarily for the purpose of making decisions but rather to provide the factual basis on which the decision-maker (usually a Minister) could reach a conclusion which, in their opinion, represented the best compromise between the private and public interests in issue. Public inquiries have long been, therefore, a typical procedural facet of those decision-making powers which involve the application of public policy to local facts or circumstances. Hence, it will be usual for a public inquiry to be convened before a ministerial decision is made to proceed with any major scheme of development involving the compulsory purchase of land (e.g. for the construction of motorways, power stations, airports or extensions to the same). Also, on a smaller and less controversial scale, thousands of local public inquiries will be convened annually to hear appeals against refusals of planning permission or the serving of compulsory purchase orders by local authorities.

Administrative tribunals

Objective 1

In addition to the virtues of speed and economy, a variety of other related reasons are often put forward to explain the legislators' preference for tribunals as the principal means of resolving disputes in the social welfare context. These include the following:

(a) Some of those politically responsible for the creation and development of the welfare state, particularly after World War II, were not convinced that judges steeped in the individualism of the common law were best qualified to identify and apply the social policy objectives behind the legislation upon which the welfare state was founded.

(b) The creation of tribunals with narrow and specific jurisdictional remits (e.g. social security entitlements) enables them to be staffed by experts in the sphere of activity in which they operate. Thus mental health tribunals will include persons with appropriate medical knowledge. This contributes to the speed of proceedings by obviating the need for expert testimony and to their quality by increasing the likelihood that the relevant legislative rules will be applied in a functionally practical way.

(c) The sheer volume of disputes arising out of the administration of the welfare state could not have been dealt with by the courts as presently constituted: '[I]f all decisions arising from new legislation were automatically vested in the ordinary courts, the judiciary would by now have been grossly overburdened' (Report of the Committee on Administrative Tribunals and Inquiries, Cmnd 218, 1957 [the Franks Committee]).

(d) Tribunals attempt to minimise the formality and procedural technicality typical of courts of law. This helps persons to more readily understand the conduct of the proceedings and thus to represent themselves more effectively.

(e) Public confidence in the welfare state would be diminished if persons claiming to be in need of benefit were kept waiting for long periods while related disputes were resolved.

(f) The administrative efficiency of government departments is improved by removing the resolution of disputes from their responsibilities.

(g) Tribunals generate an impression that government offices are answerable for their decisions and provide a forum in which 'feelings of having been treated unfairly or unjustly can be diffused' (Cane, *Administrative Law*).

(h) Tribunals also enable Ministers to 'off load responsibility for certain politically contentious decisions to a body immune from political criticism.' (ibid.)

All of this indicates that tribunals represent an attempt to give the resolution of disputes within the welfare state that degree of procedural justice which is consistent with the administrative efficiency necessary to best secure the system's overall social objectives.

Composition and independence

Objective 2

Until the Tribunals, Courts and Enforcement Act 2007, there was no general rule requiring all tribunals to be similarly constituted. The composition of each type depended on its enabling legislation and subject-matter. Some consisted of one person only (e.g. immigration adjudicators). More usually, however, there was a legally qualified chairperson with two other members appropriately qualified. In some cases these would be experts in the relevant subject-matter; in others, the members might possess some representative quality. Thus, employment tribunals consisted of a legally qualified chair sitting with two others, representative of employers' and employees' organisations, respectively.

Despite the diversity of practice in relation to the membership of tribunals, the following general principles could be extrapolated.

(a) Civil servants or other public officials were not appointed. Hence the vast majority of tribunal members had no direct links with government departments or officials.

(b) In the majority of cases the chairpersons of tribunals were appointed directly by the Lord Chancellor (i.e. chairs of mental health tribunals) or by the relevant Minister usually from panels of suitably qualified people compiled by the Lord Chancellor.

(c) The members of most tribunals were appointed in one of the following ways:

- by the relevant Minister or government department;
- by the Lord Chancellor;
- in some cases – for example, social security appeals tribunals and industrial tribunals – by the president of the particular category of tribunal.

(d) Removal of a member of a tribunal usually required the consent of the Lord Chancellor (Tribunals and Inquiries Act 1992, s 7).

(e) In the matter of the appointment of members of tribunals, Ministers were bound to have regard to the recommendations of the Council on Tribunals (ibid. s 5).

For the new standard provisions relating to tribunal appointments and composition under the Tribunals, Courts and Enforcement Act 2007, see pp. 695–8.

The above rules and practices did not guarantee the degree of independence and freedom from executive influence for tribunals that was expected of courts of law. In addition, the public conception of the independence of tribunals was not helped by the fact that many conducted their proceedings in government premises. There is, however, no record of actual or attempted executive inference with their activities or members. Were this to have been alleged in any particular case, the complainant could have sought redress by way of judicial review for illegality (acting under dictation) or bias. The matter would also have been likely to have had adverse political consequences for the Minister involved, whether personally or through their departmental officials.

Procedure

For the rules of natural justice, see Chapter 14, pp. 423–437.

The proceedings in tribunals tend to be conducted according to the adversarial model. There is an expectation, therefore, that everything will be done in accordance with the rules of natural justice. This does not mean, however, that tribunals have to act as if they were courts of law. Greater informality and procedural flexibility is the norm.

Within these general parameters, the conduct of hearings may vary slightly between the different types of tribunals. Certain minimum principles and standards may, however, be identified. These were set out by the Council on Tribunals in 2002.

- Tribunals must be independent of the state and should be perceived as such.
- Tribunals should reach their decisions according to law and without pressure from the person or body whose decision is being appealed against.
- Complainants should be given a fair hearing with access to all relevant information.
- Tribunals should be composed of persons who are entirely independent of the state or related organisations.
- Tribunal members should have security of tenure.
- Proceedings should normally take place in public.

- Hearings should be conducted with an 'appropriate degree of informality'.

- Persons without legal representation should be given 'appropriate guidance about evidence and procedure'.

- Procedural requirements should be 'appropriately modified' where a party is not legally represented.

- Special procedures should be adopted for hearings involving children.

- Presenting officers from government departments or agencies should not be present with the tribunal members in the absence of the complainant.

- Where proceedings are conducted in the absence of the complainant, the tribunal should seek to ensure that his/her side of the case is fully considered.

- Decisions should be 'soundly based' on the evidence and the law.

- Decisions should be given on the day of the hearing or as soon as possible afterwards.

- Decisions should be supported by intelligible reasons.

- Procedures for particular types of tribunals should be uniform and not subject to local variations.

- Decisions should be accompanied with information about rights of appeal.

- Complainants should be provided with 'clear and timely information' about the date and place of the hearing.

Other noteworthy procedural matters as they apply within the tribunals system would be as follows:

(a) Although most tribunals give a public hearing at which it is possible to call and cross-examine witnesses, with the consent of the claimant, routine, non-controversial cases may be disposed of through written submissions.

(b) The strict rules of evidence are generally not applicable. Hence, probative hearsay evidence may usually be admissible provided the contesting party is given the proper opportunity to challenge it (*Kavanagh* v *Chief Constable of Devon and Cornwall* [1994] 1 QB 624). Tribunal members may also rely on their own knowledge and experience. Where, however, such additional considerations are to be taken into account, the party affected should be informed and given an opportunity to make a response (*Dugdale* v *Kraft Foods Ltd* [1977] 1 ICR 48).

(c) Although seldom used, all tribunals have an inherent power to take evidence on oath.

(d) Statements made before and by tribunals are protected by qualified privilege. Whether absolute privilege extends to tribunal proceedings has not been decided conclusively. The answer would appear to depend on whether the tribunal in question may be regarded as exercising a genuinely judicial function (*Royal Aquarium Society Ltd* v *Parkinson* [1892] 1 QB 431; *Trapp* v *Mackie* [1979] 1 All ER 489).

(e) Unless judicially recognised to have the status of a court, tribunals have no power to punish for contempt. Within the new system, however, the new First Tier and Upper Tribunals have been given this status by the Tribunals, Courts and Enforcement Act 2007.

(f) Legal representation is generally permitted but is not supported by any overall entitlement to legal aid to finance it. The Council on Tribunals made frequent reference to the exclusion of tribunals from the legal aid scheme. In its 1994/95 Report, the Council suggested that legal aid for tribunal representation might be appropriate where:

- 'a significant point of law arises';
- 'the evidence is likely to be so technical or specialised that the average laymen could reasonably wish for expert help in assembling and evaluating the evidence and in its testing and interpretation';
- 'a test case arises';
- 'deprivation of liberty or the ability of an individual to follow his or her occupation is at stake'.

(g) Tribunals should give reasons for their decisions.

(h) Tribunals are not bound by any rigid system of precedent. There is, however, a perhaps inevitable tendency to build on previous decisions. This notwithstanding, tribunals do have a greater freedom than courts of law to avoid decisions which are no longer relevant or appropriate. Within the new system, as created by the Tribunals, Courts and Enforcement Act 2007, the various elements of the First Tier Tribunal will be expected to follow the decisions of the relevant Chamber of the Upper Tier Tribunal.

Public inquiries

Objective 3

Various statutes provide for the holding of public inquiries to deal with either local or national issues. This is a usual feature of legislation concerned with regulating the use of land. Under such legislation inquiries may be convened to:

- hear objections to proposals for the compulsory acquisition of land or property (usually by a local authority);
- appeal against refusals of planning permission (again, in most cases, by a local authority).

Thousands of such inquiries are held each year. Most deal with issues of no great public concern and receive little political or media interest. Those attracting attention tend to be concerned with proposals which may have significant and far-reaching environmental or social consequences – e.g. the construction or extension of a motorway, airport or nuclear power station.

Less frequently, 'one-off' public inquiries may be convened to look into:

- the causes of major accidents (e.g. the sinking of the car ferry *Herald of Free Enterprise* in 1987);
- other incidents or issues of major public concern (e.g. the Aberfan Disaster, 1966; Arms to Iraq, 1996).

Inquiries of this type may be convened under statutory powers (e.g. Merchant Shipping Act 1894 or the Inquiries Act 2005) or may simply be set up by a Minister acting administratively (also note the view that the creation of such non-statutory inquiries may derive legal authority from the royal prerogative). Table 22.1 illustrates the inquiries established under the Inquiries Act 2005 or converted into inquiries under the Act.

Land use inquiries

An Englishman's home is no longer 'his castle'. Private rights over land and property are now subject to the overriding needs of the public interest as expressed through the actions and decisions of central and local government. Thus, throughout the twentieth

Table 22.1 Table of Inquiries Established Under the Inquiries Act 2005 or Converted into Inquiries Under the Act

Inquiry	Chair	Duration	Cost	Purpose
The Billy Wright Inquiry, Northern Ireland Office	Lord MacLean, retired Scottish Appeal Judge	November 2004 to October 2010	£29.8m	To inquire into the circumstances surrounding the death of Billy Wright who was murdered at the Maze prison in Northern Ireland on 27 December, 1997. It found no evidence of collusive acts or collusive conduct in the murder of Billy Wright but identified a number of failings which facilitated his death.
The Robert Hamill Inquiry, Northern Ireland Office	Sir Edwin Jowitt, retired High Court Judge	November 2004 to February 2011	£33m	To inquire into the circumstances surrounding the death of Robert Hamill, who died from injuries he sustained during an affray in Portadown, Co. Armagh in 1997. In December 2010 criminal proceedings were commenced against three individuals on charges of perverting the course of justice in relation to Robert Hamill's death. The report will not be published until proceedings against three individuals on charges of perverting the course of justice in relation to Hamill's death have been concluded.
The *E. coli* Inquiry, National Assembly of Wales	Prof. Hugh Pennington, Professor of Bacteriology at Aberdeen University	March 2006 to March 2009	£2.35m	To investigate circumstances that led to the outbreak of *E. coli* 0175 in South Wales. It broadly found that there were system-atic failures in food safety management at the time of the out-break, with the exception of the outbreak control and clinical care systems which worked well, and that the requirements for food hygiene should have been sufficient to prevent the outbreak.
The ICL Inquiry, Scottish and UK Governments	Lord Gill, Lord Justice Clerk (now Lord President of the Court of Session)	February 2008 to July 2009	£1.91m	To carry out an investigation into an explosion in May 2004 at the ICL factory in Glasgow which killed 9 people and seriously injured a further 45. It broadly found that there were failures in appreciation of the dangers posed by Liquefied Petroleum Gas (LPG) and the condi-tion of the LPG supply at the factory over many years.
The Fingerprint Inquiry, Scottish Government	Sir Anthony Campbell, retired NI Appeal Court judge	March 2008 to December 2011	c. £4.75m estimated (media pack – no date)	To inquire into the steps taken to identify and verify the fingerprints associated with the case of *HM Advocate v McKie* in 1999, a perjury case which had given rise to questions about the correctness or otherwise of the identification of fingerprints. It broadly found that there were weaknesses in the methodology of fingerprint comparison. Fingerprint examiners are accustomed to regarding their conclusions as a matter of certainty. There is no reason to suggest that fingerprint comparison is an inherently unreliable form of evidence but practitioners should give due consideration to its limits.
The Penrose Inquiry, Scottish Government	Lord Penrose, retired Court of Session Judge	April 2008 to present (final report expected in March 2014)	£8.8m at 31/03/12 (latest figures)	To look into Hepatitis C/HIV acquired infection from blood and blood products administered by the NHS in Scotland.

(Continued)

Table 22.1 Table of Inquiries Established Under the Inquiries Act 2005 or Converted into Inquiries Under the Act   (*Continued*)

Inquiry	Chair	Duration	Cost	Purpose
The Baha Mousa Inquiry, Ministry of Defence	Sir William Gage, serving Appeal Court judge when appointed; since retired	August 2008 to September 2011	£13.0m at 31/01/12 (latest figures, exc. VAT)	To investigate the circumstances surrounding the death of Baha Mousa, an Iraqi civilian who died in Iraq in 2003 and the treatment of others detained with him by the British armed forces. It found that Baha Mousa spent most of the 36 hours after his arrest 'hooded' and forced to adopt 'stress positions'; both are banned interrogation techniques. He was subjected to violent abuse and assaults. A post-mortem examination found that Baha Mousa had sustained 93 external injuries. Nine other Iraqis were also detained; all sustained injuries, physical and/or mental.
Inquiry into the outbreak of *C. difficile* in Northern Health and Social Care Trust Hospitals. NI Department for Health, Social Services and Public Safety	Dame Deirdre Hine, former Chief Medical Officer for Wales	October 2008 to March 2011	£1.8m	To investigate the outbreak of *Clostridium difficile* infection in Northern Health and Social Care Trust Hospital in March 2009. It found that *C. difficile* infection was the underlying or a contributory cause in 31 of the deaths in the Trust during the outbreak. A total of 124 clinical records were examined.
The Bernard (Sonny) Lodge Inquiry, Ministry of Justice	Barbara Stow, former Assistant Prisons and Probation Ombudsman	February 2009 to December 2009 (ad hoc investigation began in September 2008)	Not yet known as costs for one party remain outstanding pending settlement negotiations	An *ad hoc* investigation into the death of Bernard (Sonny) Lodge at HMP Manchester in August 1998 converted into a 2005 Act inquiry to compel certain witnesses. It broadly found that the clinical care for Mr Lodge's physical health was appropriate and consistent with practice at the time and the clinical record-keeping was generally good but there were systematic failures in the psychiatric reassessment, counselling and support provided.
The Vale of Leven Hospital Inquiry, Scottish Government	Lord MacLean, retired Scottish Appeal Judge	October 2009 to present (final report expected March 2014)	£5.7m at 25/04/12, (not yet published)	To investigate the circumstances surrounding the deaths and illness which occurred at the Vale of Leven Hospital in Dunbartonshire between 1 January 2007 and 1 June 2008 attributed to *C. difficile* infection at the hospital.
The Al Sweady Inquiry, Ministry of Defence	Sir Thayne Forbes, retired High Court Judge	November 2009 to present (target end date in 2014)	£21.3m at 31/12/13 (exc. VAT)	To investigate allegations that Iraqi nationals were detained after a fire-fight with British soldiers in Iraq in 2004 during which some of those detained were unlawfully killed at a British camp and others were mistreated both at that camp and later at a detention facility.
The Azelle Rodney Inquiry, Ministry of Justice	Sir Christopher Holland retired High Court Judge	June 2010 to July 2013	c. £2.5m at 30/06/13	To investigate the death of Azelle Rodney who was shot by a police marksman in North London on 30 April 2005. (An inquest in the death could not proceed because of sensitive material which neither coroner nor inquest jury could see.) It found that Azelle Rodney died from bullet wounds to his head and chest as a result of being shot by a Metropolitan Police Officer. 'Operation Tayport' was not planned and controlled so as to minimise, to the greatest extent possible, recourse to lethal force; and the inquiry found that the force used by the Police Officer was not strictly proportionate to the aim of protecting persons against unlawful violence. The Report was also critical of what happened after Azelle Rodney was killed.

Inquiry	Chair	Duration	Cost	Purpose
Inquiry into the role of the commissioning, supervisory and regulatory bodies in monitoring of Mid-Staffordshire NHS Foundation Trust, Department of Health	Robert Francis QC	June 2010 to February 2013	£13.7m (inc. VAT)	To investigate failings in patient care at Mid-Staffordshire NHS Foundation Trust between January 2005 and March 2009. It found there had been serious systemic issues at the Trust requiring a degree of urgent and effective attention which they did not receive, despite many instances where those charged with managing, leading, overseeing or regulating the Trust's provision of services had been made aware of causes for concern.
Inquiry into the Culture, Practices and Ethics of the Press, DCMS and Home Office	Lord Justice Leveson, Court of Appeal Judge (now President of the Queen's Bench Division)	July 2011 to November 2012	£5.4m	To inquire into the culture, practices and ethics of the press and to look into the specific claims about phone hacking at the *News of the World*, the initial police inquiry and allegations of illicit payments to police by the press. The Report made 92 recommendations including the establishment of an independent self-regulatory regime, amendments to the Data Protection Act 1998 and a review of criminal and civil law.

Source: Taken from Appendix 4 of Select Committee on the Inquiries Act 2005 – *Report: The Inquiries Act 2005: Post-legislative Scrutiny.*

century numerous pieces of legislation were enacted conferring on public authorities powers to acquire land compulsorily and to control development by the grant or refusal of planning permission. From the outset, it was standard procedural practice to provide that disputes arising out of the use of such powers should be heard before a local public inquiry.

The basis of current procedure for the acquisition of land is contained in the Acquisition of Land Act 1981. Where the acquisition (compulsory purchase) is effected by a local authority the procedure is as follows:

(a) service of the compulsory purchase order on all persons whose property rights are affected;

(b) publication of the order in local newspapers;

(c) the lodging of objections (if there are any) by the parties affected;

(d) where objections have been lodged, the convening of a local public inquiry by the Secretary of State;

(e) the inquiry to be presided over by an inspector (appointed by the Minister);

(f) at the conclusion of the inquiry, the submission to the Minister of the inspector's report containing their recommendations and findings of fact;

(g) the Minister's decision whether or not to confirm the order, based on the inspector's report and government policy.

The procedure for dealing with appeals against a local planning authority's refusal of planning permission (or against grants of permission subject to conditions) is contained in the Town and Country Planning Act 1990 and the Town and Country Planning (Enforcement) (Inquiries Procedure) Rules 1992.

Where such appeal has been lodged it may be disposed of in a variety of ways. Routine cases may be decided by an inspector appointed by and acting on behalf of the Secretary of State for the Environment. Either party may insist on a public hearing. This may be by local public inquiry or a more informal hearing limited to the parties to the dispute. Otherwise, with the parties' consent, the inspector may decide the appeal purely on the basis of written submissions (over 80 per cent of cases are decided in this way).

In more controversial cases, however – as where the proposed development may have a major environmental or social impact – the Minister may reserve the right to make the final decision (i.e. whether to allow the appeal). In such cases a local public inquiry will normally be held. This will be presided over by an inspector. As with inquiries concerned with the acquisition of land, the inspector will submit a report to the Minister who will then make a final decision based on this and policy considerations.

There is considerable similarity between the way both compulsory purchase and planning inquiries are conducted. In both cases parties directly affected must be given six weeks' notice of the holding of the inquiry and four weeks' notice of the authority's case.

The procedure to be adopted at the inquiry is, to a considerable extent, within the discretion of the presiding inspector. This discretion is subject, however, to relevant statutory rules and the requirements of natural justice. In general, these may be said to impose the following procedural strictures.

(a) Persons directly affected are entitled to appear, to be legally represented and to call evidence and cross-examine witnesses.

(b) Written representations from parties not present may be admitted provided that these are put before the inquiry and an opportunity is provided to comment on them (*Miller v Minister of Housing and Local Government* [1968] 2 All ER 633).

(c) The parties to the inquiry should also be appraised of other evidence not adduced at the inquiry but upon which the inspector intends to rely, e.g. that derived from the inspector's previous experience of the subject-matter or from their inspection of the land or property in issue (*Fairmount Investments* v *Secretary of State for the Environment* [1976] 2 All ER 865).

(d) The inspector may rule inadmissible any testimony which:
  - proposes alternatives to the particular development in issue (*Wednesbury Corporation* v *Minister of Housing and Local Government (No. 2)* [1966] 2 QB 275);
  - seeks to question relevant government policy (*Bushell* v *Secretary of State for the Environment* [1981] AC 75).

(e) After the inquiry the Minister must not hear one side 'behind the back' of the other (*Errington v Minister of Health* [1935] 1 KB 249). They are bound to consider the inspector's report and to allow the parties an opportunity to comment on any fresh evidence they intend to consider (*Rea v Minister of Transport* [1984] JPL 876).

(f) The final decision should be accompanied by reasons (Tribunals and Inquiries Act 1992, s 10).

Problems associated with land use inquiries

(a) The way public inquiries are conducted may sometimes cause misconceptions as to their exact role and function. To the uninitiated it may appear that the inspector is adjudicating between the two sides of a dispute and that the decision whether to proceed with the proposed development will be determined according to which party has presented the most convincing arguments. In reality the inquiry's principal function is to assist the decision-maker (whether an inspector or the Minister) in the exercise of their discretion. This it does by providing them with all the relevant factual information so that this, along with government perceptions of wider public interests, may all be brought to bear on the final decision. The facts as elucidated at the inquiry must be taken into account but are not conclusive. Hence, it is perfectly possible for a decision to be made in favour of a particular development mainly on the basis of policy considerations notwithstanding that the opposing case was presented most convincingly at the inquiry.

> It may well be that on considering the objections, the minister may find that they are reasonable and that the facts alleged in them are true, but, nevertheless he may decide that he will overrule them. His action in so deciding is purely administrative action, based on his conceptions as to what public policy demands. The objections, in other words, may fail to produce the result desired by the objector, not because the objector has been defeated by the local authority in a sort of litigation, but because the objections have been overruled by the minister's decision as to what the public interest demands (*per* Lord Greene MR, *B Johnson Co (Builders) Ltd* v *Minister of Health* [1947] 2 All ER 395).

(b) The remit of a public inquiry is limited to information relating to the effect a particular development will have on the locality for which it is proposed. As already mentioned, therefore, wider considerations of relevant government policy (e.g. the national policy for motorways and road building) which, as indicated in (a), may be of overriding effect, cannot be raised or challenged.

> A decision to construct a nationwide network of motorways is clearly one of government policy . . . Any proposal to alter it is appropriate to be the subject-matter of debate in Parliament, not of separate investigations in each of scores of local public inquiries . . . up and down the country upon whatever material happens to be presented (*per* Lord Diplock, *Bushell* v *Secretary of State for the Environment, supra*).

(c) Major public inquiries – e.g. into the construction or extension of a nuclear power station – may raise issues of considerable technical and scientific complexity. Such inquiries may also take many months to be completed. This may cause difficulties for individual objectors and interest groups both in terms of regular attendance and finding the necessary resources to pay for expert advice and perhaps legal representation. The Sizewell B Inquiry, for example, lasted twenty-six months. Of that inquiry it has been said: 'To anyone watching the proceedings, the contrast was startling: sometimes a single person was faced by the CEGB's team of four barristers, several solicitors and other legal and administrative assistants' (Armstrong, 'The Sizewell B Inquiry' (1985) JPEL 686).

(d) The procedural format used in public inquiries is primarily adversarial rather than inquisitorial. As a result, the only facts considered by the decision-maker are those put forward in argument. Relevant information of which the parties are unaware, or which one party may not wish to use (e.g. the finding of some recent research), may not, therefore, be taken into account to the detriment of the overall quality of the decision-making exercise. In some instances, this may be exacerbated by the rule that there is no right for interested or affected third parties (e.g. neighbours or local community groups) to appeal against a planning decision although those with sufficient interest may have a right to be heard at the inquiry stage.

(e) The inspectors who preside over land use inquiries are members of the Planning Inspectorate which is an Executive Agency of the Department of Environment (now DEFRA). They are appointed by the Secretary of State and may often have a background in engineering, surveying or some related expertise. Also, where an appeal is to be decided by an inspector, they are bound to apply government policy. Despite appearances and public conceptions, therefore, inspectors cannot be regarded as performing an entirely independent role within the inquiry process.

All of this suggests that, although land use inquiries may be an appropriate forum for hearing objections to small-scale development or routine appeals against refusals of planning permission, they may not be best suited for dealing with issues of national importance where government policy will inevitably have a major impact on the final decision. Indeed, more cynical commentators have suggested that large-scale public inquiries should really be seen as little more than 'a means to neutralising public opinion, doing something about local hostility and resentment or allowing the public to let off steam' (Drapking, 'Development, Electricity and Power Stations' (1974) PL 220).

By way of response to the above criticisms, the Town and Country Planning Act 1990 provided for the creation of planning inquiry commissions to deal with proposed developments which raise issues of 'national or regional importance' or of great scientific or technical complexity (s 101). Such commissions will consist of three to five persons appointed by the Secretary of State. They are empowered to commission relevant research, to convene local public inquiries and to generally identify and investigate all matters relevant to the proposed development. Having completed their task, such commissions should submit a report to the Minister.

Inquiries into matters of public concern

Objective
4

Outside the sphere of planning and environmental control, ad hoc public inquiries may be set up for a wide variety of reasons to deal with matters of public concern or importance, e.g. major disasters, scandals, and abuses of power.

Such inquiries were originally constituted under the Tribunals of Inquiry (Evidence) Act 1921. This allowed tribunals of inquiry to be appointed by resolutions of the Houses of Parliament to investigate and report on matters of 'urgent public importance'.

Tribunals of inquiry had all the powers of the High Court in terms of requiring the attendance of witnesses and the production of documents. They sat in public unless this was against the public interest. Legal representation was at the discretion of the tribunal and proceedings were absolutely privileged. They were normally chaired by a senior judge or member of the legal profession sitting with two others.

Twenty-four major inquiries were conducted under the terms of the 1921 Act. Notable amongst these were the inquiries into the Aberfan Disaster 1966, the Bloody Sunday shootings 1972, the Dunblane shootings 1996, and the activities of Dr Harold Shipman 2002.

The 1921 Act was repealed and replaced by the Inquiries Act 2005. The Act was passed to enable Ministers to establish formal public inquiries to look into 'matters of public concern'. Unlike inquiries under the 1921 Act, such inquiries may be established without parliamentary authority – although Parliament must be informed of their creation. They do not have the status of courts of law and have no powers to determine matters of civil or criminal liability. The essential purpose is to restore public confidence in systems or services, particularly those operating in the public sector, by investigating the facts surrounding a particular event or affair and making recommendations designed to prevent recurrence of any failings or inadequacies. Inquiries of this type do, however, have the power to require the attendance of witnesses and to take evidence on oath. Their proceedings are privileged.

To date, inquiries convened under the 2005 Act include those dealing with the E-coli outbreak in Wales 2005, the explosion at ICL Plastics in Glasgow 2008, the treatment of Iraqi civilians in British military custody 2008, the standards of medical care at Mid-Staffordshire Hospital 2009 and allegations of phone-hacking by newspaper reporters (the Leveson Inquiry 2011).

The existence of such legislative powers and procedures to deal with matters of public concern does not preclude the creation of non-statutory inquiries for this purpose. Inquiries of this type are sometimes referred to as 'departmental inquiries'. These will often be used where a government department or agency is the focus of the investigation. Examples in relatively recent times would be the Hutton Inquiry 2003 (death of MOD scientist, Dr David Kelly), the Deepcut Review 2005 (deaths of soldiers at Deepcut Army barracks), and the Chilcott Inquiry 2009–16 (the decision to go to war in Iraq).

The Franks Committee

Objective 5

Post-war concerns about the ad hoc proliferation of tribunals and inquiries, their procedural standards, and the extent to which they appeared to be usurping the functions of the courts led to the creation of the Committee on Tribunals and Inquiries (the Franks Committee) in 1955. The Committee reported in 1957.

The principal findings of the Committee were:

(a) that tribunals and inquiries should be conducted with 'openness, fairness, and impartiality';

(b) that there should be a permanent body (the Council on Tribunals) to oversee their workings and attempt to ensure observance of the above standards in practical terms.

The Franks Committee and tribunals

The particular problems the Committee were asked to consider in relation to tribunals included:

- the varying standards of procedural fairness and the lack of any procedural uniformity between different types of tribunals;
- the extent to which tribunal members who were all executive appointees could be seen as performing an independent function;
- the lack of any general requirement to a right of appeal from tribunal decisions.

Perhaps the most important conclusion of the Committee in this context was that tribunals should be seen as a genuine means of independent adjudication and not simply as a device to improve the efficiency of administration and give it an appearance of procedural fairness. On this basis, the Committee's more specific recommendations for tribunals were as follows:

(a) the chairpersons of tribunals should be appointed and removed by the Lord Chancellor;

(b) members of tribunals should be appointed by the Council on Tribunals and removed by the Lord Chancellor;

(c) in general such chairpersons should be legally qualified;

(d) procedural rules for administrative tribunals should be formulated by the Council on Tribunals and should seek some degree of uniformity;

(e) apart from very exceptional circumstances, tribunals should conduct their hearings in public;

(f) legal representation should normally be allowed;

(g) reasons should be given for decisions;

(h) rights of appeal to a higher tribunal on both facts and law should normally be available with a further right of appeal on a point of law to a court.

The Committee's report was followed by the Tribunals and Inquiries Act 1958. This has subsequently been amended and consolidated by the Tribunals and Inquiries Acts of 1971 and 1992. These have given effect to some, but not all, of the Franks Committee's recommendations. Most importantly, however, the 1958 Act did create the proposed Council on Tribunals. Otherwise, the extent to which the Committee's proposals were implemented may be seen in the text above dealing with the current principles relating to the composition and procedure of tribunals.

For the Council on Tribunals, see p. 693 below.

The Franks Committee and public inquiries

The major concern in this context related to the perceived role of public inquiries and whether these should be regarded primarily as an administrative mechanism designed to assist in the exercise of executive discretion or as a quasi-judicial process for the purpose of giving full and open hearings of the cases for and against particular government schemes and projects.

The Committee decided against both extremes and sought a compromise, which should be reflected in procedural practice:

> If the administrative view is dominant the public inquiry cannot play its full part in the total process, and there is a danger that the rights and interest of the individual citizens affected will not be sufficiently protected . . . If the judicial view is prominent there is a danger that people will regard the person before whom they state their case as a kind of judge provisionally deciding the matter, subject to an appeal to the minister. This view overlooks the true nature of the proceedings, the form of which is necessitated by the fact that the minister himself, who is responsible to Parliament for the ultimate decision, cannot conduct the inquiry in person (*paras* 273–4).

The detailed proposals of the Committee in relation to inquiries were directed to achieving the best possible workable balance between these two perspectives. These were:

(a) before an inquiry, the public authority involved should be required to give full details of its case to those affected;

(b) also before the inquiry, parties affected should be given a statement of relevant government policy;

(c) the main body of inspectors for land use and related inquiries should be appointed by the Lord Chancellor and should be under the control of their department;

(d) the authority's case should be fully explained at the inquiry and supported by oral evidence;

(e) inspectors should have the power to compel the attendance of witnesses and administer the oath;

(f) the inspector's report compiled at the inquiry's conclusion should accompany the letter of decision to the parties affected and be made available both centrally and locally;

(g) evidence received after the inquiry should be submitted to the parties for their comments;

(h) the final decision should be accompanied by a statement of reasons.

Most of these recommendations have since been implemented by administrative action or statutory rules. Particular exceptions, however, have been those relating to pre-inquiry statements of government policy and the status of the inspectorate.

The Council on Tribunals

For more on the Administrative Justice Council, see pp. 699–700.

Until its replacement by the Administrative Justice and Tribunals Council in 2007, the Council on Tribunals performed a crucial and pivotal role in the supervision of the British system of statutory tribunals and inquiries.

The Council on Tribunals had 10 to 15 members appointed by the Lord Chancellor. In addition, the Parliamentary Commissioner was an *ex officio* member (1992 Act, s 2).

The principal functions of the Council were:

(a) to keep under review and report on the constitutions and working of those tribunals specified in Sched 1 to the Tribunals and Inquiries Act 1992;

(b) to consider and report on any other matters as may be referred to the Council concerning any tribunal, whether or not specified in Sched 1 (see recommendations relating to non-statutory inquiries in 1995/96 Report);

(c) to consider and report on such matters as may be referred to it or considered by the Council to be of special importance with respect to administrative procedures which may involve the holding of a statutory inquiry by or on behalf of the Minister (1992 Act, s 1).

These functions were underpinned, to a certain extent, by statutory provisions including in particular:

● the Council's right to make recommendations concerning the membership of tribunals (ibid. s 5);

● the obligation imposed on Ministers to consult with the Council when making procedural rules for most types of tribunals and inquiries.

In practice, the Council was also consulted when government departments were formulating legislation that sought to introduce a new system of tribunals or make changes affecting an existing system.

The Council met once per month. Detailed work and related recommendations were effected through a number of committees dealing with specific topics (e.g. planning procedures, and social security appeals). Members visited and observed tribunals and inquiries in action and received complaints from members of the public. Note, however, that the Council had no executive powers whatsoever and did not operate as some sort of court of appeal from tribunal decisions or those following the holding of a public inquiry. Nor had it any authority to investigate specific complaints or to initiate its own investigations. Its 'powers' were limited to making recommendations and being consulted but in neither case did its views have to be acted upon.

The Leggatt Review

Objective
6

The first major review of the tribunal system since the Franks Committee was announced by the Lord Chancellor in May 2000. The review committee was chaired by Sir Andrew Leggatt, formerly of the Court of Appeal. The review was to encompass all aspects of the workings of tribunals including their structure, jurisdiction, procedures, remedies and processes of appeal.

The review's terms of reference were 'to review the delivery of justice through tribunals other than ordinary courts of law, constituted under an Act of Parliament by a Minister of the Crown or for the purpose of a Minister's functions; in resolving disputes, whether between citizens and the state, or between other parties'. The Leggatt Review appeared in March 2001. It identified a series of key problems with the United Kingdom's tribunal network. These included:

(a) The lack of any coherent structure or system in the evolution and development of tribunals:

> . . . the present collection of tribunals has grown up in an almost entirely haphazard way. Individual tribunals were set up and usually administered by departments, with wide variations of practice and approach, and almost no coherence. The current arrangements seem to us to have been developed to meet the needs of the departments which run tribunals, rather than the need of the user (para 1.3).

(b) The lack of any clear separation between tribunals and the departments they heard appeals against:

> There is no question of the Government attempting to influence individual decisions. In that sense, tribunal decisions appear to us clearly impartial. But it cannot be said with confidence that they are demonstrably independent. Indeed the evidence is to the contrary. In most tribunals, departments provide administrative support, pay the salaries of members, pay their expenses, provide accommodation, provide IT support . . . are responsible for some appointments and promote the legislation which prescribes the procedures to be followed. At best, such arrangements result in tribunals and the department being, or appearing to be, common enterprises. At worst they make the members of a tribunal feel that they have become identified with its sponsoring department, and they foster a culture in which the members feel that their prospects of more interesting work, of progression in the tribunal, and of appointments elsewhere depend on the department against which the cases that they hear are brought (para 2.20).

(c) There was insufficient support and advice from tribunal staff and other agencies to enable individuals to present cases as effectively as possible:

> . . . the widest current theme in current tribunals is the aim that users should be able to prepare and present their own cases effectively, if helped by good quality, imaginatively presented information, and by expert procedural help from tribunal staff and substantive assistance from advice agencies . . . We have found, however, that in almost all areas the decision-making processes, and the administrative support that underlies them, do not meet the peculiar challenges the overall aim imposes (para 1.11).

(d) The lack of any right of appeal from some tribunals.

Principal recommendations

Independence

The Lord Chancellor should assume responsibility for both the administration of the tribunals system and for all appointments within it.

Structure

There should be a single tribunals system. This should be arranged into nine divisions which would group first-tier tribunals by subject-matter, e.g. Social Security and Pensions, Land and Valuation, Health and Social Services. There would be a right of appeal on a point of law from tribunals in each division to an appropriate tribunal in an appellate division and from appellate tribunals to the Court of Appeal.

Information and assistance

Basic information which should be provided to individuals should include that explaining the tribunal's jurisdiction, its procedure and any further right of appeal.

The basic agency for legal advice and assistance with tribunal hearings should be the Community Legal Service. Legal help beyond this may be provided by the contract scheme administered by the Legal Services Commission by solicitors or advice agencies. The Community Legal Service contract scheme should be extended to key advice agencies and 'the Lord Chancellor's department should consider whether the CLS's financial constraints should be adjusted so that it can fulfil the requirements of tribunal work' (para 4.20).

Tenure

All appointments to tribunals should be for five or seven years. Renewal for further such periods should be automatic except for cause. Grounds for removal should be prescribed by the Lord Chancellor.

The 2004 White Paper on tribunals

The government's response to the Leggatt Report was contained in the White Paper, 'Transforming Public Services: Complaints, Redress and Tribunals', 2004 (Cm 6243). This proposed the creation of a single, simplified system of tribunals administered by an executive agency, to be known as the 'Tribunals Service', operating under the general auspices of the Department for Constitutional Affairs.

One of the major reasons for the government's favourable response to the Leggatt proposals was a concern that the existing tribunals process did not comply with the requirements of the Human Rights Act 1998.

> Like many similar reports, the recommendations of the Leggatt inquiry might have gone unheeded, but for human rights concerns. The departments which administered tribunals were usually the rule-making authority for their tribunals and paid the salaries and fees of the tribunal members. Since those departments were usually parties to the proceedings before the tribunal, it was evident that tribunals did not have the independence which was required by Article 6 of the European Convention on Human Rights (A. Bano, Administrative Justice and Tribunals Council, Adjust newsletter, December 2007).

A new tribunal system

Objective
7

The legislative basis for reform of the tribunal system was provided by the Tribunals, Courts and Enforcement Act 2007. This created a simplified national system of independent tribunals in the form of the First Tier Tribunal and the Upper Tribunal. It was envisaged that the new system would be fully operational by the end of 2009. By then, the work and jurisdictions of most pre-existing types of tribunals were to have been subsumed within the new structure. Employment Tribunals and the Employment Appeals Tribunal were to be excluded from the system as they did not deal with disputes involving the citizen and the state.

The Upper Tribunal is largely an appellate body and hears appeals on points of law from the different elements of the First Tier Tribunal. The new system is headed by the Senior President of Tribunals appointed by the Queen on the advice of the Lord Chancellor. The Senior President must be a Justice of the Supreme Court or member of the Scottish Court of Session.

Section 2(3) of the 2007 Act imposes a duty on the Senior President to seek to ensure that:

- tribunals are accessible;
- their proceedings are fair and that cases are handled quickly and efficiently;
- their members are experts in the relevant subject-matter and law;
- innovative methods of resolving disputes are evolved.

The First Tier Tribunal

This performs the work of most pre-existing first instance tribunals. It is, therefore, a relatively large body consisting of nearly 200 'judges', and over 3,600 tribunal members. Most of these were drawn from the tribunal personnel already working within the sector. It is divided into local panels sitting throughout the country.

The First Tier Tribunal is divided into 'chambers'. Each chamber exercises a particular area of jurisdiction, e.g. social welfare benefits, health and social care. In general, related jurisdictions from the old system have been grouped within a single chamber.

Seven such chambers have been created. These, and their main areas of jurisdiction are as follows:

- General Regulatory Chamber: appeals against decisions of the Charity Commission; the Office of Fair Trading; the Environment Agency; the Gambling Commission; the Immigration Services Commission; also certain decisions relating to the freedom of information; the conduct of local councillors; postal provisions and carriers; and of Transport for London and the Registrar of approved Driving Instructors.

- Social Entitlement Chamber: appeals against decisions relating to pensions, tax credits, social welfare, child support; criminal injuries compensation; and asylum support.

- Health, Education and Social Care: appeals against decisions relating to persons working with children or vulnerable adults, persons detained under the Mental Health Acts, persons with special educational needs, and persons removed from the 'performers lists' of primary health care trusts (e.g. doctors, dentists, pharmacists).

- Immigration and Asylum Chamber: appeals against decisions of the Home Secretary relating to immigration, asylum and nationality.

- Property Chamber: appeals from residential property tribunals and those relating to land registration.

- War Pensions and Armed Forces Compensation Chamber: appeals against the Ministry of Defence relating to war pensions and compensation payments to members of the armed forces.

- Tax Chamber: appeals against tax decisions of HMRC.

Each Tribunal panel is chaired by a 'judge of the First Tier Tribunal'. Such judges must be a legally qualified person of at least five years' experience or persons with other suitable background, e.g. legal academics. New appointments are made by the Lord Chancellor, from a list drawn up by the Judicial Appointments Commission. The Lord Chancellor may also dismiss tribunal judges but only with the consent of the Lord Chief Justice and on grounds of inability or misbehaviour.

Tribunal judges and members are given a 'ticket' by the Chamber President indicating their suitability for a particular jurisdiction covered by the Chamber. With training, it is intended the judges and members will increase the number of 'tickets' held, thus widening their capacity to sit in the chamber's different jurisdictions.

The First Tier Tribunal is headed by a President who is also a member of the Upper Tribunal. Also, as indicated, there is a President for each First Tier chamber.

Appeals from the First Tier Tribunal may be made to the appropriate chamber of the Upper Tribunal. Appeal is not of right, and permission must be granted by the First Tier Tribunal which is being appealed against or by the Upper Tribunal.

The Upper Tribunal

The intention is that this will 'rationalise the hotchpotch of appeal routes from administrative tribunals'. The Upper Tribunal is divided into four chambers:

- The Administrative Appeals Chamber (appeals from the Social Entitlement, General Regulatory, Health, Education and Social Care, War Pensions and Armed Forces Compensation Chambers of the First Tier Tribunals);

- Tax and Chancery Chamber;

- the Lands Chamber (matters previously dealt with by the Lands Tribunal);

- The Immigration and Asylum Chamber.

The Upper Tribunal is, primarily, an appellate body but also has a limited judicial review jurisdiction. The latter is exercised by High Court judges only or others approved by the Lord Chief Justice and Senior President. In this context the Upper Tribunal is empowered to make mandatory, prohibiting and quashing orders, also declaratory judgments and injunctions. Decisions of the Upper Tribunal are binding on the First Tier Tribunal. A right of appeal lies to the Court of Appeal on important points of law or practice or where some other compelling reason exists.

In general, members of the Upper Tribunal are drawn from pre-existing appellate tribunals and from judges of the High Court and Scottish Court of Session. Appointments are made by the Queen on the Lord Chancellor's advice after selection by the Judicial Appointments Commission. Dismissal is limited to grounds of inability or misbehaviour and only with the concurrence of the Lord Chief Justice.

Decisions of the Upper Tribunal are subject to judicial review on grounds of excess of jurisdiction or procedural impropriety (*R (on application of Cart)* v *Upper Tribunal* [2010] EWCA Civ 859).

Figure 22.1 illustrates the structure of the tribunal system in England and Wales, and in some cases Scotland and Northern Ireland, as of September 2016.

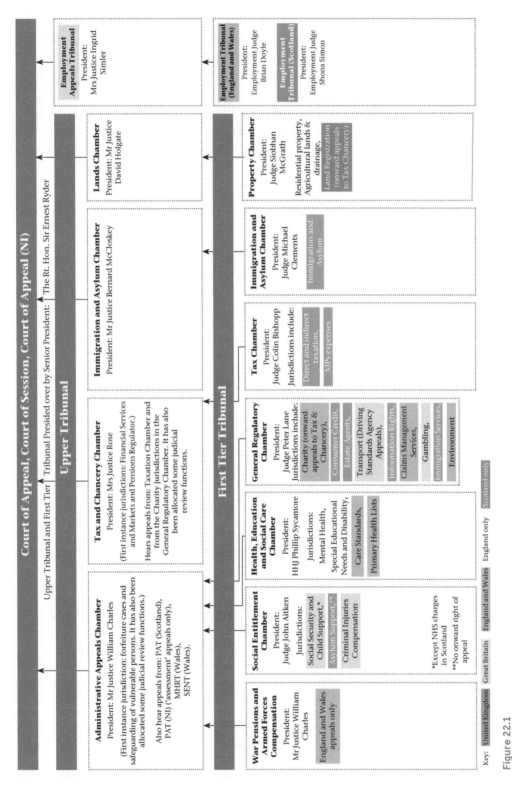

Figure 22.1

Source: https://www.judiciary.gov.uk/publications/tribunals-organisation-chart/

The Administrative Justice and Tribunals Council

Objective 8

The Council replaced and succeeded to functions of the Council on Tribunals. In addition, it was required to:

- keep the administrative justice system under review;
- consider ways to make the system accessible, fair and efficient;
- advise Ministers and the Senior President on the system's workings and development;
- make proposals for research and reform.

The Council's composition and status was similar to that attending to its predecessor, the Council on Tribunals. It consisted of between 10 and 15 members plus the Parliamentary Commissioner for Administration. Other than the Parliamentary Commissioner, its members are chosen by the Lord Chancellor in concurrence with the Scottish and Welsh Ministers.

In October 2011, and as part of its review of the utility and cost-effectiveness of public bodies in general, the government announced its intention to abolish the Council and to transfer its functions to the Ministry of Justice. The move was not supported in all quarters and, in particular, and for the following reasons, was received with some misgivings by the House of Commons Select Committee on Public Administration.

- There was no evidence on which it could have been concluded that the Council did not provide value for money.
- There were no grounds on which to base the belief that the Council's functions could be performed better or equally well by civil servants.
- The Council provided the government with an expert and independent source of advice on the workings and any perceived inadequacies of the administrative justice system.

> It is clear that there is a fundamental difference of view between the government and others from which we have heard on both the need for independent oversight of the Administrative justice system, and the extent to which the AJTC has been performing such a function. We accept that this task may be undertaken in more than one way, but consider that oversight by an independent entity independent from the government is important and should be continued in some way (Twenty-first Report, 2010–2012, HC 1621).

- Due to the high incidence of mistakes made by government departments, an effective and properly supervised tribunals system remained essential for the proper disposal of associated grievances.

> PASC regards the high level of successful appeals and complaints against decisions by government departments as an indication of widespread administrative failure. Government departments should aim to produce decisions which are right first time and command a high degree of confidence. The scale of the injustice and the cost to the taxpayer caused by this poor decision-making are wholly unacceptable . . . We also, therefore, regard the role of the AJTC as of vital importance, overseeing a system which protects the rights of millions of citizens every year (*ibid*).

An order to abolish the Council (Public Bodies (Abolition of Administrative Justice and Tribunals Council) Order 2013), made under the Public Bodies Act 2011, was laid before Parliament in December 2012.

The Tribunals Service

The administration of the reformed tribunals system is the responsibility of the Tribunals Service. This is an executive agency of the Ministry of Justice. The rules of procedure for tribunals within the reformed system are made by the Tribunal Procedure Committee.

Summary

Tribunals and inquiries provide an important extra-judicial method of dealing with disputes between individuals and public authorities. The chapter explains the emergence and growth of these procedures, and the powers and jurisdiction of the main types of tribunals and inquiries currently operating in the United Kingdom, and assesses their effectiveness.

The changes made to the systems of tribunals and inquiries following the Franks Committee Report of 1957 and the Leggatt Review of 2000 are also detailed.

References

Armstrong (1985) 'The Sizewell B Inquiry' JPEL 686.

Bano (2007) Administrative Justice and Tribunals Council, Adjust newsletter, December.

Cane (2004) *Administrative Law* (5th edn), Oxford: Oxford University Press.

Drapking (1974) *Development, Electricity and the Power Stations* PL 220.

Leggatt (2001) *Tribunals for Users: One System, One Service*, London: HMSO.

Public Administration Select Committee, Twenty-first Report 2010–2012, HC 1621.

Report of the Committee on Administrative Tribunals and Inquiries [Franks Committee] (1957) Cmnd 218.

Schwartz and Wade (1972) *Legal Control of Government*, Oxford: Clarendon Press.

Transforming Public Services: Complaints, Redress and Tribunals (2004) Cm 6243.

Further reading

Allen and Thompson (2011) *Cases and Materials on Constitutional and Administrative Law* (10th edn), Oxford: Oxford University Press, Ch. 11.

Bailey, Jones and Mowbray (2009) *Cases and Materials on Administrative Law* (6th edn), Oxford: Oxford University Press, Chs 2–3.

Craig (2016) *Administrative Law* (8th edn), London: Sweet & Maxwell, Ch. 4.

Jacobs (2016) *Tribunals Procedure and Practice* (4th edn), London: Legal Action Group.

Wade and Forsyth (2014) *Administrative Law* (11th edn), Oxford: Oxford University Press.

23

Public services ombudsmen

Objectives

After reading this chapter you should:

1. Understand the reasons for the introduction of the Parliamentary Commissioner for Administration in 1967.

2. Know the general role, status, functions and powers of the Parliamentary Commissioner for Administration.

3. Be aware of the reasons for the limits on the jurisdiction of the Parliamentary Commissioner.

4. Understand the effectiveness of the Parliamentary Commissioner.

5. Understand the extent to which the conduct and decisions of the Parliamentary Commissioner are subject to judicial review.

6. Know the role, functions and powers of the Health Service Commissioner.

7. Know the role, functions and powers of the Commissioners for Local Administration.

8. Recognise the extent to which the actions and decisions of the Commissioners are subject to judicial review.

9. Know the role, functions and powers of other public sector ombudsmen.

Background

Objective
1

In the immediate aftermath of World War II a further increase in the size and activities of government took place. The welfare state was expanded, giving greater rights of access to state benefits and services. Additional regulatory powers – particularly for the purposes of planning and urban renewal – were also entrusted to the government. Much of this was motivated by altruistic political principles and a desire to improve the quality of life of the wider community.

However, despite these overall laudable intentions, greater contact between the individual and the state and, in some cases, dependence on it, led to an increased incidence of complaints and disputes concerning the conduct of public officials and their treatment of individuals.

The creation of appropriate mechanisms to deal with grievances did not go hand in hand with the granting of powers. In some contexts (e.g. national assistance) tribunals were established to deal with complaints relating to the way an official had interpreted the relevant regulations or applied them to the facts of a particular case. Beyond this the traditional methods of dealing with a grievance against the state remained available. Hence, an individual could complain to an MP and ask for their intervention with the government department concerned or for the matter to be raised in Parliament. Also, where it appeared that a government department or official may have acted illegally, redress could be sought in the courts.

The general position was, however, unsatisfactory. Often the type of grievance felt by an individual would fall outside the jurisdiction of any tribunal and would not involve any breach of law. Examples would include such matters as rudeness, inattention, delay, inadequate or incomprehensible advice, or simply downright incompetence. The right to complain to an MP could not be regarded as a generally satisfactory or adequate means of dealing with the volume and variety of complaints arising out of the relationship between members of the public and government departments. Members of Parliament did not, and do not, have the time, resources or expertise required to deal with all such matters effectively, nor are such individual grievances matters to which Parliament can hope to devote any significant amount of time.

In the 1950s, therefore, an awareness began to develop – principally among academics and lawyers – of the need to provide the ordinary citizen with some more effective means of pursuing the type of complaint which might seem trivial in the general context of the administration of public policy but which might be of considerable importance to the individual affected.

In 1961 the British section of the International Commission of Jurists (JUSTICE) recommended the introduction of a complaints procedure modelled on that already in use in some Scandinavian countries, i.e. an independent complaints commissioner ('ombudsman') equipped with the power to investigate and secure redress for the type of grievance against officialdom not easily remedied through more traditional procedures.

Initially, the official response to the proposal was not encouraging. In particular, it was argued that investigating and reporting on the activities of civil servants would be inconsistent with, and might undermine, the convention of individual ministerial responsibility (i.e. that everything done inside a government department is done in the name of the Minister, who is answerable for the same to Parliament). Eventually, however, wiser counsels prevailed, and the incoming Labour government of 1964 gave an assurance that legislation would be formulated to deal with the problem. Their proposals were embodied in the Parliamentary Commissioner Act 1967 (subsequent references in this chapter relate to the 1967 Act, unless stated otherwise).

Since then other ombudsmen or complaints procedures have been established in both the public and private sectors. The principal public sector procedures were created as follows:

- the Health Service Commissioner (National Health Service Reorganisation Act 1973);

- the Commissions for Local Administration in England, Wales (Local Government Act 1974) and Scotland (Local Government (Scotland) Act 1975);

- the Northern Ireland Parliamentary Commissioner for Administration (Parliamentary Commissioner (Northern Ireland) Act 1969);

- the Northern Ireland Commissioner for Complaints (Commissioner for Complaints (Northern Ireland) Act 1969).

The Parliamentary Commissioner

Appointment

Objective
2

The Parliamentary Commissioner or ombudsman is appointed by the Monarch on the advice of the government. The Monarch may also exercise the power of dismissal but only pursuant to resolutions of both Houses of Parliament (s 1). This gives the Commissioner a degree of independence and security of tenure similar to that accorded to senior judges. The Commissioner should retire at 65. He/she is an *ex officio* member of the Council on Tribunals and the Commissions for Local Administration but is disqualified from membership of the House of Commons.

Jurisdiction

The Commissioner is authorised to investigate written complaints from individuals who claim to have suffered 'injustice in consequence of maladministration' in dealings with any of the government agencies or departments specified originally in the 1967 Act, Sched 2, and now contained in Sched 1 to the Parliamentary and Health Service Commissioners Act 1987 as amended by the Parliamentary Commissioner Act 1994.

Maladministration

The term maladministration was not defined in the Act. At the time of the Act's introduction, however, the Minister responsible for it said that the term would at least include 'bias, neglect, inattention, delay, incompetence, ineptitude, perversity, turpitude and arbitrariness' (Richard Crossman, House of Commons, 10 October 1966). More recently the following matters were specified by the Commissioner as falling within the definition:

> ... rudeness ...; unwillingness to treat the complainant as a person with rights; refusal to answer reasonable questions; neglecting to inform a complainant on request of his or her rights to entitlement; knowingly giving advice which is misleading or inadequate; ignoring valid advice or overrating considerations which would produce an uncomfortable result for the overruler; offering no redress or manifestly disproportionate redress; showing bias whether because of colour, sex, or any other grounds; omission to notify those who thereby lose a right of appeal; faulty procedures; failure by management to monitor compliance with adequate procedures; cavalier disregard of guidance which is intended to be followed in the interest of equitable treatment of those who use a service; partiality; failure to mitigate the effects of rigid adherence to the letter of the law where that produces manifestly inequitable treatment (PCA, *Annual Report*, 1993, para 7).

Notwithstanding this extensive definition of the term, it is generally accepted that the formation of policy and legislation do not fall within it. Hence it is not open to an individual to complain that a particular policy or legislative rule might have been different if the department concerned had consulted more widely or taken additional considerations into account. Maladministration may occur, however, if a particular policy or legislative rule appears to be causing hardship and the department responsible refuses to review its interpretation of the rule or the way it is being applied. Providing the Minister's position is not irrational and does not run counter to the objectives of the 1967 Act, he or she is not bound to accept a finding of maladministration. This follows from the general principle that the Minister is answerable ultimately to Parliament and should be free to put their own assessment of the matter before the House (*R (on application of Bradley)* v *Secretary of State for Work and Pensions* [2008] EWCA Civ 36).

The 1967 Act does make clear that the Parliamentary Commissioner was not created to act in an appellate capacity in matters of fact. The Commissioner's inquiries should concentrate, therefore, on the conduct of officials and the quality of the administrative processes through which official actions and decisions are taken. The Commissioner is thus expressly forbidden to entertain complaints relating solely to the merits of particular decisions taken without maladministration (s 12). This, however, has been interpreted to mean that where a decision is taken *with* maladministration, then its merits *are* open to comment. Also, the view has been taken that maladministration covers gross unreasonableness and irrationality.

> Either way, the parliamentary ombudsman is entitled to explore the merits of a particular decision during the course of an investigation. Were this not the case, it would often be impossible to come to a conclusion as to whether maladministration or an injustice had occurred (Kirkham, 'The Parliamentary Ombudsman: Standing the Test of Time', March 2007).

Excluded matters

Objective 3

A considerable range of activities in which central government departments are involved were, from the outset, put beyond the Commissioner's powers of investigation. The principal exclusions and the reasons given for them were as follows:

(a) Any matter in respect of which a complainant may appeal to a tribunal or seek redress in the courts (s 5) (e.g. by applying for judicial review). This was based on the principle that the Commissioner was not introduced to replace existing grievance procedures but to supplement these in areas where adequate protection for the citizen in dealings with the executive would not otherwise exist.

  Note, however, that the Commissioner has a discretion to waive this exclusion if satisfied that in the particular circumstances it would not be reasonable to expect the complainant to go before a court or tribunal, e.g. where the relevant law is uncertain or the cost of proceedings is prohibitive.

(b) Any matter or grievance which arose more than twelve months before the complaint was made ('stale' complaints) unless there are special circumstances for making an exception (s 6). This was designed to prevent a grievance being referred to the Commissioner where this did not have sufficient impact on the complainant to cause the matter to be raised at an earlier stage.

(c) Matters relating to the contractual or commercial dealings of a government department (Sched 3, para 9).

  > The original reason for this exclusion was that the PCA was intended to operate in the field of relationships between the government and the governed. Commercial judgements are by nature discriminatory . . . and so allowing the commercial judgements of departments to be open to examination by private interests while leaving those interests themselves free from investigation would amount to putting departments, and with them the taxpayer, at a disadvantage (Select Committee on the Parliamentary Commissioner for Administration, 1993/94).

(d) Matters relating to personnel issues in the public services or armed forces (Sched 3, para 10). It was felt that it would be unfair and illogical to give public sector employees a grievance procedure not available to their private sector counterparts. Also, in the case of the armed forces, it was believed that access to the Commissioner would be inimical to the maintenance of authority and discipline.

(e) Matters relating to the government's dealings with any other government or international organisation (Sched 3, para 1). Here it was argued that a decision whether or not to pursue a complaint which might involve a foreign government could often raise political considerations outwith the Parliamentary Commissioner's proper sphere of competence. Also, it was felt that, in this context, pursuit of an individual's concerns might not always be synonymous with effective protection of the wider public interest.

(f) Action taken by British diplomats outside the United Kingdom. The two reasons offered for this exclusion were that such actions might well be determined by local circumstances over which such officials had no control and that the investigation of any matter arising within the territory of a foreign state would be beset with practical difficulties (particularly in terms of access to information and official cooperation generally).

(g) Action taken relating to the investigation of crime and the protection of national security (Sched 3, para 5). It was felt that allowing information relating to the same to come into the public domain could be detrimental to the effectiveness of the law enforcement agencies and could put at risk some key prerequisites of good criminal intelligence, e.g. anonymity and confidentiality.

(h) The exercise of the prerogative of mercy (Sched 3, para 7). This was justified on the ground that royal clemency was not thought to be an appropriate issue for investigation and that, in the normal course of events, problem cases of this type would most probably have already been referred to a court for reconsideration.

(i) The grant of honours (Sched 3, para 11). Again, it was felt that it would be constitutionally improper to subject the exercise of the Monarch's powers to investigation and that, since the conferment of an honour was a privilege, nobody aggrieved in such matter could be said to have suffered injustice.

(j) The extradition process.

> In the exercise of extradition orders, the Secretary of State is acting in a quasi-judicial capacity as a final appellate authority. Adding, in effect, a further appeal – an investigation by the PCA – would, the argument ran, be inappropriate and inconsistent with the government's responsibility for compliance with international obligations (1993/94 Report).

Excluded bodies

As stated, the PCA's investigative jurisdiction extends only to those government agencies and bodies listed in Sched 2 to the 1967 Act. The Schedule currently lists some 343 of the same. Significant amongst those excluded and, therefore, not within the PCA's remit would be: the remaining public corporations, e.g. the Post Office, the Civil Aviation Authority and the Atomic Energy Authority; the Criminal Injuries Compensation Board; parole boards; the Bank of England; the Competition and Markets Authority; and various bodies operating in the sphere of education, e.g. the Higher Education Funding Council, and the National Council on Curriculum and Assessment.

Open government

The subject-matter falling within this aspect of the Parliamentary Commissioner's jurisdiction was extended as a result of the government's White Paper on Open Government published in 1993 (Cm 2290). This promised 'to establish a more disciplined framework for publishing factual and analytical information about new policies and reasons for administrative decisions'. A Code of Practice on Access to Information was introduced to secure implementation of these good intentions. A failure to supply information according to the Code's requirements amounts to injustice as a consequence of maladministration and may, therefore, be investigated by the Commissioner.

The Code of Practice divides official information into fifteen categories. Some of these are completely exempt from disclosure: communications with the royal household, public employment, public appointments and honours. Information in the other categories (e.g. defence and national security) should be disclosed unless this would harm the national interest to a degree which outweighs the national interest in making information available. The onus is, therefore, on disclosure unless it can be shown that the information falls into one of the exempted categories or there are good grounds for believing that its disclosure would do unacceptable damage to a public interest. Such official judgements may be questioned by the Commissioner – i.e. it is open to the Commissioner to dispute a government conclusion concerning the degree of harm that the disclosure of a particular piece of information might do.

The Commissioner's remit in this context extends only to those departments and bodies coming within their jurisdiction as determined by the 1967 Act.

Procedure

The 1967 Act, s 5 provided that each complaint must be made initially to an MP (not necessarily that of the complainant). This requirement is known as the 'MP filter'. It reflects the fact that the office of Parliamentary Commissioner was created to make departmental accountability to Parliament more effective rather than to replace it with an alternative mechanism. It is for the MP to decide whether the complaint should be referred to the Commissioner. Obvious considerations would be whether the complaint falls within the PCA's jurisdiction and whether it raises an issue worthy of investigation. Also, it is open to the MP to take up the complaint and pursue it personally if in their opinion this would appear to be an appropriate way of dealing with the problem. The Commissioner has no authority, therefore, to entertain a complaint which has been made to them directly by a member of the public. They may, however, communicate such complaint to an appropriate MP so that it may, at the MP's discretion, be referred back to the Commissioner and, therefore, not simply 'lost'. It should also be emphasised that the Commissioner has no authority to initiate an investigation. All is entirely dependent on a complaint being raised by an individual and being referred to the Commissioner by an MP.

Each investigation should be conducted in private (s 7). The head of the department or agency and those within it who are the subject of an investigation should be given an opportunity to comment on the complainant's allegations (*ibid*). The same persons and the Minister who referred the complaint are entitled to a report of the Commissioner's findings (*ibid*).

A general report on the performance of their functions must be laid before each House of Parliament on an annual basis (s 10). Other special reports may be laid from time to time as the Commissioner thinks fit (*ibid*). These may relate, *inter alia*, to particularly important inquiries or to instances where government departments found guilty of maladministration have refused to respond to the Commissioner's recommendations. Since 1997 such reports have been considered by the House of Commons Select Committee on Public Administration which makes recommendations concerning the Commissioner's jurisdiction, powers and investigative methods. It may also suggest changes in the administrative procedures of the government departments and bodies falling within the Commissioner's jurisdiction. This function was performed previously by the Select Committee on the Parliamentary Commissioner.

Powers and remedies

Apart from that relating to proceedings in Cabinet or Cabinet committees, any information relevant to an investigation, whether in the possession of a Minister, civil servant or any other person, must be submitted to the Commissioner on request (s 8). This includes information which is subject to the Official Secrets Acts or any other legal restriction relating to its disclosure, e.g. a duty of confidentiality or public interest immunity (*ibid*). Refusal to comply with such a request, or any other obstruction of an investigation, may be referred to the High Court and dealt with as if it were a contempt of court (s 9). The Commissioner is also empowered to demand the attendance of any person for the purpose of obtaining oral testimony and may administer the oath (s 8).

These extensive powers of access to official information are subject to the provision that the Commissioner may not include in a report anything which a Minister has certified would be damaging to the national security (s 8).

Where the Commissioner finds maladministration he/she may recommend remedial action – e.g. payment of compensation, altering of decisions or procedures, or the giving of an apology – but has no power to insist on official compliance, the sole weapon being to report the matter to the MP concerned and, in particular cases, to lay a special report before Parliament. This is another illustration that the primary purpose of the office is to assist MPs in the task of supervising the activities of government departments and agencies. It is only in relatively rare cases, however, that a government body will not respond in an appropriate fashion to an adverse finding by the Commissioner.

The judicial view on this is that, while it remains open to a Minister to reject a recommendation from the PCA, any such decision may be tested in the courts for irrationality if it appears not to be based on 'cogent reasons' (*R (on application Bradley)* v *Secretary of State for Work and Pensions* [2008]).

Evaluation

Publicity

Objective
4

A total of 6,174 complaints were made to the parliamentary ombudsman in the year 2015–16; 1,567 of these were taken forward for further assessment with 592 being accepted for formal investigation. As in other years, therefore, the vast majority of complaints were not proceeded with. This was for a variety of reasons including that the PCA felt that the body had acted correctly, reasonably or, where errors had occurred, that the complainant had been offered appropriate redress, or that the complaint was:

- 'out of remit', i.e. the matter complained about was not within the ombudsman's jurisdiction;
- 'not properly made', e.g. the complainant had not completed local resolution with the body concerned before bringing the matter to the ombudsman, or had not submitted the complaint through the MP filter;
- 'premature', i.e. the complainant had not attempted to resolve the complaint with the body concerned or had not completed the local resolution process;
- withdrawn.

Time taken for investigation

The Commissioner's record here has not always been impressive. In the early 1990s the average time taken for an investigation was in excess of 18 months. After criticism by the Select Committee, the ombudsman's 1999/2000 report recorded that this had been reduced to, on average, 44 weeks. The figures given in the 2011/12 report were that 79 per cent of complaints proceeding to investigation had been dealt with within 12 months.

The MP filter

Since the inception of the PCA in 1967 debate has continued concerning the lack of direct access and the need for a complaint to be channelled to the Commissioner through an MP. The supposed benefits of the requirement were summarised as follows in the Select Committee's Report for 1978:

- the complainant's problem could often be solved by an MP's intervention without the need for a reference to a lengthy investigation by the Commissioner;
- it helps MPs to keep in touch with the problems of constituents in the 'daily contact with the machinery of the State';
- it restricts the Commissioner's attentions to those complaints which MPs feel they would not be able to deal with competently through lack of time, expertise or resources.

It has also been emphasised that the MP filter was designed 'to allay the fears of those who thought that the Ombudsman system would detract from the traditional constitutional role of Parliament in its scrutiny of the executive' (Select Committee Report 1993/94).

Arguments against the filter include the following:

- it lowers the profile of the office of Parliamentary Commissioner and, therefore, public awareness of its existence;
- potential complainants may suspect that an MP 'of a different colour from their own political persuasion will not help them' (*ibid*);
- it imposes an additional administrative burden on MPs which some may be reluctant or unable to discharge as expeditiously as possible;
- because MPs have differing views concerning the utility of the Parliamentary Commissioner as a means of dealing with an individual's grievances, some are more likely to refer complaints to the Commissioner than others;
- 'the filter is an anomaly, almost unknown in other Ombudsmen systems' (*ibid*).

A further review of the filter system occurred in 2009. On this occasion, and despite whatever merits were originally attributed to it, the Public Administration Select Committee was persuaded that these were outweighed by the disadvantages as outlined above ('Parliament and the Ombudsman', HC 197, 2009/10). The government's response to the proposed abolition of the MP filter was as follows:

> The government believes that the filter mechanism is recognition of the constitutional nature of the Ombudsman's role as a 'servant' of Parliament. Members of Parliament hold a range of views on this issue, and some Members feel very strongly that the current arrangement is an important element of their relationship with their constituents. The government believes that this is an issue of constitutional significance that needs to be considered in the context of the wider relationship with, and responsibilities to, Parliament. Therefore, at this stage . . . the government does not believe that there is scope to take this issue forwards (HC 471, 2009/10).

Jurisdiction

Many criticisms have been made of the wide range of matters and government bodies excluded from the Commissioner's jurisdiction. The Select Committee has suggested that there should be a presumption that 'all decisions of civil servants and others within departments and appropriate public bodies involving maladministration should be subject to investigation . . . unless any constitutional principle such as independence of the judiciary dictated otherwise'. In evidence to the Select Committee in 1993, JUSTICE's proposal was that the Commissioner's jurisdiction should extend to 'all who perform a public duty and to all areas of central government administration, save of those for whom exclusion can be justified'.

The Parliamentary Commissioner and judicial review

Objective
5

From the institution of the office it was probable that the actions and decisions of the Commissioner were reviewable for simple *ultra vires* (e.g. investigating a matter not within her or his jurisdiction) and for procedural impropriety. As yet, the matter has not been settled definitively. Thus in *R v Parliamentary Commissioner for Administration, ex parte Balchin* [1999] EWHC Admin 484, a finding by the Commissioner on a crucial point was quashed for a failure to give reasons. As to the willingness of a court to review a decision of the Commissioner for abuse of discretion, the matter was shrouded in considerable uncertainty.

The first case to shed any light on the matter was *Re Fletcher's Application* [1970] 2 All ER 527, where it was held that the exercise of the Commissioner's discretion as to which complaints should be investigated could not be questioned in the courts. However, where the Commissioner has embarked upon an investigation, it would appear that decisions relating to the conduct of the inquiry may be susceptible to review if *Wednesbury* unreasonableness of a serious or gross nature can be established (*R v Parliamentary Commissioner for Administration, ex parte Dyer* [1994] 1 WLR 621). It is interesting to note that the court in the *Dyer* case refused to accept the argument that since the Commissioner is an officer of the House of Commons he/she should be answerable to Parliament, and to Parliament only, for the way they perform their functions.

A somewhat more expansive view of the courts' power of review in relation to the ombudsman, in both substantive and procedural matters, was offered by Collins J in *R (on application of Turpin) v Commissioner for Local Administration* [2001] EWHC Admin 503:

> It seems to me that if it is clear that the Ombudsman in reaching a decision has misdirected himself as a matter of law, or has failed to have regard to a relevant consideration, or has had regard to an irrelevant consideration, or has given reasons which are so defective that they indicate that his decision is bad in law, then the court can and should intervene. The court will be careful to ensure that it does so only if such errors are clear but, as it seems to me, there is nothing in the legislation to exclude the court's usual power to consider whether a discretion, however widely conferred, has been exercised in accordance with law. In addition, if the Ombudsman has conducted his investigation, or as in this case his investigation as to whether there should be an investigation, in a manner which is unfair, again the court is entitled to intervene if satisfied that there has been a risk of prejudice.

Instances of a government department refusing to follow or abide by a decision of the Parliamentary Commissioner are rare. Where, however, this occurs, the expectation is that clear and cogent reasons will be given (*R (on application of Equitable Members Action Group) v HM Treasury* [2009] EWHC 2495 (Admin)).

The Health Service Commissioner

Creation

The National Health Service was excluded from the jurisdiction of the Parliamentary Commissioner. This was because, at the time, some elements of the health service were under local government control. Central government responsibility for the entire health service was effected by the National Health Service Reorganisation Act 1973. To date the practice has been to appoint the same person who holds the post of Parliamentary Commissioner to the offices of Health Commissioner for England, Wales and Scotland.

Matters relating to the Health Commissioner's appointment, jurisdiction and powers are currently governed by the Health Service Commissioners Act 1993. Like the Parliamentary Commissioner, the Health Service Commissioner is an independent officer of Parliament appointed by the Crown but dismissible only pursuant to resolutions of both Houses of Parliament.

Jurisdiction

The Health Service Commissioner was originally empowered to investigate hardship or injustice arising from maladministration in the National Health Service or from the provision of, or failure to provide, any aspect of such service. They were not given jurisdiction, however, over complaints relating to clinical judgments or to the services provided by GPs and other family practitioners (e.g. dentists, pharmacists and opticians). These restrictions on their jurisdiction have since been removed by the Health Service Commissioners (Amendment) Act 1996.

The current remit of the Commissioner is set out in the Health Services Commissioner Act 1993. This is to investigate complaints that a person has sustained injustice or hardship in consequence of:

- a failure in a service provided by a health service body;
- a failure to provide any such service which it is the body's function to provide;
- maladministration connected with any other action taken by or on behalf of such a body.

Procedure

The MP filter does not operate in relation to the Health Service Commissioner. Complaints may be made directly to the Commissioner providing all internal health service complaints procedures have been exhausted. Also, the Health Commissioner may dispense with such preliminary proceedings if of the view that the matter is unlikely to be resolved locally or by the Health Commission. The Commissioner's reports are submitted to the Secretary of State for Health who is obliged to lay them before Parliament. Such reports are scrutinised by the Public Administration Select Committee.

Powers and remedies

The Health Commissioner's powers in the matters of access to information and the taking of oral testimony are as those of the Parliamentary Commissioner. Similarly, the assumption is that the adverse publicity caused by their reports will be sufficient to produce the necessary remedial action to secure compliance with their recommendations without the need for any formal powers of compulsion or the imposition of sanctions.

It follows that the Health Service Commissioner has no authority to make or recommend awards of compensation against private individuals, e.g. NHS doctors who, although employed by a public body, are not under any public or private law legal obligation to provide monetary recompense for alleged failures of the service (*JR 55, Re Application for Judicial Review (Northern Ireland) (Rev 1)* [2016] UKSC 22).

Judicial review

In determining the standards to be observed by the Health Commission and by like complaints commissions in general, judicial approval has been given to the Health Commissioner's 2009 policy statement that complaints should be determined according to whether there has been a 'departure from the general standards of good administration and the specific standards governing the legal, policy, and administrative framework, and the professional standards, relevant to the events in question'. The application of this standard should not be interfered with, it has been held, 'unless it reflects an unreasonable approach' (*Attwood* v *Health Service Commissioner* [2008] EWHC 2315). Little judicial support has been forthcoming for the view that, particularly in relation to complaints against medical practitioners, the standard test for determining allegations of medical negligence should be used, i.e. did the service failure fall below that which could have been provided by a reasonable doctor (often known as the 'Bolam test' from the decision in *Bolam* v *Friern Hospital Management Committee* [1957] 1 WLR 382) (*Miller* v *Parliamentary and Health Service Commissioner* [2016] EWHC 2981 (Admin)).

The work of the Health Commissioner

In the year 2015–16, there were 21,406 complaints reviewed by the Health Service Commissioner; 6,547 were taken forward for assessment and 3,746 became formal investigations. The most complained about elements within the service were hospitals, primary care trusts, GPs.

An explanation should be given to any person whose complaint has not been concluded within twelve months. In addition, the Commissioner is required to provide an annual report on how long it has taken to deal with complaints in that year, how many took more than twelve months to conclude, and what action was taken to expiate the problem (Health Service Commissioner for England (Complaint Handling) Act 2015).

Table 23.1 provides some typical examples of the types of complaint dealt with.

Table 23.1

Health authority/agency	Case ref.	Subject-matter
NHS Trust	H82503	Death of patient during emergency surgery following failure to diagnose and provide appropriate treatment for recurrent gallstone ileus, inappropriate discharge from hospital, non-reporting of x-rays, poor record-keeping, poor pain control and lack of nutritional monitoring.
NHS Trust	HS-4160	Failure to deal effectively and sensitively with complaint about the way kidney dialysis carried out and, in this, to have proper regard to the patient's learning disability.
NHS Trust	HS-8953	Failure to tell patient diagnosed in 1978 with MS that diagnosis not certain and that second opinion and/or other test might be appropriate.
NHS Trust	HS-1132	Failure to exercise flexibility in applying the six-month limit for receiving complaints and refusal to comply with NHS Commission that complaint should be investigated.

The Commission for Local Administration

Creation and appointment

Objective
7

Complaints relating to local government in England are made to the Commission for Local Administration. This was established under the terms of the Local Government Act 1974. Similar Commissioners for disposing of local government complaints in Scotland and Wales were also established. Following the 1998 devolution settlement, separate arrangements for Scotland and Wales have since been put in place. As a result, local government complaints in Scotland may now be made to the Public Service Ombudsman (Scottish Public Services Ombudsman Act 2002). Similar functions in Wales are also performed by a Public Services Ombudsman (Public Services (Ombudsman) Act 2005). The office is responsible for the jurisdictions exercised previously by the Local Government/Ombudsman for Wales, the Health Service Ombudsman for Wales, the Welsh Ombudsman for Administration, and the Social Housing Ombudsman for Wales.

A total of 20,102 complaints and inquiries were received by the Local Government Commission for England in 2015–16. Those local government services attracting the greatest proportion of complaints were education (18%), adult care services (16%), and planning and development (16%).

Jurisdiction

A complaint may be made to a Commissioner by any person who claims to have 'sustained injustice in consequence of maladministration in connection with action taken by . . . an authority . . . in exercise of [its] administrative functions'. The complaint must be lodged within twelve months from the day on which the complainant became aware of the subject-matter of the complaint.

In recent times the most common causes of maladministration have been:

- delay in taking action;
- taking incorrect action;
- failure to provide information;
- failure to complete and maintain adequate records;
- failure to take action;
- failure to take relevant matters into account;
- failure to investigate concerns or complaints;
- failure to deal with correspondence or inquiries;
- failure to comply with legal requirements;
- making misleading or inaccurate statements.

The types of injustice resulting from the above most often included:

- refusal of a benefit or other entitlement;
- financial loss;
- loss of amenity;
- missed opportunities (right of appeal, access to council housing);

- distress;
- significant inconvenience and being put to avoidable time and trouble.

A local government Commissioner has no jurisdiction to investigate:

- matters for which redress may be granted by a court, tribunal or by appeal to a Minister unless it would be unreasonable to expect the complainant to use one of these remedies;
- actions or decisions which affect all or most of the inhabitants of the authority in question (s 26) (e.g. the level of council tax);
- matters relating to the prevention and investigation of crime;
- actions taken in relation to civil or criminal proceedings in which an authority is involved;
- commercial or contractual transactions;
- personnel and disciplinary matters;
- the internal affairs of educational institutions.

The Health Act 2009 inserted a new Part 3A into the Local Government Act 1974, extending the Local Government Commission's remit to include complaints relating to adult social care not arranged or funded by a local authority. As with complaints against local councils, any such complaints may only be considered once the care provider has been given a reasonable opportunity to deal with the issue.

Procedure

A complaint may be made directly to a Commissioner or to a local councillor who may refer it to a Commissioner with the complainant's consent (s 26). Prior to this the complaint should have been brought to the attention of the local authority to which it relates and the authority must have been given a reasonable opportunity to respond to it (*ibid*).

Each investigation should be conducted in private (s 28). An opportunity to comment on the complaint should be given to the authority concerned and to any person alleged to have taken the action complained about (*ibid*). At the conclusion of an investigation a report of the Commissioner's findings should be given to the complainant, the authority, and to any local councillor through whom the complaint was referred (s 30).

Each Commissioner must submit an annual report to their local Commission and each Commission must report to a body designated by the Secretary of State as representative of the local authorities subject to its investigative powers (s 24).

Powers and remedies

A local Commissioner may require any person in possession of information relevant to an investigation to furnish them with the same. They may require the attendance of witnesses and take evidence on oath. No statutory or common law rule protecting information from disclosure (e.g. confidentiality, public interest immunity and official secrecy) may be used to deny a Commissioner access to information they consider relevant (s 29).

A local Commissioner has no power to insist on compliance with their reports. It is not open to a local authority to question a finding of maladministration (*R v Commissioner for Local Administration, ex parte Eastleigh Borough Council* [1988] QB 855). Where a report contains a finding of maladministration, the local authority concerned must, within a reasonable time, notify the Commissioner of the action it has taken or proposes to take (s 31). If the Commissioner is not satisfied with such response they may make a further report to the authority containing specific recommendations (*ibid*). A decision not to comply with such a report must be taken by the full council of the authority. Compliance is the norm.

Judicial review

Objective 8

A challenge may be made to the legality of the actions or decisions of a local government Commissioner where:

- the Commissioner has entertained a complaint which does not relate to a matter within their jurisdiction (*R v Commissioner for Local Administration, ex parte Eastleigh Borough Council*, *supra*);

- the Commissioner has made findings for which there was no reasonable factual basis (*R v Commissioner for Local Administration, ex parte Croydon London Borough Council* [1989] 1 All ER 1033);

- the Commissioner has been guilty of procedural impropriety (*R (on application of Turpin) v Commissioner for Local Administration*, *supra*).

Tenure

Commissioners are appointed by the Crown and hold office during good behaviour, retiring at 65 (s 23).

The Housing Ombudsman

Objective 9

Power for the creation of a Housing Ombudsman dealing with complaints against social landlords, including local authorities and housing associations, were provided by the Housing Act 1996. In 2016 the Housing Ombudsman remit extended to approximately 4,751,430 'housing units'.

A filter system for the making of complaints was introduced by the Localism Act 2011. This requires complaints to be made initially to a 'designated person'. This may be an MP, a councillor, or a recognised tenant panel. The designated person should decide whether or not the complaint should be submitted to the Housing Ombudsman. A tenant may complain directly to the Housing Ombudsman and without reference to a designated person where the social landlord operates a complaints procedure, this has been exhausted without satisfaction, and eight weeks have elapsed since that time.

A total of 15,988,976 determinations were made by the Housing Ombudsman in 2015–16.

The Housing Ombudsman's decisions are enforceable in County Courts.

The Office of the Independent Adjudicator for Higher Education

The office was created by the Higher Education Act 2004. It deals with impropriety or unfairness in the conduct of student complaints and appeals procedures. The jurisdiction extends to all those institutions designated for student funding support or having degree awarding powers (Consumer Rights Act 2015). It does not entertain complaints relating to matters of academic judgement. In 2015, there were 1,650 complaints made to the OIA.

Determinations of the OIA constitute recommendations only and are not legally binding or enforceable. These may often be 'brokered' by the OIA acting between the student and the university or college in question. Awards of compensation may be recommended. There were 1,850 complaints received in 2015–16. Recommendations of awards of compensation were made to a value of £485,000.

The Prisons and Probation Ombudsman

The office of Prisons and Probation Ombudsman was created in 1994 by administrative action (i.e. appointment by the Secretary of State for the Home Department) and not pursuant to any primary legislation as in the cases of all of the above.

The jurisdiction of the Prisons and Probation Ombudsman extends to all matters affecting prisoners except:

(a) those relating to litigation or criminal proceedings;

(b) those relating to persons or bodies outside the prison service – e.g. the police, courts, immigration service, the parole board;

(c) ministerial decisions concerning the release of mandatory life prisoners.

Unlike other ombudsmen, the Prisons and Probation Ombudsman may investigate the merits of decisions as well as the administrative processes through which they were made.

The government has undertaken to give the Prisons and Probation Ombudsman unfettered access to prison documents, establishments and individuals, subject to the need to withhold from complainants, and not make public, information which could be damaging to national security, to security in prisons or to the protection of individuals.

Any recommendations made by the ombudsman pursuant to an investigation must be submitted to the Director-General of the Prison Service. The ombudsman is also obliged to report annually to the Secretary of State for the Home Department, who is to lay a shortened version of the full report before Parliament.

The Legal Services Ombudsman

The Legal Services Complaints Scheme was established under the Legal Services Act 2007. It is intended principally for users of legal services who are individuals, small businesses or other small organisations including charities, clubs, societies, associations and trusts. A complaint is defined as any expression of dissatisfaction with a legal service.

As a general rule, any such complaint should be made directly to the individual or legal firm who/which is the subject of it and within fourteen months of the action or omission in question. It may then be referred to the ombudsman if it has not been resolved within eight weeks.

The Legal Ombudsman is to determine any complaint by reference to what is fair and reasonable in all the circumstances. Any determination made may involve a direction that:

- an apology be given;
- action be taken to rectify the matter complained of;
- compensation be paid (up to £50,000).

Decisions of the Legal Ombudsman are subject to judicial review on the normal public law grounds viz: illegality, procedural impropriety including breach of the rules of natural justice, and unreasonableness (irrationality) (***Stenhouse* v *Legal Ombudsman and De La Pasture*** [2016] EWHC 612 (Admin); ***Mitchell and Co* v *Legal Ombudsman and Patel*** [2016] EWHC 1933 (Admin)).

Summary

The chapter traces and explains the development of ombudsmen procedures since the inception of the Parliamentary Commissioner in 1967.

The jurisdiction and powers of the principal public sector ombudsmen are set out and followed by comment on the perceived strengths and weaknesses of this method of dealing with complaints about the process of government.

References

Kirkham (2007) *The Parliamentary Ombudsman: Withstanding the Test of Time,* HC 421.

Open Government (1993) Cm 2290.

Parliamentary Commissioner for Administration (1993) *Annual Report.*

Select Committee on the Parliamentary Commissioner for Administration, First Report 1993/94, HC 33.

Further reading

Buck, Kirkham and Thompson (2011) *The Ombudsman Enterprise and Administration,* London: Ashgate.

Gregory and Giddings (2002) *The Ombudsman and Parliament,* London: Politics Publishing.

Le Sueur, Sunkin and Murkens (2016) *Public Law, Cases and Materials* (3rdedn), Oxford: Oxford University Press.

Webley and Samuels (2015) *Complete Public Law: Text, Cases and Materials,* Oxford: Oxford University Press.

Appendix: 'Brexit'

World Wars I and II and the birth of the European ideal

The ideal of European political integration was born out of the horrors, mass killings, genocide and wholesale, wanton, mass destruction experienced on the continent of Europe in two world wars of the first half of the twentieth century. At the outset, therefore, the European project was perceived primarily as a political priority, even necessity, rather than as the means of giving practical expression to some preferred economic plan or ideology. The paramount concern was to put Europe back together again and in a way which might not so easily fall apart – at least for the foreseeable future.

At the battle of El Alamein in October 1942 the British army secured its first major victory against the forces of Nazi Germany. In the mood of national confidence thus engendered, the then Prime Minister, Mr Winston Churchill, writing to his Foreign Secretary, Anthony Eden, allowed himself a moment to contemplate, not just the prospect of an ultimate overall victory, but the possible future of the resulting post-war Europe and the means of protecting it against the chaos and conflicts of long-standing national ambitions and rivalries.

> Hard as it is to say now, I look forward to a United States of Europe in which barriers between the nations will be greatly minimised and unrestricted travel will be possible (Letter from Churchill to Eden).

Mr Churchill returned to the theme in the years immediately following the end of hostilities in 1945.

> Yet it is from Europe that have sprung that series of frightful nationalistic quarrels which we have seen even in this twentieth century wreck the peace and mar the prospects of all mankind . . . Yet all the while there is a remedy which . . . would transform the whole scene and would in a few years make all Europe . . . free and happy . . . It is to re-erect the European family . . . and provide it with a structure under which it can dwell in peace, in safety, and in freedom. We must build a United States of Europe. The structure of a United States of Europe . . . will be such as to make the material strength of a single state less important. Small nations will count as much as large ones and gain their honour by their contribution to the common cause (University of Zurich, 19 September 1946).

In a further speech on the topic two years later, Mr Churchill conceded that this would involve 'some sacrifice or merger of national sovereignty', but that it was 'also possible and not less agreeable to regard it as the gradual assumption by all the nations concerned of that larger sovereignty which can alone protect their diverse and distinctive customs and characteristics and their national traditions all of which under totalitarian systems . . . would be blotted out forever (Congress of Europe, 7 May 1948, The Hague).

Other contemporary political imperatives

Under the terms of the 'Marshal Plan', devised by the US Secretary of State, George Marshal, and in the four years from 1948 to1952, the American exchequer poured $13bn (current value approximately $185bn) into the ailing European economies (25 per cent of this to the UK). Inevitably, the view in Washington was that this could not go on indefinitely and that European political and economic reconstitution, but without the threat of wars, was a matter of urgent priority.

Other political imperatives were also at play, all of which fed into the idea of a European family of nations more united and interdependent than had existed before 1939.

There was the widely acknowledged view that European political stability and economic recovery in Europe could not be achieved by prolonged military subjugation of Germany or by the long-term suppression of its economic capacity and systems of civic administration.

And, above and beyond all this, loomed a gathering unease between the two great super-powers and the realisation that the rebuilding of Europe as an effective, functioning, political entity was essential if it was to provide a meaningful barrier to further westward expansion of the Soviet empire. Other important considerations included:

- growing awareness that the influence of European states in the world had diminished and that vis-à-vis the USA and USSR, only a united Europe could have any real effect on world affairs;
- the American preference for European integration, with its close ally the UK at the 'top table'.

The Schuman Declaration 1950

This is generally regarded as the first major step towards the creation of the initial multinational European organisation (the European Coal and Steel Community) out of which the European Community and the European Union developed subsequently. The Declaration was made by the then French Foreign Minister, Robert Schuman, on 9 May 1950. This set out the following ideals and the means of achieving them:

The contribution which an organised and living Europe can bring to civilisation is indispensable to the maintenance of peaceful relations. In taking upon herself for more than twenty years the role of champion of a unified Europe, France has always had as her essential aim the service of peace. A united Europe was not achieved and we had war . . . The coming together of the nations of Europe requires the elimination of the age-old opposition of Germany and France. Any action taken must in the first place concern these two countries . . . With this aim, the French government proposes . . . that Franco-German production of coal and steel as a whole be placed under a common High Authority, within the framework of an organisation open to the participation of the other countries of Europe . . . The policy of coal and steel production should immediately provide for the setting up of common foundations for economic development as a first step in the federation of Europe . . . The solidarity in production thus established will make it plain that any war between France and Germany becomes not merely unthinkable, but materially impossible.

The European Coal and Steel Community ('ECSC')

The Schuman Declaration was given practical effect by the Treaty of Paris 1951. This created the ECSC – the model for the pan-European organisations which followed it, viz. the European Economic Communities ('EEC'), the European Community ('EC') and the European Union ('EU').

The Treaty came into effect in early 1953. It put coal and steel production in western Europe under the supervision of a multinational European body (the 'High Authority') and thus beyond the control and possibly aggressive intentions of any state government. The High Authority was to consist of persons appointed by member states but not to 'represent' them. Preference was to be given to the common European interest. Also created were a Council of Ministers from member states, an Assembly of 76 deputies drawn from national parliaments and a Court of Justice. The free movement of products covered by the Treaty, without customs dues or taxes, was guaranteed while prohibitions were placed on state subsidies or restrictive or discriminatory trade practices.

The original members of the ECSC were France, Germany, Italy, Holland, Belgium and Luxembourg. Britain did not sign the Treaty of Paris and, therefore, was not a member. The principal reasons for this were:

- the fear that Britain's influence and freedom of action in wider international affairs might be inhibited by a permanent commitment to an inter-governmental European organisation;
- the view that Britain's trading needs could be satisfied largely by its long-established and close links with the Commonwealth (Australia, New Zealand, Canada, India, etc.) and the remaining colonies;
- the view that Britain's status as a world power might be better served by advancing its 'special relationship' with its closest wartime ally, the USA;
- the then Labour government (1946–51), under Clement Atlee, had other priorities including particularly, abroad, 'decolonisation' of the Empire and the creation of a Commonwealth of national democracies while, at home, laying the foundations of the welfare state supported by public ownership of strategically important industries;
- the fear that Britain might lose the power to prioritise its own industrial interests;
- concern about the possible moves towards a federated Europe.

Britain saw herself as much more than a European power. She was at the centre of three circles. It was said one of them was Europe, but the others were as head of the Empire, which was being transformed by the Atlee government into a multi-racial Commonwealth, and the third was the special relationship with the United States. The key to British influence and power, it was thought then, was to hold these three relationships in balance, to remain at the centre of all three and not to cut loose from any of them and any tilt in one of these directions might put the other relationships at risk and so weaken British power . . . Merging sovereignty with

Europe would compromise, it was thought, the British position as head of the Commonwealth. So, Britain could not easily converge with a European orientation (Bogdanor, 'Britain and the Continent', Gresham College lecture, 17 September 2003 www.guardian.ac.uk/lecture .transcript/print/from-the-european-coal-and-steel-community-to-the-common-market).

The European Economic Communities

Creation and objective

In 1957, by the Treaty of Rome, the six members of the ECSC agreed to establish two further pan-European organisations. These were the European Community (the 'Common Market') and the European Atomic Energy Authority ('EAEA'). These came into existence in 1958. All three were to exist side-by-side under the collective name of the European Economic Community ('EEC'). The United Kingdom took part in the discussions leading up to the EEC's foundation but, sustained by cheap, tariff-free food from the Commonwealth, still felt no pressing need to be a part of it. This caused little concern in domestic politics. There was no great public debate or media coverage. The matter was not discussed at length in Parliament or Cabinet nor was it even considered worth a mention in the political manifestos of the major parties for the 1959 General Election. The effect of the Treaty of Rome was to expand the ECSC into a broader European Common Market encompassing all cross-border trade within the six member states, eliminating all internal tariffs on imports and exports within the Common Market, and creating a customs union with a uniform tariff on all imports from outside the Community.

In this way the EEC was brought into existence with minimal impact from the UK. The rules of the 'club' were laid down, therefore, by the six founder members of the European project and were influenced particularly by the two 'great powers' within it, i.e. France and Germany. This was to prove a major problem for the UK when, eventually, it did decide to join – the main ongoing bugbear being the Common Agricultural Policy ('CAP') and its requirement that large sums of European monies should be dedicated to the support of Europe's largest agricultural sectors, i.e. those in France and Italy. At that time, agriculture accounted for 20 per cent of the French economy, 25 per cent of that of Italy, but only four per cent of the economy in the UK.

The Treaty of Rome laid down also what were to become known as the 'four freedoms' of the European project: the free movement of goods, workers, capital and the freedom of establishment of services. As the Community increased its size, and in time grew to its current complement of 28 members, the second of these, the free movement of labour, was to prove a further complication for continued British membership.

Other than the reasons already considered, the UK's decision not to join the Community at this, its inception, was influenced by the possible impact of German manufactured goods on domestic industries and the refusal of the Community to offer any compromise on Commonwealth access to European markets.

The UK seeks entry

The first application

This was lodged on 1 August 1961 by the Conservative government of Harold Macmillan. The application was vetoed by France. The principal moving figure in this was the French President, Charles de Gaulle. His views were that:

● the UK was separated from the continent of Europe by the Channel and because of centuries of war with European states, Germany, France, and Spain particularly, the British did not regard themselves as European nor were they wholly in favour of the ideal of European integration;

- the UK's close political and military relationship with the US, and its commitments to the Commonwealth, were not compatible with membership and development of the EEC;
- the UK would act as the US 'Trojan Horse' within the Community, i.e. as a conduit for American policy and influence;
- at this stage, the EEC could not be expected to change the principles on which it had been founded to facilitate the needs of a country which had, hitherto, refused to join;
- the EEC had been formed without the UK and could survive and prosper without it;
- the UK's entry could lead to modification of the Common Agricultural Policy;
- UK membership of the EEC could diminish French influence within in it.

The second application

This was made by the Labour government of Harold Wilson (Prime Minister 1964–70 and 1974–76) on 7 May 1967. The application had cross-party support and was approved by a large majority in the House of Commons (488 to 62). It was made without major preconditions and without any attempt to secure modification of the founding principles of the Treaty of Rome.

> As Britain's global role weakened, there was nowhere else to go but Europe, if Britain wished to remain a power with international reach (Parr, 'The significance of the 1967 application', UACES Conference Paper, 7–8 March 2013).

Perhaps inevitably, Mr Wilson adopted a more positive tone when he presented the case for EEC membership to the House of Commons:

> But all of us are aware of the long-term potential for Europe, and, therefore, for Britain, of the creation of a single market approaching 300 million people, with all the scope and incentive which this will provide for British industry . . . But whatever the economic arguments the House will realise that the government's purpose derives, above all, from our recognition that Europe is now faced with the opportunity of a great move forward in political unity and that we can – and indeed must – play our full part in it (Hansard, 2 May 1967).

Five of the EEC's founding six members were prepared to accept the UK's application. Not so, however, President Charles de Gaulle. In 1962 domestic economic difficulties had forced the Wilson government to devalue the pound. For de Gaulle this was more than sufficient evidence that the British economy was still not ready to cope with the added financial burden which would be imposed on it by EEC membership. President de Gaulle, therefore, had his way and the French veto was used again.

Third time lucky

The General Election of 1970 resulted in an unexpected victory for the Conservative party. The omens for EEC membership were promising. Five of the six original EEC member states remained firmly in favour of British accession and, perhaps more important than this, President de Gaulle was no longer on the scene. In 1969 he had resigned from the French presidency and had been replaced by the more amenable George Pompidou.

The newly-installed British Prime Minister, Edward Heath (Prime Minister 1970–74), was a firm European. He was convinced that EEC membership was the only option if the UK did not want to become a 'vassal state' and be condemned to permanently play 'second fiddle' in world affairs to the US:

> Many of you fought in Europe, as I did, or have lost a father or brother or husband who fell fighting in Europe. I say to you now, with that experience in my memory, that joining the Community, working together with them for our joint security and prosperity, is the best guarantee we can give ourselves of a lasting peace in Europe (Television broadcast, 7 July 1971).

From this it is clear that for Heath, as with Churchill and Macmillan before him, the main virtue and purpose of European integration was political rather than economic, i.e. the avoidance of further mass conflagration.

Mr Heath is generally agreed to have formed a good relationship with President Pompidou. And so, without the British government seeking a major concession, and with the support of the other five members, the die was cast. The 1967 application having been 'left on the table', the UK's third attempt to join the EEC began in October 1970. No French veto was forthcoming and on 2 January 1972, the Brussels Treaty of Accession was signed. The UK was 'in'. The European Economic Communities Act 1972, which gave effect to all this, was passed through Parliament with a majority of 112 (356 to 244). UK membership of the EEC became effective as from 1 January 1973.

The official position of the Labour party in opposition was that, although generally in favour of EEC membership, it was not prepared to vote in favour of the terms negotiated by Mr Heath and that, if and when returned to power, it would support membership only if more advantageous conditions could be agreed.

The 1975 EEC referendum

The winter of 1973–74 witnessed a series of prolonged, 'all-out' strikes in a number of key British industries and public utilities. Without sufficient coal for the power stations, and in order to save electricity, Mr Heath's government was forced to close down major industries for two days of every working week (the 'three day week'). Major disruption was caused. Mr Heath's response was to call what became known as the 'Who governs Britain?' General Election of February 1974. The Conservative party won more votes than any of the other major parties but did not return an overall majority. Unable to regard this as a vote of confidence, Mr Heath resigned. Harold Wilson returned to office at the head of a minority Labour government. At a second General Election in 1974, this time in October, Mr Wilson's government secured a small overall majority of three.

In the Parliament of 1974, the policy of the UK's two major parties was one of overall support for EEC membership. Both, however, contained significant contingents of those who had yet to be convinced. This was related primarily to the dilution of national sovereignty and the concern that the future relationship with the Commonwealth remained unresolved. Also, on the left of the Labour party, there were those who saw the EEC as a free-market 'capitalist club' which would inevitably be opposed to the increased regulation of capitalism, the free market and the greater protection of employment rights.

Accordingly, for the purpose of the referendum campaign, Mr Wilson suspended the convention of collective ministerial responsibility and allowed his Ministers a 'free' vote.

Twelve of the 23 Cabinet Members advocated the case for remaining within the Common Market with 11 supporting the 'leave' campaign; 145 backbench Labour MPs also voted to leave and 137 voted to remain. The figures clearly demonstrate the extent to which, at the time, the Labour parliamentary party remained 'split' on the European question.

These were the days before the internet and twenty-four-hour news and when the written media was still primarily responsible for the dissemination of information and opinion relating to public affairs. All of the major national newspapers supported the cause for remain. Only the Communist newspaper, *The Morning Star*, argued against. It was a time, also, when public deference to the wishes of the 'establishment' had not been so severely tested by public scandals, economic inequality and political disconnect and, therefore, remained an important influential factor in voting behaviour.

Beyond this, and the perhaps more mundane matters of purely domestic politics, the issue of peace in Europe still pressed heavily on many voters, considerable numbers of whom had fought in the two world wars and were still alive and active. In addition, in the background throughout this period loomed the threat of conflict between the 'East' and the 'West' with the possible use of nuclear weapons.

As in 2016, the referendum campaign was subject to misinformation, although perhaps not to the extent of the more recent vote. On the remain side this tended to be 'silence by omission' – and particularly failure to explain the possible implications for national sovereignty:

- that major EEC laws would take effect in the UK without the need for parliamentary ratification ('direct' effect);
- that the UK government would be disallowed from adopting policies incompatible with the EEC rules and decisions;
- EEC aspirations relating to monetary union and greater political unity.

For the leave side, their campaign leaflet contained the rather dubious contention that the intent of the Common Market was, by stages, to merge Britain, France, Germany Italy, Holland, Luxembourg and Belgium into a single national entity.

> The real aim of the Market is, of course, to become one single country in which Britain would be reduced to a mere province.

Immigration was not elevated into a major issue by either side.

The referendum was conducted on 5 June 1975. The question put before the electorate was:

> 'Do you think the United Kingdom should stay in the European Community (the Common Market)?'

Voting figures for the 1975 Referendum

Electorate	40,456,877
Yes	17,378,581 (67.2%)
No	8,470,073 (32.8%)
Turnout	25,848,654 (64.03%)

The 'yes' vote represented 40.9 per cent of all those entitled to vote. The 'no' vote was just 20.9 per cent of the same cohort.

Part B: Why, when and how the UK will leave the European Union

Attitudes towards Europe

'Europhobia'

Introduction

The seeds of British ambivalence towards Europe and its peoples have their origins in a rich mix of geographical, historical, political and cultural factors. A good many of these pre-date the formation of the European Community/Union and cannot, therefore, be related directly to the alleged inadequacies of that organisation. Most of the factors in issue may be subsumed under the general headings of 'europhobia' and 'euroscepticism'. The terms should, however, be distinguished as, although they relate to the same general subject-matter, each attempts to describe a different aspect of it. Hence, it is perfectly possible for a person to have great affection for all things European and, therefore, not to be europhobic, whilst, at the same time, being sceptical of the view that the EU, as currently constituted, serves the best political and/or economic interests of its member states.

Geography: 'over the sea and far away'

Britain is not part of the landmass of continental Europe. Prior to the days of mass air travel and the building of the Channel tunnel – both comparatively recent events in purely historical terms – it was accessible by sea only. For a great many British people it seemed a far distant place populated by peoples with strange eating habits and speaking impenetrable languages. Few of the general population ever set foot across the Channel unless required to do so in time of war.

For those living on the Continent, and without maritime borders, movement across state boundaries was not so difficult or infrequent and, certainly until the end of the nineteenth century, less effective restrictions on such movements had been imposed. Perhaps inevitably, therefore, many Europeans, regardless of nationality, tended to develop a less insular attitude to the other nations and peoples around them. This was particularly so pursuant to the development of the European railway system in the 1850s and the ease of travel between the European capitals thereby facilitated. From this it would hard to gainsay the view that the simple facts of physical geography have contributed significantly to the feeling amongst many British people that they are not really 'European' at all and have little enthusiasm to be part of any organisation which is.

Britain's contribution to international political, legal and industrial development – a leader, not a partner

The British can rightly claim to be the descendants of a people who, over many centuries, have been responsible for the evolution of many of the features and achievements of good government, industrial development and technological development which are currently taken for granted in the modern world. In terms of the most influential, these would include the following:

● after the Norman Conquest 1066, the emergence of one of the world's first nation states, i.e. a body of diverse peoples and communities within fixed geographical boundaries recognising the lawful authority of a single, common, central governmental authority;

- recognition of the right to trial by jury and the need for control over absolute executive power (Magna Carta 1215);
- founding of one of the world's first elected Parliaments (late twelfth century);
- creation of a system of 'national' courts and legal rules (the 'common law') to replace local customary rules (mid eleventh century);
- recognition and application of the principle of the Rule of Law, i.e. the subjection of royal and executive power to the ordinary law of the land (Bill of Rights 1689);
- creation of an independent judiciary, free of executive control (Act of Settlement 1701);
- invention of steam-powered automotive machinery and the means of industrial mass production (Industrial Revolution, late eighteenth century);
- the telephone (Alexander Graham Bell, 1847–1922); penicillin (Alexander Fleming, 1881–1955); television (John Logie Baird, 1888–1948); computers (Alan Turing, 1912–54).

These and other like events have served to underpin the widely-held view that Britain holds a special place in, and has made a unique contribution to, the history of human development. This, in turn, helps to explain the belief that Britain's international stature, prosperity and general national well-being is not dependent on relationships with others, least of all her European 'rivals' and, in some instances, erstwhile protagonists.

European wars – 'in hearts at peace, under an English Heaven'

For centuries large sections of the British people have taken the view that, far from being the domain of friendly neighbours, Europe is the place from which the greatest threats to the nation's very existence and identity have emerged. Generations of schoolchildren have been brought up on stories of heroic defence and self-sacrifice in the face of foreign, usually European, invaders and enemies. The narrative often begins with the last Saxon monarch, King Harold, falling bravely at the Battle of Hastings as he tried to hold the French forces of William the Conqueror at bay. From this, the story often moves to Philip of Spain, the Spanish Armada, and the heroics of Sir Francis Drake (1658), to the Battles of Trafalgar and Waterloo during the Napoleonic Wars with France (1803–15) and the achievements of Wellington and Nelson on land (Waterloo 1815) and sea (Trafalgar 1805). And then, of course, come the final chapters, some within living memory: the battle against the Kaiser's Germany 1914, the sacrifice at Ypres, the Somme and Passchendale, leading then to World War II (1939–45), the legends of Dunkirk, the Blitz, the Battle of Britain, El Alamein, D-Day and the final 'Victory in Europe' in May 1945.

All of these pieces of British history are deeply rooted in the national psyche and, for many, provide irrefutable graphic evidence that the English Channel should be viewed as a protection against, rather than an obstacle, to closer contact with Europe.

The British Empire – 'of their great empire where the sun never set'

Until comparatively recent times, and certainly well into the 1950s, the UK was still regarded as a major world power, still possessed the largest empire known to human history and had the world's largest naval fleet to protect it. With its colonial and Commonwealth peoples to support it and the trade, commerce, and ready supplies of cheap food and raw materials to supply its needs, imperial Britain's security and prosperity did not depend on close political alliances or trading arrangements with Europe or, indeed, the rest of the world. The sentiment that Britain's political and economic status was such that it could 'go it alone' was further reinforced by the knowledge that, with the exception of the neutral states, Britain was the sole major European nation not to be defeated on the battlefield and occupied by its enemies during World War II. There was a feeling, therefore, that whereas other European states had failed both politically and militarily, the UK had not. 'They' might be required to rebuild their political and governmental structures and to start again, but the UK did not. They might need to 'club' together to form a united Europe to maintain their place in the world, but the UK did not. All of which, it is said, has served to foster and reinforce the idea that Britain has a distinct and different role to play in the world from the nations of the rest of Europe.

Religion – 'Remember, remember, the fifth of November'

Although the immediate cause of the English break with Rome in 1534 was to facilitate the annulment of Henry VIII's marriage to the Spanish Catherine of Aragon, and to allow his remarriage to Anne Boleyn, the dispute was also about national sovereignty and who should exercise ultimate authority in domestic affairs – whether the King or the Vatican.

In subsequent times, the adoption of the reformed religion of northern Europe in opposition to the religious affiliations of France and Spain (the other 'great powers' of Europe) and the association of 'Catholic Europe' with domestic plots and subversion, became another long-standing cause of suspicion of the intentions of those across the Channel. The annual burning of Gunpowder plotter, Guy Fawkes, on the bonfires of 5 November pays ample tribute to the extent to which such suspicions have become woven into the fabric of British historical narrative in relation to Europe and its inhabitants.

In more recent times, in the context of membership of the European Union, it has been further postulated that it may have been easier for countries with a Catholic heritage, and thus accustomed to the role of the Vatican in domestic matters, education, social affairs, etc., to come to terms with the sharing of national powers and, with it, acceptance of the authority of external European bodies in these matters. According to this, therefore, and for example, the culture of the Republic of Ireland might be more amenable to the ideology of the EU than that of its neighbouring non-Catholic countries of the United Kingdom.

> Protestant countries are less likely to support European integration compared to those from traditionally Catholic countries. Protestant nations have been marked by a consensual relationship between reformist churches and national political authorities, which resulted in a strong affiliation to the nation state. Such nations also defined their national character through a strong refusal of Catholic universalism and its adherence to the Pope as a supranational power. Today this finds its expression in a rather distrustful sentiment towards internationalism and, as a result, creates a less favourable opinion towards the European political system (Scherer, 'The UK's opposition to European integration is still framed around the legacy of its past', EUROPP, LSE, 20 August 2013).

National identity – 'this island race'

The concept of national identity should not be confused with either simple nationalism or the perhaps more easily identifiable sentiments often associated with the notion of patriotism. Amongst the most quoted definitions of such terms are those of George Orwell and the American journalist and author, Sydney J. Harris. Orwell's 'Notes on Nationalism' was written in 1945. Here he explained nationalism as 'the habit of identifying oneself with a single nation or other unit, placing it beyond good or evil and recognising no other duty that that of advancing its interests.' Orwell's understanding of patriotism was that this was typified by 'devotion to a particular place and a particular way of life, which one believes to be the best in the world but has no wish to force this on other people.' Writing in 1953, Harris summarised the matter in slightly more 'acid' terms:

> The difference between patriotism and nationalism is that the patriot is proud of his country for what it does, and the nationalist is proud of his country no matter what it does; the first attitude creates a feeling of responsibility, but the second a feeling of blind arrogance that leads to war ('Strictly personal', Rigney and Co., 1953, Washington).

In contrast to these, the concept of national identity refers to a body of values, beliefs, attitudes and cultural norms held in common by a group of people usually living within a politically defined geographical area. It is perhaps a 'gentler' but more nuanced and complex aspect of human experience and awareness which cannot be understood fully by simple equation with the more emotional and politically-weighted sentiments often associated with the nationalistic or patriotic.

The national identity of the group is that which holds it together and distinguishes it from other peoples or those living within nation states. It is the feeling of commonalty which gives individuals within the group a sense of belonging and, with those feelings, of personal, cultural and ideological security, even protection, against external forces or perceived threats:

> Belonging implies some form of reciprocal commitment between the individual and the group . . . Belonging fosters an emotional attachment; it prompts the expansion of the individual's personality to embrace the attributes of the group, to be loyal and obedient to it. In return, the group offers a 'home', a familiar space – physical, virtual or imagined – where individuals share common interests, values and principles (Guibernau, 'Understanding Euroscepticism: how British hostility to the EU contrasts with opposition elsewhere in Europe', EUROPP, LSE, 12 January 2016).

National identity provides a sense of comfort and assurance in times of crisis or danger whatever its nature or source. This may be, therefore, from the threat of attack in time of war or from serious economic or cultural disruption of an established way of life and the expectations and traditions associated with it. In domestic terms, an example of this type of economic disruption might be the demise of Britain's long-established labour-intensive heavy engineering industries from the 1970s onwards or the import of 'globalisation' and the cyber-enabled international free market. All of these are matters which help to bind the group closer together and increase through consensus awareness of the need to protect their common interests from whoever or whatever might challenge them.

> In the West, material progress is considered a key objective for millions of people that will never be able to achieve it. In this environment, resentment, conflict and violence encounter a fertile ground. It is in the world of scarcity and limited resources that democracy, solidarity and freedom are in danger of being replaced by authoritarian politics. This brand of politics is almost invariably eager to point out those regarded as different as responsible for society's ills: an easy scapegoat attacked under the [pretext] that it will save and protect the community (Guibernau, *supra*).

It could be therefore that shades of europhobia, however pale these may be, comprised, for some at least, an integral element of 'Britishness' and part of the ideological justification for what may be seen as a 'last stand' against the forces of free-market globalisation, free movement of labour and modern technology which, many appear to feel, have the perceived potential to dilute them.

'Euroscepticism'

At least in the modern debate, and as indicated above, the attitudes and beliefs associated with euroscepticism tend to be related to the organisation known currently as the European Union and to its perceived failings rather than any general lack of affinity with the nations and peoples of Europe themselves. A good many of these beliefs and concerns have been referred to already in explaining the development of the EC/EU and the attitudes of British governments towards it. Suffice it, therefore, for present purposes, to draw together and catalogue these without rehearsing what has gone before:

- fear of further dilution of national sovereignty;
- apprehension concerning the effects of the free movement of workers and the influx of people from the eastern European states following the EU expansions of 2004 and 2007;
- the extension of the EU's competencies beyond those relating primarily to trade, industry, commerce, agriculture and fishing, i.e. those of the original 'Common Market';
- the perception of an EU governed by a 'disconnected' idealistic élite, out of touch with those feeling excluded from the alleged benefits of the global and European economic systems;
- increased lack of trust in national and European authorities and institutions following the banking and financial crises of 2007–08;
- association of the EU and its adherents with the policies of austerity and the reduction of public services;
- the weakness of some member states' economies and the cost of related financial 'bailouts';
- the perception of the EU institutions as being undemocratic and beyond the control of national governments;
- increased regulation by EU laws having 'direct effect' within member states;
- the attempt to introduce an EU 'Constitution' with a President, Foreign Minister, national anthem and flag;
- proposed movement for the creation of a common defence force;
- the creation of a common European currency;
- the amount of the British contribution towards the EU budget and the allocation of large parts of this to the Common Agricultural Policy ('CAP');
- free access of European fishing fleets to British waters and fishing grounds.

The road to the referendum of 2016

Amongst the UK's principal parliamentary political parties, only the Liberal Democrats, previously the Liberal party, has remained constant in its commitment to membership of the European Community and, later, the European Union. In contrast, the attitudes of both of the nation's two other leading political parties, or at least significant elements within them, have, at different times, wavered between commitment, indifference and open disillusionment.

As a broad generalisation, their policy approach to the European question has evolved in opposite directions. Hence, the Conservative direction of travel has been from largely qualified support for the European venture in the late 1950s and throughout the 1960s and 1970s, to widespread scepticism in the 1980s and onwards. During this same period, the Labour party has taken a rather different route, beginning with opposition to membership in the 1950s, a general but by no means overly-enthusiastic move towards membership in the 1960s and 1970s, back to opposition in the early 1980s but, from the middle of that decade onwards, generally commitment to a pro-European stance.

It was, of course, the Conservative government of Harold Macmillan who made the first formal, but unsuccessful, application for EC membership (this in 1962) and a subsequent Conservative Prime Minister, Edward Heath, who signed the 1972 Treaty of Accession, taking the UK into the European Community in January 1973.

Mr Heath is often said to have been the most 'pro-European' leader the Conservative party ever had. Under Mrs Thatcher, however, the general party mood began to change – although at no stage did it reach the point of favouring withdrawal. The particular causes of growing unease in this period in relation to European matters have been said to have included the following:

- a sense that the hoped for economic benefits of EC membership, for the UK at least, had not been realised to the extent anticipated;
- the level of support amongst other member states for greater political European political and economic integration – including progress towards the common currency.

The premiership of the last Conservative leader and Prime Minister of the twentieth century, Mr John Major, in office 1990–97, was particularly beset by party in-fighting over the UK's EU membership.

In 1992, Mr Major signed the Maastricht Treaty on behalf of the nation. This created the European Union with its greatly enhanced political, social and economic objectives including unequivocal commitment towards introducing a European currency, the development of common policies in relation to foreign affairs, security, home affairs and justice and the devolution of greater powers to the EU's institutions of government. In the House of Commons, a key vote to ratify the Treaty was tied, 317 for the government and 317 against. By convention, the Speaker's vote was then cast for the government side. Mr Major then made his support for the Maastricht Treaty a matter of confidence in his government and initiated a second vote a few days later. On this occasion the voting was 339 for the government and 299 against.

In this way the government survived. These events did, however, serve to illustrate the depth of divisions in the Conservative parliamentary party in matters European and the lengths to which some elements within the party were prepared to go in order to press home their point of view.

Mr Major's government was not so fortunate in the General Election of 1997 in which Mr Blair's 'New' Labour party was victorious. As ever, while there was a variety of reasons for this, most political commentators and analysts agree that the public perception of a divided party did little to improve Mr Major's electoral chances.

Following defeat in the 1997 election, the Conservative party was in opposition for the next thirteen years. The leaders of the party in this period were William Hague (in office 1997–2001), Iain Duncan Smith (2001–03), Michael Howard (2003–05) and David Cameron (in office as Leader of the Opposition, 2005–10).

None of those amongst Messrs Hague, Duncan-Smith and Howard could have been described as overly-enthusiastic proponents of the European Union's workings or of its developmental ambitions. This notwithstanding, however, none went to the point of advocating complete British withdrawal – being content instead to argue against any further extensions of the Union's competences and powers.

Mr Hague's general sentiments towards the EU were evident in a speech made in 2001:

> We're the fourth largest economy in the world. We're the fourth military power on earth. We're one of the five permanent members of the United Nations Security Council, one of the 'Group of Eight' industrial nations, we have unparalleled links with the United States, the Commonwealth and the rest of the English speaking world. How much bigger do we have to be before we're able to run our own affairs in our own interests? And don't let anyone tell you that believing in an independent Britain is anti-European or xenophobic. We are a European country. But we can never be only a European country. We are tied by our history to other continents. British people throughout the ages have settled across the seas. It's not we who are isolationists; it's those who want to lock our country into a European bloc (Election rally, Stoneleigh, Warwickshire, 16 May 2001).

An assessment of Mr Hague's European stance by a contemporary political commentator was:

> Thus by the end of 1999, Mr Hague had established the most eurosceptic policy since 1990 ironically aligning the Conservative party with the profound resentment of further European integration which precipitated Mrs Thatcher's downfall. Mr Hague has broken with the policy of the Major years [and] has thus overturned the precedent of approval for the Treaty of Rome, the Single European Act, and the Maastricht Treaty of the European Union (Homes, 'William Hague's European policy', Bruges Group, 40).

The principal immediate causes of continual and growing unease towards Europe within the Conservative parliamentary party during this time when the party was out of office, and which certainly troubled the leaderships of Mr Hague's immediate successors, could perhaps be summarised as follows:

- the introduction of the European common currency ('Euro') and 'Eurozone' in 2002;
- the proposed adoption of a European Constitution;
- the EU enlargements of 2004 and 2007;
- further increases in the powers of EU institutions, particularly those of the Parliament and of the Council of the European Union (previously Council of Ministers), effected by the Treaties of Nice (2001) and Lisbon (2007).

From the time a Common European currency was first formally promulgated in the Maastricht Treaty, the Conservative party was firmly opposed to giving up the pound sterling and permitting this to be replaced by what became known as the 'Euro'. Certainly, for all of the Conservative leaders, both in terms of political and economic sovereignty, this was a step too far and a major piece of the essential economic underpinning for what they perceived to be the foundations of a European federal state.

> Joining the Euro is not just an economic decision. It is also about democracy. If key decisions about our interest rates, our exchange rates and our tax rates were made abroad, by people over whom we have no direct control, the electoral process would be diminished. Parties would still frame their policies. Candidates would still wear rosettes. But general elections would no longer mean what they do today. So I am not choosing my words lightly when I say that this could be the last election of its kind. The last time that the people of the United Kingdom are able to elect a Parliament which is supreme in this country (William Hague, Conservative party election rally, Brighton, 29 May 2001).

As explained above (see Chapter 4, p. 93), the decision to formulate a European Constitution was taken at the Nice Intergovernmental Conference (IGC) of 2000. The eventual draft was the work of a European Convention of all member states chaired by former French President, Valéry Giscard d'Estaing. Its symbolic and, indeed, emotional significance for opponents of further EU integration cannot be underestimated. Amongst other things, the proposed Constitution made provision for:

- an EU President;
- an EU Minister of Foreign Affairs;
- an EU national anthem;
- an EU flag.

Whatever the thoughts about the proposed EU flag, for some, these ideas were like a red rag to a bull in terms of the EU's suspected direction of travel.

It fell to Iain Duncan-Smith, Mr Hague's immediate successor as Conservative leader, to give the party's overall view on this latest EU development:

> A constitution for the EU would mean that no individual nation would be able to alter the highest laws by which it is governed. It would put the making of those laws beyond nations . . . The constitution will change the European Union from being the biggest partnership of democracies in the world to an increasingly centralised and unaccountable political union. In short, a unique power, with its own constitution and supremacy over our national laws. For too long, the supranationalist agenda of the Old European mindset has been masked. That time is passed. What was once concealed is now revealed. A constitution that would lead inescapably to even more power being transferred to Brussels . . . A blueprint for a United States of Europe in all but name. One president. One currency. And now one constitution . . . An EU Constitution would thwart the will of the peoples of Europe and over-rule their national Parliaments. That's why the Conservative party's opposition to the adoption of a European constitution is a matter of principle (Prague, 10 July 2003).

The 2004 enlargement increased the size of the EU from 15 to 27 members. It was the most extensive single expansion of the organisation both up to this time and to the present. It is unlikely that many of those who were responsible for it were or, indeed, could have been aware of the extent of the movement of peoples from the east to western Europe or of the economic, social and, in time, seismic political consequences this would have for the entire European project.

In the years that immediately followed the 2004 enlargement and the admissions to membership of Bulgaria and Romania in 2007, it has been estimated that in the region of 12 million people took advantage of EU citizen status to move to the more prosperous economies of the western EU states.

At the time, the pre-existing 15 member states were allowed to opt for transitional periods of up to seven years before giving full effect to the EU requirements (i.e. free movement of workers) in relation to the nationals of the new EU states. Twelve took advantage of this and imposed limitations on the numbers that could be accepted. Three, including the UK, did not.

During the time these developments were unfolding, the leadership of the Conservative party passed from Iain Duncan-Smith to Michael Howard, a former Home Secretary, Secretary of State for the Environment, and Secretary of State for Employment in the governments of John Major. There is no detailed record of Mr Howard's then contemporary views concerning the long-term impact of the process of EU enlargement and perhaps, like most, he could not have been expected to have envisaged just how potentially significant this development would turn out to be. Accordingly Mr Howard's sentiments on matters European tended to be concerned with his party's long-standing unease relating to further European integration in general and to the implications of this for national sovereignty.

Europe isn't working properly today . . . The EU is spewing out too many regulations. It's holding our economy back . . . The British people don't want to be part of a European super-state. But other European governments are determined to press ahead with ever closer integration . . . But we must have something in return. We want to bring powers back from Brussels . . . It is not enough to say 'no' to the Euro, but a Conservative government will. It's time we went further. We want out of the Social Chapter, which is a threat to British jobs. We want out of the common agricultural policy, which is destroying communities . . . It's time to bring powers back to Britain (Speech to Conservative party conference, Bournemouth, 15 September 2004).

In 2005, the Conservative party suffered its third successive electoral defeat in eight years. Yet another change of leadership followed when the position of Leader of the Opposition passed from Michael Howard to David Cameron.

Just two years later, in 2007, the political and economic stability of the United Kingdom was seriously imperilled by an event having little to do directly with the activities of the EU. This was the international financial crisis precipitated initially by the 'collapse' of a major American investment bank (Lehman Brothers).

The bank had 'over-extended' its lending facilities in the 'sub-prime' mortgage market, i.e. it had allowed too large a proportion of its financial capital to be loaned to persons and organisations whose ability to repay could not be safely guaranteed. The bank had \$639bn in assets and \$613bn in debts and was unable to continue trading.

In the immediate aftermath of this, other leading financial houses on either side of the Atlantic were found to be in similarly weak positions in terms of the capital left available to them. The spectre loomed of an international banking failure on a scale of the Great Depression of the late 1920s and early 1930s. To avoid this, national governments all over the world were obliged to dig deep into their national finances to ensure that their banking systems had sufficient liquidity in order to continue providing essential financial and commercial services. The cost of this to the British government was estimated to have been £50bn. In the United States it was even greater, in the region of \$236bn.

It was the year neo-liberal economic orthodoxy that ran the world for thirty years suffered a heart attack of epic proportions. Not since 1929 has the financial community witnessed twelve months like it. Lehman Brothers went bankrupt. Merrill Lynch, AIG, Freddie Mac, Fannie Mae, HBOS, Royal Bank of Scotland, Bradford and Bingley, Fortis, Hypo, Alliance and Leicester all came within a whisker of doing so and had to be rescued (Nick Mathiason, *Guardian*, 28 December 2008).

While it is not possible to argue that the 2008 financial crisis was precipitated in any direct or immediate way by the policies of the European Union, it was still perceived by many as yet another indication that both the European and global economic systems, and the monetary ideologies on which they were based, could not be relied upon to guarantee the financial stability, prosperity and general all-round probity in the distribution of wealth which had been promised.

For many of those on the 'receiving end' of all this, the immediate consequences included 'cutbacks', loss of job opportunities in both the public and private sectors, wage stagnation, and reductions in public services and in the welfare state. This was allied with a growing sentiment that, faced with the increasing power of remote, disconnected and uncaring international economic forces and entities, 'ordinary' people were losing all meaningful control over their destinies.

Regardless of who was or was not to blame, the seeds of discontent had been sown.

From the beginning of his time in office as Conservative leader, David Cameron, like Messrs Major, Hague, Duncan-Smith and Howard before him, had little choice but to formulate a European policy which had some reasonable possibility of holding his party together and thereby keeping alive its ambition of being returned to power. To do so, he offered his party and the wider electorate a mixture of moderate euroscepticism, continued rejection of any greater European integration, all reinforced with promises of referendums on any future proposals for increases in the powers of the European Union's governing institutions.

> We believe in being members of the European Union but we want it to be more about trade and cooperation rather than the endless process of building a European superstate. (Cameron, Conservative Party Conference, Birmingham, 8 September 2009)
>
> A Conservative government with the first Queen's speech will pass a Bill through Parliament that says any time a government wants to pass powers from Westminster to Brussels can't do it without holding a referendum (Cameron, election rally, Chiswick, 12 April 2010).

The General Election of 2010 produced a 'hung' Parliament. Out of this emerged a coalition government headed by David Cameron and supported by 307 Conservative MPs, many of whom had fundamental misgivings about the European Union's direction of travel, and by the 59 MPs of the parliamentary Liberal Democratic party, all broadly content with it.

Thus constrained by his pro-European coalition partners, Mr Cameron's freedom of manoeuvre on the European question was severely limited.

His position vis-à-vis his own party was not an easy one and was further complicated by two factors which had not pressed so immediately on his predecessors. The first of these was that the 2010 election had propelled a new, younger and more eurosceptic element into the ranks of the parliamentary Conservative party. The second was the rise of the United Kingdom Independence Party.

In 2013, and to allay continued and heightened tensions within the Conservative party, Mr Cameron made what appeared to be a bold move. This was to promise a 'once and for all' 'in–out' referendum on membership of the European Union to be held before the end of 2017 should his party be returned to power, with an overall Commons majority, at the next general election.

> Simply asking the British people to carry on accepting a European settlement over which they have had little choice is a path to ensuring that when the question is finally put – and at some stage it will have to be – it is much more likely that the British people will reject the EU. That is why I am in favour of a referendum. I believe in confronting this issue . . . not simply hoping a difficult situation will go away (Cameron, 'The Bloomberg speech', London, 23 January 2013).

Amongst contemporary political commentators the prevailing view was that Mr Cameron and his supporters genuinely believed that, when the question was finally and unequivocally put to them, few among the broader British electorate would want to take the dramatic step of requiring the government to take the UK out of the European Union altogether.

The preponderance of public opinion polls and other forecasts for the General Election of 2015 suggested the outcome would be another hung Parliament. In the event, however, Mr Cameron's hopes were vindicated when his party gained the required Commons majority to form a Conservative administration. In the matter of the promised EU referendum, Mr Cameron announced that this would be held after negotiations between the EU and British government at which stage voters would be given a clear choice between leaving the European Union altogether or remaining within it as part of 'a new settlement subject to the democratic legitimacy and accountability of national parliaments where Member States combine in flexible cooperation, respecting national differences, not always trying to eliminate them, and in which we have proved some powers can in fact be returned to Member States' (Cameron, Bloomberg, 21 January 2013).

In February 2016 the long-awaited announcement was made. The referendum was to be held six months later on 23 June. The question to be put to the electorate was:

'Should the United Kingdom remain a member of the European Union or leave the European Union?'

The result was:

Electorate	45,500,001
Votes cast	33,551,983
Leave	17,410,742
Remain	16,141,241
Percentage of vote cast to leave	51.89
Percentage of vote cast to remain	48.10
Percentage of entire electorate voting to leave	38.26
Percentage of entire electorate voting to remain	35.47

The immediate aftermath

It was widely agreed that, in deciding to hold an 'all or nothing' referendum, and given his preference for remaining in the EU, Mr Cameron appeared to have made two major miscalculations. First, he failed to take sufficient account of the historical precedents showing:

(a) the unpredictability of referendums as mechanisms for deciding specific political or constitutional questions; and

(b) that referendum polls are often used by electorates as a means of expressing their views on a variety of issues not directly identified on the ballot paper or simply to register general dissatisfaction with the entirety of the incumbent government's economic and political strategy.

Secondly, neither Mr Cameron nor his advisers appeared to have had any real awareness of the extent of the depth of popular dissatisfaction, particularly in the less prosperous parts of the country far away from London and the south-east, with the workings of the free market neo-liberal economic models of the European and global systems of international trade.

The immediate political and constitutional consequences of the referendum vote were:

- the UK government and Parliament was politically, but not legally, bound to take the United Kingdom out of the European Union;
- until agreement had been reached between the UK and the EU as to how this should be done, and when, the UK would remain a full EU member;
- having led the campaign for continued EU membership, Mr Cameron felt his position as Prime Minister had become fatally compromised and, accordingly, he tendered his resignation to the Queen;
- Theresa May, having been elected on 17 July 2016 to lead the parliamentary Conservative party, was appointed by the Queen as the next Prime Minister.

The process for leaving the European Union

TEU Article 50

The process and procedure by which a member state may leave or 'exit' the EU is contained in the Treaty of the European Union, Article 50. It was inserted thereto by the Treaty of Lisbon 2007. The Article came into force generally in 2009 and was given effect in the United Kingdom by the EEC Act 1972 as amended by the European Union (Amendment) Act 2008.

The normal rule in international law is that a state may not withdraw unilaterally from a treaty unless there has been a fundamental change of circumstances (Vienna Convention on the Law of Treaties 1969, Art 62). It follows that TEU, Art 50 allows an exception to this. The content and requirements are procedural only. In other words these relate to the method, rather than the conditions, for making an application for leaving.

The essential provisions of Article 50 are as follows.

1 Notification of a member state's intention to withdraw from the EU should be submitted to the European Council (para 2). To be effective, any withdrawal agreement reached with the Council must be approved by a 'super qualified majority' i.e. at least 72 per cent of the members of the Council representing at least 65 per cent of the population of the member states (TFEU, Art 238) and only after consent has been given to it by the European Parliament.

2 The process of negotiations 'triggered' by the notification should continue until an agreement is reached up to a maximum period of two years (para 3). The two-year limit is, however, not absolute and may be extended for any specified period by a unanimous vote of all members of the Council (ibid.). This means that should no conclusion to the negotiations be achieved within the two-year period, or within any permitted extension to it, the state exiting the EU would be obliged to leave without an agreement in place as to its future relationship with its previous EU 'partners'. Meetings of the European Council to consider a member state's application to withdraw may be conducted without the presence of the representatives of the state concerned. This restriction would appear not to apply to proceedings of the European Parliament. Hence, although, as stated, the Parliament's consent must be given prior to the Council concluding an Article 50 agreement, MEPs from the exiting state may take part both in any related parliamentary debates and in any vote on the overall acceptability of the agreement.

The rights and duties created by the EU Treaties cease to apply to an exiting state once an Article 50 agreement has been struck and at the date which has been set for this to come into effect whether within the two-year period or any extension of it. Where no such agreement has been reached, rights emanating from the EU Treaties cease to have effect after the period set for negotiations, whether extended or not, has expired.

An agreement to withdraw from the EU is an international agreement and is, therefore, subject to judicial review by the Court of Justice of the European Union and could be challenged before the court through an action for annulment (lack of competence, infringement of an essential procedural requirement, infringement of the treaties, infringement of any rule of law relating to their application, or any other misuse of power; TFEU, Art 263). The validity of any such agreement may also be referred by any member state for a CJEU opinion.

Article 50 is silent as to the question of whether a withdrawal application once made may be withdrawn or not continued with.

A state which leaves the EU according to Article 50 is not precluded from rejoining at some later date but is required to do so by the process contained in Article 49. This is the normal procedure for any state seeking EU membership whether for the first time or not.

Brexit and the judicial process

Miller's application in the High Court

Background

As an immediate consequence of the referendum result, it was announced that the British government would submit notice of the UK's intent to withdraw from the EU by the end of March 2017 and that it would do so without reference to Parliament under the authority of the royal prerogative in foreign affairs. From this arose the legal proceedings in *R (on application of Miller and Dos Santos)* v *Minister of State for Exiting the European Union* [2016] EWHC 2768 (Admin)).

Facts and findings

The broad thrust of the complaint in *Miller* was that any such use of the prerogative to activate Article 50 would be both illegal, in the sense of an abuse of prerogative power, and would be unconstitutional, as being in breach of those long-established constitutional rules governing the relationship between Parliament and the executive and in which Parliament was to be regarded as the sovereign or ultimate legal and political authority within the state.

The case was, therefore, not concerned with the legality or wider political or economic implications of the referendum vote itself, or with the question of whether that decision should be implemented – that being purely a political matter. It follows that all media, political, or popular assertions to the contrary were, and are, incorrect.

The claimants presented five main contentions. All of these were accepted by the court.

1 It is a fundamental principle of the UK constitution that the Crown's prerogative powers cannot be used by the executive government to diminish or abrogate rights under the law of the United Kingdom (whether conferred by common law or statute), unless Parliament expressly or by necessary implication has given authority to the Crown to do so, in an Act of Parliament.

> The King by his proclamation or other ways cannot change any part of the common law, or statute law, or the customs of the realm (Coke CJ, *Case of the Proclamations* (1610) 12 Co, Rep.74).

2 Rights emanating from EU treaties and taking effect in the United Kingdom under the provisions of EC Act 1972, section 2, become part of domestic law and were, therefore, subject to the *Proclamations* principle.

> In our judgment, the clear and necessary implication from these provisions taken separately and cumulatively is that Parliament intended EU rights to have effect in domestic law and this effect should not be capable of being undone or overridden by action taken by the Crown in exercise of its prerogative powers.

3 No words could be found under which Parliament had given any such authority expressly or by necessary implication in the 1972 Act itself or in subsequent legislation relating to the European Union.

> The wide and profound extent of the legal changes in domestic law created by the EC Act 1972 makes it especially unlikely that Parliament intended to leave their continued existence in the hands of the Crown through the exercise of its prerogative powers. Parliament having taken

the major step of switching on the direct effect of EU law in the national legal system by passing the EC Act 1972 as primary legislation, it is not plausible to suppose that it intended the Crown should be able by its own unilateral action under its prerogative to switch it off again.

4   The giving of notice to leave the EU under TEU, Article 50 would directly affect any ability of Parliament to decide on which such rights should be retained, abrogated, or altered.

> Once a notice is given, it will inevitably result in the complete withdrawal of the UK from membership of the European Union . . . The effect of giving notice under Article 50 on relevant rights is direct, even though the Article 50 process will take a while to be worked through. Since the Crown will negotiate the terms of any withdrawal agreement, this means that the Crown is entitled to pick and choose which existing EU rights, if any, to preserve . . . and which to remove. Again, therefore, the effect of the Article negotiation process on relevant rights is direct.

5   No authority for the Crown to give notice of withdrawal from the EU under Article 50 could be found in the Referendum Act 2015.

> The Secretary of State's case regarding his ability to give notice under Article 50 was based squarely on the Crown's prerogative power. His counsel made it clear that he does not intend that the 2015 Referendum Act supplied a statutory power for the Crown to give notice under Article 50. He is right not to do so. Any argument to that effect would have been untenable as a matter of statutory interpretation of the 2015 Referendum Act.

Miller in the Supreme Court

Introduction and preliminary issues

The case was heard by all eleven Supreme Court Justices. Eight of these decided for the applicant and three against.

Before embarking on consideration of the main substantive issues raised by the case, the Court set about laying the ground by disposing of three preliminary, but nonetheless important, issues. These were:

(a) What, precisely, had the Court been asked to adjudicate upon?

(b) Was the subject matter of the case 'justiciable', i.e. did it raise issues which judges were not qualified or competent to pronounce upon?

(c) Could a TEU, Article 50 notice of intention to leave the European Union be withdrawn or made conditional on some future event occurring or not occurring prior to any exit agreement being reached?

The question to be answered

This was dealt with clearly and succinctly in the second paragraph of the Court's judgment.

> The question before this Court concerns the steps which are required as a matter of UK domestic law before the process of leaving the European Union can be initiated. The particular issue is whether a formal notice of withdrawal can lawfully be given by Ministers without prior legislation passed in both Houses of Parliament and assented to by HM the Queen.

Was this justiciable?

The Court emphasised that its proper remit was to consider questions of law and to determine the meaning and requirement of any legal and constitutional principles applicable to the case before it. It was not concerned with, nor would it be constitutionally acceptable, for it to be drawn into the sphere of political argument.

It is worth emphasising that nobody has suggested that this is an inappropriate issue for the Courts to determine. It is also worth emphasising that this case has nothing to do with issues such as the wisdom of the decision to withdraw from the European Union, the terms of withdrawal, the time-table or arrangements for withdrawal, or the details of any future relationship with the European Union. These are all political issues which are matters for Ministers and Parliament to resolve.

Was an Article 50 notice revocable?

The Court did not go into this question in any great detail. As with the High Court, it was 'content' to proceed on the basis that 'a notice under Article 50 cannot be given in qualified or conditional terms and that, once given, it cannot be withdrawn'.

The main issues

For the Court, the case turned on a series of key questions. These were:

(a) Could the prerogative in foreign affairs, including the power to negotiate treaties, be used to initiate a process which would inevitably abrogate, curtail or alter either domestic law or pre-existing legal rights?

(b) Could the authority of the royal prerogative be relied upon to give power to the executive government to effect major changes in British constitutional arrangements?

(c) Could the EC Act 1972 be interpreted as allowing the executive to initiate the process of withdrawing from the EU without further specific legislative authority?

(d) Could any authority to issue notification to withdraw from the EU be found in EU (Amendment) Acts 2008 and 2011?

(e) Could the authority to negate domestic legal rights be supplied retrospectively by the Great Repeal Bill?

(f) What, if any, was the legal effect of the referendum?

(g) Could the Article 50 withdrawal process be activated without the consent of the devolved assemblies in Northern Ireland, Scotland and Wales?

The Court's findings

The extent of the foreign affairs prerogative

Except in two very limited circumstances (see below), the prerogative in foreign affairs did not extend to the alteration of law or rights at the domestic level.

> As a matter of constitutional law of the United Kingdom, the royal prerogative, whilst it embraces the making of treaties, does not extend to altering the law or conferring rights upon individuals which they enjoy in domestic law without the intervention of Parliament (*dicta* of Lord Oliver in **Higgs v Minister of National Security** [2000] 2 AC 228, approved).

Accordingly, in the instant case, the rule prohibiting the government's proposed use of the foreign affairs prerogative would be applicable providing the service of notice of withdrawal would affect what could be described as 'domestic law' or the 'law of the land' and that such effects would extend to alteration or abrogation of that law or rights given by it.

As to the first of these issues the Court's view was:

> The 1972 Act provided that rights, duties and rules derived from EU law should apply in the United Kingdom as part of its domestic law . . . So long as the 1972 Act remains in force, its effect is to constitute EU law as an independent and overriding source of domestic law.

The Court was satisfied also that the direct and inevitable result of that formal notification of intent to withdraw from the EU would be the abrogation and curtailment of large parts of that law. Examples of the types of rights affected were given:

(i) Rights derived from EU law which would cease to apply in the UK unless 'replicated' by Parliament. These would include 'the rights of EU citizens to the benefits of employment protection . . . to equal treatment, to the protection of EU competition law and the rights of non-residents to the benefits of the 'four freedoms' (free movement of labour, goods and capital, and freedom to provide services).'

(ii) Rights of participation in the electoral processes of the EU, to stand for and become a member of the EU Parliament, and to petition EU institutions for the relief of grievances – none of which Parliament had any jurisdiction or authority to deal with.

The two remaining circumstances in which executive action without statutory backing may lawfully affect legal rights are:

(i) use of the prerogative relating to the management of the civil service;

(ii) use of the emergency prerogatives and application of the crime of treason and related offences following a declaration of war.

The prerogative and major constitutional change

The Court was prepared to concede that the foreign affairs prerogative might be used by the UK government to negotiate treaties and changes to EU law from within the Union as a participating member and that in so doing were 'carrying out the very functions which were envisaged by Parliament when enacting the 1972 Act'. This, it felt, however, fell far short of recognising a principle that the prerogative could be relied upon as giving Ministers the authority to take those steps required to negotiate the UK's withdrawal from its treaty obligations and consequent complete disapplication of EU law as a major source of law in the domestic legal system.

> Withdrawal is fundamentally different from variations in the content of EU law arising from further EU treaties or legislation. A complete withdrawal represents a change which is different not just in degree but in kind from the abrogation of particular rights, duties or rules derived from EU law. It will constitute as significant a constitutional change as that which was incurred when the law was first incorporated into domestic law by the 1972 Act. And, if notice is given, the change will occur irrespective of whether Parliament repeals the 1972 Act. It would be inconsistent with long-standing and fundamental principles for such far-reaching change to the UK constitutional arrangements to be brought about by ministerial action or ministerial decision alone.

The process of EU withdrawal and the EC Act 1972

In this matter the Court gave the unequivocal answer that, had Parliament intended the 1972 Act to leave in place, or to provide an executive power to initiate the process of leaving the EU and, by so doing, precipitate a change of such magnitude, it would have done so by clear words or intent and not have left this to legal argument and judicial interpretation.

> Had the Bill which became the 1972 Act spelled out that Ministers would be free to withdraw the United Kingdom from the EU treaties, the implications of what Parliament was being asked to endorse would have been clear, and the court would have so decided. But we take the legislation as it is and we cannot accept that in the 1972 Act, Parliament squarely confronted the notion that it was clothing Ministers with the far-reaching and anomalous right to use a treaty-making power to remove an important source of domestic law and important domestic rights.

The EU (Amendment) Acts 2008 and 2011

TEU, Article 50 was intended to operate on the international plain only and was not, therefore, brought into UK law through section 2 of the 1972 Act. Accordingly no domestic legal authority to withdraw from EU treaty obligations could be derived from it. Nor was there anything in the statutes enacted since Article 50 was incorporated into such treaties (viz., EU Amendment Acts 2008 and 2011) to support the contention that these could be interpreted as recognising the existence of a prerogative power to withdraw from the EU treaties 'unconstrained by parliamentary consent'.

The authority for EU withdrawal and the Great Repeal Bill

Short shrift was given to the notion that authority for the extinction of domestic legal rights could be drawn from a proposed piece of legislation to be enacted at some indeterminate date in the future. By such time, the Court pointed out, it would be too late. At that stage the withdrawal treaty, with all it's implications for the domestic law of England and Wales, would have been formulated and agreed.

> If Ministers give Notice without Parliament having first authorised them to do it, the die will be cast before Parliament has become formally involved . . . The bullet will have left the gun before Parliament has accorded the necessary leave for the trigger to be pulled. The very fact that Parliament will have to pass legislation once the Notice is served and hits the target highlights the point that the giving of Notice will change domestic law: otherwise there would be no need for new legislation.

Authority to commence withdrawal from the EU and the referendum of 2016

The process of legal reasoning chosen by the Court to deal with this aspect of the case was, in essence, little different from that already relied upon to dispose of the other matters raised, i.e. the legal consequences of a referendum, whatever the subject matter, were limited to those stipulated by Parliament in the enabling legislation. In other words, for legal purposes, it was, once again, a question of parliamentary intent.

> The effect of any particular referendum must depend on the terms of the statute which authorises it. Further, legislation authorising a referendum more often than not has provided for the consequences on the result. Thus, the authorising statute may enact a change in the law subject to the proviso that it is not to come into effect unless approved by a majority in the referendum. Thus the referendum of 2016 did not change the law in a way which would allow Ministers to withdraw the United Kingdom from the European Union without legislation.

It follows that, where a statute which enables a referendum to be held, makes no mention of the consequences which should follow from it, depending on the result, the effect of the vote is advisory only and operates purely in the sphere of politics.

The Court thus made clear that while political sovereignty, or ultimate political authority, may be with the people, sovereignty, in the sense of the overriding power to make decisions having binding legal consequences, remains with the 'Queen in Parliament, viz. Commons, Lords and Monarch.

EU withdrawal and the role of the devolved assemblies

It was accepted amongst all parties to the case that notice of withdrawal from the EU would have a direct effect on the legislative competences of the devolved assemblies of Northern Ireland, Scotland and Wales. This was particularly so, as notification would lead inevitably to the requirement in the enactments by which these assemblies established (see above, Chapter 2, p. 30) i.e. that their powers should be exercised in accordance with the law of the European Union, being rendered meaningless. It was accepted also that, according to the Sewel Convention, any such move or transgression upon the devolved assemblies' sphere of legislative authority should be preceded by the voting of a 'Legislative Consent Motion' by whichever assembly or assemblies might be affected.

Here again, the Court showed awareness that it could not allow its decision to be influenced by overtly political considerations and that it was bound, therefore, to apply the long-established rule that, while constitutional conventions might articulate normative political practice, such 'rules' were not legally enforceable and, therefore, were not matters on which a court of law could adjudicate or pronounce. It was, therefore, not open to the Court to insist that the convention be complied with.

> It is well established that the courts of law cannot enforce a political convention . . . While the UK government and the devolved executives have agreed the mechanisms for implementing the convention . . . convention operates as a political restriction on the activity of the UK Parliament. Article 9 of the Bill of Rights which provides that 'proceedings in Parliament ought not to be impeached or questioned in any court or place outside of Parliament' provides a further reason why the courts cannot adjudicate on the operation of this convention. Judges are, therefore, neither the parents nor the guardians of political conventions, they are merely observers. As such they can recognise the operation of a political convention in the context of deciding a legal question . . . but they cannot give legal rulings on its operation or scope, because these matters are determined within the political world.

Other findings relating to the role of the assemblies in the 'Brexit' process were:

(i)   The devolved legislatures do not have a parallel legislative competence in relation to withdrawal from the European Union.

(ii) The Belfast Agreement gave the people of Northern Ireland the right to determine whether to remain part of the United Kingdom or to become part of a United Ireland. It neither regulated any other change in the constitutional status of Northern Ireland nor required the consent of a majority of the people of Northern Ireland to withdrawal of the United Kingdom from the European Union.

The dissent

- As the 1972 Act did not expressly remove the relevant prerogative, i.e. that to institute proceedings to leave the EU, that executive power was left in place.

- There was no clear basis of legal validity for the view that the 1972 Act left the Crown with the prerogative to negotiate changes to EU treaties but no power to negotiate bringing the effect of those treaties in the UK to an end.

- The 1972 Act, section 2 created a legislative system for enabling EU law to take effect domestically and for withholding that effect from it if and when it was decided to bring the UK's treaty obligations to an end – a matter to be decided at international level under the prerogative. No further legislative action was required, therefore, to bring about that objective.

- Since EU law derived its authority in the UK from the EC Act 1972, it could not be regarded as a distinct and independent source of domestic law. It followed that ceasing to give effect to it, according to the statutory scheme provided, did not involve or require any great change in the UK's constitutional arrangements.

- The EU (Amendment) Act 2008 added the Treaty of Lisbon 2007, which included Article 50, to the list of treaties given effect domestically under the EC Act 1972, section 2(1).

The incorporation of a treaty providing a process for leaving the EU was not incompatible with the scheme in section 2(1) for giving effect to treaty provisions in general. Nor did this evince any indication that the process should not be exercised under the Crown's treaty prerogative.

- Service of an Article 50 notice could not have any immediate effect on, or change, any laws or rights applicable in the domestic regime. It would merely commence the political process or negotiation inherent in the Article's implementation. Although this would be carried out by the executive government, it would be answerable to Parliament for both its conduct and any resulting agreement and this, eventually, would require implementation domestically by an Act of primary legislation.

- It had been argued also that section 2(1) of the 1972 Act had given Article 50 domestic effect 'as a power exercisable by Ministers superseding the prerogative but also supplying the parliamentary authorisation desiderated by the claimants (Lord Reed).

Comment

In the Supreme Court's decision, it is possible to see the UK's most senior judges recognising and applying two of the British Constitution's most fundamental principles, i.e. those of representative democracy and the sovereignty of Parliament. Hence, as it would be impracticable to have a popular vote on all issues, general elections are held every five years through which local representatives are sent to express the popular will in the national Parliament at Westminster. Given that Parliament thus represents the UK's adult electorate, it is vested with ultimate legal and political authority to which all, including the executive government, are subject and answerable.

The case also provides a classic practical example of the independence of the judiciary and its preparedness to apply long-standing legal and constitutional principles notwithstanding the politically weighted wishes of the executive government and the clamour for a particular decision by some sections of the press and media.

At no stage were the judicial deliberations on the case, either in the High Court or the Supreme Court, directed towards the political and economic arguments for the UK leaving or remaining a member of the EU. The sole issue which the court was asked to consider was the process by which the decision to withdraw should be implemented and the extent to which the sovereign body, Parliament, should be involved in this.

The Great Repeal Bill

Main provisions

On 2 October 2016 it was announced that the formal 'Brexit' process for leaving the EU would culminate in the enactment of what was referred to as a 'Great Repeal Bill'. This, if enacted, would come into force once a withdrawal agreement had been formally ratified by the European Union's member states and institutions and, at which time, the UK would cease to be bound by the EU treaties.

The main provisions of the Bill would be to repeal the EU Act 1972 and, in particular:

(a) section 2(1) which enables those rights and obligations created by the EU treaties and all other types of EU law, e.g. regulations, required to be given direct domestic effect, i.e. to come into force without need for further legislative authority;

(b) section 2(2) which provides powers for Ministers, by way of statutory instrument, to give legal force to EU directives and any other EU rules not required to be given direct effect.

The announcement of October 2016, and subsequent statements by government Ministers, made clear also that to avoid the resulting danger of the above repeals creating enormous 'black holes' in the law applicable domestically, the Bill would include provisions:

(i)   giving statutory force and backing to the whole body of EU law already applicable in the UK;

(ii)   giving Ministers wide powers by way of statutory instrument to retain, amend or set aside aspects of that law as thought appropriate;

(iii) to disapply the House of Lords' ruling in the ***Factortame Case*** (see above, Chapter 5, p. 122), which gave EU law primacy over the requirements of Acts of Parliament;

(iv)   to remove the rule recognising the role of the Court of Justice of the European Union as the final arbiter of the requirements of the EU's law and treaties.

Leaving the EU will not affect or require any further legislative action in relation to EU law given domestic effect by statute other than the 1972 EC Act.

Some problems of transition

(a) It will not be possible for the UK to guarantee the continued effect of those legal rights and measures dependent on EU membership, e.g. right to vote for the European Parliament, the benefits of European citizenship, or the law requiring the positive cooperation of remaining EU states, e.g. those underpinning the 'four freedoms'.

(b) Nor will it be possible for the UK to ensure full application of those rules and laws dependent on the involvement of EU agencies, e.g. the European Medicines Agency, which has responsibilities relating to the evaluation of the claimed benefits of medicinal products.

(c) What level of authority should be attached to the past and future decisions of the Court of Justice of the European Union in relation to the meaning of EU law retained by the Bill?

(d) Should the judicial rules of interpretation and statutory construction for retained EU law be those of the CJEU or those traditionally relied upon by British courts?

(e) Should EU legal doctrines, like that of proportionality, continue to retain the status currently ascribed to them generally within English law?

Comment

- The volume of EU law to be transposed into English law is predicted to be enormous – the current estimate being in excess of 50,000 pieces of EU legislation and other rules. Much of this will be highly complex, technical, subject-specific and detailed. The process of sifting through all of this at the level required to ensure the process of domestic regulation is able to continue to work effectively is likely to engage those responsible for a considerable period of time.

- Given the enormity of the process of transposition, it would be impossible to remit it solely to the chamber of the House of Commons. It will be necessary, therefore, to vest Ministers with unprecedented powers to make law and to shape the content and meaning of English law for generations to come. This could diminish the role of Parliament in the legislative process and its reputation as the nation's sovereign legislative authority.

- The repeal or alteration of EU laws relating to the legislative competencies of the devolved assemblies would appear to fall within the ambit of the Sewel Convention thus requiring the consent of the assembly or assemblies affected.

⬤ References

Guibernau (2016) *Understanding Euroscepticism: How British Hostility to the EU Contrasts with Opposition Elsewhere in Europe*, LSE EUROPP, 12.1.16.

Harris (1953) *Strictly Personal*, Washington: Regnery and Co.

Holmes (2001) *William Hague's European Policy*, Bruges Group.

Mathiason (2008) *Three Days that Changed the World*, The Guardian, 28.12.08.

Orwell (1945) *Notes on Nationalism*, London: Polemic.

Parr (2013) *The Significance of the 1967 Application*, UACES Conference Paper, 7–8th March, 2013.

Scherer (2013) *The UK's Opposition to European Integration is Still Framed Around its Past*, LSE, EUROPP, 20,8.13.

Bogdanor (2013) *Britain and the Continent*, Gresham College Lecture Transcript, 17.9.13.

Bogdanor (2013) *From the European Coal and Steel Community to the Common Market*, Gresham College Lecture Transcript, 12.11.13.

Bogdanor (2014) *The Decision to Seek Entry to the European Community*, Gresham College Lecture Transcript, 14.1.14.

Bogdanor (2014) *Entry into the European Community*, Gresham College Lecture Transcript, 14.3.14.

Bogdanor (2014) *The Referendum on Europe 1975*, Gresham College Lecture Transcript, 15.4.14.

Bogdanor (2014) *The Growth of Euroscepticism*, Gresham College Lecture Transcript, 20.5.14.

Butler and Kitzinger (1976) *The 1975 Referendum*, London: Macmillan.

Craig (2017) **Miller**: *Supreme Court Case Summary*, UK Constitutional Law Association, https://ukconstitutionallaw.org/2017/01/26

Danzig (2013) *Winston Churchill: A Founder of the European Union*, https://eu-rope.ideasoneurope.eu/2013/11/10

Douglas-Scott (2016) *Brexit Article 50 and the Contested British Constitution*, MLR, 21.11.16.

Kenealy (2016) *How Did We Get Here? A Brief History of Britain's Membership of the EU*, https://www.europeanfutures.ed.ac.uk/article3278

Kasanta (2015) *British Euroscepticism*, London: Bruges Group

La Roux (2016) *The EU Referendum and the Paradoxes of Democratic Legitimacy*, https://blogs.lse.ac.uk/politicsandpolicy

House of Commons Library (2016) *Brexit: Some Legal and Constitutional Issues and Alternatives to EU Membership*, Briefing Paper No 07214, 28.7.16.

House of Commons Library (2016) *Brexit: How Does the Article 50 Process Work*, Briefing Paper No 7551, 30.6.16.

House of Commons Library (2016) *Article 50 and the EU Constitution*, Briefing Paper No 7763, 14.11.16.

House of Lords Constitution Committee (2016) *The invoking of Article 50*, 4th Report, 2016–17, HL44.

House of Lords Library Note (2016) *Leaving the EU: Parliament's Role in the Process*, LLM 2016/034

Ludlow (2016) *When Britain first Applied to Join the EU: What Can MacMillan's Predicament Teach Us*, http://blogs.lse.ac.uk.brexit/2016.04/15

Parr (2013) *The Significance of the 1967 Application*, UACES Conferences, *Treaty Years Since the First Enlargement*, Draft Paper, 7–8 March, 2013.

Sked (2015) *Why Britain Really Joined the EEC*, LSE BREXIT, https://blogs,lse,ac.uk/brexit.2015.11/26

Glossary

ab initio from the outset or from the beginning.

absolute privilege the complete legal immunity given to certain types of speech, e.g. words spoken in judicial or parliamentary proceedings.

absolute right one that permits of no exceptions or modifications to accommodate other interests, e.g. ECHR Art 3, prohibition of torture.

abuse of process use of a judicial procedure for a purpose for which it was not designed.

actio popularis literally 'popular action', used to refer to legal proceedings against a government authority commenced by an individual whose grievance is no greater than other members of the general public.

ad hoc random.

adjournment debate parliamentary debate held at the end of the day's proceedings.

Admin LR Administrative Law Reports.

administrative body government institution, usually created by statute, with responsibility for provision and running of a particular public service or function.

administrative discretion freedom to make choices about how government powers should be exercised, usually on the basis of financial, political and other public policy considerations.

administrative law the law, processes and procedures through which the powers of government are regulated and controlled.

affidavit written statement, usually for legal purposes, sworn under oath.

Alec Douglas-Home Conservative Prime Minister 1963–4.

All ER All England Law Reports.

amendment change made to an existing or proposed legislative provision.

Anthony Eden Conservative Prime Minister 1955–7.

App Cas nineteenth-century reference for law reports of courts of appeal.

aristocracy members of the social, propertied élite often possessing hereditary titles.

arrest the act of taking a person into state custody usually on suspicion of the commission of offences.

arrestable offence concept introduced by the Police and Criminal Evidence Act 1984 and abolished by the Serious Organised Crime and Police Act 2005 referring to an offence punishable by five years' imprisonment or more or for which the sentence was fixed by law, e.g. life for murder.

Art Article.

Attorney-General government's senior law officer and adviser on the legal implications of policy decisions.

Audit Commission public body created in 1992 responsible for auditing accounts of local authorities.

autocracy government by one or a limited number of persons.

backbench MP Member of Parliament who is neither a Member of the government nor one of the spokespersons of the parties of opposition and who, therefore, sits in one of the rear seats in the chamber.

bailiff person possessed of legal authority to enforce the judgments of a civil court.

Bench alternative term for a group of judges or magistrates convened to decide a particular case.

bias in the context of administrative law, favouring or disfavouring one of the parties to a decision or being prejudiced as to the outcome of a decision-making process.

Bill of Rights 1689 founding constitutional document which radically reduced the prerogative powers of the Monarch, introduced by Parliament following the overthrow of James II in 1688.

blasphemy scurrilous verbal attack on an established religious faith.

British Commonwealth the society of former British colonies which recognise the British Monarch as Head of State or Head of the Commonwealth.

Brussels capital city of Belgium and seat of the principal institutions of the European Union.

Budget the government's taxing proposals for the coming financial year.

bureaucracy process or machinery of public administration.

by-election a parliamentary election conducted in a single constituency, usually in between General Elections, and for the purpose of filling a particular parliamentary seat after the death or demise of a sitting MP.

CA Court of Appeal.

Cabinet the group of senior Ministers who meet with the Prime Minister on a weekly basis to determine government policy.

Cabinet Committee group of Ministers and civil servants who provide the full Cabinet with policy analyses, projections and proposals.

certainty principle requiring laws to be sufficiently clear and precise as to allow those affected by them to adjust their behaviour to a degree which ensures sufficient compliance.

certiorari or **quashing order** court order quashing an illegal decision of a public body.

cf. compare with.

Ch Chancery.

Chancellor of the Exchequer the senior Cabinet Minister responsible for economic policy.

Charles I King, 1625–49, executed at the end of the Civil War.

Chief Constable chief officer of a county or metropolitan police force outside London.

circuit judge judge in County Court or Crown Court.

civil proceedings general term for legal cases other than those dealt with in criminal courts.

civic relating to the process of government and citizenship.

Civil List the annual grant of moneys by Parliament to the Monarch and other members of the royal family to finance their public status and duties.

civil servants persons employed by the Crown in executive, administrative or clerical capacities.

Civil War armed conflict, 1642–51, between Charles I and II and Parliament concerning whether Monarchy or Parliament was the ultimate authority within the English constitutional structure.

class claims arguments advanced in legal proceedings, usually by a public authority, that it would be against the public interest to reveal the content of a particular class or type of document, e.g. those relating to national security.

Clerk of the House of Commons parliamentary official responsible for organising the administrative and clerical workings of the House of Commons' support staff.

closed shop agreement contractual arrangement between employer and employees whereby employer undertakes not to engage or employ persons who are not members of a particular trade union(s).

closure procedure for terminating parliamentary debate.

CLR Commonwealth Law Reports.

Cm or Cmnd or Con Command Paper or official government publication.

CMLR Common Market Law Reports.

Co Rep reports of the cases dealt with by the seventeenth-century judge, Chief Justice Coke.

codify to collect and formalise disparate constitutional rules, often found in legislation, judicial decisions and political practices, into a single, authoritative, written document.

collective ministerial responsibility constitutional convention requiring Ministers to support and take political responsibility for all government decisions and to answer for such decisions to Parliament.

comity of nations the courteous recognition extended by each state to the laws and institutions of government of other such national bodies.

common law judge-made law based on precedent.

compulsory purchase acquisition of land or property by public authority acting under statutory powers.

confidence motion parliamentary voting procedure for forcing a government to resign from office.

confidentiality the legal doctrine limiting the dissemination of information given in confidence or where this would contravene a reasonable expectation of privacy.

Congress the American bicameral legislature consisting of the Senate and the House of Representatives.

conscription compulsory induction into the armed forces: usually in time of war or national emergency.

Conservative party centre-right political party founded in 1830 in power or official opposition for almost its entire existence and traditionally associated with maintenance of the constitutional and political status quo.

Consolidated Fund the sum of government finance held by the Bank of England.

constituency one of the geographical divisions in which localities elect their Member of Parliament.

constitution the legal and political rules which regulate the process of government.

constitutional law the legal rules which specify the institutions and powers of government, and the rights of individual citizens.

constitutional Monarch a Monarch whose powers are regulated and exercised according to the provisions of the national constitution.

consultations in the context of administrative law, discussion between the parties affected and government, before a particular decision or piece of legislation is made.

contempt of court words or actions which disrupt the judicial process, bring it into disrepute, or prejudice the outcome of particular proceedings.

contents claims arguments advanced in legal proceedings, usually by a public authority, that it would be against the public interest for the contents of a particular document to be revealed and used asevidence.

contracting or signatory state those which have signed and agreed to be bound by an international covenant, treaty or convention.

conventions major rules of established political practice regarded as binding on those to whom they apply.

council in the constitutional context, a local elected body responsible for the provision of local services.

Council of the European Union (previously Council of Ministers) EU policy- and law-making body composed of Ministers from member states (one Minister from each state) with the type of Minister attending its meetings being determined by the subject-matter under consideration.

council tax charge on property levied by local councils to pay for the services they provide.

councillor elected member of body responsible for the provision of local government services.

court martial military court or tribunal.

Court of Justice of the European Union (CJEU) consisting of the European Court of Justice, the General Court and the European Union Civil Service Tribunal, and responsible for the interpretation of EU law.

covenant formal written agreement or promise usually relating to property and often involving the swearing of an oath.

Crim App Rep Criminal Appeal Reports.

Crim LR Criminal Law Review.

cross-examination questioning of witnesses in legal and related proceedings.

The Crown the amalgam of central government bodies and military services through which the United Kingdom is governed, controlled and protected.

Crown Court mainly criminal court of first instance for offences triable by judge and jury and of appeal on questions of law and fact from magistrates' courts.

Crown Proceedings private law actions by or against the Crown.

Crown Prosecution Service government agency which decides whether a person should be charged with the criminal offence of which they are suspected and, if so, conducts the subsequent prosecution.

Curia Regis literally the King's council or advisers.

declaration judicial remedy which 'declares' or sets out the law relating to a particular dispute but which gives or orders no specific redress.

declaration of incompatibility judicial statement that a particular legislative provision does not comply with the requirements of the ECHR.

delaying power provision in the Parliament Acts 1911 and 1949 that a Bill which is defeated in the House of Lords may not be presented for the Royal Assent within the next 12 months.

democracy government by the people or their chosen representatives.

Departmental Select Committees groups of MPs, usually in the region of 13 to 19, charged with scrutinising and reporting on the workings of government departments.

deportation the act of returning a person compulsorily to their country of origin.

derogation departure from the legal standards normally applicable: e.g. as imposed by the ECHR.

Dicey Albert Venn Dicey 1835–1922: author of the first authoritative work on English constitutional law (*The Law of the Constitution*, 1885).

discovery of documents judicial procedure whereby a party to legal proceedings may seek access to relevant documentary evidence.

dissolution of Parliament exercise of the royal prerogative on Prime Ministerial advice bringing a particular Parliament to an end and precipitating the next General Election.

divine law rules of conduct and belief laid down by God.

dominions former British colonies which continue to recognise the Monarch as Head of State, but which for all meaningful, political purposes are now fully independent, self-governing states.

DTI Department of Trade and Industry.

duty of care a legal obligation particularly in the law of tort, to observe a reasonable standard of care in the performance of any action or provision of any service.

EC European Community.

ECHR the European Convention on Human Rights.

ECR European Court Reports.

ECtHR European Court of Human Rights.

Edward VIII King, January–December 1936.

Edward Heath Conservative Prime Minister 1970–4.

EEC European Economic Communities formed in 1957 consisting of the European Coal and Steel Community (ECSC), the European Community (EC) and the European Atomic Energy Community (EAEC).

EHRR European Human Rights Reports.

Elizabeth I Elizabeth Tudor, daughter of Henry VIII, Queen, 1558–1603.

enabling legislation Act of Parliament conferring the power to legislate on a subordinate authority.

enactment piece of parliamentary legislation.

entrenchment the protection of fundamental constitutional principles by requiring the observance of special legislative procedures for their repeal or alteration.

equality of arms requirement of fairness in legal proceedings and, in particular, that no one party has any significant procedural advantage over another.

equitable estoppel doctrine originating from the decision in *Central London Properties Trust* v *High Trees House Ltd* [1947] KB 130, explaining the circumstances in which a person may be bound to a promise for which no consideration has been given.

Erskine May original author of *Parliamentary Practice,* the established authority on the rules and conduct of parliamentary procedure.

ERO Electoral Registration Officer, i.e. local government officer responsible for compiling the electoral register in each of the UK's parliamentary constituencies.

espionage generic term referring usually to the covert acquisition of sensitive information or material (e.g. spying) or interference with military installations, for purposes prejudicial to the interests of the state.

The Estimates the government's projected spending requirements for the coming financial year.

EU European Union.

European Commission the body which initiates EU legislation and which is responsible for the implementation of this and EU policy generally.

European Commission of Human Rights abolished in 1998, the Commission was elected by the Committee of Ministers to decide questions of admissibility.

European Court of Human Rights (ECtHR) court sitting at Strasbourg hearing applications alleging breaches of the European Convention on Human Rights.

European Court of Justice the court of the European Union which gives final rulings in matters of interpretations of EU law.

European Parliament the representative assembly of the European Union charged with scrutinising the activities of the European Commission.

EWCA England and Wales Court of Appeal.

EWHC England and Wales High Court.

ex parte of or by one party only.

exclusion refusal of entry into the state.

executive discretion in terms of authorised objectives and legitimate considerations, the decision-making parameters within which government bodies should seek to exercise the powers granted to them.

extra-curial term often used to describe comments made by members of the judiciary outside the courtroom and not in the course of formal judicial proceedings.

extradition pursuant to an extradition treaty, the act of transferring compulsorily a suspected offender to the state wishing to proceed against them.

extra-judicial that which is done other than by, or with the authority of, the judiciary.

extra-territorial outside the physical boundaries of the state as where a court or government seeks to exercise jurisdiction or power in a place beyond the internationally recognised borders of its national territory.

Factortame the judicial decision in which the House of Lords ruled that European Community law should prevail over Acts of Parliament in the event of a conflict.

fairness actions which accord with the duty to act fairly, i.e. to make decisions in compliance with the rules of procedural fairness or natural justice.

Falklands War conflict in 1982 between UK and Argentina following Argentina's invasion of the Falkland Islands, a British territory in the south Atlantic.

federalism division of sovereign legislative authority between central and regional (state) elected assemblies.

fetter restrict, limit or restrain.

First Minister the head of the executive in the devolved governments for Northern Ireland, Scotland and Wales.

first past the post popular, descriptive term for the British electoral system, otherwise known as the simple majority system, in which the person who gains more votes than any other candidate in a particular parliamentary constituency, and regardless of whether this amounts to an absolute majority, is declared the winner.

Foreign Office central government department of state responsible for foreign affairs.

franchise the legal rules determining who has the right to vote in local and general (national) elections.

freedom an area of human activity not restricted by law.

fundamental human rights those which should not be restricted save in exceptional circumstances where there is an indisputable and pressing public interest justification.

GCHQ Government Communications Headquarters, the UK's electronic communications interception and monitoring service, situated in Cheltenham, Gloucestershire.

GCHQ case the House of Lords decision that explained the test of irrationality for the purposes of judicial review (*Council of Civil Service Unions v Minister for the Civil Service* [1985] AC 374).

General Election popular, national electoral process held at least once every five years to determine the composition of the Westminster Parliament.

George V King, 1910–36.

George VI King, 1936–52.

Glorious Revolution 1688, effecting the abdication of James II and the succession of William of Orange and Mary Stuart with the support of Parliament.

good faith with honest belief and absence of any improper motive.

Good Friday Agreement agreement reached on Good Friday 1998, between the leaders of the main political parties in Northern Ireland and the British and Irish governments which brought the conflict in Northern Ireland to an end and provided for a new form of inclusive representative government for that part of the United Kingdom.

the government the Prime Minister, Cabinet and other Ministers responsible for formulating and implementing national policy.

Governor-General person who exercises the functions of Head of State on behalf of the Queen in those countries retaining dominion status, principally Australia, New Zealand and Canada.

Great Britain the constitutional, political and geographical entity formed in 1707 by the Acts of Union between England and Wales, and Scotland.

Greater London Authority the body responsible for local government in London.

Green Paper a government publication setting out its general position in a particular matter and seeking opinions before any formal legislative proposal is formulated.

guillotine parliamentary procedure for limiting the amount of time to be devoted to a particular legislative proposal.

Gulf War 1991 liberation of Kuwait by largely US and British force following its invasion by Iraq in 1990.

habeas corpus judicial order literally 'bring the body' used to secure the release of persons detained unlawfully.

Harold Macmillan Conservative Prime Minister 1957–63.

Harold Wilson Labour Prime Minister 1964–70 and 1974–6.

HC House of Commons.

Henry VIII Henry Tudor, King, 1509–47.

Henry VIII clause legislative provision which allows the statute in which it is contained to be altered by the government without reference to Parliament.

Her Majesty's Loyal or Official Opposition usually the second largest political group or party in the House of Commons.

Herbert Asquith Liberal Prime Minister 1908–16.

hereditary peer the holder of an inherited peerage which passes from generation to generation of a particular family, usually in the male line, but which since the House of Lords Act 1999, no longer gives automatic qualification to sit in the House of Lords.

HL House of Lords.

HM His or Her Majesty.

Home Office central government department of state responsible for the maintenance of law and order and the protection of national security.

horizontal effect legally enforceable by one individual against another as distinct from entitlement enforceable against the state, i.e. vertically.

House of Commons the elected Chamber of the Westminster Parliament consisting of 650 Members.

House of Lords the unelected Chamber of the Westminster Parliament consisting primarily of life peers enabled by the Monarch on the advice of the Prime Minister.

HRA the Human Rights Act 1998.

Hudoc Website of European Court of Human Rights – literally human rights documents.

human rights entitlements believed to have their origins in the integrity and dignity of the human species rather than any political dogma or legal instrument.

hung Parliament state of affairs in the House of Commons where no one party has an overall majority.

Hybrid Bill a legislative proposal containing clauses of both general and limited application.

ibid. immediately above.

ICR Industrial Court Report.

IER individual electoral registration as distinct from the registration of voters by the householder of premises where persons eligible to vote are resident.

IGC international inter-governmental conference between heads of EU states.

illegality an unlawful act or, in the context of judicial review, a general term for various types of abuse of power.

imperial to do with Empire.

in camera in closed session out of public view.

individual ministerial responsibility constitutional convention requiring each Minister to take political responsibility, and answer to Parliament, for his own actions and decisions and those of the civil servants within his department.

injunction judicial order instructing a person or body to do or not to do that which is specified.

inter alia amongst other things.

inter partes of or between the parties.

interest group organisation of persons to pursue or further a particular cause or objective.

interlocutory temporary.

International Commission of Jurists association of lawyers from various states dedicated to maintenance of the Rule of Law and recognition of human rights.

International Declaration of Human Rights United Nations Charter formulated in 1948 and generally regarded as the first comprehensive and authoritative statement of those areas of human activity which should be respected and guaranteed by national governments.

international law legal rules regulating the behaviour and activities of states rather than individuals.

IRA Irish Republican Army; that is the paramilitary organisation dedicated to the ending of the partition of Ireland and to the establishing of an independent state consisting of all of Ireland's 32 counties.

Irish Republic 26 counties of Ireland which seceded from the United Kingdom in 1922.

irrebuttable that which may not be refuted or challenged in legal proceedings.

IVF *in vitro* fertilisation.

James I James Stuart, James VI of Scotland, descendant of Henry VII, succeeded Elizabeth I to English throne, 1603–25.

James II succeeded Charles II, 1685, dethroned 1688 due to conflicts with Parliament (died 1701).

James Callaghan Labour Prime Minister 1976–9.

John Major Conservative Prime Minister 1990–7.

JP justice of the peace.

judicial of the judges or of the courts.

Judicial Committee of the Privy Council a primarily judicial body composed of the same persons who sit in the Supreme Court, which hears appeals from the courts of those Commonwealth Countries which continue to recognise its jurisdiction.

judicial independence state of legal and political affairs in which judges may reach decisions without fear of political interference or reprisals.

judicial policy underlying principles and objectives of case-law development which accord most closely with judicial perceptions of the public interest whether in matters constitutional, political, social or economic.

judicial review the legal process through which the courts assess the lawfulness or validity of the acts and decisions of government agencies and officials.

jurisdiction the geographical extent of a state's sphere of influence or of a judicial body's decision-making powers.

jurisprudence the study of the theory of law in general or the legal decisions and reasoning of a particular judicial authority, e.g. the European Court of Human Rights.

justice of the peace local, unpaid official responsible for the maintenance of law and order and for sitting in judgment in local criminal courts.

justiciability the extent to which a decision, often of government, is suited to judicial inquiry.

KB King's Bench.

Labour party centre-left political party founded in 1900, originally to pursue socialist principles through the democratic process.

Law Commission body charged with consideration of a particular area of law, often judge-made, usually prior to its reform and possible codification in statutory form.

lay magistrate person without legal qualifications who sits in judgment in a magistrates' or local criminal court for no payment.

laying before Parliament process by which subordinate legislation is presented to the appropriate officers of the House of Commons and/or the House of Lords and thereby made available for examination by members of either House.

LCJ Lord Chief Justice.

Leader of the House Cabinet member responsible for managing government business in the House of Commons.

leaks unauthorised communication by government Ministers to the media.

Legislative Consent Order a resolution by any of the devolved assemblies in Northern Ireland, Scotland or Wales requesting, or agreeing to, the enactment of legislative measures by the Westminster Parliament which relate to any matter placed within the legislative authority of any such Assembly.

legitimate aims those general objectives or courses of action which it is legally permissible for a public body to pursue.

legitimate expectation legal right to assume that a particular decision of a public authority will be made according to a certain procedure or, as promised, will be put into effect, or not revoked, unless justified by a significant change in relevant circumstances.

lethal force that which endangers or takes life.

Liberal Democratic party centre-ground political party founded in 1988 from the fusion of the pre-existing Liberal party and Social Democratic party.

licence formal grant of permission or authority.

life peer the holder of a peerage conferred for life only, thereby entitling that person to a seat in the House of Lords.

Lloyd-George Liberal Prime Minister of the First World War coalition government 1916–22.

local government the various county and district authorities providing local services under the direction of elected councillors.

locus standi or standing the position of an individual in relation to any alleged abuse of power and, in particular, whether that person's connection with the abuse is sufficiently close to justify the bringing of legal proceedings.

Lord Chancellor Cabinet Minister with responsibility for the legal system.

Lord Chief Justice (LCJ) head of the judiciary.

lower chamber with reference to Parliament, an alternative term for the House of Commons.

Loyalists general term for those in Ireland who define their national identity in terms of loyalty to the British Crown and the maintenance of the union between Northern Ireland and Great Britain.

LTR Law Times Reports.

Maastricht Treaty 1992 Treaty of European Union which transformed the European Economic Community (EEC) into the European Union (EU) with an increased political and social dimension.

mandamus or mandatory order court order instructing a public body to fulfil any of the legal duties entrusted to it for the purposes of government and administration.

mandate grant of authority to implement a particular political decision or policy usually from the electorate, in a General Election or referendum.

Margaret Thatcher Conservative Prime Minister, 1979–90.

margin of appreciation flexible standard of compliance with the ECHR which allows states a degree of national judgement in the way they observe Convention requirements.

Master of the Rolls (MR) senior judge in the Court of Appeal.

MEPs members of the European Parliament.

Metropolitan Police Commissioner the chief officer of the Metropolitan police and the senior officer in the United Kingdom.

Ministry alternative name for a central government department headed by a government Minister.

Monarch the person who occupies the throne and is recognised by law and tradition as Head of State.

Money Bill piece of proposed legislation dealing almost entirely with financial matters.

MPs Members of Parliament.

municipal that having to do with the functioning of a government body and used most frequently in the context of local administration.

municipal court court of a nation-state rather than of any international organisation.

national security the safety of the state from subversive political forces.

natural justice common law rules of procedural fairness, principally the right to a fair hearing and the rule against bias, applying to those government authorities and officials with powers to make decisions which may affect individual rights or interests.

natural law rules of conduct which are so closely related and beneficial to the well-being of mankind that they must be regarded as a natural adjunct of human existence and experience.

necessity contention that a breach of law was justified to prevent a greater evil or crime – sometimes used as a defence to a criminal charge.

negative obligation legal requirement not to act in a certain way, e.g. contrary to an Article of the ECHR.

negligence careless actions causing injury or damage.

Neville Chamberlain Conservative Prime Minister 1937–40.

NLJ *New Law Journal.*

No. 10 Downing Street official residence of the British Prime Minister.

non-derogable binding in all circumstances, permitting of no departure from the prescribed standard.

non-justiciable not suitable for judicial comment or analysis, e.g. political judgments regarding the needs of national security.

Norman Conquest invasion and conquest of England in 1066 by the followers of William of Normandy.

Northern Ireland the six Irish Counties which remained in the United Kingdom after the creation of the Irish Free State (later Irish Republic) in 1922.

objective based on facts or evidence without reference to personal or other preferences.

Oliver Cromwell commander of the parliamentary forces during the English Civil War 1642–51 and who became 'Lord Protector' and Head of State with the execution of Charles I in 1649 (died 1658).

ombudsman person to whom complaints may be made about the workings of government bodies and officials.

op. cit. the work already cited.

Order in Council piece of subordinate legislation made by the government, usually under the authority of an Act of Parliament, but also, albeit occasionally, pursuant to the royal prerogative.

ouster clause a provision in an enabling Act rendering exercise of the powers conferred immune from judicial review.

PACE Police and Criminal Evidence Act 1984.

Parliamentary Counsel specialised team of lawyers working in the Cabinet Office responsible for drafting the government's legislative proposals.

parliamentary privilege immunity from legal proceedings afforded to that said or done in the course of parliamentary proceedings.

parliamentary session House of Commons working year extending November to November.

parole early release of a prisoner on licence subject to conditions.

party political plurality a legal and political state of affairs in which electors may vote for the political party of their choice and in which there are minimal restrictions on the right to form and organise such parties.

party whip member of a political party with responsibility for persuading party colleagues to support party policy in parliamentary divisions.

PASC Public Administration Select Committee.

PCA Parliamentary Commissioner for Administration.

peerage title and elevated social status conferred by the Monarch under royal prerogative.

penal laws those which impose a penalty for breach.

per se of or through itself.

Personal Bill legislative proposal put forward by, and relating to the legal affairs of, a particular individual.

Petition of Right legal process through which permission was sought to sue the Crown.

PII public interest immunity.

planning blight devaluation of market-value of property due usually to the local planning and development proposals of a public authority, e.g. the building or widening of a highway.

planning permission grant of permission by a local council allowing the applicant to build or develop on a piece of land.

plenary in full session or with a full complement.

policy chosen method or guiding ideology for the conduct of particular government activity.

political asylum reception of a foreign national into the state for an extended period or permanently in order to protect them from persecution in their country of origin.

political culture particular society's beliefs about how the process of government should be conducted.

positive obligation legal requirement to act or use powers in a certain way, e.g. in compliance with ECHR.

prerogative of mercy prerogative power, now exercised by the Home Secretary, to pardon persons wrongly convicted of criminal offences or, before its abolition in 1965, to commute the death sentence.

presumption of innocence the legal requirement that a person should be presumed innocent of any offence unless and until proved guilty.

prima facie on the face of it.

primary legislation for instant purposes the statutes of the Westminster Parliament in the United Kingdom and for the EU, the articles of the treaties on which the EU is founded.

Private Bill legislative proposal of local or limited application initiated by a local authority, public utility or other organisation.

private law legal rules which regulate the relationships between persons rather than between the person and the state (public law).

procedural impropriety failure to comply with the prescribed procedural rules for the exercise of a particular power.

prohibition court order forbidding a public body from taking an illegal decision.

proportional representation collective term for voting systems which achieve a close relationship between the proportion of the vote cast for a particular political group and the number of seats thus acquired in the assembly for which the election was held.

proportionality legal doctrine emanating from Europe which requires that the legality of government action should be determined by the extent it was strictly necessary to achieve the objective sought.

Protestants members of Christian churches other than Roman Catholics.

protocol(s) often used to describe a provision or provisions which have been added to an international treaty or agreement.

Public Accounts Committee senior House of Commons select committee responsible for examining and reporting on government expenditure and identifying any excesses.

Public Bill legislative proposal of general application usually emanating from the government.

public body government institution usually created by statute.

public corporation government owned and managed industrial, business or commercial organisation.

public domain the area of debate and comment on matters of public interest open to individuals and the media.

public interest (public good) that which is perceived to represent the most beneficial state of affairs for the majority of the population.

public interest immunity exemption or exclusion from legal proceedings of evidence and information which could seriously prejudice the public interest, and known previously as Crown Privilege.

public law the legal rules which regulate the activities of government.

public policy that designed to serve and benefit the best interests of the majority of the population.

public sector those administrative, commercial and other activities provided by the central and local government.

QB Queen's Bench.

qualified privilege the partial or limited legal immunity afforded to certain types of speech uttered without malice, e.g. comment on parliamentary and other matters of public interest.

qualified right one that permits of exceptions or modification to accommodate other interests, e.g. ECHR Art 8, right to respect for privacy.

quash to render legally invalid and ineffective.

quasi-judicial akin or similar to that which is done by judges or the courts.

Queen's Speech delivered annually, usually in late November, at the opening of each new parliamentary session, announcing the main elements of the government's legislative programme.

Question Time parliamentary procedure of some fifty minutes' duration, usually at the beginning of the day's business, when Ministers may be questioned by backbench MPs on the floor of the House.

quorum minimum number of MPs required in the chamber for the House of Commons to conduct its business.

ratify give formal approval or effect to.

reasonableness English common law test of judicial review for determining the legality of government actions and decisions.

referendum poll or vote of the national, or of a local electorate, to decide a particular issue of public concern.

Register of Members' Financial Interests official record of MPs' sources of income and benefits.

regulatory state system of government which seeks to manage social and economic conditions.

representative parliamentary government government by a freely elected Parliament, based on universal adult suffrage and party political freedom.

Republic a form of government, whether or not democratic, according to which the head of state is not a hereditary Monarch.

responsible government government by persons who are accountable to, and may be put out of office by, the representative assembly.

Returning Officer senior local government official in each constituency for the conduct of parliamentary elections.

right an aspect or area of human activity protected by law.

RIPA the Regulation of Investigatory Powers Act 2000.

Royal Charter formal grant of legal authority made under the royal prerogative.

Royal Commission body appointed under the royal prerogative to consider and report on a matter of major public interest.

royal prerogative the remaining common law powers of the Monarch.

RPA Representation of the People Acts.

RTR Road Traffic Reports.

RUC Royal Ulster Constabulary.

Rule of Law political doctrine advocating government by law rather than political discretion.

secondary legislation law made by Ministers or public authorities pursuant to powers conferred on them by primary legislation.

Secretary of State government Minister of Cabinet rank.

Select Committee parliamentary device for inquiring into and discovering/compiling information about the conduct of government, Parliament or MPs, or any other matter of public interest.

separation of powers political doctrine which advocates that the legislative, executive and judicial branches of government should be exercised by different institutions within the overall constitutional structure.

signatory state a state whose government has signed an international treaty and which has subsequently ratified the same, e.g. by grant of parliamentary approval.

simpliciter without more.

SLT *Scottish Law Times.*

SOCPA Serious Organised Crime and Police Act 2005.

solitary confinement imprisonment of an individual without access to other prisoners.

Sovereign either the Monarch in person or the government institution which holds supreme legal authority.

sovereignty ultimate and supreme law-making authority.

the Speaker MP chosen by the House of Commons to chair its debates.

spiritual peer one of the 26 senior bishops of the Church of England thus qualified to sit in the House of Lords.

standing orders rules regulating the conduct of meetings and procedures in Parliament.

the state either the institutions of central government and law enforcement, or the geographical area under their control.

statement of compatibility ministerial statement that a piece of proposed legislation complies with the requirements of the ECHR.

statutory duty legal obligation imposed by an Act of Parliament, often on a government body, requiring it to act in a certain way or fulfil a prescribed function.

statutory instrument legislative document containing rules of subordinate legislation made by a Minister under the authority of an Act of Parliament.

statutory powers legal authority conferred by Act of Parliament, often on a government body, allowing a degree of choice in the way a particular function is performed.

statutory tribunals extra-judicial bodies for dealing with individual complaints about the decisions or actions of public authorities or officials.

stipendiary magistrate legally qualified magistrate who receives a 'stipend' or payment for his/her services.

Stormont devolved Parliament which governed Northern Ireland from 1922 to 1972.

Strasbourg French city and seat of the European Court of Human Rights.

Stuarts ruling royal family or dynasty 1603–1714.

sub judice subject to or pending determination by a court of law.

subjective based on opinion or personal judgment.

subpoena order that a person should appear in court on the date specified.

subsidiarity EU constitutional principle requiring decisions concerning the national implementation of EU law and policy to be taken by bodies accessible to EU citizens and at the lowest appropriate level of government in the systems of EU member states.

Suez Crisis invasion of Egypt by Britain and France in 1956 following Egypt's 'nationalisation' of the Suez Canal.

sufficient interest degree to which a person must be affected by a public authority's decision in order to challenge its legality by way of judicial review.

supply parliamentary process through which moneys are voted to government departments.

supra above.

tariff in relation to sentencing, the period fixed by the court as the minimum term the offender should serve for the purposes of deterrence and retribution.

terrorism acts of violence for political objectives.

TEU Treaty of the European Union setting out the institutions and powers of the EU system of law and government.

TFEU Treaty on the Function of the European Union setting out the EU's principal competence or areas of law- and policy-making jurisdiction.

Treasury central government department responsible for the nation's financial affairs.

Treaty of Rome 1957 agreement by France, Germany, Italy, Holland, Belgium and Luxembourg to form the EEC.

trespass action which takes place or involves unauthorised or unlawful entry onto or into private property.

Tudors ruling royal family or dynasty 1458–1603.

UKSC United Kingdom Supreme Court.

ultra vires Latin term used to describe actions or decisions taken by government Ministers or officials without legal authority – literally, 'beyond the powers of'.

United Kingdom constitutional, political and geo-graphical entity formed by the Act of Union 1800 between Great Britain and Ireland.

United Nations representative debating and law-making body for the international community situated in New York and established in 1946 to replace the League of Nations.

universal adult suffrage a state of legal and political conditions guaranteeing the right to vote to every person of the age of majority without reference to socio-economic status or property qualifications.

upper chamber with reference to Parliament, an alternative term for the House of Lords (also 'second' chamber).

vertical effect legally enforceable against the state, i.e. 'upwards' or vertically.

vicarious liability legal responsibility of an employer for the acts of persons under his control or direction.

vitiating rendering void or of no effect.

void of no effect, having no legal validity.

void *ab initio* used in administrative law to describe a decision which, from the outset, had no legal effect or validity.

voidable used in administrative law to describe a decision which, although legally defective when made, remains valid and enforceable unless challenged, usually by way of judicial review.

Wakeham Commission Royal Commission on Reform of the House of Lords chaired by Lord Wakeham, former Conservative Cabinet Minister, which reported in January 2000.

warrant legal order from judge or magistrate usually authorising the arrest of a specified person or the search of named premises.

Wednesbury **test** ground of judicial review based on the principles of reasonableness formulated in *Associated Picture Houses* **v** *Wednesbury Corporation* [1948] 1 KB 223.

Westminster district of London in which the UK Parliament is situated.

Westminster Hall additional Parliamentary debating chamber established in 1999.

Whitehall district of London in which the main departments of state are situated.

white noise high-pitched electronic sounds used to cause distress and disorientation intended to lower a person's resistance to interrogation.

White Paper official government publication which sets out the reasons for and the probable content of a proposed piece of legislation.

William the Conqueror member of Norman nobility who asserted his claims to the English throne by conquest in 1066 (died 1087).

Winston Churchill Prime Minister of wartime coalition government 1940–5.

WLR Weekly Law Reports.

Index

Page numbers in **bold** relate to entries in the Glossary